Dictionary of Literary Biography ● Volume Two

American Novelists Since World War II

Edited by
Jeffrey Helterman
University of South Carolina
and
Richard Layman
Columbia, South Carolina

cop 1

A Bruccoli Clark Book
Gale Research Company ● Book Tower ● Detroit, Michigan 48226
1978

Planning Board for
DICTIONARY OF LITERARY BIOGRAPHY

John Baker
William Emerson
Orville Prescott
Vernon Sternberg
Alden Whitman

Matthew J. Bruccoli, *Editorial Director*
C. E. Frazer Clark, Jr., *Managing Editor*
Richard Layman, *Project Editor*
Joel Myerson, *Series Editor*

Library of Congress Cataloging in Publication Data

Main entry under title:

American novelists since world War II.

(Dictionary of literary biography ; v. 2)
"A Bruccoli Clark book."
Bibliography: p.
1. American fiction--20th century--Bio-
bibliography. 2. Novelists, American--20th
century--Biography. I. Helterman, Jeffrey.
II. Layman, Richard, 1947-   III. Series.
PS379.A554   813'.03   77-82804
ISBN 0-8103-0914-9

For
Myron and Rae Helterman
and
Mary A. Layman

Contributors

Michael Adams	*University of South Carolina*
Steve Bannow	*University of South Carolina*
Doris Bargen	*University of Tubingen*
Joan Bischoff	*Slippery Rock State College*
Philip H. Bufithis	*Shepherd College*
Robert E. Burkholder	*University of South Carolina*
Keen Butterworth	*University of South Carolina*
Frank Campenni	*University of Wisconsin, Milwaukee*
Albert Howard Carter III	*Eckerd College*
Arthur D. Casciato	*Virginia Polytechnic Institute and State University*
Ann Charters	*New York, New York*
David Cowart	*University of South Carolina*
Thomas E. Dasher	*University of South Carolina*
Leonard J. Deutsch	*Marshall University*
Gerald Duff	*Kenyon College*
Timothy J. Evans	*University of South Carolina*
Paula R. Feldman	*University of South Carolina*
Benjamin Franklin V	*University of South Carolina*
Warren French	*Indiana/Purdue Universities, Indianapolis*
John Gerlach	*Cleveland State University*
Craig M. Goad	*Northwest Missouri State College*
William E. Grant	*University of Louisville*
Donald J. Greiner	*University of South Carolina*
John V. Hagopian	*State University of New York, Binghamton*
Jeffrey Helterman	*University of South Carolina*
Josephine Helterman	*Columbia, South Carolina*
George Jensen	*University of South Carolina*
Carol Johnston	*University of South Carolina*
Michael Joslin	*University of South Carolina*
James E. Kibler, Jr.	*University of Georgia*
Robert F. Kiernan	*Manhattan College*
Jerome Klinkowitz	*University of Northern Iowa*
Inge Kutt	*University of South Carolina*
David Madden	*Louisiana State University*
Jeanette Mann	*California State University*
Daniel B. Marin	*University of South Carolina*
Paul Marx	*University of New Haven*
Carolyn Matalene	*University of South Carolina*
John R. May	*Louisiana State University*
Jerry McAninch	*Columbia, South Carolina*

Larry McCaffery	*San Diego State University*
Thomas McClanahan	*South Carolina Arts Commission*
Robert A. Morace	*Daemen College*
Gretchen Himmele Munroe	*University of South Carolina, Sumter*
William H. Nolte	*University of South Carolina*
Cameron Northouse	*Dallas, Texas*
Robert Novak	*Indiana/Purdue Universities, Fort Wayne*
Donald Pease	*Dartmouth University*
David W. Pitre	*University of South Carolina*
Peter J. Reed	*University of Minnesota*
Jack Wright Rhodes	*Columbia, South Carolina*
Karen Rood	*University of South Carolina*
Jean W. Ross	*Columbia, South Carolina*
Hugh M. Ruppersburg	*University of Georgia*
George Edgar Slusser	*University of California*
Fred L. Standley	*Florida State University*
John Stark	*University of Wisconsin*
Howard Stringfellow	*University of South Carolina*
Stephen L. Tanner	*University of Idaho*
James W. Tuttleton	*New York University*
Ruth Vande Kieft	*Queens College*
John Vermillion	*Columbia, South Carolina*
Susan Walker	*University of South Carolina*
Richard Wertime	*Beaver College*
Everett Wilkie	*University of South Carolina*

Acknowledgments

The staff of B C Research produced this book. Glenda G. Fedricci did the paste-up; Cynthia H. Rogers and Cara L. White, the typesetting; copy editors were Anne Knox Langley and Jean W. Ross; Rhonda W. Rabon handled correspondence and record-keeping.

Jill Krementz has provided the bulk of photographs in this volume. We are indebted to her for her cooperation and expertise.

We also owe thanks for photographic work to Jerry Bauer, Jack Beech, Joan Bingham, Michael Robert Cannata, Michael Childers, Chris Corpus, Jean Faust, Alex Gotfryd, Anthony Harris, George Janoff, Daniel Kramer, Carol Lee, Duane Michals, Joel Rubiner, Layle Silbert, Nancy Sirkis, C.V. Stone, Lynn Sweigart, Richard Taylor, Michael J. Updike, Thomas Victor, Erik Weber, and Herb Weitman.

We gratefully acknowledge the assistance of the following libraries and institutions: The Alderman Library, University of Virginia; Duke University Library; Humanities Research Center, University of Texas; The Media Center of Georgia College; Mugar Library, Boston University; University of Oregon Library; Richland County Public Library; The Thomas Cooper Library, University of South Carolina; and Scientia Factum.

Thanks are due the following individuals: C. J. Cambre, Michael Havener, Dale Krueger, Susan Manakul, Jean Rhyne, Michael Strelow, Gary Treadway, and Joyce Werner.

Plan of the Work

. . . almost the most prodigious asset of a country, and perhaps its most precious possession is its native literary product—when that product is fine and noble and enduring.

Mark Twain*

The advisory board, the editors, and the publisher of the *Dictionary of Literary Biography* are joined in endorsing the truth expressed in Mark Twain's observation. The literature of a nation represents an inexhaustible resource of permanent worth. It is our expectation that this work will make the American achievement in literature better understood and more accessible to students and to the literate public, while serving the needs of scholars.

The final plan for *DLB* resulted from two years of preparation. The project was proposed to Bruccoli Clark by Frederick G. Ruffner, president of the Gale Research Company, in November 1975. After specimen entries were written and typeset, an advisory board was formed to plan and develop the series. In meetings held in New York during 1976, the publisher, series editors, and advisory board developed the scheme for a comprehensive biographical dictionary of persons who have contributed to North American literature. Editorial work on the first volume began in January 1977.

Entries range from brief notices of secondary figures (200 to 600 words) to comprehensive treatments (up to 15,000 words) of major figures. The major entries are written by authorities in their fields and intended as permanent contributions to literary history. The purpose of *DLB* is not only to provide reliable information in a clear format, but also to place literary figures in the larger perspective of North American literary history and to offer appraisals of their accomplishments by qualified scholars.

We define literature as *the intellectual commerce of a nation*: not merely as belles lettres, but as that ample and complex process by which ideas are generated, shaped, and communicated. Accordingly, entries in *DLB* will not be limited to "creative writers," but will extend to others who in their time and in their way contributed to our literature. By this means readers of *DLB* may be brought to see literature not as cult scripture in the keeping of high priests, but as at the very center of a nation's life.

DLB will include all of the major North American writers and those standing in the ranks immediately behind them. The best available scholarly and critical counsel will be sought in deciding which minor figures to include and how full the entries for them should be. Whenever possible, useful references will be made to figures who do not warrant separate entries.

In order to make *DLB* more than a reference tool and to prepare volumes that individually have claim to status as literary history, it has been decided to organize individual volumes by topic or period or genre. Thus the first five volumes are: (1) *The American Renaissance in New England*; (2) *American Novelists Since World War II*; (3) *The American Renaissance in New York and the South*; (4) *American Expatriates in Paris, 1920-1940*; and (5) *American Screenwriters*. Each of these volumes will provide a biographical-bibliographical guide and overview for a particular area of North American literature. This volume plan will require many decisions about the placement and treatment of authors who might properly be included in two or three volumes. In some instances a major author will be included in separate volumes, but with different entries emphasizing the aspect of his career appropriate to that volume. Ernest Hemingway, for example, will be represented in the *Expatriates* volume by an entry focusing on his Paris apprenticeship; he will also be included in the volume planned for the novelists of the 1920-1940 period, and there the Hemingway entry will survey his entire career. In other instances the problem will be dealt with by cross-referencing. The final volume of *DLB* will be a comprehensive index to the series.

From an unpublished section of Mark Twain's autobiography, copyright © 1972 by the Mark Twain Company.

Each *DLB* volume has a volume editor responsible for planning the volume, selecting the figures for inclusion, and assigning the entries. The volume editor is also responsible for preparing, where appropriate, appendices surveying the major periodicals and literary and intellectual movements for his volume, as well as a list of further readings. Work on the series as a whole is co-ordinated at the editorial center in Columbia, South Carolina, where the editorial staff is responsible for the accuracy of the published volumes.

One feature that distinguishes *DLB* is the illustration policy—its concern with the iconography of literature. Just as an author is influenced by his surroundings, so is the reader's understanding of the author enriched by a knowledge of his environment. Therefore *DLB* volumes include not only drawings, paintings, and photographs of authors, often depicting them at various stages in their careers, but also illustrations of their spouses, published works, and places where they lived and wrote. Specimens of the writers' manuscripts are included when feasible.

A companion volume to *DLB*—tentatively entitled *A Guide, Chronology, and Glossary for North American Literature*—will provide a sense of the frame of North American literature and trace the major influences that worked on it by means of chronologies, literary affiliation charts, glossarial entries, and entries on movements or tendencies. This supplement will be a point of reference from the *DLB* volumes, conserving space and eliminating repetition in the series. It will be planned to stand on its own as a *vade mecum*.

Samuel Johnson rightly decreed that "The chief glory of every people arises from its authours." The purpose of the *Dictionary of Literary Biography* is to trace the outlines of North American literature in the surest way available to us—by comprehensive scholarly treatment of the lives and work of those who contributed to it.

Foreword

The thirty-odd years since World War II have been extremely active ones for American novelists. As the book-reading public has increased, so has the market for fiction, and while the occupation of novelist still offers a poor chance for riches and glory, a novelist writing in the 1970s has a better chance to succeed than ever before. Between 1974 and 1976, some 1750 books of fiction were published in hardcover each year, and about the same number (many of which had already appeared in hardcover) were published in paperback. But if the market for novels has opened up, the market for short fiction has diminished. Professional fiction writers since World War II have been forced by economic pressures to concentrate on book-length works.

The proliferation of the paperback book has had a major influence on the profession of authorship in the U. S. since World War II. Low prices and huge print runs of mass-market paperbacks have given new visibility to works of fiction; marketing, once centered on the bookstore, now includes the airport and grocery. As a result, a work of fiction may sell millions of copies, particularly if there are movie or television tie-ins, making the author an instant millionaire. Paperback rights alone for a popular novel may bring as much as $2 million. But success stories are relatively rare. A novelist is still far more likely to see his book rejected, or, if it is published, a sale of perhaps 1000 copies in hardcover with no further publication.

While the publishing industry has boomed, there has been a similar increase in the field of literary criticism. Never has so much attention been paid contemporary authors; never have Americans known their living writers so well. The entries in *American Novelists Since World War II* benefit from the amount of scholarship available and serve to digest what has been written, synthesizing the best of it in a single reference book.

American Novelists Since World War II contains biographical sketches of eighty writers who either began writing novels after 1945 or have done their most important work since then. Two types of entries are used. There are eighteen master entries, which consist of extended biographical and critical essays on authors who are generally regarded as major forces in contemporary literature; the sixty-two standard entries are less elaborate and vary in length according to the author's influence and the size of his canon. In each type of entry there is a full bibliography of the author's books. Bibliographies of the author's works and of critical writings about him are selected by the contributors.

Since this volume is limited to authors who primarily wrote novels, some novelists who are better known for their work in other forms have been omitted. They will be included in other volumes of *Dictionary of Literary Biography*, as will important authors of science fiction, mystery fiction, and other sub-genres.

American Novelists
Since World War II

Dictionary of Literary Biography

JAMES RUFUS AGEE, novelist, poet, journalist, film critic, and screenwriter, is best known for a documentary study of three Alabama tenant-farming families in the midst of the Depression, *Let Us Now Praise Famous Men*, and an unfinished novel, *A Death in the Family*. Born in Knoxville, Tennessee, on 27 November 1909, Agee's childhood was marred by the death of his father, Hugh James Agee, in an automobile accident in May 1916, an event which Agee would draw on in both his published novels.

In 1919 Agee was enrolled at an Episcopalian boarding school, St. Andrews, near Sewanee, Tennessee. During his five years at St. Andrews, Agee formed a close personal friendship with one of the teachers, Father James Harold Flye. In 1924-1925 Agee attended Knoxville High School, and after a trip to Europe with Father Flye in the summer of 1925, he enrolled at Phillips Exeter Academy in Exeter, New Hampshire. It was at Phillips Exeter that Agee first became interested in writing, perhaps only because of the social distinction it afforded a poor Southern boy at an exclusive Northern school. But by the time he had matriculated at Harvard in 1928, he was committed to both the aesthetic and professional aspects of a literary career, writing poetry and prose and editing *The Harvard Advocate* during his career there.

In 1931 Agee fell under the influence of a visiting Harvard professor, I. A. Richards, whose theories about using language to embody physical reality greatly affected Agee's writing during the 1930s. The most important direct influence Richards' theories had upon Agee's approach to his art involve an increased role for the narrator in Agee's stories. Because he was impressed by Richards' idea that the final effect of any poetic endeavor depends upon the complex relationship between the poem, referent, and reader, Agee decided that it would increase chances for the original poetic experience to be communicated if his first-person narrators not only served as major characters in the chronological narrative, but also as aestheticians who explain the problems of perception involved in their secondary roles as intermediaries between the experience and the audience. From the early short story "They That Sow in Sorrow Shall Reap" (which Agee was preparing for publication during his initial exposure to Richards, and which appeared in *The Harvard Advocate* in May 1931), the technique of employing a first-person narrator with the dual functions of major character and aesthetician is a distinguishing feature of Agee's prose. It is also the technique upon which he would rely most heavily in attempting to recreate the physical reality of three tenant families in *Let Us Now Praise Famous Men*.

In 1932, after graduation from Harvard, Agee was hired by *Fortune Magazine*. Agee, whose roots were decidedly in the soil rather than the board-room, worked hard on his *Fortune* assignments, but to him the best aspect of his employment was the money and free time it allowed him to pursue his artistic interests. The outcome of this limited freedom was a book of poetry, *Permit Me Voyage* (1934), which was published as part of the Yale Series of Younger Poets. More than any volume of Agee's work, *Permit Me Voyage* demonstrates the dramatic turn Agee's aesthetic approach took following his exposure to Richards at Harvard.

On 28 January 1933, Agee married Olivia (Via) Saunders, the daughter of a Hamilton College history professor, whom Agee had met on vacation from Harvard in 1930. When his marriage to Via went through a final break in 1937, Agee was already seeing Alma Mailman, a friend of the Saunders, whose lower-class background seems to have appealed to Agee's sense of social justice. To Alma fell the thankless task of aiding Agee during the composition of *Let Us Now Praise Famous Men*. After that book was published, and shortly after the birth of their son, Joel, in 1941, Alma left Agee. Despite the fact that Agee seems to have found both his marriages too restrictive to his personal freedom, he needed the stability and companionship that marriage provided. Therefore, in 1946, he married Mia Fritsch, whom he had met at *Fortune*. Agee's marriage to Mia produced one child, Julia Teresa (born in November 1946), and lasted until Agee's death in 1955.

In 1936 *Fortune* asked Agee and photographer Walker Evans to go to Alabama and do a photo-story on tenant farming. When Agee finally finished the project more than three years later, he had channeled enough of his sensibility into the subject to produce one large book and projections for three more volumes about his Alabama experience (these projected studies never materialized). *Let Us Now Praise Famous Men* (1941) is now recognized as the centerpiece of Agee's career. Not quite a novel, but too poetic to be nonfiction, *Famous Men* is a supreme attempt at recreating the squalor and beauty of the tenant farmers' lives through use of experimental techniques, such as a shifting point of view, several narrative levels and time schemes, and a structure which combines elements of the Mass, five-act drama, and the sonata. Because of Agee's unconventional approach and subject matter far removed from the concerns of a nation preparing to enter World War II, most of the critics considered *Famous Men* a pretentious failure. When a second edition was published in 1960, the critics found it a failure still, but most were willing to grant Agee credit for an aesthetic attempt far beyond the scope of most writers.

Agee's aesthetic concerns in *Famous Men* involved his ability and the ability of his chosen medium, with all its variables, to capture the physical reality of the tenant farmers. These concerns were serious enough to make Agee consider a form of communication other than written language:

> If I could, I'd do no writing at all here. It would be photographs; the rest would be fragments of cloth, bits of cotton, lumps of earth, records of speech, pieces of wood and iron, phials of odors, plates of food and excrement.

This alternative to words is, perhaps, a much more effective way of recreating an experience in the minds of his audience, but, as Agee speculated, the American public would probably turn it into some sort of parlor game. Besides, Agee did not wish to abandon his vocation as a writer before attempting to accomplish the recreation of reality with words. Therefore he exploited his personal involvement in the lives of the three tenant families—the Woods, Gudgers, and Ricketts—by writing about that involvement and by writing about the difficulties of writing in the first person. What this technique achieves is the feeling that the writer is working from a sincere concern for the people with whom he has lived and labored. The lack of authorial detachment in *Famous Men* aids in reinforcing the sense that the artist is motivated by his desire to tell the truth. It follows that if the reader is able to appreciate the artist's desire for truth, the artist's job of communicating experience will be easier.

But communication of the experience is not enough. The reader must also understand its significance. In *Practical Criticism* (1929), I. A. Richards says that "we understand when the words prompt in us action or emotion appropriate to the attitude of the person who speaks them." Obviously, the best way to make the reader aware of the attitudes of the person speaking in a work as large as *Famous Men* is to make that speaker the center of the action. By doing this, Agee is able to post the reader on how his attitude changes from section to section with shifts in tone.

Another rhetorical stance which seems to pervade *Famous Men* follows Richards' dictum that "nearly all good poetry is disconcerting." Therefore, Agee was willing to go to any length to assure the reader that his story was both real and frightening, from the lists of the Ricketts' possessions and household decorations to his masterly description of his first sleepless night in the Ricketts' insect-infested shack. Agee simply did not wish his book to be considered an *objet d'art*, but it is too consciously artistic to fit into the "documentary" genre beside Erskine Caldwell and Margaret Bourke-White's *You Have Seen Their Faces*. The basic problem is that Agee wanted *Famous Men* to be the sort of fury that can change man's attitude toward himself. To classify such a fury as art would mean that it has been accepted, discussed at teas and cocktail parties, and its message forgotten. As Agee says in his "Preface": "The deadliest blow the enemy of the human soul can strike is to do fury honor. Swift, Blake, Beethoven, Christ, Joyce, Kafka, name me one who has not been thus castrated." This passionate intensity, so typical of *Famous Men*, disappears in most of Agee's work after 1941.

In 1938, while still hard at work on *Famous Men*, Agee began reviewing books for *Time*. Soon he shifted to reviews of movies, and in 1941 he also began writing a weekly column on film for the *Nation*. He held both posts until 1948. The distinctive quality of Agee's film criticism is the subjectivity with which he approaches his subject, reacting to each film he considers in a personal, rather than a critical or scholarly, way, and always siding with the comparatively naive movie audience. Film, in effect, was the medium for which Agee's sensibility most suited him, because it offered the artist a means of communicating a reality directly. Therefore, much of Agee's criticism suggests the potential of film as an artistic medium which, with its blending of reality and fiction, could produce works of art much more real than any other art form. As testimony to Agee's personal approach to movies, his most famous piece of criticism, "Comedy's Greatest Era" (published in *Life* magazine on 3 September 1949), actually parodies analytic criticism by grading the four stages of laughter, from titter to boffo, and then, in Agee's most evocative prose, attempts to capture the poetry of the silent comedian in brief discussions of Turpin, Sennett, Chaplin, Lloyd, Langdon, and Keaton. This evocative quality is really the essence of Agee's film criticism. His ultimate desire was to recreate the film under consideration through written language so that the audience could decide for itself.

From 1948 until his death, Agee divided his interest between writing film scripts and fiction. While he wrote several adaptations and one full-length original script, Agee's Hollywood work will always be remembered for the part he had in coauthoring *The African Queen* with director John Huston. It was while working on that film in January 1951 that Agee suffered the first of many heart attacks. But Agee's original film script *Noa Noa*, based upon the journals of Paul Gauguin, was his most ambitious project for the screen (although never produced), as well as his definitive statement about the role of the artist in society.

Probably the best way to characterize Agee after 1941 is as a man who had extended himself too far. When he accepted the job of doing movie reviews for the *Nation* in the 1940s he found that he had little time to spend on his own personal projects. For instance, in 1937 Agee had projected plans for an autobiographical novel:

> Only relatively small portions would be fiction (though techniques of fiction might be much used); and these would be subjected to non-fictional analysis. This work would contain photographs and records as well as words.

Obviously, as Agee originally planned his novel, it was intended to combine some fictional techniques with the kind proposed for *Famous Men* (records and photographs). As it turned out, Agee only published one novel during his lifetime, and it is far different from his ambitious proposal of 1937. *The Morning Watch* (first published in 1950 in the Italian journal

Botteghe Oscure, and published in America in 1951) is indeed autobiographical, but it does not employ photographs, records, or nonfictional analysis—all those things disappear from Agee's work after *Famous Men*. It is a simply-wrought tale about a young boy, Richard, who undergoes an awakening during a period of five hours on a Good Friday morning. All of the traditional Christian imagery of resurrection is here, rather heavy-handedly linked to Richard's discovery of a recently vacated locust shell, and a snake which has shed its skin, but the conventionalities of *The Morning Watch* are of little interest compared with its symmetrical structure. Richard is a sensitive child, an artist figure of sorts, and all his actions are motivated by his desire to be a saint. However, Richard is a student at a small, private religious academy in the South (not unlike Agee's own St. Andrews), and his fellow students represent a world totally unlike that of the church. Throughout the novel Richard is poised between the world of the spirit and the world of experience. This symmetrical conflict is resolved when Richard is able to find a proper balance of the two worlds. This balance is achieved when Richard kills a snake, acts against a commandment and, therefore, gives up his right to sainthood, winning the respect of his classmates, Hobe and Jimmy.

A Death in the Family (1957) is far more complex than *A Morning Watch*, and yet it seems to rely upon many of the same techniques used in the shorter novel. For instance, like *A Morning Watch*, much of the action in *A Death in the Family* is created by an exploration of tensions. In *A Death in the Family*, however, this examination of polarities takes on a new complexity. There are tensions between individuals, notably the religious differences between Jay and his wife, the different qualities of manhood displayed by Jay and his brother, Ralph, and the differences between the sensitive young Rufus and his classmates. There are also those larger tensions which seem inherent in both individuals and the society in general; such things as the difference between black and white, rich and poor, being from the country as opposed to the city, and, most important, the difference between life and death. But the structure of *A Death in the Family* depends largely upon the difference created between "then" and "now." "Then" is the reminiscences of the narrator which deal with times before his father died. Nearly all of these reminiscences involve the narrator's initiation into a new fact of life (like the meaning of parental love, pregnancy, or the problems between the races). This italicized secondary narrative is woven through the primary narrative, the story of Jay Follet's death in a freak automobile accident and the family's reaction to it. Therefore, the reader is aware of two levels of time working concurrently in the novel. This effect is created by suggestions of one level running through another, the recapitulation of past experiences in the present.

At the center of all these tensions is young Rufus Follet, whom we are led to believe is the narrator. The opening section of the novel, "Knoxville: Summer 1915," begins with these words: "We are talking now of summer evenings in Knoxville, Tennessee, in the time that I lived there so successfully disguised to myself as a child." His disguise is that of a young boy, but he is actually a fully-grown and developed artist who will not be limited by speaking through an adolescent persona. Therefore, the narrator creates the sense that he sees and understands far more than a boy Rufus's age could, and at times the narrator is even omniscient. Since we are made immediately aware of the dual identity of the narrator, we might conclude that all of *A Death in the Family* is aimed at merging these two identities: through experience the boy's disguise is slowly removed, and at the end of the novel we no longer have a boy at all, but a man. Thus the removal of disguise—Agee's trappings as a reporter for *Fortune* in *Famous Men*, Richard's saintliness in *The Morning Watch*, and Rufus's childhood innocence in *A Death in the Family*—is an important theme in all of Agee's work.

Agee's health problems, originally signalled by his first heart attack in 1951, grew progressively worse. In late 1952 he was hospitalized once more for heart trouble, but Agee found it difficult to practice the abstinence his doctors recommended, often working on several projects at the same time. By the end of 1954, after nearly a year of good health, Agee's heart attacks began again. But this time they were much more severe and frequent, occurring up to eight times a day. Another series of attacks began in March 1955. In the midst of several film projects, including a screenplay for Colonial Williamsburg, Agee suffered a series of heart attacks and died while riding in a taxicab in New York City on 16 May 1955. In 1957, McDowell and Obolensky published *A Death in the Family*, tentatively arranging Agee's unfinished, and nearly indecipherable, working draft. *A Death in the Family* was awarded the Pulitzer Prize for fiction in 1958.

Despite Agee's comparative anonymity during his lifetime, he has received both acknowledgment and respect since the publication of *A Death in the Family*. Not only did that novel win a Pulitzer Prize,

but in 1960 it was adapted for the theater by Fred Coe and Arthur Cantor, and subsequently turned into a television drama in 1961 and the movie, *All the Way Home*, in 1962. The popularity of Agee's *Letters to Father Flye* and the reevaluation of *Let Us Now Praise Famous Men* as one of the most important books of the 1930s, after its republication in 1960, have aided in advancing Agee's reputation. Finally, the publication of the two volumes of *Agee on Film* in 1958 and 1960 gave the public a new insight into the genius that motivated Agee's movie reviews and film scripts.

Agee's personality was of the iconoclastic sort which seems to draw worshipers and imitators. After his death, those closest to him tended to mythologize Agee's life in much the same way that F. Scott Fitzgerald's has been mythologized: the incredibly gifted artist drained of talent and energy by a society unable to appreciate him. But the legend of Agee is the smallest part of his legacy.

—*Robert E. Burkholder*

Books:

Permit Me Voyage (New Haven: Yale University Press, 1934);

Let Us Now Praise Famous Men, photographs by Walker Evans (Boston: Houghton Mifflin, 1941; London: Peter Owen, 1965);

The Morning Watch (Boston: Houghton Mifflin, 1951; London: Secker & Warburg, 1952);

A Death in the Family (New York: McDowell, Obolensky, 1957; London: Gollancz, 1958);

Agee on Film: Reviews and Comments (New York: McDowell, Obolensky, 1958; London: Peter Owen, 1963);

Agee on Film, Volume II: Five Film Scripts (New York: McDowell, Obolensky, 1960; London: Peter Owen, 1965);

Letters of James Agee to Father Flye (New York: Braziller, 1962; London: Peter Owen, 1964);

The Collected Poems of James Agee, ed. Robert Fitzgerald (Boston: Houghton Mifflin, 1968; London: Calder & Boyars, 1972);

The Collected Short Prose of James Agee, ed. Robert Fitzgerald (Boston: Houghton Mifflin, 1968; London: Calder & Boyars, 1972).

References:

Alfred T. Barson, *A Way of Seeing: A Critical Study of James Agee* (Amherst: University of Massachusetts Press, 1972);

Kenneth Curry, "The Knoxville of James Agee's *A Death in the Family*," *Tennessee Studies in Literature*, 14 (1969): 1-14;

Genevieve Fabre, "A Bibliography of the Works of James Agee," *Bulletin of Bibliography*, 24 (May-August 1965): 145-148, 163-166;

W. M. Frohock, "James Agee: The Question of Unkept Promise," *Southwest Review*, 42 (summer 1957): 221-229;

Victor A. Kramer, *James Agee* (Boston: Twayne, 1975);

Kramer, "Premonition of Disaster: An Unpublished Section for Agee's *A Death in the Family*," *Costerus*, N.S., 1 (1974): 83-93;

Erling Larsen, *James Agee* (Minneapolis: University of Minnesota Press, 1971);

Dwight MacDonald, "Death of a Poet," *New Yorker*, 33 (16 November 1957): 224 ff.;

MacDonald, "Some Memories and Letters," *Encounter*, 19 (December 1962): 73-84;

David Madden, ed., *Remembering James Agee* (Baton Rouge: Louisiana State University Press, 1974);

Genevieve Moreau, *The Restless Journey of James Agee* (New York: Morrow, 1977);

Peter H. Ohlin, *Agee* (New York: Obolensky, 1966);

Richard Oulahan, "A Cult Grew Around a Many-Sided Writer," *Life*, 55 (1 November 1963): 69-72;

Kenneth Seib, *James Agee: Promise and Fulfillment* (Pittsburgh: University of Pittsburgh Press, 1968).

Manuscripts:

The University of Texas has a large collection of Agee's literary manuscripts and correspondence; see Victor A. Kramer, "James Agee Papers at the University of Texas," *Library Chronicle of the University of Texas*, 8, no. 2 (1966): 33-36.

Louis Auchincloss.

Nancy Sirkis

LOUIS STANTON AUCHINCLOSS was born in Lawrence, New York, on 27 September 1917 and was reared in New York City. Related by birth to the prominent and wealthy Russell, Howland, Stanton, and Dixon families in New York City, he married Adele Lawrence in 1957 and has three sons, John, Blake, and Andrew. Far from homogeneous and far from small, the social world of these families and their affluent friends and acquaintances has provided Louis Auchincloss with a rich gallery of characters and a full range of fictional conflicts. Educated at the Bovee School for Boys and at Groton, Auchincloss matriculated at Yale in 1935 and at the University of Virginia Law School in 1938.

During World War II he served in the Naval Intelligence in the Panama Canal Zone and as gunnery officer aboard the U.S.S. *Moonstone*. Later he served as commander of an L.S.T. in England, France, and the Pacific. While at sea he read widely in the classic novelists of manners—Trollope, Thackeray, Proust, Wharton, Balzac, and especially James. The influence of Henry James has been so powerful that Auchincloss calls himself a "Jacobite." For to be exposed to the criticism, fiction, and letters of Henry James is "to be conducted through the literature of [James's] time, English, American, French, and Russian, by a kindly guide of infinitely good manners, who is also infinitely discerning,

*Mr. and Mrs. Auchincloss at
Truman Capote's Masked Ball.*

tasteful and conscientious." James, for Auchincloss, has always been a "starting point," a "common denominator." But, once started, Auchincloss has always gone his own way—often qualifying and contesting, as well as enlarging, the social and psychological insights of the nineteenth-century novelists of manners.

After the war, Louis Auchincloss returned to New York City to combine a law career with the writing of fiction, biography, and criticism. His first novel, *The Indifferent Children* (1947), provides witty and ironic pictures of New York society and society people in rear-eschelon desk jobs in the Canal Zone and at sea. Published under the pseudonym "Andrew Lee," the novel earned the disapproval of Auchincloss's parents, who feared that their friends would frown and that his law career at Sullivan and Cromwell might be damaged. The book shows many of the weaknesses of a first novel: diffuse structure, unfocused characterization, and an uncertainty of narrative voice. Even Auchincloss conceded the silliness of his nonhero, Beverly Stregelinus, and Auchincloss's resolution of the plot—disposing of

Stregelinus by throwing a "buzz bomb at him while he was on liberty from an L.S.T. in London"—was less than elegant. Even so, the novel received surprisingly high praise. William McFee remarked in the *New York Sun* that the author of this novel was "of the caliber of the Henry James who wrote *Washington Square* and *A Portrait of a Lady* rather than of the author of *The Ambassadors*. It is James alive to our times, aware of things and people James himself never even sensed, but with the psychological alertness and a mastery of English the master would have enjoyed very much indeed." Exhilarated by this tribute to his talent and by the comparison with James, Auchincloss readily embraced the life of the fiction writer, although he remained a lawyer.

Louis Auchincloss's second book, *The Injustice Collectors* (1950), a short story collection, contains eight psychological studies exploring the fate of "neurotics who continually and unconsciously construct situations in which they are disappointed or mistreated," unconscious masochists who "are looking for injustice, even in a friendly world, because they suffer from a hidden need to feel that this world has wronged them.'' The acuity of Louis Auchincloss's character analysis led one reviewer in the *Psychiatric Quarterly* to remark that Auchincloss was "still fifty years ahead of his colleagues" in psychological insight.

Sybil (1952), Auchincloss's second novel, is a deeply sympathetic study of a dissatisfied society woman which established the novelist's claim to special understanding of feminine psychology. In *A Law for the Lion* (1953) Auchincloss deepened his exploration of the woman's psyche in a penetrating study of Eloise Dilworth, who wants to discover whether there is any real "identity" beneath the various roles she has played in her lifetime—the childish niece to her aunt and uncle, the submissive wife to her indifferent husband, the taken-for-granted mother to her children. Eloise's search for an answer leads her to reject the arbitrary conventions of the elite social world in which she has been brought up, but her losses are compensated for by her discovery that a real "self" exists beneath the functions imposed on her by her social existence. The personality of Eloise Dilworth, her irreducible "I," is never fully expressed by the decor of her world or the sum of her functions.

In 1954 Auchincloss published his second collection of tales, *The Romantic Egoists*, a title taken from the unpublished version of Fitzgerald's *This Side of Paradise*. In this collection Auchincloss fictionalized some aspects of his own prep school experience at Groton ("Billy and the Gargoyles"). And in another tale he sketched out the germ of what was to be his fourth novel, *The Great World and Timothy Colt* (1956), another study of the impulse to self-punishment. In this novel the title character, Colt, punishes himself for abandoning his youthful legal idealism by confessing a misprision which could never have been proved against him. Both this novel and *Venus in Sparta* (1958) are subtle and perceptive studies of protagonists who struggle against the role assigned to each by the world in which he lives. In the latter, Michael Farish is brought up to satisfy the social expectations of his mother. A Farish leads a certain kind of life. So Michael is sent off to Averhill prep school, then to Harvard; he is taken into the Hudson River Trust Company and eventually becomes a partner. He is expected to become Director and Chairman. But Michael Farish is emotionally unequipped for the role society has fashioned for him. He has no psychological armor against the arrows of his bitch goddess Success and the socially created myth of what manhood constitutes. When a crisis occurs in his professional life and his marriage goes on the

rocks because he is unable to live up to the socially defined image of masculine virility, he runs away to Mexico. The figure of the child fearing and expecting punishment for some failure to live up to the expectations of the adult world is a recurrent image in Auchincloss's fiction. Frequently the individual welcomes punishment as a relief—such is the burden of his guilt at not successfully playing his role. If the punishment does not come, the protagonist often seeks relief from his guilt through some suicidal or self-destructive act. Timothy Colt punishes himself for abandoning his idealism by courting his own professional destruction and Michael Farish ends by drowning himself in the ocean. Such is the toll exacted of some of the characters in Auchincloss's fiction, but it is not a tragic cost. None of his characters is of tragic importance, for, as Auchincloss has conceded, "pathos has a bigger place than tragedy in the study of manners." It is, however, a poignant cost built out of the subtlety and insight of Auchincloss's characterization.

Louis Auchincloss's next three novels—*Pursuit of the Prodigal* (1959), *The House of Five Talents* (1960), and *Portrait in Brownstone* (1962)—brought to a fine point his developing powers of psychological insight and social observation. While many of Auchincloss's reviewers expressed distaste for the narrow social world of his New York aristocracy and for the novelist's apparent acceptance of the social order in which they were privileged members, others hailed him as one of the most important novelists of the mid-twentieth century. John Betjeman admired the clarity of Auchincloss's prose; Elizabeth Bowen called him "a story-teller with a beautifully clear and direct style—a classically good English style," and she remarked that he is "one of the ablest story-tellers and *direct* psychologists using the English language"; Angus Wilson called him "a very clever and subtle student of human social behavior"; and Anthony Burgess commended the power with which Auchincloss's fiction "presents the real twentieth-century world, very sharply, very subtly, very elegantly."

Portrait in Brownstone offers a bittersweet portrait of the Denisons of Fifty-third Street from the turn of the century into the 1950s. Modeled on the Dixons (on Auchincloss's grandmother's side), this family mirrors the social history of the brownstone era as told from the point of view of Ida Trask Hartley, a passive and obedient child who matures into the leader of a large and refractory family. Auchincloss's narrative of how she comes to manipulate, in her passive way, the children and grandchildren, the cousins and uncles and aunts of the tribe, is a truly impressive achievement. Ida's emergence as the dominant force for unity, in a family disintegrating from external and internal pressures, is accompanied by a perceptive study of the changing manners and morals of the American aristocracy in New York City. The novel is also a lament for New York's lost elegance and virtue, for an older social set now accessible only in *King's Notable New Yorkers*, in faded letters rescued from Newport attics, and in the distant memories of those who knew the face of New York before it began to change so rapidly.

The House of Five Talents recounts the rise of an American middle-class family from parvenu origins to aristocratic status during the period 1875-1948. It is the story of the five Millinder children, who descend from one of the most ruthless robber barons of the age of Grant, of their fortune, and of what became of it. In chronicling the story of the Millinder money, Auchincloss corrects what he believes to be some prevalent misconceptions about the relationship between wealth and American society. Told from Augusta Millinder's point of view, the novel is a series of episodes illustrating the poignant effect of the family fortune on the members of the tribe. At the same time, it is the comedy of an old maid who never married because she feared that her one suitor wanted her only for her money.

Auchincloss has remarked that "the paralyzing effect of a class-conscious background is largely illusory." Nowadays people are not as "preoccupied with their exact social niche as writers like O'Hara, for example, suggest." Consequently the novelist of manners may invest the form with a new dimension of psychology by showing that "the function of the character's background" may be "only his misconception of it. . . ." This is the case with most of Auchincloss's protagonists. The real cause of their conflicts is psychological, not social, pressure. The conventions of the aristocratic caste are utterly anachronistic, but if an individual's self-image obliges him to behave as if the obligations of caste are changeless and inflexible, he can do no other. Thus the Auchincloss novel of manners shifts its center from society to psychology: manners become the gestures by which characters, believing in the reality of their own theatrical pretense, frustrate and destroy themselves.

Powers of Attorney (1963) offers twelve interrelated stories involving office politics and legal contests won and lost in a large law office in New York City—Tower, Tilney, and Webb. Derived from Auchincloss's own observation of the workings of

the legal profession, *Powers of Attorney* (like his other fiction dealing with the legal profession) offers unparalleled insight into the workings of the law in large law firms. So acute is Auchincloss's observation of his colleagues that some of his books are recommended, if not required, reading for law students.

By most accounts, *The Rector of Justin* (1964) is Louis Auchincloss's most popular and distinguished novel. In this book he undertook to paint the portrait of a headmaster in a New England boarding school. Frank Prescott, recently deceased headmaster of a preparatory school (the resemblance to Endicott Peabody at Groton is superficial), is recreated through the differing recollections and impressions of several characters—the priggish young admirer, the irreverent daughter, the wife, the friend, the students, and the alumni. What the novel suggests is that we can never know what Prescott was really like because none of the narrators knew the real Prescott: he presented a different side to each of them. It might well be asked whether there was any "real" Prescott behind his various masks. The answer is yes, but he can never be known except as a composite of the limited points of view of his various biographers. The novel was extraordinarily successful. August Derleth and Stanton Peckham called Auchincloss "the best living American novelist." Sidney S. Thomas argued that in *The Rector of Justin* Auchincloss had left "Edith Wharton far behind. He has written a book that would forever have been beyond her." And Leon Edel remarked that Auchincloss "must be reckoned in the front rank of mid-century American novelists."

After *The Rector of Justin* Auchincloss's fiction received less acclaim from critics and reviewers. *The Embezzler* (1966) deals engagingly with Guy Prime's embezzlement of several hundred thousand dollars before the New Deal came in and hosed out the financial iniquities of old Wall Street. The events narrated in Guy's memoir, written before his death in 1962, are retold (and differently interpreted) by Rex Geer and then by Angelica, Guy's wife, who becomes Rex's mistress and later his wife. *Tales of Manhattan* (1967) contains thirteen short stories exploring from various new angles the world of wealth, power, and social distinction which Auchincloss has made his *metier*. *A World of Profit* (1968) deals with greed, with the passion for money which infects everyone when the Shalcross family decides to sell its nineteenth-century manor house in Queens to an urban developer. In this world the aristocrats are played out. Jay Livingston, a hustler and a Jew who has rejected his faith and changed his name, and the only sympathetic character, is the vortex of energy standing for the future. And in *Second Chance—Tales of Two Generations* (1970) Auchincloss offers a dozen new tales in which several characters struggle with the problem of the onset of old age and how to regenerate the self.

In *I Come as a Thief* (1972) Auchincloss investigates the impact on Tony Lowder, who takes a bribe, of a religious conversion which changes him from a rather commonplace organization man into an advocate for Christ in the Down Town Association. When the dark night of the soul descends on Lowder, he concludes that he can escape from his "surpassingly dull" if glittery world only by publicly confessing his betrayal of trust and accepting punishment for it. This confession leads to a "sense of inexpressible well-being. Of love, you might call it," but it estranges him from nearly everyone he knows.

With *The Partners* (1974), Auchincloss returned to the interrelated short story sequence—each of these fourteen tales dealing with legal, moral, sexual, and psychological crises in the lives of those connected to the Wall Street law firm of Shepard, Putney, and Cox. Chief among these tales is perhaps "The Novelist of Manners," in which Dana Clyde observes of himself: "O, I have a following yet, I grant. There are plenty of old girls and boys who still take me to the hospital for their hysterectomies and prostates. But the trend is against me. The young don't read me. The literary establishment scorns me. . . . I have always dealt with the great world. The top of the heap. How people climbed up and what they found when they got there. That was perfectly valid when the bright young people were ambitious for money and social position. But now they don't care about those things. They care about stopping wars and saving the environment and cleaning up the ghettos. And they are right, too. When the world's going to pieces, who has time to talk about good form and good taste?" Some reviewers took Dana Clyde to be Auchincloss himself. If so, the joke was on the reviewers. For *The Partners* shows that the novel of manners can still be written, even though the fictive novelist in the book denied that it is possible to do so. These tales were invariably effective and put *The Partners* on the best-seller list.

Auchincloss's most recent works of fiction have been *The Winthrop Covenant* (1976) and *The Dark Lady* (1977). In the first, Auchincloss presented a series of interlocking stories, each complete in itself, dealing with "the rise and fall of the Puritan ethic in New York and New England" from 1630 to the present. In the second, Auchincloss focused on the career of an ambitious woman, Elesina Dart, who rises, through an astute marriage, from the condition of an alcoholic actress to the role of Congresswoman from Westchester County. The point of the tale, with its Shakespearean title, is the darkness of disaster that afflicts Elesina's victims as she rises to great place.

In addition to his twenty-one works of fiction, Auchincloss has written a number of biographical and critical studies: *Reflections of a Jacobite* (1961), *Edith Wharton* (1961), *Ellen Glasgow* (1964), *Pioneers & Caretakers* (1965), *Motiveless Malignity* (1969), *Henry Adams* (1971), *Edith Wharton: A Woman in Her Time* (1971), *Richelieu* (1972), and *Reading Henry James* (1975). He has also told the story of his youth and literary apprenticeship in *A Writer's Capital* (1974). These studies reflect an acute sensibility with a deep interest in society and its intricate workings, as reflected in the lives and works of his subjects. So extensive and distinguished is Louis Auchincloss's work, in both fiction and nonfiction, that Jackson Bryer's *Louis Auchincloss and His Critics: A Bibliographical Record* (1977) argues that "With the recent deaths of Edmund Wilson and Lionel Trilling, it is not too extravagant to suggest that their logical successor as our leading man of letters, that is, a figure who is adept at various kinds of literary art, might well be Louis Auchincloss." While others may disagree with this high praise, there is no question that Auchincloss has given us a vivid picture of an exclusive social world and, in doing so, has created a gallery of memorable men and women struggling to define themselves amidst the fluidity of social change.

Auchincloss is our most important living novelist of manners and offers a glittering panorama of the world of Wall Street brokers and bankers, lawyers and corporation executives. As a lawyer himself, he knows his characters in their Park Avenue apartments and in their downtown offices. He sees the glitter and glamour of their world, its arrogant materialism, and its unexpected generosities. He knows the rigidity of the social conventions of this world and the point at which conventions give way or rebellious character breaks under the strain of social pressure. Auchincloss is able to tell the stories of his characters with penetration, psychological insight, and unusual sympathy. In recreating the contemporary *haut monde* of New York City, Auchincloss continues the tradition of the novel of manners as practiced by James, Wharton, Fitzgerald, Marquand, and O'Hara.

While Louis Auchincloss's reputation is based on his portraits of New York City society from colonial life to the present, his novels are more than

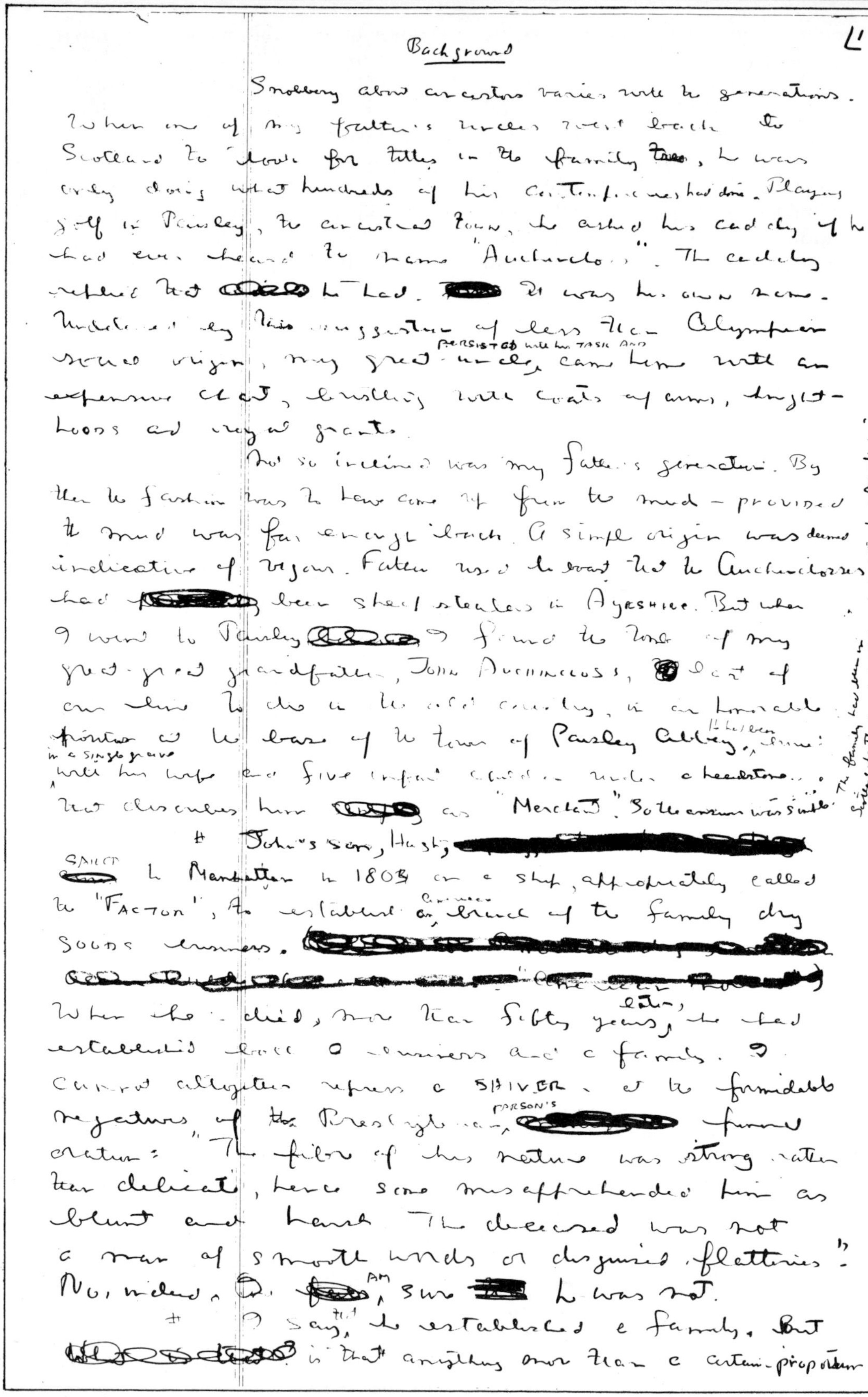

Background

Snobbery about ancestors varies with the generations. When one of my father's uncles went back to Scotland to look for titles in the family tree, he was only doing what hundreds of his contemporaries had done. Playing golf in Paisley, the ancestral town, he asked his caddy if he had ever heard the name "Auchincloss". The caddy replied that [redacted] he had. [redacted] It was his own name. Undaunted by this suggestion of less than Olympian social origin, my great-uncle persisted with his task and came home with an expensive chart, bristling with coats of arms, knighthoods and royal grants.

Not so inclined was my father's generation. By then the fashion was to have come up from the mud – provided the mud was far enough back. A simple origin was deemed indicative of vigor. Father used to boast that the Auchinclosses had [redacted] been sheep stealers in Ayrshire. But when I went to Paisley [redacted] I found the tomb of my great-great grandfather, John Auchincloss, [redacted] last of our line to die in the old country, in an honorable position at the base of the tower of Paisley Abbey, buried in a single grave with his wife and five infant children under a headstone... that describes him [redacted] as "Merchant". So the curse was [illegible]. The family had been in Scotland fairly much what they had become in New York.

John's son, Hugh, [redacted] sailed to Manhattan in 1803 on a ship, appropriately called the "Factor", to establish an American branch of the family dry goods business. [redacted] When he died, more than fifty years later, he had established both a business and a family. I cannot altogether repress a shiver at the formidable negatives of the Presbyterian parson's [redacted] funeral oration: "The fiber of his nature was strong rather than delicate, hence some misapprehended him as blunt and harsh. The deceased was not a man of smooth words or disguised flatteries." No, indeed, [redacted], I am sure [redacted] he was not.

+ I say that he established a family. But [redacted] is that anything more than a certain proportion

First page of the manuscript for A Writer's Capital *(1974).*

Duane Michals

Louis Auchincloss at home.

chronicles of manners. He is fascinated by the inexhaustible possibilities of the novel of character—character in crisis because of the imperatives of private morality in a world where social morality no longer exists. In a number of his novels, Auchincloss explores the ambiguity of selfhood, the problem of individual identity—which Ralph Ellison has called the central issue in American fiction. Most novelists of manners, profoundly influenced by the behaviorism of the natural sciences (Wharton, Wells, Bennett, O'Hara, and Marquand, for example), tend to see character as a product of the material and social environment. They create "character," as Virginia Woolf complained, in very close correlation to and through descriptions of houses, furniture, clothes, and the outward accoutrements of social class. Auchincloss rejects this method of novelistic characterization. While the interior decor of his world is described in detail, Auchincloss's characters exist independent of the web of the material environment which surrounds them. However much his fictive personae may belong to the Park Avenue–Wall Street–Long Island–Bar Harbor social set, each is a distinctly individualized character in search of self-understanding. In exploring their social ex-

perience and moral histories, Auchincloss thus writes both the traditional novel of manners—updating and sometimes arguing with Henry James and Edith Wharton—and incisive psychological studies probing the nature of the individual spirit. In an era of sometimes brilliant fictional innovations—marked by the achievement of Joyce, Woolf, Faulkner, Nabokov, Barth, and Hawkes—Louis Auchincloss offers a fiction conservative in design, orderly in structure, and civilized in style.

—*James W. Tuttleton*

Books:

The Indifferent Children, as Andrew Lee (New York: Prentice-Hall, 1947);

The Injustice Collectors (Boston: Houghton Mifflin, 1950; London: Gollancz, 1951);

Sybil (Boston: Houghton Mifflin, 1952; London: Gollancz, 1952);

A Law for the Lion (Boston: Houghton Mifflin, 1953; London: Gollancz, 1953);

The Romantic Egoists (Boston: Houghton Mifflin, 1954; London: Gollancz, 1954);

The Great World and Timothy Colt (Boston: Houghton Mifflin, 1956; London: Gollancz, 1956);

Venus in Sparta (Boston: Houghton Mifflin, 1958; London: Gollancz, 1958);

Pursuit of the Prodigal (Boston: Houghton Mifflin, 1959; London: Gollancz, 1960);

The House of Five Talents (Boston: Houghton Mifflin, 1960; London: Gollancz, 1960);

Reflections of a Jacobite (Boston: Houghton Mifflin, 1961; London: Gollancz, 1961);

Edith Wharton (Minneapolis: University of Minnesota Press, 1961);

Portrait in Brownstone (Boston: Houghton Mifflin, 1962; London: Gollancz, 1962);

Powers of Attorney (Boston: Houghton Mifflin, 1963; London: Gollancz, 1963);

The Rector of Justin (Boston: Houghton Mifflin, 1964; London: Gollancz, 1965);

Ellen Glasgow (Minneapolis: University of Minnesota Press, 1964);

Pioneers & Caretakers (Minneapolis: University of Minnesota Press, 1965; London: Oxford University Press, 1966);

The Embezzler (Boston: Houghton Mifflin, 1966; London: Gollancz, 1966);

Tales of Manhattan (Boston: Houghton Mifflin, 1967; London: Gollancz, 1967);

On Sister Carrie (Columbus, Ohio: Merrill, 1968);

A World of Profit (Boston: Houghton Mifflin, 1968; London: Gollancz, 1969);

Motiveless Malignity (Boston: Houghton Mifflin, 1969; London: Gollancz, 1970);

Second Chance—Tales of Two Generations (Boston: Houghton Mifflin, 1970; London: Gollancz, 1971);

Henry Adams (Minneapolis: University of Minnesota Press, 1971);

Edith Wharton—A Woman in Her Time (New York: Viking, 1971; London: Joseph, 1972);

I Come as a Thief (Boston: Houghton Mifflin, 1972; London: Weidenfeld & Nicolson, 1973);

Richelieu (New York: Viking, 1972; London: Joseph, 1973);

The Partners (Boston: Houghton Mifflin, 1974; London: Weidenfeld & Nicolson, 1974);

A Writer's Capital (Minneapolis: University of Minnesota Press, 1974);

Reading Henry James (Minneapolis: University of Minnesota Press, 1975);

The Winthrop Covenant (Boston: Houghton Mifflin, 1976; London: Weidenfeld & Nicolson, 1976);

The Dark Lady (Boston: Houghton Mifflin, 1977).

References:

J. Donald Adams, *Speaking of Books—and Life* (New York: Holt, Rinehart & Winston, 1965), pp. 11-14;

Jackson R. Bryer, *Louis Auchincloss and His Critics: A Bibliographical Record* (Boston: G. K. Hall, 1977);

Sandra Davis, "Best-Selling Novelist Louis Auchincloss—Urbane Echo of a Graceful Past," *Life*, 60 (15 April 1966): 53-54, 56-57;

"Dual Career," *New Yorker*, 36 (13 August 1960): 23-25;

Charles Greenwood, "A Lawyer at Large," *Law Journal*, 107 (8 November 1957): 709-710;

Patricia Kane, "Lawyers at the Top: The Fiction of Louis Auchincloss," *Critique*, 7, 2 (winter 1964-1965): 36-46;

Robie Macauley, ' "Let Me Tell You About the Rich . . . ,' " *Kenyon Review*, 27 (autumn 1965): 645-671;

Roy Newquist, *Counterpoint* (Chicago: Rand McNally, 1964), pp. 32-38;

Dennis O'Hara, "Afternoon Sketch of Louis Auchincloss," *Lynx*, 38 (spring 1966): 47-54;

Frank W. Shelton, "The Family in the Modern American Novel of Manners," *South Atlantic Bulletin*, 40 (May 1975): 33-39;

James W. Tuttleton, *The Novel of Manners in America* (Chapel Hill: University of North Carolina Press, 1972), pp. 237-261;

Tuttleton, "Louis Auchincloss: The Image of Lost Elegance and Virtue," *American Literature*, 43 (January 1972): 616-632;

Wayne W. Westbrook, "Louis Auchincloss' Vision of Wall Street," *Critique*, 15, 2 (1973): 57-66;

G. Edward White, "Human Dimensions of Wall Street Fiction," *American Bar Association Journal*, 58 (February 1972): 175-180.

James Baldwin

Fred L. Standley
Florida State University

BIRTH: New York City, 2 August 1924.

EDUCATION: P. S. 24, 139, Harlem; DeWitt Clinton High School, Bronx.

AWARDS: Eugene F. Saxton Fellowship, 1945; Rosenwald Fellowship, 1948; Guggenheim Fellowship, 1954; *Partisan Review* Fellowship, 1956; National Institute of Arts and Letters grant, 1956; Ford Foundation grant, 1959; National Conference of Christians and Jews Brotherhood Award, 1962; George Polk Award, 1963; Foreign Drama Critics Award, 1964; Elected, National Institute of Arts and Letters, 1964.

MAJOR WORKS: *Autobiographical Notes* (New York: Knopf, 1953); *Go Tell It on the Mountain* (New York: Knopf, 1953; London: Joseph, 1954); *Notes of a Native Son* (Boston: Beacon, 1955; London: Mayflower, 1958); *Giovanni's Room* (New York: Dial, 1956; London: Joseph, 1957); *Nobody Knows My Name* (New York: Dial, 1961; London: Joseph, 1964); *Another Country* (New York: Dial, 1962; London: Joseph, 1963); *The Fire Next Time* (New York: Dial, 1963; London: Joseph, 1963); *Going to Meet the Man* (New York: Dial, 1965; London: Joseph, 1965); *Tell Me How Long the Train's Been Gone* (New York: Dial, 1968; London: Joseph, 1968); *If Beale Street Could Talk* (London: Joseph, 1974; New York: Dial, 1974).

James Baldwin.

As novelist, essayist, dramatist and social critic, James Baldwin's books and numerous other pieces attest not only to a sustained prolificacy but also to a consistent perspicacity. Alternately praised and derided by blacks and whites alike, Baldwin's works have never lacked an audience. The rationale for this public interest in his work obviously consists of multiple factors, among them being his prophetic tone, moral concern, existential analysis, perceptive relevance, intense language, and poignant sincerity.

From the age of twelve, when he published a short story on the Spanish Revolution in a church newspaper, and a short time later, when he received a letter of congratulations from New York Mayor La Guardia for one of his poems, Baldwin has nurtured a passionate devotion to writing: "I consider that I have many responsibilities but none greater than this: to last, as Hemingway says, and get my work done. I want to be an honest man and a good writer."

To fulfill that ambition he recognizes that "the artist . . . cannot allow any consideration to supercede his responsibility to reveal all that he can possibly discover concerning the mystery of the human being"; and for Baldwin this means that the role of the artist is to express the existential knowledge of experience: "the states of birth, suffering, love and death . . . extreme states— extreme, universal, and inescapable. . . . The artist is present to correct the delusions to which we fall prey in our attempts to avoid this knowledge." An adequate perspective of man for our technological era is possible, in Baldwin's view, only when the artist analyzes man as not "merely a member of a society or group or a deplorable conundrum to be explained by Science . . . but something resolutely indefinable, unpredictable." Thus, in the effort to

15

confront and reveal "the disquieting complexity of ourselves," the only real concern for the artist is "to recreate out of the disorder of life that order which is art" and "to describe things which other people are too busy to describe." Baldwin is unequivocal in declaring this to be "a special function" and that "people who do it cannot by that token do many other things."

Additionally, Baldwin advocates explicitly a conception of literary art involving both personal and social responsibility. Personal responsibility implies a duty to avoid self-delusion by the "attempt to look on himself and the world as they are"; however, the writer is also "responsible to and for—the social order" by developing an ethical vision and historical orientation. In his essay "The Creative Dilemma," Baldwin describes the artist as "the incorrigible disturber of the peace" with whom "all societies have battled" because while society assumes its own stability, "the artist cannot and must not take anything for granted, but must drive to the heart of every answer and expose the question the answer hides." Hence, the writer's peculiar nature as artist imposes a condition of "warring" with his society "for its sake and for his own." Within the United States, Baldwin believes that this responsibility requires "sweat and tears" because the society seems determined to prohibit the artist's vision of human experience "in which one discovers that life is tragic, and therefore unutterably beautiful." Such a view presupposes the validity of paradox as a category of exploration, but America is a "country devoted to the death of paradox." Consequently, Baldwin eloquently advocates that "the war of an artist with his society is a lover's war, and he does at his best, what lovers do, which is to reveal the beloved to himself and, with that revelation, to make freedom real."

Within this context Baldwin's works have passionately and perceptively explored a broad spectrum of thematic concerns: the misplaced emphasis in the value systems of America; the indivisibility of the private life and the public life; the intertwining of love and power in the universal scheme of existence and in society's structures; the past historical significance and the potential explosiveness of the present racial crisis; the essential need to develop sexual and psychological consciousness and identity; and the responsibility of the artist to promote the evolution of the individual and society. For him only two options are open to all "writers, black or white—to be immoral and uphold the *status quo* or to be moral and try to change the world."

By the time of his high school graduation in 1942, Baldwin had served as editor of the literary magazine, spent three years as a Holy Roller preacher, and been indelibly influenced by Harriet Beecher Stowe and Charles Dickens. Twenty years later, as Fern Eckman has shown, "*Uncle Tom's Cabin* was to be ranked by Baldwin—along with Dostoevsky's *The Possessed, Crime and Punishment*, and *The Brothers Karamazov*, Henry James' *The Princess Casamassima* and *The Portrait of a Lady*, Dickens' *A Tale of Two Cities*, Ralph Ellison's *Invisible Man*, Richard Wright's *Black Boy* and Charles Wright's *The Messenger*—among the ten books that had helped him break out of the ghetto."

After a series of odd jobs—waiter, dishwasher, office boy, factory worker, handyman, porter, elevator operator—and writing reviews and short pieces for the *Nation* and *New Leader*, Baldwin met Richard Wright, who read part of his first novel in manuscript and helped him obtain the Saxton Award "to enable new and unrecognized authors to complete books." Finally, in 1948 he embarked for Paris and remained there for nearly a decade except for brief visits home and excursions to other European countries. Alternating between loneliness and starvation in Paris, he became acquainted with other American writers, including James Jones, Philip Roth, William Styron and Norman Mailer. It was there also that he read Henry James and began to evolve a clean conception of literary form and technique, especially what Charles Newman has described as the "dialectical art," which views the world in terms of primary conflicts and a "symmetry" based on the inherent drama of these polar conflicts.

Go Tell It on the Mountain (1953), Baldwin's first novel, focuses on the religious conversion of John Grimes. It is set in Harlem's storefront Temple of the Fire Baptised, on the fourteenth birthday of Grimes, whose experiences closely resemble those of the author's youth.

The novel is divided into three parts. Part I, "The Seventh Day," provides an introduction to the Grimes family in Harlem in 1935. John feels constricted and frustrated by the repressive, hate-suffused, hell's fire sermons of his father, Gabriel, who is the leader of the Temple of the Fire Baptised. John struggles with guilt about sex, ambivalent emotions toward his parents, and latent hatred of whites.

Part II, "The Prayers of the Saints," is a complex artistic rendering by the use of flashbacks of the Grimes's familial background centering upon three prayers: Aunt Florence, Gabriel, and Elizabeth, John's mother. Florence's prayer reminisces about the times of her and Gabriel's mother and their expectations of black family life being dominated by the male; her fleeing from the South about 1900, after having been asked by a white employer to become his "concubine"; her relationship with Frank, whose caramel color eventually led to the end of their marriage because of her disdain for his "common nigger" friends and her continued use of "them old skin-whitners," while he remarked "that black's a mighty pretty color." Florence's prayer ends "with terror and rage" as she asks God why "he preferred her mother and her brother, the old, black woman, and the low, black man, while she, who had sought only to walk upright, was come to die, alone and in poverty, in a dirty, furnished room?" Gabriel's prayer section recapitulates twenty years of his life— his earlier marriage with Deborah, "a holy fool"; the affair with Esther and the birth and death of their son, Royal; his own distaste for the "big, comfortable, ordained" evangelists at the Twenty-Four Elders Revival Meeting; his internal struggle between pietism and lust; and his ambivalence of feeling toward Elizabeth's bastard son, John. Elizabeth's prayer recounts what various experiences of love have meant to her: the "furious affectation of maternal concern" toward her; the enforced "separation of herself from her father" by the aunt; her life with Richard in New York and his ultimate suicide after being humiliated by the police; and her marriage to Gabriel after the birth of John. Elizabeth "hated it all—the white city, the white world" and finds her relief in the thought that "Only God could establish order in this chaos; to Him the soul must turn to be delivered."

Part III, "The Threshing Floor," emphasizes John's conversion on the floor before the altar surrounded by Mother Washington, Elisha, and other "saints," his mind tortured by guilt, fear, and hatred. Finally, "in the silence something died in John, and something came alive," and at dawn he emerges from the Temple, smiling and confident about the future.

In spite of the novel's numerous scriptural references and allusions, its use of Biblical names for characters, its seeming preoccupation with church practices, *Go Tell It on the Mountain* is not primarily a religious novel; rather it is a novel embodying a major cultural concept of which religion is only one element. Dr. Johnetta Cole's pervasive exploration of life-styles in "nigger culture" as being comprised of the Street, Down-home, Militant, and Upward-bound provides a significant point of entry for interpreting the novel. While "the street" or urban setting appears to be dominant, it is really the "down-home" life-style that pervades the book and occurs repetitively in the text, "indicating one's point of origin, down south, or the simple, decent way of life . . . basically rural and Southern" and centering in "the kitchens . . . the church halls . . . and the fraternal orders." Within that context this is a sociopolitical novel which is a subtly harsh indictment of a white-controlled society that has radically delimited the lives and hopes of blacks. For those whose skin color offers no hope better than "the back door, and the dark stairs, and the kitchen or basement, " the alternatives seem to be escapism through drugs, drink and sex or through the church. John Grimes must learn to accept the reality of the experiences recited in the lives of Florence, Gabriel and Elizabeth; the options open to him on the threshing floor are to leave the community of the faithful and to court disaster or to remain in the group and reduce his range of possibilities by embracing a hopeless otherworldliness divorced from reality. Thus, the novel indicts not only the white society's racism but also the black's reliance upon a religious mode of behavior that is illusory and irrelevant to his daily existence.

The primary literary technique for exhibiting the dual points of sociopolitical condemnation is irony. Despite his "religious" conversion, nothing is really changed for John Grimes at the end of this novel; "whom the son sets free is free indeed" is a scriptural illusion here. The ethical norm of the book is established and enforced by the community of saints, especially in their effort to be in the world but not of the world; yet each of the principal saints has his or her own secret code of behavior at variance with the so-called norm. Elizabeth's favorite scriptural passage is "everything works together for good for them that love the Lord," but loving the Lord has made no real change in the pain, suffering and victimization of her family in the past or present. Gabriel's favorite Biblical text is "set this house in order," yet all of the households connected with him have been in disorder and his fanatical belief structure is a rationalization for evading responsibility; the words of Gabriel as "God's messenger" are of despair, deceit, destruction, and disorder.

Go Tell It on the Mountain, then, is a prefiguration of themes and motifs that Baldwin pursues further in subsequent writing. Baldwin derides and derogates those who would oversimplify an authentic and effective mode of response to the white society's dominance over the black's existence; and he reveals that refuge in an otherworldly religion, rationalized by a conception of God borrowed from the white world, is an illusion, and therefore, damnation not salvation.

In *Notes of a Native Son* (1955) Baldwin collected ten essays that had previously appeared in *Commentary, Partisan Review,* and other magazines. This volume marked his formal entry into the literary tradition of the personal essay. These essays, primarily autobiographical and impressionistic, offer penetrating and intense comments on a variety of subjects: the novel of protest from Stowe to Wright; ghetto experiences in Harlem; black-white encounters in Europe; the film *Carmen Jones,* and other subjects that frequently overlap with the material treated in his fiction. "Stranger in the Village" has since been much anthologized. It not only reveals the author's unique experience of being the first black man encountered by a small Swiss village, but it also becomes the instrument of expressing forcefully the basic premise of the racial revolution of the twentieth century: "the people who shut their eyes to reality simply invite their own destruction. . . . The world is white no longer, and it will never be white again." For Baldwin it is the business of the writer to embark on "this journey toward a more vast reality which must take precedence over all other claims." Consequently a significant stress in this book is on the revelation of what it means to be black, especially in America, i.e., to be regarded as inferior and thus "to live in a constant state of rage." Langston Hughes contended two decades ago that the essays were "thought-provoking, tantalizing, irritating, abusing and amusing" and that "few American writers handle words more effectively in the essay form than James Baldwin."

At first glance *Giovanni's Room* (1956) would appear to be a rather complete departure from the prior books. Indeed, as Fern Eckman points out, the work "concerns itself entirely with the white world. Not a single Negro enters its radically segregated pages." The narrative focuses on David, a tall, blond, white American, who fluctuates between his fiancee, Hella, and his male Italian lover, Giovanni, until Hella discovers that David's body is "the incarnation of a mystery" manifesting itself in love for another man. Nevertheless, the principal concerns of the novel are similar to those of previous books—the search for sexual awareness and psychological identity; the complexity of the father-son relationship; the paradox of the relation between freedom and attachment; the painful and baffling complexity of relations among male and female, male and male. Critical responses have been mixed to this endeavor to treat the physical and psychological aspects of male love: Anthony West acknowledged the solemnity of the story but advocated that it "described a *passade,* a riffle in the surface of life, that completely lacks the validity of actual experience"; on the other hand, David Karp insisted that Baldwin had taken "a very special theme" and treated it with "great artistry and restraint," and Stanley Macebuh praised the work as "one of the few novels in America in which the homosexual sensibility is treated with some measure of creative seriousness."

During the five year period following his second novel, Baldwin returned from his Parisian exile, "apprenticed himself to Elia Kazan as a kind of playwright-in-training," worked on a novel, and wrote several pieces for periodicals. Then, in 1961 came *Nobody Knows My Name,* with the subtitle of *More Notes of a Native Son,* a collection of thirteen essays predominantly concerned with "the question of color" and the functions and problems of the artist in "the bottomless confusion which is both public and private of the American republic." Combining personal honesty with touches of irreverent and extravagant opinion, Baldwin commented on Harlem, the South, William Faulkner, Norman Mailer, Andre Gide, Ingmar Bergman, and other interests. "East River Downtown" exploded the naive notion that communists inspired the Negro riots at the United Nations following the death of Patrice Lumumba and asserted that any effort "to keep the Negro in his 'place' can only have the most extreme and unlucky repercussions." The frequently reprinted *apologia* entitled "The Discovery of What It Means to be an American" posits that a foreign sojourn can help the American writer to gain "a new sense of life's possibilities" and "unprecedented opportunities" in his own society because "there are no untroubled countries in this fearfully troubled world."

Another Country (1962) represents the author's *magnum opus* in fiction, though the novel has evoked considerable disapprobation. Robert Bone called the novel "a failure on the grand scale," with a plot that is "little more than a series of occasions for talk and fornication"; Howard Harper, Jr. described it as "a long playing record of frantic embraces and frantic questions"; and Eugenia Collier contended that it is "a lurid tale . . . seasoned with violence and obscenity," with "something offensive for everyone." In spite of such detractors, a small number of essays have insisted on serious critical treatment of the novel. Granville Hicks argued that it was "shaped with rigorous care" and explored the complexities of love and hate; Norman Podhoretz defended it as a "maltreated bestseller" and lauded "the militancy and cruelty of its vision of life," its "remorseless insistence on a truth," and its "element of sweet spiritual generosity."

Another Country deserves to be read as a competent and compelling book—structurally, symbolically, and thematically. Structurally, there are three sections: (1) "Easy Rider," (2) "Any Day Now," and (3) "Toward Bethlehem." The plot is comprised of four narrative strands involving two main characters in each strand: (1) Rufus Scott and Leona (black man, white woman); (2) Ida Scott and Vivaldo Moore (black woman, white man); (3) Richard and Cass Silenski (white man and woman); (4) Eric Jones and Yves (white homosexual, white male lover). These narrative accounts converge and intertwine at various points in a kind of phantasmagoria of interracial and intersexual relations among friends and strangers in New York City. The novel seems basically the story of Ida and Vivaldo; their strand is central to the movement of the work, and the conclusion focuses on their emergence as the principal norm of value, with the new mode of life for Eric and Yves embodying a subsidiary value.

Symbolically, the novel is richly suggestive in setting and title. The former is vividly described in imagery suggesting the danger, brutality, disease, lust, indifference, and despair of those who experience the ache of estrangement: "in New York, one had, still, to fight very hard in order not to perish of loneliness." The "strange climate of the city" mirrors the spiritual condition of the people in a kind of Dantesque hell of entrapment and isolation, a wasteland in which the characters struggle to live and relate to each other in order to justify self-awareness and renew the sense of being human. The title is reminiscent of Hemingway's story "In Another Country," set in the conflict of warfare and correlating the physical locale with the psychic terrain of the characters. Geographically, the title symbolizes: (1) New York, the other "country" within American society; (2) Harlem, the "other country" within a city, "which no white man can ever comprehend"; and (3) other countries, for example, France, where a black and a white can live with less guilt and dread and more possibility of joy. Ethically and philosophically, "another country" is the place wherein the values of the white majority lead to spiritual destruction because they are success

oriented and where the sense of American escapism denies the need of learning to confront the tragic— that pain, suffering, and death which belong to the essence of "the blues" that pulsate as a background in the novel. Psychologically, the title reflects the enormity of the mystery of sexual experience; to be out of touch with or to fear sensual reality is to deny the human, whether that sexual reality be expressed heterosexually, homosexually, or bisexually. It is only through the expressiveness of sexual encounter that one can overcome estrangement and experience the reality of another in that compassion and tenderness which are the essence of love. To enter "another country" is to enter that mystery in the wilderness of the love experience which is both terrifying and joyful: as Baldwin said in an earlier essay, "love takes off the masks that we fear we cannot live without and know we cannot live within. . . . Love . . . not in the infantile American sense of being made happy but in the tough and universal sense of quest and daring and growth."

Thematically, *Another Country* embodies the variety of subjects that are reiterated and modulated in the author's other works: the search for personal identity; the intensity of the emotions; the racial skirmishing of blacks and whites, involving both overt patterns of behavior and subtle psychological conditions; the need for recognition of the profound terror and joy in sexual encounter; the reality of pain, misery, and suffering in making human life tragic; and the indictment of the American dream. Within the novel, the human personality in all of its baffling mystery, its enigmatic perplexity, its web of tangled desire and frustration, is presented with force and pungency. Baldwin later confessed: "What I was trying to do was create for the first time my own apprehension of the country and the world. I understood that if I could discharge venom, I could discharge love (they frighten me equally). When I was a little boy, I hated all white people, but in this book I got beyond the hate. I faced my life by that book and it's a good book. It's as honest as I can be." From the early pages the leitmotif of aloneness and the necessity for love is explicitly expressed: "He stood there, wide legged, humping the air . . . screaming through the horn, Do you love me? Do you love me? Do you love me? . . . and yet the question was terrible and real."

From this perspective the novel becomes what Stanley Edgar Hyman calls "a parable of reconciliation, sin and forgiveness" through the central narrative strand of Vivaldo and Ida and the chief subsidiary strand of Eric and Yves. While the major characters discover ugly truths about themselves and each other, the novel concludes on a note of reconciliation; "another country" is the country of love which takes off the masks and makes reconciliation a possibility even among those of different races or of the same sex. Thus, Baldwin has been audacious enough, prior to most other artists, to grapple candidly with the usually taboo subjects of American society and culture: interracial sexual intercourse, homosexuality as a normative mode of experience, and bisexuality as a real phenomenon. This novel is an excursion into those areas of human relations about which insight is lacking and experience limited. The writer has given both in a novel that fulfills his own credo for the artistic function: "Real writers question their age. They demand Yes and No answers. Typers collaborate. You collaborate or you question."

In the intensification of the civil rights movement during the early 1960s Baldwin became an active participant. As various groups struggled to end racial discrimination and segregation, Baldwin became an increasingly ardent spokesman, enunciating in essays and speeches the agony of being black in America. While the role was not new for him, the activities of the 1960s were undertaken because of his reputation. Whether with Medgar Evers or James Meredith in Mississippi, at a session with Robert Kennedy in New York, on a speaking tour for the Congress of Racial Equality, or helping in the voter registration drive in Selma, Alabama, Baldwin was committed "to end the racial nightmare of our country and change the history of the world." The culmination of his literary effort in this era was the publication of *The Fire Next Time* (1963), a treatise which very likely helped "in restoring the personal essay to its place as a form of creative literature," as John Henrik Clarke has asserted.

The Fire Next Time consists of two essays in the form of letters, with the first as prefatory to the beliefs and concepts presented in the second. "My Dungeon Shook" contains advice to a young black male who is the author's nephew and is about to enter the domain of racial conflict on the anniversary of the proclamation that is supposed to have set him free. It is a forthright assault upon the "impertinent assumption . . . that black men are inferior to white men" and an assertion of the black's inherent "unassailable and monumental dignity."

The second essay, "Down at the Cross," is an autobiographical account in three sections: recollections of growing up in Harlem, an evaluation of the Black Muslims, and the statement of a personal credo. The Harlem section analyzes the psychological condition of learning to be black and "fighting

the man" in a "white country, an Anglo-Teutonic, anti-sexual country," of experiencing the principles of "Blindness, Loneliness, and Terror" in the Christian church, and of recognizing that "if the concept of God has any validity or any use, it can only be to make us larger, freer, and loving." The Black Muslim portion evaluates Elijah Muhammad as a charismatic and disciplined leader who "refuses to accept the white world's definitions" and therefore threatens its power. The "personal credo" posits a series of ideas relevant to contemporary America: the fact that "life is tragic"; the need "to apprehend the nature of change, to be able and willing to change"; the importance of discarding "that collection of myths to which white Americans cling"; the reality that blacks may not rise to power "but they are very well placed indeed to precipitate chaos and ring down the curtain on the American dream." Finally, in a note of compelling alarm, Baldwin prophesies that "the relatively conscious" whites and blacks may be able "to end the racial nightmare, and achieve our country, and change the history of the world"; otherwise, "no more water the fire next time."

Although this book did not offer any easy solutions to the political, social and psychological conditions of being black in America, it did suggest democracy as a means of promoting change and set forth what could be expected if such change were not forthcoming. Perhaps the greatest value of the essay's rhetorical flourishes of confession, anguish, quest and warning was its dramatization of emotional conditions with the underlying design of evoking the emotional response of empathy.

Two years elapsed between *The Fire Next Time* and the author's collection of eight short stories called *Going to Meet the Man* (1965). However, in those years the drama, *Blues for Mister Charlie* (1964), and the collaborative volume of photographs and text, *Nothing Personal* (1964, with Richard Avedon) were published. The short stories indicate clearly the influence of Henry James, and each "shows a sure sense of the short story form, a moment of illumination that has significance for the total life of the character," as George Kent phrases it. Furthermore, the stories reflect the range of Baldwin's early thematic interests and demonstrate a realistic sense of personal experiences.

The first two stories, "The Rockpile" and "The Outing," present the concern with family antagonisms and the memories of the church and thereby strongly resemble *Go Tell It on the Mountain*. "The Man Child" is a kind of horror story involving murder and illustrating Baldwin's contention in an essay on Wright that "no American Negro exists who does not have his private Bigger Thomas living in the skull." "Previous Condition" initiates a subject later treated more fully in *Tell Me How Long the Train's Been Gone* and *If Beale Street Could Talk*—the struggle for survival by the black artist and especially his ambivalent relations with whites. "Sonny's Blues" is the record of a young man's search for identity and self-expression through drugs, words and music, and "through the almost ritualistic repetition of feeling, emotion and mood the blues singer achieves," wrote Stanley Macebuh. "This Morning, This Evening, So Soon" deals with a seemingly successful black actor in a similar situation. "Come Out the Wilderness" concerns a young black woman from the South seeking love and success in the city and living with a white man, and an ambitious but lonely black actor from the South. "Going to Meet the Man" concludes the volume and coalesces the elements of history, the South, sex, violence, blacks and whites in a narrative that explores the moral, psychological and sociological roots of racism by analyzing the causes for impotency and violence in a white deputy sheriff. In this volume, as John Rees Moore says, the "people are lonely, frustrated, fearful, often angry, and above all lovelorn. . . . Most of them have a vision of a better land, a better life, but their moments of happiness are always precarious."

During the last dozen years or so, while continuing to reside in Europe with periodic treks to the United States, Baldwin has maintained an unflagging interest in the implications and effects of the civil rights movement within American society and culture. In fiction, essay, screenplay, and drama, he has reiterated the themes, motifs, and emphases of prior works—a "rap" session on race with anthropologist Margaret Mead; a television "dialogue" with poet Nikki Giovanni; an analysis of American films, both black and white, in "The Devil Finds Work"; a chronicling of and reflection about the times and the society in "No Name in the Streets"; a scenario of Malcolm X's transition from Black Muslim to spokesman for Islam; and others.

Tell Me How Long the Train's Been Gone (1968) has been denigrated as "a work of self-indulgence" and "drearily irrelevant" but commended as a realistic account of "one black man's struggle to overcome the definition of himself handed down by his white countrymen." It is the life story of a thirty-nine-year-old famous American black actor, Leo Proudhammer, who suffers a heart attack at the pinnacle of his career. During the period of his convalescence, a series of complicated flashbacks presents the momentous and significant events of his past: a childhood in Harlem; a hero-worship of his older, militant brother, Caleb; a long affair with a white actress, Barbara; police and prison guard brutality; and an attachment to a young and male black revolutionary, Christopher. The book repeats the homosexual and heterosexual, interracial lovemaking of earlier works as well as the assertive renunciation of religion and God as capable means of effective social change in the racial struggle. However, there are also distinctive changes in this novel compared to those preceding it; as Stanley Macebuh has persuasively argued, Baldwin creates for the first time a "Black Christopher" committed to "the politics of active confrontation" as an affirmation of "the essential worth of man" and makes homosexuality an intrinsic part of the revolutionary commitment so as "to present the homosexual as an authentic instrument of change in society." Thus, there appears in the novel a shift from reliance upon stressing the fictional protagonist's essential privacy as an individual to an emphasis upon the development of a "confident, proud, determined" black man devoted to public action.

Baldwin's latest novel, *If Beale Street Could Talk* (1974), also contributed to the familiar pattern of critical response, for it too has evoked not only such caustic epithets as "an almost total disaster" and "a vehemently sentimental love story" but also such complimentary descriptions as this from Joyce Carol Oates—"a quite moving and very traditional celebration of love." The story focuses upon the adversities of a young black couple: Fonny, the twenty-two-year-old sculptor and his nineteen-year-old, pregnant fiancée, Tish. Fonny is arrested and charged for a rape he did not commit, and he is capable of being freed before trial only if the bail money is raised. The novel presents the familial bond of sacrifice and love within the context of a society in which the black minority stands perpetually accused and trying to make bail for freedom. The major shift in this novel as compared to earlier works is that Baldwin concentrates for the first time on the question of what it means to be an artist in the society; previous works of fiction revealed persons of artistic sensibility, but Fonny is the closest that Baldwin has come in dealing with the common topic that nearly every twentieth-century fiction writer of stature has treated at one time or another.

Although it is somewhat premature to attempt to evaluate the literary status of James Baldwin, his accomplishments to date in fiction, drama and essay seem sufficient to assure him a ranking of considerable priority. It may be that his literary achievements are such, as Benjamin De Mott has said, that "this author retains a place in an extremely select group: that composed of the few genuinely indispensable American writers."

Other Works:

Blues for Mister Charlie (New York: Dial, 1964; London: Joseph, 1965);

Nothing Personal (New York: Atheneum, 1964);

The Amen Corner (New York: Dial, 1968; London: Joseph, 1969);

A Rap On Race, with Margaret Mead (Philadelphia: Lippincott, 1971; London: Joseph, 1971);

No Name in the Streets (New York: Dial, 1972);

One Day When I Was Lost: A Scenario Based on 'The Autobiography of Malcolm X' (London: Joseph, 1972);

A Dialogue, with Nikki Giovanni (Philadelphia: Lippincott, 1973; London: Joseph, 1975);

Little Man, Little Man (London: Joseph, 1976);

The Devil Finds Work (New York: Dial, 1976).

References:

Robert Bone, "James Baldwin," in his *The Negro Novel in America*, rev. ed. (New Haven: Yale University Press, 1965);

Maurice Charney, "James Baldwin's Quarrel with Richard Wright," *American Quarterly*, 15 (spring 1963): 65-75;

Eldridge Cleaver, "Notes on a Native Son," in *Soul on Ice* (New York: Delta, 1968);

Eugenia Collier, "Thematic Patterns in Baldwin's Essays: A Study in Chaos," *Black World*, 21 (June 1972): 28-34;

Fern Marja Eckman, *The Furious Passage of James Baldwin* (New York: Evans, 1966);

Russell G. Fischer, "James Baldwin: A Bibliography, 1947-62," *Bulletin of Bibliography*, 24 (January-April 1965): 127-130;

Addison Gayle, Jr., "Of Race and Rage," in his *The Way of the World: The Black Novel in America* (Garden City: Anchor Press, 1975);

John V. Hagopian, "James Baldwin: The Black and the Red-White-and-Blue," *CLA Journal*, 7 (December 1963): 133-140;

Calvin Hernton, "Blood of the Lamb and a Fiery Baptism: The Ordeal of James Baldwin," in *Amistad I: Writings of Black History and Culture*, eds. John A. Williams and Charles F. Harris (New York: Vintage Books, 1970), pp. 183-225;

Irving Howe, "Black Boys and Native Sons," *Dissent*, 10 (autumn 1963): 353-368;

Jennifer Jordan, "Cleaver vs. Baldwin: Icing the White Negro," *Black Books Bulletin*, 1 (winter 1972): 13-15;

George Kent, "Baldwin and the Problem of Being," *CLA Journal*, 7 (March 1964): 202-214;

Kathleen A. Kindt, "James Baldwin: A Checklist: 1947-1962," *Bulletin of Bibliography*, 24 (January-April 1965): 123-126;

Keneth A. Kinnamon, ed., *James Baldwin: A Collection of Critical Essays* (Englewood Cliffs: Prentice-Hall, 1974);

Marcus Klein, "James Baldwin: A Question of Identity," in his *After Alienation: American Novels in Mid-Century* (Cleveland: World Publishing, 1964);

Stanley Macebuh, *James Baldwin: A Critical Study* (New York: The Third Press, 1973);

Albert Murray, "Something Different, Something More," in *Anger, and Beyond*, ed. Herbert Hill (New York: Harper & Row, 1966);

Therman B. O'Daniel, ed., *James Baldwin: A Critical Evaluation* (Cambridge, Mass.: Harvard University Press, 1977);

Roger Rosenblatt, *Black Fiction* (Cambridge, Mass.: Harvard University Press, 1974);

Stephen Spender, "James Baldwin: Voice of a Revolution," *Partisan Review*, 30 (summer 1963): 256-260;

Fred L. Standley, "James Baldwin: A Checklist, 1963-67," *Bulletin of Bibliography*, 25 (May-August 1968): 135-137, 160;

Standley, "James Baldwin: The Artist as Incorrigible Disturber of the Peace," *Southern Humanities Review*, 4 (winter 1970): 18-30;

Fred L. and Nancy V. Standley, *James Baldwin: A Reference Guide* (Boston: G. K. Hall, forthcoming in 1979);

Darwin T. Turner, *Afro-American Writers* (New York: Appleton-Century-Crofts, 1970);

W. J. Weatherby, *Squaring Off: Mailer vs. Baldwin* (New York: Mason/Charter, 1977).

John Barth

Arthur D. Casciato
Virginia Polytechnic Institute and State University

John Barth.

BIRTH: Cambridge, Maryland, 27 May 1930.

EDUCATION: Cambridge High School, 1947; Juilliard School of Music, 1947; B.A., 1951, M.A., 1952, Johns Hopkins University; began Ph.D. program, Johns Hopkins.

MARRIAGE: 11 January 1950 to Harriette Anne Strickland, divorced; children: Christine, John, Daniel. 27 December 1970 to Shelly I. Rosenberg.

AWARDS: Rockefeller grant, 1965; National Institute of Arts and Letters Award for *Giles Goat-Boy*, 1966; National Book Award for *Chimera*, 1973; Honor Society, National Institute of Arts and Letters, 1974.

MAJOR WORKS: *The Floating Opera* (New York: Appleton-Century-Crofts, 1956; revised ed., Garden City: Doubleday, 1967; London: Secker & Warburg, 1968); *The End of the Road* (Garden City: Doubleday, 1958; London: Secker & Warburg, 1962; revised ed., Garden City: Doubleday, 1967); *The Sot-Weed Factor* (Garden City: Doubleday, 1960; London: Secker & Warburg, 1961; revised ed., Garden City: Doubleday, 1967); *Giles Goat-Boy or, The Revised New Syllabus* (Garden City: Doubleday, 1966; London: Secker & Warburg, 1967; revised ed., Garden City: Doubleday, 1967); *Lost in the Funhouse* (Garden City: Doubleday, 1968; London: Secker & Warburg, 1969); *Chimera* (New York: Random House, 1972; London: Deutsch, 1974).

John Barth has taken what he considers the moribund genre of the traditional novel and has revived it with a series of imaginative and inventive "fictions." Barth writes, "If I were a painter, I would attempt to be as contemporary as Frank Stella, and still paint nudes." This statement reflects his preoccupation with form and content: he is both a brilliant innovator of narrative structure and a mesmerizing storyteller. To use Robert Scholes's term, Barth is a "fabulator" who revels in weaving elaborate yarns. Often, as in *The Sot-Weed Factor* and *The Floating Opera*, Barth ironically imitates the conventions of past literary periods. In other fictions, like *Lost in the Funhouse* and *Chimera*, he solves the problem of exhausted narrative possibility by writing about that problem itself. Throughout Barth's works, intricate frame devices enclose complicated plot structures filled with mythic allusions, philosophical rhetoric, and ribald wordplay. In a recent interview, Barth offered this literary credo:

> As a writer . . . my objective has been to attempt to assimilate as well as I can the twentieth century aspects of my medium, to invent some myself, and, at the same time . . . to preserve the appeal that narrative has always had to the imagination: the simple appeals of suspense, of *story*, with which I've been in love since the beginning.

John Simmons Barth, Jr., was born 27 May 1930 in Cambridge, Maryland, to John Jacob Barth and Georgia Simmons. He was born with a twin sister named Jill. The Barth family was deeply rooted in this rural southern corner of the Old Line State. Barth's grandfather, a stone-carver by trade, also dealt in real estate, selling marshland to his fellow

23

German immigrants. The boy's father, known as "Whitey," was the proprietor of a combination candy store/restaurant. In addition, he was chief judge of the Orphan's Court in Cambridge, a small port on the Choptank River.

Barth's childhood and adolescence in Cambridge were quiet and uneventful. John Jacob Barth saw no early evidence of literary genius in his son: "This talent must have come later," he commented in 1966, "I didn't notice it when he was younger." Barth's twin sister had similar recollections; she remembered her brother as "more serious than outgoing" and recalled that "he got a lot of things without trying very hard at school." Barth's older brother, William, echoed his father and sister: "Looking back I'd never have expected him to be a writer."

Barth attended Cambridge High School where he played the drums in the band and wrote a column for the school paper under the name "Ashcan Pete." His freshman English teacher remembered that "He had depth of understanding of human nature for someone that age. His humor was a little sardonic . . . . I can see him now as a boy, so serious." Barth received little intellectual direction from the tiny faculty of his school, so he turned to the paperback rack of his father's store. He remembers reading Faulkner, Dos Passos, and Hemingway "mixed in with all the Agatha Christies and the other mysteries."

In 1947 Barth graduated from high school, and that summer, with money earned playing in local dance bands, he entered Juilliard School of Music in New York City. He studied harmony and orchestration for a few months but was forced to return home because of Juilliard's expensive tuition and the high cost of living in New York City. Barth's musical background influenced his narrative style; in fact, Barth calls himself an "arranger" of fiction, and he feels that he explores "the original conventions of the novel to discover how they might be re-orchestrated."

In the fall of 1947, Barth entered Johns Hopkins University in Baltimore on an academic scholarship. He took very few English courses, but he did manage to "discover" literature. He worked in the Classics Library of Johns Hopkins to supplement his scholarship, and while filing books in the Oriental Seminary collection, he read immense Oriental tale-cycles, including *The Ocean of Story*, the *Panchatantra*, Burton's *Arabian Nights*, and their later derivations such as the *Decameron*, the *Heptameron*, and the *Pentameron*. The effect of this "ocean of narrative" on Barth's later fiction is unquestioned; echoes can

be found throughout his mature work. Certain professors were also important to his early development. One teacher in particular, Pedro Salinas, taught him that devoting one's life to literature "could be not only a very passionate enterprise but a noble one."

On 11 January 1950, at the age of nineteen, Barth married Harriette Anne Strickland. This year also saw Barth's first appearances in print; his short stories "Fox-Island Incident" and "Parnassus Approached" were published in the Hopkins student magazine. Another story, "Lilith and the Lion," was published in the fall issue of the *Hopkins Review*. Though not especially polished, this apprentice work is noteworthy because it depicts a love triangle—the first of many triangles in Barth's fiction.

In 1951 Barth took his bachelor's degree in creative writing, graduating with the highest average of any student in the College of Arts and Sciences. Faced with the distasteful prospect of finding a job, he chose instead to enter the graduate writing program at Hopkins. His reason, he recalls, was that being a graduate assistant "would have more to do with writing than anything else I could think of which would earn my daily bread. . . . And meanwhile, I could be learning a few things too, if only by having to teach them." His "daily bread" was of particular concern now: his wife had given birth to a daughter one month after Barth took the B.A., and they were expecting a second child.

Robert Hazel, Barth's colleague and friend during these graduate school days, remembers his "fiercely humorous approach, tied to his brilliant intellectuality, towards most matters which the rest of us approached quite gravely, e.g. sexuality. Most of us were under the influence of Freud and D. H. Lawrence while Barth was laughing up his sleeve. His nascent comic genius was more influenced by Fielding, Sterne and Joyce." Barth's first lengthy fictional work was his master's thesis, a novel titled "Shirt of Nessus." The story is set in the Maryland towns "Hudson" and "Surrey." David Morrell, in *John Barth: An Introduction*, terms this unpublished novel "believable and sometimes moving. Its conflict depends on differing personalities and emotions, not on ideas as in Barth's published work, and its manner is strictly realistic. . . ." In 1952 Lurton Blassingame, Barth's first agent, tried to place this novel with a publisher but was unsuccessful. Later Barth would condemn "Shirt of Nessus" as "a neo-primitive miscarriage, justifiably unpublished."

In the spring of 1952 Barth received his master's degree in creative writing from Johns Hopkins. During the following summer he began study for a Ph.D. in the aesthetics of literature, but largely because of the financial demands of a growing family, he never completed the degree. Barth instead took a position as instructor of freshman English at Pennsylvania State University and began his teaching duties in the fall of 1953.

Speaking of this period, Barth remembered that "Even after finishing college, I was still very rooted, emotionally, in the marsh country, the swamps of the Eastern shore of Maryland. . . . At the same time, I was carrying in the back of my head . . . the memory of all those tale cycles in which stories framed other stories framing other stories and so forth." It is not surprising, then, that Barth's first serious literary endeavor at Penn State was "Dorchester Tales," a bawdy *Decameron*-like cycle of stories concerned with the history and tradition of Maryland's Eastern Shore. Barth never finished this project, abandoning it after completing fifty tales of a projected 100; but many of the characters, such as Ebenezer Cooke and Mary Mungummory, would surface again in *The Sot-Weed Factor*. One tale, "The Invulnerable Castle," was transferred almost exactly into chapter seven of the concluding section of *The Sot-Weed Factor*; and a revised version of another tale, "The Song of Algol," appeared in the *Kenyon Review* as "Landscape: The Eastern Shore."

In the fall of 1954, Barth chanced upon a photograph of *The Floating Theater*, an old showboat that had entertained in the Tidewater area during the author's childhood. Barth remembered that he saw the boat "when I was about seven. . . . I thought it would be a good idea to write a philosophical minstrel show . . . only it was going to be a work of literature." This "philosophical minstrel show" became Barth's first published novel, *The Floating Opera*.

Barth began writing the *Opera* in early January of 1955 and completed it roughly three months later, in late March. On the sixth attempt his agent finally located a publisher—Appleton-Century-Crofts. Eager to be published, Barth deferred to Appleton's demand for a new ending; or, as Barth put it, the publisher "finally agreed to launch the *Opera*, but on condition that the builder make certain major changes in its construction, notably about the stern." Appleton-Century-Crofts published *The Floating Opera* on 24 August 1956; it was a financial failure, selling only 1,682 copies, but critics and reviewers were delighted by the appearance of so obviously gifted a young writer. Ironically, though, they criticized the novel's overly sentimental ending. For his first major effort, Barth garnered critical applause, a nomination for the 1956 National Book Award, and what he terms "a boatwright little lesson" about the critical judgment of publishers.

Barth designed *The Floating Opera* to be a "nihilistic comedy," the first in a series of three such novels, unrelated except by their nihilistic themes. Barth's plans were already clearly in mind: "Each [of these novels] will concern some sort of bachelor, more or less irresponsible, who either rejects absolute values or encounters their rejection." His irresponsible bachelor in the *Opera* is Todd Andrews, a fifty-four-year-old Maryland lawyer who is writing in 1954 about the day in 1937 when he decided to commit suicide because there was "no final reason for living." Up until that June day in 1937, Andrews had successfully dulled his twentieth-century *Weltschmerz* by donning different masks (rake, saint, and cynic), but, despairing over life's irrational nature, Todd finally decides to kill himself.

Todd's stream-of-consciousness narrative imitates the wandering navigation of the showboat that inspired the novel. The showboat also functions as a metaphor for life:

> our friends float past; we become involved with them; they float on, and we must rely on hearsay or lose track of them completely; they float back again, and we either renew our friendship—catch up to date—or find that they and we don't comprehend each other any more.

At the conclusion of the novel Todd changes his mind about ending his existence. There is no optimistic yea-saying, but rather a casual, shoulder-shrugging acceptance. If there is no final reason to go on living, there is also no final reason to terminate one's life.

The Floating Opera is not merely an account of Todd's Hamlet-like musings; like "Adam's original and Unparalleled Floating Opera," the story is "fraught with curiosities, melodrama, spectacle, instruction, and entertainment." Its digressive plot includes a grisly World War I foxhole scene in which Todd bayonets a German soldier, an adulterous *menage a trois*, and a hilariously complicated legal dispute complete with seventeen wills and 129 jars of human excrement.

Most critics have noted Barth's indebtedness to Sterne's *Tristram Shandy* in the *Opera*; and certainly Todd's rambling narrative, chattiness, world view, and sickly condition echo Sterne's narrator. Barth admits his knowledge of Sterne, but adds that it was filtered through the works of the nineteenth-century

John Barth

Brazilian novelist Machado de Assis—especially his novel *Dom Casmurro*.

Barth rested during the summer of 1955 and then in early October began writing a "nihilistic tragedy" which was to be a companion piece to *The Floating Opera*. Barth's working title was "What To Do Until the Doctor Comes," but by December, when he finished the novel he had changed the title to *The End of the Road*. Appleton balked at publishing the novel because the plot was similar to that of its predecessor, so Barth instructed his agent to find him a new publisher. Eventually the agent placed the novel with Doubleday, and that firm finally published *The End of the Road* in August 1958, some two years after Barth had finished writing it. Though no more of a commercial success than his first novel (it attracted only some 3,000 buyers), *The End of the Road* was well received by the growing underground audience that admired Barth's writing. Reviewers once again heralded the author's potential.

At the conclusion of *The Floating Opera*, Todd wonders whether "in the real absence of absolutes, values less than absolute mightn't be regarded as in no way inferior and even be lived by. But that's another inquiry, and another story." *The End of the Road* is that other story. Once again the setting is the Tidewater area of Maryland where Jacob Horner, the irresponsible bachelor in this novel, teaches prescriptive grammar at Wicomico State Teachers' College. Barth has said that Horner "is supposed to remind you first of all of Little Jack Horner, who also sits in a corner and rationalizes. Then a Horner is somebody who puts horns on, who cuckolds. . . ." Horner suffers from "cosmopsis, the cosmic view," a paralytic condition arising from his inability to choose a course of action when confronted with "a multitude of desirable choices." The Black Doctor enters at this point with his pseudo-psychiatric bag-of-tricks, including Sinistrality, Antecedence, and Alphabetical Priority. After stumbling upon the immobile Horner in a Baltimore train station, the Doctor whisks him away to his Remobilization Farm. There he prescribes Mythotherapy, which, like Todd's masks, involves the changing of one's essence when necessary.

The central action of the novel takes place at Wicomico State Teachers' College where the remobilized Jake encounters the Morgans—Joe and his wife Rennie. Joe Morgan, a candidate for a Ph.D. in history and a local scoutmaster, is a relativist, a post-suicide-attempt Todd, who realizes that nothing has intrinsic value but who is satisfied to assign relative value to life's conventions, especially

to his marriage. Jake is a nihilist, a pre-suicide-attempt Todd, who views everything as equally attractive and, therefore, takes nothing seriously. The novel becomes a philosophical debate, a battle of ideas, in which Joe and Jake joust for sexual and intellectual dominance over Rennie, who may or may not be carrying Horner's child. Jake, in a frenziedly inept attempt at responsibility, arranges an abortion for Rennie with the Doctor. Barth ushers the novel's brand of rationalization to "the end of the road" when Rennie chokes to death on a supper of franks and beans during the operation. Horner, once again immobilized, manages to join the Doctor when he moves the Remobilization Farm to Pennsylvania.

In 1958 Barth completed research on an historical novel which he had begun two years earlier. He was still committed to his trilogy of nihilistic novels, but he was contemplating a change in manner: "I didn't think after *The End of the Road* that I was interested in writing any more realistic fiction—fiction that deals with Characters From Our Time, who speak real dialogue." In a lighter mood, he also claimed that he wanted to write a book fat enough to print the title horizontally across the spine. This novel, according to Barth, would have a plot fancier and more contrived than that of *Tom Jones*. Barth finished this novel, *The Sot-Weed Factor*, in March 1959, and Doubleday published the mammoth 806-page book on 19 August 1960. Like its forerunners, *The Sot-Weed Factor* (the title means tobacco merchant) was a commercial failure, selling only 5,000 copies.

The Sot-Weed Factor is based on an actual 1708 satirical poem of the same name written by Ebenezer Cooke, the self-proclaimed poet laureate of the Maryland Colony. Barth had been raised just fifteen miles from Cooke's Point where "Malden," the poet's estate, was located. Cooke himself is the main character of the novel and is Barth's third irresponsible bachelor.

Barth felt, for two reasons, that it was futile to write traditional realistic fiction: first, because all possibilities of plot had been exhausted, and second, because realism did not exactly represent reality but "a kind of true representation of the distortion we all make of life. In other words . . . a representation of a representation of life." In *The Sot-Weed Factor*, Barth gives this screw another turn, presenting his own farcical distortion of historical documents, themselves a distortion of "real" life in colonial Maryland. For example, Barth transforms the Pocahontas and Captain John Smith legend into a ribald tale of an impenetrable virgin and a Sacred

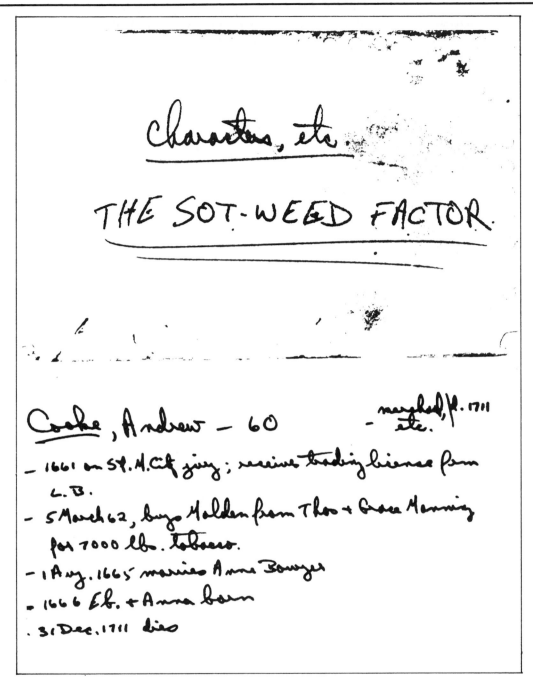

*Sample library key sort cards used by Barth
for notes on* The Sot-Weed Factor.

Eggplant. His source for this version is a document, supposedly genuine, called *The Privie Journall of Sir Henry Burlingame.* Barth accomplishes all this while imitating such conventions of the eighteenth-century novel as the convoluted plot filled with unbelievable coincidence, the journeying hero searching for his father, the nearly incestuous brother/sister relationship, and even the digressive chapter headings of this genre.

Ebenezer Cooke, gentleman, virgin, and poet, is the novel's journeying hero. Like Jacob Horner before him, Ebenezer suffers from "cosmopsis." He sits immobile in his London room, "dizzy with the beauty of the possible," unable to choose a viable course of action. But when Eben finally perceives himself as "Virgin, sir! Poet, sir!," he becomes a picaresque Joe Morgan and decides to test his assumed virtue against the legions of whores, highwaymen, and charlatans that inhabit the New World. Eben's tutor, Henry Burlingame, is, like Todd and Jake, a Protean shape-shifter and the ultimate practitioner of Mythotherapy. He disguises himself as nine different historical figures, including Eben himself. And there is yet another *menage a trois*! Burlingame, whose sexual preference is universal ("I love the world, sir, and so make love to it!"), refers to himself as the "Suitor of totality . . . the Cosmic Lover!" And he dreams of some sort of gymnastic sexual union with Eben and his twin sister, Anna.

The Sot-Weed Factor completed Barth's nihilistic series. Looking back, he realized that "What happened was, I had thought I was writing about values and it turned out I was writing about innocence." In *The End of the Road*, Barth demonstrated that Joe Morgan's unfeeling rationality was disastrous in an irrational world; in *The Sot-Weed Factor* Barth showed that any *permanent* stance, including Cooke's unflinching innocence, is untenable. In fact, mutability seems to be the key for survival in the author's cosmos.

From 1959 to 1965 Barth worked on the novel that would be his first financial success. Before it was finished, he commented that "What I really wanted to write after *The Sot-Weed Factor* was a new Old Testament, a comic Old Testament. I guess that's what the new novel *Giles Goat-Boy* is going to be. A souped-up Bible." In April 1959 Barth had begun a novel called "The Seeker," but in June 1960 he put this project aside and started work on *Giles Goat-Boy*. He completed this "souped-up Bible" later in 1965, having worked on it exclusively except for a six-month period from January to June of 1963 when he and his family toured Europe. In 1965, before completing *Giles Goat-Boy*, Barth accepted a professorship at the State University of New York at Buffalo.

The creation of *Giles Goat-Boy* took nearly six years. After publication of *The Sot-Weed Factor*, several critics suggested that Barth had relied on Lord Raglan's twenty-two points of the hero. Barth had not read Raglan's treatise, but he decided to investigate the subject thoroughly. He took notes for two years on the hero myth and related notions, especially from Raglan's *The Hero*, Joseph Campbell's *The Hero with a Thousand Faces*, and Otto Rank's *The Myth of the Birth of the Hero*. Barth also reread Homer, Virgil, and the Gospels before beginning actual composition in 1962.

Doubleday published the 710-page *Giles Goat-Boy* in August 1966. Sales reached 50,000, four times the combined sales of Barth's first three novels. *Giles Goat-Boy* even appeared briefly on the best-seller lists. The novel also gained more critical recognition for Barth. In 1966, he was cited by the Creative Arts Commission of Brandeis University for notable achievement in fiction, and the National Institute of Arts and Letters awarded him a $2,500 grant. In an interview in the *New York Times Book Review*, Barth seemed uneasy about his new prominence: "It was nice being underground. My ambition was to grow up to be a great, big truffle, but when the truffle hounds have got your scent, you can't remain underground."

In *Giles Goat-Boy*, Barth moves beyond a distortion of reality to actual fantasy. The novel is supposedly *The Revised New Syllabus of George Giles Our Great Tutor* which records the life and teachings of one George Giles as he dictated them to the *West Campus Automatic Computer*, or WESCAC. The computer then edits these memoirs, putting them in the form of printout tapes. Giles Stoker, George's son, also edits the tapes and presents them to a struggling writer-academician, "J.B.," whose literary career parallels Barth's. "J.B.," not to be outdone, makes his own emendations and sends the manuscript to his publishers, who also edit it and presumably add a Swiftian "Publisher's Disclaimer" to the entire project. One is reminded of the complicated frame-tales of Barth's collegiate reading, but this frame-tale is also a meaningful structural and thematic device which frees the author from any "realistic" restraints and reinforces his belief that reality is perpetually distorted.

The basic conceit of the novel is that the universe is a giant University. The Messiah becomes the Grand Tutor; the West and East Campuses represent the United States and Russia; the World Wars are Campus Riots and WESCAC's "EAT-waves" parallel the atomic bomb; Christ and his twelve apostles even appear as Enos Enoch and the Twelve Trustees. The novel is something of a *roman a clef*. Max Spielman, the goat-boy's mentor, resembles Robert Oppenheimer; and Lucky Rexford, the University Chancellor, reminds one of John F. Kennedy. There are also thinly-disguised satiric versions of Dwight and Milton Eisenhower (who was president of Johns Hopkins while Barth was writing the novel), of the remainder of the Kennedy clan, and even of J. Edgar Hoover.

These characters also function in a larger allegorical sense. For example, Eblis Eierkopf, who may be Barth's caricature of Einstein, represents unfeeling, eggheaded intellectuality or Pure Mind. His roommate is the huge Frumentian, Croaker, who on one level functions as the ultimate satire on the "dumb jock," but who also represents mindless sensuality or Pure Body. In a wonderfully perverse reworking of the Renaissance debate over the relationship of mind and body, Barth has Croaker carry Eierkopf on his shoulders, and thereby each character supplies the other's missing dimension.

Giles Goat-Boy is also a fanciful *Bildungsroman*. The novel chronicles George's struggles from goatdom to hero-hood. Like Ebenezer, George assumes his appointed role in life—in this case, hero-work and Grand Tutorship. His rise is opposed by a Henry Burlingame-type character, Harold Bray, George's shape-changing antithesis. George's final success and defeat of Bray is undercut by the skeptical tone of the Post-tape that completes the frame of the novel.

Reactions to *Giles Goat-Boy* have been varied. Critics have charged Barth with "pedantic puppetry," and one critic labeled *Giles Goat-Boy* an "epic snooze." But the *Goat-Boy*'s structure consciously reflects Barth's vision of the post-modernist novel. By stressing artifice, Barth feels that "you're not pretending that the novel is something it isn't. Art *is* artificial, after all." For Barth, this is "a different way to come to terms with the discrepancy between art and the Real Thing."

Because of this sudden commercial success, Barth's publishers ordered his early works republished. *The Floating Opera, The End of the Road,* and *The Sot-Weed Factor* were all republished in freshly-typeset hardcover editions, and Barth took this opportunity to revise these early works. *The Floating Opera* was reworked extensively: Barth restored its "original and correct ending" and added a number of minor passages. The other two novels were only tightened and polished. After rereading *The Sot-Weed Factor*, Barth emended and revised the original edition in order "to make this long narrative a quantum swifter and more graceful." The 806 pages of the original edition were trimmed to 756 pages in the 1967 hardcover edition.

In 1967, Barth published his influential article "The Literature of Exhaustion" in the *Atlantic Monthly*. In this essay, Barth explained his theory concerning the state of contemporary fiction and gave particular attention to the Argentine author Jorge Luis Borges. Barth wrote that "By 'exhaustion' I don't mean anything so tired as the subject of physical, moral or intellectual decadence, only the used-upness of certain possibilities." He focused on Borges because the writer illustrates the "technically up-to-date artist." Recognizing the exhaustion of narrative possibility, Borges chooses to write scholarly and philosophical footnotes to longer, imagined fictions.

In September 1968, Doubleday published Barth's fifth book, *Lost in the Funhouse*. This series of short fictions was the creative issue of Barth's long-standing love affair with oral fiction, rekindled in 1960 by his frequent speaking appearances on college campuses where *The Sot-Weed Factor* had achieved its greatest success. Later, in 1966, when Barth's English department borrowed the Music department's electronics laboratory, Barth began experimenting with fictions created especially for voice and tape.

Barth started writing *Lost in the Funhouse* early in 1966 and completed it in February 1968. This book is a series of fourteen fictions, most of which were published separately before 1968. In the prefatory note to the book Barth designated a particular medium (*Fiction for Print, Tape, Live Voice*) for each story. These directions were viewed by some critics as pretentious nonsense, causing Barth to add "Seven Additional Author's Notes" to the 1969 paperback printing (which has sold nearly 100,000 copies). Barth wrote that the original note "means in good faith exactly what it says, both as to the serial nature of the fourteen pieces and as to the ideal media of their presentation." Pretentious or not, the book was both a financial and critical success: *Lost in the Funhouse* sold 20,000 copies in its original hardcover edition and was nominated for the 1968 National Book Award.

Lost in the Funhouse is a cycle of fictions, the framing device for which is a Moebius strip, a three-dimensional geometric figure-eight that ends where it begins. Several of the fictions—"Ambrose His Mark," "Water-Message," and "Lost in the Funhouse"—return to the familiar Tidewater Maryland setting, but Barth denies that the characters in these stories are based on his own family: "Ambrose's family is a kind of traumatic ideal, the sort of family I might have enjoyed having had." Other stories, such as "Echo" and "Menelaiad," begin with classical myths, but Barth reshuffles these antique fables and presents the characters with problems that plague contemporary man. Ultimately, all the stories are related by a common theme—the plight of storyteller and story in modern society. The central characters—from Ambrose to the unnamed minstrel of the "Anonymiad"—are horrified by the world's arbitrary nature and find solace in re-imagining the universe.

In 1972 Barth accepted the position of Visiting Professor of English at Boston University. Shortly thereafter, his sixth book, *Chimera*, was published by Random House. The author summarized the

John Barth

Caricature of Barth by Kent Willis.

critical response to his latest creation as "Respectful but baffled." Barth was totally prepared, however: "It's been the general pattern with my novels that the reviews of the first edition have almost always been more unfavorable than favorable and that the books have had their real life in the paperback or later hardcover editions." Barth admits that *Chimera* is "a very complicated piece of fiction. I admire writers who can make complicated things simple, but my own talent has been to make simple things complicated. . . . If I have any single ambition it would be to become less difficult of access." Apparently, *Chimera* was more accessible than Barth imagined; it attracted 17,000 buyers and won him the National Book Award.

Chimera consists of three novellas, the "seeds" of another, as yet unpublished, longer work which Barth has been working on since the fall of 1969. The first novella, "Dunyazadiad," was taken from the story of Scheherazade, the heroine of the frame-tale of *The Thousand and One Nights*. Barth refers to Scheherazade as his "avant-gardiste." Her appeal to writer-academician Barth is that she must *literally* "publish or perish." The story is narrated by

Dunyazade, "Sherry's little sister," and it is filled with women's liberation rhetoric, academic jokes, and sexual puns. But once again, its main concern, and indeed the main concern of the entire work, is the state of narrative art in today's society.

The other two novellas, "Bellerophoniad" and "Perseid," are ostensibly the stories of middle-aged mythic heroes struggling to recapture youth and past glories. But Barth presents Perseus and Bellerophon as metaphors for storytellers who reflect his own situation as a contemporary writer. This strategy affords Barth the best of form and content: his classical subject matter is interesting, sexually titillating, and verbally resonant; and his structure and theme are technically up-to-date. Once again Barth solves the problem of exhausted narrative possibility by writing about that very problem.

Much like the Moebius strip that frames *Lost in the Funhouse*, Barth returned to where he began—the marshy Tidewater Maryland area—when he accepted the post of professor in the graduate writing seminars at Johns Hopkins in 1973. Barth has recently summed up his literary career to date:

> Having written a pair of short novels (*The Floating Opera* and *The End of the Road*) and a pair of very long ones (*The Sot-Weed Factor* and *Giles Goat-Boy*), I commenced what was to be a seven-year exploration of alternatives to long printed narratives. The issue was another pair of books: *Lost in the Funhouse* . . . and *Chimera*. . . . My interest in electronic tape was a passing one, but my conversion to the shorter forms was so complete that I have come to find it impossible to read any new fiction longer than fifty pages. If I am in fact just writing another 'novel' it is just out of a kind of perversity, so quixotic does that enterprise seem to me at this hour of the world. But Quixote is where we came in. . . .

And indeed Barth has embarked on just such a "quixotic" enterprise—another long novel. His current project, which he is calling "Letters," is the work of which *Chimera* was the "core." This work-in-progress is a re-orchestration of an earlier form—the epistolary novel. Barth's letters, though, are supposedly a combination of the real, mislaid, and forged documents of seven correspondents, some of whom have appeared in Barth's earlier fiction. (This is in keeping with Barth's aesthetic of "echoing myself without repeating myself.") "Letters" is set in contemporary Maryland. Barth had hoped that its publication would coincide with America's bicentennial, but to date he has not completed the novel. One can be certain, however, that the finished book will be challenging and unpredictable, reflecting Barth's commitment to experimentation in fictional form.

From the publication of *The Floating Opera* in 1956 to the appearance of *Chimera* in 1972, John Barth's works have unfailingly polarized critical opinion. Richard Vine has accurately characterized the response to Barth's novels as "mixed and often impassioned." Comments have ranged from Robert Scholes's glowing tribute to Barth as "a comic genius of the highest order" to Peter Ackroyd's vitriolic condemnation of *Chimera* as "an elaborate apologia for [Barth's] own apparently miserable and wasted life." Even when Barth's brilliance is recognized, one finds only qualified praise. For instance, Eliot Fremont-Smith, in his review of *Giles Goat-Boy* for the *New York Times*, writes that "(1) to recognize the genius, one must indulge the pedant; (2) John Barth is a pedant." But no one has denied Barth his place at the forefront of post-modernist fiction; in fact, Scholes calls Barth "the best writer of fiction we have at present, and one of the best we have ever had."

Reviewers agreed that Barth's first novel, *The Floating Opera*, showed considerable potential. Siegfried Mandel, in the *New York Times Book Review*, found *The Floating Opera* "amusing and revolting in turn," and praised Barth's use of "the technique and elaborate storytelling paraphernalia of such English eighteenth-century writers as Fielding and Sterne." Barth's second novel, *The End of the Road*, consolidated his reputation as underground cult figure, black humorist, and novelist of ideas. Taliaferro Boatwright, in the *New York Herald Tribune*, found the novel "amusing, occasionally brilliantly illuminating, ultimately almost physically jolting." The reviewer for *Kirkus* emphasized this last quality and said that the novel was "Sick-sick-sick, or maybe just foul . . . a real recoil." Later critics, however, have generally regarded *The End of the Road* as Barth's most successfully executed fiction.

Some reviewers were put off by the length of *The Sot-Weed Factor*, but most critics see it as Barth's finest work to date and as the fulfillment of his earlier promise. Responding to the problem of the book's length, Leslie Fiedler wrote in the *New Leader* that Barth has "talent enough to be what he has to be, against all the odds, *unfashionably*." Fiedler called *The Sot-Weed Factor* "something closer to the 'Great American Novel' than any other book of the last decades." Stanley Edgar Hyman, also in the *New Leader*, wrote that *The Sot-Weed Factor* was the funniest example of a new genre of American

novel, "the picaresque comedy of the anti-hero." One dissenter was Robert Garis, in *Commentary*, who found *The Sot-Weed Factor* (and *Giles Goat-Boy*) "about as bad as novels can be" and who accused Barth of going through an identity crisis in public. The appearance of *The Sot-Weed Factor* in contemporary fiction courses at many major universities has established the book as an important work of post-modernist literature. Its influence is reflected by a 1965 *Book Week* survey in which 200 prominent authors, critics, and editors were polled about the literature of the postwar years. *The Sot-Weed Factor* was ranked eighteenth among the twenty best books since 1945.

Giles Goat-Boy received more publicity than any other Barth novel. Robert Scholes's article "Disciple of Scheherazade," a flattering reappraisal of Barth's first three novels written for the *New York Times Book Review*, heralded the appearance of the *Goat-Boy*. This pre-publication acclaim assured *Giles Goat-Boy* of full, and occasionally scathing, attention. Some reviewers were appalled by the novel's mountain of artifice and by its length and apparent lack of depth. Denis Donoghue, in the *New York Review of Books*, called the book "too long, too tedious, a dud." Other reviewers saw *Giles Goat-Boy* as a near miss, a flawed but important work. Edward P. J. Corbett, writing in *America*, predicted that the book would establish Barth "as one of the three or four best contemporary American novelists," but Corbett complained that "One never has a clear idea of where anything is taking place, or what it looks like, or how much time an action takes, or how much time elapses between events."

Reviewers generally seemed to be confused by *Lost in the Funhouse* and by the author's directions for the multimedia presentation of his stories. Guy Davenport's reaction in the *New York Times Book Review* was typical: "In his new and thoroughly confusing work of fiction John Barth seems at first blush to be like a great architect making a batch of doll houses just to show that his virtuosity includes mastery over the elegant trifle and the deft sketch." *Life*'s Webster Schott attacked the book as "a grinding bore" and recommended that Barth "learn to spend more time looking at the world outside his study and less time poring over the yellowing clippings in which he has promised to play Che Guevara to American letters." The book was not without its champions. James Fenton, in *New Statesman*, called the book "a fascinating and highly entertaining work" and referred to Barth as "one of the most brilliant and inventive writers of our time," and Granville Hicks, in the *Saturday Review*, wrote

Jill Krementz

John Barth.

that Barth "can equal the traditionalists at their own game, and thus he has won the right to be different."

Critical reaction to Barth's latest novel, *Chimera*, followed the same pattern that greeted his first book. The reviewer for *Publishers Weekly* found the first two novellas of *Chimera* "entertaining if one has the taste for clever plays upon words and knowledge of and interest in the myths on which they are based," but he thought the involuted plot of the third novella "impenetrable." Don Crinklaw, writing in the *National Review*, found *Chimera* "a shimmering, magical book—probably the best Barth has produced so far," while Michael Wood, in his review for the *New York Review of Books*, attacked *Chimera*'s "thorough deadness of language, which belies all the book's apparent mental activity,

[making] it seem a fraud," and he accused Barth of being "a narrative chauvinistic pig."

At present, Barth's fiction is attracting a great amount of scholarly attention. Numerous Ph.D. candidates have found in Barth's novels suitable grist for their dissertations. Joseph Weixlmann's extensive primary and secondary bibliography and Richard Vine's short, annotated secondary bibliography have aided Barth studies. David Morrell's book *John Barth: An Introduction* is the best full-length critical/biographical treatment to date. Even Barth's essay "The Literature of Exhaustion" has served as the basis for John O. Stark's critical book of the same name. A working knowledge of Barth and his works would seem indispensable to any student of post-modernist fiction.

Periodical Publications:

FICTION:
"Lilith and the Lion," *Hopkins Review*, 4 (fall 1950): 49-53;
"The Remobilization of Jacob Horner," *Esquire*, 50 (July 1958): 55-59;
"Landscape: The Eastern Shore," *Kenyon Review*, 12 (winter 1960): 104-110;
"Ambrose His Mark," *Esquire*, 59 (February 1963): 97, 122-124, 126-127;
"Water-Message," *Southwest Review*, 48 (summer 1963): 226-237;
"Night-Sea Journey," *Esquire*, 65 (June 1966): 82-83, 147-148;
"Test Borings," in *Modern Occasions*, ed. Philip Rahv (New York: Noonday, 1966), pp. 247-263;
"Lost in the Funhouse," *Atlantic*, 220 (November 1967): 73-82;
"Autobiography: A Self-Recorded Fiction," *New American Review*, no. 2 (1968): 72-75;
"Petition," *Esquire*, 70 (July 1968): 68, 70-71, 135;
"Title," *Yale Review*, 57 (winter 1968): 213-221;
"Help! A Stereophonic Narrative for Authorial Voice," *Esquire*, 72 (September 1968): 108-109;
"Dunyazadiad," *Esquire*, 77 (June 1972): 136-142, 158, 160, 162, 164, 166, 168;
"Perseid," *Harper's*, 245 (October 1972): 79-96.

NONFICTION:
"My Two Muses," *Johns Hopkins Magazine*, 12 (April 1961): 9-13;
"Muse, Spare Me," *Book Week*, 26 (September 1965): 28-29;
"A Gift of Books," *Holiday*, 40 (December 1966): 171;
"Censorship—1967: A Series of Symposia," *Arts in Society*, 4 (1967): 294;
"The Literature of Exhaustion," *Atlantic Monthly*, 220 (August 1967): 29-39.

Other:

The Adventures of Roderick Random, by Tobias Smollett, afterword by Barth (New York: Signet, 1964), pp. 469-479;
"A Tribute to Vladimir Nabokov," in *Nabokov: Criticism, Reminiscences, Translations and Tributes*, ed. Alfred Appel, Jr. and Charles Newman (Evanston, Ill.: Northwestern University Press, 1970), p. 350;
"The Ocean of Story," in *Directions in Literary Criticism*, ed. Stanley Weintraub and Philip Young (University Park: Pennsylvania State University Press, 1973), pp. 1-6;

Writer's Choice, ed. Rust Hills, preface by Barth (New York: McKay, 1974), pp. 1-2.

References:

Joe David Bellamy, "Algebra and Fire," *Falcon*, 4 (spring 1972): 5-15;
Bellamy, "Having It Both Ways," *New American Review*, no. 15 (1972): 134-150;
Beverly G. Bienstock, "Lingering on the Autognostic Verge: John Barth's *Lost in the Funhouse*," *Modern Fiction Studies*, 19 (spring 1973): 69-78;
George Bluestone, "John Wain and John Barth: The Angry and the Accurate," *Massachusetts Review*, 1 (May 1960): 582-589;
Mark Bowden, "Return of the Native," *Biography News*, 1 (May 1974): 491-492;
Jackson R. Bryer, "John Barth: A Bibliography," *Critique*, 6, 2 (1963): 86-89;
Philip E. Diser, "The Historical Ebenezer Cooke," *Critique*, 10, 3 (1968): 48-59;
John J. Enck, "John Barth: An Interview," *Wisconsin Studies in Contemporary Literature*, 6 (winter-spring 1965): 3-14;
Leslie Fiedler, "John Barth: An Eccentric Genius," *New Leader*, 44 (13 February 1961): 22-24;
Frank Gado, "A Conversation with John Barth," *The Idol* (Union College), 49 (fall 1972): 1-36;
Judith Golwyn, "New Creative Writers: 35 Novelists Whose First Work Appears This Season," *Library Journal*, 81 (1 June 1956): 1496-1497;
Beverly Gross, "The Anti-Novels of John Barth," *Chicago Review*, 20 (November 1968): 95-109;
Richard Boyd Hauch, *A Cheerful Nihilism: Confidence and "The Absurd" in American Humorous Fiction* (Bloomington: Indiana University Press, 1971), pp. 201-236;
Jeffrey Helterman, *John Barth's Giles Goat-Boy: A Critical Commentary* (New York: Monarch, 1973);
Gerhard Joseph, *John Barth* (Minneapolis: University of Minnesota Press, 1970);
Jean E. Kennard, "John Barth: Imitations of Imitations," *Mosaic*, 3, 2 (1970): 116-131;
Mopsy Strange Kennedy, "Roots of an Author," *Washington Post Potomac*, 3 September 1967, pp. 17-19 (Interview with Barth's father, twin sister, brother, and high school English teacher);
David Kerner, "Psychodrama in Eden," *Chicago Review*, 13 (winter-spring 1959): 59-67;
Richard Kostelanetz, "The New American Fiction," in *The New American Arts*, ed. Richard

Kostelanetz (New York: Horizon, 1965): pp. 194-236;

James L. McDonald, "Barth's Syllabus: The Frame of *Giles Goat-Boy*," *Critique*, 13, 3 (1972): 5-10;

Phyllis Meras, "John Barth: A Truffle No Longer," *New York Times Book Review*, 7 August 1966, p. 22;

Russell H. Miller, "*The Sot-Weed Factor*: A Contemporary Mock-Epic," *Critique*, 8, 2 (winter 1965-1966): 88-100;

David Morrell, *John Barth: An Introduction* (University Park: Pennsylvania State University Press, 1976);

Richard W. Noland, "John Barth and the Novel of Comic Nihilism," *Wisconsin Studies in Contemporary Literature*, 7 (autumn 1966): 239-257;

Alan Prince, "An Interview with John Barth," *Prism* (Sir George William University) (spring 1968): 42-62;

Richard Schickel, "*The Floating Opera*," *Critique*, 6, 2 (1963): 53-67;

Robert Scholes, *The Fabulators* (New York: Oxford University Press, 1967), pp. 135-173;

Scholes, "The Allegory of Exhaustion," *Fiction International*, 1 (fall 1973): 106-108;

Israel Shenker, "Complicated Simple Things," *New York Times Book Review*, 24 September 1972, pp. 35-38;

John O. Stark, *The Literature of Exhaustion* (Durham: Duke University Press, 1974);

John C. Stubbs, "John Barth as a Novelist of Ideas: The Themes of Value and Identity," *Critique*, 8, 2 (winter 1965-1966): 101-116;

Stephen I. Tanner, "John Barth's Hamlet," *Southwest Review*, 56 (1971): 347-354;

Tony Tanner, "The Hoax that Joke Bilked," *Partisan Review*, 34 (winter 1967): 102-109;

Tanner, "No Exit," *Partisan Review*, 36, 2 (1969): 293-299;

Tanner, *City of Words: American Fiction, 1950-1970* (New York: Harper & Row, 1971), pp. 230-259;

Campbell Tatham, "The Gilesian Monomyth: Some Remarks on the Structure of *Giles Goat-Boy*," *Genre*, 3 (December 1970): 364-375;

Tatham, "John Barth and the Aesthetics of Artifice," *Contemporary Literature*, 12 (winter 1971): 60-73;

Jac Tharpe, *John Barth: The Comic Sublimity of Paradox* (Carbondale: Southern Illinois University Press, 1974);

Alan Trachtenberg, "Barth and Hawkes: Two Fabulists," *Critique*, 6, 2 (1963): 4-18;

Richard Vine, *John Barth: An Annotated Bibliography* (Metuchen, N.J.: Scarecrow, 1976);

Joseph N. Weixlmann, "John Barth: A Bibliography," *Critique*, 13, 3 (1972): 45-55;

Weixlmann, *John Barth: A Bibliography* (New York: Garland, 1976).

Manuscripts:

The Library of Congress has manuscripts and typescripts of *The Floating Opera*, *The End of the Road*, *The Sot-Weed Factor*, *Giles Goat-Boy*, and *Lost in the Funhouse*, plus working drafts and final manuscripts of various short stories and articles; see "John Barth Papers," *Quarterly Journal of the Library of Congress*, 26 (1969): 247-249. Galley proof of *Giles Goat-Boy* and *Lost in the Funhouse* are at Washington University.

DONALD BARTHELME has achieved his present eminence as one of the leading popular innovators in American fiction through the pages of the *New Yorker* magazine, where he began publishing in 1963. But, although he is best known for his stiff-upper-lip sentences and urban, upper-middle-class situations, his roots are in Texas. Born in Philadelphia on 7 April 1931, where his parents were attending the University of Pennsylvania, he moved at an early age to Houston, where his father rose to prominence as an architect in the style of Mies and Corbu. Texas language and Texas situations occasionally show up in Barthelme's stories, as do the Roman Catholicism of his youth and the experiences he had as a reporter, university publications writer, editor, and art museum director (all in Houston). He moved to New York City in 1962 to edit the only two issues of Harold Rosenberg's and Thomas Hess's art and literature journal, *Location*, and since has remained in New York to write full time, occasionally teaching as Distinguished Professor of English Prose at the City University of New York. He has been hailed by the full range of academic journals, literary quarterlies, and national news magazines as one of the most imitated and influential stylists writing today. He has received both a Guggenheim Fellowship and the National Book Award, plus numerous other literary prizes. Several times married and divorced, Barthelme writes with both deep feeling and sardonic style about the quality of personal lives, relationships, and material fortunes in contemporary America.

Because of his reliance upon language (instead of plot and character) to carry the theme of his stories, Barthelme has incurred the wrath of such

Donald Barthelme.

traditional critics as Alfred Kazin and Nathan Scott. With Barthelme we have been "sentenced to the sentence," Kazin writes in *Bright Book of Life* (1973), and further complains that, "he operates by countermeasures only, and the system that is his own joy to attack permits him what an authoritarian system always permits its lonely dissenters: the sense of their own weakness." Several of Barthelme's most severe critics base their objections on moral grounds. Joyce Carol Oates seized upon a character's statement, "Fragments are the only form I trust," and used it as the basis for Barthelme's supposed ethic, which she then attacked: "This from a writer of arguable genius, whose work reflects the anxiety he himself must feel, in book after book, that his brain is all fragments." What happens, Oates wondered,

when life came to imitate art? "And then who is in charge, who believed himself cleverly impotent, who supposed he had abdicated all conscious design?" Pearl K. Bell numbered Barthelme among "those celebrants of unreason, chaos, and inexorable decay . . . a horde of mini-Jeremiahs crying havoc in the Western world," against whom she proposed the more moral model of Saul Bellow, particularly in his novel *Mr. Sammler's Planet.* Nathan Scott complained that Barthelme's reinvention of the world "offers us an effective release from the bullying of all the vexations of history," but that such an aesthetic was too facile, the opting-out chosen "by the hordes of those young long-haired, jean-clad, pot-smoking bohemians who have entered the world of psychedelia." By 1970 the *New York Times Book*

Review began to give Barthelme longer and deeper reviews, probing the nature of his linguistic games and imaginative reinventions of social life, robbing negative critics of their strongest support. But younger critics, such as Larry McCaffery in the special 1975 issue of *Critique* devoted to Barthelme, argue that Barthelme's distrust of the ability of language to communicate any real sense, and of contemporary fiction to represent any real reality, makes him the perfect person to invent a new form of writing which will wake us up to the arbitrary nature of our conventional world.

The style Barthelme invents depends heavily on our awareness of how language has been corrupted by advertising and politics. His story "Report," from his collection *Unspeakable Practices, Unnatural Acts* (1968), features a group of military scientists who have invented such weapons as "rots, blights, and rusts capable of destroying [the enemy's] alphabet" and "the deadly testicle-destroying telegram." Their software technologists are busy working on "realtime online computer-controlled wish evaporation. Wish evaporation is going to be crucial in meeting the rising expectations of the world's peoples, which are as you know rising entirely too fast." Pieces of other realistic-sounding nonsense Barthelme invents include police bands which play cool jazz to soothe rioting crowds, amorphous balloons which cover half of New York City and provide pleasant but meaningless diversions for the populace, and even the accurate-sounding (but absurd) boxes of cereals his heroine in *Snow White* (1967) chooses for breakfast: "Chix," "Rats," and "Fear." Barthelme's genius is to take the form in which we are used to hearing something—having heard it so often that we have become anesthetized to it—and then insert a patent absurdity to shake us back to our senses and make us realize how our supposedly "realistic" lives have been conducted on the brink of pure silliness. Other stories, such as "Robert Kennedy Saved from Drowning" and "Views of My Father Weeping," are epistemological demonstrations of just how (and just how not) the world may be known; the point is always that the imagination is truer than the supposedly objective faculties of reality, and that fancy is more accurate than fact.

Snow White offers an insightful perspective on the America of the mid-1960s by retelling the Grimm Brothers' and Walt Disney's fairy tale in the language of the period—and it is the nature of that language which makes Barthelme's point. The Chief Executive of the Country is conducting "The President's War on Poetry," while Snow White sifts her way through a list of commercial-advertising princes, searching for the man "who will complete her." Her hope is for new words: "Oh I wish there were some words in the world that were not the words I always hear!" But she is chained to the same old linguistic constructions (constructions as a way of interpreting the world), such as when she drapes her tresses from Rapunzel's tower, only to have each dwarf "fail to respond to her hair initiative." Meanwhile, she herself is having her greatest impact as an object, distracting the bourgeois dwarfs from their humdrum daily business. But in such a world, she cannot expect a conventional salvation; her prince wanders in off-cue and eats the poison apple himself, earning her appellation of "pure frog."

Barthelme's second novel, *The Dead Father* (1975), resists the tendency toward fragmentation in the author's work which turns abortive novels into story collections. Instead, it adheres to a straight line of action, whereby a "dead father" (though still able to comment on the action and chase pretty girls) is hauled to burial by a crew of sons. This plot becomes the vehicle for Barthelme's observations on the role of fathers. This dead father dominates the landscape, eyes staring into the sky, smiling slightly, a bit of mackerel salad lodged between his teeth. "We think it's mackerel salad," says the narrator. "It appears to be mackerel salad. In the sagas, it is mackerel salad." The novel's situation is an adaptation of Samuel Beckett; but it exists only as a vehicle for the psychic play of action between father and son.

Barthelme's experiments with language reach their peak in his collection *City Life* (1970), where the story "Bone Bubbles" plays with almost totally meaningless juxtapositions, while its companion, "Sentence," merely speaks about itself as its words make their way across and down the page. His next assemblage of stories, *Sadness* (1972), turned back toward more recognizable situations, especially the trials of family life as detailed in "Critique de la Vie Quotidienne." In 1974 Barthelme had published *Guilty Pleasures*, a collection of satirical pieces he had been writing since his *New Yorker* debut, some of which had appeared as unsigned "Comment" contributions. Like his children's book from 1971, *The Slightly Irregular Fire Engine*, Barthelme demonstrated that he could use the artistic principle of collage to make good art from the bad refuse of contemporary language, whether it be the product ratings in *Consumer Reports* ("The world is sagging, snagging, scaling, spalling, pilling, pinging, pitting, warping, checking . . .") or the banalities of dead metaphors and dull advertisements (as in his story "A Nation of Wheels"). His

Donald Barthelme
c/o International Creative
    Management
40 W. 57
New York, N.Y.

THE NEW MUSIC

--What did you do today?

--Went to the grocery store and Xeroxed a box of English muffins, two pounds of ground veal and an apple. In flagrant violation of the Copyright Act.

--You had your nap, I remember that--

--I had my nap.

--Lunch, I remember that, there was lunch, slept with Susie after lunch, then your nap, woke up, right?, went Xeroxing, right?, read a book not a whole book but part of a book--

--Talked to Happy on the telephone saw the seven o'clock news did not wash the dishes want to clean up some of this mess?

--If one does nothing but listen to the new music, everything else drifts, goes away, frays. Did Odysseus feel this way, when he and Diomedes decided to steal Athene's statue from the Trojans, so that the latter would become dejected and lose the war? I don't think so,

-1-

novel *The Dead Father* (1975) sustains a narrative situation for 177 pages, something critics who had accused Barthelme of being a fragmentist thought he could not do. *Amateurs*, another story collection published in 1976, includes both simple situational comedy, such as "The School," where a beleaguered first-grade teacher suffers through the details of all his class's pets and nature projects, and more complex experiments with human attitudes and responses, such as "You are as Brave as Vincent Van Gogh."

The extensive popularity Barthelme enjoys, far beyond the limited audience his fellow innovationists—Ronald Sukenick, Gilbert Sorrentino, and even Ishmael Reed—share, is attributable to the ability of his fiction to operate as pure artifice, while at the same time displaying recognizable characters and situations. He is not restricted by the fragmentation of contemporary life, but rather, as Morris Dickstein says, "juxtaposes strange forms and fragments in a way that creates new forms and releases new meanings." Barthelme is more interested in human experience than in making value judgments about it, and the purpose of his writing is to exercise the full play of his own imagination in working with the materials at hand.

—*Jerome Klinkowitz*

Books:

Come Back, Dr. Caligari (Boston: Little, Brown, 1964; London: Eyre & Spottiswoode, 1966);

Snow White (New York: Atheneum, 1967; London: Cape, 1968);

Unspeakable Practices, Unnatural Acts (New York: Farrar, Straus & Giroux, 1968; London: Cape, 1969);

City Life (New York: Farrar, Straus & Giroux, 1970; London: Cape, 1971);

The Slightly Irregular Fire Engine (New York: Farrar, Straus & Giroux, 1971);

Sadness (New York: Farrar, Straus & Giroux, 1972; London: Cape, 1973);

Guilty Pleasures (New York: Farrar, Straus & Giroux, 1974);

The Dead Father (New York: Farrar, Straus & Giroux, 1975);

Amateurs (New York: Farrar, Straus & Giroux, 1976).

Periodical Publications:

"The Emerging Figure," *Forum* (Houston), 3 (summer 1961): 23-24;

"The Case of the Vanishing Product," *Harper's*, 223 (October 1961): 30-32;

"After Joyce," *Location*, 1 (summer 1964): 13-16;

"The Tired Terror of Graham Greene," *Holiday*, 39 (April 1966): 146, 148-149.

References:

John W. Aldridge, *The Devil in the Fire* (New York: Harper's Magazine Press, 1972), pp. 261-266;

Maclin Bocock, " 'The Indian Uprising'," *Fiction International*, 4-5 (1975): 134-146;

Critique, 16, 3 (1975). Special Barthelme issue, with four essays by Jerome Klinkowitz, Larry McCaffery, Betty Flowers, and Tom Whalen, plus a checklist.

William H. Gass, *Fiction and the Figures of Life* (New York: Knopf, 1970), pp. 97-103;

Francis Gillen, "Donald Barthelme's City: A Guide," *Twentieth Century Literature*, 18 (January 1972): 37-44;

Richard Gilman, *The Confusion of Realms* (New York: Random House, 1969), pp. 42-50;

Albert J. Guerard, "Notes on the Rhetoric of Anti-Realistic Fiction," *TriQuarterly*, 30 (spring 1974): 3-50;

Alfred Kazin, *Bright Book of Life* (Boston: Atlantic/Little, Brown, 1973), pp. 38, 183, 271-274;

Jerome Klinkowitz, "Literary Disruptions; Or, What's Become of American Fiction?" *Partisan Review*, 40, 3, (1973): 433-444; revised and expanded in *Surfiction*, ed. Raymond Federman (Chicago: Swallow Press, 1975), pp. 165-179;

Klinkowitz, "Donald Barthelme: A Checklist, 1957-1974," *Critique*, 16, 3 (1975): 49-58;

Klinkowitz, *Literary Disruptions* (Urbana: University of Illinois Press, 1975), pp. 62-81, 212-217;

Klinkowitz, *Donald Barthelme: A Comprehensive Bibliography and Annotated Secondary Checklist* (Hamden, Conn.: Shoe String Press/Archon Books, 1977);

Klinkowitz, *The Life of Fiction* (Urbana: University of Illinois Press, 1977), pp. 73-84;

Mark C. Krupnick, "Notes from the Funhouse," *Modern Occasions*, 1 (fall 1970): 108-112;

Robert Scholes, "Metafiction," *Iowa Review*, 1 (fall 1970): 100-115;

Earl Shorris, "Donald Barthelme's Illustrated Wordy-Gurdy," *Harper's*, 246 (January 1973): 92-94, 96;

Philip Stevick, "Lies, Fictions, and Mock Facts," *Western Humanities Review*, 30 (winter 1976): 1-12;

William Stott, "Donald Barthelme and the Death of

Fiction," *Prospects*, 1 (1975): 369-386; Tony Tanner, *City of Words* (New York: Harper & Row, 1971), pp. 141, 393, 400-406;

Alan Wilde, "Barthelme Unfair to Kierkegaard: Some Thoughts on Modern and Postmodern Irony," *Boundary*, 2, 5 (fall 1976): 45-70.

Saul Bellow

Daniel B. Marin
University of South Carolina

BIRTH: Lachine, Quebec, Canada, 10 June 1915.

EDUCATION: Tuley High School, Chicago; University of Chicago, 1933-1935; B.S., Northwestern University, 1937; graduate work in anthropology, University of Wisconsin, 1937.

MARRIAGE: 31 December 1937 to Anita Goshkin, divorced; children: Gregory. 1 February 1956 to Alexandra Tschacbosov, divorced; children: Adam; 10 December 1961 to Susan Glassman; children: Daniel.

AWARDS: Guggenheim Fellow, 1948-1949; National Institute of Arts and Letters grant, 1952; Creative Writing Fellow, Princeton University, 1952-1953; National Book Award for *The Adventures of Augie March*, 1954; Guggenheim Fellow, 1955-1956; Ford Foundation grant, 1959-1960; Friends of Literature Fiction Award, 1960; National Book Award for *Herzog*, 1965; International Literature Prize, 1965; Jewish Heritage Award from B'nai B'rith, 1968; *Croix de Chevalier des Arts et Lettres*, 1968; National Book Award for *Mr. Sammler's Planet*, 1971; Pulitzer Prize for *Humboldt's Gift*, 1975; Nobel Prize for Literature, 1976.

MAJOR WORKS: *Dangling Man* (New York: Vanguard, 1944; London: Weidenfeld & Nicolson, 1960); *The Victim* (New York: Vanguard, 1947; London: Weidenfeld & Nicolson, 1963); *The Adventures of Augie March* (New York: Viking, 1953; London: Weidenfeld & Nicolson, 1954); *Seize the Day* (New York: Viking, 1956; London: Weidenfeld & Nicolson, 1957); *Henderson the Rain King* (New York: Viking, 1959; London: Weidenfeld & Nicolson, 1959); *Herzog* (New York: Viking, 1964; London: Weidenfeld & Nicolson, 1965); *The Last Analysis*, produced New York, 1964 (New York: Viking, 1965; London: Weidenfeld & Nicolson, 1966); *Mosby's Memoirs and Other Stories* (New York: Viking, 1968; London: Weidenfeld & Nicol-

Jill Krementz

son, 1969); *Mr. Sammler's Planet* (New York: Viking, 1970; London: Weidenfeld & Nicolson, 1970); *Humboldt's Gift* (New York: Viking, 1975; London: Secker & Warburg, 1975); *To Jerusalem and Back: A Personal Account* (New York: Viking, 1976).

Saul Bellow

Saul Bellow claims the writer is a moralist, obliged to affirm the possibilities for individual life in the human community. Despite literary realism's "myth of the diminished man" and disparagement of modern civilization, Bellow finds a chance for "selfhood" in the modern world. Still he admires such modern masters as Conrad, Dreiser, Lawrence, Joyce, and Cary, and he draws materials and techniques from realism. He immerses his protagonists in a "multiplication of facts and sensations" which threatens to suffocate their selfhood. His fiction's density of specification is an analogue of the human problem it engages. In *The Adventures of Augie March* (1953), Augie articulates the dilemma: "there's too much history, too much example, too much influence, too many guys who tell you to be as they are, and all this hugeness, abundance, turbulence, Niagara Falls torrent." Bellow reassesses the human situation within this torrent.

He directs his affirmations against "a conviction that the world is evil, that it must be destroyed and rise again." In Bellow's view, man does not know enough about human existence to write it off. "Modern writers sin," he says, "when they suppose that they *know*, as they conceive that physics *knows* or that history *knows*. The subject of the novelist is not knowable in any such way." The creature's sheer biological persistence suggests that the density of modern civilization does not preclude valuable individual life. Bellow posits a tacit natural knowledge, "far deeper than head culture," and, to free himself from "the cliches of 'culture history,' " calls on "some power within us" to "tell us what we are, now that old misconceptions have been laid low."

Bellow's search for a form to express his intimate knowledge has involved the development of a style. From his "commentator within" he receives "words, phrases, syllables." In voice he finds a source of form and value. Accordingly, he has moved away from the chronology of cause-effect sequence, as in *The Victim* (1947), to fiction shaped by the dynamic of verbal gesture, as in *Henderson the Rain King* (1959). The pivotal work is *Augie March*, where with Augie's "free-style" manner Bellow began to evolve what Irving Howe calls "the first major new style in American prose fiction since those of Hemingway and Faulkner."

A persistent criticism of Bellow is that he merges with his protagonists. Bellow says, "I would have to suffer from dissociation of personality to be all these people in the books," but he confesses, "I lend a character, out of pure friendship, whatever he

needs." He lent Joseph of *Dangling Man* (1944) his Canadian birth and Chicago upbringing. With Asa Leventhal of *The Victim* he shared the editing experience he got in the editorial department of *Encyclopaedia Britannica* (1943-1946). Augie March starts out in Bellow's own 1920s Chicago and ends up, after his merchant marine stint, in France, where Bellow, after some merchant marine service of his own, started *Augie March*. The vexed and effortful hero of *Herzog* (1964) got Bellow's Chicago and Canadian roots, his bootlegging immigrant father, and his two ex-wives. Artur Sammler of *Mr. Sammler's Planet* (1970) got a trip to the Middle East for the Six Day War, which Bellow himself covered for *Newsday*. Bellow loaned Charlie Citrine of *Humboldt's Gift* (1975) his *Croix de Chevalier des Arts et Lettres*. Charlie's play, *Von Trenck*, played at the Belasco Theater, as did Bellow's *The Last Analysis*, albeit less successfully. Frequently Bellow shares with his protagonists his station in life, intellectual inclination, and cultural background. The recurrence in his fiction of tricky-talking schemers, sensually accommodating mistresses, cold-faced, aggressive-bitch ex-wives, practical, business-bent older brothers suggests that he draws heavily upon personal circumstances. There is, moreover, a correspondence between Bellow's conception of the artist and his conception of his protagonists. Just as the artist must demonstrate his trust in intuitions radically deeper than his certitude's reach, so Henderson, Herzog, Sammler, and Citrine hold themselves accountable for the utterance of what they know unaccountably. These protagonists reflect Bellow's own struggle to "express a variety of things I knew intimately." The act of affirmation is both the purpose and the substance of Bellow's fiction.

Now in his sixties, worldly and well-traveled, Bellow prefers his old haunts and friends. Although he "must have lived in upwards of 200 places," and for fifteen years resided in New York, Chicago is his center of gravity. He returned there in the early 1960s. A high school friend, Dave Peltz, who lunches with Bellow once a week, says, "I tell Saul stories that help keep him connected." Regarding his childhood feelings, Bellow says, "they were very powerful. But they were too much for me to deal with, and I covered them over with cynicism or wit or whatever. And now I realize how much emotion was invested in them, and I bring them back." The end of *Dangling Man* adumbrates an essential element in Bellow's life and fiction as Joseph returns to his childhood room where he glimpses "the ephemeral agreements by which we live and pace ourselves." In his persistent attempts to find within those "agreements" the grounds for affirmation, Bellow is a radically conservative writer.

Alfred Kazin's telling reminiscence, "My Friend Saul Bellow," recalls Bellow in 1942, a young, intellectually ambitious writer. He had published only two stories, "Two Morning Monologues" (1941) and "The Mexican General" (1942), both in *Partisan Review*. "He was," says Kazin, "measuring the world's power of resistance, measuring himself as a contender." As Bellow himself subsequently suggested in his *Paris Review* interview, he was then touching certain intellectual bases, paying his dues. And *Dangling Man* shows, in its formal and thematic similarities to Dostoevski's *Notes from Underground* and Sartre's *Nausea*, the influence of European existentialism. Its particular distinction as an American novel, however, lay in the nature of its local observation. Delmore Schwartz, the poet whose tragic career became a model for that of Von Humboldt Fleisher in *Humboldt's Gift*, noted Bellow's grasp of the "typical objects of a generation's sensibility: the phonograph records, the studio couch, the reproductions of Van Gogh, the cafeteria; and the typical relationships: the small intellectual circle which gradually breaks up, the easy and meaningless love affair, the party which ends in hysterical outbreaks or sickness of heart, the gulf separating this generation from the previous one and the family life from which it came." Schwartz thus pointed up one of the salient characteristics of Bellow's fiction: his copious documentation of the density of modern urban life.

Dangling Man (1944) illustrates, as well, a second characteristic: Bellow's concern with the plight of the intellectual. Bellow's comment on Herzog—"he comes to realize at last that what he considered his intellectual 'privilege' has proved to be another form of bondage"—also applies to Joseph, the hero of this first novel. Because he is Canadian born, his draft call has been delayed. The delay, at first a chance to read the books that had "stood as guarantors of an extended life," is, after seven months, a source of "harassment." Only nominally free, Joseph finds "not an open world, but a closed, hopeless jail," where he is "storing bitterness and spite." The more stridently Joseph asserts his freedom against the oppressive "hard-boiled-dom" of his environment, the more sharply he reveals his bondage and vulgarly betrays the selfhood he would affirm. His struggle to free himself from this bondage is the novel's central issue. The novel's denouement suggests that the cessation of such assertion is prerequisite to accurate appreciation of human possibilities. Joseph, having decided to "give myself up," finds "relief at my decision to surrender" and, after requesting immediate induction, he experiences a release from the "sure, cyclical distress of certain thoughts."

The novel's affirmation is at best provisional. Joseph's surrender leaves him vulnerable to the "flood of death" that menaces him throughout the novel. Joseph speculates that "perhaps the war could teach me, by violence, what I had been unable to learn during those months in the room. Perhaps I could sound creation through other means." And Bellow provides a basis for this tentative optimism in the irrepressible urge of Joseph's world toward life pushing through the snow, through cracks, from behind fence palings, which Joseph shares, in spite of himself, as he carries out his resolve to walk in the park on the first day of spring. But Joseph's last shrill "hurray" registers a residual irony at his surrender to what Earl Rovit has called "the realism of mortal flesh." The stridency of Joseph's final note indicates that he does not rest so easily in his "ephemeral agreements" as will Herzog in his "*occupancy.*"

The quieter conclusion of *The Victim* (1947), Bellow's next novel, bespeaks a less provisional affirmation. Asa Leventhal achieves a relative ease in the midst of his life's uncertainty and threat, even though the nature of his world and the limits of his comprehension allow no more certainty or freedom than did Joseph's "ephemeral agreements." Leventhal is fairly well-situated at Burke-Beard as editor of a small trade magazine and lives with his wife Mary in a spacious apartment, but he suspects that these circumstances are conditional. Behind a mask of indifference, he is sensitive to small slights, quick to take offense. His mother's insanity haunts him. This uneasiness impedes his sociability. He is especially uneasy in the absence of Mary, who is away helping her recently widowed mother move to Charleston. The coincidence of his nephew Mickey's illness and Kirby Allbee's appearance forces Leventhal to confront at close range the uncertainty of human circumstances. Summoned from work by his sister-in-law Elena's frantic call, he reluctantly assumes responsibilities neglected by his brother Max, who is working in Galveston, Texas. Summoned from his apartment by his door bell's unaccounted for ring to an encounter with Allbee, who emerges from the crowd in the park to charge that Leventhal ruined him in deliberate malice, Leventhal must assume responsibility for his own past actions. He becomes troubled by "the feeling that he really did not know what went on about him, what strange things, savage things." As Elena and Allbee press their claims, his sense of threat increases and the spectre of insanity draws nearer. Human affinities contingent upon love and guilt focus for Leventhal the uncertainties of his circumstances. His struggle to free himself from his uneasiness, without disavowing those human affinities, is the novel's central action.

Leventhal cannot clearly define the precise mixture of human responsibility and cosmic coincidence in Mickey's death, nor the extent of his own guilt in Allbee's affairs. The novel's language reflects Leventhal's cognitive dilemma. To Leventhal things and people "appeared," "seemed," "looked," "sounded" thus and so; they "maybe," "probably," "perhaps," "possibly" were; "must have," "might have," "may have" been; he "sensed," "felt," "thought," "guessed," "suspected," "imagined" what "could be" the case. What Keith Opdahl calls "glimpses of transcendence" do not take Leventhal beyond the sphere of uncertainty described by the novel's language. His "state of great lucidity," his "rare and pure feeling of happiness," his conviction "that he knew the truth" and "that everything . . . took place as if within a single soul or person" may suggest what Opdahl calls "something higher," but it is something of which Leventhal "had a sense," and the passage in which it occurs questions its durability, its usefulness in the daylight world to which he must wake. Aware of the danger of making metaphysical assumptions, Leventhal, to the end, confronts an ambiguous reality.

Yet, in the final chapter it is said of Leventhal that "the consciousness of an unremitting daily fight, though still present, was fainter and less troubling. . . . Something recalcitrant seemed to have left him; he was not exactly affable, but his obstinately unrevealing expression had softened." Leslie Fiedler calls the ending "an impatient . . . gesture at the sort of formal reversal and rest proper to the thick novel, but demanding to justify it a longer exposition than the rest of his book can balance." The answer to Fiedler's objection lies in an inherent plasticity in the things and people of Leventhal's world that allows them to survive. Leventhal has survived "the things that might have wrecked him." Allbee survives his bad times. Max's family survives despite Mickey's death. It is as Max has told his elder son Philip "that in a ship the plates were arranged in parts of the deck to give when there was bad weather to ride out," or as Leventhal himself reflects concerning children that "they were mauled in birth and they straightened as they grew because their bones were soft. Mauled again later, they could

recover again." Leventhal's increasing susceptibility to the claims of Elena and Allbee argues that he shares this childlike softness. Nevertheless, Leventhal is "half harsh." In his relation to his brother's family, there is a softening toward Max, Elena, even Elena's mother, but he evicts Allbee from his apartment by force. In their contrasting resolutions—the subway embrace with Max, the final fight with Allbee—the novel's parallel plots validate the mixture of softness and harshness finally attributed to Leventhal. The novel's ultimate assessment is restrained: "something recalcitrant seemed to have left him."

Bellow says that he wrote *The Victim* under "restraints." But after its publication he received a sort of certification in the form of a Guggenheim Fellowship (1948-1949), and he began *Augie March* while traveling in Europe: "I wrote it in trains and cafes. I got used to writing on the roll." When it appeared in 1953, Bellow said, "The great pleasure of the book was that it came easily. All I had to do was be there with buckets to catch it. That's why the form is loose." He "kicked over the traces, wrote catch-as-catch-can, picaresque." *Augie March* is notable for its lack of restraint, but also for its irresolution.

Augie, "varietistic" and "democratic in temperament," at the start promises something spontaneously affirmative and open, in the picaresque mode. Unlike Joseph, who claimed to talk to himself, Augie speaks—more of outward than of "inward transactions"—in a voice which answers his world's "general motion, as of people driven from angles and corners into the open, by places being valueless and inhospitable to them." In its "free-style" movement through "the whole height of space," Augie's memoir, circling out from his childhood Chicago neighborhood to Mexico to Europe, figures his disinclination "to illustrate a more and more narrow and restricted point of existence" and registers his confrontation with the "mighty free-running terror and wild cold of chaos." Critical comment, however, suggests that whatever the liberal virtues of Augie's "free-style" manner, the ease promised by his opening declaration is "forced" or "fake" and that Bellow, in his commitment to that manner, fails to provide enough form to resolve Augie's dilemma.

Certainly both Augie and Bellow came to recognize the need for restraint. But the novel's irresolution derives from the fact that Bellow, having set Augie loose, is unable to recall him. In retrospect Bellow concurred with the critics. He confessed that he "took off too many [restraints], went too far." However, his comment, "I had to tame and restrain the style I developed in *Augie March* in order to write *Henderson* and *Herzog*," argues that *Augie March*, despite its failures, was crucial to Bellow's subsequent achievement.

Augie's trip to Mexico with Thea to hunt iguanas is the novel's climactic episode. There Augie moves more centerless than ever in cosmic space. He is attracted to Thea because her particular motions imply broad reaches of space. He is stirred by her idea of ultimate release, imaged in Caligula, the eagle with which she intends to capture the iguanas. But he finally recoils from the terror of that release, as does Caligula himself. He recognizes the peril when stuck on a mountain with Stella, whom he is helping escape from her husband. He goes for help. He does not know whether what he sees in the distance "was stars or human lights." From this terrifying prospect of "light-year distances," Augie returns to lie down and make love with Stella, an act which disqualifies him from further pursuits with Thea. The mountain incident is the turning point in the episode and in the novel. After it, Augie wants to find a fixed center of existence, "the axial lines of life," where "all noise and grates, distortion, chatter, distraction, effort, superfluity, passed off like something unreal." He craves stillness.

But Augie remains "a traveling man, traveling by myself." His inability to "relax and knock off effort" to achieve the stillness upon which his "hope is based," forces him to place that hope in ironic light. And doing so he sounds the shrill notes not of "fake euphoria," as Leslie Fiedler charges, but of retrospective self-irony. On the mountain Augie turned back from the terror of the starry prospect to Stella, but married to her he finds that she has her own distances. With her he finds not a place where he can rest but space, territory to be crossed. He puts his final refusal "to lead a disappointed life" in the context of this irony when he says, "Look at me, going everywhere! Why I am a sort of Columbus of those near-at-hand and believe you can come to them in this immediate *terra incognita* that spreads out in every gaze." Augie remains "in the bondage of strangeness for a time still," trapped in the paradoxical motion of "getting to be still." His declaration of freedom becomes the revelation of his "bondage." And his final self-irony defines rather than resolves his dilemma. *Augie March* led Bellow to a deep exploration of the paradox inherent in the act of affirmation.

In a 1956 essay Bellow said that "distractions give force to a work of art by their resolution." In *Seize the Day* (1956) he turned to the coherencies of time, place, and action, and to what Alfred Kazin called a "style of definition" in order to achieve form. The neat resolution of this novella, however, comes at great expense to Bellow's affirmative impulse. The novella's hero, Tommy Wilhelm, wants to free himself from "the anxious and narrow life of the average." He wants to reduce things "to simplicity again." He searches for an elemental force beneath life's surface confusion. But Wilhelm's deepest instinct tells him that release may be worse than the vexation from which it frees him. Indeed, his past efforts to transcend the "life of the average" have merely added to his troubles. His aborted movie career "unfitted him somehow for trades and businesses." His divorce left him vulnerable to Margaret, who now cruelly exacts "the price of his freedom." At forty-four, surrounded by New York's aged, sinking under his burden at the Hotel Gloriana, where his father Dr. Adler refuses help and sympathy, Wilhelm makes one more effort. In partnership with Dr. Tamkin, who seems to reduce the mystery of "the world's business" to principle, he invests his last $700 in lard futures. But Tamkin disappears. His "truth" is ephemeral and elusive. In a world that seems "to throb at the last limit of endurance," Wilhelm finds not peace but Dr. Adler's "rule" and Margaret's "unbending voice." The progress of Wilhelm's day argues that "the easy tranquil things of life" are, like the movie career that was to have made him "a lover of the whole world," an illusion.

And yet, after this stifling day, Wilhelm seems about to obtain his release. The novella leaves him not in New York's hot and noisy press but in a chapel's "dark and cool," weeping at a stranger's funeral, sinking "deeper than sorrow, through torn sobs and cries toward the consummation of his heart's ultimate need." Can Bellow, having throughout placed Wilhelm's desire for release in ironic light, now join him in the lyricism of this ecstasy? It is difficult to believe that even the "minimal humanity" with which Leslie Fiedler credits Wilhelm at the end could survive the New York implied by the "style of definition . . . which renders the environment as a series of pressures on this all-too-feeling but never-knowing hero." When Dr. Adler, like the "electronic bookkeeping device," closes Wilhelm out, it appears that Wilhelm will be destroyed by his world's absolute unkindness. He never reenters the world "this side of the grave." For Wilhelm, then, transcendence is apparently the only answer.

His release moves him toward something less consoling than a "greater life." His final moment does not unite him with humankind, as did his momentary "blaze of love," but separates him from "the great, great crowd." Unable to leave the corpse, just as he is unable to forget the very hour of his mother's death, Wilhelm is separated from the other mourners, just as his insistence upon the memory of his mother alienates him from his father. The lyric heightening of the novella's last paragraph suggests that Wilhelm reaches a level of perception above that of the other mourners. The imagery recalls Milton's "Lycidas," a line of which—"Sunk though he be beneath the wat'ry floor"—has resonated in Wilhelm's mind during the day. However, the Miltonic imagery here consummates an irony at Wilhelm's expense that has been building throughout the narrative. The line may be consoling in the pastoral world of "Lycidas," but not in Wilhelm's pointedly non-pastoral New York. Wilhelm, at the side of the corpse, finds at "the end of all distractions" not pastoral consolation but rather the oblivion imaged in the dead man. If *Seize the Day* confirms the "conviction that the world is evil," it places in ironic light the hope that after this world's destruction it will "rise again." Critics have called *Seize the Day* Bellow's masterpiece. It is, however, the least affirmative of his major works.

Henderson the Rain King's (1959) hero discovers neither "the end of all distractions" nor stillness, but rather a relative calm within his existence's generous motions. Eugene Henderson remains in motion at the end, but his motion, less centerless and lonely than Augie's, celebrates the generosity of the horizons which circumscribe it. Henderson tells his African guide Romilayu, " 'Oh, you can't get away from rhythm. . . . You've got to live at peace with it, because if it's going to worry you, you'll lose.' " Henderson's achievement of this peace depends upon his recognition of the sustaining virtues of loyalty, love, and friendship. His achievement is dramatized as he becomes less strident and digressive and moves toward the quieter, more straightforward manner of the novel's end. This shift in Henderson's narrative mode reflects Bellow's own struggle to tame the style of *Augie March*. In Henderson's voice Bellow finds a source of form that allows him to reach a truly affirmative resolution, without surrendering to "the realism of mortal flesh."

Henderson claims that in Africa he encountered Reality and Truth. Yet this reality-affirmer narrates his travels in an Africa unlike that he read of in the accounts of nineteenth-century explorers Richard Burton and John Speke. The novel questions the reality it creates as Henderson, struggling to convey the important discovery he made in Africa, acknowledges that "not the least of the difficulties is that it happened as in a dream." Furthermore, the empty Arctic expanse of the final sequence may suggest, as Jonathan Baumbach argues, that "Henderson's ecstatic self-affirmation . . . is possible only where there is no real world about to deny it." Bellow's comment, "I feel Henderson and I are spiritually close," while not precluding a comic perspective, bespeaks a serious commitment to Henderson's affirmation. Bellow recalls that Professor Herskovits, with whom he studied African ethnology, "scolded me for writing a book like *Henderson*. He said the subject was much too serious for such fooling. I felt my fooling was fairly serious."

The central irony of Henderson's African trip is his discovery of continuity where he hoped to find discontinuity. He goes to Africa to escape the death imaged in the chaos of his life's "unbearable complications." He is looking for simplicity, essentials. But at the Arnewi village, which "looks like the original place," he is met by Itelo, who, "in his white drooping cloth and his scarf and middy, addressed me in English." Itelo underlines the irony: "You thought first footstep? Something new?" In Africa Henderson becomes more deeply immersed in chaos. His "life-pattern" stands revealed as, attempting to rid the Arnewi's cistern of the contaminating frogs, he blows up not only the frogs but the cistern too. With the Wariri King Dahfu he hopes to "approach ultimates," but his jubilation at lifting Mummah, the rain goddess, dissolves in the cosmic chaos of the wild rain ceremony and subsequent "deluge." As Rain King and successor to Dahfu, Henderson is literally implicated in "the body of this death." Death-anxiety, effort, jubilation, disaster, immersion in chaos—the rhythm Henderson cannot escape. The African experience is informative rather than transformative.

However, within that rhythm, Henderson discovers the sustaining virtue of his bond with other creatures. Whereas Wilhelm was separated from others by his "oblivion of tears," Henderson, in the "deluge," meets Romilayu, who supports him, and he reaches a moment of rest despite the whirling rain. In the end Romilayu's stabilizing influence, the loyalty and friendship he expresses, his "good sense," save Henderson. His relationship with Romilayu foreshadows his final insight. On his flight to Newfoundland, Henderson says, "I was granted certain recollections and they have made a sizable difference to me." In his youth, with an old bear, Smolak, he rode a roller coaster. Henderson and Smolak were sustained by their "common bond of despair," when "all support seemed to leave us."

The roller coaster's motion reflects the inescapable rhythm of creaturely existence, and their bond derived precisely from their participation in that rhythm. The virtue of this bond is the "something of the highest importance" that Henderson is now "obliged to communicate."

Henderson's chief problem is in the act of communication. His struggle to "make sense" in the midst of his "disorderly rush" shapes the novel. He begins by asking, "What made me take this trip to Africa?" After two chapters, having digressed about his money, his education, his suicide threat to his wife Lily, about Lily, her teeth, her father, their tour of French cathedrals, etc., he confesses, "I haven't got any closer to giving my reasons for going to Africa, and I'd better begin somewhere else." The "disorderly rush" he now engages is the verbal counterpart of the chaos which overwhelms him in Africa. But Henderson's narrative voice does not follow the rising pitch of the action he narrates, but rather reaches a crescendo as he tells of the rain ceremony and then becomes generally quieter, calmer, less digressive. In the second half of his narrative Henderson insists, with increasing frequency, upon his ties with other creatures: he asserts his loyalty and friendship for Dahfu, for Romilayu, for Lily. He enacts in the telling his trust in the bond. Both the substance and the form of his narrative earn his affirmation of "something of the highest importance."

"My life in Canada," Bellow says, "was partly frontier, partly the Polish ghetto, partly the Middle Ages. My second wife used to say I was medieval pure and simple. I've always been among foreigners, and never considered myself a native of anything. My father was the same way. In Russia he imported Egyptian onions, in Quebec he bootlegged for American rumrunners, in Chicago he sold coal. I was brought up in a polyglot community by parents who spoke many languages." Much of this background went into the creation of Moses Herzog. *Herzog* (1964) is Bellow's most autobiographical novel.

Herzog is granted a moment of complete stasis, which he celebrates in a lyric language that at once accepts and dissolves his life's vexations. His lyric moment does not move him, as did Wilhelm's, toward oblivion but rather leaves him *still on the same side of eternity as ever,*" asserting thereby his belief in the value of human life and his acceptance of the mystery of mankind. Herzog, still behaving "oddly" but nevertheless feeling "confident, cheerful, clairvoyant, and strong," is at his Ludeyville house in western Massachusetts. The novel's action,

presented retrospectively, covers a few months, during which Herzog, apprised of the long-standing infidelity of his ex-wife, Madeleine, with his ex-friend, Valentine Gersbach, "had fallen under a spell and was writing letters to everyone under the sun." He must explain, have it out, justify, put in perspective, clarify, make amends. He assumes a "posture of collapse," denying "the primitive self-attachment of the human creature." But sensing that his function is "to keep alive primordial feelings of a certain sort," he struggles to free himself from the spell. His final release, though qualified, suggests that the self's healthy instincts survive the corruptions of both urban civilization and individual consciousness.

Though the point of view is nominally third person, the novel's voice is effectively Herzog's. For Herzog language has been largely an implement of anger, sharpened by the necessities of justification. He tells his old friend Lucas Asphalter, " 'I go after reality with language. Perhaps I'd like to change it all into language, to force Madeleine and Gersbach to have a conscience.' " The novel's affirmation turns on the distinction between the strident rhetoric of Herzog's "posture of collapse" and the quiet expression of his "primordial feelings." On the one hand, Herzog's anger, manifest in the letters, recollections, and reflections that pervade the first two-thirds of the novel, marks his inability to accept even provisionally the rare moments of rest and tranquility he is offered, for example during his aborted visit to his charming friend Libby at Vineyard Haven. Libby's charm and Vineyard Haven's loveliness are submerged in a two-page rehearsal of his grievance against the cynical vision of reality advanced by his "Reality Instructors." Under the spell's influence, Herzog joins "the objective world in looking down on himself. He too could smile at Herzog and despise him." He feeds his "murdering imagination" until his rage precipitates a trip to Chicago where he intends to murder Madeleine and Gersbach. Modern civilization becomes for Herzog physically, intellectually, and morally an extension of Madeleine's "dirty way."

Herzog finds himself, however, as unable to murder as to stop breathing. Breathing is associated with "the primitive self attachment of the human creature," after all more powerful than the need to justify. This attachment asserts itself in the novel's climactic episode as Herzog, peering in through Madeleine's bathroom window, observes Gersbach bathing June, Herzog's daughter. Despite the poisonous proximity of Madeleine and Gersbach, the Herzog traits survive in June. Herzog's intended violence becomes *"theater . . . ludicrous."* The immediate scene obviates the angry rhetoric of his drive to Madeleine's. Herzog's breath comes back to him. Madeleine and Gersbach have "opened the way to justifiable murder," but the right-thinking which justifies it constitutes what Bellow (quoting R. G. Collingwood) calls " 'the worst disease of mind, the corruption of consciousness.' " Modern civilization's "dirty way" may provide grounds for "the human being's sense of a grievance," but, as Herzog now realizes, *"the chief ambiguity that afflicts intellectuals . . . is that civilized individuals hate and resent the civilization that makes their lives possible."* The angry rhetoric recedes, although the issue is not finally resolved until the passing of the spell and the cessation of Herzog's letters at Ludeyville.

Ludeyville, despite its rural location, is an extension of Herzog's "actual sphere." Urban pollution and "works of death" have counterparts there in the polluted well and the "small beaked skulls." At Ludeyville Herzog finds "the ruins of his scholarly enterprise," the relics of his marriage, including "the bed where he and Madeleine had known so much misery and hatred," and the shower built for Gersbach's convenience. At Ludeyville Herzog carries with him, as he will always carry, a residue of his own poisonous humor. Herzog finds at Ludeyville an inventory of his whole curious life. His final affirmation, then, is not, as Keith Opdahl claims, "an affirmation of a different reality" but of the conditions in which Herzog has lived and will continue to live. Indeed, the Ludeyville sequence suggests that the pollutions of contemporary human existence are not contingent upon urban civilization but inherent in creaturely being.

The juxtaposition at the novel's climactic moment of not murdering and continuing to breathe places the two on the same plane of natural occurrence. Herzog deserves no more moral credit for the former than for the latter. His "sweet instinct for the self" is the counterpart of his miraculous health. The terms of his affirmation are, accordingly, biological: *"And inside something, something, happiness. . . . 'Thou movest me.' That leaves no choice. Something produces intensity, a holy feeling, as oranges produce orange, as grass green, as birds heat."* What the creature knows as he knows his body he does not therefore cause. Implicit in the biological terms of this affirmation is the surrender of moral credit for the act of affirmation. Herzog pays tribute to that mysterious "power within us" when he accepts, as Augie March did not, the strangeness of his "immediate *terra incognita*,"

which after all is the human *"occupancy."* His final silence expresses his trust in the intuitions that motivate him, even though they lie ultimately beyond his understanding.

In 1966 Bellow observed, concerning Herzog, "Simple *aviditas vitae*. Does a man deserve any credit for this?" The observation suggests why Bellow turned next to elderly protagonists—Dr. Braun of "The Old System" (1967), Willis Mosby of "Mosby's Memoirs" (1968), and Artur Sammler. The strategy recalls Thoreau's at Walden Pond: "to drive life into a corner, and reduce it to its lowest terms." Alone in his apartment, Dr. Braun reflects that "the feeling of necessary existence might be the aggressive, instinctive vitality we share with a dog or an ape. The difference being in the power of the mind or spirit to declare *I am*. Plus the inevitable inference *I am not*." Braun is "no more pleased with being than with its opposite." After a day of rumination upon the long-past quarrel between his cousins Isaac and Tina Braun, he misvalues Tina's passionate death-bed declaration, and sees, through "closed eyes," only "red on black, something like molecular processes—the only true heraldry of being." Abdicating "the power of the mind or spirit," he makes no declaration. Willis Mosby, however, does. Mosby has spent a morning trying to put some humor into his memoirs, and "having disposed of all things human," goes to visit some ruins at Mitla. About to descend into the tomb, he is "a finished product. . . . He had completed himself in this cogitating, unlaughing, stone, iron, nonsensical form." In the tomb, however, he is "oppressed"—he cannot breathe. He rejects this death and chooses "the grace of life still there." He exercises his "power of the mind or spirit." In their contrasting resolutions these two stories point toward the distinction between that "power" and the "instinctive vitality" developed in *Mr. Sammler's Planet* (1970).

The central issue is posed in the novel's first chapter when elderly Artur Sammler, cajoled by his young friend Lionel Feffer into giving a lecture on the British Scene of the Thirties, is shouted down by "a figure of compact distortion": "Why do you listen to this effete old shit? What has he got to tell you? His balls are dry. He's dead. He can't come." Struck by this "passion to be real," Sammler regards the students as "spider monkeys in the trees . . . defecating into their hands, and shrieking, pelting the explorers below." Back on the street, he experiences "an intensification of vision." He is overwhelmed by a flood of sensations, "shining and pouring through openings in his substance, through

Saul Bellow

his gaps." This episode, shifting from drowsy remoteness to hyper-consciousness, establishes the poles between which Sammler will fluctuate. The rude student points up the central fact about Sammler: he is precisely a "diminished man"—"the human being at the point where he attempted to obtain his release from being human." He is Bellow's representative of the human species at the point of Earth-departure: when man's physical desires are at a minimum and he is powerless before the world's chaos, ready to launch from this planet, is there some essential thing that still binds him to it? And if so, how, at the last moment, can he affirm, despite the distractions of daily life and the distortions of human perception and language, its real value? Sammler, a kind of twentieth-century collective consciousness, considers it his task to condense his life experience into such a testament. His struggle to find an effective form for this mortally necessary "compassionate utterance" is the novel's central action.

By poising Sammler "between the human and not-human states," Bellow measures the precise valence of the human bond. Sammler's ambivalence is an important source of the novel's dramatic tension. On the one hand, confronted with "the free ways of barbarism," Sammler retreats. He echoes Job's petition "for a release from God's attention." He cultivates detachment. On the other hand, Sammler is "always drawn back to human conditions" by his craving for "outer forms . . . for our humanity," lacking which humankind falls back upon the "antics of failed individuality." Sammler's ambivalence is resolved in the novel's climactic episode. On the way to the hospital to see his nephew and benefactor, Elya Gruner, who is dying, Sammler is delayed when he comes upon Feffer being choked by a black pickpocket, whom Sammler had observed earlier on the Riverside bus. In the crowd, watching without interfering, is Sammler's son-in-law Eisen, an Israeli artist. As he watches the man choking Feffer, Sammler's detachment becomes a source of fear. He suddenly sees himself "freed from gravitation, light with release and dread." He turns back from this release. But when he asks Eisen to separate the combatants by taking Feffer's camera (Feffer has taken some candid camera shots of the pickpocket in action), Eisen nearly clubs the pickpocket to death. The episode's point is clear: it is precisely this distorted response, as well as Feffer's candid camera vision, that wickedly illuminates the world and obstructs "compassionate utterance." Similarly, at the hospital, Angela Gruner has magnified her quarrel with her father

and angrily rejects Sammler's suggestion of a reconciliation.

In the end "molecular processes" do not constitute "the only true heraldry of being" for Sammler. Despite the irony implicit in his diminution, he makes a declaration, affirming over Elya's body "the terms which, in his inmost heart, each man knows." His affirmation acknowledges the facts of suffocation and death, as well as "all the confusion and degraded clowning of this life"—the full range of facts, forces, and ironies he has had to confront. If Sammler's failure to "convince or convert anyone" concedes a diminution of the spirit's authority among "purposive, aggressive, business-bent, conative people," still his valuation of those "terms" is proportionate to the magnitude of the diminution Sammler himself suffers in honoring them. The paradox here reflects the mood in which the "terms" can be accepted.

The spiritual authority of the poet in "pragmatic America" is the central issue of Bellow's most recent novel, *Humboldt's Gift* (1975). Chicago, which "with its gigantesque outer life contained the whole problem of poetry and the inner life in America," is, for the most part, the scene of the novel's action. For Charlie Citrine, the narrator and protagonist, "a famous person who lives in Chicago incognito," the issue is posed by the "rise and fall" of his deceased pal, the once-promising poet Von Humboldt Fleisher. Now Charlie feels compelled to "carry on for Humboldt." It seems to be up to Charlie "to think what to do about talent in this day, in this age. How to prevent the leprosy of souls." Much of his narrative is devoted to the reconstruction of Humboldt's career. He tries to find something of persistent value that will justify, appearances to the contrary notwithstanding, Humboldt's effort.

Humboldt achieved not the spiritual revival he promised but, like Edgar Allan Poe, like Hart Crane, like Jarrell and Berryman, the poet's martyrdom in "crass America." The promise dissolved in hectic nonstop monologues, in improvisation, paranoiac detraction, madness, fanatical schemes, in the "huge volume of notions" he carried about, in pills, gin, insomnia. Humboldt thought Stevenson would bring in poetry and culture. In the Eisenhower landslide Humboldt "declined and fell." Charlie must sadly concede that all Humboldt's "thinking, writing, feeling counted for nothing, all the raids behind the lines to bring back beauty had no effect except to wear him out." Humboldt's legacy is "a question addressed to the public. The death question itself, which Walt Whitman saw as the question of

47

questions." Charlie is obsessed by his last glimpse of Humboldt, "death all over him," on a New York sidewalk. Charlie's youthful eagerness and enthusiasm have become diluted with the cynicism of "common realism." "Ah my higher life," he wails. "When I was young I believed that being an intellectual assured me of a higher life. In this Humboldt and I were exactly alike." Humboldt's career argues that this belief is nonsense.

Charlie's present circumstances point to the same conclusion. He has slipped into the "moronic inferno." He is beset by "common sense absurdities," by Rinaldo Cantabile, "demon of distraction." The novel's plot, sharply articulated and complicated with comic coincidence, shows the ascendency of "pragmatic America" and "the enormity of the awful tangle." Charlie wants to "rise above all this stuff, the accidental, the merely phenomenal, the wastefully and randomly human, and be fit to enter higher worlds." He has set himself "an indispensable metaphysical revision, a more correct way of thinking about the question of death." His pragmatic mistress Renata, however, speaks against all this. She has run off with Charlie's rival, Flonzaley, an undertaker. "I believe I live in nature," she writes. "I think that when you're dead you're dead, and that's that. Dead is dead, and the man's trade is with stiffs, and I'm his wife now. Flonzaley performs a practical service for society." Charlie's theories, his intellectual life render him no more immune to the "moronic inferno" than was Humboldt. The novel's concluding episode, wherein Charlie gets Humboldt out of Deathsville, New Jersey, and reburies him at Valhalla Cemetery, again argues the ascendancy of "pragmatic America" and the weakness of the spiritual powers. A machine lowers Humboldt's casket into the concrete bunker down in the grave: "Thus, the condensation of collective intelligences and combined ingenuities, its cables silently spinning, dealt with the individual poet." As for Humboldt's poems, "the literary funeral directors and politicians who put together these collections" have excluded them from the new anthologies.

Still, Charlie insists, this is not it. He informs us that "Humboldt acted from the grave, so to speak, and made a basic change in my life." Charlie says he has received "light" causing "an altogether unreasonable kind of joy. Furthermore, the hysterical, the grotesque about me, the abusive, the unjust, the madness in which I had often been a willing and active participant, the grieving, now had found a contrast." He announces his intention of taking up "a different kind of life" at the Swiss Steiner center.

The money from the script he and Humboldt wrote (included in Humboldt's will) will subsidize Charlie's higher activities. But Humboldt's assertion, in the accompanying letter, that "we are not natural beings but supernatural beings" seems to have convinced Charlie of the reality of the spiritual powers. The novel, moreover, endorses his conviction.

Roger Shattuck finds Charlie's declarations unconvincing. He detects "no shift in mental metabolism, no climacteric, only a stronger concern with the survival of the self." This argues that the implied "redemption" is unearned and, Charlie's assertions notwithstanding, Humboldt's efforts have indeed justified the cynicism of "common realism." The novel does not show Charlie fully achieving his "different kind of life." He has not yet straightened out his affairs. But there is a "contrast"; he has changed. There is a "shift in mental metabolism" detectable, for example, in his move away from dramatizations of Humboldt's hectic nonstop monologues to his own calmer reflections. As did Herzog's, Charlie's self-irony recedes. Humboldt's letter, expressing a final sanity, suggests that he, too, underwent a "shift in mental metabolism." Charlie's direction is clearly indicated. He has moved from the "moronic inferno" into a "reflective purgatory," where, with Humboldt's posthumous help, he has begun "to put metaphysics and the conduct of life together in some practical way." *Humboldt's Gift* is the first of Bellow's novels to base its affirmation on clear metaphysical assumptions.

The closest thing to an anthology of Bellow's nonfiction is Irving Howe's Viking Critical Library *Herzog* (1976), which includes three essays, "Deep Readers of the World, Beware" (1959), "Distractions of a Fiction Writer" (1957), and "A Comment on 'Form and Despair' " (1964), as well as his 1966 *Paris Review* interview by Gordon Harper. The selection nicely illuminates Bellow's formal and thematic intentions in *Herzog*, but still one hopes for an anthology that will measure the full range of his intellectual interests. For a full measure of the intellectual pressure Bellow can bring to bear on the particular historical moment, there is his most recent book, *To Jerusalem and Back: A Personal Account* (1976), an account of his visit to Israel during the latter part of 1975.

This book is notable for its marshalling of "dozens of books and scores of documents." Against the backdrop of written commentary, copiously quoted, we hear the voices and catch the particular gestures of Abba Eban, Yitzhak Rabin, Henry Kissinger, of a barber at the King David Hotel, a cab driver, a masseur, of Jerusalem Mayor Teddy Kollek, and others. *To Jerusalem and Back* is a book of conversation. "Here in Jerusalem," Bellow says, "when you shut your apartment door behind you you fall into a gale of conversation." Bellow is "utterly attentive." All the talk is ultimately about "the survival of the decent society created in Israel within a few decades." Always there is the paradox presented by the juxtaposition of civilization and terrorist bombings. Coffee is ordered. A bomb explodes in a coffee shop on the Jaffa Road. A cabby says, " 'So now my friend is dead. . . . And this is how we live, mister! Okay? We live this way.' "

The question of Israel's political and physical survival cannot be avoided, but Bellow, in Jerusalem "to observe, to sense a condition or absorb qualities," locates the center of the question of survival in the damaging effects upon individual consciousness of the "gale of conversation." He feels he has "dropped into a shoreless sea." The "great noise of modern life" damages the "ability to contemplate." "A life of intellectual creativity" becomes inaccessible. It is the predicament of individual consciousness in the contemporary community. It is, too, the predicament of the artist: "For a great world population, what is lingering loving contemplation, what is art? Proust, who translated Russian into French, takes up the theme of politics and art in the novelist's indirect manner: on the one side, Bergotte Vinteuil, Swann's love of music; on the other, worldliness, snobbery, the Dreyfus affair, the Great War. Proust was still able to hold the balance. That was six decades ago." Bellow's whole effort has been toward the restoration of the balance in modern consciousness destroyed by those six decades.

Periodical Publications:

"Two Morning Monologues," *Partisan Review*, 8 (May-June 1941): 230-236;

"The Mexican General," *Partisan Review*, 9 (May-June 1942): 178-194;

"Spanish Letter," *Partisan Review*, 15 (February 1948): 217-230;

"Sermon by Doctor Pep," *Partisan Review*, 16 (May 1949): 455-462;

"Dora," *Harper's Bazaar*, 83 (November 1949): 118, 188-190;

"Trip to Galena," *Partisan Review*, 17 (November-December 1950): 779-794;

"By the Rock Wall," *Harper's Bazaar*, 85 (April 1951): 135, 205, 207-208;

"Dreiser and the Triumph of Art," *Commentary*, 11 (May 1951): 502-503;

"Address by Gooley MacDowell to the Hasbeens Club of Chicago," *Hudson Review*, 4 (summer 1951): 222-227;

"Gide as Autobiographer," *New Leader*, 4 June 1951, p. 24;

"Gimple the Fool," by I. B. Singer, translation by Bellow, *Partisan Review*, 20 (May-June 1953): 300-313;

"Hemingway and the Image of Man," *Partisan Review*, 20 (May-June 1953): 338-342;

"How I Wrote Augie March's Story," *New York Times Book Review*, 31 January 1954, pp. 3, 17;

"Isaac Rosenfeld," *Partisan Review*, 23 (fall 1956): 565-567;

"A Talk With the Yellow Kid," *Reporter*, 6 September 1956, pp. 41-44;

"The Sealed Treasure," *Times Literary Supplement*, 1 July 1960, p. 414;

"Literary Notes on Khrushchev," *Esquire*, 55 (March 1961): 106-107;

"Facts That Put Fancy to Flight," *New York Times Book Review*, 11 February 1962, p. 1;

"The Writer as Moralist," *Atlantic Monthly*, 211 (March 1963): 58-62;

"Some Notes on Recent American Fiction," *Encounter*, 21 (November 1963): 22-29;

"On Jewish Storytelling," *Jewish Heritage Quarterly*, 7 (winter 1964-1965): 5-9;

"Israel Diary," *Jewish Heritage Quarterly*, 10 (winter 1967-1968): 31-43;

"Culture Now: Some Animadversions, Some Laughs," *Modern Occasions*, 1 (winter 1971): 162-178;

"Starting Out in Chicago," *American Scholar*, 44 (winter 1974-1975): 71-77;

"Nobel Lecture," *American Scholar*, 46 (summer 1977): 316-325.

Other:

Feodor Dostoevsky, *Winter Notes on Summer Impressions*, foreword by Bellow (New York: Criterion Books, 1955), pp. 9-27;

"Skepticism and the Depth of Life," in *The Arts and the Public*, eds. James E. Miller and Paul D. Herring (Chicago: University of Chicago Press, 1967);

"Literature in the Age of Technology," in *Frank Nelson Doubleday Lecture Series: Technology and the Frontiers of Knowledge* (Garden City: Doubleday, 1974), pp. 3-22;

"Zetland: By a Character Witness," in *Modern Occasions 2*, ed. Philip Rahv (Port Washington, N.Y.: Kennikat, 1974), pp. 9-30.

References:

Robert Alter, *After the Tradition* (New York: Dutton, 1969);

Jonathan Baumbach, *The Landscape of Nightmare* (New York: New York University Press, 1965);

Jo Brans, "Common Needs, Common Preoccupations: An Interview with Saul Bellow," *Southwest Review*, 62 (winter 1977): 1-19;

John Jacob Clayton, *Saul Bellow: In Defense of Man* (Bloomington: Indiana University Press, 1968);

Sarah Blacher Cohen, *Saul Bellow's Enigmatic Laughter* (Urbana: University of Illinois Press, 1974);

Robert Detweiler, *Saul Bellow: A Critical Essay* (Grand Rapids, Mich.: Eerdmans, 1967);

Robert R. Dutton, *Saul Bellow* (New York: Twayne, 1971);

John Enck, "Saul Bellow: An Interview," *Wisconsin Studies in Contemporary Literature*, 6 (summer 1965): 156-160;

David D. Galloway, *The Absurd Hero in American Fiction: Updike, Styron, Bellow, Salinger* (Austin: University of Texas Press, 1966);

Maxwell Geismar, *American Moderns* (New York: Hill & Wang, 1958);

Howard Harper, *Desperate Faith: A Study of Bellow, Salinger, Mailer, Baldwin, and Updike* (Chapel Hill: University of North Carolina Press, 1967);

Ihab Hassan, *Radical Innocence* (Princeton: Princeton University Press, 1961);

Irving Howe, ed., *Saul Bellow: Herzog: Text and Criticism* (New York: Viking, 1976);

Howe, *World of Our Fathers* (New York: Simon & Schuster, 1976);

Alfred Kazin, *Contemporaries* (Boston: Little, Brown, 1962);

Marcus Klein, *After Alienation* (New York: World, 1964);

Chirantan Kulshrestha, "A Conversation with Saul Bellow," *Chicago Review*, 23-24 (1972): 7-15;

Irving Malin, ed., *Saul Bellow and the Critics* (New York: New York University Press, 1967);

Malin, *Saul Bellow's Fiction* (Carbondale: Southern Illinois University Press, 1969);

Keith M. Opdahl, *The Novels of Saul Bellow: An Introduction* (University Park: Pennsylvania State University Press, 1967);

Norman Podhoretz, *Doings and Undoings: The Fifties and After in American Writing* (New York: Farrar, Straus & Giroux, 1964);

M. Gilbert Porter, *Whence the Power? The Artistry and Humanity of Saul Bellow* (Columbia: University of Missouri Press, 1974);

Earl Rovit, *Saul Bellow* (Minneapolis: University of Minnesota Press, 1967);

Rovit, ed., *Saul Bellow: A Collection of Critical Essays* (Englewood Cliffs: Prentice-Hall, 1975);

Brigitte Sheer-Schatzler, *Saul Bellow* (New York: Ungar, 1972);

B.A. Sokoloff and Mark Posner, *Saul Bellow: A Comprehensive Bibliography* (Folcroft, Penn.: Folcroft Library Editions, 1972);

Tony Tanner, *City of Words* (New York: Harper & Row, 1971);

Tanner, *Saul Bellow* (Edinburgh: Oliver & Boyd, 1965);

Edith Tarvoc, ed., *The Portable Saul Bellow* (New York: Viking, 1974), introduction by Gabriel Josipovici, pp. vii-xxxiv.

Manuscripts:

The University of Chicago has much of Bellow's correspondence and manuscript material for some of his novels.

THOMAS BERGER was born in Cincinnati, Ohio, on 20 July 1924. He was educated at the University of Cincinnati, where he received his B.A. in 1948, and he did graduate work at Columbia University (1950-1951). Between 1948 and 1954, Berger served as librarian at the Rand School of Social Science, staff writer for the *New York Times Index*, and associate editor of *Popular Science Monthly*. He married Jeanne Redpath in 1950. His first novel, *Crazy in Berlin* (1958), had its roots in his experiences in the United States Army between 1943 and 1946. The book was received with a modicum of critical comment, but with publication of its sequel, *Reinhart in Love* (1962), and *Little Big Man* (1964), which won the Rosenthal Award in 1965, Berger established himself as an important voice in American comic fiction.

Crazy in Berlin revolves around the experiences of Carlo Reinhart, a young American soldier in post-World War II Germany. Reinhart is swept up in a flurry of lunacy and corruption that transcends, in intensity if not duration, the physical horror that he he has witnessed in the war itself. Naive and idealistic, Carlo is initiated into a world of hatred, cruelty, and deceit, a Hobbesian jungle where every man is at war with every other man. He learns that he must divest himself of his optimism, his childlike belief in the American Dream, and replace it with a more objective attitude of complacency and

Jill Krementz

The spiritual change that prompts Reinhart's disorientation is typical of the kind of alterations that most of Berger's protagonists undergo. Berger offers a stark portrait of the common man in the twentieth century, a man who recognizes change and absurdity, but who is unable to do anything about them. And Berger himself offers no unique solutions to what he terms the "mad little private hopelessnesses." In Reinhart's case, for instance, the only "solution" is less a function of human will than it is the result of brute circumstance. Failing in his efforts to locate the ideals he once believed in, Reinhart tries to kill himself. But even this attempt is a failure, and the reader is left with a middle-aged, middle-class, middle-American man, weary and ripe for change.

In *Vital Parts* (1970), the final book of the Reinhart trilogy, Berger nurses his protagonist through middle age, a condition which finds Reinhart teetering on the edge of misanthropy, advising his daughter that "human beings are vile." Habitually assuming the worst of others, Reinhart prides himself on feeling "comfortable in a world full of malice and corruption." This "comfort," however, proves to be little more than a mask Reinhart raises to shield himself from the lack of love he receives from his wife or son. He wants to keep evil at bay by attempting to glory in its presence, an attempt that, ironically, fuels Reinhart's idealistic embers.

Reinhart's idealism is born of a need for fundamental freedom that would allow him to mingle unobtrusively with a society he neither detests nor loves. By joining Bob Sweet's Cryon Foundation, a corporate entity that claims to have developed a technique for freezing human beings, Reinhart discovers that individuality is the price for freedom. The corporation claims that their customers, by allowing themselves to be frozen for an unspecified period of time, will benefit from the advances of medical science. Once thawed, they could be cured of diseases that formerly would have proved fatal to them. But Reinhart is aware that the freezing technique is little more than a scheme to cheat people by offering them hope. By learning the game of stylistic deception and corporate flimflam, he also learns a sense of personal worth, however ill-defined or fragmented.

Reinhart's "vital parts," his individuality and sense of worth, are no longer vital. He is frozen, waiting, like those theoretical bodies who wait to be thawed once the cures for their diseases are found. If there is indeed a cure for Reinhart's suffering, it is a futuristic one, as uncertain as his own attempts to come to terms with himself.

acceptance. This tension between idealism and pragmatism foreshadows an important theme that reappears in Berger's later fiction.

The theme and mock-heroic tone of *Crazy in Berlin* are continued in *Reinhart in Love* (1963) as Carlo attempts to reconstruct his way of living in postwar America. Reinhart is confused and disoriented, fully aware of the alterations that have taken place, but hopelessly unable to gauge the dimensions or implications of the changes:

> Reinhart suddenly chose now as the time to wonder what he was doing here at all, at this precise moment in late February 1946, at 9:31 P.M., alongside an inappropriate father, bumping over streets not germane to his idea of his own identity, approaching an irrelevant home. Every atom of the human substance has been renewed in the course of seven years: a hundred of Reinhart's pounds were of another meat than he had carried away, and this change was little beside that of the spirit.

Thomas Berger
Piermont, N.Y.
ELmwood 9-1949

CUSTER'S LAST STAND

Chapter 1

A Terrible Mistake

I am a white man and never forgot it, but I was brought up by the Cheyenne Indians from the age of ten.

My Pa had been a minister of the gospel in Evansville, Indiana. He didn't have a regular church, but managed to talk some saloonkeeper into letting him use his place of a Sunday morning for services. This saloon was down by the riverfront and the kind of people would come in there was Ohio River boatmen, Hoosier fourflushers on their way to New Orleans, pickpockets, bullyboys, whores, and suchlike, my Pa's favorite type of congregation owing to the possibilities it afforded for the improvement of a number of mean skunks.

The first time he come into the saloon and started to preach, that bunch was fixing to lynch him, but he climbed on top of the bar and started to yell and in a minute or two they all shut up and listened. My Pa could handle with his voice any white man that ever lived, though he was only of the middle height and skinny as a pick handle. What he'd do, you see, was to make a person feel guilty of something they never thought of. Distraction was his game. He'd stare with his blazing eyes at some big, rough devil off the boats and shout: "How long's it been you ain't seen your old Ma?" Like as not that fellow would scrape his feet and honk his nose in his sleeve, and when my brothers and sisters carried around cleaned-out spittoons for the collection, remember us kindly for our pains.

Pa split the collection with the saloonkeeper, which was part of the reason he was let to use the place. The other part was that the bar

From typescript of Little Big Man.

Little Big Man (1964) is a mock-heroic novel about the American West. Jack Crabb—a gunfighter, buffalo hunter, scout, and adopted Cheyenne warrior—narrates the story in the local color tradition to offer a satiric glimpse into the nature of life on the western frontier. Berger's most widely read novel, *Little Big Man* holds up for ridicule the attitudes that fostered racism and hatred between Indians and whites. In so doing, the novel offers a perspective from which to view Berger's indictment of society and tradition in such works as *Reinhart in Love* and *Vital Parts*.

Old Lodge Skins, an Indian who teaches Jack Crabb the important differences between "Human Beings" (Cheyennes) and whites, is a pivotal figure in the novel. His observations shed light on the simplicity of the Indian way of life while underscoring the cruelty and inhumanity of the whites. When asked whether or not he hates his pale-skinned brothers, Old Lodge Skins replies:

> No. . . . But now I understand them. I no longer believe they are fools or crazy. I know now that they do not drive away the buffalo by mistake or accidentally set fire to the prairie with their fire-wagon or rub out Human Beings because of a misunderstanding. No, they *want* to do these things, and they succeed in doing them. . . . The Human Beings believe that everything is alive: not only men and animals but also water and earth and stones and also the dead and things from them. . . .
>
> But white men believe that everything is dead: stones, earth, animals, and people, even their own people. And if, in spite of that, things persist in trying to live, white men will rub them out.

The serious focus of *Little Big Man* is clouded by the satiric style, but Berger's obvious intent is biting ridicule aimed at ignorance and cruelty. Jack Crabb, whether "mythomaniac" or truthteller, offers "serious moral propositions" that form the backdrop for Berger's most compelling work.

With the publication of *Killing Time* in 1967, Berger put aside the satiric style employed in *Little Big Man* and concentrated on telling the story of Joe Detweiler, a murderer who believes that he has discovered absolute justice. Berger enters the mind of this "scientist of the soul," as Joe's lawyer calls him, and presents a sordid, frightening tale of murder. Berger's meticulous attention to detail underscores Joe's own meticulous attempts to justify his own acts. In so doing, the protagonist develops a system of absurdist logic that opts for murder as the only true means of coming to terms with human finitude. In effect, Joe does not see his own acts as murder, but

rather as efforts to liberate souls from their imprisonment in Time. He kills time, not people.

Killing Time opens with a gruesome description of a multiple murder. On Christmas Eve, the Arthur Baysons arrive at the apartment of a friend and find three people brutally murdered. What follows is an extended account of Joe Detweiler's incarceration and trial, an objective look at the meditative ruminations and logic of a murderer. In his story, Berger makes use of a number of familiar literary devices and themes. The protagonist is pictured as a kind of insane metaphysician whose queries about cosmic justice, sanity, and time are part and parcel of his reason for killing. He believes that the murder of three finite souls is really nothing more than an act of Divine Justice, a gesture aimed at asserting man's ability to transcend conventional morality. Detweiler's mind wavers between reality and fantasy, and his confusion resembles that of most of Berger's anti-heroes. He longs for stability amid what he sees as the chaos of "mankind in motion":

> Out in the world, try as I would, I could not get a firm grasp on experience. I was incessantly distracted by the spectacle of mankind in motion, noise, color, the flow of all the different kinds of energy. I really started choking Mrs. Starr so that I could gain a moment's peace in which to think.

In this confusion, Detweiler does occasionally see his own wrongdoing and his liability for punishment:

> God knows, I even killed three people. But the legal system is extraordinary. To be brought to justice! All this marvelous organization, so reasonable and yet compassionate, serious, grand, and precedented. Men live and die, laws change, civilizations rise and fall in the inexorable movement of Time. But justice is not transitory in concept though particulars alter . . . we have not ceased to believe that theft, treason, and murder are wrong and that their perpetrators should be brought to justice!

But as Detweiler rambles through his theories of divine and human justice, he never thoroughly comprehends the dimensions of his own personal crime because he is lost in rhetoric and abstraction, unable to "gain a moment's peace in which to think."

Killing Time is Berger's most ambitious piece of fiction, but its critical reception was disappointing. William H. Gass argued that Berger tried to accomplish too much in too short a span. As Gass puts it in the *New York Times Book Review*, Berger attempts a philosophically and psychologically profound study of murder, sex, time, responsibility, and madness—what you will—without having the talent or making the effort. Other critics, notably Stanley Kauffmann, called Berger's novel stilted and predictable, both in style and characterization. To be sure, Berger is more at home with satire than with the philosophical meanderings he affects in *Killing Time*, but the novel does mark a milestone in his literary development. If his speculations on justice, sanity, and time are sophomoric, he at least makes an effort toward serious comment.

Berger returns to the satiric mode in *Regiment of Women* (1973), a raucous, futuristic jaunt through a society dominated by women. The setting for the novel is the late twenty-first century, and the roles of male and female have undergone complete reversals, a condition which gives the novel an almost allegorical tone. Georgie Cornell, who makes his first appearance in his "baby-doll nightgown, ruffled panties and bunny slippers," is a typical Berger protagonist—inept, confused, and without direction. At the opening of *Regiment*, he is undergoing a sadistic psychological treatment that consists of anal intercourse applied with a huge dildo by Dr. Prine, the first in a series of macabre females who inflict their wills on Cornell and his male counterparts.

As the story progresses, Cornell, like Carlo Reinhart in Berger's previous novel, undergoes a series of changes that redefine his own image of himself. After his arrest for impersonating a woman (by donning trousers, sport jacket, and pipe), Cornell is involved in a jailbreak that puts him in contact with "The Movement," a dedicated group of males who are intent on breaking the chains of female domination. Cornell's own spirit, hungering for freedom from domination, is particularly receptive to the group's propaganda, and he is assigned to infiltrate the "sperm draft," a military establishment designed to "milk" the sperm of young males for procreation purposes. His specific mission is to frustrate the system by getting all the young men to masturbate "just before milking time," thereby affecting the military's supply of semen. The plan is scrapped when Cornell realizes that the men are subject to "impromptu semen milkings"; he is forced to desert the movement and attempt to gain freedom on his own.

Cornell's escape triggers personal doubts about the meaning of his life: "since birth he had lived a pointless life . . . it had been a burlesque and he a sexless monstrosity without an identifiable self." But as he conquers each obstacle that presents itself, Cornell begins to build a positive, assertive self-portrait. In the final scene, he asserts himself by making love to a woman (heretofore considered the most heinous of crimes) and he becomes "adamant, invulnerable, brutal, and masterful beyond any dream."

Unlike the imaginative futuristic setting of *Regiment of Women*, *Sneaky People* (1975), is the simple story of a man who wants to murder his wife. Buddy Sandifer is a used-car dealer whose defining characteristics are his sexual exploits and murky, fumbling attempts to free himself, both physically and emotionally, from what he considers a life of marital boredom and constraint. Like so many Berger protagonists, he is, or at least believes himself to be, imprisoned by circumstances. His ill-conceived and rather spurious scheme to have his wife murdered provides the primary plot for the novel, although as the story progresses it becomes clear that Buddy's strategy is little more than a furtive notion that demonstrates his habit of making important decisions with the casual air of one who is immune to moral guilt.

Thematically, Buddy is flanked by a cast of equally dispirited people. His wife, Naomi, is a silent shadow of a woman who goes unnoticed even by her own son: "If she were replaced with a window dummy he might not know the difference by Thanksgiving, and not then if someone else served him the plateful that matched his tastes (all white, lots of gravy because it's dry)." In her domestic solitude, and unknown to anyone else, Naomi takes to writing sado-masochistic sex novels, a pastime which gives her an outlet for her own sexual fantasies. Juxtaposed with Naomi is Laverne, Buddy's mistress, a prostitute whose extensive sexual activity belies her spiritual innocence. Her love for Buddy is a genuine concern for his happiness, although her attempts at providing this well-being are inept and childish. When she realizes the impossibility of her relationship with Buddy, she decides to join a nunnery, "To marry Christ." However, finding the old Catholic church boarded up, she gives up her idea of becoming a nun and returns to her old haunts in the downtown district.

In addition to his wife and lover, there is Leo, Buddy's employee, who sees life as "a collection of immediate problems for which simple solutions are available." Flanking Leo is Clarence, the dim-witted black handyman hired by Buddy to dispose of Naomi. Finally, there is Ralph, Buddy's fifteen-year-old son, whose pubescence counterbalances his father's psychological deterioration.

Buddy's adolescent plotting provides the thematic framework from which the personality of each character emerges. Each is a deceiver, unable or unwilling to live openly and admit need for other human beings. None of the characters is totally despicable, since none is really worthy of hatred. *Sneaky People* is a comic novel about sad and solitary individuals who search for companionship but are frustrated by nearsighted egotism. As in his earlier work, Berger writes about the real world of hard facts, the "Hobbesian jungle" that confronts such unlikely bedfellows as Carlo Reinhart, Joe Detweiler, Jack Crabb, and Buddy Sandifer, where meaningful human relationships are, at best, painful and brief.

In his most recent novel, *Who Is Teddy Villanova?* (1977), Berger returns to pure parody. This time, he is satirizing the detective story, and the perceptive reader soon recognizes the stock characterizations and plot lines. Russel Wren, Berger's 1977 counterpart of the hard-boiled detective, is a former English instructor who has turned private eye. He lives in Manhattan, has a "seedy office," and is constantly in trouble with either the police or the underworld. The entire plot consists of Wren's inept attempt to track down Teddy Villanova, archfiend and international villain. At the same time, Wren must prove that he himself is not the globe-trotting criminal.

Wren's character is portrayed by his garish use of literary imagery and comic description. His verbosity is his power, as when he discovers a dead man:

> If he was not as dead as the cold lasagna on which the tomato sauce has begun to darken, I was a Dutchman. The gaudy and, in the absence of blood, inappropriate metaphor actually came to mind at the moment, as a willed ruse to lure me away from panic—the fundamental purpose of most caprices of language, hence the American wisecrack.

The pretentious overwriting becomes trying, however, when the descriptions do nothing to advance the action. For instance, at one point Wren describes a van full of schoolgirls:

> The twin panels of the door were forthwith hurled open, and I was summoned to enter by a score of small forearms bearing fistfuls of writhing fingers, visibly an invitation to penetrate a congress of adders, while the ear was smote with the shrieking cacaphony in which bluejays couch their peeves.

Passages such as this contributed to the poor critical reception of *Who Is Teddy Villanova?* For those literary wits who appreciate verbosity for its own sake, the novel can be entertaining, but most readers are apt to view Wren's descriptive rambling as a futile effort to save a lackluster book.

From a critical standpoint, Berger can be viewed as a satirist who leans toward black humor devices for his most important statements about the nature of man's existence in twentieth-century America. His novels are signposts in modern comic fiction because they reflect the pervasive theme of man's search for individuality in a wasteland that offers technological conformity and psychological pain. As Richard Schickel said in *Commentary*, "Berger's theme is the devastation of the individual ethic by the spirit of our time . . . man is . . . hopelessly the prisoner of himself and his pathetically limited vision. All ideology, all hope of genuine change is gone." But if Berger's vision is pessimistic, it is also flavored by a comic spirit that refuses to be backed into nihilism. At his best, as in *Little Big Man*, Berger is a satirist whose concern is to offer bits of promise amidst the decay of ideals and hope.

For the most part, Thomas Berger's novels have been received with a limited amount of critical appraisal, and those who have ventured into lengthy discussions of the author's achievement have offered diverse and contradictory opinions. *Killing Time*, for instance, is simultaneously hailed as Berger's most daring achievement as well as a sophomoric attempt at psycho-drama. In large measure, Berger's reputation rests on the popular and critical success of *Little Big Man* and *Sneaky People*. The former is widely acclaimed for its brilliant satire and deft use of the mock-heroic style, while the latter is Berger's finest attempt at telling a simple story about ordinary people. Most critics believe that Berger has yet to produce a work which adequately expresses his measurable, though sporadic, literary gifts.

—*Thomas McClanahan*

Books:

Crazy in Berlin (New York: Scribners, 1958);

Reinhart in Love (New York: Scribners, 1962; London: Eyre & Spottiswoode, 1963);

Little Big Man (New York: Dial, 1964; London: Eyre & Spottiswoode, 1965);

Killing Time (New York: Dial, 1967; London: Eyre & Spottiswoode, 1968);

Vital Parts (New York: Baron, 1970; London: Eyre & Spottiswoode, 1971);

Regiment of Women (New York: Simon & Schuster, 1973; London: Eyre, Methuen, 1974);

Sneaky People (New York: Simon & Schuster, 1975);

Who Is Teddy Villanova? (New York: Delacorte/ Seymour Lawrence, 1977).

Play:

Other People, Berkshire Theatre Festival, 1970.

Periodical Publications:

"In Lieu of Doctor Goody Kuntz," *Esquire*, 55 (June 1961): 136-138;

"Professor Hyde," *Playboy*, 8, 12 (December 1961): 93, 140, 143-146;

"A Monkey of His Own," *Saturday Evening Post*, 238 (22 May 1965): 66-70;

"Son and Hair," *Esquire*, 73 (February 1970): 69-71;

"Candy Darling Is (almost) All Girl," *Esquire*, 80 (October 1973): 162, 394-396.

References:

Brian W. Dippie, "Jack Crabb and the Sole Survivors of Custer's Last Stand," *Western American Literature*, 4 (fall 1969): 189-202;

Fred M. Fetrow, "The Function of the External Narrator in Thomas Berger's *Little Big Man*," *Journal of Narrative Technique*, 5 (January 1975): 57-65;

Jay Gurian, "Style in the Literary Desert: *Little Big Man*," *Western American Literature*, 3 (winter 1969): 285-296;

Douglas Hughes, "The Schlemiel as Humanist: Thomas Berger's Carlo Reinhart," *Cithara*, 15, 1 (November 1975): 3-21;

Leo E. Oliva, "Thomas Berger's *Little Big Man* as History," *Western American Literature*, 8 (spring-summer 1973): 33-54;

Delbert E. Wylder, "Thomas Berger's *Little Big Man* as Literature," *Western American Literature*, 3 (winter 1969): 273-284.

VANCE NYE BOURJAILY was born in Cleveland, Ohio, on 17 September 1922, the son of Monte Ferris Bourjaily, a noted newspaper editor and publisher, and Barbara Webb Bourjaily. He attended Bowdoin College, but his stay was interrupted by two years in the American Field Service (1942-1944) and two years in the United States Army (1944-1946). This military service strongly influences the material of his novels. He returned to Bowdoin and graduated in 1947. Bourjaily married Bettina Yensen in 1946, and they have two children.

Vance Bourjaily.

Daniel Kramer

Bourjaily's varied writing career includes work as a newspaperman, television dramatist, playwright and lecturer. His interests in literature led to his co-founding *Discovery* (1951), a journal he edited for two years. Since 1957, he has taught at the Writers Workshop of the University of Iowa. During this period, he left Iowa briefly to serve on the United States Department of State mission to South America in 1959 and to be Distinguished Visiting Professor at Oregon State University in the summer of 1958. In addition to writing seven novels, Bourjaily has contributed to numerous magazines, including the *New Yorker*, and has written a book on hunting, *The Unnatural Enemy* (1963).

Bourjaily has not achieved the popular success merited by his sensitive and provocative depiction of post-World War II America. His novels, written since the war, explore the divisive consequences of the war on American society and the personal lives of individuals. Frequently his characters are burdened by guilt and forced to wrestle with their impassioned participation in the war effort without satisfactorily coming to terms with it. Bourjaily develops and improves his art in successive novels by experimenting with narrative and expository technique. His style is personal and distinctive without being obscure.

The End of My Life (1947) is Bourjaily's first novel and the only one which can properly be called a "war novel" as its primary subject is men in combat. Skinner Galt, the central character, is familiar in war fiction because he believes himself to be immune to the damages of war and consoles himself with youthful, romantic cynicism. Only when violent death strikes someone near to Skinner does he begin to appreciate his vulnerability. His cynicism, supported by reading Hemingway and other novelists, isolates him by precluding commitments to ideologies, friends, and lovers. Consequently he finds no interior strength binding him to people and beliefs when the horrible reality of war inescapably presents itself. On a lark, Skinner disobeys orders by taking an ambulance (he serves in a field medical unit as Bourjaily did) on a joyride to the combat zone. He accepts the risks foolishly to satisfy the whim of a nurse to whom he is loosely attached. Returning from the jaunt, Skinner swerves to avoid the fire of a German plane and the nurse is killed. The bullet which killed her would have killed him instead if he had stayed on his original course. Sent to military prison, Skinner withdraws from life, believing that war has ruined him. He also believes war is an isolated, unique event which disrupts the workings of society for a short time before peace returns.

Bourjaily rejects that view of war in *The Hound of Earth* (1955). Long after the last shots are fired, the war pursues and haunts Al Barker because he has not come to terms with his responsibility for participating in the development of the atomic bomb. The setting is a San Francisco department store during a Christmas rush in the 1950s, and the novel addresses the problems of man's obligations to himself and others. Bourjaily develops an irony between the season supposedly dedicated to peace and love, and the cruel, insensitive behavior of bitter and potentially dangerous people. Al cannot be reconciled to the war and its consequences because he learns war is not a spasmodic outburst of human perversity which gluts itself and expires, but rather a regular feature of society and an enthralling pleasure to experience. The delusion and anxiety following the war are not its legacy: they are the permanent condition of society giving life to the possibility of and desire for war. Al recognizes these frightening truths about society and himself: " 'For an instant, there, I felt myself in exultation, willing the death of the world.' " The absence of a clear link between the selfish, cruel characters and the impulse to make and use atomic weapons weakens the book, but the novel is interesting for its creation of atmosphere, the depiction of character, and the serious and intelligent attempt to deal artistically with the development and deployment of atomic weapons.

War's significance in *The Violated* (1958) is broader than in Bourjaily's previous novels. He has set aside both of his earlier treatments of war, that it is an occasional breakdown of society or a continuous and inevitable consequence of man's innate aggressiveness, in favor of a view of war as a natural and pervasive social product releasing individual aggressiveness without unleashing a power capable of shocking and changing the course of individual lives. Each of the novel's four major characters grows up just before the war, and they discover the war is an accurate representation of their own confused emotional condition. Ellen, Tom, Guy, and Eddie violate and are "violated by their inability to communicate, to love, to comprehend, to create—violated by neurotic commitments to preposterous goals or more tragically, to no goals at all." Ellen Beniger is a daughter of a loveless marriage who never is quite sure whether her daughter is the child of her Ivy League, Wall Street husband or Eddie Bissle, her brother's classmate. She begins to drink soon after college, and in her forties she suffers from confirmed alcoholism. Ellen's brother, Tom, marries an English girl during the war and gives up plans for a scholarly career. He tries a variety of occupations without making much money. He is killed accidentally by his friend Eddie Bissle just as his practical problems near solution.

Guy Cinturon, Tom's roommate in prep school, revenges himself by raping the daughter of a nurse who abused him sexually when he was a child, and then he pursues this vengeance on the female sex with a string of loveless seductions. The violations of the four characters overlap so that on the night Eddie accidentally kills Tom, Guy is in a bed in Greenwich Village, tallying seduction number 206 of his vengeful and compulsive goal of 350. Eddie's fate is just as brutal and just as characteristically that of the violator violated. When he returns from the war to find his father dead and his family fortune depleted, he takes up farming, and his cynicism meshes with Ellen's masochistic alcoholism. His shooting of Tom takes place after a drinking bout with Ellen. *The Violated*, with its considerable vitality and resourcefulness, especially in characterizations, inspires more admiration than Bourjaily's other novels. Its central situation is a stage production, in this case of *Hamlet*, a device he will repeat in *Now Playing at Canterbury*.

Confessions of a Spent Youth (1960) is Bourjaily's most experimental novel, loosely organized around the narrator's experiences, including the war. We hear of his initiations to sex, drugs, and crime, and his attempt at self-definition and friendships. Quince, the narrator, says the war's numbing effect on his generation is the loss of "part of our ability to feel. There seem, and I wish to say this without loaded words, so I shall use doctors' language—to be certain kinds of emotional stimuli to which I am not capable of responding, even now." The novel is diffuse, perhaps intentionally so, but it evokes skillfully the fear and wonder of growing up around the war. The closing section accurately and startlingly portrays the frenetic and hypertensive postwar world.

Bourjaily shifts interests in *The Man Who Knew Kennedy* (1967) from the disaffected, cynical college students and artists of his previous novels to businessmen who continue to live by cultural and ethical standards which have become fragmented in the erosion of society after the war. The novel is built around Kennedy's assassination, an event of senseless destruction which Bourjaily presents analogously in the financial demise and bizarre death of Dave Doremus, the man who knew and is like Kennedy. Dave is charming and talented; without condescension he generously devotes himself to the particular needs of people around him. His sincerity and intelligence usually uplift those whom he helps. But Dave's unreasonable obsession with straightening out a floundering and addicted girl, Sunny Brown, precipitates his death by carbon monoxide poisoning. Barney James, the narrator, relies heavily on Dave as they grow up in Missouri before the war but becomes strong as he endures the adversities of peace following the war. Barney's matured judgment enables him to help Dave with his problems and to make fittingly Bourjaily's main point in the novel: "You can be the son of a strong man . . . the youngest leader ever chosen by your people . . . and a screwy, jittering little clown can dream his hand to a gun, fantasize his way to a window, be a make-believe marksman through a nine-dollar scope . . . every man, even the most blessed, needs a little more than average luck to survive this world." Bourjaily's divided attention to Dave's dissipation and Barney's developing capacity to overcome problems is the novel's major flaw.

Brill among the Ruins (1970) is one of Bourjaily's most polished performances. The novel explores Robert Brill's return to nature and the past, his ideal of male companionship and the spiritual growth which gives him the ability to heal his emotionally broken wife. Brill is a small-town lawyer who retreats to Mexico to escape the frustrations of the 1960s. Brill goes there with Gary Pederson, who has selected him for his *compadre*, a form of close friendship and mutual support which encourages Brill to live with new purpose. Strengthened by broadening perspectives of his life, Brill understands his wife's decline and desires her as she was before life was beaten out of her. Brill wants "to go home and make love to his own wife, Pat, but not as she is now . . . Pat as she'd been fifteen years ago, before Trinket's difficult birth and the operations that followed." But it is in Oaxaca, not Illinois, that he escapes moral corruption in archaeological quests and hunting. Finally, escape fails to satisfy Brill, and he returns home, where he is needed, to "all the bargains human life is based on." This commitment to life is the novel's chief asset. The hunting sections are richly descriptive and very well written.

The premier of an opera, *$4000*, staged by a large state university is the subject of *Now Playing at Canterbury* (1976). The production is a device to gather odd and idiosyncratic people in a single effort reasonably typical of the 1970s. The diverse and volatile characters, like the pilgrims in *The Canterbury Tales*, tell their stories during the course of their mutual project. Aggression characterizes the stories. They pointedly illustrate much of American society as so thoroughly entrenched by a siege mentality and so love-starved by the sexual revolution that violence, including sexual violence, emerges as the most comprehensible mode of communication. The quality of the stories is uneven; two of the most successful are told by Billy Hoffman and Mike Shapen. The opera's director, Billy, tells a humorous tale about directing *Blithe Spirit* in Biloxi, Mississippi. Jane Lee's husband and some unsavory pals in a car chase Billy on foot around a parking lot to tell him to leave Jane alone. They crack a couple of his ribs, and Billy avenges himself by taking Jane Lee away from Biloxi, just as she requests. Jane Lee soon leaves Billy, explaining coyly in a note she would rather be chased than caught. Mike Shapen tells a story of the protest movement in the 1960s which serves to depict those confrontations as a war complete with strategies and counterstrategies. The ending has Mike in a temporary jail, while Crazy Betty is in a stolen plane dogfighting a helicopter armed with tear gas and attempting to disperse the blockade where Mike was arrested. The novel unveils several clearly chiseled characters who uncomfortably approximate the insecurities and neuroses of the 1970s. Bourjaily's cheerfulness and inventiveness distinguish this novel from his others.

Although Bourjaily's novels sometimes suffer from diffuseness caused by the absence of strong, unified plots, he successfully conveys the mystery of

60.

Skidding to an amazed stop in my sneakers to stare at

He was a man of many scars, the worst of them near the top of his head, mostly concealed by ~~the~~ thick, dark hair though he wore it short. None of the others showed when he was ~~dress~~ dressed.

We were looking at the dog book, at Curt's house. We were nine or ten, on a rainy afternoon. We found Curt, ~~Maxwaxxaxx~~ in the color pictures. He was an Irish ~~xxxxxxxxx~~ setter. Then he found a Basenji, and said, Hey, here you are. You're an African dog. Then we played dogs, all over the house, hiding, and jumping out at each other and wrestling. Curt ~~xxxxxxx~~ had to growl and bark when he heard me coming, but I didn't because ~~Xxxxxxxx~~ the book said Basenjis don't.

's profile,

I must have seen the Seurat girl for the first time that day, running through the gallery where the Strawridge Collection hung. a small canvas, nine by twelve. A young girl made with pink, yellow and a few blue dots. She glowed, on that dark afternoon, as if she held her own light.

"And nobody ever called me a remarkably handsome man, *either,* my dear," he said to Sweet Lorraine. It was altogether dark in the stall, except for ~~a little glow from the ship's running lights~~ *showed what small light showed through the cracked under the hatchway from the ship's running lights.* ~~through filitered through the hatchway.~~ "That was the first time I ever rode Whiskey. He was Mrs. Strawbridge's horse. A beautiful *little* mover. By the time ~~I was ten~~, *he was too much for her and* I was the only one ~~besides her that~~ *who* rode him."

"Once, though -- Franny, be still. There girl -- a woman told me that she thought me gorgeous." The motors throbbed along smoothly, ~~somewhere~~ *down* beneath them.

He ran his hand back and forth along Rebel Deb's flank. "You're not filling out like the others, honey. Still ~~xxxxx~~ hollow here."

"And you're quite right, Smarty," he acknowledged to Piney Brown. "The word she really used was prächtig. How would you translate it, if not 'gorgeous'?"

From discarded (first draft) revision of novel-in-progress.

man's relationship to nature, especially in *Brill among the Ruins*, with his carefully written episodes of hunting, fishing and sailing. The magnificence of the natural world is of special concern to Bourjaily, who writes about it with the conviction born of intense experience. Experiments in narrative technique keep his writing brisk. His characters are sharply defined both by thoughtful exploration of relatively few details and by precise, realistic dialogue. With little exception, each novel improves upon its predecessor, and together the novels comprise a sensitive version of the forces shaping American life in the past thirty years.

—*Howard Stringfellow*

Books:

The End of My Life (New York: Scribners, 1947; London: W. H. Allen, 1963);

The Hound of Earth (New York: Scribners, 1955; London: Spearman, 1956);

The Violated (New York: Dial, 1958; London: Barton, 1973);

Confessions of a Spent Youth (New York: Dial, 1960; London: W. H. Allen, 1961);

The Unnatural Enemy (New York: Dial, 1963; London: W. H. Allen, 1965);

The Man Who Knew Kennedy (New York: Dial, 1967; London: W. H. Allen, 1967);

Brill among the Ruins (New York: Dial, 1970; London: W. H. Allen, 1971);

Now Playing at Canterbury (New York: Dial, 1976).

References:

John W. Aldridge, *After the Lost Generation* (New York: McGraw-Hill, 1951), pp. 121-132;

Matthew J. Bruccoli, "Vance Bourjaily," in *Conversations with Writers I* (Detroit: Bruccoli Clark/Gale, 1977), pp. 2-23;

Robert W. DeLancey, "Man and Mankind in the Novels of Vance Bourjaily," *English Record*, 10 (1959): 3-4;

Harris Dienstfrey, "The Novels of Vance Bourjaily," *Commentary*, 31 (April 1961): 360-363;

Edward L. Galligan, "Hemingway's Staying Power," *Massachusetts Review*, 8 (summer 1967): 431-439;

Granville Hicks, "The Maturity of Vance Bourjaily," *Saturday Review*, 41 (23 August 1958): 13;

Hicks, "The Generation of the Assassination," *Saturday Review*, 50 (4 February 1967): 35-36;

Charles F. Madden, ed., *Talks with Authors* (Carbondale: Southern Illinois University Press,

1968), pp. 201-214;

John M. Muste, "The Second Major Subwar: Four Novels by Vance Bourjaily," in *The Shaken Realist*, ed. Melvin J. Friedman and John B. Vickery (Baton Rouge: Louisiana State University Press, 1970), pp. 311-326.

Manuscripts:

Bowdoin College has the manuscripts of five of Bourjaily's novels, including *The Man Who Knew Kennedy*, plus correspondence and manuscripts of many published and unpublished works.

RAY BRADBURY is an interesting writer who has unjustly suffered from critical neglect. In a sense he has been the victim of a genre. To consider his work as "science fiction" or "fantasy"—no matter how good—is to damn it, for invariably these modes are dismissed as secondary. Such categories and distinctions fail, however, to describe Bradbury's writing. Not only is it varied, but individual examples are hard to pigeonhole. He is a science fiction writer who knows little about science: in his tales of space and the future the emphasis is less on technology than on the abuser of technology. To Bradbury, science is the forbidden fruit, destroyer of Eden, and continuing mark of man's fall. In like manner, Bradbury is a fantasist whose fantasies are oddly circumscribed: he writes less about strange things happening to people than about strange imaginings of the human mind. Corresponding, then, to an outer labyrinth of modern technological society is this inner one—fallen beings feeding in isolation on their hopeless dreams.

Throughout his career Bradbury has also written many realistic tales, sympathetic stories about Mexicans, Irishmen, Chicanos. Though his subject matter is diverse, a native regionalism characterizes his work. Bradbury's Mars bears a similarity to the American Midwest, and behind Los Angeles and Dublin and all towns on Bradbury's map lies the archetypal village—"Green Town, Illinois." Most of the literary models identified by critics are facades too. Bradbury is only superficially in the school of Heinlein, or Poe, or O. Henry. His real affinity, in lighter moments, is with something like Steinbeck's comedies of folk tenacity. In his darker moods (and these are more numerous) he echoes the Anderson of *Winesburg, Ohio*, the writer of "grotesques." Scratch the surface in Bradbury and eminently native patterns emerge. The real Brad-

Ray Bradbury.

Michael Childers

bury is a portraitist, less the chronicler of Mars than of twisted, small-town American lives.

There is the same centripetal aspect to Bradbury's life. Born in Waukegan, Illinois, in 1920, he came west with his parents during the Depression. He has lived in Los Angeles with his wife and four daughters ever since. There was a sojourn in Ireland during the filming of *Moby Dick*, for which he wrote the screenplay; he has made frequent trips to Mexico—but he was always a tourist, even in Los Angeles, even on Mars. Though each of these places figures in his writing, they shrink too rapidly to one place. But for an occasional street name or monument, Los Angeles or Dublin is not distinguished in Bradbury's work. All of his towns are essentially faceless agglomerations of isolated houses—as in the unnamed Midwestern suburb of *Fahrenheit 451*. All places have the same geography as well. No matter what the landscape, it presses life into the same basic configuration. His Southwestern desert is no more than a ring of emptiness that forces people in on themselves and each other. Again and again his Mexican towns are encircled and isolated in a vast and hostile land. Mars only mirrors this pattern: the Martians have disappeared, the planet is a wasteland that weighs on its colonizers by its emptiness, driving them back on themselves and their past. His literary life, then, is an endless return to Waukegan. Beneath every setting is the small Midwestern town, lost in the midst of prairie or forest, in its isolation a hothouse world for strange human growths.

But Bradbury's writings are not really rooted in any specific Midwestern locale either. Like his imaginary "Green Town," his regionalism, too, is primarily a country of the mind. What is profoundly American there is less a physical than a spiritual disposition. Behind another facade—that of childhood "innocence"—lies a dark vision of the human condition deeply tainted by Calvinism. Invariably Bradbury's work turns from the future to the past, to lost Eden. Each tale is like an elaborate ritual in which man, over and over, reenacts the primal sin. Of its own, any larger social or historical projection in Bradbury breaks down into a series of these microcosmic dramas of damnation and the search for grace. In any life there may be a bright moment, a "magic summer," but it is never more than a spot engulfed in darkness. Wordsworth's "visionary gleam" has been transposed to native soil: what visits Bradbury's characters are, rather, the murky intimations of Calvinist grace. Again and again some flash of inner light, in a strange variation on the sin of intellectual pride, drives men to search, to rebel against destiny, to damn themselves even more horribly pursuing the twisted paths of darkness.

The surface fixation with childhood has led readers to consider Bradbury an "optimistic" writer. In the deepest sense, however, the opposite is true. His fiction rests on this gloomy base of the Fall. Nor is this base ever really challenged. The only change is a gradual softening of attitude toward this grim world. Already in the early tales, Bradbury's is a Calvinism in abhorrence of itself. The unrelieved tragedy of fallen man, struggling vainly with his "fault," is shown in all its horror. But things are not clear. Though Bradbury pulls at his readers' emotions, he never questions whether or not man is responsible for his fate. Later stories simply shift in direction and tone away from these parables of "sin," toward portraits of the various kinds of ingrown lives that inhabit this fallen world—men whose search for knowledge or happiness leads not outward to destruction but inward, through eccentric but often harmless byways of the isolated mind. More and more, in Bradbury's recent work, retribution is suspended, characters are treated with whimsy and tolerance instead of gruesome severity. If in Bradbury there is an evolution in attitude, it is only in terms of increasing authorial sympathy with characters that remain the grotesque products of a perverse world.

Bradbury has written in all genres—stories, novels, plays, poetry. His real mode however is short fiction. His plays, like *Pillar of Fire* (1975), are all adaptations of stories. More important, his longer prose works too (in some way or another) are derivatives of the tale. The short novel *Fahrenheit 451* (1953) expands upon an earlier story, "The Fireman." Both *The Martian Chronicles* (1950) and *Dandelion Wine* (1957) are frame collections, cycles of sketches and tales given thematic coherence (as in their model *Winesburg, Ohio*) through the basic fact of geographical situation—a town or a planet. In each case many of the stories worked into the frames were published earlier as separate entities. During the last decade Bradbury has effectively stopped writing stories. His latest collection, *Long After Midnight* (1976), is the first in seven years. A number of tales therein are old ones—written long before but never anthologized. The new ones are uninspired. Bradbury now seems to be turning his creative energies to theater and poetry. This latter, however, is not only overly sentimental and assertive, but stylistically uninteresting. Whether Bradbury will turn again to the prose story is anybody's guess. Undeniably, though, his true roots as a writer lie there. Bradbury is a master of the short form, a prose stylist in the minor modes of melancholy, fancy, and irony of the grotesque. He is not a writer of large or ponderous visions, but of quick touches.

Bradbury's career as storyteller can be divided into three periods: early, vintage, and late. The center of his early period is the Arkham House collection, *Dark Carnival* (1947). Most of the tales in this volume were reprinted in *The October Country* (1955), and several newer ones in the same vein added. In his introduction to the 1955 volume, Bradbury singles out these stories as oddities in his canon—he wrote this kind of tale before his twenty-sixth birthday (1946), and rarely since. They are pure fantasy of the "weird" sort and include some of Bradbury's most striking pieces: "The Scythe" (1943), "The Lake" (1944), "The Jar" (1944), "Skeleton" (1945), and "The Small Assassin" (1946). If these works have none of the science fiction trappings that later made Bradbury famous, they ask a question basic to this and all forms of modern fantasy: which mode of perception is superior—reason or imagination, cold logic or intuition? As he explores the implications of this question—more than the glories it is the perils of vision that interest him here—Bradbury sets the direction for his mature fictional universe. Here is the matrix for his scientific fantasies and "conventional" character studies alike, the model for future worlds as well as past.

Most of these early tales could be called expansive. They carry, however, the seed of the later contractive pattern that will become Bradbury's

trademark. In the expansive tale the hero sees some awful truth and on the strength of his vision tries to change the order of things. A similar perception, in the contractive story, brings retreat within, the creation of alternate worlds inside mind or self. "The Scythe" is the archetypal expansive tale, a Calvinist parable of an "innocent" man chosen to become the grim reaper. A fatal insight into the nature of his task leads the hero to rebel, but he refuses to cut the stalks that represent wife and children only to learn that man cannot alter the rhythms of nature—death is the ineluctable fact. What is fallen, however, can be corrupted further: under his terrible burden of knowledge and guilt the hero cracks, mows down green wheat with the ripe; war and holocaust ensue. In these stories, gradually, a shift occurs. The fall in "Skeleton" takes place more inside the hero than without: his belief that the bones are in revolt against the rest of the body leads to odd private battles. These stories are often less tragic than grotesquely comic. It is but a small step to another tale of 1945 (significantly not included in *October Country*), "Invisible Boy." If the hero of "Skeleton" probes too far into the mysteries of the body and destroys himself, here the act of imagination gives rise to a different sort of delusion. The childless old woman's acceptance of her "invisible boy" is less an assault on reality than a pathetic, if harmless, defense against it. Already the positive deed is futile. What remains for Bradbury's visionaries is the negative act, withdrawal into a fantasy world of one's own creation. From now on the study of these ingrown lives—examples of some strangely twisted fortunate fall—will be Bradbury's main concern.

The vintage period extends, roughly, from 1946 to 1955. Its focal points are the story collections *The Illustrated Man* (1951) and *The Golden Apples of the Sun* (1953), the frame collection *The Martian Chronicles* (1950), and the novella *Fahrenheit 451* (1953). It is a decade of storytelling, incredible both for the variety and quality of work produced.

Three thematic landscapes dominate this period: outer space, the future, and "odd corners" of the present or past. It is during the late 1940s that Bradbury becomes a "science fiction" writer. Tales deal with rockets, space travel, Mars, and invasion by aliens (as in "Zero Hour"). This tendency culminates in *Chronicles*. The majority of Bradbury's dystopian stories belong to the early 1950s, the period of *Fahrenheit*. Both kinds would seem projective, speculative, but in reality they narrow our vision rather than broaden it. Space travel becomes a perversion of the intellect. Bradbury's colonists, striving for new futures on Mars, are inexorably swept back to the isolation of their Midwestern past. Bradbury's studies of future society have the same pattern. There is no utopian speculation; heroes have no vision of what society might be, no plans for change. In the face of total catastrophe, the only alternative is the buried life of fantasy. The end product, then, of space tales and dystopian dramas is a twisted life. A story like "The Rocket Man," for instance, is not about rockets. It is, rather, the study of a family's disintegration. Again an Eden is destroyed by a new form of the old sin of pride—space flight.

In those tales space and future shrink to the pinpoint of private dreams or delusions. They are unstable; from them emerges the Bradbury mainstream—studies of human byways. For these there is a profusion of settings: Mexico ("El Dia de Muerte"), the Southwest ("Powerhouse"), Los Angeles ("The Cistern"), the Midwest ("Jack-in-the-Box," "The Illustrated Man," "Hail and Farewell"), the urban South ("The Dwarf"). This latter tale, in its dark Calvinist overtones, is the contractive counterpart of "The Scythe." In his misshapen being, the dwarf quite literally incarnates the primal curse or mystery. This time, however, external prying only acts as catalyst. The real center of explosion is the dwarf's mind. Once drawn beyond the harmless limits of isolation, his search to be other—be it through carnival mirrors or those of his own vicarious writings—erupts into tragic violence.

In *Fahrenheit 451* we can map the shift in emphasis that characterizes this vintage period. What in the original "Fireman" was an embryonic tale of revolution becomes in the expanded novella the story of private fall. Not only is the world destroyed by the curse of knowledge—excessive tolerance has led to book-burning, the flame of reason has become the fireman's torch—but the confused seeker, Montag, at the moment his hand compulsively closes on a book, literally falls as well. From then on he is isolated: deeds prove pointless, all attempts at communication (Faber's "seashell radio") futile. Society's course leads fatally to holocaust. The hero can only escape to a nature still fallen, where the new fire of human companionship remains a feeble spot in the dark forest. In this world of residual fragments the hero snatches one up, folds it into self—he "becomes" a book. What re-forms is less a society than a cluster of ingrown lives. Each recites his book but, out of some strange fear of the fatal intellect, refuses to interpret it.

Bradbury's late period begins with *Dandelion Wine* (1957). It evolves through the following collections: *A Medicine for Melancholy* (1959), *The Machineries of Joy* (1964), and *I Sing the Body Electric!* (1969). These titles reveal Bradbury's increasing desire to treat the light and joyous side of human existence. But though his medicine cures certain of the effects of Calvinism, it never touches the cause.

Dandelion Wine, the story of young Douglas Spaulding and his "magic summer" in Green Town, Illinois, stands at a crossroads. Geography here is the symbol of human existence itself. Not only is the town isolated in deep impenetrable woods, but its familiar world of lawns and shops is cleft by a dark ravine. *Dandelion*, as a book, is split in like manner. All the lives chronicled seem to be encapsulated by the existence of Douglas, bottled like dandelion wine for his private consumption. His final act is to stand in a cupola high above the town and, moving his arms like an orchestra leader, direct the world to sleep. This is not irony so much as ambiguity: is the boy the center of things, or is human nature as a whole? Feeding into this collection are the vintage themes of private oddities and isolated lives. Developing through and out of these themes is a different kind of study—that of collective eccentricity.

It is this pattern that dominates Bradbury's later stories. "Magic moments" are no longer (as with Douglas) personal—they become collective. Communities of the most unusual sort are formed. In "The Wonderful Ice Cream Suit" the garment itself, shared by six unemployed Mexican-Americans, becomes the brief focus of their hopeless lives, the white spot in their collective darkness. Nor are dreamer and visionary invariably alone now. Men hope together, in tales such as "The Machineries of Joy," to repair Babel, to reunite climates, regions, bloods. Or they may dream of going back in time, repeating old actions and doing them right. The classic story of this kind is "The Kilimanjaro Machine," where a man in a time vehicle returns to the past to reclaim Hemingway and give him the "right death" on that "same slope . . . on Kilimanjaro, near the leopard." The earlier grotesque is now often tempered with humor. Camillia Wilkes's magic night, in "A Medicine for Melancholy," leads not (as with Bradbury's earlier old maids) to isolation, but to marriage and life—mortality in its more common form. It is also tempered in his latest collection, *Long After Midnight* (1976), with unabashed sentimentality. In "Forever and the Earth" an act of literary body snatching brings Thomas Wolfe to a future world to write the great space novel: the only man big enough for the job lies dead in the past. Wolfe accomplishes

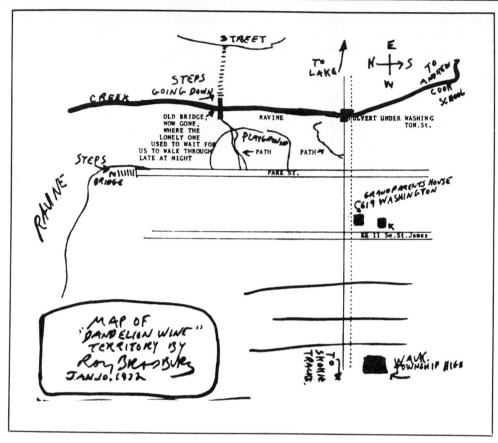

Bradbury's map of his hometown.

his task; Bradbury sings his glory. But in this misbegotten world the song is hollow, for the book must wait in the future until we catch up to it, the writer must return to the grave. Beneath a veneer of lyrical assertion lies the old fallen world, all the darker for the contrast.

The Martian Chronicles is Bradbury's undisputed masterpiece, itself a magic and ephemeral moment of balance between individual and social concerns, between fallen nature and man's ability to abide. Like the later *Dandelion Wine*, it too is inspired by the frame structure of *Winesburg, Ohio*. But what Bradbury does here with this form is more original. Contrasting tones and themes are skillfully counterpointed, longer tales of individual lives lyrically interwoven with short bridge passages that register the collective temper. Again, as everywhere in Bradbury, this is not a chronicle of human progress but of an endless cycle of falls. And yet, its pattern, in a subtle way, is both circular and open-ended. Martian civilization dies: Earthmen colonize Mars only to destroy their new home world. But when Mars dies a second time, there is a change—now it must replace Earth. Time passes from an unnatural "rocket summer" to a new summer in

autumn on Mars, where surviving man finally faces the consequences of his intellectual pride. True, this summer is born of a bleak Earth October and destruction—the fire of reason that "purified" Mars has led to atomic holocaust. But it is summer nonetheless. In the end, fire seems to regain its original use: man burns the vestiges of a bad past and starts anew. Yet, by another twist, the phoenix that rises is still fallen man. When the children ask where the Martians are, the father shows them their reflections in the water. This new paradise is a doubly barren planet: life is still firmly rooted in death. Again, the new world is one of timidity and fearful restriction. Yet there is more hope than in *Fahrenheit*. In an earlier Martian tale, "Dark They Were, and Golden-Eyed" (uncollected in *Chronicles*), Earthmen on Mars gradually take on Martian bodies and spirits, become more beautiful. Here men remain men, and the possibility of the old sin abides. But at the same time they are less alone than the hero of *Fahrenheit*, for they remain a family.

Bradbury is not a "literary" writer. He was not educated in a university and does not teach in one. On the contrary, he has worked all his life in the pulp fields of science fiction and fantasy. In the eyes of certain new writers, who bring innovations from above and without, Bradbury may seem a "primitive," when his direction is merely different—down and back. He seeks solid native roots among the shifting props of speculative fiction. Bradbury does not so much broaden the impact of his genre as redomesticate it. He reaches back not only to a physical place but to a literary time when fantasy and serious speculation on man's place in the universe coexisted, when Poe, Hawthorne, and Emerson wrote. —*George Edgar Slusser*

Books:

Dark Carnival (Sauk City, Wis.: Arkham House, 1947; London: Hamish Hamilton, 1948);

The Martian Chronicles (Garden City: Doubleday, 1950; republished as *The Silver Locusts*, London: Rupert Hart-Davis, 1951);

The Illustrated Man (Garden City: Doubleday, 1951; London: Rupert Hart-Davis, 1952);

The Golden Apples of the Sun (Garden City: Doubleday, 1953; London: Rupert Hart-Davis, 1953;

Fahrenheit 451 (New York: Ballantine, 1953; London: Rupert Hart-Davis, 1954);

Switch On the Night (New York: Pantheon, 1955; London: Rupert Hart-Davis, 1955);

The October Country (New York: Ballantine, 1955; London: Rupert Hart-Davis, 1956);

Dandelion Wine (Garden City: Doubleday, 1957; London: Rupert Hart-Davis, 1957);

A Medicine for Melancholy (Garden City: Doubleday, 1959; republished as *The Day It Rained Forever*, London: Rupert Hart-Davis, 1959);

The Small Assassin (London: Ace, 1962);

Something Wicked This Way Comes (New York: Simon & Schuster, 1962; London: Rupert Hart-Davis, 1963);

R Is for Rocket (Garden City: Doubleday, 1962; London: Rupert Hart-Davis, 1968);

The Anthem Sprinters and Other Antics (New York: Dial, 1963);

The Machineries of Joy (New York: Simon & Schuster, 1964; London: Rupert Hart-Davis, 1964);

The Vintage Bradbury (New York: Random House, 1965);

The Autumn People (New York: Ballantine, 1965);

Twice Twenty-Two (Garden City: Doubleday, 1966);

Tomorrow Midnight (New York: Ballantine, 1966);

S Is for Space (Garden City: Doubleday, 1966; London: Rupert Hart-Davis, 1968);

I Sing the Body Electric! (New York: Knopf, 1969; London: Rupert Hart-Davis, 1970);

The Wonderful Ice Cream Suit and Other Plays (New York: Bantam, 1972; London: Hart-Davis, MacGibbon, 1973);

The Halloween Tree (New York: Knopf, 1972; London: Hart-Davis, MacGibbon, 1973);

Zen and the Art of Writing and The Joy of Writing (Santa Barbara, Cal.: Capra Press, 1973);

When Elephants Last in the Dooryard Bloomed (New York: Knopf, 1973; London: Hart-Davis, MacGibbon, 1975);

Pillar of Fire and Other Plays (New York: Bantam, 1975);

Long After Midnight (New York: Knopf, 1976; London: Hart-Davis, MacGibbon, 1977);

Where Robot Mice and Robot Men Run Round in Robot Towns (New York: Knopf, 1977).

References:

Marvin E. Mengeling, "Ray Bradbury's *Dandelion Wine*: Themes, Sources, and Styles," *English Journal*, 60 (1971): 877-887;

William F. Nolan, *The Ray Bradbury Companion* (Detroit: Bruccoli Clark/Gale, 1975); updated by Donn Albright, "The Ray Bradbury Index," *Xenophile*, May 1975, p. 13; September 1976, p. 26; November 1977, p. 36;

George Edgar Slusser, *The Bradbury Chronicles* (San Bernardino, Cal.: Borgo Press, 1977).

RICHARD GARY BRAUTIGAN was born in Tacoma, Washington, on 30 January 1935, the oldest child of Bernard F. Brautigan and Lula Mary Keho Brautigan; his father was a "common laborer," his mother a housewife. On 8 June, 1957, he married Virginia Dionne Adler in Reno, Nevada; their daughter, Ianthe, was born on 25 March 1960; the Brautigans were divorced on 28 July 1970 in San Francisco. In 1967 he was poet-in-residence at the California Institute of Technology, though he had never gone to college himself. In 1968 he received a grant from the National Endowment for the Arts. Brautigan does not volunteer biographical information, and though his stories often seem to have, along with their fantasy, many autobiographical details, he obviously invents freely. In an interview he states that he wrote poetry for seven years to learn how to write a sentence because he wanted to write novels and figured that he could not write a novel until he

Richard Brautigan

Richard Brautigan.

could write a sentence: "I used poetry as a lover but I never made her my old lady."

The popularity of his books spread from California in the 1960s to a larger American audience in the wake of the popular movement often called "The Greening of America." In 1969 Kurt Vonnegut reported to Delacorte Press the West Coast popularity of Brautigan's paperbacks published by a small San Francisco press, Four Seasons Foundation (1967-1968). Delacorte successfully bargained for rights to *Trout Fishing in America, In Watermelon Sugar,* and *The Pill Versus the Springhill Mine Disaster* (the last, a book of poetry), and they appeared in 1969. Three hundred thousand copies of these three books sold that first year, and 1,390,000 copies have sold as of 1977. His new novels have been appearing yearly and now total eight.

A controversial writer because he seems to encourage the self-adoring anti-intellectualism of the young, Brautigan is commonly seen as the bridge between the Beat Movement of the 1950s and the youth revolution of the late 1960s. In the only full-length study of Brautigan's work, Terence Malley identifies the common theme of Brautigan's first four novels as "the shy loner trying to find a 'good world' in the inhospitable America of the 1960s." Josephine Hendin has noted that Brautigan's characters are marked by their lack of a passionate attachment to anyone and to any place; they never

permit themselves to feel. Perhaps an even better case can be made that Brautigan's major theme is borrowed from the Romantic poets—that of the transforming power of the imagination, that both the comedy and beauty of art lie in the power of the artist's imagination.

Trout Fishing in America (written in 1961, but not published until 1967) seems like a collage. Terence Malley, however, has explained its thematic structure and, like John Clayton, calls it an "un-novel." It has a traditional theme of American novels: the influence of the American frontier and wilderness on the American imagination, its life-style, its economics, its ethics, its therapies, its religion, its politics. The narrator as a child and, later, as a husband and father searches for the mythical Eden of the perfect trout stream that America has promised. He finds that the spirit of such a vision of America has become perverted into a legless man in a chrome-plated wheel chair, a Hollywood hero called Trout Fishing in America Shorty, and that the Cleveland Wrecking Yard has used trout streams stacked and for sale at $6.50 per foot. *Trout Fishing in America* is Brautigan's Hemingway book, a kind of "Big Two-Hearted River" as seen through the disillusioned eyes of a flower child. Its pervading tone of melancholy arises from the sense that the American child, indoctrinated by our literature, movies, and commerce to believe in the American myth of the Edenic wilderness, has been betrayed. The melancholy is saved from sentimentality by unconventional plots, exaggerated figures of speech which have become Brautigan's trademark, and a style uncomplicated by difficult syntax or logical relationships. Speaking of one trout creek, the narrator says its canyon was sometimes so narrow that the creek poured out "like water from a faucet. You had to be a plumber to fish that creek." And the Missouri River at Great Falls, Montana, "looks like a Deanna Durbin movie, like a chorus girl who wanted to go to college." The real heroes in the book are probably the sixth-graders who terrorize first-graders by chalking "Trout Fishing in America" on their backs. John Clayton praised the book's imagination but complained of its political stance of disengagement a la Woodstock. Others noted the "latency of violence and death" in the book, along with its "humor and zaniness," its pessimism about the search for the pastoral myth, and the ambivalence in Brautigan's relation to the American myths and symbols.

Based on the proposition that one can combine at the same time stories about hippies at Big Sur and San Francisco in the 1960s and a putative

Confederate general in the Battle of the Wilderness of the Civil War, Brautigan's first published novel, *A Confederate General from Big Sur* (1965), humorously portrays the life-styles of Jessie, the narrator, Lee Mellon, the man who thinks he is a Confederate general, and their hippie women. It is Brautigan's Stephen Crane Civil War book. In it, Brautigan's playful vision of America satirizes the hippie life-style.

The twenty-nine-year-old narrator "without a regular name" of *In Watermelon Sugar* (1968) is an ex-sculptor who has recently taken up writing. He describes three days in his commune at a small town oddly called iDeath [sic], population 375. A flashback describes how the town's hoodlum gang committed mass ritual suicide to restore the town. There is also an accompanying story of how the narrator grows bored with his mistress, who he feels has gone bad by consorting with the hoodlum gang, and how she commits suicide because she is displaced by a new mistress. This tragic love triangle is underplayed, and the death seems merely a sad annoyance to everybody. The real hero is the environment and the multipurpose watermelon sugar. The sun is a different color for each day of the week; there are streams everywhere, even in the living room; and houses, lighting oil, and clothes, as well as life-style, are made from processed watermelon sugar.

To Malley, this commune is a group of traumatized survivors of a holocaust, trying to cope; they are ritualized and deprogrammed from their egoism and previous ideology. He noted, however, that some people read the book as "an acid allegory of altered consciousness and 'watermelon sugar' as a euphemism for LSD or some other hallucinogen." He recognized the "curious lack of emotion" in the town and the condemnation of whiskey drinking, which is treated favorably in other Brautigan books. Such detail has led Patricia Hernlund to argue that Brautigan sees the utopian commune as an unsuccessful counterculture, without pity and joy.

The Abortion: An Historical Romance 1966 (1971) is a "love" story. It begins as if it were to tell the amusing but touching incidents in the life of a thirty-one-year-old librarian of an unusual library but ends with a trip to Tijuana for an abortion for his mistress. The mistress is the beautiful twenty-year-old Vida, who has always disliked her fabulously attractive body until she meets the hippie librarian. She is the archetypal Brautigan woman, who stirs the metaphorical imagination of the hero and is obviously the perfect companion for a gentle flower child. Their relationship liberates both of them: he

can go back into the real world again, out of the library for losers; she accepts her body enough to work in a topless bar and go back to college. The library is the most impressive invention of the book, the best artifact of the days of the San Francisco flower children. It takes and stores original manuscripts from anybody, usually the naive and childlike who need to write for private reasons. If the book is about love in 1966, then such love includes the embarrassment of the abortion trip and a relaxed, fulfilling, monogamous, unmarried sexual life. But it also includes a life-style that allows one to feel useful to his society.

Revenge of the Lawn: Stories 1962-1970 (1971) contains sixty-two vignettes and short stories which are unified by the theme of the stoicism necessary for healthy survival after one loses the easy life of a child. Many of the sketches seem to detail Brautigan's own childhood in the 1940s and 1950s in the Pacific Northwest as a lonely poor boy addicted to fishing, an enthusiasm for World War II, and writing. The humor of the title story, arising from the story's digressive structure and deadpan tone, is reminiscent of Mark Twain. Hemingway's influence on these stories is also clear in Brautigan's feeling for nature, his subdued tone, and the frequent use of the point of view of an adolescent. Those stories set in California are ambivalent about its kinky inhabitants (the man who rebuilt his house with poetry, the woman who buried her dog in an expensive Chinese rug, the Christians having outdoor services in Yosemite). The title story humorously tells about the narrator's bootlegging grandmother, her handyman who hated the lawn, and his comic troubles with drunken geese and bees which feed on rotting pears.

Perhaps the prototypal Brautigan image occurs at the end of this story: the narrator's earliest memory is of a man cutting down a pear tree, soaking it with gasoline, and setting fire to it while the pears are still green on the branches. It combines both the Brautigan surrealistic image (burning the green pears) and the uneasy relationships the Brautigan characters have with nature. Again, Brautigan's theme of the imagination's ability to reshape reality comes out in these stories in the figures of speech and the imaginative incidents, such as the geese with hangovers, the witch's bedroom filled with flowers, the child who wants to become a deer, and the customer whom the narrator sees in City Lights Bookstore debating with himself whether to buy a Brautigan book.

The Hawkline Monster (1974), set mostly in eastern Oregon in 1902, tells how two professional killers are hired to rid an isolated mansion of its monster, accidentally created by a great scientist. The humans are all amoral; only the "shadow" of the monster is moral. The book purports to be the history of an unpopular manmade recreational lake. It has fewer of the Brautigan figures of speech, and gains its power from the parody of gothic trappings and from its comic disdain for the Western life-style of the early 1900s.

Willard and His Bowling Trophies: A Perverse Mystery (1975) ties together three sets of people: the Logan Brothers, who are out to kill whoever stole their bowling trophies; Pat and John, a junior high school teacher of Spanish and her filmmaker husband, who accidentally found the trophies in an abandoned car in Marin County, California; and, upstairs in the same building as the teacher and filmmaker, a married couple, Bob and Constance, who in sexual desperation practice sado-masochism while they read poetry from the Greek Anthology. The sex is obviously meant to appear unattractive and embarrassing, though obsessive, and perhaps justifies the word "perverse" in the subtitle. Willard is a large papier-mache bird that sits in Pat and John's living room. They pretend that the bird likes to be surrounded by the trophies, and the wife arouses her tired husband by voicing her sexual fantasies with the artificial bird. Perhaps the book's mystery is how these three sets of characters will finally interact. Brautigan sees it as amusing that the Logan brothers, all-American, ideal boys, become murderers—of the wrong couple—when their bowling trophies are stolen, and he symbolizes American culture with bowling, kinky sex, Greta Garbo, Johnny Carson, and kitsch such as the papier-mache bird—all of this is the decline of the West, as one chapter labels it. The all-American Logan father understands only car transmissions, and the all-American Logan mother can only continuously bake cookies and pies for her sons, who are not even at home any longer. The theme of this novel seems to be less the celebration of the writer's imagination than it is an attack on the confusion and desperation of our culture.

Sombrero Fallout (1976) uses the omniscient point of view as it juxtaposes, chapter by chapter, the story of a ruptured love affair with events which occur when a sombrero with a temperature of minus twenty-four degrees falls out of the sky into the center of a small American town. After the writer tears up the beginning pages of the story and throws them into the wastebasket, the story continues to develop by itself. The sombrero causes strange changes in the town: the citizens break into riot among themselves, and the National Guard has

to be called in. Norman Mailer flies in as a reporter, and the President of the United States gives a Gettysburg-like address when the bloodshed is over. The protagonist of the frame story is a famous American comic novelist who personally has no sense of humor. Full of eccentric quirks, he is suffering because he has broken up with his beautiful Japanese-American mistress, a psychiatrist in San Francisco. The details of the writer's ludicrous despair cover exactly one hour of a November evening, but the flashbacks covering his affair with the woman from both his and her point of view, as well as the story of her own life, constitute five stories being told at one time. The book satirizes the media, writer's vanity, political authority, and police power. The obscene epithets in the central character's stream of consciousness and the dialogue of the President of the United States are amusing and appropriate. The heroine's beauty is romanticized by copious figures of speech. The love story has echoes of a Kurt Vonnegut novel in its simple sentence structure and its ironic motto: "There's more to life than meets the eye"; unlike Vonnegut, Brautigan in this novel tends to judge human relationships by sexual hedonism, by how good the lovers are in bed. Some of the charm and humor of the book lies in the figures of speech: the protagonist's worries follow him around "like millions of trained white mice"; two lovers undressing are described: "She took her clothes off like a kite takes gently to a warm April wind. He fumbled his clothes off like a football game being played in November mud." But Brautigan's imagination works best in this book structurally, by tying together the fantasy science fiction plot with the real love affair.

In *Dreaming of Babylon: A Private Eye Novel 1942* (1977), dedicated to his literary agent Helen Brann, Brautigan combines a parody of the hard-boiled detective novel having a 1942 San Francisco setting with subplots set in ancient Babylon. The narrator, Private Eye C. Card, twenty-eight years old, broke and in debt, a veteran of the Spanish Civil War, usually messes up his job because he begins daydreaming about being a hero in Babylon. On the single day covered by this novel, 2 January 1942, he has been hired by a rich, beautiful young woman to steal from the morgue the corpse of a murdered whore. She secretly hires two other groups also to steal the same body, and C. Card never finds out how the situation all fits together. *The New York Times Book Review* disliked the book because it seemed to be merely a 1960s cartooning of hard-boiled detective fiction. *Kirkus* called it a "cart-wheeling fantasy . . . sentimental comic book without the pictures."

The narrator is an amiable loser. Jokes are made about the early days of America's involvement in World War II and about how people relate to a young man who is broke and inept at his job. Brautigan's imagination works on the improbable events in the detective's day and his extravagant fantasies about Babylon. The theme of the San Francisco adventure is that people relate to each other only in terms of money or sex; the theme of the Babylon fantasy is prestige.

C. Card is robbed by pay telephones and hoodlums, and beaten up by bus drivers. His mother disowns him for being a detective and makes him feel guilty for the death of his father. In the Spanish Civil War, he was shot accidentally in the buttocks with his own gun. His legs were broken when a car ran over him (insurance made this his only recent luck). He has been knocked unconscious by a baseball in a practice baseball game, and he has flunked the police academy examination. But he escapes his seedy reality by fantasizing that in ancient Babylon he is a great baseball player, a distinguished detective idolized by his beautiful secretary, Nina-dirat. Or he dreams he is the Babylonian big bandleader Baby, with his own radio station.

Brautigan's novels are best appreciated by the principles of the New Fiction ("Post-Modern"), spelled out in an article in *TriQuarterly* by Philip Stevick, especially their deliberately chosen, limited audience and the joy the observer finds in the mere texture of the data of the fiction. Thomas Hearron explains how Brautigan's imagination works in his metaphors. Brautigan's theme is usually the power of the imagination to give zest, poetry, and humaneness to life as well as to literature. The youth audience reads him expecting either affirmation (unfulfilled) of the 1960s counterculture or titillation from his style and a literary equivalent of the drug experience. Professionals read him expecting enlightenment on the youth culture. He is aware of several currents of American tradition, especially that of the new American Eden as created by Thoreau in *Walden*, by Twain in Huckleberry Finn's escape to the Mississippi River, and by the Californian myth since the Gold Rush days; and Brautigan tends to condemn the new America because it has betrayed the promises of the new American Eden.

—*Robert Novak*

Books:

The Return of the Rivers (San Francisco: Inferno, 1957);

The Galilee Hitch-Hiker (San Francisco: White Rabbit, 1958);

Lay the Marble Tea: Twenty-four Poems (San Francisco: Carp, 1959);

The Octopus Frontier (San Francisco: Carp, 1960);

Please Plant This Book (San Francisco: Graham Mackintosh, 1968);

A Confederate General from Big Sur (New York: Grove, 1965; London: Cape, 1971);

All Watched Over by Machines of Loving Grace (San Francisco: Communication, 1967);

Trout Fishing in America (San Francisco: Four Seasons, 1967; London: Cape, 1970);

In Watermelon Sugar (San Francisco: Four Seasons, 1968; London: Cape, 1970);

The Pill Versus the Springhill Mine Disaster (San Francisco: Four Seasons, 1968; London: Cape, 1970);

Rommel Drives On Deep into Egypt (New York: Seymour Lawrence/Delacorte, 1970);

The Abortion: An Historical Romance 1966 (New York: Simon & Schuster, 1971; London: Cape, 1973);

Revenge of the Lawn: Stories 1962-1970 (New York: Simon & Schuster, 1971; London: Cape, 1972);

The Hawkline Monster (New York: Simon & Schuster, 1974; London: Cape, 1975);

Willard and His Bowling Trophies (New York: Simon & Schuster, 1975; London: Cape, 1976);

Loading Mercury With a Pitchfork (New York: Simon & Schuster, 1976);

Sombrero Fallout (New York: Simon & Schuster, 1976);

Dreaming of Babylon: A Private Eye Novel 1942 (New York: Delacorte/Seymour Lawrence, 1977).

References:

Kent Bales, "Fishing the Ambivalence, or, A Reading of *Trout Fishing in America*," *Western Humanities Review*, 29 (winter 1975): 29-42;

John Clayton, "Richard Brautigan: The Politics of Woodstock," *New American Review*, 11 (1971): 56-68;

John Ditsky, "The Man on the Quaker Oats Box: Characteristics of Recent Experimental Fiction," *Georgia Review*, 26 (fall 1972): 297-313;

Thomas Hearron, "Escape Through Imagination in *Trout Fishing in America*," *Critique*, 16, 1 (1974): 25-31;

Patricia Hernlund, "Author's Intent: *In Watermelon Sugar*," *Critique*, 16, 1 (1974): 5-17;

Stephen R. Jones, "Richard Brautigan: A Bibliography," *Bulletin of Bibliography*, 33 (January

1976): 53-59;

Robert Kern, "Williams, Brautigan, and the Poetics of Primitivism," *Chicago Review*, 27, 1 (summer 1975): 47-57;

Harvey Leavitt, "The Regained Paradise of Brautigan's *In Watermelon Sugar*," *Critique*, 16, 1 (1974): 18-24;

Gerald Locklin and Charles Stetler, "Some Observations on *A Confederate General from Big Sur*," *Critique*, 13, 3 (1971): 72-82;

Terence Malley, *Richard Brautigan: Writers for the Seventies* (New York: Warner Paperback Library, 1972);

Robert Novak, "The Poetry of Richard Brautigan," *Windless Orchard*, 14 (1973): 17, 48-50;

Neil Schmitz, "Richard Brautigan and the Modern Pastoral," *Modern Fiction Studies*, 19 (spring 1973): 109-125;

Kenneth Seib, "*Trout Fishing in America*: Brautigan's Funky Fishing Yarn," *Critique*, 13, 3 (1971): 63-71;

Philip Stevick, "Scheherezade Runs Out of Plots, Goes on Talking; the King Puzzled, Listens: an Essay on the New Fiction," *TriQuarterly*, 26 (winter 1973): 332-362;

John Stickney, "Gentle Poet of the Young," *Life*, 69 (14 August 1970): 49-54;

David L. Vanderwerken, "*Trout Fishing in America* and the American Tradition," *Critique*, 16, 1 (1974): 32-40;

Cheryl Walker, "Richard Brautigan: Youth Fishing in America," *Modern Occasions*, 2, 2 (1972): 308-313;

James Wanless and Christine Kolodziej, "Richard Brautigan: A Working Checklist," *Critique*, 16, 1 (1974): 41-52.

Joel Rubiner

William S. Burroughs [signature]

WILLIAM SEWARD BURROUGHS, poet and novelist, was born in St. Louis, Missouri, on 5 February 1914 to parents from two important American families. Burroughs's mother, Laura Lee, was a direct descendant of Robert E. Lee, and his father, Perry Mortimer Burroughs, was the son of the industrialist who invented the cylinder which made the modern adding machine possible. Burroughs had a restless childhood in St. Louis, dominated by his mother's obsessive Victorian prudery, and haunted by horrible nightmares. As the son of St. Louis aristocracy he attended private schools there until the age of fifteen, when he was sent to an all-male academy in Los Alamos, New Mexico. While in Los Alamos, Burroughs developed interest in two apparently unrelated areas: literature and crime. His reading in Baudelaire, Gide, and Wilde was balanced with thoughts of mobsters.

At Harvard University he studied literature with John Livingston Lowes and George Lyman Kittredge. His other primary interest in college was the study of anthropology. After graduating from Harvard with an A.B. in 1936, Burroughs traveled to Europe and briefly studied medicine in Vienna. He returned to the United States and unpredictably attempted to use a family connection to get him into the Office of Strategic Services, but after deliberately cutting off the first joint of one finger he was rejected. In 1938 Burroughs returned to Harvard to study anthropology, but a conviction that academic life was little more than a series of intrigues broken by teas led him to New York City where he worked for an advertising agency for a year and underwent psychoanalysis. He entered the army in 1942, was discharged after six months for psychological reasons, moved to Chicago, and took a series of odd jobs including exterminator and private detective.

Burroughs's move back to New York City in 1943 was most important for determining the ultimate direction of his life. In New York, Burroughs met and befriended a Columbia University coed named Jean Vollmer whom he married on 17 January 1945; they have one child, William

Seward. She was acquainted with Jack Kerouac, and when Burroughs heard her speak of Kerouac as a former seaman, he expressed an interest in meeting him. It was Kerouac who later introduced Burroughs to Allen Ginsberg. In turn, Burroughs introduced Kerouac and Ginsberg to the experimental writings of Blake, Rimbaud, and others. Burroughs's apartment on 115th Street became a literary salon, of sorts, where the Beat generation was born, and Burroughs, Kerouac, and Ginsberg emerged as the leaders of that generation.

At nearly the same moment that Burroughs's love for literature was reaching a new intensity through his friends, his attraction to the seamier side of life was also being stimulated. Herbert Huncke, a Times Square hustler, introduced Burroughs to the use of morphine and its derivatives sometime in late 1944. From that point, until the late-1950s, Burroughs was a steady drug user, and junk became the commodity that dictated how and where he would live. When police pressure became too great in New York in 1946, Burroughs moved to Waverly, Texas, where he attempted to become a farmer. In 1948 Burroughs voluntarily entered the drug rehabilitation center in Lexington, Kentucky. Returning to Waverly, already back on drugs, Burroughs was harassed by police until he moved to Algiers, Louisiana, across the river from New Orleans. After his Algiers farm was raided by police in the spring of 1949, Burroughs moved to Mexico City to avoid prosecution for illegal possession of drugs and firearms. There, while continuing his archaeological studies at Mexico City University, centering his interest on the Mayan codices, Burroughs became caught up in the street terror which was part of the Aleman regime. He found it easy enough to get drugs but felt the necessity to carry a gun with him everywhere. On the night of 7 September 1951, Burroughs accidentally shot and killed his wife. According to reports, Burroughs was playing a William Tell game, attempting to shoot a champagne glass off of her head. Burroughs later called this account "absurd and false." Mexican authorities dropped the matter, but Burroughs soon determined to leave the country. After a brief stay in Tangier, Burroughs went to South America to search for the legendary hallucinogen, yage, in the jungles of Colombia. He returned to New York City in 1953 and lived with Ginsberg before returning to Tangier. By this point in his life, writing was becoming more and more important to Burroughs. From 1955 until 1958, he worked on the manuscript that would be the source for his major literary successes: *Naked Lunch, The Soft Machine, The Ticket That Exploded,* and *The Nova Express.* But he also continued using drugs until a point in 1957 when, "after spending a month staring at [his] toe," Burroughs realized that he was, for all practical purposes, dead. He went for treatment to an English physician, John Yerby Dent, who was administering apomorphine (a blend of morphine and hydrochloric acid) as a cure intended to promote a metabolic balance in morphine users. Fortunately, Burroughs's drug addiction was replaced by an increasing addiction to the craft of writing. In 1958, Burroughs moved to Paris, ostensibly to be close to his publisher, the Olympia Press. By the mid-1960s Burroughs had moved to London, where he resides today, enjoying the increasing respectability which seems to be the reward or curse of matured former radicals.

Although he had long demonstrated an interest in writing, even to the point of composing a story called "Twilight's Last Gleaming" and submitting it unsuccessfully to *Esquire* in 1938, Burroughs admits that he did not begin writing seriously until 1950. His first effort was a book about homosexuality, "Queer," which remains unpublished. It was about this time that Burroughs also began recording his experiences as a drug addict and sending chapters to Ginsberg in New York, who was coincidentally attempting to peddle Kerouac's *Visions of Cody* to publishers. Despite the fact that Ace Books had a paperback line which Ginsberg described as "mostly commercial schlupp," he managed to persuade them to publish both Kerouac and Burroughs.

Junkie (1953), Burroughs's first novel, was published under the pseudonym William Lee. Despite the fact that *Junkie* is the most conventional of all Burroughs's books, it is important to an understanding of his later work. What gives this brutally objective tale of addiction more significance than it might otherwise deserve is Burroughs's literal description of scenes which would eventually be inflated to abstract images, ultimately becoming part of the allegorical war of control in later novels. For example, despite the simple chronology of *Junkie,* Burroughs intimates why time would eventually become nonexistent in later narratives which attempt to make the drug experience an archetype for modern man. "A junkie runs on junk-time. When his junk is cut off, the clock runs down and stops. . . . A sick junkie has no escape from eternal time." Thus in later novels, chronological time is replaced by groups of images which create the sense in the reader that he is reliving a moment frozen in inescapable, eternal time. The images of man reduced to the lowest animal form, which

Wrappers of Burroughs's first book.

of literary laudations than any piece of fiction since *Ulysses*," as *Newsweek* proclaimed. Suddenly Burroughs was elevated to membership in the literary elite, with British critic Kenneth Allsop claiming him to be "Rimbaud in a raincoat," and Norman Mailer saying he was possibly "the only American novelist living today who may conceivably be possessed by genius."

Naked Lunch was begun in Tangier in 1955. When Burroughs moved to Paris in 1958 he showed a suitcase full of manuscripts to the publisher of Olympia Press and an agreement was reached. *Naked Lunch* was selected from this mass of material and stacked upon a table. And, as if to emphasize the unconventionality of the novel, a friend suggested that the accidental order of the stack of manuscripts might be better than any order Burroughs could invent. The author agreed, and *Naked Lunch* was published.

Because there is no consistent narrative, no consistent point of view, in fact, no novel in the traditional sense, one must rely upon clues in order to orient himself in the nightmare-world of *Naked Lunch*. As Burroughs says in the "Atrophied Preface," which appears at the end of the book, "So instead of yelling 'Where am I?' cool it and look around and you will find out approximately....You were not there for *The Beginning*. You will not be there for *The End*. . . . Your knowledge of what is going on can only be superficial and relative. . . ." The primary clue to the technique of *Naked Lunch* is its title. Burroughs says that the title signifies "a frozen moment when everyone sees what is on the end of every fork." Appropriately, *Naked Lunch* is a series of such moments, image blocks, like Eliot's in *The Waste Land*, linked by theme, into a full-course, naked meal.

The dominant themes and images in this nonstructure are those delineated in *Junkie*, but in *Naked Lunch* Burroughs gives his imagination free rein to create a parable of man's struggle for freedom from the conditioned life fed to modern man on a "newspaper spoon." On its simplest level, *Naked Lunch* is the story of junkie William Lee, who begins the novel with the words, "I can feel the heat closing in." "The heat" is not only slang for the police, it also represents the pressures of the urban structure which parasitically wishes to rob him of being. The story is one of attempted escape from "the heat." After shooting two pursuing policemen and then calling the station house only to find that the policemen do not exist, Lee concludes that he has "been occluded from space-time. . . . The heat was off me from here on out." Thus escape from the space-

become an important motif in later works, are prefigured in Burroughs's vision of "Huge centipedes and scorpions" crawling in and out of buildings on 42nd Street, and his description of what he would later call a "Mugwump," a Near Eastern junkie whose eyes have "an insect's unseeing calm" and who looks as if he is fed by sucking honey "through a proboscis." The homosexual theme which becomes a major aspect of Burroughs's work after *Junkie* plays a small role in this early novel, but the auto-ejaculation motif, a symbol of man's lack of control over his own bodily functions, is prefigured in the "hair trigger orgasm" of a junk-sick William Lee, fighting vainly to master himself in Mexico City. But most important of all is Burroughs's message in *Junkie*: that junk is not merely an objective evil, but "a way of life," finally replacing being with a type of timeless contemporary hell which is nearly inescapable.

Because *Junkie* was a first novel issued by a rather inconspicuous paperback line, it received little, if any, critical notice, but Burroughs's next book, *Naked Lunch* (1959), published in Paris, reached the United States "carrying a heavier burden time controls of modern existence becomes the ultimate goal of Burroughs's art, and he steers his heroes, most notably Lee, through a maze of controls (dope, sex, language, bureaucracy) to the ultimate freedom of space-time occlusion, which is symbolized most frequently by jumping through windows.

To Burroughs's way of thinking "the Aristotelian construct with its attendant logic is one of the great shackles of Western Civilization" and Henry Luce, codifying existence by feeding experience to the monster *Time-Life-Fortune*, is its personification. In *Naked Lunch*, Burroughs fights the artificial reality of the subject-verb-object order by freeing language from its dependence upon that order. Thus another clue to understanding *Naked Lunch* is the realization that Burroughs views its incoherence as the liberator of his reader's mind.

The three novels which immediately followed the publication of *Naked Lunch* might reasonably be grouped into one block called "Naked Lunch Redivivus," or as one critic termed the four novels, including *Naked Lunch*, "a Doomsday Quartet," because it is a certainty that the material Burroughs used for these books was produced from that same suitcase from which *Naked Lunch* was selected. But *The Soft Machine* (1961), *The Ticket That Exploded* (1962), and *Nova Express* (1964) are a blending of old material with new technique. Sometime between the publication of *Naked Lunch* and the final version of *The Soft Machine*, Brion Gysin, who had helped Burroughs select *Naked Lunch*, introduced Burroughs to a technique with which he had been experimenting, and which he descriptively called "cut-up." This technique involves taking a printed or written page, cutting it up, and then rearranging it to create unusual semantic juxtapositions. Inherently distrustful of the logical sequence of language, Burroughs committed himself to the "cut-up" and even invented the "fold-in"—a technique in which one folds a page lengthwise and then places it over another page, lining up the lines to produce juxtaposition of word and image—to further confound conventional language and the false reality it produces.

The Wild Boys: A Book of the Dead (1971) represents a shift in Burroughs's career. Relying less upon the cut-up and fold-in techniques than in any of the Doomsday Quartet, Burroughs achieves a lucidity missing from his work since *Junkie*. To be sure, the book is still relatively unstructured, progressing, as the earlier books, through scenes linked by associated images. But in *The Wild Boys*, Burroughs seems to be positing a bizarre alternative to the apocalypse that consumed his preceding work.

Against a world wrecked by famine and controlled by police, Burroughs juxtaposes the wild boys, a homosexual tribe of hashish smokers who have occluded themselves from space and time through indifference, and who have developed into a world counter-culture with its own language, rituals, and self-sufficiency, to the point of producing offspring in test tubes. Of course, such self-sufficiency is dangerous to those who create the false images upon which repressive society is based. But the wild boys cannot be tamed, not even by soldiers, because their cold indifference produces a savagery that refuses to submit to control.

Exterminator! (1974) is also a book of the apocalypse. More a collection of short stories and poems than a novel, all of the stories are thematically related to the first, "Exterminator!," a straightforward narrative of Burroughs's work for a pest control company in Chicago. Death, in some form or another—by virus, nerve gas, mass murder—is the dominant theme, but in most cases the death is the product of sinister force. At its simplest, this force might be Burroughs carrying his can of bug spray into someone's home, but most often it is a force representative of power and control, like the United States Army "raping and murdering helpless civilians" in New York or the butler at the Pentagon who is really a Chinese Agent involved in mind control and secret viruses. It is clear that Burroughs's thinking became more political in *The Wild Boys* and *Exterminator!* but his primary concern for freedom from the forces of control—whether they be sexual, militaristic, journalistic, or political—has remained essentially unchanged from the beginning of his literary career.

Beginning with the publication of *Naked Lunch* in the United States in 1962, Burroughs's literary reputation was made. But despite Mary McCarthy and Norman Mailer's claims at the 1962 International Writer's Conference in Edinburgh that Burroughs was an outstanding American writer, there are dissenters. An anonymous reviewer in *Time* (30 November 1962) stated that Burroughs "cannot sustain his nightworld" in *Naked Lunch* because he is "never in control for longer than a paragraph or two"; John Wain scathingly attacked Burroughs for his "owlish seriousness" and lack of "wit and irony" in the *New Republic* (1 December 1962); and Donald Malcolm, in the *New Yorker* (2 February 1963), judged Burroughs's satire "poor" because Burroughs is "so emphatically bent on making horror stark upon the page that he accomplished very little else."

Both *The Soft Machine* and *The Ticket That Exploded* drew a somewhat baffled, if not negative, critical response. In reviewing the former, in the *Nation* (4 July 1966), Stephen W. Koch suggested Burroughs was writing to replace meaning with "meaninglessness" since the experiences of language he recorded were largely of "language without content"; and Herbert Gold noted in the *New York Times Book Review* (20 March 1966) that Burroughs's new techniques are the fingers of "arty fashion" grasping a "rabid imagination." These criticisms were carried over into notices of *The Ticket That Exploded*, with an anonymous *Time* reviewer rationalizing the incoherence by concluding that "Burroughs' work adds up to the world's greatest put-on" (5 August 1967). However, Theodore Solataroff used the publication of *The Ticket* to proclaim in the *New Republic* that Burroughs is a "vital and complex" writer whose work is closely related to both T. S. Eliot and Lenny Bruce. Because *Nova Express* relied heavily on the cut-up technique, William James Smith suggested in *Commonweal* (8 January 1965) that such techniques are "no substitute for talent, or for suffering"; and Granville Hicks, comparing *Nova Express* unfavorably to Hubert Selby's *Last Exit to Brooklyn* in *Saturday Review* (7 November 1964), finds the former a "fantasy" written "to puzzle the reader."

Of Burroughs's final two novels, *The Wild Boys* received better reviews than any other of Burroughs's works since *Naked Lunch*, with Josephine Hendin claiming in the *Saturday Review* (30 October 1971) that Burroughs "has never written better"; and Alfred Kazin calling *The Wild Boys* a "reverie in which different items suddenly get animated with a marvelously unexpected profusion of animation and disorder" in the *New York Times Book Review* (12 December 1971). *Exterminator!*, however, was viewed less favorably. An anonymous critic for the *Atlantic* (September 1973) labelled Burroughs's latest novel "the diatribe of an aging homosexual who would destroy the world because his own life is less gay than it use to be"; and Andrew C. J. Bergman, writing in the *New York Times Book Review* (14 October 1973), called *Exterminator!* "a disappointing novel of uneven parts." Despite the underground popularity Burroughs has enjoyed in the United States since the early 1960s only two of his novels—*Naked Lunch* and *The Wild Boys*—have received good reviews; the rest have remained the objects of praise in an underground cult which enjoys Burroughs's style and sympathizes with his message. It is for this cult that Burroughs continues to write. —*Robert E. Burkholder*

Books:

Junkie, as William Lee (New York: Ace, 1953, bound with Maurice Helbront, *Narcotic Agent*; reprinted under own name, Ace, 1964; reprinted as *Junky*, unexpurgated, New York: Penguin, 1977);

The Naked Lunch (Paris: Olympia, 1959; reprinted as *Naked Lunch*, New York: Grove, 1962; London: Calder, 1964);

The Exterminator, with Brion Gysin (San Francisco: Auerhahn, 1960);

The Soft Machine (Paris: Olympia, 1962; New York: Grove, 1966; London: Calder & Boyars, 1968);

The Ticket That Exploded (Paris: Olympia, 1962; New York: Grove, 1967; London: Calder & Boyars, 1968);

Dead Fingers Talk (Paris: Olympia, 1963; London: Calder, 1964);

The Yage Letters, with Allen Ginsberg (San Francisco: City Lights, 1963);

Nova Express (New York: Grove, 1964; London: Cape, 1966);

Time (New York: "C" Press, 1965);

APO-33: A Metabolic Regulator: A Report on the Synthesis of the Apomorphine Formula (San Francisco: Beach, 1968);

The Third Mind (New York: Grove, 1970);

The Last Words of Dutch Schultz (London: Cape Goliard, 1970; New York: Viking, 1975);

The Wild Boys: A Book of the Dead (New York: Grove, 1971; London: Calder & Boyars, 1972);

Exterminator! (New York: Viking/Richard Seaver, 1974; London: Calder & Boyars, 1974).

References:

Ihab Hassan, "The Subtracting Machine: The Work of William Burroughs," *Critique*, 6, 1 (spring 1963): 4-23;

Hassan, "The Literature of Silence: From Henry Miller to Beckett and Burroughs," *Encounter*, 28 (January 1967): 74-82;

Conrad Knickerbocker, "William Burroughs," *Paris Review*, 35 (fall 1965): 13-49;

Joe Maynard and Barry Miles, *William Burroughs: A Bibliography* (Charlottesville: University Press of Virginia, 1977);

Marshall McLuhan, "Notes on Burroughs," *Nation*, 199 (28 December 1964): 517-518;

Miles Associates, compilers, *A Descriptive Catalogue of the William S. Burroughs Archive*

(London: Covent Garden Press, 1973);

E. Mottram, *William Burroughs: The Algebra of Need* (Buffalo, N.Y.: Intrepid Press, 1971);

Daniel Odier, *The Job: An Interview with William Burroughs* (New York: Grove, 1970);

Tony Tanner, *City of Words: American Fiction, 1950-1970* (New York: Harper & Row, 1971), pp. 109-140;

John Tytell, *Naked Angels: The Lives and Literature of the Beat Generation* (New York: McGraw-Hill, 1976).

Thomas Victor

HORTENSE CALISHER was born in New York City on 20 December 1911, the child of Joseph Henry Calisher and Hedwig Lichstern Calisher; they were a comfortable, middle-class Jewish family. Her father was a story-telling Southerner originally from Richmond, Virginia, and her mother a German immigrant. These entangled skeins, Southern, Old World, New York, and Jewish, provide the fabric of much of her early fiction.

Calisher graduated from Barnard College in 1932, not a good year for philosophy majors. Hired by the Department of Public Welfare, she became a social worker, dispensing emergency relief in New York's tenements. This sudden shift from the world of metaphysics and timeless speculation to the realities of immediate human need again and again informs her fiction; perhaps the overriding impulse of her literary style is that her characters' carefully nurtured abstractions perpetually clash with realities.

After marriage to an engineer, she left New York City and lived in various industrial towns, while raising two children. Throughout these years, she wrote some poetry, committed herself to liberal causes, and found suburban domesticity less and less adequate. In 1948 she started writing seriously, first autobiographical family stories, then non-family stories. The first of these, "The Ginger Box," appeared in the *New Yorker* in 1948, and in 1951 her first book, a collection of short stories, most of them previously printed, was published.

In the Absence of Angels is an impressive first volume. With it, her reputation as a short story writer of importance was established. The lead story, "In Greenwich There Are Many Gravelled Walks," is one of her very finest. It contains all the marks of her storyteller's talent: control, precision, finely honed prose, careful rhythms, and a near-perfect shape. As with all of Calisher's best short fiction, the stories are about real human beings responding to real dilemmas with real emotions. Peter, the competent son of a hopelessly alcoholic mother who must periodically be checked into a Greenwich sanitorium, meets Susan, the daughter of a thrice-married mother and an aging homosexual. They are introduced just moments before the father's latest young man jumps from a fifth-story window. As they leave the scene together, hand in hand, they know they must pick their way carefully through the rubble of their elders' lives. Other stories in the volume include a careful dissection of the end of an affair, a shop girl's understanding of the aggressiveness of mediocrity, city children finding an archetype of decency in one lonely school teacher's behavior, and a middle-aged Jew's realization at a college reunion that anti-Semitism has always been a factor in his life, even during his sunny undergraduate days as an athlete. The story which gives its name to the volume is a political one about a sensitive and moral woman who is about to be tried for her sins after "the Revolution." She admits her guilt, her shame, and also her responsibility: "in the absence of angels and arbiters from a world of light, men and women must take their place."

Several of the stories are autobiographical; young Hester Elkins represents Calisher, and sometimes her brother, Joe Elkins, is also a self-portrait of the author. Joe and Hester Elkins grow up and learn about death, about peripheral persons, about female vanity, about the complicity love sometimes requires, and about the burden of parents, whether alive or dead. The Hester stories are, from one point of view, small gems of social history; the melting-pot family in a particular city at a particular time manages to snatch its pieces of the dream. And, from another point of view, they are quiet and carefully realized fictions of a young woman's growth into loving and remembering and understanding.

With the publication of *In the Absence of Angels*, Calisher had established herself publicly as a talent, and, in a more difficult sort of assertion for a responsible, well-bred wife and mother, she had defined herself privately as a writer. She was free. During the 1950s, she received a Guggenheim grant, taught writing at Barnard and the University of Iowa, toured the Far East for the State Department, and divorced and married again.

Her first novel, *False Entry* (1961), was published after seven years in the writing. It is the story of a middle-aged compiler of encyclopedias who has fallen in love with a judge's daughter, Ruth Mannix. During three months of intensive all-night writing, the narrator recollects and reorders his past to make his present, with all its complications, real and coherent to himself and to his beloved. The tension of the novel lies in the frantic imposition of limited narrative time onto the mass of persons, events, and meanings which lie unshaped and incoherent in the past. Gifted with an extraordinary memory, the narrator uses it to uncover and carve up the past so that he may select those pieces worth keeping. His task is complicated by his peculiar abilities of "false entry": "false entry into another person's life, into his present by means of his past." He is "an eternal listener at the orchestrations of others, a hoarder of what others would never dream of saving. . . ."

He has thus always played the novelist's game, but now is the moment for seriousness, for commitment, and for form. "And one night, as he sits in his evening agony of non-living, listening, hand near the dead phone, to the low mnemonic mutter of other peoples' lives, certain names, shadows, half-lights suddenly merge; all the mossy facts adhere, and he feels, formed under the hand, the stone. Shall he fling it—for if he does so, he himself will be the stone?" Writing and living are the same thing.

The separate incidents of his narrative do not add up, or at least do not form a coherent story. But in the end, the act of establishing his narrative for himself and for Ruth is an act of establishing, however tenuously, himself. From his repertoire of identities he finally selects one, and the commitment makes possible the act of love, a true entry into another's life. "This is the entry. Nothing concludes but the power to go on. We walk toward. The ordinary, advancing like lichen, covers us all." Calisher never flinches at the final smallness of human experience.

Reviewers of *False Entry* reacted to the style; some praised it as poetic, rococo writing of exquisite artistry, but more condemned it as overwritten, laden with literary embroidery. Generally, Calisher's critics are more comfortable with the terse prose of her *New Yorker* short story style than with the stylistic exuberances of her novels.

Tale for the Mirror, a collection of twelve short stories and a novella, appeared in 1962; it too is an impressive volume. The novella, "Tale for the Mirror," is about a mediocre lawyer named Garner who lives in a large, old house on the Hudson river, twenty-five miles from New York City. This setting, Calisher's own house, became one of her favorite backdrops. Away from the city, but always attached to it by a string of water and yearning, the location repeatedly reflects her characters' concurrent desires for retreat and engagement. Garner is living his ordered commuter life when a new neighbor arrives, Dr. Bhatta, an Indian doctor-guru who saves odd souls with odd techniques. As Garner and the community move to oust the fake, Garner is forced to realize that the doctor's fraudulence is no different, really, from his own. Each must manufacture every morning a tale for the mirror, a fiction to guide him through the strangeness. It is a sad and very witty story.

Other stories in the volume are about the death of love, the terror of trying it again, the nostalgia for a lost emotional vitality, the knowing acceptance of limitations, and the desperate acts of the lonely. Surely Calisher's finest examination of loneliness, perhaps one of the finest anywhere, is in her story, "The Scream on Fifty-seventh Street." A lonely widow in a borrowed New York City apartment hears a scream in the night, and its strange recurrence drives her to the brink of insanity. Finally, she realizes that she is one of the responsible ones who can hear the screams of the desolate rising from the city, and she waits in the night, yearning to hear the scream again, as she admits her own citizenship in the world of the isolated. This is Calisher at her best.

Textures of Life was published in 1963; it is a small novel, but it succeeds in fulfilling a limited purpose, to render the transformations of a young couple as they face up to the real issues of marriage and parenthood. David and Liz, who first appear as supercilious and bourgeois-baiting hippies, are eventually forced to watch themselves grow up as the isolation of marriage captures them, the remoteness creeps in, and they learn to depend upon the domestic and the ordinary. The young couple learn, like so many of Calisher's characters, that to admit their limitations is not necessarily or not only to give up; the cliches of human behavior, at least the middle-class American cliches of marriage and children and domestic retreat, are cliches for good reasons. They wall out the wilderness and sometimes enclose love.

Another volume of short stories and a novella, *Extreme Magic*, appeared in 1964. By now, Calisher had the confidence to extend her range and to be more comfortable with herself as a narrative voice—often a very female and a very funny one. In "Songs My Mother Taught Me," the narrator at a London dinner party, where the ladies are disrobing, remembers her mother's commandments about clean underwear in particular and a proper feminine image in general. The narrator has never quite succumbed to either, and when it is her turn to doff her clothes, she reveals a wickedly-black merry widow, set with a great false ruby, sparkling sensuality. Several different female voices emerge in this collection: that of "The Rabbi's Daughter" as she dwindles into wifehood with "the devious shadow of her resentment," that of a fortyish woman writer delivering a monologue to a young girl about her transformations of experience into art, that of a teacher and scholar whose support of a worthless nephew has merely affirmed his will to die, and, again, that of Hester who realizes she is caught in a double inheritance from her father and her mother and can reject neither. The stories are all competent and carefully formed; some are too clever, some are merely witty, but "The Rabbi's Daughter" is excellent. Here Calisher presents another fictional analysis of one of her central themes, the feminine retreat from public accomplishment into private rage.

Journal from Ellipsia (1965) is a complete departure from the previous fiction. Calisher says in *Herself* that she was feeling confident and was "writing her oats." A young woman anthropologist, Janice Jamison, has disappeared from her research laboratory, and it seems that Janice has not just dropped out. Yearning for a world free of messy emotions, a world of stasis and repose, she has absconded to the farthest star, Ellipsia, a perfect world where everyone is one, feelings have been dispensed with, and even awkward physical protuberances have been eliminated. The inhabitants of Ellipsia are geometrically perfect—ellipsoids. Janice has made contact with one of these creatures, Eli, who yearns for a reverse transformation from perfection of form to complexity and variety, even messiness. Eli speaks through a machine during Janet's memorial service and tells those assembled that he has come to earth to become human, to enter the fray. When he can recall the shadows of his former perfect home and can also utter a human wail, then will he be complete.

Calisher, surprised to learn that the novel was considered feminist, offered an explanation:

> . . . to me the book really takes place in that terrible but thrilling gap between word-masters of the human condition and its math-masters, between the humanists and the atomic symbolists—that gap whose consequences, pointed out to us by C. P. Snow, had been with me ever since, as a young philosophy student fresh from Kant and Hegel, Schopenhauer, and all the other beloved analogues in whose word-systems I had hoped to revolve endlessly nearer the touchstone, I had come up against the Quantum Theory and Max Planck—and had first understood the barrier nature of that other visionary side of the universe, over to which I could never travel first class unless I reversed my life, to learn *its* instruments. Expertise interests novelists, who usually despair of having all of them. Novels spring up in those gaps.

Reviewers were not sure whether to label this novel science fiction. It would seem that Calisher was not trying to interlope in science fiction but rather to defend and reaffirm the small joys and large terrors of being human, this time from the perspective of the non-human.

In 1966, two novellas were published in one volume, *The Railway Police and The Last Trolley Ride*. "The Railway Police" is Calisher's most brilliant novella to date. It is the delicately Kafkaesque story of a thirty-nine-year-old social worker who, on her way to yet another conference, sees a nonchalant vagrant arrested by the railway police. The vagrant's composure in the face of regulators and reprimands is a sign for her to begin her own vagrancy, to chuck all the rules and strip down to the bare essentials of herself. Unfortunately, her essential fact is that she is bald, as bald as the eighteen wooden globes which hold her eighteen wigs. Once she had a lover, a man found in an art gallery lauding the hairless knobs of some of Picasso's ladies. But when, locked in amorousness, she showed him her own classical skull, he was horrified, "My dear, there's a difference between art and life, you know. But women never see it. They always overdo." Now she is ready to face the world unadorned and ready to conduct her own research on the difference between art and life. She journeys into the streets of New York, into the tenements, into the parks for addicts and bums. She is almost arrested— surely there is something illegal about a bald-headed woman—but her journey is finally a success. Awakening on a park bench in the dawn, she accepts "this large, superbly bare fact on my shoulders," commits herself to uniting some of the signals of the world with her own imaginative powers, and is born.

"The Railway Police" is a perfectly realized allegory of becoming a writer. It is, of course, Calisher's own story, but as a work of fiction it is less autobiography than a step into feminism. The narrator gives up the traditional offerings—curls and counsel—of the female as social worker and accepts her own intelligence and talent joyously, "with the hilarity which comes of knowing that one's equipment is equal to one's intentions!" The problem is not being bald-headed, but being a bald-headed woman.

"The Last Trolley Ride," the longer and gentler of the two novellas in the volume, is a pleasantly nostalgic story about upper New York state. The lives of two grandfathers named Jim are recalled by a nameless grandchild for the benefit of the next generation. As the two old men review their successes and their failures, they wonder what this carving of two lives out of friendship, love, hate, war, and out of the mechanical transformations of the twentieth century all means: "It's all transport said my grandfathers." They decide on a last folly, a trip around the world. As they fly off and ascend into memory, the youthful octogenarians taunt their strangely aged heirs, "Watch our dust!" The grandfathers have always appreciated and savored the charm of life, and out of the past there is no better lesson: "you won't learn more."

The New Yorkers (1969) is Calisher's largest novel and companion to her earlier *False Entry*. The narrator in *False Entry* tells his story to Ruth Mannix, and *The New Yorkers* is Ruth's own very complicated story. At the age of twelve and at the moment of menarche, Ruth discovers her mother with a lover and murders her. Thus, for Ruth "everything has already happened." Her coalescent instant of sexuality, love, hate, murder, and death is the central event of the novel which magnetizes members of her family and defines all their social relations. Ruth grows up surrounded by a strange collection of companions; a secretive housekeeper, a deaf brother, a hunchback, a golden Quaker boy, and a bastard slum child all tell their own tales of compromise and suffering. And all sorts of weird travelers bring more personal revelations to the elegant social events of this family, privately so fiercely entwined and publicly so richly civilized. The major portion of the novel is told from the point of view of the judge, a man imbued with a rather tedious sensibility (perhaps because he is only five feet tall) who has retired from public life to devote himself to the impossible task of protecting Ruth from the knowledge of her crime. But Ruth eventually admits her guilt and reveals all to her fiance, the stalwart Quaker, and the novel concludes with her wedding, which is also a wedding of public and private, of Gentile and Jew, of the crimes of the past and the hopes of the present. Judge Mannix and his daughter at last manage to put the two halves of their lives together and to affirm both. "As our parents come to give birth to us, they died a little. We die a little giving birth to them." For Calisher, the central fact of the parent-child relationship is always the mutuality of the creation and the destruction.

The New Yorkers is one of Calisher's major works, but it cannot really be considered one of her best. The emotions and values of this select group of affluent, powerful, self-consciously Freudian, and godless New Yorkers—whose deformities seem to be literary contrivances—are made to seem not only universal but universally necessary. In fact, *The New Yorkers* is a profoundly local novel. Therein lies its real strength; Calisher knows her chosen city as few others do, and her evocations of it are stunning.

Calisher, like Virginia Woolf, likes to follow serious efforts with lighter ones. In 1971 she published the novel *Queenie* and, in 1973, *Eagle Eye*. These two works can be seen as companion pieces, a double response to the insanities of the 1960s, spoken by two members of the youth culture, the virgin Queenie, and the computer whiz, Bunty Bronstein, who grow up during the years of Vietnam. Both novels offer certain pleasures, but both now seem dated and ephemeral.

Queenie, a female Portnoy with a Woody Allen sensibility, tells her own story in a series of tape recordings. After a sunny childhood in the demimonde, Queenie as coed learns how to be unhappy, then tries the politics of envy, and finally marries a hijacker and kidnaps the President. The novel fizzles along with her cryptic commentaries and flip conclusions about sexual relationships and the private versus the public life. *Queenie* is meant to be gaily satirical, but is finally just silly.

Eagle Eye is considerably less silly and more realistic. The young person growing up is Bunty Bronstein, just back from a European *Wanderjahr* to avoid the draft. The novel opens with Bunty asleep beside the family computer, Batface, the morning after his homecoming. Calisher uses here one of her favorite narrative structures, beginning *in medias res*, then with elaborate flashbacks and shifting narrative styles or multiple narrators, enriching and complicating the narrative scene until it achieves dramatic resonance. When the opening incident has been realized or earned, so to speak, the clock starts ticking, the present takes over, and the action proceeds to the conclusions. Like a mountain climber gaining a foothold, then looking down and down and down before proceeding, Calisher likes to organize her fictions around heightened moments which force the narrators to stop and to take measure. One of the many things Bunty, the narrator of *Eagle Eye*, must measure is the current extent of his father's wealth.

The Bronstein family, Buddy and Maeve and their son Bunty, have for twenty years been rising, floating upward on a current of yearning and gratification. While Buddy made the money, Maeve did the shopping, "It was holy to shop." Calisher is very acute in describing this sad couple as they perpetually up the ante in the consumption stakes. Now, however, the sky has been reached; there is no place to go but crazy—which Maeve promptly does. And Bunty is left to make sense of it all and to deal with this preposterous excess of wealth, magically accumulated by people with no insides. Bunty is a child of the binary age, and he decides that his old friend the 7090 IBM computer can be used for a Proustian recovery. If all the events in an individual life are fed in, the fragments can be ordered, freed from time, and categorized. No one need be lost or left out. Why not provide a "universal life record" for everyone? The hero's final solution to the problem of growing up in a culture of unparalleled affluence and technological potential is unclear because the novel degenerates into cryptic dialogue and private symbols. But as Bunty flies off to California with his computer to begin anew, he seems to realize that being human means admitting attachments: "what are we here for, here for, if not to see each others' lines of force? And see them, see them pitiful."

Eagle Eye doesn't seem real. The prose covers more than it reveals; Calisher seems so afraid of being obvious that she is obscure instead, and the characters all speak an unfinished Calisher code. A fairly acute analysis of affluence turns into an identity quest in which the solution, though overlaid with chic, is the same old chestnut.

In 1972, after *Queenie* and before *Eagle Eye*, Calisher published two books, *Herself*, "An Autobiographical Work," and a short novel, *Standard Dreaming*. The first and best portion of *Herself* really is autobiographical, and Calisher's account of her own struggle to emerge from the dollhouse and enter the world of letters is as interesting and moving as one would expect from an extremely intelligent writer who never denied that she was also a woman. But then *Herself* degenerates into a random collection of personal and journalistic effluvia: a very inside "journal to a friend" written during her oriental trip, letters to assorted editors, book reviews, articles, cultural commentary, recollections of political involvements, and, it must be noted, some useful information about the imaginative sources of her works. Calisher seems to be cleaning out her desk and offering up these fragments to future scholars with a silent request: edit me, annotate me, read me.

During the writing of *Herself*, Calisher had an idea, a biological speculation in the manner of Loren Eiseley, for a novel: "One day, it crosses my mind that perhaps the race itself is now *physically middle-aged*." The result was *Standard Dreaming*, a novella as perfectly formed as "The Railway Police." A nameless narrator, who is a mediator between the medical students of the novel and the reader, relates for our benefit the writing of a medical report by a plastic surgeon named Dr. Berners. Dr. Berners, a man despised by his only son, has discovered, he thinks, a new and deadly disease. Numerous middle-aged parents, all residents of New York's Chinatown, have died inexplicably, and Berners believes that they have died of "a parental disease of the heart." "In the parentism produced by the Society of the Child, one never blames the child"; instead, the parents, rejected and scorned by their offspring, succumb to the fatal strength of their own recriminations. Thus, to Dr. Berners, his own disastrous parent-child relationship is not merely a personal failure, but rather an effect of a larger process, the decline of the species, which, according to the laws of evolution, reveals itself first in the young.

The reader of *Standard Dreaming*, carefully included in the novel as "us," might be tempted to respond to Berners's theory of species-decline with a fallacious *ad hominem* argument to the effect that bad parents naturally develop theories about the evils of children; perhaps the argument could apply as well to Calisher herself, a middle-aged novelist tired of trying to understand and affirm the youth culture. But the narrative is unfolded in the deadly serious atmosphere of a scientific report, and we know that we cannot respond to a scientist by asking him to remove his white coat. Furthermore, Berners's involvement with a group of real parents similarly rejected by their children is perfectly realized fictionally. Calisher portrays a small sample of simply rotten young people who have very familiar faces indeed, and they provide frighteningly convincing evidence that something is awry.

But is the species actually declining? Dr. Berners, after experiencing the successful resolution of a crisis in the parents group and after a trip back to his native Switzerland, a much older country than his adopted one, recovers his sense of the historical continuity of one generation nurturing the next and of the historical fraternity of medicine as well. He reaffirms his own place within the species, as a member, not an outside examiner. And he concludes that his report will be only one man's dreaming, perhaps the "standard" dreaming of every older generation and perhaps worthy of consideration, but still fictive. Actually, he does not entirely give up the possibility that his theory might be correct; he just realizes that the attempt to determine whether or not the species is declining is a non-question, unworthy of human asking because theoretical answers could only diminish the practical possibilities of being human.

Standard Dreaming is one of Calisher's best. The style is lucid and sure and elegant. The narrative technique is terse and convincing, almost frightening. It is a profound little story, a ruthless analysis of the possible causes and inevitable pains of the generation gap, and further, Dr. Berners's final report exemplifies a true synthesis of the two explanatory modes of our culture, the one bumbling and impressionistic, the other codified and rational. Calisher has worked out her own peace with both Darwin and C. P. Snow.

In 1975 *The Collected Stories of Hortense Calisher* appeared. All but one of the stories, "The Summer Rebellion," had been published previously in book form. At least one reviewer responded to this sizeable volume with the apt comment, "underrated." This would certainly seem to be the case with Calisher's short fiction. Here is a story writer recognized by fellow practitioners to be one of the finest; she is a writer's writer. She has repeatedly been invited to teach the craft and has been writer-in-residence at Barnard, Iowa, Sarah Lawrence,

Columbia, Brandeis, and Pennsylvania. She has won four O. Henry prize story awards, and her best stories have been selected for those short story collections to which writers pay attention. "In Greenwich There Are Many Gravelled Walks," for example, has been reprinted in *50 Best American Short Stories 1915-1965, Best American Short Stories 1951, Great American Short Stories*, and *Mid-Century: An Anthology of Distinguished American Short Stories*. But for reasons inexplicable, Calisher is seldom read or taught or explicated by academics. Her stories appear infrequently in college literature anthologies; she has rated only two entries in the *PMLA* Bibliography since 1951, one a doctoral dissertation, one a very brief appreciation. Perhaps her stories are somehow too simple; they offer the elusive pleasure of fine writing, perfect evocations of human conflict, rather than the allusive problems of interpretation so beloved by academics. But the time has surely come to admit her best short fiction into the canon of the classroom. And perhaps the new paperback edition (1977) of the collected stories will help.

On Keeping Women, Calisher's most recent novel (1977), is a feminist novel set in Calisher's favorite place, that large old house beside the Hudson, and the river is again a dark, fluid path, beckoning the sensibility toward the stationary configuration of the lighted city. The sensibility now beckoned is that of Lexie, a thirty-seven-year-old mother of four, who, as the novel opens, is lying naked on the river bank at dawn, trying to answer Freud's old question: What does a woman want? "What she needs most, is to find her own lingo—and have them publish the Congressional Record in it. At least half the time," says Lexie tentatively. And the rest of the novel is her attempt to find just that, without discarding any of her old vocabulary. Lexie narrates most of the novel from her prone position, "I am your representative from the Nude," and she recalls with considerable wit all of the attempts of this housed hysteric to break out. She has had babies, has gotten the house in order, has volunteered, has taken courses and lovers, has observed the crazy neighbors, and has tried a part-time job as a journalist. But now what? Before the moment on the riverbank can be fully realized, Lexie's narrative must be interrupted by the story of her absent husband, Ray, and by the activities of her children, a strange foursome who play "guerilla games" to cover the fact that one of their members is psychotic. Eventually the present is achieved, and Lexie the procreator manages to give birth to herself. When her husband does return and finds her by the river, she has found her own joy and may or may not need him.

In this novel Calisher faces up to the real problem of the modern woman, the Mrs. Ramsey syndrome. How can a woman establish a basis for valuing herself if her primary function is to perform tasks which no one values? Calisher's answer is that a woman must not stop "transliterating" experience from public to private and must not give up her own lingo, but must instead learn to shout it. Lexie, in her birth dialogue with herself, first swears, "never to swear by the cross of sexual injury," and then asks, "But what if I have only my monologue?" And a voice from somewhere replies sternly, "*Then mount it on an elephant.*"

The novel certainly has its flaws; the characters tend to speak Calisher-cryptic, the symbols begin to fly about, and the prose is fairly clogged. But the maturity of the outlook and the inclusiveness of the vision perhaps compensate for the stylistic excesses. Although most reviews were negative, the *New York Times Book Review* included *On Keeping Women* in its list of most noteworthy titles of 1977 with the comment, "always skillful and brilliant in its effect."

Hortense Calisher's future reputation will surely be based upon her short stories and perhaps a few of the novellas. In her best short fiction, her abilities as a stylist and her sense of dramatic impact unite to produce unerring portraits of ordinary people as they try to maintain for themselves a spark of creativity and a feeling of control in the composition of their lives. For Calisher, the act of writing and the act of living tend to be congruent, and perhaps this accounts for the deep feeling of sympathy with those ordinary people which her writing conveys. In the conclusion to *Herself*, she wrote: "Perhaps my own process is not so much my own as I thought, nor even one that only artists know—but one that we share with other Americans, other *people*. Less and less do I see any gap—in the process of us all." —*Carolyn Matalene*

Books:

In the Absence of Angels: Stories (Boston: Little, Brown, 1951; London: Heinemann, 1953);

False Entry (Boston: Little, Brown, 1961; London: Secker & Warburg, 1962);

Tale for the Mirror: A Novella and Other Stories (Boston: Little, Brown, 1962; London: Secker & Warburg, 1963);

Textures of Life (Boston: Little, Brown, 1963; London: Secker & Warburg, 1963);

Extreme Magic: A Novella and Other Stories (Boston: Little, Brown, 1964; London: Secker & Warburg, 1964);

Journal from Ellipsia (Boston: Little, Brown, 1965; London: Secker & Warburg, 1966);

The Railway Police and The Last Trolley Ride (Boston: Little, Brown, 1966);

The New Yorkers (Boston: Little, Brown, 1969; London: Cape, 1970);

Queenie (New York: Arbor House, 1971; London: W. H. Allen, 1973);

Herself (New York: Arbor House, 1972);

Standard Dreaming (New York: Arbor House, 1972);

Eagle Eye (New York: Arbor House, 1973);

The Collected Stories of Hortense Calisher (New York: Arbor House, 1975);

On Keeping Women (New York: Arbor House, 1977).

Periodical Publications:

Hortense Calisher has published short stories, works in progress, essays, and reviews in: *New Yorker, New World Writing, Charm, Harper's Bazaar, Harper's, The Reporter, Mademoiselle, Ladies' Home Journal, Saturday Evening Post, Gentleman's Quarterly, Evergreen Review, Kenyon Review, American Scholar, Nation,* and *New York Times Book Review.*

References:

Emily Hahn, "In Appreciation of Hortense Calisher," *Wisconsin Studies in Contemporary Literature,* 6 (summer 1965): 243-249;

David K. Kirby, "The Princess and the Frog: The Modern American Short Story as Fairy Tale," *Minnesota Review,* 4 (spring 1973): 145-149.

TRUMAN CAPOTE was born Truman Streckfus Persons, in New Orleans on 30 September 1924. His parents divorced when he was four, and some years later his mother married again, this time a well-to-do businessman named Capote, whose surname his stepson chose to adopt. In the interim the child lived a life of alternating instability and warm security as he was handed from one set of relatives to another in the rural South. Capote made up stories to help deal with his loneliness and his separation from both parents, and by age ten, or thereabouts, he had decided to become a professional writer. This determination led him to ignore formal schooling, although following his mother's second marriage he attended the Trinity School and St. John's Academy in New York and the public schools of Greenwich, Connecticut. Capote has said that all through his

Jill Krementz

Truman Capote.

adolescence he was working steadily toward becoming a writer, and that by his mid-teens he was a technically accomplished stylist.

Capote's formal schooling ended when he was seventeen. He obtained a job at the *New Yorker* magazine, where, although little more than an errand boy, he attracted attention with his mannerisms and eccentric style of dress. In the early years of World War II, Capote's central interest continued to be in his own writing. The June 1945 appearance of his short story "Miriam" in *Mademoiselle* brought him the widespread attention that his earlier publications had not attracted, and led to his signing a contract for a first novel. Selected for the O. Henry Memorial Award volume of 1946, "Miriam" typifies the early Capote manner. It is a story of isolation, dread, and psychological breakdown told in rich, precisely managed prose. There is little technical or thematic experimentation in "Miriam" and the other Capote stories that appeared regularly in the postwar years. The shadow of Edgar Allan Poe floats over the surface of these stories, and their chief aim often seems to be only to produce a

mild *frisson*. There is, however, enough psychological insight and vividness of characterization to suggest that Capote might be capable of something more than gothicism.

Capote's work has developed beyond gothicism, although sometimes masked by the courting of notoriety which has been a constant in Capote's life. Capote has gone from writing gothic stories of horror and psychological collapse at the beginning of his career to writing delicate tales of magical children and sweetly mad elderly women to writing one of the darkest and most disciplined pieces of nonfiction ever composed, all without altering his insistence on cool professionalism and perfect prose style. Unmarried, he has become the friend and confidant of some of America's most glamorous and socially prominent women, yet now he tantalizes the reading public with fragments of a work that will reveal much that is ugly about the upper reaches of society. More than once, Capote has been declared professionally dead, and each time he has proved himself not merely alive, but alive in ways his detractors had not expected.

Capote's first novel, *Other Voices, Other Rooms* (1948), demonstrated that he was capable of important work, although much of the book's initial notoriety stemmed less from its display of prose virtuosity than from the book's then-shocking homosexual theme and from the photograph of Capote on the dust jacket. The photo, which Capote has since said was chosen more or less by accident and without any intent to shock, showed him reclining on an antique settee, looking as if he were dreamily contemplating some outrage against conventional morality. Many readers assumed that Capote should be identified with the novel's protagonist and that *Other Voices, Other Rooms* constituted a confession of sexual deviance. The resulting publicity helped to make the book a best-seller and made Capote, then only twenty-three, one of the most famous of young writers.

The identification of Capote with his protagonist was, in fact, an accurate way to approach *Other Voices, Other Rooms*, but not in the simplistic way that some readers made the identification in 1948. The central character, Joel Knox, is clearly a projection of the insecurities of Capote's childhood, and the main action of the book concerns a search for a father and then, that search having failed, an attempt to come to terms with a frightening world. Joel's options are progressively closed off, so that finally he can only turn to Randolph, the grotesque transvestite who has presided over his rejection of the "normal" world. The implication is clear that *an* identity, of whatever sexual orientation, is better than *no* identity. Joel's decision to stay with Randolph seemed to many critics a horrifying one, but at least Joel is able to continue to function, in contrast to most of the characters in Capote's short stories of the same period, who usually end in a moral and psychological paralysis that is a symbolic death. Despite the qualified optimism of Joel's resolution, many critics dealt with Capote only in terms of the novel's Southern setting and its general atmosphere of decay and fear. *Time* found the book immature and its theme "calculated to make the flesh crawl." John W. Aldridge assigned Capote to permanent insignificance because of his failure to engage the problems of the real world. In his *After the Lost Generation*, Aldridge dismissed *Other Voices, Other Rooms* in language typical of Capote's detractors. The novel's characters, he said, "belong eternally to the special illusion Capote has created; outside it, they do nothing and are nothing. . . . The real world should, by rights, be part of the illusion; but it is not and cannot be." More than a quarter of a century after *Other Voices, Other Rooms* was

published, Cynthia Ozick, writing in *New Republic*, saw the book as symbolic of an attitude of retreat from reality which ultimately rendered the novel and others like it hollow and worthless.

Other critics, however, defended the novel and Capote's artistic significance. In an *American Scholar* article, Carvel Collins constructed an elaborate reading of *Other Voices, Other Rooms* as a working out of the quest for the Holy Grail, showing that the novel contained elements analogous to those identified with the Grail Quest myths by Jessie L. Weston and others. Frank Baldanza, writing in *Georgia Review*, found in Capote's work elements of Platonic thought. According to Baldanza, the world of *Other Voices, Other Rooms* is not divorced from reality, but rather is "a microcosm, symbolizing man's ordinary spiritual state." Baldanza went on to argue that throughout *Other Voices, Other Rooms* "Platonic elements dominate most of the characterization, the incident, and the style."

Perhaps the most perceptive reader of *Other Voices, Other Rooms* was Ihab Hassan. In *Radical Innocence* Hassan took into account the objections of critics like Aldridge and then argued that *Other Voices, Other Rooms* could best be understood as a "novel-romance" and that it was an attempt "to engage reality without being realistic." The realization that Capote was creating *romance*, in the sense that Hawthorne used that term in his preface to *The House of the Seven Gables*, was of considerable importance in establishing Capote's seriousness and literary worth. Such perception came, however, well after Capote's reputation as a decadent writer was fixed in the public mind, and he did not escape the Southern-gothic typecasting for many years.

A Tree of Night and Other Stories (1949) suggested little likelihood that Capote would break away from the haunted world of his first novel. The collection included "Miriam" and the first prize winner in the 1948 O. Henry awards, "Shut a Final Door." These stories, "The Headless Hawk," "Master Misery," and the title story, all center on psychological terror, and their epiphanies show the realization of character after character that his life is empty, narcissistic, meaningless. These stories are technically accomplished, but like *Other Voices, Other Rooms*, they are conservative in style, with omniscient narration and straightforward chronological order. Although the portrayals of the empty self confronting the fact of its emptiness are vivid, the stories, for the most part, ring the same note repeatedly. Milton Crane, writing in *Saturday Review*, found these dark stories the most promising aspect of Capote's talent, and predicted a successful future for Capote so long as he wrote in this "Grand Guignol" style. Crane dismissed the lighter side of Capote's talent, that revealed by "Jug of Silver" and "Children on Their Birthdays," calling the latter "derivative and pretentious."

Looked at in retrospect, however, it is clear that "Jug of Silver" and "Children on Their Birthdays" signaled an important new direction in Capote's career. The stories are light, at times almost farcical, treatments of children with the power to affect the societies in which they move. The stories are told through first-person narrators and suggest mythic dimensions for their child-protagonists. The sharp division between the haunted, nocturnal world of stories like "Shut a Final Door" and the sunlit world of the essentially comic stories was soon noted by Capote's more perceptive critics, and was articulated by Mark Schorer in his important essay "McCullers and Capote: Basic Patterns." Schorer wrote: "Capote's sensibility moves in two different directions—into the most subjective drama of all, the psychic drama far below the level of reason, on the one hand, and, on the other, into objective social drama, often fanciful. . . ." Different as the two modes are in subject matter and tone, there are links between the nocturnal and sunlit worlds of Capote's early fiction. As Hassan argued in *Radical Innocence*, in both worlds the role of the unconscious is crucial. In the dark stories the unconscious breaks through to reveal the horror of the empty personality, and often manifests itself as a seemingly supernatural phenomenon. In the light stories the unconscious becomes, as Hassan put it, "the source of our uniqueness, our insight and creativity." Throughout the 1950s the majority of Capote's work came from the sunlit side of this fictional dichotomy.

Capote sailed for Europe at almost the same time *A Tree of Night and Other Stories* was published, beginning what was to be a long exile, although an exile broken by returns to the United States. In Europe, Capote continued to write fiction as well as the nonfiction that had begun to attract increasing attention. His travel pieces, the best of them collected as *Local Color* (1950), confirm Capote's engagement with the world of society and demonstrate his eye for the precision of detail and his ear for exactness of phrase. At his best, in pieces like "To Europe" and "A Ride Through Spain," Capote showed that he could take real events and shape them into something like fiction. During these European years Capote also demonstrated his capacity for meeting and charming famous people. Capote has written of his meetings with and impressions of artists as notable and diverse as Colette, Andre Gide, Jean Cocteau, Isak Dinesen, and Cecil Beaton.

Capote settled in Sicily for two years and, as exiles often do, returned imaginatively to his native ground, writing *The Grass Harp* (1951), a novel which draws on his boyhood experiences. The book recounts an idyllic withdrawal from society by a group of gentle rebels and the beneficial effect this Edenic interlude has on all of them. The novel is parablelike in its simplicity, and is held together by its elegiac tone and by the central symbol of the harp of grass which grows in the cemetery and sings what Hassan called a "mythicized" elegy, an affirmation of human continuity. *The Grass Harp* represents a movement away from the subjectivity of *Other Voices, Other Rooms*, as William Nance noted in *The Worlds of Truman Capote*. The withdrawal into the magical, green world of romance cannot be a permanent one, and the characters must return, however regretfully, to the world of society and objective reality. The similarities between *The Grass Harp* and "Jug of Silver" and "Children on Their Birthdays" are numerous: "odd" characters opposing stiffly conventional societies, the mixing of slapstick comedy with pathos, the employment of a first-person narrator.

Capote's European years also marked the beginnings of his work for the theater and films. He wrote a dramatization of *The Grass Harp* which opened on Broadway in March 1952 to mixed reviews; it was not a financial success. A musical adaptation of another O. Henry Award-winning story, "The House of Flowers," opened on Broadway in December 1954. With a book by Capote and music by Harold Arlen, *House of Flowers* pleased some critics and ran for 165 performances, but it was not financially successful. Capote's first important film work, his collaboration with John Huston on *Beat the Devil* (1954), led to a financially unsuccessful film but one which is well-regarded by many critics and has achieved the status of an offbeat classic.

Although Capote spent much time on theatrical and cinematic work in the early 1950s, his thinking centered on the role nonfiction could have in his career and in literature in general. He began evolving a theory about the potential of nonfiction as the art of the future, and in late 1955 he began his first extensive experiment along these lines. He accompanied the touring company of *Porgy and Bess* on its historic Russian tour and reported the goings-on in two long pieces for the *New Yorker*. Combined into a book, *The Muses Are Heard* (1956), these reports show Capote's ability to control the reader's responses to characters and events by carefully selecting and organizing details. Without losing his apparent objectivity, Capote converts real events into something like a comic novel. The same seeming objectivity characterizes Capote's 1957 interview with Marlon Brando, "The Duke in His Domain." This extended interview, an experiment in raising the celebrity profile to the level of art, gave Capote the chance to practice the techniques he believed he would need in order to write a "nonfiction novel."

Following his return to the United States, Capote produced one extended piece of fiction before he began the six-years-long work on *In Cold Blood*. That was *Breakfast at Tiffany's*, published first in *Esquire* (November 1958) and then in book form along with three short stories. Like *The Grass Harp*, "Jug of Silver," and "Children on Their Birthdays," *Breakfast at Tiffany's* employs a first-person narrator and deals with the world of real life, not the haunted isolation of *Other Voices, Other Rooms*. The central character, Holly Golightly, the demi-prostitute who retains a fundamental innocence even as she accepts $50 "powder room change" from her "dates," is one of Capote's most appealing characters. More than one critic compared Holly to Christopher Isherwood's Sally Bowles, and there is no doubt that the two characters have many similarities. Although the novelette ends with Holly's flight into an uncertain and dangerous future, it clearly belongs to the lighter side of Capote's work, for Holly is another catalytic figure, able to affect the society in which she finds herself and to go on being influential in the lives of those she has touched after she is gone. Stylistically, *Breakfast at Tiffany's* is one of Capote's most perfect works, and even so severe a critic as Norman Mailer said (in *Advertisements for Myself*) that he would not change two words of it.

By late 1959 Capote was seriously searching for a subject for his proposed nonfictional novel. On 16 November of that year he read a dozen paragraphs in the *New York Times* about a multiple murder in Kansas. Within a few days he was in Holcomb, Kansas, where a wealthy farmer, Herbert W. Clutter, and three members of his family had been murdered, apparently without motive and for almost no profit. Capote chose this crime as his subject, and for the next six years devoted nearly all his energies to investigating and writing about it. The finished product, published in four long articles in the *New Yorker* in late 1965 and in book form in January 1966, was *In Cold Blood*, a work which earned Capote more money than all his previous works combined and created as much controversy as any

book published in the 1960s. Critics debated endlessly Capote's claim that he had invented a new literary form, questioned the propriety of making millions of dollars from a work that hinged on the deaths of six people (the four Clutters and their subsequently executed murderers), and deplored Capote's apparently endless promotion of his work ("A boy has to hustle his book," Capote said).

Much of the negative response to *In Cold Blood* could be explained by reference to nonliterary matters or to personal malice. Yet beyond such petty considerations serious artistic questions remained. For some, *In Cold Blood* could never achieve the status of literary art because it was a work of fact, not of the imagination. Writing in *The Spectator*, Tony Tanner credited Capote with creating "a stark image of the deep doubleness in American life," yet concluded that *In Cold Blood* suffered by comparison with other works which took their inspiration from reports of actual crimes but developed into true works of the imagination. Diana Trilling treated *In Cold Blood* even more harshly in her *Partisan Review* essay on it. She found Capote's prose "flaccid, often downright inept" and his narrative "overmanipulated." Further, she contended that the objectivity which Capote retained throughout the book served not to produce truth but to protect Capote from the need to take a stand on the issues his work raised. Robert Langbaum's *American Scholar* review found much to praise in *In Cold Blood*, but described it as finally unsuccessful, chiefly because Capote had failed to bring to bear the irony a novelist could attain, and because his portraits of the murdered Clutter family were shallow and incomplete in comparison with those of the murderers, Hickock and Smith. Langbaum concluded that "*In Cold Blood* is first-rate entertainment that at moments gives illusory promise of being something more than that."

The defenders of *In Cold Blood* were as numerous and vocal as its detractors. Rebecca West, writing in *Harper's*, called *In Cold Blood* a "formidable statement about reality" and concluded that it was a "grave and reverend book." In the *New York Review of Books*, F. W. Dupee drew comparisons between *In Cold Blood* and works by Cervantes, Hawthorne, and Henry James. The most extended analysis of *In Cold Blood* and its place in Capote's literary career came in George Garrett's *Hollins Critic* essay "Crime and Punishment in Kansas." The comparison invited by the use of Dostoyevsky's title suggested Garrett's high regard for *In Cold Blood*, which he described as "a frank bid for greatness." Garrett detailed the development of

In Cold Blood out of the tendencies of Capote's earlier work and showed that it contained elements of both the dark and light worlds that commentators like Hassan and Schorer had identified.

The controversy about the nature and literary status of *In Cold Blood* can never be wholly resolved, for it hinges on the definition of art that the individual reader accepts, but there is little doubt that the book creates a vivid portrait of western Kansas and captures the manners and speech of the people who live there. It investigates the criminal world which exists on the edges of normal society and sometimes collides with that society with disastrous results. It probes the workings of the criminal justice system and shows the difficulty that system has in dealing with sociopathic personalities. It explores the irony of the fact that the murder of the Clutters, apparently exactly the sort of crime that a prosecuting attorney can describe as being committed "in cold blood," was essentially a crime of passion, a brief explosion of repressed rage and hate, while the executions of Hickock and Smith were carried out cold-bloodedly after years of legal wrangling. Finally, and perhaps most importantly, *In Cold Blood* contains the detailed portraits of Hickock and Smith which continue to fascinate not only those with literary interests, but students of criminal psychology as well. Seldom has a writer of real ability become so involved with the mind of a murderer as Capote became with the mind of Perry Smith, and the record of Capote's long study of that distorted mind may be unique in modern literature. In a time when homicidal figures seem to hide in every shadow, the insight Capote has provided cannot be dismissed lightly.

Capote rested from his labors for a time after the success of *In Cold Blood* was assured. A televised version of Capote's 1956 short story, the autobiographical "A Christmas Memory," earned critical praise in 1967, as did the film version of *In Cold Blood* that same year. Capote became a familiar figure on the late-night television talk shows, and his views on crime, prisons, and capital punishment, backed by the expertise he had gained in the years of working on *In Cold Blood*, were frequently heard. He published hardcover versions of *A Christmas Memory* and *The Thanksgiving Visitor*, another work drawn from his childhood experiences in the rural South. In 1969 Capote prepared an autobiographical introduction for a reprinting of *Other Voices, Other Rooms;* and he continued to publish nonfiction pieces and to have earlier work produced for television and on the stage. It was not until 1973, with the publication of *The Dogs Bark*, that Capote-

watchers had a chance to see a new selection of Capote's work. Like the earlier *Selected Writings of Truman Capote* (1963), however, *The Dogs Bark* was made up of previously published material, some of it written as early as 1946. The volume gave readers an opportunity to see the range of Capote's interests and his skills in various kinds of nonfictional prose writing, but it offered nothing of a long-promised novel, *Answered Prayers*, except Capote's statements in "Self-Portrait," the final selection in *The Dogs Bark*, that he was working on *Answered Prayers* and that it would be far longer and more technically elaborate than any of his previous fiction.

The first glimpse of *Answered Prayers* finally came in the form of a short story, "Mojave," in *Esquire* (June 1975). Three more excerpts appeared over the next year and a half, and they make it clear that *Answered Prayers* will indeed be a complex work and a controversial one. Using a failed writer named P. B. Jones as his narrative persona, Capote mingles fact and fiction in a complicated and sometimes shocking way. Real people appear as characters, and other characters are clearly thinly disguised portraits of real people. Literary prediction is a dangerous game, and perhaps a useless one, but it seems safe to guess that when (and if) it is completed, *Answered Prayers* will be a major publishing event.

Today, as he approaches his mid-fifties, Capote has achieved financial success beyond the hopes of most serious writers; he enjoys a luxurious life-style, owning a number of residences and surrounding himself with the best in furnishings and art objects. He has not lost his knack for friendship and has gained a reputation as a conversationalist that has led to comparisons with Dr. Johnson. Although he has never commanded as much attention from academic critics as have some commercially less successful writers, Capote and his work have been the subjects of two books and a number of serious scholarly articles; he has always captured the attention of the popular press, and his doings (such as appearing in the film *Murder By Death*) are widely reported. He is a member of the National Institute of Arts and Letters. A handful of his stories are frequently anthologized in college fiction texts, and both *Other Voices, Other Rooms* and *Breakfast at Tiffany's* seem likely to continue to find a readership. *In Cold Blood* remains his best claim to permanence, although *Answered Prayers* may change that. Only if one accepts the claim that *In Cold Blood* is something authentically new and not simply an excellent example of nonfiction writing can Capote be regarded as a technical innovator. In general he has preferred to use available techniques, to adapt them to his own needs, and to polish them to perfection. Capote may have summed up his own standards and status in his description of his friend Humphrey Bogart: ". . .because he understood that discipline was the better part of artistic survival, he lasted, he left his mark."—*Craig M. Goad*

Books:

Other Voices, Other Rooms (New York: Random House, 1948; London: Heinemann, 1949);

A Tree of Night and Other Stories (New York: Random House, 1949; London: Heinemann, 1950);

Local Color (New York: Random House, 1950; London: Heinemann, 1955);

The Grass Harp (New York: Random House, 1951; London: Heinemann, 1952);

The Grass Harp: A Play (New York: Random House, 1952);

The Muses are Heard (New York: Random House, 1956; London: Heinemann, 1957);

Breakfast at Tiffany's (New York: Random House, 1958; London: Hamilton, 1958);

Observations (New York: Simon & Schuster, 1959; London: Weidenfeld & Nicolson, 1959);

Selected Writings (New York: Random House, 1963; London: Hamilton, 1963);

In Cold Blood (New York: Random House, 1965; London: Hamilton, 1966);

A Christmas Memory (New York: Random House, 1966);

The Thanksgiving Visitor (New York: Random House, 1967; London: Hamilton, 1969);

House of Flowers (New York: Random House, 1968);

Trilogy, with Eleanor and Frank Perry (New York: Macmillan, 1969);

The Dogs Bark (New York: Random House, 1973; London: Weidenfeld & Nicolson, 1973).

References:

John W. Aldridge, "Capote and Buechner—The Escape into Otherness," in *After the Lost Generation* (New York: McGraw-Hill, 1951), pp. 194-230;

Frank Baldanza, "Plato in Dixie," *Georgia Review,* 12 (summer 1958): 151-167;

Harvey Breit, "Talk With Truman Capote," *New York Times Book Review,* 24 February 1952, p. 29;

Carvel Collins, "Other Voices," *American Scholar,* 25 (winter 1955-1956): 108-116;

Milton Crane, "Parade of Horribles," *Saturday Review,* 26 February 1949, p. 12;

F. W. Dupee, "Truman Capote's Score," *New York Review of Books,* 6 (February 1966): 3-5;

Chester E. Eisinger, "Truman Capote and the Twisted Self," in his *Fiction of the Forties* (Chicago: University of Chicago Press, 1963), pp. 237-242;

George Garrett, "Crime and Punishment in Kansas: Truman Capote's *In Cold Blood,*" *Hollins Critic,* 3 (February 1966): 1-12;

Craig M. Goad, "Daylight and Darkness, Dream and Delusion: The Works of Truman Capote," *Emporia State Research Studies,* 16 (September 1967): 5-57;

Louise Y. Gossett, "Violence in a Private World: Truman Capote," in her *Violence in Recent Southern Fiction* (Durham: Duke University Press, 1965), pp. 145-148;

Ihab Hassan, "Truman Capote: The Vanishing Image of Narcissus," in *Radical Innocence: Studies in the Contemporary American Novel* (Princeton: Princeton University Press, 1961), pp. 230-258;

Pati Hill, "The Art of Fiction XVII: TC," *Paris Review,* 16 (spring-summer 1957): 34-51;

Jane Howard, "A Six-Year Literary Vigil," *Life,* 7 January 1966, pp. 58-69;

Jack Kroll, "*In Cold Blood* . . . An American Tragedy," *Newsweek,* 24 January 1966, pp. 59-63;

Robert Langbaum, "Capote's Nonfiction Novel," *American Scholar,* 35 (summer 1966): 570-580;

Paul Levine, "Truman Capote: The Revelation of the Broken Image," *Virginia Quarterly Review,* 34 (autumn 1958): 600-617;

Barbara Long, "In Cold Comfort," *Esquire,* 65 (June 1966): 124, 126, 128, 171-173, 178-181;

Marvin E. Mengeling, "*Other Voices, Other Rooms*: Oedipus Between the Covers," *American Imago,* 19 (winter 1962): 361-374;

William L. Nance, *The Worlds of Truman Capote* (New York: Stein & Day, 1970);

Eric Norden, "*Playboy* Interview: Truman Capote," *Playboy,* 15 (March 1968): 51-62, 160-170;

Cynthia Ozick, "Reconsideration—Truman Capote," *New Republic,* 27 January 1973, pp. 31-34;

J. Douglas Perry, Jr., "Gothic as Vortex: The Form of Horror in Capote, Faulkner, and Styron," *Modern Fiction Studies,* 19 (summer 1973): 153-167;

Donald Pizer, "Documentary Narrative as Art: William Manchester and Truman Capote," *Journal of Modern Literature*, 2 (September 1971): 105-118;

George Plimpton, "The Story Behind a Nonfiction Novel," *New York Times Book Review*, 16 January 1966, pp. 2-3, 38-43;

Mark Schorer, "McCullers and Capote: Basic Patterns," in *The Creative Present*, eds. Nona Balakian and Charles Simmons (Garden City: Doubleday, 1963), pp. 83-107;

"Spare the Laurels," *Time*, 26 January 1948, p. 102;

Tony Tanner, "Death in Kansas," *The Spectator*, 18 March 1966, pp. 331-332;

Phillip K. Tompkins, "In Cold Fact," *Esquire*, 65 (June 1966): 125, 127, 166-168, 170-171;

Diana Trilling, "Capote's Crime and Punishment," *Partisan Review*, 33 (spring 1966): 252-259;

Truman Capote's "In Cold Blood": A Critical Handbook, ed. Irving Malin (Belmont, Cal.: Wadsworth, 1968);

David L. Vanderwerken, "Truman Capote: 1943-68— A Critical Bibliography," *Bulletin of Bibliography*, 27 (July-September 1970): 57-60, 71;

Richard J. Wall and Carl L. Craycraft, "A Checklist of Works About Truman Capote," *Bulletin of the New York Public Library*, 71 (March 1967): 165-172;

Rebecca West, "A Grave and Reverend Book," *Harper's*, 232 (February 1966): 108, 110, 112-114.

Manuscripts:

The Library of Congress has manuscripts and typescripts of *Other Voices, Other Rooms, In Cold Blood*, the manuscript of *Breakfast at Tiffany's*, a number of Capote's journals, and manuscripts of various unpublished and published short fiction.

John Cheever

Robert A. Morace
Daemen College

BIRTH: Quincy, Massachusetts, 27 May 1912.

EDUCATION: Thayer Academy, South Braintree, Massachusetts (expelled at 17).

MARRIAGE: 22 March 1941 to Mary Winternitz; children: Susan, Benjamin Hale, Federico.

AWARDS: O. Henry Award, 1941, for "I'm Going to Asia"; O. Henry Award, 1951, for "The Pot of Gold"; Guggenheim Fellowship, 1951; Benjamin Franklin Award, 1954, for "The Five-Forty-Eight"; O. Henry Award, 1956, for "The Country Husband"; National Institute of Arts and Letters grant, 1956; National Book Award, 1958, for *The Wapshot Chronicle*; O. Henry Award, 1964, for "The Embarkment for Cythera"; American Academy of Arts and Letters Howells Medal, 1965, for *The Wapshot Scandal*.

MAJOR WORKS: *The Way Some People Live* (New York: Random House, 1943); *The Enormous Radio and Other Stories* (New York: Funk & Wagnalls, 1953; London: Gollancz, 1953); *The Wapshot Chronicle* (New York: Harper & Row, 1957; London: Gollancz, 1957); *The Housebreaker of Shady Hill and Other Stories* (New York: Harper & Row, 1958; London: Gollancz, 1959); *Some People, Places, and Things That Will Not Appear in My Next Novel* (New York: Harper & Row, 1961; London: Gollancz, 1961); *The Wapshot Scandal* (New York: Harper & Row, 1964; London: Gollancz, 1964); *The Brigadier and the Golf Widow* (New York: Harper & Row, 1964; London: Gollancz, 1965); *Bullet Park* (New York: Knopf, 1969; London: Cape, 1969); *The World of Apples* (New York: Knopf, 1973; London: Cape, 1974); *Falconer* (New York: Knopf, 1977).

Although some critics have dismissed Cheever as a writer of the "*New Yorker* school," a chronicler of suburbia, or a clever satirist, his impressive achievements in both the short story and the novel belie these claims and attest to his importance in American letters. Cheever, unlike many contemporary American writers, is neither stylistically flamboyant nor philosophically pessimistic. Although he has experimented with various narrative techniques, his art is essentially that of the storyteller, and while he clearly recognizes those aspects of modern life which might lead to pessimism, his comic vision remains basically optimistic. His characters all face a similar problem: how to live in a world which, in spite of its middle-class comforts

Jill Krementz

and assurances, suddenly appears inhospitable, even dangerous. Many of his characters go down in defeat, usually by their own hand. Those who survive, in mind as well as body, discover the personal and social virtue of compromise. Having learned of their own and their world's limitations, they can, paradoxically, learn to celebrate the wonder and possibility of life.

John Cheever, the second son of Frederick and Mary Liley Cheever, was born in Quincy, Massachusetts, on 27 May 1912 and grew up during what he has called "the Athenian twilight" of New England culture. His father, a self-made man, rose to become owner of a Lynn shoe factory only to lose his business in the 1929 stock market crash. His mother used the loss to assert her own independence, a decision which had a disastrous effect on her husband who, with his pride irreparably damaged, attempted suicide. Cheever was deeply disturbed by the strained family relationship from which he escaped when he was seventeen.

His story-telling gift, which his parents did little to encourage, evidenced itself early. At eight he improvised tales with which to entertain his classmates and two years later began to commit his stories to paper. His formal education ended at seventeen when Cheever, having gotten behind in his studies, was dismissed from Thayer Academy for smoking. The next year his first published work, "Expelled," appeared in *New Republic*. Although Cheever has referred to the story slightingly as "the reminiscences of a sorehead," his story is neither plaintive nor amateurish and in many ways anticipates the style that has since become Cheever's hallmark. The opening paragraph lures the reader into a story which, like many of the later works, is a series of sketches rather than a linear narrative. The narrator, who remains detached even while recounting his own expulsion, focuses on apparently disparate events which, taken together, create a single impression of what life at a prep school is like. Thematically, "Expelled" also anticipates Cheever's later work. There is the conflict between the decorum required by the school and the fervent longing for life felt by the individual. Cheever symbolizes this conflict in the school's decision to build a tower—an outward and visible sign—rather than to use the money to buy books for the library. The narrator is the first in a long line of displaced persons who make up Cheever's fiction. The displaced narrator can, at least temporarily, find his place in nature if not in society, but since he cannot live both completely and alone, he must return to the society which has cast him off and which he has just satirized.

Following his dismissal from Thayer, Cheever and his older brother Fred went to Boston and then Germany, where they spent the last of their money on a walking tour. Once back in the United States Cheever took up residence in New York City, where he lived during most of the 1930s, part of the time subsisting on bread and buttermilk in a squalid room on Hudson Street. Occasionally he visited the Yaddo writers' colony at Saratoga Springs, New York, where he did all-purpose help to pay for his board. Although there was little financial reward for him during this period, Cheever did gain the friendships of John Dos Passos, E. E. Cummings, James Agee, Paul Goodman, and James Farrell, and, more importantly, he began his relationship with the *New Yorker* magazine.

On 22 March 1941 Cheever married Mary Winternitz, who was then working for his literary agent, Maxim Lieber. Two years later, Cheever, halfway through his four-year army hitch, had his first book published. The thirty stories collected in *The Way Some People Live* (1943) had originally appeared in the *New Yorker, Story, Yale Review, Harper's Bazaar*, and *Read*. Most are either sketches or highly compressed short stories. The longer ones, such as "Of Love: A Testimony" or "The Brothers," are of interest solely as Cheever's earliest attempts at writing stories structured on a prose equivalent of incremental repetition, a form he would later perfect in "The Swimmer." The "people" whose ways of living are sketched in this collection are, except for their socioeconomic class, essentially the same Upper-Eastside and suburban residents who are found in the later fiction: those who live on the memory of past greatness in order to escape the present (the fallen aristocrats); those who try to relive their youth in order to deny their mortality (the athletes and adulterers); those who for so long have repressed their desires that their attempts to break out of the lonely world they have made for themselves are pathetically futile; those whose lives have come to nothing and who absurdly cling to a material object or to the dream of material wealth to assuage their feelings of emptiness; and those who have been jilted either by a lover or by their dreams and look for compensation in self-pity and drinking. Only a few of the stories are noteworthy—"The Cat," for example, or "Forever Hold Your Peace." The stories dealing with the war and based on Cheever's experiences as a recruit are the collection's weakest pieces. Despite the volume's shortcomings, reviewers reacted to it favorably, sensing that here was something more than just a good first book. The most perceptive was Struthers Burt, who tempered his praise with a warning: to succeed, Cheever must avoid "a hardening into an especial style that might become an affectation, and a deliberate casualness and simplicity that might become the same." Later critics have continued to debate these very points, and Cheever's literary stature depends, to some extent, on how successful he has been in avoiding these pitfalls.

Cheever's second collection, *The Enormous Radio and Other Stories* (1953), is comprised of fourteen stories, all of which had originally appeared in the *New Yorker*. Most are set in New York City, some in the kind of Sutton Place apartment house where the Cheevers lived after the war. Many of the stories deal with naifs who have arrived in the city with boundless optimism and little else. The stories are all well executed, but invariably follow the same formula and infrequently rise above the sentimental irony of an O. Henry story or the *Life With Father* television scripts Cheever was then writing. Fortunately, not all of the fourteen can be dismissed as simply the products of "a clever short-story manufacturer." In "Torch Song," for example, Jack Lorey discovers that it is not Joan Harris who has been victimized by her string of physically and spiritually infirm lovers but quite the other way around; she has used them to satisfy her bizarre vampirish craving for eternal youth. Realizing this saves Jack from falling prey to her deadly love, but whether it will also save Jack from himself—by this time he has become an alcoholic and has been twice divorced—is left unresolved.

The finest story in the collection, "The Enormous Radio," is a nearly flawless working out of one of Cheever's most prevalent themes: that beneath the surface of quotidian human life is a grotesque and destructive element that decorum (society's chief defense) can usually mask but cannot fully control. Jim and Irene Westcott are the average American couple, temperate in all things except their above-average fondness for music—that is to say, for harmony and order. But the new radio Jim buys brings disharmony rather than pleasure into their lives. Irene is dismayed by all its knobs and switches and repulsed by its ugly gumwood cabinet; when she turns it on, the radio plays not music but the cacophonous sounds of her neighbors' hidden lives. What she hears appalls her, but fascinates her too. Her hidden life is her voyeurism which she masks beneath a priggish saintliness. She soon fears that her own secret sins will become known to her neighbors. She becomes so apprehensive of the radio's power to know and tell all that she finally drives her husband to an angry outburst in which he does what she had feared the radio would do—expose her for what she is. Her sudden knowledge of the evil in the world—the world, that is, of her apartment house—causes her to adopt a false Manichean position and to then commit the worst of sins: to break, in Nathaniel Hawthorne's phrase, "the electric chain of humanity." Although the radio is described so as to suggest evil, particularly the evil of modern technology, the association between the radio and evil is all in Irene's Puritan mind. Evil, in Cheever's world, is a distinctly human trait.

Cheever continued to explore the relationship between the individual and his society in the eight stories collected in *The Housebreaker of Shady Hill* (1958). Although the characters are no longer the city dwellers of *The Enormous Radio* but instead the residents of Shady Hill (an affluent suburb modeled on Cheever's own experiences in the suburbs of New York City), they still are insecure and quietly desperate despite their outward conformity to Shady Hill's code or veneer of respectability. More pronounced in these stories is Cheever's comedy—his witty and ironic portrayal of the individual and the community—and his belief that the individual who separates himself from his family and community must learn to reintegrate himself in the group. As Cheever said shortly after the collection appeared, "There's been too much criticism of the middle-class way of life. Life can be as good and rich there as any place else. I am not out to be a social critic, however, nor a defender of suburbia." As in "The Enormous Radio," Cheever first explodes the society's hypocrisy and then turns on the person who, like Irene Westcott, loses his own humanity when he turns away from his fellow men.

The fears which plague these suburbanites are certainly real enough—unfaithful spouses, manic lovers, lost children, lost jobs—and because they are real, Cheever treats his suffering characters with compassion. Yet the ways in which they try to resolve their problems are so extreme and absurd as to force the reader to question, if not the validity of their plaints, then at least the degree to which they allow themselves to suffer. In the title story, Johnny Hake tells how after losing his job he turned to burgling his neighbors, an act which transforms Hake into a thief and his world into a world of thieves. Francis Weed (whose name suggests his position as an outsider) in "The Country Husband" discovers that neither his neighbors nor his family have any interest in his narrow escape from death in a plane wreck. Out of spite and longing he turns from all of them and falls in love with his children's babysitter.

Hake, Weed, and the husband in "The Trouble with Marcie Flint" are driven by their fantasies of self-realization into escaping their plush, suburban cul-de-sacs. Not until they realize that their fantasies are narcissistic and therefore self-destructive can they return, rejuvenated, triumphant, yet paradoxically humbled, to their family obligations.

For some, the realization does not come so easily. Charlie Blake in "The Five-Forty-Eight" is humbled at the point of a gun, not in a moment of vision. In "O Youth and Beauty!" (which anticipates "The Swimmer" and echoes Hemingway's "The Short Happy Life of Francis Macomber"), Cash Bentley experiences no moment of regenerative humiliation. His race leads not to a goal that lies ahead, but rather to one that is ironically already behind in his lost youth, and it ends when his wife fires the starter's pistol, accidentally shooting him "in midair." The desperation which drives Cash Bentley underlies life in Shady Hill, and it is precisely this underlying desperation that the community pretends does not exist. Just before the shooting, Cash's wife had been "upstairs, cutting out of a current copy of *Life* those scenes of mayhem, disaster, and violent death that she felt might corrupt her children. She always did this."

Only two of the eight stories, "The Sorrows of Gin" and "The Worm in the Apple," suffer from the sentimentality that marred the earlier collections. Otherwise *The Housebreaker of Shady Hill* evidences a significant advance in Cheever's art. Language and structure are more precise; the approaches to the material more flexible, less "slick"; the irony less pat, less a matter of formula than of vision. Moreover, Cheever has created a well-defined mythic world within which his characters—frustrated housewives and grotesques in gray flannel suits—act out the drama of American middle-class life.

Two changes occurred during the mid-1950s which radically affected Cheever's work. The decade had begun, so Cheever told fellow writer Herbert Gold, full of promise, but halfway through it, "something went terribly wrong . . . the forceful absurdities of life today find me unprepared." In order to make sense of a world that suddenly appeared absurd, Cheever began to turn his attention from the short story to the novel. "I'm still interested in the short story form," he said in 1958. "Certain situations lend themselves only to the short story. But generally it's a better form for young writers, who are more intense, whose perceptions are more fragmentary." When his first novel, *The Wapshot Chronicle* (1957), appeared, reviewers objected to the

book's episodic structure and bewildering number of characters and settings—evidence, they felt, of a short story writer's inability to adapt himself to the distinctive form of the novel. To some extent the plotlessness is intentional: "I don't work with plot. I work with intuition, apprehension, dreams, concepts." Furthermore, Cheever feels that plot is incompatible with moral conviction and masks the chaotic nature of contemporary life.

Based upon the author's own "profoundly troubled adolescence" and especially "the harm my mother's working did to my father's self-esteem," *The Wapshot Chronicle* is autobiographical but never simply a personal memoir or confession. Part One records the breakdown of the Wapshot family and focuses on the displacement and consequent loss of self-esteem suffered by the father, Leander, at the hands of his eccentric sister Honora and his strong-willed wife Sarah. Paralleling this is the larger breakdown of the old traditions and culture of St. Botolphs (Cheever's boyhood home of Quincy) before the forces of the modern world. Parts Two and Three trace the comic misadventures of Leander's sons, Moses (Cheever's brother Fred) and the "ministerial" Coverly (Cheever himself), who discover how poorly the moribund and provincial St. Botolphs has prepared them for survival in Washington and New York. In Part Four, Moses and Coverly, scarred but alive, have themselves brought forth sons, thereby ensuring the continuance of the Wapshot line.

The novel's central figure is Leander, whose triumph is the triumph of the imagination's power to transform the world. Honora and Sarah, who represent the sexless force of decorum, speak through wills and painted signs. Leander, who represents the regenerative force of the imagination and of life itself, speaks through his journal. As Cheever has said of his own journal-keeping (a family tradition), it is a way "to preserve the keenness of small daily sensations." The journal enables Leander to triumph over the loss of his self-esteem and the descent into self-pity that afflicts so many of Cheever's characters. It also transforms him into a writer, and writing is, Cheever has said, "the only coherent expression of man's struggle to be illustrious," an attempt on the writer's part "to make sense of [his] life." Leander dies, but his written words continue to turn up. At the novel's end, Coverly discovers his father's "Advice to my sons" in a copy of Shakespeare: "Bathe in cold water every morning. Painful but exhilarating. . . . Stand up straight. Admire the world. Relish the love of a gentle woman. Trust in the Lord."

The Wapshot Chronicle fully embodies Cheever's comic vision. That vision is optimistic but not, at least in this book, sentimental. Nor is *The Wapshot Chronicle* nostalgic in the pejorative sense of the word; as Cheever defines it, nostalgia means "Not regret for the past, but a keen sense of the present, saying, How splendid it was! But spoken without regret." St. Botolphs is part of "an irrecapturable past"; the images of decay in the opening chapters and Leander's death make clear that it is a world in ruins, a world that in fact never was an Eden: "if we accept the quaintness of St. Botolphs we must also accept the fact that it was a country of spite fences and internecine quarrels...." Cheever satirizes man's foibles and his tendency to wallow in his limitations; he also suggests the possibility of man's transcending his bounds, as Leander does, through a ritual celebration of life.

After completing *The Wapshot Chronicle*, Cheever used the money he had received as winner of a National Institute of Arts and Letters grant in 1956 to help finance a year-long trip to Italy. There he remained serenely unaware of how his first novel was being reviewed. Despite those reviews which sharply criticized the book's flawed structure, *The Wapshot Chronicle* won the National Book Award in 1958, thereby further establishing Cheever's place in American letters.

Prior to *The Wapshot Chronicle*, Cheever had done little experimenting with narrative points of view in his stories. Even the most successful of these, Johnny Hake's monologue in "The Housebreaker of Shady Hill," is hardly a daring innovation. Cheever became much more inventive in his first novel, where the third person narrative is interrupted by direct assaults upon the reader ("You come, as Moses did ..." and "Or you wake—like Coverly ...") and entire chapters comprised of Leander's journal entries. Cheever continued to experiment in his next book, *Some People, Places, and Things That Will Not Appear in My Next Novel* (1961). The collection's eight stories (there is also one "miscellany") are evenly divided between first and third person narration, and in one the author interrupts the story told by an American "Boy in Rome" to insert his own aside: "But I am not a boy in Rome but a grown man in the old prison and river town of Ossining...." Throughout the collection, the reader can sense Cheever's uncertainty with his methods and characters. Even in the best story, "The Death of Justina," the narrator, an advertising writer, takes time out from writing copy and arranging for the burial of his wife's cousin to deliver this line for his author: "Fiction is art and art is the triumph over

chaos (no less) and we can accomplish this only by the most vigilant exercise of choice, but in a world that changes more swiftly than we can perceive there is always the danger that our powers of selection will be mistaken and that the vision we serve will come to nothing."

For Cheever there were two formidable problems of selection to confront and resolve. One involves the exorcising of old characters and situations in order to move on to fresh ground. In "The Death of Justina," for example, Moses and Justina are partly drawn from *The Wapshot Chronicle* and the situation is simply a variation of the Remsden Park scenes in the book. On the other hand, the three stories set in Italy evidence a willingness to work with new material. The more complex problem concerns the conflict between Cheever's comic vision, which is often criticized as facile and middle-class in its values, and the naysaying, anti-bourgeois role expected of the serious contemporary American writer. Cheever fictionalized his dilemma in "The Golden Age." The main character, the writer of a popular situation comedy, "The Best Family," is so ashamed of his success that he flees to Italy "because he wants to lead a more illustrious life." His escape to Italy and withdrawal to a lonely castle tower are in vain. The natives watch the debut of his show on Italian television and love it; the Mayor tells him, "Oh, we thought, *Signore*, that you were merely a poet." Cheever's intention is "to celebrate a world that lies spread out around us like a bewildering and stupendous dream," and to accomplish this end he lists "A Miscellany of Characters That Will Not Appear" in his work: "The pretty girl at the Princeton-Dartmouth rugby game"; "all parts for Marlon Brando"; "All scornful descriptions of American landscapes ... for these are not, as they might appear to be, the ruins of our civilization but are the temporary encampments and outposts of the civilization that we—you and I— shall build"; "explicit scenes of sexual commerce"; "all lushes"; "all those homosexuals who have taken such a dominating position in recent fiction." What he proposes, in short, is nothing less than a complete break with that contemporary American fiction which thrives on despair and estrangement.

Cheever spent four difficult years in the writing of his second novel, *The Wapshot Scandal* (1964), a rather surprising fact considering the similarity between this and his first novel. Point of view remains much the same, only slightly more intimate in the sequel, especially in the Thackerayan second chapter. The four parts of the *Chronicle* are compressed into three parts in the *Scandal*, which still retains a loosely jointed, three-stranded narrative structure: Honora's ineffectual escape to Italy in order to avoid prosecution for income tax evasion; Coverly and Betsey's life in Talifer, a homogeneous middle-class community; and Moses and Melissa's life in Proxmire Manor, a well-to-do suburb. Fewer characters and settings (as compared to the *Chronicle*), the frame structure of Christmas past and Christmas present, and the thematic movement tracing Honora's and Coverly's returns to St. Botolphs work together to unify the diffuse elements of *The Wapshot Scandal*. The essential difference between the two Wapshot novels is this: while both celebrate life, the sequel portrays a world in which it has become harder to see that there is anything worth celebrating. Even Coverly has turned pessimistic; when he imagines that his father's ghost has returned to St. Botolphs, he can only wonder, "Father, Father, why have you come back." The burden of the novel is to prove to Coverly and the reader that it is possible to withstand the world's poisons and to withstand one's own poisons as well. The individual can survive, even if he cannot prevail, and he can celebrate his salvation with others.

Missiles, bombs, mad scientists, and pederasts make the modern world—the world of Talifer and Proxmire Manor—a dangerous place, but no more dangerous than the ocean where previous generations of Wapshot men were tested. Coverly survives, but Moses, broken by his wife's infidelity, turns in shame to alcohol and aimless wandering. Melissa, his wife, is the Emma Bovary of Proxmire Manor. She abandons her husband for a narcissistic teenager who in turn abandons her to drink and obscene promiscuity. Honora, one of the innocents abroad, finally returns to St. Botolphs and promptly drinks herself to death. Coverly's survival, which is both physical and spiritual, derives from the three elements of his character: his father's lusty and irrepressible vitality, his aunt's sense of decorum, and his own ability to adapt himself to the modern world. Working as a "taper," Coverly translates human language into computer language. Rather than deadening his sense of beauty as such work might do, Coverly's taping is turned to aesthetic advantage: he feeds Shelley's poetry into a computer and out come new poems. Similarly, Coverly translates his "scandalous" times and his own survival as a man, a husband, a father, a Wapshot, into a Christmas dinner celebration for himself, his family, and his aunt's eight blind guests, "the raw material of human kindness."

The Brigadier and the Golf Widow (1964), Cheever's fifth short story collection, was issued shortly after *The Wapshot Scandal*. Although it lacks the unity of *The Housebreaker of Shady Hill*, it displays a broader thematic range, greater inventiveness of style, and the perfection of Cheever's ability to invest even the most implausible, cartoon-like situation with the semblance of everyday life. In general, the collection's fourteen stories explore the contrast which exists in upper-middle-class America between the visible signs of economic security and the repressed frustrations and anxieties deriving from emotional insecurity. As Cheever has noted, "People actually sidestep the pain of death and despair by the thought of purchasing things." In these stories, Cheever forces his readers to confront "death and despair" as they observe his characters either "sidestep" that painful situation or boldly and sometimes comically meet it head on. "The Ocean," a Poe-like monologue by a mad narrator, begins, "I am keeping this journal because I believe myself to be in some danger and because I have no other way of recording my fears. I cannot report them to the police, as you will see, and I cannot confide in my friends. The losses I have suffered in self-esteem, reasonableness, and clarity are conspicuous, but there is always some painful ambiguity about who is to blame. I might be [tempted] to blame myself." In the title story, a fallout shelter symbolizes the individual's desire for physical safety in a hostile world and his desire for material proof of his economic status in an equally hostile world of downward and upward mobility. Moreover, the fallout shelter also symbolizes something the characters can feel but not understand—the frantic search for emotional security that was masked by the outwardly free-and-easy Eisenhower years. Not until a character can exorcise the fear, can he begin to live the kind of life Cheever advocates. Mrs. Pastern does this when she leaves her husband and his fallout shelter. Although there is more madness and desperation in this collection than in Cheever's previous two books, Cheever holds steadfastly to his comic vision. "The plight of man alone," he writes in "Marito in Citta," is "essentially a comic situation such as getting tangled up in a trout line."

"Clementina," one of this volume's two best stories, presents the familiar Cheever theme of the displaced person and the naif seduced by the city, but here they are given a new twist. Clementina, an Italian servant, readily adapts to American ways and eventually becomes thoroughly Americanized in her appearance. Although she is superstitious, she is not so naive as her American employer, whose ideas concerning marriage she finds boyish. His marriage, based on love, ends in divorce, while hers, to a much older man and based on practical need, is successful. Cheever's own views on marriage are neither those of the romantic employer nor those of the fatalistic Clementina, who believes that wonders are no more. When an interviewer asked Cheever for "an example of a preposterous lie that tells a great deal about life," he responded, "the vows of Holy Matrimony." The human relationship between a married couple is an entirely different matter, and Cheever has called his own marriage "a splendid example of the richness and diversity of human nature."

The collection's best story is "The Swimmer." Cheever began with the myth of Narcissus and then compiled 150 pages of notes for a story that is only fifteen pages long. Contemplating the "imponderables" made this "a terribly difficult story to write." Structurally it is his finest achievement. The story follows Neddy Merrill on his eight-mile pool-to-pool swim across Westchester. His decision to make the swim is impulsive, and the first half of the trip moves along rapidly: four miles in four pages. Then the pace becomes gradually slower, the pools farther apart, and Neddy's swimming less exhilarating, more compulsive. The final four miles take up eleven pages of text. Contemplation replaces motion, and every time Neddy climbs out of a pool the ordeal becomes greater both for him and for the reader who already knows what Neddy refuses to face: that his life is as empty as the boarded-up house he returns to at the end of his swim. The image of the athlete who returns to his past, who tries to recapture his lost youth, recurs throughout Cheever's fiction. As Cheever has recently said, "The point is to finish and go on to the next thing. I also feel, not as strongly as I used to, that if I looked over my shoulder I would die." Cheever was pleased with "The Swimmer," though not with the film version made by Frank and Eleanor Perry in 1968. His belief that the fiction writer must "avoid those experiences which can be handled most expertly on film," undoubtedly accounts for some of his dissatisfaction with the Perrys' work and perhaps also explains why although film rights for *The Housebreaker of Shady Hill* and the Wapshot novels were sold, no films were produced.

After spending six weeks in Russia in 1964 as part of a cultural exchange program, Cheever returned to his home in Ossining. In 1965 the American Academy of Arts and Letters awarded him the Howells Medal for *The Wapshot Scandal*, and four years later his third novel was published. *Bullet Park* (1969) pleased him greatly: ". . . I'd done precisely what I'd wanted: a cast of three characters, a simple and resonant prose style and a scene where a

man saves his beloved son from death by fire." The pleasure ended when Benjamin DeMott's review appeared in the 27 April 1969 issue of the *New York Times Book Review* and, in Cheever's estimation, turned the critical tide against his novel. DeMott cited poor characterization, "lax composition," and "perfunctoriness" among its weaknesses; more importantly, it was "broken-backed" and evidenced "the problem of story style vs. novel style."

Bullet Park does, at first glance, seem to be little more than two stories glued together at the end. Part One chronicles several weeks in the life of Eliot Nailles, who like his creator is a suburbanite, loves his dog and cutting wood with a chainsaw, is a writer (of mouthwash advertisements), belongs to a New York club, and has visited Italy. What Nailles gradually discovers is that he has lost control over his life. His mother has had a stroke. Neighbors come in the night to dump garbage on his property. His wife Nellie, "the raw material for a nightclub act" about the suburban housewife, seems to him no more human than a cartoon character. His son Tony is failing at school and is dropped from the football team (he is "not indispensable"). When Tony brings home the older woman he has just spent the night with, Nailles construes this as a threat to his sexual supremacy. Then Tony tells his father that he does not want to grow up in Nailles's seemingly one-dimensional image, which so provokes Nailles that he attacks his son with a golf club, precipitating Tony's Bartleby-like withdrawal from life. Outside of his home, Nailles fares no better. While waiting for a train, a man is sucked under an express and killed; the body is not found and the only evidence of his having lived at all is a shoe. Commuting to work becomes an ordeal for Nailles who begins to depend on drugs as much as the railroad to get him from Bullet Park to Manhattan. Tony is finally cured—by a guru, not drugs or modern science—and Part One ends on a faintly hopeful note.

Part Two traces the life of Paul Hammer, the illegitimate son of a wealthy, irresponsible capitalist and his secretary, a kleptomaniac from Indiana. Alone in the world, Hammer begins searching for a room with yellow walls where, he believes, his "illustrious" life will begin. After much melancholy drinking and wandering, Hammer gets his room, but not his dream. This loss, coupled with his marriage to an emasculating wife, drives Hammer insane. A combination of envy and righteousness motivates Hammer to follow the messianic plan of his virulently anti-American, expatriate mother: move to a typical American suburb, lead an inconspicuous life, find a man who is "a good example of a life lived without any genuine emotion or value" and then "crucify him," for "nothing less than a crucifixion will wake that world."

Hammer and Nailles are, Cheever has said, simply "two men with their own risks," not "psychiatric or social metaphors" or, as some reviewers have thought, allegorical personifications of good and evil. The risks they run form what Cheever has called the "perilous moral journey" that every American must face. Unlike Coverly Wapshot, Hammer and Nailles do not survive. The obsessive and extreme views they adopt in order to make sense of their lives ultimately blind them to the very reality they purport to see. Obsessions manifest themselves in action, but Cheever's concern is more with character. The strength of *Bullet Park* lies in the successful adaptation of style to character in each of its three parts. Part One is related in the third person, but the point of view is close to that of Nailles, and the confusing chronology of this section accurately reflects the confused state of Nailles's mind as he attempts to order the chaos his life has become. Part Two, related by Hammer, is a monologue in which a madman rationally recounts all of the events which led to his crime. In Part Three, the point of view alternates between Hammer and Nailles, remaining with the latter during and after the climactic scene in which Nailles—with some help from the guru and his chainsaw—saves Tony from a fire. Just before this, Nailles has resumed his sexual relationship with Nellie, an indication that he is beginning to come out of his drugged state. When he rescues his son, he is again asserting the value of life over the power of death; he saves Tony from Hammer and himself from the death-in-life state into which he has fallen. Unfortunately, his desire to celebrate life is not as strong as his desire to avoid whatever is unpleasant. "Nailles thought of pain and suffering as a principality, lying somewhere beyond the legitimate borders of western Europe," a not unreasonable idea considering the American addiction to pain-killers and the Manichean mentality fostered in the Cold War. Although Tony is saved, Hammer's cry in the suburban wilderness goes unheeded, and Hammer himself is hidden away in a state hospital. "Tony went back to school on Monday and Nailles—drugged—went off to work and everything was as wonderful, wonderful, wonderful, wonderful as it had been." This sentence, the final one in the novel, echoes the last paragraph of Part One, thus underscoring the ironic fact that perhaps not even a crucifixion will awaken Bullet Park, which prefers the soporific blandishments of Lawrence Welk ("wonderful, wonderful") to the

risks and the true wonder of life. All of Cheever's books have been critical of our modern society, but *Bullet Park*, which Wilfrid Sheed has called "a brutal vivisection of American life," is by far the most caustic and the least optimistic.

The watershed in Cheever's career is 1964, the year *The Brigadier and the Golf Widow* and *The Wapshot Scandal* appeared and, based on the few stories he has published since then, the year he completed the shift from short story writer to novelist. His next novel, *Bullet Park*, was published in 1969, but his next collection of stories did not appear for nearly a decade and even then included several pre-1964 pieces. *The World of Apples* (1973) still evidences Cheever's mastery of the short story and his continuing interest in narrative experimentation. "The Jewels of the Cabots," for example, is told as if by free association, and in another story the narrator is the belly of Lawrence Farnsworth. Although this last may seem typical of the archness which characterizes contemporary American fiction, *The World of Apples* is quite distinct from most recent work by other American writers. It is, John Wain has explained, "a book by a gifted and established writer which doesn't, for once, seem to come out of negativism, alienation, despair of the human condition and frantic self-gratification. . . ." In one story, Cheever goes so far as to explicitly disassociate himself from the kind of fiction Wain describes. In another, "Mene, Mene, Tekel, Upharsin," an American returning home after a long stay in Europe discovers this odd reversal: lavatory walls scribbled over with long, floridly written stories and book racks filled with scatological and pornographic writings.

The protagonist in the title story, Asa Bascomb, is a New England poet living in Italy who suddenly finds it impossible to write anything but obscene limericks, which he burns. Only after a Christian pilgrimage and a pagan immersion in a cold forest pool is he able to begin his "long poem on the inalienable dignity of light and air that, while it would not get the Nobel Prize, would grace the last months of his life." Celebrating life frees Bascomb from his brief but artistically deadly nightmare vision of the world as an obscenity. Equally important, it frees him from the death-fear which Americans commonly ascribe to their writers who, once they have accepted the fear, find their "esteem," their "usefulness," and finally their lives destroyed.

Few of the characters in these stories are as fortunate as Asa Bascomb. Many of them are the grotesques we expect to find in Cheever's fiction: a cigar-smoking aunt who calls herself Percy; or

"Artemis, the Honest Well Digger," whose father had chosen his name thinking it referred to artesian wells and whose search for pure water is as futile as his "looking for a girl as pure and fresh as the girl on the oleomargarine package." Their freakishness is matched by the absurdity of the situations they face and the extremes to which they go in order to make sense of their seemingly inexplicable worlds. The husband in "The Fourth Alarm" sees his wife metamorphose from lover to mother to dowdy social studies teacher to actress in a nude play; he takes to early morning gin-drinking. Other characters resort to eccentric behavior, a veneer of social respectability, imaginary lovers, even murder and the application of Euclidean geometry to human emotions. For them, as for Hammer and Nailles, there is no redemption and no celebration as there is for Coverly Wapshot and Asa Bascomb.

The antecedents for Cheever's most recent book, the highly acclaimed novel *Falconer* (1977), reach far back into his life and writings: his parents, his ambivalent relationship with his brother Fred whose murder he once contemplated, *The Wapshot Chronicle*, "The Cat," and his stories about derelict fathers. Cheever has said that *Falconer* "was not written out of a singular experience" but, rather, represents "the sum of my living." The novel's immediate foreground begins with the two years Cheever spent teaching writing at Sing Sing prison in the early 1970s. Having gone there as a "do-gooder," he soon became depressed by what he saw. He continued his teaching, however, even during the Attica riot in September 1971 ("It was very exciting. When you went in you weren't always sure you were going to get out") until a series of heart attacks forced him to stop. After a brief convalescence, he returned to a task he has never much liked—academic teaching. He had taught writing at Barnard College in 1956-1957 and now went first to the University of Iowa and then in 1974-1975 to Boston University, where he was Visiting Professor of Creative Writing. In Boston, his depression returned and led to alcoholism and a month at the Smithers Rehabilitation Center in New York City where "the dreadfulness of the place was therapeutic."

In the novel, Sing Sing, Boston, and Smithers are all fictionalized as Falconer Prison. Cheever, who eschews the documentary realist's use of circumstantial detail, creates Falconer less as a specific prison than as a state of mind, as one of the many symbols of confinement to be found in his work—St. Botolphs, Bullet Park, and marriage, among others. *Falconer* is, therefore, not a novel about prison life but, as Cheever has explained it, "the pervading sense of confinement in all apparently free behavior." This is one of the first lessons learned by Ezekiel Farragut, a forty-eight-year-old college professor and convicted fratricide, during the little more than a year he spends at Falconer. Farragut is a typical Cheever protagonist: a naif suffering the pangs of displacement. Moreover, although he has good cause to suffer—uncaring parents, a murder-minded brother, a narcissistic wife, a sadistic prison official—much of his misery is self-inflicted and derives from his own uncorrected weaknesses, particularly his drug addiction. Like Eliot Nailles in *Bullet Park*, Farragut uses drugs in order to forget a painful past and to deaden his senses to all future pain; but, also like Nailles, he has a strong desire to recall the pleasures of the past and to quicken his senses to the pleasures around him. Before Farragut can affirm life, however, he must reject the separation of mind and body theorized by Descartes, his favorite writer, and, like the Biblical Ezekiel, learn the importance of personal responsibility and the possibility of rebirth.

Farragut's journey to personal responsibility and rebirth involves four stages. The first involves his naive and selfish belief in justice and redress. He demands the right to be heard, the right to be given his daily dose of methadone, the anti-sacrament which precludes the celebration of life. In the second stage Farragut turns from the abstract to the physical. His homosexual relationship with the youthful Jody (Farragut's first) evidences his willingness to experience life, but it also forces him to question whether his desire for Jody is really love or a subconscious longing for death. Jody's escape from Falconer, a "miracle" made possible by his inverting sexuality, Christianity, and the American success ethic for his own ends, sends Farragut even deeper into his deadly self-love. Farragut has failed to learn Jody's lesson: one must transform the world in order to make both it and oneself useful. Having tried to love one man, Farragut now tries to love all mankind. His vision of social change, stimulated by the Amana (Attica) uprising, leads him to one of his first constructive, and therefore risky acts, the building of a contraband radio. Since Cheever, however, believes that individual reform must precede social reform, Farragut's grand design necessarily fails. Although Farragut perceives how the prison administration (society) sanctions and even promotes the drugged state in order to preserve the status quo, he overestimates the prisoners' desire for freedom. In the fourth stage, Farragut learns that he is free of his addiction (ironically, with the state's help). This knowledge frees him to confess the full story of his fratricide to a dying inmate who

The day was shit. He would put visibility at five
hundred feet. Could it be exploited for an escape? He didn't think
so. The chance of escape reminded him of Jody,a remembrance that
had remained light-hearted since he had and Jody has pasionately
kissed goodbye. DiMatteo,the chaplain's dude,had brought him the
facts on Jody no more than six weeks after Jody's flight. They
had met in the tunnel on a dark night when Farragut was leaving
The Valley. DiMatteo showed him a newspaper photograph of Jody.
that he had been sent in the mail. It was Jody on his wedding day--
Ody at his most beautiful and triumphant. His brightness shone
through the letter-press of a small town paper. His bride was a
demure and a pretty young Oriental and the caption said that
H. Keith Morgan had,that day,married Sally Chou Lai,the youngest
daughter of Ling Chow Lai,President of the Viaduct Wire Company
where he groom was employed. There was nothing more and nothing
more was needed. Farragut laughed,but not DiMatteo who said
angrily,"He promised to wait for me. I saved his life and he
promised to wait for me. He loved me. Oh God,how he loved me.
He gave me his golden cross." DiMatteo lifted the cross out of
the curls on his chest and showed it to Farragut. Farragut's
knowledge of the cross were intimate and his memories of his
lover were Keen but not at all sad. "He must have married her for
her money,"said BiMatteo,"she must be rich. He promised to wait
for me."

From typescript of Falconer, *"which seems to illustrate*
the fact that I use yellow paper and that, on good days, I
seldom make revisions."

represents the final result of narcissism—loneliness—just as his beautiful wife Marcia represents its cause. The inmate's death frees Farragut from the last traces of self-love, and Farragut's escape, a parody of Edmund Dantes's escape from the Chateau d'If in *The Count of Monte Cristo*, is appropriately described in terms of the birth process. Farragut emerges from Falconer psychologically whole, free of those fears which had led him to withdraw into the prison of self. Spiritually renewed, he can, with Leander Wapshot and Asa Bascomb, face his world and "Rejoice, he thought, rejoice."

Cheever's own sense of renewal was no less dramatic. After leaving Smithers, Cheever, an Episcopalian, resumed his regular practice of going to church "to make my thanksgivings," and in just ten months wrote *Falconer*, finishing it, appropriately, on Maundy Thursday. He had overcome his depression and, considering the novel's highly favorable reviews, any lingering problem with novelistic structure.

Twelve years before the publication of *Falconer*, John Aldridge called Cheever "one of the most grievously underdiscussed important writers we have at the present." This state of affairs, which has not yet been sufficiently corrected, derived, Aldridge felt, from three chief causes: Cheever's "unfortunate" association with the *New Yorker*, his failure to explore the darker implications of his work ("he does not yet disturb us enough"), and the feeling that there is "still little to convince one that Cheever is moving on." Cheever's fiction, although it has been widely reviewed, has generated only a scant amount of academic criticism, a situation for which Cheever is himself partly responsible. An intensely private writer, he avoids literary competitiveness, disassociates himself from literary schools, and even denies having any desire for posthumous fame. Believing in "the transcendent relationship between the writer and the reader," he prefers the public's acceptance of his books to what he dismisses as "academic vivisection." His stories, although often just as slick and hopeful as any *New Yorker* fiction, are generally conceded to have a significance not generally accorded to the fiction found in this magazine; "I never wrote *for* the *New Yorker*," Cheever has stated, "they bought my stories." His comic vision precludes his saying "No! In Thunder," the *sine qua non* of modern American fiction established by Leslie Fiedler, but this does not mean that Cheever's stories are "coy" and "cloying" as Aldridge suggested. Even before *Bullet Park*, Cheever had explored the darker side of middle-class

existence, and at *Esquire*'s third annual "Writing in America Today" symposium, he had said that because "life in the United States in 1960 is hell" the "only position for a writer now is negation." As a satirist, however, Cheever negates only as the precondition for the building of a better world. Although he believes in the inherent innovativeness of all fiction, his concern for the moral basis of literature puts him at odds with today's fabulators whose stylistic pyrotechnics he rejects: "experimentation, particularly that spinoff of innovation in which license is taken in using words in a nonverbal and inchoate sense . . . seems to be generally unsuccessful." Not surprisingly, his favorite among recent novels is *Humboldt's Gift* by Saul Bellow, a writer who shares many of Cheever's concerns.

One of the earliest critical pieces on Cheever, dating back only to 1961, is Ihab Hassan's discussion of *The Wapshot Chronicle* in *Radical Innocence*. Hassan, who dismissed Cheever's affirmative stance as "whimsical," was himself taken to task two years later by Frederick Bracher who pointed out that Cheever's importance derives from "the urgency of his moral insights." Clinton S. Burhans, Jr., adopting a similar position, called Cheever "a trenchant moralist who sees all too clearly the gap between men's dreams and what they make of them." He treats his characters compassionately, Burhans claimed, because they are caught in a too rapidly-changing world where the traditional values by which they wish to live are no longer operable. Alfred Kazin's discussion in *Bright Book of Life* added little to what Aldridge had already said. Kazin found Cheever precocious and provocative, but "expectable" and "never hard to take." "My deepest feeling about Cheever is that his marvelous brightness is an effort to cheer himself up." At the opposite pole from Kazin are John Leonard and novelist John Gardner. Leonard, in his review of *The World of Apples*, called Cheever "our best living writer of short stories: a Chekhov of the exurbs" and a master ironist working "on behalf of ardor and intelligence and clemency even while these words, these values really, are inadequate to cope with a world of chance, of evil." That Cheever is a master of the short story in an age devoted to the novel has, it seems, made critics seem reluctant to discuss his work and easy for them to dismiss his novels as the abortive attempts of a short story writer to work outside his chosen (and by implication inferior) field. This situation will, undoubtedly, be reversed by *Falconer* which, as Gardner noted in his review, evidences "formal and technical mastery," "educated intelligence," "artistic sincerity," "indifference to aesthetic fashion," and "the artist's correct moral relation to his material."

References:

John W. Aldridge, *Time to Murder and Create* (New York: McKay, 1966), pp. 171-177;

Frederick Bracher, "John Cheever and Comedy," *Critique*, 6, 1 (spring 1963): 66-77;

Clinton S. Burhans, Jr., "John Cheever and the Grave of Social Coherence," *Twentieth Century Literature*, 14 (January 1969): 187-198;

Susan Cheever, "A Duet of Cheevers," *Newsweek*, 89 (14 March 1977): 68-73;

Walter Clemons, "Cheever's Triumph," *Newsweek*, 89 (14 March 1977): 61-67;

John Firth, "Talking with John Cheever," *Saturday Review*, 5 (2 April 1977): 22-23;

John Gardner, "On Miracle Row," *Saturday Review*, 5 (2 April 1977): 20-23;

Annette Grant, "John Cheever: The Art of Fiction," *Paris Review*, 17 (fall 1976): 39-66;

Robert Gutwillig, "Dim Views through the Fog," *New York Times Book Review*, 13 November 1960, pp. 68-69;

Henrietta Ten Harmsel, " 'Young Goodman Brown' and 'The Enormous Radio,' " *Studies in Short Fiction*, 9 (fall 1972): 407-408;

Ihab Hassan, *Radical Innocence* (Princeton: Princeton University Press, 1961), pp. 187-201;

Alfred Kazin, *Bright Book of Life* (Boston: Atlantic/ Little, Brown, 1973), pp. 109-114;

John Leonard, "Cheever to Roth to Malamud," *Atlantic*, 231 (June 1973): 112-114;

Stephen C. Moore, "The Hero on the 5:42: John Cheever's Short Fiction," *Western Humanities Review*, 30 (spring 1976): 147-152;

Eleanor Munro, "Not only I the narrator, but I John Cheever," *Ms.*, 5 (April 1977): 74-77;

Lewis Nichols, "A Visit with John Cheever," *New York Times Book Review*, 5 January 1964, p. 28;

"Ovid in Ossining," *Time*, 83 (27 March 1964): 66-72;

Wilfrid Sheed, "Novelist of Suburbia: Mr. Saturday, Mr. Monday and Mr. Cheever," *Life*, 66 (18 April 1969): 39-46;

Rollene Waterman, *Saturday Review*, 41 (13 September 1958): 33.

Manuscripts:

Brandeis University has the typescripts of many of Cheever's short stories and books, including *The Wapshot Chronicle*.

EVAN S. CONNELL, JR. would probably rank today as the most important American novelist if critical reception were the sole criterion for determining the reputation of a writer. But the fact is that though his books have been widely reviewed and highly praised he has yet to be accorded the renown of some of his contemporaries. Reasons for this comparative obscurity are not hard to find. For one thing, he has never sought the limelight; his reputation rests on his books alone, unaided by the machinations of public relations men. For another thing, his fiction is neither so studiously obscure nor so allusive as to require the exegetical analysis that comes, as a matter of course, with being "difficult"—which is not to say that either his matter or his manner is of the sort to appeal to the average reader. As one critic remarked, Connell is "a writer whose high professionalism has not kept him from a series of increasingly ambitious and valuable experiments."

Connell was born on 17 August 1924 in Kansas City, Missouri, where he attended Southwest High School before going to Dartmouth College. Years later he noted, "While at Dartmouth I was planning to become a doctor, as my father is, and as his father was. I think that if there had not been a second World War I might have continued that direction for at least another year or so." The war was going on at the time, and he left school to enter the navy as an aviation cadet. After receiving his wings, on VE Day, he served as a flight instructor until being discharged.

He drew heavily on his experience as a pilot to write *The Patriot* (1960), in which the central protagonist was a bumbling cadet named Melvin Isaacs, who washed out of flight school a week before he was to have graduated. Following his discharge from the service, he studied art briefly at the University of Kansas. Connell, too, took a degree in English at Kansas, where he studied fiction writing under Ray B. West. Later he studied under such well-known teachers of writing as Wallace Stegner at Stanford, Helen Hull at Columbia, and finally Walter Van Tilburg Clark in San Francisco, which has been his home ever since. During that period of study he also spent two years in Europe. Although he had decided to become a writer by the time he left the navy at the age of twenty-one, he also took courses in painting and sculpture—just as Isaacs did.

Jill Krementz

Evan Connell.

Aside from the surface parallels (Isaacs was also from Kansas City), there is little resemblance between author and fictional character. If *The Patriot* has any character who might resemble Connell, that character would be Patrick Cole, an extremely skeptical and aloof young man who had learned too much from his study of history to be gulled by war-effort propaganda. One of the most memorable passages in the novel concerns Cole's debunking of Isaacs' simple-minded patriotism, which, according to Cole, was neither more intelligent nor stupid than the views of other patriots in other lands. It is not the love of one's country which so appalls Connell; rather, it is the hypocrisy which that patriotism so often breeds. Isaacs is depicted as essentially an innocent schlemiel, forever banging his shins against the hard rock of reality. He is, indeed, an object lesson in the dangers of self-delusion. The only time he succeeds in any fashion is when he purposely strives to lose. Near the end of the novel, for example, he concocts, as a joke and in defiance of the art school, a pile of junk as his entry for a sculpture contest which, to his utter amazement, he wins. By the novel's end he has succeeded in contracting a disastrous marriage—disastrous in that it can only compound his sense of defeat and helplessness. While the novel has some excellent scenes, particularly those concerned with flight training, and contains some deliciously satiric passages on modern art, it is somehow misshapen, lacking any single thread of meaning or purpose that gives unity to the best fiction. One might say that its total effect is less than its individual parts.

Connell's first published work was in the short story form. His stories appeared in various magazines and anthologies, including *Prize Stories* of 1949 and 1951 and *Best American Short Stories* of 1955 and 1957. So far two volumes have been published, *The Anatomy Lesson and Other Stories* (1957) and *At the Crossroads* (1965). If some of his stories fail, as one critic put it, "because of the heavy burden of private comment and extraneous detail carried by the stream of the narrative," his best ones stick in the memory like puzzles the reader dimly recalls having tried to solve before but never quite satisfactorily. In all of them there is playful irony, as if the author were more concerned with proving to the reader that none of us fully understands either himself or those about him than he is with explaining or simply reporting human behavior. The stories are, in effect, little lessons in our lack of understanding. Man knows little and remembers even less, Connell seems to say. If the stories baffle the reader, they also disturb him and reveal the limits of his vision. While such a lesson is doubtless important, it is easy to overestimate its value. After all, we are both better instructed and better entertained by the shared experience which all great literature provides than we are by the enigmatic or by the undeniable proposition that we cannot fully comprehend either ourselves or the world which contains us.

In his best fiction, Connell provides us with that necessary shared experience. His first published novel, *Mrs. Bridge* (1959), reveals clearly the life of a woman who is puzzled by events around her, but the reader understands, without ever being able to predict, each of the 117 brief episodic vignettes that portray Mrs. Bridge as one of the most fully realized characters in American fiction. Indeed, the novel is one of the very few written since World War II that clearly deserves to be called, as it has been, a masterpiece. In the opening chapter, entitled "Love and Marriage" (it quickly becomes apparent that the chapter titles nearly always express a muted irony), the author introduces Mrs. Bridge: "Her first name was India—she was never able to get used to it. It seemed to her that her parents must have been thinking of someone else when they named her. Or were they hoping for another sort of daughter? As a child she was often on the point of inquiring, but time passed, and she never did." In the course of the two-page vignette, she grows up, meets and marries a young lawyer named Walter Bridge, and moves with him to Kansas City. During their courtship Walter talks to her about Ruskin and Robert Ingersoll and reads verses from *The Rubaiyat* to her. He promises that he will one day take her to Europe, which in fact he does years later. In the simplicity of the account, almost shocking in its stark recording of a few important items, her whole life is outlined. It is only left for the author to fill in the details, which he does with compassion and double-edged humor.

While Mrs. Bridge is at the center of the novel, never far removed from any scene in the book, Connell depicts the small world she inhabits in an unforgettable manner. Her three children grow up, have friends, get in the kind of trouble that children have, and finally move out from under the parental influence—just as in most families. We meet various of the family friends, most of them leading lives as essentially hollow and hopeless as the life of Mrs. Bridge. The amazing thing about the novel is that we both pity and censure the characters at the same time. Nowhere else in our literature has the boredom of the leisure class been more vividly portrayed, or with more compassion and humor. With all our modern conveniences, Connell seems to be saying, we have succeeded in making life well-nigh unbearable. But not quite. Near the end of the novel, Mrs. Bridge wakes one warm, windy morning in June and listens to "the wind in the trees, to the scratching of the evergreen branches against the house, and wonders if she was about to die. She did not feel ill, but she had no confidence in her life. Why should her heart keep beating? What was there to live for? Then she grew cheerful because she recalled her husband had told her to get the Lincoln waxed and polished."

Ten years later, Connell returned to the theme and structure of *Mrs. Bridge* in the companion volume, *Mr. Bridge* (1969). Although some of the same events are described in the two novels, they might be read one after the other without any sense of repetition. *Mr. Bridge* is a more somber novel than its counterpart, and the satire has a bite that makes one wince rather than laugh. Part of the reason for the darker tone is doubtless due to Mr. Bridge's being more self-assured than his wife, and hence more unbending in his prejudices. Moreover, Mr. Bridge does have a set of values, albeit mostly false in both premise and conclusion, which sustains him after a fashion; whereas Mrs. Bridge is forever seeking, in her ineffectual way, something in which to believe, or anything that might give meaning to her admittedly meaningless life. If we laugh at her we still must sympathize with her predicament. On the other hand, the reader will, if he agrees at all with Connell, reject the insular, upper-class views of Mr.

Bridge. Although a successful man in the world's view, able to meet life on his own terms, he invariably insists on fashioning life to fit a mold so narrow as to leave out of account all that resists regimentation or reduction to a few simple formulae. He is a juiceless fellow, with no more sap to him than is contained in the legal documents that occupy his working hours. Various critics have compared *Mr. Bridge* to Sinclair Lewis's *Babbitt*. The comparison is apposite only to a point. Aside from being a hollow simpleton, almost a clown, Babbitt was a cheat and a fraud. Mr. Bridge is never dishonest, nor does he ever knowingly injure anyone. On the other hand, Babbitt does experience moments of joy and has dreams of changing his life. Mr. Bridge could never conceive of his life being anything other than it is, and his life is barren of joy. The last lines of the novel underline the fact: "He remembered enthusiasm, hope, and a kind of jubilation or exultation. Cheerfulness, yes, and joviality, and the brief gratification of sex. Gladness, too, fullness of heart, appreciation, and many other emotions. But not joy. No, that belonged to simpler minds."

Following *The Patriot* Connell wrote *Notes from a Bottle Found on the Beach at Carmel* (1963), a work that defies categorization. Most critics have called the work an epic poem, or have anyway referred to it as poetry. In testifying to its "growing underground reputation" George Garrett called it a poem "of the size and scope of Pound's *Cantos*." As he did with *Mrs. Bridge*, Connell published, ten years after *Notes*, a companion volume, entitled *Points for a Compass Rose* (1973), which was nominated for the National Book Award for Poetry in 1974. Paul Gray briefly described the two companion sets this way: "*Mrs. Bridge* (1959) and *Mr. Bridge* (1969) spun out a series of vignettes in the Midwestern lives of their protagonists; the accretions were devastating catalogues of anomie. In *Notes from a Bottle Found on the Beach at Carmel* (1963) and *Points for a Compass Rose* (1973), Connell shored fragments of history and reflection against our ruin, casting them in prose lines that rang with poetry." Gray's description is apt since only in the loosest sense of the word can either of the books be considered poetry; that they have been so considered is doubtless attributable to the typographical arrangement of the prose on the pages. It matters little, of course, what one calls the brief notes; it is their effect on the reader that matters. Moreover, the verse arrangement does add, at times anyhow, to that effect.

While the identity of the notetaker in each volume changes from section to section, he is most prominently a Magus, or kind of Wandering Jew, observing and collating ancient and modern thought and acts in order to show how repetitively absurd, in the main, are human beliefs and how tawdry are most human aspirations and deeds. We are further reminded of the reception given most of the great personages of the past who sought to break out of the anthropocentric and anthropomorphic delusions adhered to by the vast majority of mankind. The "I" paraphrases, in glistening prose, the more idiotic beliefs of the ancients—not so much to reveal the absurdity of the views as to remind us of our shaky hold on reality. The fact that we no longer hold this or that view, long since exploded, by no means protects us from believing today that which is equally at odds with reason or common sense. In making the frequently amusing comments, the speaker offers no opinion himself; indeed, he often expresses the views matter-of-factly. Mixed in with the historical or ideological "facts" are comments that defy comprehension, little puzzles for the imagination. For example:

What has grown up to the gates of the city.
An owl has flown into the garden.
At night I have listened for Cathedral bells,
remembering Saint-Etienne.

Some express an extreme solipsism, certainly not advocated by the author. For example, this one is repeated twice in *Notes*: "Nothing existed before me; nothing will exist after me." The most devastating notes concern religious beliefs and the brutality of religious fanatics. The derision can also be humorous, as in this: "How many churches count among their priceless relics/ the prepuce of Jesus Christ? The answer is twelve."

In both *Notes* and *Points* Connell surveys museums, archeological digs, civilizations, and assorted triumphs and despairs of the human animal with an eye for the more outrageous antics of the creature who, the more he changes, the more he remains the same. Both books, and particularly *Points for a Compass Rose*, read like selections from an exotic, unexpurgated *Encyclopaedia Britannica*—written by a satanic historian-scholar-philosopher intent on reminding us that yesterday's follies are the news stories of today. Because of their structure and, more obviously, their content, such books could never have a very wide appeal, but neither can they be disregarded by discerning readers.

In *The Diary of a Rapist* (1966) Connell limited his point of view to the mind of a psychopath, a

~~REGNANT~~
PUISSANT
ALEG
MAGISTERIAL(P)

FiRst dRAft NOV. 12, '72 - JAN 23, '73

The Connoisseur

UNEQUIVOCAL   *EXALTS*   *diminutive*
~~Unspeakable~~ dignity isolates and ~~augments~~ the ~~miniature~~ nobleman.

His REGNANT personality
~~It dominates the shelf,~~ ~~and while viewing,~~ ~~he~~ ignores the bric-a-brac
^*DOMINATING the shelf, his REGNANT NATURE*

RECALLS
obstructing his view. With arms ~~regally~~ folded and head lifted he

WAFTS   *FOR*
~~sits~~ cross-legged, ~~no doubt awaiting~~ the next petitioner. God help

that supplicant.
Muhlbach, Astonished, PAUSES. And all at once)

he   *with sudden passion!*
^ I want this arrogant little ~~personage,~~ ~~Muhlbach~~ thinks. But

why? Does he remind me of myself at times? Or perhaps there's

something universal in his attitude. No matter, we're kinsmen. He's

coming home with me.

The mistress of the shop approaches. She, too, has her arms

folded, either in unconscious emulation or, more likely, against

the snowy New Mexico morning ~~just outside.~~

Have you ever seen such poise? she ~~asks.~~

Though.
Quite remarkable, says Muhlbach. ^What is it?

~~and~~ bronze.
Terra cotta, she replies. People often take it for ~~metal~~ ~~bronze.~~
In fact,   *your*
~~it rings if you~~ tap it with ~~a~~ fingernail. ~~it rings like metal or~~

~~porcelain, chinaware,~~
                                                            to be polite
This is not what he wants to hear. *little statue*
^ ~~Muhlbach does so. The~~ ~~figure~~ rings like metal or chinaware.
        ~~had already guessed that it was terra cotta, but~~ he does
                                the substance
as she suggests. The little statue rings like metal or chinaware.

~~What I meant, he says, is~~

it's   *continues.*
I assume ~~this is~~ a copy of some museum piece, he ~~remarks.~~

would
Where ~~is~~ the original ~~be?~~

~~You are~~ looking at the original, she answers with a smile.

Really?

Yes. It's Mayan.

young man named Earl Summerfield, who is as convincingly real as he is frightening to behold. Unhappily married, bored with his job at a federal employment bureau, convinced that he has been badly treated by the fates, he becomes fascinated with newspaper accounts of violent crimes. One critic noted that in "the unraveling of a diseased mind capable of acts which are absolute in their extremity, Connell succeeds overpoweringly—his novel is a triumph of art over case history." Repelled by what he reads and finally convinced of the depravity of man, the somewhat fastidious and moralistic Summerfield finally convinces himself that only through violence can one revolt against one's essential helplessness. He is introspective, self-pitying, misogynistic, egotistic. His sexual crimes emphasize his belief that man, including himself, deserves damnation.

In *The Connoisseur* (1974) Connell again depicts the power of obsession—this time in the story of Karl Muhlbach, a middle-aged, conservative New York insurance executive, who, while on a brief business trip to New Mexico, purchases a small (presumably pre-Columbian) figurine. On returning to New York with his art object, he begins a search for the past which the figurine symbolizes. Himself a connoisseur of early Mexican art, Connell takes his reader on a guided tour of the literature, museums, art shops, and fakeries which now occupy his protagonist to the exclusion of everything else around him—his job, his children, his acquaintances. A widower, Muhlbach pays the inevitable price for having taken as his "mistress" that which he can never fully understand, let alone possess.

In *Double Honeymoon* (1976) the protagonist is again Karl Muhlbach. In the opening scene, by far the most vivid in the novel, Muhlbach meets Lambeth Brett at a cocktail party which both have attended for lack of an excuse to remain away. Though the much younger Lambeth represents, indeed exudes, every quality that the staid Muhlbach might be expected to dismiss as contemptible—excepting only her blonde beauty, her youthful difference from the other women of his acquaintance, and, finally, the mystery which her world-weary insouciance seems to suggest—he is interested, then desirous, and finally enthralled. The theme is found throughout Connell's opera: man's fondness for the unreal, his eternal quest for *ignes fatui*. While Muhlbach thinks of her, after a time, as one of life's "unspeakable delights and . . . deludes himself into thinking their affair has more meaning and potential than is possible," the reader is never in any doubt as to the outcome. The tale is as old as

Adam and Eve and just as predictable, and were it told by a journeyman novelist we would throw it in the fire long before the final breakup when Muhlbach is forced to see Lambeth as she is rather than as his imagination has painted her. A bad story but nevertheless told well. The novel would perhaps be less disappointing had it been written by someone else, but Connell's readers have long ago learned to expect much more from him.

But let it go. The author of the *Bridge* novels and the two volumes of notes or meditations can afford now and again to fall short of the high standard he has set. Connell clearly belongs in the front rank of American authors.

—*William H. Nolte*

Books:

The Anatomy Lesson and Other Stories (New York: Viking, 1957; London: Heinemann, 1958);

Mrs. Bridge (New York: Viking, 1959; London: Heinemann, 1960);

The Patriot (New York: Viking, 1960; London: Heinemann, 1962);

Notes from a Bottle Found on the Beach at Carmel (New York: Viking, 1963; London: Heinemann, 1964);

At the Crossroads (New York: Simon & Schuster, 1965; London: Heinemann, 1966);

The Diary of a Rapist (New York: Simon & Schuster, 1966; London: Heinemann, 1967);

Mr. Bridge (New York: Knopf, 1969); London: Heinemann, 1969);

Points for a Compass Rose (New York: Knopf, 1973);

The Connoisseur (New York: Knopf, 1974);

Double Honeymoon (New York: Putnam's, 1976).

Reference:

Gus Blaisdell, "After Ground Zero: The Writings of Evan S. Connell, Jr." *New Mexico Quarterly*, 36, 2 (summer 1966): 181-207.

Robert Coover

Larry McCaffery
San Diego State University

BIRTH: Charles City, Iowa, 4 February 1932.

EDUCATION: Southern Illinois University; B.A., Indiana University, 1953; M.A., University of Chicago, 1965.

MARRIAGE: 3 June 1959 to Maria del Pilar Sans-Mallafre; children: Diana Nin, Sara Chapin, Roderick Luis.

AWARDS: William Faulkner Award for *The Origin of the Brunists*, 1966; Rockefeller Foundation Fellowship, 1969; Guggenheim Fellowships, 1971, 1974.

MAJOR WORKS: *The Origin of the Brunists* (New York: Putnam, 1966; London: Barker, 1967); *The Universal Baseball Association, Inc., J. Henry Waugh, Prop.* (New York: Random House, 1968; London: Hart-Davis, 1970); *Pricksongs and Descants* (New York: Dutton, 1969; London: Cape, 1971); *A Theological Position* (New York: Dutton, 1972); *The Public Burning* (New York: Viking, 1977).

Lynn Sweigart

Even before the publication of *The Public Burning* (1977) made him famous, Robert Coover had already achieved a solid reputation, mostly among academics and college audiences, as one of the most original and versatile prose stylists in America. In his earlier three book-length works of fiction (*The Origin of the Brunists, The Universal Baseball Association*, and *Pricksongs and Descants*), Coover's ability to create and control a dazzling variety of styles and voices had been very evident. But it was not until *The Public Burning* appeared that Coover's place as a major figure in contemporary fiction became assured. Many of the central issues in *The Public Burning* are well in evidence in Coover's earlier fiction and were certainly clearly defined in *The Origin of the Brunists*. His new book, however, narrated in part by Richard Nixon and dealing with the highly controversial Rosenberg trial, was seen by many critics—and the general public—as being more accessible than his previous works.

What Coover returns to again and again in all his works is the concept of "man-as-fiction-maker." His characters are constantly shown in the process of inventing systems and patterns to help order their lives and give meaning to the world at large. The systems which engage his characters are often obviously artificial in nature: we observe writers trying to create stories, men struggling to break the hold of mythic patterns, desperate people inventing religious explanations for a terrible catastrophe, a middle-aged man finding love and companionship among the imaginary players of a tabletop baseball game. Yet Coover's fiction is also filled with hints that other, less obviously subjective systems—such as science, mathematics, historical and political perspectives, and myth—are also fictional at their core. In most of Coover's work there exists a tension between the process of man creating his fictions and his desire to assert that his systems are ontological rather than ideological in nature. For Coover this tension typically results in man losing sight of the fictional basis of his systems and eventually becoming controlled by or entrapped within them.

Both *The Origin of the Brunists* and *The Public Burning* have obvious and powerfully presented "social issues" to examine, but because all of Coover's work relies so heavily on artifice, games, self-reflexiveness, and other nonrealistic approaches, it is usually linked with the disruptive, metafictional methods of Barthelme, Gass, Nabokov, Pynchon, and Barth. Indeed, Coover's manipulations of style and literary conventions are often used to show the staleness and inadequacies of *any* rigid form, and his distrust of dogmatic attitudes is often reflected in the open-ended formal structures which characterize much of his work. Robert Scholes has used *Pricksongs and Descants* as an example of *metafiction*, which he defines as literature that "assimilates all the perspectives of criticism into the fictional process itself," that is, the work calls attention to itself as a made thing, and the reader, by becoming involved in the process of fiction-making, transcends the fictional work.

Robert Lowell Coover was born in Charles City, Iowa, but moved on to Bedford, Indiana during the war years and then later to Herrin, Illinois (near Carbondale), where his father became the managing editor of the *Herrin Daily Journal* at the war's end (Tiger Miller, the main character of *The Origin of the Brunists*, is also a small-town newspaper editor). Even before moving to Herrin, Coover was playing parlor baseball games as well as watching the Cincinnati Reds train at French Lick, editing school papers, and writing poems and stories. Travel was a primary ambition for Coover as a youngster; at the time, when people asked, he generally told them that he was going to be a foreign correspondent. Herrin was the scene of a mining disaster while Coover was home for the Christmas holidays in 1951, and he was to make use of this material for his first published story, "Blackdamp" (1961) and in *The Origin of the Brunists*. The parlor baseball games were to be transformed into the central metaphor of his novel, *The Universal Baseball Association*; the initial idea for this novel came to Coover when he returned home once and found one of his old games. He discovered that he still retained a remarkably vivid memory of the league and all its players—they were still as much "alive" for him as many of his "real" childhood memories.

After attending Southern Illinois University for two years, Coover moved on to Indiana University, where he received his B.A. in 1953. Receiving his draft notice on the day he graduated, he decided to join the navy, went to Officer Candidate School, and spent three years in Europe. While in Europe on a one-year tour of the Mediterranean, Coover met his wife, then a student at the University in Barcelona. The summer that Coover got out of the navy (1957) proved to be what Coover has called "the turn-around time" for his career as a writer. Before going to graduate school at the University of Chicago, he spent "a fruitful month" in a cabin on Rainy Lake in Wisconsin, where he wrote his first serious pieces, including "Panel Game," the earliest of the "Exemplary Fictions" which were collected in *Pricksongs*. Even in this very early story, many of Coover's characteristics are already evident. Set up as a kind of closet drama, "Panel Game" presents an "Unwilling Participant" who is chosen to sit on a television game show panel in the midst of several mysterious, possibly allegorical figures (an "Aged Clown," a "Lovely Lady," and "Mr. America"). Soon the "merry Moderator" is introduced and the Unwilling Participant is plunged into a complex, incomprehensible game whose rules he does not understand. Urged on by the Moderator, he senses that the game has something to do with deciphering language, but no useful rules or connections seem to emerge. This Unwilling Participant resembles many of Coover's later characters, such as the West Condonites in *The Origin of the Brunists* and Richard Nixon in *The Public Burning*, in distrusting transformation and process. He desires to assign fixed meanings, to shape patterns and create order from the mass of ambiguous, confusing signs that lie all around him.

In both 1958 and 1959 Coover made student charter trips back to Spain, the second time in order to get married. During the summer of 1959 he motorbiked all over southern Europe, an experience which provided the material for his first publication: "One Summer in Spain, Five Poems" (1960). Meanwhile Coover attended art school and wrote a number of the "Exemplary Fictions," many of which have never been published, as well as several stories which were published in magazines such as the *Evergreen Review, Cavalier,* and *Noble Savage.* At this early stage of his career, Coover reports that he never even considered working on a novel. As he has told Frank Gado in an interview, "It had never occurred to me. I thought I would always go on writing these stories." Although some of these stories proved to be quite successful (for example, "Blackdamp," and "The Marker" in 1962), Coover has said that he wrote a lot of them "not knowing at all what I was doing, not having a clue as to why I felt it was necessary to write this kind of story . . . after I would start writing them, they seldom seemed worth the effort; they were strange, incomplete things, often very shallow." During the period of roughly

1962-1965, Coover lived in his wife's hometown, Tarragona, where he did the major work on *The Origin of the Brunists*, the first draft of *The Universal Baseball Association*, and a number of stories. It was also during this time that, like Barth, he began to turn to ancient fictions to see if he could discover what had already been done and also to see what new ideas they might suggest. By going back and examining works by Ovid and *The Arabian Nights*, for example, Coover found a context which helped clarify what he was trying to do in his own fiction. Of the Ovidian concern with transformation, Coover has said that "I suddenly realized that the basic, constant struggle for all of us is against metamorphosis, against giving in to the inevitability of process."

Since the mid-1960s, Coover has spent about as much time in the United States (usually in teaching positions when he is running low on money) as in Europe (both Spain and England). By 1966, for example, his family support had run out and he applied around for teaching jobs to over 200 schools in the New York area. Luckily, Bard College accepted him and, just before the publication of *The Origin of the Brunists*, he arrived with his family in the United States, penniless and deeply in debt. At Bard he was forced into seven course preparations his first semester ("which, after Chicago, was the best education I ever got, costly as it was"). After the University of Iowa rescued him from his overload in 1967, he served briefly as a writer-in-residence at Wisconsin State University (1968) and Washington University at St. Louis (1969). From this period onward, Coover began to receive steady support from his Random House/Dutton editor, Hal Scharlett, from a Rockefeller Foundation grant (1969), Guggenheim Fellowships (1971 and 1974), and from various brief stays at universities (Princeton, 1972-1973, Columbia and V.M.I., for a semester each). It appears that Coover's financial problems should be considerably lessened by wide notoriety *The Public Burning* has already attracted. Although he ran into considerable difficulties in finding a publisher willing to accept his highly controversial novel (the completed manuscript waited several years while it was passed around several New York publishers), Coover finally found in Richard Seaver an editor and a publisher, Viking, who were willing to champion his book.

Before Coover felt he could really begin exploring fictional forms in the way that he wished, he decided he should "pay his dues" to traditional fiction by demonstrating—in *The Origin of the Brunists*—that he could handle conventional forms.

As he summarized in an interview with Alma Kadragic, "I remembered seeing some early paintings by Matisse which were old dog-eared books on a table with a candle or a lamp or some curtains, and they showed so much knowhow of the medium that they give you confidence when he sets out to attempt explorations in the later part of his work—you have some faith in him that this is not some guy who's getting by with a lack of skill, making up for it by doing something weird." Coover actually had several different options for developing a novel, including expanding his J. Henry Waugh story, "The Second Son," which had been published in 1963. Eventually, because of pressures from friends, agents, and editors and also because his mine-disaster story, "Blackdamp," had been so favorably received, Coover pushed ahead with his work on *The Origin of the Brunists*. Into this long, complex book Coover poured many of his ideas about the broad base of metaphor through which we apprehend the universe and also explored a wide variety of narrative approaches. The two books which most obviously influenced *The Origin of the Brunists* were Pynchon's *V.* (published in 1963 and read by Coover soon afterwards) and *Moby-Dick* ("I thought that if a writer could go that far in exploring an idea, then I could go the distance with my book," Coover told Gado).

Flawed in certain respects, *The Origin of the Brunists* nevertheless presents a clear, fairly comprehensive view of Coover's concept of the fiction-making process. Using the founding of the Christian religion as its primary analogue, *The Origin of the Brunists* seeks to examine the hold which the fictions of religion and history maintain over men. The plot of the book is built around a mining disaster which kills ninety-seven men in a small mining community. One of the survivors is Giovanni Bruno, a quiet, enigmatic man disliked by most of his fellow workers. Due to a complex variety of circumstances, coincidences, and local needs, Bruno becomes the unlikely center of a small religious cult ("The Brunists") whose fortunes the novel explores. The story climaxes when most of the major participants gather together on the Mount of Redemption (a small hill near the mine) in a wild, orgiastic finale. Here they wait (unsuccessfully as it turns out) for the end of the world or the coming of the White Dove—no one involved seems quite sure which. As the book concludes, we discover that despite the failure of the predicted cataclysm, the Brunists have struck a responsive chord in the world's religious needs: their cult has spread to all major areas of the United States, prospects for overseas recruitment look excellent, and the scriptural books and records are selling everywhere. Meanwhile the faithful are solemnly being prepared to meet their maker "on the 8th of January, possibly next year, but more likely in 7 or 14 years."

Such a general plot summary gives little sense of what happens in the novel because apparent digressions and subplots dominate its development. Partly because of his stated intention to "pay his dues" to traditional fiction, the strengths of this book—more than any of Coover's other works—are drawn primarily from the traditions of the realistic novel. Thus *The Origins of the Brunists* presents more than twenty vividly drawn, realistic characters and provides most of the other elements familiar to conventional fiction. Yet if Coover is paying his dues to traditional fiction here, his payments often seem to be made with ambivalent feelings. He constantly undercuts the realistic impulses of the book by borrowing elements from the surreal, the fantastic, and the absurd. Like Pynchon and Melville, he also often halts his plot to present asides such as anecdotes, jokes, and esoteric information about mining and small-town journalism.

The focus which holds the disparate parts of the novel together—and which ties this work firmly to Coover's other works—can be explained by some remarks he makes in the "Dedication" to *Pricksongs and Descants*. In this much-quoted passage, Coover says that the novelist should use "familiar or historical forms to combat the content of those forms and to conduct the reader . . . to the real, away from mystification to clarification, away from magic to maturity, away from mystery to revelation." Thus in *The Origin of the Brunists*, as in most of Coover's other works, we are presented with a familiar plot founded upon a prior "mythic or historical" source from which we will eventually be released by what Jackson Cope has termed an "anti-formal revelation." In other words, Coover hopes to use the familiar *forms*—be they Biblical patterns, the plots of fairy tales, the popular mythology of baseball or football, or the factual events of the Rosenberg case—to undercut the hold which the *content* of these forms still has on people. In *The Origin of the Brunists*, Coover uses the familiar, narrow Christian contexts, but extends them so that the book becomes a commentary on the fictive process of history itself and on the ways in which human experience is conveniently fictionalized into the dogmatic credos of society.

By focusing *The Origin of the Brunists* on religion and religious history, Coover was provided with an obvious context in which to show the way human invention is imposed upon the world to give it meaning. Coover makes it clear that the initial impetus for the Brunist development is the desire on the part of the survivors of the dead miners to attribute some purpose to the catastrophe, to justify it somehow. Faced with such a total chaotic disruption of their lives, the townsfolk find in the Brunist religion a system which provides the illusion of order and purpose to the terrible events they have experienced. As Leo Hertzel notes in his study of Coover in *Critique*, "Miners, like fishermen and every other kind of . . . folk, have always groped for a sign from beyond when confronted with the real blackness."

Not surprisingly, the Brunists are very unwilling to admit that their religion provides only fictional answers created by their own needs; faced with local opposition and laughed at nationally, they band together and gradually develop their own theology, legends, and sacred interpretations of history. As with Christianity, the Brunists are aided by a considerable number of unwitting—and even unwilling—elements. Their cause attracts answer-seeking crackpots such as Eleanor Norton and Ralph Himebaugh, whose own fictional systems (numerology and a sort of absurd empiricism, respectively) are adjusted to coincide with the Brunists' dogma. Rival church groups organize opposition, which only serves to draw the Brunists together and publicize their cause. The novel's main character, Justin "Tiger" Miller, decides to help the Brunists along as a sort of game to help relieve the boredom. Miller's name supplies the first clue about his role, for Justin was a second century writer and apologist for Christianity. But Miller is a peculiarly modern apologist, for although he becomes the Brunists' public-relations man, their historian, prophet, and gospel maker, he also recognizes them to be a hoax. In a revealing passage, we are told that games—which hold a consistent fascination for Coover—are what help provide some semblance of order to Miller's life: "Games were what kept Miller going. Games, and the pacifying of mind and organs. Miller perceived existence as a loose concatenation of separate and ultimately inconsequential instants, each colored by the actions that preceded it, but each possessed of a small wanton freedom of its own. Life then, was a series of adjustments to these actions, and if one kept his sense of humor and produced as many of these actions himself as possible, adjustments were easier." This passage helps explain Miller's role in the book as a pseudo-historian (or fiction-maker), and also offers a view of the world and man's position in it that appears in all of Coover's major works. The idea that life is a "loose concatenation of separate and ultimately inconsequential instants" directly opposes, of course, the historical view, which attempts to explain and define meaningful relationships between events. Indeed, the notion that each moment possesses "a small wanton freedom of its own" opposes *any* concept of an *externally imposed* system of order. Once this view is accepted, the alternatives are evident: either man can adopt the despairing outlook that life is fundamentally and irrevocably absurd and chaotic—an idea which rarely appeals to Coover's highly imaginative characters—or he can consider the freedom of each moment as a sign that we can create *our own* system of order and meaning. If this latter alternative is accepted—and it is accepted by Miller, J. Henry Waugh, and Richard Nixon—then the attraction of games, sports, and rituals of any kind becomes obvious: within these arenas there is order, definite sets of rules to be followed, a series of signs that can be interpreted, non-capricious rewards and punishments, and a sense of stasis and repetition that seems somehow freed from the demands of process. The meaning and order of games are fictitious and arbitrary in the sense that they are invented subjectively and then applied to the transformational possibilities within the system. But unlike the equally fictitious sense of order provided by history, politics, or religion, games allow man to act with awareness of his position, without dogmatic claims to final truths and objectivity.

A good fiction-promoter, Miller meets with great success in furthering the Brunist cause. Near the end of the novel, however, when Miller tries to remind everyone that the whole Brunist uprising has only been a sort of game, he discovers too late the tenacity with which people cling to their fictions and is nearly killed by an angry mob of Brunists. Like several later characters who do not fully understand the appeal of arbitrary systems (Lou Engels in *The Universal Baseball Association* or Julius Rosenberg in *The Public Burning*), Miller is dangerously underestimating the powerful appeal of such systems.

The critical reaction to *The Origin of the Brunists* was mixed. On the one hand, reviewers were quick to note what Emile Capouya called Coover's "imaginative exuberance"; Sol Yurick called the book "a breathtaking masterpiece on any level," and in his review in the *New York Times Book Review* Webster Schott noted that Coover "has a splendid talent" and added that "If he can somehow control his Hollywood giganticism and focus his vision of life, he may become heir to Dreiser or Lewis." From

our perspective today, it is obvious that *The Origin of the Brunists* shares with other innovative books of the time (*V.*, Barth's *Giles Goat-Boy*, Barthelme's *Snow White*, Sukenick's *Up*) a sense of self-consciousness, outrageousness, and a flaunting of artifice. But these qualities tended to bother many of the book's initial reviewers and critics, who judged the book primarily in terms of realistic biases. Thus, Capouya mistakenly termed Coover's literary attitude a "bitter" one, and suggested that "the author's literary gambit—his choice of naturalism-cum-fireworks—maneuvered him into a position that dropped a bushel over whatever sweetness and light he has." Likewise, Webster Schott complained that "Robert Coover writes his first novel as if he doesn't expect to make it to a second." At any rate, the book was certainly thought highly enough of to be awarded the William Faulkner Award for the best first novel of 1966 and helped establish many of the thematic and stylistic bases upon which Coover has built all his major works.

Coover's second novel, *The Universal Baseball Association, Inc., J. Henry Waugh, Prop.*, takes up the concept of fiction-making where *The Origin of the Brunists* left off. As Mark Taylor said of the book in *Commonweal*, "Myth, man's need for it and his creations of it from the inadequate fictions of his existence, is what the book is about." Here again Coover examines man's need for fictions, his tendency to produce from his own imaginative capacity the systems of history, myth, games, and transcendent meaning; here, too, the concepts of game and number are introduced to help clarify certain key relationships between man and his fictions; finally, as in *The Origin of the Brunists*, the central issues of the new book are developed by presenting the effects of an uncritical awareness of the fictional nature of our inventions. But whereas *The Origin of the Brunists*' focus on religion tended to narrow the scope of its probings, *The Universal Baseball Association* introduces a broader and more complex spectrum of issues. Although the novel does deal with the fictions of religion and history (mostly in terms of satire and parody), its primary focus is on the more general fiction-making activities of myth and art (this helps explain Coover's remark to Gado that "I wrote the baseball book not for baseball buffs or even for theologians but for other writers.")

The Universal Baseball Association actually evolved from a short story which Coover had published in the *Evergreen Review* in 1962. This story, "The Second Son," covers the action of what would later develop as the second chapter of the novel. It tells a fairly conventional story of a fiftyish accountant who has become fanatically obsessed with a tabletop baseball game which he has rigged up with dice and charts (real baseball he finds pretty boring). The complication arises when the hero, J. Henry Waugh, becomes so involved with the people and events of his game that he begins to believe in their literal existence. Specifically, he grows so attached to one of the imaginary players—Damon Rutherford, who has become a sort of "second son" for Henry—that when the game decrees that Damon must die (struck by a pitched ball), Henry at first becomes enraged and then collapses into uncontrollable sobs. Coover has commented that after he wrote this story, "I felt I hadn't gotten everything out of the metaphor, that I hadn't yet fully understood it. So over the years that followed I set about playing with the images, working out the Association history, searching out the structure that seemed to be hidden in it."

In his novel Coover decided to leave the basic framework of the story. As the puns of the title tell us, J. Henry Waugh (JHVH, the Jehovah of his world) is a sort of deity presiding over a universe made up of baseball players—in effect, he is the "prop" upon which the universe rests. The Universe—the "Universal Baseball Association" or the "UBA" for short—has been created by Henry partially because it provides him with many things which the real world does not, like friendship, excitement, and love. It is also an outlet for his strong imaginative and speculative tendencies which have been long stifled by his humdrum, everyday routine. So, into the foundation of his beloved Association Henry pours his wide-ranging ideas about mathematics, numerology (which obsesses many Coover characters), politics, history, philosophy, and so on. Thus, like the Brunist religion, Henry's Association can be seen as a fictional system created in response to specific needs and impulses. The relationship between Henry and his Association is very complex and intricately developed, but on the most apparent level this relationship suggests an elaborate allegory about God and our own universe, with the eight chapters of the book loosely corresponding to the seven days of creation plus an implied apocalyptic moment. As the book develops, Coover makes these Biblical parallels evident and has a great deal of fun portraying his Jehovah as a befuddled, lonely, middle-aged man who imagines beings into existence and then allows a set of dice—"heedless of history, yet makers of it"—to determine the events. More important than these allegoric implications, however, is the fact that Henry's Association is a wonderfully clear example of a fictional system created by the human mind. As such, it has certain obvious similarities to other blatantly fictional systems such as literature and myth. Henry's Association is mythically determined and derives many of its peculiar qualities from his own strong mythic orientation. This mythic orientation helps clarify some of the later relationships drawn by Coover between the UBA and other types of fictions—above all, the "aesthetic fiction" which we call the novel. The point is one familiar to many modern experts on myth: that mythic impulses lie behind the creation of *all* fictions. Henry shares with mythic thinkers a variety of views, such as his ideas concerning names ("name a man and you make him what he is"), his numerological speculations ("did you ever stop to think that without numbers or measurements, there probably wouldn't be any history?"), and his tendency to believe literally in the fictions he has invented. One crucial formal feature which Coover changed in his transition from story to novel was in allowing the "imaginary events" of the Association and the events of Henry's real life to mingle freely at times and at other times to develop autonomously—in effect, each is reported with equal objectivity. This complicated interplay between Henry and his Association formally emphasizes the difference between the boring, faceless, largely petty routines of Henry's daily world and the exciting, personal world he creates in his Association. And by allowing the Association to "come alive" just as Henry sees it, Coover forces us by his novel's structure to consider the ontological status of Henry's two worlds and the nature of his relationship to each of them.

Basically the players in Henry's Association seem to be the personae of Waugh, who mentally works out in his mind the details of what they say and do other than the specific events of the ball games, which are controlled by chance at decree of the dice. That Henry's desires, wishes, and speculations exhibit themselves in his players seems evident, and at times Henry seems to assume directly the identity of appropriate stars. Yet Coover's dual perspective allows the ballplayers also occasionally to drift free of Waugh and to adopt a reality of their own. As Frank W. Shelton suggests in *Critique*, this double perspective is especially useful to Coover in the middle portions of the book where Henry's efforts to deal with Damon's death are counterpointed to the players' own attempts to cope with it in their own terms: "The ways the players attempt to cope with disaster are paradigms of the way all men try to fit misfortune into a coherent universal scheme." These attempts also should remind us of the similar efforts of the Brunists to organize their own catastrophe. Coover therefore uses this dual framework to suggest certain important implications about man and his aesthetic creations. If we examine the Association very carefully, for example, we discover that it closely resembles a novelistic world: in both cases "players" are brought into being by an "author" who assigns perfectly free but absolute definitions (the personal characteristics of the players) to pure concepts and relationships (the players are technically only accumulations of statistics and records) which are then given names; this process parallels the situation in a novel in which characters are created by giving a name to a series of concepts and relationships. Thus Henry's Association resembles not only a novel but any invented system such as a mathematical system, a poem, or a scientific model in that once it has been constructed, it no longer relies on its creator or contact with the real world for its continued existence. Once Henry has supplied the Association's basic elements—its language, its peculiar obsessions, its names, plus the elaborate set of transformational rules—the elements undergo an ontological transformation which allows the Association to develop its own internal consistency, logic, and status as an object in the world (and by the last chapter, Henry seems to have disappeared, while his Association remains). Henry's problem, as is evidenced by his horrified reaction to Damon's death and his efforts to "right the wrong" by murdering Damon's killer, Jock Casey, is that he begins to confuse the logical and ontological dimensions of his two worlds.

The complex and puzzling last chapter of *The Universal Baseball Association* centers around "Damonsday," a yearly ritual similar to a passion play in which the players reenact a combination of the game in which Damon was killed along with the game in which Jock Casey was sacrificed to save the Association (Casey's initials have helped suggest his role). Considering Henry's confused, obsessive condition when we last saw him, it is not surprising that the game has evolved in a strange manner during the hundred years that have intervened. The result is that a variety of Henry's tendencies in the direction of muddled philosophical, religious, and ontological speculations have blossomed—or wildly mutated in some cases—into integral parts of the players' lives. Since they have no real choice in the matter, the players go along with the game and even maintain a sense of enjoyment in its ritualistic aspects, even though it seems to many of them that the game is pointless and possibly even insane. As is

typical of so many Coover characters, the players find that their efforts to uncover the meanings and patterns behind their activities are constantly thwarted by the complex, ambiguous nature of the signs which lie all around them. Gradually the chapter focuses on Paul Trench and Hardy Ingram, two rookies designated to play the roles of Royce Ingram and Damon Rutherford. Paul is a composite man of faith who has questioned the philosophical and religious opinions of his fellow ballplayers. Like the modern existentialist, he too seeks meaning in the face of absurdity, for a reason to continue playing life's senseless "game"; he too feels the dread, the sense of shame and regret: "Beyond each game, he sees another, and yet another in endless and hopeless succession. He hits a ground ball to third, is thrown out. Or he beats the throw. What difference, in the terror of eternity does it make?" Feeling "en-Trenched" in his dreary, predetermined routine, Paul's doubts have led him to a crisis stage as the moment of the ritualized game approaches. Before the first batter can step in, however, he walks out to the mound and finds Hardy now ritually transformed into Damon Rutherford. Their meeting is a moment of epiphany, for not only has a supernatural being manifested itself (Damon, now once again in his original role as savior), but Paul—now himself magically transformed into Royce Ingram—is given a sudden, transcendent insight into the nature of his universe. Damon tells Royce that all their futile arguments and questions should be ignored in the wonder and excitement of the present moment, which has plenty of room for developing all sorts of wonderful new patterns within the shifting confines of the game. "It's not a trial," says Damon, "It's not even a lesson. It's just what it is." As Frank Shelton summarizes this moment, "These two players, at least, attain a balance equivalent to a comic reconciliation: everything else is ignored in the intensity of the present." Damon's final words summarize what so much of Coover's fiction suggests: "the game" should not be viewed as a "trial" or as a "lesson"; it is filled not with messages or meaningful patterns, but with mere "being," which is always ambiguous and never reducible to dogmatic attitudes or single perspectives. His characters typically lose the all-important position of balance when they become so enraptured with their own designs and inventions that they begin to feel that the circuit is closed, that no other interpretation is possible. Indeed, many of the stories in *Pricksongs and Descants* are designed to counter any such dogmatic approaches and to demonstrate the freedom we have to operate within the patterns.

Despite the predictably limited response of many reviewers to *The Universal Baseball Association*, there were some people who saw that Coover had written more than a mere sports novel. Richard Gilman, writing in the *New Republic*, called it "the most impressive novel I've read lately, the most exciting," and Mark Taylor in *Commonweal* noted that "Anyone . . . can learn a great deal from this book, learning of a sort that we rarely get from fiction." But with the exception of Jackson Cope's perceptive article in the *Iowa Review* and Frank Shelton's in *Critique*, little critical attention was given this complex, multi-leveled novel, despite its subtle probing of such key concepts as game versus play, the ontological status of our inventions, and how to maintain a personal sense of balance in the face of apparent absurdity.

Coover's next work was *Pricksongs and Descants*, a dazzling collection of twenty-one fictions. Whereas his longer works tend to examine the broad base of metaphor through which we perceive the universe (through history, religion, art, myth, and games), his short fictions tend to deal more directly with *literary* fictions, the sources of their appeal, the problems which face those who want to create them, and the way they affect our relationship to reality. While a few of these stories rely on the quasi-realistic approaches of his novels ("Morris in Chains," "The Brother," "J's Marriage"), Coover usually presents his characters, events, symbols, and other literary devices as merely possible elements drawn from a much larger set of relationships. His short fiction starts from the premise that reader and writer must accept the work before them *as fictions*. Typically by flaunting his artifice and fictional design, Coover establishes a distance between reader and material; thus we are rarely tempted to identify with his characters or events, which are usually familiar types drawn from literature, movies, or popular culture. Instead we are offered a dialogue with the text, a dialogue which is often self-reflexively directed at the story we are reading. Coover's stories thus resemble many of the other "metafictions" created by writers such as Barth, Nabokov, Borges, and Barthelme in that they are not only about art but also strive to be their own subject. In his best stories Coover helps explore the generative potentialities of fictional patterns and also helps demonstrate his central thesis about the dangers of dogmatizing our fictions. As *The Public Burning* would examine in more detail, our ability to create adequate systems for the incredibly complex and involuted nature of human experience is feeble indeed (this is also the central idea of Coover's

novella, "Whatever Happened to Gloomy Gus of the Chicago Bears?"); as a result man needs to be constantly willing to shift perspectives, to explore new metaphors, and to accept the transformational possibilities of language and fabulation to help counter the effects of both death (stasis) and randomness (utter chaos). In many of the fictions in *Pricksongs*, Coover creates innovative narrative structures which make these ideas vital.

In order to insure that his readers respond to his stories as fictional arrangements, Coover often uses plots, characters, imagery, and other aspects of design which are drawn from a variety of well-established sources: from fairy tales, Biblical stories, tall tales, folk legends, cultural stereotypes, and other familiar literary motifs. Like other contemporary manipulators of myth, (Barth, John Fowles, Iris Murdoch, Ishmael Reed), Coover relies on this sort of material precisely because our responses to it are predetermined; since the material is familiar and our responses predictable, Coover can manipulate these expectations by transforming the familiar patterns into unfamiliar—but frequently wondrous or liberating—rearrangements. Coover hopes that his strategies will create in their formal manipulations a sort of freedom from mythic imperatives as well as a type of wonder and delight at the new patterns and perspectives presented. In the process, myth is dealt with on its own ground ("to apply reason to such beliefs," Coover tells Gado, "is like trying to solve a physics problem by psychoanalysis") by using the energy stored within these mythic residues to break up the hold which they have and redirect their force.

One of the ways Coover attempts to create new perspectives on familiar material is simply by telling the familiar story from an unfamiliar point of view. Coover's Biblical stories—"The Brother," "J's Marriage," and "The Reunion" (which appeared in the *Iowa Review* but was supposed to be included in *Pricksongs*)—rely on this method. The most effective of these stories is "The Brother," which centers not on Noah and the other survivors of God's wrath, but on Noah's brother—one of the victims. From this angle Coover capitalizes on many dramatic ironies by presenting the frightened "other sides' " point of view. Told in an unpunctuated Joycean monologue which uses an incongruously modern-sounding idiom, the story quickly wins our affection for Noah's unnamed brother. Because we know what will follow, our reaction to even the humorously reported scenes is strained; certainly the fact that there is no Biblical logic provided to help justify what is happening emphasizes the human aspects of the scene and makes Noah's refusal of aid to his brother seem cruel and cold. This variation serves as a sort of counterpoint to the familiar plot line, a musical analogy which is suggested by the title of the collection: both "pricksong" and "descant" are musical terms, referring to the form of music in which variations play against a *cantus firmus*, or basic line (the title also suggests the "death-cunt-and-prick-songs" mentioned by Granny in "The Door" and points to the primary motifs of sex, death, violence, and the grotesque found in most of the stories).

Although some are more explicit than others, many of the stories can be viewed as metafictional commentaries on the role of the artist or, more generally, on the difficulties of making any sort of sense out of the world. In "The Hat Act," for example, a magician appears on stage and performs a variety of feats of wizardry to which an impatient, highly critical audience responds with both laughter and jeers. The story serves as a sort of allegory about the role of the contemporary writer, straining to interest and amuse an audience that has become increasingly jaded, suspicious, and demanding. Coover himself is a kind of magician who continually presents the fabulous and improbable to jar us out of our expectations. In "Klee Dead," a self-conscious narrator finds it impossible to play his role as an all-knowing storyteller who is supposed to tell us why one Wilbur Klee has committed suicide. This narrator knows very well that the reasons behind a suicide are usually much too complicated to be presented neatly in a story of this sort. He does manage to point out several potentially revealing signs (Klee's dentures, a scrap of paper which may be a suicide note), but he also confesses that these may be only "lifelike forgeries"; he demonstrates at several points that he *can* present realistic stories with all the expected details and soothing illusions about cause and effect—but these stories have nothing to do with Klee and are, in fact, simply parodies of the realistic method. In the end we are left with "virtually nothing. . . . And a good fifteen, twenty minutes shot to hell." Although several other Coover stories can be similarly analyzed as metafictions (for example, "The Marker," and his plays, *Love Scene* and *A Theological Position*), probably "The Magic Poker" is his most significant treatment of this topic in his shorter work. Coover said of "The Magic Poker" in his interview with Alma Kadragic that it was "the real anchor story" of *Pricksongs* and that "When I had that one, I knew I had my book."

"The Magic Poker" is composed of various fragments and recombinations of fairy tales, legends, myths, and speculative histories. Like several other related stories ("The Elevator," "The Babysitter," "The Gingerbread House," "Quenby and Ola, Swede and Carl"), "The Magic Poker" presents a series of short paragraphs in a manner which suggests cinematic montage. A variety of potential plot lines are allowed to develop, some of which complement one another and others which contradict earlier ones. But none of these patterns are insisted upon as being the "real" one, and instead Coover allows the different elements to engage each other freely, to produce an expanding series of alternative designs. The story focuses on a godlike narrator (Prospero seems a likely model) who never allows us to forget that all the scenes and characters in the story are products solely of his imagination. From the outset we see his obsessive control over the fiction he is creating, his fumbling attempts to keep us entertained, his ambivalence to what he is doing. Somewhat like Richard Nixon in *The Public Burning*, his struggle to understand what he is putting together is often hindered by his tendency to confuse reality with his own inventions. Gradually the magical island of the narrator's imagination becomes a fictional object which takes its place in the world and slowly begins to envelop its creator (this progression is very similar to what happens with Waugh and his Association). Thus the narrator admits at one point that his metaphors seem to be developing a stubborn sense of "reality" or "hardness" of their own: "At times, I forget that this arrangement is my own invention. I begin to think of the island as somehow real, its objects solid and intractable, its condition of ruin not so much an aesthetic design as an historical denouement." Despite his effort to maintain control, the narrator begins to forget his intentions: at one point he looks between his buttocks and discovers a shag of hair which he invented for his Beast figure, and later he discovers himself impatiently tugging at the gold pants of one of his female characters. This sort of confusion, evident also in Henry and Nixon, quite properly has the effect of frightening him: "I am myself somewhat alarmed. . . . Where does this illusion come from, this sensation of 'hardness' in a blue teakettle or an iron poker, golden haunches or a green piano?" Thus, as Neil Schmitz says, "Throughout 'The Magic Poker' the narrator is . . . bemused, at once the systematizing writer and a witness to the fecundating power of words." Gradually, "by some no doubt calculable formula of event and pagination," the narrator disappears;

when the story ends and the characters have all left, the invented island remains behind to remind us of the permanency of all good fictions.

Pricksongs was immediately hailed by critics and reviewers as a remarkable achievement, in part because many felt that this collection was less sterilely involuted and repetitious than some of the works with similar intentions that had recently appeared (Barth's *Lost in the Funhouse* or Barthelme's *Snow White*, for example). Still, despite some fine reviews of the book (Coover is "a wonderful writer, and his is a miraculous imagination that synthesizes warring objects and qualities, and makes strange things seem familiar," said Geoffrey Wolff in *Time*), it was several years before critics began to really sense that Coover's tautly constructed stories suggested an important alternative to the exhausted self-consciousness of some of his contemporaries. One of the most perceptive discussions of Coover's stories was Regis Durand's essay in *Revue Francaise d'Etudes Americaines*. Durand notes that, like several other contemporary American writers, Coover was trying to discard "not only representation as a *mimesis* of 'reality', but more radically as figuration of any kind." He went on to distinguish Coover's fictions from the sterile narcissism of many other contemporary writers: "But to reduce Coover's fictions to empty manipulations of technical process would be absurd. . . . Coover's fiction is exemplary in that it invites us to reconsider the whole question: not only the exact nature of contemporary fiction but by the same token that of the nature and role of the critical discourse which is being produced in its wake. . . . Here is a fiction which makes a certain type of critical discourse appear totally superfluous, while remaining vital and dynamic *as fiction*."

From 1969 until 1977 Coover published several short stories in journals and magazines and also had two fairly substantial works appear. "Whatever Happened to Gloomy Gus of the Chicago Bears?" was a novella which appeared in the *American Review 22* and which extended Coover's exploration of history, necessity, and the aesthetic aspects of game. It also introduced a wholly imaginative, "completely metaphor-free" character named "Gloomy Gus," who turns out to bear a variety of resemblances to the Richard Nixon of *The Public Burning*. The other important work was his collection of plays, *A Theological Position* (1972). The book contains four one-act plays, "The Kid," "Love Scene," "Rip Awake," and the title play. These are outrageous satires on social standards as well as the conventions of the theater. For example,

in the title play the theological position is the impossibility of Virgin Birth which forces a priest to have sex with a pregnant maiden, and by the end of the play only the characters' genitals are speaking. "Rip Awake" has Rip Van Winkle trying to deal with the Revolution that has gone on during his sleep and with how it affects his own life. The reason that no major work appeared was partially that Coover was busy at work on several major projects, including *The Public Burning* which he began as a play in 1966. *The Public Burning* was completed and ready to be published for at least two years before it was released. Finally in August 1977 it was released amidst a swirl of controversy. The reasons for the controversy are obvious: not only does Coover deal with all the characters and events surrounding the volatile Rosenberg case in a broadly comic and often obscene manner, but he chooses then Vice-President Richard Nixon as his central narrator. As Geoffrey Wolff said in an essay in *New Times*, which also contains a brief interview with Coover, "The book's effect—but not its manner—is anarchic, subversive of public order and decency; it libels half the country and will scandalize the rest." Libelous, subversive, blasphemous: all the adjectives surely apply to *The Public Burning*, but whatever other effects the book had on the American public, the one thing it definitely did was to establish Coover as a major voice in contemporary fiction.

Although *The Public Burning* recasts a variety of Coover's favorite themes about the dangers of dogmatic thinking and the enormously complex operations of history and myth, his new book is in every respect a broader and more ambitious work than anything he had previously published. Part of the reason for the new novel's remarkable energy is the fact that the large metaphorical structures of the book—the confrontation between Uncle Sam and The Phantom, the actual "public burning" of the Rosenbergs in Time Square as a sort of saturnalian regenerative mass experience—probably seemed much closer to the public consciousness than the baseball metaphor or the elaborate Christian analogues used in his first two novels. At its most accessible level, *The Public Burning* does a brilliant job in recreating the apocalyptic mood and paranoiac spirit of the 1950s; just as remarkably, his portrait of Richard Nixon proves to be easily the most subtle, credible, and strangely compassionate characterization of the man that has yet appeared. The complexity and breadth of Coover's vision here are developed in part by his intricate interweaving of fact and fiction. As Coover comments to Wolff, *[handwritten marginalia at top: "value rarities as... Center, us edge / conspicuous & exuberant excess / magic against entropy" ; "see the electric chair (special decorations?)" ; "Betty Crocker / Foster + Al Dulles"]*

IV-1

[handwritten: "Cheer: 2468, Who - Con Ed, CE, CE! / save for lights on?"]

[handwritten box at right: "LITANY OF WEIRD PLACE NAMES / 'all the couples...' / Songs -2 / ★ SIDESHOWS / ★ MARQUEES / ★ GIMMICKS / ★ EISENHOPPERS / ★ ALTARS / ★ BARS & BOOZE / ★ ARP. FLO & DODGER ?"]

SINGALONG WITH THE PENTAGON PATRIOTS

[handwritten: "Captain Video / Old Mellow Sellers ?" ; "Nelson Eddy's michrevue + Dior!"]

[handwritten: "pathed with hardihood..."]

"Between the dark and the daylight,
When the night is beginning to lower,
Comes a pause in the day's occupations,
That is known as the Children's Hour...,"

sing the multitudes massed in Times Square--they are enjoying an old-fashioned singalong, led by Oliver XXXX Allstorm and His Pentagon Patriots, a bit of commemorative showbiz hoopla to honor the setting and get the night's entertainment underway. "I hear America singing, the varied carols I hear," cries Uncle Sam, peering out on the Sons of Light from backstage. "'Tis grand! 'tis solemn! 'tis an education of itself to look upon!" The Patriots are decked *[handwritten right: "used 1112 - see Whitman"]*

~~out in star-spangled Yankee Doodle outfits reminiscent of XXXXXXXXXXXXXXXX the uniforms worn in The Chocolate Soldier, the Revolutionary War, and by Bojangles Robinson when he danced with Shirley Temple~~

~~uniforms worn by Nelson Eddy in The Chocolate Soldier, by George Washington in the French & Indian War, and by Bojangles Robinson when he danced with Shirley Temple. A bit far out, like the Patriots themselves, not the sort of XXXXXX ge you'd find the Mills Brothers or Sammy Kaye or Bing Crosby and the Andrews Sisters wearing, but the crowd seems to like them, and join them enthusiastically as they stroll, singing their hearts out, down memory lane.~~

out in bright star-spangled Yankee Doodle outfits, complete with ~~feathers~~ macaroni and bloody bandages, reminiscent of the uniforms worn by Nelson Eddy in The Chocolate Soldier, by George Washington in the French and Indian War, ~~by Danny Kaye and Mario Lanza and~~ by Bojangles Robinson when he danced with Shirley Temple. A bit ~~far out, like the patriots themselves, not the sort of gear the country was used~~ Percy Faith and his Orchestra ~~to, you'd never find the Mills Brothers~~ or Bing Crosby out ~~and the Andrews Sisters rigged up like that. But the crowd seems to like them, to like the excitement they generate, and they all join in enthusiastically to stroll, singing their hearts out, down memory lane.~~

far out maybe, like the Patriots themselves, not the sort of gear the nation is accustomed to seeing ~~at the altars~~ in its nightclubs and churches --you'd never ~~expect to~~ find the Mills Brothers or Percy Faith and his Orchestra or ~~Bing Crosby and the Andrews Sisters~~

[handwritten bottom: "PH-FEAR out in bushes, / GUARD THE CENTER - rumors of Maumaus, Vietminh, Chinese, Gooks, Arabs etc / all trying to get in, take what we have"]

From typescript of **The Public Burning.**

116

the role of the artist is "the mythologizer, to be the creative spark in this process of renewal: he's the one who tears apart the old story, speaks the unspeakable, makes the ground shake, then shuffles the bits back together into a new story." Much like Joyce in *Ulysses*, Coover brilliantly builds his mythic framework out of an incredibly meticulous welter of facts, figures, dates, and other real data. Everything that might have a bearing on the case, from the Korean War and political intrigues in Washington right up through a wide range of cultural and pop-cultural aspects of America, is included here; as presented by Coover, everything that was going on in America at the time becomes magically relevant to the Rosenberg case (as, for example, his use of *High Noon* and *The House of Wax* as cultural analogues to the larger dramas which are unfolding). There is a deliberate strategy of excess in the book's development, an encyclopedic tendency that obviously bothered many of the book's initial reviewers. These aspects, such as the "intermezzo" sections of the book or the various lengthy lists of items, do not further the plot or heighten suspense, but are included to create a more palpable sense of exactly what was occurring in the public consciousness on 19 June 1953 when the Rosenbergs were executed.

The story of *The Public Burning* is told in twenty-eight sections which are narrated alternately by Richard Nixon and, in many disguises, Coover. Although a prologue and epilogue extend the action somewhat, the book focuses on the two days and nights that precede the execution of the Rosenbergs—an execution which Coover stages at Times Square, the "luminous navel" of the United States, a "place of feasts, spectacle, and magic . . . the ritual center of the Western World." The actual execution itself is presented in a wild, circus-like finale as a sort of public exorcism and ceremonial return to what Coover has called "dreamtime." As he explained to Wolff, "dreamtime" involves "the inner truths, legends, mythos of the race, the origins, the mysterious beginnings of the tribe. A primitive idea, maybe, but I feel we're dealing with a primitive society here. The point of a ceremonial return to dreamtime is basically regenerative: to recover belief in the tribe and get things moving again." It is crucial to understanding Coover's central intention in *The Public Burning* to see that the Rosenbergs are supposed to represent something much more than mere cogs destroyed when our judicial machinery runs amok. Instead they are archetypal victims, the central participants in a celebratory ritual which Uncle Sam (alias Sam

Slick, the wily Yankee Peddler) hopes will allow America to recapture a sense of community and the momentum it has lost in its battle with the Phantom (also a man of many disguises, but basically representing Communism, chaos, and the Devil). As Uncle Sam explains to Nixon, the execution has a specific purpose: "Oh, I don't reckon we could live like this all year round . . . we'd only expunctify ourselves. But we do need us an occasional peak of disorder and danger to keep things from just peterin' out, don't we?" Coover stages this last scene as a blatantly theatrical spectacle designed to ritualistically combine elements of entertainment (Cecil B. deMille chairs an Entertainment Committee and is assisted by Busby Berkeley, Betty Crocker, Walt Disney, Ed Sullivan, and the Mormon Tabernacle Choir—among others), religious archetypes celebrating regeneration and rebirth, and the anarchical impulses which will presumably free the populace for renewal once they have torn everything apart.

Although Coover fills nearly all the sections of the book with a bitter, ironic laughter, he also somehow manages to suggest a sympathetic understanding of the impulses which lead to such destructive results. The chief danger to which all of the major participants in the novel succumb is the familiar mistake made by so many Coover characters: the danger of dogmatizing beliefs, the danger of taking self-generated patterns and fictions too literally, the danger of relying too completely on fragile, oversimplified systems (such as historical or political perspectives) and not seeing how utterly inadequate they are to deal with the enormously complex, constantly shifting system called Reality. The central confrontation between Uncle Sam and the Phantom, for example, results directly from the failure of everyone concerned to see their struggle in any other terms than black and white. Even Uncle Sam, who seems to fully understand the inscrutable machinations of history ("Hell, *all* courtroom testimony about the past is ipso facto and teetotaciously a baldface lie, ain't that so. . . . Like history itself—all more or less bunk"), is willing to simplify the nature of his struggle with the Phantom if the propaganda value is large enough. Early in the novel, during Nixon's meeting with Uncle Sam on the golf course, Uncle Sam at first reveals the mysterious affinity that all men in power have and then goes on to suggest that his role is the protector of peace and goodness: "There's one thing about criminals and kings, priests and pariahs . . . They may be as unalike as a eagle to a rattlesnake, but they both got a piece a that dreadful mysterious power that generates the universe. The difference is what happens when they try to use it. The ones with the real stuff, the good guys, they achieve peace and prosperity with it—these are the Sons of Light. The other geezers, the Phantom's boys, well, if you don't watch out, those squonks can haul off and exfluncticate the *whole durn shootin' match!"*

Uncle Sam embodies a peculiar mixture of wild energy, folksiness, meanness and opportunism—a mixture which has helped shape the United States into what it is. In the novel's shocking "Epilogue," however, all of his folksiness disappears, and he reveals that the good-versus-evil opposition he had used in his campaign against the Phantom was all a hoax. As he prepares to sodomize Nixon—thereby touching Nixon with the "Incarnation of Power" that will manifest itself fifteen years later—Uncle Sam says: "You wanta make it with me . . . you gotta love me like I really am: Sam Slick the Yankee Peddler, gun totin' hustler and tooth-n'-claw tamer of the heathen wilderness, lusty and in everything a screamin' middler, novus ball-bustin' ordo seclorum, that's me, boy—and goodnight Mrs. Calabash to any damnfool what gets in my way! . . . You said it yourself: they's a political axiom that wheresomever a vacuum exists, it will be filled by the nearest or strongest power. Well, you're looking at it, mister: an example and fit instrument, big as they come in this world and gittin' bigger by the minute!" This frightening revelation, which seems uncomfortably accurate even as a caricature, is that the real source of evil in America grows precisely out of its strength and power, its ability to manipulate the facts to create the illusion that its wars against its enemies (like the Communists) are holy wars, struggles of good versus evil, light and darkness, form and chaos.

Caught in the midst of this titanic struggle, the Rosenbergs are presented as tragic, sympathetic victims who are perhaps too eager to accept their role as exemplary victims. Part of their trouble, as Nixon sees it, is precisely their "self-destructive suspicion that they were being watched by some superhuman presence." This suspicion—shared by Nixon as it turns out—is nurtured by their involvement with communism, with its own insistence on the inevitability of historical patterns and economic forces. At one point Nixon wonders if the whole Rosenberg case might be simply a complete fabrication, a story which the main characters have duped themselves into believing: "And then what if, I wondered, there were no spy ring at all? What if all these characters *believed* there was and acted out their parts on this assumption, a whole courtroom full of fantasists? . . . The Rosenbergs, thinking

everybody was crazy, nevertheless fell for it, moving ineluctably into the martyr roles they'd been waiting for all along, eager to be admired and pitied." Like the Brunists, the Rosenbergs are unable to see that history is "nothing but words. Accidental accretions for the most part." As a result they allow themselves to be victimized and even emphasize their "stage roles" as abstract pawns. Thus Nixon, who is well aware of the human zeal for patterns and convenient fictions, says of this desire: "And they'd [the Rosenbergs] been seduced by this. If they could say to hell with History, they'd be home free."

Remarkably, Richard Nixon emerges as perhaps the novel's most perceptive—even sympathetic—character as he lurches, clownlike, towards his destiny at "the center" of apocalypse in Times Square. Coover carefully researched Nixon's background, from his days as a youth right up through his early political career, and Coover's ability to transform the real elements of Nixon's life into his own fictional purposes makes the Nixon sections the most compelling in the novel. All of the familiar Nixon qualities are here: his smug self-righteousness, the obvious malice and insecurity masked by a phony affability, his self-pity combined with the appetite for power and success. But Coover's portrayal is no mere caricature, and Nixon emerges as a resilient figure who manages to get up after every pratfall, whose intentions are often misunderstood and misrepresented, and whose paranoia and other peculiar personality traits are convincingly explained. Nixon's role is really twofold: as clown and middleman. First of all he plays the all-important role of clown who assists the ringmaster (Coover) by creating the release of laughter which will allow the audience to refocus their attention on the main entertainment at hand. As Coover explains in his interview with Wolff, this partially explains why Nixon was ultimately created as a sympathetic character: "My interest in Nixon—or my story about him—grew out of my concept of the book as a sequence of circus acts. That immediately brought to mind the notion of clown acts, bringing the show back down to the ground. You have a thrilling high-wire number, and then the clown comes on, shoots off a cannon, takes a pratfall, drops his pants and exits. And then you can throw another high-wire act at them. So naturally I looked for the clownish aspects of my narrator, and you can't have an unsympathetic clown." Certainly the clown aspect of Nixon's role is very evident: we watch him smear himself with dog excrement, make a fool of himself on the golf course in front of Uncle Sam, play the humiliating role of puppy dog in front of his family, unwittingly hand Uncle Sam an exploding cigar, and—as a capper—he is magically transported from a sexual encounter with Ethel Rosenberg onto the stage in Times Square with his pants down (he is, however, able to recoup this last humiliation by improvising a "drop your pants for America" campaign which helps spark a wild orgy).

Nixon's second role is more difficult to define but is equally significant: it is a role as the middle-man, caught between his desire to be loyal to Uncle Sam (and perhaps move himself closer to the day he can be transformed into Sam's Incarnation) and his sympathetic identification with the Rosenbergs. What Nixon desperately wants is what all of Coover's major characters seem to want: some sort of balance, a center point which will provide them relief from apparent flux, the freedom to operate within the seemingly fixed patterns. Nixon yearns for assurances and answers, but as he begins to involve himself in the incredible labyrinth of clues and false scents of the Rosenberg case, he finds himself inundated with undecipherable signs and ambiguous messages. There is a lot of J. Henry Waugh in Coover's Richard Nixon: his numero-logical speculations, his mythic concept of names, and above all, his incredibly active imagination which is constantly at work finding links between his own situation and others (he discovers that he and the Rosenbergs are at once psychic doubles and mirror opposites) and fantasizing events which dominate his present actions. "It's not knowing what to do that tears your insides out," says Nixon at one point, and his efforts to unravel patterns and sort out meanings are both poignant and humorous. He is, after all, the only major character other than Justice Douglas who seriously doubts the Rosen-berg's guilt and is willing to do something about it. Even though his investigations lead him into some suspiciously self-centered speculations (as with his concern for Ethel Rosenberg, for example), there is also often the sense that, robbed by circumstances of the potential for warmth and sensitivity, he imaginatively projects onto others what he knows he can never possess. In these dual roles as clown and detective, Nixon is portrayed as a sensitive but bungling man against whom everything seems to conspire—even his heavy beard. "Why was I the whipping boy?" he asks, and later adds, "I'd suffered it all: the unwanted child, the unwanted boyfriend, the unwanted husband, the unwanted lawyer, the unwanted Vice Presidential candidate, the unwanted Republican leader—and now the unwanted Incarna-tion!" Coover's deft handling of the real and imaginary elements of Nixon's life makes his

portrait seem entirely credible. When Uncle Sam finally shows some real interest in Nixon as a future incarnation by raping him near the book's end, there is a pathetic but forceful glimpse into the familiar Nixon who can "at last do what I had never done before"; he confesses to Uncle Sam, "I . . . I LOVE YOU, UNCLE SAM!"

In his efforts to sort out meanings and discover his own freedom to maneuver, Nixon reminds us of the Association's ballplayers. This analogy works on several levels, for like them, Nixon is not only trying to unravel myth and separate fact from invention; unknown to Nixon—just as it was unknown to the players—everything within his sphere of action *has* been set out in advance, in part by Coover and in part by the fact that he is participating on the stage of history, which has already been written. Thus Nixon constantly senses that he is an actor in a play that has already been written: "Applause, director, actor, script: yes, it was like—and this thought hit me now like a revelation—*it was like a little morality play for our generation!*" Nixon's drive for "the center," evident within his personality since he was a child, is a fight for balance, the desire to find a position midway between utter chaos ("Ah, why did nothing in America keep its shape, I wondered? Everything was so fluid, nothing stayed the same, not even Uncle Sam") and a rigidly determined role as an actor within a play (or a character within a novel). Part of Nixon's attraction for Uncle Sam is that he views Sam as "Our Superchief in an age of Flux"; likewise, Nixon's desire to give shape to events, find connections between himself and others, and assign everything to predetermined categories is his attraction for order and stasis. In his harrowing taxi ride with the Phantom (later revealed to be "the Creator of Ambiguities"), Nixon is given a lecture which warns him to give up the "worn-out rituals" by which he has ordered his life. At this stage, Nixon is too frightened to grasp the importance of this message; but later he begins making discoveries of his own that confirm the Phantom's basic premise. Realizing that what has been bothering him all along was "that sense that everything was somehow inevitable, as though it had all been scripted out in advance," Nixon goes on to provide a neat summary of what much of Coover's work suggests:

> But bullshit! There were no scripts, no necessary patterns, no final scenes, there was just *action*, and then *more action*! Maybe in Russia History had a plot because one was being laid on, but not here—*that was what freedom was all about!* It was what Uncle Sam had been trying to tell me: *act—act in the*

living present! . . . This, then, was my crisis: to accept what I already knew. That there was no author, no director, and the audience had no memories—they got reinvented every day! . . . It served to confirm an old belief of mine: that all men contain all views, right and left, theistic and atheistic, legalistic and anarchical, monadic and pluralistic; and only an artificial—call it political—commitment to consistency makes them hold steadfast to singular positions.

Because of his recognition that "nothing is predictable, anything can happen," Nixon decides to work out his own script, to go to the Rosenbergs and try to extract a confession, even though he rightly senses that "In a sense I was no more free than the Rosenbergs were, we'd both been drawn into dramas above and beyond those of ordinary mortals." Nixon's futile fight to extract a sort of freedom within the rigid confines of his operation is at once both tragic and comic, and its portrayal is *The Public Burning*'s major triumph. It is also a key connecting point linking the concerns of his most recent novel to all his earlier work.

Although it is still too early to judge precisely how *The Public Burning* will affect Coover's literary career, it seems likely that it has pushed Coover to the forefront of contemporary American fiction. Even before it was published *The Washington Post* had hailed the book as "a great work of art . . . the kind of book you come across once in a lifetime," and Theodore Solotaroff was calling it "not just the novel of the year—it may be the novel of the decade." Thomas R. Edwards concluded his *New York Times Book Review* discussion by saying, "this book is an extraordinary act of moral passion, a destructive device that will not easily be defused." Geoffrey Wolff was also emphatic about the book's enduring importance: "I would guess that since World War II, only *Lolita, Invisible Man,* and *Catch-22* are in its class for durability. But for the risks it runs, for its capacity and reach, for its literary and probable social consequence, nothing I know of written in our language since the war can touch it." These are large claims indeed, but *The Public Burning* is clearly an important novel, a wonderfully bold working out of a set of metaphors which tells us a great deal about the paranoia and destructive self-conceptions of our age. The book may prove to be especially important for contemporary fiction because it gives at least the appearance of being accessible—and even thematically significant—to a wide range of the American public—something which cannot be said about much of the best fiction of the past fifteen years from Gass, Nabokov, Hawkes, Barth, and Pynchon.

Other Works:

The Water-Pourer (Bloomfield Hills, Mich.: Bruccoli Clark, 1972).

Periodical Publications:

"One Summer in Spain, Five Poems," *Fiddlehead* (autumn 1960): 18-19;

"Blackdamp," *Noble Savage*, 4 (October 1961): 218-219;

"The Square Shooter and the Saint," *Evergreen Review*, 25 (July-August 1962): 92-101;

"Dinner with the King of England," *Evergreen Review*, 27 (November-December 1962): 110-118;

"D.D., Baby," *Cavalier*, July 1967, pp. 53-56, 93;

"The Second Son," *Evergreen Review*, 31 (October-November 1963): 72-88;

"The Mex Would Arrive in Gentry's Junction at 12:10," *Evergreen Review*, 47 (June 1967): 63-65, 98-102;

"The Cat in the Hat for President," *New American Review*, 4 (1968): 7-46;

"The Last Quixote," *New American Review*, 11 (1970): 139-144;

"Letter from Patmos," *Quarterly Review of Literature*, 16, 1-2 (1969): 29-31;

"The Reunion," *Iowa Review*, 1, 3 (fall 1970): 64-69;

"Some Notes on Puff," *Iowa Review*, 1, 1 (winter 1970): 29-31;

"The First Annual Congress of the High Church of Hard Core (Notes from the Underground)," *Evergreen Review*, 89 (May 1971): 16, 74;

"McDuff on the Mound," *Iowa Review*, 2 (fall 1971): 111-120;

"Beginnings," *Harper's*, 244 (March 1972): 82-87;

"Lucky Pierre and the Music Lesson," *New American Review*, 14 (1972): 201-212;

"The Dead Queen," *Quarterly Review of Literature*, 8, 3-4 (1973): 304-313;

"The Public Burning of Ethel and Julius Rosenberg: an Historical Romance," *TriQuarterly*, 26 (winter 1974): 262-281;

"Whatever Happened to Gloomy Gus of the Chicago Bears?," *American Review*, 22 (1975): 31-111;

"The Fallguy's Faith," *TriQuarterly*, 35 (winter 1976): 79.

References:

Camille Blachowicz, "Bibliography: Robert Bly and

Robert Coover," *Great Lakes Review*, 3 (summer 1976): 66-73;

Jackson I. Cope, "Robert Coover's Fictions," *Iowa Review*, 2, 3 (fall 1971): 94-110;

Thomas R. Edwards, "Real People, Mythic History," *New York Times Book Review*, 14 August 1977, pp. 9, 26;

Frank Gado, *First Person: Conversations on Writers and Writing* (Schenectady, N.Y.: Union College Press, 1973), pp. 142-159;

Arlene J. Hansen, "The Dice of God: Einstein, Heisenberg and Robert Coover," *Novel*, 10 (fall 1976): 49-58;

Leo Hertzel, "What's Wrong with the Christians," *Critique*, 11, 3 (1969): 11-24;

Hertzel, "An Interview with Robert Coover," *Critique*, 11, 3 (1969): 25-29;

Alma Kadragic, "An Interview with Robert Coover," *Shanti* (summer 1972): 57-60;

Larry McCaffery, "Donald Barthelme, Robert Coover, William H. Gass: Three Checklists," *Bulletin of Bibliography*, 31 (July-September 1974): 101-106;

McCaffery, "The Magic of Fiction Making," *Fiction International*, 4-5 (winter 1975): 147-153;

Robert Scholes, "Metafiction," *Iowa Review*, 1, 3 (fall 1970): 100-115;

Neil Schmitz, "Robert Coover and the Hazards of Metafiction," *Novel*, 7 (spring 1974): 210-219;

Max Schulz, "The Politics of Parody; and the Comic Apocalypses of Jorge Luis Borges, Thomas Berger, Thomas Pynchon, and Robert Coover," in his *Black Humor Fiction of the 1960s* (Athens: Ohio University Press, 1973), pp. 66-90;

Frank W. Shelton, "Humor and Balance in Coover's *The Universal Baseball Association, Inc.*," *Critique*, 17, 1 (August 1975): 78-90;

Mark Taylor, "Baseball as Myth," *Commonweal*, 96 (12 May 1972): 237-239;

Geoffrey Wolff, "An American Epic," *New Times*, 9 (19 August 1977): 48-57.

Vogue until 1963, the year she won the Bread Loaf Fellowship in fiction. She has written articles and stories for *Mademoiselle*, the *American Scholar*, the *New York Times Magazine*, *Harper's Bazaar*, *Holiday*, and the *National Review*, where she became a contributing editor.

In 1958, she met John Gregory Dunne, a Princeton graduate from Hartford, Connecticut, and an editor at *Time* magazine. They were married 30 January 1964. Didion's first novel, *Run River*, had been published the previous year. Her collection of essays, *Slouching Towards Bethlehem*, appeared in 1968, followed in 1970 by the novel *Play It As It Lays*, her first large commercial success, and another bestselling novel, *A Book of Common Prayer*, in 1977. Her husband, himself the author of four books, *Delano, The Studio, Vegas*, and *True Confessions*, as well as numerous magazine articles, collaborated with her on several projects, including a column in the *Saturday Evening Post*, the screenplays for three films—*The Panic in Needle Park, Such Good Friends*, and *Play It As It Lays*—the early drafts of the script for *A Star Is Born*, and a screen treatment of "The Todd Dossier," with Collier Young.

Dunne and Didion moved to Los Angeles in 1964 and now reside in a home on the beach at Trancas, California, with their daughter Quintana Dunne, born in 1966. Didion has taught at UCLA, and her works in progress include *Fairytales*, a nonfiction work about California, and *Angel Visits*, a novel set in Hawaii.

Didion's novels reverberate with a sense of loss, disorder, anxiety, and destruction on both a personal and cultural scale. "Things fall apart; the center

JOAN DIDION was born on 5 December 1934 to Frank Reese and Eduene (Jerrett) Didion, a family whose roots in California's Central Valley go back five generations. She was raised in Sacramento as an Episcopalian and attended the University of California at Berkeley where she took her undergraduate degree in 1956. Winning *Vogue* magazine's Prix de Paris that same year brought her to New York. There she became associate feature editor of

Joan Didion

cannot hold; / Mere anarchy is loosed upon the world." These lines and the Yeats poem from which they come hold a special fascination for Joan Didion which is reflected in her fictional work. Her protagonists are women whose interior worlds resemble nothing so much as the arid, tortured landscapes which surround them. They feel anguish, yet they do not know why. What has fallen apart is meaning and moral responsibility. Like Nathanael West, Didion pictures the emptiness of the American dream, the cultural sickness, the uncomprehending despair. Her characters are so traumatized by experience they float through life as in a dream, or, more accurately, a nightmare, conscious only of stray, apparently unrelated details. Unable to achieve anything approaching self-respect, they exist within a private hell, albeit in sunny California or South America, numbed or indifferent to the pain of others. Marriage is for them as much a void as love and sex. In the everyday world, there is a pervasive sense of impending peril. Dams may break, rattlesnakes may bite, fires and revolutions may break out, the plumbing may begin to take on a menacing life of its own. Yet personal despair in Didion's universe has wider moral implications. In one place she defines evil as the absence of seriousness, and she is a cultural critic in whose fiction every gesture in an unserious world is morally revealing. These gestures, full of fright, show something is profoundly wrong. The past has been forgotten. Humanity is corrupt, fallen, and doomed. What has been lost is forever irretrievable. It is no wonder then that pain and disappointment prevail.

Didion's unsentimental style reflects the absurdity and alienation she sees everywhere as she recreates the nonsense and illogic of everyday conversation. She was influenced early in life by Hemingway, James, and Conrad. Her own sentences are precise, spare, and tight. She avoids melodrama by withholding emotion through understatement and indirection and achieves a surprising impact by sustaining a detachment that almost imperceptibly changes into an emotional intensity. It is this technique which provides the emotional rhythm of her prose. Her vision is as tragic, grotesque, and chilling as Faulkner's, her style as allusive and brief as West's. Sardonic and elliptical, her language is full of bitter wit and pregnant silences. The characters who populate Didion novels are sharply etched, often perfectly crystallized in a mere phrase or sentence. Her women tend to be more fully rounded than her men. But her characterizations are all carefully honed, swiftly and economically achieved. Her technique is often cinematic. Scenes and chapters end suddenly. The influence of television and popular culture is everywhere in evidence. Her irreverent humor is unnerving. Her carefully controlled prose is exact and shapely, full of symbols and recurring detail. Her rhythmic repetition of phrases brings to mind the world of dreams; her eye for the ominous detail suggests the evil lurking; her ear for social cattiness recalls the all-pervasive desolation.

Didion's first novel, *Run River* (1963), was noticed by a small coterie and a few reviewers. Guy Davenport, writing in the *National Review*, praised her superb writing and her uncommon grasp of place and character in a book he deemed reasonable and true. Yet he pronounced it "*too* even, *too* smooth. It sticks to its business with the determined regularity of minor art. All humor, all irony have been pared away. And where is invention? Must realism with all its sincerity be so flat? . . . Miss Didion has polished her prose too well for her own good." In the *New York Herald Tribune*, Robert Maurer admired her coolness and her impressive skill. He noted that "there seems to be nothing technically that she cannot do." Yet, he added, "Her reader suspects that the author, with all of her power . . . might herself not know what she wants, or might not see life, as Philip Roth does, as possessing a tang." However, Alfred Kazin, looking back in 1971 after the publication of Didion's next two books, would declare his preference for *Run River* because of its emotional depth.

The novel opens in August 1959 with a distant pistol shot which the protagonist, thirty-six-year-old Lily McClellan, hears and understands. But before she looks in the empty drawer where her husband, Everett, had kept his .38, she studies her diamond wristwatch, splashes on some *Joy* perfume and lingers until "all the *Joy* had evaporated." She finds Everett on the dock behind their seventeen-room house standing over the dead body of Ryder Channing, one of Lily's lovers. Everett "had been loading the gun to shoot the nameless fury which pursued him ten, twenty, a good many years before. All that had happened now was that the wraith had taken a name, and the name was Ryder Channing." Lily tells Everett, "We can make it all right," yet it is all beyond repair. The remainder of the novel is the chronicle of how the confusion and chaos of their lives during nineteen years of marriage has ended in murder.

"You say what you want and strike out for it," Walter Knight tells his daughter Lily. But Lily does not know what she wants, and besides she is not at all sure that getting what you ask for is much of a prize. At the age of seventeen, Lily does not know if she wants to marry Everett, but somehow, like most things in her life, she does it almost unconsciously, not realizing she has done it until after the fact and then vaguely hoping her father will rescue her from her decision or that someone will have the marriage annulled.

After three years of marriage and two children, Lily, whose wealth has shielded her from domestic responsibility, makes some attempt to figure out what the role of a young wife and mother is but gives up. Lily always fails, even as she tries, with pathetic concentration, to apprehend what is expected of her. Early in their marriage, Lily thinks of her life with Everett as "an improvisation dependent upon cues she might one day fail to hear." Except in times of crisis, like the death of her father, she can think of little to say to Everett, pretending when she is in bed with him that she is someone else. Yet she looks to him to take care of her. She is, in all senses of the word, his baby. Her first extramarital affair takes place after Everett has enlisted, with some relief, during the war, yet Lily and her lover, Joe, like Lily and Everett, do not talk much, and Lily is never certain that either derives much pleasure from the other. They inhabit a world where each person cons the other, where "everyone had his own shell game."

In the absence of Everett, whose most notable characteristic is his desire for order above all else, the McClellan ranch falls apart. Though Lily begs him to come home for Christmas, he views her letters and calls as the only disturbance in an otherwise content existence. "He missed her and the babies, but not as much as he told her he did, and then only in an abstract way." After Everett's return, the narrative follows Lily through an abortion and the events leading up to the suicide of Martha, Everett's sister and Lily's double. Martha drowns herself in the river that is a backdrop to the novel, a symbol of unbridled freedom and destruction.

Lily tries, even while failing, to fill Martha's place for Everett and takes Martha's boyfriend, Ryder Channing, as a lover. Now Everett and Lily have the same argument over and over, so that "it seemed . . . that they were condemned to play it out together all the days of their lives, raking their memories for fresh grievances, cherishing familiar ones, nourishing the already indestructible shoots of their resentment with alcohol and with the inexhaustible adrenalin generated by what she supposed was (at least she did not know any other name for it) love." When Lily finds Everett standing with a pistol over Ryder Channing's body, the implicit question is what had

it all been about, "all the manque promises, the failures of love and faith and honor," Martha's death, Lily's mother addressing invitations and watching *American Bandstand*, the whole long history of Lily's family and of Everett's. It had been, Didion points out, a history of accidents, of aimlessness, of no one knowing what he wanted— that is, until this evening when Everett refuses Lily's plea that they lie to the police and "make it all right." Instead he asks to be left alone. And it is at this point that Didion strikes the only really false note in the novel, preaches with a sledgehammer that "maybe once you realized you had to do it alone, you were on your way home. Maybe the most difficult, most important thing anyone could do for anyone else was to leave him alone; it was perhaps the only gratuitous act, the act of love."

After Lily hears the second shot, the one with which Everett takes his own life, she wonders what she can say of him to her children. She cannot decide on much except the cliche that he was a good man, though she is not certain that he was. But in the fairytale world in which she would wander, it is what she would wish for "if they gave her one wish."

When *Slouching Towards Bethlehem* (1968), Didion's collection of essays, was published, it was reviewed favorably by *Commonweal* and the *National Review*. The *Saturday Evening Post* would later recommend her "brilliant" articles over her "depressing" fiction. When her next novel came out, another review complained that "the world is already full of Morbid Female Novelists. But there is a dearth of good reporter-essayists. Skip the novel, buy *Slouching Towards Bethlehem*." As well as inspiring critical enthusiasm, this book gained for Didion a small but devoted following of readers.

It is a skeptical, wary book about cultural and spiritual malaise in America in which its author shows herself to be a perceptive, at times poetic, observer. She writes in the title essay of San Francisco hippies. "Has anyone ever written a better treatment of that overexposed topic of the year . . . ?" Melvin Maddocks asked. Other essays concern themselves with California life-styles, Las Vegas weddings and their vulgarity, Joan Baez, Howard Hughes, and John Wayne. "The future always looks good in the golden land," Didion notes, "because no one remembers the past." There is a section titled "Personals" where Didion's subject is her own private vision, life, and philosophy. Some of these essays, such as "On Self-Respect," though not exceptional in themselves, are important for an understanding of her fiction. There she says, for instance, "character—the willingness to accept responsibility for one's own life—is the source from which self-respect springs." She insists in "On Morality" that we have no way of knowing what is right and wrong, good and evil, beyond our loyalty to the social code. In "On Keeping a Notebook," Didion paints herself in a way startlingly reminiscent of her protagonists when she observes, "[I] did not like to look in the mirror, and my eyes would skim the newspapers and pick out only the deaths, the cancer victims, the premature coronaries, the suicides, and I stopped riding the Lexington Avenue IRT because I noticed for the first time that all the strangers I had seen for years . . . looked older than they once had." In a third section, "Seven Places of the Mind," Didion writes a splendid essay about Alcatraz, another about living in New York, and one about living in California. Her essay entitled "Los Angeles Notebook" concludes in a way suspiciously similar to the ending of her next novel.

Play It As It Lays (1970) was a best-seller which made Didion a six-figure sum and which catapulted her before the eye of the general public. Yet the critical reception of this book was decidedly mixed. Phoebe Adams wrote in the *Atlantic*, "The form of Miss Didion's novel is admirably lucid, vivid, and fast-paced. The context is the decline of a self-centered pseudo-actress with a crack in her head. This woman, endowed by the author with the spunk of a jelly fish and the brain of a flea, snivels her way into a mental hospital via a string of disasters that would outsuds any soap opera." In *The Midwest Quarterly*, David C. Stineback pointed to *Play It As It Lays* as a novel which "reveals precisely what a novel cannot afford to do . . . fail to make its characters . . . *worthy of being cared about* by its readers," and a reviewer for *Harper's* complained that "perhaps because of her fashionably fragmented narrative style, perhaps because she never moves beyond cliche (or is it archetype?) in inventing actions and histories for her characters, the book remains a rather cold and calculated fiction—more a problem in human geometry (to which a neat QED can be applied at the end) than a novel that truly lives." Lore Segal, writing in the *New York Times Book Review*, observed that the novel "feels as if it were written out of an insufficient impulse by a writer who doesn't know what else to do with all that talent and skill." She termed it "a bad novel by a very good writer." But David J. Geherin in *Critique* called it "a remarkable novel which never misses in its portrayal of a modern woman caught in a mid-twentieth-century crisis. She has cast anew, in her unique idiom, one of the prevailing concerns of modern literature: confrontation with the void.

Despite its preoccupation with death, suffering, boredom, and despair, *Play It As It Lays* is always fresh and alive." *Newsweek* called Didion's "honesty, intelligence, skill . . . wonders to behold," John Leonard, in the *New York Times*, said, "There is nothing superfluous, not a word, not an incident," and Guy Davenport in the *National Review* remarked, "If her vision of the world is terrifying, it is also accurate."

Maria Wyeth, the tortured protagonist of *Play It As It Lays*, learned, at the age of ten from her gambler father who could never seem to win, that life itself is a crap game, an observation which becomes the central metaphor of the novel. Thirty-one-year-old Maria, institutionalized for a mental disorder but understanding more than anyone else in the book, resents the efforts of psychiatrists to find reasons for the way she is. On tests, she prints "Nothing applies" with her magnetized IBM pencil. "What does apply?" the doctors ask "as if the word 'nothing' were ambiguous, open to interpretation." They miss the point that it is nothing which *does* apply. Maria, we learn, is an expert on nothingness. She knows "what 'nothing' means, and keep[s] on playing" the game of life, unlike her homosexual friend BZ who, before he commits suicide in Maria's arms, assures her, "Some day you'll wake up and you just won't feel like playing any more." But Maria plays for Kate, her four-year-old daughter whom she futilely hopes to rescue from the place where "they put electrodes on her head and needles in her spine and try to figure out what went wrong." It is Maria's opinion that looking for answers to anything is beside the point. "What makes Iago evil? some people ask. I never ask," she says.

She is a woman who has difficulty with what she terms "as it was." Her past includes a childhood in Silver Wells, Nevada, a town now literally nowhere, blasted off the map, then later a career as a model and actress in New York where she "knew a lot of Southerners and faggots and rich boys and that was how I spent my days and nights." As she is a woman who allows men to direct her life, it is appropriate that she marries Carter Lang, her director in two films. One film, which she likes, is a motorcycle movie in which she does not recognize herself as the woman on the screen who, unlike herself, seems to have the ability to control her own destiny. Because she cannot confront herself, she is nauseated by the other movie, titled *Maria*, in which the camera follows her through her own everyday existence.

This novel traces the degeneration of her relationship with Carter through mutual adultery, resentment, and bickering; it pictures the plastic, empty people around her who inhabit the sterile desert world of California, a microcosm of all America; but mostly it chronicles through third-person narration the subjective experience of Maria's breakdown as it progresses from one stage to another. Didion's concern is not with constructing a psychological case study (she intentionally keeps the prognosis vague) but in presenting a metaphysical reality—a spiritual and mental breakdown caused by the awareness of nothingness at the center of the world.

There is so much desolation inside and outside of Maria that she finally cannot differentiate between "where her body stopped and the air began, about the exact point in space and time that was the difference between *Maria* and *other*." She experiences, in other words, the objectification of her inability to have a sense of personal identity. Two specific events haunt Maria: the sudden violence of her mother's death in an auto accident on the desert ("the coyotes tore her up before anybody found her") and an abortion Carter blackmails her into having. A dream in which she whispers words of comfort to children being herded into a gas chamber because it was a "humane operation" demonstrates her sense of guilt associated with her own "humane operation." Despite her attempt to pretend nothing has really happened, she is plagued by thoughts of the fetus in the garbage. This novel is, in many ways, about uniquely feminine experience. One of the most vivid scenes is one in which Maria puts her head down on the steering wheel and cries for the first time since her childhood. "She cried because she was humiliated and she cried for her mother and she cried for Kate and she cried because something had just come through to her, there in the sun on the Western street: she had deliberately not counted the months but she must have been counting them unawares, must have been keeping a relentless count somewhere, because this was the day, the day the baby would have been born."

Maria's world is one with no goals, no directions, no moral standards, no meaning in life, no real human contact. All of Maria's attempts to escape her dread fail. She can find no comfort in love or drugs or sex or religion or hypnosis, though she does find temporary relief in driving the freeways. It imposes some sense of order in an otherwise chaotic life. Her father once taught her that "overturning a rock was apt to reveal a rattlesnake" but rattlesnakes pursue her everywhere, on the highway, in her dreams, in her food. Maria does not believe in rewards, "only in punishments, swift and personal" and it occurs to her that "whatever arrangements were made, they worked less well for women." Maria is suffocating. The emotional landscape (characterized by ennui, moral exhaustion, suicide, homosexuality, brain damage) reflects the physical landscape (gambling casinos, drive-in churches, freeways, motorcycle gangs, reconstituted lemon juice). In this fragmented world of chance where she cannot make the connection between cause and effect, where the will and the emotions are paralyzed, where the natural world provides no beauty and no comfort, where there are no heroes, only victims, where life is only one more grade-B picture with all its obligatory scenes involving other people only as props, BZ asks why one should go on living. Maria asks, "Why not?"

The effectiveness of this novel owes much to the restrained and matter-of-fact tone and to the staccato rhythm of the language, with chapters often just one brief scene long. Didion's technique is highly cinematic, using sharp visual images and often a series of rapid close-ups. The structure of the book itself, with juxtapositions of present and past, important and trivial events, first- and third-person narration along with the absence of continuity between chapters, suggests the disorder in Maria's world.

Didion's next novel, *A Book of Common Prayer* (1977), was a best-seller with even greater commercial success than her previous book. Its critical reception was favorable. Bruce M. Firestone, in the *Library Journal*, observed, "Didion overindulges her passion for sentence fragments, which she often uses as refrains. But the novel comes off anyway. Despite occasional excesses, *A Book of Common Prayer* ranks as Didion's best novel yet." Joyce Carol Oates wrote in the *New York Times Book Review*, "Has the novel any significant flaws? I would have wished it longer, fuller. . . . [Didion] has been an articulate witness to the most stubborn and intractable truths of our time, a memorable voice, partly eulogistic, partly despairing; always in control."

Didion claims that the source of the novel was a trip to Cartagena, Colombia, in 1973, but *A Book of Common Prayer* is as much about South America as *Moby-Dick* is about whales. It is instead concerned with the misunderstandings, misperceptions, and downright delusions that parents and children have about each other and which keep them apart. It is about the meaninglessness of revolutionary rhetoric and insurrection and the hopelessness of political solutions to human problems. It is about the life of Charlotte Douglas, a woman who "made not

286

"I can't seem to tell what you do get the real points for," Charlotte said. ~~"I mean I seem to miss getting them."~~

~~"So what."~~

"~~So what.~~" So I guess I'll stick around here a while."

And when his plane was cleared to leave she had walked out to the gate with him and he had said again don't you want to see Marin and she had said I don't have to see Marin because I have Marin in my mind and Marin has me in her mind and they closed the gate and that was the last time Leonard Douglas ever saw Charlotte, alive. ~~The last time I ever saw Charlotte was the night two weeks later when she pinned the gardenia on my dress and dabbed the Gres perfume on my wrists like a child helping her mother dress for a party.~~

VICKY: — SPACE BREAK —

¶ The last time I ever saw Charlotte alive was the night two weeks later when I left for New Orleans.

¶ When she pinned her gardenia on my dress.

¶ When she dabbed her Gres perfume on my wrists.

¶ Like a child helping her mother dress for a party.

From typescript of A Book of Common Prayer.

enough distinctions . . . dreamed her life . . . [and] died hopeful."

The narrator is Grace Strasser-Mendana, a former anthropologist from Denver dying of cancer who "lost faith in her own method, who stopped believing that observable activity defined anthropos," and who retired to marry a wealthy Bocca Grande coconut planter. At his death, she inherited 58.9% of the arable land and the same percentage of the decision-making process in an equatorial country distinguished only by its lack of anything distinctive and its obliviousness to any sense of history. Grace, unlike Charlotte, maintains that she does not dream her life and tries to make enough distinctions. She is interested in Charlotte's story because its meaning eludes her.

Charlotte is a forty-year-old woman from San Francisco, the slight disrepair of whose expensive clothes reflects an "equivalent disrepair of the morale, some vulnerability, or abandon." As a North American, Charlotte is one "immaculate of history, innocent of politics" who believes the rest of the world to be peopled by others just like herself and who lives the unexamined life. When Charlotte is confronted by an unpleasant event, she merely revises it in her mind to coincide with her notion of the way things should have been. She makes up stories, which she herself seems to believe, about her eighteen-year-old daughter Marin, their inseparability, their romantic adventures together traveling all over the globe. She stubbornly assures the FBI that Marin is away skiing, though they say she disappeared after participating in the bombing of a building and the hijacking and burning of a plane.

But Marin understands as little about her mother as Charlotte understands about her only child. Charlotte refuses to see how Marin can contemptuously call her great-grandmother's wedding bracelet "dead metal" (a bracelet the FBI finds attached like a charm to the firing pin of a bomb), just as Marin, who spouts revolutionary rhetoric, refuses to believe her mother spent much of her time in Bocca Grande giving malaria innoculations and working in a birth control clinic. She prefers to picture Charlotte in a tennis dress, just as Charlotte pictures Marin in a straw hat for Easter.

Ironically, Marin is indirectly linked to her mother's death. Like Maria Wyeth, Charlotte loves her daughter extravagantly, and her battle to fight the realization that that love is not reciprocated causes Charlotte to remain in Bocca Grande during a meaningless "revolution," a coup of which Marin later approves. Charlotte loses her life, an outsider caught in the crossfire. She is senselessly killed by the same kind of gun Marin carries. But, as Didion has said in a *New York Times* interview, Charlotte "finds her life by leaving it." She says she will not leave Bocca Grande because, "I walked away from places all my life and I'm not going to walk away from here." Finally, Grace, the narrator, who had seemed so different from Charlotte, recognizes in the telling of her story how closely she and Charlotte are connected, how similar they are in their delusions. If the book is, as Didion maintains, Grace's prayer for Charlotte's soul, it is also, finally, Grace's prayer for her own soul and Didion's prayer for all America.

Didion has already secured a place for herself in literary history as one of the most perceptive observers, both in fiction and nonfiction, of the American consciousness and culture in the last twenty years. Since she has continued to experiment with form and style, there is no reason to believe that her forthcoming productions will not surpass what she has already achieved. —*Paula R. Feldman*

Books:

Run River (New York: Obolensky, 1963; London: Cape, 1964);

Slouching Towards Bethlehem (New York: Farrar, Straus & Giroux, 1968; London: Deutsch, 1969);

Play It As It Lays (New York: Farrar, Straus & Giroux, 1970; London: Weidenfeld & Nicolson, 1971);

A Book of Common Prayer (New York: Simon & Schuster, 1977).

References:

Sara Davidson, "A Visit With Joan Didion," *New York Times Book Review*, 3 April 1977, pp. 1, 35-38;

Alfred Kazin, *Bright Book of Life: American Novelists and Storytellers from Hemingway to Mailer* (Boston: Little, Brown, 1973), pp. 189-198;

Kazin, "Joan Didion: Portrait of a Professional," *Harper's Magazine*, 243 (December 1971): 112-122;

Mark Schorer, "Novels and Nothingness," *American Scholar*, 40 (winter 1970-1971): 168-174;

David C. Stineback, "On the Limits of Fiction," *Midwest Quarterly*, 14 (1973): 339-348.

Jill Krementz

E. L. Doctorow.

EDGAR LAURENCE DOCTOROW was born in New York on 6 January 1931. He attended the Bronx High School of Science and later studied at Kenyon College, where he received his B.A. in 1952. Like the hero of *The Book of Daniel*, Doctorow did graduate work at Columbia University (1952-1953). He married Helen Setzer on 20 August 1954 and they have three children, Jenny, Caroline, and Richard. As an editor for New American Library (1959-1964) and Dial Press (1964-1969) and as a teacher at the University of California-Irvine and Sarah Lawrence, he has learned much about the development and present state of such literary subgenres as the Western, the science fiction novel, and the historical novel. His fiction is characterized by its analysis of society through the modification of these familiar literary categories. The result of these interests and experiences has been four novels which stretch the limits of the categories into which they fall. During his career he has become more specific about the causes of social problems and has drawn more definite lines between the forces of good and the forces of evil.

Only a handful of reviewers wrote about Doctorow's first novel, *Welcome to Hard Times*

(1960), but some, such as Wirt Williams in the *New York Times*, lauded it; and Kevin Starr, in a review written after it was republished in 1975, saw it as an "elemental parable of good, evil and civilization" in the tradition of Owen Wister and Walter Van Tilburg Clark. Soon after this novel begins, a roving bad man, Turner, almost destroys a small town in the Dakota Territory. Doctorow, sometimes gratuitously, includes sex and violence to show that Turner's actions are unmotivated and extreme. By making Turner little more than an embodiment of evil and by creating two-dimensional characters, Doctorow simplifies human actions. A growing accumulation of stereotyped characters helps to rebuild the town (appropriately named Hard Times), which is a paradigm of human society. Although the narrator and mayor of the town, Blue, fails to resist Turner, he does much of the rebuilding. After the town revives, however, Blue realizes that the pinnacle of its development and of his relationship with his common-law wife has been passed. Validating this realization, Turner, the Bad Man from Bodie, reappears and again lays waste to the town. As Hard Times deteriorates before Turner's reappearance, it becomes clear that many of the townspeople want him to return—that they have a death wish. Doctorow thus suggests that humans may be inherently unable to build a lasting society, much less a satisfying one. The only relief from this predicament seems to be record keeping, which occupies Blue: his chronicling of the town's rise and destructions constitutes the novel's narrative. His insistent, idiosyncratic narrative style draws attention to this compensatory act. In short, *Welcome to Hard Times* is an aptly named, bleak novel that uses some conventions of the Western.

Doctorow's second novel, *Big As Life* (1966), is a piece of science fiction about two gigantic, naked human figures who tower over the New York skyline and bring panic to the city. They appear to be motionless, but this, it is discovered, is because they exist in a time system proportionate to their size. Doctorow focuses on the reaction to the crisis by the ordinary human beings who remain in the city. *Choice* commented that "Doctorow's dead pan manner in this second novel turns from satire to tenderness and human concern. A performance closer to James Purdy than to Orwell and Huxley, but in a minor key."

The Book of Daniel (1971) is a kind of historical novel in which Doctorow fictionalizes the case of Julius and Ethel Rosenberg and their children's reaction to their execution as Communist spies. Daniel and his sister were subsequently adopted by a Boston lawyer named Lewin. In the novel, Daniel, a graduate student at Columbia University, attempts to understand his relationship to his executed parents, the Isaacsons, by writing their story. The book, as the title suggests, is ultimately the son's story.

Doctorow modifies the Rosenberg material in order to develop two interrelated themes: alienation and analysis. The alienation takes several forms. By frequently setting up resonances between the main narrative and the Biblical book of Daniel, he dramatizes the alienation of Jews. The Isaacsons are further alienated by their left-wing politics. Their hope that the political and legal systems will be just to them is in vain and finally the parents are executed and the children are psychologically damaged. The Communist Party stands by them only until it is expedient not to do so; therefore, it is not significantly more accommodating than a capitalistic democracy. Equally untrustworthy is the New Left, the radicals who break into the library at Columbia as Daniel concludes his manuscript. By their failure to recognize him, they reveal they know little about their own tradition. Daniel and his sister are also psychologically alienated—she to the point

of madness, he to the point of confusion and inability to control his aggressiveness. Whereas destruction had threatened the characters in *Welcome to Hard Times*, alienation threatens these characters. Irremediable inherent qualities had been the enemy in the earlier novel, but here specific religious, political, and psychological problems afflict the characters. The problems in *The Book of Daniel* are thus more nearly manageable. The characters, although flawed, are capable of action, so that this novel portrays the human predicament more realistically than does *Welcome to Hard Times*.

To attack his problems of alienation, Daniel has the weapon of analysis, whereas Blue in *Welcome to Hard Times* could merely record the destruction of his town. The rational characters in *The Book of Daniel*, like Daniel's stepfather, fail to understand his method of self-analysis through the creation of nonlogical images. The use of analytic images works to some extent, but it is not a panacea, as both the zaniness of Sternlicht (a creator of bizarre images) and the degrading images of Disneyland indicate. Daniel, however, by meditating on certain images, comes to terms with himself and with his parents' fate and thus is able to compose his narrative: this novel. The most important image, fire, takes many forms, such as the fiery furnace in the Biblical book of Daniel and the electric chair. To show the value of analyzing images, Doctorow writes imagistically, and this technique as well as more extensively developed characters gives the novel a richer texture than *Welcome to Hard Times*. Not surprisingly, it received enthusiastic reviews and earned its author a Guggenheim Fellowship (1972).

Doctorow is best known for his most recent novel, *Ragtime* (1975), a fictionalized account of the period just before World War I. Historical characters appear in it, although actuality does not restrict Doctorow. For example, he describes Freud and Jung in the tunnel of love at Coney Island, and he recounts a conversation between J. P. Morgan and Henry Ford about reincarnation. The historical characters interact not only with each other but also with three "fictional" families: the narrator's, a family of blacks, and a family of Jews. Doctorow's modifications of and additions to historical facts politicize history, usually by means of a Marxist class analysis. The members of the three families, as well as the historical figures, are alienated by forces, basically economic and political, which are out of their control.

To accomplish these purposes Doctorow modifies his imagistic methods. Of one character who makes a book out of silhouettes that can be flipped in order to simulate movement he writes, "thus did the artist point his life along the lines of flow of American energy." This is what Doctorow has done in *Ragtime*: create two-dimensional characters and demonstrate how historical forces— mainly economic—move them. These characters are less real than those forces and the period objects that Doctorow lavishly describes. By means of his syncopated sentences he tries to make them move to the rhythms of ragtime. Characteristically, he includes sexual and violent scenes, as well as a dose of the occult. Through much of this novel these techniques operate in vignettes, but most of the final section recounts the grievances of Coalhouse Walker, Jr., a black, and his retaliatory act of seizing and wiring for dynamite the library of *the* capitalist, J. P. Morgan. Coalhouse dies, supposedly a victim of capitalism and racism, but the narrator's Younger Brother, who has become Coalhouse's demolition expert, escapes. Younger Brother dies later fighting for Zapata. Some of Doctorow's techniques, like the fictionalizing of real historical figures and the use of vignettes as images of political truths, are innovative, but their effectiveness is open to question.

In fact, *Ragtime* has created a good deal of controversy. On the one hand, publishers and film producers greeted it with open checkbooks, many readers have bought it and a few reviewers, particularly the early ones, have extolled it. On the other hand, many reviewers have, quite rightly, complained about serious flaws in *Ragtime*. Richard Todd has called it the most overrated book of 1975 and excoriates its banal ideas and tractlike, oversimplified leftist politics. Martin Green warns that the voluptuous descriptions of objects promote purely fantastic revolutionary politics. Hilton Kramer notes that Doctorow sees value only in his black, female, and radical characters and accepts an oversimplified conception that America is totally malevolent. Kramer believes that Doctorow wants both to subvert the middle class and to flatter it with his descriptions of objects. Many of these critics are incensed because they feel that Doctorow has grossly simplified politics in order to appeal to a mass audience.

Doctorow is thus now at a crossroads. The success of *Ragtime* may lead him to use slick methods to advocate a simplistic political position or he may remember that a more complicated political and social vision worked smoothly with the literary techniques he used in *The Book of Daniel*. Difficult as it would be, forgetting *Ragtime* and trying to proceed from *The Book of Daniel* might well be a more beneficial course for him.

—*John Stark*

Books:

Welcome to Hard Times (New York: Simon & Schuster, 1960; republished as *Bad Man from Bodie*, London: Deutsch, 1961);

Big As Life (New York: Simon & Schuster, 1966);

The Book of Daniel (New York: Random House, 1971; London: Macmillan, 1971);

Ragtime (New York: Random House, 1975; London: Macmillan, 1976).

References:

Barbara L. Estrin, "Surviving McCarthyism: E. L. Doctorow's *The Book of Daniel*," *Massachusetts Review*, 16 (summer 1975): 577-587;

Martin Green, "Nostalgic Politics," *American Scholar*, 45 (winter 1975-1976): 841-845;

John Stark, "Alienation and Analysis in Doctorow's *The Book of Daniel*," *Critique*, 16, 3 (1975): 101-110.

STANLEY ELKIN was born in New York City on 11 May 1930 and was raised in Chicago. His father, a traveling salesman with a gift for storytelling, probably exerted the single most important influence on his son's literary career. Married to Joan Marion Jacobson on 1 February 1953, Stanley Elkin now lives with her and their three children in St. Louis, Missouri. From 1955-1957, he served in the United States Army where his fascination with radio and the idea of writing a novel about radio grew. During his student years at the University of Illinois, Urbana—where he received his Ph.D. in 1961 with a dissertation on Faulkner—he worked on *Accent* magazine, which published one of his earliest stories, "Among the Witnesses," in 1959. For this story and "In the Alley," published in the same year by the *Chicago Review*, the author received the Longview Foundation Award in 1962. His teaching career as a professor of English began at Washington University in St. Louis, Missouri, where he has been—except for various visiting professorships—since 1960. In 1963 he won the *Paris Review* Humor Prize for "The Great Sandusky," a selection from his then forthcoming first novel.

Elkin has been an increasingly prominent literary presence since the mid-1960s. The central themes in his work—four novels, a collection of short stories, and three novellas—dramatize contemporary conflicts in communication which derive from the effects of America's consumer culture on the one hand and popular culture on the other. The novelist fills consumer and popular culture with a poetry and meaning previously achieved in contemporary American pop art and poetry but never before brought to such a high literary level in prose. The trivia of a consumer-oriented, mass-producing, multi-media society are elevated to an epic dimension through his metaphoric inventiveness and the colorful professional jargon of his heroes. Most of Elkin's fiction is dominated by orphaned protagonists who are obsessed with a professional life they cherish in lieu of a family life. Their business is usually one that stresses oratorical skills, e.g., salesmanship or broadcasting. The episodic but carefully structured plots of the novels aptly reflect the heroes' homeless, unsettled lives and their tightly organized businessman's rounds. In pursuit of an ecstatic self-fulfillment, symbolized by their bachelor independence, they are often threatened by sickness, death, or the power of authority-figures. Because of the comic clash between their self-aggrandizement and the forces noted above, Elkin has erroneously been affiliated by some critics with the black humorists whose cultural pessimism and

Jill Krementz

disrespect for man's physical and spiritual dignity he does not share. More suitable to his idiom, humor, and shopkeeper's locale is his critical acclaim as an American-Jewish writer (although about as many of his protagonists are non-Jewish as are Jewish). Arching over Elkin's work as a whole, however, is his concern with style, which he sometimes emphasizes at the expense of the novelist's traditional focus on plot.

Elkin's first novel, *Boswell: A Modern Comedy*, was completed in Rome and London and published in 1964 by Random House, which remained his publisher until he shifted to Farrar, Straus and Giroux for his fourth novel, *The Franchiser* (1976). Greeted with critical acclaim as a hilariously funny first work of an unusually talented young writer, the novel was praised more for its poetry and style than for the episodic structure and picaresque adventures. From the present perspective of Elkin's extant work, it seems rather remarkable that his superb diction was not completely ignored by reviewers delighting in the fantastic behavior of the comic hero.

Boswell

by Stanley Elkin

I

Everybody dies, you know, everybody. Sure. Of course. And there's neither heaven nor hell. Parker says hell is six inches below the ground and heaven four above the head. So we walk between the two never quite managing to touch either, but reassured anyway because heaven is by two inches the closer. That Parker! What difference does it make? Everybody dies and that's that. But no one really believes it. They read the papers. They see the newsreels. They drive past the graveyards on the outskirts of town. Do you think that makes any difference? It does not. No one really believes in death. Except me. Boswell. I believe in it. I believe in everything. I am not a metaphysician. My metaphysics is people, the living and the dead. Ladloc, the historian, says that history is the record of all the births and deaths for which there is a record. History is dates. William Butler Yeats was born in 1865 and died in 1939. Edgar Rice Burroughs, 1875-1950. John Burgoyne, 1722-1792. Thomas De Quincey, 1785-1859. Louis XVI, 1754-1793. William Shakespeare, 1564(?)-1616. Julius Caesar, 102 (or 100)-44 B.C. I Like that. Only do you notice how when one goes back the birthdays become less certain? But the death is always absolute, fixed. There's something in that. It's that death is realer than life. I saw a sign once on U.S. 40 in Kentucky. It said REMEMBER YOU WILL DIE. I remember. But I didn't need the sign. I had my own father. In 1947 my father was a healthy man. Content. Vigorous. Powerful. Well. But when he died, he died of everything. The cancer. The blindness. The swollen heart. The failed markets. But even that, the death of one's father in a hospital room, the kiss goodbye inside the oxygen tent, isn't enough for some people. No one believes in his own death. I remember reading in The New York World Telegram an interview with the murderer, Braddock, when I was a kid. Braddock waiting in the deathhouse told Edward Renfrue, the reporter, "When they pull that switch, they'll be pulling the switch for the whole world. Nobody will outlive me. Nobody. The warden. The president. You. My girlfriends. Nobody. Everybody dies when I die." He could believe in the end of the world a fantastic short circuit that would end the world but not in his own mortality. Do you suppose only a murderer thinks that way? Listen, when they pulled that switch Braddock knew for the first time what it was like to be really

From typescript of Boswell.

James Boswell is a modern, uninhibited, comically crude parody of the eighteenth-century biographer who rose to fame pursuing the celebrity of his day, Dr. Samuel Johnson. Elkin's Boswell tries to inflate his ego by a similar quest for celebrities whom he wants to gather, under his aegis, at The Club. The project is the orphaned hero's way of escaping his fate as a loner, a theme that recurs in several variations in Elkin's fiction.

Another pattern that this novel introduces is the author's allegorical treatment of magic or death. The preposterousness of man's attempt to escape mortality is revealed through parodic allegory. Boswell, who has turned professional strong man, agrees to face John Sallow, known as the Grim Reaper, in a fixed wrestling match. When knocked out, the hero quite literally—and grotesquely—fancies himself dead. In the end, Boswell shows his true hero stature by passing up an opportunity to join his celebrities' Club. He refuses to give up his creative powers by becoming part of the establishment. Being an outsider is, after all, a respectable destiny.

Elkin's style and humor continued to be highly praised in his collection of short stories, *Criers and Kibitzers, Kibitzers and Criers* (1966), but the tragic fate and the unorthodox moral stance of his characters were often misunderstood. In the collection, Elkin exploits the more poignant "acute character" crisis typical of the short story, rather than exploring personality, the dominant organizing principle of his novels. As the title of the collection suggests, his protagonists are entangled in various dichotomous relationships, often reversible and always based on mutual need, as in the tragically revealed father-son conflict of the title story. The rebellion against authority figures does not always end in tragedy. It can also result in the triumphant self-assertion of "The Guest," a story that humorously dramatizes a drifter's rage against his patronizing hosts. As Elkin says in the *Paris Review* about his comedy: "the grand jokes of . . . whatever I've written . . . are the jokes where the character in trouble, confronted with a force much stronger than he is, mumbles *under* his breath something that is absolutely devastating to the authority which threatens him."

Yet the tragic component is undoubtedly prominent in those characters who lose their lives—metaphorically or literally—in their struggle with orphanhood ("I Look Out for Ed Wolfe") or with a terminal illness and the world's gruesome response of black humor ("In the Alley"). The fate of the heroes is always a complex one, for they are capable of gaining insights even in defeat. The protagonist of "A Poetics for Bullies," prototype of Elkin's kibitzer-victimizer, can barely hold his ground against a moralist-intruder. The bully's victims are seduced by the do-gooder's fairy tales. They do not recognize the bully's virtue of teaching them a more practical lesson—to accept their weaknesses as part of their identity.

The second novel, *A Bad Man* (1967), returns to the hard-core themes of Elkin's long fiction: personality and profession. The novel is about Leo Feldman, a department store magnate, who arranges to be put into prison for doing his customers illegal favors. He wants to experience the harder, more challenging life. In this test of strength, Feldman, like Boswell, encounters Death in various allegories and impersonations. Always keen on the salesman's self-aggrandizement, Feldman is inflicted with a grotesque growth, a homunculus, near his heart. A less obvious allegorical figure—but a more convincing one—is the prison warden whose authoritarian power has been unchallenged before Feldman's touchingly defiant bad man's tricks. In fighting Warden Fisher, the hero fights the death of the imagination. Besides having to carry the burden of a psychological and social imprisonment, Feldman also has to struggle with mortality. In solitary confinement he faces a disconnected electric chair. Tempted to sit in it, he experiences a theatrical parody of death.

As these examples show, the hero's complementary obsessions—with death and with selling himself—touch different levels of profundity. As a result of Feldman's unruly, sometimes hoaxlike, but more often startlingly self-critical behavior, the warden and the prisoners are, in the end, provoked into losing their self-control. They beat the hero, but the victory is his.

In 1971 Elkin surprised his readers with a novel about the life and career of a radio personality. *The Dick Gibson Show* features a hero who conducts a wide range of radio activities from news broadcasting to the telephone talk show. Critics were greatly impressed by Elkin's firm grip on the ramifications of a mass medium such as radio as well as by his excellent ear not only for the sales pitch displayed in other works, but also for the American voice of popular culture. Unfortunately, they once more responded unfavorably to Elkin's episodic structure which, as a rule, is perhaps too intricately woven into the crises of the hero's personality to be immediately discernible. *The Dick Gibson Show* concerns the hero's professional and personal demands; in fact, his apprenticeship in radio, his bachelor life and detachment from his show-business family are perfectly mirrored in his itinerary.

From the beginning of his career, which is also the beginning of radio broadcasting, Dick Gibson tries to establish contact with his audience—in the early days through the station owners whose authoritarian will he breaks by his idiosyncratic broadcasts; in the 1940s through army broadcasts that are intended to alert his listeners to war fears. With the technical refinements of postwar years, the hero can engage the attention of his audience more directly in the talk-show format of the 1950s and the even more confidential phone-in shows of the 1960s, in which anonymous callers articulate their despair. In these lost souls who call in, the hero finds a substitute for the family he has sought in vain. Dick Gibson does not become tragically susceptible to people's hysteria, like a Miss Lonelyhearts, but remains a sound man living "at the sound barrier."

The English edition of Elkin's three novellas, first published as *Searches and Seizures* by Random House in 1973, bears a telling title—*Eligible Men* (1974). None of the heroes—Alexander Main in "The Bailbondsman," Brewster Ashenden in "The Making of Ashenden," Marshall Preminger in "The Condominium"—escapes his bachelor mentality. Elkin returns to his favorite themes of orphanhood and the rejection of family ties.

Typically for Elkin, "The Bailbondsman" is clearly inspired by the hero's gruesome profession, which requires him to sell temporary freedom to those in trouble with the law. Alexander Main evades moral scruples by being a perfectionist at his job. Incredible as it may seem in view of Main's boastful self-confidence, the reader gradually learns that his record has not been spotless. Much about his fears and ambitions is revealed through the hero's nightmares about two bail-jumpers, Oyp and Glyp. These two seem to be forever out of his control. Not so Crainpool, Main's browbeaten secretary. Crainpool, a recaptured fugitive, is forced to play the role of a Dickensian underling. He is what the bailbondsman needs to keep alive his sense of mystery.

"The Making of Ashenden" is less dominated by profession than by social status. The first part pictures the modern aristocratic Ashenden, heir to four fortunes of earth, air, fire, and water, in search of a wife. Jane Loes Lipton, his candidate, seems inaccessible, but he finally meets her at his friend Plympton's estate. The plot is simple. Ashenden proposes to the fatally ill lady, but she will have him only when he has become "pure." In the second half,

the plot becomes more complex as Ashenden is entranced by the artful atmosphere of Plympton's private zoo, where he reconsiders his bachelorhood. The novella moves from a parody of aristocratic life to an allegory of Love as Ashenden wanders in the zoo and is seduced and raped by a bear in heat. The stylistic shifts are made with a control that is amazingly tasteful and moving.

The most realistic of the three pieces is "The Condominium." It dramatizes Marshall Preminger's inheritance of a condominium upon the death of his father. He becomes involved in life at the condominium and the intimate story of his father's past to such a degree that he loses his own identity, a loss that is symbolized by his eventual suicide. The condominium itself is a gigantic metaphor for social organization. When the hero, who remains a bachelor despite the temptations of his late father's girl friend, jumps from his balcony he escapes symbolically from the oppressive structure of the condominium into a more primitive, private notion of shelter—which is death: "the hole I'm going to make when I hit that ground!"

After ten years of public recognition, Elkin's reputation as a controversial writer suddenly plunged him into the ranks of today's foremost American novelists. His novella "The Bailbondsman" was made into a movie called *Alex and the Gypsy*. In 1976 his best book yet was published. *The Franchiser* presents a culmination of Elkin's themes and style. For the first time, critics nearly unanimously applauded his achievements in language; Thomas LeClair said, "Sentence for sentence, nobody in America writes better than Stanley Elkin. For him the novel is primarily a place for language, energized and figurative language, to happen."

In this fourth novel, the hero, a bachelor and traveling franchiser who claims responsibility for the homogenization of America, is a prototypical American. Interestingly, Ben Flesh is another orphan whose fortunes are based on the remains of the theatrical costume business of his adopted family. Julius Finsberg, his godfather, bequeaths him the privilege of borrowing for life at the then-current prime rate of interest; and the Finsberg children, some eighteen twins and triplets who all patiently suffer from grotesque diseases, inspire and endorse Ben's franchise business. In their resemblance to each other the Finsbergs are more personifications of Ben's franchises than full-fledged characters. Their stoic acceptance of the diseases that finally kill them teaches Ben to accept the energy crisis which affects his business and, moreover, to endure the energy crisis of his own body—his

Herb Weitman

Stanley Elkin.

multiple sclerosis, the most poetic, saddest metaphor in the novel. Ben's sufferings—which the author shares—are described in all their painfulness; but they are also transcended by the hero's recurrent hopes for America, for his ultimate franchise (a Travel Inn), and for himself. *The Franchiser* is the best synthesis of Elkin's art of fiction so far.

—*Doris Bargen*

Books:

Boswell: A Modern Comedy (New York: Random House, 1964; London: Hamish Hamilton, 1964);

Criers and Kibitzers, Kibitzers and Criers (New York: Random House, 1966; London: Blond, 1967);

A Bad Man (New York: Random House, 1967; London: Blond, 1968);

The Dick Gibson Show (New York: Random House, 1971; London: Weidenfeld & Nicolson, 1971);

Searches and Seizures (New York: Random House, 1973; republished as *Eligible Men*, London: Gollancz, 1974);

The Franchiser (New York: Farrar, Straus & Giroux, 1976).

References:

Jeffrey Duncan, "A Conversation with Stanley Elkin and William H. Gass," *Iowa Review*, 7 (winter 1976): 48-77;

William H. Gass, *On Being Blue: A Philosophical Inquiry* (Boston: David R. Godine, 1976), pp. 88-89;

Allen Guttmann, "Stanley Elkin's Orphans," *Massachusetts Review*, 7 (summer 1966): 597-600;

Guttmann, *The Jewish Writer in America: Assimilation and the Crisis of Identity* (New York: Oxford University Press, 1971), pp. 79-86;

Naomi Lebowitz, *Humanism and the Absurd in the Modern Novel* (Evanston: Northwestern University Press, 1971), pp. 126-129;

Thomas LeClair, "The Obsessional Fiction of Stanley Elkin," *Contemporary Literature*, 16 (spring 1975): 146-162;

Raymond Olderman, *Beyond the Waste Land:*

The American Novel in the Nineteen-Sixties (New Haven: Yale University Press, 1972), pp. 53-73, 175-181;

Olderman, "The Politics of Vitality: On Stanley Elkin," *Fiction International*, 2-3 (spring-fall 1974): 140-144;

Olderman, "The Six Crises of Dick Gibson," *Iowa Review*, 7 (winter 1976): 127-139;

Scott R. Sanders, "An Interview with Stanley Elkin," *Contemporary Literature*, 16 (1975): 131-145.

Chris Corpus

Ralph Ellison.

RALPH WALDO ELLISON was born in Oklahoma City, Oklahoma, on 1 March 1914, when the Southwest was still alive with the frontier spirit. Having become a state just seven years before, Oklahoma lacked the inexorable racial castes to be found at that time in the Deep South. As he grew up in an atmosphere that did not stifle personal aspirations, Ellison decided to become a "Renaissance Man." He was determined to devour experience and conquer all realms of knowledge.

His dreams met with uncommon success. After attending Tuskegee Institute in Alabama for three years (1933-1936), he headed north to study sculpture. In New York he met Richard Wright, who encouraged him to write a book review; before long, Ellison was writing not only reviews, but essays and short stories. He also became an editor of the *Negro Quarterly* and began thinking about a novel as he served in the Merchant Marines during World War II. Commencing in 1945, he worked on his novel, *Invisible Man*, for seven years before its publication in 1952. Following his recognition as a creative writer and critic, he was invited to lecture and teach at various colleges and universities, including Bard, Columbia, Rutgers, Yale, Chicago, and New York University, where he is currently Albert Schweitzer Professor in the Humanities. Not content with these achievements, Ellison is also an accomplished jazz trumpeter, a free-lance photographer, a furniture maker, and an expert in electronic equipment.

After the publication of *Invisible Man*, for which he received a Rosenwald Fellowship from 1945-1947, many other honors were bestowed upon Ellison. In 1953 he won the National Book Award, the Russwurm Award, and the National Newspaper Publishers' Award. He has also been the recipient of the Medal of Freedom (1969) and was made a *Chevalier de l'Ordre des Artes et Lettres* (1970). He received a fellowship to the National American Academy of Arts and Letters in Rome (1955-1957), and has been elected to offices in various national organizations, including vice-president of the American P.E.N. (1964) and vice-president of the National Institute of Arts and Letters (1967). He was a charter member of the National Council of the Arts; he served as a member of the Carnegie Commission on Educational Television, as a trustee of the John F. Kennedy Center for the Performing Arts, and on the board of advisors of the Institute of Jazz Studies.

Invisible Man, the work that garnered so many of these honors for Ellison, is about a Southern black youth who continually allows himself to be hoodwinked and who, until he learns to follow his own inner promptings, is constantly engaged in a footrace against himself. In the process of learning who he is, his experiences take the invisible man from the South to the North to, finally, an underground cellar which represents the dark recesses of his inner being. Before he sees the light—symbolized by the illumination of 1,369 bulbs—he

went back to Tatlock and others that I had had disagreements long before
college. I had always seemed to arouse the anger of some of the fellows,
though without intention at first, then later by design . It was an
antagonism that arose simply from my interest in other things, from
my ambition to put aside the things around me and take up other ways...
I'd been too clever for them though and all that was away and past.
I could not ~~xxxx~~reawaken the old anger against them now although it
would have been a relief from the bewilderment of having no one to ?
turn against in my confusion. ~~xxxxxxx~~ Suddenly as the bus came to
a stop I realized that I had been humming the tune which the man ahead
of me had been whistling, the words Now sounding in my head:

        O well they picked poor Robin clean
        O well they picked poor Robin clean
        Well they tied poor Robin to a stump,
        Lawd, they picked all the feathers round from
                                Robin's rump.

        O well they picked poor Robin
        Poor old Robin
        They picked poor Robin
        Clean.

    I yanked down upon the cord and hurried from the bus at the next
stop, looking into the man's innocent face as I went past. His thin whistle
like the sound of tissue paper blown against the teeh of a comb
~~tissue paper against the teeth of a comb~~, ~~whistling~~ followed me out ~~xxxx~~ the
through
~~xxxxxxxxxxx~~ the roar of the motor. I ~~xxxxx~~ stood watching the
off   leap from the door
bus move ~~up the street~~, half expecting the man to ~~get off behind me~~
Whistley
and follow me wherever I went ~~with his~~ old forgotten jingle about a
bare rumped robin. ~~xxxxxxxxxxxxxxxxxxxxxxxxxxxx~~ ~~I had to reassure myself~~
~~that~~ the man knew nothing about me, had never ~~seen me before and~~
~~that his whistling of that particular tune had been accidental.~~ But
that happened to me
I wasn't quiet sure. Nothing seemed accidental, only unexaplainable,
for now I was growing more and more certain that all that had happened
to me was part of a plan. It had to be; there had to be some order about

From typescript of Invisible Man.

137

stumbles through a series of experiences which are broadly and richly symbolic. The very first chapter of *Invisible Man*, which depicts the "Battle Royal" of blindfolded black youths, introduces many of the thematic materials upon which Ellison will play his endless variations: invisibility, blindness, betrayal, trickery, initiation, and violence (especially as it is self-defeatingly directed by blacks against blacks). He also introduces a number of the images and motifs that recur throughout the novel: dreams, blood, buckets, hands, food, money, masks, the boomerang, letters and documents, sexual perversity, the underground, "home," meretricious and distorted images of American institutions, circus imagery, references to Negro leaders, images of flight and "running," elements of folklore and myth, and religious and epic allusions.

This complicated panoply of imagery and symbolism conveys the book's constellation of themes, the chief of which, perhaps, is that the individual must assume responsibility for shaping his own identity; he must move beyond the condition of invisibility conferred by an indifferent and impersonal world to a sense of self that allows him to impose his own imagination on an ambiguous reality which is not only oppressive but also alive with endless and magical possibilities.

A number of readers have perceived that the novel offers a symbolic recapitulation of Afro-American history. The progression in the protagonist's experiences parallels many historical landmarks in the racial experience: there is the dilapidated promise of the Golden Day, the legacy of his Reconstruction grandfather, attendance at a Southern college for Negroes (Tuskegee), an encounter with shell-shocked black veterans of World War I, the migration from South to North, the adjustment to an urban setting and the problems of finding employment in a discriminatory and exploitive capitalistic economy, the evictions of the Depression years, the attraction to radical panaceas including Garveyism and Communism, and finally an explosive expression of frustration that issues forth in a Harlem race riot. This interpretation—that there is a common fund of experience between the main character and black people in general—is valid, just as it is true that Ellison and his hero undoubtedly shared a number of similar experiences. But the nameless narrator is not to be equated with Ellison himself. The narrator undergoes a severe identity crisis as he realizes that his humanity has been as invisible to him as it has been to the rest of the world; his journey from naivete to mature perception, from illusion to insight, is his

own, not Ellison's. To read *Invisible Man* as an autobiographical confession is to become entrapped by the biographical fallacy.

Invisible Man is an ambitious work not only in scope, but in style. As the novel's style shifts from realism in the Battle Royal scene to expressionism in the factory hospital scene to surrealism in the race riot scene, Ellison continually experiments with the resources of language and attempts nothing less than the melding of two cultural traditions: the Euro-American and the Afro-American. If the ideas and rhetoric of Booker T. Washington, Frederick Douglass, Marcus Garvey, and other well-known blacks are woven into the texture of the text, so too does one find verbal echoes of T. S. Eliot, Joseph Conrad, Mark Twain, Walt Whitman, William Shakespeare, Karl Marx, and many writers in the "western" tradition. Also incorporated are the different musical styles of Ellison's dual heritage. Structurally, *Invisible Man* resembles both a grandly orchestrated classical symphony (with its recurrent themes and leitmotifs) and an extended jazz ensemble (with its riffs, variations, chord progressions, and artistically controlled improvisations). In the rhythms and idioms of Ellison's prose, one hears not only snatches of blues, but be-bop (in Barbee's sermon) and jive (in Peter Wheatstraw's lively patter), as well as other musical voices and sounds.

The verbal brilliance, the exuberant and playful use of language, reminds the reader that, for all of its scenes of human degradation, selfish opportunism, and social oppression, *Invisible Man* is basically a comic and celebratory work, for the hero is ultimately better off at the end: he has become the shaping artist of his tale. The protagonist, in his role as writer, imposes a human pattern on chaotic reality, giving clarity and meaning to his existence.

Besides *Invisible Man*, Ellison has collected nearly two dozen of his essays in *Shadow and Act* (1964). The major concerns of this volume are art (his own as well as other writers' and artists'), racial experience, the American experience, and the human experience. Ellison has also written numerous short stories, but they have not yet been published in collected form. Some of the most frequently anthologized stories are "Flying Home," "King of the Bingo Game," and "A Coupla Scalped Indians." In each story the main character undergoes an ordeal that culminates in greater self-understanding and usually a more mature sense of responsibility to himself and to others. For many years Ellison has been at work on a novel which is reportedly well over 1000 pages long and is expected to be published as a trilogy.

Ellison was recognized as a significant literary talent as soon as *Invisible Man* appeared in 1952. Saul Bellow was not alone when he called the novel "superb." Characteristic of the majority of reviews, an early appraisal in the *Saturday Review* saw *Invisible Man* as not only "a great Negro novel" but "a work of art any contemporary writer could point to with pride." In the wake of generally laudatory notices, the book continues to sell well and is widely assigned in college English classes.

There were, however, and there continue to be detractors who find fault with the book and its author. Some critics with a politically leftist orientation have attacked Ellison for being too conservative. Marxists, for example, denounced the "vicious" portrait of the Communist Party (the *Brotherhood*) in *Invisible Man*. A liberal white critic, Irving Howe, berated Ellison for not clenching his fists and assuming a more militant stance. Similar criticism emerged from black critics who, like Ernest Kaiser, called Ellison an "Establishment writer, an Uncle Tom."

During the 1960s especially, Ellison became a controversial figure. While the prestige of his work increased in some quarters, in others it declined, and it seemed that Ellison was becoming isolated from the mainstream of the younger black writers and their more militant work. For example, in the 1965 *Book Week* poll of 200 writers and critics—predominantly white—*Invisible Man* was selected as the most distinguished novel written in the previous twenty years. This meant that Ellison's book was chosen over works by Bellow, Hemingway, Faulkner, Salinger, Mailer, Steinbeck, Styron, Wright, and Baldwin during that two-decade period. Despite these accolades—or perhaps because of them—Ellison came under increasing attack from black nationalists such as Imamu Amiri Baraka (LeRoi Jones) who thought Ellison's devotion to craftsmanship made his motives and racial allegiances suspect. Endless exegesis by the New Critics seemed to imply that Ellison was more concerned with style than substance. Instead of writing propaganda and committing himself to the revolutionary movement of the late 1960s, he was accused of self-indulgently ascending the ivory towers of Ivy League retreats.

By the 1970s, critical opinion had, in some ways, reversed itself. Many critics—predominantly white—became increasingly impatient with Ellison's apparent reluctance (or inability) to produce another novel. Some of them felt he had gotten too much mileage out of just one book and that he was destined to remain a one-novel novelist. Black critics, on the other hand, increasingly seemed to discover *Invisible Man*'s significance as a black novel. Addison Gayle Jr., applying the methodology and standards of the "Black Aesthetic" to the novel, found much to praise about the work. Larry Neal, noted for his militant criticism, thought *Invisible Man* "true" to Afro-American life, especially the positive aspects of the black experience; he proclaimed it "artistically one of the world's greatest novels." —*Leonard J. Deutsch*

Books:

Invisible Man (New York: Random House, 1952; London: Gollancz, 1953);

Shadow and Act (New York: Random House, 1964; London: Secker & Warburg, 1967).

References:

Michael Allen, "Some Examples of Faulknerian Rhetoric in Ellison's *Invisible Man*," in *The Black American Writer*, I, ed. C. W. E. Bigsby (Deland, Fla.: Everett/Edwards, 1969), pp. 143-151;

Houston A. Baker, Jr., "A Forgotten Prototype: *The Autobiography of an Ex-Colored Man* and *Invisible Man*," *Virginia Quarterly Review*, 49 (summer 1973): 433-449;

John Z. Bennett, "The Race and the Runner: Ellison's *Invisible Man*," *Xavier University Studies*, 5 (March 1966): 12-26;

William Bennett, "Black and Blue: Negro Celine," *American Mercury*, 74 (June 1952): 100-104;

Martin Bucco, "Ellison's Invisible West," *Western American Literature*, 10 (November 1975): 237-238;

David L. Carson, "Ralph Ellison: Twenty Years After," *Studies in American Fiction*, 1 (spring 1973): 1-23;

Earl A. Cash, "The Narrators in *Invisible Man* and *Notes from Underground*: Brothers in Spirit," *CLA Journal*, 16 (June 1973): 505-507;

Barbara Christian, "Ralph Ellison: A Critical Study," in *Black Expression*, ed. Addison Gayle, Jr. (New York: Weybright & Talley, 1969), pp. 353-365;

Jacqueline Covo, *The Blinking Eye: Ralph Waldo Ellison and His American, French, German and Italian Critics, 1952-1971: Bibliographic Essays and a Checklist* (Metuchen, N.J.: Scarecrow, 1974);

Leonard J. Deutsch, "Ralph Waldo Ellison and Ralph Waldo Emerson: A Shared Moral

Vision," *CLA Journal*, 16 (December 1972): 159-178;

Deutsch, "Ellison's Early Fiction," *Negro American Literature Forum*, 7 (summer 1973): 53-59;

Deutsch, *"The Waste Land* in Ellison's *Invisible Man*," *Notes on Contemporary Literature*, 7 (September 1977): 5-6;

Leigh A. Ehlers, " 'Give Me the Ocular Proof': *Othello* and Ralph Ellison's *Invisible Man*," *Notes on Contemporary Literature*, 6 (November 1976): 10-11;

Barbara Fass, "Rejection of Paternalism: Hawthorne's 'My Kinsman Major Molineux' and Ellison's 'Invisible Man,' " *CLA Journal*, 15 (December 1971): 171-196;

Russell G. Fischer, *"Invisible Man* as History," *CLA Journal*, 17 (March 1974): 338-367;

Leon Forrest, "Racial History as a Clue to the Action in *Invisible Man*," *Muhammad Speaks*, 12 (15 September 1972): 28-30;

Frances S. Foster, "The Black and White Masks of Franz Fanon and Ralph Ellison," *Black Academy Review: Quarterly of the Black World*, 1 (winter 1970): 46-58;

Donald B. Gibson, "Ralph Ellison and James Baldwin," in *The Politics of Twentieth-Century Novelists*, ed. George A. Panichas (New York: Hawthorn, 1971), pp. 307-320;

Ronald Gottesman, ed., *Studies in Invisible Man* (Columbus, Ohio: Charles E. Merrill, 1971);

Maxine Greene, "Against Invisibility," *College English*, 30 (March 1969): 430-436;

Edward M. Griffin, "Notes from a Clean, Well-Lighted Place: Ralph Ellison's *Invisible Man*," *Twentieth Century Literature*, 15 (October 1969): 129-144;

Allen Guttman, "Focus on Ralph Ellison's *Invisible Man*: American Nightmare," in *American Dreams, American Nightmares*, ed. David Madden (Carbondale: Southern Illinois University Press, 1970), pp. 188-196;

Trudier Harris, "Ellison's 'Peter Wheatstraw': His Basis in Black Folk Tradition," *Mississippi Folklore Register*, 9 (1975): 117-126;

Gary Haupt, "The Tragi-Comedy of the Unreal in Ralph Ellison's *Invisible Man* and Mark Twain's *Adventures of Huckleberry Finn*," *Interpretations*, 4 (1972): 1-12;

Peter L. Hays, "The Incest Theme in *Invisible Man*," *Western Humanities Review*, 23 (autumn 1969): 335-339;

John Hersey, ed., *Ralph Ellison: A Collection of Critical Essays* (Englewood Cliffs: Prentice-Hall, 1974);

Floyd Ross Horowitz, "The Enigma of Ralph Ellison's *Invisible Man*," *CLA Journal*, 7 (December 1963): 126-132;

David C. Howard, "Points in Defense of Ellison's *Invisible Man*," *Notes on Contemporary Literature*, 1 (January 1971): 13-14;

Abby Arthur Johnson, "Birds of Passage: Flight Imagery in *Invisible Man*," *Studies in the Twentieth Century*, 14 (fall 1974): 91-104;

John H. Johnson, ed., "Ralph Ellison: His Literary Works and Status," special issue, *Black World*, 20 (December 1970);

E. M. Kist, "A Langian Analysis of Blackness in Ralph Ellison's *Invisible Man*," *Studies in Black Literature*, 7 (1976): 19-23;

George Knox, "The Totentanz in Ellison's *Invisible Man*," *Fabula*, 12, 2-3 (1971): 168-178;

Richard Kostelanetz, "Ralph Ellison: Novelist as Brown-Skinned Aristocrat," in his *Masterminds* (New York: Macmillan, 1969), pp. 36-59;

James B. Lane, "Underground to Manhood: Ralph Ellison's *Invisible Man*," *Negro American Literature Forum*, 7 (summer 1973): 64-72;

F. H. Langman, "Reconsidering *Invisible Man*," *Critical Review*, 18 (1976): 114-127;

L. L. Lee, "The Proper Self: Ralph Ellison's *Invisible Man*," *Descant*, 10 (spring 1966): 38-48;

Howard Levant, "Aspiraling We Should Go," *Mid-Continent American Studies Journal*, 4 (fall 1963): 3-20;

Todd M. Lieber, "Ralph Ellison and the Metaphor of Invisibility in Black Literary Tradition," *American Quarterly*, 24 (March 1972): 86-100;

Marcia R. Lieberman, "Moral Innocents: Ellison's 'Invisible Man' and 'Candide,' " *CLA Journal*, 15 (September 1971): 64-79;

Stewart Lillard, "Ellison's Ambitious Scope in *Invisible Man*," *English Journal*, 58 (September 1969): 833-839;

Charles T. Ludington, Jr., "Protest and Anti-Protest: Ralph Ellison," *Southern Humanities Review*, 4 (winter 1970): 31-40;

Barbara S. McDaniel, "John Steinbeck: Ralph Ellison's Invisible Source," *Pacific Coast Philology*, 8 (1973): 28-33;

Louis D. Mitchell, "Invisibility: Permanent or Resurrective," *CLA Journal*, 17 (March 1974): 379-386;

Mitchell and Henry J. Stauffenberg, "Ellison's B. P. Rinehart: 'Spiritual Technologist,' " *Negro American Literature Forum*, 9 (1975): 51-52;

R. W. Nash, "Stereotypes and Social Types in Ellison's *Invisible Man*," *Sociological Quat-*

terly, 6 (autumn 1965): 349-360;

C. W. Nettlebeck, "From Inside Destitution: Celine's Bardamer and Ellison's Invisible Man," *Southern Review* (Australia), 7 (November 1974): 246-253;

William W. Nichols, "Ralph Ellison's Black American Scholar," *Phylon*, 21 (spring 1970): 70-76;

Therman B. O'Daniel, ed., "Special Ralph Ellison Number," *CLA Journal*, 13 (March 1970);

Raymond M. Olderman, "Ralph Ellison's Blues and *Invisible Man*," *Wisconsin Studies in Literature*, 7 (summer 1966): 149-159;

Stuart E. Omans, "The Variations on a Masked Leader: A Study on the Literary Relationship of Ralph Ellison and Herman Melville," *South Atlantic Bulletin*, 40, 2 (May 1975): 15-23;

Janet Overmyer, "The Invisible Man and White Women," *Notes on Contemporary Literature*, 6 (May 1976): 13-15;

Paul A. Parrish, "Writing as Celebration: The Epilogue of *Invisible Man*," *Renascence*, 26 (spring 1974): 152-157;

Marjorie Pryse, "Ralph Ellison's Heroic Fugitive," *American Literature*, 46 (March 1974): 1-15;

Frederick L. Radford, "The Journey Towards Castration: Interracial Sexual Stereotypes in Ellison's *Invisible Man*," *Journal of American Studies*, 4 (February 1971): 227-231;

John M. Reilly, ed., *Twentieth Century Interpretations of Invisible Man* (Englewood Cliffs: Prentice-Hall, 1970);

Stewart Rodnon, *"The Adventures of Huckleberry Finn* and *Invisible Man*: Thematic and Structural Comparisons," *Negro American Literature Forum*, 4 (July 1970): 45-51;

Rodnon, "Henry Adams and Ralph Ellison: Transcending Tragedy," *Studies in the Humanities*, 3, 2 (1973): 1-7;

Richard Ross, "*Invisible Man* as Symbolic History," *Chicago Review*, 14 (November 1967): 24-26;

Roger Sale, "The Career of Ralph Ellison," *Hudson Review*, 18 (spring 1965): 124-128;

Jerold J. Savory, "Descent and Baptism in *Native Son, Invisible Man,* and *Dutchman*," *Christian Scholar's Review*, 3 (1973): 33-37;

Hartmut K. Selke, "An Allusion to Sartre's *The Flies* in Ralph Ellison's *Invisible Man*," *Notes on Contemporary Literature*, 4, 3 (May 1974): 3-4;

Isaac Sequeira, "The Uncompleted Initiation of the Invisible Man," *Studies in Black Literature*, 6, 1 (spring 1975): 9-13;

V. D. Singh, "*Invisible Man*: The Rhetoric of Colour, Chaos, and Blindness," *Rutgers University Studies in English*, 8 (1975): 54-61;

Raney Stanford, "The Return of the Trickster: When a Not-Hero Is a Hero," *Journal of Popular Culture*, 1 (winter 1967): 228-242;

John Stark, "*Invisible Man*: Ellison's Black Odyssey," *Negro American Literature Forum*, 7 (summer 1973): 60-63;

Shelby Steele, "Ralph Ellison's Blues," *Journal of Black Studies*, 7 (1976): 151-168;

Jeffrey Steinbrink, "Toward a Vision of Infinite Possibility: A Reading of *Invisible Man*," *Studies in Black Literature*, 7 (1976): 1-5;

Carolyn W. Sylvander, "Ralph Ellison's *Invisible Man* and Female Stereotypes," *Negro American Literature Forum*, 9 (1975): 77-79;

Joseph A. Trimmer, ed., *A Casebook on Ralph Ellison's Invisible Man* (New York: Crowell, 1972);

J. M. Waghmare, "Invisibility and the American Negro: Ralph Ellison's *Invisible Man*," *Quest*, 59 (1968): 23-30;

James Walker, "What Do You Say Now, Ralph Ellison," *Black Creation*, 1 (summer 1970): 16-18 ff.;

William Walling, "Ralph Ellison's *Invisible Man*: 'It Goes a Long Way Back, Some Twenty Years,' " *Phylon*, 34 (March 1973): 4-16;

Walling, " 'Art' and 'Protest': Ralph Ellison's *Invisible Man* Twenty Years After," *Phylon*, 34 (June 1973): 120-134;

Sharon R. Weinstein, "Comedy and the Absurd in Ralph Ellison's *Invisible Man*," *Studies in Black Literature*, 3, 3 (autumn 1972): 12-16.

Irvin Faust.

Jean Faust

IRVIN FAUST began writing late in life but his literary career has been productive since that late start. He works by day as a high school guidance counselor in Garden City, Long Island, and at night as a writer of fiction in New York City. He earned an Ed.D. at Columbia University in 1960, and since 1964 he has published six volumes of fiction; he is currently at work on a novel with "a black hero." While Faust stated in 1977 that each of his careers was a therapeutic rest from the other, there are obvious relationships between his writing and counseling endeavors. For example, Faust's first published work, his revised dissertation, was *Entering Angel's World* (1963); it is a professional study of the interaction between the character and environment of adolescents of minority background. His first book of fiction, *Roar Lion Roar* (1965), contains several short stories about adolescents from similar backgrounds, most notably the title story, "Roar Lion Roar."

Faust as a writer may be viewed in three overlapping roles: as social historian; as Jewish-American writer; and as chronicler of emotional disorder amidst urban breakdown or isolation. His best fiction, such as *Roar Lion Roar, Willy Remembers* (1971), and *Foreign Devils* (1973), usually results when he integrates at least two, if not all three of these roles. He has described his fiction as comprising "a type of socio-realistic-fantastic journey from the thirties through the seventies and whatever years I am granted."

In his favored role as social historian, Faust has frequently drawn upon his own interests and experiences to summarize and symbolize the American experience. His first published story, "Into the Green Night," which appeared in the *Carleton Miscellany* when Faust was in his late thirties, deals with a youngster whose imagination is largely formed by the motion pictures of his day, a theme that is often echoed in his later stories and novels. A long chapter in *Willy Remembers* chronicles the persistence of Willy's son, a failed track-and-field performer. The episode not only reflects Faust's avid interest in sports but harks back to a story he wrote in high school about a former

Olympic track star who never won another race. After Faust received his first teaching degree (with a major in physical education), he taught in Harlem for four years. As he later said: "Much of what I experienced in Harlem later appeared in *Roar Lion Roar*—the street scene, the jargon and so on, the Puerto Rican thing."

The historical figure who has most influenced Faust's vision of the history of our time is President Kennedy. For example, the plot of *The Steagle* (1966) grows out of the Cuban missile crisis of 1962; in the first sentence of *Willy Remembers*, Willy confusedly laments the slaying of President "McKinley" by Lee Harvey Oswald; and vaudevillian Bart Goldwine of *A Star in The Family* (1975), begins to disintegrate after the assassination of John F. Kennedy. Faust sweepingly declared in a recent interview: "The great watershed for this era of American history, I believe, was November 22, 1963. I think our whole consciousness and subconsciousness were altered by that day . . . I think J. F. K.'s murder was the beginning of the breakup of the American Empire. . . ."

Faust pointed out in this same interview that he differs from the classic social-fiction writers like Howells, O'Hara, and Marquand in that they "were very—comfortable as indigenous Americans." Although he resists categorization as "a stereotyped Jewish writer" because he does not write as often about Jews as Malamud, Roth, or Bellow, he sees his work as "taking off with a great deal of fantasy involved within the realistic base . . . the combination of the fantastic, the aspiring, the yearning, the Jew turning into the American, and the realistic base." From an early short story, "Jake Bluffstein and Adolf Hitler," to *Foreign Devils* Faust deals with the theme of Jews who identify obsessively with non-Jewish, even anti-Jewish, culture-heroes. In *The Steagle*, his protagonist, Harold Weissburg, impersonates a half-dozen such culture-heroes, none of them Jewish. In this theme of self-hatred (only one of Faust's Jewish themes), the Jew must exorcise his "foreign devils" and accept his Jewish heritage. Only then can he further assimilate and understand his other heritage of American history and culture. No simple conclusions are drawn by Faust about that American heritage. Some of his characters look back with yearning to a simpler America of history and myth when hard work and willingness to fight for the known right earned glory and affluence. But twentieth-century Americans are confused and spiritually paralyzed, in part because of the darker side of that heritage which includes racism, imperialism, and violence.

In Irvin Faust's only collection of short stories, *Roar Lion Roar*, eight of the ten stories deal with teenagers. Three of these protagonists have the normal fantasies of young people molded by the sentimentalities of the mass media, and they presumably will grow beyond these imaginings of sexual conquest and athletic triumph. Not so with the others. In "Philco Baby," Morty, the stockboy, lives mentally within the glossy world of his transistor radio. Disc jockey chatter provides his "friends" in the make-believe ballroom, and radio commercials create his values and his vocabulary; his dreams have brand names. When a lonely co-worker, Miss Mandell, as short-changed physically as Morty is spiritually, determines to seduce him, she is forced to destroy his radio before she can command his attention. In "The Duke Imlach Story," Armand Imlach lives out his life as the great movie that is destined to be made about him—The Duke Imlach Story—a life filled with roadblocks and rejections cheerfully transcended in the sure knowledge of his eventual discovery and stardom. Like Morty, he is too absorbed in the happier world of dreams to notice the neurotic women who want him, but when he somehow stumbles into the world of show biz, he is in fact signed to a contract portending success. Here we encounter one of Faust's themes: so saturated are we by media fantasies and fraudulence in the age of "hype" that normal people deal with the mad on nearly equal terms. That the talentless Duke is likely to achieve his immature fantasy redirects the satirical thrust toward contemporary show business and its patrons.

In the title story, "Roar Lion Roar," a Puerto Rican high school dropout becomes so enamored of Columbia University that he commits suicide when the football team loses. The story is believably presented in Ishmael Ramos's semiliterate idiom. When this pathetic outcast merges his identity with the "ivory leak" college atmosphere where he works as a janitor, his doom is foretold, for only in his imagination could he be a citizen of that world. Less successful is "Jake Bluffstein and Adolf Hitler," in which a Jewish businessman, Jake, becomes a secret defiler of Jewish properties. Eventually, he "transforms" himself into Adolf Hitler and becomes, in the story's closing words, "free at last." Echoing the words of the freed slave, Jake has thrown off the burdens of freedom along with the remembered status of victim; the oppressed has embraced, then become, his oppressor. The transformation is too swift, however, in this relatively short story, and the reversal is too neat.

In most of these stories of schizophrenic flight in New York, Faust faithfully enters the mind and captures the idiom of his marginal characters and their sad desperation. In one exception, a social worker hires a young aide from India and then watches his protege with growing dismay. The young Indian in "The Madras Rumble" is an idealist who translates into practice those noble ideals to which he is expected to give only lip service. When the Indian aide teaches passive resistance to slum kids, the practiced ideals are, of course, legally and professionally unacceptable, and before long the disciple of Gandhi is shipped home. Nearly all the characters in these stories are isolated as members of minority groups and many—Morty, Ishmael, Jake, Duke—are further isolated in their madness. Faust's keen ear for American speech patterns serves not only to build plausible though strange characters but also to affirm the reader's sense that an authentic social milieu shapes and deforms these characters.

Faust's technique of portraying the mind's unraveling in the social breakdown of a hostile culture was applied with mixed results in his first novel, *The Steagle*. Richard Kostelanetz, feeling that Faust had very much fulfilled his early promise, pronounced this "the most perceptive breakdown in all novelistic literature," a judgment that perhaps ignores Kafka, Faulkner, and Dostoevsky. If many of the characters of the earlier short stories assumed a grandiose identity for themselves, English professor Harold Weissburg shifts from one fantasy character to another. He is, variously, Bob Hardy, brother to Andy of the movie family; Rocco Salvato, former school bully and present gangster; the fifth horseman of the famed Notre Dame football team; George Guynemer, son of the French flying ace of World War I; Cave Carson, son of Floyd Collins; and finally, Humphrey Bogart.

Weissburg's leap from suburban family man and academic hustler to high-rolling multiple-hero is precipitated by the Cuban missile crisis. He seduces a colleague, tells off his department chairman (whose scholarly papers he has meekly ghosted), and flies to Chicago, Las Vegas, and Hollywood, donning and shedding roles to match his adventures. But he is not really throwing off a dull past for an exciting present, for his assumed personalities are the detritus of his adolescent dreams, and he reverts often to imagined dialogues with his boyhood companion, Mendel. Several devices broaden the novel's scope and authenticity. Harold encounters a broad spectrum of pretenders, from the artfully normal to the completely mad, each of them uncertain and suppressed, many willing to surrender a contrived, unsatisfying personality for some other manufactured self. In Hollywood, Weissburg joins Tall Boy, an alcoholic has-been actor who relives all of Bogart's roles. Appropriately, the final episode, though far too long, takes place in the land of assumed personalities and costly dreams. The parallel between Weissburg's breakdown and the international insanity of the missile crisis is somewhat strained, and the reader needs better preparation if the political crisis is to serve as a believable spur for Weissburg's sudden departure from ambitious routine. But the richly textured details from Harold's past, blended with Las Vegas and Hollywood in the present, do convince us of the cultural wasteland that surrounds his soul and threatens his mind.

Faust takes pride in what he calls his "computer bank" memory, and also refers to "this well of New Yorkiana that's been simmering and cooking, lo these many years." But in *The Steagle*, too many of these topical references and inside jokes, however wittily employed—and Faust is very funny—threaten to escape most readers, more so as time goes by. The obscure title apparently baffled most of the novel's reviewers, few of whom risked an explanation. The merging of two football teams during World War II, the Steelers and the Eagles, allegorizes the damaging merger of past and present, or fantasy and reality, in Weissburg's mind, while a hybridization of personalities takes over completely on his present odyssey across the country. A clearer allegory emerges from the two movie personas he assumes on his trip. The personas of Andy Hardy and early Bogart epitomize the contradictory media-manufactured myths of the American character: warm-hearted, neighborly Andy Hardy and the violent, gangster-hero Bogart who intimidates the opposition. Faust implies that these contradictions of friendly neighbor and autonomous killer relate to a self-deluding American foreign policy, as with Cuba.

Faust's next novel, *The File on Stanley Patton Buchta* (1970), was his least appreciated and deservedly so. His undercover cop, Buchta, is a New York policeman, a Vietnam veteran, and a college graduate. He is, in short, a bundle of contradictions who must sort out his loyalties and his identities. Those loyalties are further complicated by his service as a triple agent: while working for the police department he infiltrates a New-Left conglomerate and also joins the Alamos, a secret rightist organization within the police force. Each group has claims upon the conscience of Buchta, who vacillates. He is also divided in love, a Hawthornesque attraction to light-lady and dark-lady; Heidi is the ultra-clean, understanding sweetheart, while Darleen is the beautiful sister of a black militant on whom he is spying. All the political activists betray their claims; the women are betrayed by Stanley; and the complicated plot confuses the reader. Buchta himself is dull and implausible, or perhaps just not clearly realized, while Faust's most conventional novel proves his discomfort with "straight" heroes and orthodox fictional techniques.

Willy Remembers makes a large leap forward. R. V. Cassill called this a "Book of Wonders" and predicted that it would "come presently to be recognized as a classic of American fiction." In his *New York Times* review of *Willy Remembers*, Cassill saw this novel as the culmination of Faust's fictional output to date:

> I assume I'm in agreement with most of the front-line critics in calling "Roar Lion Roar" one of the best short-story collections of the 1960's—and in feeling that neither "The Steagle" nor "The File on Stanley Patton Buchta" quite met the promise of Faust's first book. But—double-happy ending—those two novels now appear as projected lines that close in the fulfillment of "Willy Remembers."

At ninety-three, Willy Kleinhans, anticipating the protagonists of Thomas Berger's *Little Big Man* and Ernest Gaines's *The Autobiography of Miss Jane Pittman*, is eyewitness to late-nineteenth-century America. He, too, remembers historical events, but with a difference: although Willy can clearly recall details from long ago, chronology is hopelessly scrambled, and national history is filtered through his mesh of prejudices. Willy serves up his historical omelet with, in the same paragraph, the blizzard of '88, the pitching of Grover Cleveland Alexander (who wound up in a flea circus), Nixon versus Kennedy, the Haymarket Riot, prohibition agents Izzy and Moe, and the frame-up of Tom Mooney. The common theme here is betrayal or martyrdom, but the perceptive (and necessarily well-informed) reader must be attuned to the subtle note of historical revisionism and debunking. As a husband and businessman, Willy is very conservative and chauvinistic, but he combines simple patriotism with the cynical independence of the self-made, self-taught man. One recurring clue that we can trust Willy's honest confusions over "official" American history is his repeated complaint that Teddy Roosevelt convinced America that he rode up San Juan Hill practically by himself (Willy risked all there, not Teddy). Faust's own objectivity as social historian is neatly suggested by the presentation of

his central character. Willy is gruff, narrow-minded, and anti-Semitic, but he is also honest and thoroughly likable, an American of his time, place, and class.

One chapter of this novel can and possibly should stand alone as a powerful short story. The life and death of Willy's son, who impales himself while pole-vaulting (he is twice as old and half as talented as the other vaulters) is a moving tale of father-son rapprochement. Perhaps the only jarring note is the startling clarity with which Willy tells this poignant story, in contrast to his confused, hilarious recounting of other events in his life and times. In general, however, *Willy Remembers* shows improved, purposeful control in the handling of point of view. In *The Steagle* and *Roar Lion Roar*, Faust details his characters' longings and imaginings through the use of interior monologue verging on stream of consciousness. Occasionally, these devices, reflecting their protagonists' derangement, result in such narrative dislocation that the plot is difficult to follow, especially when social reality is heavily overlaid with fantasy. The reader must sometimes guess whether events described have taken place at all outside the mind of the central character, or whether actual events have occurred just as described. Not so in *Willy Remembers*. The author's distance from his character has here permitted greater control and objectivity. Or perhaps Willy's incipient senility, unlike madness, evokes a sense of clarity beneath confusion; he once saw things sharply and now some images blur into each other, so that Admiral Dewey dissolves into Governor Dewey, Teddy becomes Franklin Roosevelt, Grover Cleveland Alexander takes on his namesake's portly figure. The artistic use of these "overlapping stereotypes of urban and national memory" was praised by R. V. Cassill for its "Joycean complexity of ambivalences, portmanteau images and concentric legends."

With *Foreign Devils* (1973), Faust comes closest to achieving mastery of his own particular form, the blending of popular history and the disintegrating personality. Faust's new hero is, like his creator, a Jew, a writer, a New Yorker, and a veteran, but his present and past are skillfully played off against a brilliant evocation of a vanished America through the use of parody. Sidney Benson (once Birnbaum) is a guilt-ridden writer separated from his Gentile wife, and he is partly supported by his mother's earnings from the family candy store. Sidney's father had run away during the Depression years and this simultaneous breakdown of family and country is paralleled in the present by Sidney's marital troubles and the war in Vietnam. And so, as President Nixon leaves for Peking, Sidney attacks his four-year writer's block by starting a novel about the Boxer Rebellion. The adventure novel's hero, Norris Blake, will be a writer, a Gentile swashbuckling expression of Sidney himself (it is a much smaller step from Benson to Blake than from Birnbaum to Benson). This novel-within-the-novel is a nearly perfect parody, captivating as outrageous melodrama and revealing as wishful psychodrama. Faust sustains the stilted rhythms and arrogant ideology of the Richard Harding Davis school of foreign correspondence while projecting Sidney's longings for sex and danger.

The story in the present is not handled as well. It is freighted, like *The Steagle*, with hundreds of references to old movies, baseball, family history, and the friendships of the last generation. Amidst these details are one-line jokes, takeoffs, impersonations, and a running imaginary conversation between Sidney, Fletcher Christian, and Captain Bligh. Near the end, Sidney finds his mute, helpless father in Albuquerque, attended by an ancient mistress. When he tells that wrecked old sport the end of his Boxer novel, the attempted communication between father and son marks a touching, problematic resolution of the need for Sidney, and America, to come to terms with the past. In this tour de force novel, all the major themes and techniques of Faust's literary career coalesce: the search for the self in the rubbish of mass culture; the American attempt to find a usable, acceptable past; the ethnic yearning to belong and the Jew's need to survive as Jew; the wounded male ego in the turbulent city; the madness and solace of dreams; the narrative intercutting and blurring of outline by the mind in panicky flight or quest.

Faust's latest novel, *A Star in the Family* (1975) was poorly received by critics and the public. The appearance at this time of Albert Goldman's biography of Lenny Bruce and Wallace Markfield's *You Could Live If They Let You*, which seems closely modeled on Bruce, interfered with the judgment of Faust's novel. Gilbert Millstein, in the *New York Times Book Review*, found astonishing similarities in the Markfield and Faust novels and panned both. Richard Lingeman, in the *New York Times*, more correctly saw that "Bart Goldwine is not primarily the hero as Comedian, or the American as Jew, though he is both; he is the American as American . . . the good-hearted, all-American boyman with a conscience."

Verifying this intention, Faust commented:

> My comic was the all-American straight Jewish-American kid who stood up for the old-fashioned virtues and was the stand-up comic who is perhaps represented by people like Jerry Lester—if you remember him— Morey Amsterdam, a little of Berle, perhaps, but not at all the so-called modern comic. And, of course, what I was trying to do was to show the rise and fall of this nation over the last forty years, using as a vehicle the most vulnerable kind of person in our society— somebody whose business is to try and stand up and make people laugh. In my judgment, after 1963 there wasn't a hell of a lot to laugh about in America.

The novel is told through a series of interviews which Goldwine's biographer conducts, including long narrative stretches that can only be told by Goldwine. The multiple point of view allows a check on Goldwine's recollections and judgments, but Goldwine is allowed brief rebuttal to each interview and to his biographer's comments. These long backward glances by Goldwine and his associates permit Faust to capture the period flavor of the 1930s through the 1960s and to reproduce the street-talk and the show-business patter which he knows so well. Fan magazine articles, bar mitzvah speeches, Catskill resort routines, the repartee of the make-out artist, family talk, and serious courtship, all evoke an era which comes through as surprisingly innocent for all of Goldwine's hard-edged cynicism.

Goldwine grows from resort comic to stage performer, then stars in movies, radio, and television, and finally suffers a long, steady decline. He is saved for a time by his impression of John F. Kennedy that is the hit of the nightclub circuit. When the President dies the act ends and Goldwine drunkenly finishes his days doing impersonations anywhere he can get a job. But Bart Goldwine's career is really destroyed by television's insatiable appetite, and the connection Faust intends to establish between Goldwine, America, and the decline of the nation after Kennedy's death is not firmly achieved. The strength of the novel lies mainly in the character of Goldwine. The comedian, despite his failed marriages, his infidelity, and his brash conceit, has heart and has values. He cares about his family and his country in a way that Faust makes us feel is redeeming, old-fashioned and, presumably, disappearing.

Faust's main contribution to our literature lies in the portrayal of American society through representative characters. Some of these characters,

I

Well you cannot hold back any longer. Close your eyes, hold your nose, grab air and jump. Even as you did 32 years ago into Lake Powhattan at scout camp and they had to fish you out. Christ where did _that_ come from? An omen? Stop that! How many times have I told you, _ordered_ you not to be superstitious? You are a _great_ swimmer now. All right, don't yell. All right. So jump. Must I? Don't ask stupid questions. Very well; must I? YES. OK, OK, Three days ago the President's advance party left for Peking. There, that wasn't so bad. No, but I'm out of breath. Psychogenic, get on with it. Don't push so. I have to with you. All right, They left for the Forbidden City. Ah. It is the first time since '49 Americans will have pierced the holy gates. The Chien Men. The first time they will stroll up Legation Street. Don't stop. Yes, Chinese Gordon and the Opium War and Marshall and Wedemeyer and Pat Hurley and Chiang and the Long March and _The General Died at Dawn_ and the _Panay_ and Sun and the Missimo (did the boys make out with her at Wellesley? Stop!) and the Right Harmonious Fists and 1900. There you've done it! You've made the connection, that wasn't so godawful, was it? Then why am I sweating? Stop asking so damn many questions and get on with it, Yenta Telabenda. Leave the old lady out of it. All right.

From typescript of novel-in-progress.

like those in *Roar Lion Roar,* are young and socially marginal, but he has depicted with equal force the lives of a young police officer, middle-aged professor, aging vaudevillian, and senile business-man. His extraordinary memory for the details of mass culture may lead some to view him primarily as social historian of our times. What distinguishes Faust, however, is his ability to evoke a sense of social breakdown through the declining or disintegrating personality. Seeing the cultural milieu through the eyes of a schizophrenic, for example, requires a prose style that combines realism and surrealism, and a philosophic outlook that suggests both social concern and a sense of the absurd. These tensions of style and mood create the richly textured evocation sought by Faust of a "socio-realistic-fantastic journey from the thirties through the seventies."

—*Frank Campenni*

Books:

Roar Lion Roar and Other Stories (New York: Random House, 1964; London: Gollancz, 1965);
The Steagle (New York: Random House, 1966);
The File on Stanley Patton Buchta (New York: Random House, 1970);
Willy Remembers (New York: Arbor House, 1971);
Foreign Devils (New York: Arbor House, 1973);
A Star in the Family (Garden City: Doubleday, 1975).

Periodical Publications:

"The Dalai Lama of Harlem," *Sewanee Review,* 72, 2 (1964): 223-243;
"The Double Snapper," *Esquire,* 64, 6 (1965): 180-182, 304-308;
"Operation Buena Vista," *Paris Review,* 35 (1965): 87-105;
"Simon Girty Go Ape," *Transatlantic Review,* 21 (1966): 66-75.

References:

Matthew J. Bruccoli, "Irvin Faust," in *Conversations with Writers II* (Detroit: Bruccoli Clark / Gale Research, 1978), pp. 46-72;
R. V. Cassill, "Willy Remembers," *New York Times Book Review,* 29 August 1971, p. 29;
Richard Kostelanetz, "New American Fiction Reconsidered," *TriQuarterly,* 8 (winter 1967): 279-286.

SHELBY FOOTE, novelist, short story writer, and historian, was born 17 November 1916 in the Mississippi Delta town of Greenville, the son of Shelby Dade and Lillian Rosenstock Foote. His father was a Greenville businessman, his grand-father, Huger Lee Foote, an early planter near Greenville, and his great-grandfather a cavalry officer at Shiloh. Still another ancestor, Isaac Shelby, was governor of Kentucky in its early years and a participant in the Battle of Kings Mountain. Foote was educated through high school in Greenville, where he was influenced by local author William Alexander Percy and was a schoolmate of his nephew, Walker Percy. He and the younger Percy were best friends and in Percy's words, "went into the business of selling poems for 50¢ apiece." About the age of seventeen, Foote became an avid reader.

In 1935, he and Percy decided to attend the University of North Carolina. At Chapel Hill, he took only the courses he wanted and spent much of his time reading. He remained through 1937 and did not graduate. When Hitler invaded Poland, he joined the Mississippi National Guard in October 1939. In 1940, he was mobilized into the army (artillery) as sergeant and rose to captain before being "kicked completely out" during service in Northern Ireland for leaving to see his girl friend in Belfast. She became his first wife in 1944. Foote worked as an Associated Press reporter at the local desk in New York throughout the fall and winter of 1944. He lived in a third-story walk-up on the corner of Park and 86th and now mainly remembers riding the subway, eating at automats at crazy hours, and covering banquets and speeches. He recalls spending his days off reading Proust and Browning and feeling for the only time in his life "truly disoriented."

He enlisted in the Marine Corps, combat intelligence branch, in January 1945 and served until November that year. In the years after the war he held various jobs, including construction worker, radio copywriter, and reporter for Hodding Carter's *Delta Democrat-Times.* Carter called him "one of the most exasperating reporters" he ever knew because he was frequently missing at assignment time owing to his writing. Foote had been writing since the age of sixteen, when his poetry was published in the Greenville High School *Pica.* From 1935 to 1937 he worked for the University of North Carolina literary magazine and published short stories, reviews, and poetry there. He wrote his first novel before 1940, sent it out, and was told it was too experimental. After the war, Foote returned to this novel and

rewrote it so as to remove the obvious influences of James Joyce and Thomas Wolfe.

Tournament (1949) was received well as the first work of a promising young novelist, and Foote was hailed as one of America's finest young authors in the years after World War II. *Tournament,* like all of Foote's novels except *Shiloh* and *September September,* is set in Jordan County, Mississippi, modelled after Washington County, the county seat of which is Foote's hometown of Greenville, called Bristol in the fiction. Lake Washington becomes Foote's Lake Jordan. *Tournament*'s central character is Hugh Bart, roughly patterned after Foote's grandfather. The rise and fall of Bart and his plantation, "Solitaire," parallel the rise and fall of the plantation South, thus showing the beginning of the novelist's abiding interest in Southern history. Bart sells his plantation and in the hands of

unscrupulous businessmen loses everything, so that he must turn to gambling for a living. In this occupation, he betrays himself and all he has stood for in the past because he must now survive by preying off of those friends whose faith and honor he has won slowly over the years. Bart is thus a tragic hero.

As critic Thomas Landess points out, *Tournament* defines a period of change in the South's history—the transition from a farm community to a society of business and finance. With *Tournament,* Foote began a history of his region in fiction, an undertaking which was to continue through the four novels of the 1950s and the recently published *September September.* Also to be seen in *Tournament* is Foote's major theme, "that each man, even when pressed closest by other men in their scramble for the things they offer one another with so little grace, is profoundly alone." The theme of loneliness marks the tragedy of Bart's life against the backdrop of a changing era.

In his next novel, *Follow Me Down* (1950), Foote again sounds the theme that "Love has failed us. We are essentially, irrevocably alone." The central characters of the novel are Luther Eustis, a tenant farming evangelist at "Solitaire," and a young girl, Beulah, whom he seduces and then kills. It is based on a Delta trial of the 1940s, which Foote attended. The novel deals with the possibilities of moral choice in a world ordered by a merciless and inscrutable fate. As Foote remarks, he made "practically everyone in the book a victim of circumstances in one way or another, even down to the turnkey's wife's goiter, and I remember I was trying to stress the valiance of practically everyone on earth in being able to get through life at all." It is about "the terrible sadness of life, the tragedy of it." The novel, as all of Foote's work, owes no small amount to the philosophy of literary naturalism.

Follow Me Down also continues Foote's interest in Southern history. Here Eustis represents old time protestant morality in the face of Beulah's sexuality and worldliness. Beulah has been called the representative of "a force in the modern world which is something more than merely pagan—sexuality as the ultimate truth of existence." The novel contrasts the "past of moral certitude and a future of increasing decadence." Critics generally agree that this is Foote's best novel. It has been praised highly by numerous readers for its theme and mythical qualities, its "stabbing language," characterization, and structure. Foote admits that the structure owes much to a favorite literary work—Browning's *The Ring and the Book*. His idea, he says, was to "penetrate to the heart of an event and then emerge, by means of monologs that became increasingly and then decreasingly involved in the story being told. The first and last speakers, for example, are involved by their professions, and both speak in a more or less professional manner. The third and third-from-last are intimates of the principals, and their tone is lyric." The victim's monologue is central and is flanked by the two monologues of her killer. Foote's intention was to "give an impression of penetrating and emerging."

Foote's third novel, *Love in a Dry Season* (1951), captures the historical South at a crucial time of change. It takes place in Bristol from the 1920s to World War II, a time, in the words of critic Thomas Landess, when the cotton community has become no more than a business interest owned by a powerful Eastern trust. The novel again portrays an arbitrary fate and frustrated characters who have little control over their lives. As the title indicates, this work is about the lack of love, and the fundamental sterility in the hostile relationship between men and women. The theme is again loneliness, the trivialization of love, the restriction of modern man's emotional commitments. It is essentially a comedy; in this society, there can be no more tragic heroes like Hugh Bart. The characters are petty, weak, and selfish. For men like Harley Drew, woman has become a means of questing for the goal of wealth, a perversion of the chivalric tradition through materialism. As a work of art, this novel is the equal of *Follow Me Down*. It is extremely accurate as a social novel concerned with a group of people within a society in a time of change. As Foote says, "I have always been interested in society. I started out knowing that if I was going to write about a society, I had damned well better tell the truth about it." Again, this novel was well received.

Foote's fourth novel, *Shiloh* (1952), was begun prior to June 1949 and was to become his only popular success. It is an historical novel told in a series of first-person monologues somewhat reminiscent of *Follow Me Down*. As one critic sees it, the work is unique in our century's war chronicles, owing to Foote's creation of a mythic hero who embodies his society's values. That hero is Nathan Bedford Forrest, and *Shiloh* takes on an epic quality, a measuring stick by which to judge modern society. *Shiloh* was hailed by the *Saturday Review* and the *New York Times* as a "superb story of war" by a "promising novelist who has arrived."

In 1953, Foote moved to Memphis where he has lived most of the time since. The following year he published *Jordan County: A Landscape in Narrative*, a collection of thematically ordered short stories which begin in the present and work back in time to the 1600s, a history in reverse, as Foote calls it. *Jordan County* cannot be accurately designated a collection of stories because in many ways it is more closely akin to the novel. Like Joyce's *Dubliners* and Faulkner's *Go Down, Moses*, its parts may have separate existences but ideally should be read in the context of the complete work. In this novel, the author continues his major themes and his concern with the problems of Southern society. It is a key work in the Foote canon and one of the strongest. Some reviewers faulted the novel for its violence, but the violence is necessary to Foote's philosophy, mainly for its causes: the failure of love and the desire for exploitation owing to greed.

After the publication of *Jordan County*, Foote began work on the three-volume *The Civil War: A*

Narrative, a masterpiece of monumental stature. The first volume appeared in 1958, the second in 1963, the last in 1974—the entire work requiring a total of twenty years. It may be the story of the war to be remembered longest. In its composition, Foote used the techniques of novel writing to good effect; as the title indicates, the history is a narrative.

In 1956, he married Gwyn Rainer of Memphis. That year he wrote a story about Mosby's Rangers called "The Down Slope" for Stanley Kubrick but refused to move to Hollywood to pursue a career there. Kubrick did option *Love in a Dry Season,* but never produced it. Foote has been three times a Guggenheim Fellow and once a Ford Foundation Fellow. He has served as a guest lecturer at Virginia (1963) and Memphis State (1966-1967), and as writer-in-residence at Hollins (spring 1968). While associated with the Arena Stage in Washington as playwright-in-residence (1963-1964), he wrote a play, *Jordan County,* based on three sections of the novel of that title, successfully produced in 1964.

Later in 1964, he and his family moved to the Alabama coast and intended to settle, but when his stand against racial discrimination and extremism raised the ire of Klansmen, he returned to Raleigh, Tennessee, near Memphis, in 1965, before moving back to Memphis in July 1965, where he still lives.

Memphis is the setting of his sixth novel, *September September* (1978). The main characters, however, are natives of Bristol, who have come up to Memphis either to live permanently or to sojourn before moving on. Rufus is the grandson of a Bristol bank bookkeeper and is a failure in college, the Marine Corps, and life in general. Podjo is a Bristol gambler who invariably has bad luck. Reeny is the daughter of a Jordan County preacher, also down on her luck, but with an innocent optimism that things will get better. All three white characters, in fact, have this childlike faith.

The main black character is Eben Kinship, up from Bristol, the son of a cafe owner there, and now the son-in-law of wealthy Theo Wiggins of Memphis. Eben is controlled at the beginning of the novel by his father-in-law's wealth. It is his child that Rufus, Podjo, and Reeny kidnap in order to extort sixty thousand dollars.

The entire novel takes place during the month of September 1957 and revolves around this fictional kidnapping. In the background is the Little Rock integration crisis which the three kidnappers use as further intimidation of the black parents. Their crime is not racially inspired, but the three rely on the blacks' automatic assumption that it is, in order to frighten them further and not involve the white

police force, whom the black family also now fears. Foote emphasizes the psychology of the characters, particularly the sexual conflicts among the white triangle of Rufus, Reeny, and Podjo, and between Eben and Martha Kinship. Eben is fighting for his manhood by freeing himself from Martha's wealthy father. Rufus is immature; his weakness prevents his attaining manhood. He wants to get caught, even desires death, because he is afraid of being on his own. Both Rufus and Eben are alike in some ways; but whereas Rufus never matures, Eben is able to triumph, mainly as a result of the kidnapping. He finally stands up to his father-in-law and wins his wife's respect for the first time.

The reader is also encouraged to compare and contrast Podjo and Rufus. Podjo is the maturer man who is steady, strong, and self-controlled in the manner of the Hemingway code hero. Rufus is the would-be initiate, who never learns the code. Podjo sums him up perceptively:

> What he wanted was manhood — wholeness — on his own terms; that is, by sacrificing nothing to achieve it. And he not only knew he'd never have it, he also knew he'd never stop trying to get it, *his* way, till he died. That would be his release, his only possible release. He knew that, and even sought it — Catch me! Catch me! he kept shouting, whether in lies or petty crime. . . . Sooner or later he would get what he was running toward.

Foote also encourages a comparison between Reeny and Martha. Martha is sheltered and sexually repressed—that is, until the kidnapping brings her closer to Eben. Reeny enjoys as well as uses her sexuality as a means of survival. Her situation also improves as a result of the kidnapping: she is able to trade Rufus for Podjo and is put in the position of attaining her life's goal of "powing out of cakes" in Las Vegas. Although Martha's control over Eben ends, her marriage improves. Eben has grown to manhood. Rufus is where he belongs, by himself in his egocentric child's world of lies ("He wasn't just a liar. He was a lie") until he meets the death he has longed for from the beginning. Each character, therefore, benefits from the crime in his own way. Foote's novel demands a consideration of the differences and similarities among his characters. In doing so, the novelist returns to a subject which has preoccupied him from his first novel, *Tournament:* the meaning of manhood and how it is won.

In portraying his black and white characters, Foote has reversed racial stereotypes. Martha is frigid, while her white counterpart is promiscuous. The black man, not supposed to act well in the

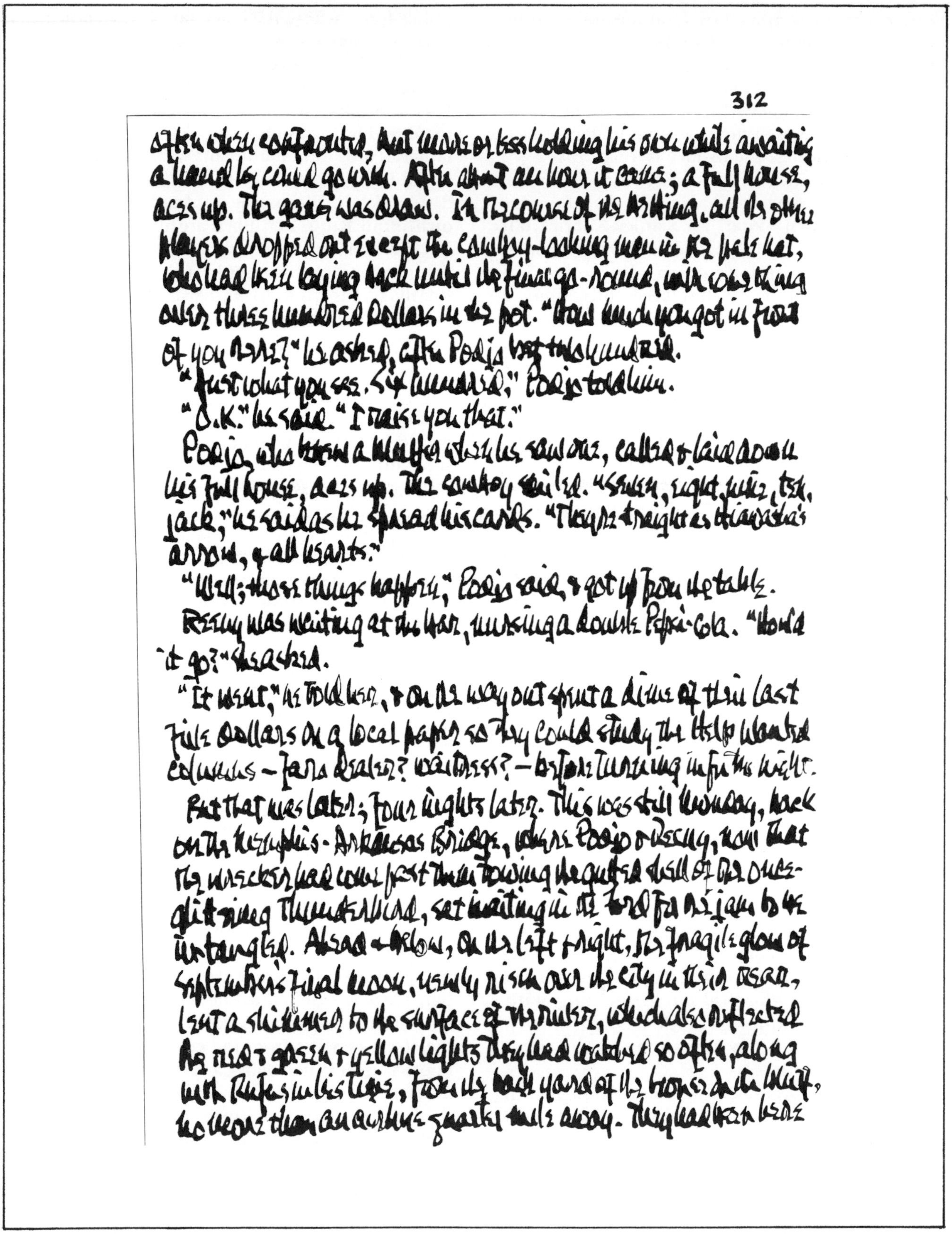
312

often when confronted, but more or less holding his own while awaiting a hand he could go with. After about an hour it came; a full house, aces up. The game was draw. In the course of the betting, all the other players dropped out except the cowboy-looking man in the pale hat, who had been laying back until the final go-round, with something over three hundred dollars in the pot. "How much you got in front of you there?" he asked, after Podjo bet two hundred.

"Just what you see. Six hundred," Podjo told him.

"O.K." he said. "I raise you that."

Podjo, who knew a bluffer when he saw one, called & laid down his full house, aces up. The cowboy smiled. "Seven, eight, nine, ten, jack," he said as he spread his cards. "They're straight as Hiawatha's arrow, & all hearts."

"Well; these things happen," Podjo said, & got up from the table.

Reeny was waiting at the bar, nursing a double Pepsi-Cola. "How'd it go?" she asked.

"It went," he told her, & on the way out spent a dime of their last five dollars on a local paper so they could study the Help Wanted columns — faro dealer? waitress? — before turning in for the night.

But that was later; four nights later. This was still Monday, back on the Memphis-Arkansas Bridge, where Podjo & Reeny, now that the wrecker had come past them towing the gutted shell of the once-glittering Thunderbird, sat waiting in the Ford for the jam to be untangled. Above & below, on the left & right, the fragile glow of September's final moon, newly risen over the city in their rear, lent a shimmer to the surface of the river, which also reflected the red & green & yellow lights they had watched so often, along with Rufus in his time, from the back yard of the house on the bluff, no more than an airline quarter mile away. They had been here

From manuscript of September September.

clutch, does, while Rufus and even Podjo fail. Eben is concerned with the future and providing for his family; whereas the white characters live only for the day. Eben worries about the things a responsible father usually does, while Rufus values his new Thunderbird above all else. Even the name "Rufus," used frequently for the black man, here is given the white. The characters' values seem to be determined more by their class than color.

September September presents a highly documented text. It is loaded, in the tradition of the Realistic novel, with more topical allusions than one would think possible in so short a novel. The effect is to depict the texture of day-to-day life, the building up of meticulous detail in order to create the reality of the day. Again, this work is a picture of the South in a transitional period. The Little Rock incident is the chief historical event which acts as a backdrop for Foote's analysis of his society in September 1957. Rising out of the text is a strong sense of the society's values. *September September* is at once a social novel, a psychological study, and an interesting narrative. It is one of Foote's best-written works and ranks with *Love in a Dry Season, Follow Me Down,* and *Jordan County.*

Foote is now at work on his seventh novel, in his words "a Mississippi Karamazov" to be entitled *Two Gates to the City.* It will treat "a struggle for values in the modern South." Again set in Bristol, the main characters are the family descended from the Lt. Lundy of "Pillar of Fire" in *Jordan County.* The novel takes place in the 1940s.

Although reviewers have praised his novels, Foote is still largely neglected by critics. He is not as yet popular with writers for the scholarly journals or with teachers in the classroom. There is some indication, however, that this situation is changing. Special issues of the *Mississippi Quarterly* (1971) and the French publication *Delta* (1977) were devoted exclusively to his work. In France particularly, Foote has a following among the scholarly community. *Jordan County* was translated and published there in 1975, and translators are presently at work on *Follow Me Down* and *Love in a Dry Season.* It is not surprising that French critics are showing an interest in him; they were largely the first to recognize the merits of William Faulkner. Like that great talent before he received the Nobel Prize, Foote deserves to be better known by his own countrymen.

—*James E. Kibler, Jr.*

Books:

Tournament (New York: Dial, 1949);
Follow Me Down (New York: Dial, 1950; London:

Hamish Hamilton, 1951);
Love in a Dry Season (New York: Dial, 1951);
Shiloh (New York: Dial, 1952);
Jordan County (New York: Dial, 1954);
The Civil War: A Narrative: Fort Sumter to Perryville (New York: Random House, 1958);
The Civil War: A Narrative: Fredericksburg to Meridian (New York: Random House, 1963);
Three Novels (New York: Dial, 1964);
The Civil War: A Narrative: Red River to Appomattox (New York: Random House, 1974);
September September (New York: Random House, 1978).

Other:

The Night Before Chancellorsville and Other Civil War Stories, edited by Foote (New York: New American Library, 1957).

References:

John Carr, "It's Worth a Grown Man's Time: an Interview with Shelby Foote," *Atlanta Contempora,* 1, 3 (July-August 1970): 2-16; reprinted in his *Kite-Flying and Other Irrational Acts* (Baton Rouge: L. S. U. Press, 1972), pp. 3-33;

Robert L. Gale, "Shelby Foote Repeats Himself: A Review Article," *Journal of Mississippi History,* 17 (January 1955): 56-60;

George Garrett, "Foote's *The Civil War:* The Version for Posterity?" *Mississippi Quarterly,* 28 (winter 1974-1975): 83-92;

John Graham, "Talking with Shelby Foote—June 1970," *Mississippi Quarterly,* 24, 4 (fall 1971): 405-427;

Evans Harrington, "Interview with Shelby Foote," *Mississippi Quarterly,* 24, 4 (fall 1971): 349-377;

James E. Kibler, Jr., "Shelby Foote: A Bibliography," *Mississippi Quarterly,* 24, 4 (fall 1971): 437-465;

Thomas H. Landess, "Southern History and Manhood: Major Themes in the Works of Shelby Foote," *Mississippi Quarterly,* 24, 4 (fall 1971): 321-347;

Allen Shepherd, "Technique and Theme in Shelby Foote's *Shiloh,*" *Notes on Mississippi Writers,* 5 (spring 1972): 3-10;

Simone Vauthier, "The Symmetrical Design: The Structural Patterns of *Love in a Dry Season,*" *Mississippi Quarterly,* 24, 4 (fall 1971): 379-403;

Vauthier, "Fiction and Fictions in Shelby Foote's 'Rain Down Home,' " *Notes on Mississippi Writers,* 8 (fall 1975): 35-50;

Shelby Foote

Wirt Williams, "Shelby Foote's *Civil War:* The Novelist as Humanistic Historian," *Mississippi Quarterly*, 24, 4 (fall 1971): 429-436.

WILLIAM PRICE FOX, novelist and short story writer, is best known for the down-home humor of his short story collection, *Southern Fried,* and his depiction of the glamorous, but dissolute Nashville music scene in the novel, *Ruby Red.* He was born in Waukegan, Illinois, on 9 April 1926 and grew up and received his education in Columbia, South Carolina. His experiences in the small backwater towns and larger urban areas of that state, as well as his father's penchant for bootlegging, seem to have been the major influences on his work. He entered the Army Air Corps in 1943 at the age of sixteen, after successfully lying about his age, and served until 1946 when he was discharged as a second lieutenant. Returning to Columbia, he put aside his uniform to become a soda jerk at a Columbia drive-in and exempting parts of his high school education through a series of tests, skipped from the tenth grade into college. He graduated from the University of South Carolina in 1950 with a B.A. in history. After stints of coaching athletics and bell hopping in Miami, Fox decided to go to New York where he worked for a while as an insurance runner and then as a salesman for a packaging company. In New York he studied writing at the New School with Caroline Gordon. When an acquaintance, Bill Manville, who worked for the *Village Voice,* asked Fox to do an article for him, Fox's piece "Moncks Corner," appeared on the front page. Its success led to the publication of Fox's first book, *Southern Fried,* in 1962. His second book, a series of letters depicting the correspondence of the aristocratic 'Dear Abby' of the golf world, *Doctor Golf,* appeared one year later. Between 1963 and 1968 he published a number of short stories in the *Saturday Evening Post, Sports Illustrated,* and *Harper's.* Of these, "Moonshine Light, Moonshine Bright," "Jack Driscoll's Revenge," and "Fast Dan" were ultimately worked into the novel *Moonshine Light, Moonshine Bright* (1967). The following year an expanded version of *Southern Fried* reappeared under the title *Southern Fried Plus Six.* Between 1968 and 1972 he taught creative writing at the graduate level at the Writers Workshop at the University of Iowa, and in 1971 his third book, *Ruby Red,* the story of a young girl's rise to success as a country and western singer, was published. In 1976, after teaching article writing at the University of Iowa School of Journalism for

William Price Fox.

two years, he became writer-in-residence at the University of South Carolina. In addition to articles published in *Travel and Leisure, Audience, Holiday, TV Guide,* the *Los Angeles Times, Harper's,* and *Esquire,* he has written screenplays for *Cold Turkey, Off We Go,* and *Southern Fried.*

Fox's themes of sex and larceny in the South have attracted minimal critical attention, perhaps because his works contain few of those nuggets of obscurity that inspire critical articles. His characters are clearly drawn and his plots are unobscured. He is that most misunderstood of contemporary writers, a traditional storyteller, and his tales resound with humor and moonshine instead of perplexity and dilemma.

Fox's works are marked by a fine sense of dialogue and detail, largely derived from the fact that the author is at home with his characters and familiar with the eccentricities of the small-town world they inhabit. In his first book, *Southern Fried,* he introduces the reader to Wilma, an oversexed young woman in a small-town trap; Logan Watts, whose hound dog, Red, pit-fights a wildcat; Senator Herman Talmadge of Sugar Hill, Georgia; Greenwood Keho, a smart-dressing card shark who sports a pompadour and quiets his nerves by hooking up to the battery of an old Buick; and the vain Fleetwood Driggers, who bases his claim to fame on having the best "soda-fountain hands" in town. The characters one roof of understanding when the great process f   was finally revealed..

He backed up and talked about mumificfcation. Hw How when the sheets

and bandages are unwrapped from the mummies there is still there on the cloth

a trace of the face. He explained it like it was a Xerox process. That all

You had to have was is sensitive enough ewuipmetn like in fingerprinting

to aise the features from the cloth. Holwy He develped the story how

Jane the winding clothes that had been around Jeus were of the finiest linen

and how carefully the disciples had taken care of the true

robe the splinter of the cross the nails the crown of thorns and the sh linen

winding clothes..Everyone was llstening. They were pressed forward as close

as they could get, and I knew we were going to sell the hellu a lot of prints

if he could keep it up/ And he did...He told them only in the past five years

had the process been perfected to the point where the was the

satisfied they could do it without harming the cloth..nd the great meeting in

Jerusalem where this was decided. Arlo like was amazing. Maybe Bridy had

sketched him in on the details and the possibilites for thu story but he had

come up with the bones of it all and the wis wise men crouched over the cloth

and flaqs finally voting and finally agreeing that he world had waited long

enough for the pix of the blessed lord...That eve even if there was a slight

rish evern I f if there till were doubting thoaes out there it was worth

it for the world was in such terrible shape they needed it...The crowd were

bobbilg their heads and as Brody said were buzzing like bees. They were ready

to be sold. With no seats he men were all stadning and they could rach their

wallebs fast...Brody caught Arlo's eye e tipped his hat but Arlo figured

th he col could get them buzzing louder, better. e could tighten them up.

and have them have their moe'y out when we came in from the back with the

pix..e kept on. How the sd wise men had deliberated and finally g v gave i

i How the pix had been smuggled into the country, and all the authorites were

denying they wre the were the real thing,...Arlo l ughed."ere they are all

lining up four blocks in Atlanta New Orlenas to see that Egyptian King

King Tuts toms. All that is is mummies. All hose pix were raised from the

cloth the same way we've done here..They admit it's trye true when it comes

to the pah pharo pharos of Egypt and they say it's all wrong when they

come to eus Christ...The crowd buzzed louder and hg ss stopped shifing

around. Brody nudged me."they are ready...Arlo felt it too. He ipped

touched his left ear and then his nose and then

of *Southern Fried* are an unusual combination of worldly sophistication and country innocence. Shrewd manipulators of copper tubing, internal combustion engines and the law, they fall easy prey to a hard-luck story, a country revival, or an over-spiced catfish stew.

In 1968 the author added six stories to this collection: "The Hair of the Dog," "Have You Ever Rode the Southern?," "Hello, New York," "Pinehurst, Due South," "200,000 Dozen Pairs of Socks," and "Room 306 Doesn't Tip" and it was published under the title *Southern Fried Plus Six*. Whereas the original *Southern Fried* tales explored a wide range of South Carolina characters from the viewpoint of a maturing Southern boy, the new tales, while maintaining the same perspective, explore other frontiers, such as New York, Miami, and the West. The world found outside South Carolina is a constant revelation of pizza, coconut juice, pastrami, paella, Fleetwood Cadillacs, big tippers, and full-dress doormen. It is, as Lamaar Peevy comments, a "fine" place, but it is not Columbia or Moncks Corner or Greenpond, and it's difficult to imagine living there as a "permanent thing."

The locale of the author's second book, *Doctor Golf*, is certainly as far removed from Moncks Corner as it is from New York and Miami, for Doctor Golf's Eagle-Ho Sanctuary is completely antithetical to the regional haunts of *Southern Fried*. The pretentious title character, a golfing aristocrat whose sole link to humanity is a series of letters and a booming mail-order business, would doubtless look as askance at the likes of Lonnie Register and Coley Mokes as he does at the heritage of one fictional correspondent, Joseph Swope of Yoknapatawpha County. His primary concern is maintaining the purity of the game (as played according to the royal and ancient code of Bonnie Prince Charles), the benevolent beating of the caddies, and the dilettantism of its followers ("Who," he asks, "is Sam Snead?"). Although he shares the often single-minded innocence of the *Southern Fried* characters, he lacks their practicality. Let loose on the world, his schemes for perfecting each golfer's game are, more often than not, disastrous. To the ailing golfer having trouble keeping his head down when he swings, Doctor Golf prescribes his steel strapping and cable arrangement #97, for securing the head and shoulders to the ground; for a wife whose marital bed has been invaded by her husband's Eagle-Ho water-filled-head putter, he suggests a set of knit golf head covers. Completely removed from society and isolated from human need, he is the perfect foil for the author's humor, a strictly one-dimensional character living in the elite, but one-dimensional world of his choosing.

Fox's colloquial style reaches its highest artistry in his third book, *Moonshine Light, Moonshine Bright*. The novel is set in and around Columbia, South Carolina, and concerns two country boys, Leroy Edge and Coley Simms, who spend a Carolina summer running moonshine, gasoline, and even butter in an effort to earn, buy, and keep their first car. The novel is largely picaresque and, in the tradition of Mark Twain's adolescent heroes, Tom Sawyer and Huck Finn, Leroy and Coley are alternately larcenous and innocent, savvy survivors of that difficult summer in which youth passes into manhood. In one scene, a screech-filled chase through Columbia, the boys try to escape the law while ridding themselves of a car filled with melting contraband butter. In another, they try to deodorize an overflow of sour mash that breaks forth from their water main still and fills an entire backyard. "How about Lysol? Bleach?," Coley suggests as the slop fills his tennis sneakers. Throughout, they are memorable and appealing characters who despite occasional setbacks continue to perceive the world with wide-eyed innocence as a place of infinite possibility and prospect.

Despite her promiscuity, Ruby Jean Jamison, the title character of Fox's best-known novel, *Ruby Red*, is as much a Carolina innocent as Leroy and Coley. She shares their belief in her own ability to create the future, and, like them, her success is dependent on her country ingenuity and persistence. Unlike them, however, she has already survived the throes of maturation and is concerned more with breaking out of the small-town pattern of her life than in functioning within it. Like *Moonshine Light, Moonshine Bright, Ruby Red* begins in Columbia in an atmosphere of moonshining and gospel singing. Ruby, however, quickly sets her sights on Nashville, and the remainder of the novel is a behind-the-scenes look at the country and western capital of the world. After a string of multiple-nighters with the bootlegger, Spider Hornsby; an albino songwriter, Jimmy Lee Rideout; and a fading country and western star, Big John Harmon, Ruby does achieve success in Nashville, her own early morning talk show.

At present, Fox is at work on a new novel, tentatively called *Dixiana Highway*, drawn from the author's experiences in the New York sales community between 1951 and 1962, as well as his travels with a circus. —*Carol Johnston*

Books:

Southern Fried (Greenwich, Conn.: Fawcett, 1962);
Doctor Golf (Philadelphia: Lippincott, 1963);
Moonshine Light, Moonshine Bright (Philadelphia: Lippincott, 1967; London: Davies, 1968);
Southern Fried Plus Six (Philadelphia: Lippincott, 1968);
Ruby Red (Philadelphia: Lippincott, 1971).

Periodical Publications:

"Moonshine Light, Moonshine Bright," *Saturday Evening Post*, 16 March 1963, pp. 45-54;
"Just a Friendly Little Game," *Saturday Evening Post*, 23 October 1965, pp. 54-57, 71-74;
"Lost Art of Moonshine," *Saturday Evening Post*, March 1966, pp. 34-35;
"Jack Driscoll's Revenge," *Saturday Evening Post*, May 1967, pp. 30-33, 68-83;
"Wild Westerns, Italian Style," *Saturday Evening Post*, April 1968, pp. 50-55.

Screenplays:

Southern Fried, 20th Century-Fox;
Off We Go, Paramount, 1968;
Cold Turkey, Paramount, 1970.

Reference:

Matthew J. Bruccoli, "William Price Fox," in *Conversations with Writers I* (Detroit: Bruccoli Clark/Gale, 1977), pp. 46-80.

BRUCE JAY FRIEDMAN was born in New York City on 26 April 1930 and was reared in the Bronx. He became interested in writing while attending DeWitt Clinton High School, where he wrote a column for *The Clinton News* called "AnyBuddy's Business," a pun on his high school nickname. At the University of Missouri in Columbia, Friedman majored in journalism, receiving his bachelor's degree in 1951. An officer in the United States Air Force from 1951-1953, he worked as a correspondent, feature writer, and photographer for the air force magazine, *Air Training*, and also wrote for the magazine some humorous fables with titles such as "Pvt. So-and-So and His Fairy Sergeant." Some of the sketches were considered "anti-establishment," and the magazine was finally told to stop printing them.

Friedman's first short story, "The Man They Threw Out of Jets," also dates from this period. His second attempt at writing short fiction, "Wonderful Golden Rule Days," was the first published, however; it appeared in the *New Yorker* on 31 October 1953. Following his marriage to Ginger Howard of St. Louis, Friedman returned to New York City where he went to work for Magazine Management Company, publishers of men's adventure magazines. He eventually became an executive editor in charge of *Men, Male,* and *Men's World* but quit the job in the spring of 1966 to devote more time to his writing. He lives with his wife and their three sons in Great Neck, New York.

Friedman's fiction is usually defined as black humor—a term which he refuses to define too precisely. In the foreword to *Black Humor*, an anthology which he edited in 1965, however, he does find one characteristic which his own work shares with that of the other writers represented. He doubts "that the writers here are bluff and hearty joke-tellers who spend a lot of time at discotheques," but, "if there is a despair in this work, it is a tough, resilient brand and might very well end up in a Faulknerian horselaugh." Yet, he refuses to see too much significance in this common approach to the world's horrors; finally, they are "thirteen writers with thirteen separate, completely private and unique visions. . . ."

Friedman's own brand of black humor eschews both the extreme technical experimentation of a Barth or a Pynchon and the traditional, well-constructed plot in favor of a looser, more picaresque structure. Nelson Algren recognizes quite early in Friedman's career that Friedman's style echoes the disorder of his world, "that he writes out of the viscera instead of the cerebrum."

Indeed, Friedman's colloquial, episodic prose echoes his vision of a world in which isolated, rootless human beings learn how to act from the mass media. He recognizes the "fading line between fantasy and reality, a very fading line, a goddamned, almost invisible line," but his characters are lost on the wrong side of a boundary they have failed to see. The world has developed a frightening new atmosphere, "a nervousness, a tempo, a near-hysterical new beat in the air, a punishing isolation and a loneliness of a strange, frenzied new kind." In this crazy environment, the *New York Times* is "the source and fountain and bible of black humor," while television news convinces Friedman "that there is a new mutative style of behavior afoot, one that can only be dealt with by a new, one-foot-in-the-asylum style of fiction." Friedman's characters

Jill Krementz

Bruce Jay Friedman.

demonstrate this behavioral deformity as they find themselves cast adrift in contemporary society.

Although they are nominally Jewish, they lack the solace of roots in religious or cultural tradition. Max Schulz calls them anti-Semites, and he points out that they sacrifice the sense of identity that being Jews could give them because it makes them different from the media images that they try to duplicate. Saul Bellow calls *Stern* a novel that examines the private life as if it were testing Socrates' saying that the unexamined life is not worth living and cannot find the life it is going to examine: "The power of public life has become so vast and threatening that private life cannot maintain a pretense of its importance." Friedman's protagonists try to deal with the complexities of modern, urban society, not with the full force of their intellectual and emotional powers, but by playing oversimplified roles which the mass media have foisted upon them.

As losers who try to cast themselves as movie versions of romantic heroes, they seek the solutions to their problems in dramatic, simple, often physical acts. The reader, however, sees how little their actions, which are usually too late, accomplish.

Despite his attempts at bravery, the typical Friedman protagonist is not a man of honor, facing and defying a corrupt world. He may be gentle and well-meaning, but his pseudo-liberalism and his ineptness in personal relationships detract from the image he would like to project. His best friends are blacks to the extent that he lets them take advantage of his patronizing geniality, but if his daughter has to go to school with them, or if his wife goes to bed with one, he dredges up all the old stereotypical prejudices.

His personal relationships within his family are especially sterile. His father is incapable of imparting manly wisdom, talking instead of such simple matters as his daily routine or the best route from one place to another; his mother is self-centered and demanding, too caught up in her own narcissistic obsessions to recognize her son's emotional needs. His wife is cold with him although she sometimes has, or appears to be having, affairs with other men, and he tends to put too much of an emotional stake on his relationship to his child, whom he barely knows. All the people in his life are shut up in isolated fantasy worlds of their own, and nothing in his own oversimplified vision of reality will help him to break through to them.

Friedman's first novel, *Stern* (1962), was highly praised by Stanley Edgar Hyman as a "superbly funny novel about suffering and misery." Although the novel did not sell particularly well, it gained a considerable underground reputation, based mainly upon Hyman's influential review.

Stern is the prototype for later Friedman protagonists. He is Jewish, but as Hyman was the first to recognize, his Jewishness is "merely a shameful inferiority and guilt." Stern buys a house in the suburbs and sets out to become the perfect middle-class homeowner, but all his attempts to conform fail and mark him even more clearly as an outsider. His real problems begin when a neighbor calls his wife and child kikes and pushes Stern's wife (who is not wearing any underwear) so that she falls down and exposes herself. Most of the plot is centered upon Stern's inability to deal both with the accident and with his anxiety about it. His anger at the man is complicated by his self-contempt; it is as if the incident is his fault because he is a Jew. Unable to handle his troubles in any other way, Stern responds in a manner which is to become typical for later characters: he develops a psychosomatic illness, in this case an ulcer. Indeed, his illness does seem to solve Stern's problems temporarily. While at the rest home where his doctor has sent him, Stern almost manages to play the hero he has hoped to be in dealing with the man who has insulted his wife. He saves the day in a baseball game, participates tentatively in a barroom fight, and makes love to a Puerto Rican girl who looks like a "battered" Gene Tierney. But when he returns home, nothing has changed, and he suffers "the mildest nervous breakdown in town." Recovering suddenly, after some meaningless advice from the cleaning lady, Stern challenges the anti-Semitic neighbor to a fight. After the man hits him first, Stern is elated that he is still alive and then sorry for the man because he could not knock Stern out. No longer angry, Stern hits back because it is expected of him, trying to imitate the style of a boxer he has seen on television. Stern's blow is weak, and the fight ends inconclusively. A man in whom public image is constantly at war with private feelings, Stern is probably Friedman's most perfectly realized character. Although his later fiction returns to the same theme, Friedman never again analyzes this paralyzing split with as much intensity.

Friedman's next book, *Far from the City of Class and Other Stories* (1963), is the result of ten years of short story writing. It contains the two stories Friedman wrote in the air force in 1953, as well as stories written much later. Max Schulz calls the early stories more realistic than Friedman's maturer style, but his first published story, "Wonderful Golden Rule Days" (1953), exhibits a pattern which recurs in later stories: a brief narrative ends with an unexpected twist. In this case, school becomes bearable for a young high school boy when he gets involved in a contest to build the best model airplane, but his hopes of winning are destroyed when his model is accidentally broken at the last minute. One of the most successful stories, "23 Pat O'Brien Movies," exhibits the same kind of trick ending. A kindly policeman tries to talk a young man out of suicide, but ends up jumping off the building himself. Other stories, most notably, "A Foot in the Door," "The Big Six," and "For Your Viewing Entertainment," follow a similar pattern but veer farther from realism to demonstrate the dangers inherent in the fulfillment of one's wildest fantasies. Another group of stories, such as "The Trip," "The Good Time," and "Far from the City of Class," contains characters and situations which reappear in *A Mother's Kisses*.

Joseph, the main character in *A Mother's Kisses* (1964), is a younger version of Stern. As the title suggests, Friedman's second novel focuses on Joseph's dependence upon his mother. The Oedipal overtones are overt. Joseph's mother brags about her attractiveness to men and flaunts her sexuality in front of her son. Her favorite joke is to insist that people probably mistake her and Joseph for lovers. Joseph's attempts at sexual activity with girls his own age are tentative and inconclusive; his mother's influence is clearly inhibiting.

What is more, his mother's control extends to all aspects of his life. Joseph seems incapable of making the simplest choices. It is his mother who finds him a summer job and a college to attend. But despite her image of herself as a person of influence who can make things happen her way, his mother is nearly as inept as Joseph. Neither the summer job nor the college is the shining opportunity for advancement she pretends it is, and her attempts to find him a place to stay at school are more misguided than helpful.

Nor is Joseph an unwilling martyr to his mother's domineering nature. While his badly infected, swollen arm is not as psychosomatic in origin as Stern's ulcer, it does give him the excuse he wants to retreat to his bed and allow his mother to handle the business of finding him a college.

Indeed, his feelings about his mother are extremely ambiguous. He resents her attempts to run his life, especially her going off to college with him and staying on and on, but when he finally confronts her with all the injustices she has done him, he is surprised to realize that the stories seem "more nostalgic than enraged." When he finally convinces her to leave, he suddenly asks her to stay a little longer, only to shout after the departing train, "I never enjoyed one second with you." Joseph may be free of his mother's physical presence, but he remains trapped in the ambiguities which their relationship has created.

Several of the short stories in *Black Angels* (1966) repeat themes from *Stern* and *A Mother's Kisses*. In "The Punch" Harris feels diminished in his wife's eyes because whenever she tells him to hit someone who makes her angry, he makes gestures of conciliation instead. Not only is he alone when he finally punches someone, but when he tells his wife, she does not react as he has expected. She says she is glad she did not see it because she might have fainted, but she also wonders why the fight did not draw a crowd. As in *Stern*, the fight does not alleviate Harris's feelings of inadequacy. The trick endings of the earlier stories are also apparent in this collection. In "Black Angels" the black gardener charges Stefano practically nothing for yard work and painting, but four hundred dollars an hour to listen to Stefano's problems. The line between fantasy and reality is blurred still farther in "The Night Boxing Ended," where one boxer literally knocks the other's head off, as well as in "The Investor," where a man's body temperature follows the fluctuations of "Plimpton Rocket Fuels" on the Dow Jones Index. Indeed, many of the stories in *Black Angels* seem to complete the move into surrealism which begins in *Far from the City of Class*.

Friedman's first play, *Scuba Duba* (1968) was a smash hit and ran off-Broadway from 10 October 1967 to 8 June 1969. Two of his short stories, "23 Pat O'Brien Movies" and "Show Biz Connections," have also been adapted for the stage, and Friedman wrote the libretto for a musical version of *A Mother's Kisses* which closed out of town in 1968. *Scuba Duba* examines the racial attitudes of middle-class liberals, an issue which first appears in *Stern*. When Harold Wonder discovers that his wife is having an affair with a black man, he immediately imagines the man to be a black skin diver who fits the typical oversexed, fast-talking stereotype. On the contrary, the man Wonder's wife has actually run off with wears Brooks Brothers suits and writes poetry for the *Partisan Review;* he is a middle-class liberal intellectual. Friedman is still examining public roles and their hidden implications.

In *The Dick* (1970) he studies the problem still farther. The idea for the novel probably arose during Friedman's research for a *Saturday Evening Post* article, "Arrested by Detectives Valesares and Sullivan. Charge: Murder." Many of his observations about the homicide division of the Chicago Police Department reappear in *The Dick*. Most important is Friedman's observation that "so profoundly have television and movies saturated the lives of [the detectives] that as they 'hit the street' and investigate 'the fresh ones,' you expect their work to be interrupted by an aspirin commercial or the latest Burt Bacharach musical theme." Friedman is attracted by their easy camaraderie, but he also realizes that they are "tough men in a bleak world."

Kenneth LePeters in *The Dick* recognizes the same dichotomy. He is both attracted and repelled by the detectives in the homicide division, where he works as a public relations man. Indeed, he is a man divided in many ways, as the scar down the middle of his face makes apparent. Having changed his name from Sussman to LePeters, he is another one of Friedman's anti-Semitic Jews. And of all Friedman's characters, he is probably the master of the grand, but pointless, gesture. Tired of being a "baby dick," he goes through detective training and graduates at the top of his class, only to turn in his badge and quit. Next, he tracks down his wife and her lover, shoots off two of the lover's toes, and refuses to let his wife come back to him. Finally, he takes his daughter out of her predominantly black school, and the two of them and her goldfish leave for undetermined destinations. As in *Stern*, LePeters has resorted to simple, dramatic actions in response to complex problems. He does not so much solve his difficulties as throw them away. While he seems more successful than Stern on the surface, LePeters is really only superior to Stern in his ability to run away, and in order to avoid new complications, he and his daughter and the goldfish must continue to run.

The main character in *Steambath* (1971), Tandy, provides a transition between LePeters and Harry Towns in Friedman's next novel. Like LePeters at the end of *The Dick*, Tandy thinks he has made some important changes in his life. But both *Steambath* and *About Harry Towns* examine the hollowness of such easy optimism. After he discovers that he and the others in the steambath are dead, Tandy tries to explain to God, the Puerto Rican attendant, why his life was so wonderful that he should be allowed to go on living. But instead he convinces himself that his life has not been so good at all—a new variation on "23 Pat O'Brien Movies." *Steambath* ran off-Broadway from 30 June 1970 to 18

October 1970. Although this play was less successful than *Scuba Duba*, Friedman has remained interested in the theater. He has since collaborated with Jacques Levy on *First Offenders*, which was produced in New York City in 1973.

More a collection of short stories with the same central character than a unified novel, *About Harry Towns* (1974) returns to the theme of the inner life lurking beneath the public image. Harry Towns is a fairly successful screenwriter in his forties, separated from his wife, who works hard at playing the swinging-bachelor role. But despite his superficial successes with women and his apartment in a "tower of steel and glass," decorated in steel and glass and leather, the symptoms of his increasing despair become apparent as he uses cocaine more and more heavily. Finally, after both his parents die "back to back," he tries an unsuccessful reconciliation with his wife. At the end of the novel, he has moved into a different kind of trendy, chic apartment—a studio with a sleeping loft in a brownstone. After a trip to the West which gives him more complications and no solutions to his problems, he develops a vague illness of the blood, which he perceives as his salvation because it forces him to reexamine his life. Occasionally he has spasms of energy, fixing up his apartment, exploring his neighborhood, taking up running, but these bursts of activity alternate with periods of lassitude. His attempt at reassessment leads to the following conclusions: that he ought to go some place without expecting travel to solve his problems, that he should look for a sweet, easygoing girl, that he should try not to get hit with a brick, and most important, that he should treat everyone generously until given some reason not to do so. While all his resolutions are admirable, it remains doubtful that Harry Towns is any more capable than Stern of coping in a world where even the best plans are at the mercy of chance.

None of Friedman's later novels has been as well received as *Stern*. One frequent criticism is that his characters lack depth. Anatole Broyard says that they have "not qualities, but *shtiks*." Max Schulz is further disturbed by the repetitiveness of character types. To criticize Friedman's fiction for its lack of "rounded" characters, however, is to ignore a number of very good novels whose characters are also unrealistic. Nor is Friedman the only novelist who repeats types from one novel to the next. Richard Todd's comments on *About Harry Towns* seem to illuminate the problem with all the later novels. Todd says that because the novel is close to Harry Towns's consciousness, it depends on the "irony of inadequate statement." Harry may be "melancholy

and self-judging," but he is not articulate. Sometimes Friedman's understatement works, and we see through to Harry's despair, but much of the time we are left with only an ironic view of the glittering surface. The same deficiency seems apparent in most of Friedman's later novels, short stories, and plays. Stern examines what Todd calls, the "sense of swallowed terror in an ordinary man's ordinary life," but in his later work Friedman seems content to satirize his characters' public roles, giving us occasional brilliant glimpses of the complex, conflicting emotions which lie beneath. In his interview with Josh Greenfeld, Friedman expresses his admiration for writers "who get as naked and as close to the bone as possible," but he seems unwilling or unable to do the same in his own writing. —*Karen Rood*

Books:

Stern (New York: Simon & Schuster, 1962; London: Deutsch, 1963);
Far from the City of Class and Other Stories (New York: Frommer-Pasmantier, 1963);
A Mother's Kisses (New York: Simon & Schuster, 1964; London: Cape, 1965);
Black Angels (New York: Simon & Schuster, 1966; London: Cape, 1967);
Scuba Duba: A Tense Comedy (New York: Simon & Schuster, 1968);
The Dick (New York: Knopf, 1970; London: Cape, 1971);
Steambath (New York: Knopf, 1971);
About Harry Towns (New York: Knopf, 1974; London: Cape, 1975).

Periodical Publications:

"The Imposing Proportions of Jean Shrimpton," *Esquire*, 63 (April 1965): 70-75, 148-150;
"Celine," *New York Times Book Review*, 5 February 1967, pp. 1, 52;
"Arrested by Detectives Valesares and Sullivan. Charge: Murder," *Saturday Evening Post*, 240 (22 April 1967): 38-42, 45-47;
"Look Mao, I'm Dancing," *Esquire*, 77 (April 1972): 55, 58;
"Hi, This is Bruce Jay Friedman, Reporting from Hollywood," *Esquire*, 86 (August 1976): 56-58.

Other:

Black Humor, edited by Friedman (New York: Bantam, 1965), pp.vii-xi;

"An Interview [with Bruce Jay Friedman]," *Notre Dame Review*, 1 (1 March 1974): 16-19.

References:

Nelson Algren, "The Radical Innocent," *Nation*, 199 (21 September 1964): 142-143;

Saul Bellow, "Some Notes on Recent American Fiction," *Encounter*, 20, 122 (1963): 22-29;

Josh Greenfeld, "Bruce Jay Friedman Is Hanging By His Thumbs," *New York Times Magazine*, 14 January 1968, pp. 30-32, 34, 36, 38, 41-42;

Charles Kaplan, "Escape into Hell: Friedman's *Stern*," *College English Journal*, 1 (1965): iii, 25-30;

Stuart A. Lewis, "Rootlessness and Alienation in the Novels of Bruce Jay Friedman," *College Language Association Journal*, 18 (1975): 422-433;

Max F. Schulz, *Bruce Jay Friedman* (New York: Twayne, 1974).

Jill Krementz

"WILLIAM GADDIS was born in New York City in 1922. His earlier and only other published work, *The Recognitions*, appeared in 1955." That is the complete biographical note on the jacket of Gaddis's second novel, *J R* (1975), and about all he would have the reader know about his life. "I have generally shied from parading personal details," Gaddis has said, "partly for their being just that, partly from the sense that one thing said leaves others equally significant unsaid, and the sense in those lines to the effect that we are never as unlike others as we can be unlike ourselves." Wyatt Gwyon, the hero of *The Recognitions*, says, "What's an artist, but the dregs of his work? The human shambles that follows it around." Gaddis has followed this credo by remaining almost as private as Thomas Pynchon and more so than the reclusive J. D. Salinger.

Gaddis was educated on Long Island and in Connecticut; he entered Harvard, where he edited the *Lampoon*, in 1941. At Harvard, he earned a reputation as a humorist, but left in 1945 without a degree. For two years, he was a checker of facts for articles at the *New Yorker*. He then spent five years traveling in Panama and other Central American countries, Mexico, the Caribbean, Spain, North Africa, and Paris, returning to New York in 1951. It was during this time that he wrote *The Recognitions*. "One aspect of this novel," Gaddis says, "was begun in 1947, in Mexico City, to be temporarily abandoned for another version that winter in Panama. *The Recognitions*, with its expanding prospects, was finally begun at the beginning in Madrid in 1948, put aside for almost a year in Paris, reconsidered and reworked again in Spain, finished after another year in America, in 1953, and cut and revised through still another winter."

Since then Gaddis has made his living as a free lance, writing speeches for corporate executives and scripts for industrial films, doing public relations for a drug company, and briefly writing for magazines and teaching, including summer writing workshops. He received a National Institute of Arts and Letters grant in 1963 and, to aid him in completing *J R*, he received a Rockefeller grant and two National Endowment for the Arts grants (1966, 1974). In 1977, he was Distinguished Visiting Professor at Bard College, where he taught writing, although he does not really enjoy talking about technique.

Gaddis now lives in a village north of New York City in a Victorian house overlooking the Hudson River. *Time* pictures him as "a small wiry man with graying hair," who "still prefers the old collegiate look of Shetland sweaters and buck shoes." He has two grown children from a previous marriage.

"I've been posthumous for twenty years," says Gaddis in reference to the fate of *The Recognitions*. A change in management at Harcourt, Brace aborted the publicity drive behind the book, and hostile, uncomprehending, or condescending reviews contributed to its failure to reach much of an audience. The meager royalties for the book were only slightly improved with a Meridian paperback reprinting in 1962, the same year the novel was first published in England. Other paperback editions appeared in 1970 and in 1974. Although Harcourt, Brace kept the book in print for many years, it became a classic example of an underground cult novel hovering on the brink of oblivion.

The commercial fate of *J R* has been only slightly better. Sixty-three pages of the opening of the novel appeared in the *Dutton Review* (1970); sections were published in *Antaeus* (1974) and *Harper's* (June 1975). Despite Knopf's effective promotion, enthusiastic reviews, and the National Book Award for 1976, the novel had sold, as of December 1976, only about 6,000 copies in hardcover and 28,000 copies in a trade paperback. Whether it will be another twenty years between novels is unknown, but in 1975 Gaddis, like Schramm in *J R*, was working on a western: "Every American writer has a western in him somewhere." Amid choices and distractions, the problem, he says, is to "decide what is worth doing." Gaddis has published no other fiction.

Each of his long, difficult novels offers even indulgent readers stretches of vexation, frustration, repetition, and boredom, but readers who stop too early miss a rich tapestry of character relationships. How complex these relationships are may be seen through a brief look at Wyatt Gwyon, forger of classic paintings, the central character of Gaddis's first novel, *The Recognitions*. Wyatt grows up in a small New England village, shaped mind and soul by his father, a Calvinist minister. He feels secure in the house because it is "saturated with priesthood," but at the same time he feels constantly watched. Eventually Wyatt quits his training for the ministry and goes to Paris to paint. Then he marries Esther, a novelist *manque*, and settles in New York. A mysterious longing from his childhood, more spiritual than artistic, still torments him and is manifested in his unfinished paintings. Even his speech is unfinished—in a novel of brilliant talk Wyatt stutters.

The figure of Wyatt looms over the intertwining stories of four other characters: Basil Valentine, a spoiled priest become an art critic who is involved in forgery schemes with Wyatt and yet aspires to protect the world's rare and beautiful things from the vulgar masses; Esme, Wyatt's model and mistress, who is a schizophrenic, heroin-addicted poetess; Otto, probably Gaddis's most fully realized character, a young playwright who parodies his hero, Wyatt; and Stanley, a simple, intensely devout Catholic, whom Gaddis places, in a seriocomic vein, somewhere between the tortured Wyatt and the ridiculous Otto. The reader is made to perceive the ways in which Wyatt affects each of these characters.

Five other characters counterpoint aspects of those five: Sinisterra, a master counterfeiter; Otto's father, Mr. Pivner, a sentimental true-believer; Recktall Brown, who markets Wyatt's forgeries and whose money touches most of the main characters; Agnes Deigh (*Agnus Dei*—"the lamb of God"), a literary agent who has undergone analysis; and Anselm, who talks and behaves out of a conviction that God has become a sentimental figure, a melodramatic device, in life as well as in art.

Wyatt leaves Esther to become a forger of old masters, but becomes possessed by an image of himself as a master painter in the Guild in Flanders. Working "in the sight of God," he says, "I don't live, I'm lived." Seeking redemption, Wyatt returns home to New England to work with his father in the ministry, but he has arrived too late because the Reverend Gwyon, obsessed with Mithraism, now worships the sun and thinks Wyatt, too, is a pagan. Wyatt, realizing that "no one knows who I am," returns to New York where he resolves to claim as his own work the paintings he has forged. He goes raving into the apartment of Recktall Brown to retrieve his paintings, but Brown, wearing ancient armor, falls down the stairs and is killed. Basil Valentine tells Wyatt that now there are just the two of them; sensing mutual spiritual depravity, Wyatt stabs Basil and flees to San Swingli, the little Spanish town where his mother is buried. In the monastery, he works patiently with a knife to scrape old masterworks down to the canvas—*tabula rasa*. Finally, he decides to return to America, to "live it through." "Now at last, to live deliberately," to "simplify."

Like *Ulysses*, *The Recognitions* is an encyclopedic novel, full of expertise on a wide range of subjects from sex to narcotics to religion and the arts. References to books, including "the first Christian novel," Clement of Rome's *Recognitions*, are numerous. Today's novelists, says Wyatt, "write for people who read with the surface of their minds," people who were brought up reading for facts, who want to know "what's going to come next." Popular and classical music, incongruously juxtaposed, assault the characters. Gaddis demonstrates ways in which popular culture intersects high culture through camp and parallels serious and avant-garde culture. In America, it is business that keeps art and literature going: "Business is co-operation with reality," Recktall Brown lectures. "Money gives significance to anything." Business controls and thrives on the mass media. Basil laments that in this age neither a painting nor a laxative can be sold without publicity. Reflecting this concern with media, the novel is loaded with ads, signs, symbols, and graffiti. Newspaper headlines graphically reflect the world in which the characters live and commit various kinds of suicide. In composing a pastiche of newspaper items and radio voices, Gaddis handles this technique as adroitly as Dos Passos. He exposes the reader to critics in all the arts. Wyatt is convinced that "criticism is the art we need most today . . . a disciplined nostalgia, disciplined recognitions."

For all its sophistication and aura of ostentatious genius, Gaddis's novel has, like Pound's *Cantos*, a redeeming air of naivete and faith. It is also a prophetic book, depicting horrors of the 1950s that anticipate realities of the 1970s. Describing the superficial religious novelist near the end, Gaddis parodies the serious experience some of his major characters have been undergoing: he "glimpsed a man having, or about to have, or at the very least valiantly fighting off, a religious experience." The novel's main theme is religion.

Chance, coincidence, accident, and repetition reign in Gaddis's field of vision; eventually each of the characters, with the "unswerving punctuality of chance," encounters or unknowingly crosses paths with most of the others. Acts of a supposed great magnitude recur on a minor scale, and minor acts are enlarged, in a new context, to a scale of great magnitude, with resultant comic absurdity. Civilization, for Gaddis, is composed of trivia, and he makes us feel the mystery of the ordinary. He stresses the triviality of the present by juxtaposing great insights and extraordinary events from the past with the mouthings and the random pseudo-events of today. Simultaneously, he implies the existential absurdity of *all* culture, yet nothing in *The Recognitions* is gratuitous, because the gratuitousness of life is, as in Gide, one of the major experiences this novel induces. These experiences of randomness are controlled, making the repetitions and returns all the more exhilarating. Everything seems familiar: Gaddis demonstrates that we are damned to experience familiar patterns and people over and over.

The blessing is that all these coincidences and resemblances can result in *recognitions*—a word repeated endlessly, with every possible denotation and connotation, along with variants and puns. And grace comes when these recognitions result in *revelation*, a word seldom used, but always implied as the reader's responsibility. Vision is contagious, as in the instance of the lunatic's seeing Christ after resurrection; Gaddis implies that life (or at least art) should be full of recognitions, visions, resurrections, and transformations—and that is what the reader's imagination, fed by *The Recognitions*, should achieve.

Gaddis's second novel, *J R* (1975), pursues the consequences of living in such a fragmented world even further. J R Vansant, the hero of the novel, a runny-nosed, eleven-year-old sixth-grader in a grammar school on Long Island, becomes a capitalist when his teacher, Amy Jourbet, takes her class on a field trip to Wall Street to "invest in a piece of America"—one share of stock. J R, a perfect product of our civilization's interlocking educational, business, and political systems, swindles his classmates out of the share and wins a minor stockholder's suit that starts him on his manic career. The free enterprise mentality is already virulent—he fanatically "sends off" for free samples of this and that and somehow manages to buy a million surplus wooden picnic forks from the navy to sell to the army. With the confidence of a true believer, J R deals out of a phone booth beside the boys' john, out of a sleazy downtown cafeteria, out of a candy store, and out of the Museum of Natural History while on another field trip.

J R's dealings soon involve the other major characters—the 1950s Greenwich Village artists, pseudo-artists, and bohemians of *The Recognitions* as they appear twenty years later. They are too busy managing their business affairs to do the one important thing that they want to do. As Jack Gibbs says, "Life is what happens to us while we're busy making other plans." One of these characters, Edward Bast, a composer who is under the delusion that writing music is "what I have to do," prostitutes his art to buy time to create it. Jack Gibbs, a physics teacher, as well as a drunken buffoon and gambler, cannot finish his "difficult" book, *Agape, Agape*, about "order and disorder, more of a, a sort of social history of mechanism and the arts, the destructive element." "You find excuses for each other's failures," Marian Eigen tells her husband, Tom, referring to the long friendship, poisoned by jealousies, of Jack and Tom, a blocked writer who published a book like *The Recognitions* but is now a corporate speech writer. Other failures include Schramm, who has tried to write a book about his experience as a front-line tank commander betrayed by his generals, but commits suicide, and Schepperman, a failed sculptor and painter. A suitable comrade for these failures is Grynszpan, who does not exist at all, but is the invention of Gibbs—concocted to confuse his creditors. The group shares a slum apartment that Bast turns into the headquarters of the J R Family of Corporations. Gaddis stresses Jack's childlike behavior, but all the men are comically and pathetically immature. Their women (Ann diCephalis, Stella Angel, Sora, and Amy) are trapped in their lovers' impotent dreams, but eventually turn on them. Marian Eigen speaks for them all when she says, "All these years I might have done something myself I might still if. . . ." Rhoda, Schramm's hippie mistress, once dreamed of becoming a model. She is an easy lay for Bast, Jack, and Al, the guitar-twanging mailman, and is the most pathetic of these used-up child-women.

J R, having cajoled amenable Bast, the school's composer-in-residence, to front for him, says ironically, "We can use each other Bast," but J R's obsession with business leads this child-capitalist to pathetic loneliness. At the end, he tells Bast, whose disloyalty hurts him most, "I had these here big plans you know hey? I mean not just for me for the both of us. . . .I just, always, I mean I always thought this is what it will be like you and, me riding in this here big limousine down, down this, this here big street. . . ." Instead, he discovers that "everybody's always getting mad at me!" To Bast, the man he has used most, he laments, "Everybody's trying to use me!" The always reluctant Bast is the only person who knows J R is a financial wizard, but many other adults, mostly through Bast, eagerly work for him. J R, the middleman, applies a few basic principles of lawful piracy to become rapidly a "ruthless corporate manipulator." He begins to believe his own public relations man's handouts that say he is a self-made man with a bulldog jaw, a "vital creative force," a "man of vision," a man celebrated for "his dedication to the traditional ideas and values that have made America what it is today. . . ." Seeing a reference in a newspaper write-up to the parent company, he exclaims, "I mean that's me the parent!"

The relationships between business concepts and procedures (generally negative) and the products (mostly useless) become metaphors for human relationships. The businesses impinge comically, sometimes farcically, upon each other and upon the lives of the characters and influence their relationships. Gaddis is particularly interested in perverted altruism. J R takes over companies to "help them out," while helping advance himself, just as he "takes over" Bast to help him write his music. Despite the intricate network of relationships, the characters are as separate from each other as the fragmented business activities and spurious products are. All these separate people are ignorant of the ways they are linked to each other through the protean outreachings of money. "It's all so, just so absurd so, lifeless," Amy says to her tycoon stockbroker uncle's head man, "there aren't any emotions it's all just reinvested dividends and tax avoidance that's what all of it is, avoidance. . . ." The most frightening implication of this massive comedy is that J R is the sanest character in the novel. "Nothing works," he says, "unless there's something in it for somebody."

"Money . . . ? in a voice that rustled" is the first line of the novel. "There's a market for everything," says Coach Vogel, referring to black market, drug-free urine. Later, he sells his own methods for freezing Beethoven's Fifth Symphony and for transporting people by telegraph. "Corporate democracy in action" places "a frenzied emphasis on the letter of the law" in "direct defiance of its spirit." Why steal, says J R, when you can get what you want by using, even making, laws? J R is a looter looting other looters. "Business in co-operation with reality," said Recktall Brown in *The Recognitions*; in *J R*, money creates its own complex, all-pervading reality. In a technocratic age, bogus paper money focuses communication and money becomes a metaphor for personal negotiations. As Isadore Duncan tells Bast, it is not an understanding of money itself, but of people's fear of money that enables men to control each other.

The same capitalist logic runs the school, where Gaddis focuses on innovative techniques, or "education enervations," to use J R's apt malaprop. These only bring the entertainment "biz" into the classroom. Using television to achieve "visual literacy" can only "key technology to the individual." Even the superintendent admits that "the function of this school is custodial and the rest is plumbing . . ." in "a system that's set up to promote the meanest possibilities in human nature and make them look good." The school ends up paying children instead of assigning them grades.

Amy and Bast try to offset those influences by teaching J R that the arts are "intangible assets," but the exploited artists, wracked with self-doubts,

7 Best - lenders banks (ie Cates) Sit him free when he pulled stunt 7 selling his stock — ie for stunt he pulled getting bank to ⑨91 sell it when he legally couldnt — how on devil Crawley let him exercise his b.t. you just to amuse my partner didnt I? option before it matured — **D**

—Full of more damn gossip I just want to know about this Bast *also taxed as regular income*
was
who's executive officer, told you to get hold of him a hundred years ago

—Yes sir, I called repeatedly but you heard foulmouthed girl on tape,

even went to the only address our sources had but it was obviously

a mistake, didnt even go in

he seems to be in a good deal of difficulty, various agencies after him

which I dont understand AFTRA, local 801?) *that there are subpenas out for him*

but mainly this insider suit regarding his sale of stock

in which I believe may have been inspired by malice since it's being

brought by a stockholder in the original Eagle Mills

[I have a large feature from newspaper here (or financial paper)

they sent looms to South America for a tax credit

leaseback arrangement they gave leases to town of UnFlls for tax credit

~~mills were torn down~~

in spite of their attempt to picture it as Leisuretown USA with gift

of park an speedway, with neither tax base nor jobs it is a ghost

town and everybody's on welfare straining the welfare rolls

EAGLE [the only industry seems to be a large cemetery since mills were trn down

—Tore down the mills how they keeping that tax umbrella going?

—That is another area of difficulty: apparently tried to sustain it

with a vast shipment of sweaters which prove to have been made in HK

also moving the mills to replacement in Georgia with cheap equipment

for fast replacement under deductible maintainance expenses

but since they were too cheap to send anyone down to oversee that

project the new facilities were erected on someone else's land

so theres another lawsuit

—Told you to get hold of him thought didnt I? never even met him?

—No sir but when I've talked with him on the phone he's seemed not

rather vague and preoccupied, nevr returned my calls (ie Btn *evr* get

him?) also Crawley spent time with him seems quite protective

Supreme Court

—Had a damn lot to be protective about, I just want him out hear me?
in it for all he can get like anybdy - wont give up easily
Out. If he wants to make trouble threaten him with suits &c
settle
probably get this (class action suit) out of court (in line with
just thrtn
debenture stock settlment or/theyll lose evrything) *if possible anticipate*
—*Old you trying to save his neck sir* *power Mrs J will have*
Not trying to save his damn neck it just looks bad for the entire *over Bast's fate*

bus community somebdy else gng to jail so damn many people off to jail
well dressed people going to jail while govn teachers & hippies mug old ladies
lately the town idiot lks like the only honst man in sight

Consent order? that he be barred permanently from evr trading on the

Exchange, harsh enough isnt it?

From "preparation for a rough draft" of J R.

went in after US Marshalls 710 = oil (avv) K466 = Bthvn weorn *attaches - cut our mountguts*

```
          INSERT    Page 9 5 1
```

—Because you know it is all of it! You know it's been
right from the start your surprise coup taking over Eagle you
were more surprised than anybody, you didn't even know what X-L
made when you bought it you asked me what's a lithograph ~~its never~~
you never thought of flooding
~~occurred to you it flood~~ the country with those damn matchbooks
                    you'd always done it
till you read ~~it someplace~~ like you read the reason you tried to
grab that insurance company was for its cash reserves, all you
wanted it for was you hated to see all these employees paying
~~out~~ premiums someplace else you wanted to pay them with one hand
and take it back with the other you know what really happened,
~~right from the start~~ that timber you didn't go after it at all
you got stuck ~~in some penny stock swindle~~ with some mining claims
and land you didn't even know where it was in a penny stock swindle like
all of it right from the start, your shrewd downstate interests
                          like at the start,
in that hopeless Union Falls paper you know it wasn't shrewd
downstate interests any more this man of vision this, these
intimate glimpses of you by that cow Virginia you know they're
not real!

        —No okay but hey Bast...? it's not okay!

        —Your suave young business exec's teetateet with funloving
somebody you know it's not real any of it!

        —No but hey Bast? I mean you never let me finish about that
hey wait up holy, my whole sneaker got wet hey wait up!

        —Finish about what, of all the stupid...

        —No but look I know it's not real hey! I mean it's just
this here idea I had where this naked girl picture I read you on
the train where they got this gossip calumnist to like fix you
up with her hey Bast? I mean just this once see this here whole
Teletravel thing once it gets like operational see she's this
like heiress of

From "draft of an insert for final page proof" of J R.

defensiveness, and impotence, plunder each other and shill for business, like "zebras grazing with lions." Education, business, politics, and mass communication make the arts trivial. Wanting art to do everything *for* them, people bring no energy to it. Gaddis ends on two contrapuntal notes: the ceiling has fallen in on both J R's paper empire and Schepperman's masterpiece painting, but both characters resolve to pick up the pieces and continue.

Language in the service of money, education, and art becomes garbage. *J R* is a compost heap of fragmented dialogues that are really monologues. These speeches are verbal versions of the many kinds of pollution in our civilization. *J R* is a Tower of Babel, "what America's all about, waste disposal and all." Characters constantly interrupt each other or themselves or are besieged by relentless distractions. They speak in sentences that do violence to grammar and syntax, and are full of cliches, evasions, euphemisms, irrelevancies, insults, mangled fragments of high and popular culture, and absurd reasoning.

Characters contribute to the miasma of verbiage in the delusion that talk is action and a means of ordering experience. "Are you listening?" J R asks Bast in the novel's final line. The implication is that neither is listening, but that the talk will never cease. If not even the speaker is really listening, can it be said that anyone is really talking? The debasement of language is both symptom and cause of corruption in every field of human endeavor.

J R is perhaps the most telling example of what John Barth calls "the literature of exhaustion." Jack Gibbs speaks often of "all this energy spilling . . . you've got entropy going everywhere"—referring to the gushing faucet and the radio that no one can reach to turn off. Entropy is "the irreversible tendency of a system, including the universe, toward increasing disorder and inertness." It is also defined as "the amount of energy unavailable for work," as "a measure of the energy inevitably lost in closed systems," and as "information lost during communication" (in cybernetics). Gaddis depicts every conceivable kind of waste of human energy. The most pathetic example of wasted energy is the tireless effort of someone on a higher floor to use chewing gum on the end of a string to pick up a quarter on the windowsill below.

As in *The Recognitions*, Gaddis throws random fragments into a vacuum, but it is his intention that in the end they do not cohere. They relate to each other only through the absurd logic that set them in motion. The interaction of chance, coincidence, accident, and repetition is even more operative in *J R*; here, all acts are minor; everything is trivia. Some concepts used to describe *The Recognitions* apply more aptly to *J R*: counterfeit, forgery, fakery, disintegration, betrayal, deception, fiction, detritus, trash. Art fails to prevent money and education from turning people, words, and things into separate pieces of junk.

J R's end is similar to *The Recognitions*': all human structures having collapsed, the slum apartment's ceiling caves in on all the trash. Bast alone may survive, may finish his work-in-progress. In the midst of this various trash, Jack's simple declaration to Amy, "I love you," is startling, but not very convincing. She is a false muse whose power fades. One should not make too much of traces of love as redemption from the holocaust of junk; both art and love fail to transcend the dump. In the machinations of business, education, and art, the medium of language turns love to junk. Only the fleeting moments of human kindness, lightly skimming the slimy surface, resemble love.

Many of the concepts that characterize *The Recognitions* illuminate by comparison or contrast *J R* as well. Unlike *The Recognitions*, however, very few of *J R*'s elements are obscure. *J R* deals consciously with elements that are painfully familiar. The surface is all. The mystery of the ordinary in *The Recognitions* becomes no longer mysterious in *J R*, just appallingly banal. One does not experience patterns, but is damned to experience familiar fragments over and over. In *J R* no one experiences revelations, visions, transformations, resurrections, profound recognitions. Religion is not a subject in *J R*; the persistent question of *The Recognitions*, "Is God watching?" becomes irrelevant. There is no reason why He should want to. Nobody wants approval from "the thing itself," because in *J R*, more than in *The Recognitions*, "Everything's sort of contraceptive," synthetic, falsified. *J R* is not a prophetic book; everything baleful foreseen in *The Recognitions* has come to pass. Everything is so grotesquely ironic that irony, paradox, and absurdity become inadequate concepts. Gaddis's vision is pure pessimism. That the only hopeful and optimistic character, as the novel ends, is J R, adds to the pessimism. *The Recognitions* was a divine comedy of religion, but *J R* is a diabolical comedy, a satire, and a burlesque of a world money has made.

Some reviewers call *J R*, like *The Recognitions*, difficult and too complex. But the complexity is not in structure or technique, rather in quantity—the problem is how to keep all its characters and episodes straight. Near the end, one federal agent asks another: "Sorted out all the players yet?" There are no conventional narrative passages amid the dialogue, and sometimes the transitions are so buried in descriptions they glide by, unnoticed. Gaddis never jumps from scene to scene; instead one scene flows or gushes into another, to make the reader feel that each character is part of a web. Jack carries a note to himself in his pocket: "a work of art has a beginning, a middle, and an end, life is all middle," and so is *J R*. *J R* may seem as chaotic as the chaos it criticizes, merely stopping at the "random climax of catastrophe," but the triumph of art is the paradox that no matter how faithfully art reproduces chaos, it emerges with a design of some kind.

The style of *The Recognitions* is sometimes precious and ostentatious, but generally brilliant. In *J R*, the author's own style, as it occasionally surfaces amidst the flotsam dialogue, is often forced, artificial, inappropriate, self-conscious. The god-like tone clashes incongruously with the dialogue, while not transcending it—if that was the intention. This example of the pathetic fallacy is typical: "morning made a tentative approach as though uncertain what it might discover." But Gaddis's stylistic brilliance is at work often enough to make this a minor flaw.

The conception that animates and controls *J R* is original. To execute that original conception, some of the techniques employed in *The Recognitions* are used differently here. In both of his massive novels, Gaddis has employed a point of view modern novelists seldom use—the omniscient, though without direct authorial comment. The devices of repetition and motif are used more often in *J R* than in *The Recognitions*, but differently; they do not contribute to organic unity; and while many things are happening simultaneously in some of the scenes, the sense of aesthetic simultaneity felt in *The Recognitions* is deliberately absent in *J R*. Organic unity and simultaneity would work against Gaddis's concept that people and things are separate objects juxtaposed or jammed together; but even the technique of juxtaposition has different effects and meanings in *J R*. The device of delayed connections is used as before, with the punch lines of jokes coming thousands of words later. To some readers the pace may seem glacial, but to others Gaddis moves with frenzied momentum from tongue to tongue within a scene and swiftly, almost imperceptibly, from one scene, time, character to another. Often the pace is frantic, farcical, slapstick. *J R* is more experimental than *The Recognitions*, most obviously in its use of graphic devices, showing, for instance, ads, musical notes, a grade school essay.

Gaddis tells everything that would be said in each scene and moves fluidly from scene to scene, giving the impression the novel is only a single monstrous scene; this new approach might be called Totalism.

The Recognitions was received with either outraged hostility or condescendingly qualified praise. Within a few years, it was revived as a cult novel, and over the quarter-century of general neglect, critics often rediscovered it. The few who read it compared it favorably and unfavorably, citing conscious influences and deliberate parallels, most often with James Joyce's *Ulysses* (which Gaddis says he has not read) and *Finnegans Wake*, as well as with Gide's *The Counterfeiters*, Eliot's *The Waste Land*, Canetti's *Auto-da-Fe*, and James Hogg's *The Private Memoirs and Confessions of a Justified Sinner*. *The Recognitions* is now regarded as an American masterpiece, but as the editors of *Writers in Revolt* said in 1963, "*The Recognitions* does not need praise; it needs to be read."

Hailed as more accessible than *The Recognitions*, and so unusual as to prevent its being compared with any other novel, *J R* received much praise, partly in atonement, one suspects, for the slighting of *The Recognitions*. Some reviewers, citing as vices what may be its virtues, argue that *J R* is a failed experiment; it lacks a strong guiding intelligence; it lacks focus, direction, control; its pretentious style is "a chore to read"; it lacks concision and contrast; it is too dense and ambiguous; its unrelievedly strident tone is oppressive—"an autistic triumph"; the talk is only chatter *ad nauseum*; *J R* strains for topical, relevant humor and satire; it shills for chaos; the endless variations on a single theme make it a minor theme; it is more difficult than *The Recognitions* (Gaddis makes fun of that charge in the novel itself); the inordinate, excessive, unjustified, arrogant length, the sheer mass of *J R* stupefies the reader. The charge of coterie appeal to the contrary, Gaddis has said that he has always wanted to reach as many readers as possible, and that any reader should be able to see and enjoy the humor in *J R*. —*David Madden*

Books:

The Recognitions (New York: Harcourt, Brace, 1955; London: MacGibbon & Kee, 1962);

J R (New York: Knopf, 1975; London: Cape, 1976).

References:

John W. Aldridge, "The Function of the Critic," in his *In Search of Heresy* (New York: McGraw-Hill, 1956), pp. 192-202;

Aldridge, "The Ongoing Situation," *Saturday Review*, 3 (4 October 1975): 27-30;

Bernard Benstock, "On William Gaddis: In Recognition of James Joyce," *Wisconsin Studies in Contemporary Literature*, 6 (summer 1965): 177-189;

David E. Gregson, *"The Recognitions,"* in *Survey of Contemporary Literature*, Supplement, ed. Frank N. Magill (Englewood Cliffs: Salem Press, 1972), pp. 243-247;

Peter William Koenig, "Recognizing Gaddis' Recognitions," *Contemporary Literature*, 16 (winter 1975): 61-72;

David Madden, "William Gaddis's *The Recognitions*, in his *Rediscoveries* (New York: Crown, 1971), pp. 291-304;

J. D. O'Hara, "Boardwalk and Park Place vs. Chance and Peace of Mind," *Virginia Quarterly Review*, 52 (summer 1976): 523-526;

Steven C. Schaber, *"J R,"* in *Literary Annual*, ed. Frank N. Magill (Englewood Cliffs: Salem Press, 1976), pp. 151-153;

John Stark, "William Gaddis: Just Recognition," *Hollins Critic*, 14 (April 1977): 1-12;

James J. Stathis, "William Gaddis: *The Recognitions*," *Critique*, 5 (winter 1962-1963): 91-94;

Tony Tanner, *City of Words* (New York: Harper & Row, 1971), pp. 393-400.

Jill Krementz

ERNEST J. GAINES, novelist and short story writer, was born to Manuel and Adrienne J. (Colar) Gaines on 15 January 1933 in the bayou country near Oscar, Louisiana, which lies about twenty-five miles northwest of Baton Rouge in Pointe Coupee parish. His father was employed on a local plantation as a laborer, and Ernest too worked in the fields until he moved away when he was fifteen. A culturally varied and complex region comprised of white, black, Cajun, and Creole communities, the bayou country has proved a rich resource for Gaines. As he says of his work, "though the places in my stories and novels are imaginary ones, they are based pretty much on the place where I grew up and the surrounding areas where I worked, went to school and travelled as a child." Though his entire adult life has been spent elsewhere, Gaines continues to maintain contact with the region of his birth and its people through regular visits. From these associations he has created the imaginary region of Bayonne, Louisiana, where all his works are set. Like Faulkner's Yoknapatawpha County to which it is frequently compared, Bayonne is Gaines's own postage stamp of native soil.

In 1948, Gaines's mother moved with his merchant marine stepfather to Vallejo, California, where Ernest subsequently joined them. There Gaines finished high school and junior college after which he spent the two years from 1953 to 1955 in the army. Military service was followed by enrollment at San Francisco State College in 1955. On graduation with a B.A. degree in 1957, Gaines was awarded a Wallace Stegner Fellowship to study creative writing at Stanford University where he spent the 1958-1959 academic year. As early as 1956, Gaines had begun publishing his work in little magazines, and in 1959 his short story "Comeback" earned him the recognition of the Joseph Henry Jackson Award. Since leaving Stanford, Gaines has been single-mindedly devoted to his craft—or as he puts it, "writing five hours a day, five days a week." This dedication has resulted in a steadily growing reputation as Gaines establishes himself as a writer of some consequence.

In an era of many literary movements, Gaines has consistently gone his own way. Surrounded by various literary groups, he has not associated himself with any current school or literary philosophy. He first began publishing his short stories in San Francisco during the mid-1950s when the literary and cultural renaissance there reached its height, but his relationship to such writers as Ginsberg, Corso, and Kerouac—who are associated with those years— is at best only coincidental. Similarly, his artistic development parallels in time the emergence of the militant black writing which grew from the Civil Rights movement. Yet, though no one would accuse Gaines of lacking sympathy for his more militant counterparts, he has not associated himself with the Black Arts Movement led by Larry Neal, Addison Gayle, Jr., LeRoi Jones, and their contemporaries. When asked if the black writer was obligated to write for a black audience, Gaines pointedly distanced himself from the basic premise of the "black aesthetic" philosophy by replying, "no more than French writers should. The artist is the only free man left. He owes nobody nothing—not even himself. He should write what he wants, when he wants, and to whomever he wants. If he is true, he will use that material which is closest to him."

Gaines's first published novel, *Catherine Carmier* (1964), is in many respects an apprentice work more interesting for what it anticipates than for its accomplishments. This story of frustrated love between Jackson Bradley, an educated young black who returns from California to his birthplace in the Bayonne area, and Catherine, the beautiful, near-white daughter of a Creole sharecropper, is thematically concerned with the inevitable conse-quences of class and caste in the Louisiana black community. Raoul, Catherine's father, is vehe-mently opposed to his family associating with anyone darker than themselves. Isolated alike from blacks, Cajuns, and whites, the Carmiers turn within for emotional sustenance. Raoul develops for his daughter a fundamentally incestuous passion which makes her the center of his life, and she answers his need with a love that precludes her ever developing a normal relationship with any man.

Into this situation comes Jackson whose experience and education have freed him from the tradition within which the Carmiers maintain their isolation. Against the advice of black friends, Jackson falls in love with Catherine; and she comes to love him in spite of her father's prohibitions.

Inevitably a confrontation develops between Raoul and Jackson, and the novel ends with a violent and primitive struggle in which Jackson beats the older man into submission. Catherine, seeing her father thus broken, sends Jackson away promising to follow him, but we, and Jackson, realize that she will remain bound to her father. Not even love, Gaines seems to imply, can triumph over the bonds of a tradition and social system which are fundamentally incestuous.

Catherine Carmier is set at the very time the South is about to undergo its most radical change since the Reconstruction period. Though the Civil Rights movement never makes itself felt in the action of the novel, several comments remind us that its forces are at work within the region. Thus, Gaines's theme of tradition and change achieves considerable irony through the distance between the actuality of his characters' lives and the concurrent process of history. Jackson, who professes no interest in the movement, is as apolitical as the Carmier family or their black, white, and Cajun neighbors who placidly accept the *status quo*. In divorcing his tale from contemporary events, Gaines declares his independence from the political and social purposes of much contemporary black writing. Instead, he elects to concentrate upon those fundamental human passions and conflicts which transcend the merely social level of human existence. But, as admirable as is Gaines's determination not to make a social document of his novel, his decision costs. Jackson loses credibility because he seems so remote from contemporary events and so uninterested in the world to which he has returned after a long absence. The novel seems to float outside time and place rather than being solidly anchored in the real world of the modern South.

Of Love and Dust (1967), Gaines's second novel, is also fundamentally a love story—"the same story you find in *Romeo and Juliet*," Gaines has said of it—based upon romance forbidden by rules of race and caste. In this case, the woman involved is a Cajun and is also married, both factors which make for a more complex situation than that in the earlier novel. Marcus Payne, the protagonist in *Of Love and Dust*, is a young black, bonded out of a prison sentence for murder by a white landowner who sets him to work under the supervision of the Cajun overseer, Sidney Bonbon. Recognizing the threat implicit in Marcus's rebellious spirit, Bonbon sets out on an unsuccessful attempt to break him. Partially to get back at Bonbon, Marcus pays attention to the overseer's wife, Louise, who is neglected by her husband in favor of a black mistress.

The inevitable happens as Marcus and Louise fall in love and try to run away together. In a confrontation even more violent than that which ends *Catherine Carmier*, Marcus is killed by Bonbon.

It is to Gaines's credit that he is able to create a far better novel from this plot than one might expect, largely through effective narration and excellent dramatic effects. The story is related by Jim Kelley, a plantation worker whose acceptance of the prevailing social conditions is in direct contrast to Marcus's rebellion. First antagonism, then respect, and finally sympathy characterize Jim's changing view of this young man whose rebellion he can never fully understand or accept. While Jim is himself too cautious to invite the inevitable destruction Marcus must bring upon himself, he nevertheless comes to recognize in the boy's unbending pride and unyielding determination to assert his manhood a spark of that human spirit which must strike out against fate even at the cost of its own existence.

Marcus, Louise, Bonbon and the other characters in *Of Love and Dust* are all caught up in a decadent social and economic system that determines their every action and limits their possibilities. After killing Marcus, for example, Bonbon claims he had no choice in the matter as the other Cajuns would have killed him if he had spared the boy. Gaines has said of the overseer, "I think . . . that Bonbon was determined by society and his environment. I suppose that the idea that man is determined by society runs through most of my work." Certainly in both *Catherine Carmier* and *Of Love and Dust* social determinism shapes the lives of all the characters, making them pawns in a mechanistic world order rather than free agents. Gaines has compared his determinism to the Fate which shapes the ends of the heroes of Greek drama, but in fact his environmental determinism flaws his early works rather than elevating them to the heights of tragedy. Though it is possible to see in Marcus's rebellion something of the *hubris* of classical tragedy, Gaines's protagonist does not reach heroic proportions. Ultimately he demonstrates, as did Catherine Carmier, that in Gaines's early fiction even the strongest are but victims of forces which control them totally.

In spite of its flaws, *Of Love and Dust* is an impressive novel. Jim Kelley's narrative voice reveals Gaines's flawless ear for the dialect of the region, while a range of minor characters and episodes provides a sense of local color which assures Gaines a place among the Southern regionalists of the Twain-Faulkner tradition. Here too the themes of a dying society's struggle against change, the Snopes-like rise of the Cajuns to displace both whites and blacks, and the conflict between the values of the past and those of the present begin to mature. Though Gaines would develop these ideas more completely in *The Autobiography of Miss Jane Pittman*, they are fully present in this work.

The five stories of *Bloodline* (1968) demonstrate that Gaines's growing control of the novel is paralleled by his mastery of the short story form. The longest story in the collection, "A Long Day in November," was published separately as a children's book in 1971, while "The Sky is Gray," technically the best piece in the collection, is Gaines's most frequently anthologized story. However, in many respects the less artistically perfect title story and "Just Like a Tree" are the more significant stories in *Bloodline* in terms of Gaines's development. In "Bloodline" a young black returns to his homeland to demand the birthright due him by the fact that his father was the white plantation owner. Though he proves finally to be quite mad, Copper's righteous demands for recognition and a place in his father's world seem a more meaningful rebellion than the petulant behavior of Marcus in *Of Love and Dust*. "Just Like a Tree" chronicles the death, on the eve of a Civil Rights demonstration, of an old black woman who clearly anticipates Miss Jane Pittman, the protagonist of Gaines's most recent and best work. In both of these stories, Gaines uses contemporary events to develop an increasingly complex representation of Southern history and culture.

The Autobiography of Miss Jane Pittman (1971) earned its author wide recognition as the subject of a popular made-for-television film but Gaines's third novel is fully deserving of attention in its own right. Adapting the oral narrative—an essential ingredient of black literary tradition from the earliest slave narratives to such recent works as *The Autobiography of Malcolm X* and Theodore Rosengarten's *All God's Dangers*—to fictional purposes, Gaines recounts the history of rural Louisiana blacks from slavery to the Civil Rights era as seen through the eyes of a woman whose life spanned those years. Over a hundred years old at the time of the telling, Miss Jane Pittman tells her story of hardship, loss, and endurance with the native wit and authentic idiom which make her one of the most successful narrative voices in recent American writing. But this novel is much more than mere fictionalized history: in *The Autobiography of Miss Jane Pittman* Gaines achieves the delicate balance of style, plot, and theme which marks the major novel.

In many respects, *The Autobiography of Miss Jane Pittman* represents a flowering of elements introduced in Gaines's early works. Such characters as Jackson, Marcus, and Copper bear a direct relationship to the more realized figures of Ned Douglass and Jimmy Aaron, both of whom turn their rebellions into positive leadership. The familiar theme of the search for manhood is continued in the story of Jane's husband, Joe Pittman, who dies proving himself. Interracial love and its tragic consequences are bluntly dramatized in the story of Tee Bob Samson and Mary Agnes. As in the other Gaines novels, the Cajuns here are represented as a rapacious element comparable to Faulkner's Snopeses as they move into the power vacuum created by the crumbling of traditional Southern aristocracy and disenfranchise the blacks from the land they have worked for generations. Interwoven with these themes is the conflict between past and present—the forces of inevitable change and the static world of the traditional South—which is a part of all Gaines's work.

The richness of this combination of elements is enough to assure a good novel, but it is the figure of Miss Jane that elevates her "autobiography" to the level of first-rate fiction. In spite of Gaines's philosophy of social determinism as Fate, he creates in Jane Pittman a character who will not be bound within these limits. In the course of the novel, Jane does not merely endure, she prevails over the forces that would contain her. The novel begins with Jane attempting to escape from Louisiana to Ohio after the Civil War. Her attempt fails and she travels in a circle back to her starting point in the plantation world into which she was born. Thereafter, Jane spends her life in that world, waiting for a black leader—"the One," she calls him—who will come to lead his people out of their bondage. Ned, her first hope, is slain during Reconstruction; Jimmy, the latest hope, is shot down during the Civil Rights movement. It is after the death of Jimmy that Jane herself, defying every rule a hundred years of survival have taught her to obey, rises to lead the people on a march to integrate the courthouse in Bayonne. In that moment of assertion, Jane transcends the limits of determinism by an act of free will that ultimately proves all human freedom. Implicitly too her act suggests that it will not be "the One" who leads the people to freedom, but the people themselves. In her moment of choice, Jane becomes the heroic affirmation of human potential, and it is that affirmation that makes *The Autobiography of Miss Jane Pittman* the first-rate fiction it is.

Gaines's literary reputation has grown steadily with each new book, reaching something of a climax with *The Autobiography of Miss Jane Pittman*. *Catherine Carmier* brought him almost no critical attention, but with the publication of *Of Love and Dust* he was recognized as a comer. Sara Blackburn wrote of the second novel in the *Nation*, "it takes a lot of nerve to write a novel like this today and a lot of skill to bring it off. Mr. Gaines has plenty of both." James Lea struck a similar note in *Saturday Review* when he wrote, "despite . . . weaknesses of technique Ernest Gaines . . . has succeeded where many others of his race and generation have failed: he has written a book about Negroes and whites as just plain people, sharing equally the blame for maintaining a worn-out tradition." However, while the work was generally well-received, Lea as well as other reviewers recognized the serious weaknesses of structure and characterization which plagued the novel. These objections are best summarized by Robert Donant's review in the *New York Times Book Review*: "Mr. Gaines's second novel is still an 'undergraduate' work in which the author trusts craft formula too much, himself too little."

With the appearance of *Bloodline*, critical reservations toward Gaines's fiction largely disappeared in a flurry of favorable responses. Robert A. Gross writing in *Newsweek* took the occasion to cite Gaines as "one of the finest American writers today" in an essay on contemporary black writing. Granville Hicks said in *Saturday Review*, "Gaines knows how to create living characters and to set them against a rich and vivid background." If the novels "are anywhere near as good as the stories," Hicks continued, Gaines "is one of the young writers . . . who will help to form the American literature of the future." In the *New York Times Book Review*, Laurence Lafore pointed out the "handsome formal designs" of Gaines's stories, and praised his "notable control . . . superb ear for speech and precisely the aim to make people seem likable, understandable and alive." Lloyd W. Griffin's comments in *The Library Journal Book Review* recognized similar qualities: "a marvelous ear for speech rhythms, content and dialect; a deep knowledge of the people . . . of the region; and a rich fund of humor, compassion and understanding."

Following the success of *Bloodline*, *The Autobiography of Miss Jane Pittman* sealed Gaines's reputation as a writer of consequence. Melvin Maddocks celebrated the occasion in *Time* by proclaiming that "Gaines . . . may just be the best black writer in America." Jerry H. Bryant hailed Jane's story as "an epic poem" in the *Nation* and claimed Gaines to be the first American novelist to "harmonize" the "discordant notes" of "propaganda and sociology that have plagued the political novel in America from the first." Geoffrey Wolfe in

125

soldier and the three flags, and walked across the sea shell

covered parking lot over to the car.

"We can get something to eat if you want to," Phillip

said. "We can pick up a box lunch and--"

But there wasn't no point going on, because the boy

wasn't listening to him. He opened the door for him to get

into the car, then he went round to the other side. He drove

out of St. Adrienne without knowing exactly where he was going.

On his left was the St. Charles River, high, muddy and gray,

the waves flowing far upon the bank, splashing against the trunks

of the cypress and willow trees before receding back into the

river again. The small black poule d'eaus

rode the high waves. They would float a while, then they would

duck under in search of food, bob up a moment later some

fifteen or twenty feet away, looking jerkily around for a second,

then go back down. On the other side of the road were the gray

unpainted farm houses, and an occasional antebellum Creole house

setting on blocks seven or eight feet above the ground. Pecan

and Live Oak trees grew in most of the yards, as well as along

side the road, and sometimes the Spanish moss hung so low over

the road that you could almost reach out and touch it.

Phillip Martin had travelled this road many times before,

and he knew it as well as he knew any place, but he paid no

attention to it today. Since getting into the car he had been

trying to think of something to say.

He caught the boy looking out at the houses on the other

side of the road.

From typescript of In My Father's House,
forthcoming 1978.

Newsweek saw Miss Jane as a "legendary figure, a magnificent creature of dignity and genius, a woman equipped to stand beside William Faulkner's Dilsey." Gaines's novel, he went on to say, "brings to mind other great works. *The Odyssey* for the way his heroine's travels manage to summarize the American history of her race, and *Huckleberry Finn* for the clarity of her voice." Comparisons to Faulkner were inevitable. Carl Sena wrote in *Commonweal*, "through Miss Jane . . . we see that the crude inventions of Faulkner and Stowe, the Topsies and rigid mammies, were all along nothing but caricatures"; while Josh Greenfeld enthused in *Life*, "no black novel about the South . . . exudes quite the same refreshing mix of wit and wrath, imagination and indignation, misery and poetry. And I can recall no more memorable female character in Southern fiction since Lena of Faulkner's *Light in August* than Miss Jane Pittman herself." The very difficulty of finding qualified responses to *The Autobiography of Miss Jane Pittman* suggests the American literary establishment was ready for a black writer to restore balance and artistry to a novel tradition which had become increasingly polemical during the troubled 1960s. At any rate, with the reception of this novel, Gaines was clearly projected into the front ranks of young American novelists.

—*William E. Grant*

Books:

Catherine Carmier (New York: Atheneum, 1964; London: Secker & Warburg, 1966);

Of Love and Dust (New York: Dial, 1967; London: Secker & Warburg, 1968);

Bloodline (New York: Dial, 1968);

The Autobiography of Miss Jane Pittman (New York: Dial, 1971; London: Joseph, 1973);

A Long Day in November (New York: Dial, 1971).

References:

Jerry H. Bryant, "Ernest J. Gaines: Change, Growth, and History," *Southern Review*, 10 (autumn 1974): 851-864;

Bryant, "From Death to Life: The Fiction of Ernest J. Gaines," *Iowa Review*, 3 (winter 1972): 106-120;

William Burke, "*Bloodline*: A Black Man's South," *CLA Journal*, 19 (June 1976): 545-558;

Ruth Laney, "A Conversation with Ernest Gaines," *Southern Review*, 10 (January 1974): 1-14;

Walter R. Macdonald, "You Not a Bum, You A Man: Ernest J. Gaines's *Bloodline*," *Negro American Literature Forum*, 9 (1975): 47-49;

John O'Brien, ed., "Ernest J. Gaines," in *Interviews with Black Writers* (New York: Liveright, 1973), pp. 79-93;

Frank W. Shelton, "Ambiguous Manhood in Ernest J. Gaines's *Bloodline*," *CLA Journal*, 19 (December 1975): 200-209;

Winifred L. Stoelting, "Human Dignity and Pride in the Novels of Ernest Gaines," *CLA Journal*, 14 (March 1971): 340-358.

JOHN CHAMPLIN GARDNER, JR., novelist, epic poet, and scholar, was born in Batavia, New York, on 21 July 1933 to John Champlin and Priscilla Jones Gardner. As a boy he lived in Batavia, attended the local schools, and worked on his father's farm. His mother was an English teacher and his father, a lay preacher, had read deeply in the Bible and Shakespeare; consequently their son was sensitive to language from the first. "Half-Welsh," he was also sensitive to music and grew up singing in various choirs. On excursions to nearby Rochester for concerts and opera he cultivated a taste for serious music, and on Saturdays his father gave him and the other hands the afternoon off to listen to the Metropolitan Opera broadcasts. Gardner still loves opera enough to insult people who say they do not, and among his many literary productions are libretti for two operas by Joe Baber: *Frankenstein* and *Rumpelstiltskin*. He also likes the Beatles.

In school he felt drawn to chemistry but did not care for the laboratory. Noticing that he always got A's in English, he decided that was his field. He attended DePauw University from 1951 to 1953, the year in which, a month shy of his twentieth birthday, he married Joan Louise Patterson. They have two children, Joel and Lucy. Gardner took an A.B. at Washington University in St. Louis in 1955, and at the State University of Iowa he took an M.A. in 1956 and a Ph.D. in 1958. For his doctoral dissertation he wrote a novel, *The Old Men*, which has not been published. He has taught medieval literature and creative writing at numerous schools including Oberlin, Bennington, Skidmore, Southern Illinois, Northwestern, Chico State College, the University of Detroit, San Francisco State, and the University of Rochester. Recently retired from teaching, Gardner lives in Cambridge, New York.

Gardner's first published novel, *The Resurrection* (1966), attracted little attention. In a waspish dismissal in *Saturday Review* Granville Hicks declared it "pretty muddled," and the novel does make many demands on the reader, including as it does a good deal of technical experimentation. Gardner reproduces, for example, an essay written on an abstruse subject by a man whose mind is deteriorating due to the deadly effects of aleukemic leukemia. The essay gradually becomes less and less coherent as its author fades mentally. The writer is James Chandler, a philosophy professor whose doctor has given him only a few months to live. The book asks the question Gardner would ask in every succeeding novel: how can existential man—under sentence of death—live in such a way as to foster life-affirming values, regardless of how ultimately provisional they may prove? *The Resurrection* is sensitive, poignant, and harrowing; it is also a good indication of the startling literary abilities of its author.

During the 1960s those abilities were becoming increasingly evident in academic publishing circles. Prior to *The Resurrection* Gardner had collaborated with Lennis Dunlap on a textbook, *The Forms of Fiction* (1961); and his translation, *The Complete Works of the Gawain-Poet* (1965), also predates his appearance as a novelist. But Gardner had been writing since childhood, and more than one of the books published in the 1970s, after he had gained recognition, was written during the lengthy rejection-slip period that is the lot of virtually every aspiring novelist. In a 1974 interview he hinted at the sequence in which he wrote his novels: "When you're sitting writing for fifteen years, and nobody liking you, you do build up a backlog. I've been publishing an early work, a late work, an early work. . . . *The Sunlight Dialogues* is an early work; *Grendel* is a late work; *Nickel Mountain* . . . is a very early work. Right after that comes my newest thing, *The King's Indian and Other Fireside Tales*, a very jazzy technical thing. That and *Jason and Medeia* are my two newest things." *October Light* (1976), he would later comment, had occupied him "for years." In the meantime he produced scholarly articles, Cliff's Notes, and books. With Nicholas Joost he co-edited *Papers on the Art and Age of Geoffrey Chaucer* (1967), and on his own he produced *The Alliterative Morte Arthure* (1971), *The Construction of the Wakefield Cycle* (1974), and *The Construction of Christian Poetry in Old English* (1975).

The remarkable thing about Gardner's fiction is its consistent clarity of purpose and moral vision. From the beginning of his career as a writer he has looked for ways to confute or reshape the fiction of exhaustion and despair now fashionable. He sought ways to follow Faulkner's lead toward some kind of credible, meaningful affirmation, something be-

Jill Krementz

yond the mere fantasies of wish-fulfillment he saw a few novelists trying to fob off as antidotes to despair. Thus in his dissertation-abstract he describes *The Old Men* in terms that could be applied to such important and typical later productions as *The Sunlight Dialogues* (1973) and *October Light*. "*The Old Men* is a novel which takes as its general theme the place of man in the universe and attempts to work out the nature and ramifications of man's two essential choices, affirmation and denial." The characters of this novel are experimenting, he explains, with "responsible" and "irresponsible" modes of affirmation; some achieve "objectification of guilt" and become "morally responsible." In doing so they adumbrate major characters in all of Gardner's novels. The same confrontation with guilt, the same aspiration to moral responsibility, exercises Henry Soames in *Nickel Mountain* (1973), James Page in *October Light*, and the doomed Hodges in *The Sunlight Dialogues*.

Fourteen years after *The Old Men*, in the essay "The Way We Write Now," Gardner would denounce black humor, nihilism, and "smart-mouth satire," declaring that the novelist must present "thought-out values" by means of "empathy and the analysis of moral and psychological process." Whatever the subject, "it's in the careful scrutiny of clearly apprehended characters, their conflicts and ultimate escape from immaturity, that the novel makes up its solid truths, finds courage to defend the good and attacks the simple-minded." Gardner's desiderata point to a conception of the novel as essentially didactic or "philosophical," but always with the stipulation that philosophy must be "dramatized." "I think I'm a philosophical novelist," he told Joe David Bellamy, "but that doesn't mean a philosopher."

Nevertheless there is perhaps too much philosophy in *The Wreckage of Agathon* (1970), Gardner's second published novel. The book attracted more attention than its predecessor, but though *Time* and *Newsweek* were kind, one reviewer lambasted it as "more hysterical than historical" and called it "a total bore." Thomas Edwards describes the book more judiciously as "an inventive if rather baroque meditation on the status of imaginative freedom within an oppressive political order." In ancient Sparta a disreputable old seer named Agathon and his sidekick, Demodokos, are jailed by Lykourgos, the tyrannical devotee of law and order. Gardner presents the philosophical impasse between the state and its laws and the individual and his freedom with high gusto, but since the narration is accomplished by Agathon and Demodokos in a series of monologues, it is hard to move beyond a kind of manic glee in disputation (Agathon has disputed even with the great Solon)—a delight in forensic and rhetorical flashiness for its own sake. This philosophical argumentation is also central to *The Sunlight Dialogues*, but when an omniscient narrator can sympathetically examine arguments against the absolute but ultimately antisocial freedom of anarchism, the result is a finer novelistic performance, one which brings mutually exclusive philosophical positions into more instructive contrast. It may be worth noting here that Gardner combines both Agathon and Lykourgos in himself. "I am on the one hand a kind of New York State Republican, conservative," he admitted in a 1977 interview in the *Atlantic*. "On the other hand, I am a kind of bohemian type. I really don't obey the laws. I mean to, but if I am in a hurry and there is no parking here, I park."

No doubt he also combines Beowulf and Grendel. His third novel, *Grendel*, which established him as an important literary figure, came out in

1971. In it he retells the *Beowulf* story from the monster's point of view, but he does so in a manner that violates neither the original tale nor the sensibilities of the twentieth-century reader. *Grendel* illustrates T. S. Eliot's dictum that the individual talent enriches and slightly modifies the literary tradition, for in this short novel Gardner burnishes the classic at the same time that he creates a new masterpiece.

The ghastly embodiment of the futility and meaninglessness of life, Grendel is the dark shape that has always waited in the shadows, the offspring of Chaos and Old Night. Wonderfully mythic, he represents "the brute existent," the unknown. An arch-nihilist, he knows that "the world is all pointless accident," and indeed, accident claims him in the end. In the time that Grendel observes humanity he witnesses the coming of one great cultural phase after another, beginning with the birth and growth of civilization itself. He sees how roving bands of hunters begin to unite, settle down, develop agriculture and animal husbandry. Kings emerge; they build roads, collect taxes, raise armies, make war on other kings. Religion waxes and wanes, from crude and primitive animism to Christianity, in both its traditional and existential forms. At each phase the people define Grendel differently: at first he is the "oaktree spirit," later Cain, or Satan, or "the Great Destroyer." Grendel also witnesses the emergence of what Gardner describes in his interview with Bellamy as "the main ideas of Western Civilization," including the heroic and courtly love ideas, Hobbesian and Rousseauesque notions of human nature, materialism, hedonism, mysticism, even *Realpolitik* and revolution-for-the-hell-of-it. Grendel recognizes the futility and absurdity of them all. None changes what he knows to be the existential truth, and he dismisses all of them as the desperate and pathetic illusions with which "pattern makers" attempt to clothe the world and their existence in meaning. But one of their activities, poetry, he finds hard to dismiss. He understands from the first that the Shaper, the Scop, is the one responsible for all the other dodges. If he sings of "the greatest of gods," man becomes monotheistic; if he sings of heroism, man becomes heroic; if he sings of courtly love, man becomes chivalrous. The Shaper is at once the greatest liar and the most puissant staver-off of despair. Thus even Grendel, who denounces illusion in tones reminiscent of Freud, Sartre, and Lord Russell, melts before the powerful magic of poetry.

It is important to note that the Shaper does not celebrate the glory and power of Hrothgar and the 𝛔

The old ram stands looking down over rockslides,

stupidly triumphant. [I blink. I stare in horror.] "Go away!" I hiss. "Go back to your

cave, ~~or~~ back to your [cow] barn‾ whatever!" He cocks his head

like an elderly, slow-witted king, considers the angles,

decides to ignore me. I stamp. I hammer the ground with

my fists. I hurl a skull-size stone at him. He will not

budge. I shake my two hairy fists at the sky and I let out

a howl so unspeaka‾ble that the water at my feet turns sudden

ice and even I myself am left uneasy. But the ram stays;

the season is upon us. And so begins the twelfth year of

my idiotic war. ~~I stomp back into the trees.~~

[The pain of it! Aaargh! The stupidity!]

~~Not that my wits~~ are squeezed shut, like the ram's, by

[Do not think my brains]

the roots of horns. Flanks atremble, eyes like ~~new-swept~~

~~cobble~~stones, he stares at as much of the world as he can

see and feels it surging in him, filling his chest as the

melting snow fills dried-out creekbeds, tickling his gross,

lop-sided balls and charging his brains with the same unrest

that made him suffer last year at this ~~same bleak~~ time, [and the year before, the year before that. (He's] ~~An~~

~~experience the ram has~~ forgotten, [them all.] His hindparts shiver with

[the usual]

~~a~~ joyful, mindless ache to mount whatever ~~is~~ [happens to bear]— the storm

piling up black towers to the west, some rotting, docile stump,

some spraddle-legged ewe. I cannot bear to look. Him too I

hate, the same as I hate these brainless budding trees, these

brattling birds.

From early draft for beginning of Grendel.

Scyldings after the fact. *He makes it happen*, and herein lies Gardner's own artistic credo, one he embraces in apostolic succession from Oscar Wilde. "Art leads, it doesn't follow," he told his *Atlantic* interviewers. "Art doesn't imitate life, art makes people do things. . . . if we celebrate bad values in our arts, we're going to have a bad society; if we celebrate values which make you healthier, which make life better, we're going to have a better world. I really believe that." Gardner's point in *Grendel* is that art is not merely our least pernicious illusion; it is our most healthy one. It can teach us ways to live and die with courage—and do so better than can other, less efficacious illusions like religion (which the Shaper created anyway).

Gardner affirms more in *Grendel* than the primacy of art. The novel contains twelve chapters, each devoted to one astrological house and each containing references to the appropriate astrological symbol. The story begins and ends in spring—Aries to Pisces—and this circularity is important, as is the number of chapters. Twelve is a mystical number symbolic of the cosmos; it is the product of three and four, the numbers symbolic of godhead and earth (Gardner uses the same numerical symbolism in the prologue to *The Sunlight Dialogues*). The twelve months described in *Grendel* comprise the twelfth year of the monster's "idiotic war" on Hrothgar and the Scyldings. In numerology a number multiplied by itself represents an intensification of the original symbolism, and Gardner's implied structure in *Grendel*, twelve-times-twelve, emphasizes the cosmic significance of the story he presents.

The circular structure is significant because in the end, grappling with Beowulf, Grendel learns that he too—death itself, symbolically—is mortal. Beowulf whispers to him: "*Though you murder the world . . . The world will burn green, sperm build again.*" It is Gardner's most beautiful way of saying "life goes on," a phrase that recurs in his novels. Life goes on, it recycles, and death's ascendancy can never be more than temporary until the culmination of the entropic drift makes the very concept of life and death irrelevant. In other words, Gardner elects not to be distressed by the Parthian shot with which Grendel expires: "Poor Grendel's had an accident. . . . *So may you all.*" His defeat, Grendel maintains, has been by "mindless chance," pure "accident." But *Grendel*'s structure is in dynamic tension with the nihilism of its narrator, for Gardner means for us to recall that in medieval iconography the circle symbolizes faith. The faith Gardner adumbrates here is of course not religious faith, but faith, simply, in life's wonderful regenerative properties—faith defined as the opposite of the despair that comes of brooding morbidly on the accidental, amoral nature of human life and of the universe that contains such an anomaly.

Gardner finds the horrors of chance harder to gainsay in his next novel, perhaps because it was written earlier than *Grendel*. The monumental scale of *The Sunlight Dialogues* (1972) contrasts even more sharply with *Grendel*'s economy. With its intricate plot and its more than eighty characters, this is Gardner's most massive novel, and possibly his finest. In Batavia, New York, during a few weeks in 1966, Police Chief Fred Clumly stakes his career and his reputation on a bizarre and protracted duel with the most extraordinary criminal he has ever encountered: the Sunlight Man. Vagrant and vandal, polymath and prestidigitator, the Sunlight Man is arrested for painting LOVE across a road. Bearded, maimed, and more than half crazy, he babbles for days in the Batavia jail, like Ezra Pound in the stockade in Pisa. Then he escapes and quickly becomes implicated in several murders and kidnappings. The police chief devotes himself more and more obsessively to tracking down the Sunlight Man, convinced that he is "the sum total of all Clumly had been fighting all his life." The quarry reciprocates by going out of his way to humiliate the hunter.

Rather glum, dumb, and clumsy, as his name implies, Fred Clumly is a fearsome figure, with his obese, pallid, and completely hairless body, his red eyes, and his mole's nose. His single-minded and unimaginative devotion to law and order hardly endears him to the reader. In his life "there was only order, lifted against the world like rusty chicken-wire. . . ." He takes a ghoulish delight in funerals and attends one after another in the course of the book, secretly pleased at their testimony to the "orderly" closure of human life. Yet even when Clumly acts viciously—smashing the jaw of a prisoner with a pistol butt—or deviously—taping, wiretapping, and eavesdropping—Gardner somehow makes us sympathize with him, or at least refuses to allow him to degenerate into that familiar figure of pasteboard villainy, the fascist policeman. As a result of his encounters with the Sunlight Man, Clumly eventually comes to question himself, his values, and the cultural order of which he is a part. Towards the end of the book he passes up a funeral, a hopeful sign which is borne out when, dismissed from his post, he finally has the Sunlight Man in his power—and lets him go. When the Sunlight Man dies, in the end, as a result of what is described on his death certificate as "police action in pursuit of order," the chief eulogizes him and gives the impression that he has learned something from the dead man.

The Sunlight Man is really Taggert Hodge, prodigal son of a prominent but declining local family. Made frantic by the deaths of his children, by the insanity of his wife, and by the refusal of his father-in-law, a sadistic tyrant, to defray the cost of the one type of therapy that might help the sick woman, he returns to Batavia to murder the old man and to terrorize the community and its police chief. As the manic and protean Sunlight Man he becomes something more than human, something beyond "the solemn judgements of psychiatry, sociology, and the like." He is a superb magician, a master pick-pocket, and a prankster—a cross between Till Eulenspiegel and the Fiend Incarnate. But like the Trickster-god described by Jung, he modulates from cruel prankster to something like a savior. He calls himself the Sunlight Man for reasons never made entirely clear, but his impact on Clumly and others is nothing less than that of the sunlight outside Plato's cave: a blinding, overwhelming, and terrible epistemological revelation. The Sunlight Man knows that "the truth is always larger than you think"; thus to Clumly he narrates a fantastic version of Plato's parable and comments: "I doubt that anything in all our system is in tune with, keyed to, reality." On finding herself a widow, his mother-in-law is disgusted at the shabbiness of her husband's corpse and observes—with unconscious irony, since she is unaware of how the old man met his end— "Sunlight in the morning shows things as they are."

Although the police chief and the Sunlight Man destroy themselves in the course of their drawn-out and obsessive duel, they eventually come to recognize that each defines the other, the one viewing order as an absolute, the other espousing absolute freedom. Cop and robber become thesis and antithesis of a profound dialectic—order versus anarchy—which the two hammer out in a series of one-sided "dialogues" in which the Sunlight Man, a brilliant rhetorician, lectures the hapless police chief on the eternally warring principles for which they stand. Moreover, in a strange way, each *is* the other, for the conjurer "was once a policeman," and the policeman, alienated from other men by his profession, "meets the world and gets along with it by means of a conjuring trick inside his brain." By means of subplots that universalize the theme of the essential identity of hunter and quarry, Gardner at once expands and undercuts this dialectic. For example a bill collector stalks—and begins to fear—a murderous swindler in whom, more and more, he recognizes himself. "We're somewhat alike, you and

I," declares his quarry. Another character actually embodies this doubling, leading two lives as Walter Boyle, housebreaker, and Walter Benson, respectable citizen.

Despite Clumly's manic devotion to order, things gradually run down in the community of Batavia. Crimes multiply, from minor hooliganism to ghastly murders, and the police sense that things are getting away from them. Disorder increases, and in disorder we see the author's resolution of the dichotomy represented by robber and cop; the Sunlight Man's anarchy shadows forth not perfect freedom but perfect randomness, which also dooms the police chief's cherished orderliness. The thesis and antithesis represented by these two characters, in other words, have their synthesis in entropy, and neither Clumly's rusty chickenwire nor the Sunlight Man's patter about *l'acte gratuit* can obscure the terrible truth. Although "human consciousness" may be "the most fantastic achievement of the whole fantastic chronicle of time and space," as the Sunlight Man says, he comes closest to the truth when he asks: "What is there in this world but accident?"

Gardner's next published work was not a novel but an epic poem, *Jason and Medeia* (1973). In this extraordinary and eclectic performance he translates, borrows, and invents new material to retell several Greek myths and merge them into a great new whole. "Parts of this poem," the author writes in a preface, "freely translate sections of Apollonios Rhodios' *Argonautica* and Euripides' *Medeia*, among other things." It is as daring a venture, in literary terms, as Jason's own. Perhaps the poem should be regarded as a vast archaeological restoration project, the forging (in both senses of the word) of an epic the ancients neglected to write. In rectifying the oversight, Gardner resembles Wyatt Gwyon, the hero of William Gaddis's *The Recognitions*, who paints forgeries that no expert can distinguish from the real thing. Like Gaddis, Gardner means for his readers to ponder the paradox of authenticity inherent in literary artifice. Opinion on *Jason and Medeia* has been sharply divided, and it is still too early to say whether it will finally be viewed as a colossal miscalculation or as an example of the kind of literary risk-taking that reveals an artist of Robert Graves's or Ezra Pound's stature.

One can, however, say that *Jason and Medeia* is light years distant from *Nickel Mountain*, the book that appeared the same year. In this novel Gardner introduces Henry Soames, the middle-aged, lonely, and very fat proprietor of a delapidated diner in the Catskills. Soames has had one heart attack and lives in dread of the little click in his chest that will announce a second, fatal one. Yet though he fears death, he feels "vaguely drawn" to the snow that surrounds and isolates him. Leading an empty life, he reads much of the night, but cannot go south in the winter. Though he pretends to like solitude, he talks obsessively and irritatingly to his infrequent patrons—the drunks who heed the plea of the diner's neon name burning into the night: Stop Off. He broods over a few shabby memories: a one-night stand spoiled by violence, a grotesquely fat and ineffectual father despised by Henry's mother, and a high school crush—his nearest encounter with love—that came to nothing. The emptiness of his life and the imminence of death fill him with a panic which he cannot name; indeed, much of Gardner's accomplishment here is his rendering of the verbal inadequacies of people painfully inarticulate, people whose lives—outwardly "simple"—are in fact chaotic.

Yet Soames is capable of great love, and his "heart trouble" suggests the damming up of what he needs to give. He offers his love to Callie Wells, a pregnant sixteen-year-old who works for him. Desperate, she takes him, and they begin to make a life. She is a hard worker, and he is good-hearted and protective. The simplicity and decency of these people are important, for Gardner describes *Nickel Mountain* in a subtitle as "A Pastoral Novel." In pastoral, as George Stade remarked in the *New York Times Book Review*, rural characters, free of the city and its ills, embody and sometimes speak for simple human virtues and wisdom. Soames has seen the city and the appalling indifference of urbanites to each other. He is haunted by a "vision of people as meaningless motion, a stream of humanity down through time, no more significant than rocks in a mountain slide. It was different in the country, where a man's life or a family's past was not so quickly swallowed up, where the ordinariness of thinking creatures was obvious only when you thought a minute, not an inescapable conclusion that crushed the soul the way pavement shattered men's arches."

Henry's embittered friend, George Loomis, believes that man's "pure meanness" underlies progress, but Henry will not accept this, believing in the possibility, at least, for human goodness. Though he recognizes the frangibility of his new family, of his happiness in it, and of his very existence, he does not allow the recognition to dampen his altruism and continually seeks, selflessly, to help his fellow man, even to the point of taking in the crazed and dangerous Simon Bale, a

religious fanatic whose wife has perished in a fire possibly of her husband's making. When Bale declares himself unwilling to have his wife properly buried, Henry quietly spends $600 on a funeral that no one attends. Henry resembles the unlikely heroes in Camus' *La Peste*, who persist in alleviating human misery, however hopeless the prospects. Henry's world picture, while hardly sophisticated, contains no illusions about religion. His father left him a Bible, but it has "a fermented, museum smell." While "the world was vastly more beautiful with angels than it was without," he knows that they and the transcendent order for which they stand are chimerical. "What was pleasant to believe was not necessarily true."

Nickel Mountain is filled with casually reported instances of violent death and dismemberment which are the more terrible for being so gratuitous, random, "accidental." Truckers die plummeting from slick mountain roads; Soames's friend Kuzitski perishes in a flaming wreck; a home owner's skull is crushed by intruders; a woman burns to death in the senseless arson of her home; a motorist dies crashing into a snowplow; a fourteen-year-old boy dies freakishly in the "dry lightning" of newly-gathered hay; George Loomis—already crippled in the Korean War—loses an arm to his corn binder; later, driving carelessly, he kills an old eccentric. These random deaths and accidents form a sinister ostinato to the book's exploration of the frailty of human life. The ability of the soft and meek Henry Soames to defy the yawning void and provide sustenance not only to his little family, but also to incidental human strays like Simon Bale, should be viewed as a poignant way of depicting a humble but very real form of heroism.

When Simon Bale dies of a broken neck sustained as he recoiled from a Soamesian outburst and fell down a staircase, Henry is profoundly distressed. The death was accidental, but he believes obsessively that he caused it. Chagrined, he goes through a bad period in which he seems to be trying to eat himself to death. Though he cannot put it into words, he understands that in contributing, however slightly, to Bale's accident he has allied himself—a human being—to chance, and he can imagine no sin more terrible. It is one thing to accept chance, another thing to conspire with it against a humanity already playing against a stacked deck.

Soames eventually transcends his guilt and achieves serenity, becoming something of a mystic and believing in "the holiness of things." He emerges finally as an almost numinous figure, his meekness and ineffectuality paradoxically balanced by an inner strength and tranquility born of his recognition and acceptance of the natural scheme of things, including his own death. Though individual men perish, "life goes on." By the end of the book Soames has matured from a feckless fat man terrorized by intimations of his own mortality and "close to a nervous breakdown" into a rustic sage, a life-affirmer chastened by an awareness of accident and strengthened by the battle with guilt. Like so many modern fictional heroes, Henry Soames has had to learn to live with the horror of the random. Like all Gardner's books, *Nickel Mountain* explores the possibilities for affirmation in the face of the world's absurdity.

Before resuming his chronicling of the simple lives and passions of Yankee rustics in *October Light*, Gardner published *The King's Indian Stories and Tales* (1974), a collection of short stories, sketches, and the title novella. Of interest here is "Sailing Through the Universe with John Napper," a sketch of the Gardner circle of home, family, and friends. As in *October Light* the author describes himself in a state of inebriation, as if he means to cultivate the image of a hard-drinking latter-day Hemingway. The John Napper of the title, an artist, did the illustrations for *The Sunlight Dialogues* (one of the extraordinary things about Gardner's novels is that they are always splendidly and copiously illustrated). Gardner admires Napper because his good-natured insouciance never falters despite his awareness—as Grendel would put it—that "things fade."

The title of "The King's Indian" refers not to a redskin but to a chess opening; the deception is part of the hoaxing this story is about. The story's narrator, Jonathan Upchurch, describes it as a thing that "has no purpose to it, no shape or form or discipline but the tucket and boom of its own high-flown language," but John Gardner, who breaks in to address the reader in *vox propria* toward the end, maintains that it is intended as "a celebration of all literature and life." The plot concerns a voyage of the whaler *Jerusalem*, which seems to be a sea-going version of John Barth's *Funhouse*, commanded by another Sunlight Man, and manned by a cast out of Coleridge, Melville, Poe, and Conrad. Basically the tale is a composite of every sea voyage in literature, from the *Odyssey* to *Moby-Dick*. The narrator-hero is at once the Ancient Mariner, Ishmael, and Arthur Gordon Pym. He also bears more than a passing resemblance to Barth's Ebenezer Cooke, for he is an innocent who gains experience through a series of brutal and comic batterings.

From the initiation of youth in "The King's Indian" Gardner turns to the trials of age in *October Light* (1976), which is actually two interlocking novels. The formal experimentation, like that of *Grendel* and "The King's Indian," indicates that this book does not come from Gardner's backlog—though apparently it was fairly long in the writing. In the frame story of *October Light* an elderly brother and sister living together in Vermont have a falling-out. James Page, the seventy-two-year-old brother, holds irascible opinions on a variety of things: welfare, social security, unions, television. Sally Page Abbot, his eighty-three-year-old sister, holds diametrically opposed opinions: she is for minority rights, the ERA, government social programs, nuclear reactors. Worst of all, she belongs to the Democratic Party, and of course few Vermonters make any distinction at all between the Democrats and the Communists. The situation in the household recalls nothing so much as the skirmishing between Squire Western and his politically-opinionated, bluestocking sister in *Tom Jones*. The real trouble starts when James blows Sally's television to smithereens with his shotgun. Shortly thereafter, irate at the very idea of a woman's holding opinions and defending them, and brandishing a piece of firewood as a club, he drives her upstairs and locks her in her room. A duel of wills ensues. Finding that she has a bedpan, a box of Kleenex, and access to the apples stored in the attic, Sally settles in for a long siege. Every bit as mulish as her brother, she locks the door from her side and refuses to leave the room, even when her niece, James's daughter, unlocks the door. Friends organize a party in hopes of luring her down, but she resists the entreaties and blandishments of everyone who comes to the door. Sally passes the time reading a "trashy" novel she finds on the floor: *The Smugglers of Lost Souls' Rock*, described in the jacket blurbs as "A Black-Comic Blockbuster" and "A sick book, as sick and evil as life in America." Though parts of the old paperback are missing, and though its text appears interwoven with the frame story, it proves easy to follow and immediately recognizable for what it is: a parody of the contemporary novel of Angst, black humor, emptiness, alienation, disenchantment, aridity, and despair. One of the first shocks of this production—at once melodramatic and heavily symbolic—is the reader's recognition of just how cliched modern fiction has become with its modish bleakness and its "existentialist" or "absurdist" outlook.

The challenge of Gardner's double novel is somehow to integrate his homely tale of domestic squabbling with his trendy novel of modern emptiness. It is a formidable task, and he brings it off beautifully. The symbolism of *Smugglers* is quite transparent, and neither Sally nor the reader has any difficulty making it out. The chief of the smugglers, Captain Johann Fist, is Faustian man in league with the devil. He and his boat, the *Indomitable*, represent capitalism, while a rival boat, the *Militant*, represents the challenge posed by minorities and the third world. The *Militant*'s crew, needless to say, is composed entirely of minorities, and some members are highly articulate, which makes for some wonderfully "dialectic" exchanges with Fist and his crew, who include an inventor named Mr. Nit (Technology), a Good Man named Goodman, a ridiculously libidinous ingenue, and a world-despairer and would-be suicide—Peter Wagner—shanghaied into service aboard the *Indomitable*. The creator of this farrago (it is, of course, Gardner himself, assisted by his wife Joan) gets all the political and philosophical mileage he can out of a confrontation on the high seas, which is followed by an alliance between the two crews.

Sally not only "solves" the symbolism, she begins to recognize people she knows in the novel. The odious Captain Fist, who seems beyond rapprochement with the crew of the *Militant*, is her nasty old Republican brother James. Mr. Nit becomes James's son-in-law, the handyman Lewis Hicks. Peter Wagner is Richard Page, James's son, whose suicide some years ago left the old man with an almost intolerable burden of guilt. The struggle between left and right in *Smugglers*, as well as the suicidal brooding, adumbrates or reflects the less baroque but no less bitter tensions in the Vermont household.

Sally's interpretations are ours as well. Gardner explains in his *Atlantic* interview: "As you read the inner and outer novels, you begin to recognize that that situation is exactly like this situation, that character is paralleled to this one." Ultimately the exotic world of *Smugglers* has been refined, so to speak, into terms at once more human and more credible, and Gardner makes—dramatically and novelistically—the points he made expositorily in his essay "The Way We Write Now." In that piece he took modern fiction to task for dwelling on bleakness and horror and for attempting occasionally to escape them by means of simple-minded and unrealistic "affirmation" (at the end of *Smugglers* a flying saucer appears to deliver the protagonists from apocalypse). Gardner is all for affirmation, but it must be reasoned and credible, growing out of "thought-out values—the solid formulations of character that Henry James or Jane Austen fictionally develop and recommend to the reader."

In the frame story of *October Light* Gardner lives up to his own exhortation. "Great novelists," he maintains, "build tight form out of singleminded psychological and moral analysis," and the reconciliation between James and Sally, when it comes, is as heartening as anything in literature. The old man, whose moral drama the book has come to emphasize, discovers that he has been guilty of a kind of inflexible righteousness that has poisoned the lives of those around him—most tragically the life of his son, driven to drink and finally suicide by the fecklessness his father had inadvertently fostered in him. In *October Light*, then, we have a rustic world where the same horrors obtain as in the black-comic, nihilistic, "smart-mouth satirical" novels typified by *Smugglers*, but Gardner convinces us that James Page can, at the age of seventy-two, come to self-knowledge—and that the thawing of this man's frozen heart holds much promise for all people who, bound in spiritual winter, have ever despaired of the spring.

Since *October Light* Gardner's *The King of the Hummingbirds, A Child's Bestiary*, and *In the Suicide Mountains*, the latest of his books for children, have been published. His other children's books are *Dragon, Dragon* and *Gudgekin the Thistle Girl*. Two more scholarly works have also appeared to mixed reviews: *The Life & Times of Chaucer* and *The Poetry of Chaucer*. He continues to produce short stories, and if the past is any index to the future, there will be many more novels to come.

As Susan Strehle has remarked, Gardner's fiction has been oddly neglected by academic critics. While books, dissertations, and whole issues of scholarly journals are being devoted to Thomas Pynchon and his three novels, Gardner stimulates the critics only to occasional articles (though his books are nearly always reviewed warmly in such intermediaries between academe and the educated public as the *New York Times Book Review*, the *Atlantic*, and *Harper's*). This neglect is probably due to a certain trepidation before the spate of major novels. The rapid-fire publication of his backlog along with his current work may not be wise, but one cannot help admiring the panache with which he storms into print, publishing as many as five books in a single year. Gardner obviously spins yarns as effortlessly as other men breathe, and no doubt we have only begun to see how prolific a writer he is. He is in the Oates class of contemporary novelists, fertile and "profluent," to use his word. The critical situation will change, for besides being prolific and

John Gardner

Jill Krementz

John Gardner.

disciplined, Gardner has a consistent moral vision which cannot fail to persuade critics—probably less dubious of his talent than awed by it—that he is one of the major novelists of our time. —*David Cowart*

Books:

The Resurrection (New York: New American Library, 1966);

The Gawain-Poet: Notes (Lincoln, Nebraska: Cliff's Notes, 1967);

Le Morte DArthur: Notes (Lincoln, Nebraska: Cliff's Notes, 1967);

The Wreckage of Agathon (New York: Harper & Row, 1970);

Grendel (New York: Knopf, 1971; London: Deutsch, 1972);

The Sunlight Dialogues (New York: Knopf, 1972; London: Cape, 1973);

Jason and Medeia (New York: Knopf, 1973);

Nickel Mountain (New York: Knopf, 1973; London: Cape, 1974);

The King's Indian Stories and Tales (New York: Knopf, 1974; London: Cape, 1975);

The Construction of the Wakefield Cycle (Carbondale: Southern Illinois University Press, 1974; London & Amsterdam: Feffer & Simons, 1974);

The Construction of Christian Poetry in Old English (Carbondale: Southern Illinois University Press, 1975; London & Amsterdam: Feffer & Simons, 1975);

Dragon, Dragon and Other Tales (New York: Knopf, 1975);

Gudgekin the Thistle Girl and Other Tales (New York: Knopf, 1976);

October Light (New York: Knopf, 1976; London: Cape, 1977);

The Poetry of Chaucer (Carbondale: Southern Illinois University Press, 1977; London & Amsterdam: Feffer & Simons, 1977);

The Life & Times of Chaucer (New York: Knopf, 1977);

The King of the Hummingbirds and Other Tales (New York: Knopf, 1977);

A Child's Bestiary, with Lucy Gardner and Eugene Rudzewicz (New York: Knopf, 1977);

In the Suicide Mountains (New York: Knopf, 1977).

Other:

The Forms of Fiction, edited by Gardner and Lennis Dunlap (New York: Random House, 1962);

The Complete Works of the Gawain-Poet, translated by Gardner (Chicago & London: University of Chicago Press, 1965);

Papers on the Art and Age of Geoffrey Chaucer, Papers on Language and Literature, III (summer 1967), edited by Gardner;

The Alliterative Morte Arthure, translated by Gardner (Carbondale: Southern Illinois University Press, 1971; London & Amsterdam: Feffer & Simons, 1971).

References:

Joe David Bellamy and Pat Ensworth, "John Gardner," *Fiction International*, 2/3 (1974): 33-49;

Bellamy, *The New Fiction: Interviews with Innovative American Writers* (Urbana: University of Illinois Press, 1974), pp. 169-193;

C. E. Frazer Clark, Jr., "John Gardner," in *Conversations With Writers I* (Detroit: Bruccoli Clark/Gale, 1977);

Don Edwards and Carol Polsgrove, "A Conversation with John Gardner," *Atlantic*, 239 (May 1977): 43-47;

Thomas Edwards, *"The Sunlight Dialogues,"* *New York Times Book Review*, 10 December 1972, pp. 1, 14;

Norma L. Hutman, "Even Monsters Have Mothers: A Study of *Beowulf* and John Gardner's *Grendel*," *Mosaic*, 9, 1 (fall 1975): 19-31;

Judy Smith Murr, "John Gardner's Order and Disorder: *Grendel* and *The Sunlight Dialogues*," *Critique*, 18, 2 (1977): 97-108;

Jay Rudd, "Gardner's Grendel and *Beowulf*: Humanizing the Monster," *Thoth*, 14, 2-3, (1974): 3-17;

George Stade, *"Nickel Mountain,"* *New York Times Book Review*, 9 December 1973, p. 5;

Susan Strehle, "John Gardner's Novels: Affirmation and the Alien," *Critique*, 18, 2 (1977): 86-96.

George Garrett.

GEORGE GARRETT was born in Orlando, Florida, on 11 June 1929, the son of George Palmer and Rosalie Toomer Garrett. His marriage to Susan Parrish Jackson in 1952 has produced three children: William, George, and Alice. He attended Sewanee Military Academy and the Hill School before going to Princeton in 1947. He took his B. A. from there in 1952 and then entered the U.S. Army where he served in the Field Artillery before returning to Princeton and earning an M.A. in 1956. He worked as an assistant professor at Wesleyan University, Middletown, Connecticut (1956-1960); visiting lecturer at Rice (1961-1962); associate professor at the University of Virginia (1962-1967); writer-in-residence at Princeton (1964-1965); director of graduate studies and writing program at Hollins College (1967-1971); and writer-in-residence and professor of English at the University of South Carolina (1971-1973). Then he left the academic profession to turn more solely to writing at his home in York Harbor, Maine.

Garrett's literary life outside the teaching profession has been distinguished. He acted as poetry editor for the *Transatlantic Review* (1958-1971). He was editor of the *Contemporary Poetry Series* of the University of North Carolina Press from 1963 to 1968. And he has served as coeditor of the *Hollins Critic*, as well as contributing editor to *Contempora* and *The Film Journal*. In addition, he has received the *Sewanee Review* Fellowship in poetry (1958), the American Academy of Arts and Letters *Prix de Rome* (1958), a Ford Foundation grant in drama (1960), and a National Endowment for the Arts grant (1967).

Although Garrett's interest in writing can be traced to his preschool years when he enjoyed dictating plays and stories about Richard the Lionhearted to his patient father, his literary career can best be said to begin in the spring of 1951 when he slipped some poems under the door of the *Nassau Literary Magazine* at Princeton. However, it is mainly his prose which has brought him fame.

His first book-length prose publication was *King of the Mountain* in 1958. Of the nineteen stories here, six are military and thirteen civilian. The military stories, most of which have their setting in post-World War II Austria (where Garrett served), concern man's deep capacity for violence and cruelty. Some of them, such as "What's the Purpose of the Bayonet?" present instances of that capacity. This grim tale is basically a description of the inside of a stockade. Especially grisly is the view we get of "the cage," two rows of individual cells, iron bars all around, where serious cases are kept until they can be sent back to the States for long terms at Leavenworth. Other of the military tales, however, emphasize the idea that the potential for violence is constant among men. In "Torment," for example, we are reminded that no matter how calm things may seem, there may be a hidden undercurrent of brutality (as when the narrator discovers that a group of arrested prostitutes is being beaten with rubber hoses in a back room of the jailhouse whose front desk bespeaks only justice).

The nonmilitary stories in this volume treat the frustration resulting from the bonds of conventional society. Of too "realistic" a mind to waste words attacking society, Garrett focuses his attention, in such works as "Four Women," on the problems of the individual whose deep inner needs are not fulfilled by society. Thus, it is almost an allegory when, in "September Morn," the professor's wife, momentarily attracted to the Italian peasant gardener who awakens sensuality in her, is interrupted from her attraction by her husband calling to make a tennis date. Her inability to identify the tune the gardener is whistling at the end signifies her ignorance of her own needs.

Garrett's first novel, *The Finished Man*, appeared in 1959. Many of the accidentals of the plot, reminiscent of *All the King's Men* by Robert Penn Warren, involve a king-pin politician running for reelection, violence and the threat of violence, a web of important personal and family relationships, a chauffeur with a taste for speed, and a strong flavor of the deep South and its ways. The novel begins *in*

medias res, and this structure reinforces one of the main themes: the determining significance of the past to the present. The events leading up to and following the assassination attempt with which the novel begins, are related by Mike Royle, and the novel as a whole can be taken as the record of his attempt to come to terms with his past, to relieve himself of the pressures it put upon him, and to channel its forces into his present self.

In different ways, each of the characters is trying to come to terms with his own nature as shaped by the past. Judge Royle, Mike's father, has a profound sense of the evil in man and in the world, and the pattern of his life seems to be a gloss on that sense. He conducts three campaigns for public office, each doomed from the start to be a lost cause, partly for the stubborn, inner purpose of reinforcing his belief that evil will prevail. And Senator Parker loses his campaign for reelection by betraying his past. Although he has always found success by being strongly in favor of equal opportunity for the races, he agrees to have his picture taken with a leader of the Ku Klux Klan in an attempt to mollify the far-right vote, thus alienating his real power base. Mike Royle, however, is more successful. When the story ends, he has discovered his directions within himself and trusts them, even though some echo his father suspiciously. It would be fair to call this a "Southern" novel, a phrase which Garrett himself probably would not gainsay, because it reflects the Southern obsession with history, tradition, and family.

Garrett's next major work was *In the Briar Patch*, a collection of short stories published in 1961. Several of the stories in this volume are developments of the kind of writing he had done before. In "The Last of the Spanish Blood," the theme of violence reappears, but with a difference: the tendency to inflict pain on others belongs not just to the crass and unenlightened "them," but to everyone, regardless of how much he may regret it. By involving his sympathetic first-person narrator in a forced act of violence, and by showing him to enjoy it in spite of himself, Garrett illustrates this human ugliness dramatically. When Harry, the narrator's tough, older cousin, pulls a gun on the bullies who have been menacing the neighborhood boys and lines them up to receive free licks, he has to force the narrator and his buddies to hit them at first; but once their instincts are aroused, he has a hard time getting them to stop.

In the Briar Patch also introduces a new element to Garrett's craft. "Thus the Early Gods," "The Gun and the Hat," and "Goodbye, Goodbye, Be Always

Kind and True'' approach the kind of Southern, almost-grotesque humor found in the works of Flannery O'Connor. In these stories we see a bulldozer operator who polishes the old wreck of a Buick convertible sitting in his front yard and pretends to be driving it; a country schoolteacher who befuddles away a would-be murderer by wearing his great-grandfather's Civil War hat—an absurd thing with ribbons and tall, bright feathers; and a one-legged World War I veteran who rigs up a family of dummies by the roadside so that he can get them to wave at passing motorists. This humorous quality combines well with Garrett's favorite themes—time and violence—to effect a real advancement in these stories.

The short stories Garrett had already published dealing with the subject of war lay the groundwork for his war novel, *Which Ones Are the Enemy?* (1961). In fact, the portion of the novel describing the formation of the outfit at Nth Field is lifted from "Hooray for the Old Nth Field," Part I of "What's the Purpose of the Bayonet?" in *King of the Mountain*. Pvt. Johnny Riche, the narrator of the story, is a study in the art of noninvolvement, and the novel is the record of his failure and its consequences. The real value of the work, however, is not in the plot, but in the concept of caring it presents. Riche, cocky and hard-boiled, realizes that caring means vulnerability, and he has no trouble staying uninvolved through much of the novel because of the phoniness he sees surrounding him. When he catches a disarming glimpse of the genuine in Angela, however, he cannot help loving her, and that love causes his arrest and her death. The essence of caring as shown here is that it is not willed; we see the foil to this quality in the shallow presumptuousness of the guards' attempt to empathize with Riche when he has to identify Angela's body. Galled by their presumption of being able to share his feelings, Riche purposely shocks them by feigning indifference. At the end of the novel the reader can see that his callous behavior all along has been a survival stratagem, a defense against caring and a barrier to bitter empathy.

True to the pattern of alternating novels with volumes of short stories, Garrett's next book was a collection of stories, *Cold Ground Was My Bed Last Night* (1964). By the mid-1960s, the military had faded somewhat from its former prominence in Garrett's works. The soldiers we find in this volume are not so often shown in combat-readiness, and there are not so many of them. The most interesting story here is the title work. Garrett evidently thought well of it, too, for he was to change the title and include it in another collection of short stories nine years later, when there were many uncollected works he might have chosen in its place.

Ike Toombs, who is being held for suspicion of murder, has all the calculated indifference of Johnny Riche, and his conflict in the story has to do with his efforts to remain uncaring so he can't be hurt. The major concern of the work, however, is Sheriff Jack Riddle, even-tempered but strong by nature, who, under the influence of his deputy's recent impulse-killing of a man in self-defense, finally straps on a gun, signifying his embrace of the violent. A *Playboy* centerfold works symbolically throughout; nakedness, for Garrett, usually indicates a state of truth, with all the false layers of protective masks stripped away. When Riddle straps on his gun, he throws away the centerfold, and the reader knows that Riddle's understanding of his own violent nature is deficient.

The publication of *Do, Lord, Remember Me* (1965) marked an advance in Garrett's narrative technique. Whereas before he had used the fairly conventional third person or the more contemporary first, in this novel he employs multiple narrators to tell the story. The events are fairly simple: Red Smalley and his tent revival come to a small Southern town, and Judith, a redhead in a sports car, follows, hoping to be healed. Red ends his revival by throwing his accumulated earnings to the crowd and shoots himself afterward as his cohorts desert him. These happenings are related mainly by the aides in Red's revival: Miami, a beautiful ex-stripper who loves Red; Cartwright, a greedy, stupid ex-pimp with a damaged ego and an obsession for sex; and Moses, an orphan, probably Jewish, who mistakenly threw a grenade into a room of children during World War II. The effect is like a hurricane, with all the minor characters whirling around the tormented center of Red Smalley. Red is torn by a deep-reaching conflict: he is a genuine instrument of God, capable of revealing glimpses of Him to eager crowds; yet he is, himself, an unworthy vessel, a drunk, a womanizer, a fake. He has real contact with God, but the problem is that it isn't constant, and the resulting tension leads him to kill himself.

In 1969 *A Wreath for Garibaldi and Other Stories* was published in England. This is largely a collection of stories already found in *In the Briar Patch* and *Cold Ground Was My Bed Last Night*, neither of which has been published in Great Britain.

His next book was *Death of the Fox* (1971), Garrett's most successful work to date. Praised by many reviewers, this novel employs the multiple

March   -1-

Late cold is a clenched fist gripping all of this island, both
these kingdoms. Days of driving rain. Wind, howling out of the
northeast, has been ~~constant~~ constant, ~~rising~~ rising and blowing
in high whining gusts ~~which~~ to twist and torment the trees, to rattle the
small panes of windows and swirl damp thick clouds of smoke ~~down~~
down the chimneys and coughing into chambers.

As Better to stand by a fire, even at the risk of being well-smoked as
a ham or a salmon, than to be outside facing this foul weather.

In the north, in Scotland, uneasy and restless in his palace of
Holyroodhouse, just a little way beyond the gates and walls of Edin-
burg, King James VI is standing now with his back to the huge fireplace
in the great hall, a crowd of his companions gathered close
around him. This Court is not stiff with old-fashioned ceremony as
is (he hears) the English Court; and considering the appearance and
condition of the king and his courtiers at this moment, any attempt
at formality maintaining could be only comic. All of them are soaked to the skin,
cold to so bone marrow. Their clothes, limp and dripping, are now
beginning to steam. No doubt some will shrink to fit tight as
a glove. All but the king have removed their hats. The feathers on
his high-crowned, broad-brimmed hunting hat have drooped like wilting,
dying flowers. Servants have hurried to heap up logs on the
fire, and others are bringing cups and bowls of strong spirits. Soon
enough, with their clothing steamed dry, skin rosy and bowels
relaxing warmly to the fumes and fires of distilled spirits, they
will be cheerful again, these Scots noblemen, able to laugh at themselves and at the folly of trying to ride out and hunt on a day like
this one. ¶ Or yesterday or the day before.....

From typescript of work-in-progress.

point-of-view technique of *Do, Lord, Remember Me* in presenting the last two days of the life of Sir Walter Ralegh from the standpoints of Ralegh himself, King James, Sir Henry Yelverton (the King's Attorney General), and others. Part of the book is narrated, but much of it is taken up with the interior monologues of these characters.

Commenting on this novel, Garrett has insisted that the proper subject of historical fiction is the human imagination in action, and that is what we find here when we listen to each of these characters think about the coming execution, try to imagine how the others may feel, and arrive at an assessment of the situation based partly on the facts and partly on an imaginative interpretation of them. Ralegh himself is shown to be a man whose actions were determined by his impelled flight from the past and his compelled avoidance of the future. Essentially a figure of the capricious court, he could neither rely on past glories to sustain his position nor depend on the future for comfort, especially as a favorite of the past queen, Elizabeth, in the new court of King James. Thus, he was driven to bold acts of the intense present.

Another book of short stories, *The Magic Striptease*, was published in 1973. The title story in this volume is a fable with human characters, different from anything Garrett had written previously. It is the fantastic tale of Jacob Quirk, a mimic who develops the ability to transform his shape totally into that of other people, animals, and even objects. Jacob's metamorphoses are a means to self-discovery, and when he dies he becomes a redemptive cult-hero.

"The Satyr Shall Cry," the last story in this work, is an expansion of "To Whom Shall I Call Now In My Hour of Need?" first published in the *Red Clay Reader* in 1965, the same year the movie *The Playground*, based on his screenplay, was released. Bosley Crowther called the film the first American black comedy cinema. Whether that's accurate or not, this short story certainly shows elements of black humor. There is much of the absurd in the fragmented and crazy bits revealed to us in multiple point-of-view chapters. The story concerns the events surrounding a double murder occurring at a tent revival in Paradise Springs, Florida.

In addition to Garrett's volumes of novels and short stories, he has published four books of poetry, written drama, screenplays, and critical articles, compiled a checklist on Federico Fellini, conducted interviews, reviewed books, translated poetry, served on discussion panels, lectured widely, and edited numerous collections of poetry and fiction by new authors in his continued support of upcoming talent. His interests run from John Cheever, Saul Bellow, and William Faulkner to *Frankenstein Meets the Space Monster*. In most of his work can be found an understated Christian viewpoint, tough, like the Old Testament, which disciplines his approach to our world. —*Jack Wright Rhodes*

Books:

Poets of Today IV (New York: Scribners, 1957), includes "The Reverend Ghost: Poems" by Garrett;

King of the Mountain (New York: Scribners, 1958; London: Eyre & Spottiswoode, 1959);

The Sleeping Gypsy and Other Poems (Austin: University of Texas Press, 1958);

The Finished Man (New York: Scribners, 1959; London: Eyre & Spottiswoode, 1960);

Abraham's Knife and Other Poems (Chapel Hill: University of North Carolina Press, 1961; London: Oxford University Press, 1961);

In the Briar Patch (Austin: University of Texas Press, 1961);

Which Ones Are the Enemy? (Boston: Little, Brown, 1961; London: W. H. Allen, 1962);

Sir Slob and the Princess: A Play for Children (New York: French, 1962);

Cold Ground Was My Bed Last Night (Columbia: University of Missouri Press, 1964);

Do, Lord, Remember Me (Garden City: Doubleday, 1965; London: Chapman & Hall, 1965);

For a Bitter Season: New and Selected Poems (Columbia: University of Missouri Press, 1967);

A Wreath for Garibaldi and Other Stories (London: Hart-Davis, 1969);

Death of the Fox (Garden City: Doubleday, 1971; London: Barrie & Jenkins, 1972);

The Magic Striptease (Garden City: Doubleday, 1973).

Play:

Garden Spot, U.S.A., Houston, Alley Theatre, 25 April 1962.

Screenplays:

The Young Lovers, Metro-Goldwyn-Mayer, 1965;

The Playground, Jerand Film Release, 1965;

Frankenstein Meets the Space Monster, Vernon-Seneca Films, 1965.

References:

John Carr, "Kite Flying and Other Irrational Acts: George Garrett," in *Kite Flying and Other Irrational Acts: Conversations With Twelve Southern Writers*, ed. John Carr (Baton Rouge: Louisiana State University Press, 1972), pp. 174-198;

Charles Israel, "Interview: George Garrett," *South Carolina Review*, 6, 1 (November 1973): 43-48;

James B. Meriwether, "George Palmer Garrett, Jr.," *Princeton University Library Chronicle*, 25, 1 (1963): 26-39;

Mill Mountain Review, In Appreciation of George Garrett, 1, 4 (1971);

W. R. Robinson, "Imagining the Individual: George Garrett's *Death of the Fox*," *Hollins Critic*, 8 (1971): 1-12;

David R. Slavitt, "History—Fate and Freedom: a Look at George Garrett's New Novel," *Southern Review* (LSU), 7 (1971): 276-294;

John Hall Wheelock, "To Recapture Delight," in *Poets of Today IV* (New York: Scribners, 1957), introduction.

WILLIAM HOWARD GASS was born in Fargo, North Dakota, on 30 July 1924 but his family almost immediately moved to Warren, Ohio, where he grew up. As a child he found it difficult to deal with an alcoholic mother and a father crippled with arthritis. His response was to reject his background as entirely as he could and to develop instead an emotional attitude that would later be reflected in his aesthetics: he detached himself, became a formalist, and in the process began to submit himself to a type of rigorous, philosophical training. He began college at Kenyon and briefly attended Ohio Wesleyan before serving as an ensign in the navy in World War II. After the war, he returned to Kenyon where he majored in philosophy (B.A., 1947). He also audited a few courses taught by New Critic John Crowe Ransom and unsuccessfully tried to publish some early work in *Kenyon Review*. In both high school and college, Gass was a voracious reader, his tastes focusing on such literary formalists as James, Faulkner, Joyce and—somewhat later—the three writers who would probably most directly influence his own writing career: Rilke, Gertrude Stein, and Valéry. Gass attended Cornell University for three years as a philosophy graduate student, but his interest in aesthetic theory was somewhat frustrated there by the lack of course offerings. Eventually he wound up working with Max Black studying the philosophy of language and the theory of metaphor. Accepting a position as a philosophy instructor at the College of Wooster in Ohio, Gass continued to work on his dissertation and received his Cornell Ph.D. in 1954. His dissertation, "A Philosophical Investigation of Metaphor," has applications which are evident in a great deal of Gass's later critical and literary output. It was also at Cornell that Gass was privileged to observe Ludwig Wittgenstein in several philosophical sessions, an experience which Gass claims "was to be the most important intellectual experience of my life." In summarizing the influence of Gass's college years on his later work, the importance of his training as a philosopher of language cannot be underestimated. Gass's insistence, for example, that fictional constructions have no necessary connection with the world and the careful manner in which he explores the way symbols operate give strong evidence of his training in the theory of models and metaphor making. This early training also helps explain his comment, "I think of myself as a writer of prose rather than a novelist, critic, or story-teller, and

I am principally interested in the problems of style.'' After receiving his Ph.D., Gass began teaching at Purdue University where he remained for fifteen years. Since 1969 he has taught a wide range of subjects in both the philosophy and English departments at Washington University at St. Louis.

Gass begins his essay, "The Medium of Fiction," by saying, "It seems a country-headed thing to say: that literature is language, that stories and the places and the people in them are merely made of words as chairs are made of smoothed sticks and sometimes of cloth or metal tubes." But appreciating this basic truth is perhaps the key to understanding the remarkable writings of William Gass who—perhaps more than any other living writer—constantly forces us to remember that novels and stories are, after all, aesthetic designs constructed out of words.

Gass has said that, partly as a result of reading Gertrude Stein in graduate school, he began his own writing career by experimenting over and over with seeing just how the basic unit of writing—the sentence—operated as a form. His first stories were accepted by *Accent Magazine*, which devoted almost an entire issue to his work (winter 1958). A notoriously slow worker, Gass labored on his first novel, *Omensetter's Luck*, for a dozen years before it was finally published in 1966. His progress on the book was hampered by having the only completed copy of his manuscript stolen (it was only in Gass's final revised version that Jethro Furber became the novel's major character). Verbally dense and experimental in form, the manuscript of *Omensetter's Luck* was rejected by a long list of publishers before The New American Library agreed to print it. Its publication immediately established Gass as a major figure in American literature.

Omensetter's Luck is set in a small Ohio river town in the 1890s. Its central conflict involves the reactions of various townspeople to the arrival of Brackett Omensetter and his family. Omensetter is a "wide and happy" man who seems to share with the prelapsarian Adam a sort of naturalness and unselfconsciousness that makes him appear admirable to some and suspicious to others. To Henry Pimber (Omensetter's landlord), Omensetter's naturalness makes him seem at first almost subhuman because he is unaware of man's separation from God. Thus an opposition is immediately established which is described by critic Richard Schneider: "Pimber and Omensetter . . . do seem to be a pair, opposite halves of the same man—Omensetter with his healthy carelessness and fertile wife, and Pimber with his weak will and barren, bitchy wife." For

Pimber, Omensetter's freedom from guilt or anxiety makes him an object of near veneration; in effect, Omensetter represents a sort of savior to Pimber and possesses an ability to experience life directly which is denied most men. But although Omensetter is once able magically to cure Pimber from lockjaw, eventually the landlord senses that Omensetter is basically indifferent to his own limited life. In despair Pimber commits suicide. The other important reaction to Omensetter is that of Jethro Furber, the town preacher, whose difficult, musical-sounding narrative takes up well over half the novel. Furber's narrative is the book's most experimental section and shifts rapidly between different styles, tempos, and orders to reveal the workings of Furber's character and obsessive consciousness. Furber sees Omensetter's mysterious unity with nature as a personal threat since Biblical logic suggests that man's Fall involves a necessary recognition of our separation from the world. Like nearly all of Gass's characters, Furber is a man isolated from those around him, and the source of this isolation lies precisely in his self-consciousness about his role as a symbol maker. Fearful and yet intrigued by the outer world, Furber retreats into his own rhetoric; indeed, like the poet in *In the Heart of the Heart of the Country*, Furber has become so obsessed with words that he finds himself totally cut off from anything outside his own mind. In creating his personal "beautiful barrier of words" which he can order and control, he makes exactly the kind of dangerous analogies between verbal resemblances and the world itself that Wittgenstein warned us of. Because Omensetter seems utterly devoid of the sort of guilt and self-consciousness that seems a necessary condition of perception, Furber distrusts him and, for a while, tries to destroy him by linking him to Pimber's death. The result of this confrontation is a sort of mutual temptation to which they both eventually succumb. As Schneider summarizes, "So Omensetter gains the mixed blessing of human perception, and Furber gains love. Both at least have the potential to be fully human, but the conflict between them has been costly to both them and the town."

Gass's first novel was immediately recognized as a stunning achievement. Writing for *New Republic*, Richard Gilman began his review of the book by calling it "the most important work of fiction by an American in this literary generation." He went on to claim that it provided "the first full replenishment of language we have had for a very long time, the first convincing fusion of speculative thought and hard, accurate sensuality that we have had, it is tempting to say, since Melville." Other reviewers were almost unanimous in their praise, frequently comparing Gass's achievements with those of Joyce and Faulkner. Certainly the book quickly established the unique verbal qualities which are so evident in all of Gass's work. As Paul West says in his review for *Book Week*, "One would have to be criminally tone-deaf and almost snowblind not to register the sonic and visual brilliance of the language . . . a pregnant, swaying physicality with an undertow of festive and smutty limericks: a delight to say aloud and a continuing sound in the mind."

Gass's second book-length work was *In the Heart of the Heart of the Country* (1968), a collection of five stories which developed the related themes of isolation and the difficulties of love in a variety of vital literary forms. The characters here are mostly outsiders, people whose alienation from a cold, often threatening environment forces them to create elaborate methods of justifying their lonely existences. Like Jethro Furber, these people tend to be brave only in the privacy of their own imaginations, and they control their lives only to the extent that they can organize their thoughts and descriptions into meaningful patterns. Not surprisingly, then, we come to know them mainly as linguistic rather than psychological selves, with their actions usually less significant to our understanding of them than the way they project their inner selves through language. The longest and most conventional story in the collection, "The Pedersen Kid," is an almost classically rendered initiation story. After Jorge (the story's adolescent narrator) and Big Hans (a hired hand) discover a neighbor's child nearly frozen to death in the snow, they listen to the boy recount a horrifying tale of his family being murdered by a mysterious stranger; frightened, but goaded on by a triangular set of male rivalries, Jorge, his father, and Big Hans set out to discover the "secret of the snow." When they arrive at the farmhouse, Jorge's father is shot and killed, Big Hans runs away, and Jorge is left alone in the basement, nearly delirious with cold and shock, the killer apparently waiting upstairs. Eventually the killer leaves, and Jorge feels satisfied that he has done "brave things well worth remembering," and the story concludes with Jorge feeling "warm inside and out, burning up, inside and out, with joy."

The sense of isolation and desire to assert oneself is equally evident in each of the remaining stories, but here the triumphs tend to be triumphs of the imagination only. In the title story of the collection nearly all the motifs and themes of the previous stories are included and developed so that it functions both structurally and thematically as the focal point of the story cycle. The form of the story is unusual: a narrator presents thirty-six titled blocks of discourse which describe different aspects of a small Midwestern town and the narrator's life there. The key to the story perhaps lies in the way it opens. After elliptically quoting from Yeats's "Sailing to Byzantium" ("So I have sailed the seas and come . . . to B . . . ") the next words appear: "a small town fastened to a field in Indiana." If "to B" is not merely a reference to Byzantium and the town in Indiana but also a pun on "to be," the central metaphor of the story becomes evident: the poet/narrator, through his words (which are all of him we will ever know), has literally become the small, dying town he is describing for us; his efforts to organize the elements of this town are also efforts at creating some sense of artistic unity about his own life. As is typical of Gass's characters, this narrator is a lonely, sensitive individual whose hauntingly beautiful blocks of discourse (prose poems, really) serve only to isolate him even further from the unresponsive world around him. As critic Frederick Busch notes, "The life he describes may be an imaginative construct, the refuge or prison he creates for himself. So we have a man who has fled the world of nature, who has somehow fallen and who is now trapped (or hiding, or both) in his imagination." There is thus a hollow sadness to his plight that dominates the mood of the story. "In the Heart" is justifiably Gass's most famous work to date, a nearly perfect work of order and beauty whose highly original form exactly suits its metafictional impulses.

As is true of all of Gass's work, *In the Heart of the Heart of the Country* was enthusiastically received by critics and reviewers, although it received little popular attention except on college campuses. Jack Richardson, in a *New York Review of Books* article, said that this collection "makes clear the rewards of an imagination which clings to the concrete world like a lover and makes of it, through near-perfect language, a renewed mystery." In a later critical essay, Frederick Busch commented on the title story that "Gass has written a short story as dense as a novel, lyrical as a poem, as veined with roads to charnel pits as a map of hell might be."

Three other works by Gass have appeared since *In the Heart*, and each of these demonstrates Gass's interest in the nature of the language and metaphor and the way in which fictions are created out of these elements. The fullest elaboration of his aesthetic principles can be found in his collection of essays, *Fiction and the Figures of Life* (1970). In Part One, the book's most theoretical and important section,

Terrific. Years ago. When he seemed a prophet, sometimes
a god. At the tip, he'd exclaim, raising his ink-stained fingers,
and a thrill would shoot through Fender, *and* he'd repeat the words
to himself, and consider again the wisdom of his teacher. Everything is property. Pearson's face would glow, his hair shake. Everything is property. Think of it. Some sort of property. And he
would rush through the office naming objects, lifting them up.
This,and this and this and that... This ear, he says triumphantly,
fingering the lobe, this ear belongs to Isabelle......

People pass on. In the midst of life, you know, Fender... well...
but property, property endures. Sure, sure, cars go to junk before
the people in them do. Sometimes... sometimes. But there's all sorts
of property, that's all, and a house will outlast its builder usually.
Lots of things outlast us, Fender. Lots of things. Lots do. Hah.
Well. That's it. Land's near immortal. Land lasts forever. That's
why it's called real, see? oh it makes sense, Fender, it makes sense!

People are property. Does that seem like a hard saying, people
are property? not even real? Oh let me tell you, Fender, we've got
it all wrong, most of us... backwards, most of us. People own property... that's what we think. Oh sure. Sure. But property owns
people. Everything's property, and the property that lasts the
longest... it owns what lasts least. Stands to reason. Hah. Wait'll
you die, you'll see! So the peroperty that lives, Fender, that
lasts and lives and goes right on, and then goes on again, well,
that's the property that's real, and it... it owns the rest... lock,
stock, and barrel... right? Makes sense.

It made sense, yes. It still made sense. But now it did seem
like a hard saying... hard to bear. His little house owned him, it
was true. He accomodated himself to its walls. He saw what was
permitted. He did not extend beyond the rooms. Up the steps of
a glowering, blind-eyed house, how many times had he led them, like
pets in search of owners? And it was right. Pearson was right.
The question his prospects should have asked - do I want to belong
to this house?- they never asked Do you want to do what this
house says? what will it make of your life? Pearson was right.

From typescript of In the Heart of the
Heart of the Country.

193

Gass returns again and again to his central thesis that, as he puts it at one point, "There are no descriptions in fiction, there are only constructions. . . . Just as the painter's designs help make his object, the lines of the novelist offer no alternatives, they are not likely interpretations of anything, but are the thing itself." Since fiction should not be viewed primarily in terms of its themes or as reportage of actual people and events, Gass hopes to direct attention to the process of how literature unfolds on the page. Taking a suggestion from Valery (whose aesthetic influence is everywhere evident in Gass's approach), Gass reminds us that words in literature differ in function from words as they are ordinarily used. Whereas in everyday activities language functions mainly as signs which are extinguished by their use, in literature the sign remains for readers to return to again and again. Aesthetic signs such as words in a novel or musical sounds have no utility except as elements within an aesthetic design, and their use only mimics their use in life. What Gass asks of both critics and readers is that they pay more attention to the building blocks of literature—to the way words are used, to the way writers develop a set of symbols. Too often, claims Gass, both readers and writers are content to view fiction as simply reproducing a preexisting order; this helps them make the related error of assuming that words in literature are mere vehicles to be "looked through" and, consequently, ignored.

These aesthetic principles are further developed and brilliantly illustrated in Gass's highly experimental "essay/novella," *Willie Masters' Lonesome Wife* (1968). This work embodies Gass's view that literature is language and that a reader should respond to the sensuous body of language with the same sort of excitement and participation that he would to any other sensual experience. Narrated by Baby Babs Masters, the lonesome wife of the title who is lady language herself, *Willie Masters* emphasizes the sensuous qualities of language—its colors, sounds, shapes, and textures—in almost every conceivable fashion. Each of the four sections of the book, for example, is printed on different-colored, different-textured pages; the photographs and the large variety of graphic and typographic experiments insure that the reader's attention never leaves the page and also free the book from most of the linear conventions of narration. Although the book is virtually plotless, the different sections roughly correspond to the different stages of the sexual intercourse that Babs is having with a particularly unresponsive lover named Gelvin. The book's central metaphor, then, is obvious: reading a book

should be a sensuous experience, but too often readers are unresponsive and ignore the physical aspects of language.

Gass's most recent book, *On Being Blue* (1976), is a work which is part history of philosophy, part metaphysical musing, and part original speculation. Its subject matter is one of Gass's favorites: the complex relationship between words and the world, the accidental process by which meanings are historically attached to words. After opening the book with a list of the ways in which the word "blue" is used ("Blue pencils, blue noses, blue movies, laws . . ."), Gass proceeds to analyze blue at various levels as word, color, state of mind, and Platonic ideal. As is true of most of his essays, *On Being Blue* is not a systematic, logical presentation but develops its own form which confounds the usual distinction between prose narration and discursive essay. By his revealing and viscerally drawn analogies, Gass demonstrates his startling ability to make us see X as Y and thus illustrates in his own prose the point that words affect our perceptions in subtle but significant ways.

Although his literary output to date is relatively small, William Gass's reputation as a critic and fiction writer is rapidly growing. Certainly no other writer in America has been able to combine his critical intelligence with a background as a student of both the literary and philosophical aspects of language and to make this synthesis vital. The excerpts which have appeared for the past decade of his current work-in-progress, *The Tunnel*, give every indication that its publication will be a major literary event. In addition, a collection of essays, *The World in the Word* is forthcoming.

—*Larry McCaffery*

Books:

Omensetter's Luck (New York: New American Library, 1966; London: Collins, 1967);

In the Heart of the Heart of the Country (New York: Harper & Row, 1968; London: Cape, 1969);

Willie Masters' Lonesome Wife (Evanston, Ill.: Northwestern University Press, 1968; New York: Knopf, 1971);

Fiction and the Figures of Life (New York: Knopf, 1970);

On Being Blue (Boston: Godine, 1976).

Periodical Publications:

FICTION:

"The Clairvoyant," *Location*, 1 (summer 1964): 59-66;

Herb Weitman

William Gass.

"The Sugar Crock," *Art and Literature*, 9 (summer 1966): 158-171;

"We Have Not Lived the Right Life," *New American Review*, 5 (1969): 7-32;

"Why Windows Are Important to Me," *Tri-Quarterly*, 20 (winter 1971): 285-307;

"The Cost of Everything," *Fiction*, 1 (1972): unpaged;

"I Wish You Wouldn't," *Partisan Review*, 42 (summer 1975): 334-360;

"Mad Meg," *Iowa Review*, 7 (winter 1976): 77-95;

"Koh Whistles up a Wind," *TriQuarterly*, 38 (winter 1977): 191-209.

NONFICTION:

"Marcel Proust at 100," *New York Times Book Review*, 11 July 1971, pp. 1-2, 12, 14;

"The Doomed in the Sinking," *New York Review of Books*, 18 May 1972, pp. 3-4;

"Paul Valery: The Later Poems and Prose," *New York Times Book Review*, 27 August 1972, pp. 6-7, 30;

"Gertrude Stein, Geographer, I," *New York Review of Books*, 3 May 1973, pp. 5-8, rpt. as part of "Introduction" to Stein's *Geographical History of America* (New York: Vintage Books, 1973);

"Gertrude Stein, Geographer, II," *New York Review of Books*, 17 May 1973, pp. 5-8;

"Groping for Trouts: On Metaphor," *Salmagundi*, 24 (fall 1973): 19-33;

"Malcolm Lowry's Inferno, I," *New York Review of Books*, 29 November 1973, pp. 26-27;

"Malcolm Lowry's Inferno, II," *New York Review of Books*, 13 December 1973, pp. 28-32;

"Freud's Fierce Science," *New York Review of Books*, 17 April 1975, pp. 3-5;

"The Scientific Psychology of Sigmund Freud," *New York Review of Books*, 1 May 1975, pp. 24-29;

"The Attack on Freud," *New York Review of Books*, 15 May 1975, pp. 9-12;

"Theatrical Sartre," *New York Review of Books*, 14 October 1976, pp. 16-24;

"Three Photos of Colette," *New York Review of Books*, 14 April 1977, pp. 11-19.

References:

Carolyn J. Allen, "Fiction and Figures of Life in

Omensetter's Luck," *Pacific Coast Philology,* 9 (1974): 5-11;

Bruce Bassoff, "The Sacrificial World of William Gass: *In the Heart of the Heart of the Country,"* *Critique,* 18 (summer 1976): 36-58;

Frederick Busch, "But This Is What It Is Like to Live in Hell: William Gass's *In the Heart of the Heart of the Country,"* *Modern Fiction Studies,* 20 (autumn 1973): 97-108;

Jeffrey Duncan, "A Conversation with Stanley Elkin and William H. Gass," *Iowa Review,* 7 (winter 1976): 48-77;

Ned French and David Deyser, "Against the Grain: A Conversation with William H. Gass," *Harvard Advocate,* 106 (winter 1973): 8-16;

French, "Against the Grain: Theory and Practice in the Work of William H. Gass," *Iowa Review,* 7 (winter 1976): 96-106;

French, "William Gass Bibliography," *Iowa Review,* 7 (winter 1976): 106-107;

Richard Gilman, "William H. Gass," in his *The Confusion of Realms* (New York: Random House, 1969), pp. 69-81.

Joseph Haas, "In the Heart of William H. Gass," *Panorama: Chicago Daily News,* 1 February 1969, pp. 4-5, 22;

Patricia Kane, "The Sun Burned on the Snow: Gass's 'The Pedersen Kid,' " *Critique,* 14, 2 (December 1972): 89-96;

Larry McCaffery, "Donald Barthelme, Robert Coover, and William H. Gass: Three Checklists," *Bulletin of Bibliography,* 31 (July-September 1974): 101-106;

McCaffery, "The Art of Metafiction: William Gass's *Willie Masters' Lonesome Wife," Critique,* 18 (summer 1976): 21-35;

McCaffery, "A William H. Gass Bibliography," *Critique,* 18 (summer 1976): 59-66;

Carole Spearin McCauley, "Fiction Needn't Say Things—It Should Make Them Out of Words: An Interview with William Gass," *Falcon,* 5 (winter 1972): 35-45;

Gary Mullinax, "An Interview with William Gass," *Delaware Literary Review,* 1 (1972): 81-87;

Richard J. Schneider, "The Fortunate Fall in William Gass's *Omensetter's Luck," Critique,* 18 (summer 1976): 5-20;

Earl Shorris, "The Well Spoken Passions of William H. Gass," *Harper's,* 244 (May 1972): 96-100;

"A Symposium on Fiction (Barthelme, Gass, Paley, Percy)," *Shenandoah,* 27 (winter 1976): 3-31.

HERBERT GOLD was born in Cleveland, Ohio, on 9 March 1924. His father, Samuel S. Gold, was a Russian immigrant who struggled to establish himself in America. In Cleveland Samuel Gold married Freida Frankel and became a successful businessman. Herbert, who was the first of the Golds' four sons, began writing in grammar school, and at Lakewood High School, from which he graduated in 1942, he wrote for the school newspaper. After graduating, he studied philosophy at Columbia University where he also contributed to student publications, but his education was interrupted from 1942 to 1946 while Gold served in the United States Army. In 1946, he received a B.A. from Columbia and in 1948, an M.A. In that year, he married Edith Zubrin, an ex-model, whom he divorced in 1956; they have two children, Ann and Judith. From 1949 to 1951, Gold studied philosophy at the Sorbonne on a Fulbright Fellowship and then from 1951 to 1953, he was a lecturer at Western Reserve University. Since lecturing at Western Reserve, he has taught as a lecturer or visiting professor at Wayne State (1954-1956), Cornell (1958), University of California at Berkeley (1963), Harvard (1964), and Stanford (1967). In 1968, he married Melissa Dilworth; they have three children, Nina, Ari, and Ethan. Gold has received, besides the Fulbright Fellowship, a *Hudson Review* Fellowship (1956), a Guggenheim Fellowship (1957), a National Institute of Arts and Letters grant (1958), a Longview Foundation Award (1959), and a Ford Theatre Fellowship (1960). In addition to writing ten novels, Gold has contributed short stories and essays to leading periodicals. He has published three volumes of short stories: *Fifteen by Three,* with R. V. Cassill and James B. Hall (1957); *Love & Like* (1960); and *The Magic Will* (1971). His essays have been collected in *The Age of Happy Problems* (1962). He has written an autobiography, *My Last Two Thousand Years* (1972), and a children's book, *The Young Prince and the Magic Cone* (1973). He has also edited *Fiction of the Fifties* (1959); *Stories of Modern America,* with David L. Stevenson (1961); and *First Person Singular: Essays for the Sixties* (1963).

Gold's novels are complex, and his characters—although their actions are occasionally melodramatic—are vital and believable. In most of his works, Gold either condemns his generation, which he portrays as blindly seeking tokens of security and success (money, power, marriage) while avoiding introspection, or contrasts his generation to his father's, which he feels knew the insecurity of life and was, therefore, willing to risk life to gain life. In

Jill Krementz

businessman, who has mastered the nine-to-five routine. During dinner on his forty-fifth birthday, he listens to the "social snickers" of his family and guests and realizes the emptiness of his life. When Reuben clumsily cuts himself with a bread knife, Lydia Fortiner, an attractive but lonely widow, tells him, "Everyman can be a hero, or at least wants to be a hero." Reuben takes the hint, and the next day he begins to romance Lydia. His character alters as the affair progresses: he begins to lie to his wife and is often late for work. Reuben's attempt to live a "heroic" life is ended when Larry, introduced as Lydia's brother, visits. Larry, a brawny sailor, is far from heroic himself. After much delay, Larry tells Mrs. Flair that Reuben is having an affair with Lydia and that he is not Lydia's brother—he is her husband. After the revelation, Larry commits suicide. At the novel's end, Reuben ends his affair with Lydia to return to his wife and his nine-to-five existence.

Harry Bowers is the overweight protagonist of *The Prospect Before Us* (1954), a novel which is Gold's most stylized. His description of Jake, Harry's clerk, shows a Joycean love for wordplay: "The eyes of Jake roamed the dogdays morning sky with a conman's monkeyshine tricks of gaze, doomed to the flesh but yearning away from it, asking faith and please-believe-me." The complex plot ends melodramatically. Harry runs a prosperous fleabag hotel that is frequented by immigrants and down-and-outers. (Gold himself managed a hotel in 1951.) When an organization fighting racial prejudice places Claire Farren, an attractive black, in the hotel, Harry's guests complain and, when Harry allows the girl to remain, they move elsewhere. Both Harry and Claire become outcasts in a nearly deserted hotel. Harry is isolated from white society (even the police mistreat him) as is Claire from black society (she lives in a white hotel). Harry is drawn to Claire, and a romance begins to develop. The romance, however, does not develop far, for Harry is nearing bankruptcy. At Jake's suggestion, Harry burns his hotel for the insurance money. Believing that Claire is still inside, Harry rushes into the burning hotel and dies.

The Man Who Was Not With It (1956), later titled *The Wild Life* in paperback, is considered by some critics to be Gold's best novel. Bud Williams narrates the novel with a mixture of street slang and carnival jargon. The language fits Bud's character. He is a runaway from Pittsburgh who has traveled with a carnival for three years and become addicted to morphine. Gracchus, or "Grack the Frenchie," the carnival barker, helps Bud break

the preface to *Fiction of the Fifties*, Gold wrote: "Indeed it is difficult not to live cautiously these days. There is so much to gain (car, house, rank); there is so much to lose (rank, house, car). And yet, what we are sure of gaining and sure of losing remains the same. We are sure of losing our lives. We are sure of the chance of gaining our lives." In his novels, Gold develops this theme with a variety of approaches and styles. Always present, however, is his love of wordplay, which has been cited as his greatest accomplishment as a fiction writer and his greatest defect. Harry T. Moore wrote, "Herbert Gold is a neat stylist, sometimes too neat. He can upon occasion master words, use them to bring out exactly what he needs to say about people and incidents; but he often slips too easily into rhetoric." Gold's wordplay is too unusual and too present to ignore; the fate of his novels rests with the acceptance or rejection of his style.

Birth of a Hero (1951) is Gold's first novel. Reuben Flair, the protagonist, is a successful lawyer-

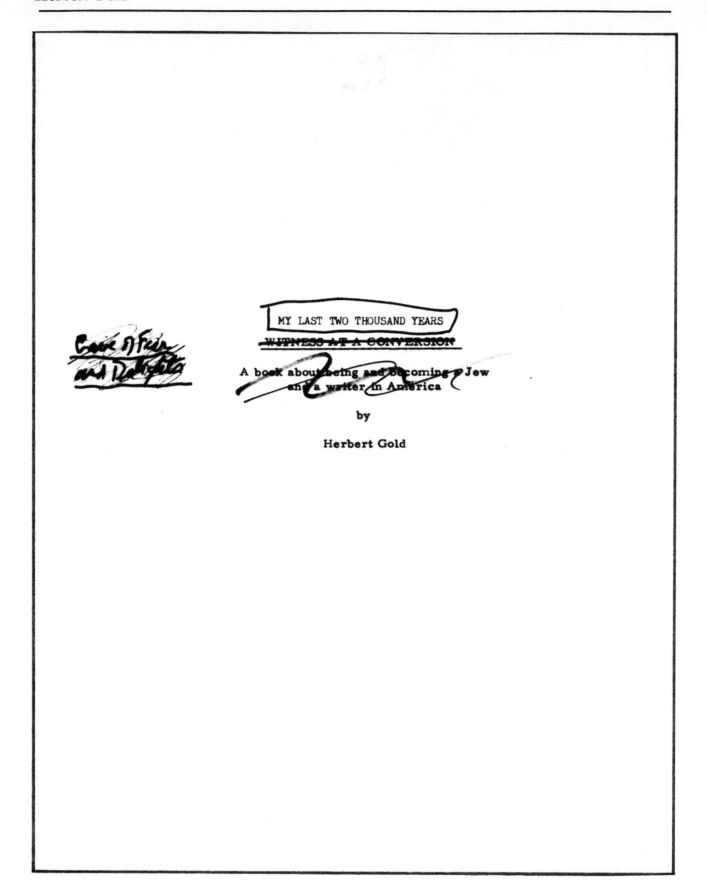

MY LAST TWO THOUSAND YEARS

~~WITNESS AT A CONVERSION~~

A book about being and becoming a Jew
and a writer in America

by

Herbert Gold

1-19

In the cathedral at Palma, on the island of Mallorca to which many Marranos fled from mainland Spain, I found Menorahs wrought in gold, stars of David, Hebrew imagery in stained mosaics which had been taken as booty into the church as the captured relics of Christianity were taken into the vodoun temples of Haiti. Of course, there was no Jewish community in Palma. But there were Jewish traditions. And when a prominent bull fight judge and architect discovered that his family was descended from Marranos, *last* *Jews,* he was so filled with shock and pride that he could not keep silent; he had to speak and he had to act; honoring his past, he and his entire family left the Church to become Protestant.

~~Why Protestant? That was the furthest distance he could imagine. Since he was a Jew, he could not be a Catholic; but since he was a Catholic, he could not be a Jew. Therefore he was a Protestant. The confusion continues, even hundreds of years after the deaths of Ferdinand and Isabella, who ordered the expulsion of the Hebrews and sped Columbus on his voyage—it is argued by some—because he really wanted to leave fast.~~

The bull fight judge continued his practice of architecture, but gave up bull fight judging. "It's not in our tradition," he said haughtily.

~~This Jewish Protestant Catholic was in shy contact with the peculiar treasure. The history of the Jews is a history of an organism, not an~~

the habit and, as a result, becomes Bud's surrogate father. Bud returns to Pittsburgh but cannot renew his relationship with his father or his girl friend Phyllis. He again leaves Pittsburgh for the carnival and marries Joy, the daughter of Palmistry Pauline. Carnival life is not, however, presented as an ideal escape. Grack becomes addicted to morphine (a habit he cannot beat even with Bud's help), robs the carnival safe, and attempts to rape Joy (who is pregnant at the time). After Grack is arrested, Bud decides that the barker is not "with it." He and Joy return to Pittsburgh and his real father.

The Optimist (1959) is Burr Fuller's story. The novel begins on Burr's seventeenth birthday as he is compiling—in the American tradition of Benjamin Franklin and Jay Gatsby—a list of resolutions; the teenager seeks nothing less than perfection. Burr enters the University of Michigan, where he joins a fraternity and becomes involved with two coeds—one promiscuous and the other a virgin whom he eventually marries. After Burr serves in the army, settles down with Laura, and becomes a successful lawyer in Detroit, he decides to run for Congress. As Burr becomes more successful, his life becomes less perfect: Laura becomes addicted to morphine; he becomes an unethical politician and takes a mistress. After Laura has an affair, Burr examines his botched life. He contemplates, but being an optimist, rejects suicide. Burr's self-scrutiny has little effect on his character; the novel ends with his words: "More. More. More! More! More!"

Therefore Be Bold (1960) appears to be a fictional treatment of Gold's teenage years in Cleveland in the late 1930s. The narrator, Dan Berman, also a character in Gold's short story "Love and Like," is a mature man looking back on and attempting to understand his awkward courtship of Eva Masters. After the romance deepens, Eva asks Dan to meet her family. Her father is anti-Semitic and demands that Eva stop seeing Dan. Eva expects Dan dramatically to defy her father; she disobeys her father and goes to the class picnic with Dan in a last attempt to save the relationship. But Dan, who is trying to understand himself and who feels pity for Eva's father, does not act. From the adolescent romance, the narrator has learned how to be bold.

Salt (1963), set in a corrupt and valueless New York, is divided into three parts. Each part develops a portion of the plot from the perspective of one of the major characters. Peter Hatten, whose story is presented first, is a stockbroker who sells his stocks short and ends romances before he is hurt. Dan Shaper, Peter's recently divorced war buddy, narrates the second section (the only section told in the first person). Dan moves to New York, and, despite Peter's attempts to teach him that love is an illusion, he falls in love with Barbara Jones, one of Peter's castoffs. After Peter tries to renew his relationship with Barbara, Dan thrashes Peter in a street fight. Barbara, whose story is told in the last section, returns to her home in Virginia. Dan follows her and proposes marriage. Barbara tells Dan that she is going to have a child (she does not say whose), and the novel ends as Dan and Barbara embrace.

Fathers: A Novel in the Form of a Memoir (1967) is, as the subtitle suggests, a novel fashioned from Gold's life and the life of his father, Samuel. In the preface, Gold establishes the novel's theme by relating a breakfast conversation he had with his father when his parents visited his San Francisco apartment. Gold cannot understand why his father, then eighty years old, will not retire and why he keeps risking his savings on real estate deals. Gold seeks security and thinks his father should seek security. His father, however, keeps repeating, "A man is never secure." The novel contrasts the two generations. Samuel Gold left Russia when he was thirteen years old. He nearly starved in New York and fought gangsters to establish his grocery business in Cleveland. He is a survivor. Gold's own trials are less formidable until he and his wife divorce. His father helps him to continue and advises him: "Next time make sure it isn't a nice Jewish girl." From his father, Gold begins to learn how to survive in an unstable world. As he writes of his father, "He thought he might as well be content in his insecurity."

The Great American Jackpot (1969), set in San Francisco during the late 1960s, is a picaresque satire. Al Dooley, clean-shaven and middle-class, is a graduate student studying sociology at Berkeley. His mentor is Jarod Howe, a respected professor and Black Muslim. Al wanders about San Francisco trying to find himself. He has a few vapid relationships, is turned down by the army, robs a bank, is convicted, and becomes a counterculture hero.

Swiftie the Magician (1974) is also a satire of the 1960s. Frank Curtis, a writer, director, and producer, is an Everyman character who leaves his New York home to wander through the California drug culture. On his journey, he encounters almost every fad and many of the celebrities of the decade. He falls in love with Swiftie Dixon, who later dies in a commune for out-of-work circus performers. Frank is as lost at the end of the novel as he was at the beginning of his journey.

Al Dooley, the protagonist of *The Great American Jackpot*, returns as the narrator of *Waiting for Cordelia* (1977), Gold's latest novel. Al is now a professor at Berkeley who must publish or perish. He is studying Cordelia, a prostitute who is trying to unionize her profession. Cordelia's nemesis is Merietta Kirwin, who is running for mayor of San Francisco on a clean up the city platform. Cordelia fights for justice; Merietta Kirwin fights to win her election.

At present, Gold's reputation as a short story writer is established; his reputation as a novelist is uncertain. Though his novels have been widely reviewed, he has received very little attention from academic critics and scholars. Even reviewers of his works are ambivalent: in general, they like his characters and plots but dislike his Joycean style. His novels tend to sell moderately well when they are published (*Fathers* was even a best-seller), but they are not long-term sellers. The fact that two of his novels were given new titles for paperback editions further indicates that his novels have not had long-range appeal. Gold is very much a part of the tradition of Theodore Dreiser and James T. Farrell; he writes about his urban environment and contemporary social problems. His novels, however, are less documentary than Dreiser's and Farrell's and may not be of interest to future generations.

—*George Jensen*

Books:

Birth of a Hero (New York: Viking, 1951);

The Prospect Before Us (Cleveland: World, 1954; republished as *Room Clerk*, New York: New American Library, 1955);

The Man Who Was Not With It (Boston: Little, Brown, 1956; London: Secker & Warburg, 1965; republished as *The Wild Life* (New York: Permabooks, 1957);

Fifteen by Three, with R. V. Cassill and James B. Hall (New York: New Directions, 1957);

The Optimist (Boston: Little, Brown, 1959);

Therefore Be Bold (New York: Dial, 1960; London: Deutsch, 1962);

Love & Like (New York: Dial, 1960; London: Deutsch, 1961);

The Age of Happy Problems (New York: Dial, 1962);

Salt (New York: Dial, 1963; London: Secker & Warburg, 1964);

Fathers: A Novel in the Form of a Memoir (New York: Random House, 1967; London: Secker & Warburg, 1967);

The Great American Jackpot (New York: Random House, 1969; London: Weidenfeld & Nicolson, 1971);

Biafra Goodbye (San Francisco: Twowindows, 1970);

The Magic Will: Stories and Essays of a Decade (New York: Random House, 1971);

My Last Two Thousand Years (New York: Random House, 1972; London: Hutchinson, 1973);

The Young Prince and the Magic Cone (Garden City: Doubleday, 1973);

Swiftie the Magician (New York: McGraw-Hill, 1974; London: Hutchinson, 1975);

Waiting for Cordelia (New York: Arbor House, 1977).

Other:

Stories of Modern America, edited by Gold and David L. Stevenson (New York: St. Martin's, 1961);

First Person Singular: Essays for the Sixties, edited by Gold (New York: Dial, 1963).

Periodical Publications:

"Obsessed by Women," *Nation*, 183 (11 August 1956): 125;

"Beckett: Style and Desire," *Nation*, 183 (10 November 1956): 397-399;

"Discovered Self," *Nation*, 183 (17 November 1956): 435-436;

"The Age of Happy Problems," *Atlantic*, 199 (March 1957): 58-61;

"Hip, Cool, Beat—and Frantic," *Nation*, 185 (16 November 1957): 349-355;

"A Short-Story Bonanza," *New Republic*, 144 (16 January 1961): 19-20;

"Haiti: Hatred Without Hope," *Saturday Evening Post*, 238 (24 April 1965): 74-80;

"Violent Jews: A Memoir," *Commentary*, 40 (December 1965): 71-74;

"Toppling the Ivory Tower," *Holiday*, 39 (May 1966): 10, 12, 16-18, 20-22;

"Artist in Pursuit of Butterflies," *Saturday Evening Post*, 240 (11 February 1967): 81-85;

"California Left: Mao, Marx, et Marcuse!" *Saturday Evening Post*, 241 (19 October 1968): 56-59;

"The Detroit Sons," *Atlantic*, 225 (February 1970): 66-67, 70;

"Culture, Counter-Culture or 'Barbaric Intrusion,' There's Something Going On in San Francisco," *Holiday*, 47 (March 1970): 56-59, 104-106;

"Marriage Is Not Enough," *Vogue*, 157 (1 February 1971): 137, 183, 187, 192;

"A Death on the East Side," *Esquire*, 75 (May 1971): 140, 60, 62-68;

"Life Among the Refuseniks," *New Republic*, 171 (24 August 1974): 15-21;

"Television's Little Dramas," *Harper's*, 254 (March 1977): 88-93.

References:

Granville Hicks, "Generations of the Fifties: Malamud, Gold, and Updike," in *The Creative Present*, ed. Nona Balakian and Charles Simmons (Garden City: Doubleday, 1963), pp. 213-237;

Robert Kiener, "An Exclusive Interview with Herbert Gold," *Writer's Digest*, 52 (September 1972): 29-31, 62;

Harry T. Moore, "The Fiction of Herbert Gold," in his *Contemporary American Novelists* (Carbondale: Southern Illinois University Press, 1964), pp. 170-181.

Manuscripts:

Columbia University has manuscripts and proofs of *The Optimist, Therefore Be Bold, Salt,* and *Fathers.*

WILLIAM GOYEN was born in Trinity, Texas, on 24 April 1915. Son of Charles Provine, a lumber salesman, and Mary Inez (Trow) Goyen, he writes of his very early years: "The world of that town, its countryside, its folk, its speech and superstition and fable, was stamped into my senses during those first seven years of my life; and I spent the first twelve years of my writing life reporting it and fabricating it in short fiction." From the age of seven, he lived in Houston, where he was educated and graduated with a B.A. and M.A. in comparative literature from Rice University. By his graduation, he had decided, despite family pressures, to become a writer, although he had once wanted to be a composer.

After teaching at the University of Houston for a year, he served in the United States Navy from 1940 to 1945 and began to write short stories and his first novel. He told Harvey Breit in 1950: "The war had a great deal to do with the writing of the novel. The war necessitated this kind of novel, which I would have written, but perhaps much later on. But all of it boiled up in me—this search for a place and an identity. So, I didn't resent the war."

After the war, Goyen settled in Taos, New Mexico, where he continued work on his first novel and met the D. H. Lawrence commune. Talking to Frieda Lawrence and reading her husband's manuscripts proved to be important influences in his life. At Taos, he met Stephen Spender, who had read parts of "The House of Breath" published in *Accent* and *Southwest Review*. Spender invited Goyen to London, where he stayed during 1949, and he visited continental Europe for the first time.

After finishing the novel, he returned to New York where *The House of Breath* was published in 1950. A considerable critical success, this first novel was awarded the MacMurray Bookshop Award in 1950 for the best first novel by a Texan; Goyen also won Guggenheim Fellowships in 1951 and 1952 and published his second book, a collection of stories, *Ghost and Flesh* (1952). In New York he began to review for the *New York Times* and met other young writers and artists, such as Truman Capote and Carson McCullers. After a year in Italy and Switzerland, he returned to New Mexico and began writing *In a Farther Country* (1955). He later became an instructor at the New School for Social Research in New York, where he taught from 1955 to 1960.

During the late 1950s, he pursued his interest in the theatre. He adapted *The House of Breath* for the stage, wrote *The Diamond Rattler*, and began work in film and television. He also had short stories published widely, leading to his second collection of stories, *The Faces of Blood Kindred* (1960). In 1963, Goyen had published his third novel, *The Fair Sister*, and on 10 November 1963, he married the actress Doris Roberts. From 1963 to 1966, he taught at Columbia University in New York. Receiving a Ford Foundation grant to novelists writing for the theatre, he was appointed Playwright-in-Residence at the Lincoln Center Repertory Company (1963-1964), where he finished *Christy*, produced in New York in 1964. He also received ASCAP Awards for musical composition in 1965, 1966, and 1968-1970. From 1966 to 1972, he was a senior editor at McGraw-Hill.

After his unhappy experience in publishing, a time when he wrote little, he taught at Brown University from 1973 to 1975 and began to write steadily once again. In 1973 he had published *A Book of Jesus*, a nonfictional account of the life of Jesus, and had produced a fourth play, *Aimee*. His fourth novel, *Come, The Restorer*, and the *Selected Writings*, appeared in 1974, and his *Collected Stories*, and a twenty-fifth anniversary edition of *The House of Breath* appeared in 1975. Since 1976, he has been writer-in-residence at Princeton University,

Michael Robert Cannata

[signature: William Goyen]

and in that year Albondocani Press published *Nine Poems*, written very early in his career. About his career he states: writing "is simply a way of life before all other ways, a way to observe the world and to move through life, among human beings, and to record it all above all and to shape it, to give it sense, and to express something of myself in it. Writing is something I cannot imagine living without."

As a novelist, William Goyen has suffered from critics' attempts to categorize him neatly. Born in Texas, he is proud of his Southern heritage and draws quite heavily from his Southern past in his fiction. Yet he does not fit into the Southern Renaissance nor in the so-called violent, grotesque-ridden fiction which has come to represent Southern literature for many people. Publishing after World War II, he has been influenced by the war, particularly its effects upon him as an individual struggling to create an identity tied to but not overcome by the past. Yet World War II fails to explain his fiction, for Goyen sees war as no more destructive than certain developments in the twentieth century. Avoiding linear plots, he challenges the reader to create, along with the author, a distinct reality of his own discoveries. Yet Goyen is not a confirmed apostle of the anti-realistic writing which has dominated much of the fiction in the last decades. Instead, he builds upon a solid background of other writers, while he also surprises his reader with new techniques which offer new ways of approaching recurring concerns.

To define these concerns, Goyen has always been especially intrigued with language, place, and people. In 1950 he said that the writer "must discover his authentic speech. Without that there can be no art. As Proust said, language is more than a style or embellishment, it is a quality of vision." Later, he stated: "There was always a sense of belonging to a place in my childhood. The place. We called the house 'the place.' 'Let's go back to the place,' we'd say. I loved that. There was such a strong sense of family and generation and ancestors in it." For Goyen, writing is a quest to capture the language of the individual, his particular song. "I think of my writing as having to do with singing people: people singing of their lives, generally, arias. The song is the human experience that attracts me and moves me to write." These emphases in his work naturally link him with the popular concept of his region's literature. Goyen agrees. Yet he views his heritage as one more closely tied with a European literary tradition. Like Pound and Eliot, he sees the need for the particular and, at the same time, the need to transcend its potential entrapment. "The story-telling method of Eliot and Pound—darting, elliptical, circular, repetitive, lyric, self-revealing, simple speech within grand cadence and hyperbole, educated me and showed me a way to be taken out of my place, away from my obsessing relations: saved me from locality, from 'regionalism.' I knew then that it was 'style' that would save me."

Goyen's strength has been in the short, unified work—the short story or segments of a novel. "It seems to me that the unified novel . . . is a series of parts. How could it not be? I generally make the parts the way you make those individual medallions that go into quilts. All separate and as perfect as I can make them, but knowing that my quilt becomes a whole when I finish the parts. It is the *design* that's the hardest. Sometimes it takes me a long time to see, or discover, what the parts are to form or make." Thus, all his books, including two early collections of short stories, are a series of these "medallions" which coalesce through juxtaposition, through the repeated efforts to find the design or the whole out of the fragments. The remnants of the past, the parables of Jesus, the members of a family represent the artist's attempt to create a unity. The discontinuity of experience and life, especially in the twentieth century, is focused upon by the technique. Goyen sees the failure to find the pattern as a type of madness; that possible failure is often found in the almost hallucinatory prose of the narrator or of a central figure struggling to tell his story or to discover a meaning. Only in *The Fair Sister* (1963) does Goyen avoid the series of parts in search of a whole, and even that novel had its beginnings in an earlier short story. Goyen comes under repeated criticism for failing to crystallize the parts into a definite unit. Yet it is in this very fragmentation, this potential madness, this courting of disaster, that he most succeeds in creating exciting fiction. The

language, the structure, and the content are consistently interwoven in each work.

An important, influential writer on Goyen's use of language and his development of subject is D. H. Lawrence, whose thought, Goyen claims, was formed by Frieda Lawrence's philosophy. Goyen returns again and again to the Lawrencian concept of the divided individual, torn by the struggle to achieve a union of masculine and feminine forces within himself, caught in a mechanized world which might allow him his quest, but which offers few possibilities for attainment. From *The House of Breath* to *Come, The Restorer*, man seeks to find a lost wholeness which civilization has stripped from him. The characters' search reflects the artist's. As Goyen says, "we speak of a lost way of life. In many of my books and stories, I've felt the need to re-create, to restore lost ways, lost places, lost styles of living." Thus Jessy says of the young narrator in *The House of Breath*: "Berryben has his hiding away and searching. But he'll redeem us all, in the end. I know he will. He only wants us all to wait and we will finally understand. He's good, Mama. He's a good thing live in this world, that's gone but coming back twofold." Likewise, the narrator in *Come, The Restorer* calls to Mr. de Persia to return, to restore that which has been lost, to "set the well house upright on its foundation, oh repairman, oh restorer." In his incantatory prose, straining to state the deepest emotions of his individuals, Goyen sees no new day. Rather, he repeatedly stresses, like Lawrence, that man has only to look within, to transcend the world around him to discover what has always been there. Although Jesus, for Goyen, is not Lawrence's "man who died," He is still the right redeemer whose message has been distorted. Isis and Christ are one. Jesus

> knew that to do something against oneself is to *break up* oneself, away from his center. Suffering follows when we divide ourselves and lose our oneness, our self-union, is what he was saying. What we seek is the solid, strong, centered self, to be of 'single purpose,' 'whole-hearted.' . . . The people of his time were very much like the people of our time. They were living in a world that was without a center and falling into pieces. They were 'dismembered.' Jesus wanted to heal up this society around him by *reforming* it, and he wanted to restore to all human beings the sense of membership, fellowship, brother-hood, kingdom.

Throughout Goyen's work runs this messianic yearning; however, the messiah lies within man himself. The journey out into the world or into the mind is a series of returnings to the center, to the individual himself, as he integrates his parts into wholeness. Like Lawrence, then, Goyen sees the spiritual and physical life as a necessary oneness within which lies man's only possible salvation. And it is the very possibility of that salvation which pervades all of Goyen's work and presents a potentially creative existence for man.

Thus Berryben, the narrator in *The House of Breath*, returns through thought and memory to the people and experiences which shaped him, which sent him on his physical journey in search of the force. "The finding of that force, the awareness of it, quivering in us, trying to turn us that we may generate, and the attempt to use it is to make oneself real. The substitution of any other force is a mechanical turning and is false; is evil." Yet his physical journey finally makes possible the spiritual journey. Like young George Willard in Anderson's *Winesburg, Ohio*, he must listen to the voices of the grotesques which he, through time and distance, has created. They have become as fragments, voices in a well, which his perceptive limitations have defined. Therefore, to make his past whole and make of himself a unity, he must create out of the ephemeral breath a reality of the word. He is told in the process:

> Go into the world, go build cities, go discover countries; go spread love, go give, go make magnificence, get and give light, save and join and piece together . . . and show a whole and put it, combined and formed and shaped, into the world like a bottle with a ship in it. Gather the broken pieces, connect them: these are the only things we have to work with. For we have been given a broken world to live in—make like a map a world where all things are linked together and murmur through each other like a line of whispering people, like a chain of whispers a full clear statement, a singing, a round, strong, clear song of total meaning, a language within language, responding to each forever in the memory of each man.

Technically quite different from *The House of Breath*, the romance *In a Farther Country* (1955) expands upon similar themes. Episodic and more dramatic, Goyen's second novel focuses upon Marietta, a Spanish-American, who devotes her life and her fantasies to restoring the wholeness of Spain. Her rather worn macaw becomes a noble road-runner; her husband's artifacts become genuine artistic creations. Each of the characters who joins her in her dream citadel tells his story, as if pilgrims on the road to Granada have chosen to entertain themselves with tales of their past fragmentation. Each has failed to be integrated into the mass society,

which has built highways through its fields. Industrialization and mechanization have dehumanized these men and women gathered around Marietta. In her dream, each undergoes a type of resurrection as they listen and understand one another. Yet the apocryphal transfiguration at the end, which ushers in a new world, vanishes in the rumbling of trucks on the New York streets, awakening Marietta. "Here, again, was the frail artifice built by the world that dreamt the solid other, the marriage and mixture of dream and circumstance that breeds back daily the pure race: the outside imitation that man had made and lived and dreamt in which the dream in the breast had, for a little while, found a bridge across to—if only a trestle of rushes." Goyen suggests that, like Marietta, man has been overwhelmed by the artificial, has been forced to desert the natural. Yet man can fight, and in his fantasy within the human heart he can win back his way to a greater reality of meaning and substance.

The Fair Sister (1963), on the surface Goyen's most unified novel, grew out of a short story which appeared in *The Faces of Blood Kindred*. Ruby Drew, the narrator, is one of Goyen's most delightful characters. She takes as her divine mission to save her fair sister, Savata. "There I saw, with my fingers in my ears, in some green kind of light, this serpent of a woman's figure. Oh 'twas wrong, 'twas evil, 'twas against God's wishes for her. But out of it came a voice that had definite evangelical possibilities. God has quite definitely mixed Good all up with the Bad . . . dross and gold, chaff and wheat . . . for good reasons. I had to separate them. Here, in this moment, squatting at a keyhole with my fingers in my ears, I saw my whole life's task brandished before me, 'Twas my Call." In his most comic novel, Goyen presents perhaps one of his most somber stories. Ruby Drew does indeed finally succeed in "saving" her sister, and, in the process, almost destroys the vital wholeness of Savata. Reflected through the eyes of her sister's religious fanaticism, Savata emerges as a pathetic victim of religion, family ties, and social pressure. She suffers a nervous breakdown and must assume Ruby's cleaning job. In the end, she vanishes, perhaps with the possibility of escaping not only Ruby, but also the distorted world Ruby represents. Ruby makes us laugh, but her mission is a chilling one, where man's faith and innocence are corrupted by money, where love and care are warped into misshapen human prisons, and where society prefers the appearance of success to the reality of the successfully integrated, whole individual.

After a break of eleven years, Goyen had published his fourth novel, *Come, The Restorer*

II.

①

Feb.19,1973

William Goyen

~~FOUR PHOTOS FOR THE RESTORER~~

~~Four Photos For The Restorer~~

Come a restorer to us, out of the Panhandle,
in those days. *Come back!*

His name was ~~Mr.~~ Mr. de Persia. Gave us no
first name as long as we knew him, which is everybody's lifetime, 's been coming here that long in everybody's memory,
and when asked said he'd never had a first name. Mr. de Persia
was his ~~xxxx~~ name, going through the little towns rescuing fading
faces of those passed away and gone.

If he'd come back now,
if he'd come back,
made Persia
man of
miracles
and
salvations

I ~~took Mr. de Persia~~ *I'd bring him* that old photo of Ace, so
handsome in his striped overalls and in his Switchman's cap,
made so long ago that ~~twas~~ *it's* hardly of him any more, so shadowy
and vanishing, like something ~~was~~ drawing him into the darkness.
I want~~ed~~ Ace restored out of the darkness.

And I'~~took~~ *take the restorer* one of me. "Save me, Mr. de Persia",
I implore~~d~~. It ~~was~~ *it's* a picture of me with a piece of blue voile
draped across my ~~bosom~~ *breasts*, then so live and sensitive 'twas a pain
to have them on me like thorns on my ~~breast~~ *bosom*, at age of 16, in
the year my womanhood took hold of me and I was in a kind of a
glory and so afraid.

And oh I ~~brought~~ the restorer one of Ace and me,
sitting on the front porch steps. Some gloom, some cloud,
some kind of a smoke ~~was~~ *is* coming in over the photo and overwhelming
it, creeping in over the picture from behind Ace and me like a
soft storm, a grey fog; restore us, Mr. de Persia; bring that back.

From the typescript of Come, The Restorer.

Courtesy of the Humanities Research Center, The University of Texas at Austin.

(1974), which harks back to *The House of Breath.* Like Christy and his unconsummated marriage to Otey in the earlier novel, Ace Adair dies, leaving his wife Jewel still a virgin. Addis Adair, their adopted son, journeys out from his home like Berryben Ganchion in search of his own fulfillment and that of those whom he has left behind, especially of his dead adopted father. Addis becomes a type of savior figure, like Berryben and Mr. de Persia, to whom people turn for spiritual salvation. Yet Mr. de Persia's power is missing from Addis's mission until he vanishes, as did Mr. de Persia, into the virgin Thicket, a doomed Eden next to the sprouting oil fields. There Addis discovers sexual passion with the transfigured Jewel and dies after a final climax which signals the end and beginning of life. Goyen comments about the progression from his first to his fourth novel: "There *is* a progression. I'm much freer. And I see a liberation of certain obsessive concerns in my work, a liberation towards joy! I feel that I'm much freer to talk about certain aspects of human relationships than I once was." More sexually explicit than his previous work, *Come, The Restorer* is also Goyen's most complex, most difficult novel. Is the joy he speaks of a discovery by father of son as represented by Mr. de Persia's discovery of Addis's grave and Jewel's hanged body? Is the circle brought complete, are the lives made whole by the penetration into the Edenic Thicket and the pure sensuality which creates and destroys? Or is the joy in the sheer telling of the story, the fabrication of the fantasy where life and death and copulation struggle against spiritual emptiness and black gold? Goyen perhaps offers clues when he says: "I think there are moments when I exceed myself as a human being, and become Ulysses, perhaps, or Zeus. It is the point of time at which the human exceeds himself, is transformed beyond himself, that I most care about writing about. This is the lyrical, the apocalyptic, the visionary, the fantastic, the symbolic, the metaphorical, the transfiguratory, transfigurational—all those terms which have been applied to my work." *Come, The Restorer* finally suggests that man's very quest for a savior, for a restorer, is futile if he looks only outside of himself. The regenerative power within the individual offers the real possibility for restoration and a saving resurrection.

Always popular in Europe, Goyen has a growing reputation in America. *The Collected Stories* and the anniversary edition of *The House of Breath* have been greeted with retrospective analyses. Critics have acclaimed his mastery of the short story almost from the beginning of his career, but his novels have only recently received attention. *Come, The Restorer,* for example, has been virtually ignored. In one of the few reviews, Shirley Ann Grau condemns the novel and still praises Goyen's courage to write the "unpopular" novel. Her condemnation and praise indicate the difficulty which critics have had with him from the beginning. Goyen, of course, seeks neither unpopularity nor obscurity. Rather he seeks an audience that comes to each of his works with only the expectation of being challenged and stimulated. —*Thomas E. Dasher*

Books:

The House of Breath (New York: Random House, 1950; London: Chatto & Windus, 1951);
Ghost and Flesh: Stories and Tales (New York: Random House, 1952);
In a Farther Country (New York: Random House, 1955; London: Peter Owen, 1962);
The Faces of Blood Kindred: A Novella and Ten Stories (New York: Random House, 1960);
The Fair Sister (Garden City: Doubleday, 1963; published as *Savata, My Fair Sister,* London: Peter Owen, 1963);
A Book of Jesus (Garden City: Doubleday, 1973);
Selected Writings of William Goyen (New York: Random House/Bookworks, 1974);
Come, The Restorer (Garden City: Doubleday, 1974);
The Collected Stories of William Goyen (Garden City: Doubleday, 1975);
Nine Poems (New York: Albondocani Press, 1976).

Plays:

The House of Breath, New York, 1956;
The Diamond Rattler, Boston, 1960;
Christy, New York, 1964;
Aimee, Providence, Trinity Square Repertory Company, 1973.

Television Scripts:

"A Possibility of Oil," *Four Star Theatre,* CBS, 1958;
"The Horse and the Day Moth," *Discovery '62,* ABC, 1961.

Other:

Albery Cossery, *The Lazy Ones,* translated by Goyen (New York: New Directions, 1952; London: Peter Owen, 1952);
The Left-Handed Gun, Warner Bros., 1958, lyrics by Goyen;

While You Were Away—a talk delivered by William Goyen (Houston: Houston Public Library, 24 April 1978).

References:

Gaston Bachelard, *The Poetics of Space* (New York: Orion Press, 1964);

Harvey Breit, "Talk with William Goyen," *New York Times Book Review*, 10 September 1950, p. 12;

Erika Duncan, "Come a Spiritual Healer: A Profile of William Goyen," *Book Forum*, 3 (1977): 296-303;

Louise Y. Gossett, *Violence in Recent Southern Fiction* (Durham: Duke University Press, 1965), pp. 131-144;

Frederick J. Hoffman, *The Art of Southern Fiction* (Carbondale: Southern Illinois University Press, 1967), pp. 124-129;

Anais Nin, *The Novel of the Future* (New York: Macmillan, 1968);

Jay S. Paul, "Marvellous Reciprocity: The Fiction of William Goyen," *Critique*, 19 (January 1978): 77-91;

William Peden, *The American Short Story* (Boston: Houghton Mifflin, 1964);

Robert Phillips, "Samuels and Samson: Theme and Legend in 'The White Rooster'," *Studies in Short Fiction*, 6 (1969): 331-333;

Phillips, "The Romance of Prophecy: Goyen's 'In a Farther Country'," *Southwest Review*, 56 (1971): 213-221;

Phillips, "Secret and Symbol: Entrances to Goyen's *House of Breath*," *Southwest Review*, 59 (1974): 248-253;

Phillips, "William Goyen The Art of Fiction LXIII" (interview), *Paris Review*, 65-68 (1976): 58-100;

Daniel Stern, "On William Goyen's *The House of Breath*," in *Rediscoveries: Informal Essays in Which Well-Known Novelists Rediscover Neglected Works of Fiction by One of Their Favorite Authors*, ed. David Madden (New York: Crown, 1971), pp. 256-261.

Jack Beech

SHIRLEY ANN GRAU was born 8 July 1929 in New Orleans to Adolph Eugene and Katherine (Onions) Grau. Her paternal grandfather came to this country from Prussia before the Civil War; the ancestry on her mother's side is a mixture of English, Scotch, and Irish. Grau spent her childhood in New Orleans and Montgomery, Alabama. She attended Booth Academy, a private school in Montgomery, where she acquired a background in math, literature, and languages, including what she calls "a good working knowledge of classical Latin." When she was a senior, the family moved to New Orleans; there she graduated from Ursuline Academy. Grau received her college education at Sophie Newcomb College, Tulane University, taking a B.A. with honors in English and remaining for a year of graduate work at Tulane.

Grau was taught to read at an early age and remembers a large family library, but writing was not a childhood ambition. It appealed to her, she has said, because there was no sexual prejudice and it didn't require the organization of many regular jobs. After her year of graduate school, she began writing full time, working first in a French Quarter apartment she took after finishing college, and later, after the sale of her first three stories, moving to New York City to make the contacts she felt necessary to a successful career.

In 1955 Grau married James Kern Feibleman, a professor of philosophy at Tulane and a prolific writer. They now have five children and make their winter home in Metarie, a New Orleans suburb, spending summers at Martha's Vineyard. Grau enjoys a number of sports, including sailing, tennis, and duck hunting.

Grau's early short stories and first three novels are decidedly Southern in locale, characterization, and the use of natural settings and detail to create atmosphere. Much of the early work centers on primitive people who live at the mercy of nature and reflect its harshness in their uninhibited behavior. But Grau also writes about whites isolated by social circumstance or pretense. In later books she has departed from the Southern tradition, while attempting a greater complexity in her work. Grau's writing is notably precise and lacking in sentiment; thus even in her most regional work she avoids the quaint and the Gothic overtones associated with much Southern writing.

Grau's first book was *The Black Prince and Other Stories* (1955). Of the nine short stories which make up the collection, only three had been published previously. The title story, the first piece of writing she sold, had appeared in *New Mexico Quarterly*. It is a Southern folktale about Stanley Albert Thompson, a black devil-figure who appears out of the morning fog, mints silver coins from wax, and wins the somewhat indifferent Alberta. Violence erupts all around Stanley Albert, but he is vulnerable only to the silver bullets a rival molds from Stanley's own magic coins. The simplicity and detachment of Grau's characterization support the folklore elements and help make this an effective fantasy. "Joshua," which first appeared in the *New Yorker*, deals with the initiation of a young bayou boy into the responsibilities of adulthood. The characters in "Joshua" are more fully drawn than those of "The Black Prince," though with a skillful economy of dialogue and situation; and Grau effectively communicates the fear Joshua tries desperately to hide.

The Black Prince was a critical success, establishing Grau as a young Southern writer of great promise. John Nerber wrote in the *New York Times*, "One has to go back to Eudora Welty's first book, *A Curtain of Green*, for a comparable performance. Without being in the least like Miss Welty—though both are Southern writers concerned with the Southern scene and people—Miss Grau has the same unmistakable authority, the instinctive feeling for form and language (obviously strengthened by a lot of hard work) and that pervasive relish for the wonderful particularities of human nature that are part of the equipment of the born writer." Already apparent in this first book were qualities which would characterize Grau's work: the lean prose which has been compared by several critics to

that of Hemingway; the precise, impersonal descriptions of nature; the meticulous craftsmanship; the use of various points of view. The subjects of the best of these stories are blacks and bayou people—people isolated by race or community. Grau depicts them realistically and honestly.

Such primitives are the characters of Grau's first novel, *The Hard Blue Sky* (1958), set on an island at the mouth of the Mississippi River before a hurricane. Again the descriptions of nature are detailed but wholly impersonal. Nature is highly important in this novel because, as the title suggests, it controls and regulates the lives of Isle aux Chiens' inhabitants. Even more than in her first book, Grau captures in *The Hard Blue Sky* a general authenticity of folkways, largely through a skilled rendition of speech patterns and customs. Her eye for this kind of detail has led certain critics to call her a fictional anthropologist.

There is no central plot in this novel, but rather a series of more or less interwoven episodes in which the islanders, an inbred assortment of French and Spanish descent, gradually take on individuality. One of the chief events centers on young Henry Livaudais, who goes into the swamp, fails to return, and is never found. The later revelation that he had run away to the swamp with a girl from the neighboring island, whose inhabitants are of Slavic descent, sets off a violent warfare between the two communities. Beginning to adjust to the certainty of her son's death, Belle Livaudais reaffirms her love for her husband by taking in his bastard son Robby, who has been living on the island with an aunt.

Annie Landry is the most fully developed character of the novel. For Annie, the difficulties of adolescence are compounded by the death of her mother and the arrival of her father's new wife. The sexual initiation Annie has so long anticipated is anything but romantic, and when she leaves the island to marry Inky D'Alfonso, she hasn't come to terms with any of her confusion. Like the islanders left behind awaiting the storm, "She was waiting. Waiting for things to happen to her."

Such fatalism is commonplace in *The Hard Blue Sky*. Shaped as it is by the vicissitudes of nature, life for the islanders is largely unquestioned. The only character in the book who deviates from this acceptance is Celine Boudreau. Though on the surface happily married, Celine has inexplicable moments of dissatisfaction. When Henry Livaudais' death in the swamp becomes apparent, she says angrily, "It don't matter why. It ends with the gars working on him." Then with tears obscuring her vision, she throws a brick at the sky and runs away. In the end, however, when the whole community is preparing for the hurricane, Celine refuses an opportunity to escape it; like the rest of the island women, she follows custom in staying behind to protect her home.

Reception of the novel was generally good. While some critics were wearied by its episodic nature and lack of climax, others felt that these qualities contributed to an effective depiction of a community in which nature plays a greater part than any individual. Elizabeth Bartelme wrote in *Commonweal,* "Above all, Miss Grau is a natural story-teller, and her novel has a kind of casual looseness that makes room for many stories, tales which, far from destroying the unity of the book, tighten the fabric of the world she constructs." The fine control and the careful natural description seen in Grau's earlier book are the real virtues of this one, a more ambitious undertaking; these strengths are not obscured by the novel's lack of dramatic force.

In her second novel, *The House on Coliseum Street* (1961), Grau departs from the primitives of her earlier work to deal with people much more sophisticated but no more in control of their lives. This book, like much of Grau's work, begins with a description of nature, a rainstorm which gathers, then spends itself. Joan Mitchell, the twenty-one-year-old protagonist of the novel, has just had an abortion, and the story unfolds as she recalls her affair with Michael Kern, a college instructor and cast-off beau of Joan's self-indulgent sister, Doris. Joan and Doris live in the house on Coliseum Street with their mother, Aurelie, who has been married five times and has had a daughter from each marriage. Doris resents Joan's financial security, a legacy from her father, and Joan's brooding loneliness is intensified by Doris's popularity. Although Fred Aleman is her steady boyfriend, Joan becomes pregnant by Michael Kern. Aurelie, rarely upset by anything that can be kept from public view, arranges an abortion with such quiet efficiency that even Joan is amazed. Although Joan has not loved Michael during their affair, she now thinks she does. She buys a car and follows him around through the course of his current affair until she thinks of a way to break it up. When she returns from an evening with Fred, with whom she has resumed a relationship, to find Doris and Michael together at the house, she decides to go to the dean of Michael's college and tell him a distorted version of her pregnancy and abortion, knowing this will cost Michael his job and possibly his career.

The strength of this novel lies primarily in Grau's depiction of Joan's withdrawal from life. Louise Y. Gossett wrote: "Miss Grau's skill in making hard and clear descriptions gives the dissociation of Joan the circumstantial vividness of a dream which cannot be forgotten." Joan completely forgets that she has signed up for a course; she follows Michael and his new love without regard for personal safety; she loses track of time until the natural order of night and day is reversed. Although the lost embryo, "the soft floating seaweed bones," becomes a recurrent image in Joan's confused thoughts, it is clear that the abortion was just another manifestation of her loneliness, her inability to find any joy in life. The novel's secondary strength is its portrayal of the meaningless, mannered world which shapes and supports a character like Joan. But the impersonality with which Grau has drawn her characters, though quite effective in evoking an atmosphere of sterility, is also a weakness in the novel. Because they consistently lust without love and act without motive or explanation, her characters seem less than real.

The Keepers of the House (1964), Grau's best work, won her a Pulitzer Prize in 1965. In this novel she returns to a rural setting, a small Alabama town. Her characters, while tied to the land by history and economics, are not the primitives of *The Black Prince* and *The Hard Blue Sky.* Nor are they the empty sophisticates of *The House on Coliseum Street.* They are roundly-drawn individuals who impose some degree of order on the elements of their world. They are related to the inhabitants of Isle aux Chiens in that they sometimes live more by instinct and desire than by reason, but they have a depth of understanding that the islanders do not approach. Their complexity makes them superior to Grau's earlier characters.

Again nature, in this case the land which comprises most of the Howland fortune, is of great importance, but with a difference: it is now bound up with the history in which the story is rooted, and it provides purpose and conflict for the central characters. Criticism of Grau's earlier work had pointed out the impersonality of nature, its indifference to the lives it regulated, its failure to impose meaning on the fiction it played so heavily in. But *The Keepers of the House,* as Ann Pearson noted in *Critique,* ". . . rises above the aimlessness of [*The Hard Blue Sky*] in that, in the best tradition of Southern fiction, the ambience of the land is incorporated with the burden of the past which Abigail Mason Tolliver must cope with in the present." The heroine, Pearson points out, finds a sense of permanence in the landscape, as well as a continuity with the ancestors who had owned the land before her; this bolsters Abigail's courage to defend the land against the townspeople's attack.

The Keepers of the House encompasses the history of three generations of Howlands, concentrating on the most recent, William Howland and his granddaughter Abigail. Years after the death of his wife, and immediately after his daughter marries and moves away, Will Howland takes a black woman into his home as mistress. In the long years of their relationship, Will and Margaret produce three children, with whom Abigail is brought up after her mother's death. Margaret's children are sent to the North to school where, since they can pass for white, they are expected to remain and make lives for themselves. Abigail marries an ambitious young politician who plays on racial prejudice and the Howland name to further his career. As their marriage progresses, it becomes increasingly apparent that Abigail, representing the Howland influence and wealth, has been as much a part of her husband's political strategy as his membership in the Klan. The marriage explodes when, on the verge of the gubernatorial primary, one of Margaret's children, long resentful of the status which society has given Abigail but denied him, releases proof that Margaret and Will Howland had actually been married. Abigail's husband promptly leaves her and their children, and Abigail returns to defend her home against the attack she knows will come from the white townspeople. What was tolerable to them as a casual relationship is intolerable as a marriage; and since Will and Margaret are both dead, they will vent their wrath on Abigail and the land she has inherited from her grandfather.

Alone except for her children and a hired man, Abigail manages to endure the burning of her barn and the slaughter of her animals and even to ward off a direct attack on the house. With a courage which arises from necessity and is shored up by the lessons of Howland history, she hides the children in the woods and sets fire to the attackers' automobiles. Weeks later, after divorce proceedings have disclosed the extent of her wealth, she announces her plan to cripple the town and its people by closing the hotel, refusing to stock the slaughterhouse, packing plant, and dairy, and withholding her timber from the market. Abigail's revenge will never alleviate her misery, but she will triumph over her enemies, as did the Howlands before her.

Grau handles the complexities of plot, character, and conflict with great clarity, building slowly to what Katherine Gauss Jackson, writing in *Harper's,* equated to ". . . the quiet edge of a whirlpool into whose pitiless center she finally sweeps one with relentless speed." Structurally, the book is divided into four parts plus an epilogue which reflect three narrative points of view: William's, Margaret's, and Abigail's. Abigail speaks briefly at the beginning and then again throughout the entire second half of the book. This device works well in setting the tone of the present conflict and then giving the chronological account of the Howland family which follows through the epilogue. It also serves to keep such a history from bogging down in the tedium of one narrative voice. The ability to arrive at a story from various points of view is one of Grau's strengths. It was foreshadowed in the use of disparate characters to create the island atmosphere of the otherwise loose *Hard Blue Sky;* it is evident in the variety of her short stories; and it is used again in her last two novels, *The Condor Passes* and *Evidence of Love.* In *The Keepers of the House,* however, it is most effective, because, in addition to its structural value, it contributes to the depth of characterization.

Grau made some enemies among both races with her treatment of characters in *The Keepers of the House.* She has said that while the book deals with segregation, it goes beyond that to consider ". . . the whole human plight of how do you cope with evil." It is her only novel in which the impersonal, sometimes cold treatment of plot and characters is replaced by a sympathetic point of view, in which observation is enhanced by the addition of meaning. There is, however, no trace of sentiment. Her characters remain tough and admirable.

Wealth and its effects on the lives it touches are the concerns of *The Condor Passes* (1971), a Book-of-the-Month Club selection. Critical reception was mixed. It is the story of a very wealthy old man, now at the point of death, as told by those closest to him: his two daughters, his son-in-law, his grandson, and his black servant, Stanley. Although the money Thomas Henry Oliver has accumulated illegally has now become respectable, its corrupting influence on his family is evident in their abnormal development.

Grau's attempt to integrate nature and meaning in this novel is seen in animal and flower imagery. The Old Man, who, it is implied, draws some kind of vitality from the greenhouse in which he spends most of his time, is described in bird imagery, including the image of the condor, a bird whose quills the Indians filled with gold and buried with their dead to provide money for the spirits. Stanley, to whom the Old Man leaves a generous sum, is also associated with the condor imagery. Although it is

THE WIND SHIFTING WEST

The wind blew out of the south, cold and wet as southern winds always were.   It had been blowing for a week, not hard but very steady. And the fog got thicker every day.   Makoniky Head and the old grey house perched on its back got dimmer and dimmer, day after day, until by Thursday morning they had disappeared completely.

"Well," said Caroline Edwards cheerfully, "there they go."

"What, honey?" Robert Edwards squatted at the far corner of the porch, his black hair glistening with damp.

He was doing something with a length of rope.   Caroline asked: "Is that the new anchor line for the Chere Amie?"

"This line?"   He didn't look up, but his tone was startled.

"Wrong?"

"Jib sheet."

"Oh.   Yes, I suppose it would have to be."

"Honey, you'll never make a sailor."

"Well, the Head has disappeared, that's all I was saying."

From typescript of **The Wind Shifting West.**

often effective in describing the Old Man, the imagery seems arbitrary and sometimes forced, as in the closing paragraph, which describes Stanley's departure after the Old Man's death: "Two floodlights from the house cast his shadow on the path ahead, a hugh broken wavery shadow, black wings fluttering on each side." Ann Pearson said of the book: "*The Condor Passes* is an ambitious work in its use of bird and nature imagery and in its scope. It also reveals Grau's perception of nature as a vitalizing force as opposed to the indifference of the hard blue sky. In spite of the strengths of the novel, one is still left without a meaningful whole, chiefly because her imagery is not extended to include other major characters whose lives run down an assortment of blind alleys." The multiple-points-of-view technique is flawed by a lack of organization which weakens the story.

After *The Wind Shifting West* (1973), a collection of short stories interesting primarily for their varied points of view, Grau attempted another family study in *Evidence of Love* (1977), again using the multiple-points-of-view technique. In this new novel, Grau ventures far from the Southern roots of previous works, placing her characters in settings which range from sophisticated Philadelphia in the 1880s to a coffee plantation in Africa. The voices are those of Edward Milton Henley, a self-indulgent old cynic who resembles the Old Man of *The Condor Passes;* Stephen Henley, the son provided Edward Milton by a carefully-chosen and well-paid Irish girl; and Stephen's wife, Lucy. The opposite image of the elder Henley, Stephen rejects his father's type of life to become a Unitarian minister and a classical scholar; his life is ordered by a set of journals outlining each task he plans to complete. The closeness of his relationship with Lucy owes nothing to sexuality, which both have largely rejected; it is a "visceral sympathy of acquired identity." Through these characters and the lesser ones whose lives they touch, Grau explores the variety and importance of love. Most of the novel's episodes suggest that these lives are shaped by love's failure. Lucy alone of the central characters senses and understands the needs of the others. This perception leads her to provide the Seconal Edward Milton wants to end his faltering life. Though Lucy has found evidences of love in both her marriages, she is content when, after Stephen's death, she can be truly alone and free.

Once again critical response was mixed, praising the variety of incidents and settings but expressing some disappointment at character-ization. Lucy is the best developed of the three main characters; Edward Milton Henley seems flat, for the most part. The sons of Stephen and Lucy, portrayed in a few brief but well-chosen incidents, are effective enough to reflect in their personalities the continuity of the novel's theme. In the best of Grau's earlier works, story and character were focused on a bond with the land. She has peopled *Evidence of Love* with characters from diverse settings and moved them around still more, thus revealing the rootlessness which forces them back on their own resources in a search for meaning. In this difference the novel is an ambitious undertaking in spite of its similarities to *The Condor Passes.* But its weaknesses are those which flawed her earlier work: a lack of dramatic force and depth of characterization.

Grau's early writing indicated that she might emerge as a major Southern writer. Her firsthand knowledge of her natural settings, the intimacy of her characters with their indifferent surroundings, the concern with manners and customs which define and often inhibit life—these qualities invite comparison with a number of Southern writers. She continues to experiment with the multiple-points-of-view technique which was most successful in *The Keepers of the House.* In her later work, with its move to remote settings and more complex characters, Grau seems to resist being categorized as a Southern writer. But this work seems inconclusive and suffers by losing touch with the Southern settings and characters which are the strengths of Grau's best writing. —*Jean W. Ross*

Books:

The Black Prince and Other Stories (New York: Knopf, 1955; London: Heinemann, 1956);

The Hard Blue Sky (New York: Knopf, 1958; London: Heinemann, 1959);

The House on Coliseum Street (New York: Knopf, 1961; London: Heinemann, 1961);

The Keepers of the House (New York: Knopf, 1964; London: Longmans, Green, 1964);

The Condor Passes (New York: Knopf, 1971; London: Longmans, 1972);

The Wind Shifting West (New York: Knopf, 1973; London: Chatto & Windus, 1974);

Evidence of Love (New York: Knopf, 1977).

Periodical Publications:

"Two Portraits of the Artist," *Carnival,* 2 (October 1949): 38-40;

"Mansions on the Mississippi," *Holiday,* 17, 3 (March 1955): 98-100, 134-135, 137, 139;

Jill Krementz

Shirley Ann Grau.

"Mississippi's Magic Coast," *Holiday*, 17, 6 (June 1955): 60-63, 145, 147, 149;

"The Felicitous Felicianas," *Venture*, 3 (August-September 1966): 73-76;

"Perfumed City," *McCall's*, 95, 7 (April 1968): 112.

Other:

George Washington Cable, *Old Creole Days*, foreword by Grau (New York: New American Library, 1961);

Marjorie Kinnan Rawlings, *Cross Creek*, introduction by Grau (New York: Time, 1966).

References:

Alwyn Berland, "The Fiction of Shirley Ann Grau,"

Critique, 6, 1 (1963): 78-84;

Jack DeBellis, "Two Southern Novels and a Diversion," *Sewanee Review*, 70, 4 (October-December 1962): 691-694;

Louise Y. Gossett, *Violence in Recent Southern Fiction* (Durham: Duke University Press, 1965), 177-195;

Margaret S. Grissom, "Shirley Ann Grau: A Checklist," *Bulletin of Bibliography*, 28, 3 (1971): 76-78;

Don Lee Keith, "A Visit with Shirley Ann Grau," *Contempora*, 2, 2 (March-July 1972): 10-14;

Ann B. Pearson, "Shirley Ann Grau: Nature is the Vision," *Critique*, 17, 2 (1975): 47-58;

Mary Rohrberger, " 'So Distinct a Shade': Shirley

Ann Grau's *Evidence of Love,"* *Southern Review*, 14, 1 (winter 1978): 195-198.

MARK HARRIS, son of Carlyle and Ruth Klausner Finkelstein, was born in Mount Vernon, New York, on 19 November 1922. He entered the United States Army in 1943 and served until 1944, when he received an honorable discharge after suffering from sustained, severe anxiety. Harris was employed primarily as a reporter between 1943 and 1950, the year he received a B.A. in English from the University of Denver. He has worked for the *Daily Item* in Port Chester, New York (1944-1945); *PM*, New York (1945), and the International News Service, St. Louis (1945-1946); and he wrote for the *Negro Digest* and *Ebony* in Chicago (1946-1951). He met Josephine Horen in October 1945, and they were married in Illinois on 17 March 1946. Mark and Josephine Harris have three children: Hester Jill, Anthony Wynn, and Henry Adam.

Mark Harris wrote his first novel, *Trumpet to the World* (1946), before he started his undergraduate career at Denver and had to balance his creative and academic interests throughout his years as a student. Although he had written four novels by the time he completed his Ph.D., his doctorate is not in creative writing. Indeed, his dissertation, "Randolph Bourne: A Study in Immiscibility," is an accomplished handling of the literary, historical, and philosophical aspects of his subject. After receiving his M.A. in English (1951) from the University of Denver and his Ph.D. in American Studies from the University of Minnesota in 1956, he made his dual commitments to writing and to teaching. Although Harris was a teaching assistant at the University of Minnesota, his rather diverse teaching career began in earnest in 1954 at San Francisco State College where he was a member of the faculty until 1968. In addition, he was a Fulbright professor at the University of Hiroshima (1957-1958), visiting professor at Brandeis University (1963), and he has taught at Purdue University (1967-1970), California Institute of the Arts (1970-1973), and Immaculate Heart College and the University of Southern California (1973-1975). He is currently a professor of English at the University of Pittsburgh. In 1960, Harris was awarded a grant from the Ford Foundation for residence with the Actor's Workshop; he won the National Institute of Arts and Letters Award for achievement in 1961; and he received a National Endowment for the Arts grant in

Anthony Harris

1966. Harris also received grants from the Guggenheim Foundation in 1965 and 1974.

Mark Harris has been a writer for virtually all of his life. From the diary he has kept since he was eleven years old, and from all of his fiction and nonfictional autobiographies, one can trace his concern for the individual's dealings with the forces of the world. Harris, in his rendering of each individual's attempt to establish his own sense of dignity and his own conception of his identity, seems to reflect, in perhaps a less tragic sense, those themes portrayed in the plays of Arthur Miller and first articulated in the playwright's famous essay, "Tragedy and the Common Man." Both writers see the potential for goodness, if not greatness, and sadness, if not tragedy, in modern man; both seem to hold to a fundamental belief in man's perfectability. Harris also shares with Miller a sense of the dramatic, and it is this that allows him to reach a certain level of complexity in his best novels. *The Southpaw, Bang the Drum Slowly*, and *Wake Up,*

Stupid effectively balance a prevailing comic tone and fundamental optimism with each book's potential for tragedy. In almost every one of his works, Harris develops carefully his central character's quest for self-discovery.

Harris is a pacifist, a believer in equality, a lover of beauty, and a man concerned with the dangers of hypocrisy on both personal and social levels. At his best, in his baseball trilogy, for example, he states his moral or philosophical case in an easy, subtle, but direct fashion. In his weaker works, like the youthfully energetic and naive *Trumpet to the World* or his unsuccessful attempt at drama, *Friedman & Son*, his potentially strong narrative becomes encumbered with moral issues. This is not to say that Harris cannot handle both humor and complex issues within the same work; he does so with great skill in novels like *Something About a Soldier*, *The Goy*, and his latest novel, *Killing Everybody*.

Harris's success as a novelist is based on his knowledge of people and his ability to relate the game-playing atmosphere within which people carry out their lives. Each character's understanding of the rules of his particular game in life and skill at putting his knowledge into action determine his success within his own area of endeavor and his worth as a human being—not necessarily a direct manifestation of his success as a "player." More than most novelists, Harris likes to think that he himself is the main character of his work, and he has commented that during the composition of his novels he is dominated by his projections. He must learn the rules, play the game, discover his identity and live according to what he finds.

The low-keyed style and the uncomplicated, often colloquial dialogue of his narratives make Harris sensitive to "stupid reviewers and critics" who dislike his works for their simplicity. He claims that all of his material is carefully written. His novels, for the most part, are well designed and skillfully crafted, and in his essay "Easy Does It Not" he aptly says to his harsher critics "I write; let the reader learn to read."

In his first novel, *Trumpet to the World* (1946), Harris projects himself into the role of Willie Jim, an articulate black man. The book deals with the intellectual development, spiritual growth, and self-discovery of its main character. The novel is the result of "the best of American social idealism" that had reached and affected the young writer. His attempts to draw a portrait of a black protagonist in other than conventional stereotypes are genuine, but he relies on sentiment and over-worn generalizations about white Southerners. One of the book's settings, Midfield College, is drawn from Harris's relatively short stay at Clemson College while he was in South Carolina during the war years.

After tracing briefly the childhood and early adolescence of Willie Jim, Harris focuses on his main character's early adulthood. The development of Willie Jim's intellect and sensibility really begins with his chance meeting of Eddie Mae, a beautiful white girl and daughter of a professor at Midfield. Working in the kitchen of the college, Willie Jim finds sanctuary from the hostile forces of Southern white society while gaining a personal education under the guidance of Eddie Mae and at the same time gathering experiences and material for his future novels. The two become increasingly involved with one another, and Eddie Mae realizes that she must leave the South to have Willie Jim's baby. With his wife in New York, Willie Jim learns that he is the father of a baby boy and moves to the ironically-named Good Hope, Georgia, where he buys a house for his new family. The local citizenry burn the house and with it some, but not all of Willie Jim's dreams. Later, still isolated from his wife and son, he becomes a good soldier who believes in the war effort. However, Willie Jim becomes disillusioned by the racism he encounters in the army. He takes an unauthorized leave, writes his second book—keeping in touch with Eddie Mae—returns to the army, and receives a prison sentence. After his release, he takes a job teaching illiterates to read and write and is promoted to sergeant. On Christmas Eve, he gets into a fight with an officer at a party for his students and knocks him out. He leaves the service, and he and his enlightened publisher organize his defense. United with his wife and child and willing to face the challenges that his complicated life will continue to present, Willie Jim decides to write yet another book on the subject. "As soon as anything happens to me I write a book about it."

Harris saw in this first effort a lack of control and tendency to fantasize that idealistic writers must learn to keep in check. It is the balance of idealism and realistic rendering of subject matter that makes many of his later novels work so well. The critical reception of *Trumpet to the World* was surprisingly positive. Most of the reviews concentrated on the novel's controversial subject matter, but at least one gave it high marks for its calm, deliberate style.

Not really a novel, yet certainly not a conventional biography, *City of Discontent* (1952), Harris's second major work, is in many ways his most ambitious effort. It is an experimental biography of Vachel Lindsay, written in the present tense, which lends a sense of immediacy and vividness to the story of a man who was himself a vital, driving force. But if the book tells the story of Vachel Lindsay, a man who needed a national audience that would demand of him his very best, it also tells us something about Harris, who also needs an audience. *City of Discontent* reflects Harris's love and respect for the power, dedication, charisma, and talent of an artist as well as his fear and resentment of those forces because they drove Lindsay to commit suicide.

Critics commented on Harris's ability to synthesize biographical fact with narrative line in order to create a tone that is almost breathless at times and an atmosphere that is full of the same movement and energy that Lindsay himself found in America. The book is both a factual, accurate biography of a famous American artist and a rather mystical account of a strangely alluring prophet-poet; it is an historical account of fifty years of America's maturation and a portrait of the vast potential for greatness and tragedy here.

With two books and a master's degree to his credit, Harris was ready to enter the phase of his career that would vault him into the position of "public" writer and cause him persistent frustrations as a "labeled" writer in the years to come. Although Harris started writing the first book of his baseball trilogy "by Henry W. Wiggen," *The Southpaw*, in 1951, the year Bobby Thomson's home run ended a great baseball season, the author's love for the game may be traced back to his childhood. His knowledge of the strategy of baseball, as well as his ability to portray the American passion for the game, combine with his ear for language, his understanding of people, and his ability to tell a good story to make the trilogy a success.

The Southpaw (1953) was widely acclaimed, not just for its realistic handling of a fundamental American institution, but also for its penetrating look into the development of a complex man. The reader follows Henry Wiggen's progress as he leaves his small-town home and baseball club and moves into the big leagues. As a member of the New York Mammoths, Henry learns through a variety of experiences—some funny, some quite painful—the finer points of pitching and becomes a sensitive human being. Wiggen's conversations with his mentor, the pacifist and intellectual Aaron Webster, with his articulate and wise catcher, Red Traphagen, and with his back-slapping, tobacco-chewing teammates, all display the maturing character of the young pitching star. Even though Harris admits the

novel is a manifestation of his own fantasy, the prevailing sense of realism is strong. The novel's real force, however, comes from its presentation as the journal of Henry Wiggen.

Henry Wiggen does just about everything a pitcher can do in *The Southpaw*. Not only do he and his team win the World Series, he is also awarded the Most Valuable Player Award. But there is more to be said about Henry Wiggen, the people, and the atmosphere that make him what he is. If Henry's character is developed in *The Southpaw*, his emotional and spiritual dimensions are tapped in Harris's next novel.

Bang the Drum Slowly (1956) is Mark Harris's best novel. It has also been a source of frustration for its author, who would love to be known as someone other than "the man who wrote *Bang the Drum Slowly*, a novel about baseball." Nevertheless, the second Henry Wiggen novel is something of special importance—not just for Harris, but for contemporary American literature. The story takes place three years after Henry's almost mythic first year. A few average seasons bring him back to the realities of a sustained career in professional athletics, and during this time he becomes a seasoned athlete. Henry's maturity is tested when he learns that his roommate, a mediocre catcher named Bruce Pearson, is dying of Hodgkin's disease.

Bang the Drum Slowly is about human relationships under the pressure of a race toward a goal. On the surface, the New York Mammoths are in a race to win the American League pennant, but at another level, Bruce Pearson races to prove himself as a man and an athlete to his friends and teammates; and finally, the wiser, more compassionate Wiggen races to develop a complete friendship with the catcher before he dies. Although some critics feel that the excitement of the close pennant race intrudes upon the more important elements of Bruce's approaching death and his growing relationships with the team members, Bruce's instrumental role in the Mammoths pennant drive adds a needed frame to the novel.

The Mammoths win the pennant, but Pearson, too ill to continue playing, must leave the team to enter the hospital. New York, with the aid of Wiggen's superb pitching, goes on to win the World Series. Harris brings us back to reality, when, with the season over and the World Series secured, Henry has to face the fact that Bruce has died, and with him, a stage of his own life. He goes to Pearson's hometown to find only a few people at the funeral— Henry is the only representative of the team. He reviews the season, his relationship with Bruce, and

25

There's a security in identity, said the Captain.

Yes sir, said Jacob.

How felicitously the Captain phrased it! Jacob resented the Captain's felicity. It was not fair that the Captain should state it so perfectly, and so deeply invade Jacob's mind, without being required, at the same time, to share with Jacob the penalty of Jewishness. Jacob resented the Captain, and in his ~~own~~ quick anger he said, In my opinion they could of followed my orders ■ if they really wanted to, but they didn't want to.

Why should they want to?

The coalsmoke smell of Smeed replaced the peanut smell of the town. Jacob heard cadence, <u>hup</u> hah <u>hup</u> hah <u>hup</u> hah, and riflefire and machinegun fire and mortarfire, and he saw an airplane towing a ~~■■■■■~~ shredded target.

~~XXXXXXXXXXXXXXXXXXXXXXXXXXXXXXXXXXXXXXXXXXXXXXXXXXXXXXXXXXXXXXXXXX~~

~~XXXXXXXXXXXXXXXXXXXXXXXXXXXX~~

(And Jacob remembered, afterward, ~~his~~ his first riflefire, how the piece recoiled, how its action and its crash of sound and its smell caught him up with truth, how he knew in that startling moment that he had never before fired, though he had seen it done in five hundred moving pictures. But it was not the same. The screen and the rifle were not the same.)

They don't ever hit the plane by mistake I hope, said Jacob. He laughed.

Not usually, said Captain Dodd.

BREAK ⟶

He was restricted to quarters in a barracks prepared for forty. Alone, ■ he saw convened in special session a military board, and he lay upon his cot and was condemned to execution, the board deeming ~~■■■■■■■■■~~ the action proper on the grounds of example, and justifying it by reference to an obscure law. Jacob often imagined himself the victim of an obscure law. "Your gracious sirs," he said, "permit me to quote to you from the Soldier's Handbook: 'A military order is usually sharp, positive, and brief.' I plead your gracious

From setting copy for Something About a Soldier.

his own character, and sums everything up succinctly, candidly, and in his own disarming style: "He was not a bad fellow, no worse than most and probably better than some, and not a bad ballplayer neither when they gave him a chance, when they laid off him long enough. From here on in I rag nobody."

The last of the Henry Wiggen baseball novels, *A Ticket for a Seamstich* (1957) was acclaimed for its humor and well-developed, smoothly sustained vernacular, but suffered critically from comparisons with *Bang the Drum Slowly*. Harris intended the novel to be lighter and less concerned with the darker side of life. The tone, theme, and focus of the novel are not centered on Henry Wiggen; he is simply the recorder of events. Harris had done as much with him as he could so he shifted the emphasis to Bruce Pearson's replacement, a young, wild, back-country boy named Piney Woods, from Good Hope, Georgia. The novel also focuses on the seamstich, a great admirer of the Mammoths and especially of Piney. She is determined to work her way across the country in order to attend the Mammoths's Fourth of July doubleheader for which she has been sent a ticket. But she is more interested in meeting Piney Woods in person. The seamstitch reaches town just in time to see the game, but although given a warm reception by the team, she is ignored by Woods, who finds her far less attractive than he had hoped. After running out on the team for a while and receiving various bits of advice, the catcher comes to accept his own condition, his place on the team, and, of course, the seamstitch. *A Ticket for a Seamstitch* is a book of self-discovery, and, as Wiggen says, "She learned. We all learned. That's what the book is about, about girls and men and learning and the 4th of July."

Also in 1957, *Something About a Soldier* was published. The break between the trilogy and the new novel is not complete: thematic concerns such as the quest of the individual for self-discovery, pacifism, and prejudice are still of great importance for Harris and his new hero—Private Jacob Epp (born Epstein). The book's comic tone and insights into people and institutions are products of Harris's own personal experiences in the army and his dedication to individualism.

Jacob, like Henry Wiggen, is a product of Perkinsville, New York, and is repulsed, if not sickened, by physical violence. Equipped with his high ideals and his *Soldier's Handbook*, Jacob enters the army and heads for camp in Cohoe, Georgia. Although Jacob is a good, likable young man, not until his whole value system is challenged by the authoritative, unyielding institution of the army, does he develop into a complete human being. Jacob falls in love with a Southern girl named Joleen, and is cared for and helped by his commanding officer, Captain Dodd, but he also experiences racial prejudice firsthand and comes to realize that he cannot accept his military role as a potential killer. Unable to kill and unwilling to be killed, Jacob goes AWOL, and during his absence he comes to terms with the forces that have confronted him. Newly enlightened and prepared for his punishment, Jacob meets Sergeant Toat, his opposite, who is to escort him back to the base. The novel pivots on Jacob's realization that while he must stay in the United States and go to prison, others will go overseas to meet their deaths. The reader is not moved to believe that Jacob is a coward who runs away from personal experience; on the contrary, he is a man who has made a sincere, highly justified moral choice.

Critically acclaimed for its epistolary style and satiric tone, *Wake Up, Stupid* (1959) covers one hectic month in the life of Lee Youngdahl, a professor of English at a San Francisco college. In writing of the trials involved in obtaining tenure, the conflicting life-styles of a successful novelist and an English teacher, and the attempts to create a successful work for the Broadway stage, Harris reveals a strong identity with the triumphs and frustrations of his protagonist.

Wake Up, Stupid consists of a series of correspondences to and from Lee Youngdahl which deal with six areas of the writer-teacher's life: (1) the practical jokes he plays on old friends through deceptive letters; (2) his attempts to publish a play for Broadway; (3) his concern that he might not be given tenure; (4) his home life as a father of seven children; (5) the possibility of a Harvard teaching position; and (6) his involvement with a Broadway actress. Although the novel contains much extraneous material and several loose ends, it is sufficiently well organized to permit the reader to arrive at an understanding of Youngdahl's exuberant personality. The protagonist emerges at the end of the book as an interesting, comic character who can cope with his problems without losing his strong sense of humor. While *Wake Up, Stupid* merits praise for its epistolary style, its successful use of satire, and its creation of a believable protagonist, it has several faults. The humor is often no more than low-grade farce and the slick diction frequently obscures the basic ribald comedy of Youngdahl's situation. Despite these flaws, the novel succeeds as a portrait of a novelist-professor and his realization that he is the stupid one who must wake up to reality.

Harris's next novel was a best-seller. *The Goy* (1970) is a telling portrayal of a Gentile who works among Jews, marries a Jew, and takes a Jewish mistress. In this novel, Westrum, a Gentile or "goy," turns to the Jewish community for warmth and humanity. Yet his attempts to assimilate himself into the Jewish community create an identity problem—he is warmly received by some Jews despite his Gentile background, but others mistrust him and consider him a dolt, a big man with a small brain. At first glance, Westrum appears to be a perfect, almost saintly human being. He is a celebrated scholar, the author of *A History of the World*, who controls those who work with him by regulating their image of him. For example, by denying he has any physical desires, he compels them to see him as an intellectual. In this way he consistently gains favor with the authorities and maintains his solid position at the school in which he works. Westrum's problem is that he cannot maintain his self-image as well as he can put on a front for others. Throughout the novel he attempts to overcome his Gentile background, and his identification with the Jewish culture grows stronger as his experiences within their community increase. Harris admits that much of the character of Westrum is drawn from the author's personal experiences as a Jew often mistaken for a Gentile. Although it becomes repetitious at times, *The Goy* exhibits Harris's deep understanding of Westrum's situation, which creates a strong sense of purpose in the novel.

Published in 1973 after being written, destroyed, and rewritten over twenty years, *Killing Everybody* portrays a man obsessed with murder. Brown, the protagonist, ponders daily the means for obliterating those people he considers enemies. Foremost on his list of candidates is McGinley, a congressional nominee who had once served as chairman of the local draft board and was thus responsible for sending Brown's "son" Junie to Vietnam to become a war casualty. Also on his list of prospects are the dog whose barking keeps him awake at night and Stanley Krannick, the real father of Junie, who abused the child as an infant and who later deserted the boy and his mother, Luella. Brown habitually writes threatening letters to all he judges to be unworthy and dangerous citizens. Renting a typewriter in the public library, he assumes the role of an anonymous public defender. His letters are sent to presidents and local officials alike and contain direct attacks on both governmental policy and personal conduct. Yet, Brown himself is an enigma. Seemingly directed by a strong sense of high personal standards, he stoops to murder and the company of prostitutes to relieve his frustrations.

The murder of McGinley is coldly premeditated; and after the politician is killed in front of a massage parlor, Brown visits his favorite masseuse-lover in an effort to soothe his troubled spirit and erase any sense of wrongdoing.

Killing Everybody fails to present a coherent portrait of Brown and those who are a part of the protagonist's life. The narration is choppy and muddled, and the plot has too many loose ends. Character development is unsuccessful, and the purpose of the novel is obscured by the contrived diction and repeated emphasis on specific plots against Brown's enemies at the expense of the overall narrative structure. The novel is nonetheless compelling at times, and it reveals a new dimension of Harris—a perverse, violent, and unrestrained energy from the man who created the Henry Wiggen baseball trilogy.

Harris's only play, *Friedman & Son*, was first performed on 6 January 1962 and published the following year with a sixty-page introduction. The play dissects the relationship between a man, Friedman, and his son, who has changed his name to Ferguson. A third major character, Schimmel, organizes and sells testimonial dinners. The three-act play takes place one day in San Francisco. Schimmel, a "shrewd businessman," is the moving force behind the conflict of the play, and he capitalizes on the guilt and the loneliness of each man in order to make a sale. He flatters Friedman into believing that he can convince a number of famous people (who, in fact, do not even know the old man) to make speeches at his dinner. The first act ends with Ferguson accusing Schimmel of conspiring to pull off a shady business transaction and Schimmel, always on the attack, countering with the charge that Ferguson has denied his own Jewish heritage.

In the second act the business motif that is so important throughout the play is intensified. The plot becomes more complicated as Friedman recalls that Schimmel was once associated with a group of businessmen involved in another dishonest transaction that Friedman was instrumental in foiling. Schimmel is successful in diverting the old man with the pleasant thought of a dinner in his honor at the expense of his son. Friedman thus allows himself to be persuaded to return with Schimmel to his son's studio.

The last act finds Friedman, Ferguson, and Schimmel gathered together for a final discussion of the father's testimonial dinner. Unable to reject his father by bluntly refusing to sponsor the dinner, Ferguson decides to try to beat Schimmel at his own game. Ferguson accepts the notion of the dinner but plans a program that is so fantastic and grandiose that the relatively conservative Schimmel withdraws his proposition. He retreats hastily, and the play ends.

For a first attempt at drama, *Friedman & Son* is a solid work. Although there is nothing profound in the play, it is humorous, witty, and absorbing, particularly in its handling of the three men within the context of the Jewish socio-business community. Unenthusiastic reviews and a tight production schedule led to a rather short run on the stage.

Although Harris sees all of his books as autobiographical to a certain degree, his canon includes three autobiographies: *Mark the Glove Boy, or The Last Days of Richard Nixon* (1964), *Twentyone Twice* (1966), and *Best Father Ever Invented* (1976). Harris has had a full, interesting life, and many readers have found these works rewarding, but the greatest beneficiary of Mark Harris's autobiographies seems to be the author himself. The books appear to be therapeutic endeavors.

Mark the Glove Boy is an account of Harris's coverage of Richard Nixon's campaign for governor of California. Throughout his works Harris is a harsh critic of Nixon, but his portrait of the then-unsuccessful candidate is incisive without being biased. The book is more than an account of the campaign and Harris's part in it; it is a brief history of a particular period in the intellectual growth of a writer and thinker. Although the book is humorous, mildly penetrating, and perhaps prophetic in its analysis of Nixon, it is of little value to the reader who has no real interest in Harris himself.

Twentyone Twice, A Journal is a reminder to Harris's reader that he shares an important characteristic with his earlier creation, Willie Jim, of *Trumpet to the World*: every time something happens to him he feels he must write a book about it. *Twentyone Twice* was not well received. It does have its humorous moments, but little more. The book is an account of Harris's trip to Sierra Leone as an investigator for the Peace Corps. It is divided into two parts: his preparations for the trip, which are made especially tiresome and tedious by the Federal Bureau of Investigation's checkup of his background, and his account of his experiences while he was in Africa.

Harris's third and supposedly last autobiography, *Best Father Ever Invented*, received high critical acclaim because of its convincing portrayal of his dedication to writing and to life. The account is consistently penetrating, self-revealing, and honest. In *Best Father Ever Invented*, Harris is finally able to establish the same sort of sustained quest for self-discovery and spiritual and intellectual growth regarding himself that he is able to portray in his most successful novels.

Best Father Ever Invented is successful on two levels. It does an excellent job of telling the story of an interesting and complex man, and it provides the reader who is interested in Harris as a writer with important background information regarding the genesis and development of all his major works. The book begins in 1942, tracing Harris's late adolescent, pre-army activities, and it ends with some reflections on his third autobiography and the state of his affairs in 1973. The book is explicit in its account of those scholars and writers who most profoundly influenced Harris. He cites Henry Nash Smith and Mulford Sibley as his greatest intellectual mentors and Robert Frost, Mark Twain, Vachel Lindsay, and Henry Adams (as well as the relatively unknown Robert Marks) as important in helping him shape his creative work.

Harris seems to have achieved the depth, candor, and honesty in *Best Father Ever Invented* that he was unable to capture completely in his earlier autobiographies. It does not attempt to disguise the less attractive, at times violent side of Mark Harris that seems so antithetical to his projection of himself through likable characters such as Henry W. Wiggen and Lee Youngdahl. Despite his proclivity toward ferocity in his personal affairs, Harris has an unyielding sense of justice and a full-time philosophical commitment to pacifism. His works repeatedly reflect these beliefs, and it is through the skillful combining of idealism, a keen understanding of the American people and their values, and the ability to tell a good story that Mark Harris has attained popular and critical acclaim as one of America's most successful contemporary novelists.

—*Steve Bannow*

Books:

Trumpet to the World (New York: Reynal & Hitchcock, 1946);

City of Discontent: An Interpretive Biography of Vachel Lindsay, Being also the Story of Springfield, Illinois, USA, and of the Love of the Poet for That City, That State, and That Nation. (Indianapolis: Bobbs-Merrill, 1952);

The Southpaw, by Henry W. Wiggen: Punctuation Freely Inserted and Spelling Greatly Improved by Mark Harris (Indianapolis: Bobbs-Merrill, 1953);

Bang the Drum Slowly, by Henry W. Wiggen: Certain of His Enthusiasms Restrained by Mark Harris (New York: Knopf, 1956);

A Ticket for a Seamstitch, by Henry W. Wiggen: But Polished for the Printer by Mark Harris (New York: Knopf, 1957);

Something About a Soldier (New York: Macmillan, 1957; London: Deutsch, 1958);

Wake Up, Stupid (New York: Knopf, 1959; London: Deutsch, 1960);

Friedman & Son (New York: Macmillan, 1963);

Mark the Glove Boy, or The Last Days of Richard Nixon (New York: Macmillan, 1964);

Twentyone Twice, A Journal (Boston: Little, Brown, 1966);

The Goy (New York: Dial, 1970);

Killing Everybody (New York: Dial, 1973);

Best Father Ever Invented: The Autobiography of Mark Harris (New York: Dial, 1976).

Screenplay:

Bang the Drum Slowly, Paramount, 1973.

Periodical Publications:

"Carmelita's Education for Living (Horatio's Dreams of Contributing to the Delinquency of a Psychology Major)," *Esquire*, 48 (October 1957): 84-85;

"Conversation on Southern Honshu," *North Dakota Quarterly*, 27 (summer 1959): 62-65;

"The Self-Made Brain Surgeon," *Noble Savage*, 1 (March 1960): 140-158;

"The Iron Fist of Oligarchy," *Virginia Quarterly Review*, 36 (winter 1960): 78-96;

"At Prayerbook Cross," *Cimarron Review*, 6 (December 1968): 6-13;

"Obituary Three for Allan Swallow," *Modern Fiction Studies*, 15 (summer 1969): 187-190.

Other:

Mark Harris, "Easy Does It Not," in *The Living Novel*, ed. Granville Hicks (New York: Macmillan, 1957), pp. 113-116;

Selected Poems of Vachel Lindsay, edited by Harris (New York: Macmillan, 1963);

Public Television: A Program for Action, by Harris and others (New York: Harper & Row, 1967);

The Design of Fiction, edited by Harris and others (New York: Crowell, 1976).

References:

Saul Bachner, "Baseball as Literature: *Bang the Drum Slowly*," *English Record*, 25, 2 (1974): 83-86;

John Enck, "Mark Harris: An Interview," *Wisconsin Studies in Contemporary Literature*, 6 (winter-spring 1965): 15-26;

Joyce R. Ladenson, "Feminist Reflections on *Bang the Drum Slowly*," *American Examiner*, 3, 3 (1974): 22-24;

William J. Schafer, "Mark Harris: Versions of (American) Pastoral," *Critique*, 19, 1 (1977): 28-42.

JOHN HAWKES was born in Stamford, Connecticut on 17 August 1925. He married Sophie Goode Tazewell in 1947, and they have four children. Hawkes took his undergraduate degree from Harvard in 1949. He has taught at Harvard, Stanford, and CCNY, and he is currently professor of English at Brown University. Although his fiction is perhaps too esoteric to generate best-seller sales, Hawkes has earned wide-ranging critical applause including the *Prix du Meilleur Livre Etranger* and fellowships from the National Institute of Arts and Letters and from the Rockefeller, Ford, and Guggenheim Foundations.

Hawkes's fiction rejects the conventions of the traditional novel which developed in the eighteenth and nineteenth centuries with such staples as round characters, realistic settings, logical plots, and recognizable themes. The discoveries of Freud and Einstein, the fury of world war, the general breakdown of civil order—in short, the chaos of the twentieth century—deny the notion of orderly processes and social reconciliation which the conventional novel illustrates. Hawkes's aggressive, even militant violations of the well-made novel occasionally mislead readers to assume that he is a "new" writer, but he has been publishing fiction since 1949.

Nevertheless his currently high critical reputation has developed slowly, probably because the theory of fiction which informs his novels is unusual and upsetting to unprepared readers. Happily, Hawkes has expressed his ideas about fiction in a series of interviews and essays. A comment published in *Wisconsin Studies in Contemporary Literature* in 1965 continues to startle the uninitiated: "My novels are not highly plotted, but certainly they're elaborately structured. I began to write fiction on the

Jerry Bauer

coherence based on verbal patterns, parallel images, and cross-references. The reader must recognize patterns which often lack chronological sequence and motive, keeping in mind recurring image and action, in order to follow the complex structure. Good fiction has about it "something new," says Hawkes. "At any rate, the function of the true innovator or specifically experimental writer is to keep prose alive and constantly to test in the sharpest way possible the range of our human sympathies and constantly to destroy mere surface morality."

Hawkes tests the range of sympathies in the sharpest way possible by involving his audience with a crazed neo-Hitler, a buried dam builder, a sexually frustrated Englishman who thinks he needs a race horse, or a protective father who defeats the king of the fat. The list goes on, and the result is often laughter—unsure and tentative, perhaps, but laughter nonetheless. The point is that a Hawkes novel often invites comic response, but the reader is not sure his laughter is appropriate. Upsetting traditional notions of comedy as consciously as he dismisses conventional elements of fiction, Hawkes startles, shocks, even enrages some readers. Aware that his untraditional fiction causes some to stress his terrifying elements at the expense of the comic, he says, "I have always thought that my fictions, no matter how diabolical, were comic. I wanted to be very comic—but they have not been treated as comedy. They have been called 'black, obscene visions of the horror of life' and sometimes rejected as such, sometimes highly praised as such." He points to Djuna Barnes, Joseph Heller, Flannery O'Connor, and Nathanael West as other comic novelists who depict extreme violence, and he argues that the good reader, when faced with the black comedy of these writers, can sense "the need for innocence and purity, truth, strength" behind the humor.

Hawkes understands, of course, that blending the comic and the nightmare has occasionally limited his appeal, but he insists that his humorous elements are not used in the traditional sense of comic relief. The role of humor in his work, he points out, is never to soften the shock of the grotesque. Indeed, comedy should force a confrontation with the nightmare: "Of course I don't mean to apologize for the disturbing nature of my fiction by calling it comic, and certainly don't mean to minimize the terror with which this writing confronts the reader—my aim has always been the opposite, never to let the reader (or myself) off the hook, so to speak, never to let him think that the picture is any less black than it is or that there is any

assumption that the true enemies of the novel were plot, character, setting, and theme, and having once abandoned these familiar ways of thinking about fiction, totality of vision or structure was really all that remained. And structure—verbal and psychological coherence—is still my largest concern as a writer. Related or corresponding events, recurring image and recurring action, these constitute the essential substance or meaningful density of my writing." In short, Hawkes resists the temptations of "familiar" fiction, the conventions of the standard novel.

His efforts to avoid the limitations of realism encourage an exchange of the documentation of reality for the created vision of imagination. Hawkes would rather make up a fictional landscape than represent one. This is not to say that *The Cannibal* or *Second Skin* ignores plot, character, setting, and theme, but only to suggest that these devices are neither the primary means of control nor the major concern. The matter is one of emphasis. Rejecting round characters, exposition, the logic of cause and effect, and easily recognizable locales as holdovers from an earlier time, Hawkes emphasizes fictional easy way out of the nightmare of human existence." The point to remember here is that Hawkes often dismisses the notion that comedy encourages a reconciliation between the wayward individual and the benevolent social norm. Thus the aim of traditional comedy to use laughter as a utilitarian means of social correction no longer applies. Individuals may be wayward in a Hawkes novel, but society is neither benevolent nor normal. To ignore the complex mixture of humor and horror is to render his fiction an exploitation of terror, for the dire events cannot be missed, whatever difficulties the reader has with the comedy. Even those who accept the laughter are likely to find Hawkes's novels rough going. Sensing the humor, they may wonder if a horrified response to the action is inappropriate, or recognizing the terror, they may doubt their first suspicions that the novels are indeed comic.

Hawkes yanks his reader into the nightmare—grinning all the way. The thing that goes bump in the night turns out to be not a passing shadow but a real threat. Thus a fat, middle-aged man named Skipper (*Second Skin*) is relieved that the projectiles wrecking his face are not enraged eaglets but iced snowballs, while a similar character in *Travesty* creates the symmetry of "design and debris" by smashing himself and his passengers to oblivion. This untraditional fiction elicits the controversial responses one would expect. Roger Sale, for example, calls *The Blood Oranges* the product of a "contemptible imagination," while Thomas McGuane, reviewing the same novel, praises Hawkes as "feasibly our best writer." Hawkes is an "American original," says Webster Schott: "As an oracle of the emotions, he has no peer writing in America today."

Such high praise—and outraged dissent—did not come easily. Beginning in obscurity in 1949 and finding little or no public reaction to his first five fictions, Hawkes started receiving the attention he deserves in the early 1960s. The publication of *The Lime Twig* (1961), a comic novel of relative lucidity, was the turning point. "Relative" is the key word, for this novel is disturbing and difficult. But in it, Hawkes shifts from brilliantly controlled individual set pieces to a less obscure narrative. In short, visual power is toned down in favor of a more sharply focused narrative element that is still demanding but more accessible, poetic, and sympathetic.

Hawkes's career began in 1949 with the publication of the novella "Charivari." A "charivari" is a mock serenade, usually for a newly married couple, and so raucous as often to signal the serenaders' disapproval. Explaining that he began his short novel while working in Montana with sore feet and general discomfort, Hawkes transports his pain and sense of dislocation into the tale. Everything does not fall into place. Most of the action remains motiveless and unexplained, contributing not to plot but to atmosphere. If "plot" means development from beginning to end, "Charivari" has plot in this elementary sense—the pregnancy crisis facing Henry and Emily is resolved during the boisterous serenade at the weekend house party. But the movement from beginning to end is so fragmented that the reader must submit to the hazy atmosphere if he hopes to enjoy the laughter while shrinking from the pain. Indeed, Emily's pregnancy is not evident at the beginning, but it assumes more importance than the riotous celebration. Unfortunately for this bewildered couple, Henry and Emily are forty years old, unable to cope with a marriage, much less a baby. Neither wants to leave the womb to find the world. When they try to emerge, Henry and Emily initiate the scenes which touch on such potentially weighty subjects as sexual sterility, suicide, unexplained motivation, and dreams. But Hawkes purposely leaves the potential in an embryo state. More interested at the beginning of his career in isolated instances of individual delusion, he leaves us with the promise of meaningful violence but never the explosion. One grins when reading "Charivari," but does not care. Distanced from the characters, placed on the side of the narrator against "them," the audience watches the characters stumble through another world that it never enters. Unlike "Charivari," most of Hawkes's other novels suggest that many people share similar fantasies and fears, thus encouraging sympathy between reader and fictional victim.

The change begins immediately with *The Cannibal* (1949) which, along with "Charivari," was written in Albert Guerard's class at Harvard. Perhaps the best, and surely the most fascinating American novel to come out of World War II, *The Cannibal* is an incredible first full-length novel. Drawing on the trauma of his experience as an ambulance driver during the war in Europe, Hawkes communicates the dislocation, fragmentation, and shock in a fiction which often stuns first readers with its complexity. The two primary strands of the action are simply described: a lone American soldier, Leevey, is left to oversee one third of Germany while an unreconstructed Nazi, Zizendorf, plots his murder; and a starving duke pursues, dismembers, and eats a young boy. These episodes are more important as illustrations of a surrealist apocalypse than as actions which develop plot and character.

Indeed, *The Cannibal* remains one of Hawkes's most fertile examples of a novel which dismisses the primacy of theme, plot, setting, and character. Structured by interlocking verbal patterns and cross-referenced images, *The Cannibal* shatters the foundations of the traditional novel. Nearly everything looks back toward an earlier scene or phrase, and yet each incident foreshadows an image or event to come. The result is a highly conscious, tightly controlled fiction which communicates not by statement but by visual power: the revolt in the asylum, the frozen monkeys, the cannibalism, the murder by tuba—all suggest sterility, despair, and annihilation.

The technique is so insistent that it blends with Hawkes's premise that World War II both reflects the assassination of Archduke Ferdinand in Sarajevo in 1914 and foreshadows the coming apocalypse. History disguised as nationalism is the main character. Portrayed as an ill-defined process, as an unstoppable force which sweeps humanity into recurring nightmares, History terrifies with irrational returns to the past and unpredictable lurches toward the unknown. In a word, History cannibalizes its participants. To convey the loss of identity, the merger of victor and vanquished, and the ubiquity of defeat, Hawkes identifies his fictional characters with the historical personages at Sarajevo, assigns rationality to animals, and gives omniscience to the outrageously comic first-person narrator Zizendorf. Hawkes says in the *Massachusetts Review*, "The writer who maintains most successfully a consistent cold detachment toward physical violence . . . is likely to generate the deepest novelistic sympathy of all, a sympathy which is a humbling before the terrible and a quickening in the presence of degradation." Degradation is everywhere in *The Cannibal*, but the imagination and verbal power which inform it are lively and well. Watching at the end the crazed and maimed line up to reenter the asylum, perhaps a signal for the next war, the reader is faced with the contradictory yet stimulating emotions of despair for the victims and admiration for the technique.

Although *The Cannibal* requires commitment and imagination from the reader, it is not as difficult as Hawkes's next fiction, *The Beetle Leg* (1951). Using once again the summer in Montana when he helped construct an irrigation dam, Hawkes creates the central incident from an account of a laborer who was accidentally buried beneath tons of excavated dirt and never found. He imagines Mulge Lampson "swimming around in that sea of mud," haunting the arid countryside while the inhabitants build up a myth about the dead. Mulge's only companion is a drowned baby, hooked by Luke Lampson who is indirectly fishing for his lost brother, and placed back into the lake made by the dam. The scene is gently described yet horrifying in both its visual impact and implications, for it underscores the sterility of an American landscape dotted with unproductive farmland, useless dams, dry sex, and unresolved violence. The dam itself is a key to the atmosphere of waste and loss, for it slithers forward toward its own destruction "a beetle leg at a time," the buried Mulge joining in the slide.

The willful experimentation of *The Beetle Leg* often sets the dividing line between critics such as David Littlejohn and Peter Brooks, who lament the novel as a decline from the triumph of *The Cannibal* and those, such as Earl Rovit, who praise Hawkes's imaginative creation of incongruous effects and apparent confusions which have an underlying coherence. *The Beetle Leg* is a parody of the Western, that peculiar American genre which normally groups the cast into good guys and bad guys while celebrating the taming of the West. But Hawkes challenges America's expression of its own innocence to expose the negation and duplicity which sully the national experience. The American dream turns into a nightmare, the dam which should supply life-sustaining water becomes a monument to death, and the good guys remain indistinguishable from the bad. *The Beetle Leg* is distinguished by its visual power, its incredible, perhaps surrealistic scenes (Luke's shower, the poker game, the shoot-out at the end) which deny motive and the normal relationships of cause and effect while communicating the betrayal of a national dream. Thus Hawkes upsets comfortable assumptions about what makes a novel and about how the West was won, simultaneously revitalizing fiction and debunking myth.

The twin themes of the violation of innocence and the ubiquity of violence are carried over to two novellas published together in 1954, *The Goose on the Grave* and *The Owl*. Set in an imaginary landscape which Hawkes calls "Italy," these short novels suggest that Hawkes is still trying to write his way out of the horror of his World War II experiences. Battles and bloodshed hover in the background, prisoners are taken and tortured, and the ancient European heritage drowns in anarchy and apathy. *The Goose on the Grave* is the less successful of the two, perhaps because its repudiation of traditional form is militant to an extreme. In one sense this novella is picaresque, for it follows the orphan Adeppi, "one of Italy's covey of fragile doves," through a war-wrecked landscape while he searches for a protector. Yet to express his outrage, Hawkes shatters time sequence, point of view, and often meaning with the result that the reader is wrenched into a whirl of obscure and despairing events. Indeed, tradition is the enemy in *The Goose on the Grave*, both in the sense of fictional form and in the theme of rituals which have degenerated to useless observances with shape but no meaning. Religion, art, and sex deteriorate to the point where "the renaissance has failed." Hawkes's contrast between the overly ritualized past and the present fragmented by war is couched in a shadowy atmosphere which consciously counters each effort by the reader to render the events logically explicable. To reveal meaning would be to propose rationality, an impossibility, Hawkes suggests, in the world of *The Goose on the Grave*.

The Owl, on the other hand, is an impressive achievement. Everything is controlled, dovetailed, as it were, to the point where incident and scene contribute to a fantastic Gothic comedy in which Hawkes again exposes the effect of the tradition-ridden past on the warring present. As in most Hawkes novels, the narrative line is simple: Il Gufo (the malevolent Owl) wards off offers of marriage because he is bound to the gallows, his dark lady, by his occupation as hangman. The plot is merely a vehicle for the visual impact of this sharply imagined world. Hawkes develops rituals and codes which govern each moment in the dying town of Sasso Fetore, and creates a ghostly atmosphere where history consumes itself because the people lack the strength to replenish their ancient decrees with life-sustaining change. Barabo tries to marry his daughter to the Owl, the last eligible male, because tradition dictates his role; Pucento performs a gavotte with a trained dog during which both are victims of the stylized dance; and the prisoner attempts to escape by flying Icarus-like from the fortress on wings made from slaughtered ganders. Love breeds terror in this novel; gesture is all. These desperate people do as they are told because they have always done so.

Following these novellas, Hawkes did not publish another novel for seven years. The silence was worth the wait. For with *The Lime Twig* (1961), he crosses a watershed, enters his major phase, and begins a series of novels which have earned him his currently high reputation. On the surface a parody of the detective thriller, *The Lime Twig* suggests that while publicly revolted, the reader privately longs for the adventure, sexual violence, and proximity to death which he vicariously experiences when relaxing with whodunits. But there is no relaxation in *The Lime Twig*. The subtly patterned images (the colors, for example), the strategically placed cross-references (the various characters are being limed), and the insistent parallel scenes (Margaret's beating, Michael's orgy) testify to the intricate structure which demands the most careful perusal by even the initiated reader.

Careful reading has its rewards, for *The Lime Twig* is more accessible than his earlier fiction. One reason is the toning down of the fantastic images used previously in such liberal quantity. The visual power, so long the trademark of a Hawkes novel, has been limited in exchange for a more sharply focused narrative line: Michael Banks wants a race horse; he gets one and is killed when a gang of hoods muscles in on the deal. Stepping closer to conventional fiction with its recognizable settings and developed characters, Hawkes makes fun of the tradition even while he reflects it. He violates anticipated probability, surprising both reader and character when events beyond the dictates of rationality occur. Although he encourages laughter at the inappropriate responses of Michael and Margaret Banks, he offers a novel full of fear, more frightening than *The Cannibal* or *The Owl* because it is easy to identify with the Banks's experiences. As the unreliable commentator Sidney Slyter says, it might be any one of us.

Indeed it might—Hawkes explores in this novel the question of what happens when a man's unconscious desires and repressed longings come true. To answer, he creates a literal dream. Michael and Margaret are jerked into their "best and worst dreams," away from preconceived distinctions between sanity and abnormality, where erotic obsession, personified in the racehorse, limes them as if they were helpless birds. Detailing the alliance between love and terror, Hawkes suggests the brutality and yet the sexual thrill lurking just beneath the surface of dreams spinning out of control when the unwary dreamer realizes that he cannot restrain what he will not acknowledge. Banks commits himself so totally to his fantasy that he dies within it, a puzzling but necessary fact for the reader to understand. Yet the ending is redemptive, as Hawkes himself has admitted. For in addition to the affirmation of the fictional rhythm, the sheer joy of beautifully rendered technique, Banks redeems himself when he plunges in front of the galloping horse to bring it down. The dreamer and the dream are one, and the sacrifice of one demands the destruction of the other. We laugh, finally, at the investigating police who putter around in the "real" world, hoping to uncover the particulars of the crime.

Hawkes's movement toward the trappings of the traditional novel takes an even greater step in *Second Skin* (1964), his finest achievement. While it is true that *Second Skin* is more conventional only when compared to a radically different fiction like *The Beetle Leg*, Hawkes's control of lyrical description, language, and imaginative vision creates an accessibility in a novel which is as violent and as experimental with time and narrative voice as the rest of his canon. His manipulation of the first-person narrator, Skipper, joins his effort to make the comedy more easily apparent as two of his announced goals: "In *Second Skin* I tried consciously to write a novel that couldn't be mistaken for anything but a comic novel. I wanted to expose clearly what I thought was central to my fictional efforts but had been generally overlooked." He succeeds.

A memoir finished just "last night" by fat, middle-aged Skipper, the novel recounts from the perspective of his tropical haven Skipper's triumph over the designs of sadistic friends and possessive lovers. He suffers an extraordinary number of personal assaults, ranging from snowball fights and bellybumping contests to the suicides of his family, but he survives with all of his love intact. Suffer and survive—Skipper does all this and more, for at the end of the novel he has created not only an imaginative reconstruction of his past of death and decay but also a lyrical evocation of his present where lovers loll in the sunlight and where virtue always wins.

His lyricism may be a key to the novel. Offering cascades of language, poetic, alliterative passages, and erotic descriptions of landscape and love, Skipper works hard to prove the suitability of his survival. Too hard, some readers observe, for it soon becomes clear that he hopes to persuade himself as well as the reader. His sustained first-person voice is a new element in Hawkes's fiction. The point of view provides a needed handle to this complicated fiction, but it also allows Hawkes to parody the novel form itself. Skipper, the main character in *Second Skin*, comments directly on the novel he is writing in which he is also the main character. The positioning of other characters and time sequences, and the allusions to motive, culpability, and effect depend not upon the claims of logical order but upon Skipper's needs as a storyteller. As author of what he calls his "naked history," he reserves the right to interrupt any chapter to direct the interpretation of his dreadful past. But he is such a bumbler, so willing to be victimized, so eager to win the praise of his audience, that the reliability of his tale becomes questionable.

Still, no one finally cares if Skipper creates a version of his history or a promise of his future from his mastery of lyrical language. Despite all the despair and defeat, he finds "love at last." For the first time in Hawkes's canon, the life forces balance the darker cycle of perversion and death. The sustaining graces of humor and language carry Hawkes, Skipper, and the reader down to the cemetery to have a fete with the dead. Pain and sorrow are forgotten as Skipper's companions celebrate a baby's birth. The redemptive power of imagination reshapes the black past into a golden promise.

Hawkes embraces life in *Second Skin*, but he does not reject his perception of private yearnings and public turmoil. The nightmare hovers always near the surface. His investigation of the kinship of love and terror, first fully explored in *The Lime Twig*, continues in the latest three novels to date, a triad of love and imagination. In *The Blood Oranges* (1971), *Death, Sleep & the Traveler* (1974), and *Travesty* (1976), Hawkes lures the reader further and further into the confidential confessions of unreliable first-person narrators until he creates one who allows no interruption in his monologue on the pleasures of "design and debris."

Cyril, the narrator of *The Blood Oranges*, would like the reader to believe that he has achieved Skipper's idyll of love and grace, but his tapestry is in ruins and his companions are dead, ill, or gone. Once again, the landscape is lush with summer, the air ripe with sun and warmth. But Cyril is no Skipper. A self-appointed "sex-singer," he tells his tale to discover why love has purged him from her field. The sexual symmetry he has created with wife Fiona and companions Hugh and Catherine in the mythical retreat of Illyria is now shattered. Cyril blames Hugh for turning their love lyric into a dissonant shriek with his onanistic releases and unexpected hanging, but we have only Cyril's word. It is not that Hugh the puritan is right and Cyril the hedonist wrong, but that Cyril tries too hard to deny his participation in pain and despair. He sees himself as a victim of Hugh's conventional ideas about monogamy; culpability is not something he can share.

Hawkes apparently supports Cyril's version, for in an interview he declares that the sex-singer is "probably right" to name monogamy the enemy. Yet the novel is delightfully ambiguous, the fun developing as Cyril goes through his paces,

For Don — this glimpse
of the crash that does not occur,
the characters who do not exist
(ha!) — with thanks and
admiration & affection
Jack

No, no, Henri. Hands off the wheel. Please. It is too late. After all, at one hundred and forty-nine kilometers per hour on a country road in the darkest quarter of the night, surely it is obvious that your slightest effort to wrench away the wheel will pitch us into the toneless world of highway tragedy even more quickly than I have planned. And you will not believe it, but we are still accelerating.

As for you, Chantal, you must beware. You must obey your Papa. You must sit back in your seat and fasten your belt and stop crying. And Chantal, no more beating the driver about the shoulders or shaking his arm. Emulate Henri, my poor Chantal, and control yourself.

11

Inscribed page proof for Travesty.

attempting to convince himself and the reader. His time sequences are jumbled, and his descriptions are poetic—as expected in a Hawkes novel. Structured by intricate patterns of cross-references and involved allusions to flowers, animals, and *Twelfth Night*, many of which are clues to Cyril's unreliability, *The Blood Oranges* continues Hawkes's bow to lucidity as well as his parody of the novel form.

The dark recesses of terror lurking in the medieval dungeon where Hugh finds a chastity belt pervade *Death, Sleep & the Traveler*. Deploring the nightmare but defending its brutal truth, Hawkes carries his narrator Allert so deep into his unexplained erotic dreams that the dreamer approaches death through orgasm. Although the novel is relatively clear and even easy to read, its meanings remain always ambiguous. More a series of astonishingly imagined visions than a fiction in the traditional sense, *Death, Sleep & the Traveler* reveals Allert as an artist figure who liberates creative energy in his nightmares to fulfill urgent but unconscious needs.

Allert is the most detached of Hawkes's narrators to this point, so remote from wife Ursula, friend Peter, and lover Ariane that he may exist only in his own dreams. Since Allert has no life beyond his narration, this novel is a fiction about fictions. It finally makes little difference whether or not Allert murders Ariane in "real" life or whether he is literally a patient at the Acres Wild asylum. Perhaps mad, surely obsessed, he pursues the equation of sex and death, relishing his autoeroticism, traveling through sleep to find his greatest erotic thrill in his own demise. The terror is overwhelming in this novel, for Hawkes sets aside the lyrical affirmation and comic tone of his most recent fictions.

Yet with *Travesty*, the final novel of the triad, the comedy reappears. A tour-de-force, a 125-page monologue in which Papa the narrator explains why he plans to crash his car and kill himself, daughter Chantal, and poet-friend Henri, *Travesty* may complete Hawkes's manipulations of the first-person narrator. Unreliability has always been a key, of course, to Papa's forerunners in the preceding novels, but in those fictions other characters besides the teller exist and other landscapes besides the visions are tread upon. In *Death, Sleep & the Traveler* the exterior landscapes are diminished, but the characters remain. *Travesty* may discard even the other people. Although this point is ambiguous, Papa may be the only character in *Travesty*, a man so proud of his fertile visions that he presents his tale as a kind of inside narrative in which he pursues his private apocalypse of "design and debris." The

suggestion that all the characters and perhaps even the destructively fast car ride are visions from Papa's obsessed mind remains enticing, fascinating, and finally uncertain. Seeking the harmony of paradox, searching for the moment of simultaneous time-lessness and cessation, Papa uses the car ride as a metaphor for a plunge into his own imagination. Perhaps the ultimate art is achieved when creator and creation become one. Those who must investigate the crash will not understand that the twisted car represents harmony as much as chaos.

The pleasures of John Hawkes continue. Rejecting representation of reality for created landscapes, he confronts terror with comedy as he leads his reader through the quagmires of the mind. Though he may startle at one turn, challenge at the next, he always rewards and renews. Hawkes reveals that the possibilities of the imagination are endless and that fiction shores up human life.

—*Donald J. Greiner*

Books:

Fiasco Hall (Cambridge, Mass.: Harvard Printing Office, 1943);

The Cannibal (Norfolk, Conn.: New Directions, 1949; London: Spearman, 1962);

The Beetle Leg (New York: New Directions, 1951; London: Chatto & Windus, 1967);

The Goose on the Grave, and The Owl (New York: New Directions, 1954);

The Lime Twig (New York: New Directions, 1961; London: Spearman, 1962);

Second Skin (Norfolk, Conn.: New Directions, 1964; London: Chatto & Windus, 1966);

The Innocent Party (New York: New Directions, 1967; London: Chatto & Windus, 1967);

Lunar Landscapes (New York: New Directions, 1969; London: Chatto & Windus, 1970);

The Blood Oranges (New York: New Directions, 1971; London: Chatto & Windus, 1971);

Death, Sleep & the Traveler (New York: New Directions, 1974; London: Chatto & Windus, 1975);

Travesty (New York: New Directions, 1976; London: Chatto & Windus, 1976).

Periodical Publications:

"Notes on Violence," *Audience*, 7 (spring 1960): 60;

"The Voice of Edwin Honig," *Voices: A Journal of Poetry*, no. 174 (January-April 1961): 39-47;

"Flannery O'Connor's Devil," *Sewanee Review*, 70 (summer 1962): 395-407;

"Notes on the Wild Goose Chase," *Massachusetts Review*, 3 (summer 1962): 784-788;

"Notes on Writing a Novel," *Tri-Quarterly*, 30 (spring 1974): 109-126;

"*The Floating Opera* and *Second Skin*," *Mosaic*, 8 (fall 1974): 17-28.

Interviews:

"John Hawkes: An Interview," *Wisconsin Studies in Contemporary Literature*, 6 (summer 1965): 141-155;

"John Hawkes on His Novels: An Interview with John Graham," *Massachusetts Review*, 7 (summer 1966): 449-461;

"Talks with John Hawkes," *Harvard Advocate*, 104 (October 1970): 6, 34-35;

"A Conversation on *The Blood Oranges* Between John Hawkes and Robert Scholes," *Novel*, 5 (spring 1972): 197-207;

"Interview," (John Hawkes and John Kuehl), in John Kuehl, *John Hawkes and the Craft of Conflict* (New Brunswick: Rutgers University Press, 1975), pp. 155-183;

Roger Sauls, "A Conversation with John Hawkes," *Charlotte Observer*, 14 March 1976;

Paul Emmett and Richard Vine, "A Conversation with John Hawkes," *Chicago Review*, 28 (fall 1976): 172-187.

References:

Lawrence Boutrous, "Parody in Hawkes' *The Lime Twig*," *Critique*, 15, 2 (1973): 49-56;

Peter Brooks, "John Hawkes," *Encounter*, 26 (June 1966): 68-72;

Jackson R. Bryer, "Two Bibliographies" [John Hawkes and John Barth], *Critique*, 6 (fall 1963): 86-94;

Frederick Busch, *Hawkes: A Guide to His Fictions* (Syracuse: Syracuse University Press, 1973);

Lois A. Cuddy, "Functional Pastoralism in *The Blood Oranges*," *Studies in American Fiction*, 3 (spring 1975): 15-25;

Robert I. Edenbaum, "John Hawkes: *The Lime Twig* and Other Tenuous Horrors," *Massachusetts Review*, 7 (summer 1966): 462-475;

Paul Emmett, "The Reader's Voyage through *Travesty*," *Chicago Review*, 28 (fall 1976): 172-187;

Leslie A. Fiedler, "The Pleasures of John Hawkes," in Hawkes, *The Lime Twig* (New York: New Directions, 1961), pp. vii-xiv;

Melvin J. Friedman, "John Hawkes and Flannery O'Connor: The French Background," *Boston University Journal*, 21, 3 (1973): 34-44;

W. M. Frohock, "John Hawkes's Vision of Violence," *Southwest Review*, 50 (winter 1965): 69-79;

Lucy Frost, "The Drowning of American Adam: Hawkes' *The Beetle Leg*," *Critique*, 14 (summer 1973): 63-74;

H. S. Garson, "John Hawkes and the Elements of Pornography," *Journal of Popular Culture*, 10 (summer 1976): 150-155;

John Graham, ed., *Studies in Second Skin* (Columbus: Charles E. Merrill, 1971);

James L. Green, "Nightmare and Fairy Tale in Hawkes' *Charivari*," *Critique*, 13, 1 (1971): 83-95;

Donald J. Greiner, "The Thematic Use of Color in John Hawkes' *Second Skin*," *Contemporary Literature*, 11 (summer 1970): 389-400;

Greiner, "Strange Laughter: The Comedy of John Hawkes," *Southwest Review*, 56 (autumn 1971): 318-328;

Greiner, *Comic Terror: The Novels of John Hawkes* (Memphis: Memphis State University Press, 1973);

Greiner, "*Death, Sleep & the Traveler*: John Hawkes' Return to Terror," *Critique*, 17 (spring 1976): 26-38;

Albert J. Guerard, "Introduction to the Cambridge Anti-Realists," *Audience*, 7 (spring 1960): 57-59;

Guerard, "Introduction," in Hawkes, *The Cannibal* (New York: New Directions, 1962), pp. ix-xx;

Guerard, "The Prose Style of John Hawkes," *Critique*, 6 (fall 1963): 19-29;

Guerard, "The Illuminating Distortion," *Novel*, 5 (winter 1972): 101-121;

Guerard, "Notes on the Rhetoric of Anti-Realist Fiction," *Tri-Quarterly*, 30 (1974): 3-50;

Ron Imhoff, "On *Second Skin* (with response by John Hawkes)," *Mosaic*, 8 (fall 1974): 51-64;

John W. Knapp, "Hawkes' *The Blood Oranges*: A Sensual New Jerusalem," *Critique*, 17 (spring 1976): 5-25;

Elisabeth Kraus, "Psychic Sores in Search of Compassion: Hawkes' *Death, Sleep & the Traveler*," *Critique*, 17 (spring 1976): 39-52;

John Kuehl, *John Hawkes and the Craft of Conflict* (New Brunswick: Rutgers University Press, 1975);

Norman Lavers, "The Structure of *Second Skin*," *Novel*, 5 (spring 1972): 208-214;

Thomas LeClair, "The Unreliability of Innocence: John Hawkes' *Second Skin*," *Journal of Narrative Technique*, 3 (January 1973): 32-39;

David Littlejohn, "The Anti-Realists," *Daedalus*, 92 (spring 1963): 250-264;

Paul Loukides, "The Radical Vision," *Michigan Academician*, 5 (spring 1973): 497-503;

Irving Malin, *New American Gothic* (Carbondale: Southern Illinois University Press, 1962);

Charles Matthews, "The Destructive Vision of John Hawkes," *Critique*, 6 (fall 1963): 38-52;

Charles Moran, "John Hawkes: Paradise Gaining," *Massachusetts Review*, 12 (autumn 1971): 840-845;

S. K. Oberbeck, "John Hawkes: The Smile Slashed by a Razor," in *Contemporary American Novelists*, ed. Harry T. Moore (Carbondale: Southern Illinois University Press, 1968), pp. 193-204;

Raymond M. Olderman, *Beyond the Waste Land: The American Novel in the Nineteen-Sixties* (New Haven: Yale University Press, 1972), pp. 150-175;

Richard Pearce, *Stages of the Clown: Perspectives on Modern Fiction from Dostoyevsky to Beckett* (Carbondale: Southern Illinois University Press, 1970);

Daniel Plung, "John Hawkes: A Selected Bibliography," *Critique*, 17 (spring 1976): 53-63;

D. P. Reutlinger, "*The Cannibal*: 'The Reality of Victim,' " *Critique*, 6 (fall 1963): 30-37;

Claire Rosenfield, "John Hawkes: Nightmares of the Real," *Minnesota Review*, 2 (winter 1962): 249-254;

Earl Rovit, "The Fiction of John Hawkes: An Introductory View," *Modern Fiction Studies*, 10 (summer 1964): 150-162;

Anthony Santore and Michael Pocalyko, eds., *A John Hawkes Symposium: Design and Debris* (New York: New Directions, 1977);

Robert Scholes, *The Fabulators* (New York: Oxford University Press, 1967);

Webster Schott, "John Hawkes, American Original," *New York Times Book Review*, 29 May 1966, pp. 4, 24-25;

John C. Stubbs, "John Hawkes and the Dream-Work of *The Lime Twig* and *Second Skin*," *Literature and Psychology*, 21, 3 (1971): 149-160;

Tony Tanner, *City of Words: American Fiction 1950-1970* (New York: Harper & Row, 1971), pp. 202-229;

Tanner, "Necessary Landscapes and Luminous Deteriorations: On Hawkes," *Tri-Quarterly*, 20 (winter 1971): 145-179;

Alan Trachtenberg, "Barth and Hawkes: Two Fabulists," *Critique*, 6 (fall 1963): 4-18;

Stanley Trachtenberg, "Counterhumor: Comedy in Contemporary American Fiction," *Georgia Review*, 27 (spring 1973): 33-48;

John M. Warner, "The 'Internalized Quest Romance' in Hawkes' *The Lime Twig*," *Modern Fiction Studies*, 19 (spring 1973): 89-95;

Richard Yarborough, "Hawkes' *Second Skin* (with a response by John Hawkes)," *Mosaic*, 8 (fall 1974): 65-75.

JOSEPH HELLER was born 1 May 1923 in Brooklyn, New York. His father died in 1927. After graduating from Abraham Lincoln High School in 1941, Heller joined the Twelfth Air Force. He was stationed in Corsica where he flew sixty missions as a wing bombardier. He married Shirley Held on 3 September 1945. They have two children, Erica Jill and Theodor Michael.

After the war, Heller attended the University of Southern California for a year before transferring to New York University in 1946. He received his B.A. in 1948 and his M.A. from Columbia a year later, where his master's thesis was "The Pulitzer Prize Plays: 1917-1935." After spending a year at Oxford on a Fulbright Scholarship, he returned to teach at Pennsylvania State University from 1950 to 1952. He spent the following four years in the same position as an advertising manager for *Time*, the next two years in the same position for *Look*, and then three years as a promotion manager at *McCall's*. He left *McCall's* in 1961 to teach fiction and dramatic writing at Yale University and the University of Pennsylvania.

Heller started writing while he was a college student. He sold a few short stories to *Esquire* in 1947 and 1948, another few to *Atlantic* in 1948. In 1954 he started working on "Catch-18," a novel which had been gestating since 1947. The first chapter was published in 1955 in *New World Writing*. In 1958 Heller signed a contract for publication of the novel with Simon and Schuster. Prior to the publication in 1961, Heller was forced to change his title to *Catch-22* to avoid confusion with Leon Uris's *Mila 18*. Heller admits that the number twenty-two had relevance to the novel "because so many things do repeat themselves. . . . For that reason the two 2's struck me as being very appropriate to the novel."

Paramount released the movie *Catch-22* in 1970 with Mike Nichols as its director. Since 1961 *Catch-22* has enjoyed a steady sale in America. The novel only began to sell strongly in hardcover in America after its publication and enthusiastic reception in England. After the movie made its appearance, *Catch-22* for the first time made the best-seller list in America. By 1975 it had sold over six million copies.

The setting of *Catch-22* is the fictional island of Pianosa, the base of the Twenty-seventh Air Force. Shimon Wincelberg sums up the story as a "sprawling, hilarious, irresponsible, compassionate, cynical, surrealistic, farcical, lacerating, and enormously readable account of what happened to some American fliers on a small island in the Mediterranean during the Italian campaign of World War II." The protagonist is a former lead bombardier, John Yossarian, who is determined to stay alive. He uses all the means at his disposal to achieve that end. He poisons his squadron with soap; he alters a combat map; he sabotages his plane; he escapes to the hospital. Finally he decides to desert to Sweden after all of his friends have been killed or have "disappeared."

The chronological structure of the plot is deliberately obfuscated. According to critic Doug Gaukroger, the reason is twofold. First, the effect created by "treating all events as equally present" confuses the reader's sense of order and upsets "his basic assumptions regarding proper form and structure." The unorthodox treatment of time in *Catch-22* is parallel to, and prepares the reader for, the unorthodox treatment of the subject matter. "It is only fitting that a novel which deals with an apparently absurd and confused world should be written in an apparently absurd and confused style." Secondly, Gaukroger believes that "Heller's obfuscation concerns itself mainly with numerous events occurring during The Great Siege of Bologna. This is part of Heller's technique to deal with a large amount of humorous material. Heller obscures and twists a chronological structure which is both plausible and logical."

The coherence, which is distorted through Heller's use of the chronological structure, is reassimilated through his use of *deja vu*. The characters in *Catch-22* have the impression that what is happening to them has happened before. The reader, like the characters, also experiences *deja vu* with what James Mellard calls the same frustrating lag between the *seeing* and the *understanding*. This lag creates "a discontinuity between a character (Yossarian), a symbol (Catch-22, which says 'they

Joseph Heller.

Jill Krementz

have a right to anything we can't stop them from doing'), a narrative event (Snowden's death), and its meaning ('the spirit is gone, man is garbage')." This technique has caused many critics to accuse Heller of needless repetition. As Mellard points out, "*deja vu* is actually neither simply repetitive nor redundant but is rather complexly incremental and progressive . . . the characters, both real and symbolic . . . gradually gain in significance, a thematic concept such as Catch-22 also changes in meaning as it recurs." The use of *deja vu* serves as a guideline through the maze of plot, characters and chronology.

In spite of the World War II setting, many critics have rejected *Catch-22* as a realistic war novel in the tradition of *From Here to Eternity* and *The Naked and the Dead*. *Catch-22* is said to represent "a satirical microcosm" of the postwar American world which not only includes the Korean and Vietnam wars but also the modern mass society. Robert Brustein stated that Heller "penetrates the surface of the merely funny to expose a world of ruthless self-advancement, gruesome cruelty, and flagrant disregard for human life." Heller has written a novel that depicts the human predicament. The climax of his vision is to be found in "The Eternal City," a Dantesque journey through the streets of Rome at night. Minna Doskow shows "how Yossarian through his participation in the archetypal pattern of the descent and renewal of the romance hero achieves his new perception which culminates quite logically in his flight to Sweden." Yet Vance Ramsey claimed that one of the flaws in *Catch-22* is its ending. "The last four chapters of the novel have a discursive quality not found in most of the other parts of the novel. The long philosophical argument between Yossarian and the ex-college professor is out of keeping with the technique of the rest of the book, in which actions and situations speak for themselves. In short, the book loses its dramatic quality." Critics claimed that Heller, faced with deadline difficulties, tucked his story-strands into a conventional and unconvincing ending. Heller insisted in an interview in *The Realist* that "the ending was written long before the middle was written . . . I couldn't see any alternative ending . . . the heavy suffusion of moral content . . . required a resolution of choice rather than by accident."

The driving force in the plot of *Catch-22* is Yossarian's determination not to die. Every logical and legal step he tries to take to leave the air force is foiled by a catch in the regulations. As Doc Daneeka patiently explains to Yossarian: "Regulations say you have to obey every order. That's the catch. Even if the colonel were disobeying a Twenty-seventh Air Force order by making you fly more missions, you'd still have to fly them, or you'd be guilty of disobeying an order of his. And then Twenty-seventh Air Force Headquarters would really jump on you." Yossarian then finds out the whole implication of that catch:

> There was only one catch and that was Catch-22, which specified that a concern for one's safety in the face of dangers that were real and immediate was the process of a rational mind. Orr [Yossarian's roommate] was crazy and could be grounded. All he had to do was ask; and as soon as he did, he would no longer be crazy and would have to fly more missions. Orr would be crazy to fly more missions and sane if he didn't, but if he was sane he had to fly them. If he flew them he was crazy and didn't have to; but if he didn't want to he was sane and had to. Yossarian was moved very deeply by the absolute simplicity of this clause of Catch-22.

Yossarian has two important alternatives in realizing his wish to stay alive without being trapped by Catch-22. One of the alternatives is offered by Milo Minderbinder, the one-man international corporation. Milo's life revolves around profits and opportunities for making them. Milo creates a syndicate in which everybody has a share; whose slogan is "what's good for M & M Enterprises is good for the country." Milo considers Yossarian a friend. He tries to initiate Yossarian to the business by explaining how to make a profit in buying eggs from Malta for seven cents apiece and selling them in Pianosa for five cents: "I make a profit of three and a quarter cents an egg by selling them for four and a quarter cents an egg to the people in Malta I buy them from for seven cents an egg . . . and a profit of two and three quarter cents apiece when I buy them back from me (I'm the people I buy them from). That's a total profit of six cents an egg. I lose only two cents an egg when I sell them to the mess halls at five cents apiece . . . I pay only one cent apiece at the hen when I buy them in Sicily . . . and transfer them to Malta secretly at four and a half cents apiece in order to get the price of eggs up to seven cents apiece." Milo also offers Yossarian the opportunity to participate in cheating the federal government out of six thousand dollars but Yossarian refuses. With that refusal Yossarian rejects the concept of profit-oriented business corporations as a mode of life for himself.

The other alternative is offered by Orr. Orr is frequently mentioned in various chapters as being small and ugly, a warmhearted, simpleminded gnome, a happy and unsuspecting simpleton, a crackpot. Orr, as his name implies, is an alternative, a means of escape for Yossarian, who does not realize this. Orr asks Yossarian: "Why don't you ever fly with me?" Yossarian is frightened by the staggering number of times Orr has been shot down. He is not convinced when Orr assures him: "I'd take care of you." Yet Yossarian knows that Orr comes "from the wilderness outside New York City and knew so much more about wild life than Yossarian did." Yossarian observes that Orr is self-reliant, patient, enduring, and adaptable, therefore excellently equipped for survival. Orr feels indebted to Yossarian. As the squadron's leading authority on internment, Yossarian tells Orr "of such sanctuaries as Spain, Switzerland, and Sweden where American fliers could be interned for the duration of the war under conditions of utmost ease and luxury." Yossarian's refusal to accept Orr's offer not only delays his escape for another fourteen chapters but also forces him to experience the painful process of growing self-awareness which culminates in his decision to desert to Sweden.

The initial criticism was mixed. Richard Stern found that "*Catch-22* has much passion, comic and fervent, but it gasps for want of craft and sensibility ... the book is no novel. ... The book is an emotional hodgepodge." Roger H. Smith claimed that "because Heller's book reads as if the pages of the manuscript had been scrambled on the way to the printer, it is viewed as experimental and 'modern'. ... By a new kind of stock response, profanity and obscenity are accepted as the signature of the literature of the elect." Nelson Algren stated that "this novel is not merely the best American novel to come out of World War II; it is the best American novel that has come out of anywhere in years." Robert Brustein called *Catch-22* an "explosive, bitter, subversive, brilliant book." Julian Mitchell wrote that *"Catch-22* is a book of enormous richness and art, of deep thought and brilliant writing." Andrew Leslie criticized: "At 443 pages, the book is rather long to sustain itself without a firmer story-line than it has. But in about one chapter in three, Mr. Heller soars sweetly up into zones of the quite brilliantly comic."

Between *Catch-22* and the publication of his next novel, *Something Happened*, in 1974, Heller worked on the scripts of movies such as *Sex and the Single Girl*, *Casino Royale* and *Dirty Dingus Magee*. In 1968 he published *We Bombed in New Haven*, a play, produced on Broadway and at the Yale School of Drama in 1967. The plot uses *Catch-22* themes and settings. A squadron is ordered to bomb Constantinople, which creates a great confusion among the fliers because Constantinople has been renamed Istanbul. Catch-22 becomes apparent as the squadron is not allowed to disobey orders and yet cannot fulfill these orders because the target, as named, does not exist. As in *Catch-22*, the characters share the audience's confusion. The actors frequently interject their own personality into their roles, thereby underlining a sense of identification between the actors and the audience. The effect is a united struggle on the part of the actors and the audience to understand the value of life and the individual's responsibility in his society.

In 1971 *Catch-22: A Dramatization* was published. The premier was at the John Drew Theater in East Hampton, New York, under the direction of Larry Arrick. The dramatization forced Heller to a "distinct, prominent narrative line accelerating toward a climactic resolution." The chronology was put in order. Many characters and scenes had to be omitted, such as Orr and "The Eternal City," both of which play crucial roles in the book. Milo Minderbinder's role was reduced; Wintergreen's was enlarged; Major Major and Major Danby were fused into one character. The play is consciously cinematic. Heller describes the technique: "Characters come in sight when they are ready to speak or be spoken to and leave the stage as soon as they are through." According to Heller, requests for permission to present the play arrive "from college theater groups and other amateur and stock companies in different cities ... there have been numerous productions . . . in this country and abroad."

In 1974 the long-awaited second novel by Joseph Heller appeared. A sequence had been published in *Esquire* in September 1966. *Something Happened* proved to be a disappointment to many readers. For them, *Something Happened* was too long, boring, and unconvincing. Calvin Bedient called it "a monstrous effort to make literature out of pettiness." According to George Searles the difficulties of *Something Happened* can be attributed to three basic features: "the extremely limited mode of narration, the unheroic nature of the protagonist, and the ostensibly pessimistic quality of the novel's message."

The narrator in *Something Happened* is the protagonist, Bob Slocum, a different kind of Mr. Everybody from Yossarian. Slocum is married, middle-aged, and a middle-management executive, the father of three children, and the owner of a comfortable house on an expensive acre of land in Connecticut. He gets along with everybody and can satisfy his sexual desires any time. He has everything, and yet the reader finds him contemptible and pitiable. He is sure of nothing and afraid of everything, even though he is not capable of defining the object of his fear. Slocum has a number of personality quirks and personal habits which, though negative, render him as much a representative man as a specific individual. Slocum is a businessman who works for a large corporation in the Market Research Department, which "is concerned with collecting, organizing, interpreting, and reorganizing statistical information about the public, the market, the country, and the world." Through Slocum's naturally limited vision, the characters that surround him become personified sociological statistics. He speaks, as Irving Malin pointed out, "in a flat, repetitive, and charted way." Through this form of limited narration, Heller has exhaustively explored "the interior psychological survival" of an outwardly successful member of the modern society.

The pessimism that suffuses the novel is created by the long lists of depressingly ordinary facts, the voluminous details of Slocum's attitudes on everything. Heller succeeds in dramatizing a condition of psychic disturbance which may well be the most common and normal condition of

Joseph Heller with packaged manuscript of Catch-22.

individuals today. For George Searles *Something Happened* is "to an alarming degree an accurate social documentary that mercilessly captures some very real elements of the contemporary American situation." Slocum is very clear-sighted and ruthlessly honest when he describes himself and his society: "I am a stick; I am a waterlogged branch floating with my own crowd in this one nation of ours, indivisible (unfortunately), under God, with liberty and justice for all those who are speedy enough to seize them first and hog them away from the rest of us. Some melting pot. If all of us in this vast, fabulous land of ours could come together and take time to exchange a few words with our neighbors and fellow countrymen, those words would be Bastard! Wop! Nigger! Whitey! Kike! Spic! . . . I float. I float like algae in a colony of green scum."

What happens when the limit of one's aspirations has been reached? Who can tell Slocum about what he should do now? Where can he discover meaning for his life? These are some of the disturbing questions Heller raises while showing the irremediable emptiness of a segment of modern life without offering any stated affirmations or even comic relief. For George Searles *Something Happened* is "in one important respect a better book than its predecessor. *Catch-22* depends . . . upon boisterous exaggeration that does not always convince, and too often verges on self-parody. . . . Heller has turned from hyperbole to implication; in opting for a less strident, less obvious statement, he has produced a more mature book." John Aldridge summarized his attitude toward Heller and *Something Happened*: "This is a remarkable and profoundly disturbing narrative. . . . Heller has confronted, with an authenticity few writers possess, some of the most unpleasant truths about our situation at this time . . . he has created a darkened, demonic, perhaps partly hallucinated fictive portrait of contemporary America, but one that has at the same time a disquieting verisimilitude."

Heller is a major novelist of our time who creates cinematic visions of American society and its individuals. Through his probing insights he reveals, captures, and focuses on those layers in individuals that are usually suppressed or artfully concealed. He has the ability to make the reader not only recognize but also identify with the protagonist, thereby deepening the individual's self-awareness. He is a novelist who rejects the world of delusion as firmly as he has refused self-imitation. He continues to probe with the skill, the patience, and the precision of a scientist beneath the camouflage of everyday life. —*Inge Kutt*

Books:

Catch-22 (New York: Simon & Schuster, 1961; London: Cape, 1962);

We Bombed in New Haven (New York: Knopf, 1968; London: Cape, 1969);

Catch-22: A Dramatization (New York: French, 1971);

Clevinger's Trial (New York: French, 1973);

Something Happened (New York: Knopf, 1974; London: Cape, 1975).

Screenplays:

Sex and the Single Girl, Warner Bros., 1964;

Casino Royale, Columbia, 1967;

Dirty Dingus Magee, MGM, 1970.

References:

John W. Aldridge, "Vision of Man Raging in a Vacuum," *Saturday Review*, 2 (18 October 1974): 18-21;

Ihab Hassan, "Laughter in the Dark," *American Scholar*, 33 (autumn 1964): 634-639;

William Kennedy, "Endlessly Honest Confession," *New Republic*, 171 (19 October 1974): 17-19;

Frederick Kiley and Walter McDonald, eds., *A 'Catch-22' Casebook* (New York: Crowell, 1973);

D. Keith Maria, "Fine Writing That Irks," *National Review*, 16 (22 November 1974): 1364;

James Nagel, ed., *Critical Essays on Catch-22* (Encino, Cal.: Dickenson, 1973);

Nagel, "The *Catch-22* Note Cards," *Studies in the Novel*, 8 (winter 1976): 394-405;

Sanford Pinsker, "Heller's *Catch-22*: The Protest of a *Puer Eternis*," *Critique*, 7, 2 (winter 1964/1965): 150-162;

Richard B. Sale, "An Interview in New York with Joseph Heller," *Studies in the Novel*, 4 (September 1972): 63-74;

Robert M. Scotto, ed., *Joseph Heller's Catch-22: A Critical Edition* (New York: Dell, 1973);

George B. Searles, "*Something Happened*: A New Direction for Joseph Heller," *Critique*, 18 (1977): 74-81;

Kurt Vonnegut, Jr., "*Something Happened*," *New York Times Book Review*, 6 October 1974, pp. 1-2;

Joseph Weixlmann, "A Bibliography of Joseph Heller's *Catch-22*," *Bulletin of Bibliography and Magazine Notes*, 31 (January-March 1974);

Alden Whitman, "Something Always Happens On the Way To the Office: An Interview with Joseph Heller," in *Pages* (Detroit: Gale Research, 1976).

Manuscripts:

Brandeis University has notes, various manuscript drafts, the final manuscript, galley proofs, and reviews of *Catch-22*, as well as the manuscript of *We Bombed in New Haven*.

GEORGE V. HIGGINS' work has two notable features: its analysis of the motives underlying human character and behavior, and its reliance on dialogue for the revelation of plot, character, and theme. Higgins is well known as the author of novels about criminals; his first, *The Friends of Eddie Coyle* (1972), a best-seller, was followed by *The Digger's Game* (1973), and *Cogan's Trade* (1974). After these, however, he moved to other subjects: Washington politics, police work, and Boston lawyers. *Dreamland* (1977), his most recent book, is a major achievement. Higgins is a master at the portrayal of character, the creation of suspense, and the designing of tight, well-plotted episodes. In his latest books he has concerned himself with characters who find it necessary to abandon idealistic ambitions in favor of more pragmatic, attainable goals which will make their lives worthwhile.

Higgins was born in Brockton, Massachusetts, on 13 November 1939. He received an A.B. in English at Boston College in 1961 and an M.A. from Stanford University in 1965. In 1967 he earned a law degree from Boston College and was admitted to the Massachusetts bar. He worked as a reporter for the Providence, Rhode Island, *Journal* and *Evening Bulletin* in 1962-1963, and the Associated Press in 1963-1964. He cites his newspaper work and his experience in courtroom cross-examination as a major source of the dialogue in his novels. From 1969 to 1970 he worked in the Massachusetts Office of the Attorney General. He was Assistant U.S. Attorney for Massachusetts from 1970 to 1973, and Special Assistant to the U.S. Attorney in 1973-1974.

Carol Lee

Since 1973 he has been president of his own law firm, based in Boston, where he writes his novels. He identifies Ernest Hemingway, James Joyce, Charles Dickens, Henry James, and especially Joseph Conrad, Graham Greene, and John O'Hara as major influences on his writing.

The early novels work according to a common formula: characters and their occupations are introduced; several plot-lines gradually develop and intermesh. One character emerges as central, primarily due to the frequency of his appearance and his involvement in the plot. It is revealed fairly early that one or more characters have committed a "sin" which will cost their lives. The narrative then chronicles, in fast-paced fashion, events which move towards the denouement of murder. These novels function on the premise that every act has a complex chain of consequences involving many people. Sooner or later, someone must assume responsibility and be punished. Life thus becomes a web of causes and effects in which the individual is inextricably tangled.

In *The Friends of Eddie Coyle* (1972), an illegal arms supplier, Coyle, is suspected of tipping off police about a series of bank robberies and is marked for murder. Ironically, though he has not exposed the bank robbers, he has implicated a young hoodlum in another crime in hopes of reducing a prison sentence which he faces. The narrative consists almost entirely of dialogue; an external narrator appears briefly at points to set the scene or introduce characters. Higgins regards dialogue as the essential key to character: "Quotes make the story," he has written, "so you damned right well better learn to listen." Thirty short, episodic chapters each describe a single conversation or event, and Higgins allows the speech of his hoods to tell the story without much help from other sources. The narrative is rife with unfolding ironies. Coyle's bartender confidant turns out to be the hitman, while one of his gun buyers is revealed as the leader of the bank robbers. The novel at first can be confusing—characters and plot are not always decipherable, but things eventually clarify and the narrative focuses in on the fate of Coyle. As the title suggests, less attention is paid Coyle than his "friends," all of whom are involved in the chain of events leading to his murder.

Higgins' prose style is largely determined by his reliance on conversation and the individual perspectives of characters. His vocabulary is generally limited to words the characters themselves would use, and with minor exceptions his novels are singularly lacking in figurative or heavily imagistic language. The result is a concrete style, economical and to the point. Prose style may vary according to the personality, vocation, and intelligence of the major characters, but even in his latest novel Higgins uses concrete language, conversational diction, and a minimum of rhetoric.

The twenty chapters of *The Digger's Game* (1973) continue to rely on dialogue as a method of exposition. Digger, a bartender and thief, loses $18,000 in Las Vegas and finds himself in debt to the Greek, a loan shark. The story details how Digger pays off the debt, and how the Greek is marked for assassination because he ignores the code of the local mob. In this and the other crime novels there is no real difference between the criminal world and normal society. Money, family pressures, and the desire for a middle-class life-style motivate the behavior of the criminal as well as the average citizen. Digger's brother, for example, is a respected Catholic priest who loves expensive cars and is ambitious to become a bishop. Higgins is especially effective at evoking tension and suspense without melodrama. The terrifying description of the murder attempt on the Greek is a masterful manipulation of narrative viewpoint—the climactic moment of violent death towards which each of the crime novels moves.

Dark humor, a penetrating analysis of character, and a growing concern with the fate of the individual distinguish *Cogan's Trade* (1974). Its plot, less complex than in previous novels, describes the fortunes of Mark Trattman, a card game operator, and an inexperienced group of young thieves. It is soon established that Trattman and the youths must die; much of the novel is devoted to a highly ironic discussion of the moral and ethical necessity for their murders—for the "public good" of the criminal world. Trattman's fate is mirrored in Dillon's fatal heart disease, and the novel's theme is succinctly summarized by one of the hoods: "We're all gonna die." Cogan frequently talks with his driver about the people and events of the narrative. The device of two characters who debate and develop ideas is common in Higgins' fiction. *Cogan's Trade* expresses an especially dim view of human nature; the hitman's ruthlessness is contradicted by his concern for the sick Dillon; Steve and Barry Caprio affectionately discuss Trattman while they wait to viciously beat him up.

Although his first three books dealt exclusively with the underworld and won him a certain degree of acclaim, Higgins has not allowed himself to become stereotyped as a crime novelist. The next three books are transitional works in which dialogue and interest in character are applied to new subjects and themes. Chapters are longer and more complex, concerned with detailed descriptions of the life and personality of one individual. The two novels focus on a central character who faces an identity crisis, who has become aware of the eventuality of his own death and is critically dissatisfied with the kind of life he is leading. The reduced emphasis on plot is compensated by an increasingly profound concern with human character.

Begun in 1973 and completed in 1975, *The Friends of Richard Nixon* is historical journalism, not fiction, but it utilizes fictional techniques and could well be termed a novel of fact. The people and events of the 1973 Senate Watergate hearings are the basis for a general discussion of the political scandal. This carefully researched book does not claim impartiality. It is couched in the lively rhetoric of a crime novel and stylistically resembles the writing of the New Journalists. It describes the personalities, motives, and deeds of those involved in the Watergate affair and the mistakes they made while trying to cover it up. Capitalizing on the title of his first novel, Higgins focuses on all the individuals who contributed, wittingly or not, to Richard Nixon's resignation from the presidency.

The Watergate scandal is an underlying motif in Higgins' fourth novel, *A City on a Hill* (1975), which contrasts the realities of political ambition and corruption with the idealism inherent in the title—an allusion to a seventeenth-century sermon mentioned in a speech by John F. Kennedy promising honest government. Hank Cavanaugh, afraid that his life has stagnated, tries to decide whether to abandon the idealistic, often unrealistic philosophy of the prominent congressman he works for in favor of the more pragmatic, less ambitious program of a Massachusetts gubernatorial candidate. The novel is not wholly successful. Political issues and the dilemmas of Cavanaugh lack the vividness of the earlier novels. Cavanaugh's problem is unconvincing: he is fairly well assured of public success—and private satisfaction—regardless of his decision. The exchange of his artistic wife Louise for the superficial, lusty (but, underneath it all, intelligent and sensitive) Sarah does not effectively symbolize his rejection of idealism for the sake of self-fulfillment.

The Judgment of Deke Hunter (1976) continues the transition, and with more success. Again a character must restructure his attitudes towards his life. Deke Hunter, a state police corporal, is unable to accept his failure as a minor league baseball player. His life is a depressing monotony. His wife constantly nags him about money; he has an affair with a court reporter who has connections with the mob; he is afraid to take the qualifying examination for promotion to sergeant. Many of his problems become apparent while he is talking to Carmody, a desk sergeant, who gradually brings him to realize what he must do to give meaning to his life. Gone are the biting ironies of the crime novels, the sudden revelations, the tension and suspense; instead, the reader is submerged in the unbearable tedium of Hunter's existence. Although dialogue is still the main source of the narrative, the external narrator plays a more prominent role than before. A number of case histories throughout the book show how events in a character's past helped influence the kind of life he leads in the present. *The Judgment of Deke Hunter* is a strong indictment of the middle-class values which encourage ambitions beyond the capabilities of the average individual, who is thus condemned to a life of continual frustration unless he can adjust. There are some rough edges—at points characters talk at such length that the convention of conversation is nearly forgotten—but the novel's portrayal of the character of Deke Hunter is highly effective.

The problems of the transitional books are solved in *Dreamland* (1977), a major achievement which places Higgins in the first rank of contemporary American authors. The external narrator is replaced by a character-narrator, Compton Wills, a respected Boston lawyer whose reminiscent first-person narrative is balanced out by his dialogue with another character, Andrew Collier. The combination works extremely well. The novel deals with Compton's discovery that his father, Cable, whom he has always revered as a lawyer and a man of probity, was possibly a World War II American spy who lost his interest in his law firm as a result. Andrew, whom Compton begrudgingly accepts as his foster brother, may well be his half brother. Compton is another Higgins character forced to reevaluate the values and beliefs of his life. Idealism, inherent in the image of his father as the respected scion of an old Massachusetts family, is undermined by the likelihood that Cable Wills violated tradition and the values of his neighbors by leading the sordid life of an espionage agent and perhaps even taking a mistress. Cable remains a respectable character nevertheless, even a patriot and hero, but on terms which are strange to Compton and which he must come to grips with, even if he cannot, as the novel hints, live up to them.

Dreamland uses the techniques of detective fiction to unravel the complexities of human character. By piecing often disparate facts together, through speculation and theorizing, Compton and Andrew eventually determine the apparent facts of Cable's past. Family documents, the testimony of friends, circumstantial evidence, all are used in revealing the truth. When an apparently complete story has emerged, a surprise "mystery" witness appears who provides information which explains the riddles of Cable Wills' character. In the process of explaining the riddles, the novel reveals that Compton built his life around a false image of his father, that his feeling of superiority over Andrew has no basis. He eventually convinces himself that what he has learned is untrue, while Andrew accepts the new version of Cable Wills as the true one because of the heritage and significance it gives to his life. It is not clear at the end of the novel which version is real. Thus, *Dreamland* is a detective novel in the richest sense of the word. Higgins has developed the technique of narration through dialogue to an original and highly powerful form. In this latest novel he has proven himself capable of tackling the most complex themes and personalities, with profound results.

Higgins has so far received virtually no attention from academic critics, though his work has been widely reviewed. His reputation rests largely on his crime novels, which won him the admiration of Ross Macdonald and Norman Mailer. Because the Massachusetts legal profession lacks popular appeal—and Higgins makes no attempt to give it appeal by sensationalizing it—*Dreamland* will likely not receive the attention it deserves, though it is a greater achievement than the earlier novels— which are praiseworthy in their own right. His skill in characterization and realistic dialogue, his success at portraying individuals in a crisis of identity, his understanding of the influences which form human character, and his development of a unique, effective novelistic form appropriate to his talents—these characteristics, especially evident in his most recent novel, establish George V. Higgins as a writer of considerable stature. —*Hugh M. Ruppersburg*

Books:

The Friends of Eddie Coyle (New York: Knopf, 1972; London: Secker & Warburg, 1972);

The Digger's Game (New York: Knopf, 1973; London: Secker & Warburg, 1973);

Cogan's Trade (New York: Knopf, 1974; London: Secker & Warburg, 1974);

A City on a Hill (New York: Knopf, 1975; London: Secker & Warburg, 1975);

The Friends of Richard Nixon (Boston & Toronto: Atlantic/Little, Brown, 1975);

The Judgment of Deke Hunter (Boston & Toronto: Atlantic/Little, Brown, 1976; London: Secker & Warburg, 1976);

Dreamland (Boston & Toronto: Atlantic/Little, Brown, 1977; London: Secker & Warburg, 1977).

Periodical Publications:

"All Day Was All There Was," *Arizona Quarterly*, 19 (spring 1963): 23-36;

"Witness: Something of a Memoir," *Massachusetts Review*, 10 (summer 1969): 596-602;

"Mass in Time of War," *Cimarron Review*, no. 9 (September 1969): 73-81;

"Something Dirty You Could Keep," *Massachusetts Review*, 10 (fall 1969): 631-644;

"Dillon Explained that He Was Frightened," *North American Review*, 255 (fall 1970): 42-44;

"The Habits of the Animals: The Progress of the Seasons," *North American Review*, 256 (winter 1971): 56-58;

"The Private Eye as Illegal Hero: How Philip Marlowe got to be Dirty Harry," *Esquire*, 78 (December 1972): 348, 350-351;

"Two Cautionary Tales: 'Donnelly's Uncle' and 'The Original Water-course'," *North American Review*, 258 (fall 1973): 40-43;

"The Judge Who Tried Harder," *Atlantic Monthly*, 233 (April 1974): 83-106;

"The Friends of Richard Nixon," *Atlantic Monthly*, 234 (November 1974): 41-52;

"Two Donnelly Stories: 'Warm for September' and 'A Place of Comfort, Light and Hope'," *North American Review*, 262 (spring 1977): 31-37.

Other:

James Ross, *They Don't Dance Much*, afterword by Higgins (Carbondale & Edwardsville: Southern Illinois University Press, 1975).

CHESTER HIMES is one of the curiosities of American literature, a fiercely independent black writer whose many faults have alienated both white and black critics, save for a few who have insisted that he is as important as Richard Wright, Ralph Ellison and James Baldwin. Only now, as he approaches his seventieth birthday, has he received serious scholarly attention: two full-length studies have recently appeared, James Lundquist's monograph, *Chester Himes* (1976) and Stephen Milliken's more complete *Chester Himes: A Critical Appraisal* (1976).

From his first novel, *If He Hollers Let Him Go* (1945), to his latest, *Blind Man With a Pistol* (1969), Himes has stressed the damage done to the black psyche as much as the viciousness of white hatred for blacks. Drawing directly upon his own experiences, Himes has portrayed a series of wounded or emotionally crippled protagonists struggling to keep from lashing back violently against a hateful environment. Several of the central characters in his early novels are black males who commit murder and who are sexually and ambivalently obsessed with white women. Nearly all are defeated or victimized by a universe that is absurd, unpredictable, and irrational.

One can best understand Himes's fictional viewpoint by beginning with his two volumes of autobiography, *The Quality of Hurt* (1972) and *My*

Chester Himes.

Life of Absurdity (1977). Making no attempt to court favor, Himes recounts the hostile, loveless family atmosphere of his youth. His father, a blacksmithing teacher at small Southern colleges, battled continuously with Himes's light-skinned mother until at last they divorced. The only solace for Himes was his love for his brilliant brother, Joe, who was blinded at an early age in an accident for which Himes partly blamed himself. Himes was thrown out of Ohio State University for his part in a speakeasy brawl in 1927 and began working as a bellhop in Cleveland. The following year he was arrested for burglary and passing bad checks, but got off with probation. At nineteen, Himes committed an armed robbery and was sentenced to twenty years in prison; he was released in 1936 at the age of twenty-six. The following year he married Jean Johnson, his longtime sweetheart, but they were divorced fourteen years later.

The important benefit of prison was that he turned from crime to writing, and thereafter expressed his emotional needs primarily through fiction. At first he published several short stories in black newspapers and magazines, including *Crisis*. Several of his prison stories were published in *Esquire* magazine and for some years Himes continued to write short stories, mostly in the naturalistic tradition of social protest fiction. A Rosenwald Fellowship in 1944 and a fellowship to Yaddo, in Saratoga Springs, in 1948 were the major encouragements offered him.

Himes drifted from job to job until he worked in a defense plant in Los Angeles during World War II. He later said of that city: "Los Angeles hurt me racially as much as any city I have ever known—much more than any city I remember from the South. It was the lying hypocrisy that hurt me." Thus, Himes's first two novels, *If He Hollers Let Him Go* (1945) and *Lonely Crusade* (1947), both feature young, black, male heroes who struggle with racism in the defense plants of Los Angeles during World War II. Although the second of these novels is better written and more ambitious in scope, his first novel is more memorable. *If He Hollers Let Him Go* narrates the racial struggles of Bob Jones, who is tormented by a white worker with whom he has a fistfight, and by Madge, a blowsy, blonde Texan, whose needling antagonism has already cost Jones a demotion on the job. Of most importance is the ambivalent sexual relationship between Jones and Madge. The white woman seems hostile to Jones and pretends great sexual fear; in reality, she is drawn to him as he is to her, and she repeatedly invites his attention. In the critical scene, she attempts to seduce him at the plant, but when they are interrupted she cries "rape." Caught in the classic terror-trap of black males, Jones panics and flees but is quickly captured; a judge allows him to join the army, but Jones has obviously been defeated in the book's central encounter.

The organization of this novel lends its stereotyped situation unexpected power. Each night during the five days encompassed, Jones has violent nightmares in which he is trapped or endangered, so that the actual events are not merely foreshadowed, but given an internalized inevitability. The surrealistic quality of these nightmares underscores vividly that the doom which hangs over Jones is the product not only of his environment but of the tortured desires and twisted fears of his damaged psyche.

In *Lonely Crusade*, Lee Gordon is the only black organizer in a Los Angeles airplane factory. His marriage to Ruth is seriously threatened by his feelings of impotence because he cannot support her and she must work. Moreover, white workers do not accept him; his boss tries to buy him out with a high-paying job and later reneges; Communists try to entice him with a white girl friend; phony intellectuals betray him. Of special interest are the portraits drawn of two warped black men: Lester, a murderous psychotic whose psychiatrist supposedly has counseled him to marry a white woman to shed his racial insecurities; and Luther, a treacherous Marxist (he also has a white mistress) who cynically sells out the union, the Communist party, and Lee. This excessively-plotted novel eventually succumbs to Himes's tendency toward melodrama and overstatement, although the tortured protagonist is complex and potentially interesting.

The novels which follow extend Himes's range and show a developing sense of craft and style, but are of less interest today. In *Cast the First Stone* (1952), Himes draws upon his own prison experiences, but while the novel was in manuscript he changed the protagonist's skin color to white in order to avoid reducing James Monroe's mental makeup and experience to racial causes. This distancing technique allows Himes to concentrate objectively on his twin themes: the demoralizing effect of prison life and Monroe's battle to understand himself and life's purpose. The prison-inferno of dagger fights, suicide, boredom, homosexuality, and institutionalized cruelty is powerfully etched, while Himes's own indomitable spirit is projected into Monroe's determined effort to survive spiritually, not merely to serve his time.

At about this time, Himes moved permanently to France, yet his next novel, *The Third Generation* (1954), draws most heavily upon his personal experiences in the United States. The novel is also based in part on a narrative history of his family written by Himes's mother. The marriage of the Taylors disintegrates as the near-white wife, hating her negroid blood, drives her husband from his teaching jobs at one agricultural college after another. Again, despite talented writing, Himes packs in far too much, proving only that autobiography is not fiction, although Milliken considers this novel the best of Himes's autobiographical fiction. The last of these "confessional" novels is *The Primitive* (1956), which Himes finished in Paris and which he has called his favorite among his works. The story is modeled on his love affair with Vandi Haygood and ends with the writer-hero murdering his white mistress, Kriss. As in *If He Hollers Let Him Go*, Himes employs the technique of violent nightmares to foreshadow the inevitable outcome of this mixed relationship. *The Primitive*, however, also includes a chimpanzee on television who predicts the news, including Jesse's trial for murder. The novel is written with surprising gusto, considering the subject matter, and foreshadows the greater use of humor in subsequent novels, especially the buffoonery of *Pinktoes* (1961).

The publishing history of Himes's remaining fiction is confusing. For example, his next novel, *Une Affaire de Viol (A Case of Rape)*, was written in 1956-1957, first published in French in 1963, and has never appeared in English. It is a complicated story of Black expatriate life in the mid-1950s in which four black men are falsely convicted of the rape-murder of a white woman. The French critic, Michel Fabre, concluded:

> *A Case of Rape* . . . deserves more than the passing glance it is usually accorded; an often scathing evocation of the prejudices encountered by Black exiles in Paris, the moving evocation of an impossible love, it constitutes a meditation that leads Himes-the-humanist to another level of awareness in his lifelong fight against man's inhumanity to man.

In 1957, Himes turned out a potboiler detective novel at the request of Marcel Duhamel for his Serie Noire. The novel, originally entitled *La Reine des Pommes*, appeared as *For Love of Imabelle* in the United States in 1957 and was reissued in slightly altered form in 1965 as *A Rage in Harlem*. This work of fiction won the Grand Prix Policier in 1958, and Himes went on to write a total of ten novels in this genre. Although Himes achieved some prominence in America when *Cotton Comes to Harlem* was released in a film version in 1970, he was as unhappy in his dealings with the film colony (and with the film version) as he has been in his dealings with publishers, both in France and in the United States. In 1972, *The Heat's On* (1966) was made into the film released as *Come Back Charleston Blue*.

Himes has described the circumstances under which these detective novels were undertaken:

> When I was writing my first detective story I was desperate. I was living in a little crummy hotel in Paris which became a beatnik hotel. I sat there in my room and worked through Christmas Day, New Year's Day and New Year's night until four o'clock. I was drinking cheap red wine, two-three bottles a day, and when I could squeeze up enough money I would go out and buy a bottle of St. James wine—drink that too and still work.

Although Himes recalls bitterly that he wrote the early novels of the series in about a month's time for seven hundred to one thousand dollars each, they may prove the works for which he is best remembered. Himes drew upon his memories of Harlem, his bellhop days in Cleveland's sleazier hotels, and his prison acquaintances for models of the bizarre characters of these works; but he freed himself from his earlier weaknesses of either telling his own life story or writing tendentious protest fiction. Instead, most of these novels feature his black detectives, Coffin Ed Johnson and Gravedigger Jones, in a series of wild exploits that almost defy summary. By objectifying and externalizing his rage against racism, Himes seems paradoxically to have liberated his imagination and his exuberant sense of life.

In the first of the detective novels, *For Love of Imabelle* (1957), Jackson, twenty-eight, who works at a funeral parlor, is in love with the unreliable Imabelle. She arranges with her friends to draw Jackson into investing his money in a machine which will change ten dollar bills to hundred dollar bills. While the money is being baked in a stove, the police burst in, the stove explodes, and everybody escapes but Jackson. He bribes the "police" to release him and is thus twice burned. Since he is forced to embezzle the bribery money, he gambles to recoup and is again bankrupted. He turns to his crooked brother Goldy for help, but Goldy (who sells tickets to heaven to gullible Harlemites) discovers that Imabelle's gang is working a lost-mine swindle, peddling shares to Eldorado. The swindlers show false gold nuggets to potential investors, but Goldy decides they have real gold hidden in a trunk. The two brothers (Goldy dressed as a black nun) search for the gang; another pair, the detectives Coffin Ed and Gravedigger, set off after the brothers and the gang. While Jackson swipes a hearse-with-corpse from his boss, Imabelle's cohorts slit Goldy's throat and then hide him in the hearse with the mysterious trunk of "gold." A wild car chase follows, in which Jackson loses trunk, corpses, and hearse; Coffin Ed is blinded by acid; Gravedigger captures the gang in an elaborate whorehouse after a shoot-out; Imabelle and Jackson are reunited, and Jackson gets his job back, since the various killings have increased business. As the French critic Rene Micha commented: "In general, the story line is so dense, the sub-plots so numerous, the purple patches so extended, that the plot soon disappears."

The density of detail in these novels may be suggested by a typical example drawn from *The Heat's On*:

> Colored people were cooking in their overcrowded, overpriced tenements; cooking in the streets, in the afterhours joints; in the brothels; seasoned with vice, disease and crime.
>
> An effluvium of hot stinks arose from the frying pan and hung in the hot motionless air, no higher than the rooftops—the smell of

sizzling barbecue, fried hair, exhaust fumes, rotting garbage, cheap perfumes, unwashed bodies, decayed buildings, dog-rat-and-cat offal, whiskey and vomit, and all the old dried-up odors of poverty.

Although there are many details of the sights and sounds of Harlem, these works are symbolic fantasies, surrealist allegories of lives in chaos. Desperate nonsense abounds as unnamed bit players cope with overwhelming circumstance. An addict squeezes a live rabbit and a glassine bag of heroin drops from its anus; on a bet, a 125-pound man wrestles with a 250-pound woman, both dressed in greased rubber suits; an old thief blows himself up along with a goat and nobody can sort out the respective meat. There is an enormous gallery of pretenders and misfits: a giant albino Negro paints himself purple; a dwarf dope pusher swallows the evidence but vomits his incriminating guilt; a tongueless thief scribbles crazy messages; the three black widows (a trio of male transvestites) prowl for victims, each with "her" separate racket. In this milieu, Coffin Ed and Gravedigger dispense their rough, unorthodox justice, often protecting Harlemites against white police. But anarchy prevails, even when order is allowed to pretend; here are myths of terrifying quests with no grail to seek. In this world of cuttings and contests, of meaningless violence and crafty signifying, it is appropriate that the detectives don't always get much done and that things go right on anyway, for these are comic dramas of proletarian endurance.

The novels in this genre are really allegories of Harlem itself, where, as Himes frequently reminds us, "anything can happen." Himes's main point is to turn the detective novel upside down, for the genre's conventions do not fit in a world where the conventions and mores are different. What are innocence and guilt, he asks, when life is lived on the margin and mere survival is triumph? In these novels, Coffin Ed and Gravedigger Jones employ torture, blackmail, illegal entry, and other criminal devices. Conversely, the real criminals in *For Love of Imabelle* and *All Shot Up* (1960) disguise themselves as police. Himes thus illustrates the thesis behind all of his work, that blacks dwell in an absurdist world where white-designed categories do not apply. The same theme, that the black man is the American writ large, and that our American absurdities surround him in exaggerated, remorseless form, underpins the work of Richard Wright, Ralph Ellison, and John A. Williams. The most violent and least humorous in the series is *Blind Man With A Pistol* (1969), where

the chaos and terror render the black detectives totally ineffectual.

The fiction of Chester Himes has moved boldly from naturalistic social protest to the more experimental autobiographical novel and finally to his manipulations of the conventions of the detective novel. Different as these genres may be, there is great continuity in his work: throughout his career, this abrasive, angry man has told his gritty truths honestly and has written unevenly with power and eloquence of the wrenching effects of being black in America. Part of the power of the novels in the closing period of his career lies in their deceptive simplicity, the lack of self-conscious attempts at "significance," and the innumerable examples of black tenacity in a mocking environment.

—*Frank Campenni*

Books:

If He Hollers Let Him Go (Garden City: Doubleday, Doran, 1945; London: Falcon Press, 1947);

Lonely Crusade (New York: Knopf, 1947; London: Grey Walls Press, 1950);

Cast The First Stone (New York: Coward-McCann, 1952);

The Third Generation (Cleveland: World, 1954);

The Primitive (New York: New American Library, 1956);

For Love of Imabelle (New York: Fawcett, 1957; republished as *A Rage in Harlem*, New York: Avon, 1965);

The Crazy Kill (New York: Berkley, 1959; London: Panther, 1968);

The Real Cool Killers (New York: Berkley, 1959; London: Panther, 1969);

All Shot Up (New York: Berkley, 1960; London: Panther, 1969);

The Big Gold Dream (New York: Avon, 1960; London: Panther, 1968);

Pinktoes (Paris: Olympia, 1961; New York: Putnam's/Stein & Day, 1965);

Cotton Comes to Harlem (New York: Putnam's, 1965; London: Muller, 1966);

The Heat's On (New York: Putnam's, 1966; London: Muller, 1966);

Run Man Run (New York: Putnam's, 1966; London: Muller, 1967);

Blind Man With a Pistol (New York: Morrow, 1969; London: Hodder & Stoughton, 1969; republished as *Hot Day, Hot Night*, New York: Dell, 1970);

The Quality of Hurt: The Autobiography of Chester Himes, volume 1, (Garden City: Doubleday,

1972; London: Joseph, 1973);

Black on Black: Baby Sister and Selected Writings (Garden City: Doubleday, 1973; London: Joseph, 1975;

My Life of Absurdity, The Autobiography of Chester Himes, volume 2 (Garden City: Doubleday, 1977).

References:

James Lundquist, *Chester Himes* (New York: Ungar, 1976);

Edward Margolies, *Native Sons* (Philadelphia and New York: Lippincott, 1968);

Margolies, "Experiences of the Black Expatriate Writer: Chester Himes," *College Language Association Journal*, 15 (1972): 421-427;

Stephen Milliken, *Chester Himes: A Critical Appraisal* (Columbus: University of Missouri Press, 1976);

Raymond Nelson, "Domestic Harlem: The Detective Fiction of Chester Himes," *Virginia Quarterly Review*, 48 (1972): 260-276;

Ishmael Reed, "The Author and His Works, Chester Himes: Writer," *Black World*, March 1972, pp. 24-38;

John A. Williams, "My Man Himes: An Interview with Chester Himes," *Amistad I* (New York: Knopf, 1970), pp. 25-95.

Manuscripts:

Yale University has a major collection of literary manuscripts and letters by Himes.

JAMES JONES was born in Robinson, Illinois, on 6 November 1921, the son of a dentist, Ramon Jones, and Ada Blessing Jones. His midwestern roots are particularly evident in his second novel, *Some Came Running*, although many of his insights into the culture of mid-America come from a later period of his life after World War II when he settled in Marshall, Illinois, and spent six years writing *From Here to Eternity* under the aegis of Mrs. Lowney Handy and her husband Harry. Jones completed his high school education in Illinois and later took some college courses at the University of Hawaii (1942) and at New York University (1945). Jones boxed as a welterweight both in the Golden Gloves and in the army, and he reveals his intimate knowledge of the sport in the fight scenes in *From Here to Eternity*. The most pervasive experience for his literary career was his hitch in the army from 1939 to 1945, during which Jones received the Bronze Star and a Purple Heart. This period in his life served as background for three of his best novels, *From Here to Eternity*, *The Thin Red Line*, and *The Pistol*. Jones married Gloria Mosolino in 1957 and they have two children, Kaylie and Jamie. The following year the Jones's moved to Paris where they remained until 1974. Jones's novel about the Paris riots of 1968, *The Merry Month of May*, was particularly praised for its knowledgeable descriptions of the city and its ambience. Of his long stay in France, Jones has said that he never felt like an expatriate, but just an American living in Paris. He and his family returned to the United States in 1974 when he was offered a teaching position at Florida International University in Miami. At the end of the 1976 school year, the Jones's moved to Southampton, Long Island, where he died on 9 May 1977.

Like Norman Mailer, Jones began his career with a spectacularly successful novel about World War II, but unlike Mailer, nothing he produced after *From Here to Eternity* was again to put him in the forefront of American letters. *From Here to Eternity* (1951) appeared with a glowing preview from Scribners which called its appearance "of comparable importance to the publication of *This Side of Paradise* or *Look Homeward, Angel*." The fact that Jones was discovered and nurtured by the great editor Maxwell Perkins (who died before the publication of the novel) did not hurt the implied similarity to Thomas Wolfe.

Charles Rolo, making the inevitable comparison in the *Atlantic*, called *From Here to Eternity* a better novel than *The Naked and the Dead* because it made its point without obviously spelling out a thesis. Rolo said "no novelist has documented army life so thoroughly or recorded the crudities of soldier talk so faithfully," but he also saw Jones as one of "those emotionally retarded he-men to whom toughness is the supreme Good, and who see life as synonymous with total war."

From Here to Eternity, which won the National Book Award in 1951, records army life in Schofield Barracks in Hawaii and ends with the attack on Pearl Harbor. The novel focuses on Private Robert E. Lee Prewitt, a man of significant talents and an idealist who will not succumb to the army system. Prewitt is a boxer, but he will not box for Captain Dynamite Holmes's "G" Company because he once blinded a man boxing and has vowed to his dying mother that he will not hurt anyone intentionally. Prewitt,

Jill Krementz

James Jones.

however, is not simply coerced by the system, he is a man who lives for confrontation. He has deliberately transferred to "G" Company with the knowledge that there will be pressure for him to box. Prewitt's transfer from the Bugle Corps was also occasioned by pride, when he felt he was displaced as the number one bugler in the corps.

The story is also that of Sergeant Milton Warden, a basically fair man who is ordered to give Prewitt "the Treatment" because of his refusal to box. Warden is torn between his duty to the system and his growing personal feeling for Prewitt. The parallel of the two men, including their love affairs, Prewitt's with a prostitute and Warden's with the captain's wife, never quite comes off, although their individual stories are brilliantly told. Both women, the prostitute Lorene (nee Alma Schmidt), who

wants to buy her way into social acceptability and Karen Holmes, the captain's wife, eventually reject love for respectability, a pattern that will be followed by many of the women in Jones's novels. As is often the case in Jones's work, the characters' names reveal a good deal about them. Alma (Latin, "fostering, nurturing") is the refuge for Prewitt that allows him to withstand "the Treatment." Prewitt, named for the Confederate general, is the idealistic hero in a losing cause, and Warden is a keeper torn between the system he serves and the men who make it up.

From Here to Eternity is an army novel, but not really a war novel, since World War II begins only as the novel ends. Nevertheless, violence is at a fever pitch from first to last. From Bloom's suicide to Fatso Judson's brutal beating of "Blues" Berry to Prewitt's murder of Judson to Prewitt's death at the hands of the military police, everything is a brutal test of manhood, yet each act is misguided. In Bloom's reaction to his own suicide the thoughts of a millisecond fill a page as he realizes the pointlessness of his one irrevocable act: "Then, as his head continued on up through the ceiling, he knew it wasn't any good. He had always wanted to commit an irrevocable act, and he had finally done it, only to find it was the wrong one. He knew a great many things that he wished he had time to say. He could explain so much. There were so many steaks to be eaten, so many whores to be laid, so much beer to be drunk. . . . What a silly thing to do, he thought." Prewitt's killing of Judson is vengeance for Fatso's sadistic attack on Berry and for the more drawn out torment of Angelo Maggio in the stockade, but Fatso never recognizes his killer's motives or the meaning of his deed. Finally Prewitt's own death occurs when he is returning from being absent without leave and is not punished for the killing of Judson. It is the ironic devaluing of such deeds of manhood which allows Jones to cultivate the endless pursuit of masculinity without falling into the trap of lauding pointless violence. Only in *The Thin Red Line* was Jones to approach this kind of control again.

After the success of *From Here to Eternity*, Jones returned to Marshall, Illinois, where Mrs. Handy had established a writers' colony in which Jones was now the star pupil and resident "priest" to a group of aspiring writers who followed the same regimen which Mrs. Handy believed had produced *From Here to Eternity*. The setting was almost monastic in its rigid discipline and consisted primarily of copying verbatim long passages from writers like Hemingway, Wolfe, Marquand, Dos Passos, and Stendhal. This was combined with Spartan eating habits and manual labor, little intellectual interchange and strict isolation. David Ray, who lived for a while in Marshall as a disciple, reports that Jones no longer followed the regimen, but spent much of his time driving about in his new sports car and eating steak with Mrs. Handy while he worked on his second novel, *Some Came Running* (1958).

The novel, a work of prodigious length (some 900 pages), was greeted with almost unanimous condemnation by the critics, who were particularly offended by Jones's disregard of syntax, his gratuitous adverbiage to describe almost every speech and action in the book, and particularly the amateur philosophizing that fills so many of the pages. *Some Came Running* recounts the return of Dave Hirsch, a war hero and ex-novelist, to his home of Parkham, Illinois, where he begins work on a war novel. The parallels between Hirsch's career and Jones's experiences with Mrs. Handy during the writing of *From Here to Eternity* are many. In the novel, Mrs. Handy is represented by Gwen French, who becomes Dave's literary mentor. Gwen speaks much of Mrs. Handy's philosophy, particularly the idea that obsession with sex is fatal to a writer's career. During the course of the novel, the young men under her tutelage all fall prey to women, and their writing careers collapse. Gwen's role is an inversion of Lorene's, the "Virgin Princess of Hawaii," the whore who longs for respectability in *From Here to Eternity*. Dave is led to believe that Gwen's frigidity is the result of her being a nymphomaniac in the past, while in fact she is a middle-aged virgin. In his frustration and as a gesture toward freedom from Gwen, Dave turns to and eventually marries Ginnie Moorhead, the town slut, who works in the brassiere factory. Ultimately, Ginnie's first husband kills Dave. It is typical of the heavy-handed irony of the novel that the virgin is named Guinevere for the ultimate heroine of romantic love, and the slut's name reminds one of the Virgin.

Throughout the novel, Dave's search for real values is contrasted with the moral emptiness of his brother Frank, a successful merchant and latter-day Babbitt, whose false values are exposed when he becomes a voyeur peeping at his own ex-mistresses. Indeed, secondhand sex, including Gwen's father's secret pornography collection and her own vicarious living through the novelists she inspires, becomes a metaphor for the inability of human beings to become truly involved in life. Jones's portrayal of all this hollowness is part of an attempt to prove that the mid-America of Sinclair Lewis and Sherwood Anderson is as decadent as Gibbons's Rome well into its decline. There are endless allusions to ancient Rome as Jones reminds his reader of the classical antecedents of American decadence. Unfortunately, Jones has not borrowed Gibbons's classically-honed style or his moral outrage in this overwritten version of the decline and fall of America.

The novel is not without its virtues, particularly the portrait of Dave's patron, 'Bama Dillert, a gambler whose dealings with Dave have many of the fine nuances of the Warden-Prewitt relationship of *From Here to Eternity*. On the whole, however, Jones seems to be trying too hard to be the great American sage, and wisdom does not come to his pen as readily as character or action.

In 1958, Jones went with his new wife, Gloria, to Paris on what was intended to be a short visit, but they bought a fine old house and spent the next sixteen years living in Paris while they refurbished and expanded their house, which became a center of the artistic community of the city. Soon after their arrival in Paris, a daughter, Kaylie, was born and they later adopted a son, Jamie, who is almost the same age as their daughter.

Jones followed the immensity of *Some Came Running* with a novella, *The Pistol* (1958), in which he returned to the familiar setting of Pearl Harbor. Before the Japanese invasion, Private First Class Richard Mast is issued a pistol for special duty, and in the ensuing confusion he is able to keep the sidearm, a sign of privilege for an infantryman. Mast begins to see the pistol as a symbol of his salvation and its ownership becomes an obsession with him, particularly after he has a dream in which a Japanese major cuts him in two when he loses the pistol. Critics have seen in the dream a fear of castration, particularly with a hero named Dick Mast, although Jones denies that such was ever his intention: "I had no ulterior motive for picking Richard Mast either, except that I wanted a hard Anglo-Saxon name and I once knew a guy in the service named Mast. So wouldn't you know it? Reviewers wrote that Richard Mast was my symbolism for an erection." Jones does not overdo the phallicism of *The Pistol*, but in view of the overt concern with penises in *Go to the Widow-Maker*, the critics do not seem too far off the mark.

Jones returned to the full scope of World War II in his next novel, *The Thin Red Line* (1962), the importance of which he revealed in the introduction to a fragment of the unfinished novel, *Whistle*. Sometime midway through the writing of *From Here to Eternity*, Jones projected a trilogy which would take his characters from the peacetime army on Hawaii through the war in Guadalcanal and New Georgia and finally "to the return of the wounded to the United States." Once he decided that Prewitt would have to be killed off in *From Here to Eternity*, Jones changed the names of his heroes, so that First Sergeant Warden becomes First Sergeant Welsh, Private Prewitt becomes Private Witt and Mess Sergeant Stark becomes Mess Sergeant Storm in *The Thin Red Line*. Jones made similar name changes in *Whistle*. He hoped his trilogy "will say just about everything I have ever had to say, or will ever have to say on the human condition of war and what it means to us, as against what we claim it means to us."

This distinction between reality and the claim of the ideal is evident in *The Thin Red Line* which sets out to debunk the glory of war. "C-for-Charley" company is involved in a mopping-up campaign in Guadalcanal, and their fighting has no place either in the grand design of the war or in the stuff of heroism. Of the some ninety characters named in the novel almost all have monosyllabic names: the roster reveals Privates "Catch, Catt, Coombs, Crown, Darl, Drake, Gluk, Gooch, Griggs." The men, though different from each other, are as plain as the dirt they march through. Only their military objectives, the things the folks back home read about in the papers, have romantic names such as the Dancing Elephant, the Sea Slug, and the Giant Boiled Shrimp. In keeping with this attempt to demythologize warfare, there are no outstanding heroes, but rather the reader's attention is spread through almost the whole company. Jones said of his technique that *The Thin Red Line* has a "fly's eye viewpoint. A fly eye is composed of 100 little cylinders and the whole viewpoint is similar, so that in the same line or paragraph the view point will change from man to man." Nonetheless, some of the characters do emerge from the novel to catch the reader's attention. Witt, the reincarnation of Prewitt, is still from Kentucky and is still coming back from being AWOL, this time across the entire island to join the company that he loves with almost doglike loyalty. Welsh is just as competent as Warden, but he has become manic and his efficiency is largely fueled by alcohol. The most interesting character, however, is not a holdover from *From Here to Eternity* but Private Don Doll, who rises to the rank of sergeant in the course of the campaign. As Peter G. Jones notes, Doll understands "that each man lives a kind of fiction about himself." Doll learns to see through the fictions of others and to use his own fictions to overcome his own weaknesses, particularly fear.

What was noted about the novel beyond its characterizations of men at war, was the absolute fidelity to the nature of war itself. Norman Mailer in *Cannibals and Christians* called it "so broad and true a portrait of combat that it could be used as a textbook at the Infantry School." Jones knew the struggles of Guadalcanal firsthand, having been wounded by shrapnel there.

Jones's next novel, *Go to the Widow-Maker* (1967) is about masculinity. Ron Grant, the most spectacularly successful playwright in the western world with the possible exception of Tennessee Williams, goes to the Caribbean to prove his manhood by skin diving and shark hunting. After hundreds of pages of sex and undersea adventure, he comes to the conclusion that each man needs to prove himself because of feelings of inadequacy acquired in boyhood upon seeing his father's penis: "Bravery. That proves they're men. So they make up games. The harder the game, the braver the man.

Politics, war, football, polo, explorers. Skin-diving. Shark-diving. All to be men. All to grow up to Daddy's great cock they remember but can never match." This sort of amateur Freudianism is grafted onto a Hemingwayesque dream of the Big Fish to produce an overblown adventure of men against the sea. (The sea is the "Widow-maker" in Kipling's "Harp Song of the Dane Women" and the men in the novel have an almost sexual preoccupation with holding their breath as long as they can in this great feminine element.)

The most comforting change in Jones's outlook is the total rejection of the possessive older woman, the Lowney Handy figure, who is represented here by Carol Abernathy, the woman who supports Ron in his down-and-out years before his success. No longer does Ron (and one must suspect, Jones) accept the notion that she was responsible for his success or that she gave up a really promising career of her own to foster his. After rejecting Carol, Grant takes up with the beautiful sexual adventuress Lucky Videndi, who claims to have slept with 400 men. Not surprisingly, Ron Grant has the exact weight, height, and build of James Jones and Lucky (Lucia) has the physical characteristics and Italian origins of Mrs. Jones. In the dedication, Jones claims that because of his marriage, he has for the first time tried to write a great love story. Unfortunately, the love affair of Ron and Lucky, if this is the one he has in mind, does not impress the reader, not even in its moments of "electrical-skin contact." Grant marries Lucky, but like most of Jones's women, she begins to restrict his freedom, particularly his masculine relationships, which she sees as "half-fag." And well she might. The real love stories in this novel are the father-son relationship of Hunt Abernathy (a Harry Handy figure) and Grant, and Grant's hero-worship of his diving instructor, Al Bonham: "Then there was Bonham's reality. Bonham leaped at a blood challenge. It was as simple as that. And thought no more about it. Grant's hero-worship for the big diver went up another notch. His love for Bonham had been increasing ponderously in three days' diving, Bonham's careful care of him, his accurate and thoughtful teaching, his so obviously sly mentorhood, who wouldn't fall in love with all of that." There is nothing about Lucky Videndi, despite her Hollywood starlet's body, that attracts Grant like this.

The problem with Grant and with Lucky is that they never convince the reader that they are what Jones claims them to be. Grant never utters a word that would convince anyone that he is an outstanding playwright and Lucky is distressingly prudish for a woman who has had 400 men. The marriage goes downhill after Lucky finds out about Ron's affair with Carol Abernathy, and her jealousy extends to Bonham and the rest of the skin diving crowd. Her vacillations on whether to have an affair with another of Grant's well-beloved buddies, Jim Grointon (sic), sounds more like something out of Richardson's *Clarissa* than the thoughts of a sexually liberated woman. Eventually Grant yields to his wife when he comes to the conclusion that his search for virility is really a childish shirking of adult responsibility.

As usual, Jones comes off badly as a philosopher and as a reporter of heterosexual love, but his descriptions of undersea adventure, shark hunting, the capture of a manta ray, and particularly the freeing of two bodies from a sunken automobile are powerfully done, as is his depiction of the spirit of camaraderie among the men in the novel.

The James Jones figure shifts from hero to narrator in *The Merry Month of May* (1971), a novel set against the 1968 student riots in Paris. *Jonathan James* Hartley is an unsuccessful writer who tries to impose his decency upon the household of Harry Gallagher, a blacklisted expatriate American who has become a success writing screenplays for European directors. Hartley says of himself, "I have always been a low-keyed man sexually; female bodies interest me less than female minds, so to speak." The novel itself is more interested in female bodies, particularly as they are engaged in lesbianism, masturbation, and triangular sex (the supreme fantasy of Harry Gallagher is making love to two women who are making love to each other).

Harry's son, Hill, becomes involved in the riots, but can never maintain his independence because his radical spirit is undermined by the sympathies of his liberal father. Hill is part of a student committee that is filming the riots for the propaganda value. Harry offers the committee his professional know-how and in a hokey son-father confrontation, Hill accuses Harry of co-opting the movement by turning the riot into a work of art, a filmed love story no less. The secondhand involvement in life that was so much a part of *Some Came Running* is extended here. Not only does Harry have a pornography collection, like Gwen French's father in *Some Came Running*, but he can only perceive the revolution in terms of camera angles, good shots, and proper lighting. The fact that Jones uses a first-person narrator who reports much of the action, particularly the sex scenes, secondhand, adds to the voyeuristic tone of the novel.

Somewhere there is supposed to be a connection between the struggle in the streets and the conflict in the Gallagher household, but the parallel remains obscure while Jones focuses on the turmoil caused in the Gallagher menage by the appearance of Samantha Everton, a young black lesbian who manages to seduce father Harry, son Hill, and finally wife Louisa, even though Paris is only a stopover on her way to Israel where her Sahbra girl friend is waiting. Only Hartley, brain-man that he is, proves impervious to her charms.

Hartley's ability to resist temptation (there is ample evidence that he is heterosexual) also proves to have tragic consequences when Louisa Gallagher calls him and asks to be seduced. She is apparently trying to prove her femininity after her affair with Samantha, but Hartley, as Harry's loyal buddy, turns her down. Louisa then attempts suicide with sleeping pills and alcohol. The attempt fails, but her brain is damaged, and she survives only as a vegetable. Harry is completely untouched by his wife's condition and rushes off to the promised land where Samantha has gone to find her Sahbra. Mercifully, the reader is spared all the details of this black, white, Irish, Jewish, homo-hetero-sexual melange-a-trois, beyond Harry's telegram from Tel Aviv, "FOUND HER."

Jones interrupted the completion of *Whistle*, the last part of his war trilogy, in order to turn a screenplay he was working on into a full-scale detective novel. *A Touch of Danger* (1973) follows the fifty-year-old private eye Lobo Davies as he tracks down some embezzled funds on a Greek island (not unlike some property Jones owned at the time). The novel, a well-done example of its genre, is interesting because it reflects Jones's own trauma of turning fifty and notable because it extends the cynical view of youthful revolutionaries in *The Merry Month of May* into a full-scale put-down of the hippies who inhabit the island. The decadent upper-class society also comes in for some of Jones's satire and reviewers seemed hopeful that the character of Lobo Davies would reappear in later novels.

In addition to his novels, Jones has published a collection of short fiction, *The Ice Cream Headache and Other Stories* (1968), which includes fiction written from 1947 to 1968. As Jones himself said, a number of the pieces had been rejected by magazines until he had made a name for himself. The best of the stories are sensitive evocations of adolescence, such as "The Valentine and a Bottle of Cream."

The mid-1970s saw Jones complete two book-length pieces of war reporting, *Viet Journal* and *WWII*. *Viet Journal* (1974) records his month-long trip to Vietnam in 1973 after the American Military Assistance Command had officially pulled out. Although more carelessly written than his war fiction because it is primarily a diary of the month's events, *Viet Journal* vividly portrays the struggle for survival among both civilians and soldiers in a country which had supposedly been brought under cease-fire. Unlike most other reporting of the Vietnam conflict, Jones does not take an ideological stand on the American involvement. He says he was "cynical about both sides," but he does give a positive account of the conduct of American military officers. In *WWII* (1975), Jones wrote the text to accompany 160 sketches and paintings of the war. The focus is on the grim details of war, particularly the emotions of individual infantrymen. Jones's prose, which is much better than in *Viet Journal*, is reflected in the gritty realism of the illustrations. Of war, Jones has said, "It is quite a romantic subject, provided it was not staring you in the face."

In a sense, it was inevitable that *Whistle* (1978), Jones's last novel, would be published posthumously. Although Willie Morris, who edited the nearly finished manuscript, reports that Jones, before his death, was working feverishly on *Whistle*, the book was begun in 1968 and had been "almost finished" for a long time. Jones let other projects, like *Viet Journal* and *WWII*, interrupt the last part of his trilogy because, just as the characters in this novel cannot exist without the army, so Jones could not bring himself to leave their story.

Whistle tells the story of Mart Winch (Milt Warden in *From Here to Eternity*) and three of his men (their names and personalities changed somewhat from both *From Here to Eternity* and *The Thin Red Line*), who have returned wounded to the United States only to find that neither their country nor their army has a real place for them any longer. The country, one feels, they could do without, but the army *is* home and family. One by one, each has his function as a soldier taken away from him, and the result is total collapse. Winch, who is facing death by congestive heart failure (the same disease that Jones knew was killing him) lives only to protect the lives of the three other men: "Somewhere down in the deepest part of his mind, in some place he wished neither to investigate nor explore, but consciously knew was there, was a strong feeling, a superstition, that if he could bring Strange and Prell and Landers through, without them dying or going crazy, and make them come out the other side intact, he himself might come through." Add Winch himself to the list and Jones's task is the same as his protagonist's: he

1/

Chapter 1

The word that they were coming reached us a month
before they arrived. Scattered all across the country in
the different hospitals as we were, it was amazing how fast
word of any change got back to us, and passed back and
forth among us. Sometimes it was by postcard, sometimes by
letter, ~~sometimes even a wire--if the news was important
enough.~~ After being back a while, we each of us acquired ~~this~~ a
picture of a strange sort of gossamer network, an
invisible spiderweb flung all across the nation tying us
together.

This time there were only four of them. Four of
them together, all in the same batch. But what an important
four they were. Winch; John Strange; Landers; and Bobby
Prell. Four of the most important men we had. Of course
we did not know then, when ~~the~~ this first news of them arrived,
that all four of them would be coming back to the exact
same place, i.e., to us in (Memphis.)

Usually it was those of us in the ~~Memphis~~ KARNAK hospital
who heard all the news the soonest. Probably that was
because we in ~~Memphis~~ KARNAK were one of the largest individual
groups. At one point there were nearly 20 of us there.

Better to fictionalize? Look up Egyptian town
of Karnak -- and impose on river btwn St. Louis
and Memphis. Will give freer play.

From typescript of Whistle.

has carried these characters for thirty years and some 1700 pages and he cannot let go of them.

It is for this reason perhaps that Jones is brilliant when he writes in retrospect of how, for example, each of the men got wounded, and is nearly as good when he writes of their present struggles against the machinations of the stateside army. The novel is weakest when his characters venture beyond the fringes of the army base into the permanent civilian world which is already looking beyond the war. Sergeant Strange's attempt at reconciliation with his now self-sufficient wife is no more than a pale echo of a similar scene in *The Best Years of Our Lives*, and Jones hardly bothers with the obligatory scenes in which Winch checks on his wife or Landers goes home to his family. On the other hand, when Winch manipulates the egos of the army brass in order to prevent the amputation of Prell's leg, Jones masterfully combines his intimate knowledge of army logic with the emotions of men in love, yet at odds, with each other.

Jones plots beautifully the tragic situation of Winch, who must save not merely the lives, but also the psyches of the other three men, yet for various reasons cannot reveal how much he is doing for them. He forces Prell, for example, to hate him because he knows that only a worthy antagonist will stir up the last reserves of energy that Prell needs to fight to save his legs. Prell fights successfully against the figment of Winch's enmity only to lose to a more insidious enemy. Jones had given Prell (as Witt) an uncanny sense of purpose in *The Thin Red Line*, but in *Whistle* when Prell wins the Congressional Medal of Honor, he becomes a kind of pin-up boy for war bond rallies, and by the end of the novel he realizes how cardboard he has become.

Similarly, Landers, the cynical company clerk, finally finds a purpose for his life when he straightens out the paperwork of an apparently hopeless company for a well-intentioned lieutenant, only to have his cause eliminated when the lieutenant is replaced because of anti-Semitic prejudice. Jones is never more at home with his subject than when he describes both the mountain of nitpicking detail and the intense energy with which Landers attacks it. When the lieutenant is replaced, Landers first goes AWOL, then, after his return, gets into a fight and strikes an officer. Winch saves Landers from a court-martial by wangling him a medical discharge, but when Landers passes the gate that separates him from the army, he deliberately steps in front of a car. After hearing of Landers's death, Prell recognizes the same emptiness in his life, goes out looking for fights in low-class bars, and

ends up getting killed in one. With the deaths of Landers and Prell, Winch's purpose in life disappears and he suffers a crack-up. The book ends with the last of the four, Strange, slipping overboard to drown in the sea.

When he breaks his own heart by deliberately antagonizing Prell, Winch says, "What Prell needed was enemies. An enemy, if he was going to fight. He wasn't complex enough to fight without an enemy there in front of him." Winch and the men of his company have run out of enemies; there are no more Fatso Judsons or Dynamite Holmeses as in *From Here to Eternity*, nor Japs as in *The Thin Red Line*; instead the men face "friends" who want to promote them, to help them, to muster them out of the army, who are always interested in changing what they are and converting them somehow into less than men. Like all of Jones's best characters, the four need something to fight against; when they are co-opted they are dead.

A proper evaluation of Jones's place among the current generation of novelists must await a more reflective judgment of *Whistle*. If the book's virtues—the incisive analysis of men removed from the only occupation they know, the powerful portrait of their attempt to give meaning to this emptiness, and the understanding of the way men fight for and love each other by indirection—all withstand further scrutiny, then Jones has written a novel as good as *The Thin Red Line* and his project of thirty years has been completed successfully. With a *Whistle* of the same calibre as the other novels, Jones has produced an immense, vital trilogy on men at war which should earn him the place he has always wanted—to be the Thomas Wolfe of his generation. Successful completion of the project would then solidify the importance of *The Thin Red Line* as the middle part of the trilogy, the actual fighting for which the peacetime army prepared and upon which the returning wounded reflect. As such it would also raise *Some Came Running* to the status of an important failure, an attempt to write a major novel which was later written. If on the other hand, the weaknesses—the inability to make any concerns but military ones vital to the readers or the characters, the inability to portray heterosexual love (though not sex), and the curious obsession with oral sex (like similar obsessions with triangular sex in *The Merry Month of May* or penis envy in *Go to the Widow-Maker*)—become more apparent on reflection and bring *Whistle* down to the level of *Go to the Widow-Maker* or *The Merry Month of May*, then Jones will be remembered as the author of a great war novel—the man whom strangers would greet, as late as 1974, with the unintentional faint praise, "I've read your book." —*Jeffrey Helterman*

Books:

From Here to Eternity (New York: Scribners, 1951; London: Collins, 1952);

Some Came Running (New York: Scribners, 1958; London: Collins, 1959);

The Pistol (New York: Scribners, 1958; London: Collins, 1959);

The Thin Red Line (New York: Scribners, 1962; London: Collins, 1963);

Go to the Widow-Maker (New York: Delacorte, 1967; London: Collins, 1967);

The Ice-Cream Headache and Other Stories (New York: Delacorte, 1968; London: Collins, 1968);

The Merry Month of May (New York: Delacorte, 1971; London: Collins, 1971);

A Touch of Danger (Garden City: Doubleday, 1973; London: Collins, 1973);

Whistle: A Work-in-Progress (Bloomfield Hills, Mich.: Bruccoli Clark, 1974);

Viet Journal (New York: Delacorte, 1974);

WWII (New York: Grosset & Dunlap, 1975);

Whistle (New York: Delacorte, 1978).

References:

Richard P. Adams, "A Second Look at *From Here to Eternity*," *College English*, 17 (January 1956): 205-210;

John W. Aldridge, *The Devil in the Fire* (New York: Harper's Magazine Press, 1972), pp. 241-248;

Chester Eisinger, "Soul-searching Under the Sea," *Saturday Review*, 50 (15 April 1967): 35;

Louis Falstein, "This is the Army," *New Republic*, 124 (5 March 1951): 20-21;

Maxwell Geismar, *American Moderns* (New York: Hill & Wang, 1958), pp. 225-238;

Charles Glicksberg, "Racial Attitudes in *From Here to Eternity*," *Phylon*, 14, 4 (1953): 384-389;

Ben Griffith, Jr., "Rear Rank Robin Hood: James Jones's Folk Hero," *Georgia Review*, 10 (spring 1956): 41-46;

Granville Hicks, "The Shorter and Better Jones," *Saturday Review*, 42 (10 January 1959): 12;

John Hopkins, *James Jones: A Checklist* (Detroit: Bruccoli Clark/Gale, 1974);

Ernest Jones, "Minority Report," *Nation*, 172 (17 March 1951): 254-255;

Peter G. Jones, *War and the Novelist* (Columbia: University of Missouri Press, 1976);

Alfred Kazin, *Bright Book of Life* (Boston: Atlantic/ Little, Brown, 1973), pp. 77-81;

John Lardner, "Anatomy of the Regular Army," *New Yorker*, 27 (10 March 1951): 117;

Michael S. Lasky, "James Jones has Come Home to Whistle," *Writer's Digest*, 56 (October 1976): 22-26, 56;

Norman Mailer, *Cannibals and Christians* (New York: Dial, 1966);

Hugh Moffett, "Aging Heavy of the Paris Expatriates," *Life*, 63 (4 August 1967): 30-32;

David Ray, "A Novel for Teacher," *Nation*, 186 (8 February 1958): 123-124;

Ray, "Mrs. Handy's Writing Mill," *London Magazine*, 5, 7 (July 1958): 35-41;

Wilfrid Sheed, "The Jones Boy Forever," *Atlantic*, 219 (June 1967): 68-72;

Allen Shepherd, " 'A Deliberately Symbolic Little Novella': James Jones's *The Pistol*," *South Dakota Review*, 10, 1 (1972): 111-129;

William J. Smith, "The Innocence and Sincerity of a Regular Guy," *Commonweal*, 62 (7 February 1958): 491;

David L. Stevenson, "James Jones and Jack Kerouac: Novelists of Disjunction," in *The Creative Present*, eds. Nona Balakian and Charles Simmons, (Garden City: Doubleday, 1963), pp. 195-212;

Harvey Swados, "Through a Glass Sourly-Darkly," *New Republic*, 138 (27 January 1958): 16-17;

Milton Viorst, "James Jones and the Phoney Intellectuals," *Esquire*, 69 (February 1968): 98-101, 131-132.

Manuscripts:

Yale University has a major collection of Jones's literary manuscripts.

ERICA JONG, American poet and novelist, was born in 1942 in New York City where she grew up on the Upper West Side. Like the protagonist of her novels, Isadora Wing, she attended the High School of Music and Art, Barnard College, and the Writing Division of the School of the Arts at Columbia University, and married and divorced a psychiatrist husband of Chinese descent. She taught English at the City College of New York before traveling in Germany, and lived in Heidelberg where she taught at the University of Maryland's Overseas Division. Her first book of poems, *Fruits & Vegetables*, was published in 1971, and two years later she won the

Erica Jong.

Alice Faye di Castagnola Award of the Poetry Society of America as well as a writing fellowship from the Creative Artists Program Service for her second book of poetry, *Half-Lives*. Poems in this collection were also awarded the Bess Hokin Prize given by *Poetry* magazine. In the spring of 1973, she received a fellowship from the National Endowment for the Arts, and in the fall of that year her controversial first novel, *Fear of Flying*, was published. Her third poetry collection, *Loveroot*, was published in 1975, and her most recent work, *How to Save Your Own Life*, appeared in 1977.

Jong's most successful subject is the predicament of the female poet in America, and her most persistent method is the redefinition of female stereotypes through the inversion of time-honored myths of human sexuality. Her blunt descriptions of sexual encounters, often phrased in the most blatantly prurient language, have alternately drawn praise and criticism from feminists and moralists. Jong's attitude toward human sexuality is, however, less clear-cut than that of many of her critics. Her most erotic scenes are parodies of contemporary pornography, her liberated woman, openly thwarted and unfulfilled.

Jong's first novel, *Fear of Flying*, revolves around themes of feminism and guilt, creativity and sex. In it Isadora Zelda White Stoller Wing,

twice-married Barnard graduate in search of an identity, leaves her husband at a Vienna psychiatrists' convention to seek the perfect sexual encounter. This ideal of sexuality in which zippers fall away "like rose petals" and underwear blows off in one breath "like dandelion fluff," an experience free of the guilt and remorse created by ties of affection and intimacy is, as Isadora soon finds, a delightful fraud. Leaving her husband, she takes up with the "beautiful," but half-impotent, Adrian Goodlove, who hypocritically exhorts Isadora to cast off her marital ties while secretly maintaining his own. After traveling with this new lover through various Continental roadside encampments for two weeks, Isadora finds his promised "liberation" to be simply a new style of confinement.

No "shy, shrinking schizoid," Isadora Wing is a streamlined, modernized version of that classically brittle literary recluse, the female poet. As poet, Isadora not only directly encounters those themes of childbirth, sexual drive, and biological need carefully sidestepped by more traditional women poets, but, as woman, she delights in all of the taboos of womanhood, masturbating, and copulating with an abandon that has alarmed rigorous moralists. Jong describes the traditional "curse" of menstruation in terms of purgation and cycles of rebirth, attacks the tendency of women to seek definition in terms of male-female relationships, conceives of penis envy in terms of misunderstood womb envy, depicts her female heroine as naturally polygamous, and pictures at least one "helpless, hopeless male" coyly staving off his lover's lust-filled advances with a feigned headache. Yet, the author is clearly aware that the freedom her heroine seeks is not to be found in the simple exchange of male and female roles. For all her sexual calisthenics, Isadora's long-sought freedom is a sham. Unveiling her passions, she is dominated by them, and torn between her erotic sensuality and her distaste for traditional female roles, she is doomed to the unfulfilled love affairs and self-defined voids that she most fears. Within the gently mocking humor of the novel, Isadora's quest for self is at once heroic and pathetic, for in seeking to redefine classical male-oriented concepts of women, she becomes more deeply identified with them. She becomes, in Jonathan Rabon's terms, "a monster . . . botheringly close to the insatiably willing dream-girl of male fantasies and male fiction."

Her second novel, *How to Save Your Own Life*, is a sequel to *Fear of Flying*, taking up Isadora's narrative three years later as she leaves her husband. The novel describes Isadora's disillusionment with

Jill Krementz

Erica Jong.

her marriage, her travels in Hollywood, a series of random heterosexual, lesbian, and group liaisons, and concludes with her discovery of love for a younger man. "I wanted to establish," Jong noted in a *Publishers Weekly* interview, "that such a woman could move on into a *good* relationship with men, that it was not impossible for her." The unfulfillment and cynicism of *Fear of Flying*, ironically, culminates in this second novel in the words of a slender Viennese doctor: "Love is everything it's cracked up to be." Isadora spends most of *How to Save Your Own Life* trying to establish those very relationships with other human beings which she had attempted to avoid in *Fear of Flying*. After a series of obstacles are overcome, she heads for Kennedy Airport, ready to fly to the West Coast and meet the man she has chosen to love. She waves good-bye to the giant balloons of Macy's Thanksgiving Day Parade, straining to pull free on helium wings. Their freedom, like her own, is ultimately an illusion. However, it may appear "to credulous little children," she comments, "the balloons don't really fly at all. In an hour or two, they will be tethered to tiny people in clown suits, and will be dragged along the avenues of New York like captured beasts of the wild, like Gullivers through a Lilliput of skyscrapers." The metaphor is a powerful one, for Isadora in attempting to soar free of human relationships only anchors herself more securely to the ground, tethered to the illusions and people who possess her. It is only through the commitment of love that she can soar free.

Many of the themes and characters of Jong's novels are foreshadowed in her poetry. Her first book, *Fruits & Vegetables*, published in 1971, is a collection of frankly sensual poems about love, feminist issues, and the workings of a woman's mind, dominated by seriocomic visions of the coupling of fruit and flesh. Poems in this series, such as "With Silk," "The Man Under the Bed," "The Heidelberg Landlady," and "Flying You Home," are early silhouettes of the motifs and characters in the novels. Her second book of poems, *Half-Lives*, is dominated by images of hunger, which are clearly muted in her third poetry collection, *Loveroot*. The defensive poetic stance adopted by Isadora Wing throughout the novels, her insistence that her sexual experiments are merely an author's search for raw data, is most clearly exposed in the poem "From the Country of Regrets." Hovering over the ocean in a doomed airplane, the poet seeks to escape personal crisis by creating a fictional objectivity. "I am the one," she counters, "with the open notebook, the one who lost her pornographic postcards, the one with thousands of mosquito bites behind each knee. Nothing bad can happen to me. I am only collecting material. I am making notes: on hell, on heaven."

—*Carol Johnston*

Books:

Fruits & Vegetables (New York: Holt, Rinehart & Winston, 1971; London: Secker & Warburg, 1973);

Half-Lives (New York: Holt, Rinehart & Winston, 1973; London: Secker & Warburg, 1974);

Fear of Flying (New York: Holt, Rinehart & Winston, 1973; London: Secker & Warburg, 1974);

Here Comes and Other Poems (New York: New American Library, 1975);

Loveroot (New York: Holt, Rinehart & Winston, 1975; London: Secker & Warburg, 1977);

How to Save Your Own Life (New York: Holt, Rinehart & Winston, 1977; London: Secker & Warburg, 1977).

References:

Josephine Hendin, "The Comestible Muse," *Nation*, 212 (28 June 1971): 828;

Ellen Hope Meyer, "The Aesthetics of 'Dear Diary'," *Nation*, 218 (12 January 1974): 55-56;

Jonathan Rabon, "Lullabies for a Sleeping Giant," *Encounter*, 43 (July 1974): 76;

Paul Theroux, "Hapless Organ," *New Statesman*, 87 (19 April 1974): 554;

John Updike, "Jong Love," *New Yorker*, 49 (17 December 1973): 149-153;

Helen Vendler, "Do women have distinctive subjects, roles and styles?" *New York Times Book Review*, 12 August 1973, pp. 6-7.

JACK KEROUAC, regarded in modern American fiction as the authentic voice of the "beat generation," thought of himself as a storyteller in the innovative literary tradition of Proust and Joyce, creating an original style that he envisioned as "the prose of the future." He wrote with the same theme of idealism as Emerson, Thoreau, Melville, and Whitman, reasserting the American dream of romantic individualism in each of his eighteen

Jack Kerouac in 1952.

published books, which he regarded as one vast autobiographical statement.

Kerouac (Jean Louis Lebris De Kerouac) was born to French-Canadian parents in Lowell, Massachusetts on 12 March 1922. He attended local Catholic grammar schools and graduated from Lowell High School with an athletic scholarship to Columbia University (he starred in football and track) after a year at Horace Mann School in New York. During his sophomore year at Columbia, he left to join the U.S. Merchant Marine and Navy during World War II. He began a novel and continued writing after his return to New York City, where he was close friends with Allen Ginsberg and William Burroughs, Jr. His first published novel, *The Town & The City* (1950) was begun after his father's death in 1946. Kerouac later dismissed it as a fiction based on the model of Thomas Wolfe, written before he had found his own voice.

In April 1951, when he spent three weeks writing an autobiographical narrative on a 120-foot roll of teletype paper that was to be published nearly seven years later as *On the Road*, Kerouac found his style. He called it "spontaneous prose," and during the period between 1951 and 1956 he wrote several books which were considered too stylistically innovative to find publishers. During the long, disheartening wait before *On the Road* was accepted by Viking Press, Kerouac worked a series of jobs as a railroad brakeman and fire lookout, traveling between the East and West Coasts, saving his money so he could live with his mother while he wrote what he conceived of as his life's work, "The Legend of Duluoz."

"The Legend of Duluoz," or "The Legend of Kerouac" (Duluoz was Kerouac's fictional name for himself in three of the novels), is a fictionalized autobiography, one of the most ambitious projects conceived by any modern American writer in its scope, depth, and variety. Kerouac intended in his old age to gather his books together in a uniform binding and insert the real names of his contemporaries into the narratives so that his larger design might be more apparent.

"The Legend of Duluoz" begins with the novel *Visions of Gerard*, which describes the first years of Kerouac's childhood and the death of his brother Gerard in 1926, when Jack was four years old. *Doctor Sax* is a fantasy of memories and dreams about his boyhood (1930-1936) in Lowell with an imaginary companion, Doctor Sax, like the pulp magazine hero The Shadow, the champion of Good in a mythic battle against the forces of Evil. *Maggie Cassidy* is a more realistic novel about his adolescence in high school and his first love (1938-1939). *Vanity of Duluoz* describes his years playing football at prep school and Columbia, and his experience in the merchant marine and navy during World War II. It was during these years (1939-1946) that Kerouac met Allen Ginsberg and William Burroughs, Jr., named "Irwin Garden" and "Will Hubbard" in the novel.

On the Road begins with Kerouac's meeting the legendary Neal Cassady, called "Dean Moriarty" in the narrative, who took Kerouac ("Sal Paradise") on the road between 1947 and 1950, hitchhiking and riding buses and cars across the United States on a search for joyful adventure. In this book Ginsberg is "Carlo Marx" and Burroughs is "Old Bull Lee." Neal Cassady was a strong personal and literary influence on Kerouac, and in *Visions of Cody* Kerouac attempted an "in-depth" description of this same period of his life with Cassady ("Cody Pomeray" here).

The Subterraneans continues the autobiography as an intense account of Kerouac's affair with a black girl in the summer of 1953; in this book he is "Leo Percepied," Ginsberg is "Adam Moorad," Burroughs is "Frank Carmody," and Gregory Corso is "Yuri Gligoric." In *Tristessa*, Kerouac describes a love affair in Mexico City during 1955 and 1956, the same time period as *The Dharma Bums*. In *The Dharma Bums* Kerouac ("Ray Smith") adventures in California with Cassady ("Cody Pomeray") and

Ginsberg ("Alvah Goldbook") and the West Coast poets Philip Whalen ("Warren Coughlin"), Michael McClure ("Ike O'Shay"), and Gary Snyder ("Japhy Ryder"), who taught Kerouac how to climb mountains, camp out with sleeping bags, and live as a Buddhist during the first year of the "Poetry Renaissance" in San Francisco.

Desolation Angels picks up the narrative in 1956, and continues until the fall, 1957, with the publication of *On the Road*, the best-selling novel that made Kerouac famous as the spokesman of the "beats." *Big Sur* and *Satori in Paris* are the last books in the narrative of "The Legend of Duluoz," chronicling 1960-1965 and Kerouac's final years of alcoholism and anger at the media's distortion of his work and refusal to regard him as a serious writer.

The larger design of Kerouac's "Legend of Duluoz" has been overshadowed by the popularity of three novels, *On the Road* (1957), *The Dharma Bums* (1958), and *The Subterraneans* (1958), that have been continuously in print since their first publication twenty years ago. In these novels Kerouac offered what a *Village Voice* reviewer saw as "a rallying point for the elusive spirit of the rebellion of these times." *On the Road* and *The Dharma Bums* are narrated in a direct prose style, telling the story of a search for a way of life in America that would fulfill an ideal of romantic individualism. In both novels Kerouac encounters "heroes" who appear to offer him alternatives to what he sees as the conformity of adult life in America after World War II.

In *On the Road* the hero is "Dean Moriarty" (actually Neal Cassady), a "young jailkid shrouded in mystery" whose energy and enthusiasm are so compelling that Kerouac follows him on a search for adventure, "because the only people for me are the mad ones, the ones who are mad to live, mad to talk, mad to be saved, desirous of everything at the same time. . . ." Dean Moriarty offers a life on the road as an alternative to settling down. As he explains, "You spend a whole life of non-interference with the wishes of others . . . and nobody bothers you and you cut along and make it your own way. . . . What's your road, man?—holyboy road, madman road, rainbow road, guppy road, any road. It's an anywhere road for anybody anyhow. Where body how?" Moriarty was "Beat—the root, the soul of Beatific," and he seemed to possess the secret of life, knowledge of the way to open the doors of experience to reveal the full richness and infinite possibilities of time itself.

Kerouac's portrait of Dean Moriarty was so compelling that most readers overlooked the conclusion of the novel, when the uncertainties and hardships of his way of life have overbalanced what

ON THE ROAD is about Sal Paradise, Dean Moriarty, and their friends -- one moment savagely irresponsible and the next touchingly responsive and gentle. The narrative of life among these wild bohemians carries us back and forth across the continent and down to New Orleans and Mexico. The characters buy cars and wreck them, steal cars and leave them standing in fields, undertake to drive cars from one city to another, sharing the gas; then for variety they go hitch-hiking or sometimes ride a bus. In cities they go on wild parties or sit in joints listening to hot trumpets. They seem a little like machines themselves -- machines gone haywire, always wound to the last pitch, always nervously moving, drinking, making love, determined to say Yes to any new experience. The writing at its best is deeply felt, poetic and extremely moving. Again at its best this book is a celebration of the American scene in the manner of a latter-day Wolfe or Sandburg. The story itself has a steady, fast, unflagging movement that carries the reader along with it, always into new towns and madder adventures.

Jack Kerouac's first novel, The Town and the City, was greeted with high praise by the critics. Three short sections from ON THE ROAD which appeared in The Paris Review, New World Writing, and New Directions attracted considerable attention and introduced the work of this author to many new readers. Through these selections and through numerous comments in magazines and newspapers, ON THE ROAD has achieved a certain pre-publication fame even as a manuscript. The appearance of the complete work in book form is a publishing event of no small interest.

This is a copy of the first edition of

ON THE ROAD

by

Jack Kerouac

It will be published in September 1957 by The Viking Press and is certain to cause violently conflicting reactions among readers and critics. We believe that readers will find truth in the book; to some this truth may be beautiful, to others it may be ugly, but no one can fail to be impressed by what this book says and the way it says it.

After World War I a certain group of restless, searching Americans came to be called "The Lost Generation." This group found its truest voice in the writings of the young Hemingway. For a good many of the same reasons after World War II another group, roaming America in a wild, desperate search for identity and purpose, became known as "The Beat Generation." Jack Kerouac is the voice of this group and this is his novel.

Review copy dust jacket for On the Road.

he seemed to be offering Kerouac, who says goodbye to his friend at the end, a sad character in a ragged, moth-eaten overcoat. The vitality of Kerouac's descriptions of their trips together through America and Mexico, and the rushing optimism of their search for identity and fulfillment, are given depth by Kerouac's poignant sense of their shared mortality. *On the Road* is an American classic.

In *The Dharma Bums* the hero is "Japhy Ryder" (actually Gary Snyder), a young poet and student of Zen Buddhism whom Kerouac meets in Berkeley, "a great new hero of American culture." The description of the banality and repression of middle-class life is more specific in this novel, and the alternative is a way of life later to be defined as a "counterculture" to the American mainstream. It is basically Dean Moriarty's life of "non-interference" presented in *The Dharma Bums* in terms of Oriental philosophy (dharma means truth) and the ecology movement. Japhy Ryder gives a political context to Kerouac's disaffiliation with his idea of a great "rucksack revolution" in American society, prophesying the hippies of the following decade.

Although the social context of Kerouac's rebellion is more clearly drawn in this novel, *The Dharma Bums* is not so substantial as *On the Road*. There is one memorable mountain-climbing episode, but there are dull scenes and mechanical passages. Kerouac later said that he wrote the book

less on the strength of a genuine creative impulse than as an attempt to have another commercial success after *On the Road*. Its ending, when Kerouac professed to feel "really free" living alone in the mountains, is contrived. In *Desolation Angels*, which closely followed the journals he kept at the time, he gave a much fuller account of his disillusionment with the experience. Kerouac was unable to live with Neal Cassady, and he also couldn't accept Gary Snyder's life-style for very long.

The third of Kerouac's most popular novels, *The Subterraneans*, is a confessional narrative, the story of his love affair with a black girl. It was written in "three full moon nights of October" on benzedrine in one of Kerouac's most astonishing creative bursts. He later said "the book is modelled after Dostoevsky's *Notes from Underground*, a full confession of one's most wretched and hidden agonies after an affair of any kind. The prose is what I believe to be the prose of the future, from both the conscious top and the unconscious bottom of the mind, limited only by the limitations of time flying by as our mind flies by with it."

The Subterraneans was closest in its narrative and its sexual detail to a Henry Miller novel, and later Miller wrote an introduction to the book saying that Kerouac's prose was as striking as his confession. There is no search for an alternative life-style in this novel. Here Kerouac confronted himself directly, and in his honesty describing his failure to love the black girl "Mardou" he created one of his most dramatic illustrations of the basic theme in his work, his belief that "All life is suffering."

The explicit sexual description of *The Subterraneans*, the social anarchy suggested by the "rucksack revolution" in *The Dharma Bums*, the use of drugs and the hedonistic "joyriding" in *On the Road* angered many reviewers in the repressive McCarthy era twenty years ago, and Kerouac's books had a stormy critical reception. *On the Road* was so distinctive that it brought him immediate acclaim from Gilbert Millstein in the *New York Times* in September 1957, who wrote that Kerouac had produced "some of the most original work being done in this country," and that the novel marked, "an historic occasion . . . the exposure of an authentic work of art."

But the controversy started immediately; the *Saturday Review* called the novel "a dizzy travelogue," and newspapers across America cried out against the "uncouth" characters, the "frantic fringe" that Kerouac celebrated in "the romantic novel's last whimper." The problem was that *On the Road* heralded a change of consciousness in American life. As Herbert Hill later wrote in *Anger and Beyond* (1966), the Beats succeeded in demonstrating in their life and work "that it was not necessary to sign up in the Establishment . . . that it was not necessary to buy all the cant that passed for serious thinking, the slop that passed for culture, the garbage that passed for statesmanship, and that even in the absence of radical political currents, it was possible to swim against the stream . . . and somehow to survive." In the uproar that followed *On the Road, The Dharma Bums*, and *The Subterraneans*, the originality of Kerouac's achievement as a writer was overlooked.

Even today, despite younger critics like John Tytell and Tony Tanner, who understand Kerouac's impact on American writing, the academic community continues to disregard him. There is finally an acceptance of the historical reality of the influence of the "beat generation" in American life; as Jess Ritter said in *The Vonnegut Statement*, "The great psychic migration of American youth since World War II can be charted by the novels they read and the novelists whose reputations they created. . . . Kerouac and the Beats represent the psychic revolt of the 1950's." However, the trend now is to give the credit to Allen Ginsberg or William Burroughs for originating the beat movement. In *Waiting for the End* Leslie Fiedler states that Ginsberg, "invented the legend of Jack Kerouac . . . into a fantasy figure

capable of moving the imagination of rebellious kids with educations and literary aspirations. . . . The legend of Kerouac is, to be sure, much more interesting than any of his books, since it is the work of a more talented writer."

The fact is that both Ginsberg and Burroughs recognized Kerouac's originality and his contribution to their own work years before they became successful writers. It was Kerouac who titled both of their major works, *Howl* and *Naked Lunch*, and he also typed Burroughs' scraps of narrative and hallucination into the manuscript of *Naked Lunch*. Two years before *On the Road* was published, Ginsberg called Kerouac a "great prose Melville Jack," and in *Howl* Ginsberg's dedication to Kerouac credited him with "creating a spontaneous bop prosody and original classic literature. Several phrases and the title of *Howl* are taken from him."

Burroughs has said that when he first met Kerouac in 1944, Jack was "completely dedicated" to being a writer: "It was Kerouac who kept telling me I should write and call the book I wrote *Naked Lunch*. I had never written anything since high school and did not think of myself as a writer and I told him so." It was Herbert Huncke, a friend of Kerouac, Burroughs, and Ginsberg, who introduced them to the word "beat," as Kerouac described in his first novel *The Town & The City* on page 402. Kerouac himself coined the term "beat generation" in 1952, when John Clellon Holmes asked him to characterize the attitude of the young hipsters on Times Square. In 1959 the American College Dictionary published Kerouac's definition of the term: "*Beat Generation*—members of the generation that came of age after World War II who espouse mystical detachment and relaxation of social and sexual tensions, supposedly as a result of disillusionment stemming from the cold war."

The technical aspect of Kerouac's writing that influenced both Ginsberg and Burroughs was what Kerouac called "sketching," an unedited and unrevised spontaneity. After finishing *The Subterraneans* in 1953, Kerouac wrote down his major aesthetic statement for Ginsberg and Burroughs, who had asked him to describe the "Essentials of Spontaneous Prose." In nine paragraphs—Set-Up, Procedure, Method, Scoping, Lag in Procedure, Timing, Center of Interest, Structure of Work, Mental State—Kerouac outlined the process of free association within which he worked. "Blow as deep as you want, write as deeply, fish as far down as you want, satisfy yourself first, then reader cannot fail to receive telepathic shock and meaning-excitement by same laws operating in his own human mind."

Kerouac compared himself to a jazz musician improvising on a musical theme: "sketching language is undisturbed flow from the mind of personal secret idea-words, blowing (as per jazz musician) on subject of image." There was to be no revision, except obvious rational mistakes such as names. "Never afterthink to improve or defray impressions . . . tap from yourself the song of yourself, *blow!—now!—your* way is your only way—good—bad—always honest. . . ." The sketch "October in the Railroad Earth," a description of his work for the railroads in San Francisco later included in *Lonesome Traveler*, is perhaps Kerouac's finest achievement with his technique of spontaneous prose.

Between 1959 and 1963, following the commercial success of *On the Road, The Dharma Bums*, and *The Subterraneans*, many of the books Kerouac had written between 1951 and 1957 were published (others still exist in manuscript): *Doctor Sax, Maggie Cassidy, Mexico City Blues* (a book of poetry where Kerouac considered himself "blowing a long blues in an afternoon jam session"), *Visions of Cody, Visions of Gerard, Book of Dreams* ("They were all written spontaneously, nonstop, just like dreams happen . . . and they continue the same story which is the one story that I always write about. The heroes of *On the Road* and *The Subterraneans* reappear here. . ."). Despite the fact that these titles included some of his strongest and most original spontaneous extended narrative, especially *Doctor Sax* and *Visions of Gerard*, the critics paid less and less attention to him as a serious writer in the furor over the emergence of the beat generation.

Kerouac had shrugged off reviewers in *Time* magazine who called him a "cut-rate Thomas Wolfe" when he made the best-seller list, but he was disheartened when *Doctor Sax* was panned as a "largely psychopathic . . . pretentious and unreadable farrago of childhood fantasy-play." Kerouac had hoped that *Mexico City Blues* would establish him as a serious poet, but Kenneth Rexroth began his review in the *New York Times* by stating, "The naive effrontery of this book is more pitiful than ridiculous." John Ciardi took him apart in the *Saturday Review*; Robert Brustein went after him in "The Cult of Unthink" in *Horizon*; John Updike parodied his style in a short story for the *New Yorker*. Most memorably, Truman Capote attacked the idea of spontaneous prose on David Susskind's television program in September 1959 by saying that what Kerouac did wasn't writing: "it's typing."

Kerouac didn't have Allen Ginsberg's skill in dealing with the mass media, but throughout the 1960s he continued to work on the "Legend of Duluoz," publishing *Big Sur, Desolation Angels, Satori in Paris* and *Vanity of Duluoz*. In 1966 he married Stella Sampas, a childhood friend from Lowell, who helped him take care of his invalid mother. In the years before Kerouac's death on 21 October 1969 in St. Petersburg, Florida, he was, as his wife said, "a very lonely man," disassociating himself from his former friends, as well as the "beatniks" and "hippies" who claimed descendancy from his books. He was politically very conservative, a patriotic American who felt that the country had given a good life to his French-Canadian ancestors, and he was unable to understand why the vision of America he had described so movingly in his books had appealed to the counterculture of the 1960s.

Probably no famous American writer has been so mishandled by the critics, who with few exceptions ignored the larger design in Kerouac's books, the integrity of his theme of individualism, his romantic optimism and his reverence for life, as well as the remarkable energy and humor of his novels, the originality of his prose method and the religious context of all of his writing. He was constantly attacked for being the spokesman for the beat movement, and only a few people listened when he protested, "I'm king of the beats, but I'm not a beatnik."

Allen Ginsberg tried to help by insisting that Kerouac was a creative writer in his review of *The Dharma Bums* for the *Village Voice* in 1958, and the following year Warren Tallman was receptive to "Kerouac's Sound" in his article for *Evergreen Review*. Although sympathetic, Tallman also understood the limitations of Kerouac's approach to writing, which was "Kerouac's almost animal suspicion of the meaning values toward which words tend. When his fictions converge toward meanings something vital in him flinches back. His sound is primarily a life sound, sensitive to the indwelling qualities of things, the life they bear. To be Beat is to be wary of moving such a sound into the meaning clutter. It might become lost, the life. So Kerouac draws back. Which is his limitation."

Since Kerouac's death in 1969 there has been a little more sympathy for his work from the critics and his influence has been noted on such writers as Ken Kesey and Richard Brautigan. He is still widely read by young readers, and *On the Road* was reissued in 1972 by Penguin Books as a "Penguin Modern Classic." What has been increasingly clear in the last twenty years is that the fabric of American culture has never been the same since "Sal Paradise" and "Dean Moriarty" went on the road. As Burroughs

said, "Kerouac opened a million coffee bars and sold a trillion Levis to both sexes. . . . Woodstock rises from his pages." The "psychic revolt of the 1950's" represented a resurgence of the dominant thread of individualism that has been present in varying hues in our history since its beginnings. Jack Kerouac was as much an American idealist as Thoreau. What he said he wanted was the same hut as Thoreau's, but in his hometown of Lowell, Massachusetts, not at Walden Pond. Something of a martyr—like Thoreau—in his own time, Jack Kerouac was a necessary hero who chronicled in his "Legend" the rewards and hazards of romantic optimism in mid-twentieth-century America. —*Ann Charters*

Books:

The Town & the City (New York: Harcourt, Brace, 1950; London: Eyre & Spottiswoode, 1951);

On The Road (New York: Viking, 1957; London: Deutsch, 1958);

The Subterraneans (New York: Grove, 1958; London: Deutsch, 1960);

The Dharma Bums (New York: Viking, 1958; London: Deutsch, 1959);

Doctor Sax: Faust Part Three (New York: Grove, 1959; London: Evergreen, 1961);

Maggie Cassidy (New York: Avon, 1959; London: Panther, 1960);

Mexico City Blues (New York: Grove, 1959);

Excerpts From Visions of Cody (New York: New Directions, 1960);

The Scripture of the Golden Eternity (New York: Totem Press in association with Corinth Books, 1960; London: Centaur, 1960);

Tristessa (New York: Avon, 1960; London: World, 1963);

Lonesome Traveler (New York: McGraw-Hill, 1960; London: Deutsch, 1962);

Rimbaud (San Francisco: City Lights Books, 1960);

Book of Dreams (San Francisco: City Lights Books, 1961);

Pull My Daisy (New York: Grove, 1961; London: Evergreen, 1961);

Big Sur (New York: Farrar, Straus & Cudahy, 1962; London: Deutsch, 1963);

Visions of Gerard (New York: Farrar, Straus, 1963; published as *Visions of Gerard & Tristessa*, London: Deutsch, 1964);

Desolation Angels (New York: Coward-McCann, 1965; London: Deutsch, 1966);

Satori in Paris (New York: Grove, 1966; London: Deutsch, 1967);

A Bibliography of Works by Jack Kerouac (New York: Phoenix Book Shop, 1967);

Vanity of Duluoz: An Adventurous Education 1935-46 (New York: Coward-McCann, 1968; London: Deutsch, 1969);

Scattered Poems (San Francisco: City Lights Books, 1971);

Pic (New York: Grove, 1971);

Visions of Cody (New York: McGraw-Hill, 1972; London: Deutsch, 1973);

Trip Trap Haiku along the Road from San Francisco to New York 1959, with Albert Saijo and Lew Welch (Bolinas: Grey Fox Press, 1973).

Periodical Publication:

"The Art of Fiction XLI," *Paris Review*, 43 (summer 1968).

References:

Ann Charters, *A Bibliography of Works by Jack Kerouac 1939-1975* (New York: Phoenix Book Shop, 1975);

Charters, *Kerouac, A Biography* (San Francisco: Straight Arrow, 1973);

Bruce Cook, *The Beat Generation* (New York: Scribners, 1971);

Frederick Feied, *No Pie in the Sky, The Hobo as American Cultural Hero in the Works of Jack*

London, John Dos Passos and Jack Kerouac (New York: Citadel Press, 1964);

Leslie A. Fiedler, *Waiting for the End* (New York: Stein & Day, 1964);

Robert A. Hipkiss, *Jack Kerouac, Prophet of the New Romanticism* (Lawrence: University of Kansas, 1977);

John Clellon Holmes, *Nothing More to Declare* (New York: Dutton, 1967);

Thomas Parkinson, ed., *A Casebook on the Beat* (New York: Crowell, 1961);

Tony Tanner, *City of Words* (New York: Harper & Row, 1971);

John Tytell, *Naked Angels: The Lives and Literature of the Beat Generation* (New York: McGraw-Hill, 1976);

KEN KESEY'S *One Flew Over the Cuckoo's Nest* (1962) was a critical success from the beginning. Its popularity, particularly among college students, has grown steadily, with paperback sales soaring into the millions. Its apparent message of contemporary man's need to get in touch with his world, to open the doors of perception, to enjoy spontaneous sensuous experience and resist the manipulative forces of a technological society, has had wide appeal. His second novel, *Sometimes a Great Notion* (1964), a larger and more complex work, also a bestseller adapted for film, has been less read and has failed to capture the college audience the way his first novel did. Aside from his novels, Kesey attained notoriety as a style setter for much of West Coast psychedelia in the 1960s. As the leader of the Merry Pranksters, described by one newspaperman as a "day-glo guerrilla squad for the LSD revolution in California," he turned from writing to search for new forms of expression induced by drugs—forms of expression in which there would be no separation between himself and the audience; it would be all one experience, with the senses opened wide. Tom Wolfe's *The Electric Kool-Aid Acid Test* (1968) chronicles this search and the escapades of the Merry Pranksters, conferring upon Kesey an almost legendary stature as the charismatic leader who transformed the Beats into the Hippies.

Kesey was born on 17 September 1935 in La Junta, Colorado. He attended public schools in Springfield, Oregon, where his father had moved to establish a dairy cooperative. He graduated from the University of Oregon, where he was involved in fraternities, drama, and athletics—as a champion wrestler he barely missed qualifying for the Olympics. In 1956, he married his high school sweetheart, Faye Haxby. The Keseys now have two sons and one daughter. After the University of Oregon, he worked for a year, toyed with the idea of being a movie actor, wrote an unpublished novel about college athletics, "End of Autumn," and then in 1958 began graduate work in creative writing at Stanford, studying with Wallace Stegner, Malcolm Cowley, Richard Scowcraft, and Frank O'Connor.

Another unpublished novel, "Zoo," which dealt with San Francisco's North Beach, was completed before he began writing *One Flew Over the Cuckoo's Nest* in the summer of 1960. About this time he was introduced to drugs, specifically LSD, through acting as a paid volunteer for government drug experiments conducted at the Veteran's Hospital in Menlo Park. Soon afterward he took a job as aide in that hospital. Both the experience with drugs and the hospital work provided material for his novel. Some of the book was written during his night shifts, and, according to Kesey, certain passages were written under the influence of peyote.

One Flew Over the Cuckoo's Nest describes how a section of a mental hospital controlled efficiently by Miss Ratched, known as Big Nurse, is disrupted by the arrival of Randle Patrick McMurphy, an exuberant, fast-talking hustler fresh from a prison work farm. The story is told from the point of view of a large, schizophrenic Indian named Bromden, an inmate pretending to be mute as a defense against a society to which he cannot adapt. In the course of the novel, McMurphy, through his irrepressible energy and laughter, helps the patients, particularly Bromden, find the self-confidence and courage to rebel against the sterile, mechanistic, manipulative forces represented by Big Nurse. McMurphy is sacrificed in the process. Allusions and motifs from the Gospels are blended with those from comic books and popular culture to lend a mythic quality to the conflict. It is a struggle between Good and Evil with McMurphy as hero. More specifically, the forces of nature, spontaneity, motion, and freedom are pitted against those of static, technological control—contemporary American society's "Combine."

One Flew Over the Cuckoo's Nest is tightly organized, consisting of four symmetrical parts linked by consistent patterns of imagery associated with the opposition of nature and the machine. A central theme is the power of laughter as a source of vitality and sanity. Bromden, the narrator, acknowledges that McMurphy taught him "you have to laugh at the things that hurt you just to keep yourself in balance, just to keep the world from running you plumb crazy." When McMurphy has finally produced spontaneous and uninhibited laughter among his fellow inmates, his purpose as hero or savior is essentially complete. The kind of salvation he brings about is most clearly seen in Bromden's recovering his ability to sense with pleasure the natural world once again. Before McMurphy came, he lived in a numbing, hallucinated fog that he imagined was produced by machines in the hospital.

Some readers see anti-feminism as an important theme in the novel. Big Nurse is certainly a personification of some negative aspects of our society, and she is just the principal figure among a number of domineering and manipulating females in the novel. One of the characters complains specifically about "the juggernaut of modern matriarchy." It can reasonably be argued, however, that Kesey's attack is not directed against women per se but against the perversion of the feminine. Big Nurse's ample breasts are tightly bound up within a starched uniform. Symbolically this suggests human warmth, tenderness, and generosity stifled by cold, sterile, technological efficiency. And the suppression or perversion of the natural in Big Nurse corresponds to a similar situation in American society: nature and the personal perverted by misguided technology and the impersonal. From this point of view, Kesey's attitude toward the feminine is as positive as his attitude toward nature.

McMurphy's refreshing vitality has been much admired and his flamboyant rebellion against repressive, depersonalizing forces in modern life is appealing, but some critics believe Kesey's treatment of moral problems is somewhat sentimentalized and oversimplified. One critic suggests that he enters the comic strip world of super heroes and arch villains too uncritically in defense of the Good. Another points out that self-assertion and freedom are good, but they cannot be attained in any meaningful way simply by casting off inhibitions.

After finishing *One Flew Over the Cuckoo's Nest* in June 1961, Kesey returned to Oregon, to logging country, and began gathering material for *Sometimes a Great Notion*. On mornings and evenings he rode in pickup trucks taking loggers to and from camps. At nights he visited bars where loggers went. After about four months of this, he returned to Stanford to write. In the summer of 1963 he moved to a mountain home in La Honda, fifteen miles from Palo Alto, which became the headquarters for the Merry Pranksters, an assortment of friends united in the bonds of drugs, rock music, and day-glo paint. There he completed the novel.

Sometimes a Great Notion is about a logging family which defies a labor union and thereby the whole community they live in by continuing their logging operations during a strike. There is also conflict within the family: Hank Stamper is in conflict with his half brother, Lee, a bookish college student who has been living in the East. As a child, Lee witnessed his mother engaged in sexual intercourse with Hank, and this has disturbed him emotionally. He returns to avenge himself by seducing Hank's wife. In the end both brothers come to understand themselves better through their conflict. Kesey once said about the novel that in writing it he wanted to find out "which side of me really is: the woodsy, logger side—complete with homespun homilies and crackerbarrel corniness, a valid side of me that I like—or its opposition. The two Stamper brothers in the novel are each one of the ways I think I am."

Despite its stylistic and psychological complexity, this novel treats an essentially simple theme: the ability of the self-reliant individual to prevail over awesome antagonistic forces. Hank Stamper, like Randle McMurphy, is big, lusty, and physically and personally vibrant. He, too, has a quarrel with civilization. Each is a version of a heroic type associated with the American frontier: the man who cherishes the freedom of life close to nature, responsible to no one but himself, considering social cooperation a weakness, possessing an indomitable will to maintain his independence. Hank is similar to the hero of the classic Western, and the oral tales sprinkled through the novel reinforce our impression of a link with the nineteenth-century West. Ostensibly, Hank is acting as a strikebreaker to save the family business, but it is obvious that it is not the business but the independence it represents that is important to him. In order to protect his independence and the natural existence that is its source, he will defy all the usual assumptions of contemporary society. Getting the logs down the river to the company is his consuming passion, and to succeed he must overcome such obstacles as union opposition, growing hostility in the community, bad weather, death in the family, and a half brother intent on settling a grudge against him. Although Hank does succeed, the reader is left pondering the cost of that victory.

Sometimes a Great Notion is a large and ambitious novel. It has some of the flavor of Faulkner, whose fiction Kesey greatly admired. In a way reminiscent of Faulkner's *Light in August*, Kesey begins his novel near the moment of climax, then shifts to the past, gradually revealing through childhood experiences and family relationships the psychological makeup of the main characters.

by pg 279
in typed revision

295

McMurphy frowned at me a minute, then asked. "Yeah? She got bigger...

How big?"

"Bigger'n pappy an' me together."

"Just took to growin', huh? How come her to swell up that way. I

never heard of a Indian woman doing somethin' like that..."

"She ~~was a Mexican woman~~ wasn't Indian. She was from The Dalles, a town woman.

"And her name was what? Sanchez? Yeah, sure. And when a ~~Mex~~ town woman marries an Indian

that's marryin' somebody the whole beneath her, ~~ain't~~ aint it? So...Yeah, I think I see. If I got it right...she made

~~you daddy get littler because, well, on account of he was an Indian and~~

~~she was a Mexican?"~~

I nodded, then told him.

"Because she was a woman, too. But it wasn't just her. Everybody

worked on him."

"Why?"

"Because he was too big. He...wouldn't give in. And everybody worked

on him, just the way they're working on you. ① They can't have somebody ~~that~~

big runnin' round...unless he's one of them. You can see that."

"Yeah, I reckon I can."

"That's why you ~~gotta~~ should ob quit lettin' 'em see ~~you're too~~ that you're big: ~~if they see~~ they thought

~~it they'll bust you!"~~ For a while you was little. Then you showed 'em you was big and

now they got to bust you.

"Like ~~bustin'~~ bustin' a mustang, huh?"

"No, listen! They don't bust you that way; they work on you ways you can't

fight! They put things in! They install things. They start as quick as

they see you're gonna be ~~x~~ big and go to fixin' you to where you can't

work right! ~~X~~ If you're too big you might turn out to be dangerous,

a Communist, or a fiend, or a ~~xxhxi fighter!~~ gangster! So they start installing

their filthy machinery when you're little, and keep on and on till your fixed...!"

Typescript page from One Flew Over the Cuckoo's Nest.

Abandoning conventional narrative chronology, he moves at will forward and backward in time, giving the reader, piece by piece, the information necessary for understanding characters, plot, and theme. Point of view is handled with similar freedom. Both Hank and Lee narrate in the first person in sections throughout the novel. From the third-person point of view family history going back to 1898 is related, and the thoughts of such characters as the union leaders are revealed. Often shifts in point of view are abrupt, sometimes occurring more than once in a single paragraph. Frequently, Kesey uses the device of presenting several incidents widely separated in space as simultaneous action. These techniques are interesting and often effective, but they make considerable demands upon the reader. Despite remarkable triumphs in language, the novel is somewhat strained and meandering, its experimental style at times difficult. Although it has sold well, it has achieved neither the enthusiastic praise nor the wide attention given to *One Flew Over the Cuckoo's Nest*.

In the summer of 1964, Kesey and the Merry Pranksters, dressed in outrageous costumes and transported in a bus painted fantastically with day-glo paint, traveled to New York for the publication of *Sometimes a Great Notion*. They shot over forty hours of film of themselves during this trip. This film came to be known as The Movie and was later used frequently at Prankster-sponsored drug and music presentations—the so-called "acid tests."

In 1965 Kesey was arrested for possession of marijuana. A year of hearings and court appearances followed, resulting in his conviction. Early in 1966 he fled to Mexico to avoid prosecution, but he returned after about six months and was arrested. Eventually he served sentences totaling about five months in the San Mateo County Jail and later at the San Mateo County Sheriff's Honor Camp. He was released in November of 1967.

In 1968 he moved to a farm in Pleasant Hills, Oregon, where he has remained. At the time of his arrest he expressed the intention of giving up writing. He wanted to move beyond writing to more "electrical forms." "I'd rather be a lightning rod than a seismograph," was his cryptic explanation. But later his interests returned once again to writing. When asked in 1971 if he had once believed writing to be an old-fashioned and artificial occupation, he replied, "I was counting on the millenium. Now I guess I'm tired of waiting."

Kesey's Garage Sale (1973), with an introduction by Arthur Miller, is a miscellaneous collection of essays, drawings, letters, interviews, and prose fiction by and about Kesey. The longest section is *Over the Border*, a movie script based on his flight to Mexico, which treats the possibilities of achieving new powers and insights through drugs. The conclusion casts doubts on such possibilities.

His renewed interest in writing has been accompanied by a turning away from drugs. He believed that drugs like LSD could open wonderful, mind-expanding experiences. Though he might not have given up that belief entirely, he has lost interest in deliberate experimenting. "There are dues," he has said, and "even if it were safe and sanctioned we just don't have the right." "The biggest thing I've learned on dope," he said in 1970, "is that there are forces beyond human understanding that are influencing our lives." His hope and fascination now seem to be the mystique of the land, the cycles of nature, and farming for awareness, not money. He has been active in arousing public interest and participation in planning for the next twenty-five years of Oregon's growth.

Currently he is editing a magazine called *Spit in the Ocean* and working on a novel titled *Seven Prayers by Grandma Whittier*, portions of which appeared in *Kesey* (1977). The central character of *Over the Border*, Devlin Deboree, appears here in a secondary role. The point of view is that of an eighty-six-year-old grandmother, a spry, self-reliant Christian woman whose compassion and understanding are brought to bear upon some unusual aspects of contemporary American society.

Kesey has called himself a "parabolist," which means, he says, "that I am not a reporter. I don't ask my reader to believe characters or situations exist anyplace other than in our minds—and there's a *possibility* for such existence in his mind and in my mind." He believes that "passing off what-might-be-true as fiction" is a better vocation than "passing off what-is-quite-possibly fiction as truth." "A single *Batman* comic book is more honest than a whole volume of *Time* magazines." He does not discount the value of reporting reality but suggests: "A writer must practice lying for a long time before he can trust himself with anything so delicate as the truth."

But he is a parabolist in another sense also. His writing and interviews are filled with little anecdotes or parables. Narrative is for him the natural and spontaneous vehicle for concepts. His insights come not as abstract ideas but radiating from story and anecdote. Similarly, he loves a tale, the type of down-home tale characteristic of the American frontier in its various phases.

At the center of his imaginative vision is fascination with the American cultural hero, particularly as he is revealed in popular art forms. Patterns in the novels suggest the patterns of popular myths in folk tales, Westerns, and comic strips. Explicit allusions are made to heroes such as Paul Bunyan, the Lone Ranger, and Captain Marvel. This fascination is perhaps at bottom a manifestation of Kesey's preoccupation with transcendence. His experimentation with drugs, his interest in psychic phenomena, his use of the I Ching, his dabbling in Eastern religions, his more recent focus on the Bible, his trip to Egypt in 1975 in search of the occult Hidden Pyramid—all such characteristically Kesey behavior is symptomatic of a transcendental quest, an inveterate faith in infinite possibility for the individual person. His tendency toward mysticism, his distrust of political movements and revolution, and his attraction to nature and simplicity are reminiscent of New England Transcendentalism. —*Stephen L. Tanner*

Books:

One Flew Over the Cuckoo's Nest (New York: Viking, 1962; London: Methuen, 1963);
Sometimes a Great Notion (New York: Viking, 1964; London: Methuen, 1966).

Other:

Ken Kesey's Garage Sale, edited by Kesey (New York: Viking; Intrepid Trips, 1973);
Whole Earth Catalog, March 1971 Supplement, edited by Kesey and Paul Krassner;
Kesey (Eugene, Oregon: Northwest Review, 1977).

References:

Richard Blessing, "The Moving Target: Ken Kesey's Evolving Hero," *Journal of Popular Culture*, 4 (winter 1971): 615-627;
John A. Barsness, "Ken Kesey: The Hero in Modern Dress," *Bulletin of the Rocky Mountain Modern Language Association*, 23 (March 1969): 27-33;
Bruce Carnes, *Ken Kesey* (Boise, Idaho: Boise State University Press, 1974);
John Wilson Foster, "Hustling to Some Purpose: Kesey's *One Flew Over the Cuckoo's Nest*," *Western American Literature*, 9 (August 1974): 115-129;
Robert Forrey, "Ken Kesey's Psychopathic Savior: A Rejoinder," *Modern Fiction Studies*, 21 (summer 1975): 222-230;
James O. Hoge, "Psychedelic Stimulation and the Creative Imagination: The Case of Ken Kesey," *Southern Humanities Review*, 6 (fall 1972): 381-391;
James R. Huffman, "The Cuckoo Clock in Kesey's Nest," *Modern Language Studies*, 7 (spring 1977): 52-72;
Barry H. Leeds, "Theme and Technique in *One Flew Over the Cuckoo's Nest*," *Connecticut Review*, 7 (April 1974): 35-50;
Terence Martin, "*One Flew Over the Cuckoo's Nest* and the High Cost of Living," *Modern Fiction Studies*, 19 (spring 1973): 43-55;
Nicolaus Mills, "Ken Kesey and the Politics of Laughter," *Centennial Review*, 16 (winter 1972): 82-90;
Raymond Michael Olderman, *Beyond the Waste Land: The American Novel in the Nineteen-Sixties* (New Haven: Yale University Press, 1972);
Carol Pearson, "The Cowboy Saint and the Indian Poet: The Comic Hero in Kesey's *One Flew Over the Cuckoo's Nest*," *Studies in American Humor*, 1 (October 1974): 91-98;
John Clark Pratt, ed., *One Flew Over the Cuckoo's Nest: Text and Criticism* (New York: Viking, 1973);
W. D. Sherman, "The Novels of Ken Kesey," *Journal of American Studies*, 5 (August 1971): 185-196;
Terry G. Sherwood, "One Flew Over the Cuckoo's Nest and the Comic Strip," *Critique*, 13, 1 (1970): 96-109;
Stephen L. Tanner, "Salvation through Laughter: Ken Kesey and the Cuckoo's Nest," *Southwest Review*, 58 (spring 1973): 125-137;
Tony Tanner, *City of Words: American Fiction, 1950-1970* (New York: Harper, 1971), pp. 372-392;
Joseph J. Waldmeir, "Two Novelists of the Absurd: Heller and Kesey," *Wisconsin Studies in Contemporary Literature*, 5 (autumn 1964): 192-204;
Bruce E. Wallis, "Christ in the Cuckoo's Nest: or, the Gospel According to Ken Kesey," *Cithara*, 12 (November 1972): 52-58;
Joseph Weixlman, "Ken Kesey: A Bibliography," *Western American Literature*, 10 (November 1975): 219-231;
Thomas Wolfe, *The Electric Kool-Aid Acid Test* (New York: Farrar, Straus & Giroux, 1968);
Eliot M. Zashin, "Political Theorist and Demiurge: The Rise and Fall of Ken Kesey," *Centennial Review*, 17 (spring 1973): 199-213.

Ken Kesey

Manuscripts:

The University of Oregon has manuscript drafts and the final manuscript of *One Flew Over the Cuckoo's Nest*, manuscript drafts of various published and unpublished works, and notebooks and recordings by Kesey.

JERZY N. KOSINSKI, novelist and essayist, was born on 14 June 1933 in Lodz, Poland, the son of Russian parents Mieczyslaw and Elzbieta. At the age of six, he was separated from his parents and wandered throughout Poland and Russia, continually suspected of being a lost Jewish or Gypsy child while being subjected to the ravishments of the Nazi holocaust and the traditional prejudice of an ignorant peasantry. Among other things, this experience caused Kosinski to lose his speech for a period of five years and produced a sense of survival-by-wits that recurs in virtually every aspect of his adult life. After six years of wandering from village to village in Eastern Europe and maturing far beyond his years, Kosinski was reunited with his parents. Of the Kosinski family, once numerous and distinguished, only two members survived the war. The situation for Kosinski at the end of World War II was problematical. Cunning, distrustful, and remarkably independent, Kosinski was enrolled in a school for the handicapped due to his muteness. After a skiing accident in 1947, he regained his speech and "armed with a distinct sense of identity" quickly worked his way through high school in less than a year.

Kosinski's sense of independence differed from the imposed conformity of postwar Poland and the state-oriented Communist ideology. His experiences during the war had undoubtedly produced a keen interest in analysis of individual behavior in situations of stress and particularly how the individual copes with situations in which he is forced to conform to a mass opinion. From 1950 to 1955, Kosinski studied at the University of Lodz, where he received two M.A. degrees, in history and political science. While studying social psychology and the sociology of literary form at the State Academy of Sciences, by his own admission Kosinski "led several lives." On one level, he appeared to be a brilliant, resourceful, and dedicated scholar, but on another level he made plans for his escape from totalitarianism.

Kosinski has described his intellectual life in Poland and the Soviet Union as being an "inner emigre." Forced by the totalitarian state to conceal his true opinions and to stifle the expression of his ideas, Kosinski rejected all thoughts of being a writer and turned instead toward a visual expression of ideas—photography. "Within the limits of photography, I could point out certain aspects of human behavior as contrasted with collective behavior." The nonverbal expression of this contrast became extremely important. Since the verbal expression of ideas could be more closely defined through convention, the nonverbal allowed Kosinski to create an explanation of what he observed in the culture and society around him, but with more freedom of interpretation in the highly politicized, Stalinist ideology. The accoutrements of photography also became important and none more so than the darkroom, a place of privacy in which the outside world could be legally excluded and the individual could preserve his own self-identity and escape from the collective state. "The photographic darkroom emerged as the perfect metaphor for my life. It was one place I could lock myself in (rather than being locked in) and legally not admit anyone else. For me it became a kind of temple.... Inside I would develop my own private images; instead of writing fiction I imagined myself as a fictional character. I identified very strongly with characters of both Eastern and Western literature [Petrourin, Romashov, Julien Sorel, and occasionally Rastignac].... I wrote my fiction emotionally; I would never commit it to paper." Thus, within a collective society, Kosinski managed at once to alienate himself from the conventions of conformity and to employ this alienation to transcend the imposed limits of this social organization. The drive for an expression of his own ideas increased, and Kosinski's development of a plan for escape became a necessity to lessen the risks to his survival (at one point he was accused by the Photographic Society of "being a cosmopolitan who sees the flesh, but not the social being"). With his own survival imperiled since any deviation from utter conformity could be a real threat if noticed by others, Kosinski decided to leave Poland for a country with a large diversified society where he could gain anonymity. He thought first of immigrating to Brazil or Argentina, but both of those countries refused to admit him because they considered him to be a potential threat since he was coming from and had been educated in a Marxist society. "And so, I started at the other end of the alphabet."

Employing the same sense of survival that allowed him to live through World War II, Kosinski learned the techniques of the totalitarian system so

266

Scientia

Jerzy Kosinski.

well that he was able to turn the system back upon itself. Discerning that the illusion of power is frequently as potent as actual power, Kosinski created a fictional situation designed to allow for his escape to the West. He created four fictitious personalities, giving them all the characteristics of distinguished scholars complete with "official seals, rubber stamps and stationary that listed their impressive titles, functions and offices." With this accomplished Kosinski and his four scholars began two years of correspondence, which culminated in Kosinski's being granted a passport to study in the United States through a grant from an American foundation—a foundation that Kosinski also created. He has said of these four scholars that "they were the four best friends I had behind the Iron Curtain."

On 20 December 1957, Kosinski arrived in the United States. At this time, he was completely unfamiliar with the English language, except for some scattered sociological jargon. Within four months, he taught himself English, assisted by his father, a philologist, who wrote a series of highly detailed letters to his son explaining the finer points of English grammar. In 1958, he received a Ford Foundation Fellowship to continue his graduate education at Columbia University (1958-1964) and the New School for Social Research (1962-1965). His studies and education in social research in Poland and the Soviet Union resulted in Kosinski's first two books, *The Future Is Ours, Comrade* and *No Third Path*, published under the pseudonym Joseph Novak. Kosinski began the first book within two years after his arrival in the United States. *The Future Is Ours, Comrade* was published by Doubleday in 1960, while Kosinski was still doing graduate work at Columbia University. The writing of this book had been preceded by a number of odd jobs—"bar cleaner, scraping paint from the hulls of ships, parking cars, racing cars, driving trucks, chauffeuring, and being a part-time movie projectionist."

Kosinski's life in the United States has retained many of the characteristics born during his years under the Stalinist regime. His first two books were published pseudonymously under the name "Joseph Novak." Kosinski has recently said that by using a pseudonym you can unabashedly recommend your book to others, but the roots of this anonymity are far deeper than merely self-promotion. Rather, self-preservation is the basic motive, with secretiveness and manipulation, both of the self and others, as concomitant results. The problem he wrestles with is to have control over his own existence, and, to an extent, this causes him to seek control over others by manipulating his behavior to gain certain ends and analyzing the behavior of others. To be sure, this is not unique. All people seek to manipulate and analyze in this manner, but Kosinski has the advantage of recognizing and employing this knowledge for his own purposes.

In a sense, Kosinski is still fleeing from imposed authority. He is reported to have had at least twenty-five New York addresses. He has several safety deposit boxes in various locations where he keeps his papers. "I am secretive. I close things. I lock them. I have fifteen different places where my things are hidden. Some of the bank vaults where I send the drafts [of novels] are almost bigger than my apartment. I am always afraid that some societal force will go after me, and will try to penetrate not only my apartment—let them do it!—but my inner life, which is reflected in my writing and in my letters." He uses disguises and attitudes to penetrate different areas of society and, one suspects, to test the reactions of those people he encounters. Finally, Kosinski turns aspects of his life into fiction and fictionalizes a reality for his own life. This occurs because of the two most important features of Kosinski's intellectual life: the inevitability of chance and the fictive nature of all explanations.

The Future Is Ours, Comrade and *No Third Path* are sociological studies of the individual in a collective society. The reviewers heaped praise upon each of these books for its incisive portrayal of the lives of people living under Communism. Both books are made up of Kosinski's conversations with people in various occupations and strata of Soviet culture. They are illuminating primarily in the sense that they show a sometimes vigorous, imaginatively alive group of individuals who are made into passive conformists because of their fear of reprisals by the state—the state both in the abstract sense of a governmental bureaucracy which is both mysterious in its workings and familiar in its effects and in the specific sense of the state as the neighbors living in the next room in the apartment house who are constantly watching for any sign of deviant behavior. The most telling images in these studies are those describing the unbearable lack of individual privacy and the dogmatic control of thought and intellectual and imaginative potential. These images, and sometimes the methods for obviating their deadly effects, are, of course, those which Kosinski has described as being the major reasons for his expatriation. With these two books, Kosinski became a best-selling author. The books were universally praised by critics, including the most distinguished intellectuals of our time, such as Bertrand Russell. *The Future Is Ours, Comrade* was condensed by *Reader's Digest*, serialized in the *Saturday Evening Post*, and has been translated into over twenty languages.

In retrospect several important characteristics emerge from Kosinski's first two books that are to be found in his later works. First, it is important to realize that Kosinski is a highly sophisticated and incisive social scientist. To read his later works without this perspective is to lose a great deal of their importance as social documents. Also, Kosinski has not left his sociological interests to be expressed solely through his novels. For example, his essay on the romance magazines and their sociological significance, "Packaged Passion," describes the influence of the contents of these magazines on reinforcing passivity in a large segment of American culture, a passivity which is already extant due to other mass forms of activity—or "entertainment"—such as television, movies, or spectator sports. The problem of passivity induced by mass social behavior is one of the subjects of Kosinski's third novel, *Being There* (1971), and plays a large role in his other works. *The Future Is Ours, Comrade* and *No Third Path* rely on the author's chance encounters with people and events. There is little information in either book to lay a basis for the revelations that Kosinski is able to make about those he meets, only vague references to introductions proffered by various people on his behalf and his own peculiar position in the Soviet system that allowed him to have easy access to all elements of the society. The nature of chance encounters with the Russian people is also exemplified in the incidental nature of the style of each book. The author encounters various people, these encounters are classified by subject and placed into chapters, and within the chapters incident is piled upon incident. At times these incidents are very brief, while other encounters are described at great length. It is the same stylistic format that Kosinski later employs in his fiction, particularly in *Steps* (1968). The focus in each of his first books is on how the individual reacts to various situations involving the impingement of social conformity upon the freedom of his own behavior. In a sense, the abstract individual composed of all the specific people Kosinski encountered is the central character of the books, and it is the reaction of the collective, central character and how he responds that is of interest. Just as the character has no name and no single, identifying characteristic, the primary characters in Kosinski's novels also remain anonymous to the reader, lacking the sense of identification provided in the typical fictional narrative.

Upon his arrival in the United States, Kosinski abandoned photography and decided to write. As he has explained, he finds the place of the writer in America to be greatly different from Europe. In "To Hold a Pen," he writes: "While Europe's political development constantly assumed her writers' innate political influence, American writers have seldom been considered political threats. Rather, they have been treated as superfluous characters, more interested in publicizing their private experiences and fantasies than in galvanizing political emotion. This attitude toward writing may be explained in part by the traditional American mistrust of novelists. Because the creation of literature is not often the means to financial success and security, is not aimed at any tangible object, and requires no special training—all important aspects of American commercialism—writing fiction is seldom considered a serious endeavor. A novelist is simply another self-styled elitist. Within this system, American writers have traditionally felt stifled, alienated from their culture and from one another." Being an author holds several advantages for Kosinski. It is a portable occupation that can be moved easily and quickly if necessary due to any complex of factors. It is potentially anonymous and reclusive. An author is never required to encounter his readers and, if he wishes, can employ a pseudonym to further insulate his privacy. With his unimpaired mobility, an author can easily come into contact with a wide variety of situations and people. In writing, the author alone is in control of the situation he inhabits and the world he creates, regardless of whether he is writing fiction or nonfiction. All of these characteristics would have great appeal for Kosinski, but there is also one other which seems to fascinate him, the indeterminate nature of writing that makes it inevitable that a writer's work is never entirely finished. As he described it in "To Hold a Pen," a writer's works:

will never be "finished," so long as they are being read; writing is a continual process of communication, which depends as much on the reader's ability to decipher the words as it does on the words themselves. A writer merely presents a framework of ideas, words and images in order to trigger the reader's imagination, but that framework itself is not the final goal; in order to be effective, writing has to transcend its physical properties. . . . Furthermore, since the only true measure of literature's effectiveness is the extent to which the reader's awareness is expanded, the writer's ultimate success or failure can never be entirely known.

After he completed *The Future Is Ours, Comrade*, Kosinski began *No Third Path*. While working on this book, he received a letter from Mary Hayward Weir praising him for his first book. The widow of Ernest T. Weir, the founder of a billion-dollar steel empire, Mary Weir and Kosinski were married in 1962. "It was a case of mutual discovery. I showed Mary the America I had come to know, and she offered me a shortcut to hers." Mary Weir's America was one of extreme wealth, power, and political and social influence. With his marriage, Kosinski entered a new world, which later would become an intrinsic part of his fiction. Six years after their marriage, Mary Weir died. It is during this period that Kosinski returned to teaching, the profession he had left behind when he came to the United States. In 1968, he accepted the position of Fellow at the Center for Advanced Studies at Wesleyan University. He later taught at Princeton University (1969-1970) and Yale University (1970-1972). He left Yale to serve for two years as the president of the American Center of P.E.N. (1973-1975).

From 1965 to 1978, Jerzy Kosinski published six novels: *The Painted Bird* (1965), *Steps* (1968), *Being There* (1971), *The Devil Tree* (1973), *Cockpit* (1975), and *Blind Date* (1977). From the very beginning, they aroused a considerable critical and reader response. The publication of *The Painted Bird* was met with acclaim for its graphic and sympathetic portrayal of a young boy, lost from his parents and wandering through Eastern Europe during World War II. The critics made the usual comparisons between the intensity and nightmarish quality of this novel and those of Kafka and Camus, while simultaneously the book was seen, at least to some degree, as a fictional parallel to *The Diary of Anne Frank*. The autobiographical implications of *The Painted Bird* did not go unnoticed. The similarity between Kosinski's own life and the life of the unnamed boy of his novel is abundantly apparent. However, Kosinski has continually asserted that the similarity is only on the surface. At one point, he said, "To say that *The Painted Bird*, for example, is nonfiction, or even autobiographical, may be convenient for classification, but it's not easily justified. What we remember lacks the hard edge of fact." The situation of the autobiographical nature of *The Painted Bird* or of the author's other novels, especially *Blind Date*, is highly problematical. It is reported that during a question period following a lecture Kosinski gave at a small Michigan college, he was asked by a student about the seemingly autobiographical nature of *The Painted Bird*. Kosinski's attitude changed dramatically to one of glaring anger when he announced that this was indeed an improper question to be asked of anyone who writes serious fiction. Although this may be true, Kosinski himself has fired the speculation. Most recently, he saw to it that the second, anniversary edition of the novel carried a dust jacket bearing a photograph of him as a young boy during World War II. The confusion is compounded, therefore, by the author's implicit assertion that the novel is autobiographical after all. The solution to this dilemma can be sought in Kosinski's background as a social scientist and his interest in studying individual behavior in response to collective, social situations.

Kosinski seems to use his own experiences as representations of collective experience in a world society or at least a Western one. In *Blind Date*, Kosinski explores a dramatic incident involving himself in the circumstances surrounding the tragic murder of Sharon Tate and others by Charles Manson's gang of killers. A friend of Roman Polanski's since their youth in Poland, Kosinski was scheduled to arrive in New York and proceed to Los Angeles on the night of the Tate murders. Because of a delay in the shipment of his luggage, he decided to remain in New York overnight and go to Los Angeles the next day. On the following morning, he was told of the murders, and, if the event in the novel is what really occurred, was asked if he knew of any relatives of a Mr. Kosinski who was believed to have been murdered. A shocking episode, but one that Kosinski is able to use to express the central concern of the novel. Namely, that we all have a blind date with life—existence is not controlled by some rational plan (or fate), but rather by chance. *The Painted Bird* is also autobiographical in this manner. The experience of the young boy in the novel is representative, in a sense, of the collective experience of World War II, both for the larger culture of the Western world in its battle for security

and a sane approach to life and also to the more brutal experiences of people living in Eastern Europe who lived through the holocaust. Kosinski uses the boy to show, among other things, a survivor, but a survivor who has been altered by his experience, who has learned that to merely react to the world is to be at its mercy, who has met with the frontier of human experience when societal forces are broken down and the only important service is the service of survival.

Personal and collective histories are explanations created by people in order to bring the past into some sense of order. The process of writing an explanation is always highly selective in using the information that is potentially available at any given moment. The nature of explanation is, therefore, fictive since an explanation can never be complete, and this fictive nature is why no explanation, historical or otherwise, can possess complete reliability or be considered as a definitive statement. For every explanation there is potentially another—sometimes many—that is equally valid and reasonable. "To help us along we create little fictions, highly subtle and individual scenarios which clarify and shape our experience. The remembered event becomes a fiction, a structure made to accommodate certain feelings. This is obvious to me. If it were not for these structures, art would be too personal for the artist to create, much less for the audience to grasp. Even film, the most literal of all the arts, is edited."

To impose a narrative structure upon past events is to give them a beginning and an end where these did not exist before. By doing so, events are made accessible, defined within certain limits. Life as it is experienced fails to meet these definable criteria, while conventional fiction meets them constantly. The more highly conventionalized a work of fiction is, the more accessible it is to a wide audience. Since *The Painted Bird* is Kosinski's most conventional novel in terms of narrative form (it has a beginning and end, chapters, clearly defined characters, a progressive movement from one point to the next), it is not surprising that this is still his most popular work. However, this is not to suggest that it is not also a disturbing novel. People have been disturbed by *The Painted Bird* since the manuscript of the novel was first completed. Among the first to read the book were four New York editors, friends of Kosinski. According to him, all of them felt that the book was unpublishable and recommended that he return to writing nonfiction where he had achieved great success. Undeterred, Kosinski asked them which publisher would be least likely to accept his manuscript. Acting on their answer, he sent the book to Houghton Mifflin, who immediately accepted it, but deleted passages from Kosinski's manuscript. Even then, the cry by critics was that the novel was too brutal, too horrifying, too intense to be realistic. Although seeing the realism of what Kosinski described, Irving Howe wrote in *Harper's* that "finally one wonders whether there is in this book a numbing surplus of brutality. *The Painted Bird* comes to seem too close to that which it portrays, too much at the mercy of its nightmare." Kosinski sees this type of response, and others far less restrained in their complaints about brutality in his novel, as peculiar, if not ignorant of what really happened in Eastern Europe. Kosinski's response to this in the "Afterward" [sic] to the second edition is worth noting:

> Whether the reviews praised or damned the novel, Western criticism of *The Painted Bird* always contained an undertone of uneasiness. Most American and British critics objected to my descriptions of the boy's experiences on the grounds that they dwelt too deeply on cruelty. Many tended to dismiss the author as well as the novel, claiming that I had exploited the horrors of war to satisfy my own peculiar imagination. On the occasion of the twenty-fifth anniversary observances of the National Book Awards, a respected contemporary American novelist wrote that books like *The Painted Bird*, with their unrelieved brutality, did not bode well for the future of the English-language novel. Other critics argued that the book was merely a work of personal reminiscence; they insisted that, given the raw materials of war-torn Eastern Europe, anyone could concoct a plot overflowing with brutal drama. In point of fact, almost none of those who chose to view the book as a historical novel bothered to refer to actual source materials. Personal accounts of survivors and official War documents were either unknown by or irrelevant to my critics.

The objections made to the brutality in the book by Western critics are clearly superceded by the violent reaction of the Communist press and its readers. Hundreds of articles and reviews denounced *The Painted Bird* as salacious Western propaganda. (Amusingly, the printing of a Library of Congress number on the book was used as evidence that it had been subsidized by the United States government.) Since the book was completely distorted in the Communist press to depict it as an anti-Polish document that slandered the people of Kosinski's homeland, the local citizenry was aroused to violence. At one point, Kosinski's mother was defamed in the newspapers as the "mother of a renegade" and crowds were incited to attack her house, a situation which was alleviated only by Kosinski gaining some support from international organizations to bring pressure on the government to protect her. Eastern Europeans living in the United States also attacked Kosinski since they apparently believed the reports in the Communist papers that the author had spoken against their country:

> On several occasions I was accosted outside my apartment house or in my garage. Three or four times strangers recognized me on the street and offered hostile or insulting remarks. At a concert honoring a pianist born in my homeland, a covey of patriotic old ladies attacked me with their umbrellas, while screeching absurdly dated invectives. Even now, ten years after *The Painted Bird*'s publication, citizens of my former country, where the novel remains banned, still accuse me of treachery unaware that by consciously deceiving them, the government continues to feed their prejudices, rendering them victims of the same forces from which my protagonist, the boy, so narrowly escaped.

The experience of the young boy in *The Painted Bird* typifies the primary concern that Kosinski has in his next four novels, *Steps, Being There, The Devil Tree*, and *Cockpit*. The boy is left alone in the world, away from his parents, lost in a situation for which his life has left him unprepared. Gradually, he begins to experience the progressive loss of all the benefits of a social system, what might best be called a buffer system that separates the people living within a society from the use of brute force. These buffers, such things as a legal system, a family and a cultural tradition, are established so that individuals within a society can function in a protected environment where, when a dispute arises, it can be resolved by many techniques before it reaches the level of the exercise of brute force. Without a social system, without a philosophy, a society or an individual is on the cultural frontier where survival is the key and the means of survival is through force or its converse, seduction. Gradually, the boy recognizes his situation and begins to create his own philosophy, a severely independent culture of one. He becomes mute at this point. Language, the vehicle for cultural communication, is no longer a useful tool. However, as he becomes recultured after the war to a broader social situation, his voice returns and in doing so repeats the stages of his experience that led to its loss. The same necessity for

A Novel by JERZY KOSINSKI

COCKPIT

Dust jacket of Cockpit, *designed by Kosinski.*

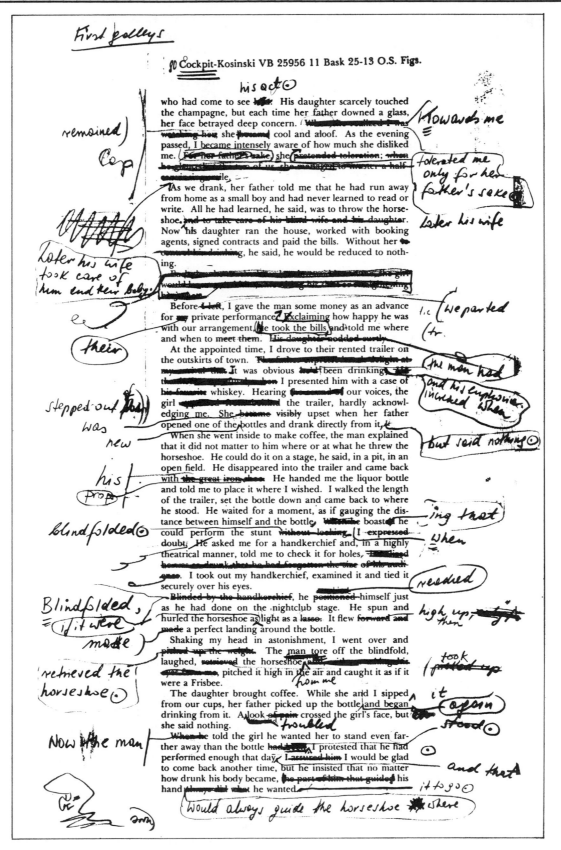

Corrected galley proof for Cockpit.

creating a personal philosophy appears in the same manner—the individual is alone, totally alienated from his past and the surrounding culture—in the next four novels. This, perhaps, is the basis for Kosinski's assertion that these books form a five-novel cycle.

With *Blind Date*, Kosinski's fictional characters enter a new phase. George Levanter is not interested in searching for a new philosophy of life. Rather, he has found one, the philosophy of chance, which he accepted from a source outside of himself. Profoundly influenced by Jacques Monod's *Chance and Necessity*, Kosinski himself seems to have undergone an experience similar to that which he ascribes to Levanter. The turns and twists of Kosinski's own life provide an ample justification for a belief (or "anti-belief") in chance. Instead of creating a philosophical structure, the individual in this situation avoids the allurements of planning his life and elects to develop strategies for strengthening his ability to deal with chance encounters so that he might best take advantage of his opportunities. He does not simply respond to situations, but creates them much in the same way that a novelist creates the situations of his characters. This attitude destroys the illusion of the metaphorical term "individual." There is no longer any rational possibility for referring to an "individual" as if we are talking about a person who is consistent in his behavior in all situations. The individual is replaced by a multi-faceted package of behaviors, some of which are employed in certain circumstances, some of which are known to a few of those that the person encounters, but none that are made to be consistent because of any overriding philosophical theory. A person, rid of the notion of a consistent personality that the word "individual" is frequently given, is able to experience a sense of self more fully, because he is more open to the unpredictable. "As a human being, I answer not only to reality but also to plausibility—to the plight of my imagination. Nothing bars me from perceiving my life as a series of emotionally charged incidents, all strung out by my memory—all dictated by chance, nature's true fantasy." —*Cameron Northouse*

Books:

The Future Is Ours, Comrade: Conversations with the Russians, as Joseph Novak (Garden City: Doubleday, 1960; London: Bodley Head, 1960);

No Third Path, as Joseph Novak (Garden City: Doubleday, 1962);

The Painted Bird (Boston: Houghton Mifflin, 1965; London: W. H. Allen, 1966);

Notes of the Author on The Painted Bird (New York: Scientia-Factum, 1965);

Steps (New York: Random House, 1968; London: Bodley Head, 1969);

The Art of the Self: Essays A Propos Steps (New York: Scientia-Factum, 1968);

Being There (New York: Harcourt Brace Jovanovich, 1971; London: Bodley Head, 1971);

The Devil Tree (New York: Harcourt Brace Jovanovich, 1973; London: Hart-Davis McGibbon, 1973);

Cockpit (Boston: Houghton Mifflin, 1975; London: Hutchinson, 1975);

Blind Date (Boston: Houghton Mifflin, 1977; London: Hutchinson, 1978).

References:

Robert Boyers, "Language and Reality in Kosinski's *Steps*," *Centennial Review*, 16 (winter 1972): 41-61;

Daniel J. Cahill, "Jerzy Kosinski: Retreat from Violence," *Twentieth Century Literature*, 18 (April 1972): 121-136;

Cahill, *et al*, "*The Devil Tree*: An Interview with Jerzy Kosinski," *North American Review*, 258 (spring 1973): 56-66;

Samuel Coale, "The Quest for the Elusive Self: The Fiction of Jerzy Kosinski," *Critique*, 14 (1973): 25-37;

Patricia Griffin, "A Conversation With Kosinski," *The Texas Arts Journal*, 1 (1978): 27-35;

Irving Howe, "The Other Side of the Moon," *Harper's*, 238 (March 1969): 102-105;

John Kane, "Jerzy Kosinski: Interview," *Yale Literature Review*, 141 (August 1972): 12-16;

William Kennedy, "Who Here Doesn't Know How Good Kosinski Is?" *Look*, 24 (20 April 1971): 12;

Douglas N. Mount, "Jerzy Kosinski," *Publishers Weekly*, 199 (26 April 1969): 13-16;

Paul S. Nathan, "Multiple Kosinskis," *Publishers Weekly*, 203 (30 April 1973): 48;

George Plimpton, "Art of Fiction," *Paris Review*, 14 (summer 1972): 183-207;

Gail Sheehy, "The Psychological Novelist as Portable Man," *Psychology Today*, 11 (December 1977): 54-56, 126, 128, 130;

Elizabeth Stone, "Horatio Algers of the Nightmare," *Psychology Today*, 11 (December 1977): 59-60, 63-64;

Thomas Walsh and Cameron Northouse, *John Barth, Jerzy Kosinski and Thomas Pynchon: A Reference Guide* (Boston: G. K. Hall, 1978);

Gerald Weales, *"The Painted Bird* and Other Disguises," *Hollins Critic*, 9 (October 1972): 1-12.

ALISON LURIE (BISHOP) was born in Chicago on 3 September 1926. She received the A.B. degree from Radcliffe College in 1947 and the following year married Jonathan Peale Bishop, Jr. They have three sons. She was the recipient of Yaddo Foundation Fellowships in 1963, 1964, and 1965, the year she was also awarded a Guggenheim Fellowship. In addition to being a housewife, she has also worked as a ghost writer and librarian. In 1968 she joined the English faculty at Cornell University, where her husband is a professor of English; she currently holds the rank of associate professor, teaching courses in narrative writing and children's literature. Her first work of fiction was published in 1962, and since then she has enjoyed a steadily increasing critical reputation on both sides of the Atlantic.

Her association with institutions of higher learning has profoundly influenced her writings, for both her experiences and her observations as an undergraduate and a faculty member have given her a great deal of the raw material which she has used in her novels and has combined with an intimate knowledge of life in the Eastern United States, where she has lived all her life. Lurie is, moreover, a highly intelligent writer, perhaps too intelligent for popular tastes since much of her satire is of a cerebral sort aimed at persons in academic life, especially those in small, prestigious colleges. Despite the lucid nature of her fiction, however, it is difficult to say precisely what course Lurie would have her characters take—one is left wondering if events have changed the characters for better or for worse.

As an observer of human events, Lurie is profoundly conservative, even pessimistic. Her environments are normally hermetic and her characters generally well educated and sophisticated by society's standards. Their isolation, breeding, and sophistication rarely save them, however, and will most likely lead to disaster. The underpinnings of society provide little support to her characters, who bumble and mumble their ways through lives in which everything that is right goes wrong and much of what seems wrong just gets worse. Even when, as in *The Nowhere City*, the values of Eastern America are mixed with the social and moral insouciance of California, the ensuing mayhem provokes the inevitable conclusion that from sea to shining sea

Joan Bingham

some great American dreams are rapidly becoming night sweats.

It is the sacrosanct things in American life that Lurie exposes—college, intelligence, culture, marriage, breeding, The Children (Lurie's emphasis), all the things that one has been taught are necessary, good, and desirable. Gazing piercingly through the pretensions of America, Lurie demonstrates how these ideals and institutions have become fetters, although it is difficult to say what, if anything, would be preferable. Aberrations such as mysticism clearly have their flaws; however, commonly accepted pursuits—history, sociology, English— have defects just as monstrous, if not worse, because they are widely accepted as desirable. Thus, in *Imaginary Friends*, a famous sociologist becomes deluded by the cult he is studying; however, the "science" of sociology seems to have set the trap which the Truth-Seekers simply spring on the hapless McCann.

Adultery is a recurrent theme in Lurie's work, figuring prominently in every novel except *Imaginary Friends*. This pernicious disease of the American marriage runs an unpredictable course, however, and Lurie prevents this common occurrence from becoming hackneyed or staid. In *The Nowhere City*, Katherine's gradual absorption into California life is helped along by frequent illicit intercourse, but she is clearly no worse off at the end of the novel than at its beginning. In her case, the Eastern values, which hold adultery taboo, have been the cause of grief. Her husband gets a broken heart for his sexual calisthenics with a young, shoplifting hippie, but is really no worse for wear. The marriage

SUNDAY, JULY 7

The wind. It slides up the flat pale sky, creaks the
trees, slaps the screen doors at Lolly, ~~front and side~~. Bang.
Bang. Sunday morning. But all empty, wrong. No Sunday
breakfast no Sunday papers. Nobody in the kitchen. Nobody
outside on the ~~terrace. Nobody i on~~ the lawn; or in the barn--
only bottles and chairs and sat-on hay and broken black pieces
of phonograph record.

'Well, come on,' Mary Ann says, ~~and she geeexback~~ turns
~~back towards the house,~~ and Lolly comes on, behind her. 'We'll
wake them up.'

Mary Ann goes into the house and climbs the stairs and
opens the door to her parents' room, Sun. A stale smell,
papers clothes crumples of sheet and blanket all over the floor
and ~~braided~~ rug, the windows rattling with wind. ~~A loud sore~~
~~sawing noise.~~ Mr. Hubbard is lying on the big bed, ~~sawing~~
with his mouth open and no clothes on. He is bright red all
over in horrible blotchy pathes like a disease, except for
his tummy that is white and hairy orange with a thing, she
can see it, ~~a pink~~ gun thing, but she won't see it, won't look.

'Hey!' Mary Ann calls out. 'We're hungry.'

Mr. Hubbard ~~isxlegsxarmsxdenitxmevex~~ doesn't move. But next
to him, curled up pink bulgy-soft with no clothes on, Mrs.
Hubbard opens one green-smudged eye.

From second draft of novel-in-progress.

is not broken up by the adultery, but rather by Katherine's adoption of a life-style in which adultery is only a small part. Conversely, *The War Between the Tates* is fought on several boudoir battlefields, but the marriage is eventually resumed. In any case, adultery has mixed effects and the outcome of such a relationship is unpredictable, contrary to conventional wisdom that adultery is always bad.

Lurie uses a variety of techniques to convey the satiric spirit of her work. Her use of names with double entendres often provides clues to the viewpoint one should adopt on certain characters and institutions, although the technique is applied at random. In *Love and Friendship*, the main character is Emily Stockwell Turner, who, though from good American stock, is hardly well; her husband, Holman, is hardly a "whole man," either. In *The Nowhere City*, Paul Cattleman writes history for a secretive company named Nutting; in *Imaginary Friends*, the Truth-Seekers are located in a town named Sophis; and all is not idyllic in Illyria, the setting of *Real People*. Finally, in *The War Between the Tates*, Erica Tate attempts an affair with an impotent mystic of dubious integrity who has chosen for himself the name Zed (British pronunciation for the last letter of the alphabet) in preference to his real name, Sandy Finkelstein, as if the distinction were of great importance in his case.

Lurie conscientiously avoids moralizing and sermonizing in her novels, a stance reinforced by her prose style, the clarity and lucidity of which keep a rigid curtain between the characters and the author, thereby preventing any significant intrusion of the author upon her material. Her style is precise and dispassionate. Lurie is not, however, the slave of her words; they are carefully controlled. But such distance is not without its difficulties, for one is sometimes tempted to view the characters as impossibly unreal. As John Leonard in the *New Republic* remarks on *The War Between the Tates*, Lurie "refuses to be sympathetic, and so this marvelously polished, splendidly crafted novel creates an antiseptic space in the mind: no one can live there." Perhaps the characters in Lurie's novels do live in their own little worlds, but the force of Lurie's style and intellect makes them live, and it is difficult to doubt their veracity.

Real People (1969) is a radical departure from Lurie's other novels. Cast in the form of a journal, it is the story of Janet Belle Smith's week-long stay at an artists' retreat, Illyria. The viewpoint of the novel is thus shifted to that of Janet, and the spectrum of experiences is seen through her prism. The novel at first appears to be about Lurie's maturation, but she is obviously too sophisticated to be identified with Janet, who is, in fact, just the sort of writer Lurie most likely despises—one who has retreated from the calling of a writer by avoiding everything that is not "nice" both in her life and in her work. The novel, which had a lukewarm reception, has often been misunderstood, for it is satire of the most corrosive sort on writers who have a lot of growing up to do. The novel is about how *not* to be a writer, and Janet is as decadent as the gaudy furnishings of Illyria. Upon Janet's departure, her view of her work has been altered for the better (perhaps, in part, because of her affair with a resident junk sculptor), but here Lurie draws the curtain, though permitting one to speculate that a novelist might do well to imitate her in some small way.

Lurie's subject is the American middle class, especially its women, who figure prominently in every novel. Inasmuch as this class is the backbone and brains of America, its sickness is that of the country. Although several of the main characters are in their twenties, Lurie's work is especially valuable for its studies of those in middle age, those of her own generation, with which *The War Between the Tates* deals. Profoundly disturbed by what she sees around her, Lurie warns us that much is in need of examination and correction and that much of what shocks us should come as no surprise at all. Blind devotion to outmoded norms of behavior and unthinking dabbling in experimental living can be equally bad. Lurie reminds us that what is to be desired is true mental agility and perspective, not the pseudo-intellectualism and false respectability that often pass for them.

—*Everett Wilkie and Josephine Helterman*

Books:

V. R. Lang: A Memoir (Munich: privately printed, 1959);

Love and Friendship (London: Heinemann, 1962; New York: Macmillan, 1962);

The Nowhere City (London: Heinemann, 1965; New York: Coward McCann, 1966);

Imaginary Friends (London: Heinemann, 1967; New York: Coward McCann, 1967);

Real People (New York: Random House, 1969; London: Heinemann, 1970);

The War Between the Tates (New York: Random House, 1974; London: Heinemann, 1974);
V. R. Lang: Poems and Plays (New York: Random House, 1975; London: Heinemann, 1976).

Manuscripts:

Manuscript collection held by the Radcliffe College Library, Cambridge, Massachusetts.

Norman Mailer

Philip H. Bufithis
Shepherd College

BIRTH: Long Branch, New Jersey, 31 January 1923.

EDUCATION: Boys' High School, Brooklyn, 1939; S.B., engineering sciences, Harvard University, 1943.

MARRIAGE: 1944 to Beatrice Silverman, divorced; children: Susan. 1954 to Adele Morales, divorced; children: Danielle, Elizabeth Anne. 1962 to Lady Jeanne Campbell, divorced; children: Kate. 1963 to Beverly Bentley; children: Michael Burks, Stephen McLeod. Common-law marriage to Carol Stevens, separated 1976; children: Maggie Alexandra.

AWARDS: *Story* magazine's annual college fiction contest for "The Greatest Thing in the World," 1941; National Institute of Arts and Letters grant, 1960; Elected, National Institute of Arts and Letters, 1967; National Book Award, Pulitzer Prize, and Polk Award for *The Armies of the Night*, 1969; MacDowell Medal, 1973.

MAJOR WORKS: *The Naked and the Dead* (New York: Rinehart, 1948; London: Wingate, 1949); *Barbary Shore* (New York: Rinehart, 1951; London: Cape, 1952); *The Deer Park* (New York: Putnam's, 1955; London: Wingate, 1957); *The White Negro* (San Francisco: City Lights, 1957); *Advertisements for Myself* (New York: Putnam's, 1959; London: Deutsch, 1961); *The Presidential Papers* (New York: Putnam's, 1963; London: Deutsch, 1964); *An American Dream* (New York: Dial, 1965; London: Deutsch, 1965); *Cannibals and Christians* (New York: Dial, 1966; London: Deutsch, 1967); *Why Are We in Vietnam?* (New York: Putnam's, 1967; London: Weidenfeld & Nicolson, 1969); *The Armies of the Night* (New York: New American Library, 1968; London: Weidenfeld & Nicolson, 1968); *Miami and the Siege of Chicago* (New York: New American Library, 1968; London: Weidenfeld & Nicolson, 1969); *Of a Fire on the Moon* (Boston: Little, Brown, 1970; London: Weidenfeld & Nicolson, 1970); *Marilyn* (New York: Grosset & Dunlap, 1973; London: Hodder & Stoughton, 1973).

Norman Mailer.

Norman Mailer's achievement lies primarily in his treatment of the conflict between man's search for self-actualization and the strictures society places upon him. Mailer has rendered this theme with an energy of style, an ideational power, and a vivid drama that has earned him an international reputation. His books have been translated into more than twenty languages. They stir foreign audiences because, notes Anthony Burgess, they are "political, which is a great recommendation to all

Europeans, and British fiction is just about unexportable manners. I mean 'political,' of course, in the widest sense—the sense of protest or counterprotest."

Mailer presents a special problem to anyone trying to arrive at a clear understanding of his work, for he has gained notoriety as a public figure as well as a writer. His extra-literary activities—acts of civil disobedience, running for mayor of New York, five tempestuous marriages, contentious remarks on television talk shows, belligerent behavior at parties—have caused him in many quarters to be more read about than read. It might appear that his public role has been a self-aggrandizing one, that since the publication of *Advertisements for Myself* (1959), he has been huckstering himself into fame, but this view is predicated on the false assumption that his public performances are strategies designed to promote his books. Actually, Mailer's escapades are crucial to the creation of his work, not to its promotion. He behaves as he does the better to write. He tries to realize in his life the beliefs, hopes, and imaginings that he expresses in his work. "Till people see where their ideas lead, they know nothing," he has said. As one would expect, the process becomes cyclical, for what Mailer discovers by testing his fictional ideas in the world is the need to modify or enlarge upon those ideas by writing more books. The important point is this: there exists in the case of Norman Mailer a symbiotic relationship between life and art. To do in one's life what one has said in one's art is an assertion of creative individuality.

By involving himself in the major crises of our time, Mailer has endeavored to reanimate for modern man a belief in the struggle between God and the Devil. Man's courage—or lack of it—against the encroachment of technology, authoritarianism, and mass values will contribute, Mailer believes, to the outcome of that struggle. His engagements in national events represent his attempts to oppose such encroachments. In 1948, at the age of twenty-five, he campaigned for Henry Wallace, the Progressive Party's candidate for President. He gave over twenty-five speeches as a member of the Progressive Citizens of America, wrote articles for the *New York Post*, and spoke on the subject of academic freedom at the convention for the National Council of Arts, Sciences, and Professions. But he soon became disillusioned with Progressivism's alliances with Communism and announced at the Waldorf Peace Conference in New York that the Russian and American governments were equally imperialistic, equally bent on securing new markets

for themselves by dominating backward countries. In 1962, to demonstrate against the desperate logic of nuclear bomb shelters, he stood in City Hall Park in New York and refused to take shelter during a civil defense drill. In 1967, while participating in the antiwar march in Washington, he crossed the United States Marshals' line and headed alone for the Pentagon. Mailer was arrested. In 1969 he announced his candidacy for mayor of New York. Running on a secessionist platform, he advocated that New York City be made into the fifty-first state and that its neighborhoods effect self-governance. He came in a distant fourth in a field of five. In 1974 he founded the Fifth Estate, a citizen's organization established to investigate the activities of the Central Intelligence Agency and the Federal Bureau of Investigation. These actions by Mailer may be put under one ideological rubric or another, but they all go beyond politics to the individual's ambition to do battle with whatever fate society has designed for him and thereby gain for himself a larger life.

The pattern of Norman Mailer's early life, however, does not prefigure with any certainty the defiant eccentricities that come later. The first child and only son (he has a sister, Barbara) of Isaac Barnett Mailer and Fanny Schneider Mailer, he was born on 31 January 1923, in Long Branch, a resort town on New Jersey's north shore, where his mother's family was in the hotel business. Isaac Mailer, of Russian-Jewish extraction, served in the British army as a supply officer and emigrated to America from South Africa via London shortly after World War I. When his son was four years old, he moved his family to the Eastern Parkway section of Brooklyn, "the most secure Jewish environment in America" Mailer recalls. Isaac (Barney) worked as an accountant in Brooklyn until his death in 1972. Mrs. Mailer still lives in Brooklyn and until recently ran a nursing and housekeeping service there. Barbara has worked from time to time as her brother's secretary.

Mailer and his sister both graduated with honors—he from Harvard and she from Radcliffe. Norman "always had the highest marks," his mother recalls. He was a confident youngster who played the clarinet and spent untold hours building model airplanes. Aeronautics was his first love, but it is noteworthy that as early as the age of nine he expressed this love in a literary way. He filled 250 notebook pages with a fantastical story called *An Invasion from Mars*. At Boys' High School in Brooklyn, Mailer published his first work, an article on how to build model airplanes. Upon graduation he set his sights on the Massachusetts Institute of Technology and the study of aeronautical engineering. Because he was only sixteen, M.I.T. wanted him to go to prep school for an additional year, so he chose Harvard instead.

In his first semester at Harvard, Mailer discovered the modern American novel—*Studs Lonigan*, *U.S.A.*, and *The Grapes of Wrath* were particularly influential. He devoted himself to writing, read Wolfe, Hemingway, and Faulkner, and vowed that he would become a major American novelist. His first short story, "The Greatest Thing in the World," was published in the *Harvard Advocate*. Derivative in conception, it was clearly written under the influence of his first masters: Farrell, Dos Passos, and Steinbeck. Encouraged by his writing professor, Robert Gorham Davis, he submitted the story to *Story* magazine's annual college contest and won first prize. Like all literary prizes, though, this one brought its weight of worry. Eighteen-year-old Truman Capote was already creating stories of consummate artistic beauty while Mailer feared that he was merely writing prose that, as he put it, "reads like the early work of a young man who is going to make a fortune writing first rate action, western, gangster, and suspense pictures."

After graduating from Harvard in 1943, Mailer set out to allay his natural feelings of callowness and garner some experiences on his own. He was inducted into the army in March 1944. That same month he married Beatrice Silverman of Chelsea, Massachusetts, who became a lieutenant in the WAVES. Sent to the Pacific, Private Mailer became by his own admission "the third lousiest GI in a platoon of twelve." Actually he was not much interested in becoming a good soldier. Rather, he was obsessed with satisfying what he called that "cold maniacal thing in my heart, sharp as a shiv"— the desire to write the definitive American novel of World War II. He went ashore with the United States infantry forces in the invasion of Luzon. Then, with his appointment to a desk job as a clerk-typist, the excitement came to a stop. Eager to get the experience necessary to write his novel, he volunteered as a rifleman with a reconnaissance platoon fighting in the Philippine mountains. After his discharge in April 1946, he settled down to fifteen months of writing. *The Naked and the Dead* achieved a remarkable critical and popular success. By 1948 Norman Mailer found himself the most celebrated young writer in America.

The Naked and the Dead tells the story of a fourteen-man infantry platoon that lands on the barren beach of a small Japanese-held island in the South Pacific. The platoon is part of a 6000-man force charged with the task of seizing control of the island in order to clear the way for a larger American advance into the Philippines. Mailer carefully delineates the differences—emotional, geographic, social, economic—of each man in the platoon, for he intends it to represent a microcosm of the American populace. The platoon includes a God-fearing Mississippi dirt farmer; a sensitive Jew from Brooklyn; a socially oppressed Mexican-American; an embittered, itinerant laborer from the coal mines of Montana; a reactionary Irishman from South Boston's working class; a dull, middle-class Kansas salesman; a cynical Chicago hoodlum; and a dissipated hedonist from Georgia.

Over the perspective of both officers and enlisted men prevails the narrative voice of Mailer, who remains a detached, omniscient observer. He conveys the tribulations of war objectively. Though his prose recalls the clarity and precision of Steinbeck's *Grapes of Wrath*, the stance he takes toward his characters resembles that of Dos Passos in his *U.S.A.* trilogy. Mailer refuses to allow the reader to get involved with a character or to imagine that any man has control over the historical moment in which he finds himself. Mailer discourages sympathy for his characters by shifting the narrative to another character or scene. In the case of Lieutenant Hearn, for example, the reader draws near only to be cut off from him with a sudden notice of his death: "A half hour later, Hearn was killed by a machine-gun bullet which passed through his chest." It seems that only the grimmest of interpretations can be drawn. In a dumb, wanton universe man labors to die. He does not really fit into the universe; he is an outlaw on an earth not designed for him. In a profoundly anti-Christian vein, Mailer concludes that God does not take any interest in man.

The compelling dramatic tension of this novel derives from Mailer's fascination with the lives of three men—General Cummings, Sergeant Croft, and Lieutenant Hearn—who press their will upon necessity. Their efforts to define themselves in opposition to a deterministic universe present all that Mailer held to be of moral value at this stage in his career. These three men, without losing their individuality, are modern incarnations of the great mythic figures of western civilization. Cummings, in his overweening urge to shape reality to his own needs and make the world answerable to them, represents Faustian man. Hearn, in his dispassionate rejection of everything that would impose conditions on the autonomy of his thought, is Socratic man. And Croft, in his irrepressible desire to climb Mount Anaka (the mountain in the center of the island), resembles the Satanic hero. The mythic heroism of these three men and the naturalistic universe they oppose constitutes the primary conflict in *The Naked and the Dead*. In thematic terms, the conflict is between romance and idealism. The interplay between these two elements gives this novel its identifying form as a work of art.

The action of the novel is both foreshadowed by and centered on Mount Anaka. When Croft undertakes to lead the reconnaissance platoon over the mountain, his rebellion attains archetypal proportions. For in climbing Mount Anaka, Croft intends to confirm that he is not what the mountain, in its aloof splendor, seems to say he is: mere flesh, a weak, transitory creature. The mountain symbolizes to Croft the deific qualities which mock man's mortality. To scale Mount Anaka would mean to him that man is more than mere flesh, that he possesses the mystical strength of the mountain. But when Croft fails to reach the summit, he despairs in the knowledge that he was wrong. Man may be *in* nature—for Mailer he is entrapped in it, embroiled in it—but he is not *of* it. No intimate kinship exists between man and nature.

Mailer chose war as the subject of his first novel because he was convinced that only in a crisis could man's real nature be revealed. In *The Naked and the Dead* Mailer dealt with two age-old human tensions—the struggle between animal desire and spiritual aspiration and the struggle between individualism and authority—in their essential pattern, with power, gravity, and veracity. A hammering scrutiny of life's damage leaves an earnest respect for the people who must sustain it.

The success of *The Naked and the Dead* allowed Mailer to cut loose from his old identity of nice-Jewish-boy-from-Brooklyn and to seek a new one. Always sympathetic to socialism, he entered first the realm of politics, but his espousal of Henry Wallace's bid for the presidency had made him realize that the end result of all governmental systems is oligarchic dominance. He traveled next to Hollywood, where he wrote an original screenplay for Metro-Goldwyn-Mayer, but it was rejected and Mailer, concluding that fiction was his proper medium after all, left Hollywood. He returned East, where he wrote the greater part of his second novel, *Barbary Shore*.

Deeply influenced by Jean Malaquais—the left-wing French intellectual who became Mailer's friend and guided him through the tortuous roadways of Marxist philosophy—*Barbary Shore* (1951) is an odd, febrile story of five desiccated lives caught between American and Soviet authoritarianism. Mailer wrote the book at an anguished pitch and came up with some starkly illuminating insights into the psyche of the fascist, the Trotskyite, the secret agent, the psychotic, the existentialist, and mass man. The critics were not impressed. Those intent on upholding the puritanism of Eisenhower-era America called the book sordid; others called it ponderous.

A divorce from Beatrice Silverman followed the publication of *Barbary Shore*. For some time Mailer had been wanting to free himself and move to Greenwich Village, where he imagined he could live a life of adventurous pleasure. When a friend introduced him to the beautiful Adele Morales, a Spanish-Peruvian painter, he found the world of lavish excitement he had been missing. They were married in 1954. In the next year Mailer founded, with Daniel Wolf and Edwin Fancher, the *Village Voice*, a pioneering weekly newspaper on politics and the arts. His use of more and more potent stimulants—liquor, marijuana, Benzedrine, Seconal—took its physical toll—appendicitis and a damaged liver. But it seemed as though Mailer was willing to rush death rather than return to normalcy, for he was convinced that experimentation with drugs had brought him Dionysian knowledge.

In the midst of his delusion, his recklessness, and what he thought of as his sloth, Mailer set out to write a novel that he hoped would regain for him the distinction he lost with the publication of *Barbary Shore*. He committed himself fully to the writing of *The Deer Park*, a novel about the symbolic hell of a Hollywood resort and the venal people in it. The novel's *raisonneur* is a movie director, Charles Eitel. Eitel directed brilliant films of honest social consciousness in the 1930s; but after World War II, when a Congressional investigative committee accuses him of Communist involvements, he refuses to become a "friendly witness" and thereby sacrifices a successful career as one of Hollywood's top box office directors. Blacklisted by every studio, Eitel tries to revive his dormant creative powers and write a screenplay that will atone for all the slick, gaudy movies he has made since his fine early work. His inability to do so constitutes the central drama of the novel.

Despite personal defeat, Eitel harbors an inviolate vision of what it is to grow—a vision that is the guiding light of the novel. He realizes his sterile condition and reflects that "there was a law of life so cruel and so just which demanded that one must grow or else pay more for remaining the same." He imparts the lessons of his self-judgments to Sergius O'Shaugnessy, the novel's narrator. The Eitel-Sergius relationship is a tutor-tyro one. Eitel frankly assesses Sergius and encourages "self-analysis." What Eitel means by self-analysis is the creation of an "art work." For he believes that only in an art work can man discover his inner self and give form to his strivings. For all *The Deer Park*'s concentration on the mores of stars, starlets, producers, sensualists, and panderers, its ethical imperative is rather outdated: only sacrifice and hard work will transcend "the mummery of what happens, passes, and is gone." The reader is led to believe that in a conformist society the creation of art is the only strategy against anonymity. An art work, Sergius eventually realizes through Eitel's sad example, will give him "dignity" and enable him to "keep in some permanent form those parts of myself which are better than me." Art teaches Sergius that only through identification with impersonal beauty can human suffering and human limitation be transcended. In Sergius's terms, the world embodied in an art work is the "real world" because it is the honest and permanent distillate of one's selfhood. Desert D'Or (the Hollywood resort of the story) is the "imaginary world" because it is devoted to that which is corporeal and therefore wholly perishable—physical beauty and material success.

Yet the problem with *The Deer Park* is that Sergius, for all his talk, is really an underdeveloped character. One does not have a sense of involvement with him because he is undersensitive and nearly devoid of tenderness; at least that is how he presents himself. Things happen to him without things happening inside him. What more than compensates for the flaws in the characterization of Sergius is the delineation of the affair between Eitel and the woman he loves—Elena Esposito, sometime actress and castoff of other men. With scrupulous honesty Mailer renders the relationship with its dynamic of sensual rapture and love, its attendant disillusionment, its deterioration, and its final stale disablement. Mailer's two characterizations are charged with life: Eitel, the suave but tortured gentleman whose perverse will compels him, despite his intelligence, to debase his artistic talents; Elena, the desperate, graceless beauty, humiliated by men and simple in her understanding of life, but valiantly in possession of self-dignity. Sergius talks about himself with a phony tartness, but he narrates the Eitel-Elena affair with dispassionate wisdom.

The novel's setting, Desert D'Or, reinforces the doomed, airless quality of the love affair. It is the center of the book which gives form to the "prisons of pain, the wading pools of pleasure, and the public and professional voices of our sentimental land." This for Mailer constitutes American culture at large. Desert D'Or is an infernal arena of "middle aged desperados of corporation land and the suburb" locked into a perpetual round of greed and lust. The desert that surrounds the resort symbolizes the spiritual wasteland within. Windowless facades and walled-in patios give sanctuary to people who have relinquished their souls to Mammon and Eros. The town possesses no tradition or heritage or recognizable past. It is a "no-man's land of the perpetual present." Sergius remarks on the "air cooled midnight" of the town's bars: "Drinking in that atmosphere, I never knew whether it was night or day.... afternoon was always passing into night, and drunken nights into the dawn of a desert morning. One seemed to leave the theatrical darkness of afternoon for the illumination of night, and the sun of Desert D'Or became like the stranger who the drunk imagines to be following him." Man has been divorced from the diurnal cycle. Symbolically, his connection with organic life has been severed. Mailer's purgatorial vision of Desert D'Or intensifies the novel's theme enunciated by Eitel: " 'One cannot look for a good time, Sergius, for pleasure must end as love or cruelty'—and almost as an afterthought, he added —'or obligation.' " *The Deer Park* is an ironic prose elegy about people seeking pleasure as though it were happiness.

When *The Deer Park* appeared, it met with mixed reviews. It was only a partial success, which, on Mailer's competitive scale of all or nothing, meant a failure. Because the world had not, he believed, tried to understand him, he resolved that he would no longer try to understand the world. Rather, he would turn inward to explore his own psyche in such a way that one would come to believe it was America's psyche itself that was being explored. He succeeded. *Advertisements for Myself* established Mailer as a writer of searing candor and oracular brilliance. He became *philosophe maudit* to the nation.

Advertisements for Myself (1959) is a compendium of Mailer's writings, almost all previously published, from the first eighteen years of his career. It is a multigeneric display of short stories, poems, plays, essays, articles, interviews, letters, excerpts from novels, and columns from the *Village Voice*. This assemblage is interlinked with commentary, what Mailer calls "Advertisements," in which he chronicles his fervent efforts—through honor and dishonor, security and paranoia, aspiration and disillusion, recklessness and remorse—to realize the best in himself through art. In writing openly and movingly about these struggles, Mailer came out from behind his fiction and established himself as a national personality, an undeniable literary presence whose admissions recalled the self-promoting strategies of Walt Whitman. An undertone of vehemence, however, balances the book's narcissism: "I have not gotten nicer as I have grown older, and I suspect that what has been true for me may be true for a good many of you."

Mailer may rather enjoy being embittered; he certainly must have gotten satisfaction from his "Advertisements" because they are written with a color, a freedom, and a brio never before found in his work:

> The shits are killing us, even as they kill themselves—each day a few more lies eat into the seed with which we are born, little institutional lies from the print of newspapers, the shock waves of television, and the sentimental cheats of the movie screen. Little lies, but they pipe us toward insanity as they starve our sense of the real. We have grown up in a world more in decay than the worst of the Roman Empire, a cowardly world chasing after a good time (of which last one can approve) but chasing it without the courage to pay the price of full consciousness, and so losing pleasure in pips and squeaks of anxiety.

"The White Negro" lies at the heart of *Advertisements for Myself*. Published originally in *Dissent*, a literary-intellectual journal of the New Left, it has gained enormous popularity and is frequently anthologized. It represents a shift in Mailer's focus, because here for the first time he concentrates on psychical rather than social reality. He takes as his province the instinctual consciousness of the urban American Negro, who operates in accordance with subliminal needs. By replacing the imperatives of society with the imperatives of the self, the urban black makes it impossible for institutions of social control to account for him in their own terms. This demonic rebel is for Mailer the essence of "hip" and the model for "a new breed of adventurers, urban adventurers who drifted out at night looking for action with a black man's code to fit their facts. The hipster had absorbed the existentialist synapses of the Negro, and for practical purposes could be considered a white Negro."

The hipster's response to experience is intuitive, sensuous, and violent. Mailer's radical assumption is that each act of individual violence, no matter how heinous it may be, subtracts from the collective violence of the state (such as the liquidation of European Jews or the nuclear bombings of Japan).

He was later to suggest, in his writings of the late 1960s for example, that the war in Vietnam was partly the result of our inhibitive lives. Mass private constraint, a population "starved into the attrition of conformity," can precipitate mass catastrophe. Unlike individual violence, no one supposedly is responsible for war; so, says Mailer, war becomes a socially acceptable means of expressing violence. It is in defiance of the "collective murders of the State" that the hipster develops into a psychopath. "The strength of the psychopath is that he knows (where most of us can only guess) what is good for him and what is bad for him at exactly those instants when . . . the potentiality exists to change [or] replace a negative and empty fear with an outward action. . . ." Mailer is saying that if violence alone will overcome fear, let violence be. Man is better off close to death than hag-ridden by the dictates of a conformist society or emasculated by an anesthetic modular world.

This hipster psychopath is an authentic existentialist because his philosophy is felt, not conceptualized. Informed by the writings of Jean Paul Sartre, Mailer contends that the only value is that value which answers one's own psychological needs. ". . . there are no truths other than the isolated truths of what each observer feels at each instance of his existence. . . ." To judge or view man "from a set of standards conceived a priori to . . . experience, standards from the past," is to preclude his right to grow according to whatever measure he sets for himself. The energy with which the hipster psychopath spurs himself on to growth is derived from a continual search for "an orgasm more apocalyptic than the one which preceded it. Orgasm is his therapy—he knows at the seed of his being that good orgasm opens his possibilities and bad orgasm imprisons him." Mailer reverses the spirit/flesh dichotomy. It is the flesh that gives sanction and value to the spirit, not vice versa. In the orgasmic moment the hipster believes he can become identical with God Who is "located in the senses of the body."

Ultimately, "The White Negro" goes beyond social psychology and sexology and turns out to be Mailer's portrait of his own psyche and of his own creative processes. Each of Mailer's subsequent protagonists in his novels is emotionally (though not factually) autobiographical and modeled on the hipster delineated in this essay. The vitalizing madness and compulsive energy that underlie *The Naked and the Dead* and *Barbary Shore* surface here.

The turbulence which expressed itself exuberantly in *Advertisements for Myself* fearsomely rocked Mailer's personal life. In 1960, after an all-night party at their new Manhattan apartment, he stabbed his wife Adele with a penknife, seriously wounding her, and entered Bellevue hospital for seventeen days of psychiatric observation. His wife did not press charges; she recovered and they were soon reconciled. But in 1962 he and Adele were divorced. That same year he married Lady Jeanne Campbell, daughter of the Duke of Argyll and granddaughter of Lord Beaverbrook. His marriage with Lady Jeanne was calamitous and short. After a year, in which a daughter, Kate, was born, they were divorced, and Mailer promptly married actress Beverly Bentley. What an astonishing departure all this is from the soft-voiced man who said in 1948, "Actually, I've got all the average middle-class fears." Now Mailer had become the terrible ruffian of American letters.

For sensation-seeking journalists Mailer became little more than material for racy copy. He was arrested in Provincetown for taunting and fighting with police officers; in a televised interview with Mike Wallace, he suggested that juvenile delinquency in New York could be decreased by holding once a year medieval jousting tournaments in Central Park between members of rival gangs; he was arrested at Birdland, a New York nightclub, in a bellicose argument over his liquor bill; at a poetry reading he had the curtain brought down on him for alleged obscenity; after Sonny Liston knocked out Floyd Patterson, he confronted the bearish Liston and told him to wise up and let him promote his next fight; he financed Jose Torres' bid for the world light-heavyweight championship and later donned a pair of boxing gloves himself to go four rounds with Torres on Dick Cavett's television show. These acts may seem exhibitionistic or absurd, but by Mailer's logic they help him to write well and therefore are not foolish.

Just how objectionable Mailer's behavior is depends then, in large part, on one's estimation of his writing, which has become more compelling since his emergence as a public personality. With the miscellanies—*The Presidential Papers* (1963) and *Cannibals and Christians* (1966)—he developed a reputation as an astute critic of politics and society in America. With *The Armies of the Night* and *Miami and the Siege of Chicago*, he gained an international reputation for a dramatic rendering of the same subjects. His two novels, *An American Dream* and *Why Are We in Vietnam?*, project the daydreams and subliminal compulsions of the American character with tonal colorations never before seen in American fiction.

An American Dream (1965) is about the dissolution of the self. It is set in New York City where Stephen Rojack, the novel's narrator, murders his diabolical estranged wife, casts off his old identities—professor, author, war hero, ex-congressman, television talk-show host, socialite—and perilously struggles toward rebirth. Rojack is the new primitive. An intellectual attuned to his nonrational being, a cultured savage, he is the type of man Mailer hopes will someday emerge in America to overcome the repressions of the state. *An American Dream* is an evolutionary novel in which, paradoxically, Rojack evolves by going back to his primordial being. The subconscious, Mailer still believes, is the mind of primordial being. It is an energy, an intelligence, existing outside time and civilization. Rojack's primary commitment is to understand this mysterious mental region and then to act eventfully in the world to substantiate his new-found knowledge.

One may well ask whether good can come from the deliberate cultivation of subconscious needs; whether this doesn't amount to insanity. Mailer would agree that it does. But his writing has always suggested that insanity is unavoidable in contemporary America. That which social tradition deems sanity, he argues, is actually sickness: the military (*The Naked and the Dead*), political parties (*Barbary Shore*), and show business (*The Deer Park*). For Mailer the social realities of our time offer a grim proposition: one's choice is not between sanity and insanity, but between static insanity and creative insanity, or what he calls "psychopathy." The theme of *An American Dream* is the clarification and intensification of the subconscious self. It is about exhuming one's primeval being so that it can invigorate and inform the conscious mind and be brought to bear upon the social and institutional arenas of America. Mailer has defined character in this novel as an endless series of second chances. His hero is trying to do what the classic American heroes of James Fenimore Cooper and Herman Melville tried to do before him—get away from the enfeeblements of civilization, the crush of history.

To give form to this struggle for unencumbered selfhood, Mailer has fashioned a polyphonic prose of remarkable metaphoric richness. *An American Dream* signifies a radical departure from Mailer's earlier, realistic novels. Literature for him became a source of mystic release and revelation. He found in this book a way to give the immediacy of direct sensation to the morbid or sensuous dream. Areas of human nature usually left unexplored—Mailer would say untapped—are now revealed.

Nowhere else in Mailer's canon is this more true than in his fifth and most recent novel, *Why Are We in Vietnam?* (1967). A hunting party of Dallas corporate executives goes to Alaska to kill grizzly bear. They hire a helicopter to flush out of the wilderness not only grizzlies but wolf, Dall ram, and caribou. Laden with guns powerful enough to drop an elephant, the huntsmen engage in a grotesque sporting holiday of blood. The parable is clear. The hunting party is the American military in miniature, replete with commanders and their GI subordinates. The crazed animals being annihilated by aerial machines are the people of Vietnam napalmed by the air force, but such pat equations do little to help one understand the art of this book.

It is the character of young D.J.'s voice that carries all of the novel's thematic, symbolic, and structural weight. "Grassed out" on marijuana at his parents' Dallas mansion and enjoying his farewell party—he will be inducted into the army the next day—D.J. narrates the events of this Alaskan odyssey in a punning prose that is a dazzling collage of speech from almost every arena of American life. In rapid-fire shifts, he speaks the language of an urban black, a pedantic psychoanalyst, a corporate bureaucrat, a Southern redneck, a revivalist preacher, an academic philosopher, a physicist, a McLuhanite media critic. The impression is of a jammed radio receiver picking up from multiple wavelengths all the ideologies, buried fantasies, fears, and desires of the collective American psyche and transmitting them across the land. D.J. calls himself "Disc jockey to the world." He is telepathically tuned in to the rumblings, the groanings, the screams, and the palpitations of our subterranean selves; and his voice, he imagines, is a "tape being made for the private ear of the Lord, Who will register it in His Univac-like celestial archives." D.J. is the recording secretary of repressed compulsions—dreams of power, ecstatic sexual hopes, hatreds, and bigotries.

D.J.'s consciousness is in the throes of trying to rid itself of that which has glutted it—namely "mixed shit," Mailer's collective symbol for all the slogans, categories, and presumptions of popular American culture. The novel is not intended to be a study of character, because it assumes that individual character cannot survive in a world where the mind control techniques of the mass media have homogenized human thought and where the value of human productivity is measured by impersonal forces such as government, business, and industry. D.J.'s consciousness has been made manic by excessive input. What particularly engorges his mind are thoughts of the violence that historically has been so large and pervasive a part of our national

character that it was eventually exported to Southeast Asia. The energetic onrush of the tale D.J. tells may be interpreted as his attempt to purge himself of his psychic overload. But even after fleeing from the hunting party and immersing himself in the pure, raw wilderness, D.J. eagerly declares at the novel's end: "Vietnam, hot damn."

What is to be made of such grotesquerie? It is Mailer's means of exploding the whole Adamic tradition of American literature. *Why Are We in Vietnam?* is a deliberate rebuttal of the revered notion that if man removes himself from the corruptness of civilization and enters the realm of unspoiled nature, he can revive within himself something of the purity of heart and nobility of spirit that Adam must have felt in that first world that God set specially before him. While Mailer believes that man does indeed divorce himself from the mystical harmonies of nature, greedily ravages it, builds war machines, and decimates his own kind, he clearly suggests, by way of D.J.'s Arctic experience, that the origin of man's barbarity is nature itself. Evil was in nature before it was in man. Such is Mailer's premise, and he shares it with William Burroughs, whose novel, *Naked Lunch*, inspired this one. "America," Burroughs writes, "is not a young land: it is old and dirty and evil before the settlers, before the Indians. The evil is there waiting." Traditional notions of a serene pastoralism, of a virgin land, are for Mailer—tough-minded urbanite that he is— nostalgic inventions of a primitive past that never was. I will be savage, D.J. seems to be saying, because I recognize that civilization is but another of savagery's masks, not an enlightened journey out of darkness.

The cultural conflicts of *Why Are We in Vietnam?*—the individual versus the corporation, independent thought versus the electronic media— are left unresolved because Mailer is inspired in this book by the impulse to escape from culture itself into a realm where nature is terrible, yet beautiful. Finally, however, the real achievement of this novel has more to do with the recreation of cultural contradictions than with escape from them; D.J.'s narrative presents the dire divisions within American society. How he renders such divisions can be seen in a passage early in the novel when, speaking in urban black vernacular, he describes the menacing interrogation of a country Negro: "Whitey the Green Eye" has a nose "red as lobster . . . a-hovering and a-plunging like a Claw, man. . . ." The narrative then modulates to the patter of a white, drug-ridden hipster: "ex-acid is my head, Love Is Death . . . it's square to be frantic. . . ." Then it shifts to the voice of an ingratiating "true-blue Wasp-ass" Texan extending a down-home Southern hospitality invitation to Jesus to "come visit." Here is capitalism trying to make its peace with Christianity. Interwoven in the passage are two threads. One is a brief excerpt from "In the Cool, Cool, Cool of the Evening," a popular song about the idyllic amicability of provincial American life. Another is a pun, "sick with the tick," which refers to time and the parasitic insect, both destroyers of life—thus D.J.'s query, "oh blood how rot is thy sting?" Encapsulated here on half a page are the hatreds and fears, delusions and dreams, weltering within American society. This novel is an oratorio for many voices, each one of which infuriates, stupefies, or calls up dark laughter. By recreating the duplicities and tensions that infect the American character, Mailer explains why we were in Vietnam.

Furthermore, just as the value of the book is that it enlarges perceptions rather than offers solutions, so the moral of the book is artistic, not ideological. Style, the very act of writing itself—of release in the form of expressive invention—is the one strategy Mailer invokes against the numbing effects of the mass media and the "communication engineers" of a programmed society. By mimicking the languages of the land, he sees through them and their beguilements and coercions. Verbal play is restorative, a spiritual tonic. Mailer suggests it is the last psychical liberty. The book's style is complex. "I say create complexities," says Mailer in *The Presidential Papers*, "let art deepen sophistication, let complexities be demonstrated to our leaders, let us try to make *them* more complex. That is a manly activity." It is an activity which can, he asserts, diminish the totalitarian forces of government, business, and mass communication that simplify life and brutalize man's mind by expunging ambiguity and diversity. A style crackling with disparate images—a style like D.J.'s—may be, Mailer hopes, the force to fight the progressive collectivism of human life. *Why Are We in Vietnam?* is a book that will not be categorized, for its intention is to subvert all category.

In its inventive prose style and in its indictment of big business and the electronic media, *Why Are We in Vietnam?* is a novelist's novel. But the general reader did not know what to make of it. To some people it was obscure, to others it was obscene, to most it was both. *The Armies of the Night* (1968), however, re-established Mailer with a wide audience and won him high critical acclaim as well. It received the National Book Award and Pulitzer Prize. Subtitled *History as a Novel, the Novel as History*,

the book is an on-the-spot account of the antiwar march on the Pentagon in October 1967. It is novelistic because it sensitively describes the effects of the march on a participant-protagonist, Mailer himself, and historical because it scrupulously describes the facts of the march.

The book's unity of time and its strict enclosure within the limits of a particular time and place give it a classical sharpness of design. Mailer was compelled to record reality rather than invent it. His previous novels shaped events; now events shape the book—events, moreover, that people know about and can therefore relate to. Tom Wolfe comments on the winning qualities of this "new journalism": it "consumes devices that happen to have originated with the novel and mixes them with every other device known to prose. And all the while, quite beyond matters of technique, it enjoys an advantage so obvious, so built-in, one almost forgets what power it has: the simple fact that the reader knows *all this actually happened*. The disclaimers have been erased. The screen is gone. The writer is one step closer to the absolute involvement of the reader that Henry James and James Joyce dreamed of and never achieved."

What makes *The Armies of the Night* so extraordinarily engaging is the characterization of the protagonist, Norman Mailer. Usually he refers to himself simply as "Mailer" or "he," but his occasional use of other names as well—the Ruminant, the Beast, the Existentialist, the Historian, the Participant, the Novelist, the General, the Protagonist, Norman—attests to the diversity of his behavior, to the fact that all along he is at will improvising identities the better to accommodate himself to the multifariousness of American society. An assumption guides him: in an extremely pluralistic nation, the self, to operate effectively, must also be pluralistic. Generally, though, Mailer is a self-preserving rogue in this book, a character of exorbitant disproportions, for always offsetting every sacrificial act of civil disobedience is some ludicrous vanity. He daringly instigates his arrest at the hands of a federal marshal, but he has engaged a filmmaker to follow him closely and take movies of his arrest. Herded into an army truck with the other prisoners, he finds it a "touch awkward" climbing over the tailgate, "for he did not wish to dirty his dark blue pinstripe suit." When he is finally put behind bars, a single thought keeps recurring to him: Can he be released in time to attend a Saturday-night party in New York "which has every promise of being wicked, tasty, and rich?" Mailer may not be convincing as an earnest radical or a "Left

Conservative" (his own term for himself) hero—but as a comic hero he is a marvel.

His self-satire is due largely to his "command of a detachment, classic in severity (for he was a novelist and so in need of studying every last lineament of the fine, the noble, the frantic, and the foolish in others and in himself)." And therein lies the power of *The Armies of the Night*—in its novelistic attributes, its evocations of character and milieu and situation. When Mailer departs from his novelistic rendering of material, the book loses its thrust. The narrative-descriptive style, in which explicit details cohere with implicit moral moments, gives way to the oracular-ruminative style which dotes on abstractions and cultural *cum* philosophical questions. The last paragraph of the book is a case in point. Mailer imagines "America, once a beauty of magnificence unparalleled," now horribly diseased because of her involvement in the Southeast Asia war. "She will probably give birth, and to what?—the most fearsome totalitarianism the world has ever known? Or can she, poor giant, tormented lovely girl, deliver a babe of a new world brave and tender, artful and wild? Rush to the locks. Deliver us from our curse. For we must end on the road to that mystery where courage, death, and the dream of love give promise of sleep." Such writing borders on cant and obscurity. How unduly apocalyptic this passage seems now that American society has settled back into relative normality. One may find Mailer, the self-styled Jeremiah, rather tiresome, but when he goes about the business of "studying" every "lineament" and exploring human behavior—his own, the demonstrators', the soldiers'—with the old-fashioned tools of the novelist, his writing incandesces.

Living and reporting the historic stresses of the 1960s, Mailer began to suspect that our national reality had become more fantastical than any fiction. His suspicion was confirmed by the National Aeronautics and Space Administration's announcement that it was ready to rocket man to the moon. Commissioned by *Life* magazine, he flew to Houston and Cape Kennedy to cover the flight of Apollo 11. As spectacular as Mailer believes the moon shot is in *Of a Fire on the Moon* (1970), he holds that the cosmic forces of existence are present just as provocatively, just as sublimely, in the relationship between man and woman as in the infinite reaches of space. Mailer contends that the interplay between the sexes is a process that God has ordained to bring symmetry and balance to creation. The heterosexual relationship "is one of the prime symbols of the connection between all things."

The chief experiences of Mailer's life have always concerned women. In 1970 he separated from Beverly Bentley and their two sons—Michael Burks and Stephen McLeod. That same year, leading exponents of the new feminists denounced him as the principal voice of male chauvinism on the American literary scene. He counterattacked with *The Prisoner of Sex* (1971). In this comically trenchant treatise he reexplores his relationship with women by examining the nature of his love for them and sets forth his own ideas on the sex game and his own sexuality. The further Mailer ponders the new feminism the more he comes to realize that it is a subject rich in possibilities. After all, he says, "the themes of his life had gathered here. Revolution, tradition, sex and the homosexual, the orgasm, the family, the child and the political shape of the future, technology and human conception, waste and abortion, the ethics of the critic and the male mystique, black rights and new thoughts on women's rights."

He first argues his position against Kate Millett. The freedom that she envisions for women once technology delivers them from the bondage of the womb, Mailer can only perceive as a deeper bondage for the whole human race. Semen banks, genetic engineering, artificial wombs, human birth by parthenogenesis—all such schemes for a scientifically immaculate conception he regards as totalitarian stratagems leading to world-wide homogeneity. On the question of the sex act itself, he scorns those feminists who applaud Masters and Johnson, the experimental sexologists who rescued their patients from frigidity and impotence by encouraging them, in comfortable laboratory conditions, to use those stimulative techniques most conducive to orgasm. All this, complains Mailer, is so clinical, so vapid, so very much beside the point. Sexuality is not genitality. Rather, he insists that it has to do—and he quotes William Blake—with "comminglings from the Head to the Feet." He implies that only a man of imagination, a novelist, can decipher the message of human orgasm.

At this juncture Mailer argues in support of two brother artists, Henry Miller and D. H. Lawrence. For Millett, Miller is America's vile pasha of depersonalized sex. She cites passages from his early novels, *Tropic of Cancer* (1934) and *Tropic of Capricorn* (1939), in which, she contends, men use women as mere carnal fodder. But Mailer accuses Millett of hypocrisy and is at his comic and mischievous best defending Miller and lampooning Millett for her dogged, tractarian approach, her insensitivity to Miller's humor and metaphoric power. As for Lawrence, Mailer refutes Millett's charge that the sexual act in Lawrence's work is a matter of male will and female submission. *Both* sexes must deliver themselves, in Lawrence's words, "over to the unknown," a mystical power far greater than themselves.

Mailer goes on to poeticize the womb as woman's alliance with eternity, her inner cosmos into which man, the striver, must make his way. Sexual intercourse becomes an apocalyptically grave engagement in which the sperm, a writhing "limb of the soul seeking to be born," takes a leap toward "every call of the woman for what was magnificent or large as her idea of future life." Mailer ecstatically visualizes the ovum as an expectant priestess choosing to receive only the most valiant of wriggling voyagers that enter through her door. The more poetically he treats sexuality the more meaning he attaches to it, until he becomes "The Prisoner." "No thought was so painful as the idea that sex had meaning: for give meaning to sex and one was the prisoner of sex—the more meaning one gave it, the more it assumed, until every failure and misery, every evil of your life, spoke their lines in its light, and every fear of mediocre death."

A year after *The Prisoner of Sex* was published Mailer again braced himself to take the plunge into the female psyche. He was offered a large sum of money to write a preface to a photographic retrospect of Marilyn Monroe. Long fascinated with persons who, like himself, have been intimate with the prizes and perils of playing to a national audience, he could not resist expanding his 25,000-word preface to a "novel biography" almost four times that length. He felt this was a chance to explore a spiritual twin. His basic contention is that if the real Monroe is to be discovered, a novelist must do it. To conceive of her novelistically, his premise goes, is to come closer than any pure biographical reportage can to the truth of what her "unspoken impulses" were. "Exceptional people have a way of living with opposites in themselves" that puts them beyond the pale of logical inquiry and renders traditional "biographical tools" insufficient. Yet his writing suffers when it moves from concrete description to abstraction. For example, what sense can be made of his explanation of how Ingmar Bergman puts his personal imprint on film? ". . . all the hoarded haunted sorrows of Scandinavia drift in to imbibe the vampires of his psyche—he is like a spirit vapor risen out of the sinister character of film itself." Such writing generates more heat than light. Another example: Monroe proves herself a "great comedian" in *Gentlemen Prefer Blondes*, "which is to say she

bears an exquisitely light relation to the dramatic thunders of triumph, woe, greed, and calculation." Hardly a clarifying definition of a great comedian. Long priding himself on being one of the fastest writers alive—he has entitled one piece in *The Presidential Papers* "Ten Thousand Words a Minute"—Mailer wrote *Marilyn* in two months in order to get it published for the summer-fall book season. It seems that the power and precision of his language have been sacrificed to the requirements of time.

And it is a pity, for the thesis of *Marilyn* is profound. Monroe's selfhood, the identity she desperately groped for all her life, was a mirage. Not able to find it by her own efforts, she sought out other people—her husbands, agents, directors—to help her find it. Unsatisfied with the results of the impossible task she set them, she sought solace in pills. Her search for an identity beneath or beyond her multiple roles was necessarily futile because, Mailer believes, identity exists *within* roles. The mask is the face. Here, then, is a clue to Mailer's own behavior. His identity is self-created and deliberately prismatic. In *The Armies of the Night*, for instance, he is master of ceremonies, actor, director, ambassador, general, banker, historian, and novelist. Since *Advertisements for Myself* the assumption of his books has been that if identity is diversified, it is more difficult for internal and external suppressors—the superego, the corporation, the state—to retard individual growth. Marilyn Monroe's problem was that, like Charles Eitel, she was caught in the corporate web, in this case Hollywood, and compelled to play the role it forced upon her, that of vibrant sex goddess. In the process—to recall an image from *The Deer Park*—the life of the "cave," of the creative mind, atrophied.

In 1974 Mailer signed a one-million dollar contract with Little, Brown to write a novel of at least two and possibly five volumes. A work of mythic themes, a family saga ranging back into ancient times and forward into the future, it will take five to seven years to write. Part of the book is set in Egypt during the Twentieth Dynasty, and part takes place in a spaceship. Some of it concerns the life of a Jewish family before World War I. A good deal of it will be contemporary. One million dollars is not as abundant a figure as it seems because, as Mailer readily admits, four ex-wives and seven children constitute a costly family enterprise. Nor do his expenses stop there; his accountant, his agent, his lawyer, and his government must be paid. He speaks from woeful experience when he says, "Economics is half of literature." Little, Brown has given him the

Jill Krementz

Norman Mailer running for mayor of New York.

chance now to keep in the black, the better to apply himself to that one grand objective that he has been trying to obtain for the past twenty years: "to hit the longest ball ever to go up in to the accelerated hurricane air of American letters. For if I have one ambition above all others, it is to write a novel which Dostoyevsky and Marx; Joyce and Freud; Stendhal, Tolstoy, Proust, and Spengler; Faulkner, and even old moldering Hemingway might come to read, for it would carry what they had to tell another part of the way."

As for Mailer's work thus far, it has shown a remarkable diversity of artistic forms and styles, but the basic theme remains the same. An essential conflict undergirds all Mailer's books and makes them indivisible: the conflict between will and external power. The only thing that operates for good in Mailer's world is the individual fighting against the institutional powers. No collective effort, no group or social program, no matter how intent on justice, can win Mailer's serious allegiance because man in the aggregate, he believes, becomes less than man; he loses his honor, his dignity, his selfhood. The Mailer protagonist is always struggling against a mighty power intent on possessing his soul.

But the struggle often turns out to be not as valiant as all that. In Mailer's world to test oneself against any implacable power is to be caught visibly in contradictions: to attempt seriousness and fall into clownishness; to become doctrinaire in defying the doctrinal; to skirt a ledge between heroism and absurdity; to shift precariously between clarity and turgidity, reason and dream, generosity and self-obsession, libertarianism and autocracy; to be Prometheus with the compulsions of Icarus. Nonetheless, Mailer does not try to neutralize any of these polarities in himself. He refuses to put together a harmonious personality because he suspects that consistency is but another name for inertia. For Mailer, life as it is lived in the modern world is degraded. His basic view has always been that the institutions of society—government, business, marriage, church, the military—are deadening and force man to adopt death as life. To resist precisely in order to make possible that awakening that literature attempts is Mailer's reason for being. A spiritual fervor kindles the heart of his rebellion; for ultimately it is not what men make or do that evokes his opposition, but the very terms of human mortality itself.

Other Works:

Death for the Ladies (New York: Putnam's, 1962; London: Deutsch, 1962);

The Bullfight: A Photographic Narrative with Text by Norman Mailer (New York: CBS Legacy Collection Book, 1967);

The Deer Park: A Play (New York: Dial, 1967);

The Short Fiction of Norman Mailer (New York: Dell, 1967);

The Idol and the Octopus: Political Writings on the Kennedy and Johnson Administrations (New York: Dell, 1968);

Maidstone (New York: New American Library, 1971);

King of the Hill (New York: New American Library, 1971);

The Prisoner of Sex (Boston: Little, Brown, 1971);

The Long Patrol (New York: World, 1971);

Existential Errands (Boston: Little, Brown, 1972);

St. George and the Godfather (New York: New American Library, 1972);

The Faith of Graffiti (New York: Praeger, 1974; reprinted as *Watching My Name Go By*, London: Matthews, Miller, Dunbar, 1974);

The Fight (Boston: Little, Brown, 1975; London: Hart-Davis, 1976);

Genius and Lust: A Journey Through the Major Writings of Henry Miller (New York: Grove, 1976);

Some Honorable Men: Political Conventions 1960-1972 (Boston: Little, Brown, 1976).

Screenplays:

Wild 90, Supreme Mix, 1968;

Beyond the Law, Supreme Mix/Evergreen Films, 1968;

Maidstone, Supreme Mix, 1971.

References:

Laura Adams, ed., *Will the Real Normal Mailer Please Stand Up?* (Port Washington, N.Y.: Kennikat, 1973);

Adams, *Norman Mailer: A Comprehensive Bibliography* (Metuchen, N.J.: Scarecrow, 1974);

Adams, *Existential Battles: The Growth of Norman Mailer* (Athens: Ohio University Press, 1976);

Leo Braudy, ed., *Norman Mailer: A Collection of Critical Essays* (Englewood Cliffs: Prentice-Hall, 1972);

Joe Flaherty, *Managing Mailer* (New York: Coward-McCann, 1970);

Richard Foster, *Norman Mailer* (Minneapolis: University of Minnesota Press, 1968);

Stanley T. Gutman, *The Individual and Society in the Novels of Norman Mailer* (Hanover, N.H.: University Press of New England, 1976);

Donald L. Kaufmann, *Norman Mailer: The Countdown (The First Twenty Years)* (Carbondale: Southern Illinois University Press, 1969);

Barry Leeds, *The Structured Vision of Norman Mailer* (New York: New York University Press, 1969);

Robert F. Lucid, ed., *Norman Mailer: The Man and His Work* (Boston: Little, Brown, 1971);

Peter Manso, ed., *Running Against the Machine: The Mailer-Breslin Campaign* (Garden City: Doubleday, 1969);

Jonathan Middlebrook, *Mailer and the Times of His Time* (San Francisco: Bay Books, 1976);

Richard Poirier, *Norman Mailer* (New York: Viking, 1972);

Jean Radford, *Norman Mailer: A Critical Study* (New York: Harper & Row, 1975);

Robert Solotaroff, *Down Mailer's Way* (Urbana: University of Illinois Press, 1974);

W. S. Weatherby, *Squaring Off: Mailer vs. Baldwin* (New York: Mason/Charter, 1977).

Bernard Malamud

Jeffrey Helterman
University of South Carolina

BIRTH: Brooklyn, New York, 26 April 1914.

EDUCATION: Erasmus Hall High School, Brooklyn; B.A., City College of New York, 1936; M.A., Columbia University, 1942.

MARRIAGE: 6 November 1945 to Ann De Chiara; children: Paul, Janna.

AWARDS: *Partisan Review* Fellowship, 1956-1957; Rosenthal Award for *The Assistant,* 1958; Daroff Memorial Award for *The Assistant,* 1958; National Bood Award for *The Magic Barrel,* 1959; Ford Foundation Fellowship, 1959; Elected, National Institute of Arts and Letters, 1964; National Book Award for *The Fixer,* 1967; Pulitzer Prize for *The Fixer,* 1967; Elected, American Academy of Arts and Sciences, 1967.

MAJOR WORKS: *The Natural* (New York: Harcourt, Brace, 1952; London: Eyre & Spottiswoode, 1963); *The Assistant* (New York: Farrar, Straus & Cudahy, 1957; London: Eyre & Spottiswoode, 1959); *The Magic Barrel* (New York: Farrar, Straus & Cudahy, 1958; London: Eyre & Spottiswoode, 1960); *A New Life* (New York: Farrar, Straus & Cudahy, 1961; London: Eyre & Spottiswoode, 1962); *Idiots First* (New York: Farrar, Straus, 1963; London: Eyre & Spottiswoode, 1964); *The Fixer* (New York: Farrar, Straus & Giroux, 1966; London: Eyre & Spottiswoode, 1967); *A Malamud Reader,* ed. Philip Rahv (New York: Farrar, Straus & Giroux, 1967); *Pictures of Fidelman: An Exhibition* (New York: Farrar, Straus & Giroux, 1969; London: Eyre & Spottiswoode, 1970); *The Tenants* (New York: Farrar, Straus & Giroux, 1971; London: Eyre Methuen, 1972); *Rembrandt's Hat* (New York: Farrar, Straus & Giroux, 1973; London: Eyre Methuen, 1973).

In recent years, it has been impossible to discuss the career of Bernard Malamud without mentioning his place as the second partner, along with Bellow and Roth, in the ruling triumvirate of Jewish-American literature, which Bellow has called the Hart, Schaffner & Marx of American letters. Those who do not discuss the Jewishness of Malamud feel obligated to explain why they have avoided the issue. It is true that most of his protagonists are Jews (only *The Natural* among his novels has nothing to do with Jews), but their Jewishness seems part of Malamud's attempt to portray a most Christ-like

figure, *homo patiens,* the man who suffers. Malamud sees this suffering for others as the ultimate test of humanity and he is only half joking when he recasts the New Testament phrase about the lilies of the field, "consider the Jewish lily that toils and spins." Malamud's heroes rarely unloose the shackles of suffering and many, like Frank Alpine and Yakov Bok, deliberately ask for more, but they acquire a spiritual freedom when they learn how their suffering relates them to the rest of mankind.

Although many of the short stories (and *The Fixer*) are structured on the model of the Yiddish folk tale, most of Malamud's longer fiction is based on non-Jewish archetypes: *The Natural* is the grail legend imposed upon the myths of baseball; *The Assistant* is a modern day life of St. Francis of Assisi; *A New Life* is a travesty of the pastoral romance; and *Pictures of Fidelman* is a neo-Jamesian view of American innocence abroad. Seen from either the Jewish or the mythic perspective, the Malamudian hero, victimized to the end, learns to cast off the prison of self and reaches out to share the suffering of at least one other human being. While Malamud does not have the intellectual range of Bellow or command of Roth's verbal pyrotechnics, his moral vision reaches depths unprobed by either of his peers.

Malamud was born in Brooklyn, New York, of immigrant parents who, like Morris and Ida Bober of *The Assistant,* ran a small grocery store which stayed open late at night, leaving Malamud with little family life. His first writing was for the literary magazine at Erasmus Hall, from which he graduated in 1932. In the middle of the Depression, he spent four relatively unhappy years at the City College of New York where he obtained a B.A. His master's degree from Columbia University in English (with a thesis on the reception of Hardy's poetry in America) gave Malamud credentials similar to those of S. Levin in *A New Life,* and in the early 1940s he started writing short stories while teaching night classes at Erasmus and later at Harlem High School. Formative influences from his reading included the Russians Chekhov, Dostoevsky, and Gogol, Yiddish writers Sholom Aleichem and I. L. Peretz, the short stories of Sherwood Anderson and Hemingway, and the novels of Mann and Joyce.

In 1949, Malamud joined the faculty of Oregon State University, where he taught for twelve years while completing his first four books. Although he was relegated to teaching composition courses even after he had attained literary recognition and although much of his satiric academic novel, *A New Life*, is based on his experiences at Oregon State, Malamud was relatively content during these years. He felt, in particular, that the security of his position allowed him to write only what he wanted to write. In 1961, Malamud joined the faculty of Bennington College in Vermont where he still teaches, although now on a part-time basis. From 1966 to 1968 he was a visiting lecturer at Harvard University.

Although not secretive like J. D. Salinger or William Gaddis, Malamud has never made himself a writing personality and rarely submits to interviews. His marriage to Ann De Chiara seems to have influenced his choice of Italian ancestry for Frank Alpine and his interest in things Italian generally. The Malamuds' year in Rome in 1956 provided the background for the stories which ultimately became *Pictures of Fidelman*. Malamud also traveled in Russia in 1965 researching *The Fixer*. His fine eye for naturalistic detail, picked up both in his travels and in observing the life around him at home, seems missing only in his first novel, where realistic texture yields to symbolic imagery.

Although Malamud has written symbolic novels throughout his career, nowhere is this so obvious as in his first novel, *The Natural* (1952), which superimposes the myth of the Wasteland upon the history of baseball. In the book, a composite of the classic lore of baseball—the Black Sox scandal, the shooting of Eddie Waitkus in a Chicago hotel, a number of events from the career of Babe Ruth, the poem "Casey at the Bat"—becomes the life of Roy Hobbs, the title character. These events are manipulated so they retell the story of the grail knight, Percival, and his attempt to heal the wounded Fisher-King which will restore plenty to the Fisher-King's land.

Roy is a "natural" in the baseball sense of having outstanding natural abilities for the game, but the title is also ironic since "natural" was the medieval term for a fool, particularly an unworldly innocent. His name carries on this duality. As Roy, he is the King (French, "roi") to restore the kingdom, but his last name suggests the country bumpkin (often called Hob in Renaissance drama) who is out of place in the sophisticated world of the city. Like Roy, Percival was also a country boy who came to the city to make good. The motif of the Wasteland as well as that of the outsider in an alien society reappears in almost all of Malamud's fiction.

At nineteen, Roy is on his way to Chicago for a tryout as a pitcher with the Cubs (the right team because he is still immature). He is shot and wounded by a young woman named Harriet Bird. The confrontation of the two, he with his lancelike bat and she with a gun in her grail hatbox, is a preliminary version of the hero's test. When Roy can explain his purpose no better than self-interest, Harriet Bird shoots him. Throughout the novel, birds symbolize the force of the destructive mother archetype. After a fourteen-year recovery, Roy returns to become a thirty-three-year-old rookie. He becomes the greatest batter in the annals of baseball and leads his team out of the cellar towards first place, but in the end, he sells out to gamblers. Roy's last minute attempt to right this wrong fails because, like mighty Casey in the poem, he is struck out by the new Young Hero, named Youngberry. This repeats the cycle; as the novel opened, the nineteen-year-old Roy had struck out the old slugger, Whammer Wambold.

The handling of the grail legend is cleverly done but is by no means subtle. Roy's team, the New York Knights, are managed by Pop Fisher, who represents the Fisher-King whose land will remain barren until his wound is cured. In this case, the wound is athlete's foot of the hand, and the team's losing streak is reflected in the parched grass of the stadium. Roy literally knocks the cover off the ball with his handmade bat, Wonderboy, and, following a marvelous comic scene where the fielders try to play the unraveling string of the ball, rain comes and Pop's miraculous cure begins. Malamud uses the sexual overtones of the myth so blatantly that they work by comic overkill: Wonderboy is so obvious a phallic symbol that it sags when Roy is in a slump.

The grail legend, as Jessie Weston has shown in *From Ritual to Romance*, grew out of primitive fertility rites in which a new young hero replaced a dying one. The old hero in *The Natural* is the Knights' batting star, Bump Bailey, whom Roy taunts into a fatal crash into the outfield wall (patterned on Pete Reiser's crash into the outfield wall). Once Roy replaces Bump as baseball hero, he also tries to take his place as sexual hero by becoming the lover of Bump's girl friend, Memo Paris. The death of Bump Bailey is more than a fertility ritual, however, because Roy never quite gets over his guilt in the matter. Furthermore, since he is ironically a middle-aged "young hero," he sees in Bump's fate his own.

Roy's tragic downfall grows out of his involvement with Memo Paris, whose name suggests Aphrodite, the goddess who tempted Paris with

Jill Krementz

Bernard Malamud.

sexual love and the gift of Helen of Troy. Memo is the protege of the Satanic figure, the gambler Gus Sands (the august Prince of the Barren Land), who dwells in the hellish nightclub, the Pot of Fire. Memo is both temptress and the deceiver whose need for money leads Roy to sell out his team to the gambler. Although she is a beauty, Memo has a "sick breast" and is associated with death and corruption. Her first tryst with Roy takes place at a polluted stream, and when she drives away from the spot, Roy believes that their car has run down a boy walking in the road. This illusion, which Roy takes as real, signifies Roy's fear of his own death, and in Memo's presence he is always mindful of his mortality. Her first name may suggest the Latin motto of man's mortality, *memento mori,* "remember you are to die." As she promises Roy when their affair begins, "I'm strictly a dead man's girl."

Roy is offered a choice of women with the appearance of the earth mother figure, Iris Lemon (both flower and fruit suggest fertility and life), a thirty-three-year-old grandmother who first appears when Roy repeats Babe Ruth's feat of hitting a home run for a sick boy in the hospital. The boy recovers and Roy is cured of a batting slump which began after the night he and Memo "ran down" the boy on the road. Iris represents the life force and the ability to turn from self to others, but Roy, who can never forget his mortality, rejects her when he realizes that marrying her would make him a grandfather.

The two women stand for two different kinds of love, love as appetite and love as responsibility for another person. Roy is always hungry around Memo and eventually, coaxed by her, almost eats himself to death in a team party which is an ironic parody of communion and the grail feast. When Roy recovers from his eating orgy, he sells out to the gamblers (who are headed by Sands and the ironically named team owner, Judge Goodwill Banner). His wondrous homemade bat (in essence the living tree of the fertility rite and Percival's lance) splits in two when its owner is no longer worthy to possess it, and, reduced to the status of an ordinary mortal with a standard Louisville slugger, Roy strikes out, trying, too late, to undo his betrayal of the Knights and Pop Fisher.

The symbolism is far more subtle in Malamud's second novel, *The Assistant* (1957), where he combines the Wasteland motif with a life of St. Francis. Frank Alpine, the assistant in the grocery store of a poor Jew named Morris Bober, lives a modern version of the life of St. Francis of Assisi. The combination of the saint's life with the grail legend yields a double perspective on the two heroes. Under the influence of St. Francis, whose idea of the good life was perfect imitation of Christ, Frank learns goodness and moral strength from the Christ figure, Morris Bober, and Frank's circumcision becomes a sign similar to the appearance of the stigmata (the five wounds of Christ) on the body of the saint. At the same time that Morris exhibits Christ-like compassion for others, both friends and enemies, he himself has fallen into almost incurable despair, and Frank heals Morris, like Percival healed the wounded Fisher-King. Since the grocery represents the ruined grail castle which can no longer even feed its own inhabitants, Frank's restoration of the shop and the addition of restaurant service make possible the symbolic renewal of the grail feast.

Frank enters the novel as a wanderer looking for an identity. His latest self-image is that of a big-time mobster, but all he can manage is the robbery of fifteen dollars from Morris, who is wounded in the holdup. Morris's physical wound is less dangerous than the despair that has ruled his life since the death of his son, Ephraim. Frank, penitent over his part in the robbery, goes to the store, where he helps out Morris until he recovers from his wound and helps him as well to overcome his despair. Frank, an orphan, is looking for a father just as Morris is looking for a son. After a great deal of mutual misunderstanding, both men find what they are looking for. Their growing love is contrasted with the breakdown of the other father-son pairs in the novel: the landlord Karp, whose lazy son, Louis, gives up the family business he inherits; Sam Pearl, whose lawyer son forgets the traditional law of religion; and Detective Minogue, whose son is an incorrigible criminal.

A third medieval myth underlies the love story of Frank and Morris's daughter, Helen. In the French *Romance of the Rose*, the lover gets a kiss from a rose and then spends the rest of his life pursuing her but is thwarted by her *daunger* ("coldness"). In *The Assistant*, Frank gets a kiss from a carnival (etymologically, "farewell to the flesh") girl, but the girl dies before he can consummate the affair, and Helen replaces the girl as his ideal. Helen is made into the rose of the romance through flower and snow imagery associated with the winter in which most of the novel takes place. As with the Frank-Morris relationship, a Franciscan story is superimposed upon this myth. Francis built himself a snow-wife to show that he had forsaken the worldly life. At first Frank pursues Helen hungrily, but love replaces desire after he destroys his self-image as knight errant: He rescues Helen from being raped by Ward Minogue only to end up making love to her himself. After this, Frank devotes himself to Helen with the same kind of selfless dedication that he has given Morris.

Although love in the novel means rising above selfish desires to something finer, it is also necessary for the characters to get rid of hollow romantic ideals. The reading habits of both Frank and Helen tell much about their ideals. Helen reads novels of tragic love affairs like *Anna Karenina* and *Madame Bovary*, while Frank reads biographies of great men. Frank yearns to be a hero while Helen's ideals are built around the dream of marriage to an extraordinary man. Even when she begins to fall in love with Frank, she dreams of an improved Frank, with straightened nose, better haircut and a college education.

Morris's problem is not finding the right ideals, but rather putting off his despair long enough to carry out what he knows is right. The moral crises faced by Morris as he tries to give his family a future are similar to those faced by the poor shopkeepers who populate *The Magic Barrel*. Morris first tries to sell the store to a poor immigrant, but he cannot let another man take up his burden, and he tells the immigrant the truth about the shop's wretched business. Then Morris goes to an old friend who had once cheated him, but he cannot bring himself to call the friend to account. Finally, he deals with a demonic fire-setter who wants to burn the store for the insurance. Although Morris turns down the fire-setter, he then tries to burn the store himself by starting a fire with a photographic negative. He changes his mind but cannot put out the fire until Frank rescues him and the store. Morris's behavior is based always on the need for honesty in his dealings with others and, beyond this, a belief in the humanity of all men. Poor as he is, he always gives credit to those poorer than himself, knowing he will never be paid back.

Morris dies from a heart attack after shoveling snow. He believes that the store has been profitably sold to Karp, but this turns out not to be the case. At the funeral, Frank falls into Morris's grave, and when he emerges he becomes the new Morris. He takes over the store, and the following Easter he becomes a convert to Judaism. The store survives and the reader is left with the impression that Helen finally understands Frank's true worth.

In *The Magic Barrel* (1958), his first collection of short stories, Malamud uses the form and rhythm of the Yiddish folk tale to explore the terrible sacrifice in one's ideals that has to be paid for love. Many of his heroes are trapped in airless, past-tormented lives that open to a breath of life for those who dare to seize the moment, or else close with the terrifying stillness of death for those who do not. Except for three Italian stories, the settings are bleak ghetto shops, tenements, and stores where most human relationships depend on a humanistic notion of credit: "After all what was credit but the fact that people were human beings, and if you were really a human being you gave credit to somebody else and he gave credit to you."

The majority of the stories are of the same lyric-naturalistic mode as *The Assistant* in which the grimy reality of poor city dwellers is made to glow with the Joycean light of epiphany while the characters learn the secrets of human love and despair. In "Take Pity," the reader is surprised to learn that the characters, a census-taker and a retired salesman, are in fact the Recording Angel and a dead man whose life is being evaluated, but Malamud handles the transition from naturalism to mystery so well that the revelation seems inevitable. The story shows how far a human being can go to offer charity to another human being and conversely how stubborn many human beings can be in refusing love which they interpret as pity. Two other stories, "The Bill" and "The Loan," show the guilt that accrues by accepting the credit of the heart when one refuses the responsibility for repayment. In "The Loan," the wife of a baker refuses to lend money to an old friend of her husband, pleading that her escape from the Nazi incinerators has left her too insecure to give up the few hundred dollars for a headstone for the friend's wife. While she is refusing her husband's moral obligation, the bread burns, and when she opens the oven she sees the objective correlative of her niggardliness: "A cloud of smoke billowed out at her. The loaves in the trays were blackened bricks—charred corpses."

Several of the stories set ordinary humanity against the inhuman idealism of the protagonists. In "The First Seven Years," Feld, a shoemaker, wants the best for his daughter but finally discovers that the proper marriage for her is with his assistant, a balding refugee twice her age. The time span mentioned in the title is the medieval period of apprenticeship, and the assistant, Sobel, not only earns the right to replace his master in his craft, but has undergone, through his dedication, an apprenticeship in love. In a similar situation in the title story, a faithless rabbinical student named Finkle finds love through a marriage broker. The object of his desires, however, is not one of the broker's clients, but the man's daughter, whose picture has accidentally slipped into his folder. The girl, who brings love and love of God to Finkle, turns out to be a whore, and in the climactic last scene, Pinye, the broker, stands in the shadows chanting the prayer for the dead (signifying that Finkle has been lost to his faith) as Finkle goes to meet his daughter under a lamp post. The merchant of romantic dreams proves incapable of believing in the reality of his own product, while the student has staked the spirit of his law against its letter and has won.

In "Angel Levine," Malamud indulges in a fantasy in which an impoverished Jewish tailor, Manischevitz, is asked to believe the unlikely story that a Negro named Alexander Levine is his guardian angel. Manischevitz rejects the angel at first but then, impelled by love for his ailing wife, makes a surrealistic journey through Harlem to express his faith in the unbelievable. The pattern of faith triumphant is inverted in "The Lady of the Lake," a story set in Italy. The hero, a Jewish-

Malamud's manuscript.

Jill Kremetz

American floorwalker in Macy's book department (this kind of existence on the margins of culture is almost always a sign of untested integrity in Malamud) falls in love with a beautiful Italian girl and denies his heritage and his identity so that she will marry him. His lie turns out to be his undoing when she proves to be a refugee from Buchenwald who treasures her suffering. She disappears into the mists that rise from the lake while he clutches vainly at the cold marble statuary of the place.

This story, like the two other Italian stories, "Behold the Key" and "The Last Mohican," shows the influence of Malamud's year in Rome while he held a Rockefeller grant and a *Partisan Review* Fellowship. "Behold the Key" is the story of a graduate student's frustrating search for an apartment in Rome, and "The Last Mohican" is the first of the Fidelman stories that were to be collected as *Pictures of Fidelman.*

Malamud's next novel, *A New Life* (1961), is based to some extent on his teaching career at Oregon State University, where, despite his growing literary reputation, he was never allowed to teach advanced literature courses because literature was for Ph.D.s. The hero's search for values is set against a satire on academic life in a "service-oriented" English department and a university that has long since gotten rid of its liberal arts program. Although the satire and the search for identity work well separately, the combination of the two undercuts the hero's dilemma because he finally has to choose between love and the academy. Since teaching at Cascadia College has already been proven worthless, his choice of love requires little moral strength.

The hero, Seymour Levin, like Roy Hobbs and Frank Alpine, is a *schlimazel*, a fool who gets into trouble by trying to improve things rather than a *schlemiel*, the passive victim of events. Levin's journey to Cascadia (Oregon) from New York reverses the paths of Frank Alpine, the Westerner who comes east, and of Roy Hobbs, the country boy who goes to New York. Levin, a Jew with a master's degree in English, goes west to the wilds of Cascadia where he hopes to overcome a past of alcoholism in a setting that he expects to nurture bucolic freedom and humanistic study. In this dream of rural self-sufficiency he is like his namesake Levin in *Anna Karenina*, but unlike Tolstoy's hero, he finds no Kitty to support him in moments of inadequacy. His ideals are quickly shattered when he discovers that Cascadia has forsaken the humanities for the regimen of composition and that the local attitude toward nature has the predatory viciousness of sporting goods salesmen.

Levin's liberal ideas about McCarthyism, the Korean War, and Alger Hiss bewilder his dull students and dismay his arch-conservative colleagues. The only excitement he ever generates in the classroom occurs after he lectures on his ability to bring his students "a better understanding of who they were and what their lives might yield, education being revelation." The class seems to respond enthusiastically and then he looks down and discovers why his promise of revelation has brought looks of joy from his students: the classic nightmare of every professor has been realized—Levin has been lecturing with his fly open.

The Cascadia faculty does not even grant Levin the dignity of being an original enemy. Rather, they treat him as a reincarnation of the preceding resident radical, an Irishman named Leo Duffy. Hoping to discover his own identity, Levin pursues the history of Duffy only to find that his predecessor had committed suicide when he found that his life was pointless.

Levin's other colleagues give him even less hope. The chairman is a martinet whose only concern is that his text, *The Elements of Grammar*, will get into its fourteenth edition. Another faculty member spends his time cutting pictures out of *Life* magazine for a projected illustrated history of the United States; the product will be, therefore, a "new Life" of sorts. More dangerous to Levin are C. D. Fabrikant, a fellow liberal, who gives up his principles when his future is at stake and, most importantly, the head of the composition program, Gerald Gilley, who becomes Levin's antagonist even before Levin seduces his wife. Gilley hates the humanities with a passion, although he still reserves the literature courses for the Ph.D.s in the department (he has a particular loathing for Thomas Hardy, the subject of Malamud's thesis). Gilley is an avid hunter and fisherman whose attitude towards his prey is one of savage antagonism, while his penchant for photography turns out to be a voyeuristic, secondhand approach to life. Symbolic of this antagonism to life, Gilley can produce no seed, and his children are both adopted.

While Levin halfheartedly copes with the endless paperwork and strict regimentation of the composition course, he attempts to fulfill himself through love. His sexual adventures are all comic disasters which play his literary idealism against the petty realities of life. He first attempts to seduce a waitress in a barn which he describes with idyllic lyricism that is lost on the waitress. Levin's pastoral romance is shattered when their clothes are stolen by his rival, a Syrian graduate student with a mania for cleaning bathrooms. Levin docs consummate his affair with a student, after a slapstick car ride across the mountains to meet her at a distant motel near the Pacific. Levin thinks of himself as a new Balboa, but the glamor of the moment disappears when the girl comes to find out how much the assignation has raised her grade. Levin again suffers an interrupted seduction after he and another faculty member arouse each other by reading Keats and Tennyson. The woman, Avis Fliss, is an echo of Memo Paris of *The Natural*. With her bird-like name and an injured breast, Avis is symbolized as a life-denying character, and she eventually betrays Levin.

After so many tries at love, Levin comes close in his affair with Pauline Gilley, the wife of his immediate supervisor. The consummation of the affair takes place in a wooded setting on a spring-like day in January, but the idyll is short-lived, and the reader soon realizes that the setting is not natural forest glade but a cultivated part of Cascadia's forestry school. Pauline is the Iris Lemon, earth mother figure, but she turns out to be flat-chested. Levin wants to see his love for Pauline as an affirmation of life, but by the time he rides off with the pregnant Pauline and her two obnoxious children in his battered Hudson, he no longer loves her and he suspects that the feeling is mutual. Furthermore, he has bargained away his future as a teacher by getting custody of Gilley's children in exchange for a vow never to teach again. Levin's new life can be seen as real only as a kind of existential commitment which ignores the value of the thing committed to. Like Frank Alpine, his future depends upon a sense of duty, but Frank cared about Helen and the memory of Morris, while Levin acts only because he has found the strength to do what he has set out to do.

The stories in *Idiots First* (1963) deal with many of the same themes as those in *The Magic Barrel*, but Malamud casts a number of his characters in an allegorical framework which gives them clearer definition but less life. In "The German Refugee," the hero, Oskar Gassner, is mired in despair because of his inability to set down roots in a new country and because he has left his Gentile wife behind in Germany. He is temporarily roused out of his gloom by the narrator, who coaches his English and helps him prepare a lecture on the influence of Whitman on German literature. The lecture, upon which most of the suspense is focused, is delivered successfully, but when Gassner discovers that his wife had converted to Judaism and was killed by the Nazis, he commits suicide. The narrator's viewpoint adds to the shock value of Gassner's death because the young

tutor's enthusiasm for the task of teaching English leads the reader to believe that Gassner's major problem is assimilation, while in fact it is isolation from the woman he loves. What distinguishes "The German Refugee" from similar tales in *The Magic Barrel* of one man trying to help another is Malamud's insistence on the similarity between the personal life of Oskar Gassner and political events in Europe. Through deft parallelism, the content of the lecture and the world political situation are epitomized in the life of one man. In *The Magic Barrel*, Malamud would have been content to tell Gassner's story without the historical overview.

The title story tells of the attempts of a dying man named Mendel to send his idiot son to an uncle in California. Mendel has made a compact with a bearded man named Ginzburg who gives him an evening to gather the money for a ticket. After being turned down by Fishbein, a wealthy man who gives charity only to institutions, Mendel gets the money in the form of the only warm coat of a sick rabbi. Mendel arrives at the station too late for the deadline, but after he struggles fiercely with Ginzburg, the latter lets the son go because of the ferocious courage love has given Mendel. Although the situation is similar to several in *The Magic Barrel*, particularly the confrontation between the dead Rosen and Davidoff, the cosmic census-taker in "Take Pity," this story has none of the well-textured humanity of the earlier collection. Instead, Malamud presents a morality play in which Mendel is abstracted to Mankind, Ginzburg to the Angel of Death, Fishbein to False Charity, and the rabbi to True Charity.

A similar demythologizing takes place in the collection's venture into fantasy. "The Jewbird" tells the adventures of a crow named Schwartz who tests the charity and wisdom of a successful Jew named Harry Cohen. Schwartz is a talking Jewish crow who moves in with the Cohens and becomes a surrogate father to Cohen's none-too-bright son, Maurie. Cohen cannot stand the bedraggled crow, whose poverty, thick accent, and old world habits remind him too much of his origins. He persecutes the bird and eventually throws him from the window to his death. Although the premise is more wildly fantastic than "Angel Levine" of the earlier collection, the story fails to capture the same mood of fantasy. Instead of focusing on the outrageous juxtaposition of man and bird, the story becomes an allegory of man's inhumanity to man, or more specifically Jews' anti-Semitism to Jews.

"Black Is My Favorite Color," a story that explores the black-Jewish relations that would become the primary concern of *The Tenants*, is entirely naturalistic in style, as a Jew recounts his relationships with blacks and particularly his love affair with a black woman. Despite his efforts to act without prejudice, the narrator can never penetrate into the alien culture, and, at the end of the story after the woman has rejected him, he tries to help a blind black man home only to discover that even a blind man can tell he is white.

Idiots First, which also contains a number of Italian stories which were to appear later as part of *Pictures of Fidelman*, is less even in quality than *The Magic Barrel*, and the stories, in general, strain too hard for their morals.

Malamud's finest novel, *The Fixer* (1966), won both the Pulitzer Prize and the National Book Award. The book is the account of a Jew in turn-of-the-century Russia who is arrested for the ritual murder of a Christian child. Malamud based his novel on an historical event, the trial of Mendel Beiliss in 1913. Beiliss was acquitted after his trial in Kiev, but Malamud ends the novel at the moment his hero, Yakov Bok, leaves for the courtroom after his two-and-a-half-year pre-trial confinement. The reader is thus left uncertain of Bok's fate.

The character of Bok (the name means "goat" and he is Malamud's ultimate scapegoat) is in many ways similar to that of Morris Bober in *The Assistant*, but the initial passive suffering of Bok is transformed into an active, deliberate suffering so that Bok adds Frank Alpine's commitment to Bober-like endurance. Unlike Bober's, Bok's prison is real, not metaphoric, and Malamud lets his readers know it. He grimly records the physical torment, mental suffering, and spiritual degradation Bok is put through in his cell. There is no relief from the insects, the pails of excrement, the beatings, and particularly the humiliating body searches in which each of Bok's orifices is probed, first two, and then six times a day. Through it all, Bok maintains his innocence, first from stubbornness, but later from a gradually emerging sense of principle. As with Bober, Bok's life is an endurance test whose only activity is suffering, but unlike Bober, Bok's actual imprisonment allows him to attain a spiritual freedom that eludes Bober. Bober finally learns to accept Frank Alpine's struggles in his behalf, but for Bok there is no one to carve some meaning out of the absolute absurdity of his existence except himself.

The technique of the novel is heavily influenced by the earthiness and mysticism of Isaac Bashevis Singer, Sholom Aleichem and I. L. Peretz, who made the Yiddish folktale into an art form. The style validates the hero's philosophic musings, which are spoken in the simplest language possible, and also accomodates the dream visions, particularly the appearance to Bok of Tsar Nicholas II, who tries to defend his realm's treatment of Jews. Although the style comes from the literate folktale, the philosophy itself often comes from Dostoevsky, particularly *The Brothers Karamazov*.

Bok, a Jew who believes little of Jewishness, attempts to escape his unpromising future as well as his self-pitying condition by leaving the Russian ghetto in which he was born and going to Kiev. He passes for a Christian, gets a good job, and lives in a sector forbidden to Jews, all of which only makes him the likely scapegoat when the murdered child is found. While he is imprisoned Bok learns that he cannot escape his fate or his history—that he is not only a Jew, but the symbol of all Russian Jews. Although it is not clear whether or not Bok believes in God at the close of the novel, it is clear he understands that the possibility of retaining his human dignity requires belief in his Jewishness.

Like Frank Alpine, Bok must discover the meaning of the suffering that seems to be the central factor in the condition of being Jewish. When he can say, as Morris does to Frank Alpine, "I suffer for you," then he has understood his heritage and himself and has achieved freedom. In order to release himself from suffering, Bok is about to goad the guards into killing him. When he thinks of his father-in-law Shmuel, however, he realizes that his suicide scheme might be taken as a tacit admission of his guilt and the cause, therefore, of a wave of pogroms. Having understood that even isolated in his cell, he is part of the human race, he chooses to go on with his suffering: "He may even die for my death if they work up a pogrom in celebration of it. If so what do I get by dying, outside of release from pain? What have I earned if a single Jew dies because I did? Suffering I can gladly live without, I hate the taste of it, but if I must suffer let it be for something. Let it be for Shmuel."

Bok extends his commitment when his wife Raisl comes to ask him to give her illegitimate child his name. He accedes to her wishes, deliberately branding himself a willing cuckold, because he realizes that her unfaithfulness was caused largely by his self-centeredness and self-pity. In acknowledging his complicity in her actions he gives up part of the guiltless-victim persona which helps most martyrs face their torments. Far from undermining his strength, however, the act of legitimizing his wife's son makes him for the first time both father and husband.

Bok spends much of his imprisonment questioning the justice of his universe and the existence of a God who rules over it. Unlike Job, however, Bok finds no voice out of the whirlwind to give form to absurdity. "To win a lousy bet with the devil he killed off all the servants and innocent children of Job. For that alone I hate him, not to mention ten thousand pogroms. Ach, why do you make me talk fairy tales? Job is an invention and so is God. Let's let it go at that."

No matter what the state does, Bok will not admit to the trumped-up charge of ritual murder—that he has killed a Christian boy to use his blood in the manufacture of matzos. The reader, who is ready to suffer with the eternally victimized Bok, is unprepared for his heroism as his staunch courage (in Yiddish, *bok* means "a piece of iron" as well as "goat") begins to drive his prosecutors into a desperate frenzy. Bok is offered all kinds of deals up to a complete pardon and physical freedom itself, if he will just sign a confession, but he insists on coming to trial. When he is given a confession to sign, he writes instead the document giving his paternity to Raisl's son, Chaim, whose name means "life." Bok's heroism proves that human dignity can be maintained even at the most minimal levels of existence and among the most brutal examples of mankind.

Pictures of Fidelman (1969) is not precisely a novel, but rather a series of vignettes built around a single character, a Jewish-American art student, who later becomes a struggling artist and finally a successful artisan, named Arthur Fidelman. The book's title is meant to suggest Joyce's *Portrait of the Artist as a Young Man*, and, like that work, *Pictures of Fidelman* follows the moral growth of its hero. Fidelman seeks the meaning of life and art in Italy, making him an inversion of Frank Alpine, the Italian-American who searches for the meaning of life in a world of Jews. Most of the book had been published previously, both as separate short stories and in the earlier collections, and Fidelman is hardly a consistent character, even granting the necessary changes that occur in the growth and aging of a man.

Fidelman is another of Malamud's *schlemiels* whose search for the meaning of life is fraught with comic suffering. His first confrontation—with Shimon Susskind, a Jewish purveyor of Catholic religious objects—concerns itself with the nature of mutual responsibility. Although Susskind's relics are false, his deceptions of Fidelman are meant to show the young student the way to truth. Susskind pesters Fidelman to give him one of his two suits and then pilfers the art history manuscript that Fidelman has been working on. Fidelman rages at Susskind when he discovers that Susskind has burned his

chapter, but he finally realizes that the act was kindness: the manuscript was as false as Susskind's relics. As Susskind says, "The words were there but the spirit was missing." As the chapter ends, Fidelman chases after his personal conscience, offering his suit.

Once Susskind has freed him from his sterile, secondhand relationship to art, Fidelman becomes a painter, but his life is complicated by his attempt at total commitment to both life and art. This leads to impossible dilemmas like having to send his mistress out into the streets so that he does not have to prostitute his talents. Fidelman is looking for love and finds that even approximations of it can be had only by compromising innumerable ideals. The wild picaresque humor of the novel points out both the absurdities and complexities of human love.

Malamud cannot resist the endless play on appearance and reality possible in a book about artists. In one episode, Fidelman falls in love with his copy of Titian's *Venus*, which he has forged so that he can steal the original. In the end, he substitutes his own painting for the Titian, steals his copy, and runs away from his conspirators. In another story, Fidelman proves a terrible failure at seducing a young woman until he paints her as the Virgin. A series of typical *schlemiel* disasters temporarily cools her ardor, but when he dresses up as a priest for a self-portrait, her passion returns while she confesses to him, and then, as her penance, he makes love to her: "pumping slowly he nailed her to the cross."

Like S. Levin, Frank Alpine and Yakov Bok, Fidelman is searching for a new life, and his change from second-rate artist begins in a ritual death and rebirth similar to Frank Alpine's fall into Bober's grave. Fidelman has been digging square holes in the ground and exhibiting them as works of pure form when he is pushed into one by a mysterious stranger who remarks that his work now has content as well as form.

Fidelman's ultimate salvation comes through perversion. He gives a private retrospective show of his life's work to Beppo, the husband of the woman he has been sleeping with. Beppo correctly sees it all as uninspired imitation of the techniques of others and destroys the whole lot. He argues that Fidelman should give up being an artist. "After twenty years if the rooster hasn't crowed she should know she's a hen. Your painting will never pay back the part of your life you've given up for it." The bisexuality is more than a metaphor—Beppo rapes Fidelman while Fidelman is making love to Beppo's wife. Beppo teaches him to create life instead of art and

Fidelman returns at last to America, a craftsman (a glass-blower) who loves both men and women. In his Italian journey, the hero has changed from a dabbler (one who fiddles around) to a man of faith *(fidel)* in love and life.

Malamud's fifth novel, *The Tenants* (1971), is an evasive answer to the question, can a liberal Jewish novelist write the great American black novel? The response is a qualified no, because although the black novel never appears, there are enough tour-de-force fragments from it to suggest that Malamud half-seriously believes that he could do it. The story is also of a confrontation whose intensity goes beyond anything that Malamud has yet written.

The protagonists, a Jew named Harry Lesser and a black named Willie Spearmint, are the last two inhabitants of an old apartment house that will be wrecked when Lesser gives up his lease. Willie is a squatter in the building; only Lesser is a tenant. Harry will not allow his landlord, Levehspiel, to tear down the building until he finishes the novel he has been working on for nine years. Lesser's dealings with the long-suffering landlord, which oppose the demands of art to those of everyday life, are familiar to readers of *Pictures of Fidelman*, but the focus of the novel, to the exclusion of everything else, is the struggle between Lesser and Spearmint.

Lesser is a writer concerned with perfect form to the point that content seems almost irrelevant. He is working on one of those reflexive novels about a novelist writing a novel which he hopes can teach him how to live, life mirroring art: "Anyway, this writer sets out to write about someone he conceives to be not he yet himself. He thinks he can teach himself to love in a manner befitting an old ideal." Like his character, Lesser is trying to use his art to teach himself how to love, which means his novel, *The Promised End*, will never be finished and, more importantly, he will never learn to love.

Lesser, the author of two somewhat successful novels, encounters Willie, who is working on his first novel, a record of the black experience in America. Spearmint's work has its own paradoxes: the most realistic portions of Willie's novel, which Harry thinks are autobiographical, turn out to be pure invention, while Willie's short stories, whose events Harry finds too artificial, are not fiction, but fact. At first glance, the two men seem polar opposites—white and black, Jew and anti-Semite, polished professional and inspired amateur—but, in fact, both suffer the same failing; their concern with their writing cuts them off from life and loving. Both stalk each other warily, first mistrusting, then learning to respect the other's strengths—Willie's emotional power and Harry's craftsmanship. Each gradually invades the other's world, although there is a greater metamorphosis in Lesser as he enters Spearmint's Harlem.

Eventually their sparring turns to all-out war when Harry steals Willie's white girl friend, Irene Bell (nee Belinski). What Lesser fails to see is that Irene has left Willie because she cannot compete with his new mistress, art. Irene begins to turn toward Lesser when Willie tells her, "I can't lay up with you tonight. You know how hard that part I am now writing on my book has got. I need my strength and juice on my work tomorrow." Lesser, the kind of man who gets upset because he does not communicate as well as he writes, who feels he would like to revise his spoken words as well as his written ones, makes the same mistake, and eventually Irene leaves him as well. Her note sums up Malamud's philosophy: "No book is as important as me."

Another love story manifests itself below the growing hate of Lesser and Spearmint. Although Willie has burned Lesser's manuscript in revenge for the seduction of Irene, Lesser yearns to communicate with Spearmint, knowing that neither can write anymore unless he knows the other is also writing:

> Hey Bill, Lesser thought in the hallway, moved by the sight of a man writing, how's it going?
> You couldn't say that aloud to someone who had deliberately destroyed the almost completed manuscript of your most promising novel, product of ten years' labor. You understood his history and possibly yours, but you could say nothing to him.
> Lesser said nothing.

The two men do forgive each other for the stealing of the girl and the destruction of the manuscript, but it is too late. They can no longer write. Lesser has made Willie too concerned with form to write with any power and Willie has freed Lesser from the well-loved burden of his endless manuscript. After Lesser destroys Spearmint's typewriter, the tension becomes unbearable, and Lesser caves in Spearmint's head with an axe, while Spearmint castrates Lesser with a razor.

Like most novels about the writing of novels, the book's central theme concerns the relative reality of life and art. Although Malamud wants to say "life," the answer is more paradoxical. Lesser's novel is about love, but his affair with Irene has more substance than the love he writes about. Nonetheless, he gives up the girl for the book in the end, and

Malamud makes Lesser's passion for writing far more convincing than his passion for Irene. Neither man would kill the other for Irene, but both become bloodthirsty when their ability to write is destroyed. Malamud undercuts his thesis by demonstrating that while art may not be life, writing *is* living.

Malamud's latest collection of stories, *Rembrandt's Hat* (1973), continues his concern with the growth or collapse of the fine bond of compassion that binds two human beings together. The collection is populated with characters who live in the margin of their chosen discipline—biology teachers, art critics, hack writers, retired doctors—and so must prove themselves by relating not to their work, but to their fellow man; some succeed, others fail. The luminous otherworldliness of Malamud's earlier stories has almost disappeared. Only one story, "The Silver Crown," approximates the mystic world of Malamud's forte, the neo-Yiddish folktale. In the story, a young biology teacher named Albert Gans goes to a rabbi to buy a "miraculous" silver crown which is supposed to cure his dying father. Gans tries to bring the irrational world of the rabbi and his crown into his own rational sphere of competence. In the process of reducing mystery to science, Gans misses the point of the crown, that it is meant to remind him of his need to love his father. The rabbi tries to calm Gans's fears that the crown will not work if he has no faith in it: "Doubts we all got. We doubt God and God doubts us. This is natural on account of the nature of existence. Of this kind doubts I am not afraid so long as you love your father." Gans buys the crown for the wrong reasons: to assuage his guilt for ignoring his father and also as a scientific experiment in another kind of epistemology. But when he feels that he has become the victim of a con man, he admits his hatred for his father and old Gans dies. Malamud teases the reader about the reality of the crown, which is fair considering the allegorical conflict between love and reason in the story, but one wonders if Malamud has lost faith in his own ability to project the miraculous. In the stories of the 1950s, the reader takes the existence of such objects as a matter of faith validated by Malamud's prose.

Three other stories are about son-father (or father figure) betrayals. In one a student carries on an abortive seduction of his old teacher's young wife through the passing of rather childish notes; in another, the reader listens to the voices of a son and a father who alternately give their versions of the other's obnoxious characteristics; and in the third, a letter with nothing written on it becomes the symbol of two people's total lack of communication.

A more ambitious story dealing with the nature of communication is "The Talking Horse," about a talking circus horse, Abramowitz, and his deaf-mute master, a clown named Goldberg. The story, told from the horse's point of view, is clearly an allegory about the nature of man. Abramowitz, with a human mind inside a horse's body, is a literal version of the way Gulliver felt among the Houyhnhnms, a confused amalgam of beast and creature of reason. The trio, Abramowitz-man, Abramowitz-horse, and Goldberg, is an inversion of Freud's notion of the psyche. In this case, it is the intellect which is repressed: Abramowitz-man is the repressed intellect (the id that threatens to burst out of control) trapped inside and kept under control by Goldberg (the superego that tries to keep the intellect from disturbing the mores of the crowd-society). Abramowitz finally discovers that he is not a talking horse, but a centaur with an artificial horse head. Through this recognition of the worth of both mind and body, he is able to free himself from the restrictions of society and his doubt about his own nature.

This optimistic note is also sounded in the title story where Arkin, an art teacher, tries to compliment a colleague, Rubin, by telling him that his hat looks like one Rembrandt had painted in a self-portrait. Rubin, a failed sculptor, is insulted, and Arkin cannot understand why until he puts himself in Rubin's place and realizes that the second-rate sculptor cannot stand the implied comparison with a great artist. The compassion grows when Arkin also learns that even as a critic he has been off the mark: in reexamining the slide of the Rembrandt, he finds that he has been mistaken about what the hat looked like. This humbling experience and his ability to perceive nuances in human behavior break down the walls preventing communication between the two men.

The longest story in the collection, "Man in the Drawer," also concerns the need to reach out and put oneself in another's place. Like "The German Refugee" in *Idiots First*, which was also about one man reluctantly taking up the responsibility for another man's life, "Man in the Drawer" gives the reader a sense of historical place and time that is absent in most of the short stories. The story is set in cold-war Russia, and the hero's dilemma is based on that time and place. Harvitz, an American free-lance journalist and something of a coward, discovers a Russian taxicab driver, Levitansky (like himself a marginal Jew), who is a writer of fiction. Levitansky's politically heterodox work can be published only if Harvitz smuggles the stories out of the country. After a great deal of wrestling with his conscience and his fears, Harvitz takes up the burden of this near stranger and goes off to the airport with the manuscript hidden in his suitcase. The synopses of the stories to be smuggled, particularly one in which a gagged writer burns his work in the sink, show why he has changed his mind.

Malamud has used medieval myths throughout his work and two medieval voices may help define the distinctive quality of Malamud's heroes. Saint Augustine, after Paul the primary architect of Christian theology, divided all mankind into two races: that of Cain which inhabited the City of Man and that of Abel which dwelt in the City of God. Three centuries later, the Beowulf Poet called his monster a *marc-stapa*, "one who walks along the borders," and Grendel is an outsider looking in, not only at the Danes, but at himself because he cannot understand how he can be both man and monster. The reason is found in his origins; he is of the race of Cain and as long as he believes in the watchword of his heritage, "I am not my brother's keeper," he must remain outside the pale of humanity.

All of Malamud's characters are "border-walkers" in this sense. They are not merely outsiders in an alien culture like Roy Hobbs, country boy in the big city; Frank Alpine, Italian among Jews; Fidelman, Jew among Italians; Seymour Levin, Easterner going west; but they also live on the borders of their own culture. If they are Jews, they are marginal Jews—Bober's eulogy must be delivered by a rabbi who has never met him; Finkle, the rabbinical student in "The Magic Barrel," doesn't believe in God; Bok leaves the *shtetl* to live like a Christian—and others are marginal artists—critics, historians, modish failures like Fidelman, novelists like Lesser who will never finish the big novel. Yet when these men commit themselves to another human being, they move from the margins of their world to the center. Bober becomes the Jew the rabbi says he is because of his commitment to Frank Alpine; Bok earns his place while denying the name of Judaism so he can save his fellow Jews from a pogrom. Lesser shows his faith in writing more when he commits himself to helping Spearmint than when he hacks away on his own endless novel, and Harvitz in "Man in the Drawer" proves himself as a writer when he rescues Levitansky's manuscript. In all cases, the question finally is not whether a man is a Jew or an artist, but whether he is a human being ready to take Abel's role rather than Cain's. It is this Augustinian duality that separates the moral failures from the successes in Malamud's fiction.

Periodical Publications:

"Benefit Performance," *Threshold*, 3 (February 1943): 20-22;

"The Place is Different Now," *American Preface*, 8 (spring 1943): 230-242;

"An Apology," *Commentary*, 12 (November 1951): 460-464;

"An Exorcism," *Harper's*, 237 (December 1968): 76-89;

"God's Wrath," *Atlantic*, 229 (February 1972): 59-62.

References:

John W. Aldridge, *Time to Murder and Create: The Contemporary Novel in Crisis* (New York: McKay, 1966), pp. 52-94;

John Allen, "The Promised End: Bernard Malamud's *The Tenants*," *Hollins Critic*, 8, 5 (1971): 1-15;

Robert Alter, "Malamud as Jewish Writer," *Commentary*, 42, 3 (September 1966): 71-76;

Richard Astro and Jackson Benson, eds., *The Fiction of Bernard Malamud* (Corvallis: Oregon State University Press, 1977);

John A. Barsness, "*A New Life:* The Frontier Myth in Perspective," *Western American Literature*, 3 (winter 1969): 297-302;

Jonathan Baumbach, "The Economy of Love: The Novels of Bernard Malamud," *Kenyon Review*, 25 (summer 1963): 438-457;

Samuel Bellman, "Women, Children, and Idiots First: The Transformational Psychology of Bernard Malamud," *Critique* (winter 1972-1973): 123-138;

Sandy Cohen, *Bernard Malamud and the Trial by Love* (Amsterdam: Rodopi, 1974);

Robert Ducharme, "Structure and Content in Malamud's *Pictures of Fidelman*," *Connecticut Review*, 5, 1 (1971): 26-36;

Edwin Eigner, "Malamud's Use of the Quest Romance," *Genre*, 1 (January 1968): 55-74;

Leslie Fiedler, *No! in Thunder* (Boston: Beacon, 1960), pp. 101-110;

Leslie A. Field and Joyce W. Field, eds., *Bernard Malamud and the Critics* (New York: New York University Press, 1970);

Field and Field, eds., *Bernard Malamud: A Collection of Critical Essays* (Englewood Cliffs: Prentice-Hall, 1974);

Alan W. Friedman, "Bernard Malamud: The Hero as Schnook," *Southern Review*, 4 (October 1968): 927-944;

Mark Goldman, "Bernard Malamud's Comic Vision and the Theme of Identity," *Critique*, 7, 1 (winter 1964-1965): 92-109;

Ralph Graber, "Baseball in American Fiction," *English Journal*, 56 (November 1967): 1107-1114;

Peter Hays, "The Complex Pattern of Redemption in *The Assistant*," *Centennial Review*, 13 (spring 1959): 200-214;

Granville Hicks, *Literary Horizons* (New York: New York University Press, 1970), pp. 65-83;

Alfred Kazin, *Contemporaries* (Boston: Little, Brown, 1962), pp. 202-207;

Marcus Klein, *After Alienation: American Novels in Mid-Century* (Cleveland: World, 1964), pp. 247-293;

Rita Kosofsky, *Bernard Malamud: An Annotated Checklist* (Kent, Ohio: Kent State University Press, 1970);

Barbara Lefcowitz, "The *Hybris* of Neurosis: Malamud's *Pictures of Fidelman*," *Literature and Psychology*, 20, 3 (1970): 115-120;

Ruth Mandel, "Bernard Malamud's *The Assistant* and *A New Life*: Ironic Affirmation," *Critique*, 7, 2 (winter 1964-1965): 110-121;

Glenn Meeter, *Bernard Malamud and Philip Roth: A Critical Essay* (Grand Rapids, Mich.: Eerdmans, 1968);

James Mellard, "Malamud's Novels: Four Versions of Pastoral," *Critique*, 9, 2 (1967): 5-19;

David R. Mesher, "The Remembrance of Things Unknown: Malamud's 'The Last Mohican,' " *Studies in Short Fiction*, 12 (fall 1975): 397-404;

Sanford Pinsker, "The Achievement of Bernard Malamud," *Midwest Quarterly*, 10 (July 1969): 379-389;

S. V. Pradhan, "The Nature and Interpretation of Symbolism in Malamud's *The Assistant*," *Centennial Review*, 16 (fall 1972): 394-407;

Marc Ratner, "Style and Humanity in Malamud's Fiction," *Massachusetts Review*, 5, 4 (1964): 663-683;

Sidney Richman, *Bernard Malamud* (New York: Twayne, 1966);

Philip Roth, "Writing American Fiction," *Commentary*, 31 (March 1961): 223-233;

Ben Siegel, "Victims in Motion: Bernard Malamud's Sad and Bitter Clowns," *Northwest Review*, 5 (spring 1962): 69-80;

Fred Standley, "Bernard Malamud: The Novel of Redemption," *Southern Humanities Review*, 5 (1971): 309-318;

Daniel Stern, "The Art of Fiction: Bernard Malamud," *Paris Review*, 61 (spring 1975): 40-64;

Tony Tanner, "Bernard Malamud and the New Life," *Critical Quarterly*, 10 (spring-summer 1968): 151-168;

Earl R. Wasserman, "*The Natural*: Malamud's World Ceres," *Centennial Review*, 9 (fall 1965): 438-460;

Christof Wegelin, "The American Schlemiel Abroad: Malamud's Italian Stories and the End of American Innocence," *Twentieth Century Literature*, 19 (April 1973): 77-88;

Ruth Wisse, *The Schlemiel as Modern Hero* (Chicago: University of Chicago Press, 1971), pp. 110-118.

Manuscripts:

The Library of Congress has manuscripts, typescripts and proofs of *The Natural, The Assistant, A New Life, The Fixer, Pictures of Fidelman*, parts of *The Magic Barrel* and *Idiots First*, and various short stories.

WALLACE MARKFIELD was born in Brooklyn, New York, on 12 August 1926. He was educated at Abraham Lincoln High School and at Brooklyn College, where he received his B.A. in 1947. Markfield also studied at New York University from 1948 to 1950. The milieu of New York and especially Brooklyn is everywhere in his work, particularly in his second novel, *Teitlebaum's Window*, which records the vicissitudes of growing up in Brooklyn in the 1930s. In the late 1940s Markfield wrote reviews for the *New Leader* and was its film critic in 1954-1955. He is a self-confessed movie nut and quite capable of both the erudition about film demonstrated by his intellectuals in *To An Early Grave* as well as the more visceral reaction to films found in the boys in *Teitlebaum's Window*. For twelve years, Markfield worked as a publicist for such organizations as the Council of Jewish Federations and Welfare Funds, the Anti-Defamation League, and the American Jewish Committee. These experiences play some part in the portrait and occupation of Morroe Rieff in *To An Early Grave*. Markfield's portraits of the other passengers of the errant Volkswagen of that novel draw on his friendships with writers for magazines such as *Partisan Review*, *Commentary*, and *Hudson Review*. Markfield has taught as a writer-in-residence at San Francisco State College, Kirkland College (New York), Queens College, and Columbia University. He has received a

Wallace Markfield.

C. V. Stone

Guggenheim Fellowship (1965) and a National Endowment for the Arts grant (1966). Markfield married Anna May Goodman in 1949 and has one child.

In *To An Early Grave* (1964), Markfield borrows Joyce's technique of converting the flotsam and jetsam of consciousness into the substructure of emotional growth. As in Joyce, the fine, everyday perceptions of the hero, Morroe Rieff, are set against sterile intellectuality, both Rieff's own and that of his friends—Barnett Weiner, "poet, critic, contributor to the literary quarterlies"; Felix Ottensteen, a writer for a Yiddish daily; and Holly Levine, a literary critic for the highbrow quarterlies. Morroe Rieff is a speech writer for Jewish causes (as was Markfield) and his quasi-literary career is not all that far from Leopold Bloom's career as a broker for want ads. The four friends are on their way to the funeral of Leslie Braverman, who has outshone them all in the literary games and gamesmanship that is their life. As Melvin J. Friedman has pointed out, the descent of these four Jewish intellectuals into the depths of Brooklyn parallels the Hades episode in *Ulysses*, where Bloom, with three acquaintances, attends the funeral of Paddy Dignam.

In this novel, which received high praise from the critics upon publication, Markfield shows a perfect ear for the cant of the highbrow intelligentsia. These men are incapable of talking about Brooklyn girls and Bronx girls without making the "sensitive" distinctions that Markfield derides even as he plays their game. He provides the perfect answer for the affected weariness of the worn-out critic who is about to say the last word on his subject:

"Then, too, what, precisely what can one find to say about Auden?"

"Say something nice. . . ."

The lives of Braverman's mourners are filled with trivial concerns for which the repeated "trivia" is an image: "By the intersection of Nostrand Avenue and Kings Highway he had named twenty-seven Mickey Rooney movies exclusive of the Andy Hardy series; nine movies wherein Harold Huber had been featured but not starred; and hummed the themes of 'Myrt and Marge,' 'Lum and Abner,' and 'Vic and Sadie.' "

Rieff's three companions absorb Braverman's death intellectually without being at all touched by it emotionally. Markfield dissects a world where brittle wit protects the inhabitants from feeling the pain of loss and, perhaps more importantly, from perceiving their own fall into polished mediocrity. Only Rieff, outwardly no better or worse than the others, feels real grief at Braverman's death, but it is as much sorrow at his own failure as it is love for a man he knows is mostly a phony. Rieff envies Braverman's success, while realizing how slight it is.

To An Early Grave begins with a brief dream in which Rieff's college dean drags him off an up escalator. Freud comments that this kind of dream of intellectual failure reflects unmerited success in the life of the dreamer. Rieff and his clique all believe they have earned the laurel of the intelligentsia, but they care no more about ideas than they do about Braverman. They are even second-rate critics: although somewhat puzzled by the rabbi's funeral oration for "Braverman," they do not realize that the speech is about someone else because they have gone to the wrong funeral. And things get worse when they do get to the right funeral; even true reminiscences become flashy, intellectual exercises: "We must first determine whether we want memoir or critique. If memoir, it behooves us to go easy on the bold and baroque. . . . If critique, it behooves us then, or it then behooves us, to find in his work what I like to think of as, ah, the double image—that which is, at once, symbolic expression of our time and tragic protest against it." Only Rieff's reflections are real, although mixed with some false sentiments. Rieff recognizes his own pretenses and reaches the feeling of honest grief that Leopold Bloom finds at Paddy Dignam's funeral.

Critical reception of Markfield's most ambitious work, *Teitlebaum's Window* (1970), was largely

Spring & Summer

- One -

There are some midsummer mornings in the Tai-tzin Province of
Northwestern Manchuria when the heavens seem to split. Rain,
sudden and slate blue and coming with a great foaming gush, can
burst the bark off trees or knock birds from the sky. Then the
tiny Wahsu sheep grazing the Mun-hang Plateau turn wild and
crazy and scramble down its rocky lip to escape the lacerating
winds. Most break their backs or rip open their bellies. But
a few nearly always make the bottom and flee in an easterly
direction till the first Soviet patrol blows them apart with
Kalashnikov rifles.

On one such morning, the Manchus say, a Russian babe will be
born to punish the world.

Even when the rain diminishes and the sky shows only leghorn
clouds and healthy pink they go about spitting toward the
Munku-tsardik Mountains and cursing this babe.

And villagers who work the fields alongside the Loo air strip
sing then of the things they anticipate at his hands -- hard
and awful things, things of darkness and filth, things which
had as yet no name. But if he is destined to come, they also
sing, well, let it be here and now so that he may all the
sooner know how we will endure him and defy him and prevail
against him.

It was a song that went to Major Wen's heart, filling him
with exalted feelings.

To the Forces of History, also to his Manchu mother, he
sent a silent message: "Praises, praises, praises upon such
people and upon my connection to them."

As the turbines came on he spoke aloud into the infernal
din: "Khruschev despised us. 'Human plankton in the colonialist
sea.' Yes and did. In Kiev the tactics instructor screamed
at me, "Masses, multitudes, waves! Your medium is people!"
'Sir,' I told him, 'Lao-tze teaches that vast populations have a music.

From typescript of work-in-progress.

- Twenty-five -

The Children's Crusade. The Treaty of Brest-Litovsk. Abraham
Lincoln's melancholy. Saul and David. Clemenceau and Landru.
The veil of Maya. 'Not once in the history of the world,' he
told me over cucumbers and yogurt, 'has there been a merciful
nation.' With the herring and slivovitz he forced me to look
through a hundred years thickness of disaster till I was
compelled to see -- but what did I not see? Neitsche taking
his whip to women. Cecil Rhodes thinking in continents and
feeling in centuries. Byron and Wagner trumpeting that man is
something to be surpassed. The Paris Commune. The Verdun and
Tannenburg. Lenin posing in his worker's cap. Trotsky
rushing to his fourteen fronts. While he ground the coffee and
quartered the heel of a hondocke.

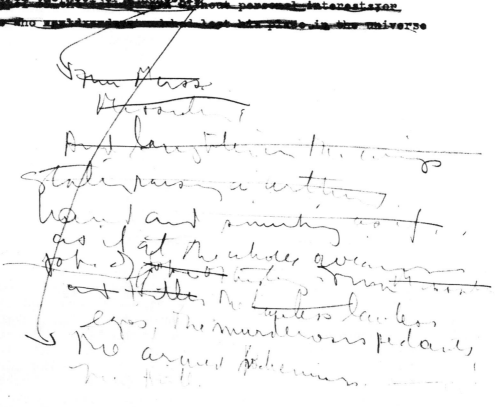

unfriendly as reviewers saw in the book one more incarnation of the Jewish-boy-grows-up novel, replete with egg creams, overbearing mother, and masturbation. The fact that Philip Roth's *Portnoy's Complaint* appeared the previous year was in no small measure responsible for this attitude. Despite external similarities, however, *Teitlebaum's Window* is no second *Portnoy*, but rather the author's Brooklyn-centered version of *A Portrait of the Artist As a Young Man*. The novel, which follows the budding intellectual, Simon Sloan, from age eight in 1932 until his first year at Brooklyn College and the attack on Pearl Harbor, is a beautifully choreographed play of change against constancy. The constancy is found first of all in a series of repeated images, including the humorous signs in Teitlebaum the grocer's window ("Forget about bringing back the N.R.A. but don't forget to start bringing back the Sheffield empties") and one-sentence fragments from the unchanging lives of a small number of people. These image clusters introduce most of the chapters with the celluloid clarity of a Movietone newsreel, and their function is to mark off the sameness in most people's lives as the years of the Depression tick away.

A more important image of constancy is the unending stream of movie heroes against which the hero and his small group of friends, the Battle Aces A.C., pattern themselves. In contrast to the intellectuals in *To An Early Grave*, the boys in *Teitlebaum's Window* care passionately about the movies they see. They worry not only about the sex life of King Kong, but, more compassionately, about how he lives: "Hymie claimed he was bothered always by something else, not that it was so important, but he would have liked them to show where exactly King Kong lives on his island, they never show you where he lives exactly."

Like the intellectual passengers in Holly Levine's Volkswagen, the boys live for their jokes, but their wit has none of the verbal brilliance of the first novel. Rather it consists of all the familiar standbys of cruelty and sexual bravado that are the staple of male adolescence everywhere. The boys play their games with the intensity necessary to ward off the crises of both adolescence and the Depression that loom everywhere in the background of the novel. Also included in the unchangeable background of the novel are the two-dimensional Dickensian characters who go through the ten years of the novel never learning anything and harping on the same themes in unchanging speech rhythms. An example of the characters bound by this kind of *idee fixe* is the delicatessen psychologist, Madame Ducoff, who attributes the language of the ghetto to the Almighty: "Mrs. Udell, I'll put it to you the way God put it to the Jews. When he was warning how they dassn't have no other gods: 'Look, I need the business.'" The tricks played on Madame Ducoff are a protest against the monomania displayed by most of the characters in the book as well as the boys' unspoken recognition that such inflexibility is part of their own future as adults.

The most important conflict of change versus constancy is the growth of the hero away from the Battle Aces A.C. itself. In the first half of the novel, Simon is, for better and worse, one of the boys, but as he grows, he wistfully leaves behind the universal sameness of adolescence and takes on an intellectual personality that is uniquely his own. This personality is recorded in the most experimental part of the novel, a documentary history of the emotional and intellectual growth of Simon Sloan, which includes his college class notes, letters from his girl friend's almost-liberal mother, his own mother's correspondence with Teitlebaum, and his own jottings on random events. As Joyce does with Stephen Dedalus, Markfield creates a portrait of intellectual growth which begins with the hero's youthful limitations and ends with the promise of maturity.

You Could Live If They Let You (1974) repeats the basic structure of *To An Early Grave* by taking stock of a dead character through the meditations of his friends. *To An Early Grave* produced only an external view of Braverman, but the reader never feels more is necessary since the primary concern is the effect of Braverman's death on Morroe Rieff. This is only partially the case in *You Could Live If They Let You*. The novel is a life of Jules Farber, a Lenny Bruce-like comedian, as seen by his Boswell, a Christian midwesterner named Chandler Van Horton. In using a *goy* to tell the story of the Jewish Farber, Markfield has a chance to observe his main character from the point of view of another culture, but he misses this opportunity because Van Horton himself admits to being adopted by "a group of toughminded New York Jewish intellectuals." The result of the "conversion" of the narrator is that the dialogue between Van Horton and Farber turns into a monologue for two voices, playing very cleverly, but nonetheless playing, with all the varieties of stereotyped Jewish-Christian relationships. Typically Farber cannot resist the one-liner so that when, *a la* Leopold Bloom-Stephen Dedalus, he begs his apprentice to cuckold him, he uses Henny Youngman's classic line, "Take my wife, please!"

A more serious flaw than the inability to view Farber from some valid external stance is the inability to view Farber from the inside, to let the reader understand the pain for which his humor is a defense and a purge. Farber plays with *tsuris*, the Jewish notion of endless trouble and aggravation, but the reader never feels the pain that should come from Farber's relationship with Mitchell, his autistic five-year-old son, or with Marlene, his *shikse* wife, who is meant to be a combination of Molly Bloom and Bellow's Madeline Herzog. Farber's sister, for example, is far more touching in her reaction to Marlene's conversion of Mitchell to the Church of Christ Therapist than is Farber. The sister dreams of airbrushing all of the Christian symbols out of the photographs of the conversion but realizes that if she could do this there would be nothing else left. Similarly, it is Van Horton, rather than Farber, who understands the I and Thou relationship (of the philosopher Martin Buber) that is meant to grow out of the Van Horton-Farber friendship. Closer to the truth is what Van Horton says about his relationship with the comedian, "we come together in the corridor, Farber and I, like knife and wound."

Markfield provides a brilliant parody of scholarly criticism as he records the academic vultures picking their livelihood off Farber's bones. He also offers the glittering monologue of Farber, as in his rap at the fabled acquisitiveness of Jews, "By the waters of Babylon I sat down and wept that I had not bought a little property." This mood reaches its climax in Farber's last performance, a manic outburst on a television talk show which ends in his death. The one-liners are perfection, but the reader searches for emotional belief in the source of Farber's outrage.

In the preface to the published fragment of an unfinished novel, *Multiple Orgasms* (1977), Markfield recognizes the crisis that he has reached in his career, "I'd grown tired, after three novels, of chronicling the Jewish experience in America." The novel was meant to be a new direction for Markfield, an erotic exercise going a step beyond Judith Rossner or Erica Jong, but it did not turn out that way: "What I intended was a good, easy, ribald read. What I got was a little more than a voice whining and carping away at my undermind." The published fragment which records Laura Pauline Goodfriend's aggravating attempt to return a sweater to Bloomingdale's is filled with the play of intellectual ironies against the everyday frustrations of life that is Markfield's forte, but rather than being a new direction, the forty-three-year-old heroine seems to be Simon Sloan grown to middle-class, middlebrow

womanhood. Markfield called *To An Early Grave* "a simple tone poem on aggravation" and *Multiple Orgasms*, despite the pornographic promise of its title, seems one more repetition of this theme. Markfield's present achievement, it can be said without facetiousness, has melded a Joycean sensibility with the wit of Henny Youngman, but he will have to find a new amalgam and a different voice if he is to escape being stereotyped as an intellectual New York Jewish writer. —*Jeffrey Helterman*

Books:

To An Early Grave (New York: Simon & Schuster, 1964; London: Cape, 1965);

Teitlebaum's Window (New York: Knopf, 1970; London: Cape, 1971);

You Could Live If They Let You (New York: Knopf, 1974);

Multiple Orgasms (Bloomfield Hills, Mich. & Columbia, S.C.: Bruccoli Clark, 1977).

Periodical Publications:

"Notes on the Working Day," *Partisan Review*, 13 (September-October 1946): 460-463;

"Ph.D." *Partisan Review*, 14 (September-October 1947): 466-471;

"The Patron," *Partisan Review*, 21 (January-February 1954): 80-86;

"The Country of the Crazy Horse," *Commentary*, 25 (March 1958): 237-242;

"The Big Giver," *Midstream*, 4 (summer 1958): 35-46;

"A Season of Change," *Midstream*, 4 (autumn 1958): 25-48;

"The Decline of Sholem Waldman," *Reconstructionist*, 17 October 1958;

"Eulogy for an American Boy," *Commentary*, 33 (June 1962): 513-518.

References:

Matthew J. Bruccoli, "Wallace Markfield," in *Conversations With Writers I* (Detroit: Bruccoli Clark/Gale, 1977), pp. 216-236;

Joseph Epstein, "Too Jewish to Love," *New Republic*, 151 (25 July 1964): 23-24;

Melvin J. Friedman, "Jewish Mothers and Sons: The Expense of *Chutzpah*," in Irving Malin, ed. *Contemporary American-Jewish Literature* (Bloomington: Indiana University Press, 1973), pp. 156-174;

Wallace Markfield

Stanley Edgar Hyman, "Jewish, All Too Jewish," in his *Standards: A Chronicle of Books for Our Time* (New York: Horizon, 1966), pp. 214-218; Marion Magid, Review of *To An Early Grave*, *Commentary*, 38 (November 1964): 81-82.

MARY McCARTHY has made her living and reputation as a writer ever since her graduation from Vassar College in 1933, Phi Beta Kappa key in hand. Beginning with book reviews for *Nation* and the *New Republic*, she allied herself with New York's left-wing writers and thinkers, eventually becoming an editor and drama critic for the *Partisan Review*, writing a weekly column, "Theatre Chronicle." She staked out a radical position contrary to the New York critical establishment, and soon her direct, intelligent, and acerbic criticism set her apart from her contemporaries, earning her their grudging respect. Not until Edmund Wilson encouraged her did she attempt to write fiction. Her first novel, *The Company She Keeps*, published in 1942, was a semi-biographical collection of loosely related short stories. With this book, Mary McCarthy's reputation as an author was established. Throughout her long career, her literary energies have remained divided between the intellectual demands of the critical essay and the creative demands of invention and fiction. Over the years, Mary McCarthy has contributed articles to numerous magazines and papers, has published books of essays and short stories, and has produced six major novels. She has been the recipient of two Guggenheim Fellowships (1949, 1959), the *Horizon* prize for 1949, and a National Institute of Arts and Letters grant for 1957. Thus honored and prolific, Mary McCarthy's fiction reflects her urbane, intellectual, sophisticated tastes and is marked by a highly comic, often satiric vision of life in post-World War II America. Nevertheless, critics of her work remain divided between those, like Harry T. Moore, who see her primarily as an essayist who "cares for ideas rather than people" and those who, like Irvin Stock, see her as a novelist with a vision which "moves us, which enlarges our sympathies, and which brings us close to complex reality." Neither group denies her importance in contemporary American writing, but each fails to resolve what exactly her contribution has been. That her work speaks to serious thinkers and writers is undeniable.

Coloring all of Mary McCarthy's work are the events of her childhood. The eldest of four children, she was born in Seattle, Washington, on 21 June 1912 to Therese Preston McCarthy and Roy Winfield McCarthy. Her maternal grandmother, Augusta Morganstern Preston, was a beautiful Jewish woman from San Francisco. Her maternal grandfather, Harold Preston, was a Seattle lawyer whose Protestant ancestors came from New England. Her paternal grandparents were wealthy Irish Catholics from Minneapolis, Minnesota, where they operated a grain elevator business. Therese Preston was a Protestant who converted to Catholicism after marrying Roy McCarthy, a man ten years her senior and a victim of progressive heart disease. The conflicts between the reactionary Catholicism of the McCarthys and the more humane Protestantism of the Prestons, as well as the Jewish heritage of her maternal grandmother, emerge as significant motifs in McCarthy's later writings. When both her parents died in the great influenza epidemic of 1918, Mary's paternal grandparents assumed the guardianship of the children and placed them in the care of a great aunt, Margaret, and her stern, authoritarian husband, Meyers Shriver. The barren conditions under which Mary and her brothers were forced to live and the harsh treatment they received are vividly recalled in *Memories of a Catholic Girlhood* (1957). Rigidly anti-Protestant, McCarthy's grandmother followed the doctrines of Catholicism in a narrow, smug fashion and generally ignored the fact that the McCarthy children lived an existence where not only were all pleasures denied them, but most of life's ordinary comforts as well. Although Mary and Kevin occasionally ran away to their grandparents' house in Minneapolis, nothing was done to change conditions for the children until 1923 when Mary's Grandfather Preston took her back to live with him in Seattle, sent Kevin and Preston to Catholic boarding schools, and left the youngest boy, Sheridan, with the Shrivers. Although life was more pleasant with her Seattle grandparents, she was never able completely to erase the memories of life in Minnesota. The sense of loss, rejection, and abandonment, and the emotional sterility of the life she endured are recurring echoes in much of McCarthy's fiction.

Her education in Seattle was more rigorous and demanding than what she had experienced in Minneapolis. She attended Forest Ridge Convent School for the remainder of her grammar school, boarding there during the week, returning to her grandparents' on weekends. Again the split between her Protestant and Catholic heritages was accentuated, and she feared for the state of her grandfather's immortal soul because he had been baptized a Presbyterian. At the convent McCarthy

Jill Krementz

Mary McCarthy.

learned rhetoric, French literature, Christian doctrine, and English history. She has stated that she lost her faith during these convent years, but the influence of the Catholic faith never left her, and through it she was drawn to Latin. Her present prose style reflects both her knowledge of Latin and of the church, as she has a tendency to formal rhetorical sentence structures, to Latinate diction, and to ecclesiastical references. She attended a public high school in Seattle, but because of poor grades due in part to her awakening interest in boys she was transferred to the Anne Wright Seminary, an Episcopal boarding school in Tacoma, where she graduated at the top of her class. Mary McCarthy headed to Vassar after a summer in which she enrolled in a drama school in Seattle. At Vassar she excelled, developing further her love for the theater, but always being recognized for her writing abilities. Other students have described her as somewhat aloof and distant, probably a result of her sense of being an orphan with no real heritage to define herself by. Later, in "The Vassar Girl," McCarthy would describe the school as a place where "the ideas of excellence, zest for adventure, fastidiousness of

mind, and humanistic breadth of feeling" were present.

After graduation from Vassar, McCarthy moved to New York City where she married an aspiring actor and unsuccessful playwright, Harold Johnsrud. Their marriage lasted only three years, but through him she was able to pursue her interest in the theater. Johnsrud confirmed her growing belief that she was not going to make a great actress, so she turned her full energies to writing. Soon she began to write book reviews for the *Nation* and the *New Republic*. Flirting with the tenets of Communism, she associated with the left-leaning New York intellectuals, finding Trotsky a romantic figure, but she was wary of the Communist Party itself. And after the war she even made anti-Communist speeches. She met Philip Rahv who eventually made her an editor of the *Partisan Review*, but she never was considered "seriously committed" to the Left's political cause and, consequently, was assigned the theater column. She continued to do "Theatre Chronicle" for the *Review* until after the war.

In 1938 Mary McCarthy married critic and essayist Edmund Wilson. Their marriage was a stormy one, but it lasted seven years, during which her only child, a son named Reuel, was born. Wilson recognized her talents for fiction and insisted she start to write. The resulting six short stories, which were collected and published as her first book, *The Company She Keeps*, were originally published separately, but Miss McCarthy maintains that "halfway through I began to think of them as a kind of unified story. The same character kept reappearing, and so on. I decided finally to call it a novel in that it does in a sense tell *a* story, one story." The heroine of the book is Margaret Sargent, a composite picture drawn from Mary's own life, the name itself a family one on her maternal grandfather's side. Margaret begins as a woman seeking an identity of her own now that she is getting a divorce. Throughout the six stories Margaret's quest for her identity is emphasized. A more basic theme is the search for truth: what is appearance and what is reality? Margaret Sargent develops from a woman bound by roles and societal values in "Cruel and Barbarous Treatment" to the tormented but courageous woman at the end of "Ghostly Father, I Confess," who understands that to survive she must compromise and frequently agree to lies. She accepts this fragmentation of spirit and flesh since she retains the ability to perceive, if not understand, the essential truth of life. The story ends on a note of heroic submission to the fact of disunity as she prays, "*O di, reddit me hoc pro pietate mea* (O gods render this to me in return for my devotion)."

The Company She Keeps had a mixed reception. Many critics felt the book was "not well put together" or was "discontinuous," ignoring precedents of novels such as Anderson's *Winesburg, Ohio* and Faulkner's *Go Down Moses*. The fact that she wrote about a specific middle, or upper-middle class, whose sophisticated and intellectual approach to life was presented in what one called "malicious accuracy of detail" bothered others. Malcolm Cowley admired her fidelity to truth and felt the book had the "unusual quality of being lived." There was general agreement that Miss McCarthy wrote intelligently and well, and critics commented on her "pointed wit and perfection of expression." Throughout the years, this book has become increasingly admired for its characterizations as well as its style. *The Company She Keeps* established Mary McCarthy as a promising writer of fiction.

Mary McCarthy and Edmund Wilson separated in 1945. McCarthy taught literature at Bard College during 1945 and 1946. She found the atmosphere at Bard stimulating, but exhausting. In the fall of 1946 her divorce from Wilson was finalized, and she married Bowden Broadwater whom she had met the previous summer in Paris. They lived in New York City where he worked for the *Partisan Review*, and they both enjoyed the left-wing friends whom McCarthy had known from the 1930s. In the spring of 1948 she taught a semester at Sarah Lawrence. Unlike Bard students, the students at Sarah Lawrence were so poor that she disliked the work and never returned.

During the time she was at Sarah Lawrence she began working on her next book, *The Oasis*, which was first published in *Horizon* under the title *A Source of Embarrassment*. The book won the *Horizon* prize for 1949 and had a mixed critical reception. Bothered by the lack of action and its episodic structure, many felt the book was not so much a novel as a group study. McCarthy sometimes described it as a philosophical landscape. Indeed, in her 1961 *Paris Review* interview she claimed: "*The Oasis* is not a novel. . . . it's a conte, a *conte philosophique*." The book grew out of her and Bowden's experiences with the European-American groups with which they were associated after World War II.

In the book McCarthy places a group of liberals in a utopian community set high on a mountain top and demonstrates how, even in their idealistic fervor, there is dissention between the group of purists led by MacDougal Macdermott (patterned after her friend Dwight MacDonald) and the realists whose leader, Will Taub, is based on Philip Rahv. The purists believe that man can achieve a perfect society, while the realists denounce that idea as naive and refuse to commit themselves to any positive belief. At the heart of the social experiment is the belief that present day society denies man his right to a "human existence." A series of crises forces the two factions of the colonists to see the weakness of their positions, and ultimately the experiment fails when they see they have violated their own principles by forcibly expelling an innocent group of strawberry pickers from the utopia's choice patch. The members of the utopia finally understand that since they, who are trying to change themselves, cannot, then utopia is not possible on earth. Reaction to the book was mixed. Philip Rahv and others who felt they were the prototypes for the book's characters were upset; Rahv even threatened to sue. Hannah Arendt praised the book highly. All critics agreed that Miss McCarthy's style was "almost perfect," but many felt the book failed both as satire and as a novel. As the *New York Herald Tribune* critic put it, the "book might best be regarded as a philosophical disquisition with fictional trimmings."

Late in 1949, when Bowden Broadwater quit the *Partisan Review*, they took some money inherited from the McCarthys and moved to a house they bought in Rhode Island. *Cast a Cold Eye*, a collection of short stories, was published in 1950. The title, which comes from Yeats, refers to the attitude which McCarthy denounces: indifference and insensitivity to the reality of the world outside the self. Unfortunately, many critics have used the phrase to describe McCarthy herself, as a person who coldly dissects, with no redeeming love or caring, the world and people around her. The book consists of four stories which follow themes similar to those of *The Company She Keeps*. There are also three versions of chapters which later appear in *Memories of a Catholic Girlhood*. The heroine of "The Weeds" resembles the Margaret Sargent of "Ghostly Father." She is trapped in a bad marriage and is forced to acknowledge that the duality of her existence cannot be escaped. The second story, "The Friend of the Family," is a development of the marriage theme, exploring the question of the nature of personal identity, as well as of reality or truth. The third story, "The Cicerone," creates a memorable comic female character, Miss Grabbe, who has come to Europe in pursuit of love. The Cicerone's mysterious character rouses the curiosity of Miss Grabbe and her companions, and they seek more information about him. Their pursuit of his identity is an interesting reversal of Miss McCarthy's identity theme. "The Old Men" is considered a less successful story, but it, too, deals with the young man's search for his identity. McCarthy suggests that the young man's solution, that the self is simply a series of roles or impersonations and that reality does not help, is wrong.

Mary McCarthy immediately began work on her next novel, *The Groves of Academe* (1952). The critics received it as another in America's tradition of academic novels. The background is the McCarthy era, during which Communists and their sympathizers were being investigated and persecuted. Miss McCarthy constructs a world where values are inverted and, in the liberal atmosphere of Jocelyn College, the apparent firing of a man for his Communist past elevates him to the status of a martyr. As the title, an epigraph from Horace, suggests, the book is about the "search for truth amid the groves of academe." The main character, Henry Mulcahy, is a despicable man by most standards, who subverts truth in order to retain his position as a member of the faculty of Jocelyn College. Opposing

him is the president of the school, Maynard Hoar, liberal, honest, good-looking, who tries to fire Mulcahy for his academic incompetence. Through the voice of Mulcahy, Miss McCarthy satirizes the academic community. In a highly comic and ironic twist of events, she demonstrates the inadequacy of the voice of reason, of sane classical notions of truth and honor, by having President Hoar resign at the moment when Mulcahy's total dishonesty has been revealed.

The critics were again divided between those who objected to the characterization, because it was either too close to stereotypes or too brutally honest in its satirical portraits of the faculty, and those who felt the book was entertaining and successful in its exposure of intellectual pretense. Some insisted on calling Mary McCarthy primarily an essayist. In recent years, her resemblance to Jane Austen has been pointed out. Irvin Stock notes "the irony, sanity, and grace of her prose, and the combination of moral concern and tough intelligence." He feels *The Groves of Academe* is a significant step forward in her art.

In 1952 the Broadwaters sold their house in Rhode Island and bought one at Wellfleet on Cape Cod, not far from where Edmund Wilson and his new wife had a home. By agreement, Mary McCarthy and Bowden Broadwater stayed away from Wellfleet when Wilson was in residence and Reuel was visiting him. For this and other reasons, namely a general *malaise* spawned by the Stevenson loss in the 1952 election, the spectacle of the McCarthy hearings, and her inability to make headway on her novel *The Group*, the couple began to travel more, spending time in Vermont, New York City, and various parts of Europe. During one of her stays at Wellfleet, she began *A Charmed Life*, submitting a portion of it as a short story, but working on the larger novel. She continued to work on the book while traveling in Portugal, and finished it in Capri in 1955, the year it was published.

Martha Sinnott, the heroine of *A Charmed Life*, is a direct descendant of earlier McCarthy heroines. She is an intellectual, a writer, faced with the problem of reconciling her dream of life to the reality which surrounds her. Her problem is compounded by the fact that she has returned with her second husband to New Leeds, a community like Cape Cod, which has a large Bohemian group of artists and thinkers who live "charmed" lives unbounded by conventional morality or traditional values, seemingly impervious to harm or the consequences of their acts. One evening when her husband is out of town, Martha has a drunken reunion with her former husband, which culminates in a comic seduction scene. Later on, Martha finds she is pregnant. Now she must decide whether to tell her husband, lie about the baby and live a falsehood with him (a course most Leedsians would take), or take the difficult but moral course by having an abortion which will thereby preserve her integrity as well as her marriage. After a long temptation scene and debate with the devil, she decides to have the abortion. While on the way to Boston she is killed by a woman, remarkably similar to her, driving on the wrong side of the road. Less a novel of ideas than earlier novels, *A Charmed Life* satirizes intellectual pretense and dramatizes the human predicament. If one is to live in society and remain aware, then he will have to come to terms with its flaws and accept the disparity between truth and reality. This awareness and acceptance removes Martha from the "charmed life" and makes her mortal. In her case, the truth is fatal.

As with her previous books, readers enjoyed hunting down the originals for the book's characters, all the while criticizing McCarthy for using autobiography in such an open way. More serious critics pointed to the ending as "unsatisfying," feeling that having Martha killed by Eleanor Considine, a woman similar to Martha yet representative of the values Martha rejects, is too contrived. Critics responded favorably to the characters in *A Charmed Life*. One noted, "Her new novel has a measure of compassion, of warmth and understanding, often lacking in her anatomy lessons of the past." Again, there was general agreement that her writing is "polished," "intelligent," and "lively."

After *A Charmed Life* was published, McCarthy and Bowden Broadwater decided that life in Wellfleet might be uncomfortable, so they sold the house and remained in Europe for the better part of the year. The relationship between them had by this time begun to deteriorate. At the end of the summer of 1955 Bowden returned to New York City where he became a teacher and Reuel a student at St. Bernard's School. Eventually Bowden was made assistant headmaster, and McCarthy joined her family in New York for the winter of 1956. In May she returned to Europe where she completed work on the commissioned book, *Venice Observed*. Reuel and Bowden went to Europe to spend the summer with her. During the next few years, the family traveled back and forth between New York and Europe, while Mary continued to write. A group of essays called *Sights and Spectacles* was issued in 1956, *Memories of a Catholic Girlhood* in 1957, and her second art

history book, *The Stones of Florence*, in 1959. The marriage continued to disintegrate. In 1959, she began working again on *The Group*, going alone to Tripoli where, in the seclusion of a wealthy friend's home, she made progress. Running into another block, she stopped work on the novel in order to go on a State Department sponsored tour of Poland, Yugoslavia, London, and some English universities. The speeches she gave on this tour resulted in the two important critical essays, "The Fact in Fiction" and "Characters in Fiction," now included in the 1961 volume, *On the Contrary*. By the end of the tour, the marriage to Bowden was over in spirit, if not in fact. McCarthy went to Rome to wait for the divorce, and once more began to work on *The Group* as a means of diverting herself from the turmoil of her personal life. In 1961 they were divorced. Two months later she married James West, a State Department official she had met while on her tour to Poland. Like Rosamund Brown in *Birds of America*, Mary McCarthy entered the marriage with nothing but a few books and her mother's silver. By the end of 1961, West had been reassigned to Paris, where he and McCarthy continue to reside.

Completed through the assistance of a Guggenheim Fellowship, *The Group* (1963) brought McCarthy financial rewards and popular acclaim, as the book moved to the best-seller list. For the very reasons it became popular, the critics denounced the book. They said she had sold out to the masses. Some called it nothing more than feminine gossip; some objected to the "shocking" sexual scenes; some maintained that while depicting the surfaces of life brilliantly, she failed to plumb the depths of her material for the larger meanings. Norman Mailer felt that the book was "full of promise," but failed to go far enough and penetrate the "central horror" of our society.

Originally intended to trace the lives of eight Vassar girls from graduation to the Eisenhower election in 1952, McCarthy narrowed the time sequence to span the seven years between the marriage of Kay Strong just after graduation from Vassar in 1933 and Kay's funeral. McCarthy says it was conceived of as a "mock-chronicle novel" detailing the "loss of faith in progress, in the idea of progress." Notable by their sense of smug superiority, each of the Vassar girls believes implicitly that "newer is better," that science and technology are creating a better life for mankind, and that she will be able to control and shape her own life since she is well equipped with both her education and her intellect. As the book progresses, Miss McCarthy delineates the "thingness" and materialism which surrounds, pervades, and, in some cases, overwhelms the group. Although criticized for her catalogues, through them she paints a portrait of the concrete reality which the girls are facing and live in. As in earlier McCarthy novels, each girl has to come to terms with reality, and the degree to which she can eliminate intellectual pretense and cut through the miasmic fogs created by ideas and abstractions is the degree to which she is an absurdly comic or a compassionately human figure. Yet there is no clearly defined growth visible in the girls, due, in part, to the fact that they are comic figures. Mary McCarthy traces her idea of comic characters back to Bergson and Dickens: "All comic characters are immortal . . . invulnerable . . . *fige*," unlike "the hero or heroine [who] exists in time . . . [and] is equipped with a purpose." This philosophy accounts for the static, episodic quality of the book. Kay Strong, the outsider, is the central figure of the group. Unlike them, she has no social position, no family, and is the strongest advocate of nonconventional morality and life-style. She is obsessed with acquiring the paraphernalia which is in keeping with the philosophy of excellence and taste she acquired at Vassar. After her marriage fails, she has a breakdown as she finds that she does not control all of her life nor can she change man's brutal nature, as evidenced by the war. Mysteriously she falls to her death during an air raid alert. Her death is compared to Martha Sinnott's, suggesting that she may have seen through the pretense, acknowledged the failure of Vassar's idealism, and therefore moved out of the charmed, protected life of illusions to reality and mortality.

Now an internationally acclaimed author, Mary McCarthy felt the need to turn away from the voice of fiction and speak again in her own voice. The war in Vietnam stirred her liberal political interests, and she took two trips to the country to get a firsthand look at the situation. Several books and articles expressing her opposition to the war resulted: *Vietnam* in 1967, *Hanoi* in 1968, and *Medina* in 1972. These were collected and published as *The Seventeenth Degree* in 1974. In an interview with Jean-Francois Revel in 1971, she expressed her general disillusionment with the war and her disappointment that Nixon hadn't been able to change things. Later on she followed the events of Watergate closely for the *London Observer*, and in 1974 those articles were published as *The Mask of State: Watergate Portraits*.

Birds of America (1971) has been Mary McCarthy's only novel since *The Group*. Begun in 1964 when the idea first struck her, the book is about the concept of equality and its effects on both society and the individual. Nature is also a central theme. Peter Levi, a twenty-year-old American college student, is the narrative voice. While in New England with his mother, twice-divorced Rosamund Brown, concert harpsichordist, Peter is obsessed with the changes they see around them, symbolized by the death of the great horned owl and the disappearance of three cormorants, an endangered species. Peter's mother is a comic character who rigidly refuses to capitulate to some changes such as sliced bread and frozen foods, while changing husbands and life-styles without regret. Peter is also comic in his naive pursuit of truth. During his junior year abroad in Paris and on a visit to the Sistine Chapel in Rome, his faith in the American notion of equality is dealt a fatal blow. When he is attacked by a black swan, his faith in nature also wavers. Finally, when he is in the hospital recuperating from the bite, he sees the philosopher Kant standing at the foot of the bed telling him that nature is dead. With this, all the abstract values by which he has lived are proven invalid.

Although frequently tediously philosophical and essayistic in style, especially in Peter's letters to his mother, *Birds of America* is a comic novel. Laughter is the only way Mary McCarthy can face her grotesque vision of reality. As she admits, she is a pessimist. She sees man destroying nature in his rush to progress, and in the process she feels he has placed himself on the endangered species list. Her message in *Birds of America* is that because his moral faculty has failed or been rendered impotent, man is doomed to extinction, just as the cormorant and the great horned owl.

Birds of America received the same mixed criticism that all of her books have. Many critics objected to the long philosophical discussions, asking her to dramatize the problem rather than tell about it. Some felt the comic elements interfered with the seriousness of the subject, while others applauded it. Many were not satisfied with Peter, finding him likeable, but not believable. Yet he was also recognized as a Candide figure who exposes society's values for what they are. None, however, criticized her style for anything more than excessive cataloguing.

Mary McCarthy's art is not a storyteller's art; instead it has its roots in a neoclassical tradition where art instructs while it delights. In a literary world influenced by romantic traditions and whose critical standards ask fiction to "show" and not "tell," her work has been labeled not courageous enough. Yet there is universal agreement that she is a master of the English sentence and her prose style is exceptionally fine. Her vision of the modern world is as bleak as any of her fellow novelists', and her sense of the grotesque and the comic also equals theirs. She is not a realist, but she is concerned with the nature of reality, a reality undisguised by illusions. The brutal honesty of her confrontations places Mary McCarthy clearly in the mainstream of modern American writing. —*Gretchen Himmele Munroe*

Books:

The Company She Keeps (New York: Simon & Schuster, 1942; London: Weidenfeld & Nicolson, 1943);

The Oasis (New York: Random House, 1949; republished as *A Source of Embarrassment*, London: Heinemann, 1950);

Cast a Cold Eye (New York: Harcourt, Brace, 1950; London: Heinemann, 1952);

The Groves of Academe (New York: Harcourt, Brace, 1952; London: Heinemann, 1953);

A Charmed Life (New York: Harcourt, Brace, 1955; London: Weidenfeld & Nicolson, 1956);

Sights and Spectacles: 1937-1956 (New York: Farrar, Straus & Cudahy, 1956; republished as *Sights and Spectacles: Theatre Chronicles, 1937-1958*, London: Heinemann, 1959; republished as *Mary McCarthy's Theatre Chronicles 1937-62*, New York: Farrar, Straus, 1963);

Venice Observed: Comments on Venetian Civilization (New York: Reynal, 1956; London: Zwemmer, 1956);

Memories of a Catholic Girlhood (New York: Harcourt, Brace, 1957; London: Heinemann, 1957);

The Stones of Florence (New York: Harcourt, Brace, 1959; London: Heinemann, 1959);

On the Contrary (New York: Farrar, Straus & Cudahy, 1961; London: Heinemann, 1962);

The Group (New York: Harcourt, Brace & World, 1963; London: Weidenfeld & Nicolson, 1963);

The Humanist in the Bathtub (New York: New American Library, 1964);

Vietnam (New York: Harcourt, Brace & World, 1967; London: Weidenfeld & Nicolson, 1967);

Hanoi (New York: Harcourt, Brace & World, 1968; London: Weidenfeld & Nicolson, 1968);

The Writing on the Wall and Other Literary Essays (New York: Harcourt, Brace & World, 1970; London: Weidenfeld & Nicolson, 1970);

Winter Visitors (New York: Harcourt Brace Jovanovich, 1970);

Birds of America (New York: Harcourt Brace Jovanovich, 1971; London: Weidenfeld & Nicolson, 1971);

Medina (New York: Harcourt Brace Jovanovich, 1972; London: Wildwood, 1973);

The Stones of Florence and Venice Observed (Harmondsworth: Penguin, 1972);

The Mask of State: Watergate Portraits (New York: Harcourt Brace Jovanovich, 1974);

The Seventeenth Degree (New York: Harcourt Brace Jovanovich, 1974; London: Weidenfeld & Nicolson, 1975);

Can There Be a Gothic Literature (Amsterdam: Vitgererijde Harmonie, 1975).

Other:

The Iliad; or, The Poem of Force by Simone Weil, translation by McCarthy (Wallingford, Pa.: Pendle Hill, 1956);

On the Iliad by Rachel Bespaloff, translation by McCarthy (New York: Pantheon, 1948).

References:

John W. Aldridge, "Good Housekeeping with Mary McCarthy," in his *The Devil in the Fire* (New York: Harper's Magazine Press, 1972), pp. 217-223;

Aldridge, "Mary McCarthy: A Princess Among the Trolls," in his *A Time to Murder and Create* (New York: McKay, 1966), pp. 95-132;

Louis Auchincloss, "Mary McCarthy," in his *Pioneers and Caretakers* (Minneapolis: University of Minnesota Press, 1965), pp. 170-186;

Brock Brower, "Mary McCarthyism," *Esquire*, 58, 1 (July 1962): 62-67, 113;

John Chamberlain, "The Novels of Mary McCarthy," in *The Creative Present*, ed. Nona Balakian and Charles Simmons (Garden City: Doubleday, 1963), pp. 241-255;

Norman Fruchter, "An Act of Comic Revenge," in *The Young American Writers*, ed. Richard Kostelanetz (New York: Funk & Wagnalls, 1967), pp. 123-127;

Sherli Evens Goldman, *Mary McCarthy: A Bibliography* (New York: Harcourt, Brace & World, 1968);

Alex Gottfried and Sue Davidson, "Utopia's Children: An Interpretation of Three Political Novels," *The Western Political Quarterly*, 15 (March 1962): 17-32;

Doris Grumbach, *The Company She Kept* (New York: Coward-McCann, 1976);

Elizabeth Hardwick, "Mary McCarthy," in her *A View of My Own: Essays in Literature and Society* (New York: Noonday Press, 1962);

Alfred Kazin, *Starting Over in the Thirties* (Boston: Little, Brown, 1965), pp. 155 ff.;

Norman Mailer, "The Mary McCarthy Case," *New York Review of Books*, 17 October 1963, pp. 1-3;

Barbara McKenzie, *Mary McCarthy* (New York: Twayne, 1966);

Elizabeth Niebuhr, "The Art of Fiction XXVII: Mary McCarthy," *Paris Review*, 27 (winter-spring 1962): 58-94;

Jean-Francois Revel, "Miss McCarthy Explains," *New York Times Book Review*, 16 May 1971, pp. 2, 24-30;

Paul Schlueter, "The Dissections of Mary McCarthy," in *Contemporary American Novelists*, ed.

Harry T. Moore (Carbondale: Southern Illinois University Press, 1964), pp. 54-64;

Elaine Showalter, "Killing the Angel in the House: The Autonomy of Women Writers," *Antioch Review*, 32 (fall 1973): 339-353;

Irvin Stock, *Mary McCarthy* (Minneapolis: University of Minnesota Press, 1968);

Eleanor Widmer, "Finally a Lady: Mary McCarthy," in *The Fifties: Fiction, Poetry, Drama*, ed. Warren French (DeLand, Fla.: Everett/Edwards, 1970), pp. 93-102.

Manuscripts:

The University of Texas has a major collection of McCarthy's manuscripts.

Carson McCullers

Robert F. Kiernan
Manhattan College

BIRTH: Columbus, Georgia, 19 February 1917.

EDUCATION: Columbus Public Schools; courses in creative writing at Columbia University and New York University.

MARRIAGE: 1937 to Reeves McCullers, divorced. 1945 remarried McCullers.

AWARDS: Guggenheim Fellow, 1942, 1946; American Academy of Arts and Letters Grant, 1943; New York Drama Critics' Circle Award, 1950; Donaldson Award, 1950; Elected, National Institute of Arts and Letters, 1952.

DEATH: Nyack, New York, 29 September 1967.

MAJOR WORKS: *The Heart Is a Lonely Hunter* (Boston: Houghton Mifflin, 1940; London: Cresset, 1943); *Reflections in a Golden Eye* (Boston: Houghton Mifflin, 1941; London: Cresset, 1942); *The Member of the Wedding* (Boston: Houghton Mifflin, 1946; London: Cresset, 1947); *The Member of the Wedding: A Play* (New York: New Directions, 1951); *The Ballad of the Sad Cafe: The Novels and Stories of Carson McCullers* (Boston: Houghton Mifflin, 1951; London: Cresset, 1952); *The Square Root of Wonderful* (Boston: Houghton Mifflin, 1958; London: Cresset, 1958); *Clock Without Hands* (Boston: Houghton Mifflin, 1961; London: Cresset, 1961); *Sweet As a Pickle and Clean As a Pig* (Boston: Houghton Mifflin, 1964; London: Cape, 1965); *The Mortgaged Heart* (Boston: Houghton Mifflin, 1971; London: Barrie & Jenkins, 1972).

With Eudora Welty, Flannery O'Connor, and Katherine Anne Porter, Carson McCullers is an explorer of the Southern grotesque, for the ambiance of her fiction is always Southern, whatever its geographic locale, and her characters are the solitary, the freakish, and the lonely. Her work is distinguished from her fellow regionalists' work in the grotesque genre, however, by a compassion for the disaffiliate so deep that she is his foremost spokesman in modern American literature. Indeed, she has transcended not only regionalism but Americanism as well and has become a spokesman for all the lonely and alienated people of the world. Her best work is tenderly lyrical rather than philosophical, but it merits a distinguished place in that eccentric, bleakly poetic body of Southern fiction that takes as its subject the dark corners of the mind.

McCullers' mother, Marguerite Smith, was clearly the dominant influence in her life, for her consuming interest in persons who feel themselves vaguely freakish was prompted by Mrs. Smith's insistence that she was different from other children and destined to become famous. Certainly the thirteen-year-old McCullers' height of 5'8½'' seemed to her to be freakish (as it was later to seem freakish to Frankie Addams in *The Member of the Wedding*) and the considerable freedom and the constant approval that her mother gave her produced an effect of aloofness and eccentricity in her behavior that was greeted by Columbus adolescents with catcalls of "Freak!"

Both McCullers and her mother thought that she was to have a career in music, for she was proficient in the piano at an early age and showed no concomitant talent for storytelling. Indeed, Marguerite Smith was herself the raconteur of the family, with a gift for storytelling so renowned that residents of Columbus refused for many years to believe that it was McCullers and not Mrs. Smith who wrote the early novels. Moreover, Mrs. Smith was famous for her technique of rearranging ordinary events into eccentric configurations that were the delight of her audiences—a technique not unlike McCullers' own, and that was probably its foundation. McCullers never acknowledged such an influence from her mother, but she liked often to say that her sense of form in literature derived from her early study of musical structure, a claim borne out by her novels.

McCullers left Columbus for New York City in 1934 at the age of seventeen, intending to study music at Juilliard and writing at Columbia, but she lost her tuition money for Juilliard on the New York subway and supported herself at such odd jobs as typing, clerking, and waiting on tables while she studied writing with Whit Burnett at Columbia and with Sylvia Chatfield Bates at New York University. These teachers have always been credited with doing much to foster her talent: it was for Bates' class that she wrote the story "Wunderkind," in fact, and she owed its publication in *Story* to Burnett.

Lula Carson Smith married Reeves McCullers, a fellow Southerner, at the age of twenty. Her family encouraged the match, believing that they would mesh well, for Reeves seemed popular, personable, and steady, while Lula Carson was reclusive and mercurial. But Reeves had grown up in an unstable home, and he desperately needed to succeed in his own right. He unfortunately chose to be a writer and therefore to compete with his wife. The newlyweds thought they would take turns writing and working until they were both established, but Reeves was always to live in his wife's shadow and never to have his turn, and it is doubtful that he had much literary talent to begin with. He never ceased to love his wife, but their marriage was to destroy his sense of sexual identity and wreak havoc on his emotional life.

Marriage to Reeves afforded McCullers the leisure to complete her first novel, however, and less than two years after her wedding day, the manuscript of *The Heart Is a Lonely Hunter* was complete. It was published in 1940 to a small number of reviews, but the critical reception was enthusiastic, and Louis Untermeyer even referred to the novel as "one of the most compelling, one of the most uncanny stories ever written in America."

The Heart Is a Lonely Hunter is the story of a deaf-mute named John Singer to whom heartfelt secrets are confided by a series of "grotesques": by Jake Blount, an embittered radical; by Benedict Mady Copeland, a disillusioned Negro doctor; by Biff Brannon, a sexually ambivalent restaurant owner; and by Mick Kelly, a twelve-year-old tomboy. The ironically named Singer is merely bewildered by these attentions, but he in turn confides in a feebleminded mute named Antonapoulos, completing the circle of desperate communication that goes nowhere. When Antonapoulos dies, Singer commits suicide, and his devotees are left to make what they can of him and to resume lives that no longer have a pressure valve. The organization of the book, as McCullers wrote to her publishers, is contrapuntal: "Like a voice in a fugue, each one of the main characters is an entity in himself—but his personality takes on a new richness when contrasted and woven in with the other characters in the book." But the book is most impressive for the maturity of its psychological understanding. Erotic and epistemological needs blend inextricably in the characters, and each character is dominated by a fixed set of ideas that makes it impossible for him to reach communion with others. Indeed, the characters are convinced they are doomed to solitude, and, out of their frustration, they tend to make antisocial gestures that compound their isolation.

The novel is sometimes thought to center on Mick Kelly and her initiation into adulthood. Mick is certainly one of McCullers' most disarming characters, and certainly her story is the most representative of the five in the novel, but the plain, grave style, a pattern of ironic religious references, and the elaborate counterpoint of the novel suggest a broader range of implication than the initiation genre affords and render it more convincingly a fable about inescapable loneliness. In many ways, of course, Mick Kelly is the young Lula Carson Smith, for Mick, like McCullers, is preoccupied with music, and she learns the same truths about loneliness that McCullers abstracted from her experience at an early age and never substantially altered. Yet, in some ways, *The Heart Is a Lonely Hunter* is the least

Carson McCullers.

immediately autobiographical of any of McCullers' works, perhaps because her emotional life with Reeves was relatively stable and satisfying during the period of *Heart*'s writing.

Reeves McCullers was increasingly restive about his own lack of a career, however, and by 1939, both husband and wife found life in Fayetteville, where Reeves was then employed, constraining. Under the pressure, their marriage began to disintegrate, and *Reflections in a Golden Eye* was McCullers' imaginative response to that disintegration. Written in two brief months during 1939, the novel seemed to McCullers to write itself, so this tale of bisexuality and estrangement might have had an emotional source in the McCullers marriage, for both Carson and Reeves were developing bisexually and were shortly to take lovers of their own sex. Indeed,

although she had not met her at the time of the novel's writing, McCullers dedicated the novel to Annemarie Clarac-Schwarzenbach, the first woman for whom she developed an uncontrolled passion, as if acknowledging the resonance of the book with her personal life.

As *Reflections in a Golden Eye* bluntly proclaims, its cast of characters includes "two officers, a soldier, two women, a Filipino, and a horse." One officer is Captain Penderton, a bisexual, a sadomasochist, and a potential drug addict; the other is Major Langdon, a man who makes love to Penderton's wife, Leonora, in a blackberry patch two hours after meeting her. Leonora Penderton is a voluptuary who "could not have multiplied twelve by thirteen under threat of the rack," and Langdon's wife Alison is a recluse, so deranged by grief over the death of her deformed child that she has cut off her nipples with garden shears. Clearly, these characters are antithetically poised one against the other, with Leonora and Major Langdon on the side of animal lust and Penderton and Alison on the side of repressed sexuality. Yet, ironically, the reader cares more for Penderton and for Alison than for their more vital spouses, simply because there is more to them and to their experiences. In the central action of the story, for instance, Penderton makes two attempts to break out of his nature: first, he attempts to ride his wife's spirited horse, Firebird, an emblem of sexual vitality; and second, he tries to break down the barriers of rank and nature between himself and Private Elgee Williams, a man who can ride Firebird bareback and who represents essential masculinity to Penderton (yet he takes his sexual pleasure with animals and spends his nights in Leonora's bedroom, voyeuristically watching her sleep: there is no such thing, we understand, as "essential masculinity"). At the end, Penderton, in an atavistic fit of jealousy, shoots Williams at his wife's bedside, all of his actions having confirmed the "queer coarse wrapper" that is his nature.

Once again, then, McCullers' themes are the utter alienation of individual natures and the absence of reciprocity in human relationships, but these themes are more insistent and more hopeless in *Reflections* than in almost any other of her novels, for her characters are given little humanity apart from their desperation and there is minimal lyricism to soften the reader's understanding of them. The critics liked the book no more than the staff at Fort Bragg (close by Fayetteville) and Fort Benning (where Reeves had earlier been stationed) or Mrs. George Patton, who denounced it in high dudgeon. Indeed, the critics charged the book with substituting caricatures for characters and adjectives for analysis, and many thought it gratuitously sensational. But the root problem of the novel is probably that McCullers attempted something beyond her—to philosophize about persons in a military world. She was always attracted by the easy, portentous abstraction, even when she did not fully understand it and when her story did not fully warrant it, and the easy abstractions of this novel are the typical failing of her work. Indeed, McCullers cared little for the literal reality of what she wrote about: she refused, for instance, to attend a convention of deaf-mutes with Reeves while writing *The Heart Is a Lonely Hunter* because she did not want her imaginative concept of a mute destroyed, and she resisted the confrontation with facts throughout her life,

preferring her imaginative concept of what the facts should be.

In 1940 McCullers' editor at Houghton Mifflin secured her a fellowship to Bread Loaf Writers' Conference, an annual summer program of Middlebury College. She was gratified to receive the fellowship, not only for the honor, but because it meant leaving Reeves temporarily. Indeed, this was the first of many periods of living apart from Reeves: she was more and more to go her own way, almost unconscious of her rejection of Reeves and of the psychic and economic damage she did him. Reeves was a necessary presence in the background of her life, but his needs and wishes rarely shaped her life after the first years of marriage, and she maintained in general a love-hate relationship with him. Reeves himself was uncannily patient with her. He always understood her mercurial temperament and her single-minded passions.

In September of 1940, on her return from Bread Loaf, McCullers moved out of the Greenwich Village apartment she shared with Reeves and into an establishment in Brooklyn which was presided over by George Davis, the fiction editor at *Harper's Bazaar*, and which was shortly to include as residents W. H. Auden, Gypsy Rose Lee, Louis MacNeice, Benjamin Britten, Paul and Jane Bowles, and the Richard Wrights. The atmosphere of the house was almost surrealistic, and it crackled with the ideas of Marx, Freud, Kierkegaard, Jung, and Nietzsche. She could not have found a friendlier atmosphere for working on the manuscript of "The Ballad of the Sad Cafe," but in fact she was distracted by the menage and did little writing.

In February 1941 during a vacation in Columbus, McCullers suffered her first cerebral stroke although it was not properly diagnosed until years later. Reeves brought her back to the Greenwich Village apartment when she was ambulatory, and they resumed living together. Her closest friend during this period was the poet Muriel Rukeyser, and it was through Miss Rukeyser that she met and fell in love with David Diamond, the composer and musician. She also met Elizabeth Ames, the executive director of the Yaddo Artists' Colony in Saratoga Springs, New York, and Miss Ames invited her to be a guest of Yaddo during the summer of 1941. Over the years, McCullers was to return to Yaddo many times, for it proved to be the place where she worked best, and Elizabeth Ames was to become one of her most trusted friends and advisors.

On her first visit to Yaddo, McCullers continued to work on the manuscript which was to become *The*

Member of the Wedding but interrupted it in order to complete "The Ballad of the Sad Cafe," a work which is often regarded as her finest. "The Ballad of the Sad Cafe" is the story of a strange and tragic love triangle, the three members of which are Miss Amelia Evans, a brooding, hardfisted Amazon; Marvin Macy, her once-loving but unloved husband; and the hunchbacked Lymon, a sickly and self-indulgent confidence man. In the course of the story, Lymon transforms Amelia into a softer and more feminine person by insinuating himself into her affections under the pretense of being her cousin, and this change is externalized by the alteration of Amelia's feed store into a cafe—"the warm center point of the town." The cafe links the entire community to Amelia's fulfillment and gives them a share in it, but love is a perverse, fragile thing, and the cafe has only a brief existence. When Macy returns from prison to his estranged wife, Lymon falls passionately in love with him, and Macy, seizing his opportunity to avenge love's imbalance, defeats Amelia in a ceremonious wrestling match with Lymon's aid. Devastated, Amelia closes the cafe and withdraws behind closed blinds, and her eyes begin to cross "as though they sought each other out to exchange a little glance of grief and lonely recognition." In the most famous passage McCullers ever wrote (it brought tears to her eyes whenever she read it), the narrator insists that love is a private rather than a mutual experience, and that there is only an accidental relationship between the experience of love and the beloved person. In justification of its title, the story uses many traditional ballad motifs, such as natural and supernatural signs mirroring human events, characters who take their keynote from animals and birds, repeated stock phrases that approach incremental refrain, and, spectacularly, an envoi entitled "The Twelve Mortal Men" which recasts the events of the story in analogous terms.

"The Ballad of the Sad Cafe" is McCullers' most daring use of the grotesque: her characters are the most extreme she ever imagined, and their actions are so bizarre as seemingly to defy her control. Yet control them she does, and much of her success must be credited to her creation of a narrator, an anonymous but sensitive member of the community who bears the same weight of time and mutability as the characters, and who discovers the meaning of his own life as he talks. In a sense, the narrator is a recasting of the voyeur figure of *Reflections in a Golden Eye*, but he is more organically useful, for he mediates between the world of the grotesques and our familiar world. And, with his quaint, story-telling language, the narrator casts the aura of folklore over the tale: the characters become archetypes in his hands rather than grotesques, and their story becomes something elemental, mysterious, and suggestive. Indeed, the tension between the grotesquerie of the story and the narrator's placid rendering is one of the most vivid effects of the story, and one of its most haunting pleasures. The story was published first in *Harper's Bazaar* in 1943 and so it was not immediately reviewed, but in 1951 it was included in an omnibus volume entitled *The Ballad of the Sad Cafe: The Novels and Stories of Carson McCullers*. The omnibus volume received fine reviews and sold well, and "The Ballad of the Sad Cafe" was singled out for special praise by many of the reviewers.

The writing of "The Ballad of the Sad Cafe" came easily to McCullers, and the reason is probably that once again she was objectifying her immediate psychic experience. There are two possible sources of the story. Annemarie Clarac-Schwarzenbach had refused to vacation with McCullers a year earlier and had seemed to take Reeves' part against her; this vaguely triangular situation seemed to McCullers to prove once again that there is no reciprocity in love. More immediately, McCullers had recently discovered that her husband loved David Diamond as deeply as she did herself and that they were living together in Rochester while she was in Yaddo. She had no objection to Reeves taking a male lover, but she did fear exclusion from their relationship—the very exclusion that she fantasized Miss Amelia suffering from the union of Lymon and Macy.

When McCullers discovered in 1941 that Reeves had been forging her name to checks, she instituted divorce proceedings almost immediately. Always careless with money herself, she nevertheless demanded strict accounts from everyone else and tended increasingly to penuriousness. Reeves rejoined the army shortly after McCullers divorced him, yet their life apart was not markedly different from their married life, for they remained in close touch and seemed as emotionally dependent on each other as ever. Indeed, McCullers stayed with Reeves at Fort Dix before his embarkation for Europe, and she had evidently no compunction about signing herself "A War Wife" in an open letter published in *Mademoiselle* in 1943. They toyed with the idea of remarriage as early as 1943 and finally remarried on 19 March 1945, after Reeves' discharge, but their marriage continued the on-again, off-again quality of their relationship.

After a bout with pleurisy, strep throat, and double pneumonia at the end of 1941, McCullers resumed work on *The Member of the Wedding*, occasionally interrupting the novel's slow progress to work on a short story. With the aid of a Guggenheim Fellowship, a National Institute of Arts and Letters grant, and summers at Yaddo between 1942 and 1945, the novel was finally completed, and upon its publication the majority of critics (who had been offended by *Reflections in a Golden Eye*) took McCullers to their hearts a second time, quibbling somewhat that the novel was short of plot, but reveling in its characterizations, its honesty, and its seriousness.

The Member of the Wedding deals once again with the tortured world of adolescence. Frankie Addams is a gawky, motherless tomboy who feels herself "an unjoined person" and "a member of nothing in the world." Her only companions are the family cook, Berenice Sadie Brown, a stoical, God-respecting woman, and John Henry West, a six-year-old neighbor who dies of meningitis before the story is over and for whom the young Truman Capote is thought to have been the model. During this "green and crazy summer" Frankie decides to be a member of the wedding between her brother Jarvis and Janice Williams, and she rechristens herself F. Jasmine so that her name will alliterate properly with theirs. Berenice tries to tell her that "Me is me and you is you and he is he," but, in a famous phrase, Frankie declares that Jarvis and Janice are "the we of me" and maintains her illusion of accompanying the newlyweds until she is dragged from their honeymoon car. Then, as a more conventionally named "Frances," she begins the process of accommodation to the reality that Berenice has tried to teach her. But the more mature Frances is less attractive than young Frankie, and, as Lawrence Graver has observed, she is "just a bit too much like everybody else."

With the possible exception of "The Ballad of the Sad Cafe," *The Member of the Wedding* is McCullers' most perfect work and her most realistic. It has been criticized as a retreat from the broader social interests of *The Heart Is a Lonely Hunter* and "The Ballad of the Sad Cafe," but the psychology of the characters is wholly under control in this novel as it is not in the earlier works, and there are none of the incoherent abstractions that so often mar McCullers' prose. Frankie's need to make connections is steadily and intricately elaborated, and allusions to music are used adroitly to bespeak the heart when words fail. The long, disjointed conversations between Berenice, Frankie, and John Henry are reminiscent of the monologues which the grotesques pour into the ear of John Singer in *The*

Heart Is a Lonely Hunter, but whereas *The Heart Is a Lonely Hunter* is elaborately contrived to allow for those monologues, they emerge effortlessly in *The Member of the Wedding*. McCullers described herself as attempting in this novel to write "a lyric tragi-comedy in which the funniness and grief coexist in the same line," an effect she really strove for in all of her fiction and which was central to her artistic aspirations, but which was never more completely realized than in this bittersweet novel of adolescence.

When McCullers joined Tennessee Williams at Nantucket for the summer of 1946, Williams proposed to her that she adapt *The Member of the Wedding* to the stage. McCullers had been annoyed by Edmund Wilson's contention that her novel lacked a sense of drama, so she responded to the challenge and completed a first draft of the play by the end of the year, before sailing with Reeves for Europe on her second Guggenheim Fellowship. A series of strokes cut short her intended stay in Europe and aborted her work on *The Member of the Wedding*, however, making it necessary for her to dictate revisions from her sickbed and leading to an unhappy attempt at collaboration with Greer Johnson. After considerable rewriting and many difficulties with casting and production, the play finally opened in New York on 5 January 1959 to glowing reviews, and it began a run of 501 performances. Harold Clurman directed Julie Harris, Ethel Waters, and Brandon de Wilde in the cast, and together they succeeded brilliantly with McCullers' fragile story and undramatic script. For Edmund Wilson was right about McCullers being no dramatist: she had seen only two Broadway plays in her life before attempting to dramatize *The Member of the Wedding*, and she was ignorant of all stagecraft. Still, miraculously, the dramatic version of *The Member of the Wedding* is one of the outstanding adaptations of a novel in the history of the American theatre. It won the New York Drama Critics' Circle Award for the best play of its season, and it was sold to Hollywood for $75,000, making McCullers financially secure for the first time in her life.

With increased financial security, McCullers indulged her wanderlust freely. Never one to stay long in a place, she had all her adult life varied her residence between Columbus and Nyack with her mother, New York with Reeves, Key West with Tennessee Williams, Yaddo with Elizabeth Ames, Brooklyn with George Davis, and wherever friends were living. But she had been unable to cross the ocean as often as she would have liked. Thus, in 1950 she visited Elizabeth Bowen in Ireland (quite uninvited) and in 1951 she traveled to England to visit with David Gascoyne and Dame Edith Sitwell, who became a much-loved friend. In 1952 she traveled with Reeves through Italy and France and then bought a home in Bachvillers, a village outside Paris, and tried to work on the manuscript of *Clock Without Hands*. Neither McCullers nor her husband was well at this time: both had been drinking heavily for many years, and McCullers' health had progressively declined since the series of strokes in 1947. Walking was difficult for her, and a spastic arm made writing a laborious process. McCullers had in fact made a suicide attempt in 1948, but that attempt cured her forever of the impulse. Reeves, on the other hand, had become actively suicidal over his relationship with his wife and his lack of career since leaving the army, and he several times proposed a double suicide to Carson. Terrified for her life after one such proposal, McCullers fled to America, leaving Reeves to kill himself a few weeks later, alone in a Paris hotel. Apparently, McCullers became so desperately afraid of her husband during their last weeks together that the emotional bond that had always survived her love-hate relationship to him snapped completely. She refused to bring Reeves' body home for burial and refused even to pay the cost of having his ashes sent to her. Many friends were alienated by her complete refusal to mourn him.

While in residence at Yaddo during the summer of 1954, McCullers wrote the first draft of her play *The Square Root of Wonderful* while continuing to work on the manuscript of *Clock Without Hands*. Arnold Saint Subber became interested in producing the play a year later, and soon he was collaborating with McCullers almost daily on the manuscript. McCullers was ill for almost the entirety of 1956, however, and she found revisions difficult, so progress was agonizingly slow. The play finally opened on 30 October 1956, with Anne Baxter in the lead, but a weak script had by that time been devastated by several changes of director, and the reviews were deservedly harsh. It closed in December after forty-five performances, when the advance ticket sales were exhausted.

The central character in the play, Molly Lovejoy, is based on Marguerite Smith. McCullers' mother had died suddenly in 1955, and she saw Molly as a memorial to her mother's "tranquil beauty and sense of joy in life." But Philip Lovejoy, the male lead in the play, is a failed novelist who is unable to come to terms with his failure and commits suicide as a final creative act: he is transparently modeled on Reeves. The action is worked out in terms of a life-death dialectic which is uncomfortably close to an apologia for the inconsistency between McCullers'

callous treatment of her husband's remains and her ample grief over her mother's death. The play is a dramatic failure in almost every way, but it offers fascinating insight into McCullers' need during this period to defend herself against the charge of callousness and to rationalize the values by which she had refused to grieve for her husband.

During the writing of *The Square Root of Wonderful*, McCullers had apparently envisioned herself as surpassing the work of her friend Tennessee Williams, and she suffered so acutely from depression after the closing of the play that her friends arranged for an interview with Dr. Mary Mercer, a psychiatrist who practiced in Nyack. Dr. Mercer concluded that McCullers did not need her professional care, but she did offer McCullers informal friendship and guidance, and she became the primary influence in McCullers' life after the death of her mother. She saw McCullers almost daily and brought a semblance of order to her very disordered life, arranging for the physical and psychic well-being of her friend until McCullers' death nine years later. Almost certainly, McCullers would not have lived as long as she did without Dr. Mercer's ministrations, and she would certainly have been unable to complete her last novel, *Clock Without Hands*, without Dr. Mercer's encouragement.

Clock Without Hands seems to have occupied McCullers' mind as early as 1941, although she did not seriously begin work on it until ten years later, and it was not completed until the end of 1960. It is the story of four men caught in the changing South of the 1950s: J. T. Malone, a small-town druggist who is dying of an incurable disease and who is distressed by the knowledge that he has never really lived; Judge Fox Clane, a senile former congressman who is indignant about the civil rights movement; Sherman Pew, the judge's black servant, who buys a home in a white neighborhood; and Jester Clane, the judge's grandson, who harbors vaguely erotic feelings for Pew. Each of these characters finds his identity challenged by the passage of time, but no one more vividly so than Malone, the man who watches the clock that for him has no hands. Malone redeems his undistinguished life, however, by opposing Judge Clane's plan to bomb Pew's home. No such redemption is accorded the judge, who is a caricature of a Southern redneck at his most ridiculous, and who refuses to acknowledge the passage of time. Sherman Pew and Jester Clane are parallel characters, both of whom try to set the clock of Southern time ahead, Pew, too quickly, by buying the house in the white neighborhood and being lynched for his effrontery, and Clane, with presumable success, in resolving to be a civil rights lawyer.

Because the delicate state of McCullers' health and the physical difficulties she encountered in writing the novel were widely known, the critics were gentle in pointing out that *Clock Without Hands* fell far below the level of her earlier work. On a thematic basis it is her most ambitious novel, for all of her familiar concerns are there—the suffering of the freak, the horror of racial and social injustice, the traumas of adolescent loneliness and sexual confusion. But it is really her weakest novel, for it fails to relate its various concerns to one another. It needs a John Singer to pull the assorted grotesques together and to keep it from seeming a series of disjointed set pieces. It needs more sustained characterization, too, for Judge Clane, Sherman Pew, and Jester Clane become merely humorous for long stretches of the text, and the effect of such easy laughter is to undercut the basic seriousness of the novel. Only the portrait of J. T. Malone is really memorable, but even Malone is unfocused, and he tends to slip out of the novel's foreground.

The original inspiration for the character of J. T. Malone was apparently Annemarie Clarac-Schwarzenbach, for McCullers understood her to have faced the ruin of her tragic life and to have transcended despair in her Congo River poems, written shortly before her death in 1942. But as the prospect of death began to loom before McCullers herself, and as the completion of her last novel began to seem improbable, the story of the dying Malone became her own story as well, and it is fitting that Malone should transcend a novel otherwise forgettable.

The last years of McCullers' life were a physical agony. She was operated on twice in 1961 after the completion of her novel, and in 1962 she underwent surgery on her left hand and for the removal of her left breast. In 1963 her aching and crippled left leg was operated on, and in 1964 she was hospitalized still again for a broken hip and a shattered left elbow, sustained in a fall. In 1965 an exploratory operation discovered that a hip pin had worked itself loose, causing her discomfort that had been dismissed by her doctors as psychosomatic, and she was compelled to spend months on a flotation pad. She was almost never without pain, and there was increasingly little difference between her postoperative weakened condition and her normal condition. Nonetheless, she interested herself during these years in Edward Albee's dramatic adaptation of "The Ballad of the Sad Cafe," in John Huston's filming of *Reflections*

in a Golden Eye, and in Thomas Ryan's scripting of *The Heart Is a Lonely Hunter,* and she herself worked with Mary Rodgers on adapting *The Member of the Wedding* to a musical treatment that eventually came to nothing. Nor did she remain quietly at home in Nyack. During ambulatory periods she visited Edward Albee on Fire Island, she attended Dame Edith Sitwell's seventy-fifth birthday celebration in England, and she entertained Isak Dinesen, whom she had long admired, during the Danish writer's visit to America. Surrounded by elaborate medical precautions, she flew to Ireland to visit John Huston in April, 1967, although she was unable to leave her bed for the entire visit. Four months later, on 15 August, she suffered a massive brain hemorrhage and lay comatose for forty-seven days, dying on 20 September in the Nyack Hospital at the age of fifty.

Although it was accepted at the time of her death that she had largely exhausted her imaginative resources, the reputation that McCullers had earned with *The Heart Is a Lonely Hunter,* "The Ballad of the Sad Cafe," and *The Member of the Wedding* was solidly established and in no way declining. Her fans were legion, both at home and abroad, and her place in modern American literature was assured. As the *New York Times* proclaimed editorially upon her death, she was "the vibrant voice of love and loneliness in the Southern novel."

Periodical Publications:

"Wunderkind," *Story,* 9 (December 1936): 61-73;

"Madame Zilensky and the King of Finland," *New Yorker,* 17 (20 December 1941): 15-18;

"A Tree. A Rock. A Cloud.," *Harper's Bazaar,* 76 (November 1942): 50, 96-99;

"The Sojourner," *Mademoiselle,* 31 (May 1950): 90, 160-166;

"A Domestic Dilemma," *New York Post,* 16 September 1951 (magazine section), pp. 10 ff.;

"Sucker," *Saturday Evening Post,* 236 (28 September 1963): 69-71.

References:

Frank Baldanza, "Plato in Dixie," *Georgia Review,* 12 (1958): 151-167;

Virginia Spencer Carr, *The Lonely Hunter: A Biography of Carson McCullers* (New York: Doubleday, 1975);

Richard M. Cook, *Carson McCullers* (New York: Ungar, 1975);

Frank Durham, "God and No God in *The Heart Is a Lonely Hunter*," *South Atlantic Quarterly*, 56 (1957): 494-499;

Dale Edmonds, *Carson McCullers* (Austin: Steck-Vaughn, 1969);

Oliver Evans, *The Ballad of Carson McCullers* (New York: Coward-McCann, 1966);

Barbara Nauer Folk, "The Sad Sweet Music of Carson McCullers," *Georgia Review*, 16 (1962): 202-209;

Lawrence Graver, *Carson McCullers* (St. Paul: University of Minnesota Press, 1969);

Ihab Hassan, "Carson McCullers: The Alchemy of Love and Aesthetics of Pain," *Modern Fiction Studies*, 5 (1959): 311-326;

Robert F. Kiernan, *Katherine Anne Porter and Carson McCullers: A Reference Guide* (Boston: Hall, 1976);

Dayton Kohler, "Carson McCullers: Variations on a Theme," *College English*, 13 (1951): 1-8;

Klaus Lubbers, "The Necessary Order: A Study of Theme and Structure in Carson McCullers' Fiction," *Jahrbuch fur Amerikastudien*, 13 (1963): 187-204;

David Madden, "The Paradox of the Need for Privacy and the Need for Understanding in Carson McCullers' *The Heart Is a Lonely Hunter*," *Literature and Psychology*, 17 (1967): 128-140;

John McNally, "The Introspective Narrator in 'The Ballad of the Sad Cafe,' " *South Atlantic Bulletin*, 38 (1973): 40-44;

Joseph R. Millichap, "Carson McCullers' Literary Ballad," *Georgia Review*, 27 (1973): 329-339;

John B. Vickery, "Carson McCullers: A Map of Love," *Wisconsin Studies in Contemporary Literature*, 1 (1960): 13-24.

Manuscripts:

The University of Texas has a major collection of McCullers' manuscripts.

THOMAS FRANCIS McGUANE III was born in Wyandotte, Michigan, on 11 December 1939. He calls his family, with its own traditions of humor and storytelling, "heavy duty Irish." He grew up mostly in Michigan, where his father manufactured auto parts, but McGuane says of himself, "As sad as it may sound, I'm pretty rootless." His father's stratum of society is often satirized in McGuane's fiction. Part of the years 1955 to 1960 was spent in Florida, where McGuane became interested in sportfishing in the Keys, an interest reflected in articles he has written for *Sports Illustrated*. He first visited the northern Rockies in 1956 and kept returning. For some years (1968 to about 1974), he alternated between Key West and Livingston, Montana, where he now lives year-round on a 700-acre ranch. Both settings figure prominently in his fiction.

McGuane was educated at Cranbrook, Michigan State University (B.A., 1962), Yale Drama School (M.F.A., 1965), and Stanford University (1966-1967). While at Yale ("chiefly avoiding the draft") McGuane read heavily in English, American, and European literature, from Thomas Nash to Cervantes, from Gogol to Rabelais, from Celine to Landolfi, from Faulkner to Biely. He especially cites Knut Hamsun, awarding him the ultimate title, "a real fiend." Thus the irreverence and experiments in McGuane's fiction have a deep literary background. As a Wallace Stegner Fellow at Stanford, McGuane wrote part of *The Bushwhacked Piano*.

Although he has had offers to teach writing at universities, McGuane has preferred to stay away from the academy. He has praised the work of John Hawkes but generally is less interested in academic writers such as William H. Gass, John Barth, or Joyce Carol Oates. Instead he prefers to place himself with such mavericks as Richard Brautigan, Ken Kesey (whom he knew at Stanford), Larry McMurtry, Hunter S. Thompson, William Eastlake ("the great"), and Jim Harrison (who helped McGuane get *The Sporting Club* published). Since he left Stanford, he has been a full-time writer of fiction, journalism, and filmscripts. He has not held a regular job and describes his general condition as "loafing."

McGuane married Portia Rebecca Crockett in 1962 and fathered Thomas Francis IV in 1967. Divorced in 1974, McGuane married Margot Kidder, the leading actress in *Ninety-Two in the Shade*. A daughter, Margaret Kidder, came from that marriage; McGuane divorced again. In 1977 he married Loraine Buffett, sister of the popular singer Jimmy Buffett.

Thomas McGuane's first three novels, *The Sporting Club*, *The Bushwhacked Piano*, and *Ninety-Two in the Shade*, have received considerable praise. They are rowdy, often irreverent, energetic, and set in a rich and quite varied style. McGuane's artistic and thematic concerns include jokes, conflicts between forceful men, the nature of language, and satire of the barbarianism of America—in contrast to the depth and power of nature.

Jill Krementz

Thomas McGuane.

McGuane has referred to *The Sporting Club* (1969) as "an experiment in political anarchy." His aesthetic for it and *The Bushwhacked Piano* is largely one of energy, a quality he admires in Celine and Hunter S. Thompson. *The Sporting Club* is about a group of sportsmen in the Michigan north woods, whose wild games escalate from hilarity to chaos, until a classical nemesis rights the balance. The protagonist, a millionaire named Vernor Stanton, decides to destroy the aristocratic Centennial Club by bringing in a red-necked criminal as caretaker for the club. The criminal, Earl Olive, and

his gang begin the destruction of the club by blowing up the lake and decimating the lodge, while Stanton lurks behind as a Satanic force. Stanton is both aided and challenged throughout the novel by the rather conservative James Quinn, and it is their struggle that provides the conflict in *The Sporting Club*. Joyce Carol Oates wrote in the *New York Times Book Review* that McGuane had "a sprightly knowing ear for dialogue, and an eye for the 'absurd,' and a light fashionably cool touch that tires us only occasionally, and an obvious intelligence that has plotted all this out, crazy pranks and jokes and all, with vigor and enthusiasm." Larry McCaffery has written: "by the time of the book's wild, orgiastic conclusion—a bizarre, almost surrealistic scene, replete with sex, tar-and-feathers, and senseless murders—McGuane has fashioned a disturbing allegory about America's inner corruption."

The Bushwhacked Piano (1971) won the Rosenthal Award from the National Institute of Arts and Letters. The novel is a picaresque tale about Nicholas Payne's travels through Michigan, Montana, and Florida in the company of C. J. Clovis, who builds "bat towers" to repel mosquitos, and in pursuit of Ann Fitzgerald, who regards the photographs she compulsively takes as proof of her experience. Jonathan Yardley wrote in the *New York Times Book Review*, "Put simply, McGuane has talent of Faulknerian potential. His sheer writing skill is nothing short of amazing. . . . At 31, McGuane is a virtuoso." The novel is intensely, brutally funny, particularly in the use of ironic characters, Ann, Clovis, and Wayne Codd, the oafish ranch caretaker with whom Payne has a "classic" Western showdown. McGuane is merciless in his excoriations of them, and even of Payne himself. Payne, at the end of the novel, is purified and renewed as a person of potential.

Ninety-Two in the Shade (1973) received high praise from many reviewers and was nominated for the National Book Award. "Thomas McGuane is one of our best young novelists, and it's cheering to watch him approach his apogee," wrote L. E. Sissman in the *New Yorker*. The tightest of the three novels, *Ninety-Two in the Shade* portrays the rivalry of two fishing guides in the Florida Keys, the veteran Nichol Dance, and the young hero Tom Skelton. Skelton has blown up Dance's boat in retaliation for a practical joke, and Dance promises death if Skelton dares guide again. Skelton takes up the challenge and is murdered in a ritual of honor. The deadly struggle is set against the background of McGuane's satire of American wealth and stupidity; we are in "Hotcakesland," where "Nobody knows, from sea to shining sea, why we are having all this trouble with our republic."

Of the three novels taken together, Larry McCaffery has written: "Although individually very different in approach, McGuane's novels are all very tightly unified in terms of theme; each of them presents main characters . . . who have recognized a defiled state of affairs around them, and who are desperately seeking out a set of values which allows them, as Skelton put it, 'to find a way of going on.' . . . One of the most gifted stylists writing today,

McGuane creates out of this sense of nothingness a sort of fun which is the stuff of all good art."

Of the three novels, *The Sporting Club* and *Ninety-Two in the Shade* have the tightest structures and the most oppressive dramatic situations, while *The Bushwhacked Piano* is rhapsodic and, until the end, open. The novels move from psychodrama to hypothesis to existential being. McGuane seems to have brought so many techniques to full fruition that it is hard to imagine what he can do next.

Currently McGuane is finishing a fourth novel, *Panama* (forthcoming from Farrar, Straus & Giroux). He has also been working on five screenplays. His earlier screenplays were for *Rancho Deluxe*, *The Missouri Breaks*, and *Ninety-Two in the Shade*, which McGuane directed himself.

McGuane inherits and extends a number of traditions: the contemporary line of Kerouac, Kesey, and Brautigan, the Hemingwayesque, tragic world of nature, and the humor and dyspepsia of Mark Twain (whom McGuane read extensively). McGuane's style is eclectic, working on many levels: loving descriptions of nature, lists of things, superb dialogue, linguistic games, technical information, and allusions to philosophers, popular culture, and classical literature. Similarly his personal aesthetic is eclectic, from highly sophisticated literary concepts to demonic slapstick; he is suspicious of neat literary theories. —*Albert Howard Carter III*

Books:

The Sporting Club (New York: Simon & Schuster, 1969; London: Deutsch, 1969);

The Bushwhacked Piano (New York: Simon & Schuster, 1971);

Ninety-Two in the Shade (New York: Farrar, Straus & Giroux, 1973; London: Collins, 1974);

The Missouri Breaks (New York: Ballantine, 1976).

Screenplays:

Rancho Deluxe, United Artists, 1974;

Ninety-Two in the Shade, United Artists, 1975;

The Missouri Breaks, United Artists, 1976.

Periodical Publications:

"Highest Price of Fish," *Sports Illustrated*, 38 (4 June 1973): 82-85;

"Ninety-six in the Shade," *Fiction*, 1, 2 (1973): unpaged.

References:

Albert Howard Carter III, "An Interview with Thomas McGuane," *Fiction International*, 4-5 (fall-winter 1975): 50-62;

Carter, "Thomas McGuane's First Three Novels: Games, Fun, Nemesis," *Critique*, 17, 1 (August 1975): 91-104;

Larry McCaffery, "Turning Nothing into Something," *Fiction International*, 4-5 (fall-winter 1975): 123-129;

Michael Tolkin, "92 in the Shade, 86'd in the Smog," *Village Voice*, 15 September 1975, pp. 122-125.

LARRY McMURTRY is closely identified with Texas. All six of his novels and a collection of essays (*In a Narrow Grave*) reflect life in his native state. Born 3 June 1936 in Wichita Falls, he was educated in Texas, receiving a B.A. from North Texas State University in 1958 and an M.A. from Rice in 1960. A Stegner Fellowship enabled him to do further graduate work at Stanford, but he returned to Texas to teach creative writing at Rice from 1963 to 1969. Since then he has left the academic world and Texas to live in Washington, D.C., where he owns a rare book store called Booked-Up.

Houston and the fictional town of Thalia recur frequently as settings in the six novels, and some of the same characters, Emma Horton, Patsy Carpenter, and Danny Deck, reappear in several different books. He has developed his stories in a number of different modes, sometimes striving for a tightly controlled single action, at times aiming for a looser, open-ended flow; sometimes seeing the action through the eyes of a sober, serious youngster, at times withdrawing to a more elevated, omniscient, and ultimately comic perspective. His first novel, *Horseman, Pass By*, is carefully controlled and economical: the central event, the discovery of hoof-and-mouth disease among cattle on Homer Bannon's ranch, develops inexorably toward the eventual destruction of the cattle and with them Homer's will to live. The story is narrated by Homer's grandson, Lonnie, who is clearly in the tradition of Huck Finn, discerning much of the falseness around him, unwilling to corrupt himself. Lonnie's voice as a narrator can be heard in his comments on Homer Bannon's funeral: "They had put paint on him, like a woman wears, red paint. I could see it on his cheeks, and caked around his mouth. I could see slick oil on his hair, and some sticky stuff like honey around his eyes. I wished I could have buried him like he died; he was better that way."

In the course of living through his grandfather's ordeal, Lonnie rejects his earlier desire to leave the ranch, rejects Hud, a cynical, brutal son of Homer's second wife, and rejects Jesse, a floating forty-year-old cowboy who has seen everything and missed everything. Ultimately he elects to stay on the land, "looking at the green grass on the ground and watching the white clouds ease into the sky from the South," in acceptance of his responsibilities to the land and his friends. Beneath these affirmations there is his unsettling attraction to Halmea, the black helper on the Bannon ranch. He desires her partly as lover, partly as mother. The tenderness, lack of fulfillment, and separation due here to differences in age and race trace out the beginning of what becomes an essential theme in later works—people's needs do not match their circumstances.

Leaving Cheyenne also explores this theme of mismatching and the isolation it ultimately brings. Two friends, Gideon and Johnny, are attracted to Molly, but Molly eventually marries a third fellow, Eddie. Instead of having children by Eddie, she has one son by Gideon and one by Johnny, and both the sons of her two lovers die in World War II. The story is told by three narrators—first by Gideon, who tells of the group as young adults, then by Molly, who narrates the middle period during which she raises the children and attends to all three of the men, and finally by Johnny, who as an old man, tells of Gideon's death. The expanded time scheme and number of narrators enrich the themes of the novel.

Both *Leaving Cheyenne* and *Horseman, Pass By* were set near the mythical town of Thalia; *The Last Picture Show* deals with Thalia itself. The effect of several levels of experience is retained, but this time transformed by the use of an omniscient narrator. The central focus is on three teenagers: Sonny, his friend Duane, and a girl they both desire, Jacy Farrow. As in *Leaving Cheyenne*, neither boy can keep the girl for himself, and the girl seems always about to slip into the hands of a third rival. The pursuits of a similar group of characters in the previous novel, *Leaving Cheyenne*, gave them a certain nobility, fully developed over time, but the characters in *The Last Picture Show* are amusingly diminished by their comic sexual-initiation rituals, Jacy by her activities at a swimming party and later in a motel with Duane, and Duane and Sonny by their frustrating visit to a whorehouse in Mexico. Their stumbling ascent to maturity runs parallel to the revelation of the past relationship between Jacy's mother and Sam the Lion, who is a father figure for

Jill Krementz

Larry McMurtry at Booked-Up.

Sonny and Duane. Her affair with Sam is now only a memory. After Sam dies, Thalia seems to rush to extinction: the movie house closes, Duane goes off to Korea, and Billy, a retard, in despair at the closing of the movie house, puts on two eye patches and is run over by a truck. The relation of Lonnie to the older black woman, Halmea, in *Horseman, Pass By* resembles Sonny's affair with Ruth Popper, the wife of the high school coach. Temporarily leaving her for Jacy, Sonny returns after a brief experience with Jacy's mother. In Mrs. Farrow's words, "Your mother and I sat next to one another in the first grade. . . . We graduated together. I sure didn't expect to sleep with her son. That's small town life for you." As Sonny is reconciled to Ruth, who is also old enough to be his mother, it is clear that love is sad, impossible, and sweet in its contrasts and absurdities.

In *Moving On* McMurtry expanded his material much further. The marriage of Jim and Patsy Carpenter is about to end, but not before it is tested by and compared to the relationship of Pete and Boots, a January-May couple; the relationship of rich Eleanor Guthrie and world champion cowboy Sonny Shanks, who has his girls in the converted hearse he lives in; the relationship of Bill Duffin, the cynical professor of modern literature who has published eight books, and his wife Lee, the campus Cassandra; and the relationship of Clara Clark, the California Girl playing at being a graduate student, and her graduate student boyfriend, Hank Malory. The setting moves through the same kind of random sequence; after several hundreds of pages of rodeo locations, the setting shifts to graduate school at Rice. McMurtry further risks losing the reader's attention by presenting very ordinary people: Patsy speaks at times with a sharp tongue, as does her friend Emma Horton, but then none of them consistently speaks with distinction over 794 pages. The character of Jim, Patsy's husband, is portrayed through his hobbies—photography, linguistics, and then graduate school. There are countless sexual arousals, a somewhat smaller number of consummations, fragments of popular songs, dozens of book titles and authors (Lumiansky, Fiedler, Tolstoy, and Ian Watt), and meals with comments on the freshness of the salad or the gristle in the steak. In his review in the *New York Times*, titled *"Moving On, and On . . . and On,"* John Leonard commented, "it's a little like turning on the radio and leaving it on for years."

And yet, by the final quarter of the book, "Summer's Lease," the very size of the book and accumulation of material do begin to work. Jim finds out about Patsy's affair with Hank; she wishes to break it off but does so in a most jagged, continuously backsliding way. In time, she breaks from Jim as well, with an equally prolonged assortment of vague reconciliations and indirections. Flap, Emma's husband, tries to commit suicide and fails. Emma's comment, "I knew the minute I started going with him years ago that I'd never get rid of him and I just couldn't believe he would die," gives some indication of McMurtry's purpose. This is a world of unshakeable banality, one that could not be represented with the normal economies of fiction. The publication of this book would seem to be coordinated with McMurtry's own break with the academic world, which *Moving On* describes in particularly dreary terms.

All My Friends Are Going to Be Strangers returns to more normal fictional dimensions, and to a wandering feast of humor wilder than that of *The Last Picture Show*. Danny Deck, who has published one novel, is working on a second book and a hopeless marriage. During pregnancy his wife turns from him to a blind man downstairs. Danny moves from one adventure to another, trying to live with a kindly and talented cartoonist named Jill, who is not interested in sex. He visits his Uncle L, who sleeps in a bedroll behind his luxurious ranch house, digs postholes indiscriminately, keeps a menagerie, including a camel, instead of cattle, and has three Mexican helpers each named Pierre. Danny drowns the manuscript of his second novel in the Rio Grande. Early in the book there is a curious image of a janitor in the Rice University Library: "Petey was not important enough to merit a giant waxer, but he didn't care. He had a middle-sized waxer and spent his evenings smoking marijuana while he followed his waxer in and out of the fifth floor stacks. He loved to get high and follow his waxer around." If the reader wishes to enjoy himself, he must assume Petey's role and follow this middle-sized plot without concern for its direction.

In *Terms of Endearment* McMurtry returns to a tighter structure by concentrating primarily on a single character, Aurora Greenwood, a widow. Originally from Boston, she has settled in Houston. Aurora, who is Emma Horton's mother, ought to be intolerable: she corrects the grammar of her friends, exploits her suitors, and calls her daughter to say "I was thinking you might want to wish me good night." But Aurora is loveable because she loves life and because she can turn a phrase. As she says of two of her suitors, "The brutal fact is that they're both old, short, and afraid of me. If I stacked them one on top of the other they might be tall enough, but they'd still be afraid of me." Her story has endless permutations but no motion; she is timeless. The last quarter of the book deals with Emma, dying of cancer, and peacefully terminates that long-suffering victim of this and two previous novels.

To date, McMurtry remains a Texas novelist. Some critics, such as Alan Crooks, have argued that he needed the sense of place to do his best work, and Charles Peavy has argued that McMurtry wrote better of the country than of the city. There have been three films made from his works, and all have been made from the novels set almost exclusively in the Texas countryside. *Hud*, starring Paul Newman, was made from *Horseman, Pass By*, and McMurtry himself collaborated with Peter Bogdanovich on the script for *The Last Picture Show*. There is some evidence in the Crooks article (based in part on interviews) that McMurtry has wished to move away from writing about Texas, and his move to Washington suggests that he may do so. The critical response to his career at this point can be summed up in Martha Duffy's review in *Time* of *All My Friends*: she claims that the book is "without discernible direction," "constructed like tumbleweed," but with "indelible people and brilliant set piece scenes." Again and again reviewers lament a general laxness, a tendency to nudge the reader, but in the same breath praise McMurtry for his memorable scenes and characters. —*John Gerlach*

Books:

Horseman, Pass By (New York: Harper, 1961; republished as *Hud*, London: Sphere, 1971);

Leaving Cheyenne (New York: Harper & Row, 1963; London: Sphere, 1972);

The Last Picture Show (New York: Dial, 1966; London: Sphere, 1972);

In a Narrow Grave (Austin: Encino Press, 1968);

Moving On (New York: Simon & Schuster, 1970; London: Weidenfeld & Nicolson, 1971);

All My Friends Are Going to Be Strangers (New York: Simon & Schuster, 1972; London: Secker & Warburg, 1972);

Terms of Endearment (New York: Simon & Schuster, 1975).

References:

Alan F. Crooks, "Larry McMurtry—A Writer in Transition: An Essay-Review," *Western American Literature*, 7 (1972): 151-155;

Kenneth W. Davis, "The Themes of Initiation in the Works of Larry McMurtry and Tom Mayer," *Arlington Quarterly*, 2, 3 (winter 1969-1970): 29-43;

James K. Folsom, "*Shane* and *Hud*: Two Stories in Search of a Medium," *Western Humanities Review*, 24 (1970): 359-372;

John Gerlach, "*The Last Picture Show* and One More Adaptation," *Literature/Film Quarterly*, 1 (April 1973): 161-166;

John Hollwedel, "*All My Friends Are Going to Be Strangers*," *MacGill's Literary Annual* (Englewood Cliffs: Salem Press, 1973): 12-16;

Thomas Landess, *Larry McMurtry* (Austin, Texas: Steck-Vaughn, 1969);

Charles D. Peavy, "A Larry McMurtry Bibliography," *Western American Literature*, 3 (fall 1968): 235-248;

Peavy, "Coming of Age in Texas: The Novels of Larry McMurtry," *Western American Literature*, 4 (fall 1969): 171-188;

Peavy, "Larry McMurtry and Black Humor: A Note on *The Last Picture Show*," *Western American Literature*, 2 (fall 1967): 223-227;

Raymond C. Phillips, Jr., "The Ranch as Place and Symbol in the Novels of Larry McMurtry," *South Dakota Review*, 13, 2 (1975): 27-47.

Manuscripts:

The University of Houston has the typescripts of *The Last Picture Show, Leaving Cheyenne,* and shorter published works; the manuscripts of two unpublished novels and an unpublished screenplay; and other miscellaneous manuscript materials.

KENNETH MILLAR, who has written under the pseudonyms John Macdonald, John Ross Macdonald, and Ross Macdonald, was born in Los Gatos, California, on 13 December 1915, but was raised in Ontario, Canada. When Millar was three years old, his father abandoned his mother and him, which has had profound thematic significance in his novels. The boy was shifted from home to home and relative to relative in what Millar in 1971 termed an "episodic and unpredictable" childhood. He calculates that by the time he graduated from an Ontario high school in 1932, he had lived in fifty rooms, and he regarded his nomadic existence and family poverty with shame and embarrassment.

Millar enrolled at the University of Western Ontario in 1932. In the winter of 1936-1937, he dropped out of college and went to Europe, where he spent two months in Nazi Germany. His impressions of the evils of the Hitlerian philosophy are passionately described in his first novel. Upon graduation from college in June, 1938, he married Margaret Sturm, who became the successful mystery novelist Margaret Millar. In 1938, Millar entered the University of Toronto, where he studied to become a high school teacher. Both husband and wife determined at that time to become writers. In the spring of 1939, Millar fathered a daughter (who died at the age of 31) and began his professional writing career by contributing verses, humorous sketches, and his first few realistic stories to *Saturday Night*, a Toronto political and literary weekly.

Largely due to his wife's professional success, Millar left high school teaching after two years to accept a full-time fellowship at the University of Michigan. The decision to return to the United

Jill Krementz

Kenneth Millar.

States in 1941 to begin work on a doctorate in English was an important one. His mother had taught him from early childhood that California was his natural home and birthplace. He was a citizen of the United States, but also of Canada, and dual citizenship had produced a psychological sense of illegitimacy which the return to Ann Arbor did not wholly alleviate, though his feeling was relieved partially by his service as a communications officer

in the United States Naval Reserve during World War II. After the war, Millar returned to the state of his birth, closing, as the author himself has said, "a physical circle, if not an emotional one, by settling in California, in Santa Barbara," where he still resides. In 1951, he was awarded a Ph.D. from the University of Michigan.

Millar's first novel, *The Dark Tunnel*, was written in Ann Arbor during the fall of 1943. It is a spy novel about a thirty-year-old college English teacher who is wrongly accused of murder, involved in an espionage plot, and obsessed with a personal manhunt to locate the real killer. It is tainted by a great deal of symbolism which frequently appears contrived and pretentious, by a dialogue that is sometimes self-consciously erudite (even in the mouth of its hero, a young Ph.D.), and by a strained use of literary quotations. In this book, Millar was already experimenting with the hardboiled genre, but he clearly had not come to terms with it. Although *The Dark Tunnel* is solidly structured and densely plotted—altogether a very good first novel—its primary importance today is as an index to Millar's development, which reached maturity in *The Galton Case.*

The Dark Tunnel was followed in rapid succession by *Trouble Follows Me* (1946), *Blue City* (1947), and *The Three Roads* (1948). The latter was the first novel to reflect the author's interest in California. *The Moving Target* (1949), the first of Millar's novels published under the pseudonym Macdonald, introduced Lew Archer as its central figure. A serious student of and a leading commentator on the detective fiction genre, Millar named his character Archer after Sam Spade's murdered partner in tribute to Dashiell Hammett.

The author's captivation with southern California has continued to be registered in his books through the present time. Millar sees southern California as an instant megalopolis in which the present crouches against the past and leans heavily upon the future. Indeed, from Millar's own home in Santa Barbara one can drive ten miles inland into a genuinely unspoiled territory where even the endangered condor can fly peacefully. He repeatedly and passionately expresses a view of California as a microcosm of America, as a land of extraordinary natural beauty sullied by the acts of hedonistic society. In a recent interview with Sam L. Grogg, Jr., Millar stated that "the destruction of Nature is a serious moral crime because it destroys man and his ability to live in the world. It's been the most important external event in my life during the last five years." He has written two books, *Sleeping Beauty* and *The Underground Man,* which directly address the problem of man's corruption of nature. An avid environmentalist and bird-watcher, he has acted vigorously on behalf of the Sierra Club and National Audubon Society.

For Millar, southern California is a pole apart from an established, traditional society. Lew Archer tries to figure out how he will preserve his personal values, and manifest them in his actions, when the society around him is largely devoid of spiritual values. Southern California in general, and Hollywood in particular, is a dreamland where vast amounts of money are in the hands of large numbers of people. Most of the characters in the Archer novels are unprepared to resist the temptations presented by the false glitter of Hollywood and twentieth-century technology; they confuse love and sex. The people who employ Lew Archer and those he meets in the cases he investigates form a cross section of this society. It is a society which equates money with happiness. Its members often are mistaken in supposing that what they are ambitious to get will be worth the cost. They believe that they live only for the present, that they are in control of their lives, and above all, that they can determine what will happen to them. They come to realize that they cannot live only for the present; they are not in control of their lives; and they cannot forecast future events. The present is closely tied to the past. Invariably, they are haunted by the phantoms of the past. The chain of cause and effect links events that occurred before the actions of the novels. It generally develops that events of the past, such as a murder which has taken place decades removed from the present action, dictate that the sins of the father be visited upon the children, even unto the second and third generation.

The narrative point of view in the Archer novels is provided by Lew Archer. Although Millar claims that "Archer is not the main object of my interest, nor the character with whose fate I am most concerned," he has made Archer the moral and psychological center of his books. The hero's clear vision into the real motives of those with whom he deals and his uncompromising honesty in expressing what he knows make him an unpopular man. Like Hammett's Sam Spade and Raymond Chandler's Philip Marlowe, Lew Archer is committed to disclosing the truth for its own sake, at whatever personal risk, and looks upon the people around him with a skeptical eye; like them also, he narrates his own experience in a highly figured, brittle, hard-boiled prose. But, like Marlowe and Spade, Archer's cynicism veils a deep idealism. In an exceedingly intricate urban environment (which Millar has called the "urban inferno"), Archer as the loner hero continues the masculine and egalitarian frontier traditions of Natty Bumpo and his nineteenth-century descendants. His personal code is highly ethical, but not squeamish; he regularly turns down bribes (including one for a million dollars). He works without a secretary out of a sparsely-furnished two-room office, drives an old Ford, owns only two suits, and is divorced. Archer possesses few material things, but he is very much his own man, a man who has come to grips with his own deficiencies, a man for whom life is lonely and frequently painful, but nonetheless strangely satisfying. The things that seem to bother his clients—envy and malice and lust and pride—do not appear to trouble Lew Archer.

Archer's divorce (on grounds of mental cruelty), his few personal attachments, his lack of friends, his modest, erratic income, and his absorption with his work have caused him to be a man without a private life. It is slightly ironic that this man who has almost no intimate connections with persons or things serves as a reminder and revealer of the past. His investigations force people to examine themselves and their links to the past, and to recognize that they are bound by past events which have fashioned their lives and will fashion their futures.

One of the distinguishing aspects of a Lew Archer novel is the complexity of its plot. Eudora Welty, in a review of *The Underground Man* (1971), wrote: "The plot is intricate, involuted, and complicated to the hilt; and this, as I see it, is the novel's point." George Grella agreed in *New Republic:* "Among their many excellences, the plots of the Lew Archer novels distinguish them from all other detective fiction." In a careful, brief study of the Archer novels, Grella observed that the plots habitually are organized as four versions of one complex sequence of events. The primary plot is concerned with the mechanical aspects of Archer's duties—that is, making telephone calls, talking to suspects and witnesses, running background checks, and examining motives. Archer usually proceeds straightforwardly toward the resolution of the case. In most cases, he fixes the object or person of his quest quickly, although he may be unable to recover the thing or person. It is at this point that the unexpected begins to occur; a crime takes place, and Archer senses that things are not as simple as he had imagined.

The simple art of detection then crosses paths with another plot development as Archer is compelled to learn about the case. His detective duties become plaited with the search for the past. Old skeletons are unearthed, people are thrown off balance, and characters begin to tell protective lies. As Archer discovers in *The Wycherly Woman*, "A repeated lie can do strange things to the mind. What you say often enough becomes a provisional truth." Guilty characters attempt to hide in the present, but the probing Archer will not let them. This search for the secrets of the past is the richest part of the plot, and the part with the greatest possibilities. The

pattern created by the synchronization of the two plots is the one most easily recognized by readers, and it is the one which has received the greatest attention from reviewers and critics. The search for the past, translated into the present, is the quest for identity. At the center of the quest is the Oedipal refrain: a boy or girl searching for his or her true parents, true self, or true name. Another habitual and vital part of this plot is the suffering child. Millar nearly always treats these young people with sympathy; however erratically or irresponsibly they behave, his young people are seldom guilty of a serious crime.

The third development of the plot deals with the process of increasing perception that Archer experiences as he moves backward in time. Things and individuals keep turning into something or someone else. For instance, Francis Martel in *Black Money* (1966) turns into Feliz Cervantes and then into Pedro Domingo, who is not a French aristocrat, it is learned, but a Panamanian peasant. Another example is found in *The Goodbye Look* (1969), in which Larry Chalmers, who is known as an ex-war hero, is finally revealed as a psychotic weakling.

The final plot development comes into play when, at the end of the case, Archer reconstructs in his memory the nightmarish, complex interactions which have brought pain and sorrow to everyone. What Archer has produced in the recounting is the myth of the Original Sin, which states that all men are guilty because of some awful past sin—everyone, not just the characters in the book.

Kenneth Millar has written at least four books which rank among the finest the detective genre has produced—*The Galton Case* (1959), *The Chill* (1964), *The Underground Man* (1971), and *Sleeping Beauty* (1973)—and many would argue that *The Goodbye Look* (1969) also belongs in this category. *The Galton Case* is the pivotal novel in the Millar canon. It was in this novel that he finally worked out the concerns which troubled him most. It is a book the author has termed his "breakthrough novel." He seemed to find out what it was about the past which so intrigued him, he began to shape carefully his mythic plot, and he fully developed his Oedipal theme, which is a variation on the traditional Oedipus story and interpretation by Sophocles and Freud.

Archer is hired to locate missing heir Tony Galton. Archer feels a great kinship with young John Galton/Theo Fredericks—his dual identity lies at the heart of the plot—who has been separated from both his money and social status since childhood. When Archer enters the well-appointed offices of a law firm in chapter one, he notes that they

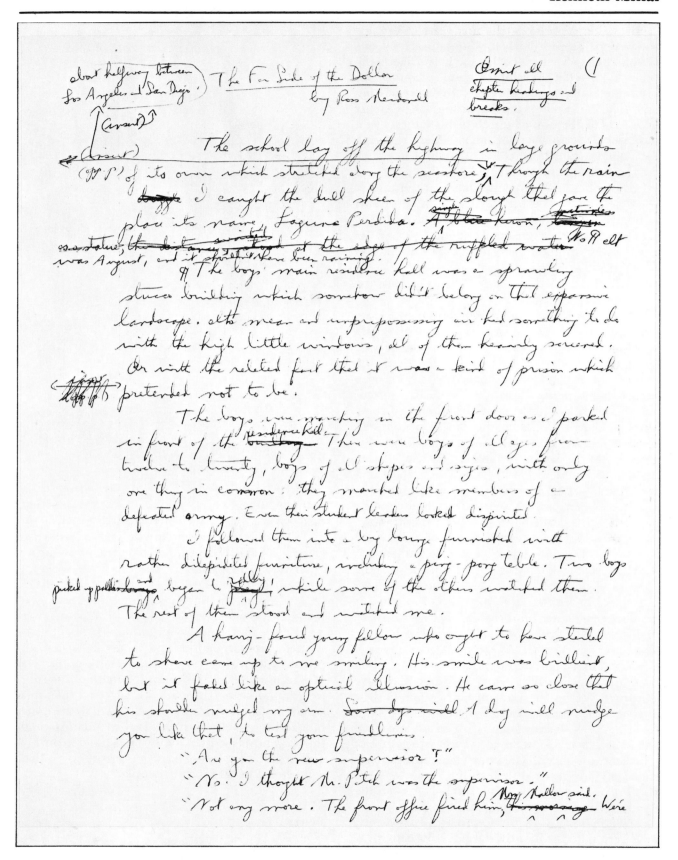

From manuscript of The Far Side of the Dollar.

"convey the impression that after years of struggle you were rising effortlessly to your natural level, one of the chosen"; when he leaves, it is "like being expelled." Archer, like John Galton, is courageous and honest but poor. In his essay, *On Crime Writing* (1973), Millar explains the shared anguish of Archer in search of the boy in search of his father: "In a puritanical society the poor and fatherless, suffering the quiet punishments of despair, may see themselves as permanently and justifiably damned for crimes they can't remember having committed."

The Galton Case was the first of Millar's books to receive respectful critical attention. In 1964, *The Chill* received even greater acclaim. Many critics again gave him high marks for his 1969 novel, *The Goodbye Look*, but it was with *The Underground Man* in 1971 that Millar finally took his place as one of our finest novelists.

With *The Underground Man*, Millar once more returned to the Oedipal theme of certain of his earlier novels, but now he was able to treat that theme with less reserve, upon a larger canvas, and with the assured power of practiced maturity. It begins with Archer encountering a small boy in the backyard of his apartment building. Together they feed some blue jays. A little later the boy's inexplicably aggressive father takes him away, ostensibly to his grandmother's home in Santa Teresa (Santa Barbara). Soon thereafter the father is murdered, and the little boy is kidnapped by a group of unfeeling adolescents. A cigarillo the victim was holding at the moment of his death ignites a raging forest fire.

It turns out that the murdered man had devoted much of his life, fifteen of his twenty-seven years, to searching for his missing father, and it was the anguish of that exhaustive quest which had made him so edgy with Archer in their earlier meeting. It develops that he was murdered because he was about to discover who had killed his father, who had not simply run off, after all. As Archer unravels the case, it is found that a host of people have been implicated in the fifteen-year-old crime, and that they have constructed elaborate mechanisms of deceit in their attempts to remain concealed. They have been teetering on the brink of madness all these years, and when Archer cracks their icy veneers, they cannot withstand the shock. The book's sad characters are shown to have reached their pitiful conditions as a result of devoting too much of their lives to guarding the unhealthy secrets of the past.

In the end, all of the recurrent Millar themes have been stated brilliantly; the past is never past; the child is father to the man; true reality resides in dreams; all men are guilty, and human actions are

Kenneth Millar.

connected; for every evil action there is a corresponding evil reaction; and everyone gets what he deserves, but no one deserves what he gets.

Over a span of more than thirty years, Millar has created a large body of fiction informed by acute observation, significant ideas, integrity, wisdom, and craftsmanship. Within and above these qualities he has found the elusive tension, emotional and imaginative, which molds the novel into an active experience. But equally important is that he has written popular fiction which may be read with profit by a cross section of the reading public. As Millar himself has said, "Ideally, a community tends to communicate through its fiction, and this communication tends to break down if there are Mandarin novels written for Mandarins and lowbrow novels written for lowbrows, and so on. My aim from the beginning has been to write novels that can be read by all kinds of people."

—*John Vermillion*

Books:

The Dark Tunnel, as Kenneth Millar (New York: Dodd, Mead, 1944; republished as *I Die Slowly*,

New York: Lion, 1955);

Trouble Follows Me, as Kenneth Millar (New York: Dodd, Mead, 1946; republished as *Night Train*, New York: Lion, 1955);

Blue City, as Kenneth Millar (New York: Knopf, 1947; London: Cassell, 1949);

The Three Roads, as Kenneth Millar (New York: Knopf, 1948; London: Cassell, 1950);

The Moving Target, as John Macdonald (New York: Knopf, 1949; London: Cassell, 1951);

The Drowning Pool, as John Ross Macdonald (New York: Knopf, 1950; London: Cassell, 1952);

The Way Some People Die, as John Ross Macdonald (New York: Knopf, 1951; London: Cassell, 1953);

The Ivory Grin, as John Ross Macdonald (New York: Knopf, 1952; London: Cassell, 1953);

Meet Me at the Morgue, as John Ross Macdonald (New York: Knopf, 1953; republished as *Experience with Evil*, London: Cassell, 1954);

Find a Victim, as John Ross Macdonald (New York: Knopf, 1954; London: Cassell, 1955);

The Name is Archer, as John Ross Macdonald (New York: Bantam, 1955);

The Barbarous Coast, as Ross Macdonald* (New York: Knopf, 1956; London: Cassell, 1957);

The Doomsters (New York: Knopf, 1958; London: Cassell, 1958);

The Galton Case (New York: Knopf, 1959; London: Cassell, 1960);

The Ferguson Affair (New York: Knopf, 1960; London: Crime Club by Collins, 1961);

The Wycherly Woman (New York: Knopf, 1961; London: Crime Club by Collins, 1962);

The Zebra-Striped Hearse (New York: Knopf, 1962; London: Crime Club by Collins, 1963);

The Chill (New York: Knopf, 1964; London: Crime Club by Collins, 1964);

The Far Side of the Dollar (New York: Knopf, 1965; London: Crime Club by Collins, 1965);

Black Money (New York: Knopf, 1966; London: Crime Club by Collins, 1966);

The Instant Enemy (New York: Knopf, 1968; London: Crime Club by Collins, 1968);

The Goodbye Look (New York: Knopf, 1969; London: Crime Club by Collins, 1969);

The Underground Man (New York: Knopf, 1971; London: Crime Club by Collins, 1971);

Sleeping Beauty (New York: Knopf, 1973; London: Crime Club by Collins, 1973);

On Crime Writing (Santa Barbara: Capra, 1973);

The Blue Hammer (New York: Knopf, 1976);

Lew Archer, Private Investigator (New York: The Mysterious Press, 1977).

References:

Matthew J. Bruccoli, *Kenneth Millar/Ross Macdonald: A Checklist* (Detroit: Bruccoli Clark/Gale, 1971);

John Carroll, "Ross Macdonald in Raw California," *Esquire*, 77 (June 1972): 148-149, 188;

William Goldman, "The Finest Detective Novels Ever Written by an American," *New York Times Book Review*, 1 June 1969, p. 1;

George Grella, "Evil Plots," *New Republic*, 173 (26 July 1975): 24-26;

John Leonard, "Ross Macdonald, his Lew Archer, and other secret selves," *New York Times Book Review*, 1 June 1969, pp. 2, 19;

Leonard, "I Care Who Killed Richard Ackroyd," *Esquire*, 84 (August 1975): 60-61, 120;

Raymond A. Sokolov, "The Art of Murder," *Newsweek*, 22 March 1971, pp. 101-104, 106, 108;

Eudora Welty, "The Stuff that Nightmares are Made Of," *New York Times Book Review*, 14 February 1971, p. 1;

Peter Wolfe, *Dreamers Who Live Their Dreams: The World of Ross Macdonald's Novels* (Bowling Green, Ohio: Bowling Green University Popular Press, 1977).

---

*All the books that follow were published under the pseudonym Ross Macdonald.

STEVEN MILLHAUSER, one of the most original novelists to emerge in the 1970s, was born on 3 August 1943 in New York and grew up in Connecticut where his father, Milton Millhauser, was an English professor at the University of Bridgeport. Millhauser received a B.A. from Columbia University in 1965 and later did graduate work at Brown University for three years. The first of his two novels, *Edwin Mullhouse: The Life and Death of an American Writer, 1943-1954, by Jeffrey Cartwright* (1972), was cited as one of the year's most notable books by *Newsweek* and *Time* and won France's *Prix Medicis Etranger*. The two main concerns of Millhauser's fiction are literature and childhood. His novels contain parodies of specific writers and genres and are heavily allusive. But more important is Millhauser's unsentimental presentation of the pains and pleasures of childhood, a period he rescues from the cliches of popular culture and the stereotypes of the sociologists and psychologists.

Edwin Mullhouse is a twelve-year-old's account of the life of his best friend who has died shortly after completing his one masterpiece, *Cartoons,* an autobiographical novel which imitates the style of animated films. *Edwin Mullhouse* is itself three novels in one: a satire of literary biographies, a detective story—since we only learn the shocking cause of Edwin's death in the final pages—and a portrait of a middle-class American childhood in mid-twentieth century. These first two qualities clearly indicate that the novel was inspired by Vladimir Nabokov's *Pale Fire,* and one reviewer has called *Edwin Mullhouse* "probably the best Nabokovian novel not written by the master himself."

Biographies from Boswell's *Life of Johnson* to Leon Edel's five-volume study of Henry James are satirized in *Edwin Mullhouse.* Jeffrey Cartwright divides the life of his friend into the Early, Middle, and Late Years and is deadly serious about his task: "it is the purpose of this history to trace not the mere outlines of a life but the inner plan, not the external markings but the secret soul." Much of the novel's humor comes from the pomposity of its precocious narrator. Inevitably, Jeffrey confesses the superiority of the watcher to the watched: "I take this opportunity to ask Edwin, wherever he is: isn't it true that the biographer performs a function nearly as great as, or precisely as great as, or actually greater by far than the function performed by the artist himself? For the artist creates the work of art, but the biographer, so to speak, creates the artist. Which is to say: without me, would you exist at all, Edwin?"

One of the pleasures of the novel is the way in which Jeffrey reveals his jealous resentment of his subject, as when he tells us that Edwin is "the brightest boy in the class (reputedly)." Similar clues are dropped about the cause of Edwin's death; in Jeffrey's "Preface to the First Edition," he thanks himself "for doing all the dirty work," and he later remarks that "a modest biographer may be driven to strange devices for the sake of his throbbing book." The most cunning clue of all is provided by Edwin himself when he has his hero, at the end of *Cartoons,* murdered by a mysterious figure in black about whose identity he teases Jeffrey.

But *Edwin Mullhouse* is more than satire and games-playing. Its primary subject is childhood, which it depicts with no condescension and a minimum of nostalgia. Millhauser's vision of childhood is hardly an idealized one, filled as it is with frustration, disease, and death; its inhabitants are not underdeveloped adults but real people confronting real problems. Yet a freshness, a playfulness, accompanies this seriousness. Boy-artist Edwin is not an aberration; as Jeffrey tells us, "The important thing to remember is that everyone resembles Edwin; his gift was simply the stubbornness of his fancy, his unwillingness to give anything up." Edwin and Jeffrey's world emphasizes the unspoiled pleasures of the everyday and the intense pain unique to this time of life. Millhauser shows how childhood—in fact, all life—cannot be reduced to stereotypes.

Portrait of a Romantic (1977) carries Millhauser's concern with childhood into adolescence as twenty-nine-year-old narrator Arthur Grumm describes his agonies from ages twelve to fifteen. The novel has similarities to *Edwin Mullhouse* but has a completely different style, tone, and comic design. If Jeffrey Cartwright is a coolly detached observer, for the most part, Arthur Grumm is the impassioned opposite, berating the "smug," "stupid" reader, babbling almost incoherently, whimpering all the way to the novel's end. Arthur says that his problem is his increasing restlessness with the boredom of growing up: "I would be assailed by illicit longings . . . oh, not those longings, but illicit longings, longings for dangerous and unknown realms of freedom at the opposite end of so-called life." Hiding from the demons of ennui, Arthur drapes the cloak of romanticism over his anguish: "I felt myself becoming a connoisseur of decay, and I dreamed of starting an autumn garden, composed of rows of ruined summer flowers."

The novel concentrates on Arthur's relationships with three fellow sufferers. William Mainwaring, "my double," is another version of Jeffrey Cartwright: a realist who collects stamps and rocks. Philip Schoolcraft, "my triple," represents the other extreme; a worshiper of Poe, more than half in love with easeful death, he leads Arthur into daily games of Russian roulette. Eleanor Schumann, "The Phantom Eleanor," is a pale beauty wilting in her dark, dusty bedroom while constructing elaborate fantasies. Arthur retreats from the latter two disastrous friendships to dependable William, once called "William Wilson" by Philip. (Poe is the restless spirit who haunts *Portrait of a Romantic;* it is full of "Poetic" allusions, parodies, and puns.) William finally jolts Arthur from his malaise by joining him in a suicide pact, just as Philip and Eleanor have done, though this one is more "successful" than the others.

Portrait of a Romantic is almost as impressive as *Edwin Mullhouse,* though it occasionally suffers from overwriting. The intense attention to detail of the first novel seems mere verbosity here. The somber comedy is often too dark, obscuring the ironies. Millhauser's triumph in these novels lies in his handling of the disparate sensibilities of his narrators and his uncovering of the violence lurking below the peaceful surface of childhood.

—*Michael Adams*

Books:

Edwin Mullhouse: The Life and Death of an American Writer, 1943-1954, by Jeffrey Cartwright (New York: Knopf, 1972);

Portrait of a Romantic (New York: Knopf, 1977).

References:

Pearl K. Bell, "It's a Wise Child," *New Leader*, 16 October 1972, pp. 15-16;

J. D. O'Hara, "Novels: Nabokovian, Plangent," *Book World*, 24 September 1972, p. 8;

O'Hara, "Two Mandarin Stylists," *Nation*, 17 September 1977, pp. 250-252;

George Stade, "Reality Gripped by Fictions," *New York Times Book Review*, 2 October 1977, p. 131.

Wright Morris

Michael Adams
University of South Carolina

BIRTH: Central City, Nebraska, 6 January 1910.

EDUCATION: Crane College, Chicago; Pomona College, Claremont, California, 1930-1933.

MARRIAGE: 1934 to Mary Ellen Finfrock, divorced 1961; 1961 to Josephine Kantor.

AWARDS AND HONORS: Guggenheim Fellowship, 1942, 1946, 1954; National Book Award, 1957; National Institute of Arts and Letters grant, 1960; Rockefeller Foundation grant, 1967; Elected, National Institute of Arts and Letters, 1970; honorary fellow, Modern Language Association, 1975; senior fellow, National Endowment for the Humanities, 1976.

MAJOR WORKS: *My Uncle Dudley* (New York: Harcourt, Brace, 1942); *The Man Who Was There* (New York: Scribners, 1945); *The Inhabitants* (New York: Scribners, 1946); *The Home Place* (New York: Scribners, 1948); *The World in the Attic* (New York: Scribners, 1949); *Man and Boy* (New York: Knopf, 1951; London: Gollancz, 1952); *The Works of Love* (New York: Knopf, 1952); *The Deep Sleep* (New York: Scribners, 1953; London: Eyre & Spottiswoode, 1954); *The Huge Season* (New York: Viking, 1954; London: Secker & Warburg, 1955); *The Field of Vision* (New York: Harcourt, Brace, 1956; London: Weidenfeld & Nicolson, 1957); *Love Among the Cannibals* (New York: Harcourt, Brace, 1957; London: Weidenfeld & Nicolson, 1958); *The Territory Ahead* (New York: Harcourt, Brace, 1958; London: Peter Smith, 1964); *Ceremony in Lone Tree* (New York: Atheneum, 1960; London: Weidenfeld & Nicolson, 1961); *What a Way to Go* (New York: Atheneum, 1962); *Cause for Wonder* (New York:

Jill Krementz

Atheneum, 1963); *One Day* (New York: Atheneum, 1965); *In Orbit* (New York: New American Library, 1967); *Fire Sermon* (New York: Harper & Row, 1971); *A Life* (New York: Harper & Row, 1973); *The Fork River Space Project* (New York: Harper & Row, 1977).

Wright Morris has had one of the most productive and enduring careers of any American novelist, winning wide praise for his nineteen novels over the past thirty-five years. His work became progressively better for almost twenty years, reaching its high point with *Ceremony in Lone Tree* in 1960. Few American novelists have written so well in the late stages of their careers, and few have been so American in their work. Morris has concentrated on Nebraska and California but has written about all parts of the nation, examining the manners and mores of his countrymen in all periods from the 1920s to the Vietnam era. He has been concerned from the beginning with defining the American character, with the hold of America's past on its citizens, and with the promise offered by the American dream. He depicts the inability of many Americans to feel, to deal honestly with emotions. His characters are in search of a connection, something which will bring about some self-knowledge. This connection can be made by acts of audacity—Morris's favorite American trait—heroism, imagination, or love. The characters may also attempt to transform some cliche, one of those life-defying aspects of American existence. Sometimes they perform these acts of symbolic exorcism while participating in some ritual such as a journey, reunion, or funeral. The success of the connection or transformation is never definite; some irony or ambiguity is usually involved. Morris's style, characters, and themes may sometimes recall those of the writers he most admires—Whitman, Twain, James, Sherwood Anderson, T. S. Eliot, Lawrence, Joyce, Mann—but he is always uniquely Wright Morris.

Morris was born 6 January 1910 in Central City, Nebraska, not far from the center of the continental land mass, prompting him to remark later, "I was born near the navel of the world." At the time of its founding, Central City had been called Lone Tree after a pony-express stop on the Platte River, but this name was felt to be forbidding to early settlers who were accustomed to more than one tree per town. Morris uses the earlier name when his home town appears in his fiction. His mother died a few days after his birth. His father, a station agent for the Union Pacific, left his position with the railroad in

order to supply the dining-car system with "day-old eggs" from his chicken farm, an ill-starred enterprise described in *The Works of Love* (1952). The writer has spoken of his father as a "Sherwood Anderson tragic figure—full of the froth of American life but few of the facts."

Morris moved with his father to Omaha in 1919 and five years later to the near-north side of Chicago at the height of the Capone era. In 1926 he and his father made the first of several car trips to and from California. These experiences formed the basis of *My Uncle Dudley* (1942), his first novel. In 1930 Morris entered Pomona College in Claremont, California, later to be the setting of *The Huge Season* (1954).

In 1933, having read a few novels and having met young men who had lived in Paris, Morris left Pomona for a year of travel in Europe. Such novels as *The Huge Season, Cause for Wonder* (1963), and *The Fork River Space Project* (1977) draw upon his experiences. Paris, as it did for so many, crystallized his intentions to become a writer. Returning to California he married Mary Ellen Finfrock, a native of Cleveland attending Scripps College. She became a teacher, and Morris began his apprenticeship as a writer.

Stimulated by what he found himself writing and remembering, Morris, in 1936, took the first of his *Inhabitants* photographs. Four years later he conceived of the word-picture relationship found in the photo-text volumes, *The Inhabitants* (1946), *The Home Place* (1948), and *God's Country and My People* (1968). During the winter of 1941, in Los Angeles, he wrote the first draft of *My Uncle Dudley*, incorporating both early and recent travels in America.

His first Guggenheim Fellowship, in 1942, enabled him to complete *The Inhabitants*. A second fellowship resulted in *The Home Place*, and a third, in 1954, allowed Morris to spend the year in Mexico, completing *The Huge Season* and beginning *The Field of Vision* (1956). His residence in suburban Philadelphia from 1944 to 1958 can be seen in *Man and Boy* (1951) and *The Deep Sleep* (1953). In 1961 he divorced his first wife and married Josephine Kantor, of Los Angeles, an art collector and dealer. The following year he began teaching in the Creative Writing Department of San Francisco State University, where he remained until his retirement from teaching in 1975. He has also taught at Princeton, the University of Nebraska, Amherst, and lectured widely on the novel.

My Uncle Dudley (1942) introduces many of the elements expanded upon in Morris's later fiction: the audacity and journey motifs, the pursuit of the

American dream, and the hero whose exploits influence the life of the witness to his deeds. Its protagonists are T. Dudley Osborn and his teenage nephew, called "the Kid," who is the first-person narrator. They have driven to Los Angeles from Chicago and are now ready to return. With seven other passengers aboard their broken-down Marmon touring car, they travel across the West, encountering adventures and speculating on the philosophical meaning of the land and the journey. For Dudley the trip is an expression of what freedom is all about. What the Mississippi is for Twain, the nation's highways are for Morris. If a man is to discover America, he must go on the road.

Dudley's adventures culminate in his most audacious act as he spits in the eye of a red-neck cop just after he has been released from jail, resulting in his return to confinement. Dudley willfully gives up his most precious possession, his freedom, in an act of protest and at the same time sets the Kid free to live his own adventures. Morris revels in renegades like Dudley, playing on the affection many Americans feel for these never-grown-up black sheep. Dudley is meant to be seen as the essence of the American character: Abe Lincoln, Will Rogers, and W. C. Fields all rolled into one.

Morris's next three novels, *The Man Who Was There* (1945), *The Home Place* (1948), and *The World in the Attic* (1949), deal with the nostalgic return of two native sons to their childhood homes and their discovery that the past cannot be recaptured, that they no longer have much in common with the land and its people. *The Man Who Was There* centers on the effect that Agee Ward, who is missing in action during World War II, has on those who know him. Morris employs his transformation theme here as Ward is somehow resurrected in his friends; he instills some emotion into their empty lives. Ward himself is incomplete because of his inability to reconcile what he was, what he is, and what he might become—a frequent dilemma for the Morris hero. Ward travels all over the world looking for himself and finally decides to return home to Lone Tree, but he does not like what he sees there. Nothing is as he remembers it. *The Man Who Was There* is apprentice fiction; Morris is still searching for a way to transform the cliches of his theme. The novel is important in his development because of his first use of the multiple point of view he is to employ more effectively in later works.

The Home Place is Morris's first and last attempt to combine photographs with fiction. The pictures are scenes of Central City and of the Norfolk, Nebraska, farm of Morris's Uncle Harry. The direct correspondence between the photographs and text is only occasional and incidental, and Morris admits that the one distracts from the other. The novel centers on the return of Clyde Muncy, with his wife and children, to his uncle's farm near Lone Tree, where he grew up. Muncy is tired of life in New York and is looking for a new home, perhaps his old one. He has either lost his sense of himself or fears doing so, and he feels a need to reestablish his roots. Quickly learning that he cannot communicate with the home folks, Muncy begins to see himself as an outsider. At the end of *The Home Place*, Muncy knows that although what he is was formed in the past, it is what he will be in the future which is important now.

In *The World in the Attic*, the most fully-developed of Morris's early novels, Muncy makes the final break with his past as he and his family stop in nearby Junction on their way back east. A major difficulty in evaluating Morris is in deciding whether he feels nostalgia or nausea or both for his Nebraska home place. *The World in the Attic* makes clear that nostalgia consists of idealized, romanticized memories of good things which seem characteristic of a better time when recollected in tranquility; but our memories and prejudices play tricks on us. The glory of the past is only an illusion, a tranquil recollection. Muncy also senses that the frontier spirit has virtually vanished. The dream of the frontier has collided with the brave new world of Sears, Roebuck. The positive, life-giving aspects of the past have not been retained. All that remains is nausea.

The one-time promise of the West, of the American dream, is symbolized in Junction by Miss Caddy Hibbard. She was brought to the frontier in 1909, and her husband built a house for her, expecting a town to spring up around it. Miss Caddy makes her home the center of a world of activity. She represents what the town wants to be and can become, and she flourishes in this role for twenty years. Then her husband dies, and she becomes a recluse. With her seclusion the town's growth stops. Miss Caddy declines from symbolizing the vibrant present and the promise of the future to being a dusty reminder of the glory of the past and a wasted future.

Yet when she dies, the rituals surrounding her death have a resurrecting effect similar to that of Agee Ward. Muncy senses a rebirth of his own. He has rediscovered his roots through Miss Caddy, whose dream he cannot reject completely, as his refusal to look at her corpse indicates. There was something good in the past and there can be something good in the present, but we must leave the former where it belongs and refrain from corrupting the latter, or we will be left with nothing from either. This is a situation facing many of the characters in Morris's subsequent novels.

In *Man and Boy* (1951), Morris uses an alternating point of view for the first time to contrast the two main characters' attitudes toward each other. The central character of the novel, set in suburban Philadelphia, is Mrs. Violet Ames Ormsby, called "Mother," a champion of all victims of injustice, who is always speaking before some organization or trying to push a bill through Congress. She treats her husband like a spineless servant and ignores their only child from his birth. The boy has been killed at Guadalcanal, dying a hero, and the Navy has decided to name a new destroyer after him. The novel consists of preparations for the christening at the Brooklyn Navy Yard and the ceremony itself intermingled with flashbacks.

Man and Boy was expanded from Morris's first published short story, "The Ram in the Thicket," and during the expansion Mother's character was softened. Morris intended to write an attack on Mother and her kind but came to realize that she is as much victim as villain. Mother defines her American dream when she says that "success is getting what you want. Happiness is wanting what you get." Morris asks whether this kind of success and happiness is worth it if the human element must be omitted. Something is missing from American life; something has been, in the terms of the novel's dominant cliche, nipped in the bud. Mother has tamed the new frontier, but has she left it too tame?

Morris spent six years on *The Works of Love* (1952), his most personal novel. Its hero is based on Morris's father, and the author is perhaps not as detached an observer as he usually is. The book is his least humorous one, and it is at times quite painful. *The Works of Love* is Morris's most detailed account of what pursuing the American dream on the plains can produce.

Will Brady, the protagonist, grows up in small Nebraska towns along the railroads which symbolize a means of escape from the desolate loneliness which kills his parents. As he gradually progresses from assistant stationmaster to hotel clerk to proprietor of Brady's Egg Empire, Brady is constantly aware that something is missing from his life. He eventually acquires two wives, both of whom leave him, and a "son," the gift of a prostitute who feels sorry for him; but he cannot communicate with any of them. Falling for the empty cliches of a wheeler-dealer, Brady tries to become a successful businessman, but nothing turns out right. He finally forsakes his dreams and leaves the plains and his past behind him, recalling Sherwood Anderson, to whose memory the novel is dedicated. In Chicago he becomes a department-store Santa Claus, trying to live up to another stereotype, a quest which leads to a bizarre death.

Will Brady is not a sentimentalized victim of the American dream but a victim of his own idealization of the dream, just as his death is brought on by his romanticized, slightly saintly conception of love. He is always too much out of the world to make the connection which can save him. Like so many Morris characters, he has no clear view of himself. He tries to become what he thinks he sees around him, and this self-blindness destroys him. *The Works of Love* is Morris's most moving novel because of the vivid portrait of Will Brady and the beautifully pathetic evocation of his world.

Like *Man and Boy*, *The Deep Sleep* (1953), which was nominated for a National Book Award, is set in Philadelphia's Main Line and centers on the rituals of death. Judge Howard Porter has died after a lengthy illness, and in the course of the novel, we view him through the consciousnesses of his wife, mother, daughter, son-in-law, and handyman, learning about his relationship with each. He emerges as a misunderstood and unfulfilled person. The primary witness to the Judge's passive heroics is Paul Webb, his son-in-law, a semi-Bohemian painter and cynical weakling. The villain is Porter's seemingly unfeeling widow.

Here in "the untamed station wagon country," the material aspects of the American dream have been attained, but the inhabitants do not know what to do next. The focal point of this deterioration of values is Mrs. Porter, who drives the Judge to bird-watching and other tame pursuits away from home. Uncovering the deep sleep into which the Judge was unwillingly returned, Webb, whose marriage has been disappointing and whose aspirations have been unfulfilled, sees the signs of his own waking, walking slumber. He gradually realizes that Mrs. Porter does care for the Judge but has been unable to find a means of communication.

The denouement of *The Deep Sleep* seems the least convincing of any in Morris's fiction. The painstakingly sculptured image of Mother-as-monster is too formidable to be crushed so easily. Morris is once again saying that all of us are victims of our conceptions of the American dream. His failure is in making Mrs. Porter a more persuasive villain than victim. His success is in showing how, as he writes elsewhere, the "American home has

From Wright Morris: Structures and Artifacts, Photographs 1933-1954.

become the deep freeze of American life, where experience is stored until the new tenants, or the undertaker, hauls it away."

In *The Huge Season* (1954) Morris combines the obsession with the past and American dream themes with his hero-witness motif. The hero, Charles Lawrence, is nearly perfect, but this "nearly" proves disastrous for both him and his witnesses. The novel consists of two interwoven stories: "The Captivity," a naive, Fitzgeraldian, first-person report of the events at Colton College in California during 1927-1929 and in Paris during 3-5 May 1929, as seen through the Lawrence-worshiping eyes of Peter Foley; and "Peter Foley," a third-person account of Foley's journey from Philadelphia to Brooklyn on 5 May 1952 for a ceremonial recognition of the anniversary of Lawrence's death. Morris's ability to manipulate the two contrasting tones, one subjec-

tive, the other objective and analytical, is one of his highest achievements. *The Huge Season* is also his first "literary" novel, filled with allusions to Fitzgerald, Hemingway, Eliot, and Joyce.

Charles Lawrence is a college student, a nationally-famous tennis player, and heir to the fortune of his grandfather, who invented barbed wire. Barbed wire led to the taming of the West, apparently in fulfillment of the American dream, but it actually destroyed the West's myth of individual freedom. This paradox is alive in Lawrence, the child of free enterprise, who yearns for perfection and yet is self-destructive. As Foley says, he is like "a firecracker that had been lit but not gone off."

The prisoners of Lawrence's aura are two of his college roommates and two other students he meets in Paris. One of the roommates, Jesse Proctor, whose head is filled with literary notions of heroism, sees Lawrence as the ideal, and his enthusiasm, because of its naive sincerity, carries over to others. No one truly knows Lawrence since he is cold and aloof, but he is a vibrant force and draws people to him. Like the American dream, he is more attractive for what he promises than for what he delivers. He is burdened by the facade of perfectibility he tries to maintain for his witnesses, and this tension leads to his suicide.

At the reunion Proctor is freed from the captivity when he fires the gun which killed Lawrence. Whether Proctor meant to shoot himself or not is left ambiguous. Either in deciding not to commit suicide or in failing to do so, Proctor knows that he can act independently of Lawrence. Peter Foley, after Proctor's escape, realizes that he is also unfulfilled, that he has been strangled by the past, that he—and his country—has been without "intention." He—and America—cannot keep feeding off the glories of the past.

The Field of Vision (1956) and *Ceremony in Lone Tree* (1960), both dealing with the same characters, are Morris's most successful novels. In them he has refined his method of employing several narrating consciousnesses viewing the same events, and he also makes use of all his major thematic concerns: the hero-witness relationship; the male-female relationship; rituals; the conflict between past, present, and future; and the American dream, scene, and character. Morris presents Americans trapped in the past, retarded by their conceptions of what life offered them and how they turned it down. The main character, Gordon Boyd, once held the promise of achieving almost anything he wanted, but unable to cope with his initial failure, he sinks into self-pity and then tries to succeed at failure and fails. Boyd's witness, Walter McKee, has attained material success but has denied his own identity for so long that he almost does not exist. McKee's wife, Lois, has suppressed her emotions until she has turned into a human ice cube. Her father, Tom Scanlon, the lone resident of a Lone Tree more desolate than Morris's earlier versions of it, has so rejected the present that he has become, in his mind, his own father.

The center of *The Field of Vision*, set at a Mexican bullfight where the characters recall the past events which made them the way they are, is Boyd, Morris's most complex character. A failure as writer and derelict, he is a prisoner of his past caught in a success-failure web of his own spinning. Eventually the lines between success and failure are engulfed by a psychic fog, and Boyd is neither in nor

out of the world. His character has been formed by three events in his youth. The first occurs when McKee introduces his best friend to his fiancee. Boyd kisses Lois, and they fall in love. She has since attempted to cover up the guilt she feels for her subconscious desires, becoming a victim of her suppressed emotions. McKee, symbol of passive, ineffectual America, realizes how she feels but is unable to help her. The second is Boyd's attempt to walk on water at a sandpit. He tries to turn failure into success by dragging himself out of the water to try to convince McKee that he can at least swim. The third is his ripping the back pocket off Ty Cobb's pants during an exhibition game in Omaha. This incident is also witnessed by McKee.

These events are repeated from several angles until they take on almost mythic proportions, forming a kind of American trinity: the kiss—belief in the Puritan ideals of love; the walk—belief in the faith which can work miracles; the pocket—belief in the heroic greatness which anyone can achieve. In reality, the kiss permanently freezes Lois; the walk proves to be prophetic of Boyd's life of audacious failure; and the pocket, which he always carries with him, comes to be a grimy, tattered symbol of the falseness of dreams. The participants are so deeply submerged in this trinity that they can never hope to escape completely. Boyd attempts to perform an exorcism of sorts by tossing the imitation coonskin cap of McKee's young grandson, Gordon McKee, Jr., into the bullring and then lowering his namesake down to retrieve it, trying to pass on his "heroism" to another generation.

Morris's purpose in *Ceremony in Lone Tree* is to try to reconcile the past, present, and future by gathering four generations in Scanlon's Lone Tree Hotel to celebrate the old man's birthday and by placing in the background a cloud of contemporary violence. Present in spirit at the ceremony are a bomb which fails to go off at a Nevada testing site the day before and two bombs which have exploded: a nephew of one of the participants who runs down three bullies with his hot rod, killing two of them; and Charlie Munger, who murders ten people during a shooting spree in Lincoln because he wants to be somebody. The implication is that the present is either seeping with the nausea of nostalgia or erupting into violence. These emotions and others are brought together in a setting where time is virtually suspended, where Boyd finds in the hotel lobby a newspaper announcing, "LINDBERGH OVER ATLANTIC." Boyd has come to Lone Tree to die a symbolic death, to seek the final break in direct confrontation with the past.

Morris depicts a society whose inhabitants have sunk into a somnambulistic state of mediocrity which even irrational violence and the threat of the Bomb cannot stir. But the deep sleep of those gathered at Lone Tree is disturbed by several acts of audacity, including McKee's finally speaking up to Boyd. The last act occurs when Lois shoots her father's ancient six-shooter. Representative of the type of people who have created Charlie Munger, she has now imitated him. The shot, which recalls Proctor's, awakens Scanlon, who has slept most of the day. He stands up only to drop dead on the morning of his ninetieth birthday.

At the end of the novel, Boyd is the one asleep. Time has finally passed by men like him and Scanlon; the McKees, for all their limitations, will determine the quality of the present and perhaps of the future. The ending is ambiguous since even Boyd and Scanlon are more alive than McKee. He may have at last awakened from his deep sleep now that he is free of his vision of Boyd as hero. Morris is not optimistic, but he does believe that the future deserves a chance, the less encumbered by the dreams of the past, the better. Between *The Field of Vision* and *Ceremony in Lone Tree*, Morris published two books which indicated that he was going to be more concerned with the present.

Love Among the Cannibals (1957) is Morris's first complete confrontation with the present, as two songwriters working on a Latin American musical in Hollywood take off for Mexico with two female acquaintances to soak up some atmosphere. Because of the use of a cynical first-person narrator, the vivid—for Morris—sexual references, and the concern with popular culture, the loyal Morris reader is bewildered at first by what is going on. The narrator, Earl Horter, loves a woman he calls "the Greek" because she represents "Life without its cliches." She "died" during a Caesarean operation at fifteen and came back to life free of the past. In taking her from the phony present of Hollywood to the then relatively unspoiled paradise of Acapulco, Horter attempts to "cannibalize" her the way all selfish lovers do. When the Greek runs away, he realizes that he must strip away the inessentials of his life in order to make the necessary connection. Thematically, the novel works, but overall it remains an interesting failure because the characters and situations lack the usual depth and credibility they have in Morris novels.

The Territory Ahead (1958) is a collection of essays on the major figures in American literature modeled upon the critical writings of Henry James and D. H. Lawrence. Morris's thesis is that American writers have made too much use of the raw material of the past and not enough use of the immediate present. *Love Among the Cannibals* represents his effort to follow his own advice, as does *What a Way to Go*, his weakest novel.

The protagonist of *What a Way to Go* (1962) is Arnold Soby, a middle-aged English professor obsessed with Mann's *Death in Venice* who decides to see Europe for himself. There he meets Cynthia, a teenage tourist who is a collection of the cliches of her age. Yet her strange beauty captivates every man who sees her, and she is compared to Eve, Nausicaa, Cleopatra, Botticelli's Primavera, Lolita, and Aschenbach's Tadzio. This mythical beauty outweighs her simple-minded vulgarity, and Soby marries her. The novel is a mixture of literary allusions, observations on the nature of art and beauty, and slapstick comedy, all in a parody of James's style. It fails primarily because the style overpowers the slight subject matter.

Morris's next novel, *Cause for Wonder* (1963), is also flawed by confused goals and self-indulgences. Part of the problem results from Morris's compulsion to write about the winter he was snowed in at a castle in Austria in 1933-1934 and his inability to develop a convincing approach for transforming the raw material. The protagonist is Warren Howe, a television scriptwriter in Hollywood, who is notified of the death of Etienne Dulac, at whose castle he passed a winter thirty years earlier. Ever since Howe has been unsuccessfully trying to write a novel about Dulac. Returning there to attempt to recapture the past, he arrives to find gathered the other inhabitants of that long-ago winter and to discover that Dulac is still alive. The senile, crippled nobleman, satisfied with his prank, does die the next day after transferring his audacity to the grandson of a former lover. At the beginning of the novel, Howe feels he would be happy in the past, and nothing seems to have changed by the end. He is the flattest of Morris's heroes, the other captives little more than stereotypes, and Dulac never approaches the charm of most of Morris's old men.

With *One Day* (1965) Morris returns to his native soil and pulls himself out of his European slump. His longest novel, it is set in a small town near San Francisco on 22 November 1963. The day opens with the discovery of an infant left at the town's ultramodern dog pound. Following are the assassination of President Kennedy and the death of one of the citizens in a freak accident. These events and reactions to them are filtered through the consciousnesses of nine characters. The main ones are Dr. Howard Cowie, the town veterinarian, and

Alec Cartwright, mother of the abandoned child. Cowie, "the maverick who never leaves the herd. The loner who does not want to be alone," identifies with the day's dominant loner, Lee Harvey Oswald. Alec's abandoning of her baby, whose father is a black man she met in Paris and pursued throughout the South, is meant to shock the complacent town but is overshadowed by the day's larger audacious act.

In responding to the events of the day, the characters muse about protest, loneliness, guilt, death, accidents, and the superficialities of life which Alec is rebelling against. Both Alec and Cowie are haunted by events in the past: Alec by her days in Paris and the south; Cowie by the summer he spent in Mexico trying to forget a broken romance, during which time he killed two men in a traffic accident and lost his ambition to be a physician. The events of the day juxtapose the concerns of time-past with those of time-present, and Alec and Cowie gain insight into themselves, especially Alec, Morris's most completely realized female character. By the end of *One Day*, she is better prepared to face the future than any of his creations have been.

In Orbit (1967) is a short, comic, ambiguous, almost poetic novel, dealing with the effects of two disasters, one natural, the other seen as supernatural, on the inhabitants of Pickett, Indiana. The natural disaster is a tornado; it is preceded by the supernatural one, Jubal Gainer, a moral descendant of Charlie Munger and Lee Harvey Oswald. Gainer gets into a violent argument with his best friend, steals the friend's motorcycle, and hits the road. Once in Pickett he rapes a mentally-retarded woman (though there is no "penetration"), smashes a sack of black cherries over a man's head, and superficially wounds another with a knife. His rather ineffectual reign of terror is not intentional; people just keep getting in his way. The tornado which allows him to escape is merely an extension of his own violence.

Gainer is representative of the shapelessness of American culture, which "seems a mindless force, like the dipping, dancing funnel of the twister, the top spread wide to spew into space all that it has sucked up." More than any of Morris's other characters, Gainer *is* the immediate present: "He is in motion. Now you see him, now you don't. If you pin him down in time he is lost in space. Somewhere between where he is from and where he is going he wheels in an unpredictable orbit. He is as free, and as captive, as the wind in his face." As Leon Howard has pointed out, Morris could have chosen "no better words to express his conception of the role of the artist in modern life": floating freely, confronting

the present, racing toward the future, leaving the past where it belongs.

But Morris is still not finished with the past. In *Fire Sermon* (1971) he performs yet another exorcism. With it he returns to his own artistic past, reworking *My Uncle Dudley* through another eastward journey across half of America by a boy and his audacious uncle. Their destination, Chapman, Nebraska, is another version of Lone Tree. Morris is recreating and reexamining earlier characters, situations, and themes for new effects.

The boy is Kermit Oelsligle, a twelve-year-old orphan who lives in California with his eighty-two-year-old granduncle, Floyd Warner. A composite of Morris's old men, Warner tries to teach the boy to hate all the right things, such as dogs and basketball players. Kermit does not allow himself to be subverted by the old man's beliefs, however, maintaining an innocent enthusiasm for and faith in the future. The 1,948-mile trip east comes about when Warner's sister dies. Driving his ancient Maxwell and towing his equally-antique house trailer, the tired Warner soon turns over the driving to Kermit, the first of many instances in which the past yields to the present. Symbolizing the immediate present are two hitchhikers they pick up, a young couple deeply immersed in the cliches of the Pepsi-and-pot generation.

They arrive in Nebraska to find the sister's home crammed with artifacts, and Warner realizes that he and the way of life represented by the house and its objects are long out of date. He knows that his relationship with the boy cannot go on as it has. Their futures are settled when the hitchhikers get into bed to smoke marijuana and set the house on fire. Warner leaves his past smoldering behind him, freeing Kermit to enter the brave new world, the territory ahead. The fire, borrowed from Buddha by way of T. S. Eliot, is of the purifying kind, a stripping down to the essentials. Kermit's new freedom is ambiguous, recalling the end of *Ceremony in Lone Tree*; it is a freedom more constricting than that with which Dudley presents the Kid.

Morris continues Warner's story in *A Life* (1973). Rushing as if in a dream toward something he cannot articulate, Warner picks up a traveling companion, George Blackbird, a more threatening version of Jubal Gainer. A monosyllabic Hopi recently returned from Vietnam, Blackbird comes to represent Warner's fate. The past, present, and future begin to merge in Warner's mind as he anticipates what awaits him at the end of his journey. The Warner of *Fire Sermon* is a pleasantly irascible old

From Wright Morris: Structures and Artifacts, Photographs 1933-1954.

geezer as seen through the eyes of his young witness. In *A Life* he is his own witness, developing, in his dream-like state, the capacity of standing outside himself and his life. Warner the witness feels a tender sympathy for Warner the hero, and he becomes reconciled to the fate of them both as Blackbird calmly, quietly murders him.

These two novels not only share a similar structure involving eventful journeys and fateful endings but reveal character development in much the same way. Just as Kermit learns to embrace the future, Warner comes to embrace death. With their similarities, repetitions, and foreshadowings, the two novels develop an almost musical quality, becoming their composer's songs of innocence and experience. The ambiguously uplifting melody of *Fire Sermon* is counterbalanced by the darker acceptances of *A Life*.

Morris's other books include *War Games* (1972), a short novel written in 1951 and partially incorporated into *The Field of Vision* and *Ceremony in Lone Tree*. His darkest novel, it deals with a murderous transvestite and is similar to his other fiction only in its exploration of loneliness. *Real Losses, Imaginary Gains* (1976) is a collection of thirteen short stories published between 1948 and 1975 and is of interest primarily for the stories' stylistic and thematic similarities to the novels. *God's Country and My People* and *Love Affair: A Venetian Journal* (1972) represent Morris's return to the photo-text form after twenty years. *A Bill of Rites, A Bill of Wrongs, A Bill of Goods* (1968) is a collection of essays of perhaps too sardonic social criticism, and *About Fiction* (1975) is his second volume of literary criticism. His most recent novel, *The Fork River Space Project*, was published in the fall of 1977, and *A Garden of Earthly Delights*, more critical commentary, is forthcoming in 1978.

Morris's critical reputation has been slow in developing. The first article analyzing his work, by Wayne Booth, did not appear until 1957, fifteen years after his first novel. That same year Morris received perhaps his greatest honor: the National Book Award for *The Field of Vision*. *Critique* devoted an issue to Morris in 1961, but since then only a trickle of articles has appeared, about one or two a year. David Madden's *Wright Morris*, the first full-length study, was published in 1964. There has been some activity in the graduate schools: eight dissertations between 1965 and 1976. The stimulus for much of the interest in contemporary writers depends upon their being taught in universities, and Morris has been handicapped in this regard because most of his books have been out of print until quite recently, when the University of Nebraska Press began reissuing all his novels.

Morris's proponents have found much to praise in his work. His novels, according to Wayne Booth, "more successfully than any other American novels in this century, render the mystical relation of time and the timeless." Discussing Morris's use of the cliche, Ralph Miller feels that "no author has done so much with dead language since Ring Lardner." For David Madden, who has written the most about him, Morris's dominant quality is his style: "the style he uses to describe disorder, chance, and contingency is the most perfectly controlled style in the United States. Everything style has been trained over the centuries to do, Morris makes it do in his novels." The quality critics most often praise is Morris's Americanness. "Wright Morris may well be the last of our novelists," says John Aldridge, "to write with a sense of the whole of America in his blood and bones, to possess a vision of the country as both a physical place and a metaphysical condition."

Morris's detractors most often accuse his work of being overwritten. British novelist John Wain, reviewing *In Orbit*, writes, "It's all so pat, so perfectly engineered: reading it is like taking the back off your watch and seeing the little wheels click round and round. A perfect small machine: but somehow too neat, too trimmed, to capture life. I suppose this is what old-fashioned critics meant when they said that a book 'smelt of the lamp.' " Alfred Kazin complains that Morris writes "the literary novel which professors like to teach and would like to write." The other major criticism is that too many of Morris's characters are mere mouthpieces, and Morris has admitted that Boyd and Webb are too close to the author.

Whatever his virtues and limitations, Morris is an important novelist with a large body of consistently interesting work which has not received widespread recognition and is often taken for granted. One cannot even assume that his books will be reviewed by the major publications. He seems damned to continuing his career as, in John Aldridge's words, "the least well-known and most widely unappreciated important writer alive in this country."

Books:

A Bill of Rites, A Bill of Wrongs, A Bill of Goods (New York: New American Library, 1968);

God's Country and My People (New York: Harper & Row, 1968);

Wright Morris: A Reader (New York: Harper & Row, 1970);

Green Grass, Blue Sky, White House (Los Angeles: Black Sparrow, 1970);

War Games (Los Angeles: Black Sparrow, 1972);

Love Affair: A Venetian Journal (New York: Harper & Row, 1972);

Here is Einbaum (Los Angeles: Black Sparrow, 1973);

About Fiction: Reverent Reflections on the Nature of Fiction with Irreverent Observations on Writers, Readers, & Other Abuses (New York: Harper & Row, 1975);

The Cat's Meow (Los Angeles: Black Sparrow, 1975);

Wright Morris: Structures and Artifacts, Photographs 1933-1954 (Lincoln: Sheldon Memorial Art Gallery, University of Nebraska, 1975);

Real Losses, Imaginary Gains (New York: Harper & Row, 1976).

References:

John W. Aldridge, "The Most Widely Un-appreciated Important Writer in the Country," *New York Times Book Review*, 11 January 1970, pp. 4, 33;

Jonathan Baumbach, "Wake Before Bomb: *Ceremony in Lone Tree*," *Critique*, 4, 3 (winter 1961-1962): 56-71;

Sam Bleufarb, "Point of View: An Interview with Wright Morris, July 1958," *Accent*, 19 (winter 1959): 34-46;

Wayne C. Booth, "The Two Worlds in the Fiction of Wright Morris," *Sewanee Review*, 65 (summer 1957): 375-399;

Booth, "The Shaping of Prophecy: Craft and Idea in the Novels of Wright Morris," *American Scholar*, 31 (autumn 1962): 608-626;

G. B. Crump, "Wright Morris's *One Day*: The Bad News on the Hour," *Midamerica*, 3 (1976): 77-91;

Crump, *The Novels of Wright Morris: A Critical Interpretation* (Lincoln: University of Nebraska Press, 1978);

Chester E. Eisinger, *Fiction of the Forties* (Chicago: University of Chicago Press, 1963);

George Garrett, "Morris the Magician: A Look at *In Orbit*," *Hollins Critic*, 4, 3 (June 1967): 1-12;

Roger J. Guettinger, "The Problem with Jigsaw Puzzles: Form in the Fiction of Wright Morris," *Texas Quarterly*, 11, 1 (spring 1968): 209-220;

Granville Hicks, Introduction to *Wright Morris: A Reader* (New York: Harper & Row, 1970);

Leon Howard, *Wright Morris* (Minneapolis: University of Minnesota Press, 1968);

John W. Hunt, Jr., "The Journey Back: The Early Novels of Wright Morris," *Critique*, 5, 1 (spring-summer 1962): 41-60;

"Interview: Wright Morris," *Great Lakes Review*, 1 (winter 1975): 1-29.

Marcus Klein, *After Alienation: American Novels in Mid-Century* (Cleveland: World, 1964);

Robert E. Knoll, ed., *Conversations with Wright Morris: Critical Views and Responses* (Lincoln: University of Nebraska Press, 1977);

David Madden, "The Hero and the Witness in Wright Morris' *Field of Vision*," *Prairie Schooner*, 34 (fall 1960): 263-278;

Madden, "The Great Plains in the Novels of Wright Morris," *Critique*, 4, 3 (winter 1961-1962): 5-23;

Madden, *Wright Morris* (New York: Twayne, 1964);

Madden, "Wright Morris' *In Orbit*: An Unbroken Series of Poetic Gestures," *Critique*, 10, 2 (fall 1968): 102-119;

Ralph Miller, "The Fiction of Wright Morris: The Sense of Ending," *Midamerica*, 3 (1976): 56-76;

Gerald Nemanic, "A Ripening Eye: Wright Morris and the Field of Vision," *Midamerica*, 1 (1974): 120-131;

Fred Pfeil, "Querencias and a Lot Else: An Interview with Wright Morris," *Place*, 3 (June 1973): 53-63;

Alan Trachtenberg, "The Craft of Vision," *Critique*, 4, 3 (winter 1961-1962): 41-55;

Arthur E. Waterman, "The Novels of Wright Morris: An Escape from Nostalgia," *Critique*, 4, 3 (winter 1961-1962): 24-40;

James C. Wilson, "Wright Morris and the Search for the 'Still Point,' " *Prairie Schooner*, 49 (summer 1975): 154-163;

Manuscripts:

The University of California at Berkeley has a major collection of Morris's correspondence and the manuscripts and typescripts of fifteen of his novels.

Vladimir Nabokov

John V. Hagopian
State University of New York at Binghamton

BIRTH: St. Petersburg, Russia, 22 April 1899.

EDUCATION: Private tutors, and Tenishev Academy, St. Petersburg, 1910-1917; Cambridge University (England), 1919-1922.

MARRIAGE: 1925 to Vera Evseevna Slonim; son: Dmitri, born 1934.

AWARDS: Research Fellow, Museum of Comparative Zoology, Harvard, 1942; Guggenheim Fellow, 1943, 1953; National Institute and American Academy Award, 1951; Award from American Academy of Arts and Letters, 1953; Brandeis University Creative Arts Medal, 1963-1964; National Institute of Arts and Letters Award of Merit, 1969; National Medal for Literature, 1973.

DEATH: Montreux, Switzerland, 5 July 1977.

MAJOR WORKS: Russian works under the pen name of V. Sirin: *Mashenka* (Berlin: Slovo, 1926; translated as *Mary* by Michael Glenny and Nabokov, New York: McGraw-Hill, 1970; London: Weidenfeld & Nicolson, 1971); *Korol, Dama, Valet* (Berlin: Slovo, 1928; translated as *King, Queen, Knave* by Dmitri and Vladimir Nabokov, New York: McGraw-Hill, 1968; London: Weidenfeld & Nicolson, 1968); *Zashchita Luzhina* (Berlin: Slovo, 1930; translated as *The Defense* by Michael Scammell and Nabokov, New York: Putnam's, 1964; London: Weidenfeld & Nicolson, 1964); *Soglyadatay* (Paris: Sovremennye Zapiski, 1930; translated as *The Eye* by Dmitri and Vladimir Nabokov, New York: Phaedra, 1965; London: Weidenfeld & Nicolson, 1966); *Podvig* (Paris: Sovremennye Zapiski, 1932; translated as *Glory* by Dmitri and Vladimir Nabokov, New York: McGraw-Hill, 1971; London: Weidenfeld & Nicolson, 1972); *Kamera Obskura* (Paris: Sovremennye Zapiski, 1932; translated as *Camera Obscura* by W. Roy, London: John Long, 1936; retranslated as *Laughter in the Dark* by Nabokov, Indianapolis: Bobbs-Merrill, 1938; London: Weidenfeld & Nicolson, 1961); *Otchayanie* (Berlin: Petropolis, 1936; translated as *Despair* by Nabokov, London: John Long, 1937; retranslated by Nabokov, New York: Putnam's, 1966; London: Weidenfeld & Nicolson, 1966); *Priglashenie na Kazn* (Paris: Dom Knigi, 1938; translated as *Invitation to a Beheading* by Dmitri and Vladimir Nabokov, New York: Putnam's, 1959; London: Weidenfeld & Nicolson, 1960); *Dar* (Paris: Sovremennye Zapiski, 1937-1938; translated as *The Gift* by Michael Scammell and Nabokov, New York: Putnam's, 1963; London: Weidenfeld & Nicolson, 1963); *The Real Life of Sebastian Knight* (Norfolk, Conn.: New Directions, 1941; London: Poetry, 1945); *Bend Sinister* (New York: Holt, 1947; London: Weidenfeld & Nicolson, 1960); *Lolita* (Paris: Olympia, 1955; New York: Putnam's, 1958; London: Weidenfeld & Nicolson, 1959); *Pnin* (Garden City: Doubleday, 1957; London: Heinemann, 1957); *Nabokov's Dozen* (Garden City: Doubleday, 1958; London: Heinemann, 1959); *Pale Fire* (New York: Putnam's 1962; London: Weidenfeld & Nicolson, 1962); Pushkin's *Eugene Onegin* (translated and annotated, 4 vols., Bollingen Series, New York: Pantheon, 1964; London: Routledge, 1964); *Speak, Memory* (memoirs originally published as *Conclusive Evidence* [1951]; New York: Putnam's, 1966); *Ada* (New York: McGraw-Hill, 1969; London: Weidenfeld & Nicolson, 1969); *Transparent Things* (New York: McGraw-Hill, 1972); *Look at the Harlequins!* (New York: McGraw-Hill, 1974; London: Weidenfeld & Nicolson, 1975).

It is a paradox that Vladimir Nabokov's life and career dramatically involved him in the most powerful socio-historical currents of the twentieth century: Marxist revolution, exile, politics, the sexual revolution, and the *poshlost* of the universities and media—and he disdained them all! Nabokov was an aristocratic snob and an aesthetic elitist—and without doubt one of the greatest literary artists of our time.

There will probably never be a definitive biography of Nabokov. The razzle-dazzle complexity of his life and his own sly, lyrical mock-true confessions—first in *Conclusive Evidence* (1951) and in two versions of *Speak, Memory* (1960, 1966)—are ultimately irrelevant as guides to his work. "I should never have tried to become an autobiographer," he said; "heart-to-heart talks, confessions in the Dostoievskian manner, are . . . not in my line." Problems begin with his birthdate, and he has not been lucky in his first biographer, Andrew Field. *Nabokov: His Life in Part* (1977) caused a break in Field's long friendship with his former teacher and prompted the family lawyers to devote "considerable attention and energy in an unsuccessful attempt to

Vladimir Nabokov and his wife, Vera.

destroy my book.'' Any capsule summary of this intricately complex life is sure to prompt protests from captious critics. Himself fascinated with ''the miracle of the lemniscate'' forms of life, he said: ''A colored spiral in a small ball of glass, this is how I see my own life. The twenty years I spent in my native Russia (1899-1919) take care of the thetic arc. Twenty-one years of voluntary exile in England, Germany, and France (1919-1940) supply the obvious antithesis. The period spent in my adopted country (1940-1960) forms a synthesis—and a new thesis.'' What followed was a not quite twenty-year period (1960-1977) in residence at the Palace Hotel (he never owned a home!) in Montreux, Switzerland. Each of those four periods is almost a separate, a unique life, with its own feeling, tone, and pace, linked and bobolinked together with a unifying consciousness constantly making ornaments of accidents and possibilities.

His childhood in Czarist Russia was Edenic, magnificently evoked in the setting and tone—but not the incidents—of *Ada*. An aristocratic family, proud of its coat-of-arms and ancestry stretching back to Nabok Murza, a fourteenth-century Russianized Tartar prince in Muscovy (though this has

been challenged by Igor Vinogradoff), provided an affluent and loving context for his idyllic boyhood. He was raised in a fashionable St. Petersburg home and a rambling country estate with a regular staff of fifty servants and a sequence of fascinating governesses and tutors. His mother, who never entered the kitchen, read bedtime stories in three languages and indulged in expensive, important luxuries like Pears soap; his father, a strong, gentle man, was a professor of criminology and a liberal member of Parliament who was sentenced to three months in solitary confinement for protesting the Czar's illegal dissolution of Parliament in 1906. In 1919 the Bolshevik Revolution brought an abrupt end to young Nabokov's two million dollar inheritance, the adolescent love to whom he wrote a hundred poems, and butterfly-chasing rambles—a hail of machine-gun fire raked his ship as it pulled out of the Yalta harbor. To Nabokov the old Russia remained an irretrievable past for which he had immense nostalgia, but he insisted that ''my old (since 1917) quarrel with the Soviet dictatorship is wholly unrelated to any question of property.''

Nabokov went to study languages at Cambridge, a place ''of no consequence,'' where he lived in squalid lodgings, never entered the library, gave the only political speech of his lifetime (losing a debate on Bolshevism), and conducted several love affairs in London. Nevertheless, he graduated with honors. In 1922 at a political rally of Russian exiles in Berlin, Nabokov's father was killed when he attempted to foil an assassin whose target was the principal speaker, a political rival.

Nabokov spent the next eighteen years on the continent, principally in Berlin where he married and had a son Dmitri, scrabbled for a living by writing for the emigre press (he composed the first Russian crossword puzzles), teaching chess, tennis, and Russian, and writing his Russian novels. The terrorism of the Nazis drove him to Paris in 1938 and to the United States in 1940; his sense of alienation was such that he made "not more than two good friends" among the Germans and French. After a brief stint as Slavic lecturer at Stanford, his skill as a lepidopterist (describing a dozen new butterfly varieties—one named after himself) earned him a research fellowship at Harvard. He also taught Russian part-time at Wellesley, but liberals sympathetic to the wartime Russian ally prevented his getting a permanent position. He was sustained during that period of anxious poverty by gifts and loans—Rachmaninoff, a fellow exile, sent him clothes and money. His book, *Nikolai Gogol* (1944), led to a professorship in comparative literature at Cornell in 1948, a position he held until the immense success of *Lolita* enabled him to quit teaching and settle down in Switzerland to full-time writing and translating his Russian works into English.

Both his scholarship and his fiction involved him in controversy. He resented the wide mis-understanding of *Lolita* as a dirty book (and was sardonically amused that Adolf Eichmann con-sidered it immoral). He was quite outspoken in his contempt for writers and critics who engaged in *poshlost*, which he defined as "corny trash, vulgar cliches, Philistinism in all its phases, imitations of imitations, bogus profundities, crude, moronic and dishonest pseudo-literature . . . Freudian symbolism, moth-eaten mythologies, social comment, human-istic messages, political allegories, overconcern with class or race, and the journalistic generalities we all know." Typical of pronouncements which raised the hackles of the literary establishment were: "I must fight a suspicion of conspiracy against my brain when I see blandly accepted as 'great literature' . . . Lady Chatterley's copulations or the pretentious nonsense of Mr. Pound, that total fake," and "I detest not one, but four doctors: Dr. Freud, Dr. Zhivago, Dr. Schweitzer, and Dr. Castro." Nabokov's polemical

disposition probably expressed itself most forcefully in his bitter dispute with his old friend Edmund Wilson, who had the effrontery to attack Nabokov's translation of Pushkin's *Eugene Onegin* in "the longest, most ambitious, most captious, and, alas, most reckless" of the reviews. Even though "a number of earnest simpletons consider Mr. Wilson to be an authority in my field," said Nabokov, "his article is a polemicist's dream come true, and one must be a poor sportsman to disdain what it offers."

In his life as well as in his work, Nabokov alienated many by his sardonic sneers at the fashionable intellectual currents of the day, especially knee-jerk, radical-chic do-gooders who demanded that the arts serve some social cause. "Nothing bores me more than political novels and the literature of social intent," he said: "I have no social purpose, no moral message; I've no general ideas to exploit." And though he believed that "all novelists of any worth are psychological," he didn't pour his heart out in fiction. "I just like composing riddles with elegant solutions." But that is a polemical exaggeration. It is true that as a passionate game-player, Nabokov loved making intricate structures because "art at its greatest is fantastically deceitful and complex." But as his observations of butterflies confirmed, that is also true of nature. His fiction is made of razzle-dazzle effects—circular time patterns, polysemantic, multilingual puns, mirror images, acrostics (the solution of "The Vane Sisters" is given in a phrase made of the first letter of each word in the last paragraph). And one of the great pleasures in reading Nabokov is the thrill of discovery—responding with "Ah, da!" (oh, yes) to *Ada*, but in a world of topsy-turvical coincidence, noting that *Ada* also means "to hell." Although a fit audience for Nabokov is indeed few, the intellectual elite who are above being titillated by nymphets (though not above being amused and fascinated by the antics of those who are titillated!), it would be a mistake to see him simply as an intricate maze-maker (he detested *Finnegans Wake*). As he said in a letter to Edmund Wilson, "The longer I live the more I become convinced that the only thing that matters in literature is the (more or less irrational) *shamanstvo* of a book, i.e., that the good writer is first of all an enchanter." And once the reader finds the essential clues, penetrates the disguises, works out the convoluted patterns, he views a human experience which is powerfully charged—emotionally and morally. The emotions are not those of a sentimental romantic nor the morals those of a *poshlost* humanitarian; they are profoundly significant—far more than elegant solutions to riddles. Nabokov was loathe to speak of these things, but on one occasion he did say that "one day a reappraiser will come and declare that, far from having been a frivolous firebird, I was a rigid moralist kicking sin, cuffing stupidity, ridiculing the vulgar and cruel—and assigning sovereign power to tenderness, talent, and pride."

Nabokov's nine Russian novels (not to mention nine plays, dozens of stories and poems) are by no means mere apprentice work. One of his earliest and most perceptive critics, Vladislav Khodasevich, said in his essay "On Sirin" (1937) that Nabokov (Sirin) "proves for the most part to be an artist of form, of the writer's device . . . distinguished by exceptional diversity, complexity, brilliance and novelty." Though Nabokov warns against identifying "the designer with the design," his Russian novels are clearly more autobiographical than any of his works in English. *Mary, Glory,* and *The Gift* are especially rich in the lore of emigre life, particularly the nostalgia for old Russia, a nostalgia which Nabokov came to realize as dangerous—"throughout one's life an insane companion." Nevertheless, though Gleb Struve is probably correct in judging the Sirin works to be "the most original and brilliant product of emigre literature," even the best of them cannot match the best of his English writings, and they will not have much appeal to readers not familiar with the strange milieu of Russian exiles in Europe.

The bare plot of *Mary* (1926), in fact, can be seen as a parable on the need to renounce a past which is irrecoverable. The setting is a Berlin pension occupied by a wide variety of Russian emigre types, including the central characters Lev Ganin and Alexei Alfiorov. Lev yearns for the woman he left behind in Russia, no doubt derived from Nabokov's adolescent love affair with Tamara, and when he discovers that the wife whom Alexei is expecting is the same woman, he plots to get him drunk, meet the train instead, and run off with her. But at the station, he realizes that time has changed everything, and, in a sad gesture of realistic renunciation, he leaves the station before she arrives.

King, Queen, Knave (1928), influenced by *Alice in Wonderland* (which Nabokov had translated into Russian), is the beginning of his long career as a gamesman novelist. "Of all my novels," he said, "this bright brute is the gayest. Expatriation, destitution, nostalgia had no effect on its elaborate and rapturous composition"—reflecting the joy of his marriage to Vera Slonim (to whom he dedicated every one of his books). The characters are pasteboard figures, face cards from a stacked deck, involved in a love triangle in which all three angles

are obtuse. A callow, bespectacled oaf named Franz is given a job in a thriving Berlin department store by his genial Uncle Dreyer. The uncle's beautiful, bored young wife Martha seduces Franz, beginning a passionate, serio-comic affair marked by burlesque escapes from detection. Martha plots with Franz to drown her husband, inherit his millions, and marry Franz, but at the last minute when she learns that Dreyer is about to make a fortune from an invention (mechanized mannequins), she aborts the plot, catches pneumonia, and dies, leaving behind an adoring husband and a relieved young lover. At the end, Franz, strolling at a seaside resort, enviously observes a loving couple and recalls the name of the man from the hotel guest book: Blavdak Vinomori (the first of many anagrammatic pseudonyms of Vladimir Nabokov). This last detail prompted William Gass to complain that a "still umbilicaled book is no more formed than a foetus. . . . Nabokov's novels are frequently formless, or when form presides, it's mechanical, lacking instinct, desire, feeling, life . . . (all) *deus ex machina.*" Gass, however, exempted from this charge Nabokov's next game book, *The Defense* (1930), "a loving exception to everything; every move is emotional, even the last one, when Luzhin flies like a Pegasus from life to death and board to board." But this concession negates Gass's general principle, for obviously intricate mechanics of form—here the form of a chess game—do not necessarily make passion impossible. *The Defense* foreshadows the fantastically symbiotic conflicting forces in *Pale Fire,* where wrapped in enigmatic layers of irony is a warm and loving hero. Grandmaster Luzhin is an ungainly, obese, sweet-natured chess fanatic, who, after his adoring father dies and his self-serving teacher abandons him, plods eternally from one international match to another and gradually loses his hold on reality. An emigre girl marries the helpless genius and tries to help him regain his sanity. Chess is forbidden, but secretly, compulsively, he continues to play games in his head until his final move, a leap to his death. Robert M. Adams's insightful comment is that the wife, "in her own endearing, well-meaning way . . . is working against the grain of his existence. . . . by being right, in a human way, [she] is wrong about Luzhin's sterile, perverted talent. . . . Luzhin is mad to think the world is a game of chess—except that the world in this novel *is* a game of chess."

The Eye (1930) is a strange novella, narrated by Smurov, a Dostoevskian underground man who, after an unsuccessful attempt at suicide, continues to live as an observer of those who observe him. Nabokov says in a foreword that the plot is not "reducible to a dreadfully painful love story in which a writhing heart is not only spurned, but humiliated and punished." In the end, Smurov proclaims, "I do not exist; there exist but the thousands of mirrors that reflect me. . . . And yet I am happy. . . . I have realized that the only happiness in this world is to observe, to spy, to watch, to scrutinize oneself and others, to be nothing but a big, slightly vitreous, somewhat bloodshot, unblinking eye."

Speaking of *Glory* (1932), Nabokov told Alfred Appel, "Not all of that stuff is as good as I thought it was 30 years ago." And Andrew Field said of the Russian version, the title of which he translated as *The Exploit*, "It is one of the least exciting of Nabokov's novels . . . with an abrupt and inconclusive ending." Nabokov uses a straight-forward, third-person narrative with all of Europe as its setting. It is (in Nabokov's words) "the story of a Russian expatriate [Martin Edelweiss], a romantic young man of my set and time, a lover of adventure for adventure's sake, proud flaunter of peril, climber of unnecessary mountains, who merely for the pure thrill of it decides one day to cross illegally into Soviet Russia, and then cross back into exile. Its main theme is the overcoming of fear, the glory and rapture of that victory." Contrary to Nabokov's wishes, Field played the only game which he thought would make the novel interesting; he compared the experiences and descriptions in *Glory* with those in Nabokov's autobiography, *Speak, Memory*.

Laughter in the Dark is an erotic black comedy which makes literal the axiom that love is blind. It opens in the manner of a parable: "Once upon a time there lived in Berlin, Germany, a man called Albinus. He was rich, respectable, happy; one day he abandoned his wife for the sake of a youthful mistress; he loved; was not loved; and his life ended in disaster. This is the whole of the story and we might have left it at that had there not been profit and pleasure in the telling. . . . detail is always welcome." Albinus Kretschmar is seduced by an usherette in a movie theater because she wants to use his influence and money to set her up as an actress in films. When he is blinded in an accident she renews her affair with Axel Rex, a cartoonist. He moves into the house where Albinus cannot see him, tiptoes about, eats at the table, sleeps with Margot, giggles silently at Albinus's every stumble—and finally murders him. The novel was made into a grotesque horror film by Edward Bond, starring Nicol Williamson.

Despair is also a comic-grotesque murder story, told by one Hermann Karlovich, a schizophrenic chocolate manufacturer whose passions in life are bourgeois luxuries, his fond, stupid wife Lydia, and his failing business. While on a trip to Prague, he encounters a tramp whom he believes resembles him and plots with his wife to lure the man to Berlin and murder him for the insurance money. Actually there was no resemblance at all and false credentials planted on the corpse fool no one. Hermann flees to Pignan, France, where he writes his story, fulminates against the perverse world that fails to appreciate the brilliance of his deceptive art, and goes mad. As the police arrive, he fantasizes that it's all a movie being filmed. The last page of his manuscript is dated April Fool's Day.

In his last two Russian novels, Nabokov loosened the tight, intricate plot structures characteristic of his earlier works to give full vent to his poetic imagination. At a time when increasing pressures of fascism were forcing him to contemplate a further move in his exile, both novels subordinate their love stories and deal with political themes but in a way which manifests the refusal of art to become political. Indeed, the escape from tyranny was psychological before it became physical. *Invitation to a Beheading* ("my dreamiest and most poetical novel") dramatizes a way to avoid the absurd horrors of a police state. Cincinnatus C. is incarcerated in a Kafkaesque prison awaiting execution for the crime of "gnostical turpitude." Powerful temptations attract him to commitment to the world—love of his wife Marthe (who openly has affairs and whose two children are not Cincinnatus's), the lures of the would-be seducer Emmie (the prison director's daughter), and the hearty sensual pleasures offered by a fellow-prisoner, Pierre (who is really the executioner). Both the narrator and Cincinnatus look upon the real world as a fake, a cheap theater where a stage manager constantly changes the two dimensional backdrops and a watchman changes the hands on the clocks. No man of imagination need remain committed to such a world. Thus, in the end when Pierre's axe swings down on him, Cincinnatus simply discards his transparent body: "Everything was failing. A spinning wind was picking up and whirling: dust, rags, chips of painted wood, bits of gilded plaster, pasteboard bricks, posters; an arid gloom fleeted; and amidst the dust and the falling things, and the flapping scenery, Cincinnatus made his way in that direction where, to judge by the voices, stood beings akin to him."

Nabokov said of his last Russian novel, *The Gift*, "It is the longest, I think the best, and the most nostalgic." Not all the critics agree that it is the best; each of the five chapters seems a self-sufficient vignette with no integral relationship to the others. Chapter One develops the character of Fyodor Godunov-Cherdyntsev, a young Russian writer who is both protagonist and sometimes narrator. He presents many of his poems and describes the Russian emigre milieu of Berlin. Chapter Two is a biography of Fyodor's father, an entomologist whose great exploit was a zoological exploration of Central Asia, an imaginative venture described in loving and beautiful detail. Chapter Three is devoted to Fyodor's love affair with Zina Mertz, the daughter of an exiled Russian woman in whose apartment Fyodor rents a room. Chapter Four (suppressed by the first emigre publishers in Paris) is the biography which Fyodor does *not* write, but contemplates. It is of the nineteenth-century pseudo-revolutionary (loathed by Tolstoy, Dostoevsky and Turgenev) who imported western Utopian socialism to Russia. The final chapter gathers together, but does not integrate all these diverse stories, plots, characters, and themes. The final paragraph opens with "Good-by, my book!" and ends with "the shadows of my world extend beyond the skyline of the page, blue as tomorrow's morning haze—nor does this terminate the phrase"—a passage that clearly foreshadows Nabokov's greatest achievement, John Shade's poem "Pale Fire." But *Pale Fire* has an implicit closed form and a coherent unity of plot; *The Gift* is unified merely by the consciousness of the central character. As Donald Malcolm said in his brilliant *New Yorker* review: "*The Gift* resembles nothing so much as a mosaic whose every tile is itself a perfect cameo. There simply is no proper distance from which to view it. If one relishes each fragment, the larger patterns are lost. If one attempts to grasp the picture in its entirety, then one finds its manifold glimmering components a great hindrance to the larger vision."

In 1938 in Paris while contemplating emigration to the United States, Nabokov wrote his first novel in English, *The Real Life of Sebastian Knight*. Not surprisingly, its principal theme is identity—posed in the form of two questions: who was he? who am I? It is an autobiography told by a narrator who is irritated by an opportunistic biography written by his brother's secretary (Mr. Goodman, a moralist). He sets out to discover the real identity of his brother Sebastian, a brilliant novelist, two months dead. The book is clearly based on, but has no one-to-one relationship with, Nabokov's own feelings about his brother Sergey (who later died in a Hamburg concentration camp in 1945). In *Speak, Memory* Nabokov wrote, "For various reasons I find it inordinately hard to speak about my other brother.

That twisted quest for Sebastian Knight (1940), with its gloriettes and self-mate combinations, is really nothing in comparison. . . ." V. is an ass and a poor writer whose relationship to the gifted Sebastian is much like Kinbote's to the great poet, John Shade in *Pale Fire* (or like Dowell's relationship to Ashburnham in Ford's *The Good Soldier*). One might say of Nabokov that the more a particular novel engages his own passions, the more he controls and conceals them by converting them into games, puzzles, and various intricate patterns; clear and obvious plots emerge from his pen only when he contemplates the experiences with a cool, dispassionate objectivity. This is not to say that the games and puzzles always have solutions; *The Real Life of Sebastian Knight* may not. Anthony Olcott observes that chess images, cued by the title, abound in the novel; there are two knights, four bishops, and V. undertakes his brother's biography in St. Damier, France ("damier" is French for chess board). But, says Olcott, "the textual games, while helpful, are not vital aspects of the book." (Incidentally, Olcott provides a useful chronology of events in *The Real Life of Sebastian Knight*.)

V. is temperamentally unsuited to understand his brother. "Time for Sebastian was never 1914 or 1920 or 1936—it was always year 1," but the narrator is always "a traveller . . . in the past." Incapable of genuine love himself, V. traces Sebastian's grand passions in life and in his novels—especially a six-year affair with Clare Bishop and a mysterious Russian woman, Nine Toorovetz (a chess castle). Nevertheless, at the end, after he rushes to his brother's deathbed only to discover that the man in bed is an Englishman and his brother is already dead, V. feels that he has become transformed into Sebastian. "Whatever his secret was, I have learned one secret, too, and namely: that the soul is but a manner of being—not a constant state—that any soul may be yours, if you find and follow its undulations. . . . Thus—I am Sebastian Knight. . . . Sebastian's mask clings to my face, the likeness will not be washed off. I am Sebastian, or Sebastian is I, or perhaps we both are someone whom neither of us knows." That is fatuous. As Kenneth Bruffee shrewdly observes, "V.'s personality has not really changed. The epilogue demonstrates in its stylistic confusion that V. is the same bumbling muddler at the end of the book that he has shown himself to be throughout."

In 1940 Nabokov went to the U. S., where "I quit smoking and started to munch molasses candy instead, with the result that my weight went up from my usual 140 to a monumental and cheerful 200. In consequence, I am one-third American—good

American flesh keeping me warm and safe"; but in another context, he made it plain that he considered the "nationality of a worthwhile author of secondary importance."

In the twenty years Vladimir Nabokov spent in the United States, he wrote only three novels: *Bend Sinister, Lolita*, and *Pnin*. Though they by no means manifest the entire spectrum of his literary techniques, they demonstrate an amazing range of matter and manner—a grim vision of the insanities of political tyranny, a compassionate but witty treatment of erotic obsessions, and a joyous comedy of academic politics. A clear, thorough understanding of *Bend Sinister* can be derived from Nabokov's own preface. Though Nabokov insists that "the story in *Bend Sinister* is not really about life and death in a grotesque police state. . . . I am neither a didacticist nor an allegorizer," the novel does reflect "the idiotic and despicable regimes that we all know" as brilliantly and powerfully as the anti-Utopian fictions of Kafka, Huxley, Orwell and Koestler. In one of its dimensions, *Bend Sinister* endorses Camus' dictum in *The Rebel* that "any type of rebellion which claims the right to destroy this solidarity [of love] simultaneously loses the right to be called rebellion and actually becomes an accomplice to murder." The central character is Adam Krug, a brilliant, internationally famous professor of philosophy, whose endorsement of the revolutionary Ekwilist regime is desperately sought by the insane homosexual dictator Paduk, who was in his youth the despised schoolmate of Krug. Krug, mourning the death of his wife, refuses: "I am not interested in politics. . . . I want to be left alone." But the regime attempts first to seduce him with women and then to intimidate him by imprisoning one by one his friends and finally holding his son David as hostage in an Institute for Abnormal Children. Krug capitulates but learns that his son has by mistake been the victim of a grotesque experiment: "The theory . . . was that if once a week the really difficult patients could enjoy the possibility of venting in full their repressed yearnings (the exaggerated urge to hurt, destroy, etc.) upon some little human creature of no value to the community, then, by degrees, the evil in them would . . . escape, and eventually they would become good citizens." The discovery drives Krug mad; he regresses to his schoolday mentality, calls to his mates to join in the run to attack Paduk and is shot. In *Speak, Memory*, Nabokov said, "Nature expects a full grown man to accept the two black voids, fore and aft, as stolidly as he accepts the extraordinary visions in between. . . . I feel the urge to take my rebellion outside and picket nature." And

here that anthropomorphic deity, the narrator, allows Krug a final escape from the pain and misery of the real world by transforming him into a moth, similar to the escape of Cincinnatus in *Invitation to a Beheading*. "The very last lap of his life had been happy and it had been proven to him that death was but a question of style. . . . A good night for mothing." The narrator's compassion for Krug no doubt stems from the fact that his passions and values—his love of family and friends, his respect for colleagues who experience "perfect felicity in specialized knowledge" and are "unlikely to commit murder," his contempt for political tyranny and moralistic *poshlost*—match exactly those of Nabokov himself.

No doubt the most terrific event in Nabokov's career was the notoriety, fame and fortune elicited by *Lolita* (and the 1962 film fiasco that followed)—it made "Nabokov" an unpronounceable household name. Refused by four American publishers, *Lolita* was first published in 1955 by a Parisian pornographic publisher, Maurice Girodias. It was smuggled into the United States and enjoyed a tremendous underground reputation until *The Anchor Review* (1957) published excerpts together with essays by Nabokov and F. W. Dupee. That prompted Putnam's to publish it in 1958, prepared for a court battle to rival that which followed the American publication of Joyce's *Ulysses* a quarter century earlier. No court battle developed, but reviewers sent shock waves throughout the reading public and established an image of Nabokov as a lewd writer and *Lolita* as a dirty book. In 1970, Alfred Appel produced the first annotated edition of a modern novel to have been published during its author's lifetime, a heavy-handed explication that spoils the fun, but emphasizes Nabokov's own intent to produce "aesthetic bliss, that is a sense of being somehow, somewhere, connected with other states of being where art (curiosity, tenderness, kindness, ecstasy) is the norm." Among other things, it was Nabokov's first book with an American setting and evokes marvelous images of the American landscape; he felt "the most affection for it" and made it the only one he has translated into Russian. A preface by a fatuous Freudian psychiatrist, John Ray, Jr., informs us that he has edited "Lolita, or the Confession of a White Widowed Male," written by the pseudonymous Humbert Humbert in prison while awaiting trial for murder, but who died of coronary thrombosis (i.e., heartbreak). Parodying the usual hypocrisy that "justifies" pornography, Ray labels the book a case study of sexual perversion and hopes that it will "help all of us . . . in bringing up a better generation in a safer world." But he knows it will not have that effect: "A desperate honesty that throbs through his confession does not absolve him from sins of diabolical cunning. He is abnormal. He is not a gentleman. But how magically his singing violin can conjure up a tendresse, a compassion for Lolita that makes us entranced with the book while abhorring its author!" A refined and scholarly European with an illicit passion for nymphets, Humbert Humbert emigrates to the United States as a condition of an inheritance from a rich uncle. In a small New England town, he boards at the home of Charlotte Haze, a widow with a twelve-year-old daughter, Lolita, so delectable that Humbert marries Charlotte to be with the girl. Upon discovering the diary in which Humbert has recorded his passion, Charlotte decides to leave him, rushes into the street to post some letters and is killed by a car. Humbert takes Lolita on a year-long drive across the continent, sleeping with her at various motels (Nabokov wrote most of the novel in a Buick that Vera drove across the country on a butterfly hunting expedition). He is astounded when Lolita, having already experienced the joys of sex at Camp Climax, seduces him at The Enchanted Hunters Inn. Returning East, they settle at Beardsley where Lolita attends a progressive girls' school and takes part in a play, *The Enchanted Hunters*, written and directed by Clare Quilty. Aware that he has a rival, Humbert takes Lolita off on another cross-country odyssey, soon notices that they are being followed, and suddenly finds Lolita gone. After a fruitless two-year search, Humbert settles down with a pathetic, childlike woman but cannot forget his nymphet. Then one day he gets a letter from Lolita announcing that she is married, pregnant, and needs money. Determined to kill his rival and take her back, Humbert discovers that Lolita has become a faded, unappealing sixteen-year-old housewife married to a young, innocent veteran. He bribes and coerces her to reveal the name of the man who had deprived him of his only love (Clare Quilty, a man who had collaborated with one Vivian Darkbloom), seeks him out, and in a scene of hilarious grotesque comedy shoots him. After his arrest he writes the memoir to be published only when Lolita is no longer alive, but by means of his prose will live in the minds of later generations: "I am thinking of aurochs and angels, the secret of durable pigments, prophetic sonnets, the refuge of art. And this is the only immortality you and I may share, my Lolita."

Insofar as the meaning lies in the plot (which it ultimately does not), the finest critical account is that of Lionel Trilling, who sees Humbert as the modern equivalent of a Provencal Troubador celebrating not sex but passion-love for the idealized and unattainable woman. Trilling observes that passion-love has disappeared from the Western world, just as Denis de Rougement said it would; it is now a possible subject for the artist only when he imagines, like Nabokov, a situation in which a man is in the grip of cruel power and slavish submission without any possibility of finding a socially sanctioned consummation of his love—certainly not in marriage to a barely pubescent nymphet. The only sexual love still taboo is that of an adult and a child. However, the ultimate meaning is not in socio-historical psychology, but in aesthetics. As Humbert himself wittily observes, "sex is but the ancilla of art," and his great achievement is in manifesting the triumph of art over life. F. W. Dupee said that "*Lolita* applies its heat to the entire sensibility, including the sense of humor"; but it's more than that—even more than Nabokov's own (surely ironic) disclaimer, "I've no general ideas to exploit, I just like composing riddles with elegant solutions." The ultimate meaning of *Lolita* lies in Humbert's demonstration of how to control and impose a meaningful shape on irrational drives; he makes a fiction out of his life and thus becomes the creator of it.

While Hurricane Lolita was moving from Paris to New York, Nabokov wrote *Pnin*, a gentle, humane novel depicting one of the most lovable schlemiels in all literature. Timofey Pnin, a kind, ineffectual emigre scholar earning a meager livelihood as teacher of Russian in an upstate New York diploma mill called Waindell College (which Pnin mispronounces "Vandal College"), has a life history—and a soul—very much like Nabokov's. He is what Nabokov would have been if he had not had such a powerful intellect, steel will, and artistic genius. Because Pnin is neither an academic fraud nor a pseudo-scholarly confidence man, he does not have tenure. (As *Lolita* showed, Nabokov's gratitude and loyalty to the U. S. did not blind him to the horror of American society.) Pnin is the kind of man who despairs when the library, at the request of another reader, demands the return of an overdue, indispensable Russian tome, only to discover that the other reader is himself. He is constantly baffled by the English language, train schedules, machinery, and the evil of the universe. A careful reader will note (from the opening of the last chapter) that Pnin's story is really being told by a man who knew him in Russia forty years before, who was once his wife's lover, and who is about to take his job at Waindell College.

As the novel opens, Pnin is en route to give a ladies' club lecture in Cremona. Though he is on the

Vladimir Nabokov

wrong train and has brought the wrong lecture, he manages to get there and deliver a speech. But he has a cardiac seizure and recalls figures and events from his past. Born in St. Petersburg in 1898, son of a prominent ophthalmologist (whom the narrator consulted to have a speck of coal dust removed from his eye in 1911), Pnin escaped the Bolsheviks via Crimea in 1919, attended the University of Prague, lived for twenty years in the emigre community in Paris, and escaped the Nazis to the U. S. where he became a naturalized citizen. He had once been married to Liza, a neurotic psychiatrist, who had left him for a "psychoasinine" Eric Wind, and had come back to him pregnant with her child Victor (to whom Pnin became a loving water-father) only to trick him into bringing her to the U. S. so that she could rejoin her new husband. In one of the central episodes, Liza visits Pnin, arousing his hopes for a reconciliation, but all she wants is for Pnin to contribute money for the education of her son. He agrees because he and the boy love each other. " 'Doesn't she want to come back?' . . . Pnin, his head on his arm, started to beat the table with his loosely clenched fist. 'I haf nofing,' wailed Pnin between loud, damp sniffs, 'I haf nofing left, nofing, nofing!' " In the end the narrator, although he does not accept "Dr. Halp's theory of birth being an act of suicide on the part of the infant," admits he does not like happy endings. "We feel cheated. Harm is the norm. Doom should not jam." Pnin is ultimately neither mawkishly sentimental nor a joke; he abruptly leaves Waindell before the end of the semester rather than work as a subordinate to the new man, the narrator, who says, "There was simply no saying what miracle might happen."

The miracle is that he turns up as a colleague of John Shade and Charles Kinbote in Nabokov's next novel, *Pale Fire*. When at the age of sixty the proceeds from *Lolita* enabled him to retire from teaching, Nabokov (for family reasons) moved to Montreux, Switzerland, and wrote the book that was interrupted forty years before by the war (originally *Solus Rex*). More than any other of his books, *Pale Fire* lives up to his dictum that "Art is never simple. . . . Because, of course, art at its greatest is fantastically deceitful and complex." Its complexity baffled and annoyed many of its first readers. Mary McCarthy hailed it as "one of the very great works of art of this century"; others, like William Peden, considered it "withdrawn from humanity, grotesque and definitely diseased, as monstrous as a three-headed calf." McCarthy was right and Peden was wrong. *Pale Fire* is a dialectic made up of a 999-line autobiographical poem in rhymed couplets by John

Shade ("the hardest stuff I ever had to compose. . . . John Shade is by far the greatest of *invented* poets") and a foreword, commentary and index by Charles Kinbote (the invented identity of a sad, mad American scholar of Russian descent named V. Botkin). To put it another way, the poem "Pale Fire" is the thesis, and Kinbote's "scholarly apparatus" is the antithesis: the reader must merge them into the synthesis of the novel. *Pale Fire* is not primarily a satire on scholarly commentaries on literary works (like Nabokov's 4-vol. ed. of Pushkin's *Eugene Onegin*), nor a view of life in an American university, nor a psycho-social study of a monarch's exile from a country overrun by a Communist revolution, nor a comic case-study of a depraved homosexual—although it includes all these motifs and more. The principal cue to its real meaning is one which Mary McCarthy missed in her first review: the title. Shade says, "But *this* transparent thingum does require/Some moondrop title. Help me, Will! *Pale Fire*." Will is, of course, Shakespeare, and the title comes from *Timon of Athens*, IV, iii:

> The sun's a thief, and with his great attraction
> Robs the vast sea; the moon's an arrant thief,
> And her pale fire she snatches from the sun.

Kinbote, a paranoid pederast who imagines himself to be the exiled king of Zembla and who distorts Shade's poem into a story of *his* life, glosses these lines as follows: " . . . in which of the Bard's works did our poet cull [the title]? My readers must make their own research. All I have with me is a tiny vest pocket edition of *Timon of Athens*—in Zemblan! It certainly contains nothing that could be regarded as an equivalent of 'pale fire.' " He goes on to describe the Zemblan translator, named Conmal ("con"—to peruse, study; "mal"—bad, evil), one of the amusing word-plays which abound in the novel. The appropriate interpretation of Shade's lines is: the sun may be a thief but is the source of vitality, drawing moisture from the sea only that it may be returned to fructify the earth; but the moon's an *arrant* thief, a parasite, a source of loony deceptions and inconstancies, a mere reflector rather than a source of light. Shade is a sun figure (there can be no shade without sun), who draws experience from reality, transforms it into genuine art, and returns it beautifully shaped to fructify human lives. Kinbote imposes his own fantasy upon reality, draws his light from Shade's poem. Ultimately, *Pale Fire* is a study of two kinds of imaginative creativity—one healthy and one sick.

Some egregious critics have been loony enough to think it is "possible, even probable," that Shade and his poem are "figments of Kinbote's imagination"; or, exactly the reverse, that "Shade has perpetrated his own 'stylistic' death within the novel, and he has then given us a new aspect of himself . . . (Kinbote and the commentary). . . . Kinbote is a pawn of Shade's design." But the title and its source properly interpreted rule out any such possibilities—suns are not moons, nor the reverse. To be sure, the two different kinds of creative imagination have a great deal in common, and the madness-poetry theme looms large in the novel—most explicitly in Kinbote's commentary on line 629, where he describes overhearing a dialogue in which Shade, obviously referring to Kinbote, says, "Madman . . . is the wrong word. One should not apply it to a person who deliberately peels off a drab and unhappy past and replaces it with a brilliant invention." When Shade is startled to see Kinbote on the scene, Eberthella H. saves the situation with the remark, "You must help us, Mr. Kinbote: I maintain that . . . [the stationmaster] who thought he was God and began redirecting the trains was technically a loony, but John calls him a fellow poet." Kinbote replies, "We are all, in a sense, poets, Madam." Here in a nutshell are the central issues of *Pale Fire's* plot and theme. The sanest and most compassionate character in the story identifies Kinbote's fantasies about being the exiled king of Zembla as merely "a brilliant invention," but understands and sympathizes with his need for such an invention. (Nabokov once said, "Some of my more responsible characters are given some of my own ideas . . . John Shade does borrow some of my opinions.") But this does not make their inventions alike. Both Shade and Kinbote present fictions, but though Shade changes names of people and places (e.g., his typist Jane Provost is renamed Jane Dean), he is creating a work of art, a poem, which is not required to have any one-for-one correspondence with historical reality. But Kinbote, who is unable to give a specific location for Zembla, is purporting to engage in scholarship which is obligated to be specific and accurate. Shade may legitimately refer to Ithaca as New Wye and Cornell as Wordsmith without in any way rendering his work suspect; but his commentator does not have that right or privilege. When Shade insists that the madman is a poet, too, he calls attention to the strange and grotesque correlation between the two imaginative modes of thought. He, too, has been tempted to see a reality in the bizarre worlds that the imagination of a sick mind conjures up. When he suffered a stroke, he had a vision of a fountain; later he read an account of a woman who while technically dead had a similar vision. But his attempt to get confirmation of the existence of a life beyond the mortal one led only to the discovery of a misprint ("mountain, not fountain"):

> Life Everlasting—based on a misprint!
> I mused as I drove homeward: take the hint,
> And stop investigating my abyss?
> But all at once it dawned on me that *this*
> Was the real point, the contrapuntal theme;
> Just this: not text, but texture! not the dream
> But topsy-turvical coincidence,
> Not flimsy nonsense, but a web of sense.
> Yes! It sufficed that I in life could find
> Some kind of link-and-bobolink, some kind
> Of correlated pattern in the game,
> Plexed artistry, and something of the same
> Pleasure in it as they who played it found.

But topsy-turvical coincidence is precisely what Kinbote converts into contingency; when he goes to assist the Shades in getting their car going, he slips and falls in the snow. "My fall acted as a chemical reagent on the Shades' sedan, which forthwith budged and almost ran me over." He constantly confuses the carousel inside and outside his head: "Let me state that without my notes, Shade's text simply has no human reality at all." On the other hand, Shade is careful not to convert topsy-turvical coincidence into cause-and-effect. For example, when he "replays" his heart attack during his poetry lecture at the Crashaw Club: "Again I stepped / Down from the platform, and felt strange and hot, / And saw that chap stand up, and toppled, not / Because a heckler pointed with his pipe, / But probably because the time was ripe / For just that bump and wobble on the part / Of a limp blimp, an old unstable heart."

Shade's poem, "Pale Fire," is among the most remarkable and most beautiful poems in rhymed couplets in the English language. The rhymes are not at all Popean; there is no iambic pentameter beating its tum-ta-tum-ta-tum to an end stop at the end of the line. The variations in rhythm and the freely modulated caesuras capture the flow of normal, though heightened, speech, and the voice of the speaker comes through—an immensely sympathetic personality. He is a man who has endured both love and anguish in their most extreme forms and has probed honestly and deeply into the meaning of life, without in the process forgetting to live it! Each of the four cantos presents an aspect of his philosophy together with the life experiences from which it is derived: Canto I, Appearance and Reality/Childhood and Illness; Canto II, Love, Death, and the After-life/Courtship, Marriage, and the Death of his child; Canto III, Time, Mutability, and Contingency/His Heart Attack and the Discovery of the Misprint; Canto IV, Aesthetics and the Relation of Art to Reality/the Composition of "Pale Fire." The whole thing is a marvelous, self-contained whole—a work of art that has a meaning of its own, while at the same time serving as the thesis which the reader merges with Kinbote's antithesis to form the synthesis of the novel. The justly famous opening lines of Canto I show how the waxwing who mistook the azure reflection of his world in the windowpane for reality smashed himself to death. But the poet who knows that the reflection of the world in that same glass is an illusion can observe its curious effects and delight in them—and survive to make further images of them in language. In Canto II, Shade tells of his daughter's death with a beautifully controlled poignancy and not a trace of sentimentality. Nothing in modern literature rivals it, except perhaps Agee's *A Death in the Family*. Canto III is, among other things, a brilliant satire on those who, like the woman in Wallace Stevens's "Sunday Morning," long for a vally-hally of changelessness. Shade goes to lecture at the Institute of Preparation for the Hereafter, I.P.H., the big IF of eternity, symbolized by the yew tree called *l'if* in French, Rabelais' grand potato (*le grand peutetre*). And in Canto IV, he makes an aesthetic rather than a metaphysic out of topsy-turvical coincidence, metamorphosing himself and his reality with his versipal verse. And in the substratum of his creative process is love, his wife Sybil (in contrast with the paranoid hatred that informs Kinbote's creativity). The poem ends on a magnificent note of *nunc dimittis*.

Kinbote, to his chagrin, discovers that he is never once cited in a poem crowded with references to Shade's colleagues and neighbors. Nothing could be farther from Shade's mind than that mad pederast—preterists are not interested in pederasts. Yet the poem does have some curious bobolinks with Kinbote's mad commentary, not the least of which is the way Shade's certainty that he will awake at 6 a.m. on July 22 and that the next day will probably be fine, is rendered ironic in the larger context of the novel, when he becomes a victim of topsy-turvical coincidence. He is shot by Jack Grey, a madman who mistakes him for the Judge Goldsworth who had sentenced him and in whose house Kinbote lives. Another madman, Kinbote, is certain that the killer is Jacob Gradus, a Zemblan assassin who was really trying to kill *him*, Charles the Beloved. Hidden in Kinbote's paranoid fantasies is a pathetic, deeply troubled, suffering soul (for whom Shade had great

compassion), but on the surface it is an intricate and amazing paper chase, a closed circle utterly without relation to reality. One of the most amusing cues to that truth is the entry "Crown Jewels" in Kinbote's index: see Hiding Place/*potaynik* (q.v.)/*taynik* (q.v.)/and finally Russ., secret place; see Crown Jewels! Unlike Shade, Kinbote does not observe, respond to, and draw from the real world; he makes of it a stage on which he enacts his own fantasies (Charles the Beloved fled from Zembla through a theater, and theatrical images abound in his account). His homosexual obsessions drive him to all sorts of paranoid distortions and misperceptions, especially in his unrequited love for John Shade and his resentment of Shade's wife Sybil. He says (note to 1.247), "From the very first I tried to behave with the utmost courtesy toward my friend's wife, and from the very first she disliked and distrusted me." But in the foreword, he reported that at their first meeting Sybil said, " 'Have a drink with us' . . . . I explained that I could not stay long as I was about to have a kind of little seminar at home followed by some table tennis, with two charming identical twins and another boy, another boy." Only when Sybil discovered that Kinbote was a pervert who plied Shade with alcohol (forbidden by his doctors) and intruded on his creativity did she adopt the role of her husband's protector.

Kinbote reports, with every confidence that the reader will regard them as preposterous, references to his madness. A woman in a grocery store said, "You are a remarkably disagreeable person. I fail to see how John and Sybil can stand you. . . . What's more, you are insane!" He once found in his coat pocket "a brutal anonymous note saying: 'You have hal . . . . . s real bad, chum,' meaning evidently 'hallucinations.' " The reference was to halitosis, but the misinterpretation is revealing, for as Kinbote writes his book he is gradually breaking down—his migraines are killing him ("Dear Jesus, do something. . . . These excruciating headaches now make impossible the mnemonic effort and eye strain. . . . My notes and self are petering out"). In fact, Nabokov told Alfred Appel that "Kinbote committed suicide."

Mirror images abound in the novel; the great mirror maker in Zembla is Sudarg of Bokay, whose name reversed yields Jacob Gradus the assassin—but both are figments of Kinbote's diseased imagination. It is possible to see Shade and Kinbote as reverse mirror images of each other, but hardly as two aspects of an individual personality. As Nabokov also said to Appel, "The *Doppleganger* subject is a frightful bore. . . . Philosophically, I am an indivisible monist." And to Herbert Gold he issued an indirect admonition to all critics when he said of Mary McCarthy, "I do think she added quite a bit of her own angelica to the pale fire of Kinbote's plum pudding." Nevertheless, whatever one makes of it, Shade and Kinbote are as opposite as two human beings can be. Shade is heterosexual, married, family-oriented; Kinbote is a homosexual with a history of family discord. Shade is gregarious, friendly and at ease with others, kind and generous; Kinbote is a social pariah, demanding and tense. Shade has a sick body, but a healthy mind in tune with nature; Kinbote has a healthy, athletic body, but a sick mind and fears nature. Shade is a scientifically oriented skeptic with a contempt for traditional religions ("No free man needs a God"); Kinbote is a Christian ("one is bound to question the wisdom of this easy aphorism"). Perhaps the ultimate difference is that Shade is a poet-creator; Kinbote is a critic-commentator.

One of the most insightful comments on Nabokov's greatest achievement is that of Robert Alter: "*Pale Fire*, written after half a century of violent revolution, world war, totalitarian terror, and the genocidal slaughter of millions . . . is very much a self-conscious novel of our times. Its display of the writer's blue magic of word-and-image play is a dazzling delight; its affirmation of the abiding beauty of life in the imagination is brilliantly enacted in the fiction; but after the last glitter of the prestidigitator's implements, it is the shadow of the assassin that falls on the final page. . . . Our vision of the imagination, through the history-haunted quixoticism of this self-conscious novel, has been both enlarged and subtly, somberly transformed; and that is precisely what the novelistic enterprise, from the seventeenth century to our own age, has at its best achieved."

As he approached the age of seventy, Nabokov pulled out all the stops and indulged himself in his longest, loosest, sexiest, most poetic and most philosophical novel, *Ada, or Ardor: A Family Chronicle*. More than any of his other works, it requires of the reader immense patience, endurance, tolerance, and knowledge—of various languages (French, German, Russian, Dutch), the history of European literature (especially Tolstoy, Flaubert, Chateaubriand, Marvell, Baudelaire, and Byron, but allusions to hundreds of writers abound), the history of art, science fiction, lepidopterology, the philosophy of time. But, as Alfred Kazin said, "*Ada* is not so much 'difficult' as wildly slippery, deceptive, a great tease of a book . . . it is preposterously erudite, showy and omniscient . . . it is enchanting even when

one is helpless skidding down VV's linguistic roller coasters."

As in the manner of several of Nabokov's earlier books, *Ada* is the memoir of Dr. Ivan (Van) Demonovitch Veen (with comments and interpolations by his sister Ada), edited clumsily after his death by one Ronald Oranger (whose name Robert Alter anagrammatizes to "angel nor ardor," a reversal of the book's title). The main action deals with the life-long passionate incest of Van and his sister, people whom Nabokov does not like. In a *Time* interview he expressed resentment of the way "Updike absurdly suggests that my fictional character, bitchy and lewd Ada, is . . . Nabokov's wife," and he said, "I loathe Van Veen." This is Van's book, not Nabokov's—a fictional *Speak, Memory* by a man who has "less control over his imagination than I." And Nabokov no more endorses the incest than he does the nympholepsy of *Lolita*: "Actually, I don't give a damn for incest one way or another. I merely like the "bl" sounds in siblings, bloom, blue, bliss, sable." He did not include in that sample list blather, blockhead, bladderwort, bleed, blind, or ablative.

Ada consists of five uneven, loosely related parts, each considerably shorter than the one preceding it. The events take place in a country called Amerussia on the planet Antiterra. Part One, more than half the novel, is a *Bildungsroman* of Van, scion of the aristocratic Veen-Durmanovs ("durman" means "narcotic"), who as a teenager in 1884 visits his uncle's opulent country home, Ardis Hall, where he falls in love with his twelve-year-old "cousin" Ada. Each seeks, but fails to find, an equivalent bliss in other lovers; both, separately and together, make love to their half-sister Lucette (who later commits suicide when she is brutally rejected by Van). Unable to bear Ada's infidelities, Van is wounded in a duel with her lover Percy de Prey, rushes off to Manhattan where he has an affair, does research in the public library and becomes "pregnant" with his first book. In Part Two, Van is tricked into returning to Ardis in 1892 by a servant, resumes his incestuous love, and is blackmailed by the servant who has made photographs of their lovemaking. In response to his father's pleas, Van once again forsakes Ada. Part Three depicts Van's academic career and Ada's marriage to Andrey Vinelander, and the reunion of the lovers in 1922 after the death of Ada's husband. Part Four is Van's account of his fantastic philosophical treatise, *The Texture of Time* (1924), in which he quotes—but misunderstands—John Shade's "Pale Fire." Van says, "I cannot imagine Space without Time, but I can very well imagine Time without Space. 'Space-Time'—that hideous hybrid whose very hyphen looks phoney. One can be a hater of Space, and a lover of Time.'' Part Five depicts a birthday party celebration of Van's completion of the memoir we are reading; he is 97, Ada is 95, and they have lived together as ardent lovers for forty-five years.

Not all the Nabokov idolators agree with Alfred Appel's judgment that ''like *The Tempest*, an earlier physics fiction, *Ada* is a culminating work . . . a great work of art . . . affirming the power of love and imagination.'' Robert Alter, though he finds it ''an achievement that has very few equals in the history of the novel,'' nevertheless feels that *Ada* ''pays a price for being an extended poetic vision of Eden: Van and Ada seem . . . less interesting individually, less engaging, than many of Nabokov's previous protagonists.'' Others have been less reserved in their condemnation. Morris Dickstein says, *''Ada* marks the betrayal of the Nabokov who wrote *Lolita* and *Pnin*, whose calculations kept touch with human feelings and predicaments, whose aestheticism could therefore issue in artistic and human wholeness. It is the hollow triumph of that other Nabokov, the formal trickster, exotic pedant, and language gamester.'' Philip Toynbee finds it ''marvellous—and appalling. *Ada* is appalling because it is a piece of unremitting exhibitionism—and in all the known senses of that compendious word.''

Ada is a loose, rambling account of the perverse triumph of antiterran vitality; *Transparent Things* is a tightly-knit account of the perverse triumph of earthly death. G. M. Hyde considers it Nabokov's real novel of valediction (and the last novel, *Look at the Harlequins!*, a sort of annotated index to his oeuvres). The central character is Hugh Person (you, nobody), an editor, among whose clients is a Mr. R. (which reversed is the Russian symbol for ''ya,'' meaning ''I''), who is a distorted mirror image of Nabokov himself—in his last book Mr. R. refers to one Adam von Librikov, a perfect anagram. The events occur primarily during Person's four visits, chronologically disarranged, to Trux, Switzerland (which, like Mont Roux in *Ada*, is obviously Montreux).

Everybody dies, each in a different way. Minor characters at a distance; one in ''a hot dirty hospital on Formosa,'' another ''buried under six feet of snow in Chute, Colorado.'' Mr. R., his ''wretched liver as heavy as a rejected manuscript,'' meditates on his deathbed: ''The entire solar system is but a reflection in the crystal of my (or your) wrist watch. The more I shrivel, the bigger I grow. Total rejection of all religions ever dreamt up by man and total

composure in the face of total death!'' When Hugh Person is twenty-two, his father dies of a heart attack while trying on a pair of trousers in a Swiss clothing store. Hugh feels liberated, picks up a prostitute and moves directly from virginity to impotence. He marries Armande Chamar, the most despicable female in all Nabokov, a woman who continues to have affairs but makes love with her husband only at teatime in the living room with both parties fully clothed. ''Our Person's capacity to condone all this . . . endears him to us, but also provokes limpid mirth, alas, at times. For example, he told himself that she refused to strip because she was shy of her tiny pouting breasts and the scar of a ski accident along her thigh. Silly Person!'' In a nightmare paroxysm of hatred, Person strangles her to death and spends five years shuttling from prison to madhouse until he is exonerated. On his last nostalgic visit to Trux to recover his past, Person finds nobody who remembers him—even the hotel director has died. In the end he dies in a hotel fire, but Nabokov, as he has done with so many of his earlier protagonists, saves him by transfiguration from the agony of total demise by making him a transparent thing: ''This is, I believe, *it*; not the crude anguish of physical death but the incomparable pangs of the mysterious mental maneuver needed to pass from one state of being to another. Easy, you know, does it, son.'' Robert Alter finds *Transparent Things* ''a beautiful instance of Nabokov's mastery—deftly controlled, amazingly inventive, and finally poignant through all the complexities of its intellectual design.''

Although *Ada* and *Transparent Things* include ironic self-portraits and allusions to Nabokov's other works, they nevertheless have a self-sufficient meaning and are a pleasure to read in their own right; not so with *Look at the Harlequins!* No one who is not intimately familiar with the Nabokov canon should bother with it. The narrator, one Vladimir Vladimirovich N————, known as Vadim McNab, cannot remember his real last name; is it Nebesnyy? Nabedrin? Nablidze? Naborcroft? After the title page appears a list of other books by the narrator, including six in Russian under the pen name of V. Irisin among which we find *Tamara*, which is the name of Nabokov's teenage sweetheart in St. Petersburg and corresponds to his first novel *Mashenka (Mary)*; *Pawn Takes Queen*, a pseudo-title for *King, Queen, Knave*; and *Camera Lucida* (Slaughter in the Sun), equivalent of *Camera Obscura* (Laughter in the Dark). The English titles include *A Kingdom by the Sea* and *Ardis*, which correspond to *Pale Fire* and *Ada*. But only a Nabokov aficionado could experience the thrill of cognition. At one point the narrator confesses, "I was bothered . . . by a dream feeling that my life was the non-identical twin, a parody, an inferior variant of another man's life, somewhere on this or another earth. A demon, I felt, was forcing me to impersonate that other man, that other writer who was and would always be incomparably greater, healthier and crueler than your obedient servant." Although there are enormous differences between Vadim McNab and Vladimir Nabokov, they share two basic characteristics: an aesthetic philosophy and a profound uxoriousness and love of family. Vadim's great-aunt tells him, "Look at the harlequins! . . . Everywhere. All around you. Trees are harlequins, words are harlequins. So are the situations and sums. Put two things together—jokes, images—and you get a triple harlequin. Come on! Play! Invent the world! Invent reality!" And that is what Nabokov has always done, what he was forced to do ever since the Bolshevik revolution evicted him from the Russian reality he so loved. In *Look at the Harlequins!* he gave us in a hermetically private, recondite manner a work that confirms his self-estimate: "While I keep everything on the brink of parody, there must be on the other hand an abyss of seriousness, and I must make my way along this narrow ridge between my own truth and the caricature of it. . . . Looking at it objectively, I have never seen a more lucid, more lonely, better balanced mad mind than mine."

R. Z. Sheppard's obituary in *Time* magazine concludes with the most appropriate final word: "Nabokov crossed too many borders to have been a winner in the geopolitics of the Nobel Prize. Yet he gave a prize greater than any he might have received: his challenging, intricate fiction, which miraculously demonstrates that art is not a mirror held up to nature, but rather a prism that refracts blinding reality into rainbows of wisdom and feeling."

Other Works:

Poems (in Russian) (St. Petersburg: privately printed, 1916);

Two Paths. An Almanac (Petrograd: M. S. Pearson, 1918);

The Empyrean Path (in Russian) (Berlin: Grani, 1923);

The Cluster (Berlin: Gamayun, 1923);

Nikolai Gogol (New York: New Directions, 1944; London: Editions Poetry, 1947);

Nine Stories (Norfolk, Conn.: New Directions, 1947);

Poems 1929-51 (in Russian) (Paris: Rifma, 1952);

Nabokov's Dozen (Garden City: Doubleday, 1958);

Poems (Garden City: Doubleday, 1959; London: Weidenfeld & Nicolson, 1961);

Nabokov's Quartet (New York: Phaedra, 1966; London: Weidenfeld & Nicolson, 1967);

Poems and Problems (New York: McGraw-Hill, 1971; London: Weidenfeld & Nicolson, 1971);

A Russian Beauty and Other Stories (New York: McGraw-Hill, 1973; London: Weidenfeld & Nicolson, 1973);

Tyrants Destroyed and Other Stories (New York: McGraw-Hill, 1975; London: Weidenfeld & Nicolson, 1975).

Other:

Lewis Carroll, *Alice in Wonderland,* translated into Russian by Nabokov (Berlin: Gamayun, 1923);

Three Russian Poets: Pushkin, Lermontov, Tiutchev, translated by Nabokov (Norfolk, Conn.: New Directions, 1944; London: Lindsay Drummond, 1947);

Mikhail Lermontov, *A Hero of Our Time,* translated by Nabokov (Garden City: Doubleday, 1958; London: Mayflower, 1958);

Anonymous, *The Song of Igor's Campaign,* translated by Nabokov (New York: Vintage, 1960; London: Weidenfeld & Nicolson, 1960).

References:

Alfred Appel, Jr., ed., *The Annotated Lolita* (New York: McGraw-Hill, 1970);

Appel and Charles Newman, eds., *Nabokov: Criticisms, Reminiscences, Translations & Tributes* (Evanston, Ill.: Northwestern University Press, 1970);

Appel, *Nabokov's Dark Cinema* (New York: Oxford University Press, 1972);

Julia Bader, *Crystal Land: Artifice in Nabokov's English Novels* (Berkeley: University of California Press, 1972);

L. S. Dembo, ed., *Nabokov: The Man & His Work* (Madison: University of Wisconsin Press, 1967);

Andrew Field, *Nabokov: His Life in Art* (Boston: Little, Brown, 1967);

Field, *Nabokov: His Life in Part* (New York: Viking, 1977);

Douglas Fowler, *Reading Nabokov* (Ithaca, N.Y.: Cornell University Press, 1974);

Jane Grayson, *Nabokov Translated: A Comparison of Nabokov's Russian and English Prose*

(London: Oxford University Press, 1976);

G. M. Hyde, *Vladimir Nabokov: America's Russian Novelist* (London: Boyars, 1978);

L. L. Lee, *Vladimir Nabokov* (Boston: Twayne, 1976);

Jessie Thomas Lokrantz, *The Underside of the Weave: Some Stylistic Devices Used by Vladimir Nabokov* (Uppsala, Sweden: Acta Universitatis Upsaliensis, 1973);

Bobbie Ann Mason, *Nabokov's Garden: A Guide to Ada* (Ann Arbor, Mich.: Ardis Press, 1974);

Donald E. Morton, *Vladimir Nabokov* (New York: Frederick Ungar, 1974);

Julian Moynahan, *Vladimir Nabokov* (Minneapolis: University of Minnesota Press, 1971);

Carl Proffer, *Keys to Lolita* (Bloomington: Indiana University Press, 1968);

Proffer, ed., *A Book of Things About Vladimir Nabokov* (Ann Arbor, Mich.: Ardis Press, 1973);

William W. Rowe, *Nabokov's Deceptive World* (New York: New York University Press, 1971);

Page Stegner, *Escape Into Aesthetics: The Art of Vladimir Nabokov* (New York: William Morrow, 1966);

Stegner, ed., *Nabokov's Congeries* (New York: Viking, 1971).

Manuscripts:

The Library of Congress has a major collection of Nabokov's correspondence and manuscript notes; drafts, typescripts, and annotated galley proofs for English and foreign language editions of eleven books; and the screenplay for *Lolita*.

ANAIS NIN, author of fiction, criticism, and diaries, was born to artistic parents in Neuilly, France, outside Paris, on 21 February 1903. Her mother, Rosa Culmell Nin, a French-Dane, sang; her Spanish father, Joaquin, was a concert pianist and composer. Nin spent her first eleven years in France: when her father deserted the family, her mother took Nin and her brothers Joaquin and Thorvald to live in New York City. Nin enrolled in the public schools, but, as legend has it, she found that education not to her liking, withdrew from John Jasper School (P.S. 9) in 1918, and became an autodidact in the public libraries. Approximately five years later, around age twenty-one, she married Hugh Guiler, a Philadelphian who, as Ian Hugo, became known as a filmmaker, engraver, and illustrator of Nin's books. She moved to Paris sometime thereafter, presumably with her husband. Little is known of Nin's life in the 1920s—where she lived, who her friends were, what she was doing, what her relationship was with her husband—but at least part of the surface of her life may be documented after 1930 in her *Diary*, although it should not be read for factual accuracy.

Nin's lifelong friendship with Henry Miller began in Paris in the early 1930s. By 1930 Nin was a published author, but she apparently had no contact with other writers. When they met, Miller, a dozen years her senior, was a penurious would-be novelist, but she saw in his work qualities others did not, assisted him in publishing his first novel, and wrote a preface to it. That book was the great and infamous *Tropic of Cancer* (1934). The two were seeming opposites: Nin was personally elegant, Miller was not; she was selective, Miller voracious; in their writings Nin was implicit, Miller explicit; she was sensual, he sexual. But despite these and other differences Nin and Miller inspired each other, and each performed as a sounding board for the other's ideas: Miller worked on Nin's *House of Incest*, and her influence is obvious in *Black Spring*, a novel he dedicated to her. Through their long friendship—the true nature of which remains unknown—their correspondence, and their interest in each other's work, this unlikely pair nourished each other for over three decades.

Two of Nin's most important acquaintances in Paris were Rene Allendy and Otto Rank, her psychiatrists. Their influence may be discerned throughout her work. Other important non-literary/artistic friends of Nin's in Paris were Miller's second wife, June, and a Peruvian Marxist, Gonzalo More, both of whom figure prominently in the *Diary*. Among Nin's other literary/artistic friends were the young Lawrence Durrell, Antonin Artaud, Alfred Perles, and Michael Fraenkel; together they and others formed a coterie—the first such group in Paris since Hemingway and Fitzgerald left that city for America—that provided the inspiration and sustenance Nin needed to develop artistically. Since none of these writers' works was then attractive to commercial publishers, certain of them established the Villa Seurat Library for Jack Kahane's Obelisk Press and published Miller's *Max and the White Phagocytes* (1938), Durrell's *The Black Book* (1938), and Nin's *The Winter of Artifice* (1939). In addition, they ran a little magazine entitled *The Booster* (later *Delta*) that Nin considered frivolous, as it was. At the outbreak of World War II, after a fruitful decade in Paris, Nin left

Anais Nin with her diary.

Jill Krementz

Europe for the United States where she would spend most of her remaining years.

Upon her return to America Nin found a pragmatic people too concerned with hostility to appreciate her fiction that deals with the human (and mostly feminine) psyche. In order to make her work available, albeit to a limited audience, she established the Gemor Press in New York and printed her own books in handsome limited editions that are now collectors' items. From the mid-1940s until the mid-1950s she had commercial publishers, but it was not until after the farsighted Alan Swallow became her publisher in 1961 that all of her fiction became available, as it remains today. She had been

writing for over thirty years to a small but devoted following when the first volume of her *Diary* was published in 1966. That and the subsequent five published volumes brought her a readership of considerable magnitude and of a quality that might be termed cultish. As a result of this popularity she frequently appeared as lecturer on college campuses and served as an introducer of works by other authors. Nin died of cancer in Los Angeles on 14 January 1977 at the height of her popularity.

Nin's major works are two volumes of quasi-literary criticism, a prose-poem, a collection of novelettes, two collections of stories, six novels, a volume of erotica, and seven volumes, so far, of her

Diary. Her first book (1932) was a modest analysis of D. H. Lawrence. She offered an appropriate description of her book, purportedly written in sixteen days, in its subtitle: an unprofessional study. *D. H. Lawrence* is valuable not so much for Nin's insights into his writings but because it reveals how much he influenced her: she shared with him belief in the value of the subconscious, myth, progression, and the recognition of the physical. Nin published two pamphlets—*Realism and Reality* (1946) and *On Writing* (1947)—in which she made her first theoretical comments on her own work, and they formed the basis for her mistitled *The Novel of the Future* (1968), a book less about the novel's future than about her own work. Her attitudes therein are idiosyncratic and occasionally self-serving. Foremost among the contemporary writers she admired most, she wrote, was Marguerite Young.

Nin was not a literary critic (nor much of a self-critic either), but she was a great writer of psychological fiction, a fact unrecognized by most, including many of her intimates who prefer the myth of the *Diary* to the truth of the fiction. Nin's fiction was never popular, but understandably so: she wrote about psychological reality, not the surface reality that she called realism and that most readers desire. Her work challenges the reader and involves him in the creative act. By far her best piece of fiction was her first, *The House of Incest* (1936). This surrealistic prose-poem relates an unnamed woman's nightmare as she encounters Sabina and Jeanne and visits the house of incest where all is death. Finally, a dancer, a woman who had lost her arms because she had been too possessive, regains them, dances *with* music (in rhythm with the nature of things), and leaves the house of incest through a tunnel that leads to daylight and life. Here Nin perfectly fused manner and matter, form and content. She published no other prose-poem, a genre she exploited once with finesse.

Her second volume of fiction, and the last of her three books first published in Paris, was *The Winter of Artifice* (1939), a collection of three novelettes: "Djuna," "Lilith," and "The Voice." Of all her creations she had the most difficulty with this one. It was the first volume she published at the Gemor Press (1942), but it then contained only two novelettes, one without title that was originally "Lilith," and "The Voice," both revised from the 1939 texts. *Winter of Artifice* next appeared in 1961 with "Stella" added as a third novelette, and since then the contents have remained uniform. Stella is a movie star dwarfed by her screen image and thus filled with self-doubt; she must attempt to develop her atrophied self into wholeness. Her problem developed when her father deserted his family during her girlhood. That same father is presented fully in "Winter of Artifice" (originally "Lilith"), and the unnamed woman resembling Stella has avoided life in order to protect herself from the pain she felt when her father deserted her. "The Voice" shows several characters attempting to find wholeness in life with the assistance of a psychiatrist, the voice.

In the late 1930s and early 1940s Nin was writing in yet another genre, short stories, and in 1944 she collected the best ones into *Under a Glass Bell*. As did *Winter of Artifice*, so, too, did this collection change contents through its various editions; here the additions were decidedly inferior to the original eight stories. "Houseboat" and "Under a Glass Bell" are among Nin's most felicitous pieces of fiction, but her best story is "Birth," the last one in the collection. This is as powerful and moving a story as has ever been written: a woman six-months pregnant experiences four hours of agony giving birth to a still-born girl. But Nin intended, as always, much more than the surface of her creations suggests. The woman's life is being threatened by the dead fetus, and she has been reluctant to pass the dead child from her protective womb. She realizes subconsciously that the girl is in fact her own undeveloped self, and after she is finally able to work with nature and rid herself of her dead past she will be able to face life's complexities as a mature woman, not as a child. This story concludes *Under a Glass Bell* on the same optimistic note that the dancer provides *House of Incest*. (*Waste of Timelessness*, a collection of Nin's early and unsatisfactory stories, was published after her death in 1977.)

Nin's most ambitious fictional effort was *Cities of the Interior*, a continuous novel of five parts published irregularly between 1946 and 1961. Each volume is a discrete unit, although each is similar in theme and character to the others. The collective title is appropriate because Nin was always concerned with the inner lives of her women characters, as she stated eloquently in the prologue to her first novel:

> I have to begin where everything begins, in the blindness and in the shadows. I have to begin the story of women's development where all things begin: in nature, at the roots. It is necessary to return to the origin of confusion, which is woman's struggle to understand her own nature. Man struggled with nature, fought the elements with his objectivity, his inventions, and mastered them. Woman has not been able to organize her own nature, her simoons, her tornadoes,

her obscurantisms, because she lacked the eye of consciousness. She was nature. Man did not help her in this because his interpretations, whether psychological, or intellectual, or artistic, did not seize her. And she could not speak for herself.

Today marvellous women speak for themselves in terms of heroic action, integrating the woman, mother, wife, in harmonious relation to history, to larger worlds of art and science. But many more, when entering action or creation, followed man's patterns and could not carry along or integrate within them the feminine part of themselves. Action and creation, for woman, was man—or an imitation of man. In this imitation of man she lost contact with her nature and her relation to man.

Man appears only partially in this volume, because for the woman at war with herself, he can only appear thus, not as an entity. Woman at war with herself, has not yet been related to man, only to the child in man, being capable only of maternity.

This novel deals with the negative pole, the pole of confused and twisted nature.

The mirrors in the garden are the mirrors women must look into before they can go further. This is only the story of the mirrors and nature in opposition, and in the mirrors is only what woman dares to see . . . so far an incomplete woman.

Nin weaves three women through *Cities of the Interior* as the major characters, each in search of her own roots. As Nin once stated, Djuna is inhibited by her reflective nature, Lillian is violent yet unaware, and Sabina acts out her fantasies to her detriment. These women interact with themselves and others (and especially with the most important man, Jay) throughout the five volumes until Lillian alone is able to perceive the unity of nature with the assistance of a Mexican doctor and therefore ceases "defending herself against her own nature. . . ."

"Lillian was always in a state of fermentation." So begins *Ladders to Fire* (1946), Nin's first novel, that develops Lillian's discontentment with her husband, Larry, her lack of satisfaction with her lover, Gerard, and her unhappiness with her family. Her quest for the ideal lover blinds her to the necessity of accepting life's imperfections. Sabina and Jay are also present, but as the novel reaches its climax in the famous party scene Djuna assumes paramount importance. All characters but she have lost contact with themselves. She is also the major figure in Nin's second novel, *Children of the Albatross* (1947). Djuna's incomplete state was caused by her father's

deserting his family when she was sixteen. From that time she failed to grow psychologically, mistrusted mature men (father figures), and kept the company of adolescent, phosphorescent, non-threatening boys. She functions with them as a mother, but at the novel's conclusion she is isolated in the cities of her interior while Sabina continues her incendiary actions and Lillian alone is making progress toward wholeness.

Djuna is again the major female character in Nin's third novel, *The Four-Chambered Heart* (1950), but she shares Nin's attention with Rango, a Guatemalan guitarist who thinks himself a political activist, who is married to the sick Zora, and who is Djuna's lover aboard a houseboat on the Seine. Theirs is a meeting of opposites: he is an unsophisticated man of the body; she is a cultivated, reflective woman. They are, symbolically, Lawrence's gypsy and the virgin, and although they cannot sustain their love, Djuna comes to a self-awareness that suggests subsequent wholeness.

Nin's most popular novel has been *A Spy in the House of Love* (1954). Sabina—a woman in search of passion, a female Don Juan—is the major character. She is married to the secure yet insensitive Alan, and to find sexual and psychological fulfillment she takes a series of lovers of diminishing quality until, at the end, she is devastated to learn from Djuna and a character named the Lie Detector that in loving many she has not loved at all.

Cities of the Interior concludes with *Seduction of the Minotaur* (1961; published in shorter form as *Solar Barque* in 1958). Lillian, a pianist, travels to Mexico for a musical engagement; there she meets Dr. Hernandez, the man whose life and death will change her life. He tends to the Mexicans' bodily ills, but he is also active in defying those who deal in illegal drugs. He has difficulties with his own family, but he is at one with nature and himself, and when the drug dealers kill him, Lillian is shocked into recognizing "the preciousness of human love and human life," returns home to her husband Larry, and with him she grows into the only complete woman in *Cities of the Interior*. She has been able to progress from childhood, as imposed upon her by her mother, into maturity. Djuna and Sabina never reach this state that is seemingly simple but is actually difficult to attain.

Nin wrote one more novel after *Cities of the Interior*. In *Collages* (1964) she attempted what was for her a new kind of novel with all of her stock characters absent: it is a pastiche of sketches (collages) with Renate as the central character. Nin intended this to be a humorous book, but it is best

Anais Nin.

Layle Silbert

considered as a light-weight and flawed extension of the themes developed fully in her first five novels.

One final volume of Nin's fiction appeared shortly after her death. *Delta of Venus* (1977) includes selections from erotica she wrote for a dollar a page in the 1940s for a patron who encouraged her to delete poetry and write sexually explicit material. Despite such desires Nin wrote in her usual manner, and what emerged was an erotica that while explicit is also elegant. She struggled for four decades to gain a wide readership; it is ironic that her erotica, written with no thought of publication, was on the best-seller list for over six months.

Before *Delta of Venus* Nin's most popular work was her *Diary*, published in six volumes between 1966 and 1976, that details highly selective aspects of her life from 1931 to 1966. These volumes, that diminish gradually yet consistently in quality as they progress, were expertly excerpted from a much larger manuscript version by Nin and her co-editor Gunther Stuhlmann, but because a hand other than the author's was present in their preparation, certain critical questions are raised that have never been answered adequately. These have to do largely with verisimilitude, honesty, hindsight, and structure. Aside from the author herself, the greatest figure therein is certainly Henry Miller, but as he and others from her early years in Paris recede, so too does the force of her writing and the magnitude of the persona, despite the fact that, in her own eyes, she grew progressively as an individual from volume to volume. The *Diary* may not, as Miller thought it would, "take its place beside the revelations of St. Augustine, Petronius, Abelard, Rousseau, Proust, and others," but it is, especially in the first two volumes, a magnificent picture of a woman and of an age.

Anais Nin's art is indebted most obviously to the surrealists, to psychoanalysis, and to Lawrence, and while her fiction may at first seem impenetrable because of its lack of surface reality, an attentive reading reveals a powerful psychological reality that is the hallmark of her writing. Her female characters are consistently ill at ease with themselves; they attempt haphazardly to find contentment in lovers, analysis, art, or some other surrogate for their inner selves. They are not presented glamorously (although their physical trappings might well be attractive); instead, they are tormented until the last pages of *Seduction of the Minotaur* when Lillian discovers her own wholeness, and with that the continuous novel necessarily ends. The fictional women reflect many of the problems faced by the persona named Anais Nin in the *Diary* as she eliminates her insecurities and moves toward completeness with time. Despite this similarity between the main women in the different genres, and despite the fact that her fiction is presented as fiction and her *Diary* as nonfiction, the author was more open and honest in her fiction than in the *Diary*. In the former she was able to deal openly with the sometimes ugly and always difficult problems confronting her women, in part because she *qua* individual was protected behind the narrator's voice, but in the *Diary* the narrator bears the author's own name; and, in order to protect the real Anais Nin who created it, she shaped the persona into an outsized extension of herself who, while having obstacles such as the demented Artaud and Gonzalo, will, the reader knows, overcome them ultimately. There is much truth in the fiction, and there is as much fiction as truth in the impressive *Diary*. Of the fiction *House of Incest* is her greatest achievement by far.

Nin has not to this day been afforded adequate critical treatment. A favorable review of *Under a Glass Bell* by Edmund Wilson in the *New Yorker* evidently helped sell the book (it quickly went into a second edition), and it also drew some general attention to this already legendary writer. After that fleeting experience with popularity she was largely and undeservedly ignored by critics and readers alike until 1966, the year the first volume of her *Diary* appeared, but after that date—and with the advent of the women's movement in recent years—her readers burgeoned in number; but they have largely been devotees of the *Diary*, not of the fiction, and their attitude toward her and her work has often been one of adolescent adoration that evinces little hint of critical insight. The only books of criticism devoted to her are by Oliver Evans (1968), Evelyn J. Hinz (1971), and Robert Zaller (1974), and all three are worthwhile, although there seems to be an unofficial boycott of Evans' book by the faithful because it does not praise her work at every turn.

Anais Nin was for too long neglected, and she has been praised to excess recently for quite the wrong reasons. Her greatest value is as a legitimate cicerone through the feminine psyche, as an author who shows both women and men that the pursuit of one's completeness is a difficult task that must be undertaken, even though it is unpleasant and even though it might not be successful in the end. She was nonetheless an optimist in a landscape of psychological despair, and her vision was augmented by her dedication to moderation and understanding.

—*Benjamin Franklin V*

Books:

D. H. Lawrence An Unprofessional Study (Paris: Titus, 1932; Denver: Alan Swallow, 1964);

The House of Incest (Paris: Siana Editions, 1936; New York: Gemor, 1947);

The Winter of Artifice (Paris: Obelisk, 1939; New York: Gemor, 1942);

Under a Glass Bell (New York: Gemor, 1944; London: Editions Poetry, 1947);

This Hunger (New York: Gemor, 1945);

Ladders to Fire (New York: Dutton, 1946; London: Peter Owen, 1963);

Realism and Reality (Yonkers, N.Y.: Alicat, 1946);

Children of the Albatross (New York: Dutton, 1947; London: Peter Owen, 1959);

On Writing (Hanover, N.H.: Daniel Oliver, 1947);

The Four-Chambered Heart (New York: Duell, Sloan & Pearce, 1950; London: Peter Owen, 1959);

A Spy in the House of Love (Paris & New York: British Book Centre, 1954; London: Spearman, 1955);

Solar Barque (Ann Arbor, Mich.: Edwards Brothers, 1958);

Cities of the Interior (n.p., 1959);

Seduction of the Minotaur (Denver: Alan Swallow, 1961; London: Peter Owen, 1961);

Collages (Denver: Alan Swallow, 1964; London: Peter Owen, 1964);

The Diary of Anais Nin 1931-1934 (New York: Swallow/Harcourt, Brace & World, 1966; London: Peter Owen, 1966);

The Diary of Anais Nin 1934-1939 (New York: Swallow/Harcourt, Brace & World, 1967; London: Peter Owen, 1967);

The Novel of the Future (New York: Macmillan, 1968; London: Collier-MacMillan, 1968);

Unpublished Selections from the Diary (Athens, Ohio: Duane Schneider, 1968);

The Diary of Anais Nin 1939-1944 (New York: Harcourt, Brace & World, 1969; London: Peter Owen, 1970);

An Interview with Anais Nin (Athens, Ohio: Duane Schneider, 1970; London: Village, 1973);

Nuances (n.p.: Sans Souci, 1970);

The Diary of Anais Nin 1944-1947 (New York: Harcourt Brace Jovanovich, 1971; London: Peter Owen, 1972);

Paris Revisited (Santa Barbara, Cal.: Capra, 1972; London: Village, 1974);

Anais Nin Reader, ed. Philip K. Jason (Chicago: Swallow, 1973);

The Diary of Anais Nin 1947-1955 (New York: Harcourt Brace Jovanovich, 1974; London: Peter Owen, 1974);

A Photographic Supplement to the Diary of Anais Nin (New York: Harcourt Brace Jovanovich, 1974);

A Woman Speaks The Lectures, Seminars, and Interviews of Anais Nin, ed. Evelyn J. Hinz (Chicago: Swallow, 1975);

Robert Snyder, *Anais Nin Observed From a Film Portrait of a Woman as Artist* (Chicago: Swallow, 1976);

The Diary of Anais Nin 1955-1966 (New York: Harcourt Brace Jovanovich, 1976; London: Peter Owen, 1977);

In Favor of the Sensitive Man and Other Essays (New York: Harcourt Brace Jovanovich, 1976);

Delta of Venus Erotica (New York: Harcourt Brace Jovanovich, 1977);

Waste of Timelessness and Other Early Stories (Weston, Conn.: Magic Circle Press, 1977);

Linotte: The Early Diary of Anais Nin 1914-1920 (New York: Harcourt Brace Jovanovich, 1978).

Periodical Publications:

"D. H. Lawrence Mystic of Sex," *The Canadian Forum*, 11, 121 (October 1930): 15-17;

"The Writer and the Symbols," *Two Cities*, 1 (April 1959): 33-40;

"Sabina," *Chicago Review*, 15, 3 (winter-spring 1962): 45-60;

"Poetics of the Film," *Film Culture*, 31 (winter 1963-1964): 12-14.

References:

Oliver Evans, *Anais Nin* (Carbondale: Southern Illinois University Press, 1968);

Benjamin Franklin V, *Anais Nin A Bibliography* (Kent, Ohio: Kent State University Press, 1973);

Evelyn J. Hinz, *The Mirror and the Garden: Realism and Reality in the Writings of Anais Nin* (Columbus: Ohio State University Libraries, 1971);

Mosaic, 11, 2 (winter 1978). Special Nin issue;

Robert Zaller, ed., *A Casebook on Anais Nin* (New York: New American Library, 1974).

Manuscripts:

A large collection of Nin's papers and literary manuscripts is at the University of California at Los Angeles, which also has her diaries. Northwestern University has a number of literary manuscripts, including the manuscript and galley proofs of *The Winter of Artifice*.

JOYCE CAROL OATES was born in the small town of Lockport, New York, on 16 June 1938 and grew up in a rural setting nearby in Erie County. Together with her brother, Frederic, and sister, Lynn Ann, she was raised as a Roman Catholic in a home free from the depressing economic problems which plague so many of her fictional families. Her father, Frederic James Oates, was employed as a tool and die designer, while her mother, Caroline Bush Oates, ran the household. Oates received her early education in a one-room country schoolhouse but attended junior and senior high school in town. In 1956 she graduated from Williamsville Central High School. Seldom does Oates discuss her growing up, and she dismissed this period of her life to a *Newsweek* interviewer as " 'dull, ordinary, nothing people would be interested in,' not because it was really dull and ordinary but because it was terrible to talk about. 'A great deal frightened me,' she said cryptically, but would not elaborate."

Traces of her early environment appear regularly in Oates's short stories and novels. Her most frequently used setting is Eden County, a fictional version of her western New York State milieu. She creates from the area near Buffalo, Lockport, and the Erie Canal a country of poor and wealthy farmers, small hamlets, towns, and growing cities. Lockport and the Erie Canal appear in *Wonderland*, while many of her other works are located in the rural areas of Eden, an allusive name, about which Oates has said, "It's not paradise at all. It's pretty bad as a matter of fact."

Creating fictional worlds has always been an obsession for Joyce Carol Oates. She began as a child—even before she could write she told her tales through pictures. During her elementary school years she wrote stories and constructed 200-page books, which she designed and bound herself. When she was fifteen her first novel submitted to a publisher was rejected as too depressing for the market of young readers; the book concerned a dope addict who is rehabilitated by caring for a black stallion.

Her writing continued after she matriculated at Syracuse University in 1956: she turned out a novel a semester while she majored in English and minored in philosophy. Her writing professor, Donald A. Dike, introduced her to Faulkner, who she admits became a major influence on her work. Another important literary influence was Kafka: "In college, I was Franz Kafka for a while." The university library magazine provided one forum for her publications, and she was co-winner of the *Mademoiselle* college fiction award in 1959 for her short story "In the Old World," which appeared in that magazine. In addition to her writing, she was an outstanding student, was elected to Phi Beta Kappa, and served as class valedictorian when she received her B.A. degree in June 1960.

After her graduation, Oates entered the University of Wisconsin's graduate English program. While working on her Master's degree, she met Raymond Joseph Smith, a doctoral candidate, whom she married on 23 January 1961. Oates received her degree in June of the same year and followed her husband to Beaumont, Texas, where he held his first teaching post.

Despite the *Mademoiselle* award, Oates lacked the confidence to become a professional author. Instead, she enrolled at Rice University in Houston, planning to commute by bus from Beaumont to work on her Ph.D. in English. In the university library she discovered that one of her short stories had been cited in the honor roll in the latest volume of Martha Foley's *Best American Short Stories*. "I hadn't known about it until I picked it up and saw it. I thought, maybe I could be a writer. . . . I went back on the bus and stopped thinking about a Ph.D."

Since that time Oates's publishing record has been overwhelming; novels, short stories, poems, plays, essays, and critical studies seem to flow effortlessly from her active mind. She readily confesses to "a laughably Balzacian ambition to get the whole world into a book." She composes her work rapidly and spends little time rewriting. "It's mainly daydreaming, I sit and look out at the river, I daydream about a kind of populated empty space. There's nothing verbal about it. Then there comes a time when it's all set and I just go write it. With a story it's one evening, if I can type that fast." Despite the rate of composition, Oates's strongly individualized writing voice carries her quickly and evenly through her novels and stories.

The presentation of a realistic sensation of life that provides a moral lesson to the reader is the intention behind her work. The concern with capturing the whole experience leads her to pile fact upon fact, to overload her fiction with detail. Often criticized for this superabundance of graphic minutiae, she answers, "One has to be exhaustive and exhausting to really render the world in all its complexities and also in its dullness." She attempts more than a detailed picture, as she has clearly explained in an interview, "What I would like to do, always, in my writing is an obvious and yet perhaps audacious feat; I would like to create the psychological and emotional equivalent of an experience, so completely and in such exhaustive detail, that anyone who reads it sympathetically will have *experienced* that event in his mind (which is where we live anyway)." The reader can then understand better, not only his own life, but also the lives of people in vastly different social situations. For Oates, "All art is moral, educational, illustrative. It instructs." The more exact her rendering of society, the more valuable it becomes.

Although she is quite certain about the intention of her work, Oates is less exact about her antecedents. A legion of writers has contributed to her development. In addition to Faulkner and Kafka, she includes as other important influences "Freud, Nietzsche, Mann—they're almost real personalities in my life. And Dostoevsky and Melville . . . and Proust. And Sartre's *Nausea*." Beyond this diverse list, she sees herself as a romantic in the tradition of Stendhal and Flaubert. She also has obvious bonds with the great American naturalists—Dreiser, Farrell, and Steinbeck–but her concern with unusual psychological states and her lyricism and vivid imagery remove her from their company. The result of this wide variety of artistic models is an original synthesis which defies simple labels—realist, naturalist, gothicist, psychologist, satirist, and journalist—that have been pinned on her. Oates has been advised by her critics to cease work for a while to allow writer and reader alike to digest and properly evaluate what has been produced. Nevertheless, she continues to create and publish at an incredible rate; each month her output grows; each year a new novel, or a volume of short stories or poems, or a critical work appears. She contributes stories and essays across the entire spectrum of periodical publications from *Playboy* and *Cosmopolitan* to the *Southern Humanities Review* and the *Shakespeare Quarterly*.

Oates's first novel, *With Shuddering Fall* (1964), sounds the themes of violence, madness, and lust which have become her trademarks. This story of a country girl, Karen Herz, and of her destructive love affair with a stock car racer, Shar Rule, demonstrates the immense power of feminine passivity in its battle with masculine violence. From the moment that the thirty-year-old Shar roars into Eden County to bury his hated, dying father until, defeated by Karen, he smashes into the wall of the Cherry River raceway, he attempts to force the eighteen-year-old girl to respond to his violence. Karen, however, acting to avenge her father whom Shar has seriously beaten, is indomitable.

While many reviewers responded favorably to this first novel, most missed the point of the story, which "was conceived as a religious work. Where the father was the father of the Old Testament who gives a command, as God gave a command to Abraham, and everything was parallel—very strictly parallel— and how we can obey or not obey it, and, if we do obey it, we're not going to get rewarded for it anyway," as Oates told Linda Kuehl, an interviewer for *Commonweal*. The parallel is explicit in the novel: Mr. Herz reads from the Bible the story of Abraham and Isaac on the day before he commands Karen, "Don't come to me until you get him. Kill him. Kill him." Karen fulfills his command, despite her growing love for Shar, filling the story with violence, riots, perverse lust, and death. This religious theme is an important aspect of *With Shuddering Fall* and indicates the religious questioning of the author, who is a lapsed Catholic, and was then questioning the role of religion in her life. That she was haunted by her Catholic upbringing is evident in much of her early writing, but her Catholic heritage grows less and less important in her later works.

Technically *With Shuddering Fall* is fairly simple and straightforward. The narrative point of view is third person, limited throughout, with Karen the center of consciousness for most of the novel, although Shar and others assume the center for certain sections. The novel is divided into three books, "Spring," "Summer," and "Fall," which coincide with Karen's meeting with, destruction of, and recovery from Shar. The prose style helps maintain control, as John Knowles in his *New York Times* review notes: "This material is not as garish as it sounds because of the clarity, grace and intelligence of the writing." On the other hand, H. G. Jackson, in *Harper's*, calls it "merely hysterically incoherent," while Dorrie Pagones, in *Saturday Review*, writes, "Miss Oates is often both esoteric and violent, adjectives seldom ascribed to women writers, and her imagination seems to have no limits."

Her second novel, *A Garden of Earthly Delights* (1967), is the opening volume of an informal trilogy which develops the dual themes of problems caused by economic circumstances and of the difficulties of young people striving to free themselves from the oppressive situations of their lives.

The chronicle of three generations, *A Garden of Earthly Delights* depicts the sordid world of the migrant laborer, the lonely world of the social

Jill Krementz

Joyce Carol Oates

outcast, and the sterile world of the comfortable middle class. The novel opens powerfully with the birth of the heroine, Clara, in the back of a decrepit transport truck for migrant workers in the 1920s. "Very much like Dreiser here, Miss Oates's honest grip on reality makes us feel but not flinch," Elizabeth Janeway writes in her *New York Times* review. Clara's father, Carleton Walpole, was forced into the migrant life by the failure of his farm and by debts which his pride requires he pay. The entire first section of the novel, told alternately from Carleton's and Clara's point of view, is remarkably well done, even though Oates has had no personal experience with the world of the seasonal laborer: the characters and their condition are as real as the gardens in which they toil.

Clara's escape from the endless road and her establishment in Tintern, a small town in Eden County, are effected by the enigmatic young man, Lowry, who fathers her son. When Lowry, not knowing that Clara is pregnant, leaves for Mexico, she decides to bring her life into control by seeking

out and surrendering to Revere, the local wealthy patrician who has been attracted to her. Taking her from her dime store saleswoman's existence in the town, he establishes her as his mistress in her own home in the country and, following his wife's death, marries her and brings her and her son, Swan, who he thinks is his, into his world. To give Swan a strong position in life is Clara's main reason for marriage, but this decision leads to disaster, as he induces a miscarriage for Clara by causing in a hunting accident the violent and bloody death of one of his stepbrothers. Finally, after destroying Revere's original family for Swan's benefit, Clara sees him shoot his stepfather and then himself. As a result, she sinks gradually into insanity, as did her migrant mother. Most of the reviewers find this ending melodramatic and contrived.

This novel again demonstrates Oates's ability to create a living world in her fiction, for she depicts brilliantly the different societies through which Clara moves. Nonetheless, there is a sense of formlessness to the novel which results from the shifting of emphasis from Carleton to Clara to Swan. Still, the novel's power cannot be denied— Carleton's steady degeneration, Clara's inability to find happiness in any of her roles, and her son's failure to benefit from her sacrifices paint a sombre picture of life at all social levels.

From the migrant world and farming community of *A Garden of Earthly Delights* Oates moves to the earthly paradise of the sheltered suburbs of wealthy America in *Expensive People* (1968). About this volume she has written, *"Expensive People* is the second of three novels that deal with social and economic facts of life in America, combined with unusually sensitive—but hopefully representative— young men and women who confront the puzzle of American life in different ways and come to different ends." Her "sensitive" but "representative" youth in this work is an eighteen-year-old, 250-pound maniac, Richard Everett, who presents the story in the first person as a memoir he is writing prior to committing suicide.

Expensive People is Richard's tale of his pitiful life. He is the child of a highly successful corporate executive, Elwood Everett, who jumps from position to position ever bettering his prestige and salary, and of a minor woman writer, Natashya Romanov, who poses as the daughter of emigre Russian nobles but who is really the daughter of poor immigrants. Richard is hopelessly neurotic, perhaps psychotic. Wallowing in self-pity, he describes the promiscuous conduct of his social-climbing mother, whom he hopelessly loves. Her periodic desertions of him and his father drive Richard to murder.

Writing about someone writing about a writer, Oates has great fun. Natashya, or Nada ("nothing") as Richard calls her, provides the plot for her own destruction by leaving behind her notebook in which she has sketched out a psychological novelette about a young man who terrorizes people by sniping at them but missing the first three times, "then the fourth, when you've been conditioned to the others, results in the murder." Interpolated in *Expensive People* is a published Oates story, "The Molesters," which is presented as one Nada contributed to the *Quarterly Review of Literature.* Richard interprets the tale to mean that his parents are knowingly "molesting" him. Richard follows the plot of the novelette and the next time that Nada packs her bags to leave, he shoots her. Or does he? The psychiatrists say that the experience is an hallucination and that someone else shot Nada. Richard insists that he did kill her; so at eighteen he writes his chronicle of disintegration, after which he begins to commit suicide by eating until he bursts.

This novel is a sharp reversal from Oates's earlier efforts. It is a satire on the moral and artistic bankruptcy of the upper middle class. This presentation is effective, although she continues to present the details of day-to-day existence. Oates undercuts the realism of the narrative by extending her descriptions to absurd lengths, as when she has Nada telephone over thirty different services necessary to suburban life. The use of the first-person narration is also a departure for Oates, one she found to be successful: "The first person was just a joy. I found it easier and more exciting to write. This feeling lasted throughout the whole book; and there was less rewriting to be done than ever before." In addition, the subject matter of this eccentric novel gives her a chance to discuss writing technique (Richard explains in great detail his theory about "How to Write a Memoir Like This," using tips from articles in *The Writer* and *Amateur Penman, Let's Write a Novel!* by Agnes Sturm, and *Waiting for the End* by Leslie Fiedler). She also introduces sample reviews of *Expensive People* (the *Time* reviewer says, "Everett sets out to outsmartre Sartre but doesn't quite make it. It is all great fun though"). The critical reception of this volume echoed the mock reviews from the novel itself; some were quite enthusiastic, while others were skeptical of the value of this unusual work.

The final volume of Miss Oates's informal trilogy is *them* (1969), her most successful work thus far and the winner of the 1970 National Book Award. In this novel, she turns to the world of the lower middle class to chronicle the survival of the Wendall family from 1937 to 1967. In an unusual admission which links this contemporary novel to those of Defoe and other early prose fiction writers, Oates states, "This is a work of history in fictional form— that is, in personal perspective, which is the only kind of history that exists. In the years 1962-1967 I taught English at the University of Detroit. . . . It was during this period that I met the 'Maureen Wendall' of this narrative." This young woman was a student and later a correspondent of Oates's, who incorporates in the body of the novel letters purportedly received from "Maureen." To buttress this assertion of authenticity, Oates describes Detroit with accuracy and a great profusion of detail, which at times encumbers the narrative, although she further states that "the various sordid and shocking events of slum life, detailed in other naturalistic works, have been understated here, mainly because of my fear that too much reality would be unbearable."

Shot through with violence from beginning to end, *them* depicts the lives of Loretta Wendall and her son, Jules, and daughter, Maureen. Early in the novel, sixteen-year-old Loretta is jolted from her sleep by the sound of a bullet crashing through the skull of her first lover. Her brother, the murderer, flees, leaving her to muddle her way through the problem; she finds a policeman, Howard Wendall, whom she knows slightly, and brings him to the sordid apartment, where he, aroused by the thoughts evoked by the body in Loretta's bed, takes her on the kitchen table. He marries her after helping to dispose of the body but is suspended from the police force, and they move to the country. Howard goes off to war, and Loretta moves back to Detroit, where she is arrested for prostitution by the first man she approaches. Ever-resilient Loretta bounces back and survives, lives through several years with Howard until he is killed in an industrial accident, and then passes from man to man, ever hopeful, never truly touched by the horrors surrounding her.

Maureen suffers from being much more sensitive than her mother. Part of her vulnerability is drawn from the author's own life; Maureen is a composite of Joyce Carol Oates and the "real" Maureen. One of the tragedies of the fictional girl's youth is the loss of her class minutes book for which she, the class secretary, is responsible. That Oates can make this insignificant event poignant and memorable is a measure of her power. Oates says this of the episode: "This is something that had happened to me too, and both of us responded in a very weak, rather victimized way, by being annihilated almost and reduced to tears and despair by a completely foolish event which is so small and yet, when you're that age, it can sort of run over you." Always the victim, Maureen turns to the library and literature to find peace and order; she reads Jane Austen and feels great sympathy for Emma but cannot feel such sympathy for her own relatives—the horrible reality of her life has become surreal to her. After literature, the only escape route she can envision is wealth.

Money is magic in *them*, and the characters pursue it almost by instinct. Maureen at fourteen begins picking up older men in her craving for money. She hides the money she earns in a book of poetry in her room, but her stepfather finds the money and beats her into a catatonic state, in which she hides from life for more than a year. Her brother Jules is similarly enthralled with money.

Jules is a hopeful young man with the resilience of his mother, but his characterization is not as convincing as that of Maureen. His early years are believably depicted, but when he reaches manhood, his bizarre adventures make him merely a name

acting through a series of unbelievable events. He has a relationship with a beautiful kept woman, who introduces him to the strange Bernard Geffen. A wealthy man trying to become a success through the gangster world, Geffen hires Jules as his chauffeur, pays him hundreds of dollars, gives him $10,000 to buy a new car for them, and finally leaves Jules sitting in the car while he goes into a decaying building and has his throat slit. During his brief career as Geffen's driver, Jules catches sight of his employer's niece, Nadine, the daughter of some wealthy people in Grosse Pointe.

Nadine, who symbolizes the riches of a world he can never enter, becomes the overriding compulsion of Jules's life. He persuades her to run away with him and while they drive to Texas, Jules commits petty crimes to support them. Nadine, however, refuses to have sex with him and when he becomes disgustingly ill, she leaves him. Several years later, they meet again and finally consummate their relationship. After an afternoon and evening of making love, Nadine shoots her lover and then herself. Jules recovers only to become a caricature of success.

At the conclusion of the novel, Jules and Maureen both escape from the horror of their lower-class backgrounds. Jules, after pimping for a young, upper-middle-class student whom he turns to prostitution, becomes involved in the Detroit riots of 1967 during which he kills a policeman and makes friends with one of the organizers of the riots. After the destruction, the organizer lands a federal grant to set up an anti-poverty program in California. Joining with him, Jules heads west in a parody of the traditional American hero striking out for new frontiers. Maureen's success is her seduction away from his wife and family of a dumpy, community college, part-time English teacher, who marries her and takes her to the haven of the suburbs. In the world of *them* these are "success" stories.

The critical reception of this work was generally favorable. Almost all reviewers were impressed by the detailed panorama displayed by Oates. Robert M. Adams, in the *New York Times*, said, "Miss Oates writes a vehement, voluminous, kaleidoscopic novel, more deeply rooted in social observation than current fiction usually tends to be," and P. E. Gray, in the *Virginia Quarterly Review*, wrote, "Of its genre she has produced a superb modern instance, certain to please those who are adherents of the pattern, approach, and style." *them* is carefully structured, and on the whole it holds together well for such an enormous novel, using, for example, motifs similar to those in long narrative poems. The narrative technique of *them* is that of her earlier works—third person limited, with the center of consciousness moving from character to character, although the inclusion of Maureen's letters, as well as some of Jules's, lends an authenticating touch. With this novel, Joyce Carol Oates became a major figure in the literary world.

Following *them*, she began a series of novels which, in her words, "deal with the complex distribution of power in the United States." The first novel of this group is *Wonderland*, which concerns the medical world and the "phantasmagoria of personality."

The "hero" of *Wonderland* is Jesse Harte/Pedersen/Vogel. His story begins in blood with his father's mass murder of the rest of the family and his suicide after wounding Jesse. Jesse Harte is eventually adopted by the famous physician and mystic, Dr. Pedersen, who awakens his slumbering intellect. Living several years in Lockport with the strange Pedersen family, all of whom are grotesquely fat, eccentric geniuses, Jesse develops a drive to emulate Dr. Pedersen. When he helps the alcoholic Mrs. Pedersen attempt to escape from the perverse domination of her husband, Jesse is ejected from the family. Without Pedersen's help, Jesse, now Vogel, struggles through medical school and internship but then marries the daughter of one of his medical professors and becomes the protege of a brilliant brain surgeon. With an inheritance, Jesse establishes a clinic and becomes himself a successful neurosurgeon. Despite his professional success, Jesse cannot control his life or his children's lives: his marriage is unhappy; his children are alienated from him; his attempt at a love affair fails; the novel ends in despair.

The catalogue of violence and perversion in this novel includes mass murder, drug addiction, castration, abortion, homosexuality, self-mutilation, the assassination of President Kennedy, cannibalism (a doctor eats a broiled uterus which he has cut from an attractive cadaver), and the more typical horrors a doctor sees in the emergency room. *Wonderland* is unrelenting in its assault on the reader. Although many of the individual episodes are magnificent accomplishments, the novel as a whole does not reach the level of Oates's other work.

The critical reception of *Wonderland* was mixed. Many reviewers were highly impressed, while others were repelled by the work. The unmitigated pessimism of the novel makes it one of the least attractive of Oates's works, but *Wonderland* has such power and intensity that it cannot be ignored.

Do With Me What You Will (1973), her next novel, presents the world of lawyers and is in Oates's words, "a celebration of love and marriage." Structured to resemble a legal presentation, *Do With Me What You Will* is divided into four parts: "Twenty-eight Years, Two Months, Twenty-six Days," "Miscellaneous Facts, Events, Fantasies, Evidence Admissible and Inadmissible," "Crime," and "The Summing Up." The first two sections are temporally parallel, with each part presenting the story of one of the two main characters; "Part One" is Elena Howe's, and "Part Two" is Jack Morrissey's. The third section documents their love affair, and the fourth neatly concludes the novel by updating all of the main characters' lives and setting them on their ways.

Elena's story is an updated Sleeping Beauty fairy tale. Kidnapped by her crazed, divorced father at age seven, Elena early withdraws into a protective shell and remains oblivious to the world. When rescued from her father, Elena, ill and confused, cannot even speak, and when she finally does, she stutters. Her mother, a cold-blooded, man-hating opportunist, never understands Elena's problems and drags Elena through childhood and adolescence until she marries her at seventeen to a famous criminal lawyer, Marvin Howe. At the end of "Twenty-eight Years, Two Months, Twenty-six Days" Elena is frozen in a trance, staring at a statue in Detroit, where she and Marvin live.

The author then returns to the beginning to tell Jack Morrissey's story, which commences when his father murders a wealthy man. Marvin Howe defends his father, and by coaching Jack as his star witness, gains an acquittal by reason of temporary insanity. Astounded by the power of the law, Jack decides to become a lawyer himself. He does, but unlike the rich and celebrated Howe, Jack crusades for the poor and downtrodden. While in the South working with the American Civil Liberties Union to help the blacks, Jack meets Rachel, whom he marries. Later they move back to Detroit, where Jack continues to help the impoverished and gains a reputation as a top lawyer for liberal causes. They never have much money because Rachel insists on sharing their money with the oppressed. When he sees Elena Howe and learns who she is, Jack feels compelled to know her. At the end of "Part Two" he is trying to awaken her from the trance which ended "Part One."

The third part of *Do With Me What You Will* depicts the progress of the love affair which develops between Jack and Elena. With her first sexual climax, she begins to awaken to reality, but because she is frightened, as well as exhilirated, by her emergence, she hides from Jack. When he forces her to choose between him and Marvin, she withdraws from him altogether, returns to Marvin, and confesses her sin. Marvin, certain he has gotten her back permanently, burns the files of evidence which his detectives have gathered since the affair began.

"The Summing Up" follows the main characters to a final decision. Elena rejects Marvin and security and pursues Jack, who has returned to his wife and the child they adopted to salvage their marriage. She succeeds. The novel ends affirmatively with Jack and Elena together.

Technically, this volume is one of Oates's most successful efforts. The critical reception of *Do With Me What You Will* was positive; after the extravagances and horrors of *Wonderland*, most welcomed the restraint and affirmation of this novel. While most of the novel is told in the third person, interspersed throughout is the first person retrospective commentary by Elena. The narrative is easy to follow, and the control and tightness of this work keep the reader's attention directed upon the twin themes of legal and amatory struggles. As the second volume of the trilogy which concerns the basis of power in the United States, *Do With Me What You Will* brilliantly reveals the complex fabric of law which envelops all of society.

Leaving the orderly world of law, Oates enters the chaotic world of politics in her next volume, *The Assassins*. There is a multiplicity of themes in this novel: politics and political assassination, art and religion, heroes and hero worship; unfortunately, none of these themes is fully developed. Critics of *The Assassins* were baffled and worn out by the narrative. J. D. O'Hara, in the *New York Times*, expressed his frustration: "Joyce Carol Oates has subtitled her novel, 'A Book of Hours.' And painfully exasperating hours they are, every one of them."

The novel chronicles three confused lives, whose center, a powerful political figure, has been destroyed. Divided into three parts, the novel gives these characters—Hugh, Yvonne, and Stephen—an opportunity to demonstrate their relationships with the assassinated ultra-right-wing hero Andrew Petrie and the ways in which the violent death has affected them. Hugh opens the novel with his first-person account of his hatred for his brother Andrew, whose death moves him toward insanity. Hugh is an artist, a caricaturist, whose savage cartoons have earned him respect, but whose disintegration isolates him from all society. The second part of the tale falls to Yvonne, Andrew's young wife, whose story is one of love and hero worship. She tries to carry on Andrew's work, but her limited ability to understand subtle differences confuses her. Third comes Stephen's narrative. He is Andrew's youngest brother, a religious mystic whose tale reveals Andrew to have been the subject of his religious compassion. Hugh ends his account by shooting himself in the head; Yvonne is shot and dismembered by an axe-wielding hunter at the conclusion of her section; and Stephen wanders off on a pilgrimage when his tale is finished.

The narratives are each individually confusing, and although they are mutually illuminating, much remains unclear. The story progresses through flashbacks and dreams whose confusion is compounded by the unreliability of the narrators. Hugh is an unabashed liar, Yvonne is often confused and is bent on protecting her husband's reputation, and Stephen lives in a world not of this earth. What is the reader to make, for instance, of Stephen's repeated episodes of astral projection? The novel is chaotic, but then Oates obviously intends to present as accurately as possible the chaos of modern life.

While employing similar techniques of stream of consciousness and shifting chronology, *Childwold* (1976) is more accessible and pleasing than *The Assassins*. *Childwold* is Oates's most free-flowing novel, the most intentionally Joycean in its structure, language, and narrative technique. Childwold is a rustic hamlet in Eden County, whose name has symbolic value: the novel is full of children and of childlike adults. Near this small town lives the Bartlett family on a decaying farm, and when Fitz John Kasch, the principal character of the novel, falls in love with fourteen-year-old Laney Bartlett, he muses over the name, composing "a litany, a sacred chant, the words of which were so beautiful I woke weeping—Childwold / Childwood / Childwide / Childworld / Childmold / Childwould / Childtold." This type of wordplay is an important part of the novel, as demonstrated by a page-length "litany" on the same word later on and by similar expansions of Kasch's name.

Many different characters—Kasch, Laney, Grandpa Hurley, Arlene Bartlett, and her two sons Vale and Brad—tell significant parts of the story, each in a distinctive voice. This narrative technique is the most sophisticated that Oates has used thus far. The intellectual, introspective Kasch employs the first person because he understands his precarious position in life and looks to his writings to help control his existence and to provide a journal for noting his progress. Laney's confusion and sense of inferiority cause her to dissociate her inner self from the Laney who acts and to analyze her actions by referring to herself in the second person throughout the novel. Presented in the third person, Grandpa Hurley's thoughts are free-flowing, roving backward and forward in time and in and out of life. His companions are more often than not the dead of his own generation; throughout the novel Oates's increasing fascination with psychic matters is manifested in the strange experiences of the characters. Arlene, Brad, and Vale complete the picture of Childwold life through their simple, third-person presentations of events.

Childwold is the story of Kasch and his interaction with the Bartlett family, a colorful menage of Arlene Bartlett, her married daughter Nancy, and their many children, legitimate and illegitimate, who provide the most obvious explanation of the title. Hovering over the novel, the not-yet-ghost of times past, is Arlene's eighty-three-year-old father, Joseph Hurley, upon whose farm the family lives. The world-traveling Kasch returns to recover his lost innocence to the nearby town of Yewville, where he meets and falls in love with Laney Bartlett, whom he pursues and instructs, lusts after and lends books to. However, when Arlene arrives to ask Kasch about his relationship with her daughter, he transfers his affection to the more mature woman. He marries Arlene and celebrates their homecoming and the consummation of the marriage through a lyric marriage song, which reveals him at the pinnacle of his physical and poetic life. However, bliss is short-lived in Oates's novels; defending his new family, Kasch smashes to pulp the skull of one of Arlene's former suitors. Tried, acquitted, hospitalized in a mental institution, Kasch withdraws from all society, and upon his release he buys the old farm and lives in the crumbling house as a hermit.

As usual with Oates's novels, plot summary leaves out much of importance: Grandpa's extraordinarily rich psychic life; Vale's brutal, degraded existence; Laney's fragile, failing child-world. The novel is full of poetry, the self-conscious rhythms of Kasch, the untutored, natural music of Grandpa. This is an excellent novel by any standard, as most critics recognized. Irene H. Chayes, in *New Republic*, wrote, "This is a novel that at last is comparable to the best of her short stories and by an evolutionary leap has already moved beyond them, into the tradition of literature, going back at least as far as the Romantics, in which the philosophical problems of man's existence and his destiny are bound up with the problems of art." *Childwold* fully demonstrates that Joyce Carol Oates is now and will remain for many years a vibrant voice in American fiction.

Novels represent only a part of Oates's literary production. Her short stories are considered by many to be her most polished pieces; she has written and published hundreds of tales and has assembled a number of them in ten volumes. Her poems, generally held to be her weakest efforts, also appear continually and have been partially collected in five volumes. Her critical essays often reveal an artist's imaginative insight into the classics of other times and into the work of contemporaries; in addition to many essays which have appeared in periodicals, she has published three critical volumes. Also, she has edited a volume of contemporary short fiction, written forewords and afterwords for fellow novelists, contributed many miscellaneous pieces to popular and scholarly magazines, and authored several plays.

In many ways, Oates's short stories are her finest works. Her style, technique, and subject matter achieve their strongest effects in this concentrated form, for the extended dialogue, minute detail, and violent action which irritate the reader after hundreds of pages are wonderfully appropriate in short fiction. The disoriented and disturbed characters whom the reader follows with exasperation and doubt through the novels captivate him when depicted concisely at the moment of crisis. Her short stories present the same violence, perversion, and mental derangement as her novels, and are set in similar locations: the rural community of Eden County, the chaotic city of Detroit, and the sprawling malls and developments of modern suburbia. An additional milieu explored in her tales is that of the academic world; many of her pieces concern the shallow nature of her fellow professors and their inability to communicate to their students or among themselves. While experimenting more freely in her stories than in her novels, Oates creates pieces of consistently high quality that the compactness of the genre enables her to maintain; however, her collected tales should be read one or two at a time rather than plowed through by the volume, because each produces such a powerful effect upon the reader that one cannot fully appreciate it without consideration and analysis.

Her poetry is not on the same level as either her tales or novels. The shock of reality which greets the reader in her prose fiction is not present in her poems, although she presents basically the same situations. The motivations and intentions of her fictional characters allow the reader to accept the horrors and to experience the terrors which all of her

26.1

life, when she had known so little, she might have rejoiced in the ~~poek~~
poet's massive vision, assuming--smugly, and wrongly--that it was a
vision one might easily appropriate. And perhaps later in her life,
near its completion, she might approach such a vision without any fear
at all. But now: no. It wasn't possible. ~~Now~~ Not now, not yet.

Instead she craved an art that defined limits, a human, humble,
~~sandxak~~ sane art, unashamed of turning away from the void, unashamed of
celebrating what was human and therefore scaled-down; an art of what
was possible, *what must be embraced.* ~~not of what was frantically desired.~~

"As you probably know, I nursed my husband for months. I was his
nurse. He didn't want anyone else and I didn't want anyone else around
him. It wasn't easy, in fact I dreaded it at first...I dreaded not only
him but myself in that role, I was afraid something irrevocable might
happen to me. After a while, though, I came to almost like it, to feel
fulfilled by nursing him. I'm ashamed of that now. I can hardly
believe it. Then, near the end, when he was very sick, I dreaded it
again and resented it, I think, and I was very, very unhappy. I was
ashamed of that too. ...But what do these emotions matter? We do what
we must do. He died. Whether I was ashamed or not, happy or unhappy,
the poor man died. ...But you're not going to."

"Of course I'm not," Beatrice said softly. "You've been so generous,
Moira, coming over here so often, fixing meals for me.... I'm not really
sick. Not really. You must be neglecting your own life, aren't you?"

Moira gazed down at herself, contemplatively. She took in the length
of her body: that day she was wearing a cable-stitched ski sweater and
faded blue jeans. So tall, so confident!--Beatrice had always admired
women like Moira. Moira said, strangely, "How can I be neglecting my own
life? This _is_ my life, here. We inhabit our own lives constantly."

From typescript of "Widows" in Night-Side.

work is based upon; however, in her poetry too often only the bloody, brutal climax flashes before us in scenes which do not appear possible but do appear repellent. Despite their philosophic truth or psychological accuracy, the images are too often unbelievable on the surface, the entrance to any poem's message. The music of poetry is also missing from Oates's verse, which is often staccato or halting. Oates herself has noted these problems. "The poems are nearly all lyric expressions of larger, dramatic, emotional predicaments, and they belong to fully-developed fictional characters who 'exist' elsewhere. The poems are therefore shorthand, instantaneous accounts of a state of mind that might have been treated in a 400-page work. I've always had a blindness for, a real inability to appreciate, the purely 'lyric.' " Easily traceable are relationships among the poems, stories, and novels; in fact, read in the context of one of her novels, some of her poems are more accessible and valuable.

As one would expect, the critical writing of Oates is imaginative and revealing. She has written on a wide variety of subjects ranging from Shakespeare to Beckett, and each of her essays elucidates both the work under discussion and her own novels, short stories and poems. While Oates's critical pieces are not examples of careful, exhaustive scholarship, they are the products of a widely-read, creative mind that considers deeply the forms and values of literature and renders erudite and fresh discussions of the works she approaches.

Despite such prolific output, Oates does not spend all of her time writing. From 1962-1967 she taught at the University of Detroit, and since 1967 she has been a full-time member of the faculty of the University of Windsor, where her husband teaches eighteenth-century English literature. They live in a house overlooking the Detroit River, directly across from the city of Detroit. Many of her short stories utilize this academic environment as the setting for the bizarre violence more typical of her Eden County and Detroit environments.

In addition to her secure academic post, Oates's writing has gained her a number of literary prizes. Three times nominated for the National Book Award, she obtained the prize in 1970 for *them*. She has held a Guggenheim Fellowship and a National Institute of Arts and Letters Rosenthal Foundation Award. Two O. Henry prizes (1967, 1973) and the Lotos Club Award of Merit have also been hers.

With each succeeding work, Oates demonstrates her growing ability to write highly artistic, yet socially relevant fiction. Still a young woman, her potential is limited only by her energy and her control. Of her energy there is no question; already her output resembles the prodigious collections of the prolific novelists of the nineteenth century. Of her control, however, many still entertain doubts; careful rewriting and precise editing are not often evident in her published novels. That Oates is today a major American novelist is an established fact, for her powerful imagination presents compelling visions of contemporary society which cannot be ignored; yet her continuing success and her position in the future depend upon her ability to impose a rigorous artistic restraint upon her compositions.

—*Michael Joslin*

Books:

By the North Gate (New York: Vanguard, 1963);

With Shuddering Fall (New York: Vanguard, 1964; London: Cape, 1965);

Upon the Sweeping Flood and Other Stories (New York: Vanguard, 1966; London: Gollancz, 1973);

A Garden of Earthly Delights (New York: Vanguard, 1967; London: Gollancz, 1970);

Expensive People (New York: Vanguard, 1968; London: Gollancz, 1969);

them (New York: Vanguard, 1969; London: Gollancz, 1971);

Anonymous Sins and Other Poems (Baton Rouge: Louisiana State University Press, 1969);

The Wheel of Love and Other Stories (New York: Vanguard, 1970; London: Gollancz, 1971);

Love and Its Derangements (Baton Rouge: Louisiana State University Press, 1970);

Cupid and Psyche (New York: Albondocani, 1970);

Wonderland (New York: Vanguard, 1971; London: Gollancz, 1972);

Marriages and Infidelities (New York: Vanguard, 1972; London: Gollancz, 1974);

The Edge of Impossibility: Tragic Forms in Literature (New York: Vanguard, 1972);

Do With Me What You Will (New York: Vanguard, 1973; London: Gollancz, 1974);

Angel Fire: Poems (Baton Rouge: Louisiana State University Press, 1973);

Sun: The Poetry of D. H. Lawrence (Los Angeles: Black Sparrow, 1973);

The Goddess and Other Women (New York: Vanguard, 1974; London: Gollancz, 1975);

The Hungry Ghosts: Seven Allusive Comedies (Los Angeles: Black Sparrow, 1974; Solihull, England: Aquila, 1975);

*Where Are You Going, Where Have You Been?
Stories of Young America* (Greenwich, Conn.:
Fawcett, 1974);

*New Heaven, New Earth: Visionary Experience in
Literature* (New York: Vanguard, 1974);

The Assassins (New York: Vanguard, 1975);

The Fabulous Beasts: Poems (Baton Rouge: Louisiana State University Press, 1975);

The Seduction and Other Stories (Los Angeles:
Black Sparrow, 1975);

*The Poisoned Kiss and Other Stories from the
Portuguese*, as Fernandes/Oates (New York:
Vanguard, 1975);

Childwold (New York: Vanguard, 1976);

Triumph of the Spider Monkey (Los Angeles: Black
Sparrow, 1976);

Crossing the Border (New York: Vanguard, 1977);

Night-Side: Eighteen Tales (New York: Vanguard,
1977).

Plays:

The Sweet Enemy, New York, Actors Playhouse,
1965;

Sunday Dinner, New York, St. Clement's Church,
1970;

Ontological Proof of My Existence, New York,
Cubiculo Theatre, 1972;

Miracle Play, New York, Playhouse 2 Theatre,
1974.

References:

Lionel Basney, "Joyce Carol Oates: Wit and Fear,"
Christianity Today, 20 (18 June 1976): 13-14,
and (2 July 1976): 20-21;

Michael and Ariane Batterberry, "Focus on Joyce
Carol Oates," *Harper's Bazaar*, 106 (September
1973): 159, 174, 176;

Warren Bower, "Bliss in the First Person," *Saturday
Review*, 51 (26 October 1968): 34-35;

Rose Marie Burwell, "Joyce Carol Oates and an Old
Master," *Critique*, 15, 1 (1973): 48-58;

Burwell, "The Process of Individuation as Narrative
Structure: Joyce Carol Oates' *Do With Me What
You Will*," *Critique*, 17, 2 (1975): 93-106;

Walter Clemons, "Joyce Carol Oates at Home," *New
York Times Book Review*, 28 September 1969,
pp. 4-5;

Benjamin DeMott, "The Necessity in Art of a
Reflective Intelligence," *Saturday Review*, 52
(22 November 1969): 71-73, 89;

Robert H. Fossum, "Only Control: The Novels of
Joyce Carol Oates," *Studies in the Novel*, 7
(summer 1975): 285-297;

James R. Giles, "From Jimmy Gatz to Jules
Wendall: A Study of 'Nothing Substantial,' "
Dalhousie Review, 56 (winter 1976-1977): 718-
724;

Howard M. Harper, "Trends in Recent American
Fiction," *Contemporary Literature*, 12 (spring
1971): 204-229;

Karl Keller, "A Modern Version of Edward Taylor,"
Early American Literature, 9 (winter 1975):
321-324;

Linda Kuehl, "An Interview with Joyce Carol
Oates," *Commonweal*, 91 (5 December 1969):
307-310;

Lucienne P. McCormick, "A Bibliography of Works
by and about Joyce Carol Oates," *American
Literature*, 43 (March 1971): 124-132;

Samuel F. Pickering, Jr., "The Short Stories of Joyce
Carol Oates," *Georgia Review*, 28 (summer
1974): 218-226;

Sanford Pinsker, "Isaac Bashevis Singer and Joyce
Carol Oates: Some Versions of Gothic," *Southern Review*, 9 (autumn 1973): 895-908;

Walter Sullivan, "The Artificial Demon: Joyce
Carol Oates and the Dimensions of the Real,"
Hollins Critic, 9, 4 (December 1972): 1-12;

Sullivan, "Gifts, Prophecies, and Prestidigitations:
Fictional Frameworks, Fictional Modes," *Sewanee Review*, 85 (January 1977): 116-125;

"Transformations of Self: An Interview with Joyce
Carol Oates," *Ohio Review*, 15, 1 (fall 1973): 50-
61;

Carolyn Walker, "Fear, Love, and Art in Oates'
'Plot' " *Critique*, 15, 1 (1973): 59-70;

G. F. Waller, "Joyce Carol Oates' *Wonderland:* An
Introduction," *Dalhousie Review*, 54 (autumn
1974): 480-490;

"Writing as a Natural Reaction," *Time*, 10 October
1969, p. 108;

Paul D. Zimmerman, "Hunger for Dreams," *Newsweek*, 23 March 1970, pp. 108, 110.

Flannery O'Connor

FLANNERY O'CONNOR'S life is best summarized in Robert Fitzgerald's introduction to *Everything That Rises Must Converge*. As friend and literary executor, Fitzgerald writes of her with candor and love: "She was a girl who started with a gift for cartooning and satire, and found in herself a far greater gift, unique in her time and place, a marvel." That gift, of course, was storytelling. She wrote two novels and thirty-one short stories and the critical response to her work has been extraordinary. Since her death in 1964, eleven books of criticism have been published, as well as two collections of essays and a major bibliographical study. In little more than two decades since her reputation began to develop in the mid-1950s, no fewer than three hundred critical essays have appeared in journals.

One of the principal reasons for this overwhelming response to her fiction is undoubtedly the fact that in an age of existential angst and the eclipse of traditional belief, Flannery O'Connor wrote brilliant stories that brought the issue of religious faith into clear dramatic focus. She was a devout Roman Catholic living in predominantly Protestant rural Georgia. Her stories are far from pious; in fact, their mode is usually shocking and often bizarre. Yet the religious issues they raise are central to her work. As Robert Fitzgerald expresses it, "she kept going deeper . . . until making up stories became, for her, a way of testing and defining and conveying that superior knowledge that must be called religious."

O'Connor's fictional world as a Catholic writer is one founded on three basic theological truths: "the Fall, the Redemption, and the Judgment." But the "modern secular world," as she was accustomed to call it, is either unprepared or unwilling to accept that vision. The would-be existentialist prophet in *Wise Blood*, Hazel Motes, in preaching his "Church Without Christ," puts it this way: "I'm going to preach there was no Fall because there was nothing to fall from and no Redemption because there was no Fall and no Judgment because there wasn't the first two." "[The Catholic fiction writer] may have to resort," O'Connor believed, "to violent literary means to get his vision across to a hostile audience." The literary genre she chose was the grotesque—"grotesque with good reason," she would claim—because "to the hard of hearing you shout, and for the almost-blind you draw large and startling figures."

Because her talent was so great, her life seemed tragically short. Born in Savannah, Georgia, on 25 March 1925, Flannery O'Connor died when she was just thirty-nine on 3 August 1964, in Milledgeville, Georgia, where her family had moved in 1938. She succumbed to a disease, disseminated lupus, that first struck in December 1950. O'Connor completed her undergraduate work at Georgia State College for Women (now Georgia College, the location of the O'Connor Collection) and two years later, in 1947, earned a Master of Fine Arts degree from the University of Iowa. Her master's thesis, entitled *The Geranium: A Collection of Short Stories*, included six stories, the last of which, "The Train," reappeared in revised form as the beginning of her first novel, *Wise Blood* (1952).

O'Connor's modest bequest to American Letters has been enough to assure her a permanent place among our greatest writers of fiction. She knew what held a good story together and expressed it this way, with characteristic reference to the element of mystery that she was convinced gave a story its worth: "I often ask myself what makes a story work, and what makes it hold up as a story," she told an audience at Hollins College in October 1963, "and I have decided that it is probably some action, some gesture of a character that is unlike any other in the story, one which indicates where the real heart of the story lies. This would have to be an action or a gesture which was both totally right and totally unexpected; it would have to be one that was both in character and beyond character; it would have to suggest both time and eternity." In terms of her Christian faith, this would be the literary analogue of the moment of grace.

It is almost invariably harder to expose the unifying structure of a novel than of a short story because the novel's greater elasticity of form diffuses its "dramatic center," yet the same pattern of saving gesture or revealing word is found in O'Connor's novels. *Wise Blood*, a novel about the Fall of man (the title is O'Connor's facetious idiom for original sin), is framed by Hazel Motes's encounter with two "ordinary" women whose interest in him is perceptive beyond their realization. The first words spoken in the novel suggest its final meaning. On the train to Taulkinham, Mrs. Wally Bee Hitchcock says to Haze, "I guess you're going home," and follows it with, "Well . . . there's no place like home." Haze, of course, does not answer. Rather than going home, Haze, like Tarwater in the second novel, is running from "the bleeding, stinking mad shadow of Jesus." His flight from Jesus is a search for "place," but flight yields no place, only emptiness and despair, as Haze himself concludes: "Where you come from is gone, where you thought you were going to never was there, and where you are is no good unless you can get away from it. Where is there a place for you to be? No place." When, finally, his lifeless body is

Flannery O'Connor with her self-portrait.

brought back to Mrs. Flood, her words connote far more than she realizes: "Well, Mr. Motes . . . I see you've come home." Haze has had, in the pattern of Oedipus, to blind himself in order to see. His act of atonement and the life of penance that leads to his death suggest that one must stop searching in order to find what one is looking for. The peace of place is within—and beyond.

In the title story of her first collection, *A Good Man Is Hard to Find* (1955), the saving gesture is the grandmother's recognition of The Misfit. This story, one of O'Connor's finest, reveals more clearly the dynamism of her fictional world in which unexpected events, usually the tragic, yield genuine human insight and the possibility of Redemption. (If her audiences considered her situations alien and offensive, she was fond of asking them simply to read the daily newspaper to see how commonplace tragedy is.) The plot is simple enough: a family on vacation is killed by an escaped convict. In preparing for and unfolding the dramatic conflict between the grandmother and The Misfit, O'Connor creates pure art out of the tragicomedy of life. She also discloses one of her characteristic signatures as a Christian writer: Good somehow is often wrenched from evil. The demonic figure of The Misfit serves as the agent of grace. O'Connor's "action of grace" is, typically, "in territory held largely by the devil."

The Misfit discloses the possibilities of existence to the grandmother when he reminds her how Jesus "thown everything off balance. If He did what He said," The Misfit claims, "then it's nothing for you to do but thow away everything and follow Him, and if He didn't, then it's nothing for you to do but enjoy

the few minutes you got left the best way you can—by killing somebody or burning down his house, or doing some other meanness to him. No pleasure but meanness." His decision to kill the grandmother and her whole family is an apparent denial then that Jesus really had "raised the dead," yet he implies the very opposite when he concludes that "it's no real pleasure in life." The grandmother's response is the perfect ironic counterpart of The Misfit's. "Not knowing what she was saying," she mumbles a denial, "Maybe He didn't raise the dead," and then reaches out to The Misfit as if she actually believes in the Resurrection when she acknowledges her responsibility for his sin, "Why you're one of my babies. You're one of my own children!" To The Misfit, her touch is like the bite of a snake. The gesture of recognition and acceptance signals her death. The Misfit denies the Resurrection in deed yet seems finally to imply a desire for acceptance; the grandmother denies it in word, perhaps, but clearly accepts it in deed.

Demonic characters are the occasion of grace or at least of judgment in three other stories in the collection. Harry Ashfield in "The River" drowns while trying to escape from the hideous Mr. Paradise and is at last received by the river whose waters, he believes, will make him "count." In "A Circle in the Fire," it is not until three young delinquents from the city wantonly set fire to Mrs. Cope's woods that she comes to appreciate the misery of the world's dispossessed. Manley Pointer, the demonic Bible salesman in "Good Country People," demonstrates the power of the evil heart over the malignant mind when he strips Hulga of the symbols of her pride, her artificial leg and her glasses—her soul and its self-styled insight.

"A Stroke of Good Fortune" and "A Late Encounter with the Enemy" show how easily man can become his own worst enemy. Ruby Hill's sloth and selfishness will kill her faster than the unwanted child she comes to discover is growing within her. "General" Sash, on the other hand, has lived for so long off of history without any genuine sense of its meaning that it is nothing more than a final enemy he succumbs to when his granddaughter uses him to add prestige to her graduation. Two other stories illustrate perfectly O'Connor's use of the grotesque as an instrument of religious vision. In both "The Life You Save May Be Your Own" and "A Temple of the Holy Ghost," it is clear that the truly grotesque are not the physically handicapped but the spiritually deformed.

The remaining stories in the first collection, "The Artificial Nigger" and "The Displaced Person," rival the title story for a place among O'Connor's very best, and appropriately enough each displays her mastery of symbolism as art's way of joining time and eternity. The first is a modern variation on the *Inferno*, dramatizing descent into self-knowledge; the other, the last story in the collection, unveils the good man who is so hard to find, a latter-day Christ who brings salvation but is rejected. Confronted with the chipped statue of the Negro boy, Mr. Head confesses his awareness of personal sin by rejecting the artificiality of discrimination. "They ain't got enough real ones here," he tells his grandson, Nelson. "They got to have an artificial one." (The relationship between an old man and a young man becomes the heart of O'Connor's second novel.) The climactic dialogue between Mrs. McIntyre and Father Flynn in "The Displaced Person" is a masterpiece of misunderstood meaning and ignored revelation. Mrs. McIntyre shores up her decision to release Mr. Guizac, the displaced person who attempts to arrange his cousin's immigration to America by having her marry a black farmhand in the segregated South: "He didn't have to come in the first place," she tells the priest. But Father Flynn, contemplating the Transfiguration of Christ in the resplendence of the peacock (O'Connor's most successful use of natural symbolism), thinks she is referring to Christ's Advent and announces the good news of salvation: "He came to redeem us."

In subtlety of symbolism and obsession with the demonic, O'Connor's short stories are descendants of Nathaniel Hawthorne's tales; the starkness of her imagery and her use of the grotesque in both the short stories and *Wise Blood* are often related with reason to Nathanael West. When it comes to her second and decidedly superior novel, *The Violent Bear It Away* (1960), the literary indebtedness that can be discerned lies closer home. Not only are the cadences of style suggestive of William Faulkner, but also some of the novel's major themes. Its preoccupation with the influence that the dead continue to exert on the living is clearly reminiscent of Addie Bundren's domination of her family in *As I Lay Dying* (Robert Fitzgerald reports that it was one of her favorite novels); there is also its pervasive concern about the relationship between words and deeds, a theme that has even deeper roots in the teaching of Jesus.

The novel abounds in images and symbols, but O'Connor is as successful here as in her richest stories in weaving them together into a harmonious whole. The principal ones are Biblical in origin: fire, water, hunger, the bread of life, prophecy, the sower, and the Word. In the final analysis, though, it is not the symbolism that puts readers off, but the central character himself, Mason, a fundamentalist backwoods prophet for whom history begins with Eden and ends with the Day of the Lord. People find it hard to be objective in the presence of fanaticism, yet be objective one must if the novel is to be understood. Mason and his nephew Rayber are locked in mortal combat for the control of young Tarwater's education. Mason stands for faith in the supernatural, Rayber for disbelief. Yet in a fictional world in which the voice of reason turns out to be the dragon of seduction, the novel makes the eminently plausible point that only the enthusiast ("the violent") can gain the kingdom ("bear it away"). It is not until Tarwater has been violated in mind and body by the homosexual stranger and has thus for the first time experienced evil himself that he accepts the prophetic mission his great-uncle has given him. As he marches toward the city at the close of the novel, he hears Mason's command again: "GO WARN THE CHILDREN OF GOD OF THE TERRIBLE SPEED OF MERCY." "The words," we are told, "were as silent as seeds opening one at a time in his blood." One has to know evil before one can understand the need to preach redemption.

If the first collection of stories sketches a world that, for O'Connor, seems almost gracious in comparison with *Wise Blood* in its evocation of mercy for the fallen—there is no redemption, of course, without a fall—the world of the posthumous collection, *Everything That Rises Must Converge* (1965), is decidedly less so. Although the stories build toward a powerful climax suggesting an affirmative interpretation of the "convergence" of the title, it is the apocalyptic moment of Judgment for an unregenerate world that abounds here, as it does in *The Violent Bear It Away.*

In the title story, however limited Julian's mother's view of reality is, it is far superior to his mindless liberalism; and her single functioning eye, which rakes Julian's face for a final time and finds nothing, implies a judgment more scathing than words can achieve. The fierce, inflamed eye of a bird in the water stain on Asbury's ceiling is the instrument of judgment in "The Enduring Chill." Asbury's interracial communion in unpasteurized milk with Randall and Morgan is the cause of the undulant fever that will return periodically to chill his body as the icy image of the Holy Ghost chastens his mind and heart. As a historian, Thomas, in "The Comforts of Home," ought to have had sufficient insight to realize that his father, the figure "squatting" in his mind, had no rights over the sanctity of the human spirit. The peace that Thomas lies to protect ends in complex tragedy; one does not connive with evil in order to end it, as Haze learns in *Wise Blood.*

Mrs. May in "Greenleaf" is the victim of a bull's irresistible attraction to cars, but more precisely of her own refusal to allow anyone—even God—to alter her view of reality. In "A View of the Woods," Mr. Fortune hopes to make his granddaughter, Mary Fortune Pitts, into a Fortune, like himself a lover of progress—drive-ins, supermarkets, gas stations, and paved roads. She prefers to give up a fortune—and her life—rather than accept his sale of the land across the road that will destroy her view of the woods. The only quality of his that she has inherited is, ironically, his irascibility, and so they struggle to the death like two titans of pride. Rufus's cry "The lame shall enter first!" in the story with the same name sounds the evangelical note of the beatitudes, condemning Sheppard for his scientific atheism and reminding us once again how Jesus has "thown everything off balance."

The title *Everything That Rises Must Converge* is borrowed from the evolutionary reflections of Pierre Teilhard de Chardin, the French paleontologist-theologian who was denied permission by Rome to publish his works. After his death in 1955, they were published by friends and colleagues; O'Connor read what was available with great interest, without, apparently, sharing fully Teilhard's optimistic view of man's rise in the evolutionary chain. The final three stories of O'Connor's second collection, nevertheless, sound an affirmative note about the human condition—

and they too rank with her most highly acclaimed. Ruby Turpin in "Revelation" places herself close to the top of life's hierarchy of classes; Mary Grace pierces through to the heart of Ruby's discriminatory attitude and opens up for her a vision of the world in which God disregards human standards of judgment and sees through to the inner value of the person. O. E. Parker in "Parker's Back" suffers, but he grows through suffering; that sort of diminishment Teilhard de Chardin accepted as a necessary part of evolution. It is the stern eyes of the Byzantine Christ in the tattooer's book of religious pictures that speaks the saving word of revelation to Parker—"GO BACK!" Parker goes back to his full name, Obadiah Elihue (which means "the servant of Yahweh, he is God"), *and* to his wife. To be rejected in an act of selfless love—the image on his back that Sarah Ruth cannot tolerate was after all for her alone—is to live unmistakably in the likeness of God's servant.

Although Flannery O'Connor undoubtedly had a great sense of the creative role of the writer, she was convinced that there were definite limits within which that creativity had to be exercised. In "The Church and the Fiction Writers," she speaks about the "what-is" that is the concrete material of the writer: "The writer learns, perhaps more quickly than the reader, to be humble in the face of what-is. What-is is all he has to do with; the concrete is his medium; and he will realize eventually that fiction can transcend its limitations only by staying within them." A writer creates by shaping reality to his purpose. "What he is rearranging *is* nature," she insisted.

The ultimate purpose of the artist's use of concrete reality is, as she saw it, to transcend it through vision. "The peculiar problem of the short-story writer," she asserts, "is how to make the action he describes reveal as much of the mystery of existence as possible. He has only a short space to do it in and he can't do it by statement. He has to do it by showing, not by saying, and by showing the concrete—so that his problem is really how to make the concrete work double time for him." For Flannery O'Connor, the mystery of existence discloses a transcendent world that is every bit as real as the visible world. On another occasion she wrote that the writer is "looking for one image that will connect or combine or embody two points; one is a point in the concrete, and the other is a point not visible to the naked eye, but believed in by him firmly, just as real to him, really, as the one that everybody sees." The writer must also have a strong sense of his own region. He leaves his region, she wrote, "at great peril to that balance between principle and fact, between judgment and observation, which is so necessary to maintain if fiction is to be true." For, "unless the novelist has gone utterly out of his mind, his aim is still communication, and communication suggests talking inside a community." She assumes, therefore, that the artist wishes to communicate. Aside from her assertion that communication works best within the community of those who share the same "manners," she speaks of the artist's communication of his prophetic vision as revelation to the reader, provided he sees the creative process as basically healthy. "Those who believe that art proceeds from a healthy, and not from a diseased, faculty of the mind," she writes, "will take what [the artist] shows them as a revelation, not of what we ought to be but of what we are at a given time and under given circumstances; that is, as a limited revelation but revelation nevertheless."

It is no surprise then that Sally and Robert Fitzgerald chose the title *Mystery and Manners* when they selected for publication and edited the collection of O'Connor's occasional prose five years after her death. The title encompasses briefly but accurately the dimensions of her art. While including a delightful piece that she wrote on peacocks and her introduction to *A Memoir of Mary Ann*, the work is principally a collection of her lectures and published essays related to the theory of fiction and to the call that she felt she had received to be, specifically, a Catholic writer.

The full legacy of O'Connor's short fiction was finally packaged in one volume and published in 1971 as *The Complete Stories*. There are thirty-one stories in the volume, twelve appearing for the first time in book form (although all twelve had been published before). The chronological sequence according to date of composition that Giroux follows provides the clearest possible index of O'Connor's growth as an artist. "Judgement Day," the last of *The Complete Stories* as well as the last in the second collection, is a revised and expanded version of the very first story O'Connor published, "The Geranium."

Both stories are concerned with exiles from their "true country," but whereas Old Dudley of "The Geranium" remains exiled from his Southern home because of his mistaken sense of place, it is perfectly clear (and confessionally appropriate) that in "Judgement Day" Old Tanner's imagined return to Corinth, Georgia, is a genuine victory over alienation—because he knows his place. O'Connor's last story is a truly distinguished American variation on the archetype of homecoming and perhaps our finest literary presentation of the significance of resurrection. Its evocation of spiritual triumph is a fitting crown for an illustrious, though regrettably short career. It is not at all strange that concern for an exile from home should be the alpha and omega of a writer whose faith was certainly as important as her art.—*John R. May*

Books:

Wise Blood (New York: Harcourt, Brace, 1952; London: Spearman, 1955);

A Good Man Is Hard to Find (New York: Harcourt, Brace, 1955; republished as *The Artificial Nigger and Other Tales*, London: Spearman, 1957);

The Violent Bear It Away (New York: Farrar, Straus & Cudahy, 1960; London: Longmans, 1960);

Everything That Rises Must Converge (New York: Farrar, Straus & Giroux, 1965; London: Faber & Faber, 1966);

Mystery and Manners (New York: Farrar, Straus & Giroux, 1969; London: Faber & Faber, 1972);

The Complete Stories of Flannery O'Connor (New York: Farrar, Straus & Giroux, 1971).

References:

Joan T. Brittain, "Flannery O'Connor—Addenda," *Bulletin of Bibliography*, 25 (1968): 142;

Brittain, "Flannery O'Connor: A Bibliography," *Bulletin of Bibliography*, 25 (1968): 98-100, 123-124;

Preston M. Browning, *Flannery O'Connor* (Carbondale: Southern Illinois University Press, 1974);

Stuart L. Burns, "The Evolution of *Wise Blood*," *Modern Fiction Studies*, 16 (summer 1970): 147-162;

Burns, "Flannery O'Connor's Literary Apprenticeship," *Renascence*, 22 (autumn 1969): 3-16;

Burns, "Structural Patterns in *Wise Blood*," *Xavier University Studies*, 8 (summer 1969): 32-43;

Brainard Cheney, "Miss O'Connor Creates Unusual Humor out of Ordinary Sin," *Sewanee Review*, 71 (autumn 1963): 644-652;

Robert Detweiler, "The Curse of Christ in Flannery O'Connor's Fiction," *Comparative Literature Studies*, 3 (1966): 235-245;

Bob Dowell, "The Moment of Grace in the Fiction of Flannery O'Connor," *College English*, 27 (December 1965): 235-239;

Robert Y. Drake, Jr., "The Bleeding, Stinking, Mad Shadow of Jesus in the Fiction of Flannery O'Connor," *Comparative Literature Studies*, 3, 2 (1966): 183-196;

Drake, "The Paradigm of Flannery O'Connor's True Country," *Studies in Short Fiction*, 6 (summer 1969): 433-442;

Leon V. Driskell and Joan T. Brittain, *The Eternal Crossroads: The Art of Flannery O'Connor* (Lexington: University of Kentucky Press, 1971);

David Eggenschwiler, *The Christian Humanism of Flannery O'Connor* (Detroit: Wayne State University Press, 1972);

Sister M. Kathleen Feeley, S.S.N.D., "Thematic Imagery in the Fiction of Flannery O'Connor," *Southern Humanities Review*, 3 (winter 1968): 14-32;

Feeley, *Flannery O'Connor: Voice of the Peacock* (New Brunswick, N.J.: Rutgers University Press, 1972);

Robert Fitzgerald, "The Countryside and the True Country," *Sewanee Review*, 70, 3 (1962): 380-394;

Melvin J. Friedman and Lewis A. Lawson, eds., *The Added Dimension: The Art and Mind of Flannery O'Connor* (New York: Fordham University Press, 1966);

Robert E. Golden and Mary C. Sullivan, *Flannery O'Connor and Caroline Gordon: A Reference Guide* (Boston: G. K. Hall, 1977);

John Hawkes, "Flannery O'Connor's Devil," *Sewanee Review*, 70 (summer 1962): 395-407;

Josephine Hendin, *The World of Flannery O'Connor* (Bloomington: Indiana University Press, 1970);

Forrest L. Ingram, "O'Connor's Seven-Story Cycle," *The Flannery O'Connor Bulletin*, 2 (autumn 1973): 19-28;

Thomas M. Lorch, "Flannery O'Connor: Christian Allegorist," *Critique*, 10, 2 (1968): 69-80;

Carter W. Martin, "Flannery O'Connor's Early Fiction," *Southern Humanities Review*, 7 (spring 1973): 210-214;

Martin, *The True Country: Themes in the Fiction of Flannery O'Connor* (Nashville: Vanderbilt University Press, 1969);

John R. May, *The Pruning Word: The Parables of Flannery O'Connor* (Notre Dame: University of Notre Dame Press, 1976);

David R. Mayer, "*The Violent Bear It Away*: Flannery O'Connor's Shaman," *Southern Literary Journal*, 4 (spring 1972): 41-54;

Dorothy Tuck McFarland, *Flannery O'Connor* (New York: Frederick Ungar, 1976);

Marion Montgomery, "Beyond Symbol and Surface: The Fiction of Flannery O'Connor," *Georgia Review*, 22 (summer 1968): 188-193;

Montgomery, "Miss O'Connor and the Christ-Haunted," *Southern Review*, 4 (summer 1968): 665-672;

Gilbert H. Muller, *Nightmares and Visions: Flannery O'Connor and the Catholic Grotesque* (Athens: University of Georgia Press, 1972);

Miles Orvell, *Invisible Parade: The Fiction of Flannery O'Connor* (Philadelphia: Temple University Press, 1972);

J(oyce Carol) Oates Smith, "Ritual and Violence in Flannery O'Connor," *Thought*, 41 (winter 1966): 545-560;

Ollye Tine Snow, "The Functional Gothic of Flannery O'Connor," *Southwest Review*, 50 (summer 1965): 286-299;

Richard Stern, "Flannery O'Connor: A Remembrance and Some Letters," *Shenandoah*, 16, 2 (winter 1965): 5-10;

Henry Taylor, "The Halt Shall be Gathered Together: Physical Deformity in the Fiction of Flannery O'Connor," *Western Humanities Review*, 22 (autumn 1968): 325-338;

Dorothy Walters, *Flannery O'Connor* (New York: Twayne Publishers, 1973);

Ralph C. Wood, "The Heterodoxy of Flannery O'Connor's Book Reviews," *The Flannery O'Connor Bulletin*, 5 (autumn 1976): 3-29.

Note: *The Flannery O'Connor Bulletin* (1972-   ) is devoted to articles about O'Connor and her work.

Manuscripts:

The Flannery O'Connor Collection was donated to the Georgia College Library by Regina O'Connor, mother of the author. It contains 328 folders of manuscript, 594 volumes from the author's personal library, audiotapes, 16 mm films, various editions and translations of the author's works, critical writings, newspaper clippings, and photographs. Research in the collection is made available to graduate students and other scholars by prearrangement.

GIL ORLOVITZ wrote in 1957 that "Too much verse is written *about* phenomena. My intent is to make the phenomena one of the symbols." Rather than writing about experience, Orlovitz made words themselves the experience. It was this very practice that was both his undoing and his lasting success, for while it alienated him from popular audiences all his life, it did establish him as a noteworthy innovator in the novel, anticipating developments made respectable in the 1960s and the 1970s by such writers as Ronald Sukenick, Gilbert Sorrentino, William H. Gass, and even by such popularly successful authors as Donald Barthelme, Richard Brautigan, and Kurt Vonnegut.

Orlovitz was born in Philadelphia, Pennsylvania, on 7 June 1918. He attended Temple University and then Columbia University in New York, where he worked most of his life as editor and free-lance television writer, with one period in Hollywood as a screenwriter for Columbia Pictures. In literary circles he was best known as a poet, publishing his first collection of verse in 1947, and as an off-Broadway dramatist. He found it extremely difficult to publish his fiction in the United States, even in avant-garde magazines, so he turned to a sympathetic British firm, Calder & Boyars, which was publishing an international series of innovative novels by Samuel Beckett, William Burroughs, Robert Creeley. Robert Pinget, Tibor Dery, Alain Robbe-Grillet, and others.

Calder & Boyars published *Milkbottle H* (1967) and *Ice Never F* (1970), the first two novels in Orlovitz's proposed trilogy. In 1968 and 1969 the first volume was reprinted in hardcover by Delacorte and then in paperback by Dell. Dell editor Richard Huett's tactic was to emphasize the controversy over Orlovitz's substitution of technique for content, his novel's self-indulgence, its alleged impenetrability, and other obstacles; negative as well as strongly positive reviews lined the book's back cover, as a challenge to both popular readers and the critical establishment. But Huett's gamble in this case failed, just as Orlovitz's personal fortunes were deteriorating. His wife Maralyn, whom he had married in 1954 and with whom he had had a daughter and two sons, demanded a separation; he also found it harder to hold a good job, moving from paperback houses to more transient firms, and finally to a position with Marvel Comics. By 1973 he was unemployed and on welfare, in ill health, living in a single room in New York City. On 9 July, returning from an unsuccessful attempt to visit his wife and two young sons, Orlovitz collapsed on the street and was taken (in a coma and with a 108° fever) to a hospital where he died the next day, never regaining consciousness. Because police were unable to trace relatives, Orlovitz was buried in a pauper's grave and remained unidentified until a missing person's report filed by his wife was collated with the death record.

The fiction of Gil Orlovitz failed among popular readers and established critics in its own day because of its aesthetic allegiance to the novelistic experiments of such fellow poets as William Carlos Williams, Kenneth Patchen, and Gilbert Sorrentino. *Milkbottle H* does have realistic components, including a setting (Philadelphia in the 1940s), a protagonist (Lee Emanuel) who is having a deep personal relationship (with Rena Goldstein), and action (resulting from complications in Lee's family and job). But Orlovitz refuses to write *about* these circumstances. To do so, even in the name of realism, would be to distort the true imaginative nature of life into artificial, conventional shapes. As author, he deliberately avoids the chronological structures of time and the linear geography of space, fearing that once his events are placed in such order they will lose their true effectiveness as objects of the mind. Instead, he presents incidents cut free of time, where plot cannot distract the reader from appreciating the writing itself. Orlovitz tries to save the power of his scenes by abstracting them from the realm of story. Such major innovations have been resisted by established critics even into the 1970s; during Orlovitz's period of greatest activity, 1945-1965, he could hope only for understanding among readers and critics of contemporary poetry. "His purpose is to distort the commonplace so that it may be newly observed," Henry Birnbaum noted in the pages of *Poetry*. "Never completely successful, he makes a trying and interesting experiment of it. Sometimes he loses his reader in one of his contrived sexual niches, and sometimes he drives him to a *non sequitur*. But as often, Orlovitz shocks his reader into awareness by striking a sleeping and satisfied nerve."

Orlovitz uses explicitly expressed sexual themes to challenge primness, and linguistic somersaults to prevent easy, unthinking identifications with the quotidian world. But although some reviewers acknowledged the need for reinvention in the novel, and a few even proclaimed *Milkbottle H* a masterpiece in this regard, most misunderstood the situation and condemned the work as unreadable. The most sympathetic American reader was Kevin Sullivan in *Book World*, who recognized that Orlovitz was creating "a genre that no longer experiments with form but discards all form and concentrates on the presentation of immediately felt experience or, more accurately, allows that experience to present itself." It is to Orlovitz's credit, Sullivan argues, that there is "no container for the verbal energies at work here, no plot, no beginning and no end to the rush and crush of language." But other critics were either blinded by their strictly Aristotelian perceptions of what literary art should be, or misled by thinking Orlovitz was trying to rewrite James Joyce's *Ulysses* in Philadelphia. Instead, he was moving a step beyond Joyce's reliance on psychology and myth into a form of narrative which presupposed neither, asking only for the play of language in the writer's and reader's minds. "Stream of consciousness," the term traditionalist critics tried to affix to *Milkbottle H,* is fully inappropriate, since Orlovitz bears no allegiance to the stream of time nor to the clinically-discoverable order of consciousness. He would never suggest that fishing in such streams would yield an insight into the underlying structure of Man. Orlovitz cared for just the opposite: the play of one man's artistic talent, adding an object of art to the things already in the world.

Ice Never F takes protagonist Lee Goldstein through marriage, career, and more family complications, most of which correspond vaguely to Orlovitz's own experiences. Events of history mix with events of the mind in an objectively contradictory but subjectively "true" manner later made popular by Robert Coover in his story "The Baby Sitter" and his novel *The Public Burning.* The foundation of the novel becomes the sense of the author's own personal associations, which are explored in their juxtapositions through language (as the most usable expression of imagination).

The only discursive essay published on Orlovitz during his lifetime, by Hale Chatfield in *Kenyon Review,* explained and justified his method as a reflection of the reinvention of painting by the Abstract Expressionists in the two decades preceding. Like Jackson Pollock, Franz Kline, Willem de Kooning, and their contemporaries, who moved beyond the self-consciously absurd juxtapositions of surrealism, Orlovitz "characterizes himself by the intensity of his search for the significance of his own associations and his militant reluctance to let them go by without explaining themselves."

—*Jerome Klinkowitz*

Books:

Concerning Man (Pawlet, Vermont: Banyan Press, 1947);
Keep to Your Belly (New York: Louis Brigants/Intro,

1952);
The Diary of Dr. Eric Zeno (San Francisco: Inferno Press, 1953);
The Statement of Erica Keith and other Stories, Poems and a Play (Berkeley: Miscellaneous Man, 1957);
The Diary of Alexander Patience (San Francisco: Inferno Press, 1958);
The Papers of Professor Bold (Eureka, Cal.: Hearse Press, 1958);
Something to Tell Mother (London: American Letters Press, 1959?);
Selected Poems (San Francisco: Inferno Press, 1960; London: Barrie & Rockliff, n.d.);
The Art of the Sonnet (Nashville, Tenn.: Hillsboro Publications, 1961);
Five Sonnets (Lanham, Maryland: Goosetree Press, 1964);
Milkbottle H (London: Calder & Boyars, 1967; New York: Delacorte, 1968);
Couldn't Say. Might Be Love (London: Barrie & Rockliff, 1969);
Ice Never F (London: Calder & Boyars, 1970);
More Poems (Fredericton, New Brunswick, Canada: Fiddlehead, 1972).

Plays:

Case of a Neglected Calling Card, New York, Dramatic Workshop, 1952;
Noone, New York, Provincetown Playhouse, 1953;
Stefanie, Philadelphia, Central Players of the YMCA, 1953; New York, Amato Theatre, 1954;
Todt and Thor (reading), New York, Gallery East.

Screenplay:

Overexposed, Columbia, 1956.

Periodical Publications:

"Two Stories: 'The Death of Sam Runnymeade' and 'Lila Bohmer'," *Quarterly Review of Literature,* 4, 1 (1947): 40-47;
"Tears from a Glass Eye," *Intro,* 1, 2 (1951): 56-64;
"A Metaphysical Inquiry into Adam Zion Davidson," *Intro,* 1, 3-4 (1951): 153-160;
"Stevie Guy," *Quarterly Review of Literature,* 6, 1-2 (1952): 245-280;
"Alice," *Whetstone,* 1 (summer 1955);
"Footnote on Willis," *Mutiny,* 1 (spring 1957): 19-30;
"A Fourth of July," *Whetstone,* 2, 2 (1957): 79-88;
"What Will You Give Our Lord Tonight,"

Colorado Quarterly, 1 (spring-summer 1957): 55-64;

"A Deposition of Ben Berman," *Mutiny*, 2 (autumn 1959): 95-102;

"Fob at Bay," *Colorado Quarterly*, 3 (winter 1958-1959): 16-24;

"Gray," *Literary Review*, 2 (winter 1959): 206-308.

Other:

"The Ubiquitous Symbol," in *The Statement of Erica Keith* (Berkeley: Miscellaneous Man, 1957), pp. 61-62;

"I'm Just in Sparta on a Visit," in *The Award Avant-Garde Reader*, ed. Orlovitz (New York: Award Books, 1965), pp. 172-187.

References:

Robert Martin Adams, "Fiction Chronicle," *Hudson Review*, 21 (spring 1968): 225-231;

Henry Birnbaum, "The Poetry of Protest," *Poetry*, 94 (September 1959): 408-413;

Hale Chatfield, "Literary Exile in Residence," *Kenyon Review*, 21, 4 (1969): 545-553.

WALKER PERCY was born in Birmingham, Alabama, on 28 May 1916. He married Mary Bernice Townsend in 1946, has two daughters, and is very much the family man and private person at his home in Covington, Louisiana. He claims to read little fiction and to associate with few other writers; he says he doesn't see himself as particularly literary. This current situation is in contrast with his upbringing.

Percy's lawyer father descended from a long line of lawyers who often wrote as an avocation; his mother came from a prominent Georgia family. When Percy was eleven, his father committed suicide; two years later his mother was killed in an auto accident. Percy and his two brothers were thereupon adopted by their father's cousin, William Alexander Percy, whose multifaceted abilities proved a strong influence on them. William Percy's house in Greenville, Mississippi, attracted many cultural enthusiasts; authors such as William Faulkner visited, and the elder Percy himself wrote a minor classic entitled *Lanterns on the Levee* (1941).

But though Walker Percy dabbled in writing during his school years (he sold sonnets to less-talented English classmates who needed them for assignments), he turned to science in college. He received a B.A. as a premed chemistry major at the University of North Carolina in 1937 and his M.D. from Columbia University in New York in 1941. It was while he was interning the next year at Bellevue Hospital in New York that serious illness ended his plans for a career in psychiatry. Performing autopsies on derelicts, Percy contracted pulmonary tuberculosis that resulted in two years of invalidism. During this illness, Percy began the extensive philosophical reading that caused him suddenly to see limitations to the scientific method and to find new values in art and humanism.

The early 1940s were a time of much significant change in Percy's personal and philosophical life. Just prior to the onset of his illness, he had ended three years of psychoanalysis; then his Uncle Will died, leaving him financially independent. He made an initial recovery from his illness and attempted to return to Columbia Medical School as a teacher of pathology; but when he suffered a relapse, he returned to a sedentary life and continued to read. He converted to Roman Catholicism and, finally, abandoned medicine for a new career in writing.

Percy has named Kierkegaard as perhaps the most influential of the philosophers he read at this time. But he was also drawn to Heidegger; he became absorbed in the existentialist ideas of Sartre and Camus and the Christian existentialism espoused by Marcel. He found that he shared the existentialist view of man as being in a predicament, troubled by uprootedness, estrangement, and anxiety. Like him, these men were interested in what it is like to be a man in a world transformed by science. And it was from these philosophers, rather than from fellow Southern writers, that Percy fashioned his literary credo.

Percy is not a typical Southern writer in the sense that he does not ape Faulknerian mannerisms or utilize Southern local color; indeed, he has declared that he thinks the age of Southern writing is over. Percy epitomizes the new Southern writer, both a descendant of the past and a man of the present. In any case, Percy specifically disavows any legacy from Southern literary tradition; rather, he declares his indebtedness to philosophers and to French and Russian novelists.

By its very communication, Percy considers art the reversal of alienation; he also believes that the writer can and should seek to influence social and political issues through his creative work. The thinly veiled religious jeremiads of his novels have caused them to be frequently grouped with modern secularized apocalyptic novels, and Percy admits that his main writing motivation is usually a desire

Jill Krementz

to correct wrongs. But he does not think that an author's philosophy should be imposed on a work; it must be an integral part of the work, as it is of the author's being.

Percy's fiction employs a special terminology, a list of concepts that appear as leitmotifs in book after book. Often the enemy is everydayness, a condition of numbness and devitalized existence resulting from routine. A second cause of modern malaise is inauthenticity, the antithesis of meaningful life, involving the surrender of personal sovereignty

through such habits as conformity. A third cause is abstraction, the absorption of concrete personality into its theoretical shadow through objectification of the self. Fortunately for troubled man, Percy posits solutions to these ills. Man can recover himself through ordeal, such as a shock that rends everydayness. Alternatively, he can attempt a rotation, experiencing the new beyond his expectations of experiencing the new; initiate a repetition, a reliving of a past experience; or cultivate intersubjectivity, nonobjective relations with other human beings. All of Percy's protagonists suffer from at least one of these causes of despair and recover, or attempt to recover, by one of these means.

Percy's first mature published writing was in essay form and primarily philosophical; he served his novelistic apprenticeship in the early 1950s, writing two unpublished novels. *The Moviegoer* (1961), written in slightly more than a year, was his first novel to achieve publication and jolted the critical world by winning the prestigious National Book Award for 1962. Percy was then forty-five years old.

The Moviegoer is an analysis of alienation, showing one man's search for a heightened reality outside everydayness and the pointlessness of so-called "meaningful lives." The setting is the South, but it is a South representative of the rest of the country. And the protagonist, "Binx" Bolling, is, despite his proud Southern heritage, a typical American outsider: for the most part, appearing conventional, acting normally, yet searching in anguish for a reality in which everything is even momentarily just as it might be.

Binx's outward daily life is unexceptional. He manages a small branch office of his uncle's brokerage firm, has pleasurable passing affairs with his secretaries, and goes to the movies. However, movie-going for Binx is more than just casual entertainment. He uses movies to keep the nightmare of life at bay. For him, movies "certify" the reality of his world; they help him hold on to his always tenuous sense of identity and place. He finds that movies, unlike actual life, are engaged in the search for meaning, even though they always disappointingly fail to attain it and sink back into the morass of everydayness, where all is figuratively dead. The world of movies offers Binx a needed haven; unable to cope with the malaise of the actual world, he settles for the cinematic one and models his behavior on that of movie actors.

The action of the novel covers one week in New Orleans during Mardi Gras when Binx is forced to answer his Aunt Emily's question about his immediate life goals. He is shown dallying with Sharon, his latest desirable secretary; trying to rouse his neurotic cousin Kate from her suicidal depression; sharing unspoken love and communion with his crippled younger half brother Lonnie. At the end of the novel, he apparently capitulates to his aunt's demand that he make something of himself: he agrees to go to medical school and to marry Kate, whose emotional instability is lessened by his caring. The epilogue shows Binx neither victorious nor defeated; he does not succumb to deadened everydayness, but he does not continue his "search" with the old intensity, either. He seems to have decided to accept the trivial outward roles of life and to maintain a meaningful life within.

Despite some surprise and disgruntlement over the awarding of the National Book Award to a new, untested author, most literary critics have in retrospect given high praise to *The Moviegoer* for its tightness and control of the material. Percy's next novel, *The Last Gentleman* (1966), has been generally deemed less satisfactory; acknowledged as a more ambitious effort, the novel is said to ramble and suffer from failure to develop its protagonist fully.

Like *The Moviegoer*, *The Last Gentleman* is comic, but the humorous strokes are broader and the satiric targets more vigorously lampooned in this later novel. Considered by some critics to be a twentieth-century *Candide*, *The Last Gentleman* borrows much from the picaresque: its protagonist, Will Barrett, is virtually adopted by the Vaught family and journeys with them from New York to their Southern home and thence westward to the ranches of New Mexico. En route, he encounters many types of men and situations for Percy to deflate: Northern housing-development blockbusters, investigative reporters, modern Southern mansions. But Will does not recognize their humor; another of Percy's serious lost young men, he is struggling to determine his own identity.

In Percy's terms, *The Last Gentleman* is a description of the process of rotation and return; Will goes back to the South, home to his roots, to better understand himself. Like Binx, he is bothered by a world of chaos and villainy and accident that cannot be easily defined. He, too, is on a pilgrim's search, but his perception is hindered by recurring attacks of amnesia and *deja vu* that give him a post-modern and post-Christian vision of life (i.e., the present world minus illusion). Will's failing is his attempt to engineer his life on scientific principles instead of living it; he is so adept at role playing that he lacks an identity and has lost access to his own inwardness. Percy's underlying question seems to be, What sort of pilgrim does a man make if he is blind and deaf to the signs and the message?

The story line of the novel is episodic. Will Barrett, transplanted Southerner, humidification-engineer at Macy's department store, falls in love with a girl he sees through his telescope. One day he follows Kitty to a hospital, where she is visiting her younger brother Jamie, who is dying of leukemia. Will meets the rest of the family: Mr. Vaught, gigantic Chevrolet agency owner; Mrs. Vaught, Civil

I

One fine day in early summer a young man lay thinking in
Central Park.

His head was propped on his jacket which had been folded
twice so that the lining was outermost and wedged into a
seam of rock. The rock jutted out of the ground in a section
of the park known as the Great Meadow. Beside him and canted up
at mortar angle squatted a telescope of an unusual design.

In the course of the next five minutes the young man was
to witness by the purest chance a ~~very~~ curious ~~little~~ happening.

It was a beautiful day, but only after the fashion of
beautiful days in New York. The sky was no more than an ordinary Eastern sky, mild and blue and hazed over, whitened under
the blue and of not much account. It was a standard sky by
which all other skies are measured. As for the park, green
leaves or not, it belonged to the animal kingdom rather than
the vegetable. It had a zoo smell. Last summer's grass was
as coarse and yellow as lion's hair and worn bare in spots exposing the tough old hide of the earth. The tree trunks were
polished /and bits of hair clung to the bark as if a large
animal had been rubbing against them. Nevertheless, thought
he
~~the young man,~~ it is a good thing to see a park put to hard
sort
use by millions of people, used and handled in its every square
inch, like a bear garden.

He was a young man of an extraordinary appearance. Of

From typescript of The Last Gentleman.

War theorist; Sutter, failed physician/pornographer; Val, member of a religious order; Rita, Sutter's divorced wife. In love with the vacuous Kitty and hired companion for the dying Jamie, Will travels with the family to their Southern home, lives with them and takes college courses with Kitty and Jamie, and eventually follows Jamie and Sutter west, where he is present at Jamie's death.

The Last Gentleman ends in ambiguity; the reader knows that Will is the "last gentleman" because the role is played out, but Percy leaves it uncertain whether, like Jamie, Will has learned to become a sovereign wayfarer, aware of his own death and in charge of his own life. Will seems to miss the point of Jamie's death; he asks Sutter, "What happened back there?" As he runs to Sutter's car at the end of the novel, Will leaves the reader uncertain whether he will save Sutter along with himself or share Sutter's planned suicidal doom.

With the publication of *Love in the Ruins* (1971), which won the National Catholic Book Award in the year it was published, Percy's ever-present apocalypticism came more obviously to the fore; the subtitle of the novel was *The Adventures of a Bad Catholic at a Time Near the End of the World*. Once again, the book is a diagnosis of the malaise of contemporary America; here, however, the world is shown as teetering on the verge of the ultimate conflagration. Notwithstanding the prospect of imminent holocaust, the rollicking humor of Percy's writing reaches new heights in *Love in the Ruins*; the novel is a comic synthesis of modern thought, a futuristic satire with something, Percy has said, to offend everybody.

In his third novel, Percy comes to terms with what it is to be a man in a world transformed by science and why it is that humanism turns to beastliness. His protagonist is Dr. Tom More, who characterizes himself as "a physician, a not very successful psychiatrist; an alcoholic, a shaky middle-aged man subject to depressions and elations and morning terrors . . . a bad Catholic; a widower and cuckold." Like Will, Tom is plagued by uncertain mental health; technically, he is still on patient-staff status at the hospital. Despite this, Tom alone among men has diagnosed the cause of modern despair—a psychic rift between man's conscience and nature—and the means of its discovery and cure—More's Qualitative Quantitative Ontological Lapsometer, a small electronic device. The suspense of the narrative results from the question of whether Tom's MOQUOL will be put into widespread use soon enough to save mankind from itself.

The cast of characters in *Love in the Ruins* includes familiar standbys: the solitary and sensitive male protagonist, more keenly attuned to the Big Questions than his fellow men are; the sensual, willing woman, like Binx's secretary, here multiplied by three; the not-fully-dimensional black and white comic stereotypes. Most notable among the others is the allegorical Art Immelmann, devil figure and Washington liaison man, who tempts Tom to the sin of hubris by holding out the promise of national funding for the production of his lapsometers.

Like *The Moviegoer*, *Love in the Ruins* ends with an epilogue that shows the main characters living almost-happily ever after. Like Binx, Tom marries, choosing the most morally upright of his three girls. Again like Binx, Tom maintains his interest in ultimate concerns, though on a slightly less intense level than before. The world does *not* come to an end on July 4; the damage done by Art's widescale distribution of lapsometers is minimal; life goes on, with the only difference being a reversal of racial discrimination patterns (Tom and his wife now live in the old slave quarters). Tom remains watching and listening and waiting as he goes about his daily life, quietly expecting the cosmic catastrophe to come. If he is able to endure the despairs of everydayness better than before, it is because he has discovered the rewards of making love "at home in bed where all good folk belong."

While *Love in the Ruins* is seen as the funniest of Percy's novels, his most recent, *Lancelot* (1977), has been described by reviewers as his bleakest, grimmest, and most pessimistic. Once more, the work is apocalyptic, but in this case the small-scale holocaust is engineered by a madman who decides to start a revolution and, Christ-like, either purify the world or totally destroy it. Other tendencies of *Love in the Ruins* are carried further here, with what many critics see as dubious results. The skewering of satiric targets is present again, but the humor is more angry Juvenalian ranting than the gentler Horatian humor of earlier novels. The slight emotional instabilities of Binx and Will and Tom here give way to the full-fledged (though perhaps temporary) insanity of Lancelot Lamar, who punishes his wife's infidelities by burning down their mansion with her and her friends in it. Finally, many critics declare, the novelistic structure does not work well. Percy employs a form similar to both the French *recit* and confession; he has Lancelot tell the story aloud to the supposedly sympathetic ears of a boyhood friend who is given no speaking part beyond a few ambiguous monosyllables at the end of the novel.

Percy apparently hoped that full characterization of Lancelot and his friend Percival would emerge from Lancelot's monologue; however, some critics charge that the characterizations remain fuzzy and the dramatic situation of the narrator is unconvincing.

Despite these critical reservations, there is agreement that certain aspects of the novel work well. The unfolding of Lancelot's story is satisfyingly suspenseful, since Lancelot's recalling of key events is frequently sidetracked by memory lapses, both windy and cogent philosophizing, and tangential anecdotes. In chronological order, the tale he relates is a simple one. Happening to notice his child's blood type on her camp application, Lancelot ascertains that a man of his blood type could not have fathered his daughter. Methodically, he sets out to prove his wife's unfaithfulness, enlisting the aid of a bright, young black servant to watch bedroom doors and install hidden TV cameras. Proof obtained, Lancelot blows up the mansion and its residents, utilizing the *deus ex machina* of a gas well under the house. He himself, burned and crazed, is admitted to a center for aberrant behavior, from which he recounts this story.

For the first time, Percy includes much heavy-handed allegory here, including the names of speaker and listener and Lancelot's quest for the reality of evil, or Unholy Grail. Other stylistic mannerisms are carry-overs. Percy's philosophical concerns are inevitably present, as when Lancelot, for example, turns his wife's sexual betrayal into a central philosophical mystery. And even in this generally somber novel, the author manages a certain number of comic shots, ridiculing wife Margot and her ambitions, movie people and their pretensions, and the modern educated black. The affirmation that usually comes at the end of a Percy novel is muted, however; the reader is left unsure that Lancelot is really going to be released, that the gang-rape victim in the adjoining cell will actually join him in Virginia to start a new life, or that the listener's final spoken "yes" suggests that some answer is possible. Given failure of communication as a key idea of the novel, justification for an optimistic reading of the ending seems shaky.

While concentrating more on novels in recent years, Percy has not entirely abandoned his non-fiction. In addition to sporadic periodical essays, in 1975 there appeared *The Message in the Bottle*, a collection of his journal articles from the past twenty years. Though some of his fictional themes are treated (e.g., the individual's loss of sovereignty), the central subject is the philosophy of language.

The development of Walker Percy's novels from 1961 evinces certain trends. His philosophical interests and religious beliefs have moved more to the foreground and are less submerged in the fiction. His predilection for comic typecasting—of women and blacks, for example—is greater in the more recent books. Yet much in his writing has remained the same. His novelistic structure most frequently features a first-person narrator, a young-to-middle-aged man of extraordinary sensitivity bordering on incapacitating emotional instability who is plagued by the despair of the modern age. He goes through life like a pilgrim seeking answers; usually he eventually learns to cope with life through the transforming power of love. Percy has said that he believes the modern novel, like today's world, is more fragmented in its plot than the nineteenth-century novel was; nonetheless, all of his fiction thus far has employed traditional story lines and characterizations easily accessible to the reader.

Although Percy's critical reputation is growing, his name is still omitted from lists of important contemporary American novelists. It is difficult to understand why this is so, for his is a unique talent: physician and author of both fiction and essays on language, philosophy, psychiatry, and science, he is a modern Renaissance man. Accordingly, he is difficult to categorize; he sees himself as a Southern "philosophical Catholic existentialist." Perhaps his most important contribution to contemporary American literature is the result of this fusion of interests: like Camus and Sartre, two writers he admires, he seeks to combine his philosophical convictions with novelistic art. —*Joan Bischoff*

Books:

The Moviegoer (New York: Knopf, 1961; London: Eyre & Spottiswoode, 1963);

The Last Gentleman (New York: Farrar, Straus & Giroux, 1966; London: Eyre & Spottiswoode, 1967);

Love in the Ruins (New York: Farrar, Straus & Giroux, 1971; London: Eyre & Spottiswoode, 1971);

The Message in the Bottle (New York: Farrar, Straus & Giroux, 1975);

Lancelot (New York: Farrar, Straus & Giroux, 1977).

Periodical Publications:

"Symbol as Need," *Thought*, 29 (autumn 1954): 381-390;

"Symbol as Hermeneutic in Existentialism: A

Possible Bridge from Empiricism," *Philosophy and Phenomenological Research*, 16 (June 1956): 522-530;

"The Man on the Train: Three Existential Modes," *Partisan Review*, 23 (fall 1956): 478-494;

"The Coming Crisis in Psychiatry," *America*, 96 (5 January, 12 January 1957): 391-393, 415-418;

"Semiotic and a Theory of Knowledge," *Modern Schoolman*, 34 (May 1957): 225-246;

"The Act of Naming," University of Houston *Forum*, 1 (summer 1957): 4-9;

"Metaphor as Mistake," *Sewanee Review*, 66 (winter 1958): 79-99;

"Symbol, Consciousness, and Intersubjectivity," *Journal of Philosophy*, 55 (17 July 1958): 631-641;

"The Loss of the Creature," University of Houston *Forum*, 2 (fall 1958): 6-14;

"Culture: The Antinomy of the Scientific Method," *New Scholasticism*, 32 (October 1958): 443-475;

"The Message in the Bottle," *Thought*, 34 (autumn 1959): 405-433;

"Naming and Being," *Personalist*, 41 (spring 1960): 148-157;

"The Symbolic Structure of Interpersonal Process," *Psychiatry: A Journal for the Study of Interpersonal Processes*, 24 (February 1961): 39-52;

"From Facts to Fiction," *Writer*, 80 (October 1967): 27-28, 46;

"Notes for a Novel about the End of the World," *Katallagete*, 3 (winter 1967-1968): 7-14;

"Toward a Triadic Theory of Meaning," *Psychiatry: A Journal for the Study of Interpersonal Processes*, 35 (February 1972): 1-19.

References:

Zoltan Abadi-Nagy, "A Talk with Walker Percy," *Southern Literary Journal*, 6, 1 (fall 1973): 3-19;

Anselm Atkins, "Walker Percy and Post-Christian Search," *Centennial Review*, 12 (winter 1968): 73-95;

Michel T. Blouin, "The Novels of Walker Percy: An Attempt at Synthesis," *Xavier University Studies*, 6 (1968): 29-42;

John M. Bradbury, "Absurd Insurrection: The Barth-Percy Affair," *South Atlantic Quarterly*, 68 (summer 1969): 319-329;

Melvin E. Bradford, "Dr. Percy's Paradise Lost: Diagnostics in Louisiana," *Sewanee Review*, 81 (autumn 1973): 839-844;

Ashley Brown, "An Interview with Walker Percy," *Shenandoah*, 18, 3 (spring 1967): 3-10;

Jerry H. Bryant, *The Open Decision: The Contem-*

porary American Novel and Its Intellectual Background (New York: Free Press, 1970), pp. 273-277;

Charles Bunting, "An Afternoon with Walker Percy," *Notes on Mississippi Writers*, 4 (fall 1971): 43-61;

Scott Byrd, "The Dreams of Walker Percy," *Red Clay Reader* (1966): 70-73;

Byrd, "Mysteries and Movies: Walker Percy's College Articles and *The Moviegoer*," *Mississippi Quarterly*, 25 (spring 1972): 165-181;

Byrd and John F. Zeugner, "Walker Percy: A Checklist," *Bulletin of Bibliography*, 30 (January-March 1973): 16-17, 44;

John Carr, "An Interview with Walker Percy," *Georgia Review*, 25 (fall 1971): 317-332;

Eugene Chesnick, "Novel's Ending and World's End: The Fiction of Walker Percy," *Hollins Critic*, 10 (October 1973): 1-11;

Carlton Cremeens, "Walker Percy, The Man and the Novelist: An Interview," *Southern Review*, 4 (April 1968): 271-290;

Bradley R. Dewey, "Walker Percy Talks About Kierkegaard: An Annotated Interview," *Journal of Religion*, 54 (July 1974): 273-298;

Ellen Douglas, *Walker Percy's "The Last Gentleman": Introduction and Commentary* (New York: Seabury, 1969);

William Dowie, S. J., "Walker Percy: Sensualist-Thinker," *Novel*, 6 (fall 1972): 52-65;

Paul L. Gaston, "The Revelation of Walker Percy," *Colorado Quarterly*, 20 (spring 1972): 459-470;

Sarah Henisey, "Intersubjectivity in Symbolization," *Renascence*, 20 (summer 1968): 208-214;

Frederick J. Hoffman, *The Art of Southern Fiction: A Study of Some Modern Novelists* (Carbondale: Southern Illinois University Press, 1967), pp. 129-137;

James Hoggard, "Death of the Vicarious," *Southwest Review*, 49 (autumn 1964): 366-374;

Stanley Edgar Hyman, "Moviegoing and Other Intimacies," in his *Standards: A Chronicle of Books for Our Time* (New York: Horizon, 1966), pp. 63-67;

Mark Johnson, "The Search for Place in Walker Percy's Novels," *Southern Literary Journal*, 8, 1 (fall 1975): 55-81;

Alfred Kazin, "The Pilgrimage of Walker Percy," *Harper's Magazine*, 242 (June 1971): 81-86;

Robert E. Lauder, "The Catholic Novel and the 'Insider God,' " *Commonweal*, 101 (25 October 1974): 78-81;

Lewis A. Lawson, "Walker Percy's Indirect Communications," *Texas Studies in Literature and*

Language, 11 (spring 1969): 867-900;

Lawson, "Walker Percy's Southern Stoic," *Southern Literary Journal*, 3, 1 (fall 1970): 5-31;

Lawson, "Walker Percy: The Physician as Novelist," *South Atlantic Bulletin*, 37, 2 (May 1972): 58-63;

Thomas LeClair, "The Eschatological Vision of Walker Percy," *Renascence*, 26 (spring 1974): 115-122;

Richard Lehan, "The Way Back: Redemption in the Novels of Walker Percy," *Southern Review*, 4 (April 1968): 306-319;

Martin Luschei, *The Sovereign Wayfarer: Walker Percy's Diagnosis of the Malaise* (Baton Rouge: Louisiana State University Press, 1972);

Robert Maxwell, "Walker Percy's Fancy," *Minnesota Review*, 7, 3 (1967): 231-237;

Herbert Mitgang, "A Talk with Walker Percy," *New York Times Book Review*, 20 February 1977, pp. 1, 20-21;

Tony Tanner, *The Reign of Wonder: Naivety and Reality in American Literature* (Cambridge: The University Press, 1965), pp. 349-356;

Tanner, *City of Words: American Fiction 1950-1970* (New York: Harper & Row, 1971), pp. 260-262;

Lewis J. Taylor, Jr., "Walker Percy and the Self," *Commonweal*, 100 (10 May 1974): 233-236;

Jerome Thale, "Alienation on the American Plan," University of Houston *Forum*, 6 (1968): 36-40;

Mary Thale, "The Moviegoer of the 1950s," *Twentieth Century Literature*, 14 (July 1968): 84-89;

Jim Van Cleave, "Versions of Percy," *Southern Review*, 6 (October 1970): 990-1010;

John F. Zeugner, "Walker Percy and Gabriel Marcel: The Castaway and the Wayfarer," *Mississippi Quarterly*, 28 (winter 1974-1975): 21-53.

(EDWARD) REYNOLDS PRICE was born in Macon, North Carolina, on 1 February 1933, the son of William Solomon and Elizabeth Rodwell Price. Both in his work and his life, he has rarely strayed far from the place of his birth. Price attended nearby Duke University (1951-1955), where he received his B.A. and was chosen a Rhodes scholar. He attended Merton College, Oxford, from which he received his B. Litt. in 1958. In that year, Price returned to Duke where he joined the English faculty. He has, with a number of interruptions to take temporary teaching posts (writer-in-residence, University of North Carolina, Chapel Hill, 1965; writer-in-residence, University of Kansas, 1969; writer-in-residence, University of North Carolina, Greensboro, 1971; Glasgow Professor, Washington and Lee University, 1971; faculty member, Salsburg Seminar, Salsburg, Austria, 1976), remained on the Duke faculty and in 1977 was named James B. Duke Professor of English.

A number of Price's short stories—"One Sunday in Late July," "The Warrior Princess Ozimba," and "Waiting at Dachau"—have been included in *Prize Stories: The O. Henry Awards*. In addition, Price won the William Faulkner Award and the Sir Walter Raleigh Award in 1962 for *A Long and Happy Life*, and the Lillian Smith Award in 1976 for *The Surface of Earth*. In 1964 he was a Guggenheim Fellow and in 1971 was given the Award in Literature from the National Institute of Arts and Letters.

As is the curse of many talented writers from the South, Price has been hailed as a "major Southern writer," a title he personally dislikes. Though his works are influenced by his native eastern North Carolina in their setting, characters, and dialogue, they transcend regionalism. His novels—with their interlacing of narrative within narrative, their biblical and mythic resonances, and their characters who seem almost a part of the land in which they live—have inevitably been compared to Faulkner's. Price denies any appreciable influence from Faulkner but does acknowledge a debt to Eudora Welty, who encouraged him in his first serious story, which later became "Thomas Egerton," while she was conducting a seminar at Duke during Price's undergraduate years. His handling of nature, his sense of "place," and his strong interest in storytelling show her influence in particular. Price's first two novels, *A Long and Happy Life* and *A Generous Man*, and the story, "A Chain of Love," all chronicle the lives of the Mustian family; and his most recent novel, *The Surface of Earth*, tells of four generations of Kendals and Mayfields; but he does not seem intent on building a private world on the pattern of Yoknapatawpha County.

Price's characters are driven by forces they cannot name, by inbred characteristics, and by ideals and traditions whose validity they must come to question in the course of their stories. The flaws and ironies of these characters are handled in a profoundly sympathetic manner, which allows his novels, despite the grisly, unfair side of life sometimes displayed in them, to be ultimately comic and optimistic.

A Long and Happy Life (1962), which Price wrote after he joined the faculty at Duke, is set in rural eastern North Carolina and concerns Rosacoke Mustian's efforts to capture the love of Wesley

Jill Krementz

Reynolds Price.

Beavers, whom she has loved for years. The novel opens with the death of Mildred Sutton, a black who dies giving birth to an illegitimate child, and ends with the death of Rosacoke's dream, when she must marry Wesley not because he has finally come to love her, but because she is pregnant by him. The novel addresses the problems posed by the conflicting demands of love and duty that arise from the situation. The relationship between Rosacoke and Wesley tilts back and forth as Rosacoke struggles with the dilemma of loving a man who has no genuine affection for her; she has always been "Rosacoke Mustian who was maybe his girl."

The novel is rich in irony and contradictions. Rosacoke, though eager to marry Wesley, has avoided consummating their relationship, and the night Wesley, armed with a condom, suggests they complete it, she refuses. When she later does submit, Wesley does not practice contraception and she becomes pregnant. Even at this point Wesley is unable to keep things quite straight and forgets Rosacoke's right name, saying politely, "I thank you, Mae." She has now surrendered everything and

it is only her condition that forces Wesley's hand. In the end a compromise is struck: her idealism is defeated in the face of Wesley's elemental force and attraction, and Wesley's freedom yields to her legitimate demands that he share responsibility for their actions.

The North Carolina countryside and its denizens, both human and animal, are accurately evoked in the novel. Broad expanses of pine forests, dusty roads, wild deer, and natural springs are all integral parts of the lives of the characters. Wesley is especially identified with the natural elements of the countryside—the hawks, snakes, and other animals that live only to live, having little conception of their purpose. Rosacoke, on the other hand, is identified closely with the people of the region—innately generous, forgiving, and loving. Thus, while Rosacoke attends Mildred Sutton's funeral, Wesley goes off on his motorcycle to fetch a condom. The fusion is so carefully managed that it is difficult to imagine the story's being set elsewhere. One must be cautious, however, not to see the animals or other natural features of the novel merely as symbols. The abundant nature in the novel is a mirror in which one may view and interpret his own experience but not replace it. The animals have their own existence quite apart from that of the human characters.

The Names and Faces of Heroes (1963), a collection of short stories Price finished while in England in 1961, generally reflects the concerns and settings which appeared in his first novel. The lead story, "A Chain of Love," is set in a Raleigh hospital where Rosacoke Mustian and her brother Rato have gone to stay with their grandfather for a week. The man in a neighboring room, Mr. Ledwell, is a stranger who has just had lung surgery, the rigors of which will combine with inoperable cancer to kill him. Rosacoke, again displayed as innately generous and loving, displays concern for Ledwell, but, ironically, it passes totally unnoticed by him. When she brings Ledwell a bouquet of flowers, brought from home for this one purpose, a priest is giving Ledwell extreme unction. No one notices her, so she lays the flowers on a chair and leaves. The validity and properness of her concern and deed are never questioned; the very act of doing is what matters. The validity of act is reaffirmed, but the act's potential for good remains unrealized, because it is both unremarked and unthanked.

The title story reveals the psychology of a nine-year-old boy who grapples with a problem of self-identification. Set primarily in the front seat of a 1939 Pontiac in which the boy and his father are returning home late one night, the story chronicles a crucial stage in the boy's maturation. The boy has heard a preacher declare that the short cut to manhood is the emulation of some hero who has the very quality one lacks. The boy is disturbed by the preacher's statement, "Personal heroes don't need to be living just so they lived once." The boy is thus confronted with the problem of deciding whether or not his father is a hero. He wonders if the man he conceives his father to be ever existed or if examination will reveal a hero who never was. Happily, his father is as he conceives him to be, but this fact emerges only after the boy realizes that it is far easier to peruse the names, faces, and deeds of heroes in books than to struggle with the face and deeds of a man whose visage is often hidden behind masks, both imagined and real, and whose deeds influence his daily life. Relationships with the living, whose faults and faces are there for personal scrutiny, are terribly difficult; however, when they arrive home, the boy senses a communion with his father: "They did not separate us tonight. We finished alive, together, whole. This one more time."

A Generous Man (1966), the story of Milo Mustian's sexual coming of age at fifteen, concerns the efforts of Milo and a posse to find a circus python named Death, Milo's retarded brother Rato, and Rato's dog Phillip, all of whom have disappeared into the woods after a struggle between Phillip and Death. In the course of the novel, all are recovered (with the snake shot dead), Milo arrives at sexual manhood and begins to mature emotionally, and a long chain of circumstances and revelations leads to the discovery of the true identity of Lois and to the recovery of nearly ten thousand dollars of GI insurance money due her.

The novel's narrative technique, which incorporates dreams and tales-within-tales, is striking, but the plot suffers from being prosaic and very nearly unbelievable. Begun as a short story, *A Generous Man* lacks the economy of plot line and the organic development of Price's other novels. Although Milo's story is clearly narrated, many of the extraneous subplots are resolved largely by coincidence. Rato, for example, the main object of the hunt, is not recovered; he simply wanders up to the house. His bloodstained shirt had been recovered earlier and construed as proof of his death.

The characterization in the novel, to a large extent, offsets the weaknesses in the plot. Milo's portrait is drawn with sensitivity and insight, and his psychological growth is well developed. Lois, the object of his affections, is a precocious, sensitive girl who accepts Milo, but only after demanding of him that he think and act as an adult. Sheriff Rooster Pomeroy is unable to make love to his young wife, Kate, with whom half the county has slept. Kate is not seen as a slut, but rather is sympathetically portrayed as a woman haunted by a man from the past and frustrated by the present, a contradiction Milo resolves, for he resembles the man for whom she has waited thirteen years. Finally, Dr. Fuller, the veterinarian, knows his liquor better than he does his veterinary science, and his faulty diagnosis that Phillip is rabid is ironically a diagnosis of his own character. With both broad characterizations and flashes of insight, Price builds his characters and peoples the novel with a community that is at once engaging and realistic.

The symbols in the novel seem so frequent that Wallace Kaufman reports a conversation in which "a man told me it was difficult to talk with women about the book because of 'the all-pervasive phallic symbol of the snake.' " Certainly a python named Death and an impotent, gun-toting sheriff named Rooster in a novel concerning Milo's first sexual encounter invite such examination, especially since

Death is shot by Rooster while coiled about Milo, who has just committed adultery with the sheriff's wife. The reality of such creatures as the python makes their symbolic function secondary, and it is more accurate to say that they serve as foils and mirrors for human conduct. As Rato, himself half-witted, remarks when Dr. Fuller pronounces Phillip rabid: "Nothing dumb about him. Smart as some folks that finished school. I ain't saying who." The point is that Phillip is about as smart as nearly everyone else in the novel, and, even if the doctor's diagnosis were correct, only half as rabid.

Love and Work (1968) examines Thomas Eborn, a novelist and teacher, who struggles after the death of his mother with the complex demands that one human may make upon another. In some ways, he is an adult Wesley Beavers, and his credo, "Work frees a man" (ironically reminiscent of the Nazi slogan *"Arbeit macht frei"*), has so fueled and ordered his life that he resents any person's making demands on him that require him to surrender anything of his elemental self; he is unwilling to strike a compromise between his needs and those of others. He calmly does his duties towards others (sends his mother money, for example) and expects that they will afford equal treatment. It is the gradual breaching of Eborn's defenses from both within and without that impels the novel.

Eborn's own growth comes from his discovery of the true nature of the relationship between his father and mother, the former dead for several years, the latter dying in the course of the novel. As he is preparing his mother's house ("excess baggage") for sale, he slowly reconstructs his parents' life together, understands in the process that each surrendered to the other the very things he so zealously guards, and comes to the realization that in fending off others he has cheated himself. Rather than the freedom he expects to find once his mother can no longer importune him, he discovers that his cherished freedom is really his own imprisonment. Because of this realization, his love of work is ultimately converted into a work of love—a novel about his parents' life, which they shared as "gift not reward."

The novel evokes a strong sense of place, for Eborn consistently views lives as connected to his own house and study (the keep of fortress Eborn) and his mother's house. The realization that one may not so facilely compartmentalize human relationships brings Eborn to his broadened perspective. In the hours before her sudden death, his mother offered to bridge the gap for him, but since he was busy writing, an activity he does not permit to be interrupted, he did not speak to her when she telephoned. As he painfully reconstructs the events of his mother's death and the secret that she wished to share with him, he realizes that his insistence on the importance of place has deprived him of the more important joy of sharing. Place, therefore, becomes a confining element; Eborn has wrongfully rooted himself in his house, thus perverting the natural strength one should properly derive from such settings.

Permanent Errors (1970), a short story collection, shows the influence of Price's sojourn in England. The theme of all the stories is "the attempt to isolate in a number of lives the central error of act, will, understanding which, once made, has been permanent, incurable, but whose diagnosis and palliation are the hopes of continuance." Thus, as one moves through the book, one has a sense of continuity and theme not often found in such collections and may often achieve different perspectives on the material simply by shifting the order of reading. As in life, errors, even if permanent, are sometimes relative, and the book's organization reflects that vicissitude.

"Waiting at Dachau," the book's most celebrated story, contains a double error on the part of the characters. The protagonist's girl friend, Sara, refuses to tour the Dachau prison camp as the couple travels through Europe. Because of her refusal the relationship eventually breaks off, but the hero regrets the occurrence and the last words of the story, which is written entirely from the first person viewpoint, are, "Sara, come back." As has been the case in the novels, nature mirrors the affairs of men. The Andromeda galaxy, which Sara points out in the sky over Munich, is, she informs him, moving away from the earth at incomprehensible speeds, although it appears quite still. He, too, was moving away from her, even then, towards freedom, a "blessed clear space at hand—empty, free—towards which I flew at stunning speeds like your galaxy." The protagonist's need for freedom was, however, fallacious, and though he grinned (like the Jewish women smiling in the ditch moments before their execution) at the prospect of release, he ultimately frowns at his foolishness and realizes, like Eborn, that if one chooses love, certain duties and compromises are involved when the relationship is assumed. Galaxies may fly away as they will; humans must pay a price.

The Surface of Earth (1975), depicting four generations of Kendals and Mayfields, is Price's most mature, complex novel in its narrative technique, strength and depth of characterization, and thematic development. Drawing together many of the

ONE

April 1903

"...was dead?" Eva asked.

"...killed her," he said. "He already knew."

Their father — from his rocker, almost sunk in the April evening — said, "Keep your voices down. Your mother's on her way. And never call him that. He was her dear father, your own grandfather, & of course he never killed her."

Kennerly said, "He gave her the baby. The baby killed her. So I think he did justice — killing himself."

"Shame," their father said. He drew at his cigar. "I hope none of you live to have such a choice." Another draw. "But one of you will. Then remember tonight — me counselling you're rushing against the helpless dead." He had started his answer to Kennerly — Kennerly was leaving home in a week: a job, his life — but he aimed it at Eva. His middle child, his choice of the three, the thing in the world (besides his own mother, dead twenty years) that he'd loved & still loved, for sixteen years.

Dark as it was, Eva met his eyes & waited him out. Then she said, "What's shameful, sir, in wanting the truth? We're all nearly grown, we've heard scraps of it all our lives — lies, jokes. We are asking to know. It's our own story."

Her mother waited. "It will kill your mother to hear it."

Eva all were silent. The street beyond was empty. The dog was surrendering to Kennerly's scratching hands. Their mother's voice came from the kitchen, still racking — "Mag, you can take this bread in with you. Bake fresh for breakfast if you get her in time." You'd...

From manuscript of The Surface of Earth.

concerns of his previous works, the novel demonstrates Price's use of irony, love of place, concern with the conflict of love and duty, and his strong sympathy for characters caught in a complex world often not of their own making. The work is remarkable not only for its breadth but also for the depth in which it probes the psychological workings of human nature. Set in North Carolina and Virginia, the novel, as Anne Hobson Freeman has pointed out, "represents a leap forward . . . into a visionary territory . . . which, if conquered, can yield the hard-won wisdom of the human heart."

The novel is biblical in theme: the sins of the fathers are visited upon the heads of their descendants, and the bitter grapes the parents tasted set the children's teeth on edge. For their "sin" of eloping, sixteen-year-old Eva Kendal and thirty-two-year-old Forrest Mayfield, her Latin teacher, live their lives separated from each other. Eva's elopement drives her mother to a particularly grotesque suicide (she drinks lye), and when faced with her own child's lingering illness, Eva simply stays at the homeplace trying to atone for her deed. In doing this, however, she gives up Forrest because he will not submit to having his wife more devoted to her family and her own sense of guilt than to him, although he loves her deeply. Their child, Rob, suffers from this situation, and the "sin" is passed on to his son, Hutch, who "kills" his mother, Rachel, in childbirth. Hutch, however, finally achieves a certain equilibrium between his own demands and those of others, and the "sin" of the fathers is expiated in him when he receives his great grandmother's wedding ring, the symbol of a desirable, necessary unity which was broken but is now partially restored.

The novel is filled with the ironies and contradictions which so often mark Price's works. Chief among them is death in childbirth, the fundamental contradiction in human experience. The situation occurs so frequently that James Ross noted dryly, "[Price] runs into a little trouble in the delivery room." The children often pose threats and contradictions beyond mere physical death. Rob's difficult birth and Eva's return home with him, for example, kill her marriage. The slaughter, both physical and emotional, continues when Rachel dies giving birth to Hutch, thereby postponing the healing of the family and the restoration of unity. Ironically, it is Hutch, unmarried and childless, who may begin to heal the fault. An unemployed artist, he senses that the healing has begun and that the power he needs "would come here if anywhere. This place was an entrance. He'd need to wait here."

The sense of place in this novel is bound up closely with the lives of the characters, so much so that it is only when Hutch is finally vested with a place of his own, separate from all the traditional family dwellings, that one may hope the future is optimistic. Place often has a damaging quality, and the actual physical locations of the characters often result in mayhem. Eva and Forrest elope, an act of escape as much as of mutual love, but their home is destroyed by Eva's return to her father's home. The Kendal homestead, one locus, and the Mayfield house in Richmond, the other locus, cast their lengthening shadows through the course of the novel. As in *Love and Work*, places produce a polarity which divides the characters and presents choices to them that are basically insoluble. Thus, Eva is caught in the contradiction of having to atone to her father for having left him and to atone to her husband for precisely the same error. Grainger, a black fathered by grandfather Mayfield, endures because his "place" is wherever he is needed or wanted. Grainger resides where he can give, because, unlike the other characters whose hearts are where their homes are, his heart is his home.

Despite its somber tones, the novel's vision of life is comic. Lives stained by guilt, blighted by terrible accidents, and driven headlong into tragedy by emotional drives are finally given some prospect of healing and redemption. Crucial to the working out of this comic vision is the continuity of the families, for despite their mischances, Hutch will atone for and justify his predecessors. A gift of the very emotions and turmoil that cause so many woes, he is the saving grace of those conflicts, and they are harmonized to some extent in him. The errors and acts of the past may not be forgotten or glossed over, but "partial amends" may be made for them.

The polarities of place and the progress of four generations require that the narrative move constantly between characters in one place and those in another, and between characters in one time and those in another. The complex narrative is held together by a liberal use of reminiscence, letters, and storytelling. Every character has a story which must be told because it makes sense of present events, and the narrative-within-narrative technique is used extensively. Price also makes sophisticated use of dreams, through which characters' futures are revealed and present events interpreted. The use of dreams makes the narrative reflect the differing views of life and experience held by the characters themselves. While the stories and dreams remain consistent with the characters' views of life, Price's control prevents the novel's viewpoint from becoming muddled or confused. However, this breadth and complicated technique have occasioned some discontent among readers of the novel.

Price's compassion and concern for his characters, one of his unfailing attributes, keeps the novel from being cynical. Despite generations of drunkenness, selfishness, pain, adultery, and turmoil, the characters persevere on the hope that relief will come in the next generation. Man may seize his destiny despite the frailties of flesh and mind, and so long as the spirit within the weak flesh be willing, a victory will be won, as Hutch and several of the peripheral characters make clear. The renewal of kind is the renewal of the spirit, an act which, itself so bound up in the flesh, produces a new generation with all the opportunities for both failure and success embodied in the old. So long as reproduction is possible, despair need be only transitory.

Despite the complexity of the novel, which Peter S. Prescott called "metaphysical molasses," the work has been admired for its ambition and the beauty of its prose. Anne Hobson Freeman found the novel "out of step with the march of most contemporary fiction" but concluded, "The fact that his Promethean effort is only partially successful should not diminish our respect for its daring and its high seriousness."

Price has also ventured into the field of translation, especially biblical passages. Although he admittedly is not sufficiently proficient in any of the original scriptural languages to permit him to translate directly from them, his main interest is in the story which runs through the passages he selects rather than in the literality of the translation. The translations bear the mark of Price's pliant, poetic prose, and in many instances, his prose is here at its best. The biblical passages, chosen for the strength of the narrative within them, are reminiscent of the King James version; however, they are really syntheses of various translations which Price studied before producing his own versions and of his own study of the original languages of the Bible.

His most important works of translation are the stories contained in *A Palpable God*, a work which reflects Price's further study of the Bible's original languages, various other translations, and biblical commentaries. Price's aim in this book is twofold. First, he desired to produce fresh, clean translations which removed the verbiage built up over centuries of scholarly efforts; and, second, he attempted to explore that aspect of man which separates him from everything else—the ability to narrate. In this latter sense, the book is also a writer's laboratory, since it is narration that permits writers to practice their trade.

The book is thus a fresh look at the roots of all narrative—the presence or absence of the deity in the affairs of men. That interest governed the stories to be included and their organization. More than this, however, these translations are the manifestation of Price's examination of his own work and life; the clarity and force which he is able to find in these admittedly ancient sources speak eloquently for the necessity and worth of the writer's craft and for the central importance of narrative in the life of the world.

Things Themselves (1972) is a collection of Price's most significant critical writing and includes a selection from his version of a proposed screenplay for *A Long and Happy Life*. Subjects covered include Eudora Welty, Hemingway, Faulkner, Rembrandt, Southern fiction, and Milton, who was the subject of his thesis at Merton College. In "Dodo, Pheonix or Tough Old Cock?" Price examines the contention that Southern fiction is exhausted and concludes that it is the readers of such fiction that are tired rather than the region, its writers, or its literature. He sees Southern literature as being relatively sane and having bright prospects for the future. The essay is particularly interesting for its insistence upon the importance of the South as basically a rural community which is based on land as opposed to the North, which is primarily an urban society based upon the city. Price views the potential for total destruction of the latter's culture in the event of holocaust as greater than the former's, for cities may be destroyed more easily than the land itself. The essay on Milton, "Poem Doctrinal and Exemplary to A Nation: A Reading of Samson Agonistes," is a lucid examination of Milton's sophisticated use of the chorus and of the blind poet's prosody through which he seeks to instruct both the England of this time and us—"That we can sit—a second audience, much like the first—and also watch the contest and deduce again its rules (announced at Creation) is one of the privileges and dangers of having survived Milton." On the whole, the essays are interesting not only for their critical insights, but also for the light they throw on the manner in which Price himself reads and teaches literature. —*Everett Wilkie*

Books:

A Long and Happy Life (New York: Atheneum, 1962; London: Chatto & Windus, 1962);
The Names and Faces of Heroes (New York: Atheneum, 1963; London: Chatto & Windus, 1963);

A Generous Man (New York: Atheneum, 1966; London: Chatto & Windus, 1967);

The Thing Itself (Durham: n.p., 1966);

Love and Work (New York: Atheneum, 1968; London: Chatto & Windus, 1968);

Permanent Errors (New York: Atheneum, 1970; London: Chatto & Windus, 1971);

Things Themselves: Essays & Scenes (New York: Atheneum, 1972);

Presence and Absence: Versions from the Bible (Bloomfield Hills, Mich. and Columbia, S.C.: Bruccoli Clark, 1973);

The Surface of Earth (New York: Atheneum, 1975);

Early Dark (New York: Atheneum, 1977);

A Palpable God: Thirty Stories Translated from the Bible with an Essay on the Origins and Life of Narrative (New York: Atheneum, 1978).

References:

John F. Baker, "PW Interviews: Reynolds Price," *Publishers Weekly*, 208 (4 August 1975): 12-13;

David R. Barnes, "The Names and Faces of Reynolds Price," *Kentucky Review*, 2, 2 (1968): 76-91;

Robert Drake, ed., *The Writer and His Tradition* (Knoxville: University of Tennessee Press, 1969);

Clayton L. Eichelberger, "Reynolds Price: 'A Banner in Defeat,' " *Journal of Popular Culture*, 1 (spring 1968): 410-417;

Anne Hobson Freeman, "Penetrating a Small Patch of *The Surface of Earth*," *Virginia Quarterly Review*, 51 (autumn 1975): 637-641;

Frederick J. Hoffman, *The Art of Southern Fiction* (Carbondale: Southern Illinois University Press, 1967);

Wallace Kaufman, "A Conversation with Reynolds Price," *Shenandoah*, 17, 4 (spring 1966): 3-25;

Allen Shepherd, "Love (and Marriage) in *A Long and Happy Life*," *Twentieth Century Literature*, 17 (January 1971): 29-35;

Shepherd, "Notes on Nature in the Fiction of Reynolds Price," *Critique*, 15, 2 (1973): 83-94;

Theodore Solotaroff, "The Reynolds Price Who Outgrew the Southern Pastoral," *Saturday Review*, 26 (26 September 1970): 27-29, 46;

John W. Stevenson, "The Faces of Reynolds Price's Short Fiction," *Studies in Short Fiction*, 3, 4 (1966): 300-306;

Simone Vauthier, "The 'Circle in the Forest': Fictional Space in Reynolds Price's *A Long and Happy Life*," *Mississippi Quarterly*, 28 (spring 1975): 123-146.

JAMES PURDY is reluctant to talk about his early years beyond acknowledging that he was born in rural Ohio on 17 July 1923 and grew up in the Midwest, which has been the setting of several of his novels. He aspired to be an artist, and he has illustrated several of his own books. He has studied at the University of Chicago, the University of Puebla in Mexico, and the University of Madrid. Before deciding to devote himself to the writings that began to appear when he was in his thirties, Purdy lived in Cuba and taught Spanish. Though he travels occasionally, he has spent the last twenty years principally in Brooklyn Heights, a restored district along the East River in New York that is the setting of some scenes in *Cabot Wright Begins*.

His first two books, privately printed—a collection of short stories, *Don't Call Me by My Right Name and Other Stories* (1956), and a novella, *63: Dream Palace* (1956)—later gathered under the title *Color of Darkness*—present the basic situations that recur throughout his fiction. Like the earlier works of Sherwood Anderson and Dreiser, most of the short stories are starkly realistic vignettes that explore the lack of communication and lack of feeling among middle-class Americans, especially parents and children, husbands and wives. In "Cutting Edge," a son tells his parents, "You never wanted anything from me and you never wanted to give me anything. I didn't matter to you." When he visits them in Florida, "a stranger who despised them," his offensive behavior forces his parents to recognize that "the fruit of their lives" is "the glacial control that had come to him out of art and New York." Caring for an invalid husband in "Sound of Talking," Mrs. Farebrother tries "to think of what she *did* want" and concludes that "one thing or another or nothing were all the same." The story that most closely foreshadows Purdy's further work thematically is "Why Can't They Tell You Why?," which introduces the persisting motif of the absent father. A young boy tries to keep memories of his father alive by brooding over photographs of him; when the vain, malicious mother forces the boy to burn them, he can retain something of the photos only by eating them. This pattern of a traumatic loss, a violent effort to keep the loser forever separated from any souvenir of his loss, with an apocalyptically violent denouement structures many of

Thomas Victor

[signature: James Purdy]

Purdy's works from *Malcolm* (1959) through *Narrow Rooms* (1978).

The pattern is apparent in *63: Dream Palace*, but the novella differs from the short stories in its haunting, nightmarish quality. The narrative concerns two parentless young boys from West Virginia who come to New York City in search of surrogate parents and encounter only decadents seeking to exploit them. Fenton Riddleway, the older, stronger, "excessive" boy, resists these forces of fragmentation, however, and persists in maintaining an affirmative relationship with his frail, visionary brother Claire. Fenton ends up, however, like many of Purdy's characters whose visions exceed their self-control, killing his brother while under the influence of drugs. This history is related by the first in a succession of "memoirists" in Purdy's fiction, Parkhearst Cratty. A failed writer, Cratty survives by catering to the whims of wealthy, eccentric, alcoholic Greatlady Grainger, who had attempted to remold Fenton into the stereotype of her departed spouse.

Like Cratty and Greatlady, many of Purdy's characters are spiritually dead and seek to stifle other life by arresting the inexorable flow of events. Cratty's recollections foreshadow the memoirs and "memorials" of Madame Girard in *Malcolm*, Aunt

Alma in *The Nephew*, Zoe Bickle in *Cabot Wright Begins*, the title character in *Eustace Chisholm and the Works*, Matt Lacey in *Jeremy's Version*, Millicent De Frayne in *I Am Elijah Thrush*, and "Lady" Nora Bythewaite in *The House of the Solitary Maggot*, all of which are examples of the traditional mode of allegory.

A static, metaphorical form, allegory is empty of the possibility for any meaning but a preassigned one; an allegorical character never really exists. This lack of life was once regarded as evidence of timelessness, of universality, for it was believed that allegories had divine sanction as the revelation of eternal truths. In modern times the belief in divine sanction has disappeared; but people still long for the permanence it offered, so that allegories assume the status of dreams without the authority of divine revelation. A memoirist becomes literary taxidermist; the revered object is drained of life in order to be possessed in memory (often as the memoirist sought to possess it in life). Consequently, the effect of reading Purdy's novels is analogous to moving from picture to picture in a shadowy museum that recalls a time when there was both a God the father and a real father of a family. The memoirist attempts to impose some order on a world in which real authority has vanished; each invents his own history and seeks to impose the authority of this private illusion on all others. As Purdy relentlessly demonstrates, however, truth eludes the memoirist, so that his thwarted efforts serve only the unexpected purpose of exposing the horrors and perversions of a community in which there is no order or authority beyond the sensual.

Assorted perversions—from incest through sado-masochism and homosexuality to vampirism and torture-deaths—are the consequences of characters' attempts to assert something resembling divine authority in a world from which it has disappeared. Practically all of Purdy's novels radiate from the central image of a father who has been killed, abandoned, exiled, divorced, or otherwise lost, leaving a black hole where once shown a divine light. In the father's absence, others attempt to usurp his role, but they succeed only in becoming allegorical monsters in a lightless, lifeless pit.

Purdy first attracted general attention with *Malcolm* (1959), the story of a helpless, confused boy who has been abandoned in "one of the most palatial hotels in the world" by a father who had heretofore sheltered the boy from all worldly experience. "I suppose if somebody would tell me what to do, I would do it," Malcolm observes. He falls into the hands of Mr. Cox, an astrologer, who advises him,

"Give yourself up to things" and then gives him a series of "addresses" of nightmarish people who either fail to communicate with the boy or seek to exploit him for their own bizarre purposes. When the world's richest man, Girard Girard, fails to fulfill a promise to make Malcolm his son, the boy, "too young for the Army, too unprepared to continue his schooling and become a scientist, too untrained for ordinary work," has no alternative but marriage. Pressured into a union with a nymphomaniacal "contemporary," "America's number one chanteuse," he soon expires of "acute alcoholism and sexual hyperaesthesia."

With its rococo decor and caricatures of representative human predators, *Malcolm* remains Purdy's prototypical realization of the American dream turned nightmare. In his next three novels, he moved in two complementary directions. On the one hand, he replaced the elegant remoteness of Malcolm's stylized world with increasingly realistic backdrops in the manner of his short stories; on the other, the situations of the victimized characters grew increasingly terrifying.

The title character of *The Nephew* (1960) is an orphan who never appears in the novel. The report that he is missing in action in Korea precipitates his Aunt Alma's efforts to put together a book as a memorial to him. Her researches in Rainbow Center, a half-American-Gothic, half-Ozlike community that is permeated by the sickly sweet odor from a ketchup factory, lead her only to discover that she has never really known Cliff, the nephew that she and her brother Boyd had cared for after his parents' deaths. Alma's memoir results not in recovering the boy, but in exposing the banal hidden secrets of her neighbors and leading them to a new apprehension of each other. As Stephen Adams has pointed out, "the novel's ultimate voice is one of affirmation," a "rare phenomenon" in Purdy's work.

Cabot Wright Begins (1964), Purdy's frontal assault on what he regards as a decadent literary establishment and the vulgarities of a culture shaped by advertising, achieves no such resolution. Cabot Wright is a "supposititious" child whose parents are killed, leaving him to be reared by Mr. Warburton, the embodiment of all the glib, hypocritical emptiness of the American businessman. After the collapse of Cabot Wright's marriage to a shallow, stereotyped model, he is turned over to a fashionable psychiatrist in the Wilhelm Reich vein, Dr. Bigelow-Martin, who uses grotesque methods to try to reduce the young man to a conforming automaton. Wright, however, reacts violently against the treatment and becomes a phantom rapist who brings into the lives of many women the first joy they have known. His career is checked only when he attempts to rape a young woman with a genuine religious faith who proves immune to his sexual magic. After imprisonment, he hides out in a room full of clocks from which he whispers to others, "Don't you begin." When at long last he learns truly to laugh, he is able to disappear from New York's encaging world to seek his own identity. His story attracts a would-be biographer, Zoe Bickle (whose husband leads an unworldly life annotating the Biblical book of Isaiah), but she is finally driven by her encounters— resembling Purdy's own—with the meretricious publishing world to abandon her invasion of Wright's privacy and to seek restorative therapy in the privacy of her marriage.

The title character of *Eustace Chisholm and the Works* (1967), who has aspired to write epic poetry, is driven to a similar solution after his pretensions to a universal voice have been discouraged by his sickening observation of the destruction of others seeking to make new worlds out of the wreckage of the American Depression. The most moving character in the novel is Daniel Haws, an army sergeant regarded by Chisholm as one of the most important of his "works," the people he befriended during the Depression. When Daniel was thirteen his coal miner father was killed in a riot. Seeking himself to become a father figure, Daniel is physically attracted to young Amos Ratcliffe; but unable to admit his homosexuality, Daniel tragically rejects Amos, only to become involved homosexually with the sadistic Captain Stadger, whose insistence on "commanding" despite his inability to deal with his own emotions leads to his brutally torturing and executing Daniel.

In brief summaries it is impossible to suggest the richness and complexity of these last three novels in which the abundance of subplots combined with Purdy's gift for memorable character names and descriptions of unusual places suggests that he may be seen as a kind of Dickens of the twentieth-century wasteland, picking up the narrative form of the panoramic nineteenth-century novel from such ominous late works as *Our Mutual Friend* and the unfinished *Mystery of Edwin Drood* and reshaping it to project his vision of a world even further decayed.

Purdy's latest work in what may be called his extravagant manner is one of the most exotic fables in our literature. *I Am Elijah Thrush* (1972), as the title suggests, is a brief, intricate tale of birds, flight, and the pursuit of freedom and art. These pursuits are embodied in "the mime," Elijah Thrush, who is trying to escape Millicent De Frayne's attempts to trammel the free spirit by, in Tony Tanner's words, "the appropriation of some vital part of a person." For her purposes, this self-styled patron, who keeps herself from aging by drinking the semen of young men, enlists a black writer to author a reductive memoir. The writer, Albert Peggs, is always in need of money to support his "habit" of keeping alive a captive golden eagle by allowing it to feed on his own "running blood." Peggs discovers that Elijah Thrush is sustained by his devotion to his great-grandchild, "Bird of Heaven," an extraordinarily pretty child incapable of any utterance but beautiful, meaningless song. Millicent De Frayne eventually captures the child and hence Elijah himself and kills Albert's eagle; but the black man survives to assume Elijah's name and to keep the mime's Arcturus Gardens theater alive—perhaps an affirmation that the aspirations of the artist survive even if they cannot triumph over gross materialistic obstacles.

Even before this fable appeared, however, Purdy turned to a remarkably different manner of narration. The terse, snide, multiple-plotted episodic novels of the 1960s gave way to less spectacular yet even more frightening tales of the South and Midwest, employing regional vernaculars to present intensive, brooding, in-depth studies of small groups of pathetic figures spotlighted against uncluttered pastoral settings.

Jeremy's Version (1970) and *The House of the Solitary Maggot* (1974) were announced as the first two parts of a continuing novel called "Sleepers in Moon-Crowned Valleys"; but they have no common characters and are related only in being set in dying rural communities. Subsequent books have not been linked with them.

The two novels mark Purdy's most extensive use of the device of the "memoirist" to reveal the hidden secrets of decayed communities. In *Jeremy's Version*, Matt Lacey, a retired actor, returns to his home town of Boutflour to dictate to the ambitious and susceptible young Jeremy the history of Wilders Fergus, a wanderer whose inability to adjust his dreams to squalid reality leads him to squander his family's fortune and to be responsible eventually for the destruction of his progeny. The revelations prompt Jeremy to flee Boutflour in the hope of finding a better life with a kinsman in Prince's Crossing.

Although *The House of the Solitary Maggot* begins in Prince's Crossing, which is no longer even marked on maps, it does not resume the story of Jeremy's wanderings. Instead, a new group of even more desperate figures is introduced in an account of the vastly wealthy Mr. Skegg's ("maggot" is a local

corruption for "magnate") refusal to acknowledge that he fathered three exceptionally sensitive and promising sons by "Lady" Nora Bythewaite. Because of the irresponsibility of the presumed parents and the inability of the sons to cope with their own emotions, all come to gruesome ends. This pathetic history of family and community destroyed is narrated—like the classic Aeneas's account of the destruction of Troy—by a hermit, Eneas Rex Harmond, over whose house a plaque reads, "Do not disturb!"

Purdy's two most recent works have been much shorter and even more concentrated than these two chapters in a history of the lurid consequences of attempts to supplant divine traditions of community with contrived "families." *In a Shallow Grave* (1976) presents one of Purdy's most macabre creations—Garnet Montrose, a veteran returned from Viet Nam, who after being buried beneath a pile of dead comrades, miraculously emerged, but with all his veins and arteries exposed on the mulberry surface of his skin, so that he sickens all who see him. After many "applicants" for the position of attending him are frightened away, two are found who are able to overcome their revulsion—Quintus Perch, a black youth who reads to Garnet, and Daventry, who seems some kind of heavenly messenger corrupted by a human crime. Garnet is restored at last to tolerable human form through Daventry's ministrations but loses in the exchange this companion who never seemed of this earth. As Stephen Adams comments, however, although this cyclical narrative begins and ends with loss, it portrays "a cycle of renewal and regeneration" as Garnet "comes to understand that the deepest love can never attain its object or arrest it from the flux of time."

As *The Nephew* was followed by two of Purdy's darkest works, so *Narrow Rooms* (1978) follows up the final spiritual affirmation of *In a Shallow Grave* with portrayals of the horrors wrought in this world by those who cannot acknowledge physical love as a momentary stay against the confusions of time's flux. The novel presents a group of young men whose lives have been destroyed by their inability to come to terms with their passionate feelings for each other. While again the grim figure of the mother of one of the sufferers causes, like Purdy's earlier "greatladies," some of the damage, the unresolvable problems and the awful consequences result from the young men's inability to follow their deepest inclinations in the face of the stultifying macho traditions of their backwoods home.

It would be foolhardy indeed to predict where Purdy will move from *Narrow Rooms*. His energies

How I Became a Shadow, how I live in the defile of mountains,
and how I lost my Cock.
                    RANGEL
        By Pablo ~~Raquel~~.

GONZAGO
~~Domingo~~ is to blame. He said, "That rooster is too good for
a pet. He belongs in the cockfight. You give him to me, you owe me
favors. I am your cousin. Give him up."

        GONZAGO
        "Never, ~~Domingo~~," I replied. ~~"Nunca.~~ I raised the little fellow
from almost an egg. I never render him to you, _primo._"

        "S̃hut your mouth that fles are always crawling in. Shut up,
you whelp, when I command. That cock is too good for a pet. Hear me.
You will give him up, and we will both make money. You bellyahce, you
say you are always broke, and then when the chance comes to make something you tell your cousin to go hang his ass up to dry. No, Pablo,
listen good. The cock is as good as mine because of all the favors
I done you, remember. _Hear me:_ ~~Listen good.~~ I am going to come take him
            fetch   _to take his place_
and will ~~bring~~ you another cock ~~as a present~~ later. Then I will enter
your cock at the fight and we will get rich."

        "I will not render him," I told ~~Domingo~~. "I will keep my pet
                                        GONZAGO
by me forever. You are not man enough anyhow to take him from me. If
Jesus Himself come down from the clouds and said, 'Pablo, I require
you to render me your cock as an offering', I would reply, "Jesus,
go back and hang again on the cross, I will not render my pet, die,
Jesus, this time for ever."

                            " GONZAGO
        "Ha, Jesus, always Him," ^~~Domingo~~ snorted. "As if He cared about
your cock or whether he fights or don't fight. You fool, even your
shit isn't brown. You were born to lose. But I will teach you yet.
You will not order your cousin about just because you have no wits
and need others to watch out for you...Hear me...Tonight I will come
for the cock. Hear? Tonight, for tomorrow is the cock fight, and we
will win, Pablo. I have been teaching your Placido to fight while you were

From typescript of "How I Became a Shadow."

seem prodigious, and he is at the height of his power as a diviner of the human condition who perceives and presents the purgative truths veiled by the lies and "versions" of his allegorical characters. Although the theme of the lack of a center—a home, a father, a guide in our modern wasteland—persists through his work, he has been unflaggingly ingenious and innovative in the vehicles through which he has communicated his vision of the self-allegorized world that he would see transcended by one in which people might learn to laugh again, as Cabot Wright did, and act naturally. Besides an extraordinary sequence of nine novels over two decades, he has produced several provocative plays about the "end" of the world, a number of poems, and further short stories, including the especially discomforting "Mr. Evening," with its implication that those without a sufficient sense of self-identity will lose even what frail identity they possess and become "curios" in the collections of such characters as Greatlady Grainger and Millicent De Frayne.

Despite the power of Purdy's work and its relevance to the modern world in which, as Madame Girard puts it in *Malcolm*, "Texture is all, substance nothing,"—perhaps because he pushes too many panic buttons—he has not only been ignored by the New York reviewing establishment, but he has received only scattered critical attention since David Daiches in 1962 seemed to be preparing the way for intensive scrutiny by praising in a preface to *Malcolm* Purdy's "special kind of literary imagination." Part of the difficulty has been that Purdy's fiction cannot be easily categorized. Eugene McNamara was quite perceptive in placing Purdy among the originators of "The Post-Modern American Novel," which this critic saw as characterized by the theme that violated love in the modern world leads to a rejection of others, causing the ultimate death of the self; but his other candidates (William Gaddis, William Styron, John Howard Griffin) have failed to develop significantly. McNamara has not pursued his original insight, and the term "post-modern" has subsequently been quite differently defined. Bettina Schwarzschild's *"The Not-Right House": Essays on James Purdy*, the first book devoted to the writer, is a collection of separate essays illuminating especially mythic parallels in his early work. Frank Baldanza has written a group of essays cataloguing major situations that recur through Purdy's fiction; and Irving Malin in *New American Gothic* links Purdy with Truman Capote, John Hawkes, Carson McCullers, Flannery O'Connor, and J. D. Salinger as writers who "image the terrors of the buried life," but his attempt to define a

new genre has not gained currency. Nearly all criticism so far has been primarily enumerative and has not posited a synthesis of the contribution of diverse elements to Purdy's emerging vision that perhaps his varied work still eludes. Even Stephen Adams's *James Purdy*, while it deals brilliantly with the occasional affirmative elements in novels such as *The Nephew* and *In a Shallow Grave*, exhibits the general reluctance to relate the grimmer side of Purdy's vision to contemporary experience. Most critics seem simply not "tough-minded" enough to cope with Purdy.

The most valuable assessment so far of his work is Tony Tanner's essay, "Frame Without Pictures," in *City of Words*, which argues that Purdy "undermines through parody, every vestigial convention of naturalistic writing," because Purdy sees a writer's confidence in an ability "to contain substantial reality . . . as a self-deception" and produces instead "the strange effect of a self-negating presence . . . in which people and things both are and are not there" (an effort that may serve to call attention to the insubstantiality of a physical reality without an authoritative spiritual center). Perhaps, as Donald Pease concludes in an earlier essay, Purdy "fights the demons of a society of sleepwalkers to evoke the real" and "challenges his readers to do the same."

—*Warren French and Donald Pease*

Books:

Don't Call Me by My Right Name and Other Stories (New York: William-Frederick, 1956);

63: Dream Palace (New York: William-Frederick, 1956; republished as *63: Dream Palace A Novella and Nine Stories*, London: Gollancz, 1957);

Color of Darkness: 11 Stories and a Novella (New York: New Directions, 1957; London: Secker & Warburg, 1961);

Malcolm (New York: Farrar, Straus & Cudahy, 1959; London: Secker & Warburg, 1960);

The Nephew (New York: Farrar, Straus & Cudahy, 1960; London: Secker & Warburg, 1961);

Children Is All (New York: New Directions, 1962; London: Secker & Warburg, 1963);

Cabot Wright Begins (New York: Farrar, Straus & Giroux, 1964; London: Secker & Warburg, 1965);

An Oyster Is a Wealthy Beast (San Francisco: Black Sparrow, 1967);

Eustace Chisholm and the Works (New York: Farrar, Straus & Giroux, 1967; London: Cape, 1968);

Mr. Evening: A Story and Nine Poems (Los Angeles:

Black Sparrow, 1968);

Jeremy's Version (Garden City: Doubleday, 1970; London: Cape, 1971);

On the Rebound: A Story and Nine Poems (Los Angeles: Black Sparrow, 1970);

The Running Sun (New York: Paul Waner Press, 1971);

I Am Elijah Thrush (Garden City: Doubleday, 1972; London: Cape, 1972);

Sunshine Is an Only Child (New York: Aloe, 1973);

The House of the Solitary Maggot (Garden City: Doubleday, 1974);

In a Shallow Grave (New York: Arbor House, 1976);

A Day After the Fair: A Collection of Plays and Short Stories (New York: Note of Hand Publishers, 1977);

Narrow Rooms (New York: Arbor House, 1978).

Other:

The Wedding Finger, Antaeus, 10 (1973).

References:

Stephen Adams, *James Purdy* (New York: Barnes & Noble, 1976);

Frank Baldanza, "James Purdy's Half-Orphans," *Centennial Review*, 18 (summer 1974): 255-272;

Baldanza, "James Purdy on the Corruption of Innocents," *Contemporary Literature*, 15 (summer 1974): 315-330;

Baldanza, "Northern Gothic," *Southern Review*, 10 (summer 1974): 566-582;

Baldanza, "The Paradoxes of Patronage in Purdy," *American Literature*, 46 (November 1974): 347-356;

Baldanza, "Playing House for Keeps with James Purdy," *Contemporary Literature*, 11 (autumn 1970): 488-510;

Douglas Bolling, "The World Upstaged in James Purdy's *I Am Elijah Thrush*," *University of Dayton Review*, 10 (summer 1974): 75-83;

George E. Bush, "James Purdy," *Bulletin of Bibliography*, 28 (January-March 1971): 5-6;

David Daiches, "A Preface to James Purdy's *Malcolm*," *Antioch Review*, 22 (spring 1962): 122-130;

Warren French, "The Quaking World of James Purdy," in *Essays in Modern American Literature*, ed. Richard E. Langford (Deland, Fla.: Stetson University Press, 1963);

French, *Season of Promise: Spring Fiction, 1967* (Columbia: University of Missouri Press, 1968);

Paul Herr, "The Small, Sad World of James Purdy,"

Chicago Review, 14 (autumn-winter 1960): 19-25;

"I Am James Purdy," *Andy Warhol's Interview*, December 1972;

Jean E. Kennard, *Number and Nightmare: Forms of Fantasy in Contemporary Fiction* (Hamden, Conn.: Archon, 1975), pp. 82-100;

Thomas Lorch, "Purdy's *Malcolm*: A Unique Vision of Radical Emptiness," *Wisconsin Studies in Contemporary Literature*, 6 (summer 1965): 204-213;

Irving Malin, *New American Gothic* (Carbondale: Southern Illinois University Press, 1962);

Eugene McNamara, "The Post-Modern American Novel," *Queen's Quarterly*, 69 (summer 1962): 265-275;

Charles Newman, "Beyond Omniscience," *Tri-Quarterly*, 10 (fall 1967): 37-52;

Donald Pease, "James Purdy: Shaman in Nowhere Land," in *The Fifties: Fiction, Poetry, Drama*, ed. Warren G. French (Deland, Fla.: Everett/Edwards, 1971);

Regina Pomeranz, "The Hell of Not Loving: Purdy's Modern Tragedy," *Renascence*, 16 (winter 1963): 149-153;

Webster Schott, "James Purdy: American Dreams," *Nation*, 198 (March 1964): 300-302;

Bettina Schwarzschild, *"The Not-Right House": Essays on James Purdy* (Columbia: University of Missouri Press, 1968);

Dame Edith Sitwell, "Introduction," *Color of Darkness* (Philadelphia and New York: Lippincott, 1961);

Joseph T. Skerrett, "James Purdy and the Works: Love and Tragedy in Five Novels," *Twentieth Century Literature*, 15 (April 1969): 25-33;

Tony Tanner, "Frames Without Pictures," in his *City of Words: American Fiction, 1950-1970* (New York: Harper & Row, 1971);

Tanner, "James Purdy's *I Am Elijah Thrush*," in *New Directions in Prose and Poetry 26*, ed. James Laughlin (New York: New Directions, 1973), pp. 62-69.

Thomas Pynchon

John Stark
University of Wisconsin

BIRTH: Glen Cove, New York, 8 May 1937.

EDUCATION: B.A., Cornell University, 1958.

AWARDS: William Faulkner First Novel Award for *V.*, 1963; Rosenthal Foundation Award for *The Crying of Lot 49*, 1967; National Book Award for *Gravity's Rainbow*, 1974.

MAJOR WORKS: *V.* (Philadelphia: J. B. Lippincott, 1963); *The Crying of Lot 49* (Philadelphia: J. B. Lippincott, 1966); *Gravity's Rainbow* (New York: Viking, 1973).

Thomas Pynchon's willingness to address the most important cultural and social issues makes him an important writer. He depicts the plight of contemporary humanity caught in, rather than sustained by, a culture that celebrates technology and death rather than humanity and life. Pynchon is a novelist of ideas and a practitioner of Menippean satire, a rich tradition that includes such masterpieces as *Candide, Gulliver's Travels* and *Gargantua and Pantagruel*. Pynchon's erudition helps him create this kind of work, which dramatizes ideas rather than faithfully imitating everyday reality. In addition, he effectively uses sophisticated literary techniques, particularly in *Gravity's Rainbow*, which, according to a growing number of critics, is one of the most important American novels.

Pynchon's desire for privacy at least saves him from being lionized, interviewed, and otherwise distracted from writing. At most it reinforces his monklike dedication to his calling, so that he could write a book as long and dense as *Gravity's Rainbow*. His cherishing of privacy, however, also frustrates biographers. Most of the facts known about him pertain to the years before he published *V.*, his first novel, and although connections can be seen between those facts and features of his work, the scarcity of corroborating biographical details and of statements by Pynchon warrant skepticism about his life's influences on his work. Nevertheless, his training in engineering at Cornell and his work as a writer for Boeing gave him some of the scientific and technological information that he uses in his fiction. Cornell also stimulated the literary side of his temperament. There he took Vladimir Nabokov's course in modern literature and became acquainted with Richard Farina, the young writer whose novel *Been Down So Long It Looks Like Up To Me* showed promise of brilliance that was cut short by a fatal accident. Pynchon's work has certain affinities with Nabokov's, such as its references to science and the enormous demands it makes on a reader. Farina's premature death seems to have been the occasion for Pynchon's meditation on death in *Gravity's Rainbow*, which he dedicated to Farina.

Pynchon's first publication was a short story, "Mortality and Mercy in Vienna," which appeared in *Epoch*, a journal published at Cornell. He based it and two other stories, "Low-lands" and "Entropy," on the Second Law of Thermodynamics: Clausius' statement that in a closed system energy will inevitably be lost, for example because of friction. In these stories entropy (lost energy) figures as a theme, an analogue of the settings—part of "Low-lands" takes place in a garbage dump, the waste of which resembles the waste that accumulates because of this principle—and as a symbol of social decadence. In addition to casting light on his novels, the three stories have substantial merit. He later revised "Under the Rose" and included it in *V.* His other two published short works appeared between *V.* and *The Crying of Lot 49*. Both "The Secret Integration," a short story, and "Journey Into the Mind of Watts," an essay assessing the condition of that neighborhood a year after its riots, demonstrate his sensitivity to racial exploitation, a prominent theme in *V.*

Pynchon's three novels, however, constitute his major achievement. *V.* is long and complex, definitely not a typical first novel. One can begin to solve its puzzles by understanding a dichotomy that is important both to this novel and to his other novels. At one point in it Weissmann, who becomes the sinister Captain Blicero in *Gravity's Rainbow*, decodes a message. After removing every third letter and rearranging them to form "Kurt Mondaugen," the name of a colleague, he is left with "Die Welt ist alles was der Fall ist": the world is everything that is the case. This theory, the opening proposition of Wittgenstein's *Tractatus*, suggests that no hidden meaning lurks beyond the reality that everyone can immediately apprehend. The letters that were juggled to form "Kurt Mondaugen," "God meant Nu Urk," however, suggest that one should be skeptical of Weissmann's decoding and the epistemological premise that he derives from it. Fausto Maijstral, a poet, also accepts Wittgenstein's proposition: "while others may look on the laws of physics as legislation and God as a human form with beard measured in light-years and nebulae for sandals, Fausto's kind are alone with the task of living in a universe of things which simply are." In contrast, Herbert Stencil believes that there are hidden meanings, specifically that a figure named V. fleetingly reveals herself behind everyday reality. His search for her is one of the two main threads of the plot.

In *V.* mankind is divided between humans who still have energy and those who through entropy have become inanimate objects. Pynchon argues that science encourages people to believe this conception of humans: "in the eighteenth century it was often convenient to regard man as a clockwork automaton. In the nineteenth century, with Newtonian physics well assimilated and a lot of work in thermodynamics going on, man was looked on more as a heat engine, about 40 per cent efficient. Now in the twentieth century, with nuclear and subatomic physics a going thing, man had become something which absorbs X-rays, gamma rays and neutrons."

Although in *V.* a counterforce opposes the degradation of the self, this novel describes an almost totally negative, more specifically decadent, society. The most extreme instances are the Whole Sick Crew, a trendy group of dabblers in intellectual matters, sensual pleasures, and social experiments. Rachel Owlglass cogently indicts them: "that Crew does not live, it experiences. It does not create, it talks about people who do.... It satirizes itself and doesn't mean it." New York City is decadent literally from top to bottom. Maddened hunters stalk alligators in its sewers, youth gangs and roisterers careen through its streets, and the Whole Sick Crew, a Psychodontist, proponents of Heroic Love, and a plastic surgeon who takes sexual pleasure in his work hold forth above street level in the buildings. The age itself is decadent; one character plausibly asks, "what was the tag-end of an age if not that sort of imbalance, that tilt toward the more devious, the less forceful?"

Although exasperating, decadence is less harmful than the exploitation described in *V.* Two groups, the Maltese and the African tribe of Hereros, are the principal victims. Although Pynchon cites only the events of World War II, Malta has been a pawn in the game of Mediterranean power politics since the Carthaginians colonized it during the eighth century B.C. As to the exploitation of the Hereros, Pynchon concentrates on von Trotha's bloody campaign against them in 1904, which he sees as a prelude to the Nazis' racial policies. The weak could plot against the exploiters, but the plots in this novel are either evil, such as the conspiracy to steal Boticelli's "Venus," or ambiguous, such as the political plots formed in Florence and Egypt, which are so arcane that it is not clear who would benefit if they were to succeed. Not only are the possible benefits of V. unclear, but also its existence is questionable. The data that Stencil finds may be merely random, or it may reveal a plot. One promising alternative to exploitation is rarely mentioned and even more rarely achieved. Of some people in Southwest Africa the narrative voice comments, "on that foggy, sweating, sterile coast there were no owners, nothing owned. Community may have been the only solution possible against such an assertion of the Inanimate."

V. does not merely deal with historical events; it analyzes the stature of history itself. Like Henry Adams, Pynchon describes historical changes in physical and mathematical terms. This method rests on the premise that history is an intellectual construct, not a set of ineluctable facts, or, less academically, that "people read what news they wanted to and each accordingly built his own rathouse of history's rags and straws."

In *The Crying of Lot 49* neither the self nor history is important, because the society depicted has nearly snuffed out the former and nearly stopped the latter. The characters are little more than bundles of anxieties, perplexities and hedonistic urges. History seems to have come to the end of its road in contemporary Southern California. Very early in this novel a metaphor communicates society's oppressiveness. First Oedipa Maas, the heroine, is said to play a "Rapunzel-like role of a pensive girl somehow, magically, prisoner among the pines and salt fogs of Kinneret." Then a painting of girls held prisoner in a tower's top room is described. They create a tapestry that "was the world." A little later this tower image is related to the Tristero, the alternative postal system whose possible existence is the central question of this novel's plot: "if one object behind her discovery of what she was to label the Tristero System or often only the Tristero . . . were to bring to an end her encapsulation in her tower, then that night's infidelity with Metzger would logically be the starting point for it."

In other words, California, which probably is what the rest of the country will become, has reached a historical cycle's nadir. As he does in *V.*, Pynchon compares the present to the Jacobean age, this time in a long plot summary of a pseudo-Jacobean play and in an account of a production of it that Oedipa sees. This play and this novel's main action have several details in common, which underscore the two era's similarities. For example, the characters in the play are fervid, exotic, and sinister, as are the characters in the main narrative. Evidence of decadence, such as obsession with popular culture and with technology, paranoia—both personal and political—and self-deluded attempts to recapture the past abounds in this novel. Several references to entropy form a thermodynamic analogue of this nearly extinguished society. Similarly, Oedipa's realization that from nearby high ground her home town looks like a circuit diagram implies that this human society has dwindled into inanimateness. Thus, using exaggeration and indirection, Pynchon scornfully castigates California's society.

No wonder that Oedipa looks for alternatives. There are other seekers, but some of them, such as the Peter Pinguid Society (Pynchon's version of the John Birch Society), clearly are paranoids. An allusion to an imaginary sect implies that for some time dissatisfaction with one's society has induced Manichaeanism: "Robert Scurvham had founded, during the reign of Charles I, a sect of most pure Puritans. . . . Creation was a vast, intricate machine. But one part of it, the Scurvhamite part, ran off the will of God, its prime mover. The rest ran off some opposite Principle, something blind, soulless; a brute automatism that led to eternal death." The Tristero, which may have begun by challenging the Thurn and Taxis, the dominant European postal system, attracts Oedipa because it may become the basis for a new society. Its existence, like that of V., remains in doubt throughout the novel. The auction of stamps that it may have issued will perhaps solve this puzzle, but offering them for sale—the crying of lot 49—does not occur until this book's final sentence. Oedipa's attempts to understand the Tristero are hampered by the interweaving of clues about it with the lives of exotic characters and especially by the fact that all the clues relate to Pierce Inverarity, the financial mogul of whose estate Oedipa and Metzger are co-executors. That is, Inverarity, a jokester, may have arranged the clues to befuddle Oedipa.

Oedipa justifiably expects a communication system to rescue her from an entropic society. Other characters tell her about Maxwell's Demon: a device that James Clerk Maxwell thought could circumvent entropy by sorting high-energy and low-energy molecules into separate containers and using the difference in potential energy to produce work. Of this machine, John Nefastis tells Oedipa, " 'entropy is a figure of speech . . . a metaphor. It connects the world of thermodynamics to the world of information flow. The machine uses both. The Demon makes the metaphor not only verbally graceful, but also objectively true.' " Nefastis means that scientists also use the concept of entropy to describe information loss. He could have added that Boltzmann's equation for heat loss is nearly identical to Shannon's equation for information loss. One mode of communication figures in a key scene and refers to the question of whether things simply are or whether they mask hidden reality, which was an important question in V. While she is comforting a drunk in one of this novel's few instances of a character's genuine concern for others, Oedipa's mind wanders from metaphor to metaphor until the narrator comments, "the act of metaphor then was a thrust at truth and a lie, depending where you were: inside, safe, or outside, lost. Oedipa did not know where she was." Pynchon thus raises but does not solve the problem of whether metaphorical communication, no doubt including writing novels, facilitates the search for truth and ultimately will help build a more satisfying society.

Gravity's Rainbow is set during World War II and the period immediately following and depicts an even grimmer society than does *The Crying of Lot 49*. The problem in *Gravity's Rainbow* is no longer a decadent society, but a culture of death. The dedication to Richard Farina and the epigraph, which quotes Wernher von Braun's statement of belief in "the continuity of our spiritual existence after death," are appropriate because this novel is a fictional elegy, a meditation on death. The war of course is a suitable occasion for such a meditation. In addition to causing death, the rocket is associated with details that connote death. The Germans fire it from Nordhausen, which means "dwellings in the north," the region, according to the Hereros, where death resides. The rocket commander, Weissmann, takes the code name Blicero from Dominus Blicero, the lord of death. The tunnels of the rocket installation, the rockets' path in flight and many other details are parabolas, the shape of the rune for the yew tree, a symbol of death. The ship of fools whose voyage constitutes part of the plot is named the *Anubis* after the ship that, the Egyptians believed, carried away the dead. Much of the plot moves forward because of efforts by Slothrop, the main character, and others to find out why rockets' approaches make him have erections. Near the end of this novel a character alleges that Slothrop "might be in love, in sexual love, with his, and the race's, death."

Several factors, *Gravity's Rainbow* suggests, cause this culture's morbidity. In a seance Walter Rathenau, the German administrative genius, identifies two: "you must ask two questions. First, what is the real nature of synthesis? And then: what is the real nature of control?" The real nature of synthesis, Pynchon's many references to plastics indicate, is that it violates nature. He develops the theme of control less extensively than the theme of synthesis, but he suggests that it, too, has frightful implications. One of the characters argues that "once the technical means of control have reached a certain size, a certain degree of *being connected* one to another, the chances for freedom are over for good."

The forces of evil, several passages in this novel suggest, have also tampered with the traditional conceptions of linear time, not to make time more meaningful, but to make it less meaningful. The rocket, for instance, travels faster than sound, so it strikes before it can be heard, thereby seeming to disrupt time. Moreover, the rocket's controls effect a double integration to transform acceleration to distance so that the fuel can be shut off at the proper time for the rocket to hit its target. As a result "time falls away: change is stilled." Not coincidentally, it is the Germans who first learned to "stop" time in order to operate rockets: "there has been this strange connection between the German mind and the rapid flashing of successive stills to counterfeit movement, for at least two centuries—since Leibniz, in the process of inventing calculus, used the same approach to break up the trajectories of cannonballs through the air." "The same approach" refers to film's counterfeiting of movement, which seems beneficial until Pynchon notes that "film and calculus [are] both pornographies of flight. Reminders of impotence and abstraction." The many references in this novel to real and imagined films and filmmakers and the uses of cinematic techniques therefore remind one of the death culture.

Pynchon notes other connections between the German mind and the death culture; in fact, this novel contains an oblique, schematic history of German thought. He calls the final scene of a movie, for example, a "Rilke-elegaic shot of weary death leading the two lovers away." *Gravity's Rainbow* makes several other references to Rilke and quotes from his work, particularly *The Duino Elegies* and *The Sonnets to Orpheus.* He usually is on the wrong side of an issue. Even more common are references to German films of the period between the two world wars, especially Fritz Lang's, mainly because most of his major characters have "yearnings aimed the same way, toward a form of death that could be demonstrated to hold joy and defiance." The Germans, therefore, are intellectual enemies as well as military enemies.

The real enemy, however, is an obscure They, an international group. The war only seems to be between the Allies and the Axis; Shell Oil, for example, operates on both sides, and Pynchon describes the fissure developing between Russia and its onetime allies even before hostilities end. As it does with many issues, the rocket clarifies this problem of They: "the rocket can penetrate, from the sky, at any given point. Nowhere is safe. We can't believe Them any more." Their weapons, military and otherwise, threaten the characters throughout this novel. They seem invincible, but Pynchon recounts the efforts of counterforces, and he describes them in more detail than he does in his earlier novels. The best organized counterforce, Enzian's black African rocket troops, searches for the mysterious rocket 00000. Pynchon frequently associates white with death, so their color suits their vitality, as does their subordinate political position, because "out and down in the colonies, life can be indulged, life and sensuality in all its forms." *Gravity's Rainbow,* among many other things, thus offers encouragement to the forlorn. Love, too, resists the death culture, because it asserts life, as a narrative comment that is reminiscent of "To His Coy Mistress" suggests: "man and woman, coupled, are shaken to the teeth at their approaches to the gates of life." Pynchon develops the love theme in many ways, including detailed and blunt descriptions of sexual variations. He also presents a running argument between proponents of Rossini and Beethoven, which he explains by having one claim that "with Rossini, the whole point is that lovers always get together, isolation is overcome. . . . Throughout the machineries of greed, pettiness, and the abuse of power, *love occurs.*" This character argues that Beethoven typifies the militancy and tragic view of life that permeate German culture.

If both force and counterforce are obscure, the ground on which they contend is even more obscure. Pynchon again shows his fascination with the questions of whether hidden meanings exist behind manifest reality and, if so, how one can discover them. The narrative voice occasionally mentions the possibility mentioned in *V.:* that the world is composed only of things that are the case, that there is no latent meaning. In *Gravity's Rainbow* this position is called anti-paranoia: the belief that nothing is connected. Paranoia, conversely, is the belief that everything is connected or that there are "other orders behind the visible," which is "a Puritan reflex." According to these definitions most of the characters are paranoids and, like Enzian, they search for texts: the rocket or anything else that they can interpret. One question haunts the interpreters: "what *is* it they know that the powerless do not? What terrible structure behind the appearances of diversity and enterprise?"

The interpreters use three main methods. Some, such as Franz Pokler, accept the older scientific belief in cause and effect. Roger Mexico, like many other contemporary scientists, depends on statistics and computes probabilities rather than certainties. Leni Pokler disputes her husband's method and then states her own, the third main method: " 'not produce', she tried, 'not cause. It all goes together. Parallel, not series. Metaphor. Signs and symptoms. Mapping on to different coordinate systems'." The literary techniques used in this novel accord best with Leni's method of finding truth. Pynchon employs juxtaposition, indirection, obscurity, piling up of details until patterns finally emerge, metaphor, all to make as much as possible go together. Many of these methods depend on his great knowledge, which encompasses such disciplines as history, literature, psychology, and film, and which includes popular culture and the everyday detritus of World War II society.

Mainly because of their difficulty, these books were given mixed reviews and then were, with increasing frequency, the subject of scholarly writing. The most extreme example of a negative review of *V.* is C. G. Gros's in *Best Sellers*. He claims, for example, that "reading *V.* is like listening to a scholarly but erratic documentation of Hell by a disinterested onlooker while verbal sewage and vignettes of all that is most disgusting in mankind alternate with sociological asides, sardonic and blasphemous attacks on Christianity, Freudian tidbits." In more contemplative reviews Whitney Balliett objects to this novel's occasional dullness and Pynchon's failure to make its meaning crystallize, and Irving Feldman complains that it is jejune and too often tongue-in-cheek. In contrast, like a few other reviewers George Plimpton warmly praises *V.*, especially its style, humor and erudition. Criticism of *V.* has taken a psychological and sociological direction and is not as impressive as the criticism of the other two novels.

Such substantial critics as Richard Poirier and Roger Shattuck reviewed *The Crying of Lot 49*, but it did not create as big a stir as did *V.* A typical reaction is Arthur Gold's, who positively reviewed *V.* and who also praises that novel in his review of Pynchon's second novel. But this time Gold concludes by saying that "one doesn't get life from a sophisticated young novelist who seems to have given up on the power of his inventions to shape it." The criticism of this novel began strongly with Anne Mangel's helpful explanation of its most important scientific references, although several later articles have gone over this same subject. A later article by Manfred Puetz is also useful, and in general this novel seems to have been explicated more thoroughly than the other two.

The reviews of *Gravity's Rainbow* are nearly unanimously positive. Bruce Allen calls it "the most demanding novel anyone has ever written and . . . surely among the most rewarding." Richard Poirier argues that this novel establishes Pynchon as "a novelist of major historical importance." W. T. Lhamon, Jr., asserts that "this novel is going to change the shape of fiction, if only because its genius will depress all competitors." Edward Mendelson writes that "few books in this century have achieved the range and depth of this one. . . . This is certainly the most important novel to be published in English in the past thirty years." Many of the reviews are long and thoughtful and the products of first-rate scholars, so they got analysis of this novel off to a strong start. Again, one of the first articles (Friedman and Puetz's) very helpfully explicates the scientific allusions, and some later articles ploughed the same ground. Other good articles have appeared, so that this novel has been the subject of more useful scrutiny than the others, but because of its difficulty it needs more work than do the other books.

What has Pynchon accomplished? *V.* is intellectually and technically mature. *The Crying of Lot 49* is admirable for its economy but also sometimes seems made up of leftovers from *V.* As the years go by and critical work on *Gravity's Rainbow* accumulates, the reviewers who hailed it extravagantly seem more likely to be correct, although it is too soon to echo their assessments. One encouraging attribute of Pynchon's career is that it develops. He has not fallen victim to the American syndrome of writing one good book and then being unable to cope with that accomplishment's results. Much of Pynchon's development is caused by his increased empathy with victims, which has balanced and humanized his increased technical control and his increased fund of information. If these lines of development continue, Pynchon, who is still a young man, will probably become an enduring classic.

Periodical Publications:

"Mortality and Mercy in Vienna," *Epoch*, 9, 4 (spring 1959): 195-213;

"Low-lands," *New World Writing*, 16 (1960): 85-108;

"Entropy," *Kenyon Review*, 22, 2 (spring 1960): 277-292;

"Under the Rose," *Noble Savage*, 3 (spring 1961): 223-251;

"The Secret Integration," *Saturday Evening Post*, 45 (19-26 December 1964): 37 ff.;

"Journey Into the Mind of Watts," *New York Times*, 12 June 1966.

References:

Peter Abernethy, "Entropy in Pynchon's *The Crying of Lot 49*," *Critique*, 14, 2 (1972): 18-33;

Alan J. Friedman and Manfred Puetz, "Science as Metaphor; Thomas Pynchon and *Gravity's Rainbow*," *Contemporary Literature*, 15, 3 (summer 1974): 345-359;

Robert E. Golden, "Mass Man and Modernism: Violence in Pynchon's *V.*," *Critique*, 14, 2 (1972): 5-17;

James Hall, "The New Pleasures of the Imagination," *Virginia Quarterly Review*, 46, 4 (autumn 1970): 596-612;

Charles B. Harris, "Death and Absurdity: Thomas Pynchon and the Entropic Vision," in his *Contemporary American Novelists of the Absurd* (New Haven: College and University Press, 1972), pp. 76-99;

Don Hausdorff, "Thomas Pynchon's Multiple Absurdities," *Wisconsin Studies in Contemporary Literature*, 7, 3 (autumn 1966): 258-269;

Jeffrey Helterman, *Thomas Pynchon's Gravity's Rainbow: A Critical Commentary* (New York: Monarch, 1976);

Roger B. Henkle, "Pynchon's Tapestries on the Western Wall," *Modern Fiction Studies*, 17, 2 (summer 1971): 207-220;

Stanley Edgar Hyman, "The Goddess and the Schlemiel," in *On Contemporary Literature*, ed. Richard Kostelanetz (New York: Avon, 1964), pp. 506-510;

David K. Kirby, "Two Modern Versions of the Quest," *Southern Humanities Review*, 5, 4 (fall 1971): 387-395;

John P. Leland, "Pynchon's Linguistic Demon: *The Crying of Lot 49*," *Critique*, 16, 2 (1974): 45-53;

George Levine, "V-2.," *Partisan Review*, 40, 3 (1973): 517-529;

Levine and David Leverenz, eds., *Mindful Pleasures: Essays on Thomas Pynchon* (Boston: Little, Brown, 1976);

R. W. B. Lewis, *Trials of the Word* (New Haven: Yale University Press, 1965), pp. 228-235;

W. T. Lhamon, Jr., "The Most Irresponsible Bastard," *New Republic*, 168, 15 (14 April 1973): 24-28;

Lhamon, "Pentecost, Promiscuity and Pynchon's *V.*," *Twentieth Century Literature*, 21, 2 (May 1975): 163-176;

Richard Locke, "Gravity's Rainbow," *New York Times Book Review*, 11 March 1973, pp. 1-3, 12, 14;

Anne Mangel, "Maxwell's Demon, Entropy, Information: *The Crying of Lot 49*," *Tri-Quarterly*, 20 (winter 1971): 194-208;

John R. May, *Toward a New Earth* (Notre Dame: University of Notre Dame Press, 1972), pp. 180-191;

John A. Meixner, "The All-Purpose Quest," *Kenyon Review*, 25, 4 (autumn 1963): 729-735;

Edward Mendelson, "Pynchon's Gravity," *Yale Review*, 62, 4 (summer 1973): 624-631;

Raymond Olderman, "The Illusion and the Possibility of Conspiracy," in his *Beyond the Waste Land* (New Haven: Yale University Press, 1972), pp. 123-149;

Lance W. Ozier, "Antipointsman/Antimexico; Some Mathematical Imagery in *Gravity's Rainbow*," *Critique*, 16, 2 (1974): 73-90;

Ozier, "The Calculus of Transformation," *Twentieth Century Literature*, 21, 2 (May 1975): 193-210;

Richard Patteson, "What Stencil Knew: Structure and Certitude in Pynchon's *V.*," *Critique*, 16, 2 (1974): 30-44;

Richard Poirier, "Embattled Underground," *New York Times Book Review*, 1 May 1966, pp. 5, 42, 43;

Poirier, *The Performing Self: Compositions and Decompositions in the Language of Contemporary Life* (New York: Oxford University Press, 1971), pp. 23-26;

Poirier, "Rocket Power," *Saturday Review of the Arts*, 1, 3 (March 1973): 59-64;

Poirier, "The Importance of Thomas Pynchon," *Twentieth Century Literature*, 29, 2 (May 1975): 151-162;

Manfred Puetz, "Thomas Pynchon's *The Crying of Lot 49*; The World Is a Tristero System," *Mosaic*, 7, 4 (summer 1974): 125-137;

Scott Sanders, "Pynchon's Paranoid History,"

Twentieth Century Literature, 21, 2 (May 1975): 177-192;

Neal Schmitz, "Describing the Demon," *Partisan Review*, 42, 1 (spring 1975): 112-125;

Robert Sklar, "New Novel, USA," *Nation*, 205, 9 (25 September 1967): 277-280;

Joseph Slade, *Thomas Pynchon* (New York: Warner Paperback Library, 1974);

John Stark, "The Arts and Sciences of Thomas Pynchon," *Hollins Critic*, 12, 4 (October 1975): 1-14;

Tony Tanner, "Caries and Cabals," in his *City of Words: American Fiction 1950-1970* (New York: Harper & Row, 1971). pp. 153-180;

William Vesterman, "Pynchon's Poetry," *Twentieth Century Literature*, 21, 2 (May 1975): 211-220;

Richard Wasson, "Notes on a New Sensibility," *Partisan Review*, 36, 3 (winter 1969): 460-477;

James D. Young, "The Enigma Variations of Thomas Pynchon," *Critique*, 10, 1 (winter 1968): 69-77.

ISHMAEL REED'S most important work has been his five novels, though he is also the author of two books of poetry, one nominated for a National Book Award. His experimental fiction has the stamp of poetry with its plots developed imagistically, its play with language for its own sake, and its continual reference to the power of ritual and ceremony. In his novels Reed breaks from the tradition of the pseudo-autobiography used by such major black writers as Richard Wright, Ralph Ellison, and James Baldwin and based on the pattern of the mostly anonymous "slave narratives" of nineteenth-century America. Instead, Reed tries to avoid the negative attitudes and philosophical despair of many modern black writers. What Reed attempts in his fiction is to explore the mythic past of the black man and restore to him his non-Western vision. Reed's aim is the establishment of a black aesthetic based on voodoo, the myth of Osiris, hoodoo, and other primordial elements of ritual belonging solely to the black character. His mode is satire aimed at the Judeo-Christian tradition, at Western science, technology, and rationalism, and his weapon in all his novels is the construction of wildly hilarious parody, allegory, and myth.

Reed was born in Chattanooga, Tennessee, on 22 February 1938 (the number 22, he has explained, is "the most powerful number in hoodoo numerology"). In a poem he declares that "goodhomefolks gave me ishmael, how/did they know he was d 'afflicted one'?" He moved with his mother to Buffalo, N. Y. at age four and lived there until he left for New York City. He had begun to write in his first year of college at the State University of New York at Buffalo, and found employment in various newspapers in New York, among them the *East Village Other*. He has continued to be interested in publishing. Along with Al Young he founded the *Yardbird Reader* in California, publishes an audio magazine (cassette recordings) called *Steve Cannon Show*, and wants to begin producing television shows. Small presses are important, he believes, because their editors can publish books "that don't fit in with the political idea of what they think black writers should be doing in the East."

Reed defines himself as publisher as much as he does as novelist. His most important recent venture, apart from his writing, is a coalition called "Before Columbus," designed to produce and distribute the work of unknown ethnic writers to an audience larger than previously possible. "Before Columbus" is "anti-Nazi," according to Reed. It is made up of Asian-Americans, Irish-Americans, Jewish-Americans, Afro-Americans—people whose literature has been suppressed. At the same time, however, Reed is concerned that he not be seen as narrow and selfish. He is proud of the fact that he is the vice-chairman of the Coordinating Council of Literary Magazines, and he sees his task to be to broaden publishing opportunities for all young writers, particularly those who have been closed off from publication because of supposed racial and ethnic bias.

Reed began his writing career with *The Free-Lance Pallbearers* in 1967. It makes use of an academic background for some of its settings and effects, but the main satiric thrust is elsewhere.

The work takes its shape from the typical black novel of identity crisis and search for selfhood. Reed's purpose, however, is to parody savagely the form and substance of novels exhibiting such definition. He goes about his task of demolition by calling up parallels between the career of his hero, Bukka Doopeyduk, and such figures as Ralph Ellison's Invisible Man. Bukka is innocent, naive, a believer in the work ethic and proper ways of acting and speaking, and he goes about his job as a Nazarene apprentice with touching and insane dedication. The course of his attempts to ingratiate himself with the power structure of Harry Sam (an urban country ruled by an LBJ-like dictator) leads him to final crucifixion suspended beneath a giant ball of human excrement. Bukka, as typical hero of the black development novel, ends up at last aware of

Ishmael Reed.

the answer to all his problems (be master of yourself) but unable to do anything with his knowledge. The plot of his progress in *The Free-Lance Pallbearers* is complex and dense, but the central symbol, excrement, defines clearly enough the theme of corruption in the self and in society which works its way throughout the book.

Neil Schmitz points out that in *The Free-Lance Pallbearers* Ishmael Reed "hoodooed those sympathetic critics who instinctively praise the first novels of young black writers. The subject of *Pallbearers* is the monstrosity of American life, but the full force of Reed's ire falls upon the conventional modes of telling the black man's role in that life. In *Pallbearers*, Reed refuses to enter Afro-American literature through the usual door."

In his next novel, *Yellow Back Radio Broke-Down* (1969), Reed utilizes the form of the American Western (the yellow-back dime novel) to further his development of the aesthetic of "Neo-HooDoo." Typically, Reed announces his interest with the first sentence: "Folks. This here is the story of the Loop Garoo Kid. A cowboy so bad he made a working posse of spells phone in sick." The difference between the Kid and Bukka Doopeyduk is that

between a mythic hero and a fool. Amalgamating the cliches of Western speech and dramatic situation with black jive, Reed allegorizes the struggle between Black Osiris (the Egyptian god) and Set, here portrayed as Drag Gibson, another LBJ-cowboy-dictator in the town of Yellow Back Radio. Loop Garoo, unlike the ineffectual Nazarene apprentice of the first novel, functions as an active representative of the power inherent in the mythic history of the black. "This time," Loop Garoo scribbles on a postcard, "the witches win." The HooDoo cowboy cleans out Drag Gibson, characterized mainly by his delight in sadomasochism, closes down the town of Yellow Back Radio, and finally, faced with the Pope, who arrives to combat the outbreak of witchcraft stirred up by the Osiris figure, drives him off as well.

Yellow Back Radio Broke-Down marks the beginning of some problems in Reed's fiction, according to several critics of the novel. Much of the difficulty with the work comes from Reed's conscious introduction of a large amount of unfamiliar material (the mythic conflict of Osiris and Set, for example) into the texture and frame of the narrative. Despite the problems in compre-

418

hension raised by Reed's attempt to construct an alternative black aesthetic in the novel, most readers find it successful, largely because it incorporates parody of the situations and language of the Western.

With *Mumbo Jumbo* (1972) Reed fully develops his aesthetic, based on a revisionist reading of the myths of ancient Egypt, the rituals of West Indian magic, and the conjuring power of dark peoples. In 1971, Reed published in *Confrontation* what he called the "Neo-HooDoo Manifesto," a program which he suggests represents the rebirth of a black spiritual-mythic vision that has long been distorted and oppressed by Judeo-Christian influences. *Mumbo Jumbo*, nominated for a National Book Award, is his most successful rendering of "Neo-HooDoo" into fiction.

The historic setting of this third novel is the Harlem Renaissance of the 1920s, complete with Hinckle Von Vampton, Reed's parody of Carl Van Vechten, the white writer and patron of black artists whose *Nigger Heaven* did so much to establish and exploit the exotic primitivistic vision of Harlem which pervaded the views and writings of the decade. Generically, *Mumbo Jumbo* is a thriller about a voodoo detective, Papa LaBas, and a strange phenomenon sweeping the nation—the outburst of Jes Grew, a spontaneous dance which renders its victims unable to function in American society. In Reed's allegory, ragtime music serves as an emblem of the dark unconscious, the Osirian element inherent in the black mind, a disruptive force which is anathema to the white rationalistic establishment.

Houston A. Baker, Jr., says that *Mumbo Jumbo* offers "a conspiracy view of history, a critical handbook for the student of the Black Arts, and a guide for the contemporary Black consciousness intent on the discovery of its origins and meaning." Other commentators have praised the novel for more stylistic reasons, citing the close cooperation between satire and mythmaking in the narrative. Unfortunately, however, much of the humor of Reed's first two novels is sacrificed in *Mumbo Jumbo* to the demands of his construction of the Neo-HooDoo aesthetic. For the first time in one of his novels, for example, Reed includes scholarly footnotes and a detailed bibliography of some 104 entries, all arguably pertinent but daunting nonetheless.

If *Mumbo Jumbo* is concerned with the black writer's need to incorporate "Jes Grew" (that awakening of Osirian consciousness) into his art, *The Last Days of Louisiana Red* (1974) carries the mythic career of Papa LaBas, cultural diagnostician

and healer, quite a few steps farther. In this novel the hoodoo detective is faced with solving the murder of Ed Yellings, developer of the Solid Gumbo Works, a business that uses spells and charms to combat the evils of Louisiana Red. Louisiana Red is literally a hot sauce, figuratively the pernicious state of mind which divides black people and sets them against each other, what Reed calls "the way they related to each other, oppressed one another, maimed and murdered one another, carving one another while above their heads, 50,000 feet, billionaires flew in custom-made jet planes. . . ."

Barbara Smith points out that "the primary targets of Reed's wit are the black revolutionary organizations that sprang up in places like Berkeley in the 1960's. . . . The posturing, the rhetoric and the exploitation that sometimes characterized actual movements symbolize the forces of foolishness and evil in Reed's hoodoo drama." With the fourth novel, Reed's reputation made a significant advance, but some critics are troubled by the implications of various of the conflicts in the work, particularly that between the sexes. At one point Papa LaBas confronts Minnie, a leader of the Moochers who are representative of the corrupt effects of Louisiana Red, and accuses her and all black women of being conspirators with white men in keeping black men in slavery. "The original blood-sucking vampire was a woman," he declares. "I can't understand why you want to be liberated. Hell, you already liberated." His prescribed method for defeating these "man-hating dykes" is attack and sexual conquest. In *The Free-Lance Pallbearers*, Bukka Doopeyduk's wife, Fanny Mae, has a female lover and makes life hell itself for her earnest Nazarene apprentice husband.

Papa LaBas, Reed's ultimate hoodoo necromancer and hero, represents a stringently patriarchal view of the relation between men and women, and Reed's approval of what he calls this "old morality" raises problems for the cultural critics who were so pleased by his earlier attacks on establishment values. A more serious flaw in the fourth novel is defined by Neil Schmitz as Reed's insistence on the construction of an "eclectic mythology. Even as it provides him with a coherent mythos, Neo-HooDoo necessarily deflects the course of his satire. . . . In *The Last Days*, Reed's mythology is used like a vacuum sweeper: it has all the answers within its system. . . . Reed has yet to . . . choose between the rigorous demands of satire and the programmatic concerns of Neo-HooDoo."

Flight to Canada (1976), Reed's most recent novel, marks a significant departure for him. The

SOUL PROPRIETORSHIP

I

Billy Eckstine, now I
understand why you
went solo, even if it meant crooning
the Pastrami and Rye circuit from
Miami to Grossinger's
Maybe you got tired of babysitting
for other people's tubas, or
running out for reeds
Maybe you got tired of the
spitballs breaking the skin
of your neck while in the midst
of one of those ostentatious supper-
club bows
The bounced checks and half-empty
seats were hard on your dignity
and the bad publicity you received
from the black eye you gave your
agent, co-hort in a secret
deal with management
didn't help

II

You always had to put ice packs
on the lead tenor's head in Chicago
when by late afternoon a concert
was scheduled for Detroit
And there was always the genius
He was avant garde
which meant he had trouble playing
in scales of five flats
he spurned your attempts to
teach him things and went out
to organize his own band

Typescript for previously unpublished poem by Reed.

SOUL PROPRIETORSHIP   2

They called their bloopers new
music and drew experimental
customers
Customers who never smiled
and owned high blood pressure
When you travel single you
can take time out to catch up
with the funnies
You no longer have to order
40 cups of coffee
10 black
5 with cream and
12 regular
You no longer have to keep
tabs on the two guys who wanted
tea

            III

And when your only companion became
your thought
You came up with the Billy Eckstine
Shirt
with prints as beautiful as
the handle of an Islamic sword
and you made a million silver dollars
And you bought an old Spanish mission
in California whose
wings could be seen from the sea
They look like two shining silver
collars, billowing, for lift off

copyright Ishmael Reed 1978

421

subject is the American Civil War rendered in typically anachronistic fashion. Arthur Swille, a Virginia planter, is a multinational businessman who watches television, hobnobs with Robert E. Lee, jets all over the world on deals, and makes long-distance telephone calls to brokers in New York and Switzerland. Raven Quickskill, his runaway slave, has written a poem titled "Flight to Canada" which functions for him as his aesthetic escape from his old slave identity. Art sets him free. Abraham Lincoln appears as a sharpster from the Midwest out for gold and glory. In short the plot is the usual dense complex of satire, allegory, and farce. The interesting difference, however, is the absence of Neo-HooDoo as primary subject. Instead, Reed has returned to the structure of a naive hero in search of an identity and makes only passing reference to voodoo, Osiris, and other constituents of the black aesthetic that he labored so to build in the previous three novels.

The result of Reed's decision to concentrate on satire at the expense of the Neo-HooDoo program is a real gain in narrative movement and a clarifying of the targets of his attack. The rich historical texture of *Flight to Canada* (the book is filled with references to fugitive slave law controversies, political details of the era, biographical knowledge of figures such as Mary Todd Lincoln) demonstrates Reed's care in sharpening the effects of his work. This most recent novel reveals Reed in the process of working his way out of the repetitious dead end he had written himself into in *The Last Days of Louisiana Red* and promises new territory for his inventive imagination.

A statement Reed made in an interview with Joe O'Brien sums up well his notions about the task of the novelist and the importance of his effort: "People go into the past and get some metaphor from the past to explain the present or the future. I call this 'necromancy,' because that's what it is. . . . Necromancers used to lie in the guts of the dead or in tombs to receive visions of the future. The Black writer lies in the guts of old America, making readings about the future. That's what I wanted to do." So far in his career Reed has done a dazzling job of "making readings" about America, and what he has accomplished with his first five novels augurs well for his attempts in the future. —*Gerald Duff*

Books:

The Free-Lance Pallbearers (Garden City: Doubleday, 1967; London: MacGibbon & Kee, 1968);
Yellow Back Radio Broke-Down (Garden City:

Doubleday, 1969; London: Allison & Busby, 1971);
Catechism of D NeoAmerican Hoodoo Church (London: Paul Breman, 1970);
Conjure (Amherst: University of Massachusetts Press, 1972);
Mumbo Jumbo (Garden City: Doubleday, 1972);
Chattanooga (New York: Random House, 1973);
The Last Days of Louisiana Red (New York: Random House, 1974);
Flight to Canada (New York: Random House, 1976).

References:

Madge Ambler, "Ishmael Reed: Whose Radio Broke Down?," *Negro American Literature Forum*, 6 (1972): 125, 131;

Houston A. Baker, Jr., Review of *Mumbo Jumbo*, *Black World*, 22 (December 1972): 63-64;

Roland E. Bush, "Werewolf of the Wild West: On a Novel by Ishmael Reed," *Black World*, 23, 3 (January 1974): 51-52, 64-66;

Gerald Duff, "Reed's *The Free-Lance Pallbearers*," *Explicator*, May 1974, Item 69;

Nick Aaron Ford, "A Note on Ishmael Reed: Revolutionary Novelist," *Studies in the Novel*, 3 (1971): 216-218;

Cameron Northouse, "Ishmael Reed," in *Conversations with Writers, II* (Detroit: Bruccoli Clark/Gale, 1978);

Ishmael Reed, "The Writer as Seer: Ishmael Reed on Ishmael Reed," *Black World*, 23, 8 (June 1974): 20-34;

Neil Schmitz, "Neo-HooDoo: The Experimental Fiction of Ishmael Reed," *Twentieth Century Literature*, 20 (April 1974): 126-140.

Philip Roth

Jeffrey Helterman
University of South Carolina

BIRTH: Newark, New Jersey, 19 March 1933.

EDUCATION: Weequahic High School, 1946-1950; Rutgers University (Newark), 1950-1951; A.B., Bucknell University, 1954; M.A., University of Chicago, 1955; further graduate work in English, University of Chicago, 1956-1957.

MARRIAGE: 22 February 1958 to Margaret Martinson Williams, divorced, 1966.

AWARDS: Houghton Mifflin Literary Fellowship, 1959; National Institute of Arts and Letters grant, 1959; Guggenheim Fellowship, 1959; Daroff Award for *Goodbye, Columbus,* 1959; *Paris Review* Aga Khan Award for "Epstein," 1959; National Book Award for *Goodbye, Columbus,* 1960; Ford Foundation grant, 1965; Elected, National Institute of Arts and Letters, 1970.

MAJOR WORKS: *Goodbye, Columbus* (Boston: Houghton, Mifflin, 1959; London: Deutsch, 1959); *Letting Go* (New York: Random House, 1962; London: Deutsch, 1962); *When She Was Good* (New York: Random House, 1967; London: Cape, 1967); *Portnoy's Complaint* (New York: Random House, 1969; London: Cape, 1970); *Our Gang* (New York: Random House, 1971; London: Cape, 1971); *The Breast* (New York: Holt, Rinehart & Winston, 1972; London: Cape, 1973); *The Great American Novel* (New York: Holt, Rinehart & Winston, 1973; London: Cape, 1973); *My Life as a Man* (New York: Holt, Rinehart & Winston, 1974; London: Cape, 1974); *Reading Myself and Others* (New York: Farrar, Straus & Giroux, 1975; London: Cape, 1975); *The Professor of Desire* (New York: Farrar, Straus & Giroux, 1977).

In 1974, Philip Roth wrote a satirical novel about baseball which he entitled *The Great American Novel.* The title refers to the parodies of a number of classic American novels in the book, but it also may be an answer to critics who keep waiting for him to write the great American novel and keep castigating him when he doesn't. From the time of the publication of his second novel, *Letting Go,* to the publication of his latest, *The Professor of Desire,* critics have been wondering aloud when Roth is going to stop squandering his enormous gifts and create the legitimate American masterpiece. The critical reaction in this regard is somewhat different than the kind that often greets second novels of promising young writers. It usually takes the form of an assertion of how good the book is of its kind and then asks why Roth would write this kind of book. This is not to say that Roth's large and varied output has been unappreciated. *Letting Go* has been seen as one of the finest achievements in the novel of manners since James; *Our Gang* has been called Swiftian and Orwellian; *Portnoy's Complaint* has been regarded as a brilliant exploitation of the new freedom in language granted to the novelist in the 1960s. Yet through more than half of the reviews of everything written after *Goodbye, Columbus,* there remains the complaint—the complaint in fact of many of Roth's heroes who have more than enough to keep them contented and yet are always asking for more.

The primary reason for the complaint is the obvious abundance of gifts Roth possesses. No one writing today is more aware of the nuances of the spoken word, of the details of everyday things which evince a life-style, of the tiny gestures that can record an attitude or a reaction, of the absurdities which can transform the crises of human life into hilarious comedy. These are all qualities of perception but they can often be combined with a bold and outrageous imagination that can dare to write a whole novella about a man transformed into a breast, that can envision an interview with Kafka's whore decked out as a decrepit tourist attraction, or can give tragic overtones to an event as ludicrous as Bill Veeck's introduction of midgets into major league baseball. Hardly a critic denies that Roth can do all these things, and yet there is the niggling suspicion that Roth has not yet set his talents to a worthy task.

Roth was born into a lower-middle-class Jewish family in Newark, New Jersey, during the heart of the Depression but grew up in the slightly more prosperous times during World War II. His memories of Newark and the social stratification in the nearby suburbs are evident particularly in *Goodbye, Columbus* and in *Portnoy's Complaint.* After two years at the Newark branch of Rutgers University, Roth finished his A.B. at Bucknell University, where he was elected to Phi Beta Kappa and edited the school's literary magazine. After

Philip Roth

Jill Krementz

Philip Roth.

receiving an M.A. in English from the University of Chicago, Roth joined the army in 1955 but was discharged after being injured in basic training. He returned to the University of Chicago in 1956, pursuing a Ph.D. and working as an instructor in English. His experiences at the University of Chicago play a large part in the background of his second novel, *Letting Go*. Roth dropped out of the Ph.D. program in 1957 and began reviewing films and television for the *New Republic*. In 1959, his career was launched auspiciously when his first book, the novella *Goodbye, Columbus* and five stories, won the National Book Award. The following two years Roth was on the faculty of the Writers' Workshop of the University of Iowa, and in 1962 he became writer-in-residence at Princeton, where he remained until 1964. Since then he has continued to teach, first at the State University of New York at Stony Brook and since 1967 sporadically at the University of Pennsylvania. The financial turning point of Roth's career was in 1969 when *Portnoy's Complaint* became the number one best-seller and the enormously successful movie version of *Goodbye, Columbus* was released.

The title novella and the stories of *Goodbye, Columbus* (1959) all involve the attempt of the hero to invade and make sense of a culture alien to his own. In each case, both the invader and the alien culture are Jewish, but aside from this they have little in common. In some cases the invasion is unsuccessful and the hero beats a somewhat hesitant retreat to his own milieu; in others the hero wins at least the admiration of the reader if not that of his contemporaries. In an interview accompanying a review of the book, Roth noted that he had already earned the distinction of being that most renegade of renegades, the anti-Semitic Jew, a charge which was to blossom with new fervor after the publication of *Portnoy's Complaint*.

In *Goodbye, Columbus*, Neil Klugman sets out from the lower-class confines of his Newark home and invades the upper-middle-class environs of Short Hills, New Jersey. He has fallen for Brenda Patimkin, the archetypal Jewish American Princess, the pampered girl who has been given everything. The Patimkin household is the gross fulfillment of the American dream of financial success, conspicuous consumption, and endless active leisure.

Neil sees its every foible, particularly in Brenda's spoiled younger sister and in her brother, whose life seems arrested in the conformity of his college days at Ohio State. Nevertheless, despite his awareness of the crassness of Brenda and everything she stands for, Neil does not transcend or reject the Patimkin world. Instead, he and Brenda break up in a silly argument, self-righteous on both sides. Neil creates a haven for himself in his job at the library, where he befriends a young Negro boy who comes to look at the lush tropical paintings of Paul Gauguin. Despite his sincerity, Neil is somewhat condescending to the boy but never realizes that the Patimkin's refrigerator is as much a false paradise for him as is Gauguin's Pacific island for the boy.

A more complete invasion of the opposing culture occurs in "Eli the Fanatic" in which the hero, a Jewish lawyer named Eli Peck, is asked by his middle-class, suburban community to get rid of the Yeshiva (a school for Orthodox Old World Jews) that is becoming a source of irritation for its assimilated neighbors. Peck finds that his legal background is no match for the unswerving belief of the Yeshiva's rabbi and eventually tries to gain some leverage by bribing the rabbi's messenger with a new suit. The messenger returns the favor by giving Peck his Old World costume, and Peck finds himself possessed by the spirit of the clothing. When he puts on the refugee's suit, Peck goes outside and sees the essence of his chrome-plated suburb—his neighbor giving her rocks a second coat of pink paint. As Eli, dressed in the ragged hand-me-downs, goes to see his newborn son at the hospital, his friends deal with him the only way they can: they declare him crazy, and the story ends with him going under from the effects of a hastily administered sedative. This story is close in tone to the mystical otherworldliness of Bernard Malamud's stories in *The Magic Barrel*.

Another story of the odd man out is "The Conversion of the Jews" in which the hero, a twelve-year-old bar mitzvah student, begins to question the values of his religion and ultimately the powers of God himself. The antagonists are the boy, Ozzie Freedman, and his rabbi, Marvin Binder, whose names suggest their opposite approaches to life. Binder can provide nothing but unexamined answers to Ozzie's questions, while Ozzie is continually looking for something more. Ozzie wants to know why, for example, the Virgin Birth can be an impossibility for a God who can create the world in six days. Binder can respond only with exasperation and a call to Ozzie's parents. Finally Ozzie forces the rabbi and the rest of the community to assent to his beliefs by climbing to the roof of the synagogue and threatening to jump. Only when he extracts a promise that no one will ever hit anyone over a question of religion does Ozzie come down, jumping into the waiting firemen's net. Unlike Neil Klugman, Ozzie has the courage of his convictions and ends the story a free man.

The most complex story in the collection is "Defender of the Faith," which concerns Sheldon Grossbart, an army recruit who uses his Jewish heritage to weasel concessions from his Jewish sergeant, Nathan Marx. Although Marx sees through most of Grossbart's tricks, at least after the fact, he lets him get away with them, primarily because he is trying to recover the humanity he feels has been lost in his front-line battle experiences. When Grossbart goes beyond hustling favors to wangle the only stateside assignment among a group of men who are being sent to fight in the Pacific, Marx uses his influence and Grossbart-like reliance on the Jewish "underground" to send Grossbart with the others to take his chances in the Pacific. Roth brilliantly sets up the mixed motivations for Marx's decision so that Marx can never be certain whether he has sent Grossbart out of spiteful vengeance or a need to see that justice is done. Marx has spent his whole stateside tour trying to relearn his grandmother's dictum that "mercy overrides justice" only to find that sometimes a man must opt for the more difficult choice of justice. In making this decision, Marx becomes the real defender of the faith—faith in human responsibility—and replaces Grossbart, whose nominal defense of his Jewish faith is simply a way to get favors and take care of himself.

After the almost unanimous praise for *Goodbye, Columbus*, Roth's second book, *Letting Go* (1962), was met with muted hostility and faint praise. Most reviewers granted Roth his undeniable eye for detail and his ear for real conversation but felt that these talents had been wasted in a large, over-written novel. *Letting Go* is a deliberately Jamesian novel, a bleak comedy of manners in which the narrator, Gabe Wallach, has to learn the value of getting involved and also of getting out of involvements. James's *Portrait of a Lady* becomes a significant stage property in the novel—a letter from Wallach's mother is left and a kind of Isabel Archer character, Libby Herz, reads it at an opportune moment. In addition, Wallach's Ph.D. dissertation is on James. If Libby finds the Jewish world of her husband Paul as much of an alien land as Isabel Archer finds Europe, then Wallach's most significant problems seem closest to those of Lambert Strether in *The Ambassadors*: Wallach tries to help out in other people's affairs without fully committing himself to anyone or anything.

The novel follows Wallach's relationships with three women: Marge Howells, a student of his with no problems other than a boring Midwestern upbringing; Martha Regenhart, a life-battered divorcee; and most importantly, Libby Herz, the troubled wife of a friend of his. As will be the case with many of Roth's heroes, Wallach is a man for whom life has not created many natural disasters and he will, therefore, have to create his own problems and test his own limits. As the novel opens he is a graduate student, but one well off enough to have no need of cashing the checks his father sends him and intellectually fluent enough not to have to struggle to get a job. Later, he does just as well teaching at college. In this he is contrasted with Paul Herz, for whom everything goes wrong. Herz is a man with a talent for misery, who wanders around in a hand-me-down coat, the smell of egg salad sandwiches wafting up from the briefcase carrying his unfinished novel-dissertation. Herz gets a job on an auto assembly line and almost immediately injures his hand. He finds the crisis of trying to get his wife an abortion confused by two men who are arguing over how to divide the profits on a stock of remaindered underwear that one has sold.

Wallach sees himself as a humanist and is proud of his clash with the faculty members who concern themselves with form and punctuation, but his humanism is less valid when concerned with real life. His affair with Marge Howells, a girl with perfect teeth who is "in revolt against Kenosha, Wisconsin," is recorded primarily to show Gabe's natural proclivity to withdraw from any human relationship at the first sign of commitment on his side. Roth gives simultaneous examples of this character flaw when he places Wallach in his father's dental office with his father working on his teeth. Wallach thinks "I could have reached up and pulled him down and kissed him. But would he understand that I was not prepared to surrender my life to his? He was a wholehearted man, and such people are hard to kiss half-heartedly." Once his teeth are clean, Wallach calls up Marge long-distance and breaks off his affair using his need to be with his father as an excuse for not returning to Chicago. Wallach is as halfhearted with her as he is with his father.

Wallach is filled with guilt about his inability to get involved and he compensates for his lack of feeling with a superabundance of charity. He helps people, using tremendous energy but little emotional commitment. His help usually causes further trouble, particularly when he tries to straighten out the troubled marriage of the Herzes. Early in the novel he tells himself "I had no business in the lives of these people and that I would not come back, no matter who invited me." Nonetheless, he feels guilty when his help does not increase the love and understanding in the Herz household and he goes off to New York to reconcile Paul's parents to the idea that their son has married a Gentile. He tries to conduct a dignified conversation with Paul's mother who talks to him while simultaneously giving her husband in the bathroom instructions for dealing with his constipation. The scene is one of many in the novel in which some minor concern undercuts the seriousness of the business at hand and often sabotages the hero's attempt to get the business of helping others done. Later, the toilet-training of a young child will interrupt Wallach's attempt to find an adoptive child for the Herzes.

In his involvement with Martha Regenhart, Wallach seems at first kind and considerate. Going beyond being merely a lover, he pays his share of the rent and food and acts as a father to her children. While this is going on, however, he never gives up his own unused apartment. He panics both when Martha lets her ex-husband take her children, leaving himself and Martha the freedom to become totally involved, and also when Martha seems ready to dismiss totally her most persistent other suitor, leaving Wallach as the man to marry her. Although Wallach sees himself as a man of sensitivity, he is instead a fault-finder who uses fine perceptions about the motivations of others to mask his boorishness. When his planned dinner for the Herzes turns into a disaster, he blames Martha for dressing the wrong way, he blames the Herzes for acting too genteelly poor, but does not admit that his subconscious motivation is both to fracture his relationship with Martha and to impress Libby with his freedom and suave worldliness.

In the most Jamesian inversion in the book, Wallach's greatest moral flaw turns out to be his failure to seduce his friend's wife. He grants Libby a stolen kiss early in the novel but then pulls back. Wallach gives Libby just enough support to allow her to question the value of staying with her doomed-to-failure husband, but he does not dare to take the step, adultery, which would free her. Wallach attempts to make up for his lack of emotional courage by working—as he sees it, crusading—to acquire a child for the couple to adopt and fill the emptiness he has helped build into Libby's life. Gabriel Wallach is ultimately satisfied with this substitution of help for commitment and feels that his name, that of the angel, is as fitting for him as is his favorite song, "Earth Angel."

Roth continued his analysis of people enamored of their own perfection in his next novel, *When She Was Good*—one of whose working titles was *Saint Lucy*. In *When She Was Good* (1967), Roth invades the American heartland the way Alexander Portnoy does when he goes off to visit his all-American girl friend, Kay Campbell. Portnoy is somewhat disappointed not to find in the Midwest the narrow-mindedness of a Sinclair Lewis or Sherwood Anderson novel, but Roth finds closed minds and a desperate lack of freedom in Liberty Center. Many reviewers noted that Roth seemed to be trying to prove that he could write about some other milieu than the urban Jewish settings that had been his forte, but far more important, although not noteworthy at the time, is that Lucy Nelson, the heroine of *When She Was Good*, remains Roth's only three-dimensional female character in some twenty years of writing.

Reviews were mixed, but most of the negative views saw the heroine as obsessive, deserving the condemnation of the novel's most despicable character, Julian Sowerby, who calls her "A little ball-breaker of a bitch. That's the saint you are, kiddo—Saint Ball-breaker." The problem for both the other characters in the novel and for the reviewers is that Lucy is not only an idealist, she is a female. Like Gabe Wallach in *Letting Go*, there is a good deal of snobbery about Lucy Nelson's attempt to improve everybody else, but Gabe draws nowhere the amount of hostility, apparently because he is a man. Lucy is a perfectionist who becomes outraged by the mediocrity, particularly the moral mediocrity, of others. She uses truth like a club, only to discover that no one in Liberty Center wants to hear it. For example, she fights back against her husband's uncle Julian, who has in effect stolen her child, by correctly accusing him of adultery but discovers that everyone, including his daughter and his wife, already know about it. What she discovers is that the truth makes no one free in Liberty Center.

When She Was Good is the only one of Roth's novels which gives a woman an independent existence, i.e., not simply a role, no matter how vividly drawn, in the life of a man. Roth begins by recording the history of the two previous generations of Lucy's family so that it is clear how she came to be the woman she is. From her grandfather, Willard Carroll, she has inherited a sense of civilized values, but unlike Willard, she has not learned to moderate these values in the face of human weakness. Willard is a figure of honesty and perspicacity, but he is too willing to excuse the flaws of others. This attitude looks like compassion but may well be weakness. For example, he continually makes excuses for Lucy's father, Whitey, in the hopes that Whitey will reform, but by taking Whitey and his family into his home, Willard effectively robs his son-in-law of the motivation to reform. Willard constantly pleads for goodness, but as his wife reminds him, he is no hero: "You are not Abraham Lincoln. You are the assistant Postmaster in Liberty Center."

Lucy has no such sense of her limits. As a teenager, she becomes a Catholic and dreams of becoming St. Teresa, but she gives this up when she finds that the passive goodness of the saint is not enough and calls for the police to keep her drunk father from attacking her mother. She had "dedicated herself to a life of submission, humility, silence and suffering. . . . After calling upon Saint Teresa of Lisieux and Our Lord—and getting no reply—she called the police."

The main action of the novel details the collapse of Lucy's marriage to Roy Bassett, an ineffectual dreamer, whom she married because she was pregnant. Roy dreams of becoming an important man but ends up with the absurd role of assistant to the "society" photographer in Fort Kean. Lucy tries to pierce Roy's empty dreams so that he might take steps to fulfill himself, but her self-righteousness only drives him and their four-year-old son out of the house. After a frantic and fruitless attempt to recover her family, Lucy walks off into the snow at Passion Paradise, where she and Roy first became involved, and there she dies of exposure.

Like Emma Bovary or Hedda Gabler, Lucy Nelson expects others to live up to her romantic high standards, particularly her obsession with truth. The weakness of the novel lies in the absence of a suitable foil for Lucy. Both her husband and her father are spineless in their own way, and her grandfather's passive endorsement of goodness does not offer a valid alternative to Lucy's moral militancy. Only Julian Sowerby faces up to Lucy, but his responses are so crass as to make her courage in the face of them meaningless.

Furthermore, Lucy's monolithic, saintlike goodness prevents her from facing any moral crises or spiritual dilemmas. She locks her father out of the house, ignoring the fact that her weak, sentimental mother would rather have him back than have him good; she fights to get her son back, but only to prove herself right—never does she weigh the importance of having him back against the importance of being right. The novel, therefore, though a fascinating portrait of the growth of an obsessive personality, fails to raise the central issues in the struggle of a morally superior person against a world of mediocrity.

Among the artifacts discovered by Alexander Portnoy in his sister's room is a copy of *A Portrait of the Artist as a Young Man*; *Portnoy's Complaint* (1969) does for the American Jewish *Bildungs-roman* what Joyce did for Irish Catholicism. Like Stephen Dedalus, Alexander Portnoy yearns for freedom from the repressive laws of his youth—and like Dedalus, Portnoy feels love as well as revulsion for that youth. In Portnoy's case, the laws are those of Jewish domesticity imposed by a mother whose domineering exterior hides a mass of guilt and fear. Her rules—eat your vegetables, beware of polio, don't fool around with shiksas, don't feel innocent when you can feel guilty—are the manifestation of a classic superego. Portnoy grows up to be not an artist, but an Assistant Commissioner of Human Opportunity, and as such he becomes the Rothian hero—the man who helps those less fortunate than himself, without ever really getting involved with them. Little is seen of Portnoy's professional role, but his involvement with women, Gentiles all (until the last few pages), is based on the same condescending need to improve the other person, combined with a fear of total commitment. Portnoy claims that it is the pull of freedom that makes him avoid complete involvement, but it is fear, guilt, and a desire to avenge his father's powerlessness in Anglo-Saxon America. Portnoy searches endlessly for girls he can improve, the prime example being Monkey, an ignorant but passionate model from the coal fields of West Virginia. When the girls do not respond sufficiently to his tutelage, he has a reason for leaving them. Typically his response to their flaws is disproportionate. He leaves Monkey largely because of her illiteracy, the documentary evidence being her dreadfully misspelled note to her maid, but he forgets that she has been brought to orgasm by his recitation of Yeats's "Leda and the Swan," surely an example of a higher literacy. Portnoy gives all of the women type names like "the Pumpkin" or "the Pilgrim," which stereotypes each as a certain kind of American conquest for him. In doing this, he ignores their humanity; each is of interest only as she becomes an extension of Portnoy.

The source of Portnoy's repression is his parents. His father is an ineffectual insurance salesman who lives in fear of the home office and its WASP managers and suffers through a lifetime of constipation. His mother, Sophie, on the other hand, seems in complete control of her environment. Not only does she impress young Portnoy with all kinds of repressive fears and compulsions toward neatness and cleanliness, but she continually strives to impress him with her patience and generosity. It is no wonder that Portnoy seeks women as unlike his mother as can be imagined, and yet it is also not surprising that he is disappointed when they are not like her.

In his youth, Portnoy's desperate search for freedom is centered around masturbation, an activity both prohibited and also exclusively devoted to the service of the id rather than the superego. The strategy does not work, however, because it only wraps Portnoy further in self and because it is never carried out without guilt. Eventually Portnoy finds himself masturbating in public places, like buses, which indicates a subconscious hope that he might get caught.

As Portnoy matures, sex with the forbidden Gentile takes the place of masturbation but does not improve upon it: the girl remains a projection of Portnoy's ego, and when she has her own personality he strives to make her as much like himself as he can. When Portnoy finally goes to Israel hoping to break out of his mold of seeking forbidden sex, the results are no better. Portnoy has become conditioned to a sense of impurity in his sexual gratification. Without it, he becomes impotent.

Portnoy's Complaint is a hilariously funny novel which is significant for its use of obscenity as part of its intrinsic meaning. Roth says "the book isn't full of dirty words because 'that's the way people talk' "; rather Portnoy "is obscene because he wants to be saved." For Portnoy, obscenity is a violation of everything his mother stands for and he hopes that by using this language he can free himself from her influence. Like Stephen Dedalus, for whom the thought of death without a Catholic afterlife is a similar obscenity, he can never be free.

In an interview following the publication of *Our Gang* (1971), Roth reveals that the immediate reason for writing this political satire was Richard Nixon's decision to free William Calley from the stockade at the same time that he was siding with anti-abortion groups whose battle cry was "the right to life." Roth says "what that statement of his on Calley 'made perfectly clear' was that if it seemed to him in the interest of his career, he would sink to *anything*. If 50.1 percent of the voters wanted to make a hero out of a convicted multiple-murderer, then maybe there was something in it—for him." The resultant book is not so much a novel but a series of satirical sketches which show the Nixon mentality at work in a number of public situations: news conferences, skull sessions, formal speeches, and finally, after the protagonist dies, on the comeback trail campaigning against Satan in Hell. Many of Roth's heroes struggle between their real selves and the fiction they have created about themselves, but Trick E. Dixon and, Roth suggests, Nixon himself have only the rhetorical persona left.

The two epigraphs of *Our Gang* invite comparison to Swift and Orwell, and it is here that the book both stands and falls. The influence of Swift's *A Modest Proposal* is pervasive, and like Swift, Roth is brilliant at building flawless logic on a basically absurd principle. The chain of logic remains intact whether the hero is distinguishing between trouble-makers among fetuses, those who kick their mothers, and rank-and-file fetuses, the silent majority who merely move in the womb; or justifying an American invasion of Denmark on the grounds that we ought to possess Elsinore Castle because Shakespeare's play about it is in English, the American language. Not only is the Nixonian logic worked out to its absurd extreme, but the rhetoric is a deft parody of Nixon's style. What Roth hasn't learned from Swift is the devastating understatement that can deliver the most scathing attack without a touch of rant.

In the interview about the novel, Roth argues that *A Modest Proposal* would have been regarded in bad taste in its day, but he doesn't see that he is talking about the idea behind the satire, that Irish babies be used for food, not about the style which is like the persona, "modest." Precisely because it proposes the most unholy of solutions in the most timorous of accents does *A Modest Proposal* succeed in revealing the horrific mentality of those who can think this way. *Our Gang* is too shrill, and the bombast undercuts the attempt to reproduce Swiftian savagery. The chapter in which Dixon compiles his enemies list and proposes the extermination of the Boy Scouts is a good example of this rhetorical overkill. Only in the final chapter where Dixon campaigns in Hell and tries to prove that Satan does not know as much about evil as he does, does the irony reach Swiftian proportion: "Much as I respect and admire his lies, I don't think that lies are something to stand on. I think they are something to build on." What more need be said about the ambitions of evil men?

No novel of Roth's has caused as much consternation about the proper critical evaluation, about how to get a grasp on it, as has *The Breast* (1972), a story of metamorphosis in which the hero, David Kepesh, finds himself transformed into a massive female breast. The novel has been seen as an over-extended single joke, whose *tour de force* qualities belong in a short story rather than a novel, and much critical rage would have been deflected if the work had appeared in a magazine as a long short story. Other reviewers such as Christopher Lehmann-Haupt or Frederick Crews saw the novel as a brilliant conception whose implementation had not been carried out properly. Finally a number of critics, including the novelists John Gardner and Margaret Drabble, saw the work as a worthy successor to the stories of Gogol and Kafka from which it germinated. R. Z. Sheppard said that Roth had outflanked reality without writing a dirty joke and found the work "more touchingly human than funny, whether read as a fable or credo." Sheppard comes close to Roth's own statement of his intentions. Roth, like Kepesh himself, notes the similarity to Kafka's story, "The Metamorphosis," and insists that the book must be taken seriously as a psychological study of the character and not as a symbolic statement about sexuality. "Not all the ingenuity of all the English teachers in all the English departments in America can put David Kepesh together again. . . . There is only the unrelenting education in his own misfortune. What he learns in the end is that, whatever else it is, it is the real thing: he *is* a breast, and must act accordingly."

What is significant about Kepesh is what he has lost—everything that has identified him in the past, everything that has made him a man—and he must come to terms with this loss in some way. His problem is how to maintain his continuity as a man and as a human being once he no longer has a man's body. Kepesh imagines completely radical solutions to his problem—sexual intercourse using his nipple and exploitation of his condition for financial gain—which call for making himself a breast rather than a man. What stops him is his fear that he might be separating himself from his own past and his own kind.

Almost as interesting as Kepesh's struggles with his identity are the reactions of those who have to deal with him. For the most part, the reactions are a commonplace sympathy that seems to signify an absurd emptiness in the lives of those who are afraid to deal with the absurdity of Kepesh's condition. Kepesh's friend and fellow academic, Schonbrunn, can do no more than visit and send a nice gift—a recording of Olivier's *Hamlet*—while Kepesh's father visits him as he would any other sick relative and regales him with tales of pregnancies, weddings, expensive caterers, and other everyday happenings. Only Kepesh's lover, Claire Ovington, seems to be able to accept Kepesh's condition for what it is, but she does not or cannot go beyond Kepesh's perceptions of his state.

Ultimately, then, it is up to Kepesh himself to face what has happened to him, and he finds himself in the paradoxical situation of not only separating dream from reality but also having the need to find himself mad rather than sane. Kepesh is a teacher of comparative literature, and it is easier for him to make intellectual sense of his going mad than it is to face the fact of his breast-reality. He posits a "mammary envy" which has manifested itself in the belief that he is a breast, and even a condition of "literary envy" where the critic out-creates his subject—by becoming a breast, he rationalizes he has out-Kafkaed Kafka. All of this is insufficient—the reality is not to be explained away, only lived, and it is by the very ordinariness of his comforters that Kepesh finally realizes that he is not mad, but far more frightening, sane. The callousness of Schonbrunn, the domesticity of his father, even the concern of Claire have none of the stuff of madness about them. The novel works only if the reader believes that Kepesh has indeed turned into a breast, and it is a tribute to Roth's skills that he can present the pyschological portrait of a man in this state without resorting to teasing questions of whether this is dream or reality as does Gogol, for example, in his story, "The Nose," in which a man loses his nose and finds it walking about by itself. Kepesh may wonder if he is mad or dreaming, but the reader never does; he knows that the hero *has* become a breast.

Roth's next novel, *The Great American Novel* (1973), is, like Bernard Malamud's *The Natural* and Robert Coover's *The Universal Baseball Association*, an attempt to mythologize the great American pastime. Although the comic touch is masterful, the mythologizing is uncertain. Roth does not stick to a central myth as does Malamud with the Wasteland motif or Coover with the Creation myth, nor does he, like Coover, get into the process of mythopoeia itself. Roth's symbols are rather superficial and dependent largely upon wordplay rather than intrinsic value. This facet of the novel may well be deliberate since the novel is a parody not only of great American (and English) novels but also the myth criticism of such novels.

The novel, after a long playful prologue which talks about other great American novels as predecessors to this one, records the history of a third major baseball league, the Patriot, and in particular, the fate of one of its teams, the hapless Ruppert Mundy's, a team of misfits created out of the few men who are left in America during World War II. The Mundy's (named ironically for Jacob Ruppert, the brewing heir who was owner of the New York Yankees during their glory years and for the team's first owner, Glorius Mundy, whose name is associated with the Latin motto for faded greatness—*sic transit gloria mundi*) have seen better days and have become the only permanent road team in the league. In their mundane existence the Mundy's are quite clearly an image of the ordinary American who is manipulated by financial interests—the League owners—beyond his reach.

One long chapter is devoted to the biographies of these wonders. They include a fourteen-year-old second baseman who is so wet behind the ears that the only nickname he has earned is Nickname; a one-legged catcher, Hot Ptah, whose great achievement is his mastery of obscene behind-the-plate chatter; and Bud Parusha, the one-armed outfielder who takes the ball out of his glove with his teeth and who occasionally gets it stuck in his mouth, causing inside-the-park home runs. Amongst these grotesques exists the perfect specimen of an athlete, Roland Agni (named for the proud hero of *The Song of Roland* and for Christ as sacrificial lamb). Roland has been relegated to the Mundy's by his father, who insists that his boy bat eighth and receive the lowest salary in order to chastise his pride.

A major chapter is built around an allegorical conflict of good and evil in which two midgets struggle against each other. As usual in this novel, it is the malicious one who is victorious. Roth has a hilarious examination of the rights of midgets which is used to establish the grounds for the conflict. One of the midgets is Bob Yamm, whose job is to do nothing but get walks. Yamm is a perfect human being, with a perfect doll-like wife, who meets his match in the person of a pitcher his own size, another midget named O. K. Ockatur. Yamm, despite his perfect nature, knows he does not exist except as a midget but asserts his personal identity when for the first time in his career, he disobeys the coach's orders, swings, and is hit in the face and blinded by Ockatur's pitch.

Yamm's self-assertion and sacrifice are paralleled by Roland Agni's. Roland, desperate to be traded, works out a deal to lead the always underdog Mundy's to a series of victories so that a seventeen-year-old genius can bet on them and win. Agni feeds his hopeless teammates scientifically developed Wheaties that really are the "breakfast of champions," but in a fit of honesty, he omits the dishonest breakfast cereal, the team loses, Isaac Ellis loses a quarter of a million dollars, and Roland is stuck with the Mundy's. Roland, like Achilles, sulks in his tent, but when he is finally convinced to win one for the losers of the world, he is shot for his troubles, the victim of a communist plot.

The investigation of the death of Agni which closes the novel is a parody of the work of the various commissions into the death of John F. Kennedy. In *The Great American Novel*, Roland Agni is the victim of a plot of incredible complexity whose ramifications are so high-reaching that the authorities find it necessary to expunge completely the record of the league, which is the reason that no one knows of its existence any longer.

In *My Life as a Man* (1974), Roth attempts to spell out what has continually obsessed his fiction—the difference between living one's life and living a fictional version of one's life. In this case, there is a playful reflex back at Roth himself. Roth is writing from the Yaddo Writers' Colony about Peter Tarnapol writing from the Quahsai Writers' Colony about a fictional character of his, Nathan Zuckerman. Zuckerman is involved in several love affairs that in some way reflect Tarnapol's life and behavior. *My Life as a Man* consists of two long short stories whose hero is Zuckerman and then Tarnapol's true story in which the failed writer tries to use his own stories to make sense of his life. The difficulty is that the stories, despite the many parallels between Zuckerman's life and Tarnapol's, are too neat and orderly to tell the novelist what is wrong with his own life.

The stories are collectively entitled "useful fictions," suggesting that Tarnapol can learn something about himself by reading or at least writing these stories. This is Tarnapol's first and biggest mistake, because seen this way the stories are useless. The first Zuckerman story, "Salad Days," finds Zuckerman torn between two loves: his teacher, Caroline Benson, who is the essence of the spirit and Sharon Shatsky, who is the flesh. It is easy enough for Tarnapol to perceive the dichotomy and understand why neither woman can completely satisfy Zuckerman, but that is just the point: reality never allegorizes itself so neatly. The fiction, then, far from being useful, encourages Tarnapol to categorize women where no such boundaries exist.

The second Zuckerman story offers a somewhat more complex heroine, but Zuckerman's relationship to her is no more complicated. The story, "Courting Disaster," tells of Zuckerman's courtship of and marriage to Lydia Ketterer, whose primary appeal to him is that she has lived a life of immense suffering, degradation, and brutality. Since literary theory has taught him to equate degradation with realism, Zuckerman courts Lydia for a taste of reality, but he finds that loving her is no more real

than his books were. Zuckerman marries Lydia to become her savior, and sex with her soon becomes merely an expression of his "goodness" and a fake one at that. After Lydia's suicide, Zuckerman runs off with his near-idiot stepdaughter, Monica ("Moonie"), for exactly the opposite reason he had married her mother—for no reason at all. He sees such a liaison as a sign of absolute existential commitment since it has no purpose. Once this theoretical stance is perceived, however, the relationship becomes just as fake as that with Moonie's mother.

The two stories, then, set up neat dichotomies by which to measure Zuckerman's behavior and mark his failures. No such neatness exists in the real life of Tarnapol, whose problem is to discover why he has married Maureen, a castrating bitch of a woman, and why, after four years of separation, he cannot ignore her. Like Lydia, Maureen is the sufferer who needs to be saved, this time from the disasters of two marriages—one to a brute and one to a homosexual. Since Tarnapol has learned from Zuckerman the foolishness of playing savior, this does not seem to be his hang-up. Maureen is a vampirelike presence who gives meaning to her life by taking away Tarnapol's existence, and it is this that obsesses Tarnapol. Maureen does literally bite him, and four years later he is still talking about getting her fangs out of him. What he doesn't see is that his real role is not to be savior, but victim. Maureen gives him what every writer with a block needs—a reason for failure other than his own inability to write: How can he finish his novel of high seriousness with her literally and figuratively sucking the blood out of him?

Tarnapol's story also includes his affair with Susan McCall, the ideal woman, like Claire Ovington in *The Breast* and *The Professor of Desire*. She has everything he wants—money, position, love to offer, but he cannot remove the shadow of the vampire, nor ultimately does he want to. Susan is a place of recovery, an island of absolute tranquility, which he cannot stand partly because he needs something on which to blame his failure, but more importantly because, being a writer, he requires crisis. As Tarnapol's brother Moe notes, the great novels of the kind he is trying write, Bellow's *Herzog* and Mailer's *An American Dream*, require a castrating bitch, a Madeleine Herzog or a Deborah Rojack. Tarnapol is caught in a dilemma—he cannot write his novel with Maureen, and without her he has no subject because his novel is ultimately to be about his own suffering.

The Professor of Desire (1977), Roth's latest novel, tells the early history of David Kepesh, the man who is turned into a breast in *The Breast*. In a recent interview in the *New York Times Book Review*, Roth denies that *The Professor of Desire* was meant to be an antecedent in the sense that it explains why Kepesh became a breast or even that the psychology is continuous from novel to novel. Rather, he says, he had sketched a brief history of Kepesh in *The Breast* and in the new novel he has brought that history forth fully articulated. The title of the new novel indicates a dichotomy in the personality that is never fully restored. Most mundanely, the title indicates Kepesh's occupation. He is a teacher of comparative literature, whose favorite course in erotic literature he calls Desire 341. As such, the novel is a fascinating and rare account of an academic who cares passionately about his subject and reveals unabashedly why Kepesh loves Chekhov and particularly Kafka. One might compare this facet of the novel to the depiction of S. Levin in Bernard Malamud's *A New Life*, where Levin's love of literature is a given rather than a thing felt and understood.

The title also indicates the split in the personality of Kepesh. He is one who professes—i.e., verbally affirms his allegiance—to desire, an emotion which has nothing to do with verbal affirmation. Kepesh is a man who would like to live with his body and tries sincerely to do so, but at every turn he finds himself analyzing what his body, and more importantly, what his emotions are doing.

Although the novel covers vast geographic space, including two trips by Kepesh to Europe and the flight of his wife to Hong Kong, it ends some thirty miles from where it begins, as Kepesh spends an idyllic summer with his mistress in a place not far from the Catskill resort where he grew up. In a long, moving self-analysis, Kepesh discovers how far he has come in his life and paradoxically how little he has changed.

In the prologue-like description of his early years in his father's hotel, the Hungarian Royale, the reader is introduced to Kepesh's first mentor, Herbie Bratasky, the hotel's social director. Bratasky's greatest talent is his ability to imitate the sound of bodily functions, particularly those related to the bathroom. Kepesh's life's task will be to free himself from Bratasky's mimesis of life, i.e., conscious playing at desire which has the appearance of the real thing.

This is not to say that Kepesh's sex life is fantasized. Far from it. Nonetheless, one finds that no matter how involved Kepesh is in sex he is always viewing it at a distance, always thinking what else it might be. For example, in his first lengthy erotic involvement in London with two Swedish girls, Kepesh watches one of them approach mental collapse from trying to be sexually abandoned. After, she returns to Sweden dreaming of the middle-class virtues of love and marriage, leaving Kepesh with the roommate. This girl is totally involved in sex and degradation, but once Kepesh discovers that there is no more "more" they can achieve, he sends her away and returns to the United States. This is the typical Roth hero, who both desires the ultimate and runs from it when he has found it.

The same duality destroys Kepesh's marriage, although the fault is not his alone. Kepesh's wife, Helen, is a man-eating bitch like Maureen Tarnapol, but much of the failure of the marriage comes from Kepesh's need to categorize Helen, to treat her as a character in some novel he knows. He sees her earlier romance with an older man as a variation on *Anna Karenina*, with her loving the Karenin-figure, not the romantic young Vronsky. Kepesh cannot deal with this twist on his literary preconceptions and half drives Helen away. He sees in Helen the self-denial and sensuousness of Anna, but this means he also believes and therefore silently promotes (to justify his theory) her deathless passion for the other man. Helen eventually goes off to Hong Kong to seek her first love and the marriage falls apart.

After a period of despair, Kepesh finds the perfect woman, Claire Ovington, a creature of adequate, but not overwhelming passion, with whom he takes off on a romantic holiday to Europe. Even having all he could want, Kepesh's imagination will not be still. He calls up the memory of the Swedish girl, now more powerful than when she was present, and finds Claire lacking in passion. He manages to cope with this crisis by visiting the grave of Kafka, and in a brilliant dream sequence he meets an ancient crone who is the whore of Kafka. In the dream, the Czech tour guide turns out to be Kepesh's old mentor, Herbie Bratasky. In addition to being the comic epitome of all grasping tour guide scenes, the dream gathers all the attitudes which control Kepesh's life. For five dollars, Kepesh is able to see the old whore's sex, perhaps the one solid reality in all the metaphysical meanderings of Kafka's life. The dream seems to say the same thing about Kepesh's relation to sex. His life has been determined almost totally in relation to sex, and yet sex itself is less important than the constructs he has built around it. Nonetheless, without the thing itself, the constructs would be worthless. As the dream closes Kepesh sees the old whore's tongue, "the pulp of the fruit, still red."

The image seems to suggest that the very core of desire will never fade, but the close of the novel casts a good deal of doubt upon this notion. Kepesh returns with Claire to the environs of his youth and in the presence of his father and his father's friend, he meditates on the nature of his life and upon the gradual dissipation of desire. The father's friend, Mr. Barbatnik, the survivor of every conceivable evil including the concentration camps, starts Kepesh's train of thought. If Barbatnik can outlive all that horror, then he, Kepesh, can outlive all this love and desire. Once again, Kepesh finds his life controlled by his theory of life. The more he tries to think about an answer to the feeling that all this will pass away, the more the feeling increases. Desperately he puts his mouth to the breast of Claire, who is lying asleep in bed with him, but the final result is not given: Will the theory destroy desire or can desire overcome the professor in him?

Periodical Publications:

FICTION:

"The Day It Snowed," *Chicago Review*, 8 (fall 1954): 34-45;

"The Contest for Aaron Gold," *Epoch*, 5-6 (fall 1955): 37-50;

"Heard Melodies Are Sweeter," *Esquire*, 50 (August 1958): 58;

"Expect the Vandals," *Esquire*, 50 (December 1958): 208-228;

"The Love Vessel," *Dial*, 1 (fall 1959): 41-68;

"Good Girl," *Cosmopolitan*, 148 (May 1960): 98-103;

"Novotny's Pain," *New Yorker*, 38 (27 October 1962): 46-56;

"On the Air," *New American Review*, 10 (10 August 1970): 7-49;

" 'I Always Wanted You to Admire My Fasting'; or Looking at Kafka," *American Review*, 17 (May 1973): 103-126.

NONFICTION:

"Mrs. Lindbergh, Mr. Ciardi, and the Teeth and Claws of the Civilized World," *Chicago Review*, 11 (summer 1957): 72-76;

"The Kind of Person I Am," *New Yorker*, 34 (29 November 1958): 173-178;

"Writing American Fiction," *Commentary*, 31 (March 1961): 223-233;

"Writing About Jews," *Commentary*, 36 (December 1963): 446-452;

"Reading Myself," *Partisan Review*, 40, 3 (1973): 404-417.

References:

Irving Buchen, "*Portnoy's Complaint* of the Rooster's Kvetch," *Studies in the Twentieth Century*, 6 (fall 1970): 97-107;

Stanley Cooperman, "Philip Roth: 'Old Jacob's Eye' With a Squint," *Twentieth Century Literature*, 19 (July 1973): 203-216;

Irving and Harriet Deer, "Philip Roth and the Crisis in American Fiction," *Minnesota Review*, 6 (winter 1966): 353-360;

John Ditsky, "Roth, Updike, and the High Expense of Spirit," *University of Windsor Review*, 5 (fall 1969): 111-120;

Margaret Drabble, "Clean Breast," *Listener*, 89 (22 March 1973): 378;

Robert Dupree, "And the Mom Roth Outgrabe Or, What Hath Got Roth?" *Arlington Quarterly*, 2 (autumn 1970): 175-189;

John Gardner, "Review of *The Breast*," *New York Times Book Review*, 17 September 1972, pp. 3, 10;

Lois G. Gordon, " 'Portnoy's Complaint': Coming of Age in Jersey City," *Literature and Psychology*, 19, 3-4 (1969): 57-60;

Allen Guttman, *The Jewish Writer in America: Assimilation and the Crisis of Identity* (New York: Oxford University Press, 1971);

Baruch Hochman, "Child and Man in Philip Roth," *Midstream*, 13 (December 1967): 68-76;

Irving Howe, "Philip Roth Reconsidered," *Commentary*, 54 (December 1972): 69-77;

Alfred Kazin, *Contemporaries* (Boston: Little, Brown, 1962), pp. 258-262;

Bernice Kliman, "Names in *Portnoy's Complaint*," *Critique*, 14, 3 (1973): 16-24;

Joseph Landis, "The Sadness of Philip Roth: An Interim Report," *Massachusetts Review*, 3 (winter 1962): 259-268;

Christopher Lehmann-Haupt, "It's Less than Meets the Eye," *New York Times*, 12 September 1972, p. 43;

John Leonard, "Cheever to Roth to Malamud," *Atlantic*, 231 (June 1973): 112-116;

Mordecai Levine, "Philip Roth and American Judaism," *College Language Association Journal*, 14 (December 1970): 163-170;

Irving Malin, *Jews and Americans* (Carbondale: Southern Illinois University Press, 1965);

John McDaniel, *The Fiction of Philip Roth* (Haddonfield, N.J.: Haddonfield House, 1974);

Sanford Pinsker, *The Comedy That "Hoits"* (Columbia: University of Missouri Press, 1975);

Bernard F. Rodgers, Jr., *Philip Roth: A Bibliog-*

raphy (Metuchen, N.J.: Scarecrow, 1974);

R. Z. Sheppard, "Braless in Gaza," *Time*, 100 (25 September 1972): 94;

Theodore Solotaroff, "Philip Roth and the Jewish Moralists," *Chicago Review*, 13 (winter 1959): 87-99;

Patricia Spacks, "About Portnoy," *Yale Review*, 58 (June 1969): 623-635;

Tony Tanner, *City of Words: American Fiction 1950-1970* (New York: Harper & Row, 1971);

Helen Weinberg, *The New Novel in America: The Kafkan Mode in Contemporary Fiction* (Ithaca,

N.Y.: Cornell University Press, 1970);

Ruth Wisse, *The Schlemiel as Modern Hero* (Chicago: University of Chicago Press, 1971).

Manuscripts:

The major collection of Roth's literary manuscripts and correspondence is at the Library of Congress; see "Philip Roth Papers," *Quarterly Journal of the Library of Congress*, 27 (1970): 343-344.

J. D. Salinger

Warren French
Indiana/Purdue Universities (Indianapolis)

BIRTH: New York, New York, 1 January 1919.

EDUCATION: Valley Forge Military Academy, 1934-1936; Ursinus College and New York University, 1937-1938; writing class at Columbia University, 1939.

MARRIAGE: 17 February 1955 to Claire Douglas, divorced; children: Margaret Ann, Matthew.

MAJOR WORKS: *The Catcher in the Rye* (Boston: Little, Brown, 1951; London: Hamish Hamilton, 1951); *Nine Stories* (Boston: Little, Brown, 1953; republished as *For Esme—With Love and Squalor and Other Stories*, London: Hamish Hamilton, 1953); *Franny and Zooey* (Boston: Little, Brown, 1961; London: Heinemann, 1962); *"Raise High the Roof Beam, Carpenters" and "Seymour: An Introduction"* (Boston: Little, Brown, 1963; London: Heinemann, 1963).

The entire body of writing by which Jerome David Salinger wishes to be known is contained in four small books—one novel and thirteen short stories. All of these were published in the eleven-and-a-half years between January 1948 and June 1959; and all but the novel and two of the stories originally appeared in the *New Yorker* magazine. Yet despite this limited body of work, Salinger remained for at least a dozen years, from 1951 to 1963, the most popular American fiction writer with serious high-school and college students, as well as many adults alienated by the stultifying conformity of the Eisenhower years; and his few publications elicited an enormous body of criticism. Few writers have developed such a major reputation for such a small body of work, largely from a single magazine noted

for its rigid formulae and chic appeal to the highly educated, upper middle class (especially since Salinger's fiction is notable for its unwavering attack on the life-style of the highly educated, urban, upper middle class). Only Salinger's last few published stories were notable for their controversial, anti-narrative structures; the novel and other stories are exemplary of the brisk, ironic *"New Yorker* style," used by other writers such as John O'Hara and John Cheever; but all Salinger's work is remarkable for his command of the brisk, nervous, defensive speech of young, upper-middle-class Manhattanites. His work is a unique phenomenon, important as the voice of a "silent generation" in revolt against a "phony world" and in search of mystical escapes from a deteriorating society rather than "causes" promising political revolution or reform.

Salinger was born and grew up in the fashionable apartment district of Manhattan, the son of a prosperous Jewish importer and his Scotch-Irish wife. In one of the few interviews he has granted, he said that his own childhood was much like that of the boy Holden Caulfield in his novel *The Catcher in the Rye*, though Salinger had only one sister. Like Holden, he was restless in fashionable prep schools, and he was finally sent to Valley Forge Military Academy, a model for Pencey Prep in his novel. Here and at nearby Ursinus College, which he attended briefly, he worked for literary magazines and wrote movie reviews. Subsequently a class in short story writing at Columbia University under Whit Burnett, founder-editor of the influential *Story Magazine*, in which many mid-century fiction writers were first published, led to his own earliest commercial publications in this magazine. He quickly graduated to the well-paying "slick" magazines of the period—*Collier's, Saturday Evening Post, Esquire, Good Housekeeping, Cosmopolitan*, and, at last, the *New Yorker*. To the first five of these and some other publications, Salinger contributed between 1941 and 1948 twenty stories that he has since 1954 refused to allow to be republished. (There does exist a pirated edition of them: *The Complete Uncollected Stories of J. D. Salinger*, 2 vols. [1974].) Most of these are very short, highly colloquial, sentimental, yet heavily ironic tales in the manner made popular by O. Henry. Many of them are the very popular "short, short stories" with a surprise ending that could be printed on a single page, although one, "The Inverted Forest," is a novelette of considerable complexity with an ambiguous ending. Several of these stories are about draftees in the army during World War II and reflect Salinger's own service between 1942 and 1945 in the Army Signal Corps and the Counter-Intelligence Corps.

After the war, Salinger published in the *New Yorker* a short story, "Slight Rebellion Off Madison," subsequently revised for inclusion in *The Catcher in the Rye*; the work by which he wishes to be known began, however, with his second contribution to the magazine, "A Perfect Day for Bananafish," an enormously popular story about the suicide of Seymour Glass, who first appears in this story.

Salinger perhaps wishes his early stories hidden away because they are apprentice work; he may be embarrassed by their slickness. A few are interesting because they introduce an earlier conception of Holden Caulfield as a rebellious young soldier who is killed in World War II; but only "The Inverted Forest" really adds anything to Salinger's stature. This is the story of a writer who "can't stand any kind of inventiveness" and his pathetic difficulties in dealing with doting and exploitative women—mother, patron, wife, and mistress. Salinger never again so specifically allegorizes the view that the artist has no obligations to society as in this caustic story of a sorely-pressed individual who withdraws from a meretricious world to live entirely within "the inverted forest" of his own imagination—an outlook that Salinger rejects in his later stories. Only some early chapters of *The Catcher in the Rye* and the short story "Pretty Mouth and Green My Eyes" among his collected works picture people without spiritual moorings in a plastic, materialistic world.

The major reason for Salinger's rejecting these early stories is that they do not reflect the Hindu-Buddhist influences that begin to color his work in "A Perfect Day for Bananafish," in which Salinger begins to depict escape from the "phony" world as not defeat, but triumph for the sensitive individual. His work thereafter can most rewardingly be perceived as colloquial, contemporary American versions of the *ko-ans* (cryptic object lessons) of the Zen Buddhist tradition.

By narrowing attention, then, to the novel and thirteen chosen stories, this whole body of work can be seen—like such other American classics as Whitman's *Leaves of Grass* and Thomas Wolfe's Eugene Gant/George Webber novel-cycle—as parts of a single statement, the theme of which is announced in the climactic moment in the last of these stories as Buddy Glass explains his older brother Seymour's suicide: "I say that the true artist-seer, the heavenly fool who can and does produce beauty, is mainly dazzled to death by his own scruples, the blinding shapes and colors of his own sacred human conscience."

Salinger's epic of the journey of the human spirit through the illusions of the material world to the transcendent spiritual Oneness beyond, which might be called "The Caulfield/Glass Saga," begins, chronologically, with a still controversial description of Seymour Glass's activities on the day of his suicide amidst the unparalleled vulgarities of Miami Beach, Florida, and ends with his disciple-brother's explanation of this action and of the unique importance of the "artist-seer." The rambling, seemingly structureless "Seymour: An Introduction" that still bothers plot-oriented readers can most satisfactorily be appreciated as Buddy Glass's petition for the sainthood of his brother by some unworldly body of right-thinking people. Seymour is indeed "a fool"—not only in the eyes of conventional, money-grubbing people, but in his own because of his romantic susceptibilities—but he does create and inspire beauty, and he does end this mortal life rather than compromise his integrity.

Using Buddy's pronouncement to make a division, a distinction can be made among Salinger's works between the stories of those who refuse to betray their sacred consciences and those who do compromise reluctantly in order to fulfill what they regard as their obligations in a conscienceless world. On the one side may be placed "A Perfect Day for Bananafish," "De Daumier-Smith's Blue Period," "Teddy," "Raise High the Roof-Beam, Carpenters," and "Seymour: An Introduction." On the other there are "Uncle Wiggily in Connecticut," "Just Before the War with the Eskimos," "The Laughing Man," "Pretty Mouth and Green My Eyes" and *The Catcher in the Rye*. In the middle—and in the middle of

J. D. Salinger

Early dust jacket for The Catcher in the Rye.

Salinger's career—is the smallest body of what has generally proved his most admired works, "Down at the Dinghy," "For Esme—With Love and Squalor," and *Franny and Zooey*—souvenirs of a fleeting time when Salinger apparently hoped that those not "seers" themselves might learn enough from these mentors to survive in "the waste land" without becoming contaminated.

As far as the published record goes, this saga began with some trial sketches for *The Catcher in the Rye,* "I'm Crazy" and "Slight Rebellion Off Madison." Comparison between the latter and the final version of Holden Caulfield's disastrous date with Sally Hayes provides the only available opportunity for studying the development in Salinger's writing. Although it has often been observed—even by Salinger himself—that there are autobiographical elements in the novel, they are finally not so important as the fact that *The Catcher in the Rye* is a story of an urban American middle-class boy who at the adolescent crisis of his life—the point at which in a communally ordered society he would undergo traditional rites of initiation into manhood—chooses, on his own and unguided, an adulterated life in the "real" world rather than an escape from it.

Holden is aware of the options, because his younger brother Allie, who wrote Emily Dickinson's poems on his baseball mitt, has escaped (though through disease not choice), and his older brother, an artist but no seer, has prostituted himself to Hollywood. When Holden fears that he may "disappear" himself, he prays to his personal saint Allie to preserve him. Holden persists in living

because, despite his frustrations in the "phony" world, he still has a naive sense of mission: in the famous passage that gives the novel its title he tells his little sister Phoebe, "I keep picturing all these little kids playing some game in this big field of rye and all. . . . And I'm standing by on the edge of some crazy cliff. What I have to do, I have to catch everybody if they start to go over the cliff." Holden learns that his dream can never be realized. Watching his little sister ride the carousel in Central Park and grab for the golden ring, he observes, "The thing with kids is, if they want to grab for the gold ring, you have to let them do it, and not say anything. If they fall off, they fall off, but it's bad if you say anything to them."

Even before acquiescing in his inability to arrest the life cycle and hold youth forever innocent, Holden has suffered another disillusionment. He has dreamed of escaping the city and going West where he could build "a little cabin somewhere . . . and live there for the rest of my life . . . near the woods, but not right *in* them, because I'd want it as sunny as hell all the time." (This description uncannily foreshadows exactly the kind of place in which Salinger has himself lived for twenty years now, not in the West, but in New England.) After he finds obscenities scratched, however, even on the walls of Phoebe's elementary school, he sadly concedes, "You can't ever find a place that's nice and peaceful, because there isn't any."

Rather than being driven out of this world by such disenchantments, Holden assures readers that he did go home after he felt "so damn happy . . . the way old Phoebe kept going around and around" while the carousel played "Smoke Gets in Your Eyes." He has made this choice after Phoebe pleads to run away with him; he must forego his own escape to do what he can for her. After this he begins "missing everybody," even those who have hurt him. He is a self-made martyr; but martyrdom in the "waste land" society means continuing to live, not accepting death. Holden chooses to live in a decadent society in order to help others live as they wish to live rather than to withdraw in order to preserve his own scruples or force his own brand of salvation on others. *The Catcher in the Rye* is a genuine initiation tale, even though it is only the candidate undergoing the ordeal who is conscious of what his final decision means; the real evidence of the decadence of his world is that the initiators who impose the ordeals upon him are too much wrapped up in themselves even to understand the meaning of their actions.

The collected *Nine Stories*, by way of contrast, ultimately climaxes in not the acceptance but the transcendence of this world. Although the stories involve different characters, they may also be read collectively as the dramatization of a progressive action, so that they exemplify what Forest Ingram calls a "short-story cycle": "a book of short stories so linked to each other by their author that the reader's successive experience on various levels of the pattern of the whole significantly modifies his experience of each of its component parts." The links between the stories in this cycle, however, do not result in the kind of narrative progression based on physical growth that we find in James Joyce's *Dubliners*, John Steinbeck's *The Red Pony*, or Dylan Thomas's *Portrait of the Artist as a Young Dog*, but rather a progression based upon spiritual enlightenment, something like the believer experiences in the Christian ritual of the Stations of the Cross or, more appropriately, the stages that the neophyte passes through in his apprehension of Zen. What is represented through this group of stories that were published—and apparently written—in the order of their presentation is the purification of the ego by the passage of the soul through an intensifying series of the torments of the hell of this mortal world to the ego-free state in which one has at last achieved total unity with the infinite so that the individual life-form no longer matters—the one has been absorbed into *the* One.

Humayun Mirza has provided the clue that has long been needed to make possible a fully coherent experience of this story-cycle in his perception that, despite the meaning of Seymour Glass's example and teachings to his sibling/disciples, Seymour is—

from the Hindu view—a false guru (teacher), because he has not been able to transcend the temptations of mortal flesh. He is like the person that Teddy McArdle (title character of the final one of the nine stories) was in his previous incarnation. This person "fell from Grace before final illumination" when he met a lady and "sort of stopped meditating." Teddy in his final incarnation, Mirza demonstrates, is a true guru.

The story-cycle thus moves from the portrayal of the dichotomized saint-in-spirit/satyr-in-the-flesh who must destroy himself to liberate his tortured conscience/consciousness to the portrayal of a person whose unified mind/body is ready for the final illumination that will result in his disappearance from the material world through no action of his own, since he has become too etherealized to persist in it.

"A Perfect Day for Bananafish" is thus misread as a moral tale, a satirical attack on our bourgeois culture, or a study of alienation. It is rather what John Steinbeck might call a "non-teleological" work, a story of what *happens* to the partially illuminated person torn between the lustings of his instincts and the dictates of his conscience. The important thing is that this story *starts* rather than *ends* the cycle. Seymour is actually not too advanced for his society, but too primitive for it. He has the purity of vision of an Old Testament prophet without the sacred purification of Jesus or Buddha. He is even less sophisticated than Holden Caulfield; he is not able to adjust to his society, but neither can he transcend it without violence.

The successive stories through "Pretty Mouth and Green My Eyes," then, represent the successive stages in the adjustment to this society that Seymour cannot make, though the central characters also progressively lose their purity of vision, the innocence that Wordsworth in "Ode on Intimations of Immortality" describes the child as bringing with him as he enters this world "trailing clouds of glory."

The next story in the cycle, "Uncle Wiggily in Connecticut," offers in a few pages the most clearly contrasting views of the "nice" and "phony" worlds that we find anywhere in Salinger's writing. Eloise, the principal character, has glimpses of the sacred world in which Seymour Glass yearns to live, but she is too mired in the phony world of Connecticut to free herself; she can only break out finally in the Wordsworthian cry, "I was a nice girl . . . wasn't I?" She is in much the same state that Holden Caulfield appears to be at the end of *The Catcher in the Rye*, although Holden has "grown up" enough to resemble more closely the sentimental Ginnie Maddox of the third story of the cycle, "Just Before the War with the Eskimos," who has become enough at home in the "phony world" to be able to make the generous gestures that elude the still embittered Eloise.

"The Laughing Man" presents a central figure another step removed from Seymour's neurotic perfectionism, another step closer to being able to make practical gestures to comfort others even in the midst of his own despair. When this "Chief" terrifies his young listeners/acolytes by letting the legendary laughing man of his seemingly endless episodic tale tear off his poppy-petal mask and die, he seems to be spitefully taking out his rage at a frustrated love affair on his helpless charges; but, paradoxically, his action is in their best interests, for the immediate pain of disillusionment is better than prolonged existence in a fantasy world that the Chief now knows must some day be dispelled painfully. But he is not yet a master of reconciliation; his technique is crude and abrupt.

The master is Boo-Boo Tannenbaum, one of Seymour Glass's two sisters. In "Down at the Dinghy," her son Lionel has cruelly had his illusions shattered at an even earlier age than the Chief's charges in "The Laughing Man." (Just what ails Lionel remains obscure; the story focuses on Boo-Boo's techniques.) Tactfully and with utmost patience rather than even well-intended harshness, Boo-Boo ends her son's attempt to withdraw from an intolerable adult world by making him accept its imperfect realities.

The master of reconciliation, the maker of as much happiness as we can ever know in the "phony world," is that proper young British girl who lends her name to the title of a great modern epithalamion, "For Esme—With Love and Squalor." Esme is able to readjust not just a young relative, but a grown man who much resembles Seymour Glass. When Sergeant X, as this character is mysteriously identified, is in Germany on the verge of a nervous breakdown after observing incredibly squalid examples of the behavior of both Hitler's Nazi minions and his boorish American fellows-in-arms, he regains his "faculties" as he receives Esme's gift of her father's wristwatch with the crystal broken and the news that she is teaching her affectionate little brother to read and write. Esme's spontaneous generosity is as much communion as we can expect to experience in this hellish life; but it is important to contemplate the nature of her gift—a *time*piece with the transparent crystal smashed. The attempted gift of time, like the unequivocal gift of letters to her

little brother, shows that Esme, for all her radiance, is completely of this linear world. Her joys are family and marriage; she has no perception of the timeless realm of Teddy McArdle.

The temporal equilibrium that Esme achieves cannot endure. This is just what happens in the plunge from the ecstatic highs of "For Esme" into the depths of Salinger's darkest, most cynical story, "Pretty Mouth and Green My Eyes," in which a naive young man desperate for success is driven to lie about his wife's behavior to the very senior member of his law firm who is in fact cuckolding him. His spiritual death is signaled by his recognition that the wife's eyes are not actually as he had fancied "green," emblematic of youth and vitality, but "like goddam *sea* shells." No single recent story better illustrates the line from T. S. Eliot's poem "Gerontion," "What is kept must be adulterated."

Many modern short-story cycles might have ended here, as James Joyce's *Dubliners* does, for example, with the completion of a movement from life-in-death to death-in-life. "Pretty Mouth and Green My Eyes" reaches the lowest pit of modern urban hell; there is no exit from here except into the extinguishing darkness of Samuel Beckett's *Endgame*—or upward by a surge of spirit into an entirely other world. One of Salinger's least comprehended stories, the genuinely mystical "De Daumier-Smith's Blue Period," makes this leap, and in so doing most conspicuously calls attention to the architectonics of *Nine Stories*. De Daumier-Smith is the first, actually the only character in Salinger's work to experience—before the reader's eyes (Teddy's illumination has preceded our acquaintance with him)—a "liminal moment," an illumination on the threshold between the sensible and supersensible.

This vain artist from a decadent background has become a teacher in a correspondence-course art school and begins to try to manage his students' lives, especially that of a talented but unself-conscious nun. He lives above an orthopedic appliances shop; gazing in its window, he recognizes that "no matter how coolly or sensibly or gracefully" he might learn to live, he "would always at best be a visitor in a garden of enamel urinals and bedpans...." One day, however, as he makes a friendly gesture to an attendant in the window, "Suddenly...the sun came up and sped toward the bridge of [his] nose at the rate of ninety-three million miles a second." He is blinded, and when his sight returns the girl is gone, "leaving behind her a shimmering field of exquisite, twice-blessed, enamel flowers." He goes home and notes in his diary, "I am giving Sister Irma her freedom to follow her own destiny. Everybody is a nun."

Scarcely another scene in literature makes so explicit the "dazzling" experience that Buddy Glass attributes to the "artist-seer." For De Daumier-Smith, however, this is only a transient experience; he returns to the great American sport of girl-watching. He is not ready to make the final, permanent move into the enamel world that Teddy does in the last story in the collection.

"Teddy" is Salinger's one story whose reception he has commented upon through the medium of Buddy Glass. In "Seymour: An Introduction," Buddy, who has spoken of what are unmistakably other of Salinger's earlier stories as his own, mentions "an exceptionally Haunting, Memorable, unpleasantly controversial, and thoroughly unsuccessful short story about a 'gifted' little boy aboard a transatlantic liner." The story has indeed proved controversial, for critics still quarrel over whether Teddy at the end jumps into an empty swimming pool or is pushed in by his spiteful little sister. Salinger has never explained why the story was "unsuccessful," but it is probably largely because readers failed to comprehend that Teddy was but a passive agent in his fate. The clue to the conclusion is his suggestion to his parents at the beginning of the story that "after I get out this door, I may only exist in the minds of all my acquaintances." When an inquisitive schoolteacher asks Teddy if he has any emotions, the boy replies, "If I do, I don't remember when I ever used them. . . . I don't see what they're *good* for." He has become detached from both the feelings of frustration that most of Salinger's other characters feel and even the feelings of joy that Esme induces and that De Daumier-Smith discovers. Teddy is no longer a part of this neurotic world, so that he is ready to depart from it—but his departure is no tragedy. Rather, since he has attained spiritual truth, his is a divine comedy. If he did not resist "dematerialization," however, neither would he—free of emotions—have taken any action of the kind that Seymour Glass did to destroy himself.

Nine Stories thus carries us through a series of emblematic tableaux of human spiritual evolution—from an opening portrait of a seer whose spiritual insight has completely outstripped his physical discipline, through the stages as one loses internal vision to gain external control of his body and emotions and then is projected suddenly into a spiritual development that provides momentary insights of timelessness, until one is absorbed altogether into the infinite. These stories should not be read, however, as models for behavior, but as what

James Joyce called "epiphanies" of manifestations of behavior at typical stages in the human fall from glory and reascension back into it.

Franny and Zooey marks a movement beyond the creation of this static portrait gallery, perhaps even a presumptuous one. In the first of these two linked stories, Seymour Glass's youngest sibling Franny has grown—like Holden Caulfield—impatient and disgusted with the meretriciousness of life in the success-seeking world and yearns to move toward spiritual purification by repeating the "Jesus Prayer" continually. She succeeds only in driving herself into a nervous breakdown. In the sequel, her brother Zooey attempts to enlighten her by making her see that she is reacting against the egotism she despises with what is only another form of egotism: "You can say the Jesus Prayer from now till doomsday, but if you don't realize that the only thing that counts in the religious life is de*tach*ment, I don't see how you'll ever even move an inch." She has been protesting the "unskilled laughter" of the audience; but Zooey, in his summoning up of a grotesque "Fat Lady," who is actually "Christ himself," tells her that depressing as the audience's reaction may be, it's none of her business: "An artist's only concern is to shoot for some kind of perfection, and *on his own terms,* not anyone else's." Zooey thus does advocate living humbly in this world, as Holden Caulfield had apparently determined to do; and by masquerading as Seymour during a phone call to Franny, he apparently succeeds in tranquilizing her into this acceptance, too.

Actually one of the last two stories collected, "Raise High the Roof Beam, Carpenters" had originally appeared between the separate publications of "Franny" and "Zooey," but it belongs with the final story, "Seymour: An Introduction," as part of Salinger's evocation through the medium of Buddy Glass of the artist whose only concern indeed is "to shoot for some kind of perfection," *on his own terms.*

That Salinger's vision of Seymour had changed from 1948 to 1959 is suggested by Buddy's observation in "Seymour: An Introduction" that the "Seymour" of the earlier story "was not Seymour at all but, oddly, someone with a striking resemblance to—alley oop, I'm afraid—myself." Coupled with the comments about the unsuccessfulness of "Teddy," this concession—following Salinger's own successful withdrawal from the "phony world" of *The Catcher in the Rye*—suggests that Salinger had begun to have a much more favorable impression of Seymour than when he wrote "A Perfect Day for Bananafish." Since Teddy's emotionless purity seemed beyond readers' comprehensions, they might identify more closely with a spiritually superior person who shares their own fleshly frailties. In "Raise High the Roof Beam, Carpenters," Buddy begins by saying of Seymour that, since his death, "I haven't been able to think of anybody whom I'd care to send out to look for horses in his stead," and in "Seymour: An Introduction," he goes on to say, "We have had only three or four *very* nearly non-expendable poets, and I think Seymour will eventually stand with those few." The curious form of the latter story, in which Buddy seeks to form an alliance with the reader against "the middle-aged hot-rodders who insist on zooming us to the moon, the Dharma Bums, the makers of cigarette filters for thinking men, the Beat and the Sloppy and the Petulant, the chosen cultists . . ." also suggests that these later Glass stories are attempts to convert readers through an embryonic saint's legend. (Buddy describes Seymour as "the only person I've habitually consorted with . . . who more frequently than not tallied with the classical conception, as I saw it, of a *mukta*, a ringding enlightened man, a God-knower.") The detachment of *Nine Stories* has been supplanted by a skillfully manipulated conversion technique. As a result, perhaps, of his own successful retreat from the world, Salinger had achieved a kind of peace that made him feel that the artist did have something more *timely* to do than point to Teddy McArdle's merger with the infinite as the culmination of man's incarnations.

He may have changed his mind again, if one can trust the limited evidence of his most recent uncollected story, "Hapworth 16, 1924," which consists mostly of a letter that Seymour writes home from summer camp at the age of seven. This letter testifies to the prodigious learning that would make Seymour the star of a 1930s children's quiz program, but it evidences also a prodigious sexuality that reinforces the early picture in "A Perfect Day for Bananafish" of the failed guru. If Salinger has swung back to a heightened appreciation of the timeless, egoless state achieved by Teddy McArdle, he has not chosen to let us know. In the one interview that he has granted in recent years (in a telephone call to San Francisco, primarily to protest the unauthorized publishing of his early stories in a collected edition), he reported that he was still writing furiously, but that he views publication as a "terrible invasion" of his privacy. He chooses to live isolated in New Hampshire, perhaps sustained by his view of the solitary splendor of neighboring Mount Ascutney.

Salinger was little known when *The Catcher in the Rye* was published; and the novel was not outstandingly acclaimed by reviewers, most of them sounding variations on Ernest Jones's theme that, although the novel was "a case history of all of us," it was "predictable and boring." Its reputation grew slowly by word of mouth, especially among college students and teachers; but little serious attention was paid to Salinger until after the publication of *Nine Stories* and "Franny." In 1956 and 1957 the first serious essays by respected scholars—Edgar M. Branch, Arthur Heiserman, James E. Miller, Jr., and Charles Kaplan—appeared, linking the novel to traditional quest myths and particularly to Mark Twain's *Adventures of Huckleberry Finn*. For the next six years, the flood of articles rose constantly, until George Steiner denounced "The Salinger Industry" for promoting Salinger to greatness for his competent rendering of "the semi-literate maunderings of the adolescent mind."

There were other skeptics: John W. Aldridge included an influential misreading of *Catcher* in *In Search of Heresy*; Leslie Fiedler said that Salinger and Jack Kerouac echoed not "the tragic *Huckleberry Finn*, but the sentimental book with which it is intertwined"; Frank Kermode supposed that Holden's attitudes pleased academics who shared these views that they could not openly express; Mary McCarthy belittled Salinger's obsessive affection for his own creations.

Many of Salinger's defenders, like Dan Wakefield and Christopher Parker, were sentimental and childishly hysterical; but a body of solid work began to appear with Donald Costello's study of Salinger's language, Carl Strauch's structural analysis of *Catcher*, and William Wiegand's sound analyses of the relationship of Salinger's art to modern Western philosophy. A landmark was Ihab Hassan's choice of Salinger as one of the four principal postwar fictionists in the pioneering study of the period, *Radical Innocence* (1961).

The peak came in 1962-1963, which saw the publication of six collections of essays about Salinger and the first book-length monograph about his work. This formidable array proved a turning point, however, coinciding, as it accidentally did, with the publication of what remains so far the last of his own books. Gradually at first, then dramatically, after 1963, new critical studies tapered off, while sales of the works themselves slowed.

Because of his lack of interest in political reforms and the passivity and escapism of his leading characters, Salinger did not appeal to young readers

This filth is being recommended to your children for extra-curricular reading in the DADE COUNTY SCHOOL SYSTEM and elsewhere. (Palmetto High School, by English Teacher WARREN, who was defended by Principal CRABTREE and sanctioned by Supt. of Schools, Joe Hall) Jack Gordon, School Board member said of "Catcher in the Rye" that anyone calling it "obscene" had misread it. Is this the kind of book that should be recommended reading by teachers in our public schools?

The Catcher in the Rye   25

"No reason. Boy, I can't stand that sonuvabitch. He's one sonuvabitch I really can't stand."

"He's crazy about *you*. He told me he thinks you're a goddam prince," I said. I call people a "prince" quite often when I'm horsing around. It keeps me from getting bored or something.

"He's got this superior *a*ttitude all the time," Ackley said. "I just can't stand the sonuvabitch, You'd think he—"

"Do you mind cutting your nails over the *table,* hey?" I said. "I've asked you about fifty—"

"He's got this goddam superior attitude all the time," Ackley said. "I don't even think the sonuvabitch is intelligent. He *thinks* he is. He thinks he's about the most—"

"*Ack*ley! For Chrissake. Will*ya please* cut your crumby nails over the table? I've asked you fifty times."

36   *The Catcher in the Rye*

It was only about a quarter to nine when we got back to the dorm. Old Brossard was a bridge fiend, and he started looking around the dorm for a game. Old Ackley parked himself in my room, just for a change. Only, instead of sitting on the arm of Stradlater's chair, he laid down on my bed, with his face right on my pillow and all. He started talking in this very monotonous voice, and picking at all his pimples. I dropped about a thousand hints, but I couldn't get rid of him. All he did was keep talking in this very monotonous voice about some babe he was supposed to have had sexual intercourse with the summer before. He'd already told me about it about a hundred times. Every time he told it, it was different. One minute he'd be giving it to her in his cousin's Buick, the next minute he'd be giving it to her under some boardwalk. It was all a lot of crap, naturally. He was a virgin if ever I saw one. I doubt if he ever even gave anybody a feel. Anyway, finally I had

46   *The Catcher in the Rye*

I didn't turn it off right away, though. I just kept laying there on Ely's bed, thinking about Jane and all. It just drove me stark staring mad when I thought about her and Stradlater parked somewhere in that fat-assed Ed Banky's car. Every time I thought about it, I felt like jumping out the window. The thing is, you didn't know Stradlater. I knew him. Most guys at Pency just *talked* about having sexual intercourse with girls all the time—like Ackley, for instance—but old Stradlater really did it. I was personally acquainted with at least two girls he gave the time to. That's the truth.

"Tell me the story of your fascinating life, Ackley kid," I said.

134   *The Catcher in the Rye*

"Maybe I'll go to China. My sex life is lousy," I said.

"Naturally. Your mind is immature."

"It is. It really is. I know it," I said. "You know what the trouble with me is? I can never get really sexy—I mean *really* sexy—with a girl I don't like a lot. I mean I have to *like* her a lot. If I don't, I sort of lose my goddam desire for her and all. Boy, it really screws up my sex life something awful. My sex life stinks."

"Naturally it does, for God's sake. I told you the last time I saw you what you need."

"You mean to go to a psychoanalyst and all?" I said. That's what he'd told me I ought to do. His father was a psychoanalyst and all.

84   *The Catcher in the Rye*

"How do you mean?" I said. I didn't know what he was driving at or anything.

"Innarested in a little tail t'night?"

"Me?" I said. Which was a very dumb answer, but it's quite embarrassing when somebody comes right up and asks you a question like that.

'How old are you, chief?' the elevator guy said.

"Why?" I said. "Twenty-two."

"Uh huh. Well, how 'bout it? Y'innarested? Five bucks a throw. Fifteen bucks the whole night." He looked at his wrist watch. "Till noon. Five bucks a throw, fifteen bucks till noon."

"Okay," I said. It was against my principles and all, but I was feeling so depressed I didn't even *think*. That's the whole trouble. When you're feeling very depressed, you can't even think.

"Okay *what?* A throw, or till noon? I gotta know."

"Just a throw."

85

women out. He said, in this one part, that a woman's body is like a violin and all, and that it takes a terrific musician to play it right. It was a very corny book—I realize that— but I couldn't get that violin stuff out of my mind anyway. In a way, that's why I sort of wanted to get some practice in, in case I ever get married. Caulfield and his Magic Violin, boy. It's corny, I realize, but it isn't *too* corny. I wouldn't mind being pretty good at that stuff. Half the time, if you really want to know the truth, when I'm hors-

86   *The Catcher in the Rye*

ing around with a girl, I have a helluva lot of trouble just *finding* what I'm looking for, for God's sake, if you know what I mean. Take this girl that I just missed having sexual intercourse with, that I told you about. It took me about an *hour* to just get her goddam brassière off. By the time I did get it off, she was about ready to spit in my eye.

Anyway, I kept walking around the room, waiting for this prostitute to show up. I kept hoping she'd be good-looking. I didn't care too much, though. I sort of just wanted to get it over with. Finally, somebody knocked on the door, and when I went to open it, I had my suitcase right in the way and I fell over it and damn near broke my knee. I always pick a gorgeous time to fall over a suitcase or something.

When I opened the door, this prostitute was standing there. She had a polo coat on, and no hat. She was sort of a blonde, but you could tell she dyed her hair. She wasn't any old bag, though. "How do you do," I said. Suave as hell, boy.

"You the guy Maurice said?" she asked me. She didn't

Pages 182-184

reveal passages even more vulgar than those reprinted here, but postal regulations would not permit the mailing of this pamphlet if they were reprinted here.

From "Are Your Children Being Brainwashed?" (Miami: Committee to Oppose the Canonization of Karl Marx, n.d.).

during the activist years of the late 1960s and early 1970s as he had earlier to members of the "silent generation" that identified with Holden Caulfield. It appears that what stands as the finest appreciation of this novelist by a distinguished American scholar, James E. Miller, Jr.'s pamphlet, *J. D. Salinger* (1965), might remain the last word on the man who possessed the singular ability to embody fictionally the alienated sensibility of the youth of a decade. Miller concludes that Salinger deserves "a place in the first rank, and even, perhaps, the preeminent position" in post-World War II American fiction.

Since then, however, there has been a rediscovery of Salinger as a writer of unique importance on different grounds. Although lately arrived critics continue to rush into print with the news that Salinger is a spokesman for America's alienated adolescents, and although some mention of the influence of Asian thought upon his writings may be found in even early criticisms, only with the elementary explanations that Bernice and Sanford Goldstein began to publish in 1966 have the influences of Zen Buddhism on Salinger's work been illustrated in detail. The first full accountings of the considerable extent of his use of oriental thought from a variety of sources appear in Humayun Mirza's dissertation and John Antush's book. The best recent essays about Salinger are by new enthusiasts such as Robert Coles and Ernest Ranly, who stress both the way in which a growing interest in Asian thought in the West has led readers back through "a passage to India" to Salinger and the way in which his colloquial embodiments of these ancient speculations have subconsciously implanted them into the minds of sensitive young Americans appalled by the increasing "phoniness" of their own materialistic culture.

Now that the early clamor over his works (including some censorious attacks upon its improprieties) has subsided, there seems little argument that Salinger, especially in *The Catcher in the Rye*, "Franny," and the more worldly of the *Nine Stories*, is unchallenged for having embedded in the amber of art the "bugs" of the depressingly paranoid McCarthy/Eisenhower years. But there is also growing evidence that his works are not just static museum pieces—like those that Holden Caulfield admires. Interest in oriental philosophies has been growing rapidly in America in recent years as we have achieved insights into their universality. Increasingly Salinger is winning recognition and acclaim as a writer thoroughly steeped in the manners and mannerisms of his own culture, who has deeply enough absorbed this traditional wisdom

from the East to be able to use it artfully in shaping legends that enable readers to appreciate through familiar icons the meaning of esoteric doctrines. Like the Phoenix of Eastern mythology, Salinger has risen from the ashes of his own *timely* reputation to assume what may prove a timeless one.

Periodical Publications:

"The Young Folks," *Story*, 16 (March-April 1940): 26-30;

"Go See Eddie," *University of Kansas City Review*, 7 (December 1940): 121-124;

"The Hang of It," *Collier's*, 108 (12 July 1941): 22;

"The Heart of a Broken Story," *Esquire*, 16 (September 1941): 32, 131-133;

"The Long Debut of Lois Taggett," *Story*, 21 (September-October 1942): 28-34;

"Personal Notes of an Infantryman," *Collier's*, 110 (12 December 1942): 96;

"The Varioni Brothers," *Saturday Evening Post*, 216 (17 July 1943): 12-13, 76-77;

"Both Parties Concerned," *Saturday Evening Post*, 216 (20 February 1944): 14, 47-48;

"Soft-Boiled Sergeant," *Saturday Evening Post*, 216 (15 April 1944): 18, 82-85;

"Last Day of the Last Furlough," *Saturday Evening Post*, 217 (15 July 1944): 26-27, 61-64;

"Once a Week Won't Kill You," *Story*, 25 (November-December 1944): 23-27;

"A Boy in France," *Saturday Evening Post*, 217 (31 March 1945): 21, 92;

"Elaine," *Story*, 26 (March-April 1945): 38-47;

"This Sandwich Has No Mayonnaise," *Esquire*, 24 (October 1945): 54-56, 147-149;

"The Stranger," *Collier's*, 116 (1 December 1945): 18, 77;

"I'm Crazy," *Collier's*, 116 (22 December 1945): 36, 48, 51;

"Slight Rebellion Off Madison," *New Yorker*, 22 (21 December 1946): 76-79;

"A Young Girl in 1941 with No Waist at All," *Mademoiselle*, 25 (May 1947): 222-223, 292-302;

"The Inverted Forest," *Cosmopolitan*, 113 (December 1947): 73-109;

"A Girl I Knew," *Good Housekeeping*, 126 (February 1948): 37, 186-196;

"Blue Melody," *Cosmopolitan*, 125 (September 1948): 50-51, 112-119;

"Hapworth 16, 1924," *New Yorker*, 41 (19 June 1965): 32-40, ff.

References:

Jonathan Baumbach, "The Saint as a Young Man: A Reappraisal of *The Catcher in the Rye*," *Modern Language Quarterly*, 25 (December 1964): 461-472;

William F. Belcher and James E. Lee, eds., *J. D. Salinger and the Critics* (Belmont, Cal.: Wadsworth, 1962);

Edgar M. Branch, "Mark Twain and J. D. Salinger: A Study in Literary Continuity," *American Quarterly*, 9 (summer 1957): 144-158;

James E. Bryan, "J. D. Salinger: The Fat Lady and the Chicken Sandwich," *College English*, 23 (December 1961): 226-229;

Bryan, "A Reading of 'For Esme—With Love and Squalor,'" *Criticism*, 9 (summer 1967): 275-288;

Bryan, "A Reading of Salinger's 'Teddy,'" *American Literature*, 40 (November 1968): 352-369;

Bryan, "The Psychological Structure of *The Catcher in the Rye*," *PMLA*, 89 (October 1974): 1065-1074;

Robert Coles, "Reconsideration: J. D. Salinger," *New Republic*, 168 (28 April 1973): 30-32;

Donald P. Costello, "The Language of *The Catcher in the Rye*," *American Speech*, 34 (October 1959): 172-181;

Robert Detweiler, *Four Spiritual Crises in Mid-Century American Fiction* (Gainesville: University of Florida Monographs, 1964), pp. 36-43;

Donald M. Fiene, "J. D. Salinger: A Bibliography," *Wisconsin Studies in Contemporary Literature*, 4 (winter 1963): 109-149;

Warren French, *J. D. Salinger* (New York: Twayne, 1963; Boston: Twayne, 1976);

French, "The Age of Salinger," in his *The Fifties: Fiction, Poetry, Drama* (Deland, Fla.: Everett/Edwards, 1971), pp. 1-39;

French, "Steinbeck and J. D. Salinger," in *Steinbeck's Literary Dimension*, ed. Tetsumaro Hayashi (Metuchen, N. J.: Scarecrow, 1973), pp. 105-115;

Barbara Giles, "The Lonely War of J. D. Salinger," *Mainstream*, 12 (February 1959): 2-13;

Lyle Glazier, "The Glass Family Saga: Argument and Epiphany," *College English*, 27 (December 1965): 248-251;

Bernice and Sanford Goldstein, "Zen and Salinger," *Modern Fiction Studies*, 12 (autumn 1966): 313-324;

Goldstein and Goldstein, "Zen and *Nine Stories*," *Renascence*, 22 (summer 1970): 171-182;

Goldstein and Goldstein, "Some Zen References in Salinger," *Literature East and West*, 15, 1 (1971): 83-95;

Goldstein and Goldstein, "Ego and 'Hapworth 16, 1924,'" *Renascence*, 24 (spring 1972): 159-167;

Goldstein and Goldstein, "Seymour's Poems," *Literature East and West*, 17 (June-September-December 1973): 335-348;

Henry A. Grunwald, ed., *Salinger: A Critical and Personal Portrait* (New York: Harper, 1962);

Frederick L. Gwynn and Joseph L. Blotner, *The Fiction of J. D. Salinger* (Pittsburgh: University of Pittsburgh Press, 1958);

Kenneth Hamilton, *J. D. Salinger: A Critical Essay* (Grand Rapids, Mich.: Eerdmans, 1967);

Ihab Hassan, "J. D. Salinger: Rare Quixotic Gesture," *Western Review*, 21 (summer 1957): 261-280;

Arthur Heiserman and James E. Miller, Jr., "J. D. Salinger: Some Crazy Cliff," *Western Humanities Review*, 10 (spring 1956): 129-137;

Charles Kaplan, "Holden and Huck: The Odysseys of Youth," *College English*, 28 (November 1956): 76-80;

Alfred Kazin, "J. D. Salinger: Everybody's Favorite," *Atlantic*, 158 (August 1961): 27-31;

Arthur F. Kinney, "J. D. Salinger and the Search for Love," *Texas Studies in Literature and Language*, 5 (spring 1963): 111-126;

Marvin Laser and Norman Fruman, eds., *Studies in J. D. Salinger* (New York: Odyssey, 1962);

Paul Levine, "J. D. Salinger: The Development of the Misfit Hero," *Twentieth Century Literature*, 4 (October 1958): 92-99;

Levine, "The Politics of Alienation," *Mosaic*, 2 (fall 1968): 3-17;

Malcolm M. Marsden, ed., *"If You Really Want to Know": A Catcher Casebook* (Chicago: Scott, Foresman, 1963);

Mary McCarthy, "J. D. Salinger's Closed Circuit," *Harper's* (October 1962): 46-48;

James E. Miller, Jr., *J. D. Salinger* (Minneapolis: University of Minnesota Press, 1965);

Arthur Mizener, "The Love Song of J. D. Salinger," *Harper's*, 218 (February 1959): 83-90;

Richard W. Noland, "The Novel of Personal Formula: J. D. Salinger," *University Review*, 33 (autumn 1966): 19-24;

Carol and Richard Ohmann, "Reviewers, Critics, and *The Catcher in the Rye*," *Critical Inquiry*, 3 (autumn 1976): 15-38;

Bernard Oldsey, "The Movies in the Rye," *College English*, 23 (December 1961): 209-215;

Anthony Quagliano, "'Hapworth 16, 1924': A Problem in Hagiography," *University of Dayton Review*, 8 (fall 1971): 35-43;

Ernest W. Ranly, "Journey to the East," *Commonweal*, 97 (23 February 1973): 465-469;

Max F. Schulz, "J. D. Salinger and the Crisis of Consciousness," in his *Radical Sophistication: Studies in Contemporary Jewish-American Novelists* (Athens: Ohio University Press, 1969), pp. 198-217;

Daniel Seitzman, "Salinger's 'Franny': Homoerotic Imagery," *American Imago*, 22 (spring-summer 1965): 57-76;

Seitzman, "Therapy and Antitherapy in Salinger's 'Zooey,' " *American Imago*, 25 (summer 1968): 140-162;

Peter J. Seng, "The Fallen Idol: The Immature World of Holden Caulfield," *College English*, 23 (December 1961): 203-209;

Harold P. Simonson and E. P. Hager, eds., *Salinger's "Catcher in the Rye": Clamor vs. Criticism* (New York: Heath, 1963);

Robert M. Slabey, *"The Catcher in the Rye:* Christian Theme and Symbol," *College Language Association Journal*, 6 (March 1963): 170-183;

Gordon E. Slethaug, "Seymour: A Clarification," *Renascence*, 23 (spring 1971): 115-128;

"Special Issue: J. D. Salinger," *Modern Fiction Studies*, 12 (autumn 1966);

"Special Number: Salinger," *Wisconsin Studies in Contemporary Literature*, 4 (winter 1963);

William Bysshe Stein, "Salinger's 'Teddy': *Tat Tvam Asi* or That Thou Art," *Arizona Quarterly*, 29 (autumn 1973): 253-265;

George Steiner, "The Salinger Industry," *Nation*, 189 (14 November 1959): 360-363;

Carl F. Strauch, " 'Kings in the Back Row': Meaning through Structure—A Reading of Salinger's *The Catcher in the Rye*," *Wisconsin Studies in Contemporary Literature*, 2 (winter 1961): 5-30;

Clinton W. Trowbridge, "The Symbolic Structure of *The Catcher in the Rye*," *Sewanee Review*, 74 (summer 1966): 681-693;

Kermit Vanderbilt, "Symbolic Resolution in *The Catcher in the Rye:* The Cap, the Carousel, and the American West," *Western Humanities Review*, 17 (summer 1963): 271-277;

Dan Wakefield, "Salinger and the Search for Love," *New World Writing*, 14 (December 1958): 68-85;

Helen Weinberg, *The New Novel in America: The Kafkan Mode in American Fiction* (Ithaca, N. Y.: Cornell University Press, 1970);

William Wiegand, "J. D. Salinger's Seventy-Eight Bananas," *Chicago Review*, 11 (winter 1958): 3-19;

Wiegand, "The Knighthood of J. D. Salinger," *New Republic*, 141 (19 October 1959): 19-22;

Wiegand, "Salinger and Kierkegaard," *Minnesota Review*, 5 (May-July 1965): 137-156.

HUBERT SELBY, JR., came into prominence in 1964 with the publication of *Last Exit to Brooklyn*, a collection of violent, interrelated stories depicting homosexuals, thugs, drunks, whores, and others engaged in acts of perverse brutality and blind self-destructior *Last Exit to Brooklyn* was the subject of an obscenity trial in England, banned in Italy, and given a mixed reception in the United States. Selby, then 36, had drawn on his personal experience for the stories of life in the lower depths. Some critics found the work self-indulgent, obscene, and unliterary, while others rose to its defense. The reactions were strong on both sides, but the critics were in agreement on at least two points—that Selby knew his material and that his style was energetic and uninhibited.

Two novels have followed *Last Exit to Brooklyn*. The first of these, *The Room* (1971), about an imprisoned psychopath awaiting trial, extends the themes and actions of *Last Exit to Brooklyn*, though within a narrower compass. It was greeted enthusiastically by a number of reviewers. Selby's latest novel, *The Demon* (1976), was given very little attention. It is an effort to portray a man possessed by ambition, lust, and violence, but it is murky in its intentions and execution.

A largely self-taught writer with little formal education, Hubert Selby, Jr., was born on 23 July 1928 in Brooklyn. He attended Peter Stuyvesant High School there for one year before joining the merchant marine in 1944. Between 1946 and 1950, he was hospitalized for tuberculosis. Selby worked for six years on *Last Exit to Brooklyn*, holding in the meantime a variety of jobs and publishing in such journals as the *Black Mountain Review*, *New Directions Annual* and the *Provincetown Review*. He currently lives in Los Angeles with his third wife and their children where he is at work on a novel, "A Pound of Pure" (described by Selby as focusing on the problems of addiction to drugs, food, television—"That is, the American way of life"). Selby also writes scripts for film and TV (a recent script for a television special on the Third Commandment was not used; he has said his next script will be "an investigation of faith").

Selby has said of *Last Exit* that he was attempting to "portray the horrors of a loveless world," "to overwhelm the reader with truth, like

H. Selby Jr.

Beethoven, so that weeks, months, or any damn time after he has finished the book and whether he liked it or it disgusted him, he will be forced to think." Selby cites the composer as one of his two major influences; the other is Isaac Babel, whose writing he admires for its power. Relentless brutality and shock are characteristic devices in all three of Selby's works. Although his style is paratactic and full of energetic run-ons, it is tightly controlled in both *Last Exit* and *The Room*. His handling of form is equally rigorous in these novels; three of the stories in *Last Exit* have in common a spiralling structure which deserves close attention, and *The Room*, like "Landsend," which is the "Coda" of *Last Exit*, has a form very similar to that of a musical rondo.

Classifying Selby is a difficult matter. Having been on the fringes of the literary establishment has kept him, perhaps as much as the violence of his works, from being given much attention in formal academic journals, and so the number of serious critical studies devoted to him is small. It would seem most proper to regard him as a moralist—as a moralist primarily and a social critic only secondarily. He indicts his characters sternly for their grave and multiple failings, especially in *Last Exit*. He deserves to be compared with Flannery O'Connor, whose stories, like his, often engender in the reader an antipathy toward the characters and end with violent retributions. Selby takes his own Christianity very seriously, and in *Last Exit* it is expressed almost as harshly as Flannery O'Connor's Catholicism.

Of Selby's works so far, *Last Exit* is clearly the most exciting and most significant. It is both an obsessed and a deceptively variegated book, as much a whole, coherent novel as an aggregate of stories. Described in some reviews as being a journey into hell, it opens to the reader a world of tedium and depravity, of drug abuse and viciousness, of self-exploitation and abysmal ignorance that seems at once unbearable and all too real. What gives this work its power is less fidelity to fact than an unremitting energy. As Selby hoped, it overwhelms; it denies the reader the distance which usually goes with aesthetic pleasure, and it does so by detailing explicitly the thoughts and actions of its characters. Some reviewers responded with outrage or self-protective sarcasm. One critic noted that *Last Exit* is not a book for the fainthearted.

Although *The Room* is not as rich a book or quite as unerring as *Last Exit*, it, too, is dreadfully plausible. The protagonist is a bleak, unnamed prisoner who alternately has fantasies of reprisal against his captors and imagines himself as the spearhead of a judicial reform campaign. He is frightful and pathetic. He is made universal by the bewilderment he feels in trying to assess his actions and feelings, a bewilderment which fatally cripples his sense of responsibility as well as his self-esteem. His desire to be acceptable to himself is so desperate that he forcibly rejects the idea of his wrongdoings, and yet his guilt is a merciless weight. Like Harry Black in *Last Exit*, who is the epitome, perhaps, of Hubert Selby's suffering characters, this man is on the rack every second of his life. Vomiting, masturbating, pinching a deeply-rooted pimple—these are the climactic actions that give his life shape. His dreams of revenge against the policemen who apprehended him are so savage as to risk seeming gratuitous at times. Selby manages, though, to make this material real and functional. He is not quite so convincing when his character is imagining himself as a reformer; the projected alter ego has a verbal tone and a cleverness which seem, at least in some ways, beyond the prisoner's imagination.

The failure of *The Demon* to measure up to Selby's other novels is a consequence of its scattering its energies broadly. Its hero, Harry White, is intended as a counterpart of some sort to Harry Black of "Strike." But the construction falters seriously. Selby seems unable to decide whether Harry is to be pitied or despised, and what results is a muddled portrait of a brilliant young executive whose larcenous, lecherous, and murderous pursuits do not

Hubert Selby, Jr.

achieve dramatic or psychological coherency. Nothing about this Harry ever quite comes into focus. His supposed business acumen is suggested, not portrayed; his marital relationship retains an implausible decency even during the period of his most degraded and sordid actions. Stylistically as well, *The Demon* is perplexing; the tone vacillates between the coarse, pungent crudity so proper to *Last Exit* and an embarrassing bland idiom which is incompatible with that crudity. The range of tone which is midway between these two extremes—uncliched but common-sounding—eludes Selby here, as does the bedrock credibility of his other works. *The Demon* is melodramatic, overlong, and arbitrary.

Selby has said, however, in response to this criticism, that *The Demon* is "a morality play rather than a novel about a man's success and failure. . . . Harry White fought his obsession with his ego, rather than surrendering his problems to God, and when he utters those famous last words in the hotel room, One wont hurt, his life becomes a shambles and his destruction is inevitable." Selby has also said that "the entire book is an extended cliche"—one whose stylistic mixture is intended, not accidental. Still, the reader finds it difficult to know from the text that his usual novelistic expectations are out of order here; and one cannot help feeling that the author's intentions are somehow overly intellectual. *Last Exit* and *The Room* are both written from the gut, and they more readily succeed because their "meanings" are less imposed upon the fabric of the action. —*Richard Wertime*

Books:

Last Exit to Brooklyn (New York: Grove, 1964; London: Calder & Boyars, 1968);
The Room (New York: Grove, 1971; London: Calder & Boyars, 1972);
The Demon (New York: The Playboy Press, 1976).

Periodical Publications:

"Fat Phil's Day," *Evergreen Review*, 11 (August 1967): 53;
"Solving the Ice-Cream Cone Problem," *Evergreen Review*, 12 (August 1968): 57-58;
"Happy Birthday," *Evergreen Review*, 13 (August 1969): 35-37;
Review of *Lament*, by David Carson, *Village Voice*, 1 November 1973, p. 28.

References:

Frank Kermode, " 'Obscenity' and the 'Public Interest,' " *New American Review*, 3 (April 1968): 229-244;
James B. Lane, "Violence and Sex in the Post-War Popular Urban Novel: with a Consideration of Harold Robbins's *A Stone for Danny Fisher* and Hubert Selby, Jr.'s, *Last Exit to Brooklyn*," *Journal of Popular Culture*, 8, 2 (fall 1974): 295-308;
Charles D. Peavy, "Hubert Selby and the Tradition of Moral Satire," *Satire Newsletter*, 6, 2 (spring 1969): 35-39;

Peavy, "The Sin of Pride and Selby's *Last Exit to Brooklyn,*" *Critique,* 11, 3 (1969): 35-42;

Gilbert Sorrentino, "The Art of Hubert Selby," *Kulchur,* 13 (spring 1964): 27-43;

Richard A. Wertime, "Psychic Vengeance in *Last Exit to Brooklyn,*" *Literature and Psychology,* 24 (4 November 1974): 153-166.

SUSAN SONTAG, cultural critic, essayist, novelist, and filmmaker, was born 16 January 1933 in New York City. She grew up in Tucson, Arizona, and Los Angeles, California, and at the age of fifteen (1948) entered the University of California at Berkeley. She transferred after a year to the University of Chicago, where in 1950 she met and subsequently married Philip Rieff, a social psychologist, with whom she had a son in 1952. In 1951 she took her B.A. in philosophy and continued her studies at Harvard, where she took an M.A. in English in 1954, an M.A. in philosophy in 1955, and was a Ph.D. candidate from 1955-1957. In 1957 she attended St. Anne's College, Oxford, to pursue graduate study, and in 1957-1958 she studied at the University of Paris on a grant from the American Association of University Women. After her divorce in 1959, Sontag spent a brief time as an editor at *Commentary* and then resumed her academic interests as a lecturer in philosophy at the City College of New York and Sarah Lawrence. From 1960-1964 she was an instructor in the religion department of Columbia University and after that was writer-in-residence for one year at Rutgers. In 1965 she received a Rockefeller Fellowship. In 1966 she received the George Polk Memorial Award "for contribution toward better appreciation of theatre, motion pictures, and literature," and was also awarded a Guggenheim Fellowship. Another Rockefeller Fellowship followed in 1974, and a second Guggenheim in 1975. In 1976 she was the recipient of the Ingram Merrill Foundation Award in Literature in the field of American Letters, the Brandeis University Creative Arts Award, and the Arts and Letters Award of the American Academy of Arts and Letters. *On Photography* received the National Book Critics' Circle Award for the Best Work of Criticism in 1977.

Susan Sontag's career has been marked by a seriousness of pursuit and a relentless intelligence that analyzes modern culture on almost every possible level: artistic, philosophical, literary, political, and moral. Although she began writing essays, stories, poems, and plays at about the age of eight, not until she was twenty-eight did she begin her career as a writer in earnest, with the publication of *The Benefactor.* Sontag later made her popular reputation as an incisive and controversy-provoking essayist, although she rejects this easy and apparently outdated label: ". . . it's somewhat of a burden to be thought of primarily as an essayist. . . . I'm interested in leaving my past work behind." In comparing her approach to fiction and essays, Sontag comments: "It's always a relief to do fiction; it's always a trial to do essays. They're much harder for me. An essay can go through 20 drafts, a work of fiction rarely goes through more than three or four drafts. With fiction, I'm almost there after the first draft." Her essays and short stories have appeared in such journals as *Harper's Bazaar, Harper's, Partisan Review, Nation, New York Review of Books,* and *Commentary.* Since 1968 Sontag has concentrated her energies on filmmaking and photography as well as literature, with screenplays, films, and a collection of essays on photography to her credit. At present, Sontag has a collection of short stories entitled *I, etcetera* slated for publication in fall 1978, and is writing a story and continuing a novel on which she has been working for several years.

Susan Sontag's first novel, *The Benefactor* (1963), treats the relationship between the day-self and the night-self, the conscious and the unconscious, reality and dream. The protagonist, Hippolyte, is a withdrawn young man who suddenly becomes aware of the stirring, liberating effect of his dreams and who seeks actively to pursue them, "not looking for my dreams to interpret my life, but rather for my life to interpret my dreams." This attitude leads him to recreate as closely as possible in his life the situations he encounters in his dreams, and from his dreams he takes the cues that enable him to solve current personal problems. But never at any time does he confuse the relative merits of his two worlds: even his mistress, Frau Anders, does not possess him as utterly as does his dream of her. Hippolyte rejects all conventional and unconventional explanations for his spate of dreams: the priest advises confession, the arcane mystic tries to convert him, the writer/homosexual suggests that Hippolyte participate in his nightly forays that obviate the need to dream, his mistress is convinced that his dreams are rooted in sex.

Not only his life, but also the novel, take their patterns from dreams. Selling Frau Anders to the Arab, attempting to murder her and then rewarding her with the gift of a specially furnished house—bizarre and apparently unmotivated events happen throughout the book. But the novel is anything but formless. Instead of imposing a mechanical,

Jill Krementz

Susan Sontag

arbitrary plot upon the work, Sontag weaves a pattern of recurring images, symbols, and allusions into the organic unity of a dream. Frau Anders—at once Hippolyte's patroness, his mistress, his mother, his tormentor—is the strongest unifying element of Hippolyte's life and the novel, and her appearances and disappearances occur in the uncanny fashion of a disturbing dream. Hippolyte's final confusion of Frau Anders with his old housekeeper illustrates the extent to which his unconscious state has appropriated his everyday existence. Did he, in fact, go mad? Not even the Hippolyte who narrates the novel thirty years later can verify the events of his earlier dreaming days.

The Benefactor has been called a "European novel," and it certainly is to the extent that it is highly introspective, more concerned with defining the particular self than the world. John Wain went so far as to say: "This Continental flavor seems to me more eye-catching and more important than anything intrinsic to the book itself. . . . It owes nothing to any American author or to any American

way of looking at things. Its ancestors are Baudelaire, Kafka, and perhaps . . . Dostoevsky and Proust." Yet *The Benefactor* has the limitations of such a novel—little surface action and an almost exquisite sense of self. Wain commended her "sureness of touch very unusual in a first novel," yet he found, "The trouble is that one has the impression of delighted skill applied to an end which doesn't, finally, much interest the writer." Daniel Stern wrote, "Miss Sontag is an intelligent writer who has, on her first flight, jettisoned the historical baggage of the novel. However, she has not replaced it with material or insights that carry equal, or superior, weight."

Against Interpretation (1966), Sontag's first collection of critical essays on the modern sensibility, is a broad selection of her contributions to magazines such as *Partisan Review, New York Review of Books,* and *Film Quarterly* from 1961 to 1965. It was nominated for the National Book Award. As Sontag acknowledges in the headnote to the collection, ". . . in the end, what I have been

448

writing is not criticism at all, strictly speaking, but case studies for an aesthetic, a theory of my own sensibility," and the underlying tenets of her aesthetic are propounded in the opening section of the book. This essay, "Against Interpretation," calls for a sensual experience of art, rather than the analytical dissection of the artwork to reach the "meaning," which is the typically modern response to art. Her approach to art is further defined in "On Style," which attacks the traditional distinction between form and content. Although she has been criticized for "lobotomizing" art, she defends her approach to art through the aesthetic rather than the critical faculty by maintaining, "I think the aesthetic experience is a form of intelligence, and that a great deal of what people call intellectual activity is aesthetic experience."

The essays range from those on the works of Sartre, Cesare Pavese, and Simone Weil, to criticism of films by Godard, Resnais, and Robert Bresson, to a short but perceptive critique of Ionesco, to other aspects of the theatre, to her famous "Notes on 'Camp,' " for which she is probably best known in popular culture. If, as Benjamin DeMott observed, *Against Interpretation* ". . . may well rank among the invaluable cultural chronicles of these years," it is surely because of Susan Sontag's inexhaustible curiosity and hard, almost brittle intellect, which is better suited to her criticism than her novels.

Sontag's second novel, *Death Kit* (1967), is a reexamination and a refocusing of some of the major themes in *The Benefactor*: the makeup of subjective reality, the pursuit of the unconscious, the attempt to get "completely inside one's own head." Dalton Harron (or Diddy) is the lethargic and passive "hero" of the novel, a man who pursues his death instead of his dreams: "The deliquescent running-down of everything becomes co-existent with Diddy's entire span of consciousness, undermines his most minimal acts." Did he actually leave the stalled train and kill the surly worker in the tunnel? The blind girl in his compartment says he didn't. Is the woman he tracks down the widow of the man he may have killed? There's a possibility she isn't. Why did the Catholic workman request cremation? Why doesn't the railroad investigate the possibility of murder? Will he be discovered? Will he be absolved? Did he do it? Diddy's life, and, by extension, his world, have so succumbed to entropy that the possibility that he *didn't* kill a man becomes his *raison d'etre*.

The pattern of the novel resembles the structure of a chambered nautilus, one large space enclosing many smaller successive ones. Diddy moves from the train tunnel to fantasies of life in a shell, to his self-sufficient apartment, and finally back to the train tunnel—the chamber of his death—making at last a discovery that he probably has sensed all along: "Life=the world. Death=being completely inside one's own head." Inside his own head is probably where Diddy and the reader have been throughout, for the closing lines suggest that the "events" of the novel are but his dying fantasies as his suicide attempt—briefly alluded to in the beginning—is accomplished. In accordance with her belief that there is no "one way of rendering experience which is correct," Sontag commented to Joe David Bellamy: "I like the idea that *Death Kit* can be read in that way [as "a second story of dying"] and that it can also be read as a straight narrative in which certain magical events take place on exactly the same level as those events which are convincing in terms of everyday life. . . . You can say it's all a dream. But at the same time, it should be felt as an experience that was actually happening. . . . I want the book to exist on both levels of reading."

Death Kit is much more absorbing, less academic, more alive than *The Benefactor*. Yet it still lacks a dynamic quality—an ability to make the reader care about the protagonist. While Sontag is capable of passages of great perception and brilliance, on the whole her tone is too objective, her treatment of Diddy too generalized, her own interest in him perhaps not as sustained as it should be.

Styles of Radical Will (1969), a collection of criticism, reflects the shift in Sontag's interest away from literature to cinema, which she considers the "most alive, the most exciting, the most important of all art forms." Section II of the book, for example, is devoted entirely to cinema: "Theatre and Film," "Bergman's Persona," and "Godard," which Richard Gilman called "a masterly long study and appreciation of Godard, the best I know of." "Trip to Hanoi" (first published in *Esquire* and then in paperback), the longest essay and the coda to the collection, is, according to Emile Capouya, "the story of a religious conversion." Although a member of the independent political left and "passionately opposed to the American aggression in Vietnam," Sontag steered clear of overt partisanship in previous works. But in her recollections and journals of her 1968 trip to North Vietnam she, according to Capouya, "invites us to re-imagine the America once conceived by the Founding Fathers and now abandoned by the Americans, a land of permanent revolution in the interests of a human polity." Lawrence M. Bensky considered it a "triumph that by being true to what she sees and feels—her first concern—she is able to transfer her artistic and philosophical values to politics without distorting them or losing herself, and find value and meaning where others have lapsed into political cliches or been struck dumb with horror."

Sontag's long-standing interest in cinema attested to by essays published in *Against Interpretation* and *Styles of Radical Will*, led her in 1968 to write and direct a screenplay, *Duet for Cannibals*, which was filmed in Stockholm and first screened at the New York Film Festival in 1969. It was published in 1970. She wrote a second screenplay, *Brother Carl*, in 1969 and directed its filming in Stockholm in 1970. It was released in 1972 and published in 1974. Also in 1974, Sontag directed a documentary film, *Promised Lands*, about the Yom Kippur War of 1973. She explains her fascination with filmmaking as "the chance to exercise a part of my imagination and my powers in a way that I can't as a writer. A visual sense, a plastic sense, a structural sense, a musical sense. . . . I'm not interested in films as a *writer*, but as a director and an editor."

On Photography, published in 1977, is a collection of six previously published essays on individual photographers such as Diane Arbus and Richard Avedon, as well as on the art of photography. Sontag concentrates on what William Gass called "the act of photography," which encompasses discussion of the gray area between the amateur and professional photographer, the value of and relationship between the photographic image and the object it represents, and the status accorded the photographer in our society. In an interview with Charles Simmons, Sontag commented on her work: ". . . I came to realize that I wasn't writing about photography so much as I was writing about modernity, about the way we are now. The subject of photography is a form of access to contemporary ways of feeling and thinking. And writing about photography is like writing about the world." Calling the collection "brilliant," Gass notes that "Every page of 'On Photography' raises important and exciting questions about its subject and raises them in the best way. In a context of clarity, skepticism and passionate concern . . . Sontag encourages the reader's cooperation in her enterprise."

In his review of *On Photography* Alfred Kazin categorized Sontag as a "cafe intellectual" inhabiting some rarefied atmosphere outside of the real world; Sontag's "real world" is in fact the world of ideas and their relationships, which she pursues both in her essays and in fiction. Although critical reception of her fiction is mixed, even her detractors do not fail to note that her work is "full of brilliant statements." Her dual career of commentator and artist has encompassed the polarities of such criticism. Sontag has produced a stimulating and varied body of work which entertains the issues of art while satisfying the rigors of her own intellect.

—*Susan Walker*

Books:

The Benefactor (New York: Farrar, Straus, 1963; London: Eyre & Spottiswoode, 1964);

Against Interpretation (New York: Farrar, Straus & Giroux, 1966; London: Eyre & Spottiswoode, 1967);

Literature (n.p., 1966);

Death Kit (New York: Farrar, Straus & Giroux, 1967; London: Secker & Warburg, 1968);

Trip to Hanoi (New York: Farrar, Straus & Giroux, 1968; London: Panther, 1969);

Styles of Radical Will (New York: Farrar, Straus & Giroux, 1969; London: Secker & Warburg, 1969);

Duet for Cannibals (New York: Farrar, Straus & Giroux, 1970; London: Allen Lane, 1970);

Brother Carl (New York: Farrar, Straus & Giroux, 1974);

On Photography (New York: Farrar, Straus & Giroux, 1977);

I, etcetera (New York: Farrar, Straus & Giroux, 1978);

Illness as Metaphor (New York: Farrar, Straus & Giroux, 1978).

Screenplays:

Duet for Cannibals, 1969;

Brother Carl, New Yorker Films, 1972;

Promised Lands, New Yorker Films, 1974.

Periodical Publications:

FICTION:

"Man With a Pain," *Harper's*, 228 (April 1964): 72-75;

"The Will and the Way," *Partisan Review*, 33 (summer 1965): 373-396;

"Project for a Trip to China," *Atlantic*, 231 (April 1973): 69-77;

"Debriefing," *American Review 18* (New York: Bantam, 1973), pp. 68-85;

"Baby," *Playboy*, 21 (February 1974): 74 ff.;

"Old Complaints Revisited," *American Review 21* (New York: Bantam, 1974), pp. 213-252;

"Doctor Jekyll," *Partisan Review*, 41 (winter 1974):

539-552, 586-603;

"Unguided Tour," *New Yorker*, 53 (31 October 1977): 40-45.

NONFICTION:

"Feast for Open Eyes," *Nation*, 198 (13 April 1964): 374-376;

"Opinion, Please, from New York: Susan Sontag," *Mademoiselle*, 60 (April 1965): 58, 60;

"Theatre," *Vogue*, 146 (August 1965): 51-52;

"The Role of the Writer as Critic," *Publishers Weekly*, 189 (28 March 1966): 36-37;

"The Avant-Garde and Contemporary Literature," *Wilson Library Bulletin*, 40 (June 1966): 930-932, 937-940;

"Trip to Hanoi," *Esquire*, 70 (December 1968): 131-141, 287-290;

"Some Thoughts on the Right Way (for us) to Love the Cuban Revolution," *Ramparts Magazine*, 7 (April 1969): 6, 10, 14, 16, 18-19;

"Letter from Sweden," *Ramparts Magazine*, 8 (July 1969): 23-38;

"The Double Standard of Aging," *Saturday Review*, 55 (23 September 1972): 29-38;

"Reflections," *New Yorker*, 49 (19 May 1973): 39-44, ff.;

"The Third World of Women," *Partisan Review*, 40 (summer 1973): 180-206;

"Photography," *New York Review of Books*, 18 October 1973, pp. 59-63;

"Freak Show," *New York Review of Books*, 15 November 1973, pp. 13-19;

"Shooting America," *New York Review of Books*, 18 April 1974, pp. 17-24;

"Make a Movie," *Vogue*, 164 (July 1974): 84-85;

"Photography: The Beauty Treatment," *New York Review of Books*, 28 November 1974, pp. 35-39;

"Fascinating Fascism," *New York Review of Books*, 6 February 1975, pp. 23-30;

"Francis Bacon: About Being in Pain," *Vogue*, 165 (March 1975): 136-137;

"Feminism and Fascism: An Exchange," *New York Review of Books*, 20 March 1975, pp. 31-32;

"Woman's Beauty: Put-Down or Power Source?," *Vogue*, 165 (April 1975): 118-119;

"Beauty: How Will It Change Next?," *Vogue*, 165 (May 1975): 116-117, 174;

"Can Rights Be Equal?," *Vogue*, 166 (July 1976): 100-101;

"Photographic Life/Death," *Vogue*, 166 (September 1976): 348-349;

"Photography in Search of Itself," *New York Review of Books*, 20 January 1977, pp. 53-59;

"Illness as Metaphor," *New York Review of Books*, 26 January 1978, pp. 10-16;

"Images of Illness," *New York Review of Books*, 9 February 1978, pp. 27-29.

Other:

Antonin Artaud: Selected Writings, translated by Helen Weaver, edited with introduction by Sontag (New York: Farrar, Straus & Giroux, 1976).

References:

Joe David Bellamy, "Susan Sontag," *The New Fiction* (Chicago: University of Illinois Press, 1974), pp. 113-129;

Robert Boyers, "Women, the Arts, and the Politics of Culture: An Interview with Susan Sontag," *Salmagundi*, 31-32 (1975): 29-48;

Emile Capouya, "The Age of Allegiance," *Saturday Review*, 52 (3 May 1969): 29;

Benjamin DeMott, "Lady on the Scene," *New York Times Book Review*, 23 January 1966, pp. 5, 32;

William H. Gass, "A Different Kind of Art," *New York Times Book Review*, 18 December 1977, pp. 7, 30-31;

Richard Gilman, "Susan Sontag and the Question of the New," *New Republic*, 160 (3 May 1969): 23-26, 28;

Charles Simmons, "Sontag Talking," *New York Times Book Review*, 18 December 1977, pp. 7, 31, 33;

Sharon Smith, "Susan Sontag," in her *Women Who Make Movies* (New York: Hopkinson & Blake, 1975), pp. 52-54;

Theodore Solotaroff, "Interpreting Susan Sontag," in his *The Red Hot Vacuum* (New York: Atheneum, 1970), pp. 261-268;

Daniel Stern, "Life Becomes a Dream," *New York Times Book Review*, 8 September 1963, p. 5;

Tony Tanner, "Space Odyssey," *Partisan Review*, 35 (summer 1968): 446-451;

John Wain, "Song of Myself," *New Republic*, 149 (21 September 1963): 26-27, 30.

Terry Southern

TERRY SOUTHERN was born in Alvarado, Texas, on 1 May 1924. He was educated at Southern Methodist University, the University of Chicago, Northwestern University, where he received his B.A. in 1948, and the Sorbonne, where he studied from 1948 to 1950. He served in the U.S. Army from 1943 to 1945. In 1956 he married Carol Kauffman; they have one son, Nile. Although primarily known as a novelist, Southern also has written a number of screenplays. He won the British Screen Writers' Award in 1964 and was twice nominated for an Academy Award: in 1963 for *Dr. Strangelove* and in 1968 for *Easy Rider*.

Flash and Filigree (1958), the first of Southern's novels, is, like the others, satiric black comedy. There are two parallel plots which occasionally intermingle but which are, for the most part, separate stories working themselves out simultaneously. The characters in each are only marginally influenced by one another, primarily because of their occupations. The principal character in one plot is Dr. Frederick Eichner, the world's foremost dermatologist and an avid racing car enthusiast. He works at the same clinic where Babs Mintner is a fledgling nurse. Presumably he is the "Flash" of the title, while she is the "Filigree." One story revolves around Eichner, while Babs is at the heart of the other. Both lose their innocence, but in quite different ways. Eichner, a calculating but unabashed speedster behind the wheel, has a bizarre accident and finds himself involved in a Kafkaesque trial as a result. His efforts to clear himself with the aid of an alcoholic private detective result in a series of ridiculous mishaps which poke fun at a number of institutions and types. Among them are cosmetic medicine, the police, the jury system, the unfeeling physician, and the tough, hard-drinking private eye. There is also one most unusual character: a Mr. Felix Treevly, whose behavior never fails to astound. He is the catalyst for the action of the "Flash" plot.

The "Filigree" plot is concerned with sex. The first of Southern's numerous ingenues, Babs's innocence is lost in a long, hilarious, pitched battle at a drive-in theater. The Babs sequence also allows Southern to satirize several types, perhaps the most interesting of which is the head nurse, a suppressed lesbian whose special pleasure is in watching Babs change from her uniform to street clothes.

Painstakingly conventional description alternates with absurd satiric scenes, the conventional writing making the satire even funnier by contrast. It is in isolated scenes that the novel is most memorable: the automobile accident; Dr. Eichner's description of his amazing driving habits to an astonished jury; the attempt to hide the body of a man disguised as a woman; and Babs's sexual vacillations in the back seat of a convertible. Certain keynotes of style, theme, and character type which recur in other Southern novels are first struck here: the disjointed narrative, the parallel plot, and, perhaps most importantly, the sexual ingenue. Babs Mintner obviously intrigued Southern, for in his next novel she became the heroine and protagonist, Candy.

Southern and his particular brand of heroine first became widely known through *Candy* (1958). Written jointly with Mason Hoffenberg, *Candy* was seen by a number of critics and reviewers, such as Albert Goldman and William Styron, as a fresh, clever piece of satire, though not one with any particular literary distinction. Nevertheless, reviewers applauded its refreshing boldness. *Candy*, like *Flash and Filigree*, satirizes a number of institutions and types as the heroine makes her way through a bizarre series of picaresque adventures culminating in an outrageous scene of incest in a Tibetan temple. The targets of Southern's satire in *Candy* are wide ranging. He aims his barbs in some new directions—social do-gooders, college professors, the American brand of Zen—as well as in some old ones. The medical profession is a recurring favorite with Southern; here he pokes fun at doctors in general, psychiatrists and gynecologists in particular. In addition, Albert Goldman claims that, intentionally or not, *Candy* also satirizes a number of its critics and readers: "Taken not as a book but as an act in the current cultural situation, *Candy* is a perfect Put On of that liberal, intellectual audience of readers and critics who are forever trying to understand and explain everything, and who seem constitutionally incapable of enjoying fantasy or humor without indulging in the cant of 'redeeming social value.' "

The form of the novel is disjointed as Candy wends her way through a series of sexual encounters, ever willing to supply her body to the lustful lechers whom she excuses because she feels they "need" her. "Well, it's my own fault, darn it!" is her recurrent response. Rarely aggressive though never unwilling to submit, she is the principal target of Southern's satire. Candy Christian, an updated female Candide with a touch of DeSade's Justine and a bow to John Bunyan's hero, cheerfully insists on sacrificing herself to the masses of lecherous males who parade through the novel, most of whom represent the same deadly sin, lust. She is the American dream, the ideal girl-next-door, all witless innocence and virginal submission, all body and no brains.

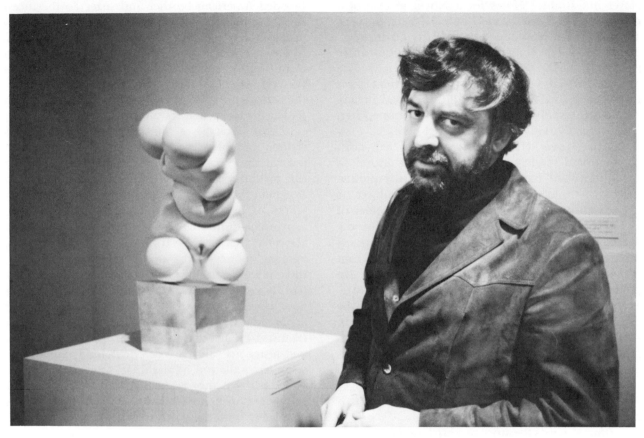

Terry Southern at the Museum of Modern Art.

Southern also parodies the pornographic style, dutifully presenting a sex act every few pages replete with lustful language and explicit detail. William Styron calls *Candy* "a droll little sugarplum of a tale and a spoof on pornography itself," but *Time* magazine says that *Candy*'s "most conspicuous intent is to be more outrageous in detail than what it is satirizing." *Candy*, at any rate, has the dubious distinction of being one of the few books in English banned by the French for indecency.

The style of *The Magic Christian* (1959) is even more disjointedly picaresque than *Candy* and, like *Flash and Filigree*, it has two interrelated plots. This time both plots revolve around the same character, Guy Grand, but one is set in the present, the other in the past. Southern opens each chapter with a brief scene occurring on a single afternoon and, for the most part, set in the drawing room of Guy's two doting, elderly aunts; the scene frequently shifts to the past to describe one of Guy's previous financial escapades. Guy Grand, a billionaire, is "one of the last of the big spenders." The hobby on which he spends roughly ten million a year is "making it hot" for people, sometimes literally as well as figuratively. He is a practical joker who, for example, buys

a building in downtown Chicago and in less than a day tears it down and erects a huge vat of boiling stockyards offal in which he floats 10,000 $100 bills free to anyone willing to jump in and collect them. In other escapades he buys a newspaper and devotes it to printing only letters to the editor—after having sufficiently provoked its readers by other antics; he pays a well-known dog trainer to enter a black panther in a dog show; he buys a movie theater and inserts suggestive scenes of his own manufacture into familiar family films; he designs a luxury car to cater to snob appeal but makes it too long to turn corners; he buys a cosmetics firm and promotes products which do the opposite of their advertised function; and on and on. In his final prank he purchases a luxury passenger liner, the *Magic Christian*, which literally falls to pieces under its wealthy. passengers. As with all of Guy's other schemes, "it cost him a pretty penny" to buy his way out of trouble afterward. The book describes a series of some fifteen such sketches designed to expose the snobbishness, silliness, and materialism of people in general.

Critical opinion on the novel is mixed. Many critics found *The Magic Christian* amusing and clever but slight: "Notes for a Novel instead of a novel," wrote Keith Waterhouse. Others, such as John Coleman, applauded the "thrifty distinction" of the style. The slapstick satire and the caricature portraits, like the style, received mixed reviews. *The Magic Christian* was published in the United States four years before *Candy*, though *Candy* had already been on the shelves for two years in Europe when *The Magic Christian* was published here.

Blue Movie (1970) is written in the most conventional style of all Southern's novels—straightforward narrative. It is more fully plotted than its three predecessors, but its subject is unconventional. It picks up the sexual themes of *Flash and Filigree* and *Candy* rather than the materialism of *The Magic Christian*. Perhaps because of its more conventional style, some felt that it crossed the line that divides a satire on pornography from pornography disguised as satire. However, R. R. Harris observes that although the novel "fails as a satire of the Hollywood motion picture industry . . . Southern's dialogues are often sharp and witty, and some of his characterizations are extremely funny." Though Southern is credited with having a keen eye for the most noxious of Hollywood types, in the end most critics found this novel disappointing and dull.

Blue Movie is the story of a brilliant Hollywood director, Boris, who believes that explicit sex in films can be beautiful, artistic, and sensitive if done by a dedicated and talented group of moviemakers and actors. He sets about getting the best in the business to make his movie, *The Faces of Love*, a series of short tales each examining a different sexual preference. The movie is to be largely financed by Liechtenstein, which will have exclusive exhibiting rights for ten years in order to attract the tourist trade. Citizens of Liechtenstein, naturally, will not be allowed to attend such a filthy decadent film themselves.

The American ingenue appears again in the person of Angela Sterling, a young Marilyn Monroe. She plays a Southern belle who gets back at her wealthy daddy, a plantation-owning bigot, by escaping to the Casbah and having sexual relations, both individually and en masse, with black Morrocans. Another of Boris's performers is the famous French actress Arabella, a lesbian who reenacts those events from her childhood which served as the catalysts for her lesbian leanings. A beautiful, aloof, aristocratic British actress for whom Arabella has a yen is cajoled into playing Arabella's delectable teenage cousin, while Boris's producer, Sid Krassman, plays her lecherous uncle. A red-

blooded American brother and sister do the incest sketch, reluctantly at first, but apparently developing a liking for it as the filming progresses. Meanwhile Boris must keep his American backers from finding out just what is afoot, not to mention the ever-watchful church, and, in a number of cases, the performers themselves. But it is the Vatican with which the moviemakers must do battle in the end.

This book gives Southern, who himself has written more than a dozen screenplays, a chance to portray some traditional movieland types. There is the brilliant and beloved director, an American Bergman or Fellini, whose films are invariably works of art and for whom performers will do anything—quite literally—simply for the honor of appearing in one of his films. There is also the gross, vulgar, money-mad, woman-chasing producer; there is the sex star who is worshipped by men the world over yet who is a sweet, shy, fearful girl-next-door at heart and who wants more than anything to achieve fame as an artist; there is the beautiful, liberated French actress; there is the cutesy brother and sister act; and so on. Movieland cliches and stereotypes abound. While the characters are indeed types, perhaps they are a little more human, more fully developed, more complex than most of the characters from Southern's earlier novels. But he is far more concerned with satire than with character development, and satire, after all, depends at least in part upon a type with which the reader is already familiar.

The sex, explicit and varied, is as regular as in an authentic pornographic movie, and several critics feel that it finally becomes tedious. "This is one of the longest peep shows ever made, and the dullest," wrote David Dempsey. One rather surprising break in this tedium comes with a death. Death and injury are certainly not new to Southern's novels; however, in *Flash and Filigree*, for example, death has merely comic value. Here, though, the death is a real and unpleasant event, both tragic and shocking. Nevertheless, the other characters waste little time in mourning. Instead, true to Hollywood tradition, they prepare to exploit it.

Red Dirt Marijuana and Other Tastes (1967) is a wide-ranging but uneven collection of short stories and essays, most of which were originally published in periodicals. In this book Southern is concerned with topics which remain largely undeveloped in his novels.

One of these topics, as the title of the book suggests, is drugs. Both the casual use of drugs and the world of the drug culture are examined in a number of stories throughout the book. One story describes four stoned Americans in Paris and seems more than anything to suggest that reading about a drug experience is likely to be a great bore. One of the funniest and liveliest stories in the book, however, is about drugs. It is the title story, wherein twelve-year-old Harold Stevens, the son of a white Texas farmer, is initiated into the curing and use of marijuana by his father's black farmhand, C. K. Crow. In this delightful tale, Southern proves he has an excellent ear for dialogue. Not so amusing is the tale that follows, "Razor Fight," in which C. K. presides at Harold's initiation into the adult world of violence. In the process C. K. and his brother, Big Nail Crow, slash each other to ribbons. A number of tales, in fact, focus with sensitivity on the world of the child, particularly as he encounters drugs, violence, and weapons for the first time and must learn to face a harsher reality than he has previously known.

The settings in the book range from Mexico and Texas to New York and Paris, and the focus in the stories and essays is wide ranging as well. Southern reveals an unexpected interest in music, particularly jazz, and a not-so-unexpected interest in young ladies. The book is uneven, yet it shows a range that Southern's novels do not. Some of the tales and essays are mere throwaways, while others are clever and thought-provoking.

In addition to his fiction, Southern has written a number of screenplays, many of which show clear evidence of his satiric hand even though they are often co-authored with the director, the original novelist, or others. Southern's wildly satiric style—that same black humor that we see in his fiction—marks *Dr. Strangelove or How I Learned to Stop Worrying and Love the Bomb* (1964) and *The Loved One* (1965).

Southern's early novels, though often slight and somewhat underdeveloped, were seen as the promising works of a young writer by many critics who found them fresh, clever, bold, and often very funny pieces of satire. His development, however, seems to have been arrested. His last and most conventional novel was also his least popular. It is a falling off from his previous work. He has, perhaps, overworked his favorite topic, sex, and has failed to go on and explore new fields, or even to explore that one as deeply as he might, preferring instead a superficial treatment of his subject and his well-established character types. Though he is a rather slight novelist and a frequent collaborator with others, nevertheless Southern's writing—both in prose and in films—shows a certain originality, a daring, a clever exploitation of types which, at its

best, can be quite witty, incisive, and very funny.
—*Jerry McAninch*

Books:

Flash and Filigree (London: Deutsch, 1958; New York: Coward-McCann, 1958);

Candy, as Maxwell Kenton, pseud. for Southern and Mason Hoffenberg (Paris: Olympia Press, 1958; New York: Putnam's, 1964; republished as *Lollipop*, Paris: Olympia Press, 1959);

The Magic Christian (London: Deutsch, 1959; New York: Random House, 1960);

The Journal of the Loved One: The Production Log of a Motion Picture (New York: Random House, 1965);

Red-Dirt Marijuana and Other Tastes (New York: New American Library, 1967; London: Cape, 1971);

Blue Movie (New York: World, 1970; London: Calder & Boyars, 1973).

Screenplays:

Dr. Strangelove or How I Learned to Stop Worrying and Love the Bomb, with Stanley Kubrick and Peter George, Columbia, 1964;

The Loved One, with Christopher Isherwood, MGM/Filmways, 1965;

The Cincinnati Kid, with Ring Lardner, Jr., MGM/Filmways, 1966;

Barbarella, with Roger Vadim, Brian Degas, Claude Brule, Jean-Claude Forest, Tudor Gates, Clement Biddle Wood, and Vittorio Bonicelli, Marianne, 1967;

Easy Rider, with Dennis Hopper and Peter Fonda, Columbia, 1968;

End of the Road, Allied Artists, 1969;

The Magic Christian, Commonwealth United/Grand Films, 1971.

Other:

William S. Burroughs, *Naked Lunch*, reviews by Southern and others (New York: Grove, 1962).

References:

D. M. Murray, "Candy Christian as a Pop-Art Daisy Miller," *Journal of Popular Culture*, 5 (1971): 340-348;

Edward T. Silva, "From *Candide* to *Candy*: Love's Labor Lost," *Journal of Popular Culture*, 8 (1974): 783-791.

JEAN STAFFORD has defined the role of the novelist as that of telling the truth: "the problem is how to tell the truth so persuasively and vividly that our readers are taken in and made to believe that the tale is true, that these events have happened and could happen again and do happen everywhere all the time." Firmly rooted within the forms of the traditional, realistic novel of Flaubert and James and the post-Joycean short story, as well as within the conventional expression of American experience and themes in a period of literary innovation and social change, Stafford's contribution to American letters is in the truth that she has told and in the sureness of the telling. Although neither a feminist nor the "exceptional and original feminine talent" she was labeled in a major review of her first novel, she is a woman writer who portrays real women in real situations. Within the basic setting of the period immediately preceding and following World War II, a period marked by cultural dissolution, mindless violence, and individual isolation, she presents the survival of inflexible, inexorable cultural modes of experience which restrict, confine, and destroy the individual. A Westerner by birth and upbringing, Stafford identifies her fiction with that of Twain and James both in their firm sense of place and in their portrayal of the dislocation of innocence. Her major themes are the common search for self-survival in an alien, and often hostile, culture and the inordinate price which the individual must pay for a small measure of freedom and knowledge. With brilliant irony she depicts a capitalistic society where the market is rigged, where the greatest price must be paid for the smallest measure by those who choose the cultural values of self-sacrifice and abnegation over the human ones of affirmation and knowledge of the self.

All the figures of Stafford's imagination—her major themes, character types, method, and style—are fully presented in her first novel, *Boston Adventure* (1944). The critical response to this novel was typical of that to all her novels. Although favorably received, in general, as being one of the best first novels of the decade, it was considered in some sense alien, not really a novel. Those critics who have addressed it since have had to come to terms with the novel's neglect and have attributed it to a failure in Stafford's vision, a too-narrow limiting of scope, an incompatibility with the popular imagination, or a lack of distance from the autobiographical material in the second part. Born in California, raised in Colorado, and educated at the University of Colorado (B.A., M.A., 1936) and Heidelberg University (1936-1937), Stafford, like her central character, Sonia Marburg, was an alien to Boston society. In 1940, the year she began *Boston Adventure*, she married the poet Robert Lowell, a member of one of the city's first families; they were divorced in 1948. She has since married Oliver Jensen—they were divorced in 1953—and A. J. Liebling, who died in 1963.

Boston Adventure is structured around Sonia's quest for selfhood and her initiation into Boston society. It is generally agreed that the novel is loose and disjointed, divided into two distinct parts: "Hotel Barstow," a resort patronized by elderly Bostonians in the poor fishing village of Chichester, and "Pickney Street," where Miss Pride, the aging defender of conservative values who serves as Sonia's mentor, lives across the Bay. These parts function either as the disparate terms of a single metaphor or as the opposing poles which pull the novel apart. As the central consciousness of the novel, Sonia must function as the synthesizing force and the bridge between these two worlds. Herself an outsider, she is the daughter of a beautiful but mad Russian chambermaid, Shura, and a tormented, guilt-ridden German shoemaker, Hermann. However, her "adventure" does not follow a traditional pattern. As a child in Chichester she dreams not of marriage but of adoption into the world of Miss Pride's beautiful niece, Hopewell Mather, who functions as Sonia's psychic ideal. Sonia's journey across the Bay is due to her intelligence, hard work, and Miss Pride's snobbery. The males in the novel whom Sonia loves (her father, her brother Ivan, Nathan Kadish, the iconoclastic student, and Philip McAllister, the society doctor) are peripheral to Sonia's quest. Cripples all, they turn to her for nurturing and sustenance, but she views them only in terms of the conflict which dominates the novel, the struggle between Shura and Miss Pride for Sonia's soul. Each woman demands that Sonia sacrifice her youth and her identity and devote her life to total submission and service. Thus, although obsessed by her love for Ivan, Sonia loves him only as part of her duty to her mother.

In a structurally brilliant turn, Sonia sacrifices her sexuality and her innermost being, symbolized in her vision of the "red room" and identified by Sonia with her mother's soulless beauty and madness, to Miss Pride's sterile, rigid cultural asceticism. Hope Mather had sacrificed her social identity and her life through an affirmation of her vital sexuality and exotic beauty in a love affair with Harry Morgan. Trapped by her pregnancy in a loveless marriage with Philip, she remains true to her own nature, even in the mode of her death, a riding accident. Sonia,

Jean Stafford.

who is terrified of her vision of her own nature and repelled by Hope's sexuality, relinquishes her quest and retreats to the security of Miss Pride's money. She agrees to serve Miss Pride for life in the conventional role of secretary-companion in exchange for the permanent incarceration of her mother in a private hospital. At the end of the novel Sonia is integrated into Boston society, but with full knowledge of its sterility and arid decadence. Trapped by Miss Pride's golden eyes, she has achieved an understanding of her predicament; she knows that there is no escape, neither through madness like her mother's nor through death like Hope's.

In Stafford's second novel, *The Mountain Lion* (1947), she presents an alternative to Sonia's choice in Molly Fawcett. Much of Stafford's own childhood experience is incorporated into the novel through the dual California and Colorado settings and through the character of Molly, a lonely child who spends her time reading and writing poems and stories which nobody understands. The daughter of a writer of Western stories, Stafford began writing at the age of six. One of Molly's poems was actually composed by Stafford as a child. Her narrative method, although more consciously symbolic, is that of the earlier novel: a realistic presentation, in Ihab Hassan's words, of an "ironic vision of the external world of manners and the internal world of psychological process." The novel has received little critical attention.

The Mountain Lion is also structured around a psychic quest and a cultural initiation through the presentation of a dual society. In this novel, however, the two cultures are fully integrated within the characters' experience because they are represented by Molly's and her brother Ralph's two grandfathers: Grandfather Bonney, a conventional, middle-class manufacturer of buttons who knew President Cleveland and was an avid admirer of Tennyson, and Grandfather Kenyon, a crude, wealthy, almost illiterate owner of four cattle ranches and friend of Jesse James. Molly and Ralph, sickly and ugly children, are alienated from both cultures through their staunchly defended innocence and their love and devotion to each other. Although using a contrapuntal movement through a dual initiation, Stafford does not present either child as the psychic complement to the other; rather, she uses Ralph's conventional initiation as a foil for Molly's estrangement. Only Ralph can accept Uncle Claude as the mentor who initiates him into the world of Grandfather Kenyon and, in doing so, prepares him for life in Grandfather Bonney's world. Ralph is perfectly happy to leave Colorado at the end of their year's visit and to matriculate at an Eastern college, if he can take as a trophy the body of the mountain lion, Goldilocks, the embodiment of freedom, beauty, and virility, as the symbol of his achievement.

For Molly there is no possibility of psychic or cultural integration. Her only mentor at the ranch, Winifred, betrays her by growing into a fresher version of her older sisters, Leah and Rachel. Repelled by her sisters' continual primping and obsession with attracting young men, and unable to accept her own sexuality or the brutal fecundity of ranch life, she can only survive by withdrawing further into the extremely limited world of her imagination, peopled by parts of bodies posing as men, and populated by her two grandfathers, the only ones who are forgiveable because they are both dead. Burdened by the weight of Molly's love and unable to carry her beyond childhood, Ralph destroys his sister—first when he asks her to tell him all the dirty words she knows, and finally when he, mistaking her for the mountain lion, shoots and kills her. Molly achieves no understanding of the social and natural forces which destroy her and exercises no choice. Blinded in her refusal to sacrifice any part of her inner self, even for Ralph, she can only retain her innocence and psychic identity through death.

In Stafford's third novel, *The Catherine Wheel* (1952), she presents a character who chooses to accept all that Molly rejects and is also rewarded by death. Her method in this novel is much closer to the romance of Hawthorne than to the contemporary novel. In the first two novels she uses a conventional structure in which significant dramatic action occurs in the foreground and is the product of common social and mythical patterns. In *The Catherine Wheel* she uses a closed symbol system and concentrates on the consequences of the act rather than the act itself. This difference in method may partially account for the general critical neglect of this novel which has, if anything, exceeded that of the other two, although it is the most brilliant in concept and the finest in execution.

Katherine Congreve, the central character of *The Catherine Wheel,* is the most fully developed of all Stafford's characters who have made the conscious decision to sacrifice their psychic identity and freedom to a cultural role and have lived with the consequences of this decision. She can become the perfect daughter, cousin, mistress, and friend because she has committed spiritual self-immolation twenty years before the action of the novel begins. By stopping time on her seventeenth birthday when she sees, by the light of a catherine wheel, that John Shipley, whom she loves, loves her cousin Maeve, she refuses to taste the knowledge of failure and defeat. Living in a state of spiritual death, symbolized by her white hair, she creates a life of static perfection for John and Maeve's children and her friends, The Ancients, in the perpetual summer of Congreve House.

Totally absorbed in her love for the middle-aged, bored dabbler which John has become, she betrays the deep, pure love of his son, the twelve-year-old Andrew. Not only does she fail to see the boy's distress and despair at the loss of his only friend, Victor Smithwick, to his older brother Charles, she also projects her guilt onto the child. Having sacrificed her own spirit by denying its reality, she violates the boy's spirit: she misinterprets his fear that she has heard his inner-voice which cries for Charles's death as evidence that the boy knows of her love for his father. Even in death, when, engulfed in flames while trying to save Charles's life, she becomes a living catherine wheel, she interprets his expression of love as a statement of her guilt. Stafford clearly condemns Katherine's sacrifice through her portrayal of her self-immolation. When she asks the boy to destroy her secret diary, the only remnant of her inner self which she could not force into her given role, he obeys, and in doing so, not only destroys the sacred symbol of the martyrdom of St. Catherine of Alexandria, the patron saint of knowledge, but also sets into motion the catherine wheel of guilt which will bind him as she had bound his father and herself.

Stafford's first published short story, "The Darkening Moon," appeared in the same year as *Boston Adventure*. Over the next thirty years she published regularly in many leading periodicals, including the *New Yorker, Harper's Bazaar,* and the *Sewanee Review.* Her stories are frequently anthologized, and in 1955 she received the O. Henry Prize. In 1970 she was awarded a Pulitzer Prize for her *Collected Short Stories.* She has also published a children's book, *Elephi, the Cat With a High I.Q.* (1962), and a nonfictional study of Lee Harvey Oswald's mother, *A Mother in History* (1966). She regularly reviews books and publishes other short pieces of nonfiction.

Stafford works within the traditional forms of Chekhov and James in her short fiction. Some critics believe that this form is more compatible to her than is that of the novel. In each story she creates a moment of experience, through the use of realistic settings, characters, and dialogue, so as to present, often through the device of dramatic irony, the sudden illumination or understanding, the symbolic crisis, or the unresolved glimpse into the heart of the situation. She relies heavily upon the use of the symbolic object and often uses it to reflect changes and development within the characters. In her short stories she has introduced no new character types nor themes, although she has deepened and enriched those of the novels.

Stafford's major literary contribution has been as an interpreter of human experience within a conventional social system in the period immediately preceding and following World War II, and through the conventions, modes, and forms of the realistic tradition. Her reputation rests solely upon the stylistic brilliance and the psychological sureness of her short fiction. Because of general critical neglect of her work, particularly of the novels, her influence can not yet be measured.

—*Jeanette Mann*

Books:

Boston Adventure (New York: Harcourt, Brace, 1944; London: Faber, 1946);

The Mountain Lion (New York: Harcourt, Brace, 1947; London: Faber, 1948);

The Catherine Wheel (New York: Harcourt, Brace, 1952; London: Eyre & Spottiswoode, 1952);

Children Are Bored on Sunday (New York: Harcourt, Brace, 1953; London: Gollancz, 1954);

The Interior Castle (New York: Harcourt, Brace, 1953);

Elephi, the Cat With a High I.Q. (New York: Farrar, Straus, 1962);

Bad Characters (New York: Farrar, Straus, 1964; London: Chatto & Windus, 1965);

A Mother in History (New York: Farrar, Straus & Giroux, 1966; London: Chatto & Windus, 1966);

Collected Stories (New York: Farrar, Straus & Giroux, 1969; London: Chatto & Windus, 1970).

Periodical Publication:

"The Psychological Novel," *Kenyon Review,* 10 (spring 1948): 224.

References:

Stuart L. Burns, "Counterpoint in Jean Stafford's *The Mountain Lion*," *Critique,* 9, 2 (1969): 20-32;

Richard Condon, "Stafford's *The Interior Castle*," *Explicator,* 15 (October 1956): 6;

Ihab H. Hassan, "Jean Stafford: The Expense of Style and the Scope of Sensibility," *Western Review,* 19 (spring 1955): 185-203;

Jeanette W. Mann, "Toward New Archetypal Forms: *Boston Adventure*," *Studies in the Novel,* 8 (fall 1976): 291-303;

Mann, "Toward New Archetypal Forms: Jean Stafford's *The Catherine Wheel*," *Critique,* 17, 2 (December 1975): 77-92;

Olga W. Vickery, "Jean Stafford and the Ironic Vision," *South Atlantic Quarterly,* 61, (autumn 1962): 484-491;

Vickery, "The Novels of Jean Stafford," *Critique,* 5, 1 (spring-summer 1962): 14-26.

William Styron

Keen Butterworth
University of South Carolina

BIRTH: Newport News, Virginia, 11 June 1925.

EDUCATION: Christchurch Preparatory School; Davidson College, 1942-1943; A.B., Duke University, 1947; New School for Social Research, 1947.

MARRIAGE: 4 May 1953 to Rose Burgunder; children: Susanna, Paola, Thomas, and Alexandra.

AWARDS: American Academy of Arts and Letters Prix de Rome for *Lie Down in Darkness*, 1952; Pulitzer Prize for *The Confessions of Nat Turner*, 1968; Howells Medal of American Academy of Arts and Letters, 1970.

MAJOR WORKS: *Lie Down in Darkness* (Indianapolis: Bobbs-Merrill, 1951; London: Hamish Hamilton, 1952); *The Long March* (New York: Random House, 1956; originally published in *Discovery*, No. 1, New York: Pocket Books, 1953; London: Hamish Hamilton, 1961); *Set This House on Fire* (New York: Random House, 1960; London: Hamish Hamilton, 1961); *The Confessions of Nat Turner* (New York: Random House, 1967; London: Cape, 1968); *In the Clap Shack* (New York: Random House, 1973).

The critics received *Lie Down in Darkness* (1951) as an auspicious first novel, perhaps the best to appear since World War II. Its style, if reminiscent of Faulkner, was distinctly the author's own; its psychological insights, accurate; and its moral vision, mature. It was, in fact, an astonishingly good novel for an author only twenty-six at the time of its publication. Styron was immediately placed in the top rank of writers of his generation; he was awarded the Prix de Rome; and his subsequent work was awaited anxiously by critics and readers alike. The wait was a long one. Between 1951 and the appearance of his second novel in 1960, Styron's only published fiction was the novella, *The Long March* (1953), and an excerpted episode from his work-in-progress. When *Set This House on Fire* finally appeared, it was not well received, primarily because the story seemed to sprawl out of control, with wildly allegorical episodes obviously satirical in intent. It was not the kind of book *Lie Down in Darkness* had led one to expect. However, the poetic power of description and the dramatic power of narration and characterization were evident, more refined, and the story was far less derivative than the first novel. Some felt

that perhaps this was the book Styron needed to get out of his system before going on to his best work. Again the public waited—seven years this time, filled with a trickle of essays, reviews, and excerpts from work-in-progress—for the appearance of the next novel, *The Confessions of Nat Turner*. When it was published in 1967, the critics generally agreed that this one had been worth the long wait. Styron had found his subject—a subject his style and moral vision were perfectly suited for. The novel received a great deal of publicity and favorable criticism, and Styron was awarded the Pulitzer Prize in 1968. Since *Nat Turner*, Styron has published "Marriott, the Marine," an excerpt from "The Way of the Warrior," a novel which he has since put aside; a play, *In the Clap Shack* (1973); and "The Seduction of Leslie," an excerpt from another work-in-progress, which is projected for publication in the near future.

Styron's production of novels has been slow, particularly compared to most of his contemporaries. He began writing *Lie Down in Darkness* in 1947, and he has produced only three full-length novels in thirty years, this in the face of a tendency among American critics to measure an artist not only by the quality of his work but by the quantity as well. It is significant that Styron has resisted the pressure to produce his fiction more rapidly, for it is improbable that he could turn out the high quality work that he has at a faster rate. He has stated in interviews that writing is an agonizing process for him, that he must wrestle with every word, and that he cannot go on to the next paragraph until he has perfected the present one. In the four or five hours he devotes to writing each day, he usually produces only two legal-sized pages of holograph manuscript. At times he has had to halt work on a novel for considerable periods to resolve technical problems before continuing his composition. Styron has thus limited his production, but his labors are evident in the highly polished prose of all his work.

This polish, as well as power, in Styron's writing has been recognized since the publication of *Lie Down in Darkness*, and Styron has generally been accorded a place among the most accomplished stylists of contemporary American letters. However, there are other aspects of Styron's writing which have not been so widely agreed upon. One of these has to do with his "Southern-ness." The similarities

Jill Krementz

between *Lie Down in Darkness* and Faulkner's fiction, particularly *The Sound and the Fury* and *As I Lay Dying*, caused many to see Styron as Faulkner's literary heir. Malcolm Cowley even suggested that in some ways Styron had improved on Faulkner's handling of several motifs. And there is much in the novel—its setting, its characters, its themes—to indicate that Styron was consciously working in the tradition of Faulkner, Wolfe, and Warren. But, given Styron's Southern background, this was to be expected. Styron's father, William Clark Styron, was a North Carolinian, a marine engineer, whose career had taken him to Newport News, Virginia. Styron grew up there on the banks of the James, and when his mother (Pauline Margaret Abraham Styron) died in 1938, Styron's father sent him off to Christchurch, an Episcopal preparatory school for boys on the south bank of the Rappahannock. The school was not as elite as several other of the Virginia prep schools, but it was respectable, and it carried on the traditions of the Tidewater gentry. Styron also attended two prominent Southern colleges: he spent one year at Davidson before transferring to Duke in 1943. Only after his graduation from Duke in 1947 did Styron leave the South. Although he has chosen to live in the North since then (New York City, Martha's Vineyard, Roxbury, Connecticut), his formative years were definitely Southern years, and they are reflected in his fiction. The scenes and characters of *Lie Down in Darkness* are largely Southern, *Nat Turner* is entirely Southern, and even though the major action of *Set This House on Fire* takes place in Italy, the two major characters are Southern, and they meet in Charleston, South Carolina, to reconstruct their story. (Although both *The Long March* and *In the Clap Shack* are set in the South they are about the military and so are not Southern in the sense of the three major novels.) Despite his Southern characters and settings, Styron stated in an interview early in his career that he did not consider himself a writer of the Southern school. Of course he had been influenced by Faulkner, Warren, and Katherine Anne Porter, but so had nearly every other American writer of his generation. And he has pointed out other influences which he considers as important as the Southern ones: Fitzgerald and Dos Passos in America; Conrad and Joyce in Britain; Flaubert, Dostoevsky and Camus on the continent. (These of course are the modern influences. Among the traditional ones he has indicated are the Bible, Shakespeare, Marlowe, Donne, Browne, and Blake.) These influences were cosmopolitan, not sectional. However, Styron is no cosmopolitan writer; he is a national one and wants to be thought of as such. There are good reasons why he and other Southerners, Walker Percy, for instance, wish to avoid the tag "Southern writer." First is the fact that the Southern Renaissance, if not entirely over, is far into its last phase. As Shelby Foote has put it, Faulkner stifled it with his sheer excellence. Another reason is that American life, along with its milk, has become irrevocably homogenized. Consequently, sectional literature, like that of the nineteenth century and the first half of this century, is no longer possible. Attempts to perpetuate it as such are doomed to degenerate into

nostalgia. Styron is obviously aware of this. But it has not been necessary for him to avoid sectionalism consciously. He merely had to observe and describe accurately the life he saw about him. *Lie Down in Darkness*, for all its seeming Southern-ness, could have been set in Cincinnati, Ohio, nearly as well as in Port Warwick, Virginia. The American expatriates of *Set This House on Fire* are in the tradition of Hemingway and Fitzgerald, not Faulkner or Wolfe or Warren. *Nat Turner* is Southern only because Styron chose to meditate upon a historical event which he felt significant to the country as a whole, and particularly relevant to the national racial tensions of the 1960s. It is also about the modern world, in the sense that any historical novel is about the age in which it is written rather than the age in which it is set. *The Long March, In the Clap Shack,* and the aborted novel, "The Way of the Warrior," are about the American military establishment because Styron's generation, having been forced into the ranks in mass, was more profoundly influenced by the military experience than any other generation in American history. It was a national experience, unlike that of the Civil War, which was truly sectional. In fact, World War II was the force that effectively ended sectionalism in America by creating a common national experience and hastening the process of homogenization which had been slowly at work since the founding of the country.

Another aspect of Styron's fiction that sets him apart from his Southern predecessors is his attitude towards community. Nowhere in his work does he depict a strong, vital community, as there is in Faulkner, Wolfe, Warren, or Welty. Port Warwick society in *Lie Down in Darkness* is solipsistic, vain, and hedonistic. The wanderers of *Set This House on Fire* exist outside the community, and the few glimpses we get of society indicate that it is greedy, hedonistic, and in a state of chaotic flux. Of course, the military establishment of *The Long March, In the Clap Shack,* and "Marriott, the Marine" is highly structured, but its rigid strength has been achieved at the expense of human values; thus it is destructive to life, both in its rigidity and purpose. Even the early nineteenth-century society of Tidewater Virginia depicted in *Nat Turner* is incoherent and dehumanized. It has been enervated and degraded by the conflict between the values of the slave system which it defends through economic necessity and the traditional Christian values it pretends to embrace. Even though there are hints in Styron's fiction that society may have been more cogent and vital at times in the past, he does not emphasize the fact. The juxtaposition of a troubled present to a tranquil past as an artistic strategy does not interest him, for it seems Styron disbelieves man can recover the stability of a more slowly moving world. And even though Styron has been outspoken on political and moral issues in his essays and public statements, he does not allow his fiction to concern itself with solutions to contemporary social and ethical problems. His concern is rather with what effect the modern world has on morally sensitive individuals who must live in it, and with investigating the possibilities those individuals have of maintaining their moral integrity and thus asserting their personal dignity in the midst of hypocrisy and chaos. Therefore Styron's protagonists are outsiders. They may live in the society and take from it what they need for subsistence, but they can never accept its values and become a part of it. They must, finally, rebel, for only through rebellion can they establish their moral integrity and dignity: to remain mute would imply assent. Moral resolution in Styron's novels, then, is not a question of the individual's reconciling himself with society, but involves rather his ability to resolve the internal moral conflicts caused by his isolation and rebellion. Salvation in Styron's novels is, indeed, an individual matter. Because of their corruption, hypocrisy and incredibility, the community and its institutions have forfeited their right to participate in individual salvation. One may regret this loss, particularly of the security that a coherent community offered, but we cannot deny the accuracy of Styron's vision. He strikes sharply through modern life and lays bare his cross sections for all to see.

Styron's apprenticeship as a writer began during his college years. Although he had made early ventures into fiction, they were the usual boyhood attempts at storytelling, and he did not consider writing as a career until he began studying with Professor William M. Blackburn at Duke University. Blackburn published two of Styron's stories in his anthology of Duke narrative and verse and urged him to continue his writing. Styron's education was interrupted by a stint in the Marine Corps toward the end of the war. However, he returned to Duke, and after his graduation in 1947, he went to New York to work as a reader for McGraw-Hill; but he disliked the job immensely and left the company after four months. In the same year he enrolled in Hiram Haydn's short story course at the New School for Social Research. Haydn saw that Styron was not comfortable with the constrictions of the short story form and suggested that he try writing a novel. As a consequence, Styron began work on *Lie Down in Darkness*. Even though he published two more short stories in *American Vanguard* (1948 and 1950), he must have found Haydn's advice good, for he has published no more stories since then: the short fiction that has appeared in magazines since 1950 was excerpted from his novels-in-progress. However, Styron did not find novel writing easy. He has said recently that he wasn't mature enough, or didn't know enough in 1947 to write the story. But his experiences over the next two or three years, during which he established a bohemian existence in Greenwich Village, provided him with what he needed, and he was able to finish the novel in 1950.

Lie Down in Darkness is an impressive book, a much better one than Styron's four early short stories—indicative of his talent but clearly apprentice work—would have led one to expect. Styron's greatest problem in his short stories had been with characterization, but the expansive form of the novel, which suited his abilities much better, allowed him to create a number of interesting, fully-developed characters to whom one can react imaginatively. His talent for poetic description, which had been evident in his apprentice work, was further developed and refined in the novel. And the story is replete with vividly presented and memorable scenes. It is an emotionally charged book: Styron has said that he wrote his heart into it, that he had been more completely absorbed in its creation than he ever was again with any of his later work. But it is a young man's book, and it has flaws which result from its youthful subjectivity: the imagery at times is too personal, and the metaphors sometimes will not carry the load Styron wished them to carry. In short, the physical matter was not shaped quite well enough to a metaphysical purpose. For instance, Styron opens the book with an interesting strategy to involve the reader directly in the story, to invite him inward through the frame: he does this by projecting a train trip from Richmond to Port Warwick, and he places the reader ("you") on the train; then he describes the passengers, the landscape of passage and the entry into the town. This device is quite personal, not only because Styron speaks directly to the reader, but also because it is apparently Styron himself who is taking the final leg of a trip from New York to Port Warwick to tell the story of the Loftis family. (This becomes apparent in the final passage of the book when a train leaves Port Warwick headed toward Richmond and the North—evidently Styron returning to New York after having told the story.) It is an effective device, and an appropriate one for a novel which requires a very subjective involvement in its action. Ultimately however, it must be considered extraneous because it does not integrate with the literal or metaphorical concerns of the story.

Another related problem is Styron's having Peyton Loftis commit suicide on the day the United States dropped the first atom bomb on Japan. A coincidence of this sort must mean something, but what is not apparent. The novel is certainly not concerned with politics; in fact, the characters, caught up in their own personal problems, are nearly oblivious to the war. About the only answer one can come up with is that some parallel is intended between the state of affairs in the Loftis family and the state of affairs of the world. But the novel does not develop that analogy. Thus the coincidence must be considered gratuitous, a misdirected attempt to give another dimension to the novel.

These are artistic flaws, certainly, but they are the kinds of flaws that reveal themselves only after one has finished the novel and contemplates it in retrospect. Also, they are the kinds of flaws one is willing to forgive in a young writer. Yet, in spite of its flaws, *Lie Down in Darkness* has worn well over the quarter-century since its publication. It has been republished in several paperback editions and is probably the most often taught of Styron's novels in college English courses.

Styron has said that after the idea for the book came to him, the most difficult technical problem he faced was the handling of time. His solution was to present the action within the frame of a single day, and then fill in the necessary background through a series of flashbacks. This method was certainly not new with Styron, but it is an effective strategy for his purposes in the novel. The day which frames the story is that of Peyton's funeral. As the narrative begins, Milton Loftis, the father; Dolly Bonner, his mistress; Ella Swan, the family servant; and the undertaker and his understrapper are waiting on a sultry August day at the Port Warwick train station for the arrival of Peyton's body. During the course of the novel the body arrives, is carried, despite a series of automotive mishaps, to the graveyard, and is buried. But this is only the aftermath; the climax of the story has already occurred, and most of the novel is occupied with explaining how the characters arrived at this dreadful state of affairs. One of the most impressive aspects of the book is how well Styron handles the shifts in time and makes the present situation a believable outcome of the history he presents through the flashbacks. He evokes a sense of inevitability, an essential element of the tragic mode. And, indeed, the novel is a tragedy, not in the classical or Elizabethan sense, perhaps, for every age

dictates its own terms for tragedy, but certainly in the tradition of *Sister Carrie, The Great Gatsby,* and *The Sound and the Fury.*

The central and most fully developed character of the novel is Milton Loftis, and essentially the tragedy is his, for although it is Peyton who comes to a tragic end when she flings herself, naked, from the window of a Harlem sweatshop, it is Milton who must mourn and acknowledge his large share of responsibility for her suicide. He has spoiled her and almost literally stifled her to death with love. Milton is a charming and handsome man, but a feckless one. Once an ambitious young lawyer with political aspirations, he has slowly let his law practice dissipate until he makes barely enough for his family's subsistence and depends on his wife's inheritance for the amenities. Helen, whose father and model of manhood had been an army officer, a man of strength and authority, reacts to Milton's ineffectuality early in their marriage and begins to withdraw herself from him. The affection she withdraws from Milton is transferred to Maudie, their retarded daughter. In reaction, Milton begins to lavish his love on their other child, the normal and lovely Peyton. Thus the family is polarized—and neither parent is equipped to deal with the problem. Helen becomes unreasonably jealous of Peyton, and her incipient emotional imbalance is aggravated into a psychotic rigidity. Milton, who still loves his wife, would like to reconcile their marriage but finds he cannot cope with Helen's frigid inaccessibility. Consequently, he turns more to Peyton and whiskey and finally initiates an affair with Dolly Bonner, the sensual and willing wife of an acquaintance. The situation is untenable yet irresolvable, and herein lies the tragedy of the book, for Peyton, who is not only beautiful but intelligent, and possesses a great potential for love and life, must grow up in and is finally destroyed by this fractured world. No matter how she tries to escape it—at college in the mountains of Virginia, in the homes of friends during the summers, or, finally, by rebelling against not only her family but the entire culture of her childhood by going to New York and marrying a Jewish artist—she cannot. She must finally admit both her hatred for her mother and incestuous love for her father and, what is more damaging to her psyche, that she suffers from the same weaknesses as they—her father's promiscuity and dependence on alcohol and her mother's insane jealousy and vindictiveness.

Lie Down in Darkness is a pessimistic novel, a deterministically pessimistic novel. Peyton, Helen, and Milton are trapped by circumstance and biology, and there is no salvation available to them through a society whose selfishness and hedonism Styron captures vividly at Peyton's wedding reception. This society cannot, does not even care to exert the moral pressure to forbid the relationship between Milton and Dolly. Nor is salvation available through religion, the ineffectuality of which is manifest in the Episcopal minister, Carey Carr, and the charlatanism of Daddy Faith. Nor is there salvation in love in a world that has forgotten love's proper forms. Styron is saying what tragedians in all times have said: even those in apparently the most favorable circumstances are not immune to the direst suffering at the hands of an inscrutable fate. If there is any indication of hope in the world of this novel, it lies with two characters: Peyton's Jewish husband, Harry Miller, who can love and knows its proper meaning even though he cannot save his already doomed Peyton; and the Loftis's black servant La Ruth—not Ella Swan, who is as much as the whites a victim of a false respectability and who is hoodwinked by the religious huckster Daddy Faith. La Ruth, Ella's simple daughter, loved Peyton simply for what she was. Though neither Harry nor La Ruth can save her, they can mourn her death honestly without self-pity.

Much has been made of Styron's indebtedness to Faulkner in *Lie Down in Darkness*, particularly to *The Sound and the Fury* and *As I Lay Dying*. Styron has admitted that before he wrote the novel he had gorged himself on Faulkner's works. But, in fact, Faulkner is not the only modern American author to whom Styron is indebted. The country club life of Port Warwick and the several parties are reminiscent of Fitzgerald, and there are similarities in the characterizations of Milton Loftis and Dick Diver of *Tender Is the Night*. Furthermore, Peyton's experiences in New York are certainly indebted to Dos Passos' *Manhattan Transfer*. But nearly all writers appropriate from others' works. It is not that they do, but what they do with it that is important. Perhaps Styron would have been well advised to have avoided close parallels with Faulkner. But he never follows Faulkner or his other sources slavishly. Even where the parallels are closest, as in the similarities between the final section of *Lie Down in Darkness* and the Dilsey section of *The Sound and the Fury*, Styron has put the material to his own use—the differences in his treatment are more significant than the similarities. And if Styron is to be accused of stealing from Faulkner, it should be pointed out that Faulkner seems to have stolen from Styron also: Linda Snopes's journey to New York and her marriage to a Jew who becomes involved in the

Spanish Civil War certainly owe something to Peyton's experiences.

In 1950, shortly after *Lie Down in Darkness* had been accepted for publication by Bobbs-Merrill, Styron was recalled to active service by the Marine Corps because of the United States' involvement in Korea. It was a traumatic experience for him, he has said, and for those others like him who had remained in the inactive reserve after World War II. They had believed their ordeals in Europe and the Pacific were to end war for a long time to come. They had fallen back into the comparatively careless routines of civilian life; many had families and businesses; but suddenly here they were again back in uniform, torn from their families, their businesses disrupted. Styron had neither wife nor business, but he did have a craft and he resented bitterly finding himself again at Camp Lejeune, North Carolina, reft of his artist's life in Greenwich Village, away from the literary circles of New York, where he had hoped to reap the benefits of a hard-earned fame when his novel came out the next year. There he was, instead, making a forced march through the fierce summer heat of coastal Carolina. When he was released from the Marines the following year, he decided to write about that experience, to capture the bitterness and frustration that he and his fellow reservists had felt. The result was *The Long March*, published in 1953.

Styron has said that of all his work this novella was perhaps the easiest for him to write, that once he got started it seemed almost to write itself. He wrote the entire story in about six weeks in Paris in the summer of 1952. His facility is explained largely by the fact that *The Long March* is really an extended short story rather than a novel. It is concerned with a single event, and the history of the characters is not particularly important to understanding their behavior during the course of the story. That is not to say that it is merely an expose of military life or simply an effort on Styron's part to purge himself of his bitterness. Nor does the story lack complexity. Styron has transmuted his experience and given it a larger significance: the story becomes a metaphor for the human condition itself, and its complexity derives from symbolic interaction rather than from psychological development. In fact, the story has a classical neatness and efficiency, for its form and execution owe a large debt to Sophoclean drama.

There are three major characters: Lieutenant Culver, from whose point of view most of the action is seen; Captain Mannix, a Jew from Brooklyn, who is the protagonist of the story; and Colonel Templeton, the battalion commander, a regular officer who believes in putting his troops through hell to prepare them for combat. As the novel begins, the bodies of eight dead marines lie strewn about the pine woods. Two mortar shells have misfired during an exercise and fallen among the troops. Culver, who has not witnessed the incident but arrives on the scene to observe the aftermath, stumbles away from the corpses to retch in the leaves nearby. Thus the tone of the novel is set. Shortly after, Colonel Templeton orders a forced march for his battalion—thirty-six miles back to base. The march would be ordeal enough for seasoned troops, but these are reserves, still poorly conditioned, and even though the march is to begin at night, it will extend through the torturous heat of the following day. There is the usual bitching among the troops, but most, like Culver, accept the inevitability of the march and reconcile themselves to the protracted suffering of their impending ordeal. Mannix, however, having already shown signs of incipient rebellion, decides that he will not accept lightly what he considers an inhuman abuse of authority. Since overt revolt would be senselessly futile, Mannix inverts his rebellion: he promises himself that he will complete the march at all costs and warns the company he commands that it, to a man, must complete the march also. For Mannix, the march becomes a contest with Templeton, in which he defies the colonel's authority by following his commands to the letter. It is a familiar form of rebellion, a childish defiance, but it is the only form available to Mannix in these circumstances. The situation is aggravated when Mannix finds a nail protruding into his boot, which during the course of the march punctures his foot and causes it to swell. Mannix hobbles on through the night and the next day, exhorting his men to do the same. And increasingly he makes his defiance known to Templeton. The story reaches its climax when Templeton, seeing Mannix's condition, orders him to board a truck. But Mannix will have none of it: he speaks his contempt for the colonel and disobeys his command by continuing the march. Templeton has no choice save to order him court-martialed. Though Mannix completes the thirty-six miles himself, he relents, at Culver's prompting, in his demands on his company and allows those who are exhausted or injured to ride into camp on trucks provided for that purpose.

The focus of the story is the conflict between Mannix, the individual, and Templeton, the figure of authority and representative of the system. Culver functions merely as a control figure, an observer who is not directly involved in the conflict, whose normality provides a point of reference, and whose sensitivity to what he witnesses informs and gives meaning to the action. Although Culver does not join Mannix's revolt, he sympathizes with it; yet he also senses the paradox and irony of Mannix's position. He can see what Mannix fails to see: that Templeton is indifferent to Mannix's rebellion so long as it does not directly challenge his own authority. Further, Culver realizes that Mannix's particular form of rebellion has turned him into a tyrant even more inflexible than Templeton himself. Only after his confrontation with Templeton does Mannix's humanity return. He is purged of his rage and is able to perceive his situation objectively once again.

The Long March suggests two important sources in myth. The first is implied by Mannix's swollen foot: he is Oedipus; Templeton, Laius. Of course, the parallels are only loose ones, and the implications of the Oedipal motif are more Freudian than classical. The other myth suggested is that of Sisyphus, particularly in Camus' redaction and interpretation. Again the parallels are loose, but the march is much like Sisyphus' task of rolling the stone uphill. Both are senseless, absurd, but inescapable. If a man accepts the task unquestioned, he is less than a man. Only by questioning, seeing the task for what it really is, and then, paradoxically, rebelling against his condition by accepting it, can man assert his dignity in the face of absurdity and become the moral creature he is capable of being. Both parallels imply that Mannix's rebellion is metaphorically a metaphysical revolt against a universe that makes no sense, which seems even inimical to man: eight men die for no reason; a battalion must walk thirty-six torturous miles while trucks that could carry them follow, empty, at the rear. And as Culver lies awake in the radio tent at night, he hears only static, the chaotic sounds of a universe without an understandable message, interrupted occasionally by the puny voices of men. The final scene of the book, however, is not a despairing one. Back at the BOQ, now confined to quarters, Mannix prepares to shower—a physical cleansing to signify the emotional and spiritual ones he has just undergone. As he limps toward the bath, he passes a black maid, who sees his suffering and sympathizes with him. "You poor man. . . . Do it hurt?" she says. Mannix stops, his towel falls from around his waist, and standing naked to the world he says, without self-pity, "Deed it does." The Southern black and the Jew—both know suffering and can understand one another. In American Indian myth an old woman says, "It is best we die forever, so that we can feel sorry for each other." In order to comprehend that old woman's meaning one must meet the reality of man's condition head on, must understand suffering and futility before he can rise above it and sympathize with his fellow creatures: It seems that Mannix and the black maid have.

When Styron was released from active duty in 1951, he returned to New York. There he helped found the *Paris Review*, which began publication in the spring of 1952. Also in 1952, having won the Prix de Rome, Styron left for Europe. In 1953 he married Rose Burgunder, and the next year they returned to America, to Roxbury, Connecticut, where Styron began work on *Set This House on Fire*. For the scenes of this novel he drew on his boyhood experiences at Christchurch School in Virginia, his bohemian life in Greenwich Village, and his sojourn in Europe, particularly on his brief visit in 1953 to Rapallo, Italy, where the American movie *Beat the Devil* was on location. Styron worked hard on the book for the next six years, but when it was published in 1960, it was not well received. And even, though a few have admired and defended it over the last eighteen years, it is still generally considered the least successful of his novels. Styron himself has indicated, however, that it is, perhaps, his favorite. Although, as he has said, he put more of himself into *Lie Down in Darkness*, and even though *Nat Turner* is probably a more even and perfect work of art, he finds himself going back to *Set This House on Fire* again and again. In this novel he seems to have given his imagination freer reign than he had in *Lie Down in Darkness* or *The Long March*, or would in *Nat Turner*. An indication that Styron did not control the writing as closely as was his wont is the revision, or excision, which he performed after he had completed and turned the manuscript over to his publisher. A great deal of material was removed by Styron and his editor, Bob Loomis, and still the novel remains by far his longest. Perhaps it is an apparent looseness, a. tendency to wild flights of imagination, that has caused critics to overlook the very solid basic structure of the novel.

There are two other major differences between *Set This House on Fire* and the earlier work. The first concerns narration. Although there is a long interior monologue by Peyton in *Lie Down in Darkness* and *The Long March* uses Culver as a center of consciousness, this was Styron's first book to use the first-person narrator, an important development in his technique since all of his subsequent work has been in the first person also. Styron has said that he likes the method because of its immediacy. The second difference is in tone. Although there are elements of satire in his earlier

work, the dominant mode is that of tragedy. In *Set This House on Fire* satire prevails, and the mode is that of tragicomedy. This makes for a different kind of book; and possibly its very difference frustrated the expectations of critics and readers and accounted for its poor reception.

Peter Leverett, the narrator, tells the story by recounting conversations which took place between him and Cass Kinsolving at Cass's home in Charleston, South Carolina. There, over a period of several weeks, they reconstruct the events at Sambuco, where, it is learned, Cass has killed Mason Flagg. In the course of their conversation it is revealed that Peter has known Mason since boyhood, when they attended prep school together in Virginia. Mason is an intruder, a Northerner whose wealthy father has bought an old plantation on the York River near Gloucester. Mason's looks, money, and self-assurance attract Peter and they become friends, but Peter soon learns that Mason is a liar and a coward. Finally, Mason is dismissed from the school for seducing a half-witted thirteen-year-old girl in the chapel. After the war Peter encounters Mason again in New York, and the two spend a sybaritic week together. Here Peter learns a great deal more about Mason's compulsive lying and shallowness, even though he is still attracted by Mason's glib charm. Peter's final encounter with Mason is in Sambuco, where Mason has invited him for a visit. When Peter arrives, however, he finds an American movie company on location, many of the principals staying in Mason's rented palace. Peter enters this scene of frivolous and hedonistic chaos to renew their friendship, but within twenty-four hours Mason is dead, apparently by suicide; the movie company has abruptly departed; and Peter is left to clean up the mess.

Cass, in contrast to Peter's normality, is a guilt-ridden expatriate painter. A North Carolina country boy whose parents were killed when he was a child, he has been raised by a poor uncle near Wilmington. During the war he saw action with the Marines in the Pacific, an experience that triggers his mental breakdown. After psychiatric treatment by the Navy, Cass studies painting, marries a pretty, guileless Catholic girl, and moves to Paris to practice his art. But Cass's guilt, the source of which he does not yet recognize, drives him to incessant drinking, and he does little painting. Finally, he moves his family, which by now includes children, southward, ending in Sambuco, where he establishes residence. Here he meets Mason and, later, Peter. Mason takes advantage of Cass's alcoholism, uses him, and finally degrades him publicly. Cass, in his drunken

3

Lest from the above I be accused at the outset of sounding too portentous, I will say that these events were a murder
and a rape which ended, too, in death, along with a series of
other incidents not so violent yet grim and distressing. They
took place, or at least had their origins, at the Palazzo
d'Affitto ("⌃ curious group of Arab-Norman structures rendered
specially picturesque and evocative by the luxurious vegetation
by which they are framed. The garden-terrace commands a wonderful panorama.") and they involved more than a few of the
townspeople and at least three Americans. One of these Americans, Mason Flagg, is now dead. Another, Cass Kinsolving, is
alive and flourishing, and if this story has a hero it is he,
I suppose, who fits the part. It is certainly not myself,
whom the events in Sambuco touched only tangentially. I am
self-possessed enough not to despise myself, which is something.
Yet while I have a hunch that in some unforeseeable mettle= and =
spine-testing situation I would acquit myself as well as many
of the people I know, I have strong doubts as to the limits of
my endurance. ~~This alone, I suspect, is enough to disqualify
me from the hero role. Let us say that I am not of the heroic
mold -- a solid middle-class American of the twentieth century.
Gallant struggles are not for me. I observe and I record.~~

~~Although I am uncertain of myself, I am a member of that
communion of young men who like to say: "I wish I were not as
glib and sophisticated as I am." when in many ways, really, I'm
quite shaky. I have the feeling already, for instance, that this
story is going to be cumbersome, disjointed, and -- certainly in
an age of digests -- overlong. I ask you to stick with it: that is
my private. In another time I would not have to ask you that,~~

From setting copy for Set This House on Fire.

masochism, seems to enjoy this degradation, but when Mason rapes the Italian girl with whom Cass has fallen in love (and, Cass believes, fatally beats her too), Cass chases Mason down, smashes his head with a rock, and throws him from a precipice.

This is the sprawling and complex story Peter and Cass reconstruct. In some ways their collaboration is like that of Quentin Compson and Shreve McCannon in *Absalom, Absalom!*, but the similarity is only superficial, for Peter and Cass are piecing together things they know from their own past, not hypothesizing about someone else's. A more important parallel exists between Peter and Nick Carraway of *The Great Gatsby*. They are both observer-narrators (only peripherally involved in the action) through whom the two strands of their respective stories are tied together. They have similar backgrounds, and their moral sensibilities are basically the same. Styron has drawn on Fitzgerald in this way, it seems, to call our attention to the parallels between Jay Gatsby and Mason Flagg, not that they are alike—both represent rather what their creators saw as the prevailing American sensibility of their time. Thus it is their differences that are telling. Whereas Gatsby, for all his faults, is an idealist, a man of powerful imagination and will whom we can admire, Mason has no redeeming virtues. Unlike Gatsby he has not had to struggle for his wealth but has inherited it from his father; although he has a more worthy object of love than Daisy Buchanan in his wife Celia, he cannot love her, for he knows only self-love; and his imagination, although active, begets little more than self-glorifying, vicarious fantasy. Mason is a degraded Gatsby, because Styron sees the American dream of the post-World War II era as a degraded dream. He has ensured in other ways that the reader does not miss this point. For instance, Mason Flagg's surname itself associates him with American ideals. His connection with Hollywood (his father's money was made in the movie distribution business) associates him with that materialistic-fantasy aspect of modern American life. Furthermore, Mason's interest in the arts and his pose as a playwright are entirely superficial—in fact, Mason says he believes that art has no future. Even his interest in jazz is faddish. He is a racist. He is obsessed with sex—but sex for Mason exists outside the context of love—it is, he says, the new frontier, a thing to be pursued for itself. The list of Mason's faults could go further, but these are his major ones. The significant thing to note is that with this burden of symbolism, Mason is less than a real character: he is a villain. And this, too, is a part of Styron's strategy. When Mason is killed the reader is glad that he is dead. This is a necessary characteristic of tragicomedy.

Cass, the hero, on the other hand, is a very real character. He is a complicated bundle of faults and virtues. His greatest virtue is his sense of integrity: he is earnest in whatever he does, even his drinking and fornication. He is also a country boy, whereas Mason is an urbanite, and this seems to be one key to the difference in their values. Since Cass hates everything in American life that Mason stands for, particularly its self-indulgent and cosmetic affluence, he attempts to escape it by expatriating himself in Europe. But, of course, he cannot, since in the post-World War II world America is everywhere. It follows him—it brings him home to it, first in the form of the McCabes in Rome, and then, more emphatically, in Mason at Sambuco. But there is more to it than that. For Cass, America is not only external—it is internal as well: he carries America around in him, both the bad and the good of it. Cass is living off America when he accepts his pension checks; he is also living off the spoils of capitalism when he uses Poppy's (his wife's) earnings from her inheritance. He carries also the guilt of the racism of his youth, a guilt he attempts to expiate by helping the peasants at Tramonti. Styron thus develops this irony: in trying to escape America, Cass is trying to escape himself—through expatriatism, through alcohol and hallucination, and, finally, by trying to recapture a prelapsarian world with Francesca, the innocent and beautiful Italian girl Mason rapes. But Cass's integrity, engendered by his puritan, rural-American background, will not let him escape; therefore, he must finally come to terms with his guilt or be destroyed. By killing Mason, Cass takes the first step toward his salvation. Metaphorically, by destroying the symbol of all he hates in American life, he accepts the burden of guilt for it. This becomes apparent when Luigi, the Italian policeman, will not let Cass expiate his crime by confessing it publicly. More importantly, when Luigi reveals that it is not Mason but Saverio, the half-wit, who has killed Francesca, it is clear that Mason as a symbol of evil is merely a chimera—it is the human condition itself that is at fault, not Mason and his ilk. Cass learns another important lesson after killing Mason. As he lies on the ledge above the villa of Emilio Narduzzo (from West Englewood, New Jersey), watching the family in the intimacy of its backyard, he must realize that even behind this crass show of wealth, fellow humans live. Thus, what Cass accepts finally is humanity, his own as well as others'—the burden of an imperfect world. This does not mean, however, that he must accept it indiscriminately.

When he returns to America, he chooses to live in old Charleston, a city of tradition, one of the most beautiful in the world. He becomes a cartoonist, satirizing, we assume, from the vantage point of his hard-earned knowledge, those things which he finds repulsive and ludicrous in American life.

Two other literary allusions also seem important in *Set This House on Fire*. The first is to Hawthorne's *The Marble Faun*, another American novel set in Italy. Both have murders in which the victims are thrown from a precipice, and which draw from the archetypal image of God hurling Satan from Heaven. The similarity is unimportant; the difference in the punishments of the two murderers, however, is significant. Donatello, who lives in a stable and viable society, must expiate his crime publicly. Cass, on the other hand, lives in the modern existential world, the society of which is unfit to bear the burden of his guilt; thus Cass must bear it himself. The other allusion is to Roethke's "The Waking," the last stanza of which Styron uses as an epigraph to Part Two of the novel, and which is the modern equivalent to the passage from Donne that introduces the book and supplies its title. It applies to Cass, of course, who must, in this relativistic modern world, follow his instincts blindly toward salvation. Whether the force that leads one be named God, as in Donne's age, or given no name, as in Styron's and Roethke's, the journey and ordeal are the same.

After *Set This House on Fire*, Styron turned to a subject that had been on his mind since his studies with Hiram Haydn in the 1940s. In 1831, in Southampton County, Virginia, across the James River but not far from the place Styron was to be born nearly one hundred years later, Nat Turner led the most successful slave rebellion in United States history. However, the rebellion was aborted, and Turner was captured, tried, and executed. Although Turner's full confession, which included some important autobiography, was published in the same year, little was known about the man. Styron felt that this was promising material for fictional treatment, but in the 1950s he was not ready to tackle the subject and put it aside. The racial tensions of the 1960s, however, started Styron thinking about the rebellion again, and he decided to write Turner's story. The problem for Styron was deciding how the narration should be handled. He found a solution in *The Stranger*, which dealt with a condemned man meditating on his life and impending death: Camus had Meursault narrate his own story. It would be a bold strategy for a white man to attempt to enter the mind of a black, but Styron decided that this was the way

the story should be told. At first he thought the material would make at most a novella, and he wrote what is now part one of the book. The story was obviously incomplete and seemed to demand full novelistic treatment, but Styron did not know where to go from there. This time it was a movie rather than a book which came to his aid. He saw *Citizen Kane* and realized that he could use a similar technique. He would reconstruct Nat's past to account for the man who led the bloody insurrection and who met his death with equanimity. He would use the few facts that were known about Turner, and for the rest he would allow his imagination free reign to construct whatever seemed necessary to the task. He worked on the novel over the next several years, publishing excerpts and an essay, "This Quiet Dust," about his researches in Southampton County, as he worked toward completion.

The novel was published, with much fanfare, in 1967 and was favorably received by critics and the public. Many considered its appearance the literary event of the decade. Shortly thereafter, however, a reaction developed in the black intellectual community and to some extent among white liberals. In 1968 a collection of essay attacks on the novel was published under the title *William Styron's Nat Turner: Ten Black Writers Respond*. The charges against Styron were many. He was accused of falsifying details of Turner's life, ignoring known facts, misrepresenting the institution of slavery, and, ultimately, of misrepresenting Turner himself. Styron was condemned as a Southerner and racist and for the audacity of trying to write from a black man's (and a slave's, besides) point of view. In retrospect the reasons for these attacks are understandable, but in the charged atmosphere of the late 1960s it was difficult to cope with them. Styron, who was anything but a racist and whose intention was obviously to bridge the gap between the races by becoming, himself, a black man as he wrote the book, was disturbed and thrown off balance. He answered the attacks as best he could. He argued for his interpretation of the slave society, and he was supported by such noted historians as Eugene Genovese and C. Vann Woodward. He also argued for his use of the known facts of Turner's life, and in 1971 Seymour Gross and Eileen Bender published a well-researched article in *American Quarterly* which defended the factual accuracy of Styron's treatment. For several years criticism of the novel was polarized and sidetracked: the book was being considered as history rather than fiction, although it was evident that many of the blacks were also criticizing it as propaganda—or, rather, for its not being propa-

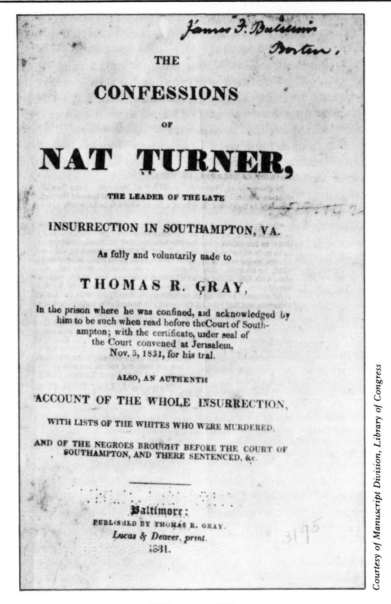

Title page, 1831.

ganda. They wanted Turner presented as a heroic figure—Styron had presented him as a human being. They wanted a militant slave population—Styron had presented them as docile, or at least subdued; and historical research has generally supported Styron's view. As he has pointed out, American slavery and the concentration camps of Hitler's Germany, although they were different in many ways, had much in common. Both successfully demoralized their victims by reducing them through dependency to a state equivalent to childhood. Thus there was little—and no successful—rebellion in either institution.

Since Styron's choosing a historical figure and event as the subject for his novel and since his calling it "a meditation on history" suggest that it is in some way a historical study, it is important that he get his facts right and have an understanding of the period he is writing about. He seems to have fulfilled that obligation—still *Nat Turner* is fiction, and it must finally be judged as such: those who have read the 1831 *Confessions* know that Styron's Nat is not Turner. Turner was a narrow fanatic; Nat has poetic and moral breadth. This is as it had to be. For Nat is not only the main character—his is the book's controlling vision. Thus Styron must give Nat the moral capacity and power to transcend the very particularities of his life and time.

At the center of Nat's psychological development is his relationship with his white owners.

Styron has pointed out, and this is supported by the surviving statements of slaves themselves, that those who were treated with the most indulgence were the very slaves who rebelled or ran away—a result, one would assume, of their seeing more clearly the very arbitrariness of their relationship to their owners. Nat is not only indulged by his first owners, the Turners, he is also taught to read, taught a trade, and promised freedom when he comes of age. In effect, he is given the knowledge and skills to grow out of this childish state of dependency which keeps the other slaves in psychological, as well as physical, bondage. Nat is a precocious child, and because his mother is a house servant of a liberal and benevolent master, his precocity is discovered early. The master, Samuel Turner, has his family teach Nat to read; in adolescence Nat is taught carpentry. Turner's idea is to prepare Nat for freedom. He is a well-intentioned master, but he is also a naive, idealistic one; and what he accomplishes in essence is placing Nat in racial limbo, for Nat's accomplishments and position on the plantation have separated him from his fellow blacks, yet he cannot enter the world of the whites except on their limited terms. But Nat accepts this ambivalent position in plantation society because his callowness allows him to believe that his promised emancipation will solve his problems. When the plantation fails and Turner puts Nat into the Reverend Epps's hands, Nat is abruptly awakened to the reality of the slave's true condition. He is worked at menial tasks until he is numb; and Epps, whom Turner has so egregiously misjudged, sells him, rather than free him as Turner had directed.

During his childhood, Nat, cut off from the other slaves and without a father, naturally adopts the Turners as substitute family and as role models. This also causes a number of psychological problems for him. He comes to scorn the field slaves for their squalid living and ignorance. As a consequence, he is never, even when he is forced among his fellow blacks, able to accept them as fellow creatures. Those few he does make friends with he attempts to reshape through training and education into suitable companions. More damaging to his development, he is cut off from sexual contact with women—from those of his own race by his scorn, and from the white women by the codes of the society. His masturbatory fantasies are filled with white women, not black ones. (The only sexual contact Styron allows Nat is a homosexual one with Willis, a boy Nat has groomed to meet his own standards of behavior.) Eventually this isolation from his own race and his adulation of the whites causes in Nat a traumatic sense of betrayal. His idealized concept of womanhood is shattered when he overhears its embodiment, Emmeline Turner, cursing and fornicating with her cousin in the bushes. When Turner surreptitiously sells Nat's friend Willis, Nat is abject in his disillusionment. The ultimate betrayal comes when Turner delivers Nat into the sordid clutches of Epps. Nat is so outraged that he swears never to think of Turner again.

Nat's life with the Turners is definitive: his Bible reading, his isolation, his celibacy, his betrayals, have turned him inward upon himself; and after Epps sells him, he realizes that the freedom he had expected is lost forever. These are the factors that eventually cause Nat to conceive of the rebellion. The vengeance of the Old Testament God becomes the vengeance Nat envisions himself wreaking on the white community that has caused his suffering. The more ascetic Nat becomes, the more powerful his vision and his desire to destroy the whites. And because he has gained the confidence of the slaves in the community through his preaching, he is able to put his plan into effect.

Styron's psychology is convincing. Given the circumstances of Nat's life, his insurrection was inevitable; if, however, that were all, Nat would be a mechanically developed character indeed. But Nat has depth. And that depth derives from the Turner family as well, for Nat has absorbed during his life with them their humanistic idealism, along with a concept of love, which he is able to realize. Though he tries to ignore these qualities in himself, tries to sublimate them to his vengeance, he never can. One way in which Styron manifests this theme is through the imagery. There is a preponderance of earthy imagery associated with the body and body functions: defecation, urination, the smells of sweat and secretion, fornication, the details of death. The effect of this imagery is to ground the book solidly in the physical world of human flesh, a world that Nat's dehumanizing idealism would like to escape. Nat cannot accept his body because he cannot accept the human condition itself. On the other hand, Nat's need to love finds an object in Margaret Whitehead. She, unlike Emmeline Turner, is a worthy object of his love. His relationship to her, however, is complex: he hates her for her whiteness but loves her for herself; yet her whiteness is symbolic of her purity, which he loves, and he hates her for the degradation of his sexual attraction to her. His attitude toward her is as ambivalent as post-Freudian psychology can make it. But ultimately her symbolism becomes very simple: she represents love.

Styron has said that the movement of the book is from Old Testament to New Testament. In these terms it is a movement from vengeance to love—from Yahweh to Christ. And though Margaret is not Christ, she is a sacrificial figure. She is the only person Nat kills. Through her he sins yet is paradoxically purged of sin. And through her he is finally redeemed. The terms of their relationship are solidly in the tradition of romantic love, which holds that the souls of lovers who have been separated in this life by insurmountable obstacles will be joined in a spiritual realm beyond this world. At the end of the book Nat believes he is going to join Margaret: he has not recovered God, but he has discovered Love.

On a metaphorical level, *Nat Turner* is as much about the condition of modern man as any other of Styron's novels. Analogically Nat's world is the modern world in its instability. Economic forces have disrupted a formerly stable society. And Nat's life has a universal quality—in childhood we feel restricted, enslaved, and we look forward to the freedom of adulthood; but that freedom never comes, for, like Nat, we are enslaved by other masters. We stand cowed before them—or we rebel. The rebellion is ultimately against the human condition itself. It may, through knowledge gained by suffering, reconcile us to our condition, as it does Mannix and Cass; or it may destroy us if it is too extreme, as it does Peyton and Nat. But there is a difference between Peyton's end and Nat's. Although Nat is not reconciled to this life—for he says he would do it all again—he is redeemed by love, and that is an important difference.

After *Nat Turner*, Styron began work on a novel to be entitled "The Way of the Warrior," about a professional Marine officer, a Virginian and VMI graduate, who maintains an interest in the liberal arts and wants to humanize the armed services through reform. However, the one excerpt that appeared in print, "Marriott, the Marine," does not indicate very clearly how the story would be developed. It is a first-person narrative, drawn apparently from Styron's experiences at Camp LeJeune in 1950. The material is autobiographical to such an extent that it is difficult to separate Styron from his fictional narrator. Marriott himself is handled obliquely in the excerpt, and we learn more about the narrator than we do of him. In this way its technique is similar to that of *Set This House on Fire*. Styron gave the novel up, he says, because the material ceased to move him. During the following year he worked on a play, *In the Clap Shack*, which was first presented on 15 December 1972 at the Yale Repertory Theatre in New Haven. Although several critics liked the play, Clive Barnes wrote an unfavorable review of the performance and seems to have killed any chances the play had of going to New York. As Styron has said, a play is a collaborative enterprise of playwright, director, and actors. Perhaps flaws in the original production caused the play's lack of success. (Styron has said that the lead was not cast properly, although he liked several of the other roles.) But it seems that the play itself must bear the final responsibility. The scene of the play is a urological ward of a hospital on a Marine base in the South. The year is 1943. The main character is a young Marine, Magruder, who has been confined to the "clap shack" by mistake. Because an acute case of trench mouth has caused a positive reading on his Wasserman test, he is believed to have a rampant case of syphilis. The error is finally discovered, but not before Magruder has suffered considerable anguish. When he learns that he is well, that really he has never been "sick," he rebels against the system and its representative—the perverted doctor who is responsible for his suffering—by speaking his anger. As a consequence, he is court-martialled, but he is willing to pay that price to have his say. Magruder is another of Styron's rebels. But Magruder's rebellion is not convincing, because there is too little preparation for it, and when it comes, it seems out of character. It appears that Styron's imagination needs room to work itself out: the compression of drama does not suit his talent. Even though the play has some fine comic moments, the comedy is undermined by its serious concerns: the racial conflict, the rigid institution, inhuman technology, perverted authority, and the pervasive "sickness" of society itself. In short, it is too busy with these various themes to succeed as drama. *In the Clap Shack* is more interesting as a microcosmic study of Styron's novelistic work than it is as a self-contained work of art.

For the past several years Styron has been working on a novel which he has tentatively entitled "Sophie's Choice." It is about a Polish Catholic girl living in New York City who was imprisoned in Auschwitz during the war. However, the one excerpt that has been published, "The Seduction of Leslie," does not concern her at all. It is about the narrator's attempted seduction of a svelte, rich Jewish girl. As in "Marriott, the Marine," the first-person narrator seems to be Styron himself. Another excerpt from the novel that he has read publicly is based directly on his experiences at McGraw-Hill in 1947. Styron has said in an interview that the novel will contain the young man who wrote *Lie Down in Darkness*. One of the reasons he has chosen to adopt an autobiographical approach in his fiction, he says, is to gain credibility. This is certainly an interesting strategy in an age when authors are busily inventing devices to announce their work as fiction or fantasy. Styron remains in the line of traditional storytellers: he wants to gain the reader's confidence, because he feels his stories are important enough, serious enough, to warrant and demand our belief in them.

Periodical Publications:

FICTION:
"The McCabes," *Paris Review*, 6 (autumn-winter 1959-1960): 12-28;

"Runaway," *Partisan Review*, 33 (fall 1966): 574-582;

"Virginia: 1831," *Paris Review*, 9 (winter 1966): 13-45,

"The Confessions of Nat Turner," *Harper's*, 235 (September 1967): 51-102;

"Novel's Climax: The Night of the Honed Axes," *Life*, 63 (13 October 1967): 54-60;

"Marriott, the Marine," *Esquire*, 76 (September 1971): 101-104, ff.;

"The Seduction of Leslie," *Esquire*, 86 (September 1976): 92-96, ff.

NONFICTION:
"Letter to an Editor," *Paris Review*, 1 (spring 1953): 9-13;

"The Prevalence of Wonders," *Nation*, 176 (2 May 1953): 370-371;

"The Paris Review," *Harper's Bazaar*, 87 (August 1953): 122, 173;

"What's Wrong with the American Novel?" *American Scholar*, 24 (autumn 1955): 464-503;

"If You Write for Television. . . ." *New Republic*, 140 (6 April 1959): 16;

"Mrs. Aadland's Little Girl, Beverly," *Esquire*, 56 (November 1961): 142, 189-191;

"The Death-in-Life of Benjamin Reid," *Esquire*, 57 (February 1962): 114, 141-145;

"As He Lay Dead, A Bitter Grief," *Life*, 53 (20 July 1962): 39-42;

"Aftermath of Benjamin Reid," *Esquire*, 58 (November 1962): 79, ff.;

"Two Writers Talk It Over," *Esquire*, 60 (July 1963): 57-59;

"This Quiet Dust," *Harper's*, 230 (April 1965): 135-146;

"Truth and Nat Turner: An Exchange—William Styron Replies," *Nation*, 206 (22 April 1968): 544-547;

"Oldest America," *McCall's*, 95 (July 1968): 94, 123;

"Symposium: Violence in Literature," *American Scholar*, 37 (summer 1968): 482-496;

"In the Jungle," *New York Review of Books*, 26 September 1968, pp. 11-13;

'My Generation," *Esquire*, 70 (October 1968): 123-124;

"On Creativity," *Playboy*, 15 (December 1968): 138;

"The Uses of History in Fiction," *Southern Literary Journal*, 1 (spring 1969): 57-90;

"Kuznetsov's Confession," *New York Times*, 14 September 1969, sec. 4, p. 13.

Other:

"Autumn," in *One and Twenty: Duke Narrative and Verse, 1924-1945*, ed. William Blackburn (Duke University Press, 1945), pp. 36-53;

"The Long Dark Road," in *One and Twenty*;

"A Moment in Trieste," in *American Vanguard*, ed. Don Wolfe (Ithaca, N.Y.: Cornell University Press, 1948), pp. 241-247;

"The Enormous Window," in *1950 American Vanguard*, ed. Charles I. Glicksberg (New York: School for Social Research, 1950), pp. 71-89;

Introduction to *Best Short Stories from "The Paris Review*," (New York: Dutton, 1959), pp. 9-16;

"Writers under Twenty-five," in *Under Twenty-five: Duke Narrative and Verse, 1945-1962*, ed. William Blackburn (Durham: Duke University Press, 1963), pp. 3-8.

References:

John W. Aldridge, *In Search of Heresy* (New York: McGraw-Hill, 1956);

Aldridge, *Time to Murder and Create: The Contemporary Novel in Crisis* (New York: McKay, 1966);

John Baker, "William Styron," in *Conversations With Writers II* (Detroit: Bruccoli Clark/Gale, 1978);

Jonathan Baumbach, *The Landscape of Nightmare: Studies in the Contemporary Novel* (New York: New York University Press, 1965);

Robert Canzoneri and Page Stegner, "An Interview with William Styron," *Per/Se*, 1 (summer 1966): 37-44;

John H. Clark, ed., *William Styron's Nat Turner: Ten Black Writers Respond* (Boston: Beacon, 1968);

Robert Gorham Davis, "The American Individualist Tradition: Bellow and Styron," in *The Creative Present: Notes on Contemporary Fiction*, ed. Nona Balakian and Charles Simmons (Garden City: Doubleday, 1963), pp. 111-114;

Harriet Doar, "Interview with William Styron," *Red Clay Reader*, 1 (1964): 26-30;

Sidney Finkelstein, "Cold War, Religious Revival, and Family Alienation: William Styron, J. D. Salinger, and Edward Albee," in his *Existentialism and Alienation in American Literature* (New York: International Publishers, 1965);

Ben Forkner and Gilbert Schricke, "An Interview with William Styron," *Southern Review*, 10 (autumn 1974): 923-934;

Robert H. Fossum, *William Styron: A Critical Essay* (Grand Rapids, Mich.: Eerdmans, 1968);

Melvin J. Friedman, *William Styron* (Bowling Green, Ohio: Bowling Green University Press, 1974);

Friedman and Irving Malin, eds., *William Styron's "The Confessions of Nat Turner"—A Critical Handbook* (Belmont, Cal.: Wadsworth, 1970);

David D. Galloway, *The Absurd Hero in American Fiction* (Austin: University of Texas Press, 1966);

Eugene D. Genovese, *In Red and Black—Marxian Explorations in Southern and Afro-American History* (New York: Pantheon, 1968);

Louise Y. Gossett, *Violence in Recent Southern Fiction* (Durham: Duke University Press, 1965);

Marvin Klotz, "The Triumph Over Time: Narrative Form in William Faulkner and William Styron," *Mississippi Quarterly*, 17 (winter 1963-1964): 9-20;

Wesley A. Kort, *Shriven Selves—Religious Problems in Recent American Fiction* (Philadelphia: Fortress Press, 1972);

Cooper R. Mackin, *William Styron* (Austin, Texas: Steck-Vaughn, 1969);

Peter Matthiessen and George Plimpton, "William Styron," *Paris Review*, 2 (spring 1954): 42-57;

Robert K. Morris and Irving Malin, eds., *The Achievement of William Styron* (Athens: University of Georgia Press, 1975);

Marvin Mudrick, *On Culture and Literature* (New York: Horizon Press, 1970);

Richard Pearce, *William Styron* (Minneapolis: University of Minnesota Press, 1971);

Marc L. Ratner, *William Styron* (New York: Twayne, 1972);

David L. Stevenson, "William Styron and the Fiction of the Fifties," in *Recent American Fiction: Some Critical Views*, ed. Joseph J. Waldmeir (Boston: Houghton Mifflin, 1963);

Gunnar Urang, "The Voices of Tragedy in the Novels of William Styron," in *Adversity and Grace: Studies in Recent American Literature*, ed. Nathan A. Scott (Chicago: University of Chicago Press, 1968), pp. 183-209;

James L. W. West, *William Styron: A Descriptive Bibliography* (Boston: G. K. Hall, 1977).

Manuscripts:

Duke University has correspondence, clippings, scrapbooks, drafts of many of Styron's writings, and miscellaneous items relating to his personal life and career as an author.

HARVEY SWADOS' collection of essays, *A Radical's America* (1962), has as its epigraph a sentence from Chekhov: "There ought to be, behind the door of every happy, contented man, someone standing with a hammer, continuously reminding him with a tap that there are unhappy people." Harvey Swados was continuously aware of the suffering and unhappiness in the world, and his two most important novels, *Standing Fast* (1970) and *Celebration* (1975), are about people who want to make a better world. These two books, like all his writing, are realistic, earnest, and ultimately optimistic.

Swados was born in Buffalo, New York, on 28 October 1920, the son of a physician. He once defined himself in four facets: Jew, socialist, novelist, and "middle-class man of the mid-century, born and brought up in a middle-sized American city." He graduated from the University of Michigan in 1940. Between 1942 and 1945 he served as a radio officer in the merchant marine. As a struggling young writer he worked on automobile assembly lines. As his writing became known, he was the recipient of a number of fellowships and grants and academic appointments. He taught at the State University of Iowa, Sarah Lawrence College, New York University, San Francisco State College, and Columbia University. At the time of his death, 11 December 1972, he taught at the University of Massachusetts.

Although Swados was born into and died a member of the middle class, his loyalty was to the working class; working-class lives were more in need of help. He once wrote of his dismay that "among the men on the assembly line there was a near unanimity of contempt for what they did and a shame at their inability to earn their livings in a better way." His middle-class friends, he wrote, "were frankly ignorant of the working lives of their fellow-Americans, and they were as eager for me to bring them the news as they had been to learn my reactions to the Australians, the Yugoslavs, or the Venezuelans back in the days when I had been a merchant seaman.''

Swados is seldom mentioned with the other Jewish-American novelists of mid-century. He does not have the dazzling style or intellectual depth of Bellow, nor the imaginative power of Malamud, nor even a trace of the humor of Roth. Swados' life and work are marked by courage, compassion, serious-ness, selflessness, and honesty. His commitment to political activism goes far beyond that of most writers. While he is dedicated to the task of the novelist, winning critical acclaim for his novels concerns him little; helping men to see each other as brothers is his greatest concern. Joe, the Vanishing American, the compassionate assembly-line worker of Swados' most important short story, tells a young man who will soon be leaving the factory to return to college that he must not forget what he has seen; he must remember after he has escaped "what it was like for the people who made the things you'll be buying . . . the sweat, exhaustion, harrying, feverish haste, and stupid boredom.''

In contemporary America, living with boredom is often a much more acute problem than putting bread on the table. Along with the problem of effecting sympathetic, congenial relations with the people who are a part of one's work life, day after day of mind-deadening work is a major cause of unhappiness. Swados believed that work does not have to be the most dismal part of life. He believed that socialism could humanize work in ways that would be impossible under capitalism. But the growth of socialism depends on gaining political power for those who are sympathetic. Swados believed unequivocally that it is right for a writer to be a political activist. And during the last year of his life, he was a speech writer for Democratic vice-presidential candidate Sargent Shriver.

Swados stated that "the main line" of his development as a writer dates from the series of interrelated stories about factory life published as *On the Line* (1957). It is from that point on that Swados concentrated on the social and economic forces shaping individual human development. His earlier novel, *Out Went the Candle* (1955), dealt with the rise and fall of a self-made businessman, Herman Felton, and the complexities of relations within a family and between generations. The story takes place during World War II and the decade following. It is told from the point of view of a young newspaperman. "So well is his story told," wrote P. F. Quinn, "So perceptively . . . has Swados imagined this man and devised means to place him fully before us, that we put the book down with something like a

sense of knowledge. In his simplicity and complexity Herman Felton comes through to us, not just as one more character in one more novel, but as a human being, admirable, pitiable, and above all, under-stood.'' On the other hand, Brendan Gill found the book "long, earnest, ambitious, intelligent, and, alas, not very appealing.''

In *The Will* (1963), Swados again dealt with the subject of the family. The focus here is on three brothers who have grown up to be very different men—a recluse, a convict, a bourgeois. The plot revolves around their claims to an inheritance. Hilton Kramer wrote that *The Will* was a novel "whose social meaning transcends the psychology of its individual characters." While characterization remains strong in this book, Swados made his plot move much more swiftly than he previously had done. R. V. Cassill, however, thought that all Swados did was to trot out the "machinery of Dumas and Scott" for "one more wheezing try."

False Coin (1959) is a novel about a special kind of work, the work of the artist. It is about Ben Warder's attempt to keep his work and that of others meaningful. Perhaps there is no other kind of work that provides as great an opportunity for a vital connection between the person and the objects the person makes than art. The corrupting forces within the American art world are the focus of *False Coin*. The continuing existence of the vital connection in the life of the artist depends on his being utterly incorruptible, on his not allowing anything to obtrude between his personality and vision and the forms which he feels compelled to shape. But Ben Warder sees how wealthy patrons tempt artists to betray that vital connection. In protest, Ben quits his job as a sound engineer at a retreat for artists and musicians. The reviewer for *Booklist* thought *False Coin* a "tough, realistic rendering of personalities, motivations, and background," typical of Swados' fiction. Other reviewers thought the plot contrived and Swados mistaken in treating his characters with his usual realism instead of venturing into satire.

Standing Fast (1970) is by far Swados' most important novel. It is a panoramic novel that focuses on the lives of a group of young socialists who come together in Buffalo in the late 1930s. While the focus for the most part remains on these people and follows them through their twenties and thirties and into middle age, the novel also deals with their parents and with a third generation, their children. During World War II and for eighteen years following it, the scene frequently shifts from Buffalo, to the South Pacific, to Israel, to California, to Alabama, to Long Island, to Washington, D.C., as the group's commitment to the capital-labor issue of the 1930s is swept over by the tide of history and new concerns are forced upon them.

Swados has great respect for almost all the characters in this large cast: the talented, irrepressible Norm and the stoical, dedicated Vera; enthusiastic, hard-working Sy and Bernice; the union leader Bill and his lawyer wife Margaret; the blacks, Big Boy and Hamilton Wright; and Joe Link, the all-American boy turned devout socialist. They all stand ready to commit their lives to the building of socialism. But between the 1930s and the 1960s far-reaching changes took place in American life. Depression and poverty gave way to a prosperity that unexpectedly continued well into the postwar years; America became the affluent society. Socialism as a scheme for redistributing wealth and ending poverty became irrelevant. But socialism signifies other goals as well—humanizing work, for one—and for a while Joe Link remains determined to help bring on the revolution. In an affluent America, his gallant commitment to the old ideals almost leads to his ruin and to that of his family. Norm, also blessed with great leadership ability, realizes immediately after the war that the Marxist model is no longer applicable. But even if it were, Norm has learned that "you can't persuade people to do what you think they ought to simply because it's moral or logical.... People are going to react from a whole series of motives—most of which have no relation to logic." Norm closes his Marx and becomes one of the breed of journalists Marx despised, a liberal reformist. Similarly, preserving the Jewish remnant and leading the Negro civil rights movement for Sy and for Ham Wright assume higher priorities than socialism.

Standing Fast is in the tradition of the novels of the great English writer of a century ago, George Eliot. Eliot and Swados both see the broad picture. They place the lives of their characters in the context of their times and show the impact made by powerful social forces. And like Eliot, Swados follows the lives of his people with sympathetic understanding. Swados, however, does suffer lapses. *Standing Fast* is weakest in those sections in which characters such as Fred Vogel/Byrd, the socialist professor who has become a TV quiz-master, and Harry Sturm, the party functionary who has used his devious ingenuity to become a millionaire, are revealed as simply cowardly and self-seeking. Swados does not like these men who have been too ready to abandon their prewar ideals. Swados' own idealism intrudes too blatantly, making it difficult for some reviewers to like the book. "Too many characterizations are

leftist cliche, too much of the plot is soap opera," wrote Josh Greenfield.

Standing Fast is an intensive study of how the Depression shaped the lives of a group of young people committed to making a better America and how America has evolved with only minimal impact from those commitments. This has led many reviewers to admire the book despite their misgivings about Swados' skill with plot and characterization. Harding Lemay's response is typical: "In presenting with uncommon generosity of spirit his chronicle of what it has meant, since 1939, to care more about what happens to others than what happens to oneself, Swados achieves what more sophisticated and accomplished novelists have failed to do. He rubs our noses in our failures and deceits and forces us to care."

None of Swados' first four novels was as well received as the novel that was published after his death, *Celebration* (1975). The cordial reception of this book was, perhaps, the result of two innovations. The central intelligence of the novel is that of a ninety-year-old man. Samuel Lumen is among the oldest major characters in American literature. What with the new interest in the elderly in the 1970s and the fact that Swados was diligent in attempting to render accurately the mental state and the various physical disabilities of a very old person, reviewers were certain to be favorably inclined. In addition, Swados dispensed with the usual narrative. The novel is powered by entries Lumen makes in his diary.

Lumen decides to begin keeping a diary at such a very advanced age because he is determined not to forget who he really is. Over the decades he has become renowned for his radical ideas on child raising and education and he has become one of the world's foremost spokesmen on behalf of children—a combination of A. S. Neill of Summerhill School and Danny Kaye of UNICEF. As his life draws to a close he is being seen more and more as a Grand Old Man. He is going to be the subject of a series of television specials. He knows that the television shows will reinforce the legend of the Grand Old Man, so he begins to write down all those things about himself and his past that he will not tell the TV interviewers, the things he has done that he is not proud of, such as seducing his son's wife.

What little plot the novel has revolves around the struggle between an associate who would have Lumen be faithful to his image of the Grand Old Man and another who would have him revert to his old roles of radical and iconoclast. This struggle generates "the many moments of self-indulgent and melodramatic attitudinizing " which J. L. Crain thought weakened the novel. But the novel's quality lies in the reflections of Lumen. During his long life Lumen knew many a defeat on the way to attaining his fame. Much of his public activity produced ambiguous results at best; much of his private behavior still causes him pain. At ninety, he sees a very mixed harvest.

Swados probably admired Lumen more than any of his other characters, for Lumen is one of those rare men who, despite his own serious flaws and a succession of disillusionments, continues to believe the world could be made better and keeps up the good fight. Thus, Irving Malin's comments on *Celebration* were particularly appropriate. *Celebration*, he wrote, is a "wonderfully serene novel" that accepts conflict and "acknowledges the need for liberation of fathers and sons. It refuses to flee from political, sexual, and educational strife. It is an appropriate testament— not only to Lumen but to Swados himself."

—*Paul Marx*

Books:

Out Went the Candle (New York: Viking, 1955);
On the Line (Boston: Atlantic/Little, Brown, 1957);
False Coin (Boston: Atlantic/Little, Brown, 1959);
Nights in the Gardens of Brooklyn (Boston: Atlantic/Little, Brown, 1960);
A Radical's America (Boston: Atlantic/Little, Brown, 1962);
The Will (Cleveland: World, 1963);
A Story for Teddy and Others (New York: Simon & Schuster, 1965);
A Radical at Large (London: Hart-Davis, 1968);
Standing Fast (Garden City: Doubleday, 1970);
Standing Up for the People: The Life and Work of Estes Kefauver (New York: Dutton, 1972);
Celebration (New York: Simon & Schuster, 1975).

Periodical Publications:

"Work As a Public Issue," *Saturday Review*, 12 December 1959, pp. 13-15;
"Is Work for Squares?," *Mademoiselle*, March 1961, pp. 140-141;
"Utopia's Children: An Interpretation of Three Political Novels," *Western Political Quarterly*, March 1962, pp. 17-32;
"Revolution on the March," *Nation*, 7 September 1963, pp. 104-107;
"What's Left of the Left?," *Nation*, 20 September 1965, pp. 108-114;

"Ambivalent Scholars: Marx and Shame," *Nation*, 10 October 1966, pp. 347-351.

Other:

Years of Conscience: The Muckrakers: An Anthology of Reform Journalism, edited by Swados (Cleveland: Meridian, 1962);
The American Writer and the Great Depression, edited by Swados (Indianapolis: Bobbs-Merrill, 1966).

References:

Paul Cowan, "*Standing Fast*," *Village Voice* (New York), 22 October 1970, p. 6;
Hilton Kramer, "Remembering Harvey Swados," *Massachusetts Review*, 14 (1973): 226-228;
Paul Marx, "Harvey Swados," *Ontario Review*, 1, 1 (fall 1974): 62-66;
Charles Shapiro, "Harvey Swados: Private Stories and Public Function," in *Contemporary American Novelists*, ed. Harry T. Moore (Carbondale: Southern Illinois University Press, 1966).

Manuscripts:

Columbia University has a large collection of letters by Swados.

PAUL THEROUX, an American novelist who has lived and written as an expatriate since 1963, was born in Medford, Massachusetts, on 10 April 1941, to Albert Eugene and Anne Dittami Theroux. Following his graduation from Medford High School in 1959, he briefly attended the University of Maine, transferring the next year to the University of Massachusetts. There, he immediately refused to join the ROTC, declaring himself to be a pacifist; later he wrote that it was actually cowardice, a trait he finds admirable, which motivated him. In 1962 he was arrested for leading an antiwar demonstration, not the last time that his politics got him into trouble.

Following his graduation from Massachusetts in 1963, and a brief period of graduate study at Syracuse, he joined the Peace Corps and was sent as a lecturer in English to Malawi in eastern Africa. He taught at Soche Hill College in Limbe, Malawi, until the fall of 1965. On 20 October 1965 he was arrested for spying and for aiding revolutionaries who were attempting to overthrow the dictator of the

Paul Theroux.

country. Convicted within hours, he was placed on the only plane leaving Malawi that day and ended up in Rhodesia. Many of the problems which led to his deportation were not his fault. For instance, a man claiming to be an agent for a German monthly asked him to write a regular column on Malawi political and social affairs. It turned out that his reports, instead of being published by any periodical, were being handed over to the German equivalent of the CIA. But Theroux was not entirely blameless: he volunteered to be a messenger for the leading political opponent of the Malawi dictator, not realizing that the message was the go-ahead for an assassination attempt on the dictator. His experiences are reflected somewhat in *Jungle Lovers*

(1971), where the dictator, Hastings Banda, becomes Hastings Karryama Osbong.

After coming to the United States briefly, so that he could be questioned by the State Department, and be expelled from the Peace Corps, he returned to Africa. He became a lecturer in English at Makerere University in Kampala, Uganda, where he remained from 1965 to 1968. While in Uganda he married Anne Castle, another teacher, on 4 December 1967. In that same year he published *Waldo*, his first novel. Theroux left Africa in 1968 to go to the University of Singapore, where he taught Jacobean drama until 1971.

At the end of the 1971 school year Theroux decided that he could not teach and write at the same time. In "Love Scenes after Work" he says writers like Anthony Trollope, whose *Autobiography* described the difficulties of writing love scenes after a hard day's work, could handle two careers, but he himself is not one of these men. He decided in 1971 to try to live by writing alone and has published at least one book every year since he made his decision. Additionally he has become a prolific writer of book reviews. He frequently writes reviews for the *New York Times Book Review, Book World* in the *Washington Post,* and occasionally for *New Statesman, Encounter,* and other journals. Except for being writer in residence for the fall semester of 1972 at the University of Virginia, Theroux has lived in England since he decided to quit teaching. He has two sons, Marcel Raymond and Louis Sebastian.

Recognition for Theroux, critical as well as popular, has been growing slowly but steadily. In 1960, when he was nineteen, he won the Robert Hamlet one-act play award. He was the 1971 and 1976 winner of *Playboy* magazine's Writing Award for Best Fiction. In 1977 he received the Academy-Institute Award in Literature from the American Academy and Institute of Arts and Letters. He also had his short story "The Autumn Dog" chosen for *Prize Stories 1977: The O. Henry Awards.* Evidence of his popular acceptance is indicated by the fact that *The Family Arsenal* (1976) was chosen to be a main selection of the Book-of-the-Month Club.

Theroux's writing contains little technical innovation, an attribute often associated with contemporary novelists. There is some manipulation of the chronology in *Jungle Lovers,* but it adds little to the novel. What Theroux does seem to share with other contemporary writers is a vision of a meaningless, chaotic world enveloping his characters. They are unable to draw meaning from their lives or surroundings, and therefore they attempt to impose some kind of order, generally either through violence, or through writing, or both. Theroux says in his poem "Man Alone in a Garden" that the poet must smash and destroy things, like a man shredding a flower. Only then can he control whatever he faces enough to understand it:

He does not hold the whole bloom
in still hands, does not restore
or celebrate the form, but shuffles,
cuts, then broods on the new order.

Most of his protagonists are writers or artists who attempt to understand what they cannot control, and who frequently resort to violence in an attempt to establish an order of their own.

Waldo (1967), Theroux's first novel, deals with the theme of a man trying to find or create order in his life, and the method he eventually chooses is journalism. The title character begins the novel in a glass cage in the Booneville School for Delinquent Boys, and ends in a glass cage in a night club. In between these two imprisonments, he is engaged in furious, though usually pointless, activity. He has trouble communicating with family and friends, and his inability to discover any meaning to his existence is a continual frustration. Partially due to his own instincts, and partially due to the advice of his psychiatrist/optometrist, he uses his continuous activity as a means of alleviating this frustration.

Much of his activity is in conjunction with or support of Mrs. Clovis Techy, a middle-aged, wealthy nymphomaniac who becomes his patron. He spends several weeks locked in a motel room with her before deciding to become a journalist. He also flirts with the idea of writing esoteric novels for the appreciation of a select few, but journalism offers more activity, and he hopes it will offer him a chance to create an order out of the chaos he perceives. He has one successful story, and it deals with a mother's account of her ten-year-old son's terminal illness. She and Waldo form a nightclub act, in which she moves her lips while a tape recording plays her story and he sits in the suspended glass cage pretending to type it. None of this helps Waldo, however, and he returns to Clovis and his dreams of a novel.

The novel presents themes that Theroux continues to use, and has the open, inconclusive ending which is typical of his work. Order is not discovered by the characters, and it is not imposed by the writer on the novel. Waldo occasionally resorts to violence, but his principal resort is to continuous activity. By the end of the novel he is bald, old, and burnt out from this ceaseless motion. Critical opinion has ranged from Martin Levin's assessment that it is "pointless and witless," to Roderick Cook's evaluation of *Waldo* as "a good funny novel." The truth is somewhere between these two viewpoints. The novel does have a point, and it has some humorous, satiric passages which make it worth reading, but it is very episodic, with vignettes of uneven quality.

Fong and the Indians (1968), set in Kenya, is a much more unified work. It deals with Sam Fong, a Chinese Catholic living in Africa. He is a carpenter by trade, but he quickly discovers that Asians living in Africa are subject to prejudice and harassment from all directions. The British, Americans, Communists, and native Africans all work against him. Unable to find work as a carpenter, he is forced into the grocery business, where he loses money. He is constantly being threatened with deportation, although the only crime he and the Indians in the title have committed is being from the wrong cultural background. Fong resorts to daydreams in an attempt to establish some control over the situation. He wishes that the milk train from the coast will wreck, thus forcing people to buy from his store. The train has never wrecked before, but it does this time, and, for the moment at least, Sam experiences some peace and success.

From its ironic title to the last grisly paragraphs, nothing could have less peace and success in it than *Girls at Play* (1969). Indeed, the only success in the novel, the Peace Corps worker's attempt to eliminate class differences in her area of eastern Africa, precipitates the tragedy. The novel concerns a boarding school in Malawi where there are five women teaching the native girls. There are three Englishwomen, an Indian, and the idealistic American Peace Corps worker. They hate each other almost as much as all of them (except the American) hate the blacks. To establish some order in their existence, they have weekly meetings, with each woman sending elaborate invitations to all of the other teachers except the Indian.

The American girl is upset by the prejudice and hatred she finds and sets out to rectify the situation. She tries to convince the natives that the white women are not different, are not superior, are not goddesses. She succeeds only too well. The Africans, convinced they have been lorded over by impostors, react violently. The school is eventually destroyed, and two of the teachers are raped. The American girl, in despair at what her attempts at egalitarianism have produced, commits suicide. The novel is well written, and the satire is bitter. The women's attempt to order their environment is too flimsy to withstand the meddling of one idealistic girl.

In *Jungle Lovers* (1971), also set in Malawi, the protagonist, Calvin Mullet, is an American from Massachusetts who has been forced to travel to Africa to earn a living. (These correspondences to Theroux's life are coincidental, and the few autobiographical details are insignificant.) Mullet and another American, Marais, are both attempting to alter the lives of the people of Malawi, the former through selling insurance, and the latter through revolution. Neither is able, though, to overcome the inertia of African life, the resistance to change, the total disregard for the future. Both men are also hampered by their racial difference from the people whose lives they attempt to change. The picture drawn of the blacks is generally unflattering, and the narrator's opinion of Africans seems identical to that of Alfred Munday, the anthropologist in *The Black House* (1974): a repeated assertion of empathy for the blacks does not convincingly cover an attitude of paternalism. In *Jungle Lovers*, though, the British and American settlers are also viewed with ridicule, and Theroux seems content to leave the merits of the Americans' plans for change open to question.

In the end the government swallows all opposition. The revolution fails, and Marais either is killed or simply disappears. The insurance company, which had sold only five policies, is nationalized. Mira, Calvin's mistress, gives birth to a child which may or may not be Calvin's, and the insurance salesman dreams of returning with a black wife and son to Massachusetts now that his company no longer has a branch in Malawi. Nothing alters, and the foreigners are driven out of the country they planned to change.

Both of these men are also writers, and Calvin, at least, leaves some impression on the country, although it is by accident. In an attempt to discover why his frustration is so complete, Mullet writes a long story called "The Uninsured." It is narrated by a black man who is the spokesman for blacks who have suffered from discrimination and other frustrations beyond their control. They are uninsured against what life and history have done to them. Whenever the salesman becomes frustrated, he adds to the story. When the company is nationalized the diatribe is found and published. It becomes a handbook for dissidents and for blacks looking for reasons to hate Asians and whites who have entered their country. Calvin himself is scorned by his black insurance trainee, who has read the pamphlet but who, of course, rejects all suggestions that Calvin wrote it. Marais, too, writes, but his journal of the revolution he precipitates is never to be seen. Realizing that he has failed in his goals because he cannot understand the culture of the blacks he wants to lead, he destroys all of his writing and resigns any attempt to create or describe a new order.

Another frustrated writer is Jack Flowers, the title character of *Saint Jack* (1973). He wishes to be a novelist, famous, rich, and, perhaps, sainted. But instead he is a middle-aged man who ostensibly works for a merchant named Hing in Singapore, while he makes his real living as a pimp and hustler. He is always trying to figure an angle and is so willing to cater to the desires of his clients that "anything at all" becomes a catch phrase for him in the novel. He continually daydreams about what he is doing and even makes up biographical sketches for the actors in the pornographic movies he shows his clients. He wishes to write a novel, but his writing is restricted to composing letters to himself. The reader only sees the first lines of these letters, but all of them deal with sudden windfalls, great wealth which will deliver Jack from pandering for a living.

Actually, however, Jack could never change, because he represents life in Singapore. As Jonathan Rabon says, *Saint Jack* is "a bubbling crucible of large hopes and small failures." Jack may dream of an ideal existence and wish that he could write the novel which would depict it, but he cannot. Just like Waldo in Theroux's first novel, Jack is doomed to a frenetic, meaningless existence. He will occasionally try to do something else, but he cannot get through to anyone with his dreams. He tells an Irish seaman that he is crazy about Joyce, to which the sailor replies that she is one of the better whores. Jack is in his fifties, and his existence is already too rigid to change, even though that rigidity itself is too complex for him to understand. Life will always be a treadmill for him.

Theroux's sixth novel, *The Black House* (1974), is a study of a man, Alfred Munday, who intentionally separates himself from everything and everyone ever connected with him. He leaves England to live in Uganda, ostensibly so that he can study the Bwamba tribe. He stays until he has lost all contact with the people he knew, and then, told by his doctor that he has a heart condition, he returns to England. Actually it is his wife whose heart is failing, but she and the doctor know that Alfred will return to England only if he is convinced that his own health is failing.

Once in England Alfred proceeds to alienate people: his neighbors in the village where he settles; those he knew in Africa, who now also reside in England; his former lover; and he begins to separate himself from his wife, Emma. He is so arrogant, pretentious, obnoxious, and cowardly that even the reader soon wishes to disassociate himself from Munday. The method he uses to estrange his wife is an affair he begins with Caroline Summers. Emma believes the house they live in, the Black House of the title, is haunted, and fears Caroline because she looks like the ghost Emma has seen. Caroline does seem to exercise some control over Emma, and her love-making with Alfred, passionate and described in detail, occurs only in the Black House and only when Emma is nearby. Alfred finally discovers that though he says he has "mastered solitude," it is only because of the strength Emma gives him. He banishes Caroline, who he believes is a figure created by his own mind, and looks forward to life with his freshly discovered source of strength. He plans to draw on

Emma to enable him to satisfy the great scholarly and personal ambitions that previously seemed too difficult for him to manage. The final irony, although never directly stated, is that Emma is dead, dying in her sleep during Alfred's final encounter with Caroline.

The strengths of this novel are two. The first is the relaxed style which allows the tension of the ghost story to build slowly but inexorably. The second is that, as with most successful ghost stories, there is a careful blending of the mood with the physical surrounding. The Black House, like the House of Usher, radiates evil, and even the simplest of descriptions adds to the emotional impact of the story. The final blow struck on Alfred while he is in the Black House will happen after the novel ends, but the novel, both in tone and in its use of description, has prepared the reader for this final shock.

Alfred is also a writer, although in this case he is a scholarly rather than a creative writer. He is attempting to explain an order in the life of the African tribe, but what he is actually doing, what he admits to himself he is doing, is creating an order which he hopes will in some way capture the tribal life he spent ten years observing. His book is necessarily a simplification and condensation of his observations, and at the same time, it becomes a guide for him in understanding his life wherever he lives. He begins to believe that he can order and even create his own existence according to his own desires, as long as he has Emma to help him. After all, he reasons, the two of them created Caroline. The novel ends before his realization that all such order is impossible; the chaos of life is always present and always defies human attempts at structure.

Theroux's seventh novel, *The Family Arsenal* (1976), deals with London terrorists and their attempt to order the society that surrounds them through violence. Two of the characters, Murf and Brodie, believe they "can possess a city only by incinerating it." They are wrong, of course; there is no way for them to possess it. Even with the help of the rich and powerful, represented by the lecherous aristocrat, Lady Arrow, and the actress, Araba Nightwing, they cannot force their surroundings to conform to their wishes. Valentine Hood, the American in the group, seems to realize this fact, but he is helpless. He would be a man of continuous action like Waldo or Jack, but his attempt to become part of a group, this band of urban guerrillas, has temporarily taken his options away.

Hood and Gawber, an accountant, are the most persistent in attempting to create order. Hood attempts to find order by viewing a stolen self-portrait by a Dutch master, and by smoking opium. He continually makes up new names for the painting, although the one he keeps returning to is "Death Eating a Cracker." Most of his dreams end in violence, and he, like the poet in the garden of Theroux's poem, hopes to destroy what he finds and then to create an order he perceives and understands from the pieces. Destruction and violence become art forms. Gawber comes to much the same conclusion, but from a drastically different direction. He has a completely rigid life. He lives in the house he was born in. He always eats the same food. His only variation in his schedule is what brings him into contact with Hood. But Gawber's one persistent dream, indeed his hope, is his belief that financial collapse is imminent for England. He awaits with eager anticipation a time when the figures he works with daily show him that the order he has always lived by has been destroyed. What he then expects, if he expects anything at all, is not stated.

Theroux's writing has become persistently more satirical and less humorous with each novel. His view of the chaos of society has remained consistent, but his view of the malignancy of that chaos has become increasingly bitter. For a writer who lists his politics as socialist, he has a very dim view of government. Indeed, if he were a native of Britain, he could be a Tory, viewing society as decayed, and all changes as encouragements to that decay. Like the poet in the garden, he tears at what he views in order to show its distinctive parts. Whatever new order he intends to create from the parts is not yet apparent. —*Timothy J. Evans*

Books:

Waldo (Boston: Houghton Mifflin, 1967; London: Bodley Head, 1968);

Fong and the Indians (Boston: Houghton Mifflin, 1968; London: Hamish Hamilton, 1976);

Girls at Play (London: Bodley Head, 1969; Boston: Houghton Mifflin, 1969);

Murder in Mount Holly (London: Alan Ross, 1969);

Jungle Lovers (Boston: Houghton Mifflin, 1971; London: Bodley Head, 1971);

Sinning with Annie, and Other Stories (Boston: Houghton Mifflin, 1972; London: Hamish Hamilton, 1974);

V. S. Naipaul: An Introduction to His Works (New York: Africana Publishing, 1972; London: Deutsch, 1972);

Saint Jack (Boston: Houghton Mifflin, 1973; London: Bodley Head, 1973);

The Black House (Boston: Houghton Mifflin, 1974; London: Hamish Hamilton, 1974);

The Great Railway Bazaar: by Train through Asia (Boston: Houghton Mifflin, 1975);

The Family Arsenal (Boston: Houghton Mifflin, 1976; London: Hamish Hamilton, 1976);

The Consul's File (Boston: Houghton Mifflin, 1977);

Picture Palace (Boston: Houghton Mifflin, 1978).

Periodical Publications:

FICTION:

"Two in the Bush," *Atlantic*, 222 (July 1968): 74-79;

"The Man Who Read Graham Greene," *North American Review*, 6 (summer 1969): 62-65;

"Odd-job Man," *Atlantic*, 237 (April 1976): 94-96.

NONFICTION:

"On Cowardice," *Commentary*, 43 (June 1967): 41-44;

"Burma," *Atlantic*, 228 (November 1971): 37-47;

"The Killing of Hastings Banda," *Esquire*, 76 (December 1971): 22-40;

"Love-scene After Work: Writing in the Tropics," *North American Review*, 9 (winter 1972-1973): 75-78;

"Desert at the Belvedere," *Playboy*, 20 (January 1973): 83, ff.;

"In Darkest Afghanistan," *Harper's*, 252 (March 1976): 89-98.

John Updike

Jerome Klinkowitz
University of Northern Iowa

BIRTH: Shillington, Pennsylvania, 18 March 1932.

EDUCATION: A.B., Harvard University, 1954; study on Knox Fellowship at the Ruskin School of Drawing and Fine Arts in Oxford, England, 1954-1955.

MARRIAGE: 26 June 1953 to Mary Entwistle Pennington, divorced; children: Elizabeth Pennington, David Hoyer, Michael John, and Miranda. 30 September 1977 to Martha Ruggles Bernhard.

AWARDS: Guggenheim Fellow, 1959; Rosenthal Award, National Institute of Arts and Letters, 1959; National Book Award in Fiction, 1964; O. Henry Prize, 1967-1968; Elected, National Institute of Arts and Letters, 1964; Elected, American Academy of Arts and Letters, 1977.

MAJOR WORKS: *The Carpentered Hen and Other Tame Creatures* (New York: Harper, 1958; republished as *Hoping for a Hoopoe*, London: Gollancz, 1959); *The Poorhouse Fair* (New York: Knopf, 1959; London: Gollancz, 1964); *The Same Door* (New York: Knopf, 1959; London: Deutsch, 1962); *Rabbit, Run* (New York: Knopf, 1960; London: Deutsch, 1961); *Pigeon Feathers* (New York: Knopf, 1962; London: Deutsch, 1963); *The Centaur* (New York: Knopf, 1963; London: Deutsch, 1963); *Telephone Poles* (New York: Knopf, 1963; London: Deutsch, 1964); *Olinger Stories* (New York: Vintage, 1964); *Assorted Prose* (New York: Knopf, 1965; London: Deutsch, 1965); *Of the Farm* (New York: Knopf, 1965; London: Deutsch, 1966); *The Music School* (New York: Knopf, 1966; London: Deutsch, 1967); *Couples* (New York: Knopf, 1968; London: Deutsch, 1968); *Midpoint* (New York: Knopf, 1969; London: Deutsch, 1969); *Bech: A Book* (New York: Knopf, 1970; London: Deutsch, 1970); *Rabbit Redux* (New York: Knopf, 1971; London: Deutsch, 1972); *Museums and Women* (New York: Knopf, 1972; London: Deutsch, 1973); *Buchanan Dying* (New York: Knopf, 1974; London: Deutsch, 1974); *A Month of Sundays* (New York: Knopf, 1975; London: Deutsch, 1975); *Picked-Up Pieces* (New York: Knopf, 1975; London: Deutsch, 1976); *Marry Me* (New York: Knopf, 1976); *Tossing and Turning* (New York: Knopf, 1977; London: Deutsch, 1977).

John Updike.

During his college years John Updike was a graphic artist, especially adept as a cartoonist and draftsman, and this very literal sense of style has been the most distinguishing factor in his novels and stories. He is a master of the well-crafted sentence, composed of words often as interesting for their sound and physical texture as for the ideas they convey. But unlike some of his more innovative contemporaries (Barthelme, Sukenick, Major) who occasionally focus on language alone, Updike keeps a sense of story in his works. His reputation was built in the *New Yorker* magazine, and his short fictions of the 1950s, 1960s, and 1970s chart the fortunes of two major geographical groups among whom Updike has lived: the small-town folk of eastern Pennsylvania and the urban and suburban populace of New York City and New England. His novels often attend to the relationships between lovers but also carry explicit theological themes, centering on the shabbiness of modern life and the attempts to construct religious meaning out of secular materials. Hence, Updike deserves the badge of contemporary moralist worn by such writers as Saul Bellow and Bernard Malamud, while still representing the tradition of suburban manners described by John O'Hara and John Cheever. Through his essays for the *New Yorker*, Updike has expressed a serious interest in contemporary religious thought; originally an advocate of the uncompromising Karl Barth (and Barth's spiritual ancestor Kierkegaard), Updike's sentiments have lately embraced the more liberal theology of Paul Tillich (and his predecessor Schleiermacher), who believed that the truly religious could have a valid counterpart in the material world. This thematic progression is established in the movement from *Rabbit, Run* (1960) to *A Month of Sundays* (1975), and demonstrates Updike's continued affinity with cultural changes in America.

In 1973, after John Updike had achieved the stature of a major American author, columnist and fellow-novelist Wilfrid Sheed asked him if he ever wanted to be "something else." Replying in the pages of the *New York Times Book Review*, Updike confessed that, "My true and passionate ambition— though as a badly hooked movie-goer I did have yearnings toward being a private detective, a test pilot, or Errol Flynn—was to be a cartoonist, first for Walt Disney, then for the syndicates, lastly for the *New Yorker*. What I have become is a sorry shadow of those high hopes."

As a boy growing up in Shillington, Pennsylvania, Updike had admired cartoons, essays, poems, and stories in the *New Yorker*. At age thirteen, as an only child, he moved out into the nearby countryside with his parents and commuted daily to the school in Shillington where his father worked as a science teacher; living away from town gave Updike even more time for fashioning his own insights, then comparing them with those of the professionals he saw published in the national magazines. After high school in Shillington, Updike attended Harvard, where he majored in English, contributed to and then edited the *Harvard Lampoon*, and graduated *summa cum laude* in 1954. The year before, he had married an art student from Radcliffe, Mary Pennington, and together they spent the academic year of 1954-1955 at the Ruskin School of Drawing and Fine Art in Oxford, England (Updike on the Knox Fellowship), beginning his career in art. But on 30 October 1954, the *New Yorker* had published his first national story, "Friends from Philadelphia," and Updike wrote more for publication during his year in England. In 1955, he returned to settle with Mary in Manhattan, joined the *New Yorker* staff (many of his "Talk of the Town" contributions have been identified and reprinted in *Assorted Prose*), and continued with his poetry and short fiction. By 1957, when he left the magazine's staff and moved with his family to Ipswich, Massachusetts, to write full time, he had accumulated enough *New Yorker* contributions to begin planning collections of poetry (*The Carpentered Hen*) and short fiction (*The Same Door*). These two books flanked his first novel, *The Poorhouse Fair* (1959), and served to launch his critical reputation.

In each genre, Updike identifies himself as a student not only of the world, but of how that world expresses itself in language. *The Carpentered Hen*, which collects light verse prompted by the idiosyncracies of daily life, contains many poems which take their cue from the words of advertisements, editorials, atlas notes, column fillers, or even dictionary words themselves. Comically demonstrating that even the most mundane object may inspire the loftiest language, Updike describes himself as "The Sensualist" who can (from the poem's epigram) invoke the ingredients of a box of Parke-Davis throat discs ("Come Capsicum, cast off thy membranous pods; Thy Guinea girlhood's blossoms have been dried./Come, Peppermint, beloved of the gods . . ."). The stories of *The Same Door* contain narrative, but never at the expense of fine language; Updike demonstrates that the materials of a sensitive but unexceptional boyhood in the small cities and countryside of southeastern Pennsylvania and of a middle-class courtship and marriage in the suburbs and larger cities farther east can serve as the occasion for insights not just into life, but into how we react to life in words. Of the Pennsylvania stories from *The Same Door* and from *Pigeon Feathers* (1962) which were again collected in 1964 as *Olinger Stories: A Selection*, Updike has remarked that both in such lives and in such stories, "*We are rewarded unexpectedly* [his italics]. The muddled and inconsequential surface of things now and then parts to yield us a gift. In my boyhood I had the impression of being surrounded by an incoherent generosity, of—to quote a barefaced reminiscence I once wrote ["The Dogwood Tree: A Boyhood," collected in *Assorted Prose*], 'a quiet but tireless goodness that things at rest, like a brick wall or a small stone, seem to affirm. A wordless reassurance that these things are pressing to give.'" Stories such as "Pigeon Feathers," "Flight," and "Friends from Philadelphia" have easily recognized narrative structures, while others, including "In Football Season" and "Packed Dirt, Churchgoing, A Dying Cat, A Traded Car" seem plotless to the point of being mere sketches. The true plot of many of Updike's early stories is best described in his own words: "the horse-chestnut trees, the telephone poles, the porches, the green hedges recede to a calm point that in my subjective geography is still the center of the world."

The Poorhouse Fair is not only Updike's first novel, but is his first major statement against the blank materialism of secular life—a theme which has been closely identified with his writing in years since. Published in 1959, its action is projected several decades into the future, presumably the imagined 1970s. From the author's point of view, however, we see the emptiness of the Eisenhower years projected as an anti-utopia, where every temporal care of its retirement-age citizens is satisfied, except for the biggest one: their fear of approaching death. The administrator of the county home where they live is a technologically efficient man named Conner who dreams of a perfectly organized welfare state, answering all the material needs of its citizens from birth until death. His own idea of death is a cleansing renewal, clearing the way for newer and better improvements in society's life. But his plan disregards the deeper needs of the old people, as pathetically expressed in the handicrafts fair they mount each year. An indictment of the behavioristic psychology of B. F. Skinner and his colleagues, *The Poorhouse Fair* contains much political and psychological thought (in the form of debates among the residents and between them and their administrator), but Updike's gift of style manages to locate these abstractions solidly within the sensations of the surrounding world. As Updike describes a scene following one discussion, "In ones and twos more inmates were drifting from spots around the Home into the room, shuffling amusedly through the screen of uniforms drawn up like a guard. It was as if the world had been holding its breath while Hook and Conner debated its condition, and now resumed bumping onwards." Waiting only to die, Conner's charges have American health, but no heart, since the mores of their children's new society have taken that away from them. Though his first novel is heavily allegorical, Updike's indictment of the present society is clear. His heavily stylized prose, noticeable from the very first, takes root in the baroque quality of these old people's lives and is played against the sterile efficiency of the world their prefects would impose.

Rabbit, Run (1960) is a more culturally immediate test of Updike's theme and style, and for its setting returns to the southeastern Pennsylvania country which in other books holds the mythical Olinger, and which here features the imaginary "town of Mt. Judge, suburb of the city of Brewer, fifth largest city in Pennsylvania." There, Harry "Rabbit" Angstrom is setting out on the life of a

lower-middle-class family man, demonstrating gadgets in a five-and-ten store, and regretting that the quality of this life doesn't measure up to the graceful success of his high school basketball career, where the artificial rules of the basketball court prescribed a neat and orderly world. But the opportunities for graceful or saintly conduct in his new life are minimal: hanging up his coat neatly, avoiding heavy foods, not smoking, and so forth. Viewing the TV game show "Queen for a Day," he realizes that "The idea is all these women have tragedies they tell about and then get money according to how much applause there is, but by the time the M.C. gets done delivering commercials and kidding them about their grandchildren and their girlish hairdos there isn't much room for tragedy left."

Updike's reaction against the sterility of secular society is expressed by Rabbit's needs, and Updike's stylistics become the vehicle for Rabbit's protest against a world which offers him no good. Rabbit feels that his own worth adds up to little more than the shabbiness of his dowdy wife Janice, their unpleasant apartment, and his own broken ideals. The stern faith of his childhood, characterized by the Karl Barthian minister Kruppenbach, is replaced by the "ping-pong religion" of young Jack Eccles, the minister who would presumably save him (but who can hardly save himself). Eccles is the religious counterpart to Conner of *The Poorhouse Fair*, and, despite his collar, is just as sterile and secular. The best that Rabbit can do is flee this world which offers him no avenue to the spiritual or meaningful. Rabbit doubts his own existence (characterized as it is by such shabby materialism) and can confirm it only in love. But the love he finds is pagan or erotic, leading to a dead end and to death itself—saintly love tempts, but eludes him.

In addition to expressing Rabbit's own yearning for style and grace, Updike's language catches up the trivia of the times and memorializes it beyond the value of its content, but in a way which reflects its influence on his characters' lives. A typical scene finds Rabbit coming home to find Janice sitting stupefied before the afternoon TV; the "Mickey Mouse Club" show is described in compelling detail, not for its own trivial content, but as an element of contemporary secularization which Rabbit will later try to fashion into religious meaning. When he makes his first attempt to flee, driving through the night, his car radio plays a sequence of popular and jazz songs (and finally static) which reflect the spirit of his quest. Later, the romance of Rabbit and his new lover is catalogued by the current films they see, all of which mirror the spiritual desolation of their lives. The contemporary may be useless to Rabbit, but for Updike it is the building blocks of style.

The Centaur (1963), a highly acclaimed book, expresses his same attitude toward life developed in the earlier novels and stories. The fear of death, as examined in *The Poorhouse Fair*, in *Rabbit, Run*, and in the story "Pigeon Feathers" is repeated. Once again, death is more than the cessation of physical life; it is the vacancy of beauty and value as well. As protagonist, high school student Peter Caldwell is grateful for his teacher-father's gift of life. But the elder Caldwell's steps are marked by a mortality which Updike conveys by telling the story with parallel chapters: the first series set in a Pennsylvania high school, the second transmogrified into the Chiron myth. The boy sees his father mocked and the myth debased, all to emphasize the fear of nothingness that stands behind human (and godly) mortality. Yet Mr. Caldwell teaches life over death, by being realistic about the conditions of his school, by his unselfish charity, and by his ultimate measure of the worth of man. The novel's question is, will Peter, his son, find grace to live, or will each of them suffer in a sickness unto death? The answer is that salvation comes not from a doctrine of works (at which the father pathetically fails), but from a doctrine of grace. Underscoring this American Puritan concept is the book's epigraph, from the sternly conservative theologian Karl Barth: "Heaven is the creation inconceivable to man, earth is the creation conceivable to him. He himself is the creature on the boundary between heaven and earth." And as with Rabbit's quest in the previous novel, Peter will suffer from the very ambivalence which is his own hope of happiness. By accepting this paradox—the paradox of life in death itself—Peter overcomes the nihilistic view that death is nothingness and realizes that his father has served as a counterforce to the son's persistent fear of life.

Peter's perceptions in *The Centaur* evoke the best points of Updike's style. His adolescent terror is captured in montages of sight and sound, while strongly physical images express the sense of the material world which underlies the psychological. Purely lyrical images—such as hallucinations which are allowed to enter the actual world and wreak their havoc as if they are paranoiac fears come true—work dramatically to express the struggle within Peter's mind to come to terms with life and with his fears about it. Such movements as these between the subjective and the objective, between the imagined and the real, strengthen the bonds between the two

stories Updike interpolates: of Chiron the Centaur and of Mr. George Caldwell the father and teacher.

Beyond the expressed correlations of classical myth and contemporary story are the correspondences with Updike's own biography, as the son of a Pennsylvania high school teacher who, like the son, Peter Caldwell, opted for the life of a graphic artist, but who ends up examining the meaning of his father's life and death by finding their expression in words. Peter Caldwell's contemplation becomes John Updike's novel. The settings and themes of *Olinger Stories*, selected and republished during the year of *The Centaur's* acclamation, grounded the Updike canon in the Pennsylvania of his boyhood. The following year Updike published *Of the Farm* (1965), a short novel about the length of *The Poorhouse Fair* which used some settings from *The Centaur*, notably the farm to which the protagonist's family has moved at his mother's behest (as did Updike's family when he was thirteen). The time is much later; the boy, this time called Joey, is full grown, and he is an advertising man, not an artist. He and his newly acquired second wife and stepson visit his widowed mother on the farm. Joey's second marriage may go wrong, as did the first, because there is ambivalence about how he makes his living: he "supports himself" not by art (like Peter Caldwell), but by simple capitalistic service. His mother always hoped he would be a poet, and now she disagrees with his new wife, Peggy, about the best ways to handle life and marriage. The mother's initial decision to give up town life for the ancestral farm, a minor theme in *The Centaur*, becomes the dominant interest in *Of the Farm*, for by the end the mother has explicitly cut off Joey from the orderly mythology by which she has sustained her life. The farm becomes not "ours" but "hers." It is the last of the formal "Olinger stories" that Updike has written; in the preface to his 1964 collection of that name, he confessed that "in my novel *The Centaur*, by turning Olinger explicitly into Olympus, I intended to say the final word, and farewell. . . . I offer this book in the faith that it is a closed book." But between his own past experience in Shillington and his present life in Ipswich lay his years in Manhattan, and *Of the Farm* becomes the novel corresponding to that experience.

After closing his Olinger stories, Updike began writing stories about a couple called the Maples, Boston suburbanites not distantly removed from the experiences of Updike's own family life in Massachusetts. The rise and fall of their marriage is catalogued in a special section of *Museums & Women* (1972), which collected fiction from the mid-

1960s on. But more central to Updike's literary career during these years was the imaginary village of Tarbox, Massachusetts, lying just south of the Boston urban sprawl (Ipswich lies north), the setting for his novel *Couples* (1968). Updike's narrative of sexual exchanges among the young-to-middle-aged couples of Tarbox takes place in 1963, and its happenings are counterpointed with actual news reports of the Kennedy family fortunes and tragedies. *Couples* reestablishes Updike's concern with sexual relations between men and women, the initial subject of *Rabbit, Run*, which served as the allegorical anchor to the search for spiritual identity. The subject of marital infidelity had great popular currency in the 1960s, and Updike works hard to correlate the microcosmic happenings among the couples to the larger fortunes of the country, and beyond that to the thematics of life and death, salvation and grace. Ever present in Tarbox is the Puritan landscape Updike's moderns occupy. His protagonist, the carpenter Piet Hanema, alone recognizes the legacy of craftsmanship and stern Calvinistic moralism, but not enough to keep him from the same fall into *eros* which damned Rabbit Angstrom. His lofty intentions are lost amid the carnal, a theme Updike exploited throughout the first decade of his novelistic career. But once more his style argues against the harsh morality of his subject, celebrating instead the natural instincts of his characters, which too often run against their better fortunes. The simplest of physical acts prompts Updike's finest prose, as when Piet's first shared infidelity with Foxy Whitman occasions a description equal to a transcendental sermon. It is the hallmark of Updike's style, and a clue to the intentions of his characters, that he can routinely insert one hundred words of stylistic exercises in finely wrought prose just as his lovers' clothing falls away.

Thematically, Updike uses *Couples* to show how there are social consequences of certain beliefs and choices, just as he did in *Rabbit, Run*. But just as Rabbit sought to fashion a world of higher meaning out of the imperfect materials of contemporary life, so too does Piet Hanema seek a more spiritual quality to his life. Their intentions are noble, and Updike as stylist demonstrates how the shabbiest of material circumstances can be rhapsodized, but because their love cannot advance from *eros* to *agape* (which Updike adopts from the theologian Reinhold Niebuhr) or from the Kierkegaardian initial steps of aesthetic and ethical (which precede the leap of faith), each is swallowed up in pagan lust. And the final issue of that lust is not only a loss of spirit, but a

decay of their own stylistic lyricism which first promised a road to the infinite.

In 1969 Updike published *Midpoint*, a collection which included a section of his typical "Light Verse," but also more serious "Poems" followed by "Love Poems"; and leading off the volume was the heavily personal and introspective title work itself, which brought the writer into very intimate confrontation with the themes and techniques he had been developing in his fiction. The poet speaks directly of his parents, his wife, and his children—and of the unions, reunions, and separations among those relationships. "Midpoint" refers to the midpoint of Updike's life, and he is practicing an examination of conscience before he begins its second half. But it is also the occasion for his reaffirming what had already become his imaginative credo. "An easy Humanism plagues the land," he states in conclusion. "I choose to take an otherworldly stand." Yet he still pledges to celebrate the sunsets and dawns within this worldly life, and his collection *Bech: A Book* (1970) examines the professional life of a writer as if checking over his own ability. Henry Bech is seen worrying about his exhausted theme and technique (a popular pose in literature of this period), but through Bech, Updike acknowledges the lesson: one of his own imaginative values, Kierkegaardian "dread," has reached the limits of its efficacy for American culture. As Updike begins the 1970s, *Bech* is his admission that large parts of his own aesthetic may have been weakened by time and circumstance.

Rabbit Redux (1971) discusses Rabbit's own exhaustion. There has been a dissipation of energy between his younger and middle years, Rabbit admits; whereas a decade before Rabbit could at least be anti-heroic, in 1969 (the time of the novel) he is simply pathetic. The materialism of 1950s life was at least concrete and definable; Rabbit had his own grace as an athlete and aesthete to place against it. But the coming 1970s strike him as inexplicable: he can't possibly understand the physics of outer space, for instance, nor can he invent a mythology for it. He feels tired enough to retire. Rabbit pursues an ambivalent affair with a "hippie" girl and engages the dialectic of a young black revolutionary. But no real themes develop from this surface topicality. *Rabbit Redux* shows two things: that Updike's classic protagonist has been outdated by the new thematics of the time, and that the story of his present life does not provide the makings of good Updike-style fiction. It is best regarded as Updike's experiment with his old themes and techniques amid the times; the result of the experiment is that they do not mix. Therefore it is no surprise that Updike's next books make a decided turn in thematics, in order to maintain both the author's stylistics and his commitment to the quotidian facts and experiences of current American life. *Museums & Women* contains deliberately experimental stories in the mode of John Barth, and while Updike's own style and devotion to narrative maintain themselves, it is noteworthy that he remains open to new and developing influences. Even in conventional stories, his new self-consciousness allows him to use his stylistics in a novel way. For one story, "The Day of the Dying Rabbit," he casts his protagonist as a creative photographer, whose own imagination visualizes things in terms of the author's language as he takes photographs "of grass and sand and shadows, close-up, using the ultraviolet filter, trying to get what may be ungettable, the way the shadow edges stagger from grain to grain on the sand, and the way some bent-over grass blades draw circles around themselves, to keep time away." Here the thematics of theology are replaced by a simple aesthetic problem, voiced by an aesthetician in terms proper to his (and to Updike's) art. But Updike also reveals a movement away from strict religion as the necessary counterpart to his natural descriptions; early in his title story he makes a distinction, quite new for the imaginative center of his writing, that "What we seek in museums is the opposite of what we seek in churches—the consoling sense of previous visitation. In museums, rather, we seek the untouched, the never-before-discovered; and it is their final unsearchability that leads us to hope, and return."

Yet Updike remains fascinated by religion, and *A Month of Sundays* (1975) shows his resolution to adapt this interest to his developing theme and technique. The secularization of our culture now pains Updike less and fascinates him more; and in terms of structure, he has discarded strong narrative in favor of a quiet, hopeful examination of subjects in stasis—almost as if they are tucked away for study in a museum. Most of the stories in *Museums & Women* were static affairs: the examination of an "orphaned" swimming pool, of a curious street corner, or of a carol sing at church. Theological debates now interest Updike less than the mundane business of what to do with a disgraced minister (disgraced for secular, not theological reasons), or simply the day-to-day running of the church. Even sexuality becomes a representation simply of itself, especially in his novel of 1976, *Marry Me*. This work details the affair of Jerry Conant and Sally Mathias, who are distinguished by their involvement in the

physical, rather than the metaphysical. They desert their own families for reasons of no real depth— Updike emphasizes their inconclusiveness by providing the novel with three different endings. But it is *A Month of Sundays* which signals the ultimate secularization of Updike's fiction. Its disgraced minister, Thomas Marshfield, has been exiled to a western retreat house for physical and spiritual rebuilding. But instead, he fashions the materials of his religion into a physical seduction (through words) of the retreat housekeeper—just the opposite strategy of the earlier novels. An epigraph by the liberal Paul Tillich, "This principle of soul, universally and individually, is the principle of ambiguity," stands at the head of *A Month of Sundays* and informs its every chapter. Reverend Marshfield has neither the stern religion of Kruppenbach nor the social eagerness of Eccles, but instead follows his ambiguity of soul to its grounding in the physical—the "double proof" of Tillich and Schleiermacher. Marshfield must create his own religion from the secular history of his life, since the Bible has been banned from this psychological retreat. His self-created words rebuilt his bridge to the world, just as Updike creates a life of fiction through the novel. His minister is now not only the reflector of the heavenly realm, but the fashioner of his own reality—a role which Updike as fictionist can share.

The first reviews of John Updike discussed his volume of poetry, *The Carpentered Hen*; among these early commentaries are hints of how Updike's fiction would be received by the reviewing media. G. D. McDonald noted how the author could be inspired by "a quotation found in some unlikely source" within the absurdities of modern life, but that "he employs no poison pen or arrows of sarcasm. The mood is one of amiable deflation." Nearly all reviewers praised Updike's mastery of technique, but some added the disclaimer that this very mastery exceeded the worth of its subject—that Updike was overwriting his material, and taking too easy a moral stance. Richard Gilman amplified this charge when reviewing *The Poorhouse Fair*: "It relies more directly on language than on thought," he observed, "takes the closest insight as most useful and permits to metaphors a stabbing or flashing action but never an all-encompassing one." The novel suffered from the burden of continued eloquence, Gilman complained, and warned Updike that "He would profit from knowing that it is in the spaces between images that their resonance is nurtured and maintained." The majority of critics, however, were generous and friendly, remarking that

John Updike

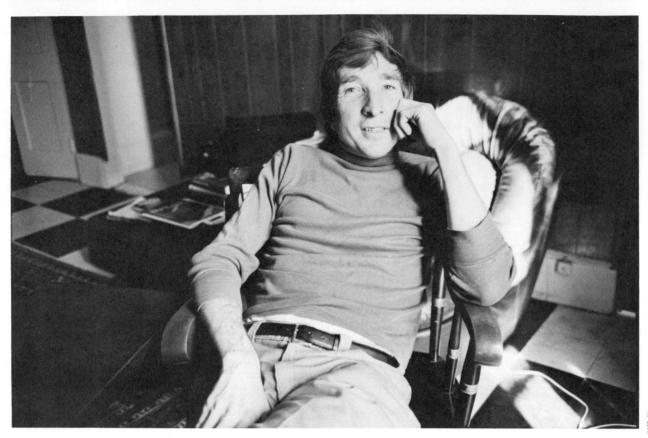

John Updike.

the birth of a major talent was at hand. "The book's strength lies in its many carefully developed and skillfully wrought pieces," Peter Salmon wrote. "That they do not cohere into what we ordinarily think of as a novel is probably attributable less to the author's ability than to the publisher's insistence upon the novel form. But when they are set down with such skill as John Updike's only the most rigorous purist (which this reviewer certainly is not) could complain."

The critical and popular success of *Rabbit, Run* moved Updike a step closer to the eminence he presently enjoys. Granville Hicks, who had worried that the allegedly thin story of *The Poorhouse Fair* was made to bear too heavy a weight, now admitted that, "Updike seizes upon qualities in Harry Angstrom that are of large significance, and, with his stylistic resources, he makes them real to us"; yet *Time* magazine demurred, arguing that "For all its excellence, it would have been a bigger book if Rabbit had been a bigger man." Melvin Maddocks, reviewing *Pigeon Feathers*, voiced the most serious complaint about Updike's work, that "When the time comes to touch the essential, the writer's grip slips, almost from embarrassment, into rhetoric, and feelings become aesthetic sensations."

Because Updike was making so much of the Kierkegaardian progression from aesthetic to ethic to religious faith, and by his own stylistics demonstrating his protagonists' danger of becoming bogged down in that aesthetic, it is understandable how reviewers might be confused and accuse Updike himself of the same mistake. Publication of *The Centaur*, which won the National Book Award in fiction, silenced this debate for a time; by separating his story into classical and contemporary components, Updike demonstrated his ability to style both sentences and thoughts in a manner less confusing to transient reviewers. With his growing body of works, Updike began to present a higher profile to critics, and it became apparent that while in subject matter he was extending the suburban tradition of John O'Hara and John Cheever, his moral stances placed him in the company of such novelists as Saul Bellow and Bernard Malamud. Since the mid-1960s each of his books has been received as the work of a major writer, and although there have been persistent complaints about the lushness of his style, more radical experiments with pure style (and almost no content) by more innovative fictionists have taken some of the pressure from Updike. *Couples* occasioned some sensationalism because of its sexual theme, and *Rabbit Redux* took some blows for its "tedious topicality," but both enlarged Updike's popular audience beyond his *New Yorker* beginnings. By the early 1970s Richard Locke could "think of no stronger vindication of the claims of essentially realistic fiction than [Updike's] extraordinary synthesis of the disparate elements of contemporary existence."

Academic criticism was from the start more respectful of Updike's work, and a growing number of studies praise his writing. The first book-length study, by Alice and Kenneth Hamilton, relied heavily on the theological interpretations Updike had encouraged by his advocacy of Karl Barth and Reinhold Niebuhr. But even before this, in their early chapters on Updike's fiction, David Galloway and Howard Harper chose to interpret the author in strongly philosophical terms. Book-length studies by Rachael Burchard and Edward P. Vargo emphasize Updike's affirmative Christianity and ideal of transcending the material, while those by Robert Detweiler and Joyce Markle give more attention respectively to his structural use of myth and his theme of love and lovers. The critics who fault Updike for his overuse of myth and style are hence answered by detailed studies. Tony Tanner's complaint that Updike's theology is extraneous to his plot is debated by Robert Detweiler, who demonstrates how Updike's theme grows directly from metaphysical concerns; Alfred Kazin's charge that Updike's style is overwrought is disputed by Larry Taylor, who shows how this style is at the heart of a new pastoral vision. Only a strong new school of revisionist criticism could unseat Updike from his present eminence among academics.

Other Works:

The Magic Flute (New York: Knopf, 1962; London: Deutsch & Ward, 1964);

The Ring (New York: Knopf, 1964);

Verse (Greenwich, Conn.: Fawcett, 1965);

A Child's Calendar (New York: Knopf, 1965);

Bath After Sailing (Stevenson, Conn.: Country Squires Books, 1968);

Three Texts From Early Ipswich (Ipswich, Mass.: 17th Century Day Committee, 1968);

Bottom's Dream (New York: Knopf, 1969);

The Indian (Marvin, S.D.: Blue Cloud Abbey, 1972);

Seventy Poems (London: Penguin, 1972);

Warm Wine (New York: Albondocani Press, 1973);

A Good Place (New York: Aloe Editions, 1973);

Six Poems (New York: Aloe Editions, 1973);

Cunts (New York: Hallman, 1974);

Query (New York: Albondocani Press, 1974).

References:

Jerry H. Bryant, *The Open Decision* (New York: The Free Press, 1970), pp. 240-245;

Rachael C. Burchard, *John Updike: Yea Sayings* (Carbondale, Ill.: Southern Illinois University Press, 1971);

Robert Detweiler, *John Updike* (New York: Twayne, 1972);

David D. Galloway, *The Absurd Hero in American Fiction*, revised edition (Austin: University of Texas Press, 1970), pp. 21-50;

Richard Gilman, *The Confusion of Realms* (New York: Random House, 1970), pp. 62-68;

Alice and Kenneth Hamilton, *The Elements of John Updike* (Grand Rapids, Mich.: Eerdmans, 1970);

Hamilton and Hamilton, *John Updike* (Grand Rapids, Mich.: Eerdmans, 1967);

Howard M. Harper, Jr., *Desperate Faith* (Chapel Hill: University of North Carolina Press, 1967), pp. 162-190;

Leo J. Hertzel, "Rabbit in the Great North Woods," *University Review* (Kansas City), 33 (December 1966): 143-147;

Granville Hicks, *Literary Horizons* (New York: New York University Press, 1970), pp. 107-133;

John S. Hill, "Quest for Belief: Theme in the Novels of John Updike," *Southern Humanities Review*, 3 (September 1969): 166-178;

Jane Howard, "Can a Nice Novelist Finish First?," *Life*, 61 (4 November 1966): 74-82;

Alfred Kazin, *Bright Book of Life* (Boston: Atlantic/ Little, Brown, 1973), pp. 119-124;

Joyce B. Markle, *Fighters and Lovers: Theme in the Novels of John Updike* (New York: New York University Press, 1973);

Arlin G. Meyer with Michael Olivas, "Criticism of John Updike: a Selected Checklist," *Modern Fiction Studies*, 20 (spring 1974): 121-133;

Arthur Mizener, *Sense of Life in the Modern Novel* (Boston: Houghton Mifflin, 1963), pp. 247-266;

Modern Fiction Studies, 20 (spring 1974), John Updike number, with eleven essays and a critical checklist;

Joyce Carol Oates, "Updike's American Comedies," *Modern Fiction Studies*, 21 (autumn 1975): 459-472;

Michael Olivas, *An Annotated Bibliography of John Updike Criticism 1967-1973, and a Checklist of His Works* (New York: Garland, 1975);

William Peden, *The American Short Story*, 2nd edition (Boston: Houghton Mifflin, 1975), pp. 47-53, ff.;

Richard H. Rupp, *Celebration in Postwar American Fiction* (Coral Gables, Fla.: University of Miami Press, 1970), pp. 41-57, 210-218;

Charles Thomas Samuels, *John Updike* (Minneapolis: University of Minnesota Press, 1969);

B. A. Sokoloff and David E. Arnason, *John Updike: A Comprehensive Bibliography* (Norwood, Penn.: Norwood Editions, 1973);

William T. Stafford, "The 'Curious Greased Grace' of John Updike: Some of His Critics and the American Tradition," *Journal of Modern Literature*, 2 (November 1972): 569-575;

Fred L. Standley, "*Rabbit, Run*: An Image of Life," *Midwest Quarterly*, 8 (1967): 371-386;

Tony Tanner, *City of Words* (New York: Harper & Row, 1971), pp. 141-152;

C. Clarke Taylor, *John Updike: A Bibliography* (Kent, Ohio: Kent State University Press, 1968);

Larry E. Taylor, *Pastoral and Anti-Pastoral Patterns in John Updike's Fiction* (Carbondale: Southern Illinois University Press, 1971);

Edward P. Vargo, *Rainstorms and Fire: Ritual in the Novels of John Updike* (Port Washington, N.Y.: Kennikat, 1973).

NOTE: The vast field of secondary work on Updike is listed in the *Modern Fiction Studies* number and in the bibliographies cited above. Updike himself has collated the major interviews with himself in *Picked-Up Pieces* (New York: Knopf, 1975), pp. 491-519.

Manuscripts:

The major collection of Updike's papers is at the Houghton Library of Harvard University. The Library of Congress has manuscripts, typescripts, and proofs of *The Poorhouse Fair, The Centaur, Of the Farm*, and other works.

Kurt Vonnegut, Jr.

Peter J. Reed
University of Minnesota

BIRTH: Indianapolis, Indiana, 11 November 1922.
EDUCATION: Cornell University, 1940-1942, 1945; University of Chicago, 1945-1947, M.A. (anthropology), awarded, 1971.
MARRIAGE: 1 September 1945 to Jane Marie Cox; children: Mark, Nannette, Edith.
AWARDS: Guggenheim Fellowship, 1967-1968; National Institute of Arts and Letters grant, 1970; Elected vice-president, National Institute of Arts and Letters, 1975.
MAJOR WORKS: *Player Piano* (New York: Scribners, 1952; London: Macmillan, 1953); *The Sirens of Titan* (New York: Dell, 1959; London: Gollancz, 1962); *Mother Night* (Greenwich, Conn.: Fawcett, 1962; London: Cape, 1968); *Cat's Cradle* (New York: Holt, Rinehart & Winston, 1963; London: Gollancz, 1963); *God Bless You, Mr. Rosewater; or, Pearls Before Swine* (New York: Holt, Rinehart & Winston, 1965; London: Cape, 1965); *Slaughterhouse-Five; or, The Children's Crusade* (New York: Seymour Lawrence/Delacorte, 1969; London: Cape, 1970); *Breakfast of Champions; or, Goodbye, Blue Monday* (New York: Seymour Lawrence/Delacorte, 1973; London: Cape, 1973); *Slapstick; or, Lonesome No More* (New York: Delacorte/Seymour Lawrence, 1976).

Kurt Vonnegut, Jr.

Jill Krementz

As of 1977, Vonnegut's work includes eight novels, a play and a television play, two collections of short stories, a collection of essays, and a number of uncollected shorter pieces of fiction and non-fiction. He is himself the subject of a number of books, critical articles, theses, and dissertations, as well as many reviews, interviews, and features in the popular press. Although he began publishing in 1950, it was really in the 1960s that he made his impact. His immediate appeal was to youth, partly because he espoused pacifism in the era of the Vietnam War. Besides peace, Vonnegut speaks of everyone's need for treatment with decency, respect, and compassion in a lonely, incomprehensible world. While his plots often seem pessimistic they are nevertheless funny, and he has been called a Black Humorist. He also has been tagged a science-fiction writer, a satirist, and a surrealist, but perhaps he might better be seen as using all of these techniques.

The release of the film *Slaughterhouse-Five* in 1972 completed the emergence of Kurt Vonnegut, Jr., from the obscurity of ten years before to a level of fame rivaled by few contemporary American authors. From 1950 to 1960 he remained virtually a literary unknown, despite stories in large circulation glossy magazines and two novels; from 1960 to 1970 his following swelled from a loyal but small "underground" coterie to a steadily expanding college-age audience to encompass finally a broad, heterogeneous, and perhaps truly national readership. Now it is accurate to speak of his appeal as international. That an international audience should develop is appropriate, for although in some ways, such as in his humor, he seems particularly American, and although he has been an astute observer and diagnostician of the American scene, Vonnegut's perspective remains essentially international. He makes it clear that he distrusts nationalism. He is the product of an era in which world war and nuclear explosion have made most parochial nationalism obsolete, in which humans have for the first time seen their own planet from space and recognized the imperative of mutual dependence. Yet Vonnegut's vision must surely be shaped by more humble influences. For, to return to *Slaughterhouse-Five*, the special anguish that Vonnegut felt over the firebombing of Dresden arose partly from his peculiar situation of being under attack by his own forces and sharing the sufferings of his "enemies," and in part from the fact that his own family was of German origin. Family remains an important concept for Vonnegut, from his assertion of the family's value for the individual, to his belief that we must all see ourselves as part of a larger human family. It is in family, then, that we can look for the beginnings of much that emerges later in his fiction.

Vonnegut's ancestors were prominent members of Indianapolis's large German-American community. Vonnegut's grandfather, Bernard Vonnegut, and his father Kurt were both architects and men of artistic sensibility, while on the Lieber side came prosperity from a successful brewery. Edith Lieber married Kurt Vonnegut, the author's father, on 22 November 1913, and for a short time they lived well.

The outbreak of World War I seriously changed the fortunes of the family. Vonnegut speaks of the impact of the war and of its residual anti-German feelings on his family in the opening of *Slapstick*. He dwells there on the psychological and cultural effects of being treated with prejudice and suspicion and of having a native language and artistic tradition denied. After the war, the family suffered economically, as well. First, Prohibition effectively ended all income from the brewing of beer. Then the Depression meant a drastic slowdown in the construction of houses—and in the need for architects to design them. For the ten years before World War II, Vonnegut's father was almost constantly unemployed. By that time there were three children: Bernard was born in 1914, Alice in 1917, and Kurt, Jr., in 1922. For the two elder children there were at first governesses and then private schools, but Kurt, Jr., went to public schools.

In 1940 Vonnegut went to Cornell University to major in biochemistry. By the beginning of his sophomore year he was writing for the student newspaper, the *Cornell Sun*, where several of his articles opposed American entry into the war. In particular he appealed for rationality and humanity in resisting German-baiting jingoism or any such talk that exalts brutality in the name of patriotism. But the Japanese attack on Pearl Harbor lessened his reservations about the war, and Vonnegut volun-

teered for military service in January 1943. Though he was at first rejected for health reasons, he finally entered the army in March, knowing that descendants of his great-grandfather were German officers.

Meanwhile, the problems faced by Vonnegut's parents mounted. In 1941 they moved to a new, smaller house designed and built by Kurt, Sr., in the northern suburbs of Indianapolis. Vonnegut's father is described as having become increasingly fatalistic about the ruin of his career. Vonnegut's mother also found their sinking fortunes hard to endure. She tried to make money by writing short stories, and when this failed she became prone to depression. In 1944, Vonnegut obtained special leave to return home for Mother's Day. The night before he arrived, she took an overdose of sleeping pills and died in her sleep.

In the Battle of the Bulge, Vonnegut was among large numbers of Americans taken prisoner. He was sent to Dresden where, like Billy Pilgrim in *Slaughterhouse-Five*, he worked making a diet supplement for pregnant women. On 13 February, Royal Air Force bombers made a heavy raid on Dresden which was continued during the following day by the United States Air Force. Through this devastating raid Vonnegut, again like Billy Pilgrim, was sheltered in a meat storage cellar below a slaughterhouse. The devastation brought on Dresden was almost total as the compounded fires became one huge conflagration. The horrors intensified when the prisoners were employed to dig through the rubble for corpses.

It is commonplace for critics to dwell on the effects of the Dresden firebombing in Vonnegut's work, but he has denied that his war experiences were pivotal:

> The importance of Dresden in my life has been considerably exaggerated because my book about it became a best seller. If the book hadn't been a best seller, it would seem like a very minor experience in my life. And I don't think people's lives are changed by short-term events like that. Dresden was astonishing, but experiences can be astonishing without changing you. It did make me feel sort of like I'd paid my dues—being as hungry as I was for long as I was in prison camp. Hunger is a normal experience for a human being, but not for a middle-class American human being. I was phenomenally hungry for about six months.

In April 1945 Soviet troops occupied Dresden and Vonnegut was liberated and repatriated to the United States where he was awarded the Purple Heart. On 1 September he married Jane Marie Cox and that fall enrolled at the University of Chicago to study anthropology. During 1946 he supplemented his family income by working as a police reporter for the Chicago City News Bureau. In the following year he finished his M.A. thesis, "Fluctuations Between Good and Evil in Simple Tales," only to have it unanimously rejected by the faculty of the Chicago anthropology department. In 1971, the anthropology department accepted *Cat's Cradle* in lieu of a thesis and he was awarded the degree.

In 1947 one of the more important episodes in Vonnegut's life began. He went to work for General Electric Research Laboratory in Schenectady, New York, as a public relations writer. Vonnegut draws directly on this experience in several of his works, perhaps most conspicuously in the story "Deer in the Works" and his first novel, *Player Piano*. The Ilium of the latter is an ironically named parody of Schenectady, and the Ilium Works a hyperbolically rendered version of the General Electric plant. Vonnegut worked at writing in Schenectady, at first trying unsuccessfully to recount some aspect of his Dresden experience. Success came in 1949 with the acceptance of his first short story, "Report on the Barnhouse Effect," which appeared in the February 1950 *Collier's*, soon to be followed by others and by *Player Piano*. In 1951, Vonnegut made the decisive step; he resigned his job with General Electric and moved to Provincetown, Massachusetts (and later to West Barnstable), to devote himself to full-time writing.

The short stories that Vonnegut wrote during these early years of his career were quite widely varied in nature and subject. He was to speak of them later as inconsequential works written to support himself while he wrote novels. Whether he really thought so lightly of them is uncertain, but it is true that he achieved commercial success with the short stories almost instantly, whereas it would be almost twenty years before he began to earn much from his novels. *Collier's, Ladies' Home Journal, Cosmopolitan, Esquire*, and *Saturday Evening Post* were among the prominent magazines which published stories by Vonnegut during the 1950s. Although several of these stories used Vonnegut's knowledge of science or technology, few would qualify as science fiction. Rather, they represent the author's attempt to relate a world he has experienced, one in which technology plays a large and daily increasing role. The stories which have such technology-related plots are generally set in recognizable, mundane worlds rather than the exotic settings frequently common to science fiction. Their purpose often seems to be, in fact, to cause reflection on what the impact of technological innovations might

be on the daily lives of ordinary people. In "EPICAC," for instance, the developing trend toward having computers do everything for us is taken to the extreme when EPICAC's operator uses the machine to help him win a woman's affections with love poetry. The message about the dehumanization of modern man is delivered through an ironic reversal: the computer "humanizes," falls in love, despairs, and commits suicide.

Vonnegut later had a few short stories published in *Galaxy Science Fiction* and *Magazine of Fantasy and Science Fiction*, which, along with the technological content of other stories and of *Player Piano*, helped earn him the label of science-fiction writer. A glance at stories like "Long Walk to Forever," "Miss Temptation," "Next Door," "More Stately Mansions," or "The Hyannis Port Story" reveals this generalized label as misleading. While Vonnegut's work for General Electric, his earlier education, and perhaps his scientist brother are evident in some stories, at least equally evident is a reportorial sense for human interest. The stories often deal with quite ordinary lives, which are perceived with a mix of compassion and ironic humor, and, in the end, extol homespun middle-class values. In fact, his inclusion of the technological, especially in the earlier stories and *Player Piano*, is not a reaching toward the exotic but a continuation of his concern with the level of reality which touches many daily lives. "I supposed," he has said of *Player Piano*, "that I was writing a novel about life, about things I could not avoid seeing and hearing in Schenectady, a very real town, awkwardly set in the gruesome now."

In *Player Piano* (1952) Schenectady becomes the Ilium of a fictional, if still gruesome, future. The General Electric plant has become the great Ilium Works, one-time home of Edison but now under the direction of Paul Proteus. In his late thirties, Proteus is still on the way up, and at the opening of the novel appears poised between the decision to push for the next promotion or to succumb to a troubling malaise which makes him question not just the promotion but even his present status. A visit by an old friend proves crucial in deciding which way Proteus will go. Ed Finnerty is a contemporary who has also been an engineer and manager and who has received rapid promotions. Yet now he has actually quit the company. More dramatically, he effectively has rejected the whole social system and soon becomes a sought-after outlaw. Proteus dismisses the course of the outspoken, hard-drinking, and grubby Irishman as too extreme. Yet through Finnerty, Proteus is introduced to persons and circumstances which lead

CHAPTER ONE

Yes.

In the spring of 1977 I was wearing olive drab overalls.
I was sitting alone on one of twenty narrow cots on the second
floor of a wooden barracks that had been built for an Air
Force recruits in World War Two.   On my lap were two white bedsheets
and a pillowcase.   That quilt, and eight others just like it,
were on the edge of Charlotte Air Force Base near Atlanta,
Georgia.   They constituted a Federal minimum security prison camp for white collar criminals.

I had not committed a violent crime. No one there had
committed a violent crime.

My name is Walker Kelvin. I am a graduate of Harvard and
Oxford. I was then sixty two.

And I would have told you then that life was total nonsense
from start to end.

xxxxxxxx * * * * * * *

There were no bars on the windows or locks on the doors.
The only fence started nowhere and ended nowhere, and was intended
to keep us prisoners from wandering out onto an active runway
nearby.   I was alone because all the other prisoners had chores
to do, whereas I was about to be set free.   I had served eighteen
months for my preposterous contributions to the already forgotten
American political scandals known collectively as "Watergate."

I was bored stupid to tears.

I had stripped my cot, as ordered, and was waiting for a
guard to fetch me to the supply room, where I would turn in my

From early draft typescript of novel-in-progress.

JAN 14, 1978

CHAPTER ONE

Life goes on. Yes. And a fool and his good reputation are soon parted.

In the spring of 1977, there was a fifty-two year old graduate of Harvard and Oxford who had lost his good reputation -- and his money and his friends. Not even his only child, his grown son, would speak to him any more. His son was a book reviewer for The New York Times.

His name was Walker Kelvin. He was sitting alone now on one of twenty cots on the second floor of a wooden barracks that had been built for Army Air Force recruits during World War Two. The building, and six others just like it, were on the edge of Finletter Air Force Base near Atlanta, Georgia. They now constituted a Federal minimum security prison camp for white collar criminals.

There were no bars on the windows. The only fence was intended to keep prisoners from wandering out onto the tip of an active airplane runway nearby. Kelvin was all alone because all the other prisoners had chores to do, whereas he was about to be set free. He had served eighteen months for his own preposterous contributions to the already forgotten American political scandals known collectively as "Watergate."

Kelvin had been an athlete in college -- before he gave up athletics for radical politics. Before he became co-chairman of the Harvard Chapter of the Young Communist League, he had been stroke of the second boat of the Harvard Crew.

At least he was lean again, thanks to prison -- and his muscle

"It is my custom to doodle on superseded drafts, and to sign and date the doodles."

Kurt Vonnegut, Jr.

to his rejecting the company and the system, and ultimately to his leading an armed rebellion. The rebellion fails, but in the novel's terms, that may be less important than the fact that Proteus does not fail himself. In the end he achieves much self-perception and makes a stand for his values.

Though Proteus's decision to turn against the company clearly has a relationship to Vonnegut's life in the period preceding the novel, equating Vonnegut with Proteus alone might be misleading. Like many good writers, Vonnegut writes a part of himself into various characters; there is obviously a great deal of the Ed Finnerty in Vonnegut. Finnerty is the practical joker, the iconoclast, the one who loves fun and life and freedom, and all these things characterize Vonnegut, too. A key event in the novel concerns a cat which tries to escape from the fully-automated Ilium factory. At the last it scales a high fence, is killed by the electrified wires at the top, and falls "dead and smoking, but outside." Proteus and Finnerty fight to escape that fence, and although they appear to be condemned to death, they are outside the confines of the moribund, mechanized society at the end.

By using the name "Ilium" Vonnegut invites an ironic contrast between modern cities like Schenectady (or the Utopian vision of what technology can make them) and the Troy of Homer. The name "Proteus," from the god who could change his appearance at will, shows the same interest in myth and the ironic use of names. Vonnegut continues to make much play with the use of names in later fiction. Sometimes they are, as here, allusive, sometimes punning, and often satirical. *Player Piano* contains a good deal of satire—of the army, of the business leader's retreat, of college "amateur" athletics, to name a few—which underlines its serious purpose as social commentary. Certainly the depiction of what happens to persons deprived of useful social function, of the psychological cost to the individual of Utopian schemes to make the masses placidly happy, serves as a kind of sociological editorializing.

While the satire entertains and at the same time carries the novel's message, there is besides something about *Player Piano* which other anti-utopian or satiric novels often lack and which becomes more evident in Vonnegut's later works. There is a personal touch, an element of human warmth, even the suggestion of authorial concern in the kind of novel which is often distanced, objective-seeming, and generalized. In part that human touch shows up in the faltering uncertainty of Paul Proteus, in his yearning for something earthy and homey. Perhaps Paul's urge toward the old Gottwald farm owes much to the impulse that led Vonnegut away from General Electric and Schenectady to a big old house on Cape Cod. Certainly something like Paul's nostalgia for a time when social values were different and seemed to offer the individual more sense of belonging emerges frequently both in Vonnegut's fiction and in what he has said in interviews. And yet another personal touch in this novel which recurs is talk of the writer and his place in society. In *Player Piano*, of course, the writer is satirized—he has let his wife go on the street rather than give up his artistic integrity by writing what the market demands. Obviously, the treatment of this writer involves some self-parody in its mockery, yet the satire also works in the other direction at the expense of the commercial and philistine elements of society which can make a writer's life misery. Writers, almost invariably suggesting some form of self-parody, reappear in many of Vonnegut's novels. The self-deprecating humor, compassion, nostalgia, and hint of long-suffering fatalism heard in the narrative voice of *Player Piano* become recognizable as Vonnegut's characteristic tone. As he writes more novels, he continues to show these qualities and enters into his novels increasingly directly.

Player Piano attracted no critical acclaim at publication, and to this day seldom wins praise equal to that reserved for some subsequent novels. During the seven years that lapsed between the publication of *Player Piano* and the appearance of *The Sirens of Titan*, Vonnegut worked on another never-to-be-finished novel, "Upstairs and Downstairs," wrote short stories, and sought to supplement his income with activities such as opening a Saab dealership and writing advertising copy. In 1957 his father died of lung cancer, and this is reported to have caused a writing block which lasted for a year. Another death which profoundly affected him was that of his sister Alice. This coincided closely with the death of her husband (as recounted in the introduction to *Slapstick*) and led to Vonnegut's adopting three of his four nephews.

By the late 1950s some of the magazines such as *Collier's*, which had formed a ready market for Vonnegut's stories, were struggling. Partly because of this change, Vonnegut turned to writing novels for the paperback market. *The Sirens of Titan*, which does have certain affinities with the "space opera," further added to the branding of Vonnegut as a science-fiction writer. He was not anxious to be so categorized, wishing rather to be recognized as someone who wrote about contemporary existence in realistic terms—which included taking into account scientific and technological advances and their intrusions into the average citizen's life. In that respect there is little doubt Vonnegut felt much of what he has Eliot Rosewater voice: "I love you sons of bitches," Eliot says to science fiction writers, "You're the only ones who'll talk about the *really* terrific changes going on . . . the only ones with guts enough to *really* care about the future, who *really* notice what machines do to us, what cities do to us. . . ." At the same time, Vonnegut saw the classification as an impediment and a kind of discrimination, remarking subsequently that the critics who put him in the science fiction drawer often subsequently mistook that drawer for a urinal.

The Sirens of Titan (1959) has won the respect of many readers, some of whom regard it as the author's best book. It is basically the story of a playboy millionaire, Malachi Constant, who is told he will become a space traveler—and does, even though he has no real wish to. He is whisked off by Martians with a society woman named Beatrice Rumfoord. Despite their mutual contempt, they conceive a child, a son they call Chrono. After a brutal period of victimization on Mars, and years trapped on Mercury, Malachi at last returns to earth. There he is hailed by the new religion, the Church of God the Utterly Indifferent, as the long-promised Space Wanderer when he speaks the foretold words, "I was a victim of a series of accidents, as are we all." Soon after, however, he is made the religion's scapegoat, reviled, and hurled back into space. He ends his days, as has been promised from the start, on Titan, in the company of Beatrice, Chrono, and a Tralfamadorian robot named Salo. There the once-embittered Chrono joins the beautiful giant bluebirds and learns to thank his parents for the gift of life, Beatrice turns from resenting having been used all her life to being glad she was of some use, and the egocentrically loveless Malachi learns the value of loving "whoever is around to be loved." He also learns to his dismay that the earth and all its civilizations are no more than a message center for the Tralfamadorians. Stonehenge, for example, is a kind of note telling Salo that a missing part is on the way.

This second novel contains much that is repeated or amplified in subsequent novels. Simple repetitions include Tralfamadorians (although they change in appearance and nature) and the Rumfoord family, while conceptions like that of nonlinear time ("everything that ever has been always will be, and everything that ever will be always has been"), of the futility of searching for existential meaning outside of self when the answer can only be found within, or of the superiority of a charitable love between any or all humans to a narrower conjugal love also reappear with variation. The relationship between Malachi and Beatrice goes beyond the commonplace inadequacies of the Paul-Anita marriage of *Player Piano*. An important conception of love is affirmed through them. And yet, there is really no romantic love story here, and Beatrice hardly emerges as a fully developed female character. In later years Vonnegut was to admit that neither a real woman nor a romantic love relationship has appeared in his novels. Father and son relationships reemerge, as, in a lesser way, does the role of the writer. Once again the main character becomes involved in a form of quest for meaning in his own life and undergoes several stages of change in himself, coming to a level of understanding he lacked at the outset. While the protagonist changes, however, there is a sense that the world cannot be changed, that existence is governed by inevitability. Despite the strong element of fatalism in the book, it contains more humor than *Player Piano*. *The Sirens of Titan* is rich in contrasts, its humor and its pathos mutually sharpened by their juxtaposition, its portrayals of scarcely-relieved suffering and the cold wastes of space heightening its affirmation of the joy of life and the value of love.

For all this, and for all its subsequent recognition, *The Sirens of Titan* brought no great change to Vonnegut's reputation. In the meantime, however, Vonnegut had signed a two-book contract with Fawcett, a paperback house, which was to cover *Canary in a Cat House* and *Mother Night*. *Canary in a Cat House* (1961) was a collection of twelve short stories previously published in magazines between 1950 and 1958. This collection quickly went out of print, though all but one of the stories were reprinted in *Welcome to the Monkey House*.

The second book of the Fawcett contract was *Mother Night* (1962), the story of an American playwright with a German wife living in Germany before World War II. Howard W. Campbell, Jr., is persuaded to remain in Germany during the war as an American agent. His cover involves becoming a Nazi propagandist, in which role he remains hated and hunted after the war without being able to reveal his other identity as spy. Caught and tried by the Israelis, he appears to be saved when his American control breaks all security to verify Campbell's secret activity, but then Campbell apparently commits suicide. The novel represents his memoirs written during those final days in an Israeli prison. What troubles Campbell most is a search for his own true identity; was he really the Nazi or really the spy?

Vonnegut supplied the novel with a simple moral when he added an Introduction to it in 1966: "We are what we pretend to be, so we must be careful about what we pretend to be."

In its plot, *Mother Night* is strikingly different from the two previous novels. *Player Piano* and *The Sirens of Titan*, of course, are widely different, but they share such basic plot elements as the use of a fictional future and an emphasis on technology. *Mother Night* has no future, no technology, nothing science-fictional. It is the first of the novels to be written with a first-person narrator, and that helps to deepen the characterization of the protagonist and to intensify the inward reaching, on both his part and the author's, that goes on in this book. Partly for these reasons, *Mother Night* has been seen as "different" by several commentators and is regarded by many as marking a transition in Vonnegut's work or as being his best. Vonnegut himself admits to the book's difference, partly because at the time his head was filled with the work of the British playwright Harold Pinter, "so I was rather gloomy as I finished up the book," and partly "because of the war and because of my German background, and that sort of thing." Despite these differences, there are nevertheless strong lines of continuity to the other stories. Campbell becomes the most intense rendition yet of the protagonist in quest of meaning in an absurd world. Like his predecessors he begins as a rather shallow and unappealing person who suffers and learns and finally becomes a character who has won our involvement if not our affection. Like the others he feels the desire to call "Olly-olly-ox-in-free" and resign from life, but like them he finds that he cannot. Typically the point of resignation seems to be a necessary step toward a limited recognition of his relationship to life. Since Campbell is a writer, the writers-and-artists theme receives more extensive treatment than ever in *Mother Night*. In particular it is with the writer as deceiver, the creator of fictional worlds who makes his audiences believe, that Vonnegut seems most concerned here. Ironically, Campbell himself has difficulty deciding what is true.

Cat's Cradle, the next novel, appeared in 1963 in hardcover, thanks largely to the efforts of Samuel Stewart, who had recently joined Holt, Rinehart & Winston. The return to hardcover would eventually mean that Vonnegut's work would be taken seriously, but *Cat's Cradle* was another of those works which reviewers could classify as science fiction. The story focuses on the three children of a scientist named Felix Hoenikker who, Vonnegut says, owes much of his characterization to Dr. Irving Langmuir, a researcher at General Electric in Schenectady. Thus, when in the story Hoenikker leaves a tip for his wife under his breakfast plate, or when he becomes preoccupied with whether turtles buckle or compress their spines when they retract their heads, it is because Langmuir is reputed to have done both those things. Likewise, the central plot device of the novel, *ice-nine*, owes its existence to the same source. Vonnegut tells the story that when H.G. Wells, the British novelist who wrote some compelling science fiction, came to visit the Schenectady laboratory

> Langmuir thought he might entertain Wells with an idea for a science-fiction story—about a form of ice that was stable at room temperature. Wells was uninterested, or at least never used the idea. And then Wells died, and then, finally, Langmuir died. I thought to myself: "Finders, keepers—the idea is mine." Langmuir, incidentally, was the first scientist in private industry to win a Nobel Prize.

Ice-nine becomes the cause of the end of the world. The narrator of *Cat's Cradle*, who calls himself John or Jonah, has set out originally to write a book called *The Day the World Ended*, meaning his subject to be the day Hiroshima was atom-bombed. In this concern with bombings and apocalyptic ends, one senses that Vonnegut is edging closer to talking about Dresden.

With the use of the General Electric laboratory, Langmuir, and the Dresden experience all evident, it is apparent that *Cat's Cradle* continues Vonnegut's tendency to become increasingly autobiographical in his novels. There is other evidence of that, too. Hoenikker resembles other father-figures in Vonnegut, and may owe almost as much to Kurt, Sr., as to Langmuir. Like the Vonnegut family, Hoenikker's three children include an older son who is a scientist, a tall middle daughter, and a younger son who joins Delta Upsilon. In this there is a correspondence between Vonneguts and Hoenikkers. And once again Vonnegut makes the writer within the novel the focus of some self-deprecating humor. Jonah becomes a follower of Bokonon, who is also a writer and who warns, "All the truths you are about to read are shameless lies." The writer-as-deceiver theme moves a step beyond *Mother Night*.

In 1965, Holt, Rinehart & Winston published a second Vonnegut novel in hardcover, *God Bless You, Mr. Rosewater*, the story of a shell-shocked multimillionaire who seeks to realize the motto, "Goddamn it, you've got to be kind." Many have seen that motto as the essence of Vonnegut. What the novel reveals, however, is that even such a simple

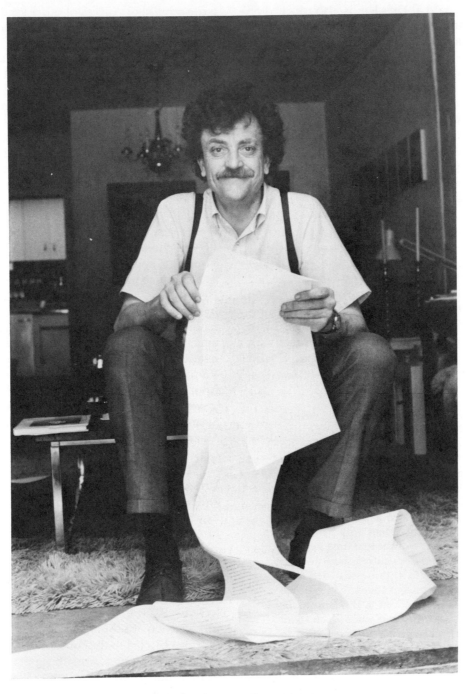

Jill Krementz

Kurt Vonnegut with manuscript.

sounding objective becomes difficult and complicated in the contemporary world. Eliot Rosewater makes an interesting variation on the Vonnegut protagonist for he, under the kinds of stresses that drive the others to the point of resignation, falls into a Lear-like madness. Sanity and questions of what constitutes insanity in an absurd environment become fully developed theses in this novel. There is another semi-autobiographical, tongue-in-cheek

portrait of the writer in *Rosewater,* too. This comes in the figure of Kilgore Trout, perhaps the most famous of all Vonnegut's characters. He is a science fiction writer who has published countless stories—which are frequently shelved with pornography—and who remains destitute and unknown while working at various menial jobs. Trout is, as Vonnegut has admitted, a vision of what the author feared he might become. Another previously seen theme, the great raid at Dresden, is also touched on several times, and at one point Rosewater hallucinates that Indianapolis is consumed in a Dresden-style firestorm.

It might seem that at this point Vonnegut's career should have reached a plateau from which to launch the final climb to success. He had written three of the novels most often named as his best (*The Sirens of Titan, Mother Night,* and *God Bless You, Mr. Rosewater*—the other would be *Slaughterhouse-Five*) and had returned to publication in hardcover. Yet in fact his situation was far from ideal. The once-remunerative short story market was gone, his science fiction reputation was keeping him from being seriously reviewed, the two hardcover novels had sold only a few thousand copies, and the only work he had left in print was *Rosewater*. Besides having his own three children to provide for, he had adopted three of his sister Alice's four sons. It was in this situation that Vonnegut accepted an appointment at the Writers Workshop at the University of Iowa. The position brought him into contact with other writers and with students and faculty, with consequences which Jerome Klinkowitz has described:

> The first result for Vonnegut's own writing was a startling self-consciousness. For earlier novels, *Cat's Cradle* in particular, his publishers had warned him not to use his own name or personality in fiction. In Iowa City Vonnegut learned there were no real reasons not to, and so for the hardcover issue of *Mother Night* he added a personal preface about his own involvement with "the Nazi monkey-business." For the first time in print, he told about the Dresden massacre and his own act of witness to it. Two years later, as he left Iowa City, Vonnegut added a confessional preface to his story collection *Welcome to the Monkey House,* which explained much about how his own personality expressed itself in stories and novels. And by then he had figured out *Slaughterhouse-Five.*

By the time he left Iowa in 1967, the upturn was under way. His "underground" following, mainly among college students, was beginning to break through to a larger audience, Dell and Avon republished his novels in paperback, Harper & Row republished *Mother Night,* and Holt, Rinehart & Winston reprinted *Player Piano*—all this in 1966 and 1967.

Vonnegut, meanwhile, had not ceased writing shorter prose entirely as his production of novels increased. Rather, in the mid-1960s, he began to write more short pieces of other kinds than the now largely marketless short stories, including essays, reviews, short travel accounts, and human-interest stories. "Brief Encounters on the Inland Waterway" (1966) recounts a journey from Massachusetts to Florida on the Kennedy yacht crewing for their captain, Frank Wirtanen (whose name had been borrowed for the character of an American intelligence office in *Mother Night*). "Oversexed in Indianapolis" (1970) is a review of a novel written by another graduate of Shortridge High School, *Going All the Way* by Dan Wakefield. A couple of pieces in 1969 deal with witnessing the launching of space rockets. Many of these were later to be collected in *Wampeters, Foma & Granfalloons,* published in 1974. A characteristic of this short nonfiction is that Vonnegut frequently includes himself directly, just as he starts to in his novels from about 1966 onward. He may write reportage, but he lets us know who is reporting and how he feels about what he is reporting. One of the most interesting aspects of this material for the reader becomes the emergent relationship between observer/writer and subject. Vonnegut's association with the short story was far from over, however, and he prepared and introduced a new collection which was published in 1968 by Seymour Lawrence/Delacorte. *Welcome to the Monkey House* included eleven of the stories from *Canary in a Cat House,* plus fourteen more.

The year after leaving Iowa, Vonnegut visited Dresden with the assistance of a Guggenheim Fellowship, gathering material for the novel on that experience which was to emerge as *Slaughterhouse-Five.* In the course of preparing the novel, Vonnegut visited his old friend Bernard O'Hare, who had been a scout, then a prisoner, with him in Germany, and who is now an attorney in Pennsylvania, to see if together they could uncover more specific recollections. It was then, as Vonnegut notes in the introduction to *Slaughterhouse-Five,* that Mary O'Hare objected to the conception of the story which seemed to be afoot as something that could be turned into a movie starring John Wayne and Frank Sinatra. Vonnegut comments, "She freed me to write about what infants we really were: 17, 18, 19, 20, 21. We were baby-faced, and as a prisoner of war I don't think I had to shave very often. I don't recall that was a problem." The description fits the kind of character Vonnegut places at the center of the novel; the bemused, "eager to please," naive Billy Pilgrim. Many things which happened to Vonnegut are made to happen to Billy Pilgrim. He gets caught up in the Battle of the Bulge, wanders between the lines searching for his own forces, meets up with some other Americans, is taken prisoner, spends a long time packed in cattle cars with little food and sleeping standing up, becomes employed in Dresden making a vitamin-supplemented malt syrup for pregnant women, escapes the great air raid of 13 February by taking shelter in a meat storage locker deep underground, comes up to be used by the Germans in digging corpses from the ruins of the city, and finally is repatriated. All of that happened to Kurt Vonnegut, too, although the specific details of biography and novel sometimes vary. Many other things happen to Billy Pilgrim, of course, which Vonnegut has never claimed happened to him: he visits Tralfamadore, he "time trips" into the future and back, he becomes a kind of preacher. Yet through these multiple roles and situations, Billy Pilgrim's characterization retains a thread of consistency, and he emerges as a modern Everyman who is part innocent, part fool, part victim. He becomes a pilgrim who is lost, an innocent Jesus who suffers without having a purpose, and yet, like the other protagonists, through losing all, even at times his wits, he comes in the end to a species of knowledge that brings him the ability to live in peace with a world whose madness and cruelty were epitomized in the blasting of Dresden. Perhaps the most striking thing is that in this book in which Vonnegut at last confronts the Dresden experience the dominant tones are not of anger or bitterness nor even of pain so much as of compassion and sorrow.

Slaughterhouse-Five fascinates not just in its content but in the ways in which it is put together. There are multiple plot lines, just as there were in *Player Piano*, but here their interrelationship is much more complicated in that it is temporal as well as spatial. On the title page Vonnegut describes the novel as "somewhat in the telegraphic schizophrenic manner of tales from the planet Tralfamadore, where the flying saucers come from." Later the Tralfamadorian novel is described as being made up of "clumps of symbols" each of which "is a brief, urgent message," which the Tralfamadorians read simultaneously rather than consecutively. That seems to be almost what Vonnegut attempts in constantly juxtaposing brief scenes from different plot lines, places, and times, all of which flow together to cohere at the focal event, time, and place: Dresden. The novel integrates in other ways, too. Vonnegut integrates himself into the novel more directly and extensively than in any previous book. The whole story is framed by the autobiographical beginning and ending, so that from the mind of the author we are "merged," as it were, into the world of the novel. And that relationship is maintained throughout with interjected moments where Vonnegut appears as a character, noting, "That was me," or, "I said that." And finally, the novel integrates a great deal that has gone before, from familiar characters, names, and places to catch-phrases, ideas, and themes. This well-constructed work seems to pull together all that Vonnegut had been reaching toward in the previous novels.

Slaughterhouse-Five enjoyed a greater commercial success than had any of the previous novels. By now Vonnegut was emerging from the "underground" of a largely youthful audience to a wider recognition. Much of the developing interest in Vonnegut was not simply with the literary man, but with the social observer and commentator on life as a popular philosopher. Many of his views struck a sympathetic chord in this era of the Vietnam War, not as merely relating to war itself, but to such issues as over-population, ecology preservation, and the consumer protection which were also enjoying popularity. This popularity was to grow even greater in the next few years, hastened in part by the making of the film *Slaughterhouse-Five*. He now became much more the public figure. In 1969, for example, he was invited to a symposium on the novel at Brown University; in the following year he gave the commencement address to the graduating class of Bennington College, won a grant from the National Institute of Arts and Letters, and spent a term teaching creative writing at Harvard University. In January of 1970, he flew into Biafra, a part of Nigeria fighting for independence, accompanying an aircraft load of medical and food supplies. Scarcely was his visit over when Biafra fell. His moving account of the suffering of the Biafrans and of the beauty and strength of their family system was published in *McCall's* (and later included in *Wampeters, Foma & Granfalloons*), though these impressions emerge most profoundly in *Slapstick*.

Despite success and recognition, Vonnegut experienced a rather troubled phase in his life, marked by some severe depression. Possibly contributing may have been the fact that now at last the Dresden book was finished, perhaps leaving the kind of flatness which often follows the attainment of a goal. Perhaps he had, in effect, purged himself of the major motivational drive for his writing. Factors which he has mentioned himself include his children's ages, now all leaving or having left home, and his own age, approaching fifty. And Vonnegut seems to have been uncomfortable with his new found popularity and visibility. Doubtless he was glad to escape the Kilgore Trout fate he earlier had feared, yet the new role imposed strains, too.

the trousers were wet in the center. In the last newspaper
photographs taken of me as I sat at the back of a Federal Marshal's car after a sentencing, I appeared to be hanging my
head in shame. I was in fact noticing that I had just
set my pants afire.

****

Back in the White House, in the basement of the Executive Office
Building, I used to smoke three and four packages of cigarettes
a day -- especially after my wife died. Few people complained. I
had no associates -- not even a secretary. People entered my
office only by mistake, and seldom stayed long. Emil Larkin
looked in one day, I remember, and asked if I knew where he could
find a volleyball. He was still a great athlete then.

In the four years I was there, my most intimate visit came from
three of the so-called "Plumbers". They were a special espionage
service operating on orders from the White House, and their office
was right above mine. They wanted to know who I was, and they
performed some experiments, yelling and stamping around upstairs,
to see if I could possibly hear anything through the floor.
I could not.
I remember one of them asked way come the panes in my little
window, which was way up high, right under the ceiling, were amber.
I myself hadn't noticed, and was then at a loss for an answer.

I have an answer now: The panes were thickly coated with cigarette tar.

************************************* JAN. 9, 1978

Did I notice how useless I was? Did I notice that no one ever
had a question for the President's Special Advisor on Youth Affairs?
No.

From early draft typescript of novel-in-progress.

504

4

the trousers, very near the crotch. In the last newspaper pictures

graph taken of me, as I sat in the back of a Federal Marshal's

sedan after being sentenced, I appeared to be hanging my head

in haggard shame. I was in fact noticing that I had set my

suitpants on fire with a cigarette.

Back in the White House, especially after my wife died, I used

to smoke three and four packages of cigarettes a day. It did not

matter to anybody but myself, since I had no associates -- not

even a secretary. Only once in four years was I asked to say

anything about youth.

But I was so humorless back then -- and, I have to think, senile,

too. I was capable, at any rate, of endless seriousness about

a job which had no connection with the rest of the world whatsoever.

I subscribed to hundreds of college newspapers and magazines, and

read them all. In the name of the White House, I asked the Federal

Bureau of Investigation to furnish me with a weekly summary of

student radical activities anywhere in the country, and dossiers

of the seeming leaders. I kept all this in burglar-proof file

cabinets. *Only I had the keys*

And let me lapse back into that period of senile humorlessness

for a moment in order to say this: I thought of those rioting young

people not as felons but as my own children, who were too ignorant

to know how wrong they were. I myself had been a radical in my

time, and a noisy one -- co-chairman of the Young Communist League

at Harvard, co-editor of The Commonwealth Progressive, a frankly

Marxist weekly newspaper, edited by students for Cambridge and

Boston working people. I had been co-chairman of a fund drive

that raised money for two ambulances which were sent to the Inter-

national Brigade then fighting the Fascists in the Spanish Civil

JAN. 10, 1978

From early draft typescript of novel-in-progress.

505

Vonnegut discusses that problem (largely through making Trout suddenly rich and famous) and others reflecting this troubled period in his life in *Breakfast of Champions*, a book already begun but not to be finished and published until 1973.

Saying that he was dissatisfied with insubstantial characters who existed only on paper and that he would therefore write no more novels, Vonnegut cast about for a new direction. He found solid characters, and a new family to replace his own dissolving one, in the theatre. On 7 October 1970, his play *Happy Birthday, Wanda June* opened on Broadway and was to run until 14 March 1971. It was based on one he had written some fifteen years earlier, derived from two attitudes. One is an impatience with the figure of the Hemingway-type hero who demonstrates his manhood by killing beautiful and rare animals that never harmed him and by abusing women. The other is an interest in Penelope of Homer's *Odyssey*, one of the works included in the Great Books program which Vonnegut and his wife had conducted on Cape Cod. Indeed, the original play carried the title "Penelope." *Slaughterhouse-Five* makes the point that all people need to feel they retain some dignity; *Wanda June* shows a proud "hero" whose false sense of dignity denies any kind of dignity to women, nonwhite races, and a good many other men.

By 1971 he had moved, alone, to New York. The next year saw the performance on public television of a ninety-minute screenplay, *Between Time and Timbuktu*, which collects scenes, characters, and themes from various pieces of Vonnegut's work. Like *Happy Birthday, Wanda June*, it was also published in the same year that it was performed, by Seymour Lawrence/Delacorte.

Breakfast of Champions, which appeared in 1973 but had been begun soon after *Slaughterhouse-Five* and laid aside, marked its author's return to the novel. Theatre and screen were appealing and interesting, but for Vonnegut they imposed an important limitation; they made it much harder for him to appear as a character in his work. In the preface to *Between Time and Timbuktu*, he says, "I want to be a character in all of my works. . . . I have always rigged my stories so as to include myself, and I can't stop now. And I do this so slyly, as do most novelists, that the author *can't* be put on film." Vonnegut puts himself very firmly into this novel, for he appears directly in it as both character and author. He appears as Philboyd Studge, the "author" of this novel which details how Dwayne Hoover, a Pontiac dealer, runs amok after reading a science-fiction novel by Kilgore Trout, another Vonnegut surrogate. The subtitle, *Goodbye Blue Monday!* suggests the author's reemergence here from a period of malaise and uncertainty, and that he is indeed writing the book as a fiftieth birthday present to himself. He also claims that the book clears all the clutter of the past from his mind, including his old characters. Indeed Vonnegut casts Kilgore Trout loose, as indeed he must, with a degree of regret on both sides. Trout's last request is, "Make me young!" But the young Vonnegut and the Vonnegut who might have become a Kilgore Trout are gone. Instead Vonnegut has to grapple with the problem of the now famous and "fabulously-well-to-do" Kilgore Trout, of having people take what was only "solipsistic whimsey" as gospel. For good measure, Vonnegut tosses more "solipsistic whimsey" into the book in the form of drawings which adorn nearly every page.

Although it drew frequently unfavorable reviews, *Breakfast of Champions* became Vonnegut's greatest publishing success to that date, with a first printing of 100,000 copies. His popularity was now at its height, and he had achieved more serious critical and scholarly recognition as well. Two critical quarterlies, *Summary* and *Critique*, ran special Vonnegut numbers in 1971, and two book-length studies, *Writers for the 'Seventies: Kurt Vonnegut, Jr.*, by Peter Reed and *The Vonnegut Statement*, edited by Jerome Klinkowitz and John Somer, came out of academe. Vonnegut won honorary degrees from Indiana University (1973) and Hobart and William Smith College (1974), appointment as Distinguished Professor of English Prose by the City University of New York (Fall 1973—he left in February 1974), and election to vice-president of the National Institute of Arts and Letters (1975).

While *Breakfast of Champions* seemed quite different from most of the fiction that had gone before it, *Slapstick* (1976) appears to reach back in thought if not in style. It is the memoir of Dr. Wilbur Daffodil-11 Swain, a 100-year-old ex-president, who with his twin sister has written the most popular child care book ever. His presidential program consists of giving everyone new middle names so that they will become part of elaborate extended families. Unfortunately, a plague and other disasters turn the United States into an anarchic collection of states and make the plan and the presidency meaningless. The book in its grotesque way is meant as a tribute to Vonnegut's sister Alice. Its dominant theme is suggested by the subtitle, *Lonesome No More!* In the introduction Vonnegut talks about that large old German family in Indianapolis from which he is

Jill Krementz

Kurt Vonnegut with his grandson, Zachary.

descended, and how it gave love and comfort and stability to its members. Once most Americans had such families, but now the generations are separated, and the remaining nuclear family is overloaded with the burdens once assumed by a larger and more heterogenous group. The main problem with modern Americans, he concludes, is that they are lonely. This is an old theme, though it has not been quite so overt before, having taken the form of people feeling purposeless and therefore unwanted. *Breakfast of Champions* talked of people as slaves and robots, and of how once they are so viewed they lose value to themselves and to others. *Slapstick* also has slaves, human robots as it were, and characters who are not valued because they are hideous freaks. In big families—or in artificial extended families, such as Vonnegut proposes here—such people are still loved, valued, and cared for. *Slapstick* is dedicated to Laurel and Hardy, and here, too, the book reaches back. Vonnegut speaks of the importance of Laurel and Hardy and contemporary comedians of radio and film to people during the Depression and therefore to himself in his formative years. One might recall how he wrote a joke column

in his college newspaper, and that he has referred to his novels as mosaics built out of numerous small tiles, each tile a joke.

Vonnegut lives in New York and is writing a novel called *Spit and Image*. His son Mark, now recovered from the schizophrenic breakdown described in his book *The Eden Express* (1975), is in medical school. Despite some negative reviews of both *Breakfast of Champions* and *Slapstick*, the reputation of Kurt Vonnegut continues to solidify in this country. Two essays in the recent collection *Vonnegut in America*, one by Jerome Klinkowitz and one by Donald M. Fiene, survey Vonnegut's reception in Europe and the Soviet Union and indicate his growing international stature. The man who parodied himself as Kilgore Trout and deprecated his own style as "like Philboyd Studge" has unmistakably transcended all that these two figures represent, yet his writing continues to embody the humility and humor that gave rise to them. Those are qualities which, over the years, have done much to endear Vonnegut to his readers and to give his works their distinctive tone.

Other Works:

Canary in a Cat House (Greenwich, Conn.: Fawcett, 1961);

Welcome to the Monkey House (New York: Seymour Lawrence/Delacorte, 1968; London: Cape, 1969);

Happy Birthday, Wanda June (New York: Seymour Lawrence/Delacorte, 1971; London: Cape, 1973);

Between Time and Timbuktu (New York: Seymour Lawrence/Delacorte, 1972; St. Albans: Panther, 1975);

Wampeters, Foma & Granfalloons (New York: Seymour Lawrence/Delacorte, 1974; London: Cape, 1975).

References:

Richard Giannone, *Vonnegut: A Preface to His Novels* (Port Washington, N.Y.: Kennikat, 1977);

David H. Goldsmith, *Kurt Vonnegut: Fantasist of Fire and Ice* (Bowling Green, Ohio: Bowling Green University Popular Press, 1972);

Donald J. Greiner, "Vonnegut's *Slaughterhouse-Five* and the Fiction of Atrocity," *Critique*, 14, 3 (1973): 38-51;

Betty L. Hudgens, *Kurt Vonnegut, Jr.: A Checklist* (Detroit: Gale, 1972);

Jerome Klinkowitz, "The Literary Career of Kurt Vonnegut, Jr.," *Modern Fiction Studies*, 19 (spring 1973): 57-67;

Klinkowitz and Donald L. Lawler, *Vonnegut in America* (New York: Seymour Lawrence/Delacorte, 1977);

Jerome Klinkowitz and John Somer, eds., *The Vonnegut Statement* (New York: Delacorte/Seymour Lawrence, 1973);

"Kurt Vonnegut, Jr.: A Symposium," *Summary*, 1, 2 (1971);

John R. May, "Loss of World in Barth, Pynchon, and Vonnegut: The Varieties of Humorous Apocalypse," in his *Toward A New Earth: Apocalypse in the American Novel* (Notre Dame: University of Notre Dame Press, 1972), pp. 172-200;

Raymond M. Olderman, "Out of the Waste Land and into the Fire: Cataclysm or the Cosmic Cool," in his *Beyond the Waste Land: The American Novel in the Nineteen-Sixties* (New Haven: Yale University Press, 1972), pp. 189-219;

Peter J. Reed, *Kurt Vonnegut, Jr.* (New York: Warner, 1972);

Stanley Schatt, *Kurt Vonnegut, Jr.* (Boston: Twayne, 1977);

Schatt, "The World of Kurt Vonnegut, Jr.," *Critique*, 12, 3 (1971): 54-69;

Robert Scholes, " 'Mithridates, He Died Old': Black Humor and Kurt Vonnegut, Jr.," *Hollins Critic*, 3 (October 1966): 1-12;

Peter A. Scholl, "Vonnegut's Attack Upon Christendom," *Newsletter of the Conference of Christianity and Literature*, 22 (fall 1972): 5-11;

Max F. Schulz, "The Unconfirmed Thesis: Kurt Vonnegut, Black Humor, and Contemporary Art," *Critique*, 12, 3 (1971): 5-28;

Tony Tanner, "The Uncertain Messenger: A Study of the Novels of Kurt Vonnegut, Jr.," *Critical Quarterly*, 11 (winter 1969): 297-315;

"Vonnegut," *Critique*, 12, 3 (1971), special number, with bibliography.

EDWARD LEWIS WALLANT wrote four novels which attracted a small but enthusiastic readership. Born 19 October 1926 in New Haven, Connecticut, Wallant died young on 5 December 1962. As a modern novelist, Wallant is important for his thoughtful but cautious refusal to accept as insuperable the existential despair and the universal isolation of modern man so often encountered in his contemporaries' works. Wallant's quiet affirmation of the worth and joy of life is often contrasted, for example, with the absurdist vision of Bruce Jay Friedman and the implacable bitterness of Nathanael West. Wallant differs further from his contemporaries in his Romantic temperament. Though Wallant attended the University of Connecticut and studied at both the Pratt Institute and the New School for Social Research, his heroes are mostly from uneducated lower-class society. Despite Wallant's profession as a graphics artist for several advertising agencies, he seldom introduces characters who are either professionals or businessmen. Indeed, Wallant shares an artistic kinship with the English Romantics of the early nineteenth century, as well as with D. H. Lawrence early in this century. Wallant finds his heroes among the unfortunate, the outcast, the seemingly common. In portraying "common" men and women as sensitive and dignified, in asserting a heedful optimism, and in his nonsaccharine perception of life and its often painful demands, Wallant further warrants description as a Romantic novelist. Edward Lewis Wallant has appropriately been termed a "new Romantic" by several critics, and his four novels attest to the accuracy of the term and to the distinct philosophical and esthetic temperament which makes him an important if generally unknown modern novelist.

Joseph, or Yussel, Berman of *The Human Season* (1960) epitomizes Wallant's heroes: at the novel's beginning, Berman is embittered (by his wife's death), wrapped in a cloak of voluntary indifference and cruelty, sequestered from his family, his friends, his God, and his self. Like all of Wallant's heroes, Berman must die emotionally and spiritually and then must be reborn. The power of *The Human Season* rests as much on the reader's accompanying Berman from death-in-life to life as on the character of Berman, fine though that character is. Berman is a self-made plumber whose thoughts on God, however profound and piercing they may be, are phrased in terms appropriate to such a man: "Such a deal you gave me, all my life. My eyes are open, you. You watched me pray every day of my life, saw me fast all the holy days, saw me be kind, loving, honest, you saw me take all the other rotten things and still go on loving you. And then you. . . you figured you could do anything to me. . . . that I was a hopeless sucker. . . . And then you do this." Typical of Wallant's writing, this passage realistically establishes Berman as a thoughtful but unpolished man.

Joe Berman's progress toward life and the living is clearly marked for the reader; a date heads each chapter. Wallant's skills as a visual artist manifest themselves in the careful chronological structuring of *The Human Season*: each chapter set in the present (1956) is counterpointed with a chapter which reaches. further into Berman's past. These contrapuntal chapters simultaneously mark Berman's increasing despair and the life he will eventually find in exploring the reality of past joy. As the time elapses since his wife's death, Berman's routine becomes more rigid, his intercourse with other people more infrequent. This is as Berman wishes; only a numbness to all emotion, all thought, all human events will do. Wallant's richly figurative style superbly captures the deadness of Berman's life: "Going up his front steps he almost had the feeling of being physically engaged in some worn piece of machinery. There was a sense of automation, of knowing exactly what each movement would be, one after another, like a movie he had sat through innumerable times. There was no pleasure in it, only a sort of bleak ease, for it demanded nothing from him." Yet, the poignant scenes from Berman's earlier life constantly cast off glimmers of his inescapable entanglement with the glory and

mystery of life: in a flashback scene of remarkable lyrical beauty, Berman recalls how, as a child, he came to what can only be described as a mystical understanding of the preciousness of human existence:

> Berman gasped as though transfixed by something beyond naming. His little sound brought the father's head around, eyes red rimmed from the night of looking at darkness. Berman pointed in apology toward the man holding the fish aloft on the river. His father followed his gesture, studied the simple sight with an expression of perplexity as though he had just come back from a vastly different consideration. Finally he turned back to his son. They held their eyes locked for just a few seconds, both puzzled now in the gently rocking wagon with the other boy and the woman asleep and only the two of them awake in that morning light. Until finally the father nodded slowly at the boy, confirming something wondrous to him, something he would have all the time in the world to find out.

In this haunting scene, Wallant demands, as always, that his character embrace life.

Juxtaposed with the memories of Berman's youth is the painful, enervating reality of the present. If Wallant lovingly depicts Berman's childhood in poor but pastoral Russia, and his youth as one of unbounded hope and energy, he also unflinchingly lays bare a frightening, solipsistic Berman who abortively slashes his wrists with a simple "Oh, well." And Wallant also includes a scene which conveys the theme found in all of his novels: man realizing the horror of being alone, a horror always worse than death, always more appalling than the absence of even a malicious or indifferent Hardyesque God. Berman is at his lowest when he realizes, "there was no Enemy, no Betrayer, no bearded Torturer. . . . He was alone. How could death measure up to that blackness!" As in all of his novels, Wallant insists in *The Human Season* that his hero "die" completely before he is reborn. Berman must plummet into the abyss and wallow there in the misery of his own making, but once he realizes his utter loneliness, he is constantly in expectation of *something*: " 'So what is it all about?' he asked in his old man's American bed. And he realized that he had at least a little of the answer to find." The answer is provided when Berman finds himself expectantly going to the beach and waiting, all day, on a sea wall (in three of Wallant's novels, the hero's return to or entrance into life involves water). When Berman returns to the city that night, he finds himself again involved with people (he witnesses a fight) and, symbolically, he must once again partake of life. Significantly, a cloudburst drenches Berman as he willingly gives information to the bored policeman investigating the fight: "He felt an immeasurable relief, as if something that had been of great value, and pain, too, was removed from him, and he could dwell in the calm of contemplation."

Joseph Berman's rebirth comes from realizing, and ultimately appreciating, that no one can disengage himself from humankind. If life thrusts as much sorrow at people as it does happiness, man must comprehend that these contraries are intertwined. Similarly, Berman's responsibility is to answer the pleas of his living; Wallant insists that people respond to each other's loneliness. At the novel's conclusion, Berman objects to "the emptiness. And how come, then, that there had been the lined, beautiful face of his wife to fill him with passion, the awkward, soft incompleteness of his children to make him tremble with tenderness?" If Berman must content himself with "Answers [which] come in little glimmers to your soul," Wallant assures us, in his first novel, that "It *is* enough!" This cautious but unshakeable optimism will be restated in Wallant's subsequent novels.

The Human Season won Wallant the National Jewish Book Award in 1961, and his second novel, *The Pawnbroker* (1961), probably Wallant's finest, won him both a nomination for the National Book Award and, in 1962, a Guggenheim Fellowship (*The Pawnbroker* was also made into a widely-acclaimed film released in 1966). Solomon Nazerman, the hero of *The Pawnbroker*, is a former instructor at the University of Cracow in Poland and a survivor of the Nazi concentration camps. His job as a pawnbroker causes him no embarrassment, for he has retreated not only from the affairs of his fellow humans but also from their emotions. As he says throughout the book, his job allows him "to be left alone," it pays well, and it serves as a means to blur the events of the concentration camps. Except for his assistant, Jesus Ortiz, who irritates and makes Sol vaguely uncomfortable for most of the novel, and for his sister and her family, who freely exploit Sol's finances in order to live "American," Sol leads a bland life which suits him perfectly. And since he has nothing to do with human affairs, human emotions, or human morality, Sol's dealings with gangster Albert Murillio, who procured the pawnshop for Sol (or at least it is in Sol's name), cause no shame, prompt no regret. In fact, if it were not for a "deep, unlocalized ache, a pain that was no real pain but only the vague promise of suffering," life would be as Sol desires.

But like a monolith which only seems intact, Sol has several chinks in the face he presents. Ortiz's energy and vitality irritate Sol; his assistant's "peculiar beauty" and "volatile innocence" make Sol uncomfortable and peevish at times. Sol "was huge and ugly, and he wished his ugliness to pierce the smallest of dreams." On his part, Ortiz resents his employer because Sol knows whatever it is that makes people financially successful; yet, he finds Sol undeniably appealing somehow, finds himself "involved in an odd current of emotions, softened and blinded and bound." Neither employer nor employee can escape the other's influence, and an unwilling intimacy springs from their attraction-repulsion relationship.

The Pawnbroker also introduces one of Wallant's most impressive techniques, that of parading an array of the downtrodden and the pariahs. Into Sol's pawnshop trudge junkies half-wild for money, deserted women stoically selling all they own to support born and unborn babies, geniuses whose work has been unrecognized or unwritten, hoodlums who cannot tolerate the drudgery of "honest" work, lovely and loving young women who turn to prostitution to escape a squalid environment. The list of flawlessly drawn minor characters is endless. They appear also in Wallant's last two novels, and they are never depicted as "lesser" humans because of a lack of money, social status, or education. These many characters may appear only briefly, but their impact on the reader is profound. Mabel Wheatly, Jesus Ortiz's whore-girl friend, would happily sacrifice all she has earned to be his wife. George Smith is a sexual pervert who has "abandoned himself to fantastic dream-ravishing of young boys and girls." But Wallant devotes several pages in several chapters to showing that this unseemly deviant has the potential to be a fine scholar, and Smith's struggle against sick lust takes on a pathetic nobility as he uses "the books and the towering aspiration of his intellect" to confine "his rapes . . . to his dreams." Among the harmless is Mrs. Harmon, who chooses impregnable joviality over despair and madness.

In demonstrating the unmistakable air of tragedy about these sad slum-dwellers' struggles, Wallant proclaims a dignity, an integrity, an unflagging vitality which cannot but evoke admiration from his readers. Wallant argues that there is a tragic and incessant struggle which attests to the irrevocable majesty of life. Scores of minor characters in Wallant's novels prove he is right.

Sol Nazerman tries, and fails, to convince himself that the unfortunates who shuffle in and out of his pawnshop, hocking bits of their lives, are "animals." Though he assures himself that "they mean nothing," the cracks in his impressive facade widen. Buxom, vivacious Marilyn Birchfield, a social worker who tries to befriend Sol, reminds him of his dormant manhood. Jesus Ortiz becomes important to Sol apart from his efficiency as assistant. The abjectly poor but marvelously alive customers begin to seem like people rather than objects; their cares and woes insinuate themselves into Sol's consciousness. As Sol finds himself drifting closer to humankind, his mysterious ailments worsen: "There was this pressure in him, a feeling of something underneath, which caused the growing tremors on the surface of him, perhaps heralding some great and awful thrust which would rend him, destroy him." And Sol's "anniversary," the date of his wife's dehumanized murder in the concentration camp, approaches, bringing horrific nightmares in graphic detail. Finally, he confronts Murillio when he learns that some of the pawnshop money may be tied in with a brothel Murillio owns. This act of defiance, a sure sign that Sol cannot remain aloof from human events, is prompted by his nightmare recollection of his wife's forced prostitution in the concentration camp.

These building pressures culminate with an unsuccessful armed robbery of the pawnshop. Three losers, playing on Ortiz's wish for financial success, convince him to participate in robbing Sol, but when Sol refuses to cooperate and one of the men fires at him, Ortiz leaps in between and is mortally wounded. In this emotionally wrenching scene, Wallant reveals the father-son love Sol and Jesus have sought to extinguish or at least to bury: "There was a strange struggle between them, a silent tugging that left them both bewildered and dazed looking." Sol Nazerman is violently thrust back into the turmoil of life; his defenses crumble before the onslaught of emotions brought on by Ortiz's self-sacrifice and love: "And then the dry-retching sound of weeping, growing louder and louder, filling the Pawnbroker's ears, flooding him, drowning him back to that sea of tears he had thought to have escaped. And he sat hunched against that abrasive roar, his body becoming worn down under the flood of it, washed down to the one polished stone of grief, of *grief*." Wallant's theme of emotional and spiritual complicity is stated again at the end of *The Pawnbroker*. Sol comes to this realization through Ortiz's death: "All his anesthetic numbness left him.... What was this great, agonizing sensitivity and what

was it for? Good God, what was all this? *Love?* Could this be *love?*" At long last, Sol can mourn for the deaths of the many people he has lost. Ever careful to avoid the sentimental and the trite, Wallant has his character accept the pain and the responsibility of life "if not happily, like a martyr, at least willingly, like an heir." Accepting the pain and the responsibility is awesome, certainly frightening, but Wallant's novels insist that it be done.

Wallant died in a coma, the result of an aneurism, in December 1962, and both of his last two books appeared posthumously. *The Tenants of Moonbloom* (1963) was actually written after *The Children at the Gate* (1964), but the latter required more revision and was ready for publication after the former. Wallant left the manuscripts, both written within one year, with his publisher before leaving for Europe as a result of receiving his Guggenheim grant. *The Tenants of Moonbloom*, like both *The Pawnbroker* and *The Children at the Gate*, has been called Wallant's "masterpiece," but the lighter tone and treatment of the lives of tenement dwellers lessen the power of Wallant's message. Tragedy, or at least the *tragic*, is more appropriate for the themes of Wallant's novels. To be sure, the novelist's hand is unerring in creating the modern Everyman, Norman Moonbloom. But the near-comic tone, restrained as it may be, still seems slightly inappropriate: sometimes it is too trying to smile at the misfortunes of the tenants, and only a few innocuous scenes—like Norman's long-delayed loss of virginity, his baptism by filth, or the building superintendent's lack of ambition and mutinous threats of quitting—are comfortably humorous. Though this novel, like the other three, traces the development of a dissociated character through forced intimacy with his tenants, the theme of necessary involvement is less movingly and therefore less powerfully conveyed. The throng of unfortunates, again treated with respect and admiration and endowed with vitality, humanity, genius, and noble endurance, steals many of the scenes.

In *The Children at the Gate* (Wallant's personal favorite), Wallant returns to his tragic mode. If the tone is not as relentlessly austere as that of *The Human Season* and *The Pawnbroker*, it is due to the benevolent insanity and levity of Sammy Kahan, the Jewish orderly who befriends the saturnine, cynical protagonist, Angelo DeMarco. Sammy, a major character in his own right, counterbalances the gloominess of skeptical Angelo. Together, they provide a story which is a sad, often funny, ultimately solemn affirmation of Wallant's *caritas* theme. Angelo's routine includes working at his cousin's drugstore, reading scientific textbooks, and debunking all "myths" (including human emotion). On one of his daily trips to a nearby hospital, where he blinds himself to the misery around him as he insouciantly solicits orders for ice cream cones and sodas, Angelo meets Sammy, the charismatic orderly. From this first meeting, Angelo, despite his swaggering independence, cannot free himself of Sammy's influence. The "regular scientist," as Sammy sarcastically refers to Angelo, is juxtaposed with the orderly who preaches heart over head. When Angelo once spouts the scientific facts he has just read, Sammy responds with a catalogue (three pages' worth) of appalling, moving, phenomenal incidents which reduces Angelo's "science" to ludicrous and empty parroting. Or, as Sammy succinctly puts it, "What do the scientists know about *love*?"

Sammy shakes Angelo out of his smug belief that he has no delusions, that he is forever steeled against meddling in petty human affairs. The orderly frightens Angelo because he freely admits his love for mankind, and his aggressive personal campaign to save the human race leads Angelo, Judas-like, to report Sammy anonymously for administering drugs to relieve the patients' suffering. The many allegorical overtones of this novel (the title is from T. S. Eliot's "Ash Wednesday") have raised mild objections from some critics, for the Christ figure, Sammy, is at the same time a lunatic, and the uncertainty of what, exactly, he is makes some readers apprehensive. But it seems clear that Wallant would have the qualities of savior and lunatic blurred intentionally. His heroes are, after all, commoners, and it is appropriate to offer Sammy, the widely traveled and experienced orderly, as a modern savior-figure, replete with contradictory traits.

Paradoxically, as Sammy's shenanigans and proselytizing become increasingly febrile, the nearer comes Angelo's involvement with human events, and the more clearly Wallant's theme emerges: " 'Love one another, love me, love you.... What is it otherwise, *kinderlach?* Alone all nasty, alone pain shit dark and *nothing*!' " Angelo resists but finds no alternative to Sammy's demand that people love, that they care, even that they hate, so long as they are involved and recognize each other's yearnings and needs. Sister Louise, the hospital administrator and Angelo's longtime enemy, offers only another cold religion far removed from the arena of animated human emotions and affairs. Not until Angelo witnesses Sammy's painful death (fraught with sacrificial overtones) does he understand the orderly's message: "He wanted Sammy to stay there,

to stay and suffer that immolation over and over and over. Oh, yeah, Sammy, I get it, I get it." Like Joe Berman, Sol Nazerman, and Norman Moonbloom, Angelo DeMarco realizes that if being immersed in human events means being made very dirty, it also means being alive. The novels of Edward Lewis Wallant are important because they defiantly affirm that modern man need not and must not despair, for life, with all of its vicissitudes, offers so much.

—*David W. Pitre*

Books:

The Human Season (New York: Harcourt, Brace, 1960; London: Gollancz, 1965);

The Pawnbroker (New York: Harcourt, Brace & World, 1961; London: Gollancz, 1962);

The Tenants of Moonbloom (New York: Harcourt, Brace & World, 1963; London: Gollancz, 1964);

The Children at the Gate (New York: Harcourt, Brace & World, 1964; London: Gollancz, 1964).

Other:

"I Held Back My Hand," *New Voices 2: American Writing Today*, ed. Don M. Wolfe (New York: Hendricks House, 1955), pp. 192-201;

"The Man Who Made a Nice Appearance," *New Voices 3: American Writing Today*, ed. Charles I. Glicksberg (New York: Hendricks House, 1958), pp. 336-353;

"When Ben Awakened," *American Scene: New Voices*, ed. Don M. Wolfe (New York: Lyle Stuart, 1963), pp. 94-100;

The Artist's Eyesight (New York: Harcourt, Brace & World, 1963).

References:

James Angle, "Edward Lewis Wallant's 'Trinity of Survival,' " *Kansas Quarterly*, 7 (1975): 106-118;

Nicholas Ayo, "Secular Heart: the Achievement of Edward Lewis Wallant," *Critique*, 12, 2 (1970): 86-94;

Ayo, "Edward Lewis Wallant, 1926-1962," *Bulletin of Bibliography*, 28 (1971): 119;

William M. Davis, "A Synthesis in the Contemporary Jewish Novel: Edward Lewis Wallant," *Cresset*, 31 (1968): 8-13;

Davis, "Fathers and Sons in the Fiction of Edward Wallant," *Research Studies*, 40 (1972): 53-55;

Davis, "The Renewal of Dialogic Immediacy in Edward Lewis Wallant," *Renascence*, 24 (1972): 56-69;

Davis, "The Sound of Silence: Edward Lewis Wallant's *The Children at the Gate*," *Cithara*, 8 (1969): 3-25;

Charles Alva Hoyt, "The Sudden Hunger: An Essay on the Novels of Edward Lewis Wallant," in his *Minor American Novelists* (Carbondale & Edwardsville: Southern Illinois University Press, 1970), pp. 118-137;

Marcus Klein, "Further Notes on the Dereliction of Culture: Edward Lewis Wallant and Bruce J. Friedman," in *Contemporary Jewish Literature: Critical Essays*, ed. Irving Malin (Bloomington and London: Indiana University Press, 1973), pp. 243-247;

Robert W. Lewis, "The Hung-up Heroes of Edward Lewis Wallant," *Renascence*, 24 (1972): 70-84;

Thomas M. Lorch, "The Novels of Edward Lewis Wallant," *Chicago Review*, 19 (1967): 78-91;

Joseph Lyons, "*The Pawnbroker*: Flashback in the Novel and Film," *Western Humanities Review*, 20 (1966): 243-248;

Harold U. Ribalow, "The Legacy of Edward L. Wallant," *Chicago Jewish Forum*, 22 (1964): 325-327;

Max F. Schulz, "Edward Lewis Wallant and Bruce Jay Friedman: the Glory and the Agony of Life," in his *Radical Sophistication: Studies in Contemporary Jewish/American Novelists* (Athens: Ohio University Press, 1969), pp. 172-197;

Schulz, "Wallant and Friedman: The Glory and Agony of Love," *Critique*, 10, 3 (1968): 31-47;

Raney Stanford, "The Novels of Edward Wallant," *Colorado Quarterly*, 17 (1969): 393-405.

Robert Penn Warren

Everett Wilkie
University of South Carolina
Josephine Helterman
Columbia, S. C.

BIRTH: Guthrie, Kentucky, 24 April 1905.

EDUCATION: B.A. (summa cum laude), Vanderbilt University, 1925; M.A., University of California, 1927; Yale University, 1927-1928; B.Litt., Oxford University as a Rhodes Scholar, 1930.

MARRIAGE: 12 September 1930 to Emma Brescia, divorced 1950. 7 December 1952 to Eleanor Clark; children: Rosanna Phelps and Gabriel Penn.

AWARDS: The Caroline Sinkler Award, 1936, 1937, 1938; Levinson Prize, 1936; Houghton Mifflin Literary Fellowship for *Night Rider*, 1939; Guggenheim Fellowship, 1939-1940, 1947-1948; Shelley Memorial Award, 1943; Pulitzer Prize in the Novel for *All the King's Men*, 1947; Southern Prize, 1947; Robert Meltzer Award from the Screen Writers' Guild, 1949; Union League Civic and Arts Foundation Prize, 1953; Prix du Meilleur Livre Etranger for *All the King's Men*, 1953; Sidney Hillman Prize for *Segregation*, 1957; Edna St. Vincent Millay Memorial Prize, National Book Award, and Pulitzer Prize in Poetry for *Promises*, 1958; *New York Herald Tribune* Van Doren Award for *Who Speaks for the Negro?*, 1965; Bollingen Prize in Poetry, 1966-1967; Van Wyck Brooks award for poetry, 1970; National Medal for Literature, 1970; Emerson-Thoreau Medal, 1975; the Copernicus Award, 1976; honorary degrees from University of Louisville (1949), Kenyon College (1952), University of Kentucky (1955), Colby College (1956), Swarthmore College (1958), Yale University (1959), Bridgeport University (1965), Fairfield University (1969), and Wesleyan University (1970).

MAJOR WORKS: *John Brown: The Making of a Martyr* (New York: Payson & Clark, 1929); *Thirty-Six Poems* (New York: Alcestis Press, 1935); *Night Rider* (Boston: Houghton Mifflin, 1939; London: Eyre & Spottiswoode, 1940); *Eleven Poems on the Same Theme* (Norfolk, Conn.: New Directions, 1942); *At Heaven's Gate* (New York: Harcourt, Brace, 1943; London: Eyre & Spottiswoode, 1943); *Selected Poems, 1923-1943* (New York: Harcourt, Brace, 1944; London: Fortune Press, 1951); *All the King's Men* (New York: Harcourt, Brace, 1946; London: Eyre & Spottiswoode, 1948); *Blackberry Winter* (Cummington, Mass.: Cummington Press, 1946); *The Circus in the Attic and Other Stories* (New York: Harcourt, Brace, 1947; London: Eyre & Spottiswoode, 1952); *World Enough and Time: A Romantic Novel* (New York: Random House, 1950;

London: Eyre & Spottiswoode, 1951); *Brother to Dragons: A Tale in Verse and Voices* (New York: Random House, 1953; London: Eyre & Spottiswoode, 1954); *Band of Angels* (New York: Random House, 1955; London: Eyre & Spottiswoode, 1956); *Segregation: The Inner Conflict in the South* (New York: Random House, 1956; London: Eyre & Spottiswoode, 1957); *Promises: Poems, 1954-1956* (New York: Random House, 1957; London: Eyre & Spottiswoode, 1959); *Selected Essays* (New York: Random House, 1958; London: Eyre & Spottiswoode, 1964); *The Cave* (New York: Random House, 1959; London: Eyre & Spottiswoode, 1959); *The Gods of Mount Olympus* (New York: Random House, 1959; London: Frederick Muller, 1962); *All the King's Men (A Play)* (New York: Random House, 1960); *You, Emperors, and Others: Poems, 1957-1960* (New York: Random House, 1960); *Wilderness: A Tale of the Civil War* (New York: Random House, 1961; London: Eyre & Spottiswoode, 1962); *Flood: A Romance of Our Time* (New York: Random House, 1964; London: Collins, 1964); *Who Speaks for the Negro?* (New York: Random House, 1965); *Selected Poems: New and Old, 1923-1966* (New York: Random House, 1966); *Incarnations: Poems 1966-1968* (New York: Random House, 1968; London: Allen, 1970); *Audubon: A Vision* (New York: Random House, 1969); *Homage to Theodore Dreiser: August 27, 1871-December 28, 1945, on the Centennial of His Birth* (New York: Random House, 1971); *Meet Me in the Green Glen* (New York: Random House, 1971; London: Secker & Warburg, 1972); *Or Else—Poem/Poems 1968-1974* (New York: Random House, 1974); *Democracy and Poetry* (Cambridge: Harvard University Press, 1975); *A Place to Come To* (New York: Random House, 1977; London: Secker & Warburg, 1977); *Selected Poems, 1923-1975* (New York: Random House, 1977).

Warren has spent his entire professional career associated with institutions of higher education. After graduation from Oxford, he joined the faculty, as an assistant professor, at Southwestern College, Memphis, Tennessee, in 1930. He stayed only one year before accepting a position as acting assistant professor at Vanderbilt, where he remained until 1934. In 1934, he went to Louisiana State University, Baton Rouge, as an assistant professor and was promoted to associate professor in 1936. It was at LSU that Warren met Cleanth Brooks, and their association continued unbroken even after Warren moved to Yale University as a professor of playwriting in 1950. At Yale, he became professor of English in 1961, and, finally, professor emeritus in

1973. Warren has also served writing conferences at the University of Colorado, Boulder (1936, 1937, 1940), and at Olivet College, Olivet, Michigan (1940); he was a visiting lecturer in 1941 at the State University of Iowa, Iowa City, and Poetry Consultant to the Library of Congress from 1944 to 1945.

Warren's reputation as one of the most versatile and talented of America's men of letters has grown steadily since the publication of his first work in 1929. Although he achieved instant recognition among scholars as a critic, poet, and essayist, popular acceptance of his work was not forthcoming until the 1946 publication of *All the King's Men*. As Leonard Casper and Charles H. Bohner have noted, this situation was the probable result of financial disasters at home and wartime conditions abroad. Warren's first book, *John Brown: The Making of a Martyr* (1929), reached bookstores during the stockmarket crash; *Night Rider* (1939) was published as Hitler entered Prague; and *At Heaven's Gate* (1943) was largely ignored at the height of America's military involvement in Europe during World War II. Many of Warren's contributions have gained for him international literary fame, especially his contributions to literary criticism. In many ways, however, he has never wandered far from his Southern heritage, often drawing upon it for the framework of his novels, which stress the painful acquisition of knowledge and the brutish state of ignorance. Despite his Southern settings, Warren has so constructed his material that it easily transcends any narrow, sectional view of life and arrives, instead, at a universal view from which many of the basic facets of human experience may be viewed. There is to date no comprehensive evaluation of his total contributions to the fields in which he has worked, and it will probably be years from now before his influence can be adequately assessed.

A would-be chemist, Warren turned to poetry and poetics through his association with Vanderbilt English professor John Crowe Ransom, which led to his introduction to the "Fugitives," an informal group of such poet-critics as Donald Davidson, Allen Tate, and Ransom himself. The *Fugitive* magazine (1922-1925) published Warren's initial efforts as early as the summer of 1923, although he was not included in the group's membership until February 1924. His most notable contribution to the *Fugitive*, "To a Face in the Crowd," appeared in June 1925 and was subsequently reprinted in his first volume of poetry, *Thirty-Six Poems* (1935), and in his *Selected Poems, 1923-1943* (1944).

Robert Penn Warren and his wife, Eleanor Clark.

The poems in these early volumes illustrate the formulation and development of Warren's aesthetic, a Naturalistic approach he expounds in his essay, "Pure and Impure Poetry" (1943). Warren's poems abound with apparently "unpoetic" images and paradoxes; for Warren, however, the "impure" juxtaposition, for example, of redemption imagery and rotting garbage creates a poetic tension, resulting in "purer" and more realistic verses than those influenced by nineteenth-century Romanticism. Insisting upon T. S. Eliot's autotelic principle as the basis for a poem, Warren also counterpoints formal and colloquial language, melody and cacophony, and unexpected images in the manner of such French poets as Mallarme and Baudelaire in order to explore his existential concern with modern man's alienation and dual nature. The promise of his early poems is fulfilled in *Brother to Dragons* (1953), with its rich combination of rhetoric and dialect and in *You, Emperors, and Others: Poems 1957-1960* (1960), with its mature use of irony.

The Fugitives turned their attention in the late 1920s to social phenomena and evolved a philosophy that Warren and eleven others voiced in *I'll Take My Stand* (1930), an attack on the encroaching Northern industrialism and science in favor of a return to the Jeffersonian theory of Agrarianism, which urged a reliance on the older, more enduring virtues of the rural life and religion. Warren's contribution, "The Briar Patch," indicted the North for worsening the plight of the Negro by taking him from the land and plunging him into the unrelieved misery of the Northern factories, for which he was unprepared.

Despite the impact of Agrarianism, the most influential movement in which Warren was to be involved was "New Criticism." Warren's association with Cleanth Brooks while both were at Louisiana State University proved to be a crucial connection in the history of American letters. In 1936 they had published *An Approach to Literature* and in 1938, *Understanding Poetry: An Anthology for College Students*. These volumes became the bedrock of the new critical school, which advocated the examination of literature in order to perceive its psychological foundations and effects rather than merely studying its historical and generic qualities. According to New Criticism, the language of poetry should not serve as a vehicle for scientific and technological data; rather a poem's words are necessarily imprecise, imaginative, and suggestive of abstract thought, thereby reflecting the abstractions of the poet's own imagination.

While still at Louisiana State University, Warren and Brooks founded the *Southern Review*, a literary-cultural journal which introduced the public to the talents of such writers as Eudora Welty and Randall Jarrell. They have since collaborated on anthologies and books concerning rhetoric, approaches to the various genres, and aesthetics.

With his first novel, *Night Rider*, Warren took historical facts and created a fictional context for the interpretation and redefinition of the event, a pattern which was to become the hallmark of his fiction. Set in Kentucky in the first years of the twentieth century, the novel offers a vivid picture, with moralistic overtones, of the Association formed by local tobacco growers in an attempt to wrest higher prices from the large tobacco companies. When non-Association farmers accept only slightly higher prices for their tobacco, the Association's "night riders," a secret organization using Ku Klux Klan tactics, retaliate by destroying the unfortunate farmers' crops.

Warren's novel, superficially a story of only regional implications, invites interpretations of universal scope in its portrayal of attorney and night rider Percy Munn ("Mr. Munn" throughout the novel), a modern man in search of selfhood. Barnett Guttenburg emphasizes, "He is not Man, but Munn," a distinction which in Munn's mind exempts him from the problems of this world. Even when all his pretenses are stripped away and he stares directly into the existential void, Munn cannot clearly perceive his moral dilemma. For Warren, selfhood is achieved when man looks into the void and accepts his Sartrian responsibility, thereby having knowledge of it in a manner reminiscent of the "Fortunate Fall."

The traditional dichotomies of light/dark and good/evil are woven into the fabric of the novel in such a manner that they become the compelling metaphors in the work. Darkness and evil are represented in Mr. Munn, and his consistent refusal to respond to the knowledge symbolized in the light imagery leads to his ultimate destruction "in the woods, the absorbing darkness." His refusal naturally colors all he perceives. Thus, May, who is basically innocent, is raped by Munn in the night, an extension of the violence still raging in him after he has committed a murder. Even Lucille Christian, whose name means "Light of Christ," is perverted in Munn's own mind into a creature of the night, one

identified "with all the small night noises." It is Munn's resounding rejection of knowledge and its responsibility that leads to his violent deeds and his violent death. Despite the existential overtones, living by the sword brings its promised conclusion, and, ultimately, Munn must inherit man's fate.

Warren's second novel, *At Heaven's Gate* (1943), bridges the simple chronology of *Night Rider* and the more elaborate time juxtapositions of *All the King's Men*. Although his more complex structural techniques do not approach the maturity of his craft in *All the King's Men*, they do anticipate his extensive use of flashback and demonstrate his experimentation with second-person narration. In this second novel, Warren counterpoints time past with time present to emphasize the futility of defining oneself through an alter ego. Set in Tennessee in the 1920s, *At Heaven's Gate* is based on the career of Luke Lea, a wealthy and unscrupulous financier prominent during Warren's undergraduate years at Vanderbilt. Like Lea, Warren's Bogan Murdock, with his corrupt machinations, represents to the Agrarian mind the evils of a spiritually empty urban world. Contrasted to Murdock is Ashby Wyndham, a farmer and visionary, whose combination of stoicism and traditional Christianity provides Agrarianism's answer to the corruptions of a modern age. One must, as Wyndham's life makes clear, not only accept oneself, but other people, and also recognize the legitimacy of their existence.

Warren's most celebrated novel is *All the King's Men* (1946), which was made into a movie in 1949. This work, which has received the bulk of critical attention given Warren's novels, is based on the story of Huey Long, the celebrated Louisiana governor who rose to national prominence through his populist politics, only to be gunned down in mid-career by Dr. Carl A. Weiss, who acted from motives still unclear. Warren has denied that the novel is based directly on Long, insisting instead that Long's story simply gave him the "line of thinking and feeling" he used to construct the novel.

As he often does, Warren shifts the natural historical focus of the story. *All the King's Men* does not concentrate on Willie Stark (Long's counterpart), but rather on Jack Burden, the governor's sycophant who does much of Stark's gumshoe work. As Stark requires one manipulation after another, Burden always rises to the occasion. It is Burden's gradual realization of his own true position and the consequences of his actions that lead to his heightened, more nearly correct perception of his role in this life.

The temptation is to point to the role of lies and deceit in this novel; however, it is not deceit *per se* which is the book's basis, but rather the uses to which truth may be legitimately put. Burden's major task is not to fabricate lies, but to discover truth and to put it into the hands of those who can use it to their own ends and to the purposes of their political ideology. Judge Irwin, whose lack of cooperation infuriates Stark, has, in fact, committed a crime which Burden discovers; however, Stark attempts to use this knowledge to forestall a blackmail attempt aimed at him personally. When the judge is confronted with the proof of his guilt, he commits suicide rather than face the consequences or support Stark in fending off the blackmail attempt. By posing such situations, Warren explores the difficult problems presented when one tries to transform an intellectual idea of what is "right" into a reality encompassing it.

Burden has, for the most part, lived his life believing he is exempt from both time and responsibility. His explanation for the events of this world is "The Big Twitch," or alternately, "The Big Sleep." He is slow to perceive causal relationships between what he does and ensuing events and ascribes chains of events to the Twitch itself rather than to anything he does, where the responsibility properly belongs. It may be that no greater force does shape this world; however, as Burden discovers, that fact does not exempt him from responsibility for what he does. Nor is he exempt from time, as he initially believes. All his actions are on a continuum of existence, and Burden must gradually realize that all his beliefs have no validity in the face of certain realities, of which time is the most real of all.

The complex interweavings of several dimensions of time reinforce Burden's realizations. *All the King's Men* is a masterpiece of narrative technique. The flashbacks reinforce the idea that all existence is on the continuum Burden seeks so desperately to avoid or escape and that events of the past reach forward to shape present events, which will themselves have ramifications in the future. However, it is also clear in the technique that time will not save one, either; it always comes for a person, that moment when his time in this world ceases. Stark dies with dramatic suddenness from a bullet, as does Judge Irwin. Burden is given a respite to live a little longer and to reflect further on the awful responsibility time imposes.

The so-called Kentucky Tragedy forms the basis for *World Enough and Time*, although Warren expertly moves the tale from the melodramatic confines often given it by other writers to a realm of universal significance. In many respects the physical details remain the same, and Warren loudly echoes his source. For example, the historic Colonel Sharp becomes Colonel Fort; Jeroboam Beauchamp becomes Jeremiah Beaumont; and both tales are set in Kentucky during the first quarter of the nineteenth century. But Warren has managed to imbue the old story with new life and has expanded his fictional version of it far beyond the original boundaries.

The point of view from which the story is told is crucial to the success of the novel. Rather than permitting one of the characters to control the narrative, Warren places that role in the hands of an unnamed historian who has discovered the truth of the matter among the papers of the now dead Wilkie Barron, a principal in the novel. The crucial document is Jeremiah's diary, from which the bulk of the information is derived; however, its contents are not served up in a raw, undigested state. Rather, the scholarly narrator chooses which elements to show us and connects the parts with his own comments, which give insight into the moral dilemmas posed by the history.

This technique gives Warren three stages of control over the vocabulary, that element upon which the success of such a narrative must rest. The first stage, that of the primary sources such as the diary and letters, reflects the preoccupations and concerns of the characters, who themselves are not totally blind to the implications of their deeds and whose developing awareness the reader may view. The second stage, that of the connecting passages, allows the impartial observer to correct the characters' impressions and to become involved himself, to a certain extent, in the incredible tale of love, revenge, and politics he has discovered, and of which "We have what is left, the lies and half-lies and the truths and half-truths." The interplay between the narrator and the characters forms one of the salient features of the novel's technique.

Of most importance is the third level of vocabulary, that which describes all of life, including that with which the reader might describe his own. One is not particularly inclined to see his own life in terms of "blood," "revenge," or "murder," as is the case in this novel; however, everyone may well question the consequences of his actions and the horrible weight which they often compel him to bear, as when Beaumont, reflecting on the enormity of his deeds, sums up the response in his journal entry for 20 October: "Drunk." He later concludes, "It is the crime of self, the crime of life. The crime is I."

The Cave, based on the real story of Floyd Collins, is not so much the story of Jasper Harrick, who is trapped in a cave he was exploring, as it is the tale of his rescuers. Warren is able to explore not only the individual consciousnesses of each character, but also to reveal the groping and struggling of the entire community as it wrestles with its own preoccupations and helplessness in the face of disaster.

This work is unusual among novels in that the main character and object of the rescue is never seen or heard from. Trapped far below ground, he is never reached alive, despite false reports from the cowardly, grandstanding Isaac Sumpter, and dies alone and unrelieved in the darkness of his underground tomb. Although he is lost from view, his plight is never forgotten and serves as a foil to the machinations of the would-be rescuers whose lives are revealed through their schemings.

The novel is explicitly a tale of knowledge, self-discovery, and communal responsibility. The epigraph of the novel links the story to a scene in Plato's *The Republic*, the famous metaphor of the cave. The question naturally arises whether any of the characters in the novel have struggled up the long road to the pure sunlight and to real appreciation of reality or whether they have simply perverted the concepts of truth and justice to make them fit their own ends. Thus, the cave metaphor operates on two levels in the novel. The first is the obvious one of Jasper trapped below, with no one above of sufficient fortitude or knowledge to save him. The second level is that of the metaphysical cave in which the whole community and all mankind is trapped. In reality, it is not Jasper who is trapped, it is everyone else. They are chained and unable to glimpse anything but the most perverted images of reality, like Isaac, who ends up pursuing money and makes publicity for himself from Jasper's plight.

In many respects, the knowledge gained is of a negative nature; it is not so much the knowledge of what we are, but rather the realization of what we are not. This is knowledge gained by the process of elimination rather than an aggressive examination of the human condition. After Jasper is declared dead, the crowd goes off into an orgy of drinking and intercourse. The commissioner observes, "They have enthusiasm." The lieutenant replies: "It is the same old kind . . . Red-eye and nookie. They are also enthusiastic about not being dead in the ground." As Plato makes clear, and Warren with him, knowledge is a hurtful thing and often odious to him who acquires it. It is far simpler to stare at the shadows of reality dancing before our eyes than to see it revealed clearly in the bright light of perfect truth.

Band of Angels (1955) is a novel rich in complex ironies and sudden reversals of fortune. Told from the first-person view of Amantha Starr, the tale explores the painful acquisition of the answer to the question "Who am I?" as Amantha's fortunes sink when she is gradually caught up in the lost cause of the Old South, at first by no fault of her own, later by a deliberate choice on her part. It is a world where nothing is really as it seems and Amantha has stripped away from her the physical attributes by which she formerly defined her own nature and the meaning of existence. It is a world of masks.

The question "Who is everybody else?" is posed as well and becomes a significant feature in the novel. Amantha's father, though he tried to protect and educate her, ended up laying a trap for her by concealing her birth and then by failing to rectify the deceit before his death. The kindly Hamish Bond, who at first pitied her and to whom she becomes devoted, in fact uses her instead of feeling any true affection for her. He was previously a dealer in slaves. Seth Parker, a wild-eyed idealist at Oberlin, where Amantha was taught "the vanity of this, our perishing world," eventually deserts his calling to follow the lures of this world instead. Finally, Tobias Sears, a Union officer, marries her, and, after some wandering, both real and symbolic, the couple begins to resolve the problems of identity which have plagued them. It is in this resolution that the key to the novel lies. Amantha learns that she is the only one in this world who can solve the problems of self-knowledge in a manner that gives them meaning to her own life.

In a world of pretending, it is important that one not pretend, for such action is only deceptive and self-defeating. Amantha runs speedily from her own origins, but finds that they pursue faster than she can escape and must, as everyone must, come to grips with the reality of who she really is. The slave mentality is not only symbolic, it is real, and even the emancipation following the Civil War does not set Amantha free; only she can do that, for freedom is a relative concept, not truly dependent upon circumstances of birth or position. This world is not constituted of bands of angels, only bands of humans struggling on the face of this earth. God is not coming to set you free; there is no one to do that "except yourself."

Warren's latest novel, *A Place to Come To* (1977), is in many respects his most personal. The story of a renowned medieval scholar who has come far from his humble beginnings in Dugton,

Jill Krementz

Robert Penn Warren in his study.

Alabama, the novel poses many of the questions Warren has explored in his earlier works and shows the futility of seeking to escape the past and the flux of time. The work is apparently autobiographical to a certain extent and Warren's use of history in this case seems to lean heavily on his own experiences as a scholar and teacher.

The main character, Jed Tewksbury, narrates the story in the first person and everything is filtered through his enlightened, though somewhat confused, view of the world and the events that have shaped his life. Whereas Jack Burden in *All the King's Men* ascribed events to "The Big Twitch," Jed sees the world in terms of "The Great Avalanche" or what might be called the "Great Dong Theory." Jed's father died in a particularly obscene accident and as the story of his death passed into local legend, Jed found he could not escape it and eventually tried to sublimate the effects of the incident by telling the tale, complete with gestures, to his friends at parties. All of his maneuverings, however, prove futile, for his past continues to come back on him when he least suspects it, and it is not until he integrates his heritage into his life that he can hope to find some peace with himself and the world.

The narrative technique of the novel is a complex web of narrative-within-narrative and flashbacks, which reinforces the awful presence of the past. Moreover, Jed's work as a medievalist makes him even more sharply aware of the past, for he not only wonders why a man who is supposedly in control of his life prefers such ancient history, but he also sees in the medieval texts situations and phrases which apply to his present condition. One may not, as Jed learns, live his life divorced from what has come before. As he states early in the novel: "Something is going on and will not stop. You are outside the going on, and you are, at the same time, inside the going on. In fact, the going on is what you are. Until you can understand that these things are different but are the same, you know nothing about the nature of life. I proclaim this." The narrative technique is itself a "going on" that embodies the complexities of Jed's experiences.

The novel clearly expounds an existential view of existence. In one of the more moving passages, Jed's wife concludes even as she dies that there is no God. Indeed there is no God in this work except the one of knowledge and knowing, from whom Jed constantly turns his face. Even as Jed struggles to persuade his lover, whom he first met in high school, to leave her husband, the chiming of the clock interrupts his speech, "words fraught with the authority of passion," and he feels that each of them is "like a grasshopper that, impaled on a boy's fishhook, is swung out, twitching, kicking, spitting, and gesticulating, over the dark water." Only Jed's gradual realization and acceptance of his condition in a world where all time is realized in the present allow him to view the world with the dispassionate sobriety required truly to know one's condition.

Warren's contributions to the field of American novels have been immense, and it will be many years before his influence is fully known. Warren's hallmark is the extreme intelligence he brings to his work, which allows him to order his novels in complex patterns that are intriguing without being confusing or difficult. His main obsession is knowledge; his works reflect the many forms in which he himself has found knowledge, and are, therefore, to some extent autobiographical. In the novels one may discover existentialism, agrarianism, and traditional religious values, often bound closely together as they often are in life itself. Warren's wisdom is the wisdom of interpretation; his main question, "How is one to look at life?" From an elaboration of the complex forces which shape both our lives and our perceptions, he shows us history as a living force which can yet tell us something about ourselves.

Other Works:

An Approach to Literature, with Cleanth Brooks and John Thibaut Purser (Baton Rouge: Louisiana State University Press, 1936);

Understanding Fiction, with Cleanth Brooks (New York: Crofts, 1943);

Modern Rhetoric, with Cleanth Brooks (New York: Harcourt, Brace, 1949);

Fundamentals of Good Writing: A Handbook of Modern Rhetoric, with Cleanth Brooks (New York: Harcourt, Brace, 1950; London: Dobson, 1952);

To a Little Girl, One Year Old, in a Ruined Fortress (New Haven: Yale School of Design, 1956);

Remember the Alamo! (New York: Random House, 1958);

How Texas Won Her Freedom: The Story of Sam Houston & The Battle of San Jacinto (San Jacinto Monument, Texas: San Jacinto Museum of History, 1959);

The Scope of Fiction, with Cleanth Brooks (New York: Appleton-Century-Crofts, 1960);

Conversations on the Craft of Poetry, by Warren, *et al.* (New York: Holt, Rinehart & Winston, 1961);

The Legacy of the Civil War: Meditations on the Centennial (New York: Random House, 1961);

A Plea in Mitigation: Modern Poetry and the End of an Era (Macon, Ga.: Wesleyan College, 1966).

Periodical Publications:

"T. S. Stribling: A Paragraph in the History of Critical Realism," *American Review*, 2 (February 1934): 463-486;

"John Crowe Ransom: A Study in Irony," *Virginia Quarterly Review*, 11 (January 1935): 93-112;

"Dixie Looks at Mrs. Gerould," with Cleanth Brooks, *American Review*, 6 (March 1936): 585-595;

"Some Don'ts for Literary Regionalists," *American Review*, 8 (December 1936): 142-150;

"The Reading of Modern Poetry," with Cleanth

Brooks, *American Review*, 8 (February 1937): 435-439;

"The Situation in American Writing, Part II," *Partisan Review*, 6 (fall 1939): 112-113;

"The Present State of Poetry: In the United States," *Kenyon Review*, 1 (fall 1939): 384-398;

"Pure and Impure Poetry," *Kenyon Review*, 5 (spring 1943): 228-254;

"Melville the Poet," *Kenyon Review*, 7 (spring 1946): 208-223;

"A Note to *All the King's Men*," *Sewanee Review*, 61 (summer 1953): 476-480;

"Knowledge and the Image of Man," *Sewanee Review*, 62 (winter 1955): 182-192;

"*All the King's Men*: The Matrix of Experience," *Yale Review*, 53 (December 1964): 161-167;

"Faulkner: The South and the Negro," *Southern Review*, 1 (July 1965): 501-529;

"Uncorrupted Consciousness: The Stories of Katherine Anne Porter," *Yale Review*, 55 (December 1965): 280-290;

"Melville's Poems," *Southern Review*, 3 (October 1967): 799-855;

"Notes on the Poetry of John Crowe Ransom at his Eightieth Birthday," *Kenyon Review*, 30, 3 (1968): 319-349;

"The Uses of History in Fiction," with Ralph Ellison and William Styron, *Southern Literary Journal*, 1 (spring 1969): 57-90;

"Andrew Lytle's *The Long Night*: A Rediscovery," *Southern Review*, 7 (January 1971): 130-139;

"Mark Twain," *Southern Review*, 8 (July 1972): 459-492;

"Hawthorne Revisited: Some Remarks on Hellfiredness," *Sewanee Review*, 81 (winter 1973): 75-111;

"Theodore Dreiser: *An American Tragedy*," in *Der Amerikanische Roman im 19. und 20. Jahrhundert*, ed. Edgar Lohner (Berlin: Erich Schmidt, 1974): 152-161;

"Life and Death with Agnes," *Ohio Review*, 18 (1977): 49-74.

Other:

"The Briar Patch," in *I'll Take My Stand: The South and the Agrarian Tradition* (New York: Harper, 1930);

A Southern Harvest: Short Stories by Southern Writers, edited by Warren (Boston: Houghton Mifflin, 1937);

Understanding Poetry: An Anthology for College Students, edited by Warren and Cleanth Brooks (New York: Holt, 1938);

"A Poem of Pure Imagination," in *The Rime of the Ancient Mariner* (New York: Reynal & Hitchcock, 1946);

An Anthology of Stories from the Southern Review, edited by Warren and Cleanth Brooks (Baton Rouge: Louisiana State University Press, 1953);

Short Story Masterpieces, edited by Warren and Albert Erskine (New York: Dell, 1954);

Six Centuries of Great Poetry: From Chaucer to Yeats, edited by Warren and Albert Erskine (New York: Dell, 1955);

A New Southern Harvest, edited by Warren and Albert Erskine (New York: Bantam, 1957);

Selected Poems by Dennis Devlin, edited by Warren and Allen Tate (New York: Holt, Rinehart & Winston, 1963);

Faulkner: A Collection of Critical Essays, edited by Warren (Englewood Cliffs: Prentice-Hall, 1966);

Randall Jarrell: 1914-1965, edited by Warren, Robert Lowell and Peter Taylor (New York: Farrar, Straus & Giroux, 1967);

Selected Poems of Herman Melville: A Reader's Edition, edited by Warren (New York: Random House, 1970);

John Greenleaf Whittier's Poetry: An Appraisal and a Selection, edited by Warren (Minneapolis: University of Minnesota Press, 1971);

American Literature: The Makers and the Making, edited by Warren, Cleanth Brooks and R. W. B. Lewis (New York: St. Martin's Press, 1973).

References:

Charles A. Allen, "Robert Penn Warren: The Psychology of Self-Knowledge," *Literature and Psychology*, 8 (spring 1958): 21-25;

Charles R. Anderson, "Violence and Order in the Novels of Robert Penn Warren," *Hopkins Review*, 6 (winter 1953): 88-105;

John Baker, "Robert Penn Warren," in *Conversations with Writers I* (Detroit: Bruccoli Clark/Gale, 1977);

Eric Bentley, "*All the King's Men*," *Theatre Arts*, 31 (November 1947): 72-73;

Bentley, "The Meaning of Robert Penn Warren's Novels," *Kenyon Review*, 10 (summer 1948): 407-424;

Charles H. Bohner, *Robert Penn Warren* (New York: Twayne, 1964);

John M. Bradbury, *The Fugitives: A Critical Account* (Chapel Hill: University of North Carolina Press, 1958);

Bradbury, "Robert Penn Warren's Novels: The Symbolic and Textural Patterns," *Accent*, 13 (spring 1953): 77-89;

Frederick Brantley, "The Achievement of Robert Penn Warren," in *Modern American Poetry*, ed. B. Rajan (London: Dennis Dobson, Ltd., 1950), pp. 66-80;

Cleanth Brooks, "Brooks on Warren," *Four Quarters*, 21, 4 (1972): 19-22;

Brooks, *The Hidden God* (New Haven: Yale University Press, 1963);

Brooks, *Modern Poetry and the Tradition* (Chapel Hill: University of North Carolina Press, 1939);

Clifford Byrne, "The Philosophical Development in Four of Robert Penn Warren's Novels," *McNeese Review*, 9 (winter 1957): 56-58;

Leonard Casper, *Robert Penn Warren: The Dark and Bloody Ground* (Seattle: University of Washington Press, 1960);

Casper, "Trial by Wilderness: Warren's Exemplum," *Wisconsin Studies in Contemporary Literature*, 3, 3 (1962): 45-53;

Marden J. Clark, "Religious Implication in the Novels of Robert Penn Warren," *Brigham Young University Studies*, 4, 1 (1961): 67-79;

George Core, "In the Heart's Ambiguity: Robert Penn Warren as Poet," *Mississippi Quarterly*, 22 (fall 1969): 313-326;

Louise Cowan, *The Fugitive Group* (Baton Rouge: Louisiana State University Press, 1959);

Donald Davidson, "The Thankless Muse and Her Fugitive Poets," *Sewanee Review*, 66 (spring 1958): 201-228;

Ralph Ellison and Eugene Walter, "The Art of Fiction XVIII: Robert Penn Warren," *Paris Review*, 4 (spring-summer 1957): 112-140;

Ruth Fisher, "A Conversation with Robert Penn Warren," *Four Quarters*, 21, 4 (1972): 3-17;

F. Cudworth Flint, "Mr. Warren and the Reviewers," *Sewanee Review*, 64 (autumn 1956): 632-645;

Newell F. Ford, "Kenneth Burke and Robert Penn Warren: Criticism by Obsessive Metaphor," *Journal of English and Germanic Philology*, 53 (April 1954): 172-177;

Norton R. Girault, "The Narrator's Mind as Symbol: An Analysis of *All the King's Men*," *Accent*, 7 (summer 1947): 220-234;

James A. Grimshaw, Jr., "Robert Penn Warren's *All the King's Men*: An Annotated Checklist of Criticism," *Resources for American Literary Study*, 6 (spring 1976): 23-69;

Seymour L. Gross, "The Achievement of Robert Penn Warren," *College English*, 19 (May 1958): 361-365;

Barnett Guttenburg, *Web of Being: The Novels of Robert Penn Warren* (Nashville: Vanderbilt University Press, 1975);

John A. Hart, "Some Major Images in *All the King's Men*," in *All the King's Men: A Symposium*, ed. A. Fred Sochatoff, et al. (Pittsburgh: Carnegie Press, 1957), pp. 63-74;

Robert B. Heilman, "Melpomene as Wallflower; or, The Reading of Tragedy," *Sewanee Review*, 55 (January-March 1947): 154-166;

Heilman, "The Tangled Web," *Sewanee Review*, 59 (summer 1951): 107-119;

Irene Hendry, "The Regional Novel: The Example of Robert Penn Warren," *Sewanee Review*, 53 (winter 1945): 84-102;

H. P. Heseltine, "The Deep, Twisting Strain of Life: The Novels of Robert Penn Warren," *Melbourne Critical Review*, 5 (1962): 76-89;

John Hicks, "Exploration of Value: Warren's Criticism," *South Atlantic Quarterly*, 62 (autumn 1963): 508-515;

Mary N. Huff, *Robert Penn Warren: A Bibliography* (New York: David Lewis, 1968);

Charles Humboldt, "The Lost Cause of Robert Penn Warren," *Masses and Mainstream*, 1 (July 1948): 8-20;

Nicholas Joost, " 'Was All for Naught?': Robert Penn Warren and New Directions in the Novel," in *Fifty Years of the American Novel—A Christian Appraisal*, ed. Harold C. Gardiner (New York: Scribners, 1951), pp. 273-291;

James H. Justus, "On the Politics of the Self-Created: At Heaven's Gate," *Sewanee Review*, 82 (spring 1974): 284-299;

Norman Kelvin, "The Failure of Robert Penn Warren," *College English*, 18 (April 1957): 355-364;

Roma A. King, Jr., "Time and Structure in the Early Novels of Robert Penn Warren," *South Atlantic Quarterly*, 56 (autumn 1957): 486-493;

John Lewis Longley, Jr., "Robert Penn Warren: American Man of Letters," *Arts & Sciences*, spring 1965, pp. 16-22;

Longley, *Robert Penn Warren* (Austin, Texas: Steck-Vaughn, 1969);

James Magmer, "Robert Penn Warren's Quest for an Angel," *Catholic World*, 183 (June 1956): 179-183;

F. O. Matthiessen, "American Poetry Now," *Kenyon Review*, 6 (autumn 1944): 683-696;

Frederick P. W. McDowell, "Psychology and Theme

in *Brother to Dragons*," *PMLA*, 70 (September 1955): 565-586;

McDowell, "Robert Penn Warren's Criticism," *Accent*, 15 (summer 1955): 173-196;

McDowell, "The Romantic Tragedy of Self in *World Enough and Time*," *Critique*, 1 (summer 1957): 34-49;

Jerome Meckier, "Burden's Complaint: The Disintegrated Personality as Theme and Style in Robert Penn Warren's *All the King's Men*," *Studies in the Novel*, 2, 1 (1970): 7-21;

L. Hugh Moore, Jr., *Robert Penn Warren and History: "The Big Myth We Live"* (The Hague: Mouton, 1970);

Moore, "Robert Penn Warren and the Terror of Answered Prayer," *Mississippi Quarterly*, 21 (winter 1968): 29-36;

Tatsuo Namba, "Regionalism in Robert Penn Warren's *All the King's Men*," *Studies in American Literature*, 8, 1 (1972): 63-79;

William Van O'Connor, *An Age of Criticism: 1900-1950* (Chicago: Henry Regnery, 1951);

O'Connor, "Robert Penn Warren: 'Provincial' Poet," in *A Southern Vanguard: The John Peale Bishop Memorial Volume*, ed. Allen Tate (New York: Prentice-Hall, 1947);

O'Connor, "Robert Penn Warren's Short Fiction," *Western Review*, 12 (summer 1948): 251-253;

Rob Roy Purdy, ed., *Fugitives' Reunion: Conversations at Vanderbilt* (Nashville, Tenn.: Vanderbilt University Press, 1959);

Robert J. and Ann Ray, "Time in *All the King's Men*: A Stylistic Analysis," *Texas Studies in Literature & Language*, 5, 3 (1963): 452-457;

Louis D. Rubin, Jr., "All the King's Meanings," *Georgia Review*, 8 (winter 1954): 422-434;

Rubin, "The Eye of Time: Religious Themes in Robert Penn Warren's Poetry," *Diliman Review*, 4 (July 1958): 215-237;

Rubin, *The Faraway Country* (Seattle: University of Washington Press, 1963);

Alvan S. Ryan, "Robert Penn Warren's *Night Rider*: The Nihilism of the Isolated Temperament," *Modern Fiction Studies*, 7 (winter 1961-1962): 338-346;

Richard Sale, "An Interview in New Haven with Robert Penn Warren," *Studies in the Novel*, 2, 3 (1970): 325-354;

Joseph N. Satterwhite, "Robert Penn Warren and Emily Dickinson," *Modern Language Notes*, 71 (May 1956): 347-349;

Allen Shepherd, "Robert Penn Warren as Allegorist: The Example of *Wilderness*," *Rendezvous*, 6, 1 (1971): 13-21;

Shepherd, "Robert Penn Warren as a Philosophical Novelist," *Western Humanities Review*, 24 (spring 1970): 157-168;

Shepherd, "Toward an Analysis of the Prose Style of Robert Penn Warren," *Studies in American Fiction*, 1 (autumn 1973): 188-202;

Malcolm O. Sillars, "Warren's *All the King's Men*: A Study in Populism," *American Quarterly*, 9 (autumn 1957): 345-353;

W. P. Southard, "The Religious Poetry of Robert Penn Warren," *Kenyon Review*, 7 (autumn 1945): 653-676;

Robert Stallman, "Robert Penn Warren: A Checklist of His Critical Writings," *University of Kansas City Review*, 14 (autumn 1947): 78-83;

John L. Stewart, "The Achievement of Robert Penn Warren," *South Atlantic Quarterly*, 47 (October 1948): 562-579;

Stewart, *The Burden of Time* (Princeton: Princeton University Press, 1965);

Stewart, "Robert Penn Warren and the Knot of History," *ELH*, 26 (March 1959): 102-136;

Victor Strandberg, *A Colder Fire* (Lexington: University of Kentucky Press, 1965);

Strandberg, "Robert Penn Warren: The Poetry of the Sixties," *Four Quarters*, 21, 4 (1972): 27-44;

Strandberg, "Theme and Metaphor in *Brother to Dragons*," *PMLA*, 79 (September 1964): 498-508;

Jerome Thale, "The Narrator as Hero," *Twentieth Century Literature*, 3 (July 1957): 69-73;

William Tjenos, "The Poetry of Robert Penn Warren: The Art to Transfigure," *Southern Literary Journal*, 9, 1 (1976): 3-12;

Parker Tyler, "Novel into Film: *All the King's Men*," *Kenyon Review*, 12 (spring 1950): 369-376;

Reino Virtanen, "Camus' *Le Malentendu* and Some Analogues," *Comparative Literature*, 10 (summer 1958): 232-240;

Marshall Walker, "Robert Penn Warren: An Interview," *Journal of American Studies*, 8 (August 1974): 229-245;

Floyd C. Watkins, "Thomas Wolfe and the Nashville Agrarians," *Georgia Review*, 7 (winter 1953): 410-423;

Dennis M. Welch, "Image Making: Politics and Character Development in *All the King's Men*," *Hartford Studies in Literature*, 8, 3 (1976): 155-177;

Robert White, "Robert Penn Warren and the Myth of the Garden," *Faulkner Studies*, 3 (winter 1954): 59-67;

Curtis J. Whittington, "The 'Burden' of Narration: Democratic Perspective and First-Person Point of View in the American Novel," *Southern Humanistic Review*, 2 (spring 1968): 236-245.

Manuscripts:

Warren's manuscripts are held by the Beinecke Library at Yale University.

Eudora Alice Welty

Ruth Vande Kieft
Queens College, City University of New York

BIRTH: Jackson, Mississippi, 13 April 1909.

EDUCATION: Mississippi State College for Women, 1925-1927; B.A., University of Wisconsin, 1929; Columbia University School of Business, 1930-1931.

AWARDS: O. Henry Memorial Contest Award, 1942, 1943, 1968; Elected, National Institute of Arts and Letters, 1952; William Dean Howells Medal of American Academy of Arts and Letters for *The Ponder Heart*, 1955; Creative Arts Medal for Fiction from Brandeis University, 1966; Edward MacDowell Medal, 1970; Elected, American Academy of Arts and Letters, 1971; Gold Medal for Fiction of National Institute of Arts and Letters, 1972; Appointment to National Council of the Arts, 1972; Pulitzer Prize for *The Optimist's Daughter*, 1973.

MAJOR WORKS: *A Curtain of Green* (Garden City: Doubleday, Doran, 1941; London: Bodley Head, 1943); *The Robber Bridegroom* (Garden City: Doubleday, Doran, 1942; London: Bodley Head, 1944); *The Wide Net and Other Stories* (New York: Harcourt, Brace, 1943; London: Bodley Head, 1945); *Delta Wedding* (New York: Harcourt, Brace, 1946; London: Bodley Head, 1947); *The Golden Apples* (New York: Harcourt, Brace, 1949; London: Bodley Head, 1950); *The Ponder Heart* (New York: Harcourt, Brace, 1954; London: Hamish Hamilton, 1954); *The Bride of the Innisfallen and Other Stories* (New York: Harcourt, Brace, 1955; London: Hamish Hamilton, 1955); *Losing Battles* (New York: Random House, 1970); *The Optimist's Daughter* (New York: Random House, 1972).

Eudora Welty's importance lies in the fact that during the past four decades she has produced an original and enduring body of fiction. Independent of any specific literary group, clear even of the influence of her most illustrious fellow Mississippian, William Faulkner, she stands preeminent among living writers of the Southern Renascence, and high, indeed, among all living American writers

of fiction. Her best work is as difficult to describe or "place" as it is remarkable and secure in its excellence. If there is any key to her importance, it exists in the faithful exercise of a creative imagination which sees, hears, and celebrates the myriad life of humankind, suffers through a dilemma, probes a mystery, and fuses inner and outer reality, transmuting it into the language and forms of fiction. Her works are mostly short stories or novellas, though two are novels, one long (*Losing Battles*). These works are largely Mississippian in setting and atmosphere, for an important tenet of Eudora Welty's fictional theory is that attachment to place, or "regionalism," is not restrictive, but becomes a means to universality in great literature, a way of getting to the roots of what is constant in human experience. She has produced a body of work which often seems more like a precious and alluring collection of smaller art objects than a great artistic *oeuvre*. Yet the whole is greater than the sum of its parts, much as they defy the process of summing up, and nothing could fairly be said of one work that might not be contradicted in another.

Eudora Welty has been full and generous in discussing her art, its motivating force, methods, and aims, but she backs off from the idea of her own biography. The prospect, she told an interviewer in 1972, made her "shy, and discouraged at the very thought, because to me a writer's work should be everything. A writer's whole feeling, the force of his whole life, can go into a story—but what he's worked for is to get an objective piece down on paper. That should be read instead of some account of his life.... Your private life should be kept private. My own I don't think would particularly interest anybody, for that matter. But I'd guard it; I feel strongly about that. They'd have a hard time trying to find something about me."

What they've found is, for a contemporary writer in an era of accessible and often confessional

Jill Krementz

private histories, refreshingly simple. Her story would go like this: A happy, free, nurturing childhood; a good education; early artistic promise and experiment; enough experience—personal and observed—for the makings of stories; initial difficulties in getting published, but, with the proverbial "little help from friends," publication, and critical acclaim. A successful career, ordinary in having its ups and downs, yet full of surprises. A large number of honors and awards. Generally harmonious relationships with the literary and home community. A continuing joy in creation—a life's *raison d'etre*, deeply fulfilling and sustaining.

Eudora Alice Welty was the only daughter, with two brothers, of Mary Chestina Andrews and Christian Webb Welty. Her mother, the Southern parent, a Virginian by descent, was of English, Irish, Scottish, and French Huguenot ancestry; she moved to Jackson from West Virginia soon after her marriage in 1904. Her father, the Northern parent, was of German Swiss ancestry, though both families had come to America before the Revolutionary War. They were similar in being country people whose

relatives often were schoolteachers, preachers, or country lawyers. Eudora Welty has presented these types, especially teachers, with great insight in her fiction—Miss Julia Mortimer, the dedicated country schoolteacher of *Losing Battles*, being an example. She has also stated that many details of the life of Becky McKelva in *The Optimist's Daughter* resemble those of her own mother as a young woman in West Virginia, where life was actually a sort of pioneer existence, both rough and tender.

Her happy early life, as well as her dedication to the South, have been pointed up humorously in the statement that her only source of childhood suffering was her father's having been a Yankee from Ohio. But he became a very solid Southern citizen as president of an important firm, the Lamar Life Insurance Company. He was apparently gentle and indulgent, while her mother provided the energy and adventuresome spirit to encourage her daughter in her evolving artistic and educational pursuits. She was an avid reader and later described her early and continuing satisfaction of the appetite for books as "A Sweet Devouring." The legends, classical myths, fairy tales, tall tales, family tales, Mississippi and frontier history, as well as serious adult literature, were to become an influential part of her imaginative furnishings, summoned often to service in a tale of her own. So also were her love of gardening, nature study, music lessons, and her work as an amateur watercolorist.

After attending a public high school in Jackson, Eudora Welty went to Columbus to attend the Mississippi State College for Women, where she contributed drawings, prose, and poetry to student publications. From there she transferred to the University of Wisconsin, from which she graduated two years later as an English major. Her earlier interest in painting and sketching, later supplemented with photography, gave way to concentration on the writing she was bound for; however, she has always retained a painter's eye in her fiction, which excels in descriptive detail and visual effects. After college she studied advertising for a year at the Columbia School of Business, an attempt on her part, made at her father's urging, to find a means of practical employment. Coming onto the job market in 1931 at the height of the Depression, she returned to Jackson. In the same year her father died, a heavy loss to her and her family. She was able to find part-time work with radio and newspapers, and she put her father's typewriter to good use by writing stories. By 1933 she had found a job which was to prove more formative to her writing career than the techniques of advertising: as publicity agent for the State Office of the Works Progress Administration, she traveled for three years around the eighty-two counties of Mississippi doing feature stories on local projects, meeting and conversing with many different types of people, gathering impressions of the varied persons, groups, landscapes, and towns she visited. It was these impressions which were to feed her imagination for many years: pictures taken, literally and figuratively, set in "that time, that place" (Mississippi in the Depression), formed the basis of much of her fiction from her earliest stories to *Losing Battles*.

Often fascinated, troubled, or horrified by what she saw and photographed, she would develop her own prints in the kitchen at night and study them. These pictures seemed initially more successful than the stories she had started writing privately, some of the best of which met with dozens of rejection slips. Undiscouraged, she continued writing and trying to place her stories. Her first modest success came in 1936, not only in having a show of her unposed photographs of Mississippi blacks shown in a small New York camera shop, but more importantly, in the publication of "Death of a Traveling Salesman,"

in *Manuscript*. Soon her talent was discovered and her stories published by Robert Penn Warren and Cleanth Brooks, then editors of *The Southern Review*; the discriminating and influential Diarmuid Russell became her literary agent and loyal supporter. In a couple of years *Atlantic* was publishing her stories, Ford Madox Ford took up the cause of her fiction and pressed for its publication, and Katherine Anne Porter wrote an introduction to the first collection of Welty's stories, *A Curtain of Green* (1941). O. Henry Memorial Contest short story awards for "A Worn Path" and "The Wide Net" helped to establish her reputation, and she soon had a national audience.

Her first three major publications—*A Curtain of Green, The Robber Bridegroom,* and *The Wide Net,* all of which appeared within a three-year period—established the most distinguishing marks of her fiction: the importance of place; the impulse to celebrate life; the exploration of human mystery; the theme of love and separateness; the sense of multiplicity in life; and an elusive, changing, and lyrical style.

The stories were set in and around the towns and countryside of Mississippi. "Place in fiction," she declared later in an essay by that title, "is the named, identified, concrete, exact and exacting, and therefore credible, gathering-spot of all that has been felt, is about to be experienced. . . ." Many of the stories take place, within a time spectrum of over a century, on or near the Natchez Trace. This was a path originally traced through the wilderness by animals, later followed by Indians, and then literally carved into the forest bed as it was traveled by river men on their way home after coming down the Mississippi, by traders, settlers, mail carriers, all cutting northeast or southwest between Natchez and Nashville. It is on the Trace that the story "A Still Moment" takes place. In it, Miss Welty uses three actual historical characters from the early nineteenth century; Lorenzo Dow, circuit-riding evangelist; James Audubon, the naturalist and painter of birds; and James Murrell, an outlaw horse thief and murderer. In the story, which includes specific biographical details and even a few words from writings by and about Audubon and Dow, these three driven souls meet for a shared moment of private revelation centered on a snowy white heron. The Trace is also a setting for stories which take place in the twentieth century. Old Phoenix Jackson makes her journey on "The Worn Path" to fetch the "soothing medicine" for her little grandson, though Phoenix herself, the courageous old black woman born "before the Surrender" (at the close of the Civil

War), seems as ancient and timeless as the Trace. It is on the Trace that dignified old Solomon carries his young wife to his "nice house" in the story named "Livvie." It is the Trace that William Wallace and his large entourage follow on their way to the Pearl River in the title story of *The Wide Net*. These stories are mostly about country people, black and white, though others are placed in small towns and cities. Whatever the setting, Eudora Welty has been accurate in her depiction of the social structures that go with place and time.

Local customs of speech and language have also had a marked influence on her fiction. She has described the Southern penchant for talking and listening as "a treasure I helped myself to." Southerners are "born reciters" and "great memory retainers. . . . Southern talk is on the narrative side." Eudora Welty has an impressive command of colloquial speech—apparent early in stories using dramatized narration, such as the conversational satire of "Petrified Man" and the monologues of "Why I Live at the P. O." and *The Ponder Heart*. Miss Welty has referred to these stories as having been written "by ear," her ears being like "magnets." She writes stories emphasizing speech from what she calls the "outside" point of view, dramatic in technique. They are usually comic in their effect, though rarely without serious implications.

Family continuity in Southern life has also provided Eudora Welty with a natural basis for her fiction. She told an interviewer that "if you grew up in the South when things were relatively stable, when there was a lot of talk and so on, you got a great sense of the person's whole life. This is because you know all of the families. You know several generations because they all live together." Family histories lend themselves to novels more than to short stories, and in her novels, accordingly, they chiefly appear. Yet "Why I Live at the P. O." swiftly conveys the sense of family, and a kind of "extended family" of a rural community drags the river in "The Wide Net." In a later prizewinning story, "The Demonstrators," she conveys with remarkable economy the sense of a highly organized, subtly stratified, yet deeply interdependent community over a period of years. The clannishness of traditional Southern society has provided her with ample material for fictionalizing community ceremonies. Though human foibles are often shown, the tone of this group comedy is usually tolerant, detached, amused, and occasionally even hilarious.

Not all of Eudora Welty's stories have Southern settings. "Music from Spain" (from *The Golden Apples*), set in San Francisco, contains a splendid evocation of that exotically "foreign" American city. In the collection titled *The Bride of the Innisfallen* (1955) we find some of the fruits of what her "traveling self" discovered on ocean liners, trains, ferries, and cities among the Irish or Italian-Americans. It was on her second Guggenheim Fellowship (1949) that Miss Welty traveled to Europe and met, among others, the Anglo-Irish writer Elizabeth Bowen, who became a close friend. She shared an affinity of artistic aims and techniques with this writer, dedicated *The Bride of the Innisfallen* to her, and is said to have written the title story at Bowen's Court. The success of these stories shows how place has always sparked the imagination of Eudora Welty, whether or not that place has been her Mississippi home.

In "How I Write," she describes the emotional fuse to her imagination as the lyrical impulse of the mind, "the impulse to praise, to love, to call up, to prophesy"; it is "the outside signal that has startled or moved the creative mind to complicity and brought the story to active being: the irresistible, the magnetic, the alarming (pleasurable or disturbing), the overwhelming person, place, or thing." In the first two collections of her stories, the overwhelming person most impresses the casual reader. Powerhouse, the fantastic jazz musician, excites, outrages, terrifies, and delights both of his admiring audiences, the whites and the blacks, with the sheer energy of his talent and personality. She wrote that story one night after having been at a concert and dance where black jazz musician Fats Waller played, though the story is not especially about Fats Waller, but rather any artist in an "alien world," whose life she had "tried to put . . . in the words and plot suggested by the music I'd been listening to." Phoenix Jackson of "A Worn Path" is overwhelming in her great age and fidelity, a solitary old black woman moving across the winter fields; she is a memorable figure Eudora Welty had once seen, and then provided with incidental adventures and a mission of continuing, dedicated love. The three characters in "A Still Moment" are overwhelming in their urgent, single-minded pursuit of their disparate life goals and enigmas. Some of these early characters are overwhelming because they are grostesques or victims: the man-destroying women in the beauty parlor of "Petrified Man"; the little, club-footed Negro snatched from home to become "Keela, the Outcast Indian Maiden" in a carnival show and made to bite off the heads of live chickens; the heroine of "Clytie," born in a gothic household, frustrated in her attempts to find love, ending upside down, drowned in a rain barrel; deaf mutes in "The

Key" and "First Love." Later Eudora Welty was to make less use of grotesque types, though at the time they served to point up the eloquent loneliness of their characters' inner lives. Yet many of the characters are ordinary, and no less remarkable for that; the ordinary is often turned into the fantastic or legendary in her fiction. There are the rootless protagonists of "Death of a Traveling Salesman" and "The Hitchhikers"; the romantic young country wife, Ruby Fisher, of "A Piece of News," fighting against her confined existence; and old Mr. Marblehall, leading a shocking double life in his fantasies. No "ordinary" person exists, once you get a look inside.

Inside is where all the mystery lies, and Eudora Welty's great pursuit has been to explore the mysteries of identity and meaning—of the essential self, which is inviolable. She gently probes the puzzles which human beings have about their thoughts and feelings as individuals, separated from others, resisting and rebelling against loneliness; needing love yet also needing the privacy and inner space to live as free, exploring individuals. Conveying these mysteries requires the capacity to "slip into" others, to find there the most elusive of human feelings. Eudora Welty has admitted the difficulty of conveying them. She believes that the peculiar, apparently perverse habit of the best artists is to be "obstructive"; they seem to "hold back their own best interests." This is because "beauty is not a . . . promiscuous or obvious quality—indeed, at her finest she is somehow associated with obstruction— with reticence of a number of kinds." The stories in which Eudora Welty deals most directly with these mysteries, written chiefly from the "inside" point of view (through the introspection of a central character), include some of the best known of her early stories: "Death of a Traveling Salesman," "A Still Moment," "A Curtain of Green," "First Love," "At the Landing." In the title story of *A Curtain of Green* a young woman whose husband is killed in a freakish accident when a tree falls and crushes him in his car, tries to part the curtain of green, the veil of mystery cast over nature, by plunging herself into the wild fecundity of her garden. She learns only that the curtain cannot be lifted, that life and death seem to be capriciously interchangeable, that there is nothing a strong protective love can do but submit to the mystery of an unknowable and unaccountable universe.

Even when love seems to be fulfilled in marriage and family relationships, the mysteries remain; in several stories Eudora Welty shows that lovers and mates should not assume knowledge of each other,

and members of a family must stand apart now and then to see others as inviolable, changing, growing, surprising. Families may be hard on outsiders, especially in-laws from another type of family or class structure; they may try to assimilate these outsiders into the family, devouring their identity in the process, even robbing them of their mates. This happens to the young wives in *Delta Wedding* and *Losing Battles*. The larger families of small towns and communities may be equally hostile to the independence of outsiders: a German music teacher, Miss Eckhart, suffers that fate in "June Recital." Provincial communities may also resist the efforts of a teacher, such as Miss Julia Mortimer in *Losing Battles*, to educate them and extend their hopes and visions.

In her fiction, Eudora Welty shows how the most public things in life, love and death, are also the most mysterious and private, and must be kept so. Though privacy requires the risk of isolation and loneliness, it is a risk worth taking in order to achieve the proper balance between love and separateness. The failure to put a proper value on persons, places, and things, the violations of human privacy and dignity, is the essence of vulgarity in Eudora Welty's fiction and has drawn satire from her. The best known of her satirical stories is "Petrified Man," an account of a group of women in a cheap beauty parlor. They are crude; their tastes run to the freakish and sensational, and they reveal many perverted attitudes and practices relating to marriage, sex, and maternity. Most characteristically, her fiction is neither tragic, comic, nor satiric, but a blend of these elements. Though her earlier stories tended to concentrate on a single tonal effect, the mixtures and rapid shifts of human feeling and response have always been apparent in her fiction, making for a Chekhovian kind of realism in which the fluctuations of fiction are as rapid and subtle as they are in life, and the fact of mutability tempers any rapture or dream. Eudora Welty's own "double vision" is like that of one of her characters from *The Golden Apples*, Virgie Rainey, who "never saw it differently, never doubted that all the opposites on earth were close together, love close to hate, living to dying; but of them all, hope and despair were the closest blood—unrecognizable one from the other sometimes, making moments double upon themselves, and in the doubling double again, amending but never taking back."

The "double vision" has also given her a genial tolerance and humanity; her fiction is notably lacking in villainous characters and behavior, and in strong moral judgments. In her work she has never undertaken, as did Faulkner and Robert Penn Warren, the burden of Southern history. To apply her own designations of "inside" and "outside" stories, the "inside" stories, sensitive and introspective, would link her with such modern writers as Katherine Mansfield, Chekhov, Virginia Woolf, and Elizabeth Bowen, from whom she probably learned more about the possibilities of fiction than from any Southern writer. The "outside" stories, comic and brilliantly colloquial, seem more indigenous, less personal, and might link her with the Southwest humorists, Twain, Ring Lardner, the comic and colloquial Faulkner. ("Faulkner taught me," she said on one occasion, "that you can much better suggest the way we speak by cadences and punctuation than by any sort of spelling.") With equal justice, then, her style could be described as poetic, delicate, and intuitive, as robust, humorous, and tough. Her style can be as luminous and clear as a Vermeer and as impressionistic as a Turner painting. As surprise, chance, and experimentation play a thematic role in her fiction, so do they in her style and the whole body of her work. She has spoken of "the lure of *possibility*, all possibilities" in describing her experience of writing stories.

It was the lure of possibilities in form that led Eudora Welty to the writing of longer fictional works. Of her first novella, *The Robber Bridegroom* (1942), she said, "Everything in it is something I've liked as long as I can remember. . . ." It included "a lifetime of fairy-tale reading," folklore, tall tales, Southwest humor, legends of the Mississippi River during pioneer days, and a collection of indigenous character types. Among them were Natchez Indians; Mike Fink, champion keelboatman; the Harpe brothers, bandits noted for their cruelty; Clement Musgrove, an innocent and peaceful planter; the heroine, his beautiful daughter Rosamond and her bandit lover Jamie; and New Orleans merchants. Time is compressed in this historical fantasy— Indians, bandits, and planters scarcely coexisted on the Southwest frontier—yet the novella manages to convey the sense of mutability as one culture displaces another, and the theme of "doubleness" is seriously explored. *The Robber Bridegroom* has been listed in an *Encyclopedia Americana* bibliography on the state of Mississippi, which attests to its historical fidelity. In the novella Eudora Welty also tapped some deep source of American folk art, as has recently been evidenced by the popularity of a "country musical" based on the work which was first produced in 1974 and enjoyed a successful run on Broadway.

Delta Wedding (1946) was Eudora Welty's initial experiment with a full-length novel. She chose for its setting a Mississippi place not immediately familiar to her—the delta country. The events transpire in 1923, a year free of war, depression, or natural catastrophe, which gave her the opportunity to explore both the potentials and limitations of love within a large Southern family, the Fairchilds of Shellmound. Plot is tenuous in this novel; the central event is not, as the title suggests, the wedding of Dabney Fairchild to a plantation overseer named Troy, but rather an incident in which the bride's uncle, George Fairchild, saves a simple-minded cousin from being killed by a local train. His action sets off a complex of reactions, most importantly that of his young wife Robbie Reid in protest against the strongly matriarchal family domination of her husband. In the novel Eudora Welty extends her technique of fusing internal and external reality, for the members of this burgeoning household are seen as a group of introverts, drawing toward and pushing away from each other as though in some balletic interplay of psyches. Amplitude is what the novel gives her: the opportunity to present, in the full panoply of aunts, cousins, and a dead soldier hero, the large Southern legend-making family in all its formidable pride and solidarity; and within that family, to explore personal crises and relationships. Introspection predominates; clannishness is implicitly criticized, though not from the perspective of a social historian: rather from the point of view of an outsider who is also insider, Ellen Fairchild, wife, sister, mother. A town-loving Virginian, Fairchild only by marriage, Ellen is both clear-eyed and sympathetic, sensitive to individual needs but working for harmony—the sort of person in whose sensibility Eudora Welty has always seemed most familiar and effective as a writer. *Delta Wedding* was read by a larger audience than her earlier works had been—proving, perhaps, only that novels have always been more popular than collections of short stories.

In *The Golden Apples* (1949) experimentation is once more evident. It consists of stories written and published individually in various magazines and journals over a period of about two years, then revised by Miss Welty, arranged in loosely chronological order, extended with one major story and a cast of characters ("Main Families in Morgana"), and published as a short story cycle which may be read as though it were a novel. Covering a time-span of forty years, it focuses on some leading characters and families in the delta town of Morgana, whose lives and destinies flow together and apart (for many of its inhabitants are wanderers who come and go) as each searches for the golden apples of fulfillment through love or the art of music. The stories are told from different narrative vantage points, variants of "inside" and "outside" narration: the first, "Shower of Gold," is a dramatic monologue in which garrulous Katie Rainey plunges us into Morgana life by telling the story of King MacLain's amorous career, his wife Snowdie's patience and the town's shocked but admiring response to it, and a Halloween trick played on him by his mischievous twin sons. "June Recital," as moving as it is technically brilliant, makes use of multiple points of view, playing various kinds of innocence against experience. It tells the story of a German music teacher, Miss Eckhart, and her tragic attempt to pass her musical passion and talent on to the one gifted student in Morgana, Kate's daughter Virgie, who rejects the gift and the discipline required to express it beautifully for the easier satisfactions of sex. Other stories deal with the frustrations in marriage of the MacLain twins; the experiences of Morgana girls in summer camp; and in the final story, "The Wanderers," we find Virgie Rainey, now a woman of forty, a detached participant in her mother's funeral rites. As an adult she finally *receives* the gift and meaning of Miss Eckhart's music through an evolved understanding of humanity in which heroic action, or hometown smugness, or even love may be seen as victimizing, though the search for the golden apples, ideally caught in the music of Beethoven, continues so long as hope and joy persist.

In *The Golden Apples* Eudora Welty makes more use of classical myth and symbolism as unifying devices than in any of her other works. Behind King MacLain is the Zeus who took Danae, Leda, and other dazzled mortal women as sexual partners; behind Loch Morrison, youthful hero of "Moon Lake," and the Spanish guitarist of "Music from Spain," is Perseus; and behind all of these figures stand both the change and constancy of nature. Human beings are seen as stars and constellations in slow revolutions; they are like lost beasts, "terribly at large, roaming on the face of the earth," prehistoric and timeless. The perspective and wisdom achieved in this book, its technical virtuosity and mingled tragedy and comedy, its pervasive sense of time and mutability, make it one of Eudora Welty's greatest achievements, and one of her avowed favorites.

Another novella, *The Ponder Heart* (1954), was both a popular and critical success. It is the dramatic monologue of Edna Earle Ponder, small-town hotel manager and niece of her generous, fond, and foolish conveyor of love and money, Uncle Daniel Ponder. He literally tickles his silly little wife to death when a lightning fireball rolls into the room, and his trial turns into farce when he actually throws his money away in the courtroom. Because of its comic high spirits and adroit use of the Southern colloquial idiom, the novella won Eudora Welty the William Dean Howells Medal of the American Academy for the most distinguished work of American fiction between 1950-1955. It also brought her work to the attention of the general public through the medium of theater, for in 1956 Jerome Chodorov and Joseph Fields made a play of *The Ponder Heart*, which had a successful run on Broadway and has since been revised and produced in Jackson and elsewhere.

During the next fifteen years Eudora Welty published no longer works, but there was in the making a fiction which grew in length and complexity as she worked on it. Originally conceived as a novella, it was finally completed and published as her longest novel, *Losing Battles* (1970), and her first to appear on the best-seller lists. In it she tried something new for her: "translating every thought and feeling into action and speech, speech being another form of action"; dropping introspection and extensive description, she tried to "make everything shown . . . without benefit of the author's telling any more about what was going on inside the characters' minds and hearts." It was, in short, her most extensive work of "outside" narrative. In the novel the Vaughn-Beecham-Renfro clan from the hill country of northwestern Mississippi meet for a reunion to celebrate the ninetieth birthday of Granny Vaughn and the homecoming (from prison) of the hero, Jack Renfro. The novel is a cornucopia of talk and action, much of it farcical; family stories are told in a rambling and contrapuntal manner by members of the clan, the history of which spans over six generations. The "losing battles" of the title are both comic and serious; they include Jack Renfro's attempt to save Judge Moody's Buick from plunging over "Lover's Leap"; the schoolteacher Miss Julia Mortimer's battle against ignorance and provincialism, and her lonely death; the clan's struggle against the Depression which threatens their survival as farmers. Despite its length, Eudora Welty retains firm control of the themes and action of the novel, which takes place in a day and a half.

A long private ordeal, ending in her mother's death, led to a somewhat autobiographical novella, in that she made use of scenes and recollections from her mother's youth in West Virginia. Once again using the introspective form of narration, in *The*

6

"I won't do it harm coming on this excursion withyou," she said.
"I know I wouldn't do a thing like that."

"And your same old satchel over your shoulder! Are we marching
back to school!"

"Joe ~~Ray~~, what I'm bringing with us is baby needs," she said.

"Carry her too, for a while, if you want to," he offered, ~~ready
to go~~. "She's hotter than any stove."

~~"This tea is cold. Swap."~~
~~Could not give swap to her?"~~ "Now You don't know anything."

Among the standing trees could be seen, scattered, gray whole
naked fallen trees, ~~then the church, white as a table with a cloth
over it.~~

Joe ~~Ray~~ and Willowdene, while she clasped the baby well, went
lightly running and soberly through the sweet high shade, and jumping back and
forth over the ~~long~~ red Shallow gullies ~~creases in the floor~~ that rayed down from
the top of the next hill. They followed-the-leader around a grandfather
pine where a family of locust-shells went praying wide open up the
trunk.

"How much did you miss me, then?" he cried, as they ~~both walked~~
on their knees ~~and~~ dipped side to side, dodging each other and
balancing with arms spread. "How much?"

They touched shoulders. A long glittering dragonfly held.
dagger high, above Willowdene's serious forehead before a word was spoken.

"Remember when I ask you to marry and come on home with me?"
he cried then with his face rushing past hers behind hers. The noise of the river
when swollen with rains came rushing to her ears where his ears were.
She could smell the gaseous fumes of the first daffodils in the
schoolyard, growing by the bunch, as if, just under the clay, red
fists kept tight hold on them. X

From typescript of Losing Battles.

Optimist's Daughter Miss Welty presents the painful inner journey of Laurel McKelva, the daughter of "optimist" Judge McKelva. For reasons Laurel finds difficult to imagine or accept, the judge married a vulgar, selfish younger woman, Fay Chisom, shortly after his wife's long illness and death. Since Fay has already violated her mother's memory, position, and home, Laurel faces the final ordeal of leaving that home to Fay, with all its treasures of memory and experience, after her father's death. This causes Laurel to review her parents' relationship and her own with her husband—brief and happy, perfected in time since his early death in World War II. She is forced to the conclusion that no one can be "saved" from others; that the more intense love is, the more it consumes what it seizes on. Even she and her parents had not been exempt from that destructive power of love. Yet Laurel proves herself transcendent over Fay, and an optimist in regaining her faith in the heart that "can empty but fill again, in the patterns restored by dreams."

The Optimist's Daughter, though relatively spare and clear in style, is a difficult work because of the emotional complexities presented, but that did not prevent it from appearing on the best-seller lists. It also won Eudora Welty a Pulitzer Prize—the prize some critics felt she should have been awarded for *Losing Battles*. Of a fiction so various and steadily excellent in form and style, it is difficult to say whether her achievement has been greater in the "outside" or "inside" kind of narrative. Not only aesthetic but temperamental preferences are involved in such judgments. But probably the critics chose wisely.

As might be expected, an art so difficult to assess as Eudora Welty's had its effect on her reputation, the course of which has been traced by Victor Thompson in *Eudora Welty: A Reference Guide*. Potential editors were initially reluctant to publish her work because, as one of them responded to Ford Madox Ford upon his effort to get a first collection published in 1939, "These highly developed, sensitive, elusive, tense and extremely beautiful stories will certainly appeal to discriminating readers but we haven't the hope that it would be possible to sell even the modest first edition of the book." When a collection did appear in 1941, it was to generally high critical acclaim, and though the audience was to become larger than predicted, it did remain, for many years, small and discriminating. One sector or another of that audience has always been critical of some facet, stage, or tendency of Miss Welty's work. One objection was to Southern "gothic" decadence in *A Curtain of Green*. Then, beginning with stories in *The Wide Net*, some critics raised objections to what seemed a needless obscurity, a portentous, dreamlike quality, a confusing blend of reality and fantasy. They complained that at its worst, the style seemed precious, suggestive of a rich meaning too tenuous to capture. These tendencies persisted in some of the stories of *The Golden Apples* and reached their peak in *The Bride of the Innisfallen*. Elaborateness, subtlety, sophistication of narrative technique, what Reynolds Price once called a "slow, dissolving impressionism," are distinguishing marks of those stories. Though some critics savored this style, others did not. To them the earliest stories remained the best, and Eudora Welty's reputation to the end will rest on her great achievement in the stories of *A Curtain of Green* and *The Wide Net*. To most of her readers, however, the changes and developments in Miss Welty's fictional techniques and forms have added to her artistic stature, each new award a recognition not only of past triumphs but also of fresh and continuing achievement.

In the 1960s an objection flared up which had first been kindled among a few liberals with the publication of *Delta Wedding*: they found it a hopelessly regional exercise in nostalgia for the lost life of the Southern plantation. Then as the issue of race relations pricked the national conscience, Eudora Welty was accused by such Northern liberals as Diana Trilling and Isaac Rosenfeld of a lack of social consciousness. She was expected, as a notable and enlightened Mississippian, to employ her talents in the cause of civil rights. Her response to this attack was characteristically oblique. It came, at first, in an article titled "Must the Novelist Crusade?" which appeared in the *Atlantic Monthly* of October 1965. Her answer was that he must not, even granting the fact that "morality as shown through human relationships is the whole heart of fiction." Crusades spring from crisis; they must deal in arguments and speak in generalities; they must be clear; they must label. Writers of fiction, with an equal commitment to truth and morality, must deal with the interior life of particular, complex human beings, with all the confusions of actuality, where "people are not Right and Wrong, Good and Bad, Black and White personified." Crusades must be effected in public, while "fiction has, and must keep, a private address. For life is *lived* in a private place; where it means anything is inside the mind and heart." The raw materials of fiction change rapidly, but the instruments of perceiving—the way the artist looks—stay the same. What is perceived, despite all the changes, is that "there is a relationship in

Jill Krementz

*Eudora Welty and Reynolds Price
at the Algonquin Hotel in New York.*

progress between ourselves and other people; this
was the case when the world seemed stable, too.
There are relationships of the blood, of the passions
and affections, of thought and spirit and deed. There
is the relationship between the races. How can one
kind of relationship be set apart from the others?
Like the great root system of an old and long-
established growing plant, they are all tangled up
together; to separate them you would have to cleave
the plant itself from top to bottom.''

A story she wrote during the same general
period, "The Demonstrators," was Eudora Welty's
other, even more oblique response to those critics
who required of her a crusading fiction. The story,
also an O. Henry Memorial Contest prize winner,
shows the intricate social structure of Holden,
Mississippi. The enveloping action, the "issues" in
the background suggested by the title, are very much
those of the 1960s: racial tension, the "generation
gap," a general challenging of all authority figures
and the clash of radical and conservative attitudes.
Everyone in the story is a demonstrator, making a
private claim to rights and privileges belonging to
the self by reason of position, authority, or group

membership. These demands are often made with
hostility: the atmosphere is full of various kinds of
social friction. And yet all of the people of Holden
are linked together by society, tradition, common
responsibility and service, personal and impersonal
forms of love. Within this network of inter-
dependence stands the inviolable personal self,
"savage, death-defying, private." The story served
for its author—perhaps unconsciously—both as a
declaration of life and a declaration of independence:
of the right to remain private as an artist, to choose
her own subjects and treat them in her own way,
which would be complex and truthful rather than
tailored to any cause, however noble its aims.

It is interesting that this very private writer who
has kept for years the same private address in the
family home in Jackson, initially became more
widely known to the general public through the
medium of theater than she ever had through her
early fiction. The Broadway production of *The
Ponder Heart* helped to make Jacksonians aware of
the celebrity who lived and worked among them. She
had never been withdrawn or hostile to her home
community: in fact, she has always been deeply

involved in local Southern life as, for example, a sustaining member of the Junior League, winner of the First National Bank Award (1964), sponsor of various public and private events. Yet within a decade (from 1957-1967) she passed from a state of relative local obscurity to being, as a *Jackson Daily News* reporter infelicitously described her, "one of Mississippi's better known products." By the time the governor of Mississippi proclaimed 2 May 1974 Eudora Welty Day, an event duly celebrated in the chamber of the House of Representatives of the Old State Capitol, at which Miss Welty read from *Losing Battles*, Mississippians must have been sufficiently aware of her fame, and justifiably proud.

Eudora Welty has been the recipient of a large number of honors, awards, and fellowships. In addition to those mentioned, she has received the M. Carey Thomas Award from Bryn Mawr, the Hollins Medal, the first Annual Award of Excellence by the Mississippi Arts Commission, two Guggenheim Fellowships, and writing grants from the Rockefeller and Merrill Foundations. Honorary degrees have been conferred on her by Smith, the University of Wisconsin, Western College for Women, Millsaps College, University of the South, Denison University, Washington and Lee, Mount Holyoke College, Tulane University, Washington University, Harvard, and Yale. A three-day symposium honoring Eudora Welty inaugurated the Center of Studies in Southern Culture at the University of Mississippi on 10-12 November 1977. It was one of a number of such meetings which have been held over the past several years. However, as she sprung from no particular "school" of writers, she has not established one, though Reynolds Price has professed a general debt to her work, and a variety of writers, including Joyce Carol Oates, Toni Morrison, Walker Percy, and others, have expressed their admiration of it.

In her introduction to *One Time, One Place*, Eudora Welty spoke of the "living relationship between what we see going on and ourselves," the necessity of both "exposure" to the outside world and "reflection" on it. Reflection is a slow process, demanding the gift of sympathy: both writer and reader need it. "We struggle through any pain or darkness in nothing but the hope that we may receive it, and through any term of work in the prayer to keep it." There has been no quick, easy way for her to perceive and communicate what people reveal of themselves, nor is there any shortcut for the reader of her stories. Any single approach to her work may be distorting; only by attentive reading and the exercise of a sympathetic imagination will the reader find the fiction of Eudora Welty slowly yielding its precious treasure of secrets and truths. As an eager and ignorant young photographer she learned something "away off one day up in Tishomingo County . . . that my wish, indeed my continuing passion, would be not to point a finger in judgment but to part a curtain, that invisible shadow that falls between people, the veil of indifference to each other's presence, each other's wonder, each other's human plight." If, as seems likely, Eudora Welty's fiction will be read well into the future, it will be for the same reason that Faulkner's is read: for their mutual, though different, faithfulness to "the old verities and truths of the human heart."

Other Works:

Short Stories (New York: Harcourt, Brace, 1950);

Place in Fiction (New York: House of Books, 1957);

Three Papers on Fiction (Northampton, Mass.: Smith College, 1962);

The Shoe Bird (New York: Harcourt, Brace & World, 1964);

One Time, One Place: Mississippi in the Depression, A Snapshot Album (New York: Random House, 1971);

The Eye of the Story (New York: Random House, 1978).

Periodical Publications:

"The Reading and Writing of Short Stories," *Atlantic*, 183 (February, March 1949): 54-58, 46-69;

"How I Write," *Virginia Quarterly Review*, 31 (spring 1955): 240-251;

"The Eye of the Story," *Yale Review*, 55 (1966): 265-274;

"Some Notes on Time in Fiction," *Mississippi Quarterly*, 26 (1973): 483-492;

"Artists on Criticism of Their Art: 'Is Phoenix Jackson's Grandson Really Dead?' " *Critical Inquiry*, 1 (1974): 219-221.

References:

John W. Aldridge, "The Emergence of Eudora Welty," in his *The Devil in the Fire* (New York: Harper's Magazine Press, 1972), pp. 249-256;

John A. Allen, "Eudora Welty: The Three Moments," *Virginia Quarterly Review*, 51 (autumn 1975): 605-627;

Alfred Appel, Jr., *A Season of Dreams: The Fiction of Eudora Welty* (Baton Rouge: Louisiana State University Press, 1965);

Louise Blackwell, "Eudora Welty: Proverbs and

Proverbial Phrases in *The Golden Apples*," *Southern Folklore Quarterly*, 30 (December 1966): 332-341;

M. E. Bradford, "Miss Eudora's Picture Book," *Mississippi Quarterly*, 26 (fall 1973): 659-662;

Fredrick Brantley, "*A Curtain of Green*: Themes and Attitudes," *American Prefaces*, 7 (spring 1942): 241-251;

Cleanth Brooks and Robert Penn Warren, eds., *The Scope of Fiction* (New York: Appleton-Century-Crofts, 1960), pp. 108-113;

Brooks, "The Past Reexamined: *The Optimist's Daughter*," *Mississippi Quarterly*, 26 (fall 1973): 577-587;

J. A. Bryant, Jr., *Eudora Welty* (Minneapolis: University of Minnesota Press, 1968);

William F. Buckley, Jr., "The Southern Imagination: An Interview with Eudora Welty and Walker Percy," *Mississippi Quarterly*, 26 (fall 1973): 493-516;

Charles T. Bunting, " 'The Interior World': An Interview with Eudora Welty," *Southern Review*, 8 (October 1972): 711-725;

Nash K. Burger, "Eudora Welty's Jackson," *Shenandoah*, 20, 3 (spring 1969): 8-15;

Charles C. Clark, *The Robber Bridegroom*: Realism and Fantasy on the Natchez Trace," *Mississippi Quarterly*, 26 (fall 1973): 625-638;

Eleanor Clark, "Old Glamour, New Gloom," *Partisan Review*, 16 (June 1949): 631-636;

Walter Clemons, "Meeting Miss Welty," *New York Times Book Review*, 12 April 1970, pp. 2, 46;

Daniel Curley, "Eudora Welty and the Quondam Obstruction," *Studies in Short Fiction*, 5 (spring 1968): 209-224;

Robert Daniel, "The World of Eudora Welty," in *Southern Renascence: The Literature of the Modern South*, eds. Louis D. Rubin, Jr., and Robert D. Jacobs (Baltimore: Johns Hopkins Press, 1953), pp. 306-315;

Charles E. Davis, "The South in Eudora Welty's Fiction: A Changing World," *Studies in American Fiction*, 3 (autumn 1975): 199-209;

Albert P. Devlin, "Eudora Welty's Historicism: Method and Vision," *Mississippi Quarterly*, 30 (spring 1977): 213-234;

Robert Y. Drake, Jr., "Comments on Two Eudora Welty Stories," *Mississippi Quarterly*, 13 (summer 1960): 123-131;

Drake, "The Reasons of the Heart," *Georgia Review*, 11 (winter 1957): 420-426;

Chester E. Eisinger, "Eudora Welty and the Triumph of the Imagination," in his *Fiction of the Forties* (Chicago: University of Chicago

Press, 1963), pp. 258-283;

Marvin Felheim, "Eudora Welty and Carson McCullers," in *Contemporary American Novelists*, ed. Harry T. Moore (Carbondale: Southern Illinois University Press, 1964), pp. 41-53;

John F. Fleischauer, "The Focus of Mystery: Eudora Welty's Prose Style," *Southern Literary Journal*, 5 (spring 1973): 64-79;

Jean Todd Freeman, "Eudora Welty," in *Conversations with Writers II* (Detroit: Bruccoli Clark/Gale, 1978), pp. 284-316;

Eunice Glenn, "Fantasy in the Fiction of Eudora Welty," in *A Southern Vanguard*, ed. Allen Tate (New York: Prentice-Hall, 1947), pp. 78-91;

Louise Y. Gossett, "Eudora Welty's New Novel: the Comedy of Loss," *Southern Literary Journal*, 3 (fall 1970): 122-137;

Gossett, "Violence as Revelation: Eudora Welty," in her *Violence in Recent Southern Fiction* (Durham: Duke University Press, 1965), pp. 98-117;

R. J. Gray, *The Literature of Memory: Modern Writers of the American South* (Baltimore: Johns Hopkins University Press, 1977), pp. 150-152, 174-185;

Benjamin W. Griffith, " 'Powerhouse' As a Showcase of Eudora Welty's Methods and Themes," *Mississippi Quarterly*, 19 (spring 1966): 79-84;

Seymour L. Gross, "Eudora Welty's Comic Imagination," in *The Comic Imagination in American Literature*, ed. Louis D. Rubin, Jr. (New Brunswick, N.J.: Rutgers University Press, 1973), pp. 319-328;

John Edward Hardy, "The Achievement of Eudora Welty," *Southern Humanities Review*, 2 (summer 1968): 269-278;

Hardy, "*Delta Wedding* as Region and Symbol," *Sewanee Review*, 60 (summer 1952): 397-417;

Hardy, "Eudora Welty's Negroes," in his *Images of the Negro in American Literature* (Chicago: University of Chicago Press, 1966), pp. 221-232;

Wendell V. Harris, "The Thematic Unity of Welty's *The Golden Apples*," *Texas Studies in Literature and Language*, 6 (spring 1964): 92-95;

Robert B. Heilman, "Salesmen's Deaths: Documentary and Myth," *Shenandoah*, 20 (spring 1969): 20-28;

Donald Heiney, "Eudora Welty," in his *Recent American Literature* (Great Neck, N.Y.: Barron's Educational Series, 1958), pp. 255-261;

Frederick J. Hoffman, "Eudora Welty and Carson McCullers," in his *The Art of Southern Fiction* (Carbondale: Southern Illinois University Press, 1967), pp. 51-73;

Robert B. Holland, "Dialogue as a Reflection of Place in *The Ponder Heart*," *American Literature*, 35 (November 1963): 352-358;

Neil Isaacs, *Eudora Welty* (Austin: Texas: Steck-Vaughn, 1969);

Isaacs, "Life for Phoenix," *Sewanee Review*, 71 (January 1963): 75-81;

Alun R. Jones, "The World of Love: The Fiction of Eudora Welty," in *The Creative Present*, eds. Nona Balakian and Charles Simmons (Garden City: Doubleday, 1963), pp. 175-192;

Madison Jones, "One Time, One Place," *New York Times Book Review*, 21 November 1971, pp. 60, 62, 64;

William M. Jones, "Name and Symbol in the Prose of Eudora Welty," *Southern Folklore Quarterly*, 22 (December 1958): 173-185;

Smith Kirkpatrick, "The Anointed Powerhouse," *Sewanee Review*, 77 (January 1969): 94-108;

Michael Kreyling, *Eudora Welty* (Jackson: Mississippi Library Commission, 1976);

Kreyling, "Life with People: Virginia Woolf, Eudora Welty and *The Optimist's Daughter*," *Southern Review*, 13 (April 1977): 250-271;

Linda Kuehl, "The Art of Fiction XLVII: Eudora Welty," *Paris Review*, 55 (fall 1972): 72-97;

Thomas H. Landess, "The Function of Taste in the Fiction of Eudora Welty," *Mississippi Quarterly*, 26 (fall 1973): 543-557;

Ruth Ann Lief, "A Progression of Answers," *Studies in Short Fiction*, 2 (summer 1965): 343-350;

Anne M. Masserand, "Eudora Welty's Travellers: The Journey Theme in Her Short Stories," *Southern Literary Journal*, 3 (spring 1971): 39-48;

W. U. McDonald, Jr., "Eudora Welty Manuscripts: An Annotated Finding List," *Bulletin of Bibliography*, 24 (September-December 1963): 44-46;

McDonald, *Eudora Welty Newsletter* (Toledo: University of Toledo), 1 (winter 1977): 1-11; 2 (summer 1977): 1-15;

Thomas L. McHaney, "Eudora Welty and the Multitudinous Golden Apples," *Mississippi Quarterly*, 26 (fall 1973): 589-624;

William E. McMillan, "Conflict and Resolution in *Losing Battles*," *Criticism*, 15 (first quarter 1973): 110-124;

Harry C. Morris, "Eudora Welty's Use of Mythology," *Shenandoah*, 6 (spring 1955): 34-40;

Morris, "Zeus and the Golden Apples: Eudora Welty," *Perspective*, 5 (autumn 1952): 190-199;

Joyce Carol Oates, "The Art of Eudora Welty," *Shenandoah*, 20 (spring 1969): 54-57;

Kurt Opitz, "Eudora Welty: The Order of a Captive Soul," *Critique*, 7 (winter 1964-1965): 79-91;

Walker Percy, "Eudora Welty in Jackson," *Shenandoah*, 20 (1969): 37-38;

Nell A. Pickett, "Colloquialism as a Style in the First-Person-Narrator Fiction of Eudora Welty," *Mississippi Quarterly*, 26 (fall 1973): 559-576;

Noel Polk, "A Eudora Welty Checklist," *Mississippi Quarterly*, 26 (fall 1973): 663-693;

Katherine Anne Porter, "Introduction" to *A Curtain of Green* (Garden City: Doubleday, Doran, 1941), pp. i-xix; reprinted in her *The Days Before* (New York: Harcourt, Brace, 1952), pp. 101-108;

Peggy Prenshaw, "Cultural Patterns in Eudora Welty's *Delta Wedding* and 'The Demonstrators,'" *Notes on Mississippi Writers*, 3 (fall 1970): 51-70;

Reynolds Price, "The Onlooker Smiling: An Early Reading of *The Optimist's Daughter*," *Shenandoah*, 20 (spring 1969): 58-73;

Price, "Frightening Gift," in his *Things Themselves: Essays and Scenes* (New York: Atheneum, 1972), pp. 139-142;

John Crowe Ransom, "Delta Fiction," *Kenyon Review*, 8 (summer 1946): 503-507;

Isaac Rosenfeld, "Consolations of Poetry," *New Republic*, 109 (18 October 1943): 525-526;

Rosenfeld, "Double Standard," *New Republic*, 114 (29 April 1946): 633-634;

Louis D. Rubin, Jr., "Everything Brought Out into the Open: Eudora Welty's *Losing Battles*," *Hollins Critic*, 7 (June 1970): 1-12;

Rubin, "The Golden Apples of the Sun," in his *The Faraway Country* (Seattle: University of Washington Press, 1963), pp. 131-154;

Richard H. Rupp, "Eudora Welty: A Continual Feast," in his *Celebration in Postwar American Fiction 1945-1967* (Coral Gables, Fla.: University of Miami Press, 1970), pp. 59-75;

Diarmuid Russell, "First Work," *Shenandoah*, 20 (spring 1969): 16-19;

Lewis Simpson, "The Chosen People," *Southern Review*, 6 (July 1970): xxii-xxiii;

Merrill Maguire Skaggs, *The Folk of Southern Fiction* (Athens: University of Georgia Press, 1972), pp. 234-248;

William J. Stuckey, "The Use of Marriage in Welty's *The Optimist's Daughter*," *Critique*, 17, 2 (1975): 36-46;

Victor H. Thompson, *Eudora Welty: A Reference Guide* (Boston: G. K. Hall, 1976);

Diana Trilling, "Fiction in Review," *Nation*, 162 (11 May 1946): 578;

Robert Van Gelder, "An Interview with Eudora Welty," *New York Times Book Review*, 14 June 1942, p. 2;

Ruth M. Vande Kieft, *Eudora Welty* (New York: Twayne, 1962);

Vande Kieft, "Introduction," in *Thirteen Stories by Eudora Welty* (New York: Harcourt, Brace & World, 1965), pp. 3-14;

Vande Kieft, "The Vision of Eudora Welty," *Mississippi Quarterly*, 26 (fall 1973): 517-542;

Robert Penn Warren, "The Love and Separateness in Miss Welty," *Kenyon Review*, 6 (spring 1944): 246-259; reprinted in his *Selected Essays* (New York: Random House, 1958), pp. 156-169;

John W. Wilson, "Delta Revival," *English Journal*, 38 (March 1949): 117-124.

Manuscripts:

The Mississippi Department of Archives and History has the major collection of Welty's manuscripts, including correspondence, literary manuscripts, and proofs of her published works.

JOHN ALFRED WILLIAMS was born near Jackson, Mississippi, on 5 December 1925. His parents, who were living in Syracuse, New York, at the time, went to their native Mississippi for his birth but then returned to Syracuse where Williams was raised and where he graduated from Central High School. Williams joined the Navy before his eighteenth birthday, and after the service he married his first wife, Carolyn Clopton (1947); they have two children, Gregory and Dennis. Williams went to Syracuse University where he received his B.A. in 1950. He worked for the county welfare department in Syracuse before moving into public relations and then journalism.

Williams worked as a staff member for special events programs at the Columbia Broadcasting System (1954-1955) and then became the publicity director for Comet Press Books. A fictional version of his experiences at Comet appears in his first novel, *The Angry Ones* (1960, reprinted with his original title, *One for New York*, in 1975). In the novel, Steve Hill struggles with various kinds of racial prejudice in housing and employment, but the focus is on his growing realization of the way his employers at Rocket Press destroy the dreams of would-be authors. A second theme which will persist through Williams's work is the way that people use love, particularly interracial love, as a tool or a weapon.

As Steve tells Lois, his white girl friend, "You used me as a tool against your parents. . . . Your mother gave you a hard time. . . . but, boy, if she knew you were sleeping with a Negro, wouldn't she be fit to be tied." Although the novel was finished soon after he left Comet, it was not published until 1960, and the editor's choice for a marketable title shifted the focus of the novel. Although Steve is angry about the way he is manipulated by whites, the novel is about a man's frustration caused by spending a year compromising his artistic integrity for a dishonest publisher.

After he left Comet, Williams moved closer to legitimate publishing, first by becoming the editor and publisher of the *Negro Market Newsletter* and then by becoming the assistant to the publisher at Abelard-Schuman. In 1958, Williams went to Europe as a correspondent for *Ebony* and *Jet*, and in the 1960s he traveled extensively throughout Europe for a number of magazines, particularly *Holiday* and *Newsweek*. His intimate knowledge of European locales is evident in the experiences of Iris Stapleton in *Sissie* and especially in the expatriate world in *The Man Who Cried I Am*.

In 1962, Williams became the first nominee for the Prix de Rome to be turned down by the American Academy. Williams had been informed that he would win the prize and then was told without explanation that he would not receive it. Whether racial reasons or Williams's political activism was involved (he had been involved with the Committee for a Sane Nuclear Policy) was never known, but Alan Dugan, the poet who eventually was awarded the prize, courageously made public the issue at the presentation ceremony. Williams gives a fictional version of the incident in *The Man Who Cried I Am*, where it becomes part of the life of Harry Ames.

In 1965, Williams married Lorrain Isaac and they have a son, Adam. In addition to his work in welfare, publishing, and journalism, Williams has taught in the English Department of Laguardia Community College (New York, 1973-1975) and at the University of Hawaii in the summer of 1974.

Night Song (1961), Williams's second novel, is a fictional life of a jazz saxophonist who greatly resembles Charlie "Yardbird" Parker. As is the case in many of his subsequent novels, Williams starts with a man near death who will have to evaluate his past and also cram as much significant living as possible into his remaining days. The hero's actions will influence the lives of those who are dependent on him.

The point of view is not that of the saxophonist, Richie "Eagle" Stokes, but of two men whose lives

Layle Silbert

circle around his: David Hillary, a white ex-college professor who is trying to overcome alcoholism, and Keel Robinson, a friend who has always lived in Eagle's shadow. Keel spends so much of his emotional energy trying to support the life and music of the drug-addicted Eagle that he almost ruins his own life, particularly his love affair with Della. Although his virility returns only with the death of Eagle, Keel never regrets his commitment to the saxophonist. In the relationship of Hillary and Eagle, Eagle is the teacher, and the ex-teacher, nicknamed Prof, is the student. Eagle tries to bring Hillary back to involvement in life and succeeds to the point where Hillary fights for what he believes in, but when Hillary is rehabilitated enough to get his job back, he fails Eagle. Hillary is daydreaming about showing off the famed musician on campus when he comes upon Eagle being beaten by a policeman. Because he once again has something to lose, Hillary walks on, deserting the man who put him in the position to hold a job. Although Eagle later listens to Hillary's well-rationalized confession, both know he has failed.

In the portrait of Richie Stokes, Williams is completely at home in the contemporary jazz scene and presents a man who has come to terms with his successes and failures and particularly his place as a black. The scene in which Eagle is beaten by the policeman is an almost allegorical presentation of personal passive resistance. Eagle, who could escape the beating simply by announcing who he is, takes the blow as part of his community with black men who could not escape a similar fate through the celebrity resulting from a God-given talent. The Eagle remains plain Richie Stokes while the cop rains down blow after blow on his head. The grimness of this incident is counterbalanced by a scene in which Eagle calls on the reserves of talent which once made him great and turns a jam session in a small club into a moment of soaring wizardry. Williams handles both the mundane troubles and the flashes of brilliance with equal dexterity.

Williams's third novel, *Sissie* (1963), tells of the conflict between two generations of a black family. Again the crisis in the lives of the main characters is precipitated by the approaching death of a major character and the effect that death will have on those around her. In this case, it is Sissie Joplin, the mother of Ralph Joplin, a successful playwright, and of Iris Stapleton, a well-known pop singer, who is dying. Brother and sister are on their way to their mother's bedside, and the novel is almost entirely a retrospective look at the lives of the three characters. The focus is first on the children who have made it in the worlds of theatre and music, Ralph in New York and Iris in Europe. Both, however, are rootless and cannot explain why they feel this way until they understand the effect their mother has had upon their lives. The story of Iris takes place among expatriate Americans after World War II, where the success of her singing career is contrasted with her inability to make a marriage and then a love affair work. Some hidden shadow makes it impossible for Iris to commit herself fully to her lover, and it is only when she reaches her mother's bedside that she understands what it is. Iris is nicknamed "Home-folks," but she can never bring herself to go home.

Equally adrift is Ralph, and his story features a comic patient-analyst relationship where both patient and doctor are sure that their half of the story is the whole. Ralph believes that his problems are purely racial in origin, and the psychiatrist is sure that Ralph is suffering from a classic Oedipal complex. What neither sees is the way the two problems are inseparable for Ralph.

Behind the children is the figure of Sissie, who is able to survive a life of poverty and emotional privation through strength, cunning, and primal endurance, yet unable to communicate her love for her children until they finally perceive it as hate. The portraits of Sissie and her husband, "Big Ralph," for all their tribulations, show a sense of connectedness, of strength garnered from suffering that is not acquired by the children. Only as Sissie dies does Ralph see in his mother's choice of his now dead brother as her favorite a subconscious attempt to free Ralph from the confines of her world and does Iris discover that her mother's love affair, which put a shadow on Iris's paternity, was the result not of a casual fling, but of Sissie's passionate attempt to rescue the lives of herself, her husband, and her lover. Nonetheless, she has become too hardened by years of hate to say the words of forgiveness that will allow Sissie to die in peace.

Williams's next novel, *The Man Who Cried I Am* (1967), marks a departure from his earlier aims in fiction. *Sissie* and *Night Song* had been attempts to write about the lives of black men in a white society, but starting with *The Man Who Cried I Am*, the next three novels are about the life of the black man as a tool of white society and are filled with elaborate, nearly plausible conspiracies which allegorize the fates of his characters. The characters of these later novels are often as real as his earlier ones, but they are dwarfed by the imagined political circumstances in which they find themselves: a plan for racial extermination in *The Man Who Cried I Am*, racial civil war in *Sons of Darkness, Sons of Light*, and a vast military conspiracy in *Captain Blackman*.

The protagonist of *The Man Who Cried I Am* is another of Williams's dying heroes who tries to put his life in order before he dies. In this case, Max Reddick, a black writer living in Europe, is dying of rectal cancer and makes a last attempt to straighten out his relationship with his Dutch wife, Margrit. The marriage had fallen apart from the pressure of interracial tensions which, Max finally discovers, he had injected into the relationship himself. He realizes that his first motive for marrying, beyond the love he felt for her, was the chance to prove his manhood constantly: "His possible vulnerability, with Margrit at his side would be publicized, his manhood put on the line as never before, for now it would always be challenged." The novel is at its best when Max reflects on his life with Margrit and also when he recalls his relationship with his chief literary rival, Harry Ames (modeled upon Richard Wright, although with a good deal of Williams himself in the portrait), who finds Harry dishonest because he packages racial anger and sells it in his books: "I want people to jerk up and look for trouble; I want trouble to be my middle name when I write about America."

Max stops in Paris for Harry's funeral and discovers that Harry has been killed because he has uncovered a secret European and American conspiracy, the *Alliance Blanc* which was organized to keep the emerging black African nations from uniting into a powerful black Africa. A far more sinister plot also emerges, the King Alfred Plan, which is a plot to detain and then exterminate the blacks in the United States in case of war with the African states. Max's knowledge of these schemes makes him the target of those who killed Harry. In hopes of passing along his secret he telephones the story to Minister Q, a Malcolm X-like figure. Both Minister Q and Max are captured, and Max is put to death with an overdose of the morphine he uses to fight the pain of his cancer. Williams uses his journalistic skills to "document" the King Alfred Plan so that it almost seems real.

Williams continues his invention of complex conspiracies in his next novel, *Sons of Darkness, Sons of Light* (1969), which he subtitles *A Novel of Some Probability*. Eugene Browning, who works for the Institute of Racial Justice, decides to move from his theoretical world to direct action after a white policeman named Carrigan shoots a Negro boy. In a rather absurd chain of events, Browning embezzles some of the Institute's funds to pay a Mafia don to hire an Irgun (Israeli) hit man to kill the Irish policeman. Whatever probability these events have comes from Williams's ability to supply real lives for the characters involved in the scheme. The history of the don, particularly his hatred of the Irish and sympathy with Negroes, gives some credence to his bending strict Mafia rules and taking on an outside contract at "cost." The most realized character in the novel is not any of the blacks, who seem stereotypes of various shades of political thought from liberal to radical, but the Israeli killer, Itzhak Hod, who plans to use his payment to start a chain of jewelry shops in Israel in order to convince his American father-in-law-to-be that he is a solid businessman.

Although Browning manifests some guilt when his plan goes beyond his expectations and his "simple, selective violent act" becomes the spark for racial war in the United States, his most interesting reaction is his jealousy of the radical who claims responsibility for the murder of Carrigan. "In less hectic moments Browning found that he envied Greene. He had done nothing, but he took the blame; he, Browning had had it done, but in such a way that he would not have to take the blame. He approached each day's news with quickening breath; *he* could have been in Greene's place with the history of the United States howling down *his* back."

The plot takes another fantastic turn when Hod goes off to Alabama to kill the white bomber of three black girls and finds himself, almost comically, hiding in a closet with a black there for the same purpose. The black kills the bomber with Hod's gun—perhaps a symbol of the passing of the torch, as it were, to a new generation of freedom fighters—but Browning's attitude toward the incident should have been the novelist's: "It's too much, just too much."

In *Captain Blackman* (1972), Williams takes his technique of flashback to its ultimate extreme. The allegorically named Captain Abraham Blackman (Abraham, the father of a new nation), a soldier wounded in Vietnam, is The Black Soldier, and so Blackman's reveries trace not his personal history, but the history of the black soldier from the revolutionary war to the War of 1812, the Civil War, the Indian Wars, San Juan Hill, the Spanish Civil War, and World Wars I and II. The technique as fiction is somewhat disconcerting because Blackman is a developing character in the flashbacks, but he grows and learns only as fast as black people have grown in their knowledge of whites. The result is that Blackman, particularly in the second half of the book, is too naive, considering what he has already been through. If he were simply an allegorical figure the reader might accept his inability to see through the deceptions practiced upon him, but because Williams makes Blackman a flesh-and-blood character, it is hard to believe that as late as World War II he is still worried about the "honor" of dying side-by-side with white men.

As history the book is fascinating, both for the account of the important part in American military history played by black soldiers like the Buffalo Soldiers and the Abraham Lincoln Brigade, and for the chilling view of the official attitude toward the Negro "problem" in the military. Williams intersperses real documents with an imaginary 200-year-long staff meeting to portray the Army's policy toward blacks: both the need to keep them under control and the growing fear of a large armed minority within the United States. In his role as the black man in the military, Blackman is granted both great personal courage and a tremendous amount of pride, which allows him to be manipulated by the white officer staff of whatever generation he lives in.

Only in his incarnation of the Vietnam veteran does Blackman finally realize what has been done to him. "We insisted that we belonged, that we were Americans. Oh, yeah, we ran that down for a long time, without once realizing what the enemy always knew: the most basic instrument of warfare was

-121-

Yes, there was something about being in dress blues. Briskly now
he strode toward his place on the parade grounds, knowing that each
man behind him was skip-hopping into step.

It pleased him to be standing before the regiment, or what was
here of it on the fine May day. The colors whipped and skipped in
the hot Texas wind, and the line of troopers in full dress, sat stiffly
on their well-controlled, handsomely groomed horses, the detachments
told their companies by the colors of their animals, bay, sorrel, black
and calico.

Sweetly to Grierson came the the drumtaps and bugle calls; the
commands from the captains, lieutenants, sergeants; they echoed down
the line of black, brown, ginger and high-yellow men. The Colonel
felt then, as he always did at dress parades, when the flag whipped
and the lines moved evenly, that the Army was a special thing for
special men. There was honor here, he thought, and courage, and
devotion to duty, and enough glory for every man in an Army uniform,
regardless of his color. And Grierson was confident then, so much so
that for seconds at a time his eyes grew wet, that the Army would
one day soon sing of these black men and their bravery, and take them
to its bosom without reservation for, even excluding the Civil War in
which they'd done well, they'd been outstanding in this No Man's-Land.
He had the faith that his Army would make up for its past deeds.

Now Alvord with his heavy-butted walk, came over the grass to
within five precise paces of Grierson, threw a salute and bellowed:

"All present or accounted for, Sir."

Grierson returned the salute, wheeled, and squared and walked
to the reviewing position, his aides at his heels. Once again the

From typescript of Captain Blackman.

possession of terrain from which to either launch an attack or to fight a defensive action. We don't have any. American terrain wasn't ours; it was in our possession only as a figment of the imagination." Seeing this, Blackman concocts a plot as sinister as the King Alfred plot that Williams developed in *The Man Who Cried I Am*. In the same language used to describe the historical sequences, the reader is told of the ultimate fate of the black presence in the military: A cadre of mulattoes passing for white takes over the nuclear defense system and in essence captures the United States.

Mothersill and the Foxes (1975) represents a turn by Williams away from the pseudo-historical novel and back to his forte, the examination from a point of crisis of a man's entire life. Odell Mothersill, in his mid-forties, looks back at his successful life, growing up in the Depression, getting a doctorate in the following decade, becoming a welfare worker in the 1950s and finding an important place in the bureaucracy of the Great Society—in order to find out why, after affairs with many women, he cannot love. He discovers as do many of Williams's characters that he has used sex, although not consciously or maliciously, as a tool for asserting his masculinity. As he reevaluates his relations with women from his first experience at age nine to the time he is almost murdered by a jealous woman, he realizes that he has used the "foxes" to counterbalance the emasculating equivocations needed for "making it" in a white world.

Although often misguided, Mothersill's relationships with women are never crass or casual. He is a fully realized individual whose strengths and weaknesses are shared by the women in his life. Like the best of Williams's characters he is never free of his history, and his former lovers press upon his conscience by committing suicide, by becoming insane, or just by enduring when they ought to crack.

In counterpoint to the multiplicity of "foxes" are the abandoned children whom Mothersill remembers from his own youth and whom he tries to help in his career as a social worker. In them, as in the women, he finds an extension of himself, and his name seems to be a pun on the classic blues image of loneliness, the "motherless child." Despite his trials, Mothersill does come to understand the relation of love to sex, and this is among the most upbeat of Williams's novels.

Williams's latest novel, *The Junior Bachelor Society* (1976), tells of the reunion of a group of middle-aged ex-high school athletes who meet to celebrate the seventieth birthday of their coach, Chappie Davis. In the first part of the novel,

Williams does what he does best as he watches each of the men, all successes in a middle class that ranges from blue-collar worker to concert pianist, reflect upon his life. Their histories reveal pressure from marriage, illness, and jobs which the reunion heightens by forcing each to compare his situation to those of his peers.

To the reunion comes one uninvited guest, Moon, the only "black sheep" of the group. Moon is a pimp on the run because he has accidentally killed a crooked white detective. Although the comfortable middle-class characters at first reject Moon despite the fact that he was once the best of them on the football field, eventually they all regain their team spirit and join to protect him from a corrupt black policeman. The policeman wants a bribe, but his primary motivation is his jealousy of the Junior Bachelor Society (as the group called itself in high school), from which he was excluded.

By far the strongest part of the novel is the first half, in which the characters take stock of their lives. In a short chapter for each man, Williams paints a picture of the frustrations of the black middle class and of the dues paid for success. The conclusion, particularly a complex plot about the bribe, seems contrived, and the sparks that fly between the characters at the reunion seem put in just so differences can be overcome when Coach Davis's boys unite behind their man. Although there is some variety of response to the crisis, all of the men manifest a youthful core of courage untouched by age or change. Williams has done too good a job showing the weaknesses of his characters for this unanimity to be believable.

Williams has not allowed his well-honed journalistic skills to dull while producing eight novels. He has written a biography of Richard Wright, *The Most Native of Sons* (1970), which expands upon the fictional portrait of Wright as Harry Ames in *The Man Who Cried I Am*. Williams has said that Wright, along with Chester Himes, is the most important influence on his literary career. A far less flattering portrait, of Martin Luther King, appears in *The King God Didn't Save* (1970), and Williams's attitude toward King as being out of step with the times can be seen earlier in the character of Reverend Paul Durrell, also in *The Man Who Cried I Am*. Williams has also written a history of Africa and has given his views of the black experience in America in *This is My Country, Too* (1965) and *Minorities in the City* (1975). A retrospective of his nonfiction can be found in *Flashbacks: A Twenty-Year Diary of Article Writing* (1973).

Noel Schraufnagel cites Williams as a prime example of a black writer who has moved in his career from apology to protest, and it is ironic that the least "angry" of Williams's novels (*The Angry Ones* and *Sissie*, whose British title is *Journey Out of Anger*) have been given titles designed to play upon a quality that is only a minor note in them. Williams's interest in biography is evident in his fiction, where his strength has always been the creation of character. He can put a dozen major characters in a novel, as he does in *The Junior Bachelor Society*, and give each of them totally believable histories. Williams's reportorial tactics give the most fantastic of plots verisimilitude, particularly in his "angry" novels—*The Man Who Cried I Am, Sons of Darkness, Sons of Light,* and *Captain Blackman.*

—*Jeffrey Helterman*

Books:

The Angry Ones (New York: Ace, 1960; republished as *One for New York*, Chatham, N.J.: Chatham Bookseller, 1975);

Night Song (New York: Farrar, Straus & Cudahy, 1961; London: Collins, 1962);

Africa: Her History, Lands and People (New York: Cooper Square, 1962);

Sissie (New York: Farrar, Straus & Cudahy, 1963; republished as *Journey Out of Anger*, London: Eyre & Spottiswoode, 1965);

The Protectors, by Harry J. Anslinger and Williams under pseudonym J. Dennis Gregory (New York: Farrar, Straus, 1964);

This is My Country, Too (New York: New American Library/World, 1965; London: New English Library, 1966);

The Man Who Cried I Am (Boston: Little, Brown, 1967; London: Eyre & Spottiswoode, 1968);

Sons of Darkness, Sons of Light: A Novel of Some Probability (Boston: Little, Brown, 1969; London: Eyre & Spottiswoode, 1970);

The Most Native of Sons, with Dorothy Sterling (Garden City: Doubleday, 1970);

The King God Didn't Save (New York: Coward-McCann, 1970; London: Eyre & Spottiswoode, 1971);

Captain Blackman (Garden City: Doubleday, 1972);

Flashbacks: A Twenty-Year Diary of Article Writing (Garden City: Anchor/Doubleday, 1973);

Mothersill and the Foxes (Garden City: Doubleday, 1975);

Minorities in the City (New York: Harper & Row, 1975);

The Junior Bachelor Society (Garden City: Doubleday, 1976).

Other:

The Angry Black, edited by Williams (New York: Lancer, 1962; republished with new material as *Beyond the Angry Black*, New York: Cooper Square, 1966);

Amistad I, edited by Williams and Charles F. Harris (New York: Knopf, 1970);

Amistad II, edited by Williams and Charles F. Harris (New York: Knopf, 1971).

References:

David Boroff, "Blue Note for Bigotry," *Saturday Review*, 46 (30 March 1963): 49;

W. Francis Browne, "The Black Artist in New York: An Interview with John A. Williams," *Centerpoint*, 1, 3 (1975): 71-76;

Jerry H. Bryant, "John A. Williams: The Political Use of the Novel," *Critique*, 16, 3 (1975): 81-100;

William M. Burke, "The Resistance of John A. Williams: *The Man Who Cried I Am*," *Critique*, 15, 3 (1973): 5-14;

Earl Cash, *John A. Williams: The Evolution of a Black Writer* (New York: Third Press, 1974);

Addison Gayle, Jr., *The Way of the New World* (Garden City: Anchor/Doubleday, 1975), pp. 277-288;

David Henderson, "*The Man Who Cried I Am*: a Critique," in *Black Expression*, ed. Addison Gayle, Jr. (New York: Weybright & Talley, 1969), pp. 365-371;

Clarence Major, *The Dark and the Feeling* (New York: Joseph Okpaku, 1974), pp. 85-94;

John O'Brien, "Seeking a Humanist Level: Interview with John A. Williams," *Arts In Society*, 10 (1973): 94-99;

Noel Schraufnagel, *From Apology to Protest: The Black American Novel* (Deland, Fla.: Everett/Edwards, 1973), pp. 147-151, 189-193;

Catherine Starke, *Black Portraiture in American Fiction* (New York: Basic Books, 1971), pp. 231-240;

Ronald Walcott, "The Man Who Cried I Am: Crying in the Dark," *Studies in Black Literature*, 3, 1 (1972): 24-32.

CALDER BAYNARD WILLINGHAM, JR., was born in Atlanta, Georgia, on 23 December 1922, the son of Calder and Eleanor Willingham. His father was a hotel manager, a fact which certainly influenced the setting of two of his novels, *Geraldine Bradshaw* and *Reach to the Stars*. A fictional view of the depression years in the Willingham household is found in the largely autobiographical *Rambling Rose*. Willingham was educated at the Citadel (1940-1941), which is a model for the Academy in *End as a Man*, and at the University of Virginia (1941-1943). His first marriage, to Helene Rothenberg in 1945, produced one child, Paul, and he has five children from his second marriage (1953) to Jane Marie Bennett. Since the auspicious appearance of his first novel, *End as a Man*, Willingham has been busy producing ten novels and some half dozen screenplays.

End as a Man (1947) was greeted by James T. Farrell as a "permanent contribution to American literature." The novel is a satiric portrait of life in a Southern military academy, and the title carries the ironic theme of the novel. The words of the title come from the commanding officer's speech in which he exhorts his charges to use their training properly so that each of them will "end as a man," but, in fact, each of the characters undergoes a transformation into something more brutish, so that his years at the academy mark each cadet's end as a man. The commanding officer dreams of his boys becoming gentlemen, but the rigid code of the academy fosters sadism, since the cadets learn to respect only what they fear.

Willingham took a dangerous but successful step in choosing as his protagonist Robert Marquales, a glib, self-pitying, self-serving boy. The use of such an unattractive character works well as the reader sees even greater evil than Marquales's from the point of view of his weakness. The corruption in the academy is complete. Marquales becomes the toady of Sergeant Jocko de Paris, but when de Paris is caught in a gambling scandal, Marquales saves himself by becoming an informer, and this betrayal seems dishonorable even in a world whose favorite pastime is the sadistic mistreatment of overweight cadets such as Sowbelly Simmons.

Willingham is able to turn his Southern academy into a hell on earth,and nowhere is he more successful than in the episode in which Marquales visits the injured, voluble homosexual, Perrin McKee. The scene, in part a parody of the Southern Gothic novel, takes place in an old mansion filled with every staple of that genre—a weak, aristocratic father, a homosexual friend, a ferocious mammy—

and yet it works not merely as parody, but as a genuine portrayal of satanic hatred. McKee and Marquales verbally annihilate each other, rubbing raw nerves through comic indecency and spiting each other over the subject of their mutual affection, the school's hero, Jocko de Paris.

The brilliance of this first novel, combined with the imprimatur of Farrell and the notoriety gained from two unsuccessful obscenity prosecutions, catapulted Willingham to national attention and to the best-seller lists. The flawless ear for dialogue and the deep South setting marked Willingham as that most enviable of creatures, the Southern novelist, who writes as naturally as other people eat, fornicate, vomit, or curse. The fact that the characters in *End as a Man* spend most of their time doing the last four did not hurt sales, but what is remarkable is the uniformity with which the reviewers of the next nine novels insist that no matter what his flaws, Willingham is a "natural" writer.

Willingham's next two novels, *Geraldine Bradshaw* (1950) and *Reach to the Stars* (1951), have the same hero, a rather literate bellhop named Dick Davenport, who is a quester after truth but who finds nothing but lies in the world. The earlier novel records Dick's two-day pursuit of Geraldine Bradshaw, a girl whose defense of her virtue consists of creating a string of lies about herself: at first she pleads virginity, then that she was raped at thirteen by a hobo, then that she was raped by her brother-in-law during her sister's pregnancy. Geraldine becomes more convincing with each story until she has not only Dick believing her, but the reader as well.

The novel begins by giving the impression that the somewhat worldly Dick is seducing a rather innocent and ignorant young girl, but as the novel progresses, it becomes clear that it is Dick who is being deceived by Geraldine and not the other way around. It is ironic that Dick, who fancies himself a somewhat educated character, is taken in by Geraldine's stories, which are ultimately nothing more than slightly refined versions of the "true confessions" that she reads and for which Dick has only contempt. The reader watches in fascination as Dick builds Geraldine's psychology out of a matrix of false information. By the end, he is hopelessly balancing one lie against another in an attempt not merely to understand Geraldine but to salve his own ego, which is suffering from his inability to seduce her.

Reach to the Stars is the continuation of Dick Davenport's story in which the bellhop has moved from Chicago to a plush California hotel, the

George Janoff

Calder Willingham, Jr.

Goncourt, which is filled with faded movie stars, ravishing starlets, aged and eccentric homosexuals, a sadistic house detective, and other expected inhabitants of such baroque surroundings. The hero is once again trying to find himself, but he becomes even more disillusioned than he had been with Geraldine. The title of the novel bears several meanings; it refers first of all to the movie stars who inhabit the hotel and seem out of reach of the hero: "Davenport hadn't believed that stars lived at the Goncourt, even though the boy had mentioned specific stars, including this one. He hadn't really believed it; the stars were too remote to live on earth like anyone else, too remote even to live in such a place as this." Dick soon learns, to his chagrin, that the stars are far more human and frail than he has believed.

The title also refers to the science fiction stories that are interchapters in the novel and stand as ironic comment and to the comic goings-on in the everyday world. The pretensions of the characters and of Dick himself are deflated in the science fiction chapters so that the story, for example, of Gloria, the buxom starlet who tries to be taken seriously, is echoed by the story of an alien creature who appears on earth in the form of a luminous blue globe. The creature vainly tries to get the attention of a dull, stolid farmer, just as Gloria tries to be recognized by real people. Gloria remains in the eyes of the Goncourt's residents no more than a pneumatic object, and the creature, in exasperation, can do no more than give the farmer an interplanetary raspberry: "a great pinkish tongue protruded from the lower half of the globe, then there were huge white teeth, and suddenly two enormous saucer eyes peered at him. 'Bd-dl-n-dl-b-dl-bdlbdlbdlbdlbdlbdl!' said the mouth."

Dick's contact with what he had expected to be an infinitely exciting world of wealth and power leads him to boredom, and he almost believes that the story of an extraterrestrial creature who is ridiculously proud of his huge antennae is a fair image of human pride. After some necessary deflation of his own ego, Dick raises himself in the reader's estimation by managing to maintain his integrity in the course of a hilarious cross-examination by the house detective who is trying to get him fired. Having fought to save his job because of the principle involved, Dick then leaves the hotel under his own initiative. The novel ends with the strangely prosaic tale of the mass rape of one of the movie stars. The stars have come down to his level and Dick has no more to reach for.

The two Dick Davenport novels were originally intended to be part of a trilogy, but Willingham abandoned the effort after *Reach to the Stars*. For the English edition in 1964, Willingham revised *Geraldine Bradshaw* so that it could stand alone, and in 1975 he published *The Big Nickel*, a third Dick Davenport novel which is probably a version of his planned third volume of the trilogy.

Perhaps tired of the frustrations of his characters in these first novels, Willingham tells a story of fulfillment in *Natural Child* (1952). The novel revolves around George and Phil, two New York "intellectuals," and their relationships with Bobbie and Sue, two girls from the provinces who become part of their pseudo-bohemian world. The novel is filled with the fine dialogue that made the previous novels, particularly *End as a Man*, so successful. The reader hears the inanities, this time about art and writing, out of which the characters fashion their hollow version of reality. Although the characters, particularly the men, think of themselves as tough-minded and able to cope, they are soon revealed as innocents in the world they inhabit. The satiric edge of the novel is softened as the story of Bobbie and her relationship to George develops. Her pregnancy seems like an impossible obstacle for the couple, but they come to terms with it, and a real maturity replaces the egotistical bombast of the early days of their encounter. Bobbie, from whose point of view the story is told, is the most attractive of the young girls who populate Willingham's novels, at least until the appearance of Rose in *Rambling Rose*.

To Eat a Peach (1955) is another story of late adolescent love, this time set in a ramshackle summer camp in Tennessee. The characters are primarily the male staff of the camp, and the title, from T. S. Eliot's "Love Song of J. Alfred Prufrock," refers to their ability, or rather inability, to become involved in love. Although many of the staff members yearn for Madeleine Jerome, another of Willingham's irresistible females, only the sardonic Jimmy McClain, editor of the camp newspaper, "dares to eat a peach." Although the possibilities of the devastating satire of *End as a Man* exist in the portrait of Camp Walden and its bombastic director, Daddy Tom, Willingham views the foibles of the characters with affectionate bemusement rather than scathing irony. What is missing is a real sense of the boys, whose lack of the "Walden spirit" seems a virtue of omission in light of the pompous orations of Daddy Tom. The camp seems finally little more than a background for the love story, and Willingham seems primarily interested in chronicling the intrusion of a female presence in a male world (Madeleine is the riding instructor because it is wartime and a male is not available).

After a hiatus from novel-writing while he wrote screenplays for *The Strange One* (the movie version of *End as a Man*, which Willingham had already turned into a play that had been produced in New York in 1953), *Paths of Glory*, *The Vikings*, and *One-Eyed Jacks*, Willingham produced a major novel which has been viewed as either his most important or his most pretentious. *Eternal Fire* (1963) is the epitome of the Southern Gothic novel. "Faulknerian" is the favorite adjective of those who see this tale of sex, incest, murder, miscegenation, suicide, and voyeurism as a parable of good and evil. One can hardly take the work seriously and believe in its importance, but taken comically it becomes an almost satanic parody of the genre.

The story, briefly, concerns the efforts of Judge Micah V. Ball to prevent the marriage of his ward, Randy Shepherdson, to Laurie Mae Lytle, the sweet and innocent schoolteacher. If Randy marries he will inherit Ball's estate and discover that Judge Ball has already pilfered most of it. To prevent the marriage the judge plans to tarnish the reputation of Laurie Mae by having her seduced by the ultimate lecher, Harry Diadem, who, as it turns out, has a taint of Negro blood in him.

The entire novel is written, or rather, deliberately overwritten in the purplest prose conceivable. When young Randy dreams of his pure love, allegorical forces are being marshalled for an epic struggle: "She had lifted his life from an empty darkness into a transcendent light. . . . He knew himself to be the most fortunate of men, blessed by

God and ennobled by his love, which he felt strong enough to withstand any evil put upon it. The sad truth was that evil had already been put upon his love. The egg-tooth of the buzzard had pecked through the shell." Critics point out that the young lovers are pure not by intention but by external restraint and by social convention, and therefore the attempt to besmirch their purity is meaningless. That, however, is the point. That is why Willingham gives his young hero the antithetic names Randy and Shepherdson: never has an innocent lamb been more randy. The characters are comic because they exaggerate the moral significance of everything they do.

Harry Diadem, the great lover who boasts of his 603 conquests (he seems to forget that his idol Don Giovanni had 1003 in Spain alone), gives up his pursuit of Laurie Mae the moment he is spurned— and bitten on the thumb—by the girl. Even though he has managed to get almost all of the clothes off the pure, young heroine on his first attempt, the Mephistophelean (a word sprinkled like saffron through the novel) seducer has to be coaxed into trying again. Willingham gets great fun out of the Archetype of Evil near tears over his injured thumb.

Many of the scenes include a prejudiced observer who creates a comic distance on the overwrought intensity of the stereotype. For example, the prurience of Harry's first wooing of Laurie Mae is undercut by the presence of Judge Ball and his henchman who are trying to see, through rain that falls with ever greater opacity, if they have enough evidence to end the marriage. The eavesdroppers' combination of clinical observation, libidinous cheerleading, desire to be in Harry's place, and inability to trust in the evidence of their own eyes produces comic chaos. Similarly, the successful deflowering of Laurie Mae takes place after he has seduced her in a cemetery and they are locked in a cotton warehouse (where else but upon the accumulated labor of hundreds of blacks would a blood-tainted villain seduce the angelic virgin?). Again Willingham has introduced peripheral concerns to undercut the sexual frankness of the scene: Harry cannot quite concentrate on his task because he is worried about changing his image to that of shining white knight, about how to rate Laurie Mae in his little black book, and about a dwarf with superhuman strength who is the defender of the angelic Laurie Mae and who is waiting outside the warehouse. Throughout the novel, Willingham has taken every stereotype of the Southern Gothic novel and compounded it and expanded it until it becomes a comic extrapolation. He even contrives a

happy ending in which the faithful Negro retainers reconcile the apparently distraught couple.

In *Providence Island* (1969), Willingham attempts to stave off criticism that he is pandering to the popular taste, by having his protagonist, a television executive named Jim Kittering, lash out at pandering to the popular taste. Kittering has invented a term, "gluck," to describe the product of the mass media that is used to sell the garbage of the advertisers. Kittering says, "We have learned from bitter experience gluck contains nothing disturbing, controversial, exceptional, depressing, exciting, true or beautiful." Unfortunately, Willingham's novel is gluck. He presents Kittering's idyllic year in which he is marooned, after a shipwreck, with two women on a deserted island. The island is Kittering's paradise, filled with endless sex and a convenient stand of marijuana, for highs beyond the alcoholic haze that often blurs the characters' vision. After a year of this nonsense, pretentiously marked by chapters named for significant holidays—May Day, Labor Day, Midsummer Night, Easter—as if some primal rite were being enacted, Jim finds true love with his more intellectual companion.

Early in the novel, Kittering makes a fine distinction: "The dividing line between dream and reality is as subtle and elusive as a cherub's fart. It is *there* and yet it is *not* there. A little stinky wisp of purity, if you know what I mean." Despite Kittering's lip service to beauty and reality, Willingham has not found his elusive breath of truth; the novel is *Robinson Crusoe* drowned in gluck.

Rambling Rose (1972) is a comfortable change of pace from Willingham's two blockbuster novels of the 1960s. The story, told from the viewpoint of a thirteen-year-old boy (the narrator technically is the boy grown into a Willingham-like, self-conscious novelist), is that of a sensuous nineteen-year-old girl and the impact she makes when she comes to live, in 1935, with the Hillyers, a middle-class Southern family. The work is largely autobiographical, and the humanity of the family into which Rose comes is felt everywhere. Rose is as nubile as any of Willingham's young heroines, but she is more attractive than most. Despite a history of degradation—incest at eleven, gonorrhea at fourteen, prostitution at nineteen—Rose is basically an innocent because of her refusal to recognize the cruelty and brutality that surround her. This quality endears her particularly to the mother of the family, who has much the same attitude.

The mother is a slightly batty liberal who believes "that to hire a person to do household work is a criminal practice" and who therefore takes Rose in "as a friend, as a guest and hopefully as a member of this family." Despite the many catastrophes brought upon the family by Rose's promiscuity, this code is followed to the letter, and Rose is given both protection and love. Mrs. Hillyer is a creature of unshakable intellectual attitudes, the most important of which is her absolute disagreement with Freud. This stance allows her to put Rose's amoral sexuality in the proper perspective: "The man [Freud] is a total learned idiot and it would be laughable that he's taken seriously, if it wasn't such a pathetic comment on our civilization itself. Imagine, sex determining the human spirit instead of vice versa!"

The warm, comic mood extends to the father, who has to reconcile his rational cynicism and his personal desire with the sensuous naivete of his boarder and the liberal Christianity of his wife. Mr. Hillyer's rages, fueled by both his lust for Rose and his need to be reasonable, are constantly defused by the pathetic crises into which Rose gets herself. More than Mr. and Mrs. Hillyer, however, it is the narrator, Buddy, who is in love with Rose, and the novel is ultimately a retrospective love letter written by the boy to Rose, with whom he spends a comic, yet lovely, night of sexual awakening, and to his family, who had the compassion to take Rose in. The possible sentimentality of such a work is controlled by the Fielding-like narrative voice, although this voice does become a little too intrusive and coy toward the end of the book.

Willingham resurrects Dick Davenport a third time in his latest novel, *The Big Nickel* (1975). No longer an aspiring writer, Dick has written a successful first novel and is reaping the harvest of early notoriety—money, fame, women—in short, "the big nickel." The result of this is not joy, but terror. Dick has reached near-desperation because, like many first novelists, he cannot begin his second novel and must listen almost mutely as the "giants" warn him of imminent disaster. Daniel J. Hennessy (a James T. Farrell figure) doubts Dick's ability to go beyond his first success, and a Norman Mailer type harangues Dick about genius and courage, while producing nothing. Beau St. John, Dick's companion from the earlier novels, has suffered a nervous breakdown because of his inability to turn his literary fragments into a whole work, and Dick seems headed in the same disastrous direction.

Paralleling Dick's growing despair is the story of Polly Dawn, a Junoesque creature of his fantasy. Dick struggles with the unfed maw of his typewriter during the day and creates wild dreams about Polly at night. Polly has come to New York looking for wealth but finds herself trapped in incredibly degrading sexual adventures. In *Reach to the Stars*, the science fiction interchapters had threatened to dominate the realistic story they were meant to counterpoint; here the stories of Polly and Dick are told in alternating chapters, and the comic pornography of the fantasy soon outshines the realistic psychological terror of the stifled novelist. The stories are meant to be parallel and of equal value, but they are not. The reader believes in Polly's ability to turn the tables on her antagonists but has to take Willingham's word that Dick has overcome his block.

It seems curious that Willingham would reach back to recreate a character he had dropped some twenty years earlier, a character who is like Willingham at age twenty-five—the creator of a first novel of amazing promise and the fair-haired boy of James T. Farrell. Perhaps Willingham sees in Dick's ability to start his second significant novel the possibility of fulfilling his own promise with less gaudy but more substantial success than he has had.

—*Jeffrey Helterman*

Books:

End as a Man (New York: Vanguard, 1947; London: Lehmann, 1952);

Geraldine Bradshaw (New York: Vanguard, 1950; London: Barker, 1964);

The Gates of Hell (New York: Vanguard, 1951; London: Mayflower, 1966);

Reach to the Stars (New York: Vanguard, 1951; London: Barker, 1965);

Natural Child (New York: Dial, 1952; London: Mayflower, 1968);

To Eat a Peach (New York: Dial, 1955; London: Mayflower, 1966);

Eternal Fire (New York: Vanguard, 1963; London: Barker, 1963);

Providence Island (New York: Vanguard, 1969; London: Hart-Davis, 1969);

Rambling Rose (New York: Delacorte, 1972; London: Hart-Davis, MacGibbon, 1973);

The Big Nickel (New York: Dial, 1975).

Screenplays:

The Strange One, Columbia, 1957;
Paths of Glory, United Artists, 1957;
The Vikings, United Artists, 1958;
One-Eyed Jacks, Paramount, 1961;

The Graduate, with Buck Henry, Avco-Embassy, 1967;
Little Big Man, Cinema Center, 1970;
Thieves Like Us, United Artists, 1973.

Reference:

J. L. Parr, "Calder Willingham: The Forgotten Novelist," *Critique*, 11, 3 (1969): 57-65.

RICHARD YATES has enjoyed the strong personal advocacy of critics and fellow writers, among them John Ciardi, William Styron, Tennessee Williams, Dorothy Parker, Vance Bourjaily, and Kurt Vonnegut, who called his first novel, *Revolutionary Road* (1961), "*The Great Gatsby* of my time." From his first stories to his most recent novels, Yates's work is characterized by a profound sadness; his themes of disappointment and disillusion are expressed in the lives of closely familiar characters, such that the average reader would find it difficult to distance himself from the action, and, as a result, large popular audiences have shied away from this sensitive author.

Richard Yates was born on 3 February 1926 in Yonkers, New York. His father was a sales executive, as are John Wilder in *Disturbing the Peace* (1975) and Frank Wheeler's father in *Revolutionary Road*, and Yates's early years were spent moving from home to home in and around New York, much like his protagonist, Emily Grimes, in *The Easter Parade* (1976). He graduated from Avon School in 1944 and served as an infantry private in World War II, collecting experiences similar to those of his characters in *A Special Providence* (1969). Following the war he worked as a rewrite man for United Press (Emily's father in *The Easter Parade* is a headline writer), as a publicity writer for Remington Rand (in *Revolutionary Road* Frank Wheeler does the same work for "Knox Business Machines, Inc."), and then (following two years off in Europe writing fiction, something Frank Wheeler hoped to do, as well) as a freelance ghostwriter until 1959, when a series of university teaching positions at Columbia, Iowa, and the New School for Social Research helped him build an academic reputation.

In terms of prizes and recognition, Yates is a well-endowed author. *Revolutionary Road* was nominated for the National Book Award in fiction, a rare honor for a first novel, and one year later Yates won a Guggenheim Fellowship. His stories have appeared in several prize collections, and the National Institute of Arts and Letters has honored him twice, in 1963 and in 1975. Brandeis University and the National Arts Council made substantial awards, and all of his books have benefited from strong, supportive reviews.

Each of his books speaks to a special kind of sadness, even from its title or first sentence. From "The final dying sounds" which begin *Revolutionary Road*, to the *Eleven Kinds of Loneliness* enumerated in his short story collection of 1962, the disappointing trips "On Saturday" in *A Special Providence*, the fact that "Everything began to go wrong for Janice Wilder in the late summer of 1960" recounted in *Disturbing the Peace*, and the foreboding opening phrase of *The Easter Parade* ("Neither of the Grimes sisters would have a happy life"), Richard Yates presents a picture of unrelieved sadness, redeemed only by his excellent literary style.

Yates's achievement has been to take characters so average that they tend to be flat and uninteresting and—by his management of imagery and style—capture the truth of their lives, all in a manner which makes the writing itself interesting and optimistic to read, at the same time that the materials described are not. His first novel, a study of the empty fates hopelessly challenged by Frank and April Wheeler, succeeds as a series of slight hopes followed by crushing disappointments. Frank feels superior to his office job, while April feels she is a great actress. Both pride themselves on their deeper spirits, but neither can rise above plain selfishness. "Every phrase reflects the highest degree of integrity and stylistic mastery," said Jeremy Larner. He continued, "To read *Revolutionary Road* is to have forced upon one a fresh sense of our crucial modern shortcomings: failures of work, education, community, family, marriage . . . and plain nerve." "Yates can take a threadbare suburban cliche," David Boroff wrote, "and endow it with stinging new life." When *Eleven Kinds of Loneliness* appeared the next year, some critics were disappointed by the unrelieved sadness of its theme, and especially by its narrowness of application over eleven different situations. But Hollis Alpert, who voiced some of the strongest complaints, also admitted that, "Mr. Yates depends on our recognizing his characters, and many of his stories gain strength not because they are unique, but because he has thrown a searchlight on the lives of more or less anonymous ones."

By 1969, when *A Special Providence* appeared, critics recognized that Yates was resisting the urge toward innovation (as represented by John Barth, Thomas Pynchon, Kurt Vonnegut, and others) and

Richard Yates

Jill Krementz

Richard Yates.

maintaining instead "a leisurely and direct manner, more in the tradition of Bennett than of Barth," as Robert Phillips said. "And in a time of hysterical experimentation in the novel," he concluded, "his is a triumph of lucidity—utterly lacking in stylistic gymnastics or self-conscious mannerism. Which is not to say that Yates's technique is artless. Within the limits of quotidian detail he is especially skillful at devising symbolic acts that reverberate with meaning." *A Special Providence* is set in World War II, to which the protagonist feels superior. But his prejudice and aloofness make him lonely, all the more sad because his alienation derives from his very sense of worth. Richard Todd summed up how moderate the criticism of Yates has been when he said of *Disturbing the Peace*, "Every page, flawed or not, bears the mark of comprehended pain. . . . *Disturbing the Peace* reminds you of the considerable courage that can sometimes be found in unselfconscious art." This novel portrays the disillusion and ultimately the breakdown of John Wilder, a successful salesman who identifies his own higher aspirations with those of the Kennedy years. But once more, Yates shows how a character's will to do better makes him do worse—human aspirations

are not to be trusted. *The Easter Parade* is based on even slimmer hopes—of two sisters, Sarah and Emily Grimes, one of whom gets her picture in the newspaper as a young, attractive girl. The rest of their lives decline from this one happy memory—so viciously that Emily resents the happiness of others. Only sadness is within her reach.

While Yates is not an innovationist in the sense of Barth, Pynchon, or Vonnegut, neither is he a social realist in the tradition of John Steinbeck or John O'Hara. His sense of literary style moves him closer to John Updike, but without Updike's brilliantly sensitive characters. Instead, Yates writes of people who aren't witty, attractive, charming, or deep—just unexceptional people, whose lives have no hold on us beyond the fact that they are so recognizable. They occupy a small universe; and by strictly limiting himself to the microcosm of their lives, Yates manages to present them in a fullness which compels our interest. Most importantly, he styles his writing so the reader must face the kind of sadness he describes. A rich comparison can be made between Yates's work and Joseph Heller's achievement in *Something Happened* (1974), which showed the same ability to take the conventional suburban life of a New York City advertising man and, by the rigors of literary style, capture the very essence of married middle-class life in comfortable America. It may be an important measure of Yates's significance in the developing tradition of contemporary American fiction that Joseph Heller, an acknowledged innovator with *Catch-22* in 1961 (the same year as *Revolutionary Road*), adopted Yates's method for his second novel thirteen years later.

—*Jerome Klinkowitz*

Books:

Revolutionary Road (Boston: Atlantic/Little, Brown, 1961;

Eleven Kinds of Loneliness (Boston: Atlantic/ Little, Brown, 1962);

A Special Providence (New York: Alfred A. Knopf, 1969);

Disturbing the Peace (New York: Delacorte/ Seymour Lawrence, 1975);

The Easter Parade (New York: Delacorte/Seymour Lawrence, 1976).

Other:

Stories for the Sixties, edited by Yates (New York: Bantam, 1963).

Left to right: John Gardner, Kurt Vonnegut, Jr., Bernard Malamud, and John Barth.

This is a selective list of general studies relating to the contemporary novel. Fuller bibliographies may be found in Lewis Leary, *Articles on American Literature, 1950-1967* (Durham, N.C.: Duke University Press, 1970), the annual MLA International Bibliographies, and *American Literary Scholarship: An Annual* (Durham, N.C.: Duke University Press, 1965-).

Aldridge, John W. *In Search of Heresy: American Literature in an Age of Conformity*. New York: McGraw-Hill, 1956.

Aldridge. *Time to Murder and Create: The Contemporary Novel in Crisis*. New York: McKay, 1966.

Aldridge. *The Devil in the Fire: Retrospective Essays on American Literature and Culture, 1951-1971*. New York: Harper & Row, 1972.

Allen, Mary. *The Necessary Blankness: Women in Major American Fiction of the Sixties*. Urbana: University of Illinois Press, 1976.

Alter, Robert. *After the Tradition: Essays on Modern Jewish Writing*. New York: Dutton, 1969.

Auchincloss, Louis. *Pioneers & Caretakers: A Study of Nine American Women Novelists*. Minneapolis: University of Minnesota Press, 1965.

Bachelard, Gaston. *The Poetics of Space*. New York: Orion Press, 1964.

Balakian, Nona and Charles Simmons, eds. *The Creative Present: Notes on Contemporary American Fiction*. Garden City: Doubleday, 1963.

Baumbach, Jonathan. *The Landscape of Nightmare: Studies in the Contemporary American Novel*. New York: New York University Press, 1965.

Bellamy, Joe D. *The New Fiction: Interviews with Innovative American Writers*. Urbana: University of Illinois Press, 1974.

Bergman, Ronald. *America in the Sixties: An Intellectual History*. New York: Free Press, 1968.

Bigsby, C. W. E., ed. *The Black American Writer*. Deland, Fla.: Everett/Edwards, 1969.

Blotner, Joseph. *The Modern American Political Novel, 1900-1960*. Austin: University of Texas Press, 1966.

Bone, Robert A. *The Negro Novel in America*, Rev. ed. New Haven: Yale University Press, 1965.

Bradbury, John M. *Renaissance in the South: A Critical History of the Literature, 1920-1960*. Chapel Hill: University of North Carolina Press, 1963.

Bryant, Jerry H. *The Open Decision: The Contemporary American Novel and Its Intellectual Background*. New York: Free Press, 1970.

Carr, John, ed. *Kite-Flying and Other Irrational Acts: Conversations with Twelve Southern Writers*. Baton Rouge: Louisiana State University Press, 1972.

Conversations with Writers, 2 Vols. Detroit: Bruccoli Clark/Gale, 1977, 1978.

Cook, Bruce. *The Beat Generation*. New York: Scribners, 1971.

Cook, M. G., ed. *Modern Black Novelists*. Englewood Cliffs: Prentice-Hall, 1971.

Core, George, ed. *Southern Fiction Today: Renascence and Beyond*. Athens: University of Georgia Press, 1969.

Cowan, Louise. *The Fugitive Group: A Literary History*. Baton Rouge: Louisiana State University Press, 1959.

Cowley, Malcolm. *The Literary Situation*. New York: Viking, 1954.

Drake, Robert, ed. *The Writer and His Tradition*. Knoxville: University of Tennessee Press, 1969.

Eisinger, Chester E. *Fiction of the Forties*. Chicago: University of Chicago Press, 1963.

Federman, Raymond, ed. *Surfiction: Fiction Now and Tomorrow*. Chicago: Swallow Press, 1975.

Feldman, Gene and Max Gartenberg, eds. *The Beat Generation and the Angry Young Men*. New York: Citadel, 1958.

French, Warren, ed. *The Fifties: Fiction, Poetry, Drama*. Deland, Fla.: Everett/Edwards, 1970.

Friedman, Melvin J. and John B. Vickery. *The Shaken Realist*. Baton Rouge: Louisiana State University Press, 1970.

Fuller, Edmund. *Man in Modern Fiction: Some Minority Opinions on Contemporary American Writing*. New York: Random House, 1958.

Gado, Frank. *First Person: Conversations on Writers and Writing*. Schenectady, N.Y.: Union College Press, 1973.

Galloway, David D. *The Absurd Hero in American Fiction: Updike, Styron, Bellow, Salinger*, Rev. ed. Austin: University of Texas Press, 1970.

Gass, William H. *Fiction and the Figures of Life*. New York: Knopf, 1970.

Gass. *On Being Blue: A Philosophical Inquiry*. Boston: Godine, 1976.

Gayle, Addison, Jr., ed. *Black Expression: Essays by and About Black Americans in the Creative Arts*. New York: Weybright & Talley, 1969.

Gayle. *The Way of the New World: The Black Novel in America*. Garden City: Anchor Press, 1975.

Geismar, Maxwell. *American Moderns: From Rebellion to Conformity*. New York: Hill & Wang, 1958.

Gerstenberger, Donna and George Hendrick. *The American Novel 1789-1959: A Checklist of Twentieth-Century Criticism*. Denver, Col.: Swallow, 1961.

Gilman, Richard. *The Confusion of Realms*. New York: Random House, 1969.

Glicksberg, Charles I. *The Sexual Revolution in Modern American Literature*. New York: Humanities Press, 1972.

Gold, Herbert, ed. *First Person Singular: Essays for the Sixties*. New York: Dial, 1963.

Gossett, Louise Y. *Violence in Recent Southern Fiction*. Durham: Duke University Press, 1965.

Green, Martin. *Re-Appraisals: Some Commensense Readings in American Literature*. London: Hugh Evelyn, 1963.

Gruen, John. *The Party's Over Now: Reminiscences of the Fifties*. New York: Viking, 1972.

Guttmann, Allen. *The Jewish Writer in America: Assimilation and the Crisis of Identity*. New York: Oxford University Press, 1971.

Handy, William J. *Modern Fiction: A Formalist Approach*. Carbondale: Southern Illinois University Press, 1971.

Hardwick, Elizabeth. *A View of My Own: Essays in Literature and Society*. New York: Noonday Press, 1962.

Harper, Howard M., Jr. *Desperate Faith: A Study of Bellow, Salinger, Mailer, Baldwin, and Updike*. Chapel Hill: University of North Carolina Press, 1967.

Harris, Charles B. *Contemporary American Novelists of the Absurd*. New Haven: College and University Press, 1971.

Hassan, Ihab. *Radical Innocence: Studies in the Contemporary American Novel*. Princeton: Princeton University Press, 1961.

Hassan. *Contemporary American Literature, 1945-1972: An Introduction*. New York: Ungar, 1973.

Hauck, Richard Boyd. *A Cheerful Nihilism: Confidence and "The Absurd" in American Humorous Fiction*. Bloomington: Indiana University Press, 1971.

Hicks, Granville. *The Living Novel: A Symposium*. New York: Macmillan, 1957.

Hill, Herbert, ed. *Anger and Beyond: The Negro Writer in the United States*. New York: Harper & Row, 1966.

Hoffman, Frederick J. *The Art of Southern Fiction: A Study of Some Modern Novelists*. Carbondale: Southern Illinois University Press, 1967.

Jones, Peter G. *War and the Novelist: Appraising the American War Novel*. Columbia: University of Missouri Press, 1976.

Kazin, Alfred. *An Interpretation of Modern American Prose Literature*. Garden City: Doubleday, 1956.

Kazin. *Contemporaries*. Boston: Little, Brown, 1962.

Kazin. *Bright Book of Life: American Novelists and Storytellers from Hemingway to Mailer*. Boston & Toronto: Atlantic/Little, Brown, 1973.

Kennard, Jean E. *Number and Nightmare: Forms of Fantasy in Contemporary Fiction*. Hamden, Conn.: Archon, 1975.

Klein, Marcus. *After Alienation: American Novels in Mid-Century*. Cleveland & New York: World, 1964.

Klein, ed. *The American Novel Since World War II*. Greenwich, Conn.: Fawcett, 1969.

Klinkowitz, Jerome. *Literary Disruptions: The Making of a Post-Contemporary American Fiction*. Urbana: University of Illinois Press, 1975.

Klinkowitz. *The Life of Fiction*. Urbana: University of Illinois Press, 1977.

Kort, Wesley A. *Shriven Selves: Religious Problems in Recent American Fiction*. Philadelphia: Fortress, 1972.

Kostelanetz, Richard, ed. *On Contemporary Literature: An Anthology of Critical Essays on the Major Movements and Writers of Contemporary Literature*. New York: Avon, 1964.

Kostelanetz. *The New American Arts*. New York: Horizon, 1965.

Kostelanetz, ed. *The Young American Writers: Fiction, Poetry, Drama, and Criticism*. New York: Funk & Wagnalls, 1967.

Kostelanetz. *Master Minds: Portraits of Contemporary American Artists and Intellectuals*. New York: Macmillan, 1969.

Kostelanetz. *The End of Intelligent Writing: Literary Politics in America*. New York: Sheed & Ward, 1974.

Krim, Seymour. *Shake It for the World, Smartass*. New York: Dial, 1970.

Lebowitz, Naomi. *Humanism and the Absurd in the Modern Novel*. Evanston, Ill.: Northwestern University Press, 1971.

Lehan, Richard. *A Dangerous Crossing: French Literary Existentialism and the Modern American Novel*. Carbondale: Southern Illinois University Press, 1973.

Lipton, Lawrence. *The Holy Barbarians*. New York: Messner, 1959.

Litz, A. Walton. *Modern American Fiction: Essays in Criticism*. New York: Oxford University Press, 1963.

Lord, William J., Jr. *How Authors Make a Living: An Analysis of Free Lance Writers' Incomes, 1953-1957*. New York: Scarecrow, 1962.

Ludwig, Jack. *Recent American Novelists*. Minneapolis: University of Minnesota Press, 1962.

Lutwack, Leonard. *Heroic Fiction: The Epic Tradition and American Novels of the Twentieth Century*. Carbondale: Southern Illinois University Press, 1971.

Madden, Charles F., ed. *Talks with Authors*. Carbondale: Southern Illinois University Press, 1968.

Madden, David, ed. *American Dreams, American Nightmares*. Carbondale: Southern Illinois University Press, 1970.

Madden. *Rediscoveries: Informal Essays in Which Well-Known Novelists Rediscover Neglected Works of Fiction by One of Their Favorite Authors*. New York: Crown, 1971.

Malin, Irving. *New American Gothic*. Carbondale: Southern Illinois University Press, 1962.

Margolies, Edward. *Native Sons: A Critical Study of Twentieth-Century Negro American Authors*. Philadelphia & New York: Lippincott, 1968.

May, John R. *Toward a New Earth: Apocalypse in the American Novel*. Notre Dame: University of Notre Dame Press, 1972.

Moore, Harry T., ed. *Contemporary American Novelists*. Carbondale: Southern Illinois University Press, 1964.

Myers, Carol Fairbanks. *Women in Literature: Criticism of the Seventies*. Metuchen, N.J.: Scarecrow, 1976.

Newquist, Roy. *Counterpoint*. Chicago: Rand McNally, 1964.

Nin, Anais. *The Novel of the Future*. New York: Macmillan, 1968.

O'Brien, John, ed. *Interviews with Black Writers*. New York: Liveright, 1973.

Olderman, Raymond M. *Beyond the Waste Land: A Study of the American Novel in the Nineteen-Sixties*. New Haven: Yale University Press, 1972.

Panichas, George A. *The Politics of Twentieth-Century Novelists*. New York: Hawthorn, 1971.

Parkinson, Thomas, ed. *A Casebook on The Beat*. New York: Crowell, 1961.

Pearce, Richard. *Stages of the Clown: Perspectives on Modern Fiction from Dostoyevsky to Beckett*. Carbondale: Southern Illinois University Press, 1970.

Peden, William. *The American Short Story: Front Line in the National Defense of Literature*. Boston: Houghton Mifflin, 1964.

Pinsker, Sanford. *The Schlemiel as Metaphor: Studies in the Yiddish and American Jewish Novel*. Carbondale: Southern Illinois University Press, 1971.

Podhoretz, Norman. *Doings and Undoings: The Fifties and After in American Writing*. New York: Farrar, Straus, 1964.

Rosenblatt, Roger. *Black Fiction*. Cambridge: Harvard University Press, 1974.

Rubin, Louis D., Jr., and Robert D. Jacobs, eds. *South: Modern Southern Literature in its Cultural Setting*. Garden City: Doubleday, 1961.

Rubin. *The Faraway Country: Writers in the Modern South*. Seattle: University of Washington Press, 1963.

Scholes, Robert and Robert Kellogg. *The Nature of Narrative*. New York: Oxford University Press, 1966.

Scholes. *The Fabulators*. New York: Oxford University Press, 1967.

Schulz, Max F. *Radical Sophistication: Studies in Contemporary Jewish-American Novelists*. Athens: Ohio University Press, 1969.

Schulz. *Black Humor Fiction of the Sixties: A Pluralistic Definition of Man and His World*. Athens: Ohio University Press, 1973.

Spiller, Robert, ed. *A Time of Harvest: American Literature, 1910-1960*. New York: Hill & Wang, 1962.

Stark, John. *The Literature of Exhaustion: Borges, Nabokov, and Barth*. Durham: Duke University Press, 1974.

Stuckey, W. J. *The Pulitzer Prize Novels: A Critical Backward Look*. Norman: University of Oklahoma Press, 1966.

Sutherland, William O. S., ed. *Six Contemporary Novels: Six Introductory Essays in Modern Fiction*. Austin: University of Texas Department of English, 1962.

Tanner, Tony. *The Reign of Wonder: Naivety and Reality in American Literature*. Cambridge: The University Press, 1965.

Tanner. *City of Words: American Fiction, 1950-1970*. New York: Harper & Row, 1971.

Tilton, John W. *Cosmic Satire in the Contemporary Novel*. Lewisburg, Pa.: Bucknell University Press, 1977.

Turner, Darwin T. *Afro-American Writers*. New York: Appleton-Century-Crofts, 1970.

Tuttleton, James W. *The Novel of Manners in America*. Chapel Hill: University of North Carolina Press, 1972.

Tytell, John. *Naked Angels: The Lives and Literature of the Beat Generation*. New York: McGraw-Hill, 1976.

Waldmeir, Joseph J., ed. *Recent American Fiction: Some Critical Views*. Boston: Houghton Mifflin, 1963.

Watkins, Floyd C. *The Death of Art: Black and White in the Recent Southern Novel*. Athens: University of Georgia Press, 1970.

Weber, Ronald, ed. *America in Change: Reflections on the 60's and 70's*. Notre Dame: University of Notre Dame Press, 1972.

Westbrook, Max, ed. *The Modern American Novel: Essays in Criticism*. New York: Random House, 1966.

Williams, John A. and Charles F. Harris, eds. *Amistad I: Writings of Black History and Culture*. New York: Knopf, 1970; *Amistad II*. New York: Knopf, 1971.

Writers at Work: The "Paris Review" Interviews, 4 Vols. New York: Viking, 1958, 1963, 1967, 1976.

running out for reed[s]
[m]aybe you got tired of the
spitballs breaking the skin
of your neck while in the midst
of one of those ostentatious suppe[r]
club bows
The bounced checks and half-empty
seats were hard on your dignity
and the bad publicity you received

---

the last newspaper pictures
of a Federal Marshal's
to be hanging my head
[think]ing that I had set my

[af]ter my wife died. I used
[cig]arettes a day. It did not
[dis]associate — not
[the] years was I [afraid] to say

and I have to think, senile,
endless seriousness about
rest of the world whatsoever.
college newspapers and magazines, and

I subscribed to hundreds of college newspapers and
read them all. In the case of the White House. I asked the Federal
Bureau of Investigation to furnish me with a weekly summary of
student radical activities throughout the country, and dossiers
[on a] burglar-proof file

---

of senile humorlessness
[sigh]t of those rioting young
who were too ignorant
been a radical in my
Young Communist League
[p]rogressive, a frankly
for Cambridge and
man of a fund drive
[w]ere sent to the Inter-
in the Spanish Civil

[O]scars, the worst of them near the top
[the] thick, dark hair though he wore it
showed when he was [xxxxx] dressed.
[the] dog book, at Curt's house. We were
[a]fternoon. We found Curt, [xxxxxxxx] in
[w]as an Irish [xxxxxxxx] setter. Then he
[sai]d, Hey, here you are. You're an African
all over the house, hiding, and jumping
[w]restling. Curt [xxxxx] had to growl and
[be]coming, but I didn't because [xxxxx] the
I must have seen the Seurat girl for the
[isn']t. first time that day, running through the
[xx]ridge Collection hung. small canvas, nine by
[m]ade with pink, yellow and a few blue dots. She
afternoon, as if [it] held its own light.
[he] called me a remarkably handsome man,
Sweet Lorraine. It was altogether dark in
after a little glow from the ship's running lights
the ship's running lights. That was the first time
[th]rough the hatchway.
He was Mrs. Strawbridge's horse. A beautiful little
I was ten, I was the only one besides her that who
h — Franny be still. There girl — a woman told
[me] gorgeous." The motors throbbed along
beneath them.
[s] hand back and forth along Rebel Deb's flank. Still
[mo]thers, honey. Still

Terrific. Years ago. When he seemed a prophet, som[e]
a god. At the tip, he'd exclaim, raising his ink-stained
and a thrill would shoot through Fender, and he'd repeat
to himself, and consider again the wisdom of his teacher.
thing is property. Pearson's face would glow, his hair s[...]
thing is property. Think of it. Some sort of property.
would rush through the office naming objects, lifting the
[...]s and this and that... This ear, he says tri[...]
[...] lobe, this ear belongs to Isabelle......
pass on. In the midst of life, you know, Fe[...]
property endures. Sure, sure, cars go to
them do. Sometimes... sometimes. But the[...]
that's all, and a house will outlast its bu[...]
outlast us, Fender. Lots of things. Lot[...]
it. Land's near immortal. Land lasts for[...]
[...]d real, see? oh it makes sense, Fender, it[...]
[...]e property. Does that seem like a hard sa[...]
not even real? Oh let me tell you, Fender[...]
most of us... backwards, most of us. Peop[...]
[...]at we think. Oh sure. Sure. But proper[...]
[...]thing's property, and the property that la[...]
[...] owns what lasts least. Stands to reason.
see! So the property that lives, Fend[...]
and goes right on, and then goes on aga[...]
[...]erty that's real, and it... it owns the
[...]l... right? Makes sense.
[...]se, yes. It still made sense. But no[...]
[...]ng... hard to bear. His little h use[...]
[...]commodated himself to its walls. He s[...]
[...]d not extend beyond the rooms. Up th[...]
[...]d-eyed house, how many times had he [...]
[...] owners? And it was right. Pearson
[...] prospects should have asked - do I w[...]
[...] never asked Do you want to do[...]

Characters

THE SOT-WE[ED]